W9-BLD-822

**ANOTHER RECORD-SMASHING YEAR
AT GUINNESS!**

THE 1993 EDITION OF
THE GUINNESS BOOK OF RECORDS
IS BURSTING WITH BREATHTAKING
RECORDS SUCH AS . . .

- GESUNDHEIT! . . . The girl who sneezed for 977 straight days. [p. 173]
- SOLE POWER! . . . The company that manufactures mink-lined golf shoes costing $23,000 a pair. [p. 553]
- CAREER CRIMINAL! . . . The man who was arrested nearly 3,000 times. [p. 491]
- STANDING OVATION! . . . The man who stood continuously for over 17 years. [p. 173]

PLUS!!!

- THE 74-FOOT SNOWGIRL! [p. 266]
- THE 21-POUND CAR! [p. 297]
- THE $675 TRILLION LAWSUIT [p. 482]
- THE 13-MILE-LONG SAUSAGE [p. 542]

AND

- THE LARGEST APPLE PIE, THE LONGEST BANANA SPLIT, AND THE HEAVIEST EASTER EGG! [pp. 537, 539]

All this and much more . . . the best and the worst, the most beautiful and the most grotesque, the most memorable, all captured in one spectacular book!

THE GUINNESS BOOK OF RECORDS

Bantam Books in the Guinness Series

GUINNESS BOOK OF OLYMPIC RECORDS
THE GUINNESS BOOK OF RECORDS 1993

THE GUINNESS BOOK OF RECORDS 1993

EDITOR
Peter Matthews

EXECUTIVE EDITOR, U.S. EDITION
Michelle Dunkley McCarthy

EDITOR, U.S. EDITION (NEW YORK)
Mark Young

FOUNDING EDITOR
Norris D. McWhirter

BANTAM BOOKS
NEW YORK • TORONTO • LONDON • SYDNEY • AUCKLAND

This edition contains the complete text of the original hardcover edition.
NOT ONE WORD HAS BEEN OMITTED.

THE GUINNESS BOOK OF RECORDS 1993
*A Bantam Book / Published by arrangement with
Guinness Publishing, Ltd.*

Bantam edition/April 1993

World rights reserved.
Revised American editions copyright © 1993, 1992, 1991, 1990, 1989,
1988, 1987, 1986, 1985, 1984, 1983, 1982, 1981, 1980, 1979, 1978, 1977,
1976, 1975, 1974, 1973, 1972, 1971, 1970, 1969, 1968, 1966, 1965, 1964,
1963, 1962, 1960 by Guinness Publishing, Ltd.

*No part of this book may be reproduced or transmitted in any form or by
any means, electronic or mechanical, including photocopying,
recording, or by any information storage and retrieval system, without
permission in writing from the publisher.*

Art spreads by State of the Art/Robert D. Roe

*If you purchased this book without a cover you should be aware
that this book is stolen property. It was reported as "unsold and
destroyed" to the publisher and neither the author nor the
publisher has received any payment for this "stripped book."*

ISBN 0-553-56257-6

Published simultaneously in the United States and Canada

*Bantam Books are published by Bantam Books, a division of Bantam Dou-
bleday Dell Publishing Group, Inc. Its trademark, consisting of the words
"Bantam Books" and the portrayal of a rooster, is Registered in U.S.
Patent and Trademark Office and in other countries. Marca Registrada.
Bantam Books, 666 Fifth Avenue, New York, New York 10103.*

PRINTED IN THE UNITED STATES OF AMERICA

OPM   0 9 8 7 6 5 4 3 2 1

The name Guinness is a registered trademark and should not be used in publicity for, or otherwise in the context of, a record attempt without our prior written consent.

The publishers do not normally supply personnel to supervise record attempts but reserve the right to do so.

All record attempts are undertaken at the sole risk of the (potential) claimant. The publishers cannot be held responsible for any (potential) liability, howsoever arising out of any such attempt, whether to the claimant or any third party.

We are likely to publish only those records that improve upon previously published records and we reserve the right to determine at our sole discretion the records to be published.

CONTENTS

Records for 17 major animal orders, from mammals to sponges, extinct animals, plus a new section on rare and endangered flora and fauna. The Plant Kingdom features giant fruits, vegetables and flowers. Also included are the Kingdoms Protista, Fungi and Procaryota, as well as Parks, Zoos, Oceanaria and Aquaria.

THE GUINNESS BOOK OF RECORDS

INTRODUCTION

This is the 32nd American edition of *The Guinness Book of Records*. Regular readers will note some changes in the order of contents, and as always the book has been completely reillustrated. The text has been thoroughly revised and thousands of changes made.

The book was first produced in 1955 to assist in resolving arguments that might take place on matters of fact. In 1951, Sir Hugh Beaver (1891–1967), the then managing director of Guinness, was out shooting on The North Slob, in County Wexford in the southeast of Ireland. Some golden plover were missed by the shooting party, and later Sir Hugh discovered that reference books in the library of his host at Castlebridge House could not confirm whether the bird was Europe's fastest game bird. Then, in August 1954, argument arose again, this time as to whether grouse were even faster than golden plover. Sir Hugh thought that there must be many other such questions debated nightly, but there was no book with which to settle the arguments about records.

On 12 Sep. 1954, Sir Hugh challenged Norris and Ross McWhirter, who ran a fact and figure agency in London, England, to compile a book of records. An office was set up in Fleet Street, London, and work began on the initial 198-page edition. The first copy was bound by the printers on 27 Aug 1955. Well before Christmas, *The Guinness Book of Records* was No. 1 on the British best-seller lists, and every subsequent edition has been similarly represented.

The Guinness Book of Records began its worldwide expansion in 1956, when the first United States edition was published in New York City, followed by editions in French (1962) and German (1963). In 1967 there were first editions in Japanese, Spanish, Danish and Norwegian, and in the 1970s editions were published in Portuguese, Czechoslovakian, Hebrew, Serbo-Croat, Dutch, Icelandic and Slovene. In the 1980s there were translations into Greek, Indonesian, Chinese, Turkish, Hindi, Malay, Arabic, Tamil, Thai, Telugu, Malayalam, Kannada and Hungarian. More recently, in the

1990s, editions have been published in Bulgarian, Korean, Macedonian, Polish, Romanian and Russian.

This 1993 edition marks the thirty-second published in the United States overall and the third by Facts On File, Inc. Our hope remains that, as with the first edition, this new edition will assist in resolving questions of fact.

EDITORIAL POLICY

Since its inception in 1955 in Great Britain, *The Guinness Book of Records* has become the authoritative source on facts, feats and exploits of the world and its inhabitants. The book records the ultimate achievements of men and women as well as the superlatives of the world around us. Many such achievements are obvious entries; for others we have to exercise our editorial judgment as to what to include and what to exclude from the variety of activities that are presented to us, or that we and our expert advisors research.

Each year we vary the contents by resting some categories and introducing new ones, and we also review every entry in the book and revise where appropriate. We pride ourselves on our attention to detail, and take much care to check the facts that we present in this book. We are, however, always pleased to hear from readers who may be able to supply improvements to the text or to suggest new categories, and we welcome direct contributions from new record breakers.

If you feel that your particular achievement should be considered for inclusion in the book, you should make contact in writing with this office and include a business-size self-addressed stamped envelope. We will advise you regarding any rules and guidelines. Because of the large volume of mail that we receive, we would be grateful if you could make contact at least two months before any record attempt. In addition, a last-minute check should be made in case the published record has recently been broken.

Please bear in mind that we are much more likely to publish a record that betters a previous record in an existing category. Occasionally we do introduce new categories if they relate to an activity that has become the subject of widespread interest, but pressure of space usually means that if we do this an existing category has to be dropped. We reserve the right to determine at our sole discretion the records to be published.

Contact Address: Facts On File, Inc.
  460 Park Avenue South
  New York, NY 10016

THE
GUINNESS
BOOK OF
RECORDS
1993

EARTH
AND SPACE

Plateau in the *Lost World* region of Venezuela.
(Photo: Domingo Luis Pérez Pino)

THE UNIVERSE

Large structures in the Universe Our own Milky Way galaxy is only
one of 10 billion galaxies. It is part of the so-called Local Group of galaxies
moving at a speed of 370 miles/sec. with respect to the cosmological frame
in the general direction of a dense concentration of galaxy clusters known as
the "Great Attractor" (a term coined by Alan Dressler [USA]).

In November 1989 Margaret Geller and John Huchra (USA) announced
the discovery of a "Great Wall" in space, a concentration of galaxies in the
form of a "crumpled membrane" with a minimum extent of 280×800 mil-
lion light years (1.6×10^{21} miles $\times 4.7 \times 10^{21}$ miles) and a depth of up to 20
million light years (9.6×10^{19} miles).

Based on the effect of line of sight on the spectra of distant quasars, Josef
Hoell and Wolfgang Priester (Germany) suggested in July 1991 that the large-
scale structure of the Universe consists of "bubbles" each up to 100 million
light years (5.8×10^{20}) in diameter with galaxies being formed on the "surfaces" of the "bubbles" and with the interiors being virtually devoid of matter.

Galaxies The possible existence of galaxies external to our own Milky
Way system was mooted in 1789 by Sir William Herschel (1738–1822).
These extra-galactic nebulae were first termed "island universes."

In July 1990 Juan M. Uson, Stephen P. Boughn and Jeffrey R. Kuhn (USA)
announced the discovery of the largest galaxy—the central galaxy of the
Abell 2029 galaxy cluster, 1,070 million light years (6.3×10^{21} miles) distant
in Virgo. The galaxy has a major diameter of 5.6 million light years ($3.3 \times
10^{19}$ miles), which is eighty times the diameter of our own galaxy (see page
5), and has a light output equivalent to 2 trillion Suns.

The brightest galaxy (or galaxy in the process of forming) is IRAS F10214
+ 4724, which was detected as a faint source by IRAS (Infra Red Astronomy
Satellite) in 1983 but was shown in February 1991 to have a far-infrared luminosity 3×10^{14} times greater than that of the Sun. It has a red shift of 2.286,
equivalent to a distance of 11.6 billion light years (6.8×10^{22} miles), but the
remotest galaxy is the radio source 4C 41.17, determined by K. Chambers,
G. Miley and W. Van Bruegel in January 1990 to have a red shift of 3.800,
equivalent to a distance of 12.8 billion light years (7.5×10^{22} miles).

Age of the Universe For the age of the Universe a consensus value of
14 ± 3 eons or gigayears (an eon or gigayear being 1 billion years) is obtained
from various cosmological techniques. The equivalent value of the Hubble
constant based on a Friedman model of the Universe without cosmological
constant is Mpc43±9 m/s. In 1973 an *ex nihilo* creation was postulated by
Edward P. Tryon (USA). Modified versions of the Inflationary Model, originally introduced by Alan Guth (USA) in 1981, now complement the Big
Bang theory of creation. In order to explain their observations of the large
scale structure of the Universe, Hoell and Priester (see above) have made the
bold suggestion that the Universe must be at least twice as old as currently
considered and that the cosmological constant must be nonzero.

Remotest object The interpretation of the red shifts of quasars in terms

FARTHEST VISIBLE OBJECT. The remotest heavenly body that can be seen with the naked eye is the Great Galaxy in Andromeda. This image was produced by combining observations made by the Infrared Astronomical Satellite in three infrared wavelengths. The overall dark area represents the warmest material and the circular gray area the coldest. The light ring of clouds marks areas where star formation is occurring. (Photo: NASA)

of distance is limited by a lack of knowledge of the Universal constants. The record red shift of 4.897 for the quasar PC 1247 + 3406 as determined by Donald P. Schneider, Maarten Schmidt (Netherlands) and James E. Gunn and announced in May 1991, following spectroscopic and photometric observations made in February and April of the same year using the Hale Telescope at Palomar Observatory, CA. If it is assumed that there is an "observable horizon," where the speed of recession is equal to the speed of light, i.e., at 14 billion light years or 82.3 million trillion miles, then a simple interpretation would place this quasar at 94.4 percent of this value or 13,200 million light years distant (7.8×10^{22} miles).

Farthest visible object   The remotest heavenly body visible to the naked eye is the Great Galaxy in *Andromeda* (mag. 3.47), known as Messier 31. It was first noted from Germany by Simon Marius (1570–1624). It is a rotating nebula in spiral form at a distance from the Earth of about 2,309,000 light

Largest scale model The largest scale model of the Solar System was inaugurated by the Futures' Museum, Falun, Sweden on 29 Nov. 1986. A model of the Earth with a diameter of ½ in. was placed in the museum. The Sun (diameter 5 ft.), and the planets (with diameters ranging from ⅛ in. to 5 ½ in.) were positioned in the nearby city of Borlange some 10 miles away. *Proxima Centauri* was sited to scale in the Museum of Victoria, Melbourne, Australia.

Age of the Universe It was announced on 23 Apr. 1992 that the COBE (Cosmic Background Explorer) satellite, launched by NASA on 18 Nov. 1989, had detected minute fluctuations from the cosmic microwave background temperature of $-454.745°F$. This has been interpreted as evidence for the initial formation of galaxies within the Universe only a million years after the Big Bang. (See also *Age of the Universe* on page 2.)

years, or 1.36×10^{19} miles (13 million trillion miles), and our galaxy is moving towards it. It is just possible that under ideal conditions for observations, Messier 33, the Spiral in Triangulum (mag. 5.79), can be glimpsed by the naked eye of keen-sighted people at a distance of 2,509,000 light years.

Quasars An occultation of 3C 273, observed from Australia on 5 Aug. 1962, enabled the existence of quasi-stellar radio sources ("quasars" or QSOs) to be announced by Maarten Schmidt (Netherlands, b. 1929). The red shift proved to be $z = 0.158$.

Quasars have immensely high luminosity for bodies so distant and of such small diameter. The discovery of the most luminous object in the sky, the quasar HS 1946 + 7658, which is at least 1.5×10^{15} times more luminous than the Sun, was announced in July 1991 following the Hamburg Survey of northern quasars. This quasar has a red shift of 3.02 and is therefore at a distance of 12,400 million light years (7.3×10^{22} miles).

The first double quasar (0957 + 561) among well over 2,000 known quasars was announced in May 1980.

The most violent outburst observed in a quasar was recorded on 13 Nov. 1989 by a joint US–Japanese team which noted that the energy output of the quasar PKS 0558-504 (which is about 2 billion light years distant) increased by two-thirds in three minutes, equivalent to the total energy released by the Sun in 340,000 years.

STARS

The first direct measurement of the distance of a star was made in 1838 when Friedrich W. Bessel (1784–1846) of the Königsberg Observatory, Germany used the parallax method to measure the distance of 61 Cygni to be about six light years (modern value 11.08 light years).

Nearest Except for the special case of our own Sun, the nearest star is the very faint *Proxima Centauri*, discovered in 1915, which is 4.225 light years (25 trillion miles) away.

The nearest star visible to the naked eye is the southern hemisphere binary *Alpha Centauri*, or *Rigel Kentaurus* (4.35 light years distant), with an apparent magnitude of −0.29. It was discovered by Nicolas L. de Lacaille (1713–62) in *c.* 1752. By A.D. 29,700 this binary will reach a minimum distance from the Earth of 2.84 light years and should then be the second brightest star, with an apparent magnitude of −1.20.

Farthest   The Solar System, with its Sun's nine principal planets, 61 satellites, its asteroids and comets, is located in the outer regions of our Milky Way galaxy, orbiting the center of the galaxy at a mean distance of 29,700 light years and with an orbital eccentricity of 0.07. The present distance from the center is 27,700 light years and it will reach the minimum distance of 27,600 light years (perigalacticon) in about 15 million years, on the last day of the year.

The Milky Way galaxy has a diameter of about 70,000 light years, so the most distant star will be at 66,700 light years when the Solar System is farthest from the center (apogalacticon). At present the most distant stars are at 62,700 light years.

The present orbital velocity of the Sun and a large number of nearby stars has been averaged to 492,000 mph (the "Local Standard of Rest"), which would lead to an orbital period of 237 million years. However, the Sun's actual velocity is 60,400 mph faster than this average, reaching 552,400 mph.

Largest, heaviest and most luminous   The largest star is the M-class supergiant *Betelgeux* (Alpha Orionis—the top left star of Orion), which is 310 light years distant. It has a diameter of 400 million miles, which is about 500 times greater than that of the Sun. In 1978 it was found to be surrounded not only by a dust "shell" but also by an outer tenuous gas halo up to 5.3 × 10^{11} miles in diameter or over 1,100 times the diameter of the star.

The heaviest star is the variable *Eta Carinae*, 9,100 light years distant in the Carinae Nebula, with a mass 200 times greater than that of our own Sun. If all the stars could be viewed at the same distance it would also be the most luminous star, with a total luminosity 6,500,000 times that of the Sun. However, the *visually* brightest star viewed through a telescope is the hypergiant Cygnus OB2 No. 12, which is 5,900 light years distant. It has an absolute visual magnitude of −9.9 and is therefore visually 810,000 times brighter than the Sun. This brightness may be matched by the supergiant IV b 59 in the nearby galaxy Messier 101. During the year 1843 the absolute luminosity and absolute visual brightness of *Eta Carinae* temporarily increased to values 60 and 70 million times the corresponding values for the Sun.

Brightest (as seen from Earth)   Sirius A (*Alpha Canis Majoris*), also known as the Dog Star, is the brightest star of the 5,776 stars visible to the naked eye. It has an apparent magnitude of −1.46 but because of the relative motions of this star and the Sun this should rise to a maximum value of −1.67 in about 61,000 years. *Sirius* is 8.64 light years distant and has a luminosity 26 times greater than that of the Sun. It has a diameter of 1.45 million miles and a mass 2.14 times that of the Sun. The faint white dwarf companion *Sirius B* has a diameter of only 6,000 miles, which is less than that of the Earth, but its mass is slightly greater than that of the Sun. *Sirius* is in the constellation *Canis Major* and is visible in the winter months of the northern hemisphere, being due south at midnight on the last day of the year.

Youngest and oldest   The youngest stars appear to be two protostars known collectively as IRAS – 4 buried deep in dust clouds in the nebula NGC 1333 which is 1100 light years 6.5×10^{15} miles distant. Announced in May 1991 by a combined British, German and American team, these protostars will not blaze forth as fully fledged stars for at least another 100,000 years.

The oldest stars in the galaxy have been detected in the halo, high above the disc of the Milky Way, by a group led by Timothy Beers (USA) that discovered 70 such stars by January 1991 but eventually expect to detect 500. These stars are characterized by having the lowest abundances of heavy elements, whereas later generation stars (such as our own Sun) have higher heavy element abundances because of a build-up of such elements in galaxies from the successive explosions of supernova stars.

Longest star name *Torcularis Septentrionalis* is the name applied to the star *Omicron Piscium* in the constellation *Pisces*.

Smallest, lightest and dimmest star A mass 0.014 that of the Sun is estimated for RG 0058.8-2807, which was discovered by I. Neill Reid and Gerard Gilmore using the UK Schmidt telescope (announced in April 1983). It is also the faintest star detected, with a total luminosity only 0.0021 that of the Sun and an absolute visual magnitude of 20.2, so the visual brightness is less than one millionth that of the Sun. The smallest star appears to be the white dwarf L362-81 with an estimated diameter of 3,500 miles or only 0.0040 that of the Sun.

Pulsars The earliest observation of a pulsating radio source, or "pulsar," CP 1919 (now PSR 1919 + 21), by Dr. Jocelyn Burnell (nee Bell, b. 1943) was announced from the Mullard Radio Astronomy Observatory, Cambridgeshire, Great Britain on 24 Feb. 1968. It had been detected on 28 Nov. 1967.

For pulsars whose spin rates have been accurately measured, the fastest-spinning is PSR 1937 + 214, which was discovered by a group led by Donald C. Backer in November 1982. It is in the minor constellation *Vulpecula* (the Little Fox), 16,000 light years (9.4×10^{16} miles) distant, and has a pulse period of 1.557806449 millisec, which is equivalent to a spin rate of 641.9282573 revolutions per sec. However, the pulsar that has the slowest spin-down rate, and is therefore the most accurate stellar clock is PSR 1855 + 09 (discovered in December 1985) at only 2.1×10^{-20} sec. per sec.

Brightest and latest supernova The brightest supernova ever seen in historic times is believed to be SN 1006, noted in April 1006 near *Beta Lupi*. It flared for two years and attained a magnitude of –9 to –10. The remnant is believed to be the radio source G.327.6 + 14.5, nearly 3,000 light years distant. Others have occurred in 1054, 1604, 1885, and most recently on 23 Feb. 1987, when Ian Shelton sighted the one designated –69°202 in the Large Magellanic Cloud 170,000 light years distant. This supernova was visible to the naked eye when at its brightest in May 1987.

Black holes The concept of super-dense bodies was first proposed by the Marquis de LaPlace (1749–1827). This term for a star that has undergone complete gravitational collapse was first used by John Archibald Wheeler at an Institute for Space Studies meeting in New York City on 29 Dec. 1967.

The first tentative identification of a black hole was announced in December 1972 in the binary-star X-ray source Cygnus X–1.

The best black hole candidate is the central star of the binary (or triple) star system V404, which is 5,000 light years (2.9×10^{16} miles) distant in the constellation Cygnus and which first showed a possible black hole signature as the transient X-ray source GS 2023 + 338 discovered by the Ginga satellite in May 1989. In September 1991 J. Casares, P.A. Charles and T. Naylor firmly established the mass as being greater than six times that of the Sun (and more likely eight to fifteen times) and for the first time obtained a black hole candidate mass unequivocally above the maximum value of five solar masses for a neutron star. The masses of other black hole candidates such as Cygnus X–1 (see above) and AØ620–00 in our galaxy and X–3 in the Large Magellanic Cloud are still so poorly known that their minimum possible values do not rule out the possibility that these objects could be neutron stars. For a black hole weighing ten times the mass of our Sun, light cannot escape (i.e., the point at which the black hole becomes "black") if it is within 18.3 miles of the center (the Schwarzschild or gravitational radius named after the German astronomer Karl Schwarzschild).

Evidence continues to accumulate to suggest that galaxies are powered by super massive black holes at their centers. In the case of our own galaxy there is increasing evidence of a 2 million solar mass black hole in the region of the radio point source Sagittarius A*.

Stellar planets   All claims to have discovered planetary systems around other stars must be treated with caution. There has been confusion with small, dim stellar companions known as "brown dwarfs" that are failed stars since they are too cool to trigger the fusion of hydrogen.

However, detection of variations in the pulse period of pulsar stars is capable of being used to detect planets down to one hundredth the mass of the Earth, but to date claims for discoveries of planets around pulsars remain tentative. Such planets almost certainly could not have survived the violent supernova explosions that lead to the formation of such neutron stars but could have been formed from the debris that exists after such explosions.

Constellations   The largest of the 88 constellations is *Hydra* (the Sea Serpent), which covers 1302.844 deg.^{2} or 6.3 percent of the hemisphere and contains at least 68 stars visible to the naked eye (to 5.5 mag.). The constellation *Centaurus* (Centaur), ranking ninth in area, however, embraces at least 94 such stars.

The smallest constellation is *Crux Australis* (Southern Cross), with an area of only 0.16 percent of the sky, or 68.477 deg.^{2} compared with the 41,252.96 deg.^{2} of the whole sky.

THE SUN

Distance extremes   The true distance of the Earth from the Sun is 1.00000102 astronomical units—the distance from the center of the Earth to the center of the Sun as defined in 1938, equivalent to 92,955,807 miles—or 93 million miles. Our orbit being elliptical, the distance of the Sun varies between a minimum (perihelion) of 91.5 million miles and a maximum (aphelion) of 94.5 million miles. Based on an orbital circumference of 58.4 million miles and an orbital period (sidereal year) of 365.256366 days, the average orbital velocity is 66,620 mph, but this varies between a minimum of 65,520 mph at aphelion and a maximum of 67,750 mph at perihelion.

Temperature and dimensions   The Sun has a stellar classification of a yellow dwarf type G2, although its mass at 2 octillion tons is 332,946.04 times that of the Earth and represents over 99 percent of the total mass of the Solar System. The solar diameter at 865,040 miles leads to a density of 1.408 times that of water or a quarter that of the Earth.

The Sun has a central temperature of about 15,400,000 K (Kelvins) and a core pressure of 1.65 million tons/in.^{2}. It uses up about 4.4 million tons of hydrogen per sec., equal to an energy output of 3.85×10^{26} watts, although it will have taken 10 billion years to exhaust its energy supply (about 5 billion years from the present). The luminous intensity of the Sun is 2.7 octillion candela, which is equal to a luminance of 290,000 candela/in.^{2}.

Sunspots   To be visible to the *protected* naked eye, a sunspot must cover about 1/2,000th part of the Sun's disc and thus have an area of about 0.5 billion miles^2. The largest sunspot ever noted was in the Sun's southern hemisphere on 8 Apr. 1947. Its area was about 7 billion miles^2 with an extreme longitude of 187,000 miles and an extreme latitude of 90,000 miles. Sunspots appear darker because they are more than 2,700° F. cooler than the rest of the Sun's surface temperature of 9,945° F.

In October 1957 a smoothed sunspot count showed 263, the highest recorded index since records started in 1755. In 1943 one sunspot lasted for 200 days, from June to December.

PLANETS

Largest   The nine major planets (including the Earth) are bodies within the Solar System and revolve round the Sun in definite orbits.

Jupiter, with an equatorial diameter of 88,846 miles and a polar diameter of 83,082 miles, is the largest of the nine major planets, with a mass 317.828 times, and a volume 1,323.3 times, that of the Earth. It also has the shortest period of rotation, resulting in a Jovian day of only 9 hrs. 50 min. 30.003 sec. in the equatorial zone.

Smallest, coldest and outermost   Pluto was first recorded by Clyde William Tombaugh (b. 4 Feb. 1906) at Lowell Observatory, Flagstaff, AZ on 18 Feb. 1930 from photographs he took on 23 and 29 January. His find was announced on 13 March.

The discovery of Pluto's companion Charon was announced on 22 June 1978 from the US Naval Observatory, Flagstaff, AZ. Pluto, with a mass about 1/500th of that of the Earth, has a diameter of 1,429 miles, while Charon has a diameter of 737 miles. Their mean distance from the Sun is 3,674,488,000 miles, with a period of revolution of 248.54 years. Because of their orbital eccentricity they are temporarily closer to the Sun than Neptune in the period from 23 Jan. 1979 to 15 Mar. 1999. The lowest observed surface temperature of any natural body in the Solar System is −391° F. in the case of Neptune's large moon *Triton*, although a refined surface temperature of Pluto and Charon remains to be measured.

Fastest   Mercury, which orbits the Sun at an average distance of 35,983,100 miles, has a period of revolution of 87.9686 days, so giving the highest average speed in orbit of 107,030 mph.

Hottest   For Venus a surface temperature of 864° F. has been estimated from measurements made from the Russia *Venera* and US *Pioneer* surface probes.

HOTTEST PLANET. Venus, the second closest planet to the Sun after Mercury, has an estimated surface temperature of 864° F., based on measurements made from the Russian *Venera* and US *Pioneer* surface probes. (Photo: NASA)

Nearest planet   The fellow planet closest to the Earth is Venus, which is, at times, only 26 million miles inside the Earth's orbit, compared with Mars' closest approach of 35 million miles outside the Earth's orbit. Mars, known since 1965 to be cratered, has temperatures ranging from 85° F to –190° F.

Densest and least dense planet   Earth is the densest planet, with an average density 5.515 times that of water, while Saturn has an average density only about one-eighth of this value or 0.685 times that of water.

Surface features   By far the highest and most spectacular is *Olympus Mons* (formerly *Nix Olympica*) in the Tharsis region of Mars, with a diameter of 310–370 miles and a height of 75,450–95,150 ft. above the surrounding plain.

Venus has a canyon some 1,000 miles south of the Venusian equator that is 21,000 ft. deep and 250 miles long.

The ice cliff on the Uranian moon Miranda is 3.23 miles high.

Brightest and faintest   Viewed from the Earth, by far the brightest of the five planets visible to the naked eye is Venus, with a maximum magnitude of –4.4. Uranus, the first to be discovered by telescope when it was sighted by Sir William Herschel (Great Britain) from his garden at 19 New King St., Bath, Great Britain on 13 Mar. 1781, is only marginally visible, with a magnitude of 5.5.

The faintest planet is Pluto, with a magnitude of 15.0.

Conjunctions   The most dramatic recorded conjunction (coming together) of the other seven principal members of the Solar System (Sun, Moon, Mercury, Venus, Mars, Jupiter and Saturn) occurred on 5 Feb. 1962, when 16° covered all seven during an eclipse in the Pacific area. It is possible that the sevenfold conjunction that occurred in September 1186 spanned only 12°. The next notable conjunction will take place on 5 May 2000.

SATELLITES

Most and least   The Solar System has a total of 61 satellites, with Saturn having the most at 18 while Earth and Pluto have only one satellite each and Mercury and Venus none. The most recently discovered, announced on 16 July 1990 by Mark R. Showalter (USA), is the Saturnian satellite Pan (Saturn XVII) temporarily designated 1981 S13, which was found on eleven *Voyager 2* photographs taken during the close approach in August 1981. It has a diameter of only about 12 miles and orbits within the 200-mile Encke gap in the A ring. E.A. Marouf and G.L. Tyler have predicted the existence of two further Saturnian satellites in the Cassini Division between the A and B rings.

Largest and smallest   The largest and heaviest satellite is *Ganymede* (Jupiter III), which is 2.017 times heavier than the Earth's Moon and has a diameter of 3,273 miles. Of satellites whose diameters have been measured the smallest is *Deimos*, the outermost moon of Mars. Although irregularly shaped, it has an average diameter of 7.8 miles. The diameter of *Leda* (Jupiter XIII) is estimated to be less than 9 miles.

Distance extremes of satellites   The distance of satellites from their parent planets varies from the 5,827 miles of *Phobos* from the center of Mars to the 14,700,000 miles of Jupiter's outer satellite *Sinope* (*Jupiter IX*).

ASTEROIDS

Number and distance extremes   There are estimated to be about 45,000 asteroids, but the orbits of only about 5,300 have been accurately computed. While most orbit between Mars and Jupiter, average distances from the Sun vary between 72,200,000 miles (just outside of Venus's orbit) for the Aten asteroid 1954XA (discovered 5 Dec. 1954 but currently lost) and 1,902 million miles (just outside of Uranus' orbit) for 1992AD (discovered 9 Jan. 1992).

Because of the asteroids' large orbital eccentricities the closest approach to the Sun is by the Apollo asteroid Phaethon (discovered 11 Oct. 1983) to within 12,980,000 miles at perihelion, while the farthest distance is achieved by 1992AD (see above), which reaches to 2,997 million miles from the Sun at aphelion (beyond the orbit of Neptune). The closest known approach to the Earth by an asteroid was to within 105,600 miles on 18 Jan. 1991 by 1991BA (the day after its discovery).

Largest and smallest   The largest and first discovered (by G. Piazzi in Palermo, Sicily on 1 Jan. 1801) is 1 *Ceres*, with a diameter of 582 miles. The smallest asteroid is 1991BA (see above) with a diameter of 30 ft. The only asteroid visible to the naked eye is 4 *Vesta* (discovered 29 Mar. 1807), which is 323 miles in diameter and has a maximum apparent magnitude as viewed from the Earth of 5.0.

THE MOON

The Earth's closest neighbor in space and its only natural satellite is the Moon, which has an average diameter of 2,159.3 miles and a mass of 8.1×10^{19} tons, or 0.0123 that of the Earth, so its density is 3.344 times that of water.

The Moon orbits at a mean distance from the Earth of 238,854.5 miles center-to-center, although the center of mass is displaced from the center of figure by 1.1 miles toward the Earth so that the distance surface-to-surface is 233,813 miles. In the present century the closest approach (smallest perigee) was 221,441 miles center-to-center on 4 Jan. 1912 and the farthest distance (largest apogee) was 252,718 miles on 2 Mar. 1984. The orbital period (sidereal month) is 27.321661 days, giving an average orbital velocity of 2,289 mph.

The currently accepted "giant impact" theory of lunar origin suggests that the Moon was formed just outside the Earth's Roche Limit (about 11,500 miles from the Earth's center) from the debris resulting from a glancing collision between the Earth and a Mars-size planetesimal. That this event must have occurred in the early history of the Solar System is indicated by the fact that the oldest lunar rocks and soils brought back to Earth by the Apollo program crews are of a similar age to the oldest known meteorites (about 4.5 billion years).

The first direct hit on the Moon was achieved at 2 min. 24 sec. after midnight (Moscow time) on 14 Sep. 1959, by the Soviet space probe *Lunar II* near the *Mare Serenitatis*. The first photographic images of the hidden side of the Moon were collected by the USSR *Lunar III* from 6:30 A.M. on 7 Oct. 1959 from a range of up to 43,750 miles, and transmitted to the Earth from a distance of 292,000 miles.

Craters   Only 59 percent of the Moon's surface is directly visible from

THE MOON. The Earth's closest neighbor in space and its only natural satellite is the Moon. These images were obtained by the Galileo spacecraft in December 1990. On the right, the near side of the Moon and about 30 degrees of the far side (left edge) are visible. In the full disk on the left a little less than half the far side (to the right) can be seen. (Photo: NASA)

the Earth because it is in "captured rotation," i.e., the period of rotation is equal to the period of orbit. The largest wholly visible crater is the walled plain Bailly, toward the Moon's South Pole, which is 183 miles across, with walls rising to 14,000 ft. The Orientale Basin, partly on the averted side, measures more than 600 miles in diameter.

The deepest crater is the Newton Crater, with a floor estimated to be between 23,000 and 29,000 ft. below its rim and 14,000 ft. below the level of the plain outside. The brightest (most reflective) directly visible spot on the Moon is Aristarchus.

Highest mountains In the absence of a sea level, lunar altitudes are measured relative to an adopted reference sphere with a radius of 1,080 miles. The greatest elevation attained on this basis by any of the 12 US astronauts who have landed on the moon has been 25,688 ft. on the Descartes Highlands by Capt. John Watts Young (USN) and Major Charles M. Duke, Jr. on 27 Apr. 1972.

Temperature extremes When the Sun is overhead the temperature on the lunar equator reaches 243° F. (31° F. above the boiling point of water). By sunset the temperature is 58° F., but after nightfall it sinks to −261° F.

ECLIPSES

Earliest recorded For the Middle East, lunar eclipses have been extrapolated to 3450 B.C. and solar ones to 4200 B.C.

The oldest record of a total solar eclipse is on a clay tablet found in 1948 among the ruins of the ancient city of Ugarit (now in Syria). A reassessment in 1989 suggests that this records the eclipse of 5 Mar. 1223 B.C.

Longest duration   The maximum *possible* duration of an eclipse of the Sun is 7 min. 31 sec. The longest actually *measured* was on 20 June 1955 (7 min. 8 sec.), seen from the Philippines. An eclipse of 7 min. 29 sec. should occur in the mid-Atlantic Ocean on 16 July 2186.

Most and least frequent   The highest number of eclipses possible in a year is seven, as in 1935, when there were five solar and two lunar eclipses. In 1982 there were four solar and three lunar eclipses.
   The lowest possible number in a year is two, both of which must be solar, as in 1944 and 1969.

Eclipses   Although normally the maximum possible duration of an eclipse of the Sun is 7 min. 31 sec., durations can be "extended" when observers are airborne. On 30 June 1973, for example, an eclipse was "extended" to 72 min. aboard a Concorde.

AURORAE

Most frequent   Polar lights, known since 1560 as aurora borealis or northern lights in the northern hemisphere, and since 1773 as aurora australis in the southern, are caused by electrical solar discharges in the upper atmosphere and occur most frequently in high latitudes. Aurorae are visible at some time on *every* clear dark night in the polar areas within 20 degrees of the magnetic poles. The extreme height of aurorae has been measured at 620 miles, while the lowest may descend to 45 miles.

Lowest latitudes   Extreme cases of displays in very low latitudes were recorded at Cuzco, Peru (2 Aug. 1744), Honolulu, HI (1 Sep. 1859), and questionably Singapore (25 Sep. 1909).

Noctilucent clouds   These remain sunlit long after sunset because of their great altitude, and are thought to consist of ice crystals or meteoric dust. Regular observations (at heights of *c.* 52 miles) in Western Europe date only from 1964; since that year the record high and low number of nights on which these phenomena have been observed have been 43 (1979) and 15 (1970).

COMETS

Earliest recorded   Records date from the 7th century B.C. The speeds of the estimated 2 million comets vary from 700 mph in outer space to 1.25 million mph when near the Sun. The successive appearances of Halley's Comet have been traced back to 467 B.C. It was first depicted in the Nuremberg Chronicle of A.D. 684.
   The first prediction of its return by Edmund Halley (1656–1742) proved true on Christmas Day 1758, 16 years after his death. On 13–14 Mar. 1986, the European satellite *Giotto* (launched 2 July 1985) penetrated to within 335 miles of the nucleus of Halley's Comet. It was established that the core was 9 miles in length and velvet black in color.

EARLIEST RECORDED COMETS. Records of comets date from the 7th century B.C. The first comet whose return was predicted was Halley's Comet. Its successive appearances have been traced back to 467 B.C. It most recently appeared in 1986, with this shot being taken from New Zealand. The Moon is behind the cloud at the bottom right. (Photo: Science Photo Library)

Closest approach   On 1 July 1770, Lexell's Comet, traveling at a speed of 86,100 mph (relative to the Sun), came within 745,000 miles of the Earth. However, more recently the Earth is believed to have passed through the tail of Halley's Comet on 19 May 1910.

Largest   The tail of the brightest of all comets, the Great Comet of 1843, trailed for 205,000,000 miles. The bow shock wave of Holmes Comet of 1892 once measured 1.5 million miles in diameter.

Shortest period   Of all the recorded periodic comets (that are members of the Solar System), the one that returns most frequently is Encke's Comet, first identified in 1786. Its period of 1,206 days (3.3 years) is the shortest established. Only one of its 53 returns has been missed by astronomers; that was in 1944. Now increasingly faint, it is expected to die by February 1994.

The most frequently observed comets are Schwassmann-Wachmann I, Kopff and Oterma, which can all be observed every year between Mars and Jupiter.

Longest period   At the other extreme is Delavan's Comet of 1914, whose path was not accurately determined. It is not expected to return for perhaps 24 million years.

METEOROIDS

Meteoroids are of cometary or asteroidal origin. A meteor is the light phenomenon caused by the entry of a meteoroid into the Earth's atmosphere.

Meteor "shower" The greatest shower on record occurred on the night of 16–17 Nov. 1966, when the Leonid meteors (which recur every 33¼ years) were visible between western North America and eastern Russia. It was calculated that meteors passed over Arizona at a rate of 2,300 per min. for a period of 20 min. from 5 A.M. on 17 Nov. 1966.

METEORITES

Meteorites When a *meteoroid* (consisting of broken fragments of cometary or asteroidal origin and ranging in size from fine dust to bodies several miles in diameter) penetrates to the Earth's surface, the remnant, which may be either aerolite (stony) or siderite (metallic), is described as a *meteorite*. Such events occur about 150 times per year over the whole land surface of the Earth.

The most anxious time of day for meteorophobes should be 3 P.M. In historic times, the only recorded person injured by a meteorite was Mrs. Ann Hodges of Sylacauga, AL. On 30 Nov. 1954 a 9-lb. stone, some 7 in. in length, crashed through the roof of her home, hitting Mrs. Hodges on the arm and bruising her hip. The physician who examined her, Dr. Moody D. Jacobs, declared her fit but she was subsequently hospitalized as a result of the publicity.

Oldest A revision by T. Kirsten in 1981 of the age estimates of meteorites that have remained essentially undisturbed after their formation suggests that the oldest accurately dated is the Krahenberg meteorite at 4600 ± 20 million years, which predates the Solar System by about 70 million years.

It was reported in August 1978 that dust grains in the Murchison meteorite, which fell in Australia in September 1969, may also be older than the Solar System.

Largest There was a mysterious explosion of 12½ megatons at Lat. 60° 55′N, Long. 101° 57′E, in the basin of the Podkamennaya Tunguska River, 40 miles north of Vanavar, in Siberia, Russia, at 00 hrs. 17 min. 11 sec. UT (Universal Time) on 30 June 1908. The cause was variously attributed to a meteorite (1927), a comet (1930), a nuclear explosion (1961), and antimatter (1965). The explosion devastated an area of about 1,500 miles[2] and the shock was felt as far away as 600 miles. The theory now favored is that it was the terminal flare of stony debris from a comet, possibly Encke's comet, at an altitude of 20,000 ft. or less.

A stony meteorite with a diameter of 6.2 miles striking the Earth at 55,925 mph would generate an explosive energy equivalent to 100 million megatons. Such events should not be expected to recur more than once in 75 million years.

The largest known meteorite was found in 1920 at Hoba West, near Grootfontein in Namibia, and is a block 9 ft. long by 8 ft. wide, estimated to weigh 65 tons. The largest meteorite exhibited by any museum is the "Tent" meteorite, weighing 68,085 lbs., found in 1897 near Cape York, on the west coast of Greenland, by the expedition of Commander Robert Edwin Peary (USA; 1856–1920). It was known to the Inuits as the Abnighito and is now exhibited in the Hayden Planetarium in New York City. The largest piece of stony meteorite recovered is a piece weighing 3,902 lbs., part of a 4.4-ton shower that struck Jilin (formerly Kirin), China on 8 Mar. 1976.

Lunar Twelve known meteorites are believed to be of lunar origin as distinguished by characteristic element and isotopic ratios. The first 11 were found in Antarctica but the most recently discovered, which has only a 1 in. diameter and weighs 0.67 oz., was found at Calcalong Creek on the Nullarbor Plain to the north of the Great Australian Bight by D.H. Hill, W.V. Boynton and R.A. Haag (USA), with the discovery being announced in January 1991. The name "Calcalong" is a corruption of the Aboriginal word meaning "seven sisters went up to the sky, chased by the moon."

Tektites The largest tektite (a class of small natural glassy objects of uncertain origin found only in certain areas of the Earth's surface) of which details have been published weighed 7 lbs. and was found in 1932 at Muong Nong, Saravane Province, Laos. It is now in the Louvre Museum, Paris, France. Eight SNC meteorites (named after their find sites at Shergotty in India, Nakla in Egypt and Chassigny in France) are believed to have emanated from Mars.

Fireball The brightest fireball ever photographically recorded was by Dr. Zdenek Ceplecha over Sumava, Czechoslovakia on 4 Dec. 1974; it had a momentary magnitude of −22 or 10,000 times brighter than a full Moon.

Remotest spot from land The world's most distant point from land is a spot in the South Pacific, approximately 48° 30′ S, 125° 30′ W, which is about 1,660 miles from the nearest points of land, namely Pitcairn Island, Ducie Island and Cape Dart, Antarctica. Centered on this spot is a circle of water with an area of about 8,657,000 miles² — about 2 million miles² larger than Russia, the world's largest country.

Craters It has been estimated that some 2,000 asteroid–Earth collisions have occurred in the last 600 million years. One hundred and two collision sites or astroblemes have been identified.

In 1962, a crater 150 miles in diameter and ½ mile deep in Wilkes Land, Antarctica was attributed to a meteorite. Such a crater could have been caused by a meteorite weighing 14,329,900,000 tons striking at 44,000 mph. Soviet scientists reported in December 1970 an astrobleme with a diameter of 60 miles and a maximum depth of 1,300 ft. in the basin of the River Popigai.

There is a crater-like formation or astrobleme 275 miles in diameter on the eastern shore of Hudson Bay, Canada, where the Nastapoka Islands are just off the coast.

One of the largest and best-preserved craters is the Coon Butte or Barringer Crater, discovered in 1891 near Canyon Diablo, Winslow, AZ. It is 4,150 ft. in diameter and now about 575 ft. deep, with a parapet rising 130–155 ft. above the surrounding plain. It has been estimated that an iron-nickel mass of some 2,204,600 tons and a diameter of 200–260 ft. gouged this crater in c. 25,000 B.C.

Evidence was published in 1963 discounting a meteoric origin for the crypto-volcanic Vredefort Ring (diameter 26 miles), to the southwest of Johannesburg, South Africa, but this has now been reasserted. The New Quebec (formerly the Chubb) Crater, first sighted on 20 June 1943 in northern Ungava, Canada, is 1,325 ft. deep and measures 6.8 miles around its rim.

THE EARTH

The Earth is approximately 4,500 million years old. It is not a true sphere, but is flattened at the poles and hence an oblate spheroid. The polar diameter of the Earth, 7,899.806 miles, is 26.575 miles less than the equatorial diameter (7,926.381 miles). The Earth has a pear-shaped asymmetry, with the north polar radius being 148 ft. longer than the south polar radius. There is also a slight ellipticity of the equator, since its long axis (about longitude 37° W) is 522 ft. greater than its short axis. The greatest departures from the reference ellipsoid are a protuberance of 240 ft. in the area of Papua New Guinea and a depression of 344 ft. south of Sri Lanka, in the Indian Ocean.

The greatest circumference of the Earth, at the equator, is 24,901.46 miles, compared with 24,859.73 miles at the meridian. The area of the surface is estimated to be 196,937,400 miles². The period of axial rotation, i.e., the true sidereal day, is 23 hrs. 56 min. 4.0996 sec., mean time.

The mass of the Earth was first assessed by Dr. Nevil Maskelyne (1732–1811) in Perthshire, Great Britain in 1774. The modern value is 6.6 sextillion tons and its density is 5.515 times that of water. The volume is an estimated 0.26 trillion miles³. The Earth picks up cosmic dust, but estimates of the amount vary widely, with 36,375,000 tons a year being the upper limit.

Modern theory is that the Earth has an outer shell or lithosphere 50 miles thick. The outermost part of this lithosphere forms the crust which is some 22 miles thicker beneath continents than beneath oceans (around 6¼ miles). The lithospheric crust and outer mantle ride on the asthenosphere, which extends to a depth of some 155 miles. Below this the mantle continues to a depth of 1,745 miles, where it gives way to an iron-rich core with a radius of 2,160 miles. If the iron-rich core theory is correct, iron would be the most abundant element in the Earth. At the center of the core, the estimated density is 0.4729 lb./in.³, the temperature 8,132° F. and the pressure 364 GPa or 26,432 tons f./in.².

STRUCTURE AND DIMENSIONS

OCEANS

The area of the Earth covered by water (the hydrosphere) is estimated to be 139,781,000 miles² or 70.98 percent of the total surface. The mean depth of the hydrosphere was once estimated to be 12,450 ft., but recent surveys suggest a lower estimate of 11,660 ft. The total weight of the water is estimated to be 1.45 quintillion tons, or 0.022 percent of the Earth's total weight. The volume of the oceans is estimated to be 323.9 million miles³ compared to 8.4 million miles³ of fresh water.

**LARGEST GULF. The Gulf of Mexico has an area of 596,000 miles²
and a shoreline of 3,100 miles, the Gulf Stream being the main
current moving oceanic waters into and out of it. The continent
of North America and the Gulf are clearly visible in this satellite
image. (Photo: Science Photo Library)**

Largest   The largest ocean in the world is the Pacific. Excluding adjacent
seas, it represents 45.9 percent of the world's oceans and covers 64.2 million miles² in area. The average depth is 13,740 ft.

The shortest navigable transpacific distance, from Guayaquil, Ecuador to
Bangkok, Thailand, is 10,905 miles.

Deepest   The deepest part of the ocean was first pinpointed in 1951 by the
British Survey Ship *Challenger* in the Mariana Trench in the Pacific Ocean.
The depth was measured by wide-band sounding at 35,639 ft. Subsequent
visits have resulted in slightly deeper measurements. A survey by the Soviet
research ship *Vityaz* in 1957 produced a depth that was later refined to 36,200
ft., and on 23 Jan. 1960 the US Navy bathyscaphe *Trieste* descended to the
bottom at 35,813 ft. A more recent visit produced a figure of 35,839 ft. ± 33
ft., from data obtained by the survey vessel *Takuyo* of the Hydrographic Department, Japan Maritime Safety Agency in 1984, using a narrow multi-beam
echo sounder.

A metal object, for example, a 2.2-lb. ball of steel, dropped into water
above this trench would take nearly 64 min. to fall to the seabed, where hy-
drostatic pressure is over 18,000 lbs./in.².

United States   Defining US waters as within 200 nautical miles of any US
territory (Economic Exclusive Zone [EEZ]), the deepest point in American
waters is Challenger D in the Mariana Trench in the Pacific Ocean. Challenger D is 5,973 fathoms (35,838 ft.) deep, 170 nautical miles SW of Guam
at 11° 22.4 N, 142° 35.5 E.

The deepest point from an American state is the Vega Basin in the Aleutian Trench, which is 4,198 fathoms (25,188 ft.) deep at 50° 51 N, 177° 11 E, 60 nautical miles south of the Aleutian Islands, AK.

Largest sea   The largest of the world's seas is the South China Sea, with an area of 1.1 million miles².

Largest bay   The largest bay in the world measured by shoreline length is Hudson Bay, northern Canada, with a shoreline of 7,623 miles and an area of 476,000 miles². The area of the Bay of Bengal, in the Indian Ocean, is larger, at 839,000 miles².

Largest gulf   The largest gulf in the world is the Gulf of Mexico, with an area of 596,000 miles² and a shoreline of 3,100 miles from Cape Sable, FL, to Cabo Catoche, Mexico.

Longest fjord   The world's longest fjord is the Nordvest Fjord arm of the Scoresby Sound in eastern Greenland, which extends inland 195 miles from the sea.

Highest seamount   The highest known submarine mountain, or seamount, is one discovered in 1953 near the Tonga Trench, between Samoa and New Zealand in the South Pacific. It rises 28,500 ft. from the seabed, with its summit 1,200 ft. below the surface.

Most southerly   The most southerly part of the oceans is located at 85° 34' S, 154° W, at the snout of the Robert Scott Glacier, 305 miles from the South Pole.

Sea temperature   The temperature of water at the surface of the Earth's seas varies greatly. It is as low as 28° F. in the White Sea and as high as 96° F. in the shallow areas of the Persian Gulf in summer.

The highest temperature recorded in the ocean is 759° F., for a hot spring measured by an American research submarine some 300 miles off the west coast of the United States, in an expedition under the direction of Prof. Jack Diamond of Oregon State University in 1985. Remote probes measured the temperature of the spring, which was only kept from vaporizing by the weight of water above it.

Clearest   The Weddell Sea, 71° S, 15° W off Antarctica, has the clearest water of any sea. A Secchi disc was visible to a depth of 262 ft. on 13 Oct. 1986, as measured by Dutch researchers at the German Alfred Wegener Institute. Such clarity corresponds to what is attainable in distilled water.

STRAITS

Longest   The longest straits in the world are the Tatarskiy Proliv or Tartar Straits between Sakhalin Island and the Russian mainland, running from the Sea of Japan to Sakhalinsky Zaliv—500 miles, thus marginally longer than the Malacca Straits, between Malaysia and Sumatra.

Broadest   The broadest *named* straits in the world are the Davis Straits between Greenland and Baffin Island, Canada, with a minimum width of 210 miles. The Drake Passage, a deep waterway between the Diego Ramirez Islands, Chile and the South Shetland Islands, is 710 miles across.

Narrowest The narrowest navigable straits are those between the Aegean island of Euboea and the mainland of Greece. The gap is only 131 ft. wide at Khalkis.

WAVES

Highest The highest officially recorded sea wave was calculated at 112 ft. from trough to crest; it was measured by Lt. Frederic Margraff, USN from the USS *Ramapo* proceeding from Manila, Philippines to San Diego, CA on the night of 6–7 Feb. 1933, during a 68-knot hurricane. The highest instrumentally measured wave was one 86 ft. high, recorded by the British ship *Weather Reporter*, in the North Atlantic on 30 Dec. 1972 at Lat. 59° N, Long. 19° W. It has been calculated on the statistics of the Stationary Random Theory that one wave in more than 300,000 may exceed the average by a factor of four. On 9 July 1958 a landslip caused a 100 mph wave to wash 1,720 ft. high along the fjord-like Lituya Bay in Alaska.

Highest seismic The highest estimated height of a *tsunami* (often wrongly called a tidal wave) was one of 1,180 ft., which struck the northern Shetland Isles *c.* 4950 B.C. at 110 mph. It was generated by a massive undersea landslip from the Storegga area of the South Norwegian Sea involving 430 miles^2 of mud and rock. The highest known in modern times appeared off Ishigaki Island, Ryukyu Chain on 24 Apr. 1771. It tossed a 826.7-ton block of coral more than 1.3 miles. Tsunami (a Japanese word: *nami*, a wave; *tsu*, overflowing) have been observed to travel at 490 mph, and are usually caused by a submarine earthquake.

CURRENTS

Greatest The greatest current in the oceans is the Antarctic Circumpolar Current or West Wind Drift Current. On the basis of four measurements taken in 1982 in the Drake Passage, between South America and Antarctica, it was found to be flowing at a rate of 4.3 billion ft.^{3} per sec. Results from computer modeling in 1990 estimate a higher figure of 6.9 billion ft.^{3} per sec. Its width ranges from 185–1,240 miles and it has a proven surface flow rate of $^4/_{10}$ of a knot.

Strongest The world's strongest currents are the Nakwakto Rapids, Slingsby Channel, British Columbia, Canada (Lat. 51° 05′ N, Long. 127° 30′ W), where the flow rate may reach 16 knots.

TIDES

Extreme tides are due to lunar and solar gravitational forces affected by their perigee, perihelion and syzygies. Barometric and wind effects can superimpose an added "surge" element. Coastal and sea-floor configurations can accentuate these forces. The normal interval between tides is 12 hrs. 25 min.

Greatest The greatest tides occur in the Bay of Fundy, which divides the peninsula of Nova Scotia, Canada from Maine and the Canadian province of New Brunswick. Burncoat Head in the Minas Basin, Nova Scotia, has the greatest mean spring range, with 47 ft. 6 in. A range of 54 ft. 6 in. was recorded at springs in Leaf Basin, in Ungava Bay, Quebec, Canada in 1953.

Least   Tahiti, in the mid-Pacific Ocean, experiences virtually no tide.

ICEBERGS

Largest   The largest iceberg on record was an antarctic tabular iceberg of over 12,000 miles², 208 miles long and 60 miles wide, sighted 150 miles west of Scott Island, in the South Pacific Ocean, by the USS *Glacier* on 12 Nov. 1956. The 200 ft. thick arctic ice island T.1 (140 miles²), discovered in 1946, was tracked for 17 years.

Tallest   The tallest iceberg measured was one of 550 ft. reported off western Greenland by the US icebreaker *East Wind* in 1958.

Most southerly arctic   The most southerly arctic iceberg was sighted in the Atlantic by a USN weather patrol at Lat. 28° 44′ N, Long. 48° 42′ W, in April 1935.

Most northerly antarctic   The most northerly antarctic iceberg was a remnant sighted in the Atlantic by the ship *Dochra* at Lat. 26° 30′ S, Long. 25° 40′ W, on 30 Apr. 1894.

LAND

There is satisfactory evidence that at one time the Earth's land surface comprised a single primeval continent of 80 million miles², now termed Pangaea, and that this split about 190 million years ago, during the Jurassic period, into two supercontinents, which are called Laurasia (Eurasia, Greenland and North America) and Gondwana (Africa, Arabia, India, South America, Oceania and Antarctica), named after Gondwana, India, which itself split 120 million years ago. The South Pole was apparently in the area of the Sahara as recently as the Ordovician period of *c*. 450 million years ago. Consequently the Sahara, now one of the hottest areas of the world, was at one time the coldest.

United States   On 18 Dec. 1991 the Census Bureau reported that the total land area of the United States is 3,787,425 miles².

Largest state   The largest state in land area is Alaska, with 591,004 miles². The largest in the 48 coterminous states is Texas, with 267,017 miles² of land.

Land remotest from the sea   The point of land remotest from the sea is at Lat. 46° 16.8′ N, Long. 86° 40.2′ E in the Dzungarian Basin, which is in the Xinjiang Uighur Autonomous Region (Xinjiang Uygur Zu zhi ju), China's most northwesterly province. It is at a straight-line distance of 1,645 miles from the nearest open sea—Baydaratskaya Guba to the north (Arctic Ocean), Feni Point to the south (Indian Ocean) and Bo Haiwan to the east (Yellow Sea).

UNITED STATES EXTREME POINTS

Geographic Center	Butte County, SD (west of Castle Rock)
(50 states)	Lat. 44° 58′ N, Long. 103° 46′ W
Geographic Center	Smith County, KS (near Lebanon)
(48 coterminous states)	Lat. 39° 50′ N, Long. 98° 35′ W
Northernmost Point	Point Barrow, AK
	Lat. 71° 23′ N, Long. 156° 29′ W
Easternmost Point	West Quoddy Head, ME
	Lat. 44° 49′ N, Long. 66° 57′ W
Southernmost Point	Ka Lae (South Cape), HI
	Lat. 18° 55′ N, Long. 155° 41′ W
Westernmost Point	Pochnoi, AK (Semisopochonoi Island)
	Lat. 51° 17′ N, Long. 172° 09′ E

Smallest state   The smallest state is Rhode Island, with 1,212 miles^2.

Coastline   According to the measurements of the National Oceanic and Atmospheric Administration (NOAA), the entire coastline of the United States, including Hawaii, Alaska and the Great Lakes states, is 94,112 miles. Excluding Hawaii and Alaska, the coastline equals 59,156 miles. The state with the longest coastline is Alaska; it measures ±3,904 miles.

ROCKS

The age of the Earth is generally considered to be within the range of 4,500 ± 70 million years, based on the lead isotope systematics. However, no rocks of this great age have yet been found on the Earth since geological processes have presumably destroyed them.

Oldest   The greatest reported age for any scientifically dated rock is 3,962 million years in the case of the Acasta Gneisses, found in May 1984. The rocks were discovered approximately 200 miles north of Yellowknife, Northwest Territories, Canada by Dr. Samuel Bowring as part of an ongoing Canadian geology survey mapping project. When the samples were analyzed in June 1989, Dr. Bowring and scientists from the Australian National University in Canberra established their age, using a machine called SHRIMP (Sensitive High-mass Resolution Ion MicroProbe).

Older minerals that are not rocks have also been identified. Some zircon crystals discovered by Bob Pidgeon and Simon Wilde in the Jack Hills, 430 miles north of Perth, Western Australia in August 1984 were found to be 4,276 million years old, again using SHRIMP. These are the oldest fragments of the Earth's crust discovered so far.

United States   The oldest rocks in the United States are the Morton Gneisses, found in 1935 by G.A. Phiel and C.E. Dutton scattered over an area of 50 miles from New Ulm, Brown Co. to Renville Co. in Minnesota. In 1980 these rocks were dated at 3.6 billion years by Sam Goldrich of the US Geological Survey in Denver, CO, using the uranium-lead dating method.

Largest   The largest exposed monolith in the world is Ayers Rock, which rises 1,143 ft. above the surrounding desert plain in Northern Territory, Australia. It is 1.5 miles long and 1 mile wide. The nearest major town is Alice Springs, which is 250 miles to the northeast.

It was estimated in 1940 that La Gran Piedra, a volcanic plug located in the Sierra Maestra, Cuba, weighs 67,632 tons.

CONTINENTS

Largest   Of the Earth's surface, 41.25 percent, or 81.2 million miles², is covered by continental masses of which only about 57,151,000 miles² (about two-thirds, or 29.02 percent of the Earth's surface) is land above water, with a mean height of 2,480 ft. above sea level. The Eurasian landmass is the largest, with an area (including islands) of 20.7 million miles². The Afro-Eurasian landmass, separated artificially only by the Suez Canal, covers an area of 32.7 million miles² or 57.2 percent of the Earth's landmass.

Smallest   The smallest continent is the Australian mainland, with an area of 2,941,526 miles², which, together with Tasmania, New Zealand, Papua New Guinea and the Pacific Islands, is sometimes described as Oceania.

Peninsula   The world's largest peninsula is Arabia, with an area of about 1.25 million miles².

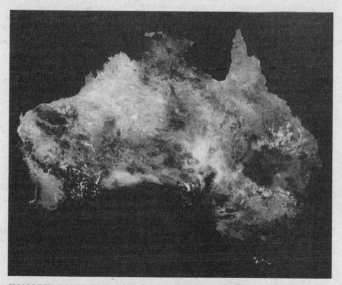

SMALLEST CONTINENT. The smallest continent is the Australian mainland, with an area of 2,941,526 miles². This satellite picture is a mosaic of images made by Advanced Very High Resolution Radiometer equipment. (Photo: Science Photo Library)

ISLANDS

Largest   Discounting Australia, which is usually regarded as a continental landmass, the largest island in the world is Greenland, with an area of about 840,000 miles^2. There is evidence that Greenland is in fact several islands overlaid by an ice cap, without which it would have an area of 650,000 miles^2.

The largest sand island in the world is Fraser Island, Queensland, Australia with a sand dune 75 miles long.

The largest island in North America is Newfoundland, Canada, with an area of 42,030 miles^2.

Freshwater   The largest island surrounded mostly by fresh water (18,500 miles^2) is the Ilha de Marajó in the mouth of the River Amazon, Brazil.

The world's largest inland island (i.e., land surrounded by rivers) is Ilha do Bananal, Brazil (7,000 miles^2). The largest island in a lake is Manitoulin Island (1,068 miles^2) in the Canadian section of Lake Huron.

Remotest   The remotest island in the world is Bouvet Island (Bouvetøya), discovered in the South Atlantic by J. B. C. Bouvet de Lozier on 1 Jan. 1739, and first landed on by Capt. George Norris on 16 Dec. 1825. Its position is 54° 26′ S, 3° 24′ E. This uninhabited Norwegian dependency is about 1,050 miles from the nearest land—the uninhabited Queen Maud Land coast of eastern Antarctica.

The remotest inhabited island in the world is Tristan da Cunha, discovered in the South Atlantic by Tristão da Cunha, a Portuguese admiral, in March 1506. It has an area of 38 miles^2. The first permanent inhabitant was Thomas Currie, who landed in 1810. The island was annexed by Great Britain on 14 Aug. 1816. After evacuation in 1961 (due to volcanic activity), 198 islanders returned in November 1963. The nearest inhabited land to the group is the island of St. Helena, 1,315 nautical miles to the northeast. The nearest continent, Africa, is 1,700 miles away.

Greatest archipelago   The world's greatest archipelago is the crescent of more than 13,000 islands, 3,500 miles long, that forms Indonesia.

Highest rock pinnacle   The world's highest rock pinnacle is Ball's Pyramid near Lord Howe Island in the Pacific, which is 1,843 ft. high, but has a base axis of only 660 ft. It was first scaled in 1965.

Northernmost land   On 26 July 1978 Uffe Petersen of the Danish Geodetic Institute observed the islet of Oodaq Ø, 100 ft. across, 0.8 miles north of Kaffeklubben Ø off Pearyland, Greenland at Lat. 83° 40′ 32.5″ N, Long. 30° 40′ 10.1″ W. It is 438.9 miles from the North Pole.

Southernmost land   The South Pole, unlike the North Pole, is on land. The Amundsen–Scott South Polar station was built there at an altitude of 9,370 ft. in 1957. The station is drifting bodily with the ice cap 27–30 ft. per year in the direction 43° W and was replaced by a new structure in 1975.

DEPRESSIONS

Deepest   The deepest depression so far discovered is the bedrock of the Bentley subglacial trench, Antarctica at 8,326 ft. below sea level. The great-

Newest island   The world's newest island is Pulau Batu Hairan ("Surprise Rock Island"), some 40 miles to the northeast of Kudat, in Sabah, Malaysia. It was first sighted by three local fishermen on 14 Apr. 1988. A week later it had doubled in height and now has an area of 1.9 acres and a maximum height of 10 ft.

Largest atoll   The largest atoll in the world is Kwajalein in the Marshall Islands, in the central Pacific Ocean. Its slender coral reef 176 miles long encloses a lagoon of 1,100 miles².

The atoll with the largest land area is Christmas Atoll, in the Line Islands in the central Pacific Ocean. It has an area of 251 miles², of which 124 miles² is land. Its principal settlement, London, is only 2½ miles distant from another settlement, Paris.

Longest reef   The Great Barrier Reef off Queensland, northeastern Australia is 1,260 miles in length. It is not actually a single reef, but consists of thousands of separate reefs. Between 1959 and 1971, and again between 1979 and 1991, corals on large areas of the central section of the reef—approximately between Cooktown and Proserpine—were devastated by the crown-of-thorns starfish (*Acanthaster planci*).

---

est submarine depression is an area of the northwest Pacific floor that has an average depth of 15,000 ft.

The deepest exposed depression on land is the shore surrounding the Dead Sea, now 1,310 ft. below sea level. The deepest point on the bed of this saltiest of all lakes is 2,388 ft. below sea level. The rate of fall in the lake surface since 1948 has been 13¾ in. per year.

The deepest part of the bed of Lake Baikal in Russia is 4,872 ft. below sea level.

United States   The lowest-lying area in the United States is in Death Valley, CA at 282 ft. below sea level.

Largest   The largest exposed depression in the world is the Caspian Sea basin in Azerbaijan, Russia, Kazakhstan, Turkmenistan and Iran. It is more than 200,000 miles², of which 143,550 miles² is lake area. The preponderant land area of the depression is the Prikaspiyskaya Nizmennost, lying around the northern third of the lake and stretching inland for a distance of up to 280 miles.

CAVES

Longest   The most extensive cave system in the world is that under the Mammoth Cave National Park, KY, first entered in 1799. Explorations by many groups of cavers have revealed the interconnected cave passages beneath the Flint, Mammoth Cave and Toohey Ridges to make a system with a total mapped length that is now 348 miles.

Largest   The world's largest cave chamber is the Sarawak Chamber,

Lubang Nasib Bagus, in the Gunung Mulu National Park, Sarawak, Malaysia, discovered and surveyed by the 1980 British-Malaysian Mulu Expedition. Its length is 2,300 ft.; its average width is 980 ft.; and it is nowhere less than 230 ft. high. It would be large enough to garage 7,500 buses.

Underwater cave   The longest explored underwater cave is the Nohoch Na Chich cave system in Quintana Roo, Mexico, with 43,600 ft. of mapped passages. Exploration of the system, which began in November 1987, has been carried out by the CEDAM Cave Diving Team under the leadership of Mike Madden.

The longest dive from the bottom of a cave, following the water out to a daylight spring, was made by Geoff Yeadon and Geoff Crossley in August 1991. They took five hours to dive the 10,006 ft. from King Pot to Keld Head in the Yorkshire Dales, Great Britain.

Greatest descent   The world depth record was set by the Groupe Vulcain in the Gouffre Jean Bernard, France at 5,256 ft. in 1989. However, this cave, explored via multiple entrances, has never been entirely descended, so the "sporting" record for the greatest descent into a cave is recognized as 4,947 ft. in the Shakta Pantjukhina in the Caucasus Mountains of Georgia by a team of Ukrainian cavers in 1988.

Longest stalactite   The longest known stalactite in the world is a wall-supported column extending 195 ft. from roof to floor in the Cueva de Nerja, near Málaga, in Spain.

The longest freehanging stalactite in the world is one of 20 ft. 4 in., in the Poll an Ionain cave in County Clare, Ireland.

Tallest stalagmite   The tallest known stalagmite in the world is one in the Krásnohorska cave in Czechoslovakia, which is generally accepted as being about 105 ft. tall.

The tallest cave column is considered to be the Flying Dragon Pillar, 128 ft. high, in Nine Dragons Cave (Daji Dong), Guizhou, China.

Deepest   The deepest cave in the United States is Lechuguilla Cave in Carlsbad Caverns, Carlsbad, NM, which currently measures 1,565 ft.

MOUNTAINS

Highest   An eastern Himalayan peak known as Peak XV on the Tibet–Nepal border (in an area first designated Zhu-mu-lang-ma on a map of 1717) was discovered to be the world's highest mountain in March 1856 by the Survey Department of the Government of India, from theodolite readings taken in 1849 and 1850. Its height was computed to be 29,002 ft. It was named Mt. Everest after Col. Sir George Everest (1790–1866), formerly surveyor-general of India, who pronounced his name "Eve-rest."

The status of Everest (Eve-rest) as the world's highest mountain was challenged after 131 years by K2 (formerly Godwin Austen), also known as Chogori, in the disputed Kashmiri northern areas of Pakistan, in an announcement on 6 Mar. 1987 by the US K2 Expedition. Their satellite transit surveyor yielded altitudes of between 29,064 and 29,228 ft. for K2 as against the official 19th-century figure of 28,250 ft., and the 20th-century proposed height of 28,740 ft. However, on 13 Aug. 1987 Chinese authorities reaffirmed their own July 1973 height measurements of 29,029 ft. 3 in. for Everest and

US—HIGHEST ALTITUDES

STATE*	HIGHEST POINT	ELEVATION (FEET)
Alaska	Mt. McKinley	20,320
California	Mt. Whitney	14,494
Colorado	Mt. Elbert	14,433
Washington	Mt. Rainier	14,410
Wyoming	Gannett Peak	13,804
Hawaii	Mauna Kea	13,796
Utah	Kings Peak	13,528
New Mexico	Wheeler Park	13,161
Nevada	Boundary Peak	13,140
Montana	Granite Peak	12,799
Idaho	Borah Peak	12,662
Arizona	Humphrey's Peak	12,633
Oregon	Mt. Hood	11,239
Texas	Guadalupe Peak	8,749
South Dakota	Harney Peak	7,242
North Carolina	Mt. Mitchell	6,684
Tennessee	Clingmans Dome	6,643
New Hampshire	Mt. Washington	6,288
Virginia	Mt. Rogers	5,729
Nebraska	Johnson Township	5,426
New York	Mt. Marcy	5,344
Maine	Mt. Katahdin	5,267
Oklahoma	Black Mesa	4,973
West Virginia	Spruce Knob	4,861
Georgia	Brasstown Bald	4,784
Vermont	Mt. Mansfield	4,393
Kentucky	Black Mountain	4,139
Kansas	Mt. Sunflower	4,039
South Carolina	Sassafras Mountain	3,560
North Dakota	White Butte	3,506
Massachusetts	Mt. Greylock	3,487
Maryland	Blackbone Mountain	3,360
Pennsylvania	Mt. Davis	3,213
Arkansas	Magazine Mountain	2,753
Alabama	Cheaha Mountain	2,405
Connecticut	Mt. Frissell	2,380
Minnesota	Eagle Mountain	2,301
Michigan	Mt. Arvon	1,979
Wisconsin	Timms Hill	1,951
New Jersey	High Point	1,803
Missouri	Taum Sauk Mount	1,772
Iowa	Sec. 29, T 100N, R 41W	1,670
Ohio	Campbell Hill	1,549
Indiana	Franklin Township	1,257
Illinois	Charles Mound	1,235
Rhode Island	Jerimoth Hill	812
Mississippi	Woodall Mountain	806
Louisiana	Driskill Mountain	535
Delaware	Ebright Road	442
Florida	Sec. 30, T 6N, R 20W	345

* Pete Allard, Jim Grace, Shuan Lacher, David Sandway and Dennis Stewart reached each highpoint of the 48 contiguous states in a record time of 30 days 10 hours 51 minutes and 55 seconds 1–31 July 1991.

28,250 ft. for K2. The Research Council in Rome, Italy announced on 23 Oct. 1987 that new satellite measurements restored Everest to primacy at 29,078 ft., and put K2 down to 28,238 ft. (For details of ascents of Everest, see Mountaineering.)

The mountain whose summit is farthest from the Earth's center is the Andean peak of Chimborazo (20,561 ft.), 98 miles south of the equator in Ecuador, South America. Its summit is 7,057 ft. farther from the Earth's center than the summit of Mt. Everest.

The highest mountain on the equator is Volcán Cayambe (18,996 ft.), Ecuador, at Long. 77° 58′ W. A group of mountaineers on the summit would be moving at 1,038 mph relative to the Earth's center, due to the Earth's rotation. If they were just south of the summit, passing through a glacier at 16,000 ft., they would be on the only spot on earth where both latitude and temperature would be 0°.

The highest insular mountain (of, relating to, or resembling an island) in the world is Puncak Jaya (formerly Puncak Sukarno, formerly Carstensz Pyramide) in Irian Jaya, Indonesia. A survey by the Australian Universities' Expedition in 1973 yielded a height of 16,023 ft. Ngga Pulu (also in Irian Jaya), which is now 15,950 ft., was in 1936 possibly 16,110 ft. before the melting of its snow cap.

United States   The highest mountain in the United States is Mt. McKinley in Alaska, with a highest point of 20,320 ft. McKinley, so named in 1896, was called Denali (Great One) in the Athabascan language of North American Indians. The highest mountain in the 48 contiguous states is Mt. Whitney in California, with a highest point of 14,494 ft.

Unclimbed   The highest unclimbed mountain is Namcha Barwa (25,531 ft.), in the Great Bend of the Cangpo (Brahmaputra), China. It is the 32nd highest mountain in the world. The highest unclimbed summit is Lhotse Middle (27,605 ft.), one of the peaks of Lhotse, in the Khumbu district of the Nepal Himalaya. It is the tenth highest individually recognized top in the world, Lhotse being the fourth highest mountain.

Tallest   The world's tallest mountain measured from its submarine base (3,280 fathoms) in the Hawaiian Trough to its peak is Mauna Kea (White Mountain) on the island of Hawaii, with a combined height of 33,480 ft., of which 13,796 ft. are above sea level.

Another mountain whose dimensions, but not height, exceed those of Mt. Everest is the volcanic Hawaiian peak of Mauna Loa (Long Mountain) at 13,680 ft. The axes of its elliptical base, 16,322 ft. below sea level, have been estimated at 74 miles and 53 miles. It should be noted that Cerro Aconcagua (22,834 ft.) is more than 38,800 ft. above the Pacific abyssal plain (16,000 ft. deep) or 42,834 ft. above the Peru–Chile Trench, which is 180 miles distant in the South Pacific.

Greatest ranges   The greatest of all mountain ranges is the submarine Mid-Ocean Ridge, extending 40,000 miles from the Arctic Ocean to the Atlantic Ocean, around Africa, Asia and Australia, and under the Pacific Ocean to the west coast of North America. It has a greatest height of 13,800 ft. above the base ocean depth.

The world's greatest land mountain range is the Himalaya-Karakoram, which contains 96 of the world's 109 peaks of over 24,000 ft. *Himalaya* derives from the Sanskrit *him*, snow; *alaya*, home. The longest range is the Andes of South America, which is approximately 4,700 miles in length.

Longest lines of sight Vatnajökull (6,952 ft.), Iceland has been seen by refracted light from the Faeroe Islands 340 miles distant.

United States In Alaska, Mt. McKinley (20,320 ft.) has been sighted from Mt. Sanford (16,237 ft.), a distance of 230 miles. (See also Mountains, Highest.)

Greatest plateau The most extensive high plateau in the world is the Tibetan Plateau in Central Asia. The average altitude is 16,000 ft. and the area is 77,000 miles².

Sheerest wall Mt. Rakaposhi (25,550 ft.) rises 3.72 miles from the Hunza Valley, Pakistan in 6.2 miles with an overall gradient of 31°.

The 3,200-ft.-wide northwest face of Half Dome, Yosemite, CA is 2,200 ft. high but nowhere departs more than 7° from the vertical. It was first climbed (Class VI) in 1957 by Royal Robbins, Jerry Gallwas and Mike Sherrick.

Highest halites Along the northern shores of the Gulf of Mexico for 725 miles there exist 330 subterranean "mountains" of salt, some of which rise more than 60,000 ft. from bedrock and appear as the low salt domes first discovered in 1862.

WATERFALLS

Highest The highest waterfall (as opposed to vaporized "bridal-veil fall") in the world is the Salto Angel (Angel Falls) in Venezuela, on a branch of the Carrao River, an upper tributary of the Caroni, with a total drop of 3,212 ft.—the longest single drop is 2,648 ft. The Angel Falls were named after the US pilot Jimmy Angel (d. 8 Dec. 1956), who recorded them in his log book on 14 Nov. 1933. The falls, known by the Indians as Cherun-Meru, had been reported by Ernesto Sanchez La Cruz in 1910.

United States The tallest continuous waterfall in the United States is Ribbon Falls in Yosemite National Park, California, with a drop of 1,612 ft. This is a seasonal waterfall and is generally dry from late July to early September.

Yosemite Falls, also in Yosemite National Park, has the greatest *total* drop at 2,425 ft., but actually consists of three distinct waterfalls. These are the Upper (1,430 ft.), Middle (675 ft.) and Lower falls (320 ft.).

Greatest On the basis of the average annual flow, the greatest waterfalls in the world are the Boyoma (formerly Stanley) Falls in Zaïre with 600,000 cusec.

The flow of the Guaíra (Salto das Sete Quedas) on the Alto Paraná River between Brazil and Paraguay did on occasions in the past attain a peak rate of 1.75 million cusec. However, the completion of the Itaipú dam in 1982 ended this claim to fame.

It has been calculated that a waterfall 26 times greater than the Guaíra and perhaps 2,620 ft. high was formed, when some 5.5 million years ago the

Mediterranean basins began to be filled from the Atlantic through the Straits of Gibraltar.

Widest   The widest waterfalls in the world are the Khône Falls (50–70 ft. high) in Laos, with a width of 6.7 miles and a flood flow of 1.5 million cusec.

RIVERS

Longest   The two longest rivers in the world are the Nile (*Bahr el-Nil*), flowing into the Mediterranean, and the Amazon (*Amazonas*), flowing into the South Atlantic. Which is the longer is more a matter of definition than of simple measurement.

Not until 1971 was the true source of the Amazon discovered, by Loren McIntyre (USA) in the snow-covered Andes of southern Peru. The Amazon begins with snowbound lakes and brooks—the actual source has been named Laguna McIntyre—which converge to form the Apurimac, a torrent in a deep canyon. This joins other streams to become the Ene, the Tambo and then the Ucayali. From the confluence of the Ucayali and the Marañón above Iquitos, Peru the river is called the Amazon for the final 2,300 miles as it flows eastward through Brazil into the Atlantic Ocean. The Amazon has several mouths that widen toward the sea, so that the exact point where the river ends is uncertain. If the Pará estuary (the most distant mouth) is counted, its length is approximately 4,195 miles. Because of seasonal flooding and changes in channels, geographers tend to round off the length at 4,000 miles.

The length of the Nile watercourse, as surveyed by M. Devroey (Belgium) before the loss of a few miles of meanders due to the formation of Lake Nasser, behind the Aswan High Dam, was 4,145 miles. This course is unitary from a hydrological standpoint and runs from the source in Burundi of the Luvironza branch of the Kagera feeder of the Victoria Nyanza via the White Nile (*Bahr el-Jebel*) to the delta in the Mediterranean.

United States   The longest river in the United States is the Mississippi, with a length of 2,348 miles. It flows from its source at Lake Itasca, MN through 10 states before reaching the Gulf of Mexico. The entire Mississippi River system, including the eastern and western tributaries, flows through 25 states in all.

Submarine river   In 1952 a submarine river 250 miles wide, known as the Cromwell Current, was discovered flowing eastward 300 ft. below the surface of the Pacific for 3,500 miles along the equator. Its volume is 1,000 times that of the Mississippi.

Subterranean river   In August 1958 a crypto-river, tracked by radio isotopes, was discovered flowing under the Nile with six times its mean annual flow, or 20 trillion ft^3.

Shortest   As with the longest river, two rivers could also be considered to be the shortest river with a name. The Roe River, near Great Falls, MT., has two forks fed by a large freshwater spring. These relatively constant forks measure 201 ft. (East Fork Roe River) and 58 ft. (North Fork Roe River) respectively. The Roe River flows into the larger Missouri River. The D River, located at Lincoln City, OR, connects Devil's Lake to the Pacific Ocean. Its length is officially quoted as 120 ± 5 ft.

Largest basin   The largest river basin in the world is that drained by the Amazon (4,007 miles), which covers about 2,720,000 miles². It has some 15,000 tributaries and sub-tributaries, including the Madeira, which at 2,100 miles in length is the longest tributary in the world.

Longest estuary   The world's longest estuary is that of the often frozen Ob, in the north of Russia, at 550 miles. It is up to 50 miles wide.

Largest delta   The world's largest delta is that created by the Ganges (Ganga) and Brahmaputra in Bangladesh and West Bengal, India. It covers an area of 30,000 miles².

Greatest flow   The greatest flow of any river in the world is that of the Amazon, which discharges an average of 4.2 million cusec into the Atlantic Ocean, increasing to more than 7 million cusec in full flood. The lower 900 miles of the Amazon average 55 ft. in depth, but in some places the river reaches a depth of 300 ft.

Largest swamp   The world's largest tract of swamp is the Gran Pantanal of Mato Grosso state in Brazil. It is about 42,000 miles² in area.

RIVER BORES

The bore (an abrupt rise of tidal water) on the Qiantong Jiang (Hangzhou He) in eastern China is the most remarkable of the 60 in the world. At spring tides the wave attains a height of up to 25 ft. and a speed of 13–15 knots. It is heard advancing at a range of 14 miles.

The annual downstream flood wave on the Mekong, in southeast Asia, sometimes reaches a height of 46 ft.

The greatest volume of any tidal bore is that of the Furo do Guajarú, a shallow channel that splits Ilha Caviana in the mouth of the Amazon.

LAKES AND INLAND SEAS

Largest   The largest inland sea or lake in the world is the Caspian Sea (in Azerbaijan, Russia, Kazakhstan, Turkmenistan and Iran). It is 760 miles long and its total area is 143,550 miles². Of the total area, some 55,280 miles² (38.5 percent) are in Iran, where it is named the Darya-ye-Khazar. Its maximum depth is 3,360 ft. and the surface is 93 ft. below sea level. Its estimated volume is 21,500 miles³ of saline water. Its surface has varied between 105 ft. (11th century) and 72 ft. (early 19th century) below sea level. (See also Depressions, largest.)

United States   The largest lake in the United States is Lake Michigan, with a water surface area of 22,300 miles², a length of 307 miles, a breadth of 118 miles and a maximum depth of 923 ft. Both Lake Superior and Lake Huron have larger areas, but these straddle the Canadian/American border.

Excluding the Great Lakes, the largest natural lake wholly within the United States is the Great Salt Lake, UT, which has a water surface area of 1,361 miles².

The Amazon

Longest River

If the Pará estuary (the most distant mouth) is counted, the Amazon is the longest river in the world, at approximately 4,195 miles. This photograph from space shows approximately 150 miles of the Juruá, the Amazon's and the world's second longest tributary (2,040 miles in length), marked as ✖ on the map.

The longest tributary is the Madeira (2,100 miles), marked as ✔. The view is of an area of western Brazil in which the confluence of the Juruá—which flows from west to east , or top left to bottom right—and the Tarauacá, one of the Amazon's many subtributaries, is clearly visible.

(Photo: NASA)

Subterranean river
In August 1958 a crypto-river, tracked by radio isotopes, was discovered flowing under the Nile with six times its mean annual flow, or 20 trillion ft^3.

Deepest   The deepest lake in the world is Lake Baikal in central Siberia, Russia. It is 385 miles long and between 20–46 miles wide. In 1957 the lake's Olkhon Crevice was measured and found to be 6,365 ft. deep and hence 4,872 ft. below sea level. (See also Depressions.)

United States   The deepest lake in the United States is 6-mile-long Crater Lake, in Crater Lake National Park in the Cascade Mountains of Oregon. Its surface is 6,176 ft. above sea level and its extreme depth is 1,932 ft., with an average depth of 1,500 ft. The lake has neither inlets nor outlets; instead it is filled and maintained solely by precipitation.

Highest   The highest navigable lake in the world is Lake Titicaca (maximum depth 1,214 ft., with an area of about 3,200 miles²) in South America (1,850 miles² in Peru and 1,350 miles² in Bolivia). It is 110 miles long and is 12,506 ft. above sea level. There are higher lakes in the Himalayas, but most are glacial and of a temporary nature only. A survey of the area carried out in 1984 showed a lake at a height of 17,762 ft., named Panch Pokhri, which was 1 mile long.

Freshwater   The freshwater lake with the greatest surface area is Lake Superior, one of the Great Lakes of North America. The total area is 31,800 miles², of which 20,700 miles² are in Minnesota, Wisconsin and Michigan and 11,100 miles² in Ontario, Canada. It is 600 ft. above sea level. The freshwater lake with the greatest volume is Lake Baikal in Siberia, Russia, with an estimated volume of 5,500 miles³.

Largest lagoon   Lagoa dos Patos in southernmost Brazil is 158 miles long and extends over 4,110 miles².

Underground lake   The world's largest underground lake is believed to be that in the Drachenhauchloch cave near Grootfontein, Namibia, discovered in 1986. The surface of the lake is some 217 ft. underground, and its depth 276 ft.

Reputedly the United States' largest underground lake is the Lost Sea, 300 ft. subterranean in the Craighead Caverns, Sweetwater, TN, measuring 4½ acres and discovered in 1905.

Largest marsh   The Everglades is a vast plateau of subtropical saw-grass marsh in southern Florida, covering 2,185 miles². Fed by water from Lake Okeechobee, the third largest freshwater lake in the United States, the Everglades is the largest subtropical wilderness in the continental United States.

Lake in a lake   The largest lake in a lake is Manitou Lake (41.09 miles²) on the world's largest lake island, Manitoulin Island (1,068 miles²), in the Canadian part of Lake Huron. The lake itself contains a number of islands.

OTHER FEATURES

Desert Nearly an eighth of the world's land surface is arid, with a rainfall of less than 10 in. per year. The Sahara in North Africa is the largest desert in the world. At its greatest length it is 3,200 miles from east to west. From north to south it is between 800 and 1,400 miles. The area covered by the desert is about 3,579,000 miles². The land level varies from 436 ft. below sea level in the Qattára Depression, Egypt to the mountain Emi Koussi (11,204 ft.) in Chad. The daytime temperature range in the western Sahara may be more than 80 deg. F. Desert surfaces have been known to heat up to 180° F.

United States The largest desert in the United States is the Chihuahuan in Texas, New Mexico and Arizona, which extends into Mexico. It covers an area of approximately 140,000 miles².

Sand dunes The world's highest measured sand dunes are those in the Saharan sand sea of Isaouane-N-Tifernine of east-central Algeria at Lat. 26° 42′ N, Long. 6° 43′ E. They have a wavelength of 3 miles and attain a height of 1,410 ft.

Largest mirage The largest mirage on record was that sighted in the Arctic at 83° N 103° W by Donald B. MacMillan in 1913. This type of mirage, known as the Fata Morgana, appeared as the same "hills, valleys, snow-capped peaks extending through at least 120 degrees of the horizon" that Peary had misidentified as Crocker Land six years earlier.

On 17 July 1939 a mirage of the mountain Snaefells Jokull (4,715 ft.) on Iceland was seen from the sea at a distance of 335–350 miles.

Largest gorge The largest land gorge in the world is the Grand Canyon on the Colorado River in north-central Arizona. It extends from Marble Gorge to the Grand Wash Cliffs, over a distance of 277 miles. It varies in width from 4–13 miles and is 1 mile in depth. The submarine Labrador Basin canyon is *c.* 2,150 miles long.

Deepest canyon The deepest canyon is El Cañón de Colca, Peru, which is 10,574 ft. deep. It was first traversed by the Polish Expedition CANOAN-DES' 79 kayak team from 12 May–14 June 1981.

The deepest submarine canyon yet discovered is one 25 miles south of Esperance, Western Australia; it is 6,000 ft. deep and 20 miles wide.

United States The deepest canyon in the United States is Kings Canyon, East Fresno, CA, which runs through Sierra and Sequoia National Forests. The deepest point, which measures 8,200 ft., is in the Sierra National Park Forest section of the canyon.

The deepest canyon in low relief territory is Hell's Canyon, dividing Oregon and Idaho. It plunges 7,900 ft. from the Devil Mountain down to the Snake River.

Deepest valley The Kali Gandaki valley lies 14,436 ft. deep between the Dhaulagiri and Annapurna ranges of the Nepal Himalayas. The closest bastions of these ranges are Tukuche Peak (22,703 ft.) and Nilgiri North Peak (23,166 ft.), just 11.3 miles apart, with the Gandaki River in between, at an elevation of 8,464 ft.

DEEPEST VALLEY. The Kali Gandaki valley is 14,436 ft. deep between the Dhaulagiri and Annapurna ranges of the Nepal Himalayas. Tukuche Peak (22,703 ft.) and Nilgiri North Peak (23,166 ft.), on either side of the valley, are just 11.3 miles apart. This view is from Dhaulagiri. (Photo: Dr. A.C. Waltham)

Cliffs   The highest sea cliffs yet pinpointed anywhere in the world are those on the north coast of east Moloka'i, HI near Umilehi Point, which descend 3,300 ft. to the sea at an average gradient of more than 55°.

Natural arches   The longest natural arch in the world is the Landscape Arch in the Arches National Park, 25 miles north of Moab in Utah. This natural sandstone arch spans 291 ft. and is set about 100 ft. above the canyon floor. In one place erosion has narrowed its section to 6 ft. Larger, however, is the Rainbow Bridge, UT, discovered on 14 Aug. 1909, which although only 278 ft. long, is more than 22 ft. wide.

Longest glaciers   It is estimated that 6.02 million miles^2, or 10.5 percent of the Earth's land surface, is permanently glaciated. The world's longest known glacier is the Lambert Glacier, discovered by an Australian aircraft crew in Australian Antarctic Territory in 1956–57. It is up to 40 miles wide and, with its upper section, known as the Mellor Glacier, it measures at least 250 miles in length. With the Fisher Glacier limb, the Lambert forms a continuous ice passage about 320 miles long.

The longest Himalayan glacier is the Siachen (47 miles) in the Karakoram range, though the Hispar and Biafo combine to form an ice passage 76 miles long.

The fastest-moving major glacier is the Quarayaq in Greenland, flowing 65–80 ft. per day.

United States   The largest glacier in the United States is the Malaspina glacier, 30 miles north of Yakutut, AK. It measures 850 miles^2 and is part of the 2,000-mile^2 Malaspina Glacier Complex.

Thickest ice   The greatest recorded thickness of ice is 2.97 miles, measured by radio echo soundings from a US Antarctic research aircraft at 69° 9′38″ S, 135° 20′25″ E, 250 miles from the coast of Wilkes Land on 4 Jan. 1975.

Deepest permafrost   The deepest recorded permafrost is more than 4,500 ft., reported from the upper reaches of the Viluy River, Siberia, Russia in February 1982.

NATURAL PHENOMENA

EARTHQUAKES

(Seismologists record all dates with the year *first*, based not on local time but on Universal Time/Greenwich Mean Time).

Greatest   It is estimated that each year there are some 500,000 detectable seismic or microseismic disturbances, of which 100,000 can be felt and 1,000 cause damage. The deepest recorded hypocenters are of 447 miles in Indonesia in 1933, 1934 and 1943.

The scale most commonly used to measure the size of earthquakes is Richter's magnitude scale (1954). It is named after Dr. Charles Richter (USA; 1900–85), and the most commonly used form is M_S, based on amplitudes of surface waves, usually at a period of 20 sec. The largest reported magnitudes on this scale are about 8.9, but the scale does not properly represent the size of the very largest earthquakes, above M_S about 8, for which it is better to use the concept of seismic moment, M_O, devised by K. Aki in 1966. Moment can be used to derive a "moment magnitude," M_W, first used by Hiroo Kanamori in 1977. The largest recorded earthquake on the M_W scale is the Chilean shock of 22 May 1960, which had $M_W = 9.5$, but only 8.3 on the M_S scale. For the largest events, such as the Chilean 1960 earthquake, the energy released is more than 10^{19} joules.

United States   The strongest earthquake in American history, measuring 8.4 on the Richter scale, was near Prince William Sound, AK (80 miles east of Anchorage) on 27 Mar. 1964. It killed 131 people and caused an estimated $750 million in damage; it also caused a tsunami 50 feet high that traveled 8,445 miles at 450 mph. The town of Kodiak was destroyed, and tremors were felt in California, Hawaii and Japan.

Worst death toll   The greatest chronicled loss of life occurred in the earthquake that rocked every city of the Near East and eastern Mediterranean *c.* July 1201. Contemporary accounts estimate the loss of life at 1.1 million. Less uncertain is the figure of 830,000 fatalities in a prolonged earthquake (*dizhen*) in the Shaanxi, Shanxi and Henan provinces of China, of 1556 Feb. 2 (new style; January 23 old style).

The highest death toll in modern times has been in the Tangshan earthquake (Mag. $M_S = 7.9$) in eastern China on 1976 July 27 (local time was 3 A.M. July 28). The first figure published on 4 Jan. 1977 revealed 655,237

WORST NATURAL DISASTERS IN THE WORLD

TYPE OF DISASTER	NUMBER KILLED	LOCATION	DATE
Earthquake	1,100,000	Near East and E. Mediterranean	c.July 1201
Circular Storm[1]	1,000,000	Ganges Delta Islands, Bangladesh	12–13 Nov. 1970
Flood	900,000	Hwang-ho River, China	Oct. 1887
Landslides (triggered off by single earthquake)	180,000	Kansu Province, China	16 Dec. 1920
Volcanic Eruption	92,000	Tambora, Sumbawa, Indonesia	5–7 Apr. 1815
Avalanches[2]	c. 18,000	Yungay, Huascarán, Peru	31 May. 1970
Dam Burst[3]	c. 5,000	Machhu River Dam, Morvi, Gujarat, India	11 Aug. 1979
Smog	2,850	London fog, Great Britain (excess deaths)	5–13 Dec. 1952
Fire[4] (Single building)	1,670	The Theatre, Canton, China	May 1845
Tornado	c. 1,300	Shaturia, Bangladesh	26 Apr. 1989
Hail	246	Moradabad, Uttar Pradesh, India	20 Apr. 1888
Lightning	81	Boeing 707 jet airliner, struck by lightning near Elkton, MD	8 Dec. 1963
Mountaineering	43	Lenin Peak, Tajikistan/Kyrgyzstan border (then USSR)	13 July 1990

FOOTNOTES

[1] This figure published in 1972 for the Bangladeshi disaster was from Dr. Afzal, Principal Scientific Officer of the Atomic Energy Authority Centre, Dacca. One report asserted that less than half of the population of the four islands of Bhola, Charjabbar, Hatia and Ramagati (1961 census 1.4 million) survived. The most damaging hurricane recorded was Hurricane Hugo from 17–22 Sep. 1989, which was estimated to have done $7 billion worth of damage.

[2] A total of 18,000 Austrian and Italian troops were reported to have been lost in the Dolomite valleys of northern Italy on 13 Dec. 1916 in more than 100 snow avalanches. Some of the avalanches were triggered by gunfire.

[3] The dynamiting of a Yangtze Kiang dam at Huayuan Kow by the Kuomintang during the Sino-Japanese war in 1938 is reputed to have resulted in 900,000 deaths.

[4] 200,000 killed in the sack of Moscow, as a result of fires started by the invading Tartars in May 1571. Worst-ever hotel fire, 162 killed, Hotel Daeyungak, Seoul, South Korea 25 Dec. 1971, Worst circus fire killed 168 in Hartford, CT 6 July 1944.

killed, later adjusted to 750,000. On 22 Nov. 1979 the New China News Agency inexplicably reduced the death toll to 242,000.

United States   The highest death toll for the United States is 503 in the Great San Francisco Earthquake of 1906 Apr. 18, which measured an estimated 8.3 on the Richter Scale. Accurate records were not kept at that time, and some experts believe the 503 deaths to be a low calculation. There was also no Richter Scale, and this measurement, although it is the consensus, is debated.

VOLCANOES

The total number of known active volcanoes in the world is 1,343, of which many are submarine. The greatest active concentration is in Indonesia, with some 200 volcanoes. The word *volcano* derives from the now-dormant Vulcano Island (from the Roman god of fire *Vulcanus*) in the Mediterranean.

Greatest explosion   The greatest explosion in historic times (possibly since Santorini in the Aegean Sea, 60 miles north of Crete, in 1628 B.C.) occurred at *c.* 10 A.M. (local time), or 3:00 A.M. GMT, on 27 Aug. 1883, with an eruption of Krakatoa, an island (then 18 miles^2) in the Sunda Strait, between Sumatra and Java, in Indonesia. One hundred and sixty-three villages were wiped out and 36,380 people killed by the wave it caused. Pumice was thrown 34 miles high and dust fell 3,313 miles away 10 days later. The explosion was recorded four hours later on the island of Rodrigues, 2,968 miles away, as "the roar of heavy guns," and was heard over one-thirteenth of the surface of the globe. This explosion, estimated to have had about 26 times the power of the greatest H-bomb test (by the USSR; for details of thermonuclear explosions, see Bombs, Chapter 4), was still only a third of the Santorini cataclysm.

Greatest eruption   The total volume of matter discharged in the eruption of Tambora, a volcano on the Indonesian island of Sumbawa, 5–10 Apr. 1815, was 36–43 miles^3. This compares with a probable 14–16 miles^3 ejected by Santorini (see above) and 5 miles^3 ejected by Krakatoa (see above). The energy of the Tambora eruption, which lowered the height of the island by 4,100 ft. from 13,450 ft. to 9,350 ft., was 8.4×10^{19} joules. A crater 5 miles in diameter was formed. More than 92,000 people were killed or died as a result of the subsequent famine.

The ejecta in the Taupo eruption in New Zealand *c.* A.D. 130 has been estimated at 33 billion tons of pumice moving at one time at 400 mph. It flattened 6,200 miles^2 (over 26 times the devastated area of Mt. St. Helens, which erupted in Washington State on 18 May 1980). Less than 20 percent of the 15.4 billion tons of pumice carried up into the air in this most violent of all documented volcanic events fell within 125 miles of the vent.

Largest active   Mauna Loa in Hawaii has the shape of a broad gentle dome 75 miles long and 31 miles wide (above sea level), with lava flows that occupy more than 1,980 miles^2 of the island. It has a total volume of 10,200 miles^2, of which 84.2 percent is below sea level. Its caldera (Spanish *caldaria*, boiling pot) or volcano crater, Mokuaweoweo, measures 4 miles^2 and is 500–600 ft. deep. Mauna Loa rises 13,680 ft. and has averaged one eruption every 4½ years since 1843, although none have occurred since 1984.

LARGEST ACTIVE VOLCANO

The largest active volcano is Mauna Loa, on Hawaii. In the past 150 years it has erupted 33 times, or on average every 4½ years. Below is a list of these, from which it is clear that the eruptions have become increasingly infrequent in recent times.

Year and duration (at summit)	Volume of matter discharged ($m^3 \times 10^6$)
1843 (5 days)	202
1849 (c. 15 days)	25
1851 (4 days)	35
1852 (1 day)	182
1855 (<1 day)	280
1859 (<1 day)	383
1865 (c. 125 days)	50
1868 (<1 day)	123
1871 (c. 20 days)	20
1872 (c. 1200 days)	630
1877 (<1 day)	8
1879 (<1 day)	1
1880 (Jan. 6 days)	10
1880 (Nov.*)	130
1887 (<1 day)	128
1892 (3 days)	12
1896 (16 days)	25
1899 (4 days)	81
1903 (Sep. 1 day)	3
1903 (Oct. 61 days)	70
1907 (<1 day)	121
1914 (48 days)	55
1916 *	31
1919 (<1 day)	183
1926 (<1 day)	121
1933 (17 days)	100
1935 (6 days)	87
1940 (134 days)	110
1942 (2 days)	176
1949 (145 days)	116
1950 (1 day)	376
1975 (1 day)	30
1984 (<1 day)	220

* flank only

Highest active   The highest volcano regarded as active is Ojos del Salado (which has fumaroles), at a height of 22,595 ft., on the frontier between Chile and Argentina.

Northernmost and southernmost   The northernmost volcano is Beeren Berg (7,470 ft.) on the island of Jan Mayen (71° 05′ N) in the Greenland Sea. It erupted on 20 Sep. 1970, and the island's 39 inhabitants (all male) had to be evacuated. It was possibly discovered by Henry Hudson, the English navigator and explorer (d. 1611), in 1607 or 1608, but was definitely visited by Jan Jacobsz Mayen (Netherlands) in 1614. It was annexed by Norway on 8 May 1929. The Ostenso seamount (5,825 ft.), 346 miles from the North Pole at Lat. 85° 10′ N, Long. 133° W, was volcanic. The most southerly known active volcano is Mt. Erebus (12,450 ft.), on Ross Island (77° 35′ S) in Antarctica. It was discovered on 28 Jan. 1841 by the expedition of Capt. (later Rear-Admiral Sir) James Clark Ross of the British Navy (1800–62), and first climbed at 10 A.M. on 10 Mar. 1908 by a British party of five, led by Prof. Tannatt William Edgeworth David (1858–1934).

Largest crater   The world's largest caldera (Spanish *caldaria*, boiling pot) or volcano crater is that of Toba, north-central Sumatra, Indonesia, covering 685 miles^2.

Longest lava flow   The longest lava flow in historic times is a mixture of *pahoehoe,* ropey lava (twisted cordlike solidifications) and *aa,* blocky lava, resulting from the eruption of Laki in 1783 in southeast Iceland, which flowed 40½–43½ miles. The largest-known prehistoric flow is the Roza basalt flow in North America *c.* 15 million years ago, which had an unsurpassed length (190 miles), area (15,400 miles^2) and volume (300 miles^3).

AVALANCHES

Greatest   The greatest natural avalanches, though rarely observed, occur in the Himalayas, but no estimates of their volume have been published. It was estimated that 120 million ft.^{3} of snow fell in an avalanche in the Italian Alps in 1885.

The 250-mph avalanche triggered by the Mt. St. Helens eruption in Washington State on 18 May 1980 was estimated to measure 96 billion ft.^{3} (see Accidents and Disasters).

GEYSERS

Tallest   The Waimangu (Maori "black water") geyser, in New Zealand, erupted to a height in excess of 1,500 ft. in 1904, but has not been active since it erupted violently at 6:20 A.M. on 1 Apr. 1917 and killed four people.

Currently the world's tallest active geyser is the National Park Service's Steamboat Geyser, in Yellowstone National Park, WY. During the 1980s it erupted at intervals ranging from 19 days to more than four years, although there were occasions in the 1960s when it erupted as frequently as every 4–10 days. The maximum height ranges from 195–380 ft.

The greatest measured water discharge was an estimated 740,000–1,000,000 gallons by the Giant Geyser, also in Yellowstone National Park. However, this estimate, made in the 1950s, was only a rough calculation.

The Geysir (Icelandic *geysa*, to gush) near Mt. Hekla in south-central Iceland, from which all others have been named, spurts on occasions to 180 ft., while the adjacent Strokkur, reactivated by drilling in 1963, spurts at 10–15 min. intervals.

WEATHER

The meteorological records given below necessarily relate largely to the last 140–160 years, since data before that time are both sparse and often unreliable. Reliable registering thermometers were introduced as recently as *c.* 1820. The longest continuous observations have been maintained at the Radcliffe Observatory, Oxford, Great Britain since 1815, though discontinuous records have enabled the Chinese to assert that 903 B.C. was a very bad winter. (See also Weather Feature.)

Most equable temperature   The location with the most equable recorded temperature over a short period is Garapan, on Saipan in the Mariana Islands, Pacific Ocean. During the nine years from 1927–35, inclusive, the lowest temperature recorded was 67.3° F. on 30 Jan. 1934 and the highest was 88.5° F. on 9 Sep. 1931, giving an extreme range of 21.2° F.

Between 1911 and 1966 the Brazilian offshore island of Fernando de Noronha had a minimum temperature of 65.5° F. on 17 Nov. 1913 and a maximum of 89.6° F. on 2 Mar. 1965, an extreme range of 24.1° F.

Greatest temperature ranges   The greatest recorded temperature ranges in the world are around the Siberian "cold pole" in the east of Russia. Temperatures in Verkhoyansk (67° 33′ N, 133° 23′ E) have ranged 188° F., from –90° F. to 98° F.

Highest shade temperature   The highest shade temperature ever recorded is 136° F. at Al'Azīzīyah, Libya (alt. 367 ft.) on 13 Sep. 1922.

Hottest place   On an annual mean basis, with readings taken over a six-year period from 1960 to 1966, the temperature at Dallol, in Ethiopia, was 94° F.

At Marble Bar, Western Australia (maximum 121° F.), 162 consecutive days with maximum temperatures of over 100° F. were recorded between 30 Oct. 1923 and 8 Apr. 1924.

At Wyndham, also in Western Australia, the temperature reached 90° F. or more on 333 days in 1946.

Driest place   The annual mean rainfall on the Pacific coast of Chile between Arica and Antofagasta is less than 0.004 in.

Longest drought   Desierto de Atacama, in Chile, experiences virtually no rain, although several times a century a squall may strike a small area of it.

Least sunshine   At the South Pole there is zero sunshine for 182 days every year, and at the North Pole the same applies for 176 days.

Lowest screen temperature   A record low of –128.6° F. was registered at Vostok, Antarctica (alt. 11,220 ft.) on 21 July 1983.

The coldest permanently inhabited place is the Siberian village of Oymyakon (pop. 4,000), 63° 16′ N, 143° 15′ E (2,300 ft.), in Russia, where the temperature reached –90° F. in 1933, and an unofficial –98° F. has been published more recently.

Coldest place   Polus Nedostupnosti (Pole of Cold), Antarctica at 78° S, 96° E, is the coldest place in the world, with an extrapolated annual mean of –72° F.

The coldest measured mean is –70° F., at Plateau Station, Antarctica.

Wettest place   By average annual rainfall, the wettest place in the world is Tutunendo, in Colombia, with 463½ in. per year.

DRIEST PLACE. The driest part of the world is the Pacific coast of northern Chile between Arica and Antofagasta, where the annual mean rainfall is less than 0.004 in. (Photo: Science Photo Library)

Weather Records

In this era of ozone holes, El Niño and the greenhouse effect, weather records are frequently being set—the winter of 1991–92, for example, was the warmest ever recorded in the United States, with an average temperature of 36.87 degrees. This feature illustrates a variety of American weather extremes and natural phenomena.

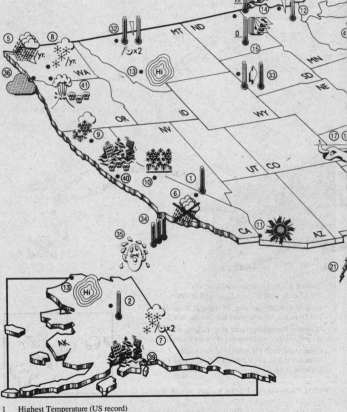

1   Highest Temperature (US record)
    134 degrees F at Greenland Ranch, Death Valley, CA on 10 Jul 1913

2   Lowest Temperature (US record)
    -79.8 degrees F at Prospect Creek, AK on 23 Jan 1971

3   Greatest Rainfall (24 hours) (US record)
    42 inches fell at Alvin, TX 25–26 Jul 1979

State Abbreviations

		CA	California	IA	Iowa	NH	New Hampshire
AK	Alaska	CO	Colorado	ID	Idaho	NJ	New Jersey
AL	Alabama	CT	Connecticut	IL	Illinois	NM	New Mexico
AR	Arkansas	DE	Delaware	IN	Indiana	NV	Nevada
AZ	Arizona	FL	Florida	KS	Kansas	NY	New York
		GA	Georgia	KY	Kentucky	OH	Ohio
		HI	Hawaii	LA	Louisiana	OK	Oklahoma
				MA	Massachusetts	OR	Oregon
				MD	Maryland	PA	Pennsylvania
				ME	Maine	RI	Rhode Island
				MI	Michigan	SC	South Carolina
				MN	Minnesota	SD	South Dakota
				MO	Missouri	TN	Tennessee
				MS	Mississippi	TX	Texas
				MT	Montana	UT	Utah
				NC	North Carolina	VA	Virginia
				ND	North Dakota	VT	Vermont
				NE	Nebraska	WA	Washington
						WI	Wisconsin
						WV	West Virginia
						WY	Wyoming

Note: Alaska and Hawaii are shown out of position

4. Greatest Rainfall (one year) (US record)
   704.83 inches fell at Lae a Kuikui, HI in 1982

5. Greatest Rainfall (one year, 48 states) (US record)
   184.56 inches fell at Wynoochee Oxbow, WA in 1931

6. Minimum Precipitation (one year) (US record)
   No precipitation was recorded in Death Valley, CA in 1929

7. Greatest Snowfall (24 hours) (World record)
   78 inches fell on 7 Feb 1963 at Mile 47 Camp, Cooper River
   Division 4, AK

8. Greatest Snowfall (one year) (World record)
   1,224.5 inches at Paradise, Mt. Rainier, WA in 1972

9. Greatest Snowfall (one storm) (World record)
   189 inches at Mt. Shasta Ski Bowl, CA 13–19 Feb 1959

10. Greatest Depth of Snow on the Ground (World record)
    37 ft 7 in at Tamarac, CA in March 1911

11. Maximum Sunshine (World record)
    90 percent for Yuma, AZ (highest annual average)

12 Annual Mean Temperature Readings (US record)
    Highest: 78.2 degrees F at Key West, FL Lowest: 36.5 degrees F at International Falls, MN

13 Highest Barometric Pressure (US record)
    Overall: 31.43 inches, Barrow, AK 3 Jan 1970 In 48 states: 31.40 inches, Helena, MT 9 Jan 1962

14 Most Days Below 32 Degrees F Consecutively (US record)
    92 days 30 Nov 1935–29 Feb 1936 at Langdon (Cavalier County), ND

15 Most Days Below 0 Degrees F Consecutively (US record)
    41 days 11 Jan–20 Feb 1936 at Langdon (Cavalier County), ND

16 Highest Surface Wind Speed (World record)
    231 mph at Mt. Washington, NH 12 Apr 1934

17 Worst Drought (US record)
    Commonly referred to as "Dust Bowl Days," the Great Plains suffered from drought conditions
    from the Summer of 1930 to the Fall of 1940. At its height, in the Winter of 1935–36, it affected
    50 million acres in parts of New Mexico, Texas, Oklahoma, Kansas and Colorado. During August
    1934, in Western Kansas, the Drought Severity Index reached -5.96. Below -4.0 on this index
    indicates extreme drought conditions

18 Most Intense Drought (US record)
    57-month drought from May 1952 to March 1957 in Western Kansas. Drought Severity Index
    reached lowest point ever of -6.2, in September 1956

19 Lightning (most people killed) (World record)
    81 people killed when airplane struck by lightning crashed near Elkton, MD on 8 Dec 1963

20 Lightning (most deaths—state) (US record)
    313 in Florida since 1959 (when records were first kept)

21 Lightning (most deaths—month) (US record)
    874 in July—the worst month for reports of death by lightning since 1959

22 Tornadoes (most deaths—one tornado) (US record)
    695 people were killed on 18 Mar 1925 in Missouri, Illinois, and Indiana.
    4 each killed in Annapolis & Biehle, MO
    234 killed in Murphysboro, IL
    148 killed in West Frankfurt, IL
    69 killed in De Soto, IL
    37 killed in Gorham, IL
    45 killed in Princeton, IN
    25 killed in Griffen, IN
    129 victims in rural areas of these states. At 219 miles, this tornado ranks first as a tornado with
    the longest continuous track on the ground; first with a 3.5-hour continuous duration on the
    ground; first in total area of destruction, covering 164 sq miles; first in dimensions, with the funnel
    sometimes exceeding 1 mile wide; and third in forward speed, reaching a maximum of 73 mph,
    while averaging 62 mph over its duration.

23 Tornadoes (most recorded—one state, one year) (US record)
    232 tornadoes were reported in Texas in 1967.

24 Tornadoes (highest death rate per 10,000 miles^2) (US record)
    120 deaths per 10,000 miles^2 from 1953–90 in Massachusetts (statistics have been gathered since
    1953).

25 Tornadoes (fastest speed) (World record)
    280 mph at Wichita Falls, TX on 2 Apr 1958

26 Hurricanes (lowest barometric pressure) (US record)
    26.35 for the 1935 Labor Day Hurricane which crossed the US coastline at Matecumbe Key, FL at
    10:00 p.m. on 2 Sep 1935.

27 Hurricanes (fastest sustained winds) (US record)
    200 mph sustained windspeed and 210 mph gusts were recorded on 17–18 Aug 1969 when
    Hurricane Camille hit the Mississippi/Alabama coast at Pass Christian, MS

28 Hurricane (greatest storm surge) (US record)
    24.6 ft by Hurricane Camille in August 1969

29 Hurricane (fastest forward speed) (US record)
    Great New England Hurricane on 21 Sep 1938 had a forward speed which exceeded 60 mph
    (average speed equaled 58 mph) when it struck central Long Island at Babylon, NY; continued on
    to landfall at Milford, CT

30 Hurricane (greatest damage) (US record)
Hurricane Hugo slammed into the coast of South Carolina in September 1989 and caused $7.1 billion worth of damage.

31 Hurricanes (most deaths) (US record)
6,000 people were killed by a hurricane that hit Galveston Island, TX on 8 Sep 1900

32 Greatest Temperature Variation (one day) (World record)
100 degrees F at Browning, MT on 23–24 Jan 1916 (a fall from 44 degrees F to -56 degrees F).

33 Most Freakish Rise in Temperature (World record)
49 degrees F in two minutes at Spearfish, SD on 22 Jan 1943 (from -4 degrees F at 7:30 a.m. to 45 degrees F at 7:32 a.m.)

34 Highest Temperature—consecutive (World record)
43 consecutive days with a maximum temperature of over 120 degrees F at Death Valley, CA from 6 July to 17 August 1917

35 Humidity (World record)
Highest level registered on the Temperature Humidity Index is plus 15, which has been recorded twice at Death Valley, CA—on 27 Jul 1966 (119 degrees F and 31 percent) and on 12 Aug 1970 (117 degrees F and 37 percent).

36 Fog—most (US record)
The international definition of fog states that it exists when horizontal visibility is below 0.62 miles (1 km); while heavy fog takes place when there is less than 0.25 miles (0.4 km) of visibility. Cape Disappointment, WA averages 2,552 hours (or 106 complete days) of heavy fog per year.

37 Fog—least
Key West, FL averages less than 1 day a year with heavy fog.

38 Hailstone (largest) (US record)
Diameter 5.62 inches; circumference 17.5 inches; weight 1.671 lb. in Coffeyville, KS on 3 Sep 1970.

39 Earthquake (severest on Richter scale) (US record)
Most violent recorded earthquake in the US hit near Prince William Sound, 80 miles east of Anchorage, AK on 27 Mar 1964 and measured 8.4 on the Richter Scale.

40 Earthquake (most deaths) (US record)
An earthquake in San Francisco, CA on 18 Apr 1906 caused a fire that razed an area of four square miles, killing over 500 people.

41 Volcanic Eruption (most deaths) (US record)
The eruption of Mt. St. Helens, WA on 18 May 1980 killed 60 people.

42 Fire (most deaths) (US record)
The worst fire in US history occurred on 8 Oct 1871 in Peshtigo, WI where 1,182 people were killed. According to survivors, a tornado-like column of intensely hot air rushed through the parched area causing the fire.

43 Flood (most deaths) (US record)
More than 2,000 people were killed in a flood at Johnstown, PA on 31 May 1889. First the Conemaugh River, just above Johnstown, overflowed its banks, reaching 20 ft above low water before the flood gauge swept away. Four hours later, a dam gave way at the South Fork Creek of the Little Conemaugh River 15 miles upstream from Johnstown. This combination of water formed a wall 20 to 30 ft high, rushing through the valley on the way to Johnstown at a rate of 15 mph.

44 Highest Property Damage from Floodstorm
$2.1 billion (122 deaths) on 22 Jun 1972 when the remains of Hurricane Agnes brought heavy rains (12 inches) to Pennsylvania and New York. Wilkes-Barre, PA on the Susquehanna River suffered most.

Sources:

National Climatic Data Center

National Oceanic and Atmospheric Administration

National Hurricane Center

The American Weather Book

Geography on File–World Climate

Facts On File, Inc.

Artwork: Maltings Partnership (UK) for Guinness Publishing

Most intense rainfall   Difficulties attend rainfall readings for very short periods, but the figure of 1½ in. in one min. at Barst, Guadeloupe on 26 Nov. 1970 is regarded as the most intense recorded in modern times.

Greatest rainfall   A record 73.62 in. of rain fell in 24 hours in Cilaos (alt. 3,940 ft.), La Réunion, Indian Ocean on 15 and 16 Mar. 1952. This is equal to 8,327 tons of rain per acre.

For a calendar month, the record is 366 in., at Cherrapunji, Meghalaya, India in July 1861.

The 12-month record was also at Cherrapunji, with 1,041.8 in. between 1 Aug. 1860 and 31 July 1861.

Highest surface wind speed   The fastest speed at a low altitude was registered on 8 Mar. 1972 at the USAF base at Thule, Greenland (145 ft.), when a peak speed of 207 mph was recorded.

Longest-lasting rainbow   A rainbow lasting over three hours was reported from the coastal border of Gwynedd and Clwyd, North Wales, Great Britain on 14 Aug. 1979.

Windiest place   The Commonwealth Bay, George V Coast, Antarctica, where gales reach 200 mph, is the world's windiest place.

Hurricanes   The most commonly used scale to measure the size of a hurricane is the Saffir-Simpson Scale, which rates hurricanes on a scale of one to five, five being the most severe.

The most damaging hurricane in the United States was Hurricane Hugo, which hit the mainland 21–22 Sep. 1989 after devastating a number of islands in the Caribbean. The storm made landfall at Sullivan Island, northeast of Charleston, SC. On crossing the mainland, Hugo measured four on the Saffir-Simpson Scale. Winds measured 135 mph and 28 people were killed.

The greatest number of fatalities from an American hurricane is an estimated 6,000 deaths on 8 Sep. 1900 in Galveston Island, TX.

Highest waterspout   The highest waterspout of which there is a reliable record was one observed on 16 May 1898 off Eden, New South Wales, Australia. A theodolite reading from the shore gave its height as 5,014 ft. It was about 10 ft. in diameter.

Heaviest hailstones   The heaviest hailstones on record, weighing up to 2¼ lbs., are reported to have killed 92 people in the Gopalganj district of Bangladesh on 14 Apr. 1986.

Cloud extremes   The highest standard cloud form is cirrus, averaging 27,000 ft. and above, but the rare nacreous or mother-of-pearl formation may reach nearly 80,000 ft. (see also Noctilucent clouds). A cirrus cloud is composed almost entirely of ice crystals at temperatures of –40° F. or below. The lowest is stratus, below 3,500 ft. The cloud form with the greatest vertical range is cumulonimbus, which has been observed to reach a height of nearly 68,000 ft. in the tropics.

Upper atmosphere   The lowest temperature ever recorded in the atmosphere is –225° F. at an altitude of about 50–60 miles, during noctilucent cloud research above Kronogård, Sweden from 27 July to 7 Aug. 1963.

Thunder-days   In Tororo, Uganda an average of 251 days of thunder per year was recorded for the 10-year period 1967–76.

Between Lat. 35° N and 35° S there are some 3,200 thunderstorms every 12 nighttime hours, some of which can be heard at a range of 18 miles.

Lightning   The visible length of lightning strokes varies greatly. In mountainous regions, when clouds are very low, the flash may be less than 300 ft. long. In flat country with very high clouds, a cloud-to-Earth flash may measure 4 miles, though in the most extreme cases such flashes have been measured at 20 miles. The intensely bright central core of the lightning channel is extremely narrow. Some authorities suggest that its diameter is as little as ½ in. This core is surrounded by a "corona envelope" (glow discharge), which may measure 10–20 ft. in diameter.

The speed of a discharge varies from 100–1,000 miles/sec. for the downward leader track, and reaches up to 87,000 miles/sec. (nearly half the speed of light) for the powerful return stroke.

Every few million strokes there is a giant discharge, in which the cloud-to-Earth and return strokes flash from and to the top of the thunderclouds. In these "positive giants" energy of up to 3 billion joules (3×10^{16} ergs) has been recorded. The temperature reaches about 54,032° F., which is higher than that of the surface of the Sun.

Longest sea-level fogs   Sea-level fogs—with visibility less than 3,000 ft.—persist for weeks on the Grand Banks, Newfoundland, Canada, with the average being more than 120 days per year.

Barometric pressure   The highest barometric pressure ever recorded was 32 in. at Agata, Siberia, Russia (alt. 862 ft.) on 31 Dec. 1968.

The lowest sea-level pressure was 25.69 in. in Typhoon Tip, 300 miles west of Guam, Pacific Ocean, at Lat. 16° 44′ N, Long. 137° 46′ E, on 12 Oct. 1979.

Humidity and discomfort   Human comfort or discomfort depends not merely on temperature but on the combination of temperature, humidity, radiation and wind speed. The United States Weather Bureau uses a Temperature–Humidity Index (THI), which equals two-fifths of the sum of the dry and wet bulb thermometer readings plus 15. A THI of 98.2 has been twice recorded in Death Valley, CA—on 27 July 1966 (119° F. and 31 percent) and on 12 Aug. 1970 (117° F. and 37 percent). A person driving at 45 mph in a car without a windshield in a temperature of –45° F. would, by the chill factor, experience the equivalent of –125° F., i.e., within 3.6° F. of the world record.

GEMS, JEWELS AND
PRECIOUS STONES

DIAMOND

Largest   The largest diamond is 3,106 carats and was found on 25 Jan. 1905 in the Premier Mine, Pretoria, South Africa. It was named *The Cullinan* after the mine's discoverer, Sir Thomas Cullinan, and was presented to Britain's King Edward VII in 1907. Currently the largest uncut stone is of 599 carats, found near Pretoria, South Africa in July 1986, although its existence was announced by De Beers only on 11 Mar. 1988. It is expected to yield a 350-carat cut stone.

Largest cut   The largest cut diamond is the 530.2-carat, 74-facet pear-shaped gem named *The Star of Africa*, that was cleaved from *The Cullinan* by Jak Asscher and polished by Henri Koe in Amsterdam, Netherlands in 1908. It is now in the Royal Sceptre, Great Britain.

Largest natural intense fancy blue   The largest diamond that is a natural intense fancy blue is the 136.25 carat *Queen of Holland* cushion-shaped brilliant-cut diamond, which was found in 1904. It was cut by F. Freedman & Co. in Amsterdam, Netherlands, and was exhibited at the Paris Exhibition in 1925. It was then sold to an Indian maharaja, but its current owner is unknown.

Largest natural intense fancy green   The largest natural intense fancy green diamond is 41-carats. It is located in the Green Vaults in Dresden, Germany.

Smallest   The smallest diamond is 0.0001022 carat. D. Drukker & Zn NV of Amsterdam, Netherlands has produced a 57-facet brilliant with a diameter of 0.009 in.

Rarest color   The rarest diamond color is blood red. The largest is a 5.05-carat flawless stone found in Tichtenburg, South Africa in 1927 and now in a private collection in the United States.

Highest-priced   A superb 11-sided pear-shaped mixed-cut diamond of 101.84 carats was sold to Robert Mouawad at Sotheby's, Geneva, Switzerland on 14 Nov. 1990 for $12,760,000. The record per carat is $926,315 for a 0.95-carat purplish-red stone sold at Christie's, New York on 28 Apr. 1987. A record price of $10 million was paid for a rough uncut diamond by Chow Tai Fook of Hong Kong on 4 Mar. 1989.

RUBY

Largest star   The *Eminent Star* ruby, believed to be of Indian origin, is the largest ruby, at 6,465 carats. It is an oval cabochon with a six line star cut in it, and measures $4\frac{1}{4} \times 3\frac{5}{8} \times 2\frac{1}{4}$ in. It is owned by Eminent Gems Inc. of New York.

Largest double star A 1,370-carat cabochon cut gem, *Neelanjali*, also owned by G. Vidyaraj of Bangalore, India, displays 12 star lines and measures 3 in. in height and 2 in. in diameter.

Largest In July 1985 jeweler James Kazanjian of Beverly Hills, CA displayed an 8,500-carat 5½-in.-tall red corundum (Al_2O_3) carved to resemble the Liberty Bell.

Highest-priced A ruby and diamond ring made by Chaumet, in Paris, France, weighs 32.08 carats and was sold at Sotheby's, New York on 26 Oct. 1989 for $4,620,000. The record per carat is $227,300 for a ruby ring with a stone weighing 15.97 carats, which was sold at Sotheby's, New York on 18 Oct. 1988.

EMERALD

Largest cut An 86,136-carat, 37-lb. 15.6 oz. natural beryl was found in Carnaiba, Brazil in August 1974. It was carved by Richard Chan in Hong Kong and valued at £718,000 ($1,120,080) in 1982.

Largest single crystal The largest single emerald crystal of gem quality was 7,025 carats. It was found in 1969 at the Cruces Mine, near Gachala, Colombia, and is owned by a private mining concern. Larger Brazilian and Russian stones do exist, but they are of low quality.

Highest-priced The highest price paid for a single lot of emeralds was $3,080,000, for an emerald and diamond necklace made by Cartier, London, Great Britain in 1937 (a total of 12 stones weighing 108.74 carats), which was sold at Sotheby's, New York on 26 Oct. 1989. The highest price for a single emerald is $2,126,646, for a 19.77-carat emerald and diamond ring made by Cartier in 1958, which was sold at Sotheby's, Geneva, Switzerland on 2 Apr. 1987. This also represented the record price per carat for an emerald, at $107,569.

Crystal ball The world's largest flawless rock crystal ball is 106.75 lbs. and 13 in. in diameter, and was cut in China from Burmese rough material. It is now in the Smithsonian Institution in Washington, D.C.

Largest topaz The rectangular, cushion-cut 22,892.5 carat *American Golden Topaz* with 172 facets and 5⅞ in. in overall width has been on display at the Smithsonian Institution, Washington, D.C. since 4 May 1988.

Largest jade A single boulder of nephrite jade was found in northeast China in March 1990. It measured 23 × 20 × 16 ft. and weighed 291 tons.

SAPPHIRE

Largest carved   The largest carved sapphire was 2,302 carats and was found at Anakie, Queensland, Australia in *c*. 1935. This corundum (Al_2O_3) was carved into a 1,318-carat head of Abraham Lincoln and is now in the custody of the Kazanjian Foundation of Los Angeles, CA.

Largest star sapphire   The largest star sapphire, *The Lone Star*, was 9,719.50 carats and was cut in London, Great Britain in November 1989. It is owned by Harold Roper.

Highest-priced   A step-cut stone of 62.02 carats was sold as a sapphire and diamond ring at Sotheby's, St. Moritz, Switzerland on 20 Feb. 1988 for $2,791,723.

OPAL

Largest   The largest single piece of gem-quality white opal was 26,350 carats, found in July 1989 at the Jupiter Field at Coober Pedy in South Australia. It has been named *Jupiter-Five* and is in private ownership.

Largest polished opal   The largest free-form cabochon cut precious opal, *Galaxy*, is 3,749 carats and measures 5½ × 4 × 1⅝ in. It was excavated in Brazil in 1976 and was displayed by Steven Sodokoff at the Tucson Gem Show at Tucson, AZ in February 1991.

Largest black opal   A stone found on 4 Feb. 1972 at Lightning Ridge in Australia produced a finished gem of 1,520 carats, called the *Empress of Glengarry*. It measures 4¾ × 3⅛ × ⅝ in., and is owned by Peter Gray.

Largest rough black opal   The largest gem-quality uncut black opal was also found at Lightning Ridge, on 3 Nov. 1986. After cleaning, it weighs 2,020 carats and measures 4 × 2⅝ × 2½ in. It has been named *Halley's Comet* and is owned by a team of opal miners known as The Lunatic Hill Syndicate.

PEARL

Largest   The 14 lb. 1 oz. *Pearl of Lao-tze* (also known as the *Pearl of Allah*) was found at Palawan, Philippines on 7 May 1934 in the shell of a giant clam. The property of Wilburn Dowell Cobb until his death, this 9½-in. long by 5½-in. diameter molluscan concretion was bought at auction on 15 May 1980 in San Francisco, CA by Peter Hoffman and Victor Barbish for $200,000. An appraisal by the San Francisco Gem Laboratory in May 1984 suggested a value of $40–42 million.

Largest abalone pearl   A baroque abalone pearl measuring 2¾ × 2 × 1⅛ in. and 469.13 carats was found at Salt Point State Park, CA in May 1990. It is owned by Wesley Rankin and is called the *Big Pink*. It has been valued in the United States at $4.7 million.

Largest cultured pearl   A 1½-in. round, 138.25-carat cultured pearl weighing 1 oz. was found near Samui Island, off Thailand, in January 1988. The stone is owned by the Mikimoto Pearl Island Company, Japan.

Highest-priced   *La Régente*, an egg-shaped pearl weighing 302.68 grains and formerly part of the French crown jewels, was sold at Christie's, Geneva, Switzerland on 12 May 1988 for $864,280.

AMBER

Largest   The largest amber, *Burma Amber*, is 33 lbs. 10 oz. and is located in the Natural History Museum, London, Great Britain. Amber is a fossil resin derived from extinct coniferous trees, and often contains trapped insects.

GOLD

Largest nugget   The 7,560-oz. *Holtermann Nugget*, found on 19 Oct. 1872 in the Beyers & Holtermann Star of Hope mine, Hill End, New South Wales, Australia, contained some 220 lbs. of gold in a 630-lb. slab of slate.

Largest pure nugget   The *Welcome Stranger*, found at Moliagul, Victoria, Australia in 1869, yielded 2,248 troy oz. of pure gold from 2,280 ¼ oz.

LIVING WORLD

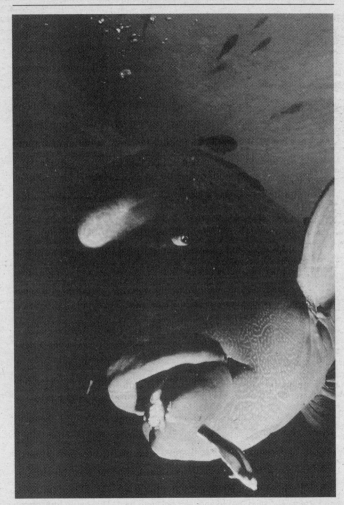

The giant Maori wrasse (*Cheilinus undulatus*).
(Photo: Spectrum Colour Library)

ANIMAL KINGDOM

Unless otherwise stated, all measurements refer to adult specimens.

GENERAL RECORDS

Largest   The discovery of the world's largest living organism was reported on 2 Apr. 1992. Scientists from the University of Toronto, Canada and Michigan Technological University, MI showed that the network of filaments of the fungus *Armillaria bulbosa* found in the forests of Michigan represents an individual organism originating from a single fertilized spore at least 1,500 years ago. It covers some 37 acres and calculations suggest a weight of over 100 tons, comparable with the blue whale (*Balaenoptera musculus*). Giant redwood trees can attain greater weights, but much of this is dead wood. (See Largest mammal and Kingdom Fungi, Largest.)

Noisiest   The noisiest land animals in the world are the howling monkeys (*Alouatta*) of Central and South America. The males have an enlarged bony structure at the top of the windpipe that enables the sound to reverberate, and their fearsome screams have been described as a cross between the bark of a dog and the bray of a donkey increased a thousandfold. Once they are in full voice they can be clearly heard for distances up to 10 miles.

The low-frequency pulses made by blue whales when communicating with each other have been measured up to 188 decibels, making them the loudest sounds emitted by any living source. They have been detected 530 miles away.

Most fertile   It has been calculated that a single cabbage aphid (*Brevicoryne brassica*) can give rise in a year to a mass of descendants weighing 906 million tons, more than three times the total weight of the world's human population. Fortunately the mortality rate is tremendous!

Strongest   In proportion to their size, the strongest animals are the larger beetles of the family Scarabaeidae, which are found mainly in the tropics. In tests carried out on a rhinoceros beetle (*Dynastinae*) it was able to support 850 times its own weight on its back (compared with 25 percent of its body weight for an adult elephant).

Strongest bite   Experiments carried out with a Snodgrass gnathodynamometer (shark-bite meter) at the Lerner Marine Laboratory in Bimini, Bahamas revealed that a 6-ft.-6¾-in.-long dusky shark (*Carcharhinus obscurus*) could exert a force of 132 lbs. between its jaws. This is equivalent to a pressure of 22 tons/in.^{2} or 22 tons at the tips of the teeth.

Suspended animation   In 1846 two specimens of the desert snail *Eremina desertorum* were presented to the British Museum (Natural History) in London as dead exhibits. They were glued to a small tablet and placed on display. Four years later, in March 1850, the museum staff, suspecting that one of the snails was still alive, removed it from the tablet and placed it in tepid water. The snail moved and later began to feed. This hardy little creature lived for another two years before it fell into a torpor and then died.

MOST FERTILE ANIMAL. A single cabbage aphid (*Brevicoryne brassica*) can give rise to a mass of 906 million tons of descendants in one year. (Photo: Jacana Agence de Presse/R. Dulhoste)

Regeneration The sponge (Porifera) has the most remarkable powers of regeneration of lost parts of any animal, as it can regrow its entire body from a tiny fragment of itself. If a sponge is squeezed through a fine-meshed silk gauze, each piece of separated tissue will live as an individual.

Most dangerous The world's most dangerous animals (excluding human beings) are the malarial parasites of the genus *Plasmodium* carried by mosquitoes of the genus *Anopheles*, which, if we exclude wars and accidents, have probably been responsible directly or indirectly for 50 percent of all human deaths since the Stone Age. Even today, despite major campaigns to eradicate malaria, at least 200 million people are afflicted by the disease each year, and more than one million babies and children die annually from it in Africa alone.

Most poisonous The most active known poison found naturally among animals is the batrachotoxin derived from the skin secretions of the golden poison-dart frog (*Phyllobates terribilis*) of western Colombia, which are at least 20 times more toxic than those of any other known poison-dart frog (human handlers have to wear thick gloves); an average adult specimen contains enough poison (0.000067 oz.) to kill nearly 1,500 people. This species is preyed upon by the frog-eating snake (*Leimadophis epinephelus*), which is thought to be immune to its poison.

Largest colonies The black-tailed prairie dog (*Cynomys ludovicianus*), a rodent of the family Sciuridae found in the western United States and northern Mexico, builds the largest colonies. One single "town" discovered in 1901 contained about 400 million individuals and was estimated to cover 24,000 miles².

Greatest concentration   The greatest concentration of animals ever recorded was a huge swarm of Rocky Mountain locusts (*Melanoplus spretus*) that passed over Nebraska on 15–25 Aug. 1875. According to one local scientist who watched their movements for five days, these locusts covered an area of 198,600 miles² as they flew over the state. If he over-estimated the size of the swarm by 50 percent, it still covered 99,300 miles², which is approximately the area of Colorado or Oregon. It has been calculated that this swarm of locusts contained at least 12.5 trillion (10^{12}) insects, with an aggregate weight of 27.5 million tons. For unexplained reasons, this pest mysteriously disappeared in 1902 and has not been seen since.

Most prodigious eater   The larva of the Polyphemus moth (*Antheraea polyphemus*) of North America consumes an amount equal to 86,000 times its own birth weight in the first 56 days of its life. In human terms, this would be equivalent to a 7-lb. baby taking in 301 tons of nourishment!

Weight loss   During the 7-month lactation period, a 132-ton female blue whale (*Balaenoptera musculus*) can lose up to 25 percent of her body weight nursing her calf.

Most valuable   The most valuable animals in cash terms are thoroughbred racehorses. The most ever paid for a yearling was $13.1 million on 23 July 1985 at Keeneland, KY by Robert Sangster and partners for Seattle Dancer. (See Horse Racing.)

Size difference   Although many differences exist in the animal world between the males and females of species, the most striking difference in size can be seen in the marine worm *Bonellia viridis*. The females of this species are 4–40 in. long compared with just 0.04–0.12 in. for the male, making the females millions of times heavier than the males.

Slowest growth   The slowest growth in the animal kingdom is that of the deep-sea clam *Tindaria callistisormis* of the North Atlantic, which takes *c*. 100 years to reach a length of 0.31 in.

Largest eye   The Atlantic giant squid has the largest eye of any animal, living or extinct. It has been estimated that the one recorded at Thimble Tickle Bay had eyes 15.75 in. in diameter. (See Mollusks.)

MAMMALS *Mammalia*

Largest   The longest and heaviest mammal in the world, and the largest animal ever recorded, is the blue or sulphur-bottom whale (*Balaenoptera musculus*), also called Sibbald's rorqual. Newborn calves measure 21 ft. 3½

DEEPEST DIVE. A welcome breather for this sperm whale (*Physeter catodon*), which may descend to depths of over 9,840 ft., for dives lasting almost two hours. (Photo: Planet Earth Pictures)

in.–28½ ft. in length and weigh up to 6,614 lbs. The barely visible ovum of the blue whale, weighing a fraction of a milligram, grows to a weight of *c.* 29 tons in 22¾ months, made up of 10¾ months' gestation and the first 12 months of life. This is equivalent to an increase of 30 billion. (See General records.)

Despite being protected by law since 1967 and the implementation of a global ban on commercial whaling, the population of the blue whale has declined to tens of thousands from peak estimates of about 200,000 at the turn of the century.

Heaviest   A female blue whale measuring 90 ft. 6 in., caught in the Southern Ocean by the Soviet Slava whaling fleet on 20 Mar. 1947, weighed 209 tons.

Longest   The longest specimen ever recorded was a female blue whale landed in 1909 at Grytviken, South Georgia, Falkland Islands in the South Atlantic; it measured 110 ft. 2½ in. in length.

Deepest dive   In 1970 American scientists, by triangulating the location clicks of sperm whales, calculated that the *maximum* depth reached by this species was 8,202 ft. However, on 25 Aug. 1969 another bull sperm whale was killed 100 miles south of Durban, South Africa after it had surfaced from a dive lasting 1 hr. 52 min., and inside its stomach were found two small sharks that had been swallowed about an hour earlier. These were later identified as *Scymnodon sp.*, a type of dogfish found only on the seafloor. At this point from land the depth of water exceeds 9,876 ft. for a radius of 30–40 miles, which suggests that the sperm whale sometimes descends to a depth of over 9,840 ft. when seeking food and is limited by pressure of time rather than by water pressure.

Largest on land   The largest living land animal is the African bush elephant (*Loxodonta africana*). The average adult bull stands 10 ft. 6 in. at the shoulder and weighs 6.3 tons. The largest specimen ever recorded was a bull shot in Mucusso, Angola on 7 Nov. 1974. Lying on its side this elephant measured 13 ft. 8 in. in a projected line from the highest point of the shoulder to the base of the forefoot, indicating that its standing height must have been about 13 ft. Other measurements included an overall length of 35 ft. (tip of extended trunk to tip of extended tail) and a forefoot circumference of 5 ft. 11 in. The weight was computed to be 13.5 tons.

Tallest   The endangered desert elephant of Damaraland in Namibia (reduced to 84 individuals in August 1981) is the tallest species of elephant in the world because it has proportionately longer legs than other elephants.

The tallest elephant ever recorded was a bull shot near Sesfontein in Damaraland, Namibia on 4 Apr. 1978 after it had reportedly killed 11 people and caused widespread crop damage. Lying on its side, this mountain of flesh measured 14½ ft. in a projected line from the shoulder to the base of the forefoot, indicating a standing height of about 13 ft. 10 in. Other measurements included an overall length of 34 ft. 1 in., and a forefoot circumference of 5 ft. 2 in. This particular animal weighed an estimated 8.8 tons.

Largest marine   The largest toothed mammal ever recorded is the sperm whale (*Physeter catodon*), also called the cachalot. In the summer of 1950 a record-sized bull measuring 67 ft. 11 in. was captured off the Kurile Islands in the Pacific by a Soviet whaling fleet, but much larger bulls were reported in the early days of whaling. The 16-ft.-4¾-in.-long lower jaw of a sperm whale exhibited in the British Museum (Natural History) in London belonged to a bull measuring nearly 84 ft., and similar lengths have been reported for other outsized individuals killed.

Tallest on land   The giraffe (*Giraffa camelopardalis*), which is now found only in the dry savannah and semidesert areas of Africa south of the Sahara, is the tallest living animal. The tallest ever recorded was a Masai bull (*G. camelopardalis tippelskirchi*) named George, received at Chester Zoo, Great Britain on 8 Jan. 1959 from Kenya. His "horns" *almost* grazed the roof of the 20-ft.-high Giraffe House when he was nine years old. George died on 22 July 1969. Less-credible heights of up to 23 ft. (measured between pegs) have been claimed for bulls shot in the field.

Smallest on land   Kitti's hog-nosed bat (*Craseonycteristhonglongyai*), also called the bumblebee bat, has a wing span of about 6.3 in. and weighs 0.06–0.07 oz. It is confined to about 21 limestone caves on the Kwae Noi River, Kanchanaburi, Thailand. (See Bats.)

The smallest land mammal in terms of length is Savi's white-toothed pygmy shrew, also called the Etruscan shrew (*Suncus etruscus*), which has a head and body length of 1.32–2.04 in., a tail length of 0.94–1.14 in. and weighs 0.05–0.09 oz. It is found along the Mediterranean coast and southward to Cape Province, South Africa. (See Insectivores.)

Smallest marine   In terms of weight, the smallest totally marine mammal is probably Commerson's dolphin (*Cephalorhynchus commersonii*), also known as Le Jacobite, which is found off the tip of South America. The weights of a group of six adult specimens ranged from 50.7 lbs. to 77.1 lbs. The sea otter (*Enhydra lutris*) of the North Pacific is of comparable size (55–81.4 lbs.), but this species sometimes comes ashore during storms.

Fastest on land   Over a short distance (i.e., up to 1,800 ft.) the cheetah or hunting leopard (*Acinonyx jubatus*) of the open plains of East Africa, Iran, Turkmenistan and Afghanistan has a probable maximum speed of 60–63 mph on level ground.

The fastest land animal over a sustained distance (i.e., 3,000 ft. or more) is the pronghorn antelope (*Antilocapra americana*) of the western United States. Specimens have been observed to travel at 35 mph for 4 miles, at 42 mph for 1 mile, and at 55 mph for ½ mile.

Fastest marine   On 12 Oct. 1958 a bull killer whale (*Orcinus orca*), measuring an estimated 20–25 ft. in length, was timed at 34.5 mph in the east Pacific. Similar speeds have also been reported for Dall's porpoise (*Phocoenoides dalli*) in short bursts.

Slowest   The ai or three-toed sloth (*Bradypus tridactylus*) of tropical South America has an average ground speed of 6–8 ft. per minute (0.07–0.1 mph), but in the trees it can "accelerate" to 15 ft. per minute (0.17 mph).

Sleepiest   Some armadillos (Dasypodidae), opossums (Didelphidae) and sloths (Bradypodidae) spend up to 80 percent of their lives sleeping or dozing, while it is claimed that Dall's porpoise (*Phocoenoides dalli*) never sleeps at all.

Oldest   No other mammal can match the extreme proven age of 120 years attained by humans (*Homo sapiens*; see Chapter 3). It is probable that the closest approach is made by the Asiatic elephant (*Elephas maximus*). Sri Lanka's famous bull elephant Rajah, which had led the annual Perahera procession through Kandi carrying the Sacred Tooth of the Buddha since 1931, died on 16 July 1988, reportedly at the age of 81 years. The greatest age that has been verified with certainty is 78 years in the case of a cow named Modoc, which died at Santa Clara, CA on 17 July 1975. She was imported into the United States from Germany in 1898 at the age of two.

Highest-living   The yak (*Bos grunniens*), of Tibet and the Sichuanese Alps, China, occasionally climbs to an altitude of 20,000 ft. when foraging.

Largest herds   The largest herds on record were those of the springbok (*Antidorcas marsupialis*) during migration across the plains of the western parts of southern Africa in the 19th century. In 1849 John Fraser observed a herd that took three days to pass through the settlement of Beaufort West, Cape Province, South Africa. Another herd seen moving near Nels Poortje, Cape Province in 1888 was estimated to contain 100 million head, although 10 million is probably a more realistic figure. A herd estimated to be 15 miles wide and more than 100 miles long was reported from Karree Kloof, Orange River, South Africa in July 1896.

Longest gestation period   The Asiatic elephant (*Elephas maximus*) has an average gestation period of 609 days (over 20 months) and a maximum of 760 days—more than two and a half times that of a human.

Shortest gestation period   The gestation periods of the American opossum (*Didelphis marsupialis*), also called the Virginian opossum, the rare water opossum or yapok (*Chironectes minimus*) of central and northern South

HIGHEST-LIVING MAMMAL. A head for heights is useful to the yak (*Bos grunniens*) when foraging for food at altitudes of 20,000 ft. (Photo: Jacana Agence de Presse/E. Dragesco)

America, and the eastern native cat (*Dasyurus viverrinus*) of Australia are all normally 12–13 days but can be as short as eight days.

Largest litter   The greatest number of young born to a *wild* mammal at a single birth is 31 (30 of which survived) in the case of the tailless tenrec (*Tenrec ecaudatus*) found in Madagascar and the Comoro Islands. The normal litter size is 12–15, although females can suckle up to 24.

Youngest breeder   The streaked tenrec (*Hemicentetes semispinosus*) of Madagascar is weaned after only five days, and females can breed 3–4 weeks after their birth.

CARNIVORES

Largest on land   The average adult male Kodiak bear (*Ursus arctos middendorffi*), native to Kodiak Island and the adjacent Afognak and Shuyak islands in the Gulf of Alaska, has a nose-to-tail length of 8 ft., with the tail measuring about 4 in. It stands 52 in. at the shoulder and weighs 1,050–1,175 lbs. In 1894 a weight of 1,656 lbs. was recorded for a male shot at English Bay, Kodiak Island, whose *stretched* skin measured 13½ ft. from nose to tail. This weight was exceeded by a "cage-fat" male in the Cheyenne Mountain Zoological Park, Colorado Springs, CO, which weighed 1,670 lbs. at the time of its death on 22 Sep. 1955.

Heaviest   In 1981 an unconfirmed weight of over 2,000 lbs. was reported for a peninsula giant bear (*Ursus a. gyas*) from Alaska on exhibition at the Space Farms Zoological Park in Beemerville, NJ.

Largest litigon An adult male litigon (a hybrid of an Indian lion and a tigon—itself the offspring of a tiger and a lioness) named Cubanacan at Alipore Zoological Gardens, Calcutta, India is believed to weigh at least 800 lbs. This animal stands 52 in. at the shoulder (compared with 44 in. for the lion Simba) and measures a record 11½ ft. in total length. This animal, the first and only one of its kind, was reported to have died on 12 Apr. 1991.

Weights exceeding 2,000 lbs. have also been reported for the polar bear (*Ursus maritimus*), but the average adult male weighs 850–900 lbs. and measures 7 ft. 9 in. from nose to tail. In 1960 a polar bear reportedly weighing 2,210 lbs. was shot at the polar entrance to Kotzebue Sound, AK. In April 1962 the 11-ft.-1¼-in.-tall mounted specimen was put on display at the Seattle World's Fair.

Smallest The smallest living member of the order Carnivora is the least weasel (*Mustela rixosa*), also called the dwarf weasel, which is circumpolar in distribution. Four races are recognized, the smallest of which is *Mustela r. pygmaea* of Siberia, Russia. Mature specimens have an overall length of 6.96–8.14 in. and weigh 1¼–2½ oz.

Largest feline The largest member of the cat family (*Felidae*) is the protected long-furred Siberian tiger (*Panthera tigris altaica*), also called the Amur or Manchurian tiger. Adult males average 10 ft. 4 in. in length from the nose to the tip of the extended tail, stand 39–42 in. at the shoulder and weigh about 585 lbs. In 1950 a male weighing 846.5 lbs. was shot in the Sikhote Alin Mountains, Maritime Territory, Russia.

An outsized Indian tiger (*Panthera tigris tigris*) shot in northern Uttar Pradesh in November 1967 measured 10 ft. 7 in. between pegs (11 ft. 1 in. over the curves) and weighed 857 lbs. (compared with 9 ft. 3 in. and 420 lbs. for an average adult male). Its stuffed body is now on display in the Museum of Natural History at the Smithsonian Institution, Washington, D.C.

Captive The largest tiger ever held in captivity, and the heaviest "big cat" on record, is a nine-year-old Siberian male named Jaipur, owned by animal trainer Joan Byron-Marasek of Clarksburg, NJ. This specimen measured 10 ft. 11 in. in total length and weighed 932 lbs. in October 1986.

Lions The average adult African lion (*Panthera leo*) measures 9 ft. overall, stands 36–38 in. at the shoulder and weighs 400–410 lbs. The heaviest wild specimen on record weighed 690 lbs. and was shot near Hectorspruit, Transvaal, South Africa in 1936.

In July 1970 a weight of 826 lbs. was reported for a black-maned lion named Simba (b. Dublin Zoo, Ireland, 1959) at Colchester Zoo, Essex, Great Britain. He died on 16 Jan. 1973 at the now-defunct Knaresborough Zoo, North Yorkshire, Great Britain.

Smallest feline The smallest member of the cat family is the rusty-spotted cat (*Felis rubiginosa*) of southern India and Sri Lanka. The average adult male has an overall length of 25–28 in. (the tail measures 9–10 in.) and weighs about 3 lbs.

PRIMATES

Largest living   The average adult male eastern lowland gorilla (*Gorilla g. graueri*) of the lowland forests of eastern Zaïre and southwestern Uganda stands 5 ft. 9 in. tall and weighs 360 lbs.

The mountain gorilla (*Gorilla g. beringei*) of the volcanic mountain ranges of western Rwanda, southwestern Uganda and eastern Zaïre is of comparable size, i.e., 5 ft. 8 in. tall and 343 lbs., and most of the exceptionally large gorillas taken in the field have been of this race.

Tallest   The greatest height (top of crest to heel) recorded for a gorilla in the wild is 6 ft. 2 in. for a male of the mountain race shot in the eastern Congo (Zaïre) *c.* 1920. The tallest gorilla ever kept in captivity is reportedly an eastern lowland male named Colossus (b. 1966), who is currently on display at a zoo in Gulf Breeze, FL. He reportedly stands 6 ft. 2 in. tall and weighs 575 lbs., but these figures have not yet been confirmed.

Heaviest   The heaviest gorilla ever kept in captivity was a male of the mountain race named N'gagi, who died in San Diego Zoo in California on 12 Jan. 1944 at the age of 18. He weighed 683 lbs. at his heaviest in 1943, and 635 lbs. at the time of his death. He was 5 ft. 7¾ in. tall and boasted a record chest measurement of 78 in.

Monkey   The only species of monkey reliably credited with weights of more than 100 lbs. is the mandrill (*Mandrillus sphinx*) of equatorial West Africa. The greatest reliable weight recorded is 119 lbs. for a captive male, but an unconfirmed weight of 130 lbs. has been reported. (Adult females are about half the size of males.)

Oldest   The greatest age recorded for a nonhuman primate is 59 years 5 months for a chimpanzee (*Pan troglodytes*) named Gamma, who died at the Yerkes Primate Research Center in Atlanta, GA on 19 Feb. 1992. Gamma was born at the Florida branch of the Yerkes Center in September 1932. A similar age was reached by a male orangutan (*Pongo pygmaeus*) named Guas, who died in Philadelphia Zoological Garden, PA on 9 Feb. 1977. He was at least 13 years old on his arrival at the zoo on 1 May 1931.

Monkey   The world's oldest monkey, a male white-throated capuchin (*Cebus capucinus*) called Bobo, died on 10 July 1988 at the age of 53 following complications related to a stroke.

Smallest monkey   Adult specimens of the rare pen-tailed shrew (*Ptilocercus lowii* — classified by some experts as part of the Insectivore family instead of the Primate family) of Malaysia have a total length of 9–13 in. (head and body 4–5½ in.; tail 5–7½ in.) and weigh 1.23–1.76 oz.

The pygmy marmoset (*Cebuella pygmaea*) of the upper Amazon basin and the lesser mouse-lemur (*Microcebus murinus*) of Madagascar are of comparable length to the shrew but heavier, with adults weighing 1.75–2.65 oz. and 1.6–2.8 oz. respectively. The pygmy marmoset is also the smallest monkey.

PINNIPEDS *Seals, Sea Lions, Walruses*

Largest   The largest of the 34 known species of pinniped is the southern elephant seal (*Mirounga leonina*) of the sub-Antarctic islands. Adult bulls average 16½ ft. in length from the tip of the inflated snout to the tips of the outstretched tail flippers, have a maximum girth of 12 ft. and weigh about 5,000 lbs. The largest accurately measured specimen was a bull that probably weighed at least 4.4 tons and measured 21 ft. 4 in. after flensing (stripping of the blubber or skin). Its original length was about 22½ ft. It was killed in the South Atlantic at Possession Bay, South Georgia on 28 Feb. 1913.

Live   The largest recorded live specimen is a bull nicknamed "Stalin" from South Georgia. It was tranquilized by members of the British Antarctic Survey on 14 Oct. 1989 when it weighed 5,869 lbs. and measured 16½ ft.

Smallest   The smallest pinnipeds are the ringed seal (*Phoca hispida*) of the Arctic and the closely related Baikal seal (*P. sibirica*) of Lake Baikal and the Caspian seal (*P. caspica*) of the Caspian Sea, Asia. Adult males measure up to 5½ ft. in length and can weigh up to 280 lbs.

Oldest   A female gray seal (*Halichoerus grypus*) shot at Shunni Wick, Shetland, Great Britain on 23 Apr. 1969 was believed to be "at least 46 years old" based on a count of dentine rings. The captive record is an estimated 41 years (1901–42) for a bull gray seal named "Jacob" held in Skansen Zoo, Stockholm, Sweden.

Most abundant   The total population of the crabeater seal (*Lobodon carcinophagus*) of Antarctica was estimated in 1977 to be nearly 15 million.

Fastest   The highest swimming speed recorded for a pinniped is a short spurt of 25 mph by a California sea lion. The fastest-moving pinniped on land is the crabeater seal, which has been timed at speeds up to 12 mph.

Deepest dive   In May 1988 a team of scientists from the University of California at Santa Cruz tested the diving abilities of the northern elephant seal (*Mirounga anguistirostris*) off Ano Nuevo Point, CA. One female reached a record depth of 4,135 ft., and another remained submerged for 48 minutes. Similar experiments carried out by Australian scientists on southern elephant seals (*M. leonina*) in the Southern Ocean recorded a dive of 3,720 ft., with other dives lasting nearly two hours also observed. It was discovered that the seals regularly swam down to about 2,500 ft. and when they resurfaced apparently had no "oxygen debt."

BATS

Largest   The only flying mammals are bats (order Chiroptera), of which there are about 950 species. The largest in terms of wingspan is the Bismarck flying fox (*Pteropus neohibernicus*) of the Bismarck Archipelago and New Guinea. One specimen preserved in the American Museum of Natural History in New York City has a wing spread of 5 ft. 5 in., but some unmeasured bats probably reach 6 ft.

United States   Mature specimens of the large mastiff bat (*Eumops pero-*

tis), found in southern Texas, California, Arizona and New Mexico, have a wingspan of 22.04 in.

Smallest   The smallest bat in the world is Kitti's hog-nosed bat at 6.3 in. and 0.06–0.07 oz. (See Smallest land mammal.)

United States   The smallest native bat is the Western pipistrelle (*Pipistrellus hesperus*), found in the western United States. Mature specimens have a wingspan of 7.9 in.

Bats' highest detectable pitch   Because of their ultrasonic echolocation, bats have the most acute hearing of any terrestrial animal. Vampire bats (family Desmodontidae) and fruit bats (Pteropodidae) can hear frequencies as high as 120–210 kHz, compared with 20 kHz for the adult human limit and 280 kHz for the common dolphin (*Delphinus delphis*).

Fastest   Because of the great practical difficulties, little data on bat speeds has been published. The greatest velocity attributed to a bat is 32 mph in the case of a Mexican free-tailed bat (*Tadarida brasiliensis*), but this may have been wind-assisted. In one American experiment using an artificial mine tunnel and 17 different kinds of bat, only four of them managed to exceed 13 mph in level flight.

Oldest   The greatest age reliably reported for a bat is 32 years for a banded female little brown bat (*Myotis lucifugus*) in the United States in 1987.

Largest colonies   The largest concentration of bats found living anywhere in the world today is that of the Mexican free-tailed bat (*Tadarida brasiliensis*) in Bracken Cave, San Antonio, TX, where up to 20 million animals assemble after migration.

Deepest   The little brown bat (*Myotis lucifugus*) has been recorded at a depth of 3,805 ft. in a zinc mine in New York State. The mine serves as winter quarters for 1,000 members of this species, which normally roost at a depth of 650 ft.

RODENTS

Largest   The capybara (*Hydrochoerus hydrochaeris*), also called the carpincho or water hog, of tropical South America, has a head and body length of 3¼–4½ ft. and can weigh up to 250 lbs. (cage-fat specimen).

Smallest   The northern pygmy mouse (*Baiomys taylori*) of central Mexico and southern Arizona and Texas measures up to 4.3 in. in total length and weighs 0.24–0.28 oz.

Oldest   The greatest reliable age reported for a rodent is 27 years 3 months for a Sumatran crested porcupine (*Hystrix brachyura*) that died in the National Zoological Park, Washington, D.C. on 12 Jan. 1965.

Longest hibernation   The barrow ground squirrel
(*Spermophilus parryi barrowensis*) of Point Barrow, AK
hibernates for nine months of the year. During the remaining three
months it feeds, breeds and collects food for storage in its burrow.

Fastest breeder   The female meadow vole (*Microtus agrestis*), found in
Great Britain, can reproduce from the age of 25 days and can have up to 17
litters of 6–8 young in a year.

INSECTIVORES

Largest   The moon rat (*Echinosorex gymnurus*), also known as Raffles'
gymnure, which is found in Myanmar (formerly Burma), Thailand, Malaysia,
Sumatra and Borneo, has a head and body length of 10½–17½ in., a tail measuring 7.9–8.3 in. and weighs up to 3.1 lbs.

Heaviest   The European hedgehog (*Erinaceus europaeus*) is much shorter
overall (7.7–11.7 in.), but well-fed examples have been known to weigh as
much as 4.19 lbs.

Smallest   The smallest insectivore is Savi's white-toothed pygmy shrew
(*Suncus etruscus*). (See Smallest land mammals.)

**LIGHTEST ANTELOPE. Salt's dik-dik (*Madoqua saltina*), so named
because of the noise it makes when alarmed, may well look
apprehensive, as it weighs a mere 8 lbs. and stands only 14 in. tall.
(Photo: Jacana Agence de Presse/François Gohier)**

Oldest The greatest reliable age recorded for an insectivore is over 16 years for a lesser hedgehog-tenrec (*Echinops telfairi*), which was born in Amsterdam Zoo, Netherlands in 1966 and was later sent to Jersey Zoo, Channel Islands, Great Britain. It died on 27 Nov. 1982.

ANTELOPES

Largest The rare giant eland (*Taurotragus derbianus*) of western and central Africa may surpass 2,000 lbs. The common eland (*Taurotragus oryx*) of eastern and southern Africa has the same shoulder height of up to 5 ft. 10 in. but is not quite so massive, although there is one record of a 5 ft. 5 in. bull shot in Malawi *c.* 1937 that weighed 2,078 lbs.

Smallest Mature specimens of the royal antelope (*Neotragus pygmaeus*) of western Africa measure 10–12 in. at the shoulder and weigh only 7–8 lbs., which is the size of a large brown hare (*Lepus europaeus*).

Lightest Salt's dik-dik (*Madoqua saltina*) of northeastern Ethiopia and Somalia weighs only 5–6 lbs. when adult, but this species stands about 14 in. at the withers (highest part of the back of an animal).

Oldest The greatest reliable age recorded for an antelope is 25 years 4 months for an addax (*Addax nasomaculatus*) that died in Brookfield Zoo, Chicago, IL on 15 Oct. 1960.

DEER

Largest The largest deer is the Alaskan moose (*Alces alces gigas*). Adult bulls average 6 ft. at the shoulder and weigh *c.* 1,100 lbs. A bull standing 7 ft. 8 in. between pegs and weighing an estimated 1,800 lbs. was shot on the Yukon River in the Yukon Territory, Canada in September 1897. Unconfirmed measurements of up to 8 ft. 6 in. at the shoulder and estimated weights of up to 2,600 lbs. have been claimed.

Smallest The smallest true deer (family Cervidae) is the northern pudu (*Pudu mephistopheles*) of Ecuador and Colombia. Mature specimens measure 13–14 in. at the shoulder and weigh 16–18 lbs.

The smallest ruminant is the lesser Malay chevrotain (*Tragulus javanicus*) of southeast Asia, Sumatra and Borneo. Adults measure 8–10 in. at the shoulder and weigh 6–7 lbs.

Oldest The world's oldest recorded deer is a red deer (*Cervus elaphus scoticus*) named Bambi (b. 8 June 1963), owned by the Fraser family of Kiltarlity, Great Britain.

United States The greatest reliable age recorded for a deer is 26 years 8 months for a red deer (*Cervus elaphus scoticus*) that died in the Milwaukee Zoo, WI on 28 June 1954.

MARSUPIALS

Largest The adult male red kangaroo (*Megaleia rufa* or *Macropus rufus*) of central, southern and eastern Australia stands up to 7 ft. tall, measures up to 8 ft. ½ in. in total length and weighs up to 187 lbs.

> **Oldest marsupial**   The greatest reliable age recorded for a marsupial is 26 years 22 days for a common wombat (*Vombatus ursinus*) that died in London Zoo, Great Britain on 20 Apr. 1906.
>
> **Fastest speed**   The fastest speed recorded for a marsupial is 40 mph for a mature female eastern gray kangaroo (*Macropus giganteus* or *M. canguru*). One large male red kangaroo died from his exertions after being paced for one mile at 35 mph.

Smallest   The smallest-known marsupial is the rare long-tailed planigale (*Planigale ingrami*), a flat-skulled mouse of northeastern and northwestern Australia. Adult males have a head and body length of 2.16–2.48 in., a tail length of 2.24–2.36 in. and weigh 0.13–0.19 oz.

Highest jump   A captive eastern gray kangaroo once cleared an 8-ft. fence when an automobile backfired, and there is also a record of a hunted red kangaroo clearing a stack of timber 10 ft. high.

Longest jump   During the course of a chase in New South Wales, Australia in January 1951, a female red kangaroo made a series of bounds that included one of 42 ft. There is also an unconfirmed report of an eastern gray kangaroo jumping nearly 44 ft. 8½ in. on level ground.

TUSKS

Longest   The longest recorded elephant tusks (excluding prehistoric examples) are a pair from Zaïre preserved in the National Collection of Heads and Horns kept by the New York Zoological Society (Bronx Zoo), New York City. The right tusk measures 11 ft. 5½ in. along the outside curve and the left tusk measures 11 ft. Their combined weight is 293 lbs. A single tusk of 11 ft. 6 in. has been reported.

Heaviest   A pair of tusks in the British Museum (Natural History), London collected from an aged bull shot at the foot of Mt. Kilimanjaro, Kenya in 1897 originally weighed 240 lbs. (length 10 ft. 2½ in.) and 225 lbs. (length 10 ft. 5½ in.) respectively, giving a total weight of 465 lbs., but their combined weight today is 440½ lbs. A single elephant tusk collected in Benin, Africa and exhibited at the Paris Exposition, France in 1900 weighed 258 lbs.

HORNS

Longest   The longest horns grown by any living animal are those of the water buffalo (*Bubalus arnee=B. bubalis*) of India. One huge bull shot in 1955 had horns measuring 13 ft. 11 in. from tip to tip along the outside curve across the forehead. The longest single horn on record measured 81¼ in. along the outside curve and was found on a specimen of domestic ankole cattle (*Bos taurus*) near Lake Ngami, Botswana.

Domestic animal   The largest spread recorded for a Texas longhorn steer is 10 ft. 6 in. The horns are currently on exhibition at the Heritage Museum, Big Springs, TX.

ANTLERS

Largest   The record antler spread or "rack" is 78½ in. (skull and antlers 91 lbs.) for a set taken from a moose killed near the headwaters of the Stewart River in the Yukon Territory, Canada in October 1897. The antlers are now on display in the Field Museum, Chicago, IL.

HORSES AND PONIES

There are approximately 5.25 to 6.0 million domestic horses in the United States. The documented population of wild horses on public lands in the United States is 47,720, of which 33,987 can be found in Nevada. The population of wild burros in the nation stands at 7,241, with 3,018 in Arizona.

Earliest domestication   Evidence from the Ukraine indicates that horses may have been ridden by at least 4000 B.C. (See Agriculture.)

Largest   The tallest and heaviest documented horse was the shire gelding Sampson (later renamed Mammoth), bred by Thomas Cleaver of Toddington Mills, Bedfordshire, Great Britain. This horse (foaled 1846) measured 21.2½ hands (7 ft. 2½ in.) in 1850 and was later said to have weighed 3,360 lbs.

Boringdon Black King (foaled 1984), a shire gelding born and bred at the National Shire Horse Center in Plymouth, Great Britain, stands 19.2 hands (6½ ft.), making him the world's tallest living horse.

Thoroughbred   The tallest recorded non-draft horse was a Canadian thoroughbred gelding named Tritonis, owned by Christopher Ewing of Southfield, MI. This show jumper, which died in September 1990 at the age of 7, stood 19.2 hands (6½ ft.) and weighed 2,100 lbs. (For record horse prices see Agriculture.)

Oldest living pony   The oldest living pony in the United States is Trigger, at 47 years of age on 26 Feb. 1992. He is owned by Dorothy B. Cruise in Whiteside, MO.

Smallest   The Falabela of Argentina was developed over a period of 70 years by inbreeding and crossing a small group of undersized horses originally discovered in the southern part of the country. Most adult specimens stand less than 30 in. and average 80–100 lbs. in weight. The smallest mature horse bred by Julio Falabela of Recco de Roca before he died in 1981 was a mare that stood 15 in. and weighed 26¼ lbs.

The stallion Little Pumpkin (foaled 15 Apr. 1973), owned by J.C. Williams Jr. of Della Terra Mini Horse Farm, Inman, SC, stood 14 in. and weighed 20 lbs. on 30 Nov. 1975.

Oldest   The greatest age reliably recorded for a horse is 62 years in the case of Old Billy (foaled 1760), believed to be a cross between a Cleveland and eastern blood, bred by Edward Robinson of Wild Grave Farm, Woolston, Great Britain. Old Billy later worked along the local canals until 1819 and died on 27 Nov. 1822.

Thoroughbred   The greatest age recorded for a thoroughbred racehorse is 42 years, in the case of the chestnut gelding Tango Duke (foaled 1935), owned by Mrs. Carmen J. Koper of Barongarook, Victoria, Australia. The horse died on 25 Jan. 1978.

Pony   The greatest reliable age recorded for a pony is 54 years for a stallion owned by a farmer in central France (foaled 1919).

Mules   Apollo (foaled 1977) and Anak (foaled 1976), owned by Herbert L. Mueller of Chicago, IL, are the largest mules on record. Apollo measures 19.1 hands (6 ft. 5 in.) and weighs 2,200 lbs., with Anak at 18.3 hands (6 ft. 3 in.) and 2,100 lbs. Both are the hybrid offspring of Belgian mares and mammoth jacks.

DOGS

The canine population of the United States for 1991 was estimated by the Pet Food Institute at 53.3 million. There was at least one dog as a pet in 39 percent of the households in the United States.

Largest   The heaviest breeds of domestic dogs (*Canis familiaris*) are the Old English mastiff and the St. Bernard, with adult males of both species regularly weighing 170–200 lbs. The heaviest (and longest) dog ever recorded is Aicama Zorba of La-Susa (whelped 26 Sep. 1981), an Old English mastiff owned by Chris Eraclides of London, Great Britain. Zorba stands 37 in. at the shoulder and weighed 343 lbs. in November 1989. Other statistics include a chest girth of 58¾ in., a length of 8 ft. 3½ in. and a neck measurement of 37½ in.

Tallest   The Great Dane and the Irish wolfhound can exceed 39 in. at the

---

Guide dog   The longest period of *active service* reported for a guide dog is 14 years 8 months (August 1972–March 1987) in the case of a Labrador retriever bitch named Cindy-Cleo (whelped 20 Jan. 1971), owned by Aron Barr of Tel Aviv, Israel. The dog died on 10 Apr. 1987.

Largest dog show   The centennial of the annual Crufts show, held at the National Exhibition Center, Birmingham, Great Britain on 9–12 Jan. 1991, attracted a record 22,993 entries.

Longest jump   A greyhound named Bang jumped 30 ft. while chasing a hare at Brecon Lodge, Gloucestershire, Great Britain in 1849. He cleared a 4-ft.-6-in. gate and landed on a hard road, damaging his pastern bone.

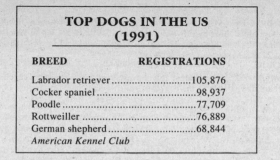

TOP DOGS IN THE US (1991)

BREED	REGISTRATIONS
Labrador retriever	105,876
Cocker spaniel	98,937
Poodle	77,709
Rottweiller	76,889
German shepherd	68,844

American Kennel Club

shoulder. The tallest dog ever recorded was Shamgret Danzas (whelped 1975), owned by Wendy and Keith Comley of Milton Keynes, Great Britain. He stood 41½ in., or 42 in. when his hackles were raised, and weighed up to 238 lbs. He died on 16 Oct. 1984.

Smallest *Miniature* versions of the Yorkshire terrier, the chihuahua and the toy poodle have been known to weigh less than 16 oz. as adults.

The smallest mature dog on record was a matchbox-sized Yorkshire terrier owned by Arthur Marples of Blackburn, Great Britain, a former editor of *Our Dogs*. This tiny atom, which died in 1945 at the age of nearly two years, stood 2½ in. at the shoulder and measured 3¾ in. from the tip of its nose to the root of its tail. Its weight was just 4 oz.

The smallest living adult dog is a miniature chihuahua named Peanuts (whelped 23 Sep. 1986), owned by Grace Parker of Wilson's Mills, NC. She measures 9.84 in. from head to tail, 5.5 in. at the shoulder and weighed 18 oz. on 25 Oct. 1988.

Oldest Most dogs live between 8 and 15 years, and authentic records of dogs living over 20 years are rare. They are generally the smaller breeds. The greatest reliable age recorded for a dog is 29 years 5 months for an Australian cattle-dog named Bluey, owned by Les Hall of Rochester, Victoria, Australia. The dog was obtained as a puppy in 1910 and worked among cattle and sheep for nearly 20 years. He was put to sleep on 14 Nov. 1939.

Most prolific The greatest sire ever was the champion greyhound Low Pressure, nicknamed Timmy (whelped Sep. 1957), owned by Bruna Amhurst of London, Great Britain. From Dec. 1961 until his death on 27 Nov. 1969 he fathered 2,414 registered puppies, with at least 600 others unregistered.

Most valuable The largest legacy devoted to a dog was by Miss Ella Wendel of New York, who bequeathed her standard poodle Toby $75 million in 1931.

Highest jump The canine "high jump" record for a leap and a scramble over a smooth wooden wall (without ribs or other aids) is held by a German shepherd dog named Volse, who scaled 11 ft. 9 in. at a demonstration in Avignon, France in November 1989. The dog is owned by Phillipe Clement of Aix-en-Provence, France.

Duke, a three-year-old German shepherd dog, handled by Cpl Graham Urry of the Royal Air Force base at Newton, Great Britain, scaled a ribbed wall with regulation shallow slats to a height of 11 ft. 9 in. on the British Broadcasting Corporation *Record Breakers* TV program on 11 Nov. 1986.

Tracking   In 1925 a Doberman pinscher named Sauer, trained by Detective-Sergeant Herbert Kruger, tracked a stock thief 100 miles across the Great Karroo, South Africa by scent alone.

Top show dogs   The greatest number of Challenge Certificates won by a dog is the 78 compiled by the famous chow chow Ch. U'Kwong King Solomon (whelped 21 June 1968). Owned and bred by Mrs. Joan Egerton of Bramhall, Great Britain, Solly won his first CC at the Cheshire Agricultural Society Championship Show on 4 June 1969, and his 78th CC was awarded at the City of Birmingham Championship Show on 4 Sep. 1976. He died on 3 Apr. 1978.

The greatest number of Best-in-Show awards won by any dog in all-breed shows is 203, compiled by the Scottish terrier bitch Ch. Braeburn's Close Encounter (whelped 22 Oct. 1978) by 10 Mar. 1985. She is owned by Sonnie Novick of Plantation Acres, FL.

Drug sniffing   The greatest sniffer-dogs on record are a pair of malinoises

CAGED PET LONGEVITY

ANIMAL/SPECIES	NAME (OWNER), ETC.	YEARS	MONTHS
BIRD *Canary*	*Joey* bought 1941, died 8 Apr. 1975 (K. Ross) Hull, Great Britain	34	—
Budgerigar	*Charlie* April 1948–20 June 1977 (J. Dinsey) London, Great Britain	29	2
RABBIT *Wild*	*Flopsy* caught 6 Aug. 1964 d. 29 June 1983 (L.B. Walker) Longford, Tasmania, Australia	18	10¾
GUINEA PIG	*Snowball* d. 14 Feb. 1979 (M.A. Wall) Bingham, Great Britain	14	10½
GERBIL *Mongolian*	*Sahara* May 1973–4 Oct. 1981 (Aaron Milstone) Lathrup Village, MI	8	4½
MOUSE *House*	*Fritzy* 11 Sep. 1977– 24 Apr. 1985 (Bridget Beard) West House School, Birmingham, Great Britain	7	7
RAT *Common*	*Rodney* b. Jan. 1983 (Rodney Mitchell) Tulsa, OK	7	1

called Rocky and Barco. These Belgian sheepdogs (whelped 1984) are members of an American stop-and-search team that patrols the Rio Grande Valley ("Cocaine Alley") along the southern Texas border. In 1988 alone they were involved in 969 seizures of drugs worth $182 million, and they are so proficient at their job that Mexican drug smugglers have put a $30,000 price on their heads. Rocky and Barco were awarded honorary titles of sergeant major and always wear their stripes when on duty.

CATS

The feline population of the United States for 1991 was estimated by the Pet Food Institute to be 62.4 million. There was at least one pet in 32 percent of the households in the United States.

Largest   The largest of the 330 breeds of domestic cat is the ragdoll, with males weighing 15–20 lbs. In the majority of domestic cats (*Felis catus*) the average weight of the adult male (tom) is 8.6 lbs., compared with 7.2 lbs. for female or queen. Neuters and spays are generally heavier.

In February 1988 an unconfirmed weight of 48 lbs. was reported for a cat named Edward Bear, owned by Jackie Fleming of Sydney, New South Wales, Australia.

The heaviest reliably recorded domestic cat was a neutered male tabby named Himmy, owned by Thomas Vyse of Redlynch, Queensland, Australia.

LARGEST PET LITTERS

ANIMAL/BREED	NO.	OWNER	DATE
CAT *Burmese/Siamese*	19[1]	Mrs. Valerie Gane, Church Westcote, Great Britain	August 1970
DOG *American foxhound*	23	Cdr. W.N. Ely, Ambler, PA	June 1944
DOG *St. Bernard*	23[2]	R. and A. Rodden, Lebanon, MO	February 1975
DOG *Great Dane*	23[3]	Mrs. Marjorie Harris, Little Hall, Great Britain	June 1987
FERRET	15	John Cliff, Denstone, Great Britain	1981
GERBIL *Mongolian*	14[4]	Sharon Kirkman, Bulwell, Great Britain	May 1983
GUINEA PIG (CAVY)	12	Laboratory specimen	1972
HAMSTER *Golden*	26[5]	L. and S. Miller, Baton Rouge, LA	February 1974
MOUSE *House*	34[6]	Marion Ogilvie, Blackpool, Great Britain	February 1982
RABBIT *New Zealand white*	24	Joseph Filek, Sydney, Nova Scotia, Canada	1978

[1] 4 stillborn [2] 14 survived [3] 16 survived [4] Litter of 15 recorded 1960s by George Meares, geneticist-owner of gerbil-breeding farm, St. Petersburg, FL. Used special food formula [5] 18 killed by mother [6] 33 survived .

At the time of his death (from respiratory failure) on 12 Mar. 1986 at the age of 10 years 4 months he weighed 46 lbs. 15¼ oz. (neck 15 in., waist 33 in., length 38 in.).

Oldest   Cats generally live longer than dogs. The average life expectancy of intact (unaltered) well-fed males raised under household conditions and receiving good medical attention is 13–15 years (15–17 years for intact females), but neutered males and females live on the average one to two years longer.

A tabby named Puss, owned by Mrs. T. Holway of Clayhidon, Great Britain, reportedly celebrated his 36th birthday on 28 Nov. 1939 and died the next day, but conclusive evidence is lacking. The oldest reliably recorded cat was the female tabby Ma, owned by Alice St. George Moore of Drewsteignton, Great Britain. This cat was put to sleep on 5 Nov. 1957 at the age of 34.

Largest cat show   The largest cat show ever held in the United States was at the Cerrantes Convention Center, St. Louis, MO from 19–20 Nov. 1988; it attracted a record 814 entries.

Best climber   On 6 Sep. 1950 a four-month-old kitten belonging to Josephine Aufdenblatten of Geneva, Switzerland followed a group of climbers to the top of the 14,691 ft. Matterhorn in the Alps.

Smallest cat   The smallest breed of domestic cat is the Singapura or drain cat of Singapore. Adult males average 6 lbs. in weight and adult females 4 lbs.

A male Siamese cross named Ebony-Eb-Honey Cat, owned by Angelina Johnston of Boise, ID, weighed only 1 lb. 12 oz. in February 1984 at the age of 23 months.

TOP CATS IN THE US
(1991)

BREED	REGISTRATIONS
Persian	
Traditional	20,109
Pointed Pattern	19,730
Colorpoint Carrier	12,998
Siamese	3,188
Maine Coon	2,844
Abyssinian	1,688
Exotic Shorthair	1,329

Cat Fanciers' Association, Inc.

Most prolific   A tabby named Dusty (b. 1935) of Bonham, TX produced 420 kittens during her breeding life. She gave birth to her last litter (a single kitten) on 12 June 1952.

In May 1987 Kitty, owned by George Johnstone of Croxton, Great Britain, produced two kittens at the age of 30 years, making her the oldest feline mother on record. She died in June 1989, just short of her 32nd birthday, having given birth to a known total of 218 kittens.

RABBITS AND HARES

According to the American Rabbit Breeders Association, as of 1 Jan. 1992 there were at least 250,000 families in the United States with at least one pet rabbit.

Largest   The largest breed of domestic rabbit (*Oryctolagus cuniculus*) is the Flemish giant. Adults weigh 15.4–18.7 lbs. (average toe-to-toe length when fully stretched is 36 in.), but weights of up to 25 lbs. have been reliably reported for this breed. In April 1980 a five-month-old French lop doe weighing 26.45 lbs. was exhibited at the Reus Fair in northeast Spain.

The heaviest recorded wild rabbit (average weight 3½ lbs.) weighed 8 lbs. 4 oz. and was killed on 20 Nov. 1982.

Smallest   The Netherland dwarf and the Polish dwarf both have a weight range of 2–2½ lbs. when fully grown. In 1975 Jacques Bouloc of Coulommière, France announced a new cross of the above breeds that weighed 14 oz.

Most prolific   The most prolific domestic breeds are the New Zealand

LONGEST-EARED RABBIT. Therese Seward (left) holds up the record-breaking 28½ in. ears of her champion English lop "Sweet Majestic Star," whose record will no doubt soon be challenged by the ears of son "Easter Magic," shown off by Therese's daughter, Cheryl. (Photo: Therese and Cheryl Seward)

white and the Californian. Does produce 5–6 litters a year, each containing 8–12 kittens during their breeding life (compare with five litters and 3–7 young for the wild rabbit).

Longest ears   The longest ears are found in the Lop family (four strains), and in particular the English Lop. The ears of a typical example measure about 24 in. from tip to tip (taken across the skull), and 5.51 in. in width. In 1901 a specimen was exhibited in England that had 30.5-in. ears; it is not known, however, if this was a natural attainment or if weights had been used to stretch the ears and left the veins inside badly varicosed.

"Sweet Majestic Star," a black English lop rabbit owned by Therese and Cheryl Seward of Exeter, Great Britain, has ears measuring 28½ in. long and 7.4 in. wide.

Largest hare   In Nov. 1956 a Brown hare weighing 15 lbs. 1 oz. was shot near Welford, Great Britain. The average adult weight is 8 lbs.

BIRDS *Aves*

Largest ratite   The largest living bird is the North African ostrich (*Struthio c. camelus*), which is found in reduced numbers south of the Atlas Mountains from Upper Senegal and Niger across to the Sudan and central Ethiopia. Male examples (adult hens are smaller) of this flightless (ratite) subspecies have been recorded up to 9 ft. in height and 345 lbs. in weight. The heaviest subspecies is *S. c. australis*, which can weigh 330 lbs., although there is an unsubstantiated record of 353 lbs.

Largest carinate   The world's heaviest flying birds are the Kori bustard or paauw (*Ardeotis kori*) of northeast and southern Africa and the great bustard (*Otis tarda*) of Europe and Asia. Weights of 42 lbs. have been reported for the former, and there is an unconfirmed record of 46.3 lbs. for a male great bustard shot in Manchuria that was too heavy to fly. The heaviest reliably recorded great bustard weighed 39.7 lbs.

The mute swan (*Cygnus olor*), which is resident in Britain, can reach 40 lbs. on very rare occasions, and there is a record from Poland of a male weighing 49.6 lbs. that had temporarily lost the power of flight.

Bird of prey   The heaviest bird of prey is the Andean condor (*Vultur gryphus*), adult males averaging 20–25 lbs. A weight of 31 lbs. has been claimed for an outsized male California condor (*Gymnogyps californianus*) now preserved in the California Academy of Sciences at Los Angeles. This species is appreciably smaller than the Andean condor and rarely exceeds 23 lbs.

Largest wingspan   The wandering albatross (*Diomedea exulans*) of the southern oceans has the largest wingspan of any living bird, adult males averaging 10 ft. 4 in. with wings at full stretch. The largest recorded specimen was a very old male with a wingspan of 11 ft. 11 in., caught by members of the Antarctic research ship USGS *Eltanin* in the Tasman Sea on 18 Sep. 1965.

MOST ABUNDANT BIRD. Gazelle and ibex in Botswana veiled by just a few of the estimated breeding population of 1.5 billion red-billed queleas (*Quelea quelea*). (Photo: Jacana Agence de Presse/P. Jaunet)

Unconfirmed measurements up to 13 ft. 10 in. have been claimed for this species.

The only other bird reliably credited with a wingspan exceeding 11 ft. is the vulturelike marabou stork (*Leptoptilus crumeniferus*) of tropical Africa.

Smallest   The smallest bird in the world is the bee hummingbird (*Mellisuga helenae*) of Cuba and the Isle of Pines. Adult males (females are slightly larger) measure 2.24 in. in total length, half of which is taken up by the bill and tail, and weigh 0.056 oz. (females are slightly heavier).

Bird of prey   The smallest bird of prey is the 1.23 oz. white-fronted falconet (*Microhierax latifrons*) of northwestern Borneo, which is sparrow-sized.

United States   The smallest American bird is the calliope hummingbird (*Stellula calliope*). Adult specimens measure 2 ¾–3 ½ in. from bill to tail with a wingspan of 4 ½ in. and an approximate weight of ¹/₁₀ oz. The calliope is found in the western United States.

Most abundant   The red-billed quelea (*Quelea quelea*), a seed-eating weaver of the drier parts of Africa south of the Sahara, has an estimated adult breeding population of 1.5 billion, and at least 1 billion of these "feathered locusts" are slaughtered annually without having any impact on the population. One huge roost in the Sudan contained 32 million birds.

United States   The red-winged blackbird (*Agelaius phoeniceus*) had a population of 25.6 million birds as of January 1983. The US Fish and Wildlife

Service estimates the current total is at least 30 million. The blackbird is found throughout the country, except for desert and mountainous regions.

Fastest-flying   The fastest creature on the wing is the peregrine falcon (*Falco peregrinus*) when swooping from great heights during territorial displays. In one series of German experiments, a velocity of 168 mph was recorded at a 30° angle of descent, rising to a maximum of 217 mph at an angle of 45°.

The fastest fliers in level flight are found among the ducks and geese (Anatidae); some powerful species such as the red-breasted merganser (*Mergus serrator*), the eider (*Somateria mollissima*), the canvasback (*Aythya valisineria*) and the spur-winged goose (*Plectropterus gambiensis*) can probably exceed an airspeed of 65 mph.

United States   America's fastest bird is the white-throated swift (*Aeronautes saxatilis*), which has been estimated to fly at speeds of 200 mph. The peregrine falcon (*Falco peregrinus*) has been credited with a speed of 175 mph while in a dive. The dunlin (*Calidris alpina*) has been clocked from a plane at 110 mph.

Fastest wing-beat   The wing-beat of the horned sungem (*Heliactin cornuta*) of tropical South America is 90 beats/sec.

Slowest-flying   Probably at least 50 percent of the world's flying birds cannot exceed an air speed of 40 mph in level flight. The slowest-flying bird is the American woodcock (*Scolopax minor*), which, during courtship flights, has been timed at 5 mph without stalling.

Oldest   An unconfirmed age of *c*. 82 years was reported for a male Siberian white crane (*Crus leucogeranus*) named Wolf at the International Crane Foundation, Baraboo, WI. The bird was said to have hatched in a zoo in Switzerland *c*. 1905. He died in late 1988 after breaking his bill while repelling a visitor near his pen.

The greatest irrefutable age reported for any bird is over 80 years for a male sulfur-crested cockatoo (*Cacatua galerita*) named Cocky, who died at London Zoo, Great Britain in 1982. He was presented to the zoo in 1925, and had been with his previous owner since 1902 when he was already fully mature.

Domestic   The longest-lived domesticated bird (excluding the ostrich, which has been known to live up to 68 years) is the domestic goose (*Anser anser domesticus*), which may live about 25 years. On 16 Dec. 1976 a gander named George, owned by Florence Hull of Thornton, Great Britain, died at the age of 49 years 8 months. He was hatched in April 1927.

Brooding   A female royal albatross (*Diomedea epomophora*) named Grandma (Blue White), the oldest ringed seabird on record, laid an egg in November 1988 at the age of 60. She was first banded as a breeding adult in 1937 (such birds do not start breeding until they are 9 years old). She has raised 10 chicks of her own and fostered three others with her mate Green White Green, who is 47.

Longest flights   The greatest distance covered by a ringed bird is 14,000 miles by an arctic tern *(Sterna paradisea)*, which was banded as a nestling

Most talkative bird   A number of birds are renowned for their talking ability (i.e., the reproduction of words) but the African gray parrot (*Psittacus erythacus*) excels in this ability. A female named "Trudie," formerly owned by Lyn Logue (died January 1988) and now in the care of Iris Frost of Seaford, Great Britain, won the "Best talking parrot-like bird" title at the National Cage and Aviary Bird Show in London each December for 12 consecutive years (1965–76). "Trudie," who has a vocabulary of nearly 800 words, was taken from a nest at Jinja, Uganda in 1958. She retired undefeated.

Fastest swimmer   The gentoo penguin (*Pygoscelis papua*) has a maximum burst of speed of *c.* 17 mph.

Deepest dive   In 1969 a depth of 870 ft. was recorded for a small group of 10 emperor penguins (*Aptenodytes forsteri*) at Cape Crozier, Antarctica by a team of US scientists. One bird remained submerged for 18 minutes.

on 5 July 1955 in the Kandalaksha Sanctuary on the White Sea coast, Russia, and was captured alive by a fisherman 8 miles south of Fremantle, Western Australia on 16 May 1956. The bird had flown south via the Atlantic Ocean and then circled Africa before crossing the Indian Ocean. It did not survive to make the return journey.

In 1990 six foraging wandering albatrosses (*Diomedea exulans*) were tracked across the Indian Ocean by satellite via radio transmitters fitted by Pierre Jouventin and Henri Weimerskirch of the National Center for Scientific Research at Beauvoir, France. Results showed that the birds covered anywhere between 2,240 and 9,320 miles in a single feeding trip and that they easily maintained a speed of 35 mph over a distance of more than 500 miles, with the males going to sea for up to 33 days while their partners remained ashore to incubate the eggs.

Highest-flying   Most migrating birds fly at relatively low altitudes (i.e., below 300 ft.) and only a few dozen species fly higher than 3,000 ft.

The highest irrefutable altitude recorded for a bird is 37,000 ft. for a Ruppell's vulture (*Gyps rueppellii*), which collided with a commercial aircraft over Abidjan, Ivory Coast on 29 Nov. 1973. The impact damaged one of the aircraft's engines, causing it to shut down, but the plane landed safely without further incident. Sufficient feather remains of the bird were recovered to allow the US Museum of Natural History to make a positive identification of this high-flier, which is rarely seen above 20,000 ft.

United States   The highest verified altitude record for a bird in America is 21,000 ft. for a mallard (*Meleagris gallopavo*) that collided with a commercial jet on 9 July 1963 over Nevada. The jet crashed, killing all aboard.

Most airborne   The most aerial of all birds is the sooty tern (*Sterna fuscata*), which, after leaving the nesting grounds, remains continuously aloft from 3–10 years as a sub-adult before returning to land to breed.

The most aerial land bird is the common swift (*Apus apus*), which remains

MOST AIRBORNE BIRD. An adolescent sooty tern (*Sterna fuscata*) can remain aloft continuously for up to 10 years before landing to breed. (Photo: Jacana Agence de Presse/François Gohier)

airborne for 2–3 years, during which time it sleeps, drinks, eats and even mates on the wing.

Vision Birds of prey (Falconiformes) have the keenest eyesight in the avian world, and large species with eyes similar in size to those of humans have visual acuity at least twice that of human vision. It has also been calculated that a large eagle can detect a target object at a distance 3–8 times greater than that achieved by humans. Thus a peregrine falcon (*Falco peregrinus*) can spot a pigeon at a range of over 5 miles.

In experiments carried out on the tawny owl (*Strix aluco*) at the University of Birmingham, Great Britain in 1977, it was revealed that the bird's eye on average was only 2½ times more sensitive than the human eye. It was also discovered that the tawny owl sees perfectly adequately in daylight and that its visual acuity is only slightly inferior to that of humans.

Longest bills The bill of the Australian pelican (*Pelicanus conspicillatus*) is 13.3–18.5 in. long.

The longest bill in relation to overall body length is that of the sword-billed hummingbird (*Ensifera ensifera*) of the Andes from Venezuela to Bolivia. It measures 4 in. in length and is longer than the bird's actual body if the tail is excluded.

Shortest bills The shortest bills in relation to body length are found among the smaller swifts (Apodidae) and in particular that of the glossy swiftlet (*Collocalia esculenta*), whose bill is almost nonexistent.

Longest feathers The longest feathers grown by any bird are those of the phoenix fowl or onagadori (a strain of red jungle fowl *Gallus gallus*), which has been bred in southwestern Japan since the mid-17th century. In

1972 a tail covert measuring 34 ft. 9½ in. was reported for a rooster owned by Masasha Kubota of Kochi, Shikoku, Japan.

Among flying birds the tail feathers of the male crested pheasant (*Rheinhartia ocellata*) of southeast Asia regularly reach 5 ft. 8 in. in length and 5 in. in width, and the central tail feathers of the Reeves' pheasant (*Syrmaticus reevesi*) of central and northern China have reached 8 ft. in exceptional cases.

Largest egg   The average ostrich (*Struthio camelus*) egg measures 6–8 in. in length, 4–6 in. in diameter and weighs 3.6–3.9 lbs. (around two dozen hens' eggs in volume). The egg requires about 40 min. for boiling, and the shell, though only 0.06 in. thick, can support the weight of a 280 lb. man. On 28 June 1988 a 2-year-old cross between a northern and a southern ostrich (*Struthio c. camelus* and *Struthio c. australis*) laid an egg weighing a record 5.1 lbs. at the Kibbutz Ha'on collective farm, Israel.

United States   The largest egg on the list of American birds is that of the trumpeter swan; it measures 4.3 in. in length, 2.8 in. in diameter. The average California condor egg measures 4.3 in. in length and 2.6 in. in diameter and weighs 9.5 oz.

Smallest egg   Eggs emitted from the oviduct before maturity, known as "sports," are not considered to be of significance. The smallest egg laid by any bird is that of the vervain hummingbird (*Mellisuga minima*) of Jamaica. Two specimens measuring less than 0.39 in. in length weighed 0.0128 oz. and 0.0132 oz. (See Smallest nest.)

United States   The smallest egg laid by a bird on the American list is that of the Costa hummingbird (*Calypte coastae*); it measures 0.48 in. in length and 0.33 in. in diameter with a weight of 0.017 oz.

Longest incubation   The longest normal incubation period is that of the wandering albatross (*Diomedea exulans*), with a normal range of 75–82 days. There is an isolated case of an egg of the mallee fowl (*Leipoa ocellata*) of Australia taking 90 days to hatch, against its normal incubation of 62 days.

---

g force   Experiments have revealed that the beak of the red-headed woodpecker (*Melanerpes erythrocephalus*) hits the bark of a tree with an impact velocity of 13 mph. This means that when the head snaps back the brain is subject to a deceleration of about 10 *g*.

Most and least feathers   In a series of feather counts on various species of bird, a whistling swan (*Cygnus columbianus*) was found to have 25,216 feathers, 20,177 of which were on the head and neck. The ruby-throated hummingbird (*Archilochus colubris*) has only 940.

Shortest incubation   The shortest incubation period is 10 days in the case of the great spotted woodpecker (*Dendrocopus major*) and the black-billed cuckoo (*Coccyzus erythropthalmus*).

Largest nest   A nest measuring 9½ ft. wide and 20 ft. deep was built by a pair of bald eagles (*Haliaeetus leucocephalus*), and possibly their successors, near St. Petersburg, FL. It was examined in 1963 and was estimated to weigh more than 2.2 tons. The golden eagle (*Aquila chrysaetos*) also constructs huge nests, and one 15 ft. deep was reported from Scotland in 1954. It had been used for 45 years.

The incubation mounds built by the mallee fowl (*Leipoa ocellata*) of Australia are much larger, measuring up to 15 ft. in height and 35 ft. across, and it has been calculated that the nest site may involve the mounding of 900 ft.³ of material weighing 330 tons.

Smallest nest   The smallest nests are built by hummingbirds (*Trochilidae*). That of the vervain hummingbird (*Mellisuga minima*) is about half the size of a walnut, while the deeper one of the bee hummingbird (*M. helenea*) is thimble-sized. (See Smallest egg.)

Bird-watchers   The world's leading bird-watcher or "twitcher" is Harvey Gilston (b. 12 Oct. 1922) of Lausanne, Switzerland, who had logged 7,085 of the 9,672 known species, representing over 73 percent of the available total. (The exact number of species at a given time can vary because of changes in classifications.)

The greatest number of species spotted in a 24-hour period is 342, by Kenyans Terry Stevenson, John Fanshawe and Andy Roberts on day two of the Birdwatch Kenya '86 event held on 29–30 November. The 48-hour record is held by Don Turner and David Pearson of Kenya, who spotted 494 species at the same event.

Peter Kaestner of Washington, D.C. was the first person to see at least one species of each of the world's 159 bird families. He saw his final family on 1 Oct. 1986. Since then Dr. Ira Abramson of Miami, FL, Dr. Martin Edwards of Kingston, Ontario, Canada and Harvey Gilston (last family seen in December 1988) have also succeeded in this achievement.

REPTILES *Reptilia*

CROCODILIANS

Largest   The largest reptile in the world is the estuarine or saltwater crocodile (*Crocodylus porosus*) of southeast Asia, the Malay Archipelago, Indonesia, northern Australia, Papua New Guinea, Vietnam and the Philippines. Adult males average 14–16 ft. in length and weigh about 900–1,150 lbs. There are four protected estuarine crocodiles at the Bhitarkanika Wildlife Sanctuary, Orissa State, eastern India that measure more than 19 ft. 8 in. in length. The largest individual is over 23 ft. long.

Captive   The largest crocodile ever held in captivity is an estuarine/Siamese hybrid named Yai (b. 10 June 1972) at the Samutprakarn Crocodile Farm and Zoo, Thailand. He measures 19 ft. 8 in. in length and weighs 2,465 lbs.

Smallest   Osborn's dwarf crocodile (*Osteolaemus osborni*), found in the upper region of the Congo River, West Africa, rarely exceeds 3 ft. 11 in. in length.

Oldest   The greatest age authenticated for a crocodile is 66 years for a female American alligator (*Alligator mississipiensis*) which arrived at Adelaide Zoo, South Australia on 5 June 1914 as a two-year-old, and died there on 26 Sep. 1978.

LIZARDS

Largest   The largest of all lizards is the komodo monitor or ora (*Varanus komodoensis*), a dragonlike reptile found on the Indonesian islands of Komodo, Rintja, Padar and Flores. Adult males average 7 ft. 5 in. in length and weigh about 130 lbs. Lengths up to 30 ft. have been claimed for this species, but the largest specimen to be accurately measured was a male presented to an American zoologist in 1928 by the Sultan of Bima which was taped at 10 ft. 1 in. In 1937 this animal was put on display in St. Louis Zoological Gardens, MO for a short period. It then measured 10 ft. 2 in. in length and weighed 365 lbs.

Longest   The slender Salvadori monitor (*Varanus salvadori*) of Papua New Guinea has been reliably measured up to 15 ft. 7 in., but nearly 70 percent of the total length is taken up by the tail.

Smallest   *Sphaerodactylus parthenopion*, a tiny gecko indigenous to the island of Virgin Gorda, one of the British Virgin Islands, is believed to be the world's smallest lizard. It is known only from 15 specimens, including some pregnant females found between 10–16 Aug. 1964. The three largest females measured 0.70 in. from snout to vent, with a tail of approximately the same length.

It is possible that another gecko, *Sphaerodactylus elasmorhynchus*, may be even smaller. The only known specimen was an apparently mature female with a snout-vent measurement of 0.67 in. and a tail of the same length. This specimen was found on 15 Mar. 1966 among the roots of a tree in the western part of the Massif de la Hotte in Haiti.

Oldest lizard   The greatest age recorded for a lizard is over 54 years for a male slow worm (*Anguis fragilis*) kept in the Zoological Museum in Copenhagen, Denmark from 1892 until 1946.

Fastest reptile   The fastest speed measured for any reptile on land is 18 mph for a six-lined race runner (*Cnemidophorus sexlineatus*) near McCormick, SC in 1941.

CHELONIANS

Largest   The largest living chelonian is the leatherback turtle (*Dermochelys coriacea*), which is circumglobal in distribution. The average adult measures 6–7 ft. from the tip of the beak to the end of the tail (carapace 5–5½ ft.), about 7 ft. across the front flippers and weighs up to 1,000 lbs.

The largest leatherback turtle ever recorded is a male found dead on the beach at Harlech, Great Britain on 23 Sep. 1988. It measured 9 ft. 5½ in. in total length over the carapace (nose to tail), 9 ft. across the front flippers and weighed an astonishing 2,120 lbs. It is now in the possession of the National Museum of Wales, Great Britain and was put on public display on 16 Feb. 1990.

United States   The greatest weight reliably recorded is 1,908 lbs. recorded for a male captured off Monterey, CA on 29 Aug. 1961, which measured 8 ft. 4 in.

Tortoise   The largest living tortoise is the Aldabra giant tortoise (*Geochelone gigantea*) of the Indian Ocean islands of Aldabra, Mauritius and the Seychelles (introduced 1874). A male tortoise named Esmerelda, a longtime resident on Bird Island in the Seychelles, recorded a weight of 657 lbs. on 26 Feb. 1989.

Fastest   The fastest speed claimed for any reptile in water is 22 mph by a frightened Pacific leatherback turtle.

Deepest dive   In May 1987 it was reported by Dr. Scott Eckert that a leatherback turtle (*Dermochelys coriacea*) fitted with a pressure-sensitive recording device had dived to a depth of 3,973 ft. off the Virgin Islands in the West Indies.

Smallest turtle   The smallest marine turtle in the world is the Atlantic ridley (*Lepidochelys kempii*), which has a shell length of 19.7–27.6 in. and does not exceed 80 lbs.

Oldest tortoise   The greatest authentic age recorded for a tortoise is over 152 years for a male Marion's tortoise (*Testudo sumeirii*), brought from the Seychelles to Mauritius in 1766 by the Chevalier de Fresne, who presented it to the Port Louis army garrison. This specimen, which went blind in 1908, was accidentally killed in 1918. The greatest proven age of a continuously observed tortoise is more than 116 years for a Mediterranean spur-thighed tortoise (*Testudo graeca*).

Oldest snake   The greatest reliable age recorded for a snake is 40 years 3 months 14 days for a male common boa (*Boa constrictor constrictor*) named Popeye, who died at the Philadelphia Zoo, PA on 15 Apr. 1977.

Longest amphibian gestation   The viviparous alpine black salamander (*Salamandra atra*) has a gestation period of up to 38 months at altitudes above 4,600 ft. in the Swiss Alps, but this drops to 24–26 months at lower altitudes.

SNAKES, GENERAL

Longest The reticulated python (*Python reticulatus*) of southeast Asia, Indonesia and the Philippines regularly exceeds 20 ft. 6 in. In 1912 a specimen measuring 32 ft. 9½ in. was shot near a mining camp on the north coast of Celebes in the Malay Archipelago.

Captive The longest (and heaviest) snake ever held in captivity was a female reticulated python named Colossus who died in Highland Park Zoo, PA on 15 Apr. 1963. She measured 28 ft. 6 in. in length, and weighed 320 lbs. at her heaviest.

United States Three species, in the southeastern United States, have average measurements of 8 ft. 6 in. These include the indigo snake (*Drymarchon corais*), the eastern coachwhip (*Masticophis flagellum*) and the black ratsnake (*Elaphe obsoleta*).

Shortest The shortest snake in the world is the rare thread snake (*Leptotyphlops bilineata*), which is known only from the islands of Martinique, Barbados and St. Lucia in the West Indies. In one series of eight specimens the two longest both measured 4.25 in.

Heaviest The anaconda (*Eunectes murinus*) of tropical South America and Trinidad is nearly twice as heavy as a reticulated python (*Python reticulatus*) of the same length. A female shot in Brazil *c.* 1960 was not weighed, but as it measured 27 ft. 9 in. in length with a girth of 44 in., it must have weighed nearly 500 lbs. The average adult length is 18–20 ft.

VENOMOUS SNAKES

Longest The longest venomous snake in the world is the king cobra (*Ophiophagus hannah*), also called the hamadryad, of southeast Asia and the Philippines; it has an average adult length of 12–15 ft. A 18-ft.-2-in. specimen, captured alive near Fort Dickson in the state of Negri Sembilan, Malaya in April 1937, later grew to 18 ft. 9 in. in London Zoo, Great Britain. It was destroyed at the outbreak of war in 1939.

Shortest The namaqua dwarf adder (*Bitis schneider*) of Namibia has an average adult length of 8 in.

Heaviest The heaviest venomous snake is probably the eastern diamondback rattlesnake (*Crotalus adamanteus*) of the southeastern United States. One specimen, measuring 7 ft. 9 in. in length, weighed 34 lbs. Adult examples average 5–6 ft. in length and weigh 12–15 lbs.
    The West African gaboon viper (*Bitis gabonica*) of the tropical rain forests is probably bulkier than the eastern diamond, but its average length is only 4–5 ft. A female 6 ft. long was found to weigh 25 lbs., and another female measuring 5 ft. 8½ in. weighed 18 lbs. with an empty stomach.

Most venomous The sea snake (*Hydrophis belcheri*) has a myotoxic venom a hundred times as toxic as that of the Australian taipan (*Oxyuranus scutellatus*). The snake abounds in the Ashmore Reef in the Timor Sea, off the coast of northwest Australia.
    The most venomous land snake is the 6-ft.-6¾-in.-long smooth-scaled

snake (*Parademansia microlepidotus*) of the Diamantina River and Cooper's Creek drainage basins in Channel County, Queensland and western New South Wales, Australia, which has a venom nine times as toxic as that of the tiger snake (*Notechis scutatus*) of South Australia and Tasmania. One specimen yielded 0.00385 oz. of venom after milking, enough to kill 125,000 mice, but so far no human fatalities have been reported.

More people die of snakebites in Sri Lanka than in any comparable area in the world. An average of 800 people are killed annually on the island by snakes, and more than 95 percent of the fatalities are caused by the common krait (*Bungarus caeruleus*), the Sri Lankan cobra (*Naja n. naja*), and Russell's viper (*Vipera russelli pulchella*).

The saw-scaled or carpet viper (*Echis carinatus*) bites and kills more people in the world than any other species. Its geographical range extends from West Africa to India.

United States   The most venomous snake in the United States is the coral snake (*Micrurus fulvius*). In a standard LD99–100 test, which kills 99–100 percent of all mice injected with the venom, it takes 0.55 grain of venom per 2.2 lbs. of mouse weight injected intravenously. In this test, the smaller the dosage, the more toxic the venom. However, the teeth of the coral snake point back into its mouth, and therefore it cannot inject the venom until it has a firm hold on the victim.

Longest fangs   The longest fangs of any snake are those of the highly venomous gaboon viper (*Bitis gabonica*) of tropical Africa. In a specimen of 6 ft. length they measured 1.96 in. On 12 Feb. 1963 a gaboon viper under severe stress sank its fangs into its own back at the Philadelphia Zoo, PA and died from traumatic injury to a vital organ. It did not, as has been widely reported, succumb to its own venom.

Fastest   The fastest-moving land snake is probably the slender black mamba (*Dendroaspis polylepis*) of the eastern part of tropical Africa. It is possible that this snake can achieve speeds of 10–12 mph in short bursts over level ground.

LONGEST VENOMOUS SNAKE. The king cobra (*Ophiophagus hannah*), which has an average length of up to 15 ft., is unusual among snakes, in that it uses twigs and leaves to build a nest in which to lay its eggs. (Photo: Planet Earth Pictures/Ken Lucas)

AMPHIBIANS *Amphibia*

Largest   The largest species of amphibian is the Chinese giant salamander (*Andrias davidianus*), which lives in northeastern, central and southern China. The average adult measures 3 ft. 9 in. in length and weighs 55–66 lbs. One specimen collected in Hunan province weighed 143 lbs. and measured 5 ft. 11 in. in length.

Smallest   The smallest-known amphibian is the tiny Cuban frog (*Sminthillus limbatus*), which is less than ½ in. long.

Oldest   The greatest authentic age recorded for an amphibian is 55 years for a Japanese giant salamander that died in Amsterdam Zoo in the Netherlands in 1881.

Highest and lowest   The greatest altitude at which an amphibian has been found is 26,246 ft. for a common toad (*Bufo bufo*) collected in the Himalayas. This species has also been found at a depth of 1,115 ft. in a coal mine.

FROGS

Largest   The largest-known frog is the rare African giant frog or goliath frog (*Conrana goliath*) of Cameroon and Equatorial Guinea. A specimen captured in April 1989 on the Sanaga River, Cameroon by Andy Koffman of Seattle, WA had a snout-to-vent length of 14.5 in. (34.5 in. overall with legs extended) and weighed 8 lbs..1 oz. on 30 Oct. 1989.

Smallest   The smallest frog in the world is *Sminthillus limbatus* of Cuba. (See Smallest amphibians.)

Longest jump   (*Competition frog jumps are the aggregate of three consecutive leaps.*)
   The greatest distance covered by a frog in a triple jump is 33 ft. 5½ in. by a South African sharp-nosed frog (*Ptychadena oxyrhynchus*) named Santjie at a frog derby held at Lurula Natal Spa, Paulpietersburg, Natal, South Africa on 21 May 1977.

United States   At the annual Calaveras Jumping Jubilee held at Angels Camp, CA on 18 May 1986, an American bullfrog (*Rana catesbeiana*) called Rosie the Ribeter, owned and trained by Lee Giudicci of Santa Clara, CA, leapt 21 ft. 5¾ in. Santjie would have been ineligible for this contest because entrants must measure at least 4 in. "stem to stern."

TOADS

Largest   The largest-known toad is the marine toad (*Bufo marinus*) of tropical South America and Queensland, Australia. An average adult specimen weighs 1 lb. The largest ever recorded was a male named Prinsen (The Prince), owned by Hakan Forsberg of Akers Styckebruk, Sweden. The toad weighed 5 lbs. 13½ oz. and measured 15 in. from snout to vent (21 ⅕ in. when extended) in March 1991.

Smallest   The smallest toad in the world is the subspecies *Bufo taitanus beiranus*, originally of Mozambique, the largest specimen of which was 1 in. long. (See Smallest amphibians.)

FISHES *Gnathostomata, Agnatha (See Fishing)*

GENERAL RECORDS

Largest   The largest fish in the world is the rare plankton-feeding whale shark (*Rhincodon typus*), which is found in the warmer areas of the Atlantic, Pacific, and Indian Oceans. The longest scientifically measured one on record was a 41½-ft. specimen captured off Baba Island near Karachi, Pakistan on 11 Nov. 1949. It measured 23 ft. around the thickest part of the body and weighed an estimated 16.5 tons.

Bony   The longest of the bony or "true" fishes (Pisces) is the oarfish (*Regalecus glesne*), also called the "King of the Herrings," which has a worldwide distribution. In *c.* 1885 a specimen 25 ft. long, weighing 600 lbs., was caught by fishermen off Pemaquid Point, ME, but unconfirmed claims of 50 ft. have been made.

Heaviest   The heaviest bony fish in the world is the ocean sunfish (*Mola mola*), which is found in all tropical, subtropical and temperate waters. On 18 Sep. 1908 a specimen accidentally injured off Bird Island near Sydney, New South Wales, Australia weighed 4,927 lbs. and measured 14 ft. between the anal and dorsal fins.

Carnivorous   The largest carnivorous fish (excluding plankton-eaters) is the comparatively rare great white shark (*Carcharodon carcharias*), also called the "man-eater." Adult females (males are smaller) average 14–15 ft. in length and generally weigh between 1,150–1,700 lbs. The largest example accurately measured was 20 ft. 4 in. long and weighed 5,000 lbs. It was harpooned and landed in the harbor of San Miguel, Azores in June 1978. (See Fishing.)

Smallest   The shortest recorded marine fish—and the shortest known vertebrate—is the dwarf goby (*Trimmatom nanus*) of the Chagos Archipelago, central Indian Ocean. In one series of 92 specimens collected by the 1978–79 Joint Services Chagos Research Expedition of the British Armed Forces, the adult males averaged 0.338 in. in length and the adult females 0.35 in.

Lightest   The lightest of all vertebrates and the smallest catch possible for any fisherman is the dwarf goby *Schindleria praematurus* from Samoa, which weighs only 2 mg. (equivalent to 14,184 fish to the ounce) and is ½–¾ in. long.

Shark The spined pygmy shark (*Squaliolus laticaudus*) of the western Pacific matures at 6 in. in length.

Fastest The maximum swimming speed of a fish is dependent on the shape of its body and tail and its internal temperature. The cosmopolitan sailfish (*Istiophorus platypterus*) is considered to be the fastest species of fish over short distances, although the practical difficulties of measuring make data extremely difficult to secure. In a series of speed trials carried out at the Long Key Fishing Camp, FL, one sailfish took out 300 ft. of line in 3 sec., which is equivalent to a velocity of 68 mph (compare with 60 mph for the cheetah).

Oldest Aquaria are of too-recent origin to be able to establish with certainty which species of fish can be regarded as being the longest-lived. Early indications are, however, that it may be the lake sturgeon (*Acipenser fulvescens*) of North America. In one study of the growth rings (annuli) of 966 specimens caught in the Lake Winnebago region in Wisconsin between 1951 and 1954, the oldest sturgeon was found to be a male (length 6 ft. 7 in.) that gave a reading of 82 years and was still growing.

In 1948 the death was reported of an 88-year-old female European eel (*Anguilla anguilla*) named Putte in the aquarium at Hälsingborg Museum, southern Sweden. She was allegedly born in the Sargasso Sea, in the North Atlantic, in 1860, and was caught in a river as a 3-year-old elver.

In July 1974 a growth ring count of 228 years was reported for a female koi fish (a form of fancy carp) named Hanako living in a pond in Higashi Shirakawa, Gifu Prefecture, Japan, but the greatest authoritatively accepted age for this species is "more than 50 years."

The perch-like marine fish *Notothenia neglecta* of the Antarctic Ocean, whose blood contains a natural antifreeze, is reported to live up to 150 years, but this claim has not yet been verified.

Oldest goldfish Goldfish (*Carassius auratus*) have been reported to live for over 50 years in China.

A goldfish named "Fred," owned by A.R. Wilson of Worthing, Great Britain, died on 1 Aug. 1980 at 41 years of age.

Shortest-lived The shortest-lived fish are probably certain species of the suborder Cyprinodontei (killifish), found in Africa and South America, which normally live about eight months.

Deepest Brotulids of the genus *Bassogigas* are generally regarded as the deepest-living vertebrates. The greatest depth from which a fish has been recovered is 27,230 ft. in the Puerto Rico Trench (27,488 ft.) in the Atlantic by Dr. Gilbert L. Voss of the US research vessel *John Elliott*, who took a 6½-in.-long *Bassogigas profundissimus* in April 1970. It was only the fifth such brotulid ever caught.

Dr. Jacques Piccard and Lt. Don Walsh of the US Navy reported seeing a sole-like fish about 1 ft. long (tentatively identified as *Chascanopsetta lugubris*) from the bathyscaphe *Trieste* at a depth of 35,820 ft. in the Challenger Deep (Mariana Trench) in the western Pacific on 24 Jan. 1960. This sighting, however, has been questioned by some authorities.

Most eggs   The ocean sunfish (*Mola mola*) produces up to 30 million eggs, each of them measuring about 0.05 in. in diameter, at a single spawning.

Fewest eggs   The mouth-brooding cichlid *Tropheus moorii* of Lake Tanganyika, East Africa, produces seven eggs or less during normal reproduction.

Most valuable   The world's most valuable fish is the Russian sturgeon (*Huso huso*). One 2,706-lb. female caught in the Tikhaya Sosna River in 1924 yielded 541 lbs. of best-quality caviar, which would be worth $330,000 on today's market.

The 30-in.-long Ginrin Showa koi, which won the supreme championship in nationwide Japanese koi shows in 1976, 1977, 1979 and 1980, was sold two years later for 17 million yen. In March 1986 this ornamental carp was acquired by Derry Evans, owner of the Kent Koi Centre near Sevenoaks, Great Britain, for an undisclosed sum, but the 15-year-old fish died five months later. It has since been stuffed and mounted to preserve its beauty.

Most venomous   The most venomous fish in the world are the stonefish (Synanceidae) of the tropical waters of the Indo-Pacific, and in particular *Synanceja horrida*, which has the largest venom glands of any known fish. Direct contact with the spines of its fins, which contain a strong neurotoxic poison, often proves fatal.

Most ferocious   The razor-toothed piranhas of the genera *Serrasalmus, Pygocentrus* and *Pygopristis* are the most ferocious freshwater fish in the world. They live in the sluggish waters of the large rivers of South America, and will attack any creature, regardless of size, if it is injured or making a commotion in the water. On 19 Sep. 1981 more than 300 people were reportedly killed and eaten when an overloaded passenger-cargo boat capsized and sank as it was docking at the Brazilian port of Obidos. According to one official, only 178 of the boat's passengers survived.

Most electric   The most powerful electric fish is the electric eel (*Electrophorus electricus*), which is found in the rivers of Brazil, Colombia, Venezuela and Peru. An average-sized specimen can discharge 400 volts at 1 amp, but measurements up to 650 volts have been recorded.

MOST ELECTRIC FISH. The electric eel (*Electrophorus electricus*) of South America can produce an electrical discharge of up to 650 volts, enough to stun a man but used mainly to immobilize fish and other prey. (Photo: Jacana Agence de Presse/ T. McHugh)

MARINE

Largest   The largest marine fish is the whale shark (*Rhincodon typus*), which can reach 30 ft. in length. (See Fishes, General records.)

Smallest   The shortest recorded marine fish is the dwarf goby (*Trimmatom nanus*) of the Chagos Archipelago in the Indian Ocean. (See Fishes, General records, Smallest.)

FRESHWATER

Largest   The largest fish that spends its whole life in fresh or brackish water is the rare pla beuk (*Pangasianodon gigas*). It is confined to the Mekong River and its major tributaries in China, Laos, Cambodia and Thailand. The largest specimen, captured in the River Ban Mee Noi, Thailand, was reportedly 9 ft. 10¼ in. long and weighed 533½ lbs. This was exceeded by the European catfish or wels (*Silurus glanis*) in earlier times (in the 19th century lengths up to 15 ft. and weights up to 720 lbs. were reported for Russian specimens), but today anything over 6 ft. and 200 lbs. is considered large.

The arapaima (*Arapaima glanis*), also called the pirarucu, found in the Amazon and other South American rivers and often claimed to be the largest freshwater fish, averages 6½ ft. and 150 lbs. The largest authentically recorded specimen measured 8 ft. 1½ in. in length and weighed 325 lbs. It was caught in the Rio Negro, Brazil in 1836.

Smallest   The shortest and lightest freshwater fish is the dwarf pygmy goby (*Pandaka pygmaea*), a colorless and nearly transparent species found in the streams and lakes of Luzon in the Philippines. Adult males measure only 0.28–0.38 in. in length and weigh 0.00014–0.00018 oz.

The world's smallest commercial fish is the now-endangered sinarapan (*Mistichthys luzonensis*), a goby found only in Lake Buhi, Luzon, Philippines. Adult males measure 0.39–0.51 in. in length, and a dried 1-lb. fish cake contains about 70,000 of them!

STARFISHES *Asteroidea*

Largest   The largest of the 1,600 known species of starfish in terms of total arm-span is the very fragile brisingid *Midgardia xandaros*. A specimen collected by the Texas A & M University research vessel *Alaminos* in the southern part of the Gulf of Mexico in the late summer of 1968 measured 4½ ft. tip to tip, but the diameter of its disc was only 1.02 in. Its dry weight was 2.46 oz.

Heaviest   The heaviest species of starfish is the five-armed *Thromidia catalai* of the western Pacific. One specimen collected off Ilot Amédée, New Caledonia on 14 Sep. 1969 and later deposited in Nouméa Aquarium weighed an estimated 13.2 lbs. (total arm span 24.8 in.).

Smallest   The smallest-known starfish is the asterinid sea star *Patiriella* *parvivipara*, discovered by Wolfgang Zeidler on the west coast of the Eyre peninsula, South Australia in 1975. It has a maximum radius of only 0.18 in. and a diameter of less than 0.35 in.

Most destructive   The crown of thorns (*Acanthaster planci*) of the Indo-Pacific region and the Red Sea has 12–19 arms and can measure up to 24 in. in diameter. It feeds on coral polyps and can destroy 46½–62 in.^{2} of coral in one day. It has been responsible for the destruction of large parts of the Great Barrier Reef off Australia.

Deepest   The greatest depth from which a starfish has been recovered is 24,881 ft. for a specimen of *Porcellanaster ivanovi* collected by the USSR research ship *Vityaz* in the Mariana Trench, in the western Pacific, *c*. 1962.

CRUSTACEANS *Crustacea*

---

*(Crabs, lobsters, shrimps, prawns, crawfish, barnacles,
water fleas, fish lice, woodlice, sandhoppers, krill, etc.)*

Largest marine   The largest of all crustaceans (although not the heaviest) is the takashigani or giant spider crab (*Macrocheira kaempferi*), also called the stilt crab, which is found in deep waters off the southeastern coast of Japan. Mature specimens usually have a body measuring 10 × 12 in. and a claw-span of 8–9 ft., but unconfirmed measurements up to 19 ft. have been reported. A specimen with a claw-span of 12 ft. 1½ in. weighed 41 lbs.

Largest concentration of crustaceans   The largest single concentration of crustaceans ever recorded was an enormous swarm of krill (*Euphausia superba*) estimated to weigh 11 million tons and tracked by US scientists off Antarctica in March 1981.

Fastest spider   The fastest-moving arachnids are the long-legged sun spiders of the order *Solifugae*, which live in the arid semidesert regions of Africa and the Middle East. They feed on geckos and other lizards and can reach speeds of over 10 mph.

Largest webs   Aerial webs spun by the tropical orb weavers of the genus *Nephila* have been measured up to 18 ft. 9¾ in. in circumference.

Smallest webs   The smallest webs are spun by spiders such as *Glyphesis cottonae* and cover about 0.75 in.^{2}.

Heaviest The heaviest of all crustaceans, and the largest species of lobster, is the American or North Atlantic lobster (*Homarus americanus*). On 11 Feb. 1977 a specimen weighing 44 lbs. 6 oz. and measuring 3 ft. 6 in. from the end of the tail fan to the tip of the largest claw was caught off Nova Scotia, Canada and later sold to a New York restaurant owner.

Largest freshwater The largest freshwater crustacean is the crayfish, or crawfish (*Astacopsis gouldi*), found in the streams of Tasmania, Australia. It has been measured up to 2 ft. in length and may weigh as much as 9 lbs. In 1934 an unconfirmed weight of 14 lbs. (total length 29 in.) was reported for an outsized specimen caught at Bridport.

Smallest Water fleas of the genus *Alonella* may measure less than 0.01 in. in length. They are found in British waters.

Oldest Very large specimens of the American lobster (*Homarus americanus*) may be as much as 50 years old.

Deepest The greatest depth from which a crustacean has been recovered is 34,450 ft. for *live* amphipods from the Challenger Deep (Mariana Trench), western Pacific by the US research vessel *Thomas Washington* in November 1980.

Highest Amphipods and isopods have also been collected in the Ecuadorean Andes at a height of 13,300 ft.

ARACHNIDS *Arachnida*

SPIDERS *(Araneae)*

Largest The world's largest-known spider is the goliath bird-eating spider (*Theraphosa leblondi*) of the coastal rain forests of Surinam, Guyana and French Guiana, northeastern South America; isolated specimens have also been reported from Venezuela and Brazil. A male example collected by members of the Pablo San Martin Expedition at Rio Cavro, Venezuela in April 1965 had a leg span of 11.02 in.

Heaviest Female bird-eating spiders are more heavily built than males, and in February 1985 Charles J. Seiderman of New York City captured a female example near Paramaribo, Surinam which weighed a record peak 4.3 oz. before its death from moulting problems in January 1986. Other measurements included a maximum leg span of 10½ in., a total body length of 4 in., and 1-in.-long fangs.

United States The *Rhecosticta california*, a type of tarantula found in the Southwest, is the heaviest spider and has the longest body. However, the orb web spider (*Nephila clavipes*) of the family *Araneidae*, found in the southern Gulf states, and the wolf spider (*Lycosa carolinensis*) of the family *Lycosidae*, found in the Southeast, equal its leg span.

Smallest   The smallest-known spider is *Patu marplesi* (family Symphytognathidae) of Western Samoa in the Pacific. The type specimen (male), found in moss at *c.* 2,000 ft. in Madolelei, Western Samoa in January 1965, measured 0.017 in. overall, which means that it was about the size of a period on this page.

United States   The *Troglonata paradoxum* of the family *Mysmmenidae* is the smallest spider in the United States.

Oldest   The longest-lived of all spiders are the primitive *Mygalomorphae* (tarantulas and allied species). One female therasophid collected in Mexico in 1935 lived for an estimated 26–28 years.

United States   The longest-lived species of American spider is the *Rhecosticta californica* of the family *Theraphosidae*, which has an average life span of 25 years.

Most venomous   The world's most venomous spiders are the Brazilian wandering spiders of the genus *Phoneutria*, and particularly *P. fera*, which has the most active neurotoxic venom of any living spider. These large and highly aggressive creatures frequently enter human dwellings and hide in clothing or shoes. When disturbed they bite furiously several times, and hundreds of accidents involving these species are reported annually. When deaths do occur, they are usually in children under the age of seven. Fortunately, an effective antivenin is available.

SCORPIONS *(Scorpiones)*

Largest   The largest of the 800 or so species of scorpion is the tropical "emperor" *Pandinus imperator* of Guinea, adult males of which can attain a body length of 7 in. or more.

Smallest   The smallest scorpion in the world is *Microbothus pusillus* from the Red Sea coast, which measures about 0.5 in. in total length.

Most venomous   The most venomous scorpion in the world is the Palestine yellow scorpion (*Leiurus quinquestriatus*), which ranges from the eastern part of North Africa through the Middle East to the shores of the Red Sea. Fortunately, the amount of venom it delivers is very small (0.000009 oz.) and adult lives are seldom endangered; however, it has been responsible for a number of fatalities among children under the age of five.

INSECTS *Insecta*

It is estimated that there may be as many as 30 million species of insect—more than all other phyla and classes put together—but thousands are known only from a single or type specimen.

Earliest   A shrimp-like creature from Western Australia found in 1991 in rocks dated at 420 million years is the oldest known insect. A euthycarci-noid, the insect was a large (5 in. long) freshwater predator.

Heaviest   The heaviest living insects are the Goliath beetles (family Scarabaeidae) of Equatorial Africa. The largest members of the group are *Goliathus regius, G. goliathus* (= *G. giganteus*) and *G. druryi*, and in one series of fully-grown males (females are smaller) the lengths from the tips of the small frontal horns to the end of the abdomen measured up to 4.33 in. and the weights ranged from 2.5–3.5 oz.

The elephant beetles (*Megasoma*) of Central America and the West Indies attain the greatest dimensions in terms of volume, but they lack the massive build-up of heavy chiton forming the thorax and anterior sternum of the goliaths, and this gives them a distinct weight advantage.

Longest   The longest insects in the world are stick-insects (walking sticks), especially of the African species *Palophus*, which can attain lengths of 15¾ in. in the case of *Palophus leopoldi*.

Smallest   The smallest insects recorded so far are the "feather-winged" beetles of the family Ptiliidae (= trichopterygidae) and the "battledore-wing fairy flies" (parasitic wasps) of the family Mymaridae; they are smaller than some species of protozoa (single-celled animals).

Lightest   The male bloodsucking banded louse (*Enderleinellus zonatus*) and the parasitic wasp (*Caraphractus cinctus*) may each weigh as little as 5,670,000 to an oz. Eggs of the latter each weigh 141,750,000 to an oz.

Largest cockroach   The world's largest cockroach is *Megaloblatta longipennis* of Colombia. A preserved female in the collection of Akira Yokokura of Yamagata, Japan measures 3.81 in. in length and 1.77 in. across.

Loudest insect   The loudest of all insects is the male cicada (family Cicadidae). At 7,400 pulses/min. its tymbal organs produce a noise (officially described by the US Department of Agriculture as "Tsh-ee-EEEE-e-ou") detectable more than a quarter of a mile distant.

Largest termite mound   In 1968 W. Page photographed a specimen south of Horgesia, Somalia estimated to be 28.5 ft. tall.

Mantle of bees   Jed Shaner was covered by a mantle of an estimated 343,000 bees weighing an aggregate of 80 lbs. at Staunton, VA on 29 June 1991.

Highest g force   The click beetle (*Athous haemorrhoidalis*) averages 400 *g* when "jack-knifing" into the air to escape predators. One example measuring ½ in. in length and weighing 0.00014 oz. that jumped to a height of 11¾ in. was calculated to have "endured" a peak brain deceleration of 2,300 *g* by the end of the movement.

Fastest-flying Acceptable modern experiments have now established that the highest maintainable air speed of any insect, including the deer botfly, hawkmoths (Sphingidae), horseflies (*Tabanus bovinus*) and some tropical butterflies (Hesperiidae) is 24 mph, rising to a maximum of 36 mph for the Australian dragonfly *Austrophlebia costalis* for short bursts. Experiments have proved that the widely publicized claim by an American scientist in 1926 that the deer botfly (*Cephenemyia pratti*) could attain a speed of 818 mph at an altitude of 12,000 ft. was wildly exaggerated. If true, the fly would have had to develop the equivalent of 1.5 hp and consume 1½ times its own weight in food per second to acquire the energy that would be needed and, even if this were possible, it would still be crushed by the air pressure and incinerated by the friction.

Fastest-moving The fastest-moving insects are certain large tropical cockroaches, and the record is 3.36 mph, or 50 body lengths per second, registered by *Periplaneta americana* at the University of California at Berkeley in 1991.

Oldest The longest-lived insects are the splendor beetles (Buprestidae). On 27 May 1983 a *Buprestis aurulenta* appeared from the staircase timber in the the home of Mr. W. Euston of Prittlewell, Great Britain, after 47 years as a larva.

Fastest wing-beat The fastest wing-beat of any insect under natural conditions is 62,760 per min. by a tiny midge of the genus *Forcipomyia*. In experiments with truncated wings at a temperature of 98.6 ° F. the rate increased to 133,080 beats/min. The muscular contraction–expansion cycle in 0.00045 or 1/2218th of a sec. represents the fastest muscle movement ever measured.

Slowest wing-beat The slowest wing-beat of any insect is 300 per min. by the swallowtail butterfly (*Papilio machaon*). The average is 460–636 per min.

DRAGONFLIES *(Odonata)*

Largest *Megaloprepus caeruleata* of Central and South America has been measured up to 4.72 in. across the wings and 7.52 in. in body length.

United States The giant green darner (*Anax walsinghami*), found in the West, has a body length of up to 4½ in.

Smallest The smallest dragonfly in the world is *Agriocnemis naia* of Myanmar (formerly Burma). A specimen in the British Museum (Natural History), London, Great Britain had a wing expanse of 0.69 in. and a body length of 0.71 in.

United States The smallest dragonfly in the United States is the elfin skimmer (*Nannothaemis Bella*), which has a body length of ⁴/₅ in.

FLEAS *(Siphonaptera)*

Largest Siphonapterologists recognize 1,830 varieties, of which the largest-known is *Hystrichopsylla schefferi*, which was described from a single specimen taken from the nest of a mountain beaver (*Aplodontia rufa*) at Puyallup, WA in 1913. Females measure up to 0.3 in. in length.

Longest jump The champion jumper among fleas is the common flea (*Pulex irritans*). In one American experiment carried out in 1910, a specimen allowed to leap at will performed a long jump of 13 in. and a high jump of 7¾ in. In jumping 130 times its own height a flea subjects itself to a force of 200 *g*.

BUTTERFLIES AND MOTHS (*Lepidoptera*)

Largest The largest-known butterfly is the protected Queen Alexandra's birdwing (*Ornithoptera alexandrae*), which is restricted to the Popondetta Plain in Papua New Guinea. Females may have a wingspan exceeding 11 in. and weigh over 0.9 oz. (See Species on the Brink, Insects.)

The largest moth in the world (although not the heaviest) is the Hercules moth (*Cosdinocera hercules*) of tropical Australia and New Guinea. A wing area of up to 40.8 in.² and a wingspan of 11 in. have been recorded. In 1948 an unconfirmed measurement of 14.2 in. was reported for a female captured in Innisfail, Queensland, Australia.

The rare owlet moth (*Thysania agrippina*) of Brazil has been measured up to 12.2 in. wingspan in the case of a female taken in 1934.

United States The largest *native* butterfly in the United States is the giant swallowtail (*Papilio cresphontes*), found in the eastern states.

Smallest The smallest of the 140,000 known species of Lepidoptera is *Stigmella ridiculosa*, which has a wingspan of 0.079 in. with a similar body length and is found in the Canary Islands.

United States The smallest butterfly in the United States is the pygmy blue (*Brephidium exilis*), found in the Southeast.

Most acute sense of smell The most acute sense of smell exhibited in nature is that of the male emperor moth (*Eudiapavonia*), which, according to German experiments in 1961, can detect the sex attractant of the virgin female at the almost unbelievable range of 6.8 miles upwind. This scent has been identified as one of the higher alcohols ($C_{16}H_{29}OH$), of which the female carries less than 0.0000015 grain.

Migration A tagged female monarch butterfly (*Danaus plesippus*) released by Donald Davis at Presqu'ile Provincial Park near Brighton, Ontario, Canada on 6 Sep. 1986 was recaptured 2,133 miles away, on a mountain near Angangueo, Mexico on 15 Jan. 1987. This distance was obtained by measuring a line from the release site to the recapture site, but the actual distance traveled could be up to double that figure.

Largest butterfly farm The Stratford-upon-Avon Butterfly Farm, Warwickshire, Great Britain can accommodate 2,000 exotic butterflies in authentic rain forest conditions. The total capacity of all flight areas at the farm, which opened on 15 July 1985, is over 141,258 ft.³. The complex also comprises insect and plant houses and educational facilities.

United States Butterfly World, in Coconut Creek, FL, accommodates between 2,000 and 3,000 butterflies in authentic rain forest or North American conditions. About 80 species of butterfly can be seen at any one time, and in the course of a year up to 300 species are shown in the 37 screened enclosures. The museum, founded by Ron Boender, Clive Farrell, and John Chalk, cost $1.5 million and was built in five months to open in March 1988.

CENTIPEDES *Chilopoda*

Longest   The longest-known species of centipede is a large variant of the widely distributed *Scolopendra morsitans*, found on the Andaman Islands in the Bay of Bengal. Specimens have been measured up to 13 in. in length and 1½ in. in breadth.

United States   *Tomotaemia parviceps*, found in California and Washington, has been measured up to 5.9 in. in length and 0.1 in. in diameter.

Shortest   The shortest recorded centipede is an unidentified species that measures only 0.19 in.

United States   *Nampabius georgianus*, found in Georgia, measures up to 0.19 in. in length and 0.03 in. in diameter. *Poaaphilus keywinus*, found in Iowa, is smaller in diameter at 0.007 in., but has a length of 0.25 in.

Most legs   *Himantarum gabrielis*, found in southern Europe, has 171–177 pairs of legs when adult.

Fastest   The fastest centipede is probably *Scrutigera coleoptrata* of southern Europe, which can travel at 1.1 mph.

MILLIPEDES *Diplopoda*

Longest   Both *Graphidostreptus gigas* of Africa and *Scaphistostreptus seychellarum* of the Seychelles have been measured up to 11 in. in length and 0.8 in. in diameter.

United States   *Orthoporus ornatus*, found in Texas and Arizona, measures up to 7.28 in. in length and 0.55 in. in diameter.

Shortest   The shortest millipede in the world is the British species *Polyxenuslagurus*, which measures 0.082–0.15 in.

United States   *Polyxenus fasciculatus*, found in the Southeast, measures only 0.07 in. in length and 0.03 in. in diameter. The next-shortest millipede is *Buotus carolinus*, found in North Carolina and Virginia, which has been measured at 0.11 in. in length and only 0.01 in. in diameter.

Most legs   The greatest number of legs reported for a millipede is 375 pairs (750 legs) for *Illacme plenipes* of California.

SEGMENTED WORMS *Annelida*

Longest   The longest-known species of earthworm is *Microchaetus rappi* (= *M. microchaetus*) of South Africa. In *c.* 1937 a giant earthworm measuring 22 ft. in length when naturally extended and 0.8 in. in diameter was collected in the Transvaal.

Shortest   *Chaetogaster annandalei* measures less than 0.02 in. in length.

Worm-charming   At the first World Worm Charming Championship held at Willaston, Great Britain on 5 July 1980, Tom Shufflebotham (b. 1960) charmed a record 511 worms out of the ground (a 9.84 ft.² plot) in the allotted time of 30 min. Garden forks or other implements are vibrated in the soil by competitors to coax up the worms, but water is banned.

MOLLUSKS *Mollusca*

CEPHALOPODS

Largest invertebrate   The Atlantic giant squid, *Architeuthis dux*, is the world's largest-known invertebrate. The heaviest ever recorded was a 2.2-ton monster that ran aground in Thimble Tickle Bay, Newfoundland, Canada on 2 Nov. 1878. Its body was 20 ft. long and one tentacle measured 35 ft.

Longest   There are numerous types of squids, ranging in size from 0.75 in. to the longest ever recorded—a 57-ft. giant *Architeuthis longimanus* that was washed up on Lyall Bay, Cook Strait, New Zealand in October 1887. Its two long slender tentacles each measured 49 ft. 3 in.

Largest octopus   The largest-known octopus is the Pacific giant (*Octopus dofleini*), which ranges from California to Alaska and off eastern Asia south to Japan. It is not known exactly how large these creatures can grow but the average mature male weighs about 51 lbs. and has an arm span of about 8 ft. The largest recorded specimen, found off western Canada in 1957, had an estimated arm span of 31½ ft. and weighed about 600 lbs.

Smallest   The smallest cephalopod is the squid *Idiosepius*, which rarely reaches 1 in. in length.

Oldest   The longest-lived mollusk is the ocean quahog (*Arctica islandica*), a thick-shelled clam found in the mid-Atlantic. A specimen with 220 annual growth rings was collected in 1982.

Most tentacles   Most cephalopods have eight or 10 tentacles, but some types of *Nautilus* use up to 94 suckerless tentacles for catching prey on the ocean floor.

BIVALVES

Largest   The largest of all existing bivalve shells is that of the marine giant clam *Tridacna gigas*, found on the Indo-Pacific coral reefs. An outsized specimen measuring 45.2 in. in length and weighing 734 lbs. was collected off Ishigaki Island, Okinawa, Japan in 1956 but was not scientifically examined until August 1984. It probably weighed just over 750 lbs. when alive (the soft parts weigh up to 20 lbs.).

Longest   Another giant clam collected at Tapanoeli (Tapanula) on the northwest coast of Sumatra, Indonesia before 1817 and now preserved at Arno's Vale measures 54 in. in length and weighs 507 lbs.

Smallest   The smallest bivalve shell is the coinshell *Neolepton sykesi*, which is known only from a few examples collected off Guernsey, Channel Islands, Great Britain and western Ireland. It has an average diameter of 0.047 in.

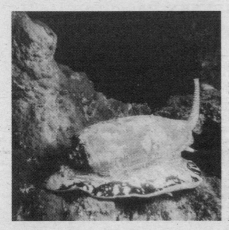

MOST VENOMOUS MOLLUSK. The geographer cone (*C. geographus*) delivers its neurotoxin through a unique harpoon-like proboscis and one in five of its known victims has died after being stung. (Photo: Jacana Agence de Presse/P. Laboute)

Most venomous   There are some 400–500 species of cone shell (*Conus*), all of which can deliver a poisonous neurotoxin. The geographer cone (*Conus geographus*) and the court cone (*C. aulicus*), marine mollusks found from Polynesia to East Africa, are considered to be the most deadly. The venom is injected by a unique, fleshy harpoon-like proboscis, and symptoms include impaired vision, dizziness, nausea, paralysis and death. Of the 25 people known to have been stung by these creatures, five have died, giving a mortality rate exceeding that for common cobras and rattlesnakes.

GASTROPODS

Largest   The largest-known gastropod is the trumpet or baler conch (*Syrinx aruanus*) of Australia. One specimen collected off Western Australia in 1979 and now owned by Don Pisor of San Diego, CA measures 30.4 in. in length and has a maximum girth of 39.8 in. It weighed nearly 40 lbs. when alive.

The largest-known land gastropod is the African giant snail (*Achatina sp.*). A specimen named Gee Geronimo owned by Christopher Hudson (1955–79) of Hove, Great Britain, measured 15½ in. from snout to tail when fully extended (shell length 10¾ in.) in December 1978 and weighed exactly 2 lbs. The snail was collected in Sierra Leone in June 1976.

Fastest   The world's fastest gastropods are probably banana slugs of the species *Ariolimax*. The fastest recorded speed was 0.28 in./sec. over 36 in. set by a specimen of *A. columbianus* in a slug race at Northwest Trek, WA in July 1983.

Snail   The fastest-moving species of land snail is probably the common garden snail (*Helix aspersa*). It is probable, however, that the carnivorous (and cannibalistic) snail *Euglandina rosea* could outrun other snails in its hunt for prey. The snail-racing equivalent of a four-minute mile is 24 in. in 3 min., or a 5½-day mile.

Snail racing   On 20 Feb. 1990 a garden snail named Verne completed a 12.2 in. course at West Middle School in Plymouth, MI in a record 2 min. 13 sec. at 0.233 cm/sec.

Smallest gastropod   The smallest-known shellbearing species is the gastropod *Ammonicera rota,* which is found in British waters. It measures 0.02 in. in diameter.

RIBBON WORMS *Nemertina*

Longest   The longest of the 550 recorded species of ribbon worm, also called nemertines (or nemerteans), is the "boot-lace" worm (*Lineus longissimus*), which is found in the shallow waters of the North Sea, Great Britain. A specimen that washed ashore at St. Andrews, Fife, Great Britain in 1864 after a severe storm measured more than 180 ft. in length.

JELLYFISHES AND CORALS *Cnidaria*

Largest jellyfish   The largest jellyfish is the Arctic giant jellyfish (*Cyanea capillata arctica*) of the northwestern Atlantic. One that washed up in Massachusetts Bay had a bell diameter of 7 ft. 6 in. and tentacles stretching 120 ft.

Most venomous   The beautiful but deadly Australian sea wasp (*Chironex fleckeri*) is the most venomous jellyfish in the world. Its cardiotoxic venom has caused the deaths of 66 people off the coast of Queensland since 1880, with victims dying within 1–3 minutes if medical aid is not available. One effective defense is women's pantyhose, outsize versions of which are now worn by Queensland lifesavers at surfing tournaments.

Coral   The world's greatest stony coral structure is the Great Barrier Reef off Queensland, northeast Australia. It stretches 1,260 miles and covers 80,000 miles². (See Most destructive starfish.)

The world's largest reported example of discrete coral is a stony colony of *Galaxea fascicularis* found in Sakiyama Bay off Irimote Island, Okinawa on 7 Aug. 1982 by Dr. Shohei Shirai of the Institute for Development of Pacific Natural Resources. It has a long axis measurement of 23 ft. 9 in., a height of 13 ft. 1½ in. and a maximum circumference of 59 ft. 5 in.

SPONGES *Porifera*

Largest   The largest-known sponge is the barrel-shaped loggerhead sponge (*Spheciospongia vesparium*) of the West Indies and the waters off Florida. Individuals measure up to 3 ft. 6 in. in height and 3 ft. in diameter. Neptune's cup or goblet (*Poterion patera*) of Indonesia grows to 4 ft. in height, but it is a less bulky animal.

Heaviest   In 1909 a wool sponge (*Hippospongia canaliculatta*) measuring

6 ft. in circumference was collected off the Bahamas. When taken from the water it weighed between 80–90 lbs. but after it had been dried and relieved of all excrescences it weighed 12 lbs. (This sponge is now preserved in the National Museum of Natural History, Washington, D.C.)

Smallest   The widely distributed *Leucosolenia blanca* measures 0.11 in. in height when fully grown.

Deepest   Sponges have been recovered from depths of up to 18,500 ft.

SPECIES ON THE BRINK

LAND MAMMALS

A number of mammals are known only from a single or type specimen.

General   The Javan rhinoceros (*Rhinoceros sondaicus*), the solitary, single-horned species, is the world's rarest large mammal (it is up to 5½ ft. tall at the shoulder and weighs 3,086 lbs.). Once widely distributed, its population has declined to just 50–70 wild specimens, mainly as a result of illegal hunting of its horns for use in traditional Oriental medicines and the destruction of its habitats. There are none held in captivity.

The red wolf (*Canis rufus*) of the southeast United States became extinct in the wild in the early 1970s, but there are now over 125 individuals (not all of them genetically pure) held by the US Fish and Wildlife Service. In June 1988 it was announced that two pairs released in North Carolina by the captive breeding program had produced cubs.

The black-footed ferret (*Mustela nigripes*) of the northern United States is also extinct in the wild, but in 1988 the captive population of 25, housed in a special center in Cheyenne, WY, more than doubled when the second breeding season produced 38 pups. There are now at least 300 individuals in captivity and the ferret will be reintroduced to the wild in Wyoming in the early 1990s.

Felines   The Irimote cat (*Felis iriomotensis*), confined to the small (113 miles^2) Japanese-owned island from which it takes its name, was only discovered in 1967; since then its population has fallen to about 80. A nocturnal animal, the Iriomote, which is the size of an average domestic cat, is protected by Japanese law and has been declared a national monument.

The general population of the tiger in the wild, estimated at about 1,000,000 in 1900, has fallen to some 7,000, and three of the eight subspecies, the Bali, Caspian and Javan tigers, are already extinct.

Primates   The greater bamboo broad-nosed gentle lemur (*Hapalemur simus*) of Madagascar reportedly became extinct in the early 1970s, but in 1986 a group consisting of 60–80 individuals was found living in a remote rain forest near Ranomafana in the southeastern part of the island by an expedition from Duke University, Durham, NC.

The golden-rumped tamarin (*Leontopithecus chrysopygus*), which is now restricted to two areas of forest in the state of São Paulo, Brazil, is also on the verge of extinction, with only 75–100 individuals surviving in 1986.

Bats   At least three species of bat are known only from the type specimen. They are: the small-toothed fruit bat (*Neopteryx frosti*) from Tamalanti, Sulawesi (Celebes; 1938–39); *Paracoelops megalotis* from Vinh, Vietnam (1945); and *Latidens salimalii* from the High Wavy Mountains, India (1948).

Rodents   The rarest rodents in the world are Garrido's hutia (*Capromys garridoi*) of the Canarreos Archipelago, Cuba, and the little earth hutia (*C. sanfelipensis*) of Juan Garcia Cay, an islet off southern Cuba. The latter species has not been recorded since its discovery in 1970.

Antelopes   The Arabian oryx (*Oryx leucoryx*) has been saved from the brink of extinction by a captive breeding program at San Diego Zoo, CA and strict protective measures in the wild, resulting in its successful reintroduction into the deserts of Oman and Jordan, where the population has reached at least 1,500.

Deer   Until recently, Fea's muntjac (*Muntiacus feae*) was known only from two specimens collected on the borders of southern Myanmar (formerly Burma) and western Thailand. In December 1977 a female was received at Dusit Zoo, in Bangkok, followed by two females in 1981 and three males and three females from Xizang, Tibet between February 1982 and April 1983.

Marsupials   The thylacine or tasmanian wolf or tiger (*Thylacinus cynocephalus*), feared extinct since the last captive specimen died in Beaumaris Zoo, Tasmania, Australia on 7 Sep. 1936, was possibly identified in July 1982 when a wildlife ranger claimed he saw one of these predatory marsupials in the spotlight of his parked car. Since then, however, there have been no more positive sightings.

New and recent discoveries   One new discovery reported in June 1991 was a moth of the genus *Monochroa,* found in Great Britain and subsequently named *Monochroa moyses*. Moyses, the Greek version of Moses, was chosen because the moth spends its youth hidden in rushes.

The three-banded armadillo of the species *Tolypeutes* was rediscovered in Brazil in 1991 after being thought extinct following no sightings of it for 20 years. One of the two species able to roll itself into a ball when threatened, this armadillo is a poor digger and therefore easy prey for humans hunting for food, a situation which has prompted the launch of a captive breeding program.

The elusive plankton-feeding megamouth shark has been recorded off Los Angeles, CA. After its rescue from a gill net, the shark was fitted with a transmitter before being released and tracked by researchers. It was only the fifth specimen seen since its discovery in 1976.

MARINE MAMMALS

Cetaceans   Longman's beaked whale (*Indopacetus pacificus*) is known only from two skulls. The type specimen was discovered on a beach near MacKay, Queensland, Australia in 1922, and the second near Muqdisho, Somalia in 1955.

Sightings of the vaquita or gulf porpoise (*Phocoena sinus*) in the Gulf of California in 1986 (the first since 1980) suggest an estimated population of just 30, making this now the most probable contender for the rarest cetacean.

The Baiji, or Yangzi River, dolphin (*Lipotes vexillifer*) is probably the most endangered of all the cetaceans (whales, dolphins and porpoises), with a population estimated at about 300 and falling due to competition for fish supplies with China's human population (dolphins are often caught up in fishing gear) and the reduction of overall food supplies because of environmental degradation.

Pinnipeds   The last reliable sighting of the Caribbean or West Indian monk seal (*Monachus tropicalis*) was on Serranilla Bank off the coast of Mexico's Yucatan Peninsula in 1952, and this species is almost certainly extinct. Monk seals were once common throughout the Pacific, the Caribbean and the Mediterranean. The first pinnipeds recorded by Aristotle (384–322 B.C.), monk seals were the first to be spotted by Christopher Columbus (1451–1506) in the New World.

BIRDS

General   The number of threatened bird species worldwide has risen in the past 10 years from 290 to 1,029 as a result of human activity, according to a survey published in October 1988. Many species are now extinct in the wild but may be surviving in captivity, usually as a result of breeding programs. Because of the practical difficulties in assessing bird populations in the wild, it is virtually impossible to establish the identity of the world's rarest living bird. The most probable contender, however, is Spix's macaw (*Cyanopsitta spixii*) of Brazil, the world's most endangered parrot, which was reduced to a single specimen in the wild in July 1990. There are only 15 left in captivity around the world.

The Kakapo (*Strigops habrotilus*), a flightless parrot from New Zealand, is also in imminent danger of extinction from hunting and predation by introduced alien species, despite several attempts to relocate it to increasingly inaccessible islands. In 1990 there were 43 known survivors but, as the Kakapo breeds somewhat sporadically (only once in 4 or 5 years), it may go the way of the dodo, the only bird with which it apparently shares any features.

REPTILES

Crocodilians   The total wild population of the protected Chinese alligator (*Alligator sinensis*) of the lower Yangtze River in the Anhui, Zhejiang and Jiangsu provinces of China is currently estimated at no more than a few hundred. Although captive breeding programs are proving successful, the alligator cannot be reintroduced into the wild because of the destruction of its habitats and its extinction outside captivity is expected before the end of the century, if not sooner.

Chelonians   The world's rarest chelonian is the protected short-necked swamp tortoise (*Pseudemydura umbrina*), which is confined to Ellen Brook and Twin reserves near Perth, Western Australia. The total wild population is now only 20–25, with another 22 held at Perth Zoo.

Snakes   The world's rarest snake is now considered to be the St. Lucia racer or couresse (*Liophis ornatus*), found only on Maria Island, off St. Lucia, West Indies. Estimates by Dr. David Corke of the Polytechnic of East London, Great Britain put its population at under 100 in 1989, with no specimens held in captivity.

The Round Island boa (*Bolyeria multicarinata*) is known from only two specimens collected in the past 40 years and probably became extinct in 1980.

FISHES

Marine   A coelacanth, a large, deep-water fish formerly known only from fossilized remains dating from 400 to 65 million years old, was landed at East London, South Africa on 22 Dec. 1938 and only later identified as such and named *Latimeria chalumnae*. It has been claimed to be the "missing link" between man and fish. Since this discovery, living coelacanths were observed in their natural habitat 656 ft. below the waters off the Comoros in the Indian Ocean in the late 1980s.

INSECTS

General   It is estimated that there may be as many as 30 million species of insect—more than all other phyla and classes put together—but thousands are known only from a single or type specimen.

The current status of the St. Helena earwig of the order Dermaptera (about 1,100 species) is unknown and, as the last reliable sightings were between 1965 and 1967, this nocturnal insect may be on the brink of extinction. It is the largest of the order Dermaptera, with a maximum recorded total length (body and tail pincers) of 3 in. Its decline is a result of the accidental intro-

---

Rarest amphibians   Only five specimens of the painted frog (*Discoglossus nigriventer*) of Lake Huleh, Israel have been reported since 1940.

Rarest arachnids   The most elusive of all spiders are the rare trapdoor spiders of the genus *Liphistius,* which are found in Southeast Asia.

Rarest trees   The palm tree genus *Hyophorbe* contains only five species and is endemic to the Mascarene Islands. All five species are considered endangered, but especially the Mauritius palm (*H. Amaricaulis*), whose once abundant population has been reduced to a single specimen, probably planted deliberately, at the Curepipe Botanic Garden, Mauritius. Attempts at propagation have so far proved unsuccessful and this species faces certain extinction.

duction of rats to its habitat and predation by the fearsome Giant centipede, which can attack the earwigs deep in their protective burrows.

Butterflies and moths   The rarest butterfly is considered to be Queen Alexandra's birdwing (*Ornithoptera alexandrae*), which is found with its only source of nutrition, the vine *Aristolochia dielsiana*, in Papua New Guinea. Its population is extremely difficult to estimate as it flies very high and is seldom seen. The caterpillars are also somewhat elusive in their habitat 131 ft. above the ground in the vine leaves. However, only three individuals were sighted in 1990 during surveys of an area covering 220–320 acres. (See Largest butterfly.)

Another birdwing, *Ornithoptera (= Troides) allottei* of Bougainville, Solomon Islands, is known from less than a dozen specimens. This is not a true species, but a natural hybrid of *Ornithoptera victoriae* and *O. urvillianus*.

PLANTS

General   Plants that had been thought to be extinct are rediscovered each year, and there are thus many plants that are found in only a single locality.

The last surviving specimen (a female) of the cycad *Encephalartos woodii*, a palmlike tropical plant of a group known to have existed for 65–225 million years, is held at the Royal Botanic Gardens, Kew, Great Britain. It is possible that this plant is a hybrid of the specimen *Encephalartos altensteinii*, also at Kew. (See Plant Kingdom, Oldest pot plant.)

Pennantia baylisiana, a tree found in 1945 on Three Kings Island off New Zealand, also exists only as a female and cannot bear fruit.

In May 1983 it was reported that there was a sole surviving specimen of the lady's slipper orchid (*Cypripedium calceolus*) in Britain.

Rothschild's slipper orchid (*Paphiopedilum rothschildianum*) was discovered in 1888 and thought to be extinct until its rediscovery in 1959. The spectacular beauty of this plant has, naturally, contributed greatly to its imminent extinction at the hands of illegal collectors and traders, although its highly specific ecological requirements are also a major force. Seeds were gathered in 1982 and its only chance for survival in the wild is propagation and re- release in new and highly secret locations.

EXTINCT ANIMALS

DINOSAURS

Part of the reptile order, dinosaurs are undoubtedly the best-known group of extinct animals. The first dinosaur to be scientifically described was *Megalosaurus bucklandi* ("great fossil lizard") in 1824. The remains of this bipedal flesh-eater were found by workmen before 1818 in a slate quarry near Woodstock, Great Britain and later placed in the University Museum, in Oxford, Great Britain. The first fossil bone of *Megalosaurus* was actually illustrated in 1677, but its true nature was not realized until much later. It was not until 1841 that the name Dinosauria ("terrible lizards") was given to these newly discovered giants.

Disappearance   No wholly satisfactory theory has been offered for the dinosaurs' sudden extinction 65 million years ago. Evidence from the Hell Creek Formation of Montana suggests that dinosaurs dwindled in importance over a period of 5–10 million years and were replaced progressively by mammals, possibly because of long-term climatic changes. Another theory is their sudden elimination by the impact of an asteroid, which would have had a diameter of some 5.6 miles, or by a shower of comets causing clouds of dust to block out the sun. The asteroid theory is supported strongly by the discovery of significant levels of the element iridium, a good indicator of extraterrestrial impact, at numerous locations around the world. A further hypothesis is that of a period of severe volcanic activity, which would also result in darkness caused by dust, and acid rain and iridium.

Earliest-known   The earliest dinosaur is believed to be the *Herrerasaurus*, a carnivore known from an almost complete skeleton discovered in 1989 in the foothills of the Andes in Argentina. *Herrerasaurus* is thought to date from 230 million years ago and stood about 6½–8 ft., with a weight of over 220 lbs. Its evolutionary importance is suggested by its dual-hinged jaw, a feature that did not appear in other dinosaurs for another 50 million years. Other dinosaurs of a similar age from the Late Triassic are known from incomplete remains found in Brazil, Argentina, Morocco, India and Scotland.

United States   The earliest dated remains of dinosaurs found in the United States are those of *Coelophysis*, found at Ghost Ranch, MI in 1947. They are slightly younger than the *Herrerasaurus* remains found in Argentina. The creatures ranged in size from smaller than a chicken to larger than a turkey. The find represents the largest concentration of skeletal remains, over 1,000, of meat-eating dinosaurs in the world.

Largest   The largest-ever land animals were sauropod dinosaurs, a group of long-necked, long-tailed, four-legged plant-eaters that lumbered around most of the world during the Jurassic and Cretaceous periods 208–65 million years ago. However, it is difficult to determine precisely which of these sauropod dinosaurs was the largest (longest, tallest or heaviest). This is because many of the supposed giants are based only on incomplete fossil remains, and also because many discoverers have tended to exaggerate the sizes of their dinosaur finds. Estimating dinosaur lengths and heights is relatively straightforward when there is a complete skeleton. Sauropods are divided into five main groups: cetiosaurids, brachiosaurids, diplodocids, camarasaurids, and titanosaurids. The world's biggest dinosaur has been identified at different times as a brachiosaurid, a diplodocid or a titanosaurid.

Tallest   The tallest and largest dinosaur is the *Brachiosaurus (Giraffatitan) brancai* from the Tendaguru site in Tanzania, dated as Late Jurassic (150 million years ago). The site was excavated by German expeditions during the period 1909–11 and the bones prepared and assembled at the Humboldt Museum in Berlin. A complete skeleton was constructed from the remains of several individuals and put on display in 1937. It is the world's largest and tallest mounted dinosaur skeleton, measuring 72 ft. 9½ in. in overall length (height at shoulder 19 ft. 8 in.), a raised head height of 46 ft., and a likely weight of 30–40 tons. However, larger sizes are suggested by an isolated fibula from another *Brachiosaurus* in the same museum.

Oldest land animals   Animals moved from the sea to the land 414 million years ago, according to discoveries made in 1990 near Ludlow, Great Britain. The first land animals include two kinds of centipede and a tiny spider found among plant debris, suggesting that life moved onto land much earlier than previously thought.

Earliest reptile fossil   The oldest reptile fossil, nicknamed "Lizzie the Lizard," was found on a site in Scotland by palaeontologist Stan Wood in March 1988. The 8-in.-long reptile is estimated to be 340 million years old, 40 million years older than previously discovered reptiles.

Most brainless   *Stegosaurus* ("plated lizard"), which roamed across Colorado, Oklahoma, Utah and Wyoming about 150 million years ago, measured up to 30 ft. in total length but had a walnut-sized brain weighing only 2½ oz. This represented 0.004 of 1 percent of its computed body weight of 1.9 tons (compare with 0.074 of 1 percent for an elephant and 1.88 percent for a human).

Heaviest   The largest-known sauropods appear to have weighed around 55–110 tons, but this does not necessarily represent the ultimate weight limit for a land vertebrate. Theoretical calculations suggest that some dinosaurs approached the maximum body weight possible for a terrestrial animal, namely 120 tons. At weights greater than this, the legs would have to be so massive to support the bulk that the dinosaur could not have moved!

The main contenders for the heaviest dinosaur are probably the titanosaurid *Antarctosaurus giganteus* ("Antartic lizard") from Argentina and India, at 45–88 tons; the brachiosaurid *Brachiosaurus altithorax* (49–59 tons); the diplodocids *Seismosaurus halli* and *Supersaurus vivianae* (both over 50 tons).

Longest   Based on the evidence of footprints, the brachiosaurid *Breviparopus* attained a length of 157 ft., which would make it the longest vertebrate on record. However, a diplodocid from New Mexico named *Seismosaurus halli* was estimated in 1991 to be 128–170 ft. long based on comparisons of individual bones.

Complete   The longest dinosaur known from a complete skeleton is the diplodocid *Diplodocus carnegii* ("double beam"), assembled at the Carnegie Museum in Pittsburgh, PA from remains found in Wyoming in 1899. *Diplodocus* was 87½ ft. long, with much of that length made up of an extremely long whiplike tail, and probably weighed 6.4–20.4 tons, the higher estimates being the more likely. The mounted skeleton was so spectacular that casts were requested by other museums, and copies may be seen in London, Great Britain; La Plata, Argentina; Washington, D.C.; Frankfurt, Germany; and Paris, France.

Largest predatory dinosaur   The largest flesh-eating dinosaur recorded so far is *Tyrannosaurus rex* ("king tyrant lizard"), which seventy million years ago reigned over what are now the states of Montana, Wyoming and Texas and the provinces of Alberta and Saskatchewan, Canada. The largest and heaviest example, as suggested by a discovery in South Dakota in 1991, was 19½ ft. tall, had a total length of 36½ ft. and weighed an estimated 6–8 tons.

A composite skeleton of a slightly smaller specimen of this nightmarish beast can be seen in the American Museum of Natural History, New York City.

Longest The discovery of the allosaur *Epanterias amplexus* from Masonville, CO has suggested that this theropod reached a length of 50 ft. and a weight of 4.4 tons, but remains are incomplete. Similar lengths were also attained by *Spinosaurus aegyptiacus* ("thorn lizard") of Niger and Egypt.

Tallest *Dynamosaurus imperiosus* ("dynamic lizard") of Shandong Province, China had a bipedal length of 20 ft. and an overall length of 46 ft., but these tyrannosaurids were not as heavily built as those from North America.

Smallest The chicken-sized *Compsognathus* ("pretty jaw") of southern Germany and southeast France, and an undescribed plant-eating fabrosaurid from Colorado, measured 29.5 in. from the snout to the tip of the tail and weighed about 15 lbs.

Longest tracks In 1983 a series of four *Apatosaurus* (= *Brontosaurus*) tracks that ran parallel for a distance of over 705 ft. were recorded from 145-million-year-old Morrison strata in southeast Colorado.

Fastest Tracks can be used to estimate dinosaur speeds, and one from the Late Morrison of Texas discovered in 1981 indicated that a carnivorous dinosaur had been moving at 25 mph. Some ornithomimids were even faster, and the large-brained, 220-lb. *Dromiceiomimus* ("emu mimic lizard") of the Late Cretaceous of Alberta, Canada could probably outsprint an ostrich, which has a top speed of 40 mph.

Largest footprints In 1932 the gigantic footprints of a large bipedal hadrosaurid ("duckbill") measuring 53½ in. in length and 32 in. wide were discovered in Salt Lake City, UT, and other reports from Colorado and Utah refer to footprints 37.5–39.5 in. wide. Footprints attributed to the largest brachiosaurids also range up to 40 in. wide for the hind feet.

Longest neck The sauropod *Mamenchisaurus* ("mamenchi lizard") of the Late Jurassic of Sichuan, China had the longest neck of any animal that has ever lived. It measured 36 ft.—half the total length of the dinosaur.

Largest skull The skulls of the long-frilled ceratopsids were the largest of all known land animals and culminated in the long-frilled *Torosaurus sp.* ("piercing lizard"). This herbivore, which measured *c.* 25 ft. in total length and weighed up to 8.8 tons, had a skull measuring up to 9 ft. 10 in. in length (including fringe) and weighing up to 2.2 tons. It ranged from Montana to Texas.

Largest claws The therizinosaurids ("scythe lizards") from the Late Cretaceous of the Nemegt Basin, southern Mongolia, had the largest claws of any known animal, and in the case of *Therizinosaurus cheloniformis* the claws measured up to 36 in. around the outer curve (compare with 8 in. for *T. rex*). It has been suggested that these sickle claws were designed for grasping and tearing apart large victims, but this creature had a feeble skull partially or entirely lacking teeth and probably lived on termites.

Largest eggs   The largest-known dinosaur eggs are those of *Hypselosaurus priscus* ("high ridge lizard"), a 40-ft.-long titanosaurid that lived about 80 million years ago. Examples found in the Durance valley near Aix-en-Provence, France in October 1961 would have had, uncrushed, a length of 12 in. and a diameter of 10 in. (capacity 5.8 pt.).

OTHER REPTILES

Largest predator   The largest-ever land predator may have been an alligator found on the banks of the Amazon in rocks dated as 8 million years old. Estimates from a 5-ft.-long jaw (complete with 4-in.-long teeth) indicate a length of 40 ft. and a weight of about 13 tons, making it even larger than the fearsome *Tyrannosaurus rex*. However, this find has yet to be studied in detail.

Longest   Other fossil crocodiles suggest that the longest predator was probably the euschian *Deinocheirus mirificus* ("terrible crocodile") from the lakes and swamps of what is now Texas about 75 million years ago. Fragmentary remains discovered in Big Bend National Park, TX indicate a hypothetical length of 52 ft. 6 in.

Largest chelonians   The largest prehistoric chelonian was *Stupendemys geographicus*, a pelomedusid turtle that lived about 5 million years ago. Fossil remains discovered by Harvard University palaeontologists in northern Venezuela in 1972 indicate that this turtle had a carapace (shell) measuring

---

Earliest mammals   The first true mammals appeared about 220 million years ago during the Late Triassic, and by the end of the Cretaceous period, 65 million years ago, the first primate, *Purgatorius,* had emerged. This creature was similar in appearance to modern tree shrews of the order Scandentia.

Largest antlers   The prehistoric giant deer (*Megaloceros giganteus*), which lived in northern Europe and northern Asia as recently as 8000 B.C., had the longest horns of any known animal. One specimen recovered from an Irish bog had greatly palmated antlers measuring 14 ft. across, which corresponds to a shoulder height of 6 ft. and a weight of 1,100 lbs.

Oldest insect   A shrimp-like creature found in 1991 in rocks dated as 420 million years old may be the world's oldest insect. Found in Western Australia, this euthycarcinoid was a large (5 in. long) freshwater predator.

Largest insect   The largest prehistoric insect was the dragonfly *Meganeura monyi,* which lived about 300 million years ago. Fossil remains (impressions of wings) discovered at Commentry, France indicate a wing extending up to 27½ in.

---

7 ft. 2 in.–7 ft. 6½ in. in mid-line length, measured 9 ft. 10 in. in overall length and had a computed weight of 4,500 lbs.

Tortoise   The largest prehistoric tortoise was probably *Geochelone* (= *Colossochelys*) *atlas*, which lived in what is now northern India, Myanmar (formerly Burma), Java, the Celebes and Timor, about 2 million years ago. In 1923 the fossil remains of a specimen with a carapace 5 ft. 11 in. long (7 ft. 4 in. over the curve) and 2 ft. 11 in. high were discovered near Chandigarh in the Siwalik Hills, India. This animal had a total length of 8 ft. and is computed to have weighed 2,100 lbs.

Longest snake   The longest prehistoric snake was the pythonlike *Gigantophis garstini*, which inhabited what is now Egypt about 38 million years ago. Parts of a spinal column and a small piece of jaw discovered at Fayum in the Western Desert indicate a length of about 37 ft.

Largest marine reptile   *Kronosaurus queenslandicus,* a short-necked pliosaur from the Early Cretaceous period (135 million years ago) of Australia, measured up to 50 ft. in length and had a 10-ft.-long skull containing 80 massive teeth.

Largest flying creature   The largest-ever flying creature was the pterosaur *Quetzalcoatlus northropi* ("feathered serpent"). About 70 million years ago it soared over what is now Texas, Wyoming and New Jersey; Alberta, Canada; and Senegal and Jordan. Partial remains discovered in Big Bend National Park, TX in 1971 indicate that this reptile must have had a wingspan of 36–39 ft. and weighed about 190–250 lbs.

MAMMALS

Largest   The largest land mammal ever recorded was *Paraceratherium* (= *Baluchitherium*), a long-necked, hornless rhinocerotid that roamed across western Asia and Europe (Yugoslavia) about 35 million years ago and was first known from bones discovered in the Bugti Hills of Baluchistan, Pakistan in 1907–1908. A restoration in the American Museum of Natural History, New York City measures 17 ft. 9 in. to the top of the shoulder hump and 37 ft. in total length, and this gigantic browser must have weighed about 36 tons.

Mammoths   The largest prehistoric elephant was the steppe mammoth (*Mammuthus [Parelephas] trogontherii*), which, one million years ago, roamed what is now central Europe. A fragmentary skeleton found in Mosbach, Germany indicates a shoulder height of 14 ft. 9 in.

Tusks   The longest tusks of any prehistoric animal were those of the straight-tusked elephant (*Paleoloxodom antiquus germanicus*), which lived in northern Germany *c.* 300,000 years ago. The average length for tusks of adult bulls was 16 ft. 5 in. A single tusk of a woolly mammoth (*Mammuthus primigenius*) preserved in the Franzens Museum at Brno, Czechoslovakia measures 16 ft. 5½ in. along the outside curve.

Heaviest   The heaviest single fossil tusk on record weighed 330 lbs. with a maximum circumference of 35 in. and is now preserved in the Museo

Civico di Storia Naturale, Milan, Italy. The specimen, which is in two pieces, measures 11 ft. 9 in. in length.

Primates   The largest-known primate was *Gigantopithecus* of the Middle Pleistocene in what is now northern Vietnam and southern China. Males would have stood an estimated 9 ft. tall and weighed about 600 lbs. It is risky, however, to correlate tooth size and jaw depth of primates with their height and body weight, and *Gigantopithecus* may have had a disproportionately large head, jaws and teeth in relation to body size. The only remains discovered so far are three partial lower jaws and more than 1,000 teeth.

Largest marine mammal   The serpentine *Basilosaurus* (*Zeuglodon*) *cetoides*, which swam in the seas that covered modern-day Arkansas and Alabama 50 million years ago, measured up to 70 ft. in length.

MAMMOTHS. The largest of the prehistoric elephants, mammoths are believed to have been hunted to extinction by Ice Age people. A single tusk from a specimen of this woolly mammoth (*Mammathus primigenius*) measured a record 16 ft. 5½ in. long. (Photo: Syndication International Ltd.)

BIRDS

Earliest The earliest fossil bird is known from two partial skeletons found in Texas in rocks dating from 220 million years ago. Named *Protoavis texensis* in 1991, this pheasant-sized creature has caused much controversy by pushing the age of birds back 45 million years from the previous record, that of the more familiar *Archeopteryx lithographica* from Germany.

Largest The largest prehistoric bird was the flightless *Dromornis stirtoni*, a huge emulike creature that lived in central Australia 11 million years ago. Fossil leg bones found near Alice Springs in 1974 indicate that the bird must have stood *c.* 10 ft. tall and weighed about 1,100 lbs.

The giant moa *Dinornis maximus* of New Zealand was even taller, attaining a maximum height of 12 ft., though 8 ft. is the maximum accepted by most experts. It weighed only about 500 lbs.

Flying bird The largest-known flying bird was the giant teratorn (*Argentavis magnificens*), which lived in Argentina about 6 million years ago. Fossil remains discovered at a site 100 miles west of Buenos Aires, Argentina in 1979 indicate that this gigantic vulture had a wingspan of over 19 ft. 8 in., up to possibly 25 ft., and weighed 220–265 lbs.

Largest amphibian The largest amphibian ever recorded was the gharial-like *Prionosuchus plummeri*, which lived 270 million years ago. Fragmented remains were discovered in northern Brazil in 1972. These were reported in 1991 and the total body length was estimated at 30 ft. based on a 5-ft.-3-in.-long skull.

Largest fish No prehistoric fish larger than living species has yet been discovered. Modern estimates suggest that the great shark *Carcharodon megalodon*, which abounded in Miocene seas some 15 million years ago, did not exceed 43 ft. in length, far less than the 80 ft. claimed in early, erroneous estimates based on ratios from fossil teeth.

PLANT KINGDOM *Plantea*

GENERAL RECORDS

Oldest "King Clone," the oldest-known clone of the creosote plant (*Larrea tridentata*), found in southwest California, was estimated in February 1980 by Prof. Frank C. Vasek to be 11,700 years old. It is possible that crustose lichens in excess of 19.6 in. in diameter may be as old.

Most massive The most massive tree on earth is the biggest-known giant sequoia (*Sequoiadendron giganteum*), a tree named the General Sherman, standing 274.9 ft. tall, in the Sequoia National Park, CA. In 1989 it had a girth of 83 ft. 2 in., measured 4.5 ft. above the ground. (See Trees and Wood.)

Northernmost The yellow poppy (*Papaver radicatum*) and the Arctic willow (*Salix arctica*) survive, the latter in an extremely stunted form, on the northernmost land at Lat. 83° N .

Southernmost   Lichens resembling *Rhinodina frigida* have been found in Moraine Canyon at Lat. 86°09′S, Long. 157°30′W in 1971 and in the Horlick Mountain area, Antarctica at Lat. 86°09′S, Long. 131°14′W in 1965.

The southernmost recorded flowering plant is the Antarctic hair grass (*Deschampsia antarctica*), which was found at Lat. 68° 21′ S on Refuge Island, Antarctica on 11 Mar. 1981.

Highest   The greatest certain altitude at which any flowering plants have been found is 21,000 ft. on Kamet (25,447 ft.) by N.D. Jayal in 1955. They were *Ermania himalayensis* and *Ranunculus lobatus*.

Deepest   The greatest depth at which plant life has been found is 884 ft. by Mark and Diane Littler off San Salvadore Island, Bahamas in October 1984. These maroon-colored algae survived although 99.9995 percent of sunlight was filtered out.

Roots   The greatest reported depth to which roots have penetrated is an estimated 400 ft. for a wild fig tree at Echo Caves, near Ohrigstad, Transvaal, South Africa. A single winter rye plant (*Secale cereale*) has been shown to produce 387 miles of roots in 1.83 ft.³ of earth.

Fastest-growing   Some species of the 45 genera of bamboo have been found to grow up to 3 ft. per day (0.00002 mph). (See Fastest-growing and Tallest grass.)

BLOOMS AND FLOWERS

Earliest flower   A flower believed to be 120 million years old was identified in 1989 by Dr. Leo Hickey and Dr. David Taylor of Yale University, New Haven, CT from a fossil discovered near Melbourne, Victoria, Australia. The flowering angiosperm, which resembles a modern black pepper plant, had two leaves and one flower and is known as the Koonwarra plant.

United States   The oldest fossil of a flowering plant with palmlike imprints in America was found in Colorado in 1953 and dated about 65 million years old.

Largest   The largest of all blooms are those of the parasitic stinking corpse lily (*Rafflesia arnoldii*), which measure up to 3 ft. across and ¾ in. thick, and attain a weight of 15 lbs. The plants attach themselves to the cissus vines in the jungles of southeast Asia. True to its name, the plant has an extremely offensive scent.

Inflorescence   The largest-known inflorescence (as distinct from the largest of all blooms) is that of *Puya raimondii*, a rare Bolivian monocarpic member of the Bromeliaceae family. Its erect panicle (diameter 8 ft.) emerges to a height of 35 ft. and each of these bears up to 8,000 white blooms. (See Slowest-flowering plant.) The flower-spike of an agave measured in Berkeley, CA in 1974 was found to be 52 ft. long.

Blossoming plant   The giant Chinese wisteria (*Wisteria sinensis*) at Sierra

Madre, CA was planted in 1892 and now has branches 500 ft. long. It covers nearly 1 acre, weighs 248 tons and has an estimated 1.5 million blossoms during its blossoming period of five weeks, when up to 30,000 people pay admission to visit it.

Smallest flowering and fruiting
The floating, flowering aquatic duckweed (*Wolffia angusta*) of Australia, described in 1980, is only 0.0236 in. long and 0.0129 in. wide. It weighs about $\frac{1}{100,000}$ oz. and its fruit, which resembles a minuscule fig, weighs $\frac{1}{400,000}$ oz.

United States   The smallest plant regularly flowering in the United States is *Wolffia globosa*, which is found in the San Joaquin Valley, central California, and rivers draining the Sierra Nevada Mountains. The plant weighs about 150 micrograms, and is listed as 0.015 in. to 0.027 in. in length and 0.011 in. in width.

Fastest-growing
It was reported from Tresco Abbey, Isles of Scilly, Great Britain in July 1978 that a *Hesperoyucca whipplei* of the family Liliaceae grew 12 ft. in 14 days, a rate of about 10 in. per day.

Slowest-flowering
The slowest-flowering of all plants is the rare *Puya raimondii*, the largest of all herbs, discovered at 13,000 ft. in Bolivia in 1870. The panicle emerges after about 80–150 years of the plant's life. It then dies. One planted near sea level at the University of California's Botanical Garden, Berkeley in 1958 grew to 25 ft. and bloomed as early as August 1986 after only 28 years. (See Largest blooms.)

Longest daisy chain   The longest daisy chain measured 6,980 ft. 7 in. and was made in 7 hrs. by villagers of Good Easter, Great Britain on 27 May 1985. The team is limited to 16.

Orchids *Tallest*   The tallest of all orchids is *Grammatophyllum speciosum*, a native of Malaysia. Specimens have been recorded up to 25 ft. in height.

A height of 49 ft. has been recorded for *Galeola foliata*, a saprophyte of the vanilla family. It grows in the decaying rain forests of Queensland, Australia, but is not freestanding.

Largest flower   The largest orchid flower is that of *Pathiopedilum sanderianum*, whose petals are reported to grow up to 3 ft. long in the wild. It was discovered in 1886 in the Malay Archipelago. A plant of this variety grown in Somerset, Great Britain in 1991 had three flowers averaging 2 ft. from the top of the dorsal sepal to the bottom of the ribbon petals, giving a record stretched length of 4 ft.

The largest flowering orchid in the United States is the yellow ladyslipper (*Cypripedium calceolus*) of the Pubsecens variety. Its petals grow up to 7 in. long.

Tallest   The tallest of all American orchids is the *Eulophia ecristata*, with a recorded height of 5.6 ft. There are five species of vanilla orchids that are vines and can spread to almost any length depending on the environment. These include *Phaeantha*, *Planifolia*, *Inodora*, *Dilliana*, and *Barbellata*. These orchids root in the ground and will grow in any direction over their surroundings.

Smallest The smallest orchid is *Platystele jungermannoides*, found in Central America. Its flowers are just 0.04 in. in diameter.

The smallest orchid in the United States is *Lepanthopsis melanantha*, with a petal spread of 0.02 in. and a maximum height of 1.6 in.

Largest cactus The largest of all cacti is the saguaro (*Cereus giganteus* or *Carnegiea gigantea*), found in Arizona, southeastern California and Sonora, Mexico. The green fluted column is surmounted by candelabra-like branches rising to a height of 57 ft. 11¾ in. in the case of a specimen discovered in the Maricopa Mountains, near Gila Bend, AZ on 17 Jan. 1988.

An armless cactus 78 ft. in height was measured in April 1978 by Hube Yates in Cave Creek, AZ. It was toppled in a windstorm in July 1986 at an estimated age of 150 years.

Largest rhododendron Examples of the scarlet *Rhododendron arboreum* reach a height of 65 ft. on Mt. Japfu, Nagaland, India. The cross-section of the trunk of a *Rhododendron giganteum*, reputedly 90 ft. high, from Yunnan, China, is preserved at Inverewe Gardens, Highland, Great Britain.

Largest rose tree A Lady Banks rose tree at Tombstone, AZ has a trunk 40 in. thick, stands 9 ft. high and covers an area of 5,380 ft.^{2}. It is supported by 68 posts and several thousand feet of piping, which enables 150 people to be seated under the arbor. The cutting came from Scotland in 1884.

Biggest aspidistra The biggest aspidistra in the world measures 56 in. and belongs to Cliff Evans of Kiora, Moruya, New South Wales, Australia.

Oldest pot plant The world's oldest, and probably rarest, pot plant is the single cycad *Encephalartos altensteinii* brought from South Africa in 1775 and now housed at the Royal Botanic Gardens Kew, Great Britain. (See Species on the Brink, Plants.)

Hanging basket A giant hanging basket measuring 20 ft. in diameter and containing about 600 plants was created by Rogers of Exeter Garden Centre, Great Britain in 1987. Its volume was approximately 4,167 ft.^{3} and weighed an estimated 4.4 tons. Another example from France with the same diameter but more conical in shape was smaller in terms of volume.

Clovers A fourteen-leafed white clover (*Trifolium repens*) was found by Randy Farland near Sioux Falls, SD on 16 June 1975. A fourteen-leafed red clover (*T. pratense*) was reported by Paul Haizlip at Bellevue, WA on 22 June 1987. Clovers are not invariably three-leafed, and their collection is not considered to be botanically significant.

Vegetables, Fruits & Flowers World Records

Garlic
2 lb 10 oz
R. Kirkpatrick, Eureka,
California, 1985

Apple
3 lb 1 oz
V. Loveridge, Ross-on-
Wye, Great Britain, 1965

Pineapple [2]
17 lb 8 oz
Dole Philippines Inc., South
Cotabato, Philippines, 1984

Tomato Plant [5]
53 ft 6 in
G. Graham,
Edmond,
Oklahoma,
1985

Melon (Cantaloupe)
62 lb
G. Daughtridge, Rocky
Mount, North Carolina, 1991

US NATIONAL RECORDS

Apple	2.73 lb	C. Bender	Cashmere, WA	1991
Beet	45 1/2 lb.	R. Meyer	Brawley, CA	1984
Collard Plant	35 ft tall	B. Rackley	Rocky Mount, NC	1980
Corn Stalk	31 ft high	D. Radda	Washington, IA	1946
Dahlia	16 ft 5 in	S.&P. Barnes	Chattahoochee, FL	1982
Eggplant	5 lb 5.4 oz	J. & J. Charles	Summerville, SC	1984
Lima Bean	14 in	N. McCoy	Hubert, NC	1979
Okra Stalk [8]	17 ft 6 1/4 in	C.H. Wilber	Crane Hill, AL	1983
Onion	7 1/2 lb	N.W. Hope	Tempe, AZ	1984
Peanut	4 in	E. Adkins	Enfield, NC	1990
Pepper	13.1/2 in	J. Rutherford	Hatch, NM	1975
Pepper Plant	8 ft 1 in	R. Allen	Gillespie, IL	1987

Sunflower [4]
25 ft 5 1/2 in
M. Heijms,
Oirschot,
Netherlands,
1986

Parsnip
14 ft 3 3/4 in
B. Lavery,
Llanharry,
Great
Britain,
1990

Celery
46 lb 1 oz
B. Lavery, Llanharry,
Great Britain, 1990

Turnip
48 lb 12 oz
A. Foster, Alnwick, Great
Britain, 1980

Marrow
108 lb 2 oz
B. Lavery, Llanharry,
Great Britain, 1990,

Radish
28 lb 1 oz
B. Lavery, Llanharry, Great
Britain, 1990

Vegetables, Fruits & Flowers World Records, Continued...

In the interests of fairness and to minimize the risk of mistakes, all plants should, where possible, be entered in official international, national or local garden contests. Only produce grown primarily for human consumption will be considered for publication. The assistance of Garden News and the World Pumpkin Confederation is gratefully acknowledged.

Grapefruit
6 lb 8 ½ oz
J. and A. Sosnow,
Tucson, Arizona, 1984

Rhubarb
5 lb 14 oz
E. Stone,
East Woodyates,
Great Britain, 1985

Potato [3]
7 lb 1 oz
J. East, Spalding, Great Britain, 1963
J. Busby, Atherstone, Great Britain, 1982

Strawberry
8.17 oz
G. Anderson, Folkestone,
Great Britain, 1983

Watermelon [6]
262 lb
B. Carson, Arrington,
Tennessee, 1990

Pumpkin
816 lb 8 oz
E. and R. Gancarz,
Wrightstown, New Jersey
1990

US NATIONAL RECORDS, *continued*

Rutabaga	39 lb	R.&J. Towns	Gresgham, OR	1979
Sweet Potato	40 ¾ lb	O. Harrison	Kite, GA	1982
Tomato				
(Cherry) Plant	28 ft 7 in	C.H. Wilber	Crane Hill, AL	1985
Zucchini	19.92 lb	W.C. Nicholas	Hartley, WI	1984

[1] A Vietnamese variety 6 ft long was reported by L. Szabo of Debrecen, Hungary in September 1976. [2] Pineapples weighing up to 28 lb 11 oz were reported from Tarauca, Brazil in 1978. [3] One weighing 18 lb 4 oz was reported dug up by T. Siddal in his garden in Chester, Great Britain in 1978. [4] A sunflower with a head measuring 32 ¼ in in diameter was grown by E. Martin of Maple Ridge, British Columbia, Canada in September 1983. [5] It was reported at the Tsukuba Science Expo Center, Japan on 28 Feb 1988 that a single plant produced 16,897 tomatoes. [6] B. Rogerson of Robersonville, NC grew a watermelon that weighed 279 lb on 3 Oct 1988, but this was not measured under competition conditions. [7] A gourd weighing 196 lb was grown in Herringfleet, Great Britain, by J. Leather in 1846. [8] This record was tied in 1986 by B. and E. Crosby of Brooksville, FL.

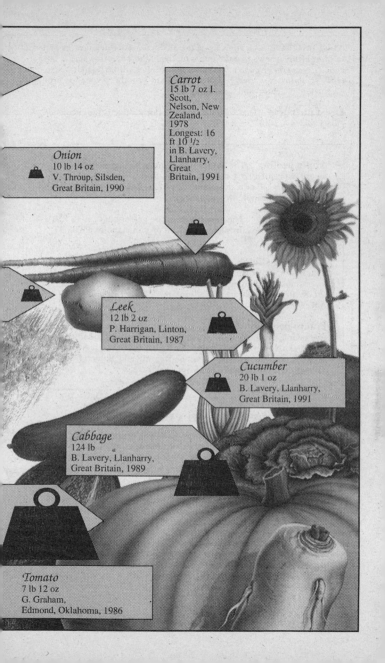

Carrot
15 lb 7 oz I.
Scott,
Nelson, New
Zealand,
1978
Longest: 16
ft 10 ½
in B. Lavery,
Llanharry,
Great
Britain, 1991

Onion
10 lb 14 oz
V. Throup, Silsden,
Great Britain, 1990

Leek
12 lb 2 oz
P. Harrigan, Linton,
Great Britain, 1987

Cucumber
20 lb 1 oz
B. Lavery, Llanharry,
Great Britain, 1991

Cabbage
124 lb
B. Lavery, Llanharry,
Great Britain, 1989

Tomato
7 lb 12 oz
G. Graham,
Edmond, Oklahoma, 1986

FRUITS AND VEGETABLES

Most nutritive An analysis of the 38 commonly eaten raw (as opposed to dried) fruits shows that the one with the highest caloric value is the avocado (*Persea americana*), with 741 calories per edible pound; it also contains vitamins A, C and E and 2.2 percent protein. Avocados probably originated in Central and South America.

Least nutritive That with the lowest caloric value is the cucumber (*Cucumis sativus*), with 73 cal./lb.

Apple peeling The longest single unbroken apple peel on record is one of 172 ft. 4 in., peeled by Kathy Wafler of Wolcott, NY in 11 hrs. 30 min. at Long Ridge Mall, Rochester, NY on 16 Oct. 1976. The apple weighed 20 oz.

Apple picking The greatest recorded performance is 15,830 lbs. picked in 8 hrs. by George Adrian of Indianapolis, IN on 23 Sep. 1980.

Cucumber slicing Norman Johnson of Blackpool College, Lancashire, Great Britain set a record of 13.4 sec. for slicing a 12-in. cucumber, 1½ in. in diameter, at 22 slices to the inch (total 264 slices) at West Deutscher Rundfunk in Cologne, Germany on 3 Apr. 1983.

Potato peeling The greatest quantity of potatoes peeled by five people to an institutional cookery standard with standard kitchen knives in 45 min. is 830 lbs. 11 oz. (net) by Lia Sombroek, Marlene Guiamo, Ria Grol, Yvonne Renting and Nguyet Nguyen at Emmeloord, Netherlands on 15 Sep. 1990.

VINES AND VINEYARDS

Largest vine This was planted in 1842 at Carpinteria, CA. By 1900 it was yielding more than 9.9 tons of grapes in some years, and averaged 7.7 tons per year until it died in 1920. A single bunch of grapes (Red Thompson seedless) of 20 lbs. 11½ oz. was weighed in Santiago, Chile in May 1984.

Largest vineyard The world's largest vineyard extends over the Mediterranean slopes between the Pyrenees and the Rhône in the *départements* Gard, Hérault, Aude and Pyrénées-Orientales. It covers an area of 2,075,685 acres, 52.3 percent of which is *monoculture viticole*.

United States The largest continuous vineyard in the United States is Minor Thornton Ranch in Fresno, CA. Owned by the Golden State Vintners Corp., the vineyard covers 5,200 acres and produces 6,500 tons of grapes each year.

Most northerly vineyard   There is a vineyard at Sabile, Latvia just north of Lat. 57° N.

Most southerly vineyard   The most southerly commercial vineyards are to be found in central Otago, South Island, New Zealand, south of Lat. 45° S.

LEAVES

Largest   The largest leaves of any plant belong to the raffia palm (*Raphia farinifera = R. raffia*) of the Mascarene Islands in the Indian Ocean, and the Amazonian bamboo palm (*R. taedigera*) of South America, whose leaf blades may measure up to 65 ft. in length with petioles up to 13 ft.

Undivided   The largest undivided leaf is that of *Alocasia macrorrhiza*, found in Sabah, Malaysia. A specimen found in 1966 was 9 ft. 11 in. long and 6 ft. 3½ in wide, with a surface area of 34.12 ft.^{2}. A specimen of the water lily *Victoria amazonica* (Longwood hybrid) on the grounds of the Stratford-upon-Avon Butterfly Farm, Warwickshire, Great Britain measured 8 ft. in diameter on 2 Oct. 1989.

United States   The largest leaves to be found in outdoor plants in America are those of the climbing fern (*Lygodium japonicum*) of the Gulf coast, with leaves of 23 ft.

SEEDS

Largest   The largest seed in the world is that of the double coconut or coco de mer (*Lodoicea maldivica = L. callipyge, L. seychellarum*), the single-seeded fruit of which may weigh 44 lbs. This grows only in the Seychelles in the Indian Ocean.

Smallest   The smallest are those of epiphytic (nonparasitic plants growing on others) orchids, at 35 million/oz. (compare with grass pollens at up to 6 billion grains/oz.).

Most viable   The most conclusive claim for the viability of seeds is that made for the Arctic lupine (*Lupinus arcticus*) found in frozen silt at Miller Creek in the Yukon, Canada in July 1954 by Harold Schmidt. The seeds were germinated in 1966 and were radiocarbon dated to at least 8000 B.C., and more probably to 13,000 B.C.

FERNS

Largest   The largest of the more than 6,000 species of fern is the tree fern (*Alsophila excelsa*) of Norfolk Island in the South Pacific, which attains a height of 60–80 ft.

United States   The highest in America is the giant fern (*Acrostichum danaeaefolium*) of the Gulf coast, which measures up to 16.4 ft. However, the bracken fern (*Pteridium aquilinum*) is the largest fern plant. It grows to a height of 4.9 ft. above ground, but also grows giant clones or stem systems underground that can reach up to a quarter of a mile. This fern is found throughout the United States.

Smallest   The world's smallest ferns are *Hecistopteris pumila*, found in Central America, and *Azolla caroliniana*, which is native to the United States and has fronds as small as ½ in.

GRASSES AND MOSSES

Commonest   The world's commonest grass is Bermuda grass (*Cynodon dactylon*), which is native to tropical Africa and the Indo-Malaysian region, but which extends from Lat. 45°N to 45°S. It is possibly the most trouble-some weed of the grass family, affecting 40 crops in over 80 countries. The Callie hybrid, selected in 1966, grows as much as 6 in. a day and stolons reach 18 ft. in length.

Mosses   The tallest variety of moss is the Australian species *Dawsonia Superba*, which can reach a height of 12 in. The longest is the mainly aquatic species *Fontinalis*, especially *F. antipyretica*, which forms streamers well over 3 ft. long in flowing water.

The smallest variety of moss is the microscopic pygmy moss (*Ephemerum*) and the longest is the brook moss (*Fontinalis*), which forms streamers up to 3 ft. long in flowing water. Its leaves are notable, however, for their large cells, which can measure up to 120 μm long and 25 μm wide.

Tallest grass   A thorny bamboo culm (*Bambusa arundinacea*) felled at Pattazhi, Travancore, India in November 1904 was 121½ ft. tall.

Fastest-growing grass   Some species of bamboo have a growth rate of 3 ft. per day. (See also Plant Kingdom, General records.)

WEEDS

Largest   The largest weed is the giant hogweed (*Heracleum mantegaz-zianum*), originally from the Caucasus. It reaches 12 ft. tall and has leaves 3 ft. long.

Most damaging   The virulence of weeds tends to be measured by the number of crops they affect and the number of countries in which they occur. On this basis, the worst would appear to be the purple nutsedge, nutgrass or nutsedge (*Cyperus rotundus*), a land weed which is native to India but which attacks 52 crops in 92 countries.

United States   The most damaging and widespread weed in America is the purple nut sedge (*Cyperus rotundus*), primarily found in the southern states.

WORST AQUATIC WEED. The rapid growth of aquatic plants in man-made lakes is exemplified by the free-floating fern *Salvinia auriculata,* which choked about 10 percent (200 miles²) of Lake Kariba in just 13 months. (Photo: Bruce Coleman Collection)

Its seeds can germinate at 95°F. and will withstand temperatures of –68°F. for two hours and remain viable. The purple nutsedge will grow to 39 in. in height and speeds underground through its system of rhyzomes and tubers. It remains dormant underground in extreme weather conditions.

Tallest weeds The tallest weed in the United States is the Melaleuca tree (*Melaleuca quinquenervia*), introduced to the Florida and Gulf coasts from Australia in 1900. Growing to an average of 39 ft., the weed has infested 3.7 million of the 4.7 million acres of Florida wetlands. Very dense and resistant to fire, the crowns are destroyed but the stem survives. It is a fire hazard in that it contains "essential" petroleums that spread fire quickly.

Most spreading The greatest area covered by a single clonal growth is that of the wild box huckleberry (*Gaylussacia brachycera*), a mat-forming evergreen shrub first reported in 1796. A colony covering about 100 acres was found on 18 July 1920 near the Juniata River, PA. It has been estimated that this colony began 13,000 years ago.

Aquatic weeds The worst aquatic weeds of the tropics and subtropics is the water hyacinth (*Eichhornia crassipes*), which is a native of the Amazon basin but extends from Lat. 40° N to 45 ° S. The intransigence of aquatic plants in man-made lakes is illustrated by the mat-forming water weed *Salvinia auriculata*, found in Africa. It was detected when Lake Kariba, which straddles the border of Zimbabwe and Zambia, was filled in May 1959, and within 11 months had choked an area of 77 miles², rising to 387 miles² in 1963.

SEAWEED

Longest The longest species of seaweed is the Pacific giant kelp (*Macrocystis pyrifera*), which, although it does not exceed 215 ft. in length, can grow 18 in. in a day.

TREES AND WOOD

Earliest The earliest species of tree still surviving is the Maiden-hair tree (*Ginkgo biloba*), of Zhexiang, China, which first appeared about 160 million years ago, during the Jurassic era. It has been grown since *c*. 1100 in Japan, where it was known as *ginkyō* ("silver apricot") and is now known as *icho*.

United States The oldest species is the bristlecone pine, which grows in the desert regions of southern California and Nevada. The exact date of the oldest tree is not known; however, some living species are believed to be at least 4,000 years old.

Oldest Dendrochronologists estimate the *potential* life span of a bristle-cone pine at nearly 5,500 years, and that of a giant sequoia (*Sequoiadendron giganteum*) at perhaps 6,000 years. No single cell lives more than 30 years. The oldest recorded tree was a bristlecone pine (*Pinus longaeva*) designated WPN-114, which grew at 10,750 ft. above sea level on the northeast face of Mt. Wheeler, NV. It was found to be 5,100 years old.

Living The oldest known *living* tree is the bristlecone pine named Methuse-lah, growing at 10,000 ft. on the California side of the White Mountains, con-firmed as 4,700 years old. In March 1974 it was reported that this tree had produced 48 live seedlings.

Most massive The most massive tree on earth is the biggest-known giant sequoia (*Sequoiadendron giganteum*), a tree named the General Sherman, standing 274.9 ft. tall, in the Sequoia National Park, CA. In 1991 it had a girth of 83 ft. 2 in., measured 4.5 ft. above the ground. The General Sherman has been estimated to contain the equivalent of 600,120 board feet of timber,

---

Christmas tree The world's tallest cut Christmas tree was a 221 ft. Douglas fir (*Pseudotsuga menziesii*) erected at Northgate Shopping Center, Seattle, WA in December 1950.

Tree topping Guy German climbed a 100-ft. spar and sawed off the top in a record time of 53.35 sec. at Albany, OR on 3 July 1989.

Tree climbing The fastest time up a 100-ft. fir spar pole and back down to the ground is 24.82 sec., by Guy German of Sitka, AK on 3 July 1988 at the World Championship Timber Carnival in Albany, OR.
    The fastest time up a 29.5-ft. coconut tree barefoot is 4.88 sec., by Fuatai Solo, 17, in Sukuna Park, Fiji on 22 Aug. 1980.

Tree sitting The duration record for staying in a tree is more than 21 years, by Bungkas, who went up a palm tree in the Indonesian village of Bengkes in 1970 and has been there ever since. He lives in a nest which he made from branches and leaves. Repeated efforts have been made to persuade him to come down, but without success.

---

sufficient to make 5 billion matches. The foliage is blue-green, and the red-brown bark may be up to 24 in. thick in parts. Estimates place its weight, including its root system, at 2,756 tons, but the timber is light (18 lbs./ft.³).

The seed of a "big tree" weighs only ¹/₆,₀₀₀ of an oz. Its growth at maturity may therefore represent an increase in weight of 13×10^{11}.

Greatest spread　The tree canopy covering the greatest area is that of the great banyan (*Ficus benghalensis*) in the Indian Botanical Garden, Calcutta, with 1,775 prop or supporting roots and a circumference of 1,350 ft. It covers some 3 acres and dates from before 1787. However, it is reported that a 550-year-old banyan tree known as "Thimmamma Marrimanu" in Gutibayalu village near Kadiri Taluk, Andrha Pradesh, India spreads over 5.2 acres.

Greatest girth　A circumference of 190 ft. was recorded for the pollarded (trimmed to encourage a more bushy growth) European chestnut (*Castanea sativa*) known as the "Tree of the Hundred Horses" (*Castagno di Cento Cavalli*) on Mt. Etna, Sicily, Italy in 1770 and 1780. It is now in three parts, widely separated.

"El Arbol del Tule" in the state of Oaxaca, Mexico is a 135-ft.-tall Montezuma cypress (*Taxodium mucronatum*) with a girth in 1982 of 117.6 ft., measured 5 ft. above the ground. Generally speaking, however, the largest girths are attributed to African baobob trees (*Adansonia digitata*), trunks of which have measured 180 ft. in circumference.

United States　The Giant Sequoia in the Sequoia National Park, CA has a girth of 83 ft. 2 in. (See Most massive).

Tallest　A *Eucalyptus regnans* at Mt. Baw Baw, Victoria, Australia is believed to have measured 470 ft. in 1885. According to the researches of Dr. A.C. Carder, the tallest tree ever measured was an Australian eucalyptus (*Eucalyptus regnans*) at Watts River, Victoria, Australia, reported in 1872 by forester William Ferguson. It was 435 ft. tall and almost certainly measured over 500 ft. originally.

Living　The tallest tree currently standing is the "National Geographic Society" coast redwood (*Sequoia sempervirens*) in Humboldt Redwoods State Park, CA. Its revised height, following earlier miscalculations, was 365 ft. in October 1991, according to Ron Hildebrant of California.

The tallest nonconiferous flowering tree is an Australian mountain ash, or giant gum (*Eucalyptus regnans*), which grows to over 315 ft. The tallest is currently one of 312 ft. in the Styx Valley, Tasmania, Australia.

Fastest-growing　Discounting bamboo, which is not botanically classified as a tree but as a woody grass, the fastest rate of growth recorded is 35 ft. 3 in. in 13 months by an *Albizzia falcata* planted on 17 June 1974 in Sabah, Malaysia.

Slowest-growing　Excluding *bonsai*, the 14th century Oriental art of cultivating miniature trees, the extreme in slow growth is represented by the *Dioon edule* (Cycadaceae), measured in Mexico between 1981 and 1986 by Dr. Charles M. Peters, who found the average annual growth rate to be 0.03 in.; a specimen 120 years old measured 3.9 in. in height.

GIANT TREES OF THE UNITED STATES

The National Register of Big Trees, a program of the American Forestry Association (AFA), sponsored by The Davey Tree Expert Company, officially recognizes the largest "champion" tree of each species in the United States. Trees are measured in three sections: circumference (of the tree in inches at 4½ ft. from the ground); total vertical height; average diameter of the crown to the nearest foot (calculated by measuring the widest spread and the narrowest, adding them together and dividing by two). To calculate the champion tree the AFA uses a point system based on the following calculation: circumference + height + ¼ of the crown spread.

TREE	CIRC. (inches)	HEIGHT (feet)	SPREAD (feet)	POINTS (AFA)	LOCATION
Ash (White)	304	95	82	420	Palisades, NY
(Fraxinus americana)					
Beech (American)	222	130	75	371	Ashtabula County, OH
(Fagus grandifolia)					
Birch (Yellow)	252	76	91	351	Deer Isle, ME
(Betula alleghaniensis)					
Cedar (Port-Orford)	451	219	39	680	Siskiyou National Forest, OR
(Chamaecyparis lawsoniana)					
Cherry (Black)	181	138	128	351	Washtenaw County, MI
(Prunus serotina)					
Chestnut (American)	202	110	108	339	Grand Traverse, MI
(Castanea dentata)					
Cypress (Monterey)	341	93	83	455	Mendocino, CA
(Cupressus macrocarpa)					
Dogwood (Pacific)	169	60	58	244	Clatskanie, OR
(Cornus nuttalli)					
Douglas-Fir (Coast)	438	329	60	782	Coos County, OR
(Pseudotsuga menziesii)					
Elm (American)	312	100	95	435	Louisville, KS
(Ulmus americana)					
Fir (Noble)	300	272	49	584	Mt. St. Helens National Monument, WA
(Abies procera)					
Hemlock (Western)*	316	202	47	530	Olympic National Park, WA
(Tsuga heterophylla)					
Hemlock (Western)*	291	227	49	530	Olympic National Park, WA
(Tsuga heterophylla)					

Tree					Location
Hickory (Pignut)	157	190	78	367	Robbinsville, NC
(Carya glabra)					
Juniper (Western)	480	86	58	581	Stanislaus National Forest, CA
(Juniperus occidentalis)					
Magnolia (Cucumbertree)	293	75	83	389	Waukon, IA
(Magnolia acuminata)					
Maple (Norway)	235	137	116	401	New Paltz, NY
(Acer platanoides)					
Maple (Red)	222	179	120	431	St. Clair County, MI
(Acer rubrum)					
Maple (Sugar)	269	91	80	380	Norwich, CT
(Acer saccharum)					
Oak (White)	374	79	102	479	Wye Mills State Park, MD
(Quercus alba)					
Oak (Swamp Chestnut)	197	200	148	434	Fayette County, AL
(Quercus michauxii)					
Pecan	231	143	115	403	Cocke County, TN
(Carya illinoensis)					
Pine (Sugar)	348	270	68	635	Yosemite National Park, CA
(Pinus lambertiana)					
Redcedar (Western)	732	178	54	924	Forks, WA
(Juniperus virginiana)					
Redwood (Coast)	638	363	62	1,017	Humboldt Redwoods State Park, CA
(Sequoia sempervirens)					
Sequoia (Giant)	998	275	107	1,300	Sequoia National Park, CA
(Sequoiadendron giganteum)					
Spruce (Sitka)	707	191	96	922	Seaside, OR
(Picea sitchensis)					
Spruce (Blue)	186	122	36	317	Ashley National Forest, UT
(Picea pungens)					
Sycamore	582	129	105	737	Jeromesville, OH
(Platanus occidentalis)					
Walnut (Black)	278	130	140	443	Sauvie Island, OR
(Juglans nigra)					
Willow (Black)	379	114	136	527	Grand Traverse County, MI
(Salix nigra)					

*Two trees listed as largest

Source: National Register of Big Trees

Most leaves Little work has been done on the laborious task of establishing which species has the most leaves. A large oak has perhaps 250,000 but a cypress may have some 45–50 million leaf scales.

Remotest The tree believed to be the remotest from any other is a sole Norwegian spruce on Campbell Island, Antarctica. Its nearest companion would be over 120 nautical miles away on the Auckland Islands.

Largest forest The largest forested areas in the world are the vast coniferous forests of northern Russia, lying between Lat. 55°N and the Arctic Circle. The total wooded area amounts to 2.7 billion acres (25 percent of the world's forests), of which 38 percent is Siberian larch. The former USSR is 34 percent forested. In comparison, the largest area of forest in the tropics remains the Amazon basin, amounting to some 815 million acres.

United States The largest forest in the United States is the Tongass National Forest (16.7 million acres), in Alaska. The United States is 32.25 percent forested.

Longest avenue The world's longest avenue of trees is the Nikko Cryptomeria Avenue, comprising three parts converging on Imaichi City in the Tochigi Prefecture of Japan and measuring a total of 22 miles. It was planted in the period 1628–48, and over 13,500 of its original 200,000 Japanese cedar (*Cryptomeria japonica*) trees survive, at an average height of 88.6 ft.

Wood cutting The first recorded lumberjack sports competition was held in 1572 in the Basque region of Spain. Records set at the Lumberjack World Championships at Hayward, WI (founded 1960):

Power saw (three slices of a 20-in. diameter white pine with a single-engine saw from a dead start)—8.71 sec. by Ron Johnson (USA) in 1986.

One-man bucking (one slice from a 20-in. diameter white-pine log with a crosscut saw)—18.96 sec. by Rolin Eslinger (USA) in 1987.

Two-man bucking (one slice from a 20-in. diameter white-pine log with a crosscut saw)—7.27 sec. by Jim Colbert and Mike Sullivan (both USA) in 1988.

Standing block chop (chopping through a vertical 14 in. diameter white-pine log 30 in. in length)—22.05 sec. by Melvin Lentz (USA) in 1988.

Underhand block chop (chopping through a horizontal 14 in. diameter white-pine log [length 30 in.])—17.84 sec. by Laurence O Toole (Australia) in 1985.

Springboard chopping (scaling a 9 ft. spar pole on springboards and chopping a 14 in. white pine log)—1 min. 18.45 sec. by Bill Youd (Australia) in 1985.

KINGDOM PROTISTA

Protista were discovered in 1676 by microscopist Antonie van Leeuwenhoek of Delft, Netherlands (1632–1723). Protista are one-celled or acellular organisms with characteristics common to both plants and animals. The more plant-like are termed Protophyta (protophytes), including unicellular algae, and the more animal-like are placed in the phylum Protozoa (protozoans), including amoeba and flagellates.

Largest The largest protozoans in terms of volume that are known to have existed were calcareous foraminifera (Foraminiferida) belonging to the genus *Nummulites*, a species of which, in the Middle Eocene rocks of Turkey, attained 8½ in. in diameter.

The largest existing protozoan, a species of the fan-shaped *Stannophyllum* (Xenophyophorida), can exceed this in length (9¾ in. has been recorded) but not in volume.

Smallest protophytes The marine microflagellate alga *Micromonas pusilla* has a diameter of less than 2 microns or micrometers (0.00008 in.).

Fastest The protozoan *Monas stigmatica* has been found to move a distance equivalent to 40 times its own length in a second. No human can cover even seven times his own length in a second.

Fastest reproduction The protozoan *Glaucoma*, which reproduces by binary fission, divides as frequently as every three hours. Thus in the course of a day it could become a great-great-great-great-great-great-grandparent and the progenitor of 510 descendants!

KINGDOM FUNGI

Fungi were once classified in the sub-kingdom Protophyta of the kingdom Protista.

Largest The discovery of a clonal growth of the parasitic fungus *Armillaria bulbosa* covering an area of 37 acres and weighing over 100 tons, and therefore representing possibly the world's largest living organism, was reported on 2 Apr. 1992. (See Animal Kingdom, General records.)

The largest record tree fungus is the bracket fungus *Rigidoporus ulmarius* growing from dead elm wood on the grounds of the International Mycological Institute at Kew, Great Britain. It measured $59 \times 56^{7}/_{10}$ in. with a circumference of 178¾ in. in January 1992 and is growing at a ráte of 9 in. per year.

Most poisonous The yellowish-olive death cap (*Amanita phalloides*), which can be found in England, is regarded as the world's most poisonous fungus and is responsible for 90 percent of all fatal cases of poisoning caused by fungi. The total toxin content is 7–9 mg. dry weight. The estimated lethal amount of amatoxins for humans, depending on body weight, is only 5–7 mg.—equivalent to less than 1¾ oz. of a fresh fungus. From 6–15 hours after eating, the victim experiences vomiting, delirium, collapse and death. Among its victims was Cardinal Giulio di' Medici, Pope Clement VII (b. 1478) on 25 Sep. 1534.

Aeroflora   The highest total fungal spore count was 5,686,861/ft.³ near Cardiff, Great Britain on 21 July 1971. The lowest counts of airborne allergens are zero.

KINGDOM PROCARYOTA

The earliest life-form reported from Great Britain is *Kakabekia barghoorniana*, a microorganism similar in form to an orange slice, found near Harlech, Great Britain in 1964 and dated in July 1986 to 4 billion years ago.

BACTERIA

Antonie van Leeuwenhoek (1632–1723) was the first to observe bacteria, in 1675.

Oldest   Viable bacteria were reported in 1991 to have been recovered from sediments 3–4 million years old from the Sea of Japan.

Living   In 1991 it was reported that live bacteria were found in the flesh of a mastodon (an ancestor of the elephant) from Ohio, which died 12,000 years earlier and which, on the evidence of spear marks found in the ribs, represented the first proof of humans killing a prehistoric animal.

Largest   The largest of the bacteria is the sulfur bacterium *Beggiatoa mirabilis*, which is 16–45 micrometers in width and may form filaments several millimeters long.

Smallest free-living entity   The smallest of all free-living organisms are the pleuro-pneumonia-like organisms (PPLO) of the *Mycoplasma*. One of these, *Mycoplasma laidlawii*, first discovered in sewage in 1936, has a diameter during its early existence of only 10^{-7} m. Examples of the strain known as H.39 have a maximum diameter of 3×10^{-7} m and weigh an estimated 10^{-16} g. A 209.4-ton blue whale weighs 1.9×10^{24} times as much.

Highest   In April 1967 the National Aeronautics and Space Administration (NASA) reported that bacteria had been discovered at an altitude of 25½ miles.

Fastest   The rod-shaped bacillus *Bdellovibrio bacteriovorus*, by means of a polar flagellum rotating 100 times/sec., can move 50 times its own length of 2 micrometers per sec. This would be the equivalent of a human sprinter reaching 200 mph or a swimmer crossing the English Channel between England and France in 6 min.

Toughest The bacterium *Micrococcus radiodurans* can withstand atomic radiation of 6.5 million roentgens or 10,000 times the dose that would be fatal to the average person. In March 1983 John Barras (University of Oregon) reported bacteria from sulfurous seabed vents thriving at 583°F. in the East Pacific Rise at Lat. 21°N.

VIRUSES

Dmitriy Ivanovsky (1864–1920) first reported filterable objects in 1892, but Martinus Willem Beijerink (1851–1931) first confirmed the nature of viruses in 1898. These are now defined as aggregates of two or more types of chemical (including either DNA or RNA) that are infectious and potentially pathogenic.

Largest The longest-known virus is the rod-shaped *Citrus tristeza* virus with particles measuring 2×10^{-5} m.

Smallest The smallest known viruses are the nucleoprotein plant viruses, such as the satellite of tobacco *Necrosis virus* with spherical particles 17 nm in diameter.

VIROIDS

Viroids were discovered by Theodor O. Diener (USA) in Feb. 1972. They are infectious agents of plants, are smaller than viruses, and consist only of nucleic acid (RNA) cores.

A putative new infectious submicroscopic organism without nucleic acid, named a "prion," was announced from the University of California in February 1982.

First chemical description of a virus The first chemical description of a living entity was published in Dec. 1991 by A. Molla, A.V. Paul and Eckard Wimmer of the State University of New York. The formula for the organic matter of poliovirus is $C_{32,652} H_{92,388} N_9 8,245 O_1 31,196 P_7,501 S_2,340$ and it is believed to be the largest empirical formula ever reported.

PARKS, ZOOS, OCEANARIA, AQUARIA

PARKS

Largest   The Wood Buffalo National Park in Alberta, Canada (established 1922) has an area of 17,375 miles^2.

United States   The largest public park in the United States is Wrangell-St. Elias National Park and Preserve in Alaska. Of the 13.2 million acres, the National Park section is 8.33 million acres and the Preserve comprises 4.88 million acres.

Largest game reserve   The world's largest zoological reserve is the Etosha National Park, Namibia. Established in 1907, its area has grown to 38,427 miles^2.

ZOOS

It has been estimated that throughout the world there are some 757 zoos with an estimated annual attendance of 350 million.

Oldest   The earliest-known collection of animals was the one set up by Shulgi, a third-dynasty ruler of Ur from 2097–2094 B.C., at Puzurish in southeast Iraq. The oldest-known zoo is the one at Schönbrunn, Vienna, Austria, built in 1752 by the Holy Roman Emperor Franz I for his wife Maria Theresa.
   The oldest existing public zoological collection in the world is that of the Zoological Society of London, Great Britain, founded in 1826. In January 1989 the collection comprised 11,108 specimens, housed in Regent's Park, London, Great Britain (36 acres) and at Whipsnade Park, Bedfordshire, Great Britain (541 acres; opened 23 May 1931). The record annual attendances are 3,031,571 in 1950 for Regent's Park and 756,758 in 1961 for Whipsnade.

United States   The Philadelphia Zoo received its charter from the state of Pennsylvania in 1859, but did not open to the public until 1874. Lincoln Park Zoo, a 60-acre public park owned by the city of Chicago, received a gift of two swans from Central Park, New York City in 1868. By 1870 a "small barn and paddocks" had been built to house additional animals that had been donated by the public. The current facility covers 35 acres.
   According to the American Association of Zoological Parks and Aquariums, the top zoo for attendance is Lincoln Park Zoo with 4 million visitors each year. The next largest total is the San Diego Zoo, CA, which hosts 3.2 million visitors per year. San Diego's top attendance was in 1987, with 3,808,600.

Without bars   The earliest zoo without bars was that at Stellingen, near Hamburg, Germany. It was founded in 1907 by Carl Hagenbeck (1844–1913), who made use of deep pits and large pens instead of cages to separate the exhibits from visitors.

LARGEST PARK. The Wood Buffalo National Park (in both photos above), in Alberta and Northwest Territories, Canada was originally established to protect the last remaining herds of bison in Canada. It covers 17,375 miles² and is also home to a variety of flora and fauna, including the endangered whooping crane (*Grus americana*), the tallest American bird at almost 5 ft. (Photos: Wood Buffalo National Park/J. Langille)

OCEANARIA

Earliest   The world's first oceanarium is Marineland of Florida, opened in 1938 at a site 18 miles south of St. Augustine, FL. Up to 5.8 million gals. of seawater are pumped daily through two major tanks, one rectangular (100 ft. long by 40 ft. wide by 18 ft. deep) containing 375,000 gals., and one circular (233 ft. in circumference and 12 ft. deep) containing 330,000 gals. The tanks are seascaped, including coral reefs and even a shipwreck.

AQUARIA

Largest   In terms of the volume of water held, the Living Seas Aquarium, opened in 1986 at the EPCOT Center, FL is the world's largest, with a total capacity of 6.25 million gals. It contains over 3,000 fish representing 90 species.

The Monterey Bay Aquarium in California has the most tanks, specimens and species. The aquarium was opened on 20 Oct. 1984 at a cost of $55 million. It now has 95 tanks with a capacity of 750,000 gallons on 2.2 acres of land. It contains over 6,500 specimens of 525 species of fauna and flora. The two largest tanks hold 335,000 and 326,000 gallons. The average annual attendance is 1.7 million visitors; however, in 1985 there were 2.3 million visitors, the highest for any aquarium in the United States.

HUMAN BEINGS

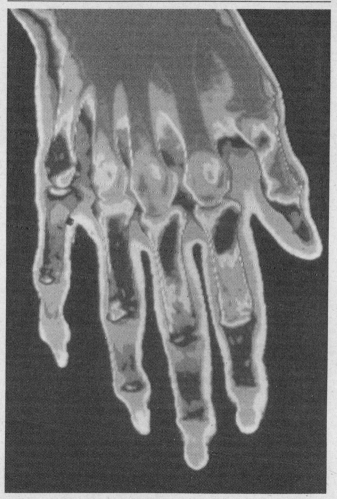

An arthritic hand as revealed by tomography.
(Photo: Zefa Picture Library Ltd.)

ORIGINS

EARLIEST HUMANS

SCALE OF TIME *If the age of the Earth–Moon system (latest estimate 4.45 billion years) is likened to a single year, hominids appeared on the scene at about 7:40 P.M. on 31 Dec., the Christian era began nearly 14 seconds before midnight, and the life span of a 120-year-old person would be about 84/100ths of a second. Present calculations indicate that the Sun's increased heat as it becomes a "red giant" will make life on Earth untenable in about 5.5 billion years. Meanwhile there may well be colder epicycles. The period of 1 billion years is sometimes referred to as an eon.*

Human beings (homo sapiens) *are a species in the subfamily Homininae of the family Hominidae of the superfamily Hominoidea of the suborder Simiae (or Anthropoidea) of the order Primates of the infraclass Eutheria of the subclass Theria of the class Mammalia of the subphylum Vertebrata (Craniata) of the phylum Chordata of the subkingdom Metazoa of the animal kingdom.*

Earliest primates Primates appeared in the Paleocene epoch about 65 million years ago. The earliest members of the suborder Anthropoidea are known from both Africa and South America in the early Oligocene, 30–34 million years ago, when the two infra-orders, Platyrrhini and Catarrhini, from the New and Old Worlds respectively, were already distinct. New finds from the Fayum, in Egypt, are being studied and may represent primates from the Eocene period, as old as 38 million years.

Earliest hominoid The earliest hominoid fossil is a jawbone with three molars, discovered in the Otavi Hills, Namibia on 4 June 1991 by Martin Pickford (b. 1943) of the *Muséum Nationale d'Histoire Naturelle*, Paris, France and provisionally dated at 10–15 million years, but later refined to 12–13 million years and named *Otavipithecus namibiensis*.

Earliest hominid The characteristics typical of the Hominidae include a large brain and bipedal locomotion (walking on two legs). The earliest hominid relic is an Australopithecine jawbone with two molars, each 2 in. long, found by Kiptalam Chepboi near Lake Baringo, Kenya in February 1984 and dated to 4 million years ago by associated fossils and to 5.4–5.6 million years ago through rock correlation by potassium-argon dating.

The most complete of the early hominid materials is the skeleton of "Lucy" (40 percent complete), found by Dr. Donald C. Johanson and T. Gray at Locality 162 near the Awash River, Hadar, in the Afar region of Ethiopia on 30 Nov. 1974. She was estimated to be *c.* 40 years old when she died 3 million years ago, and she was 3 ft. 6 in. tall.

Parallel tracks of hominid footprints extending over 80 ft. were first discovered at Laetoli, Tanzania in 1978, by Paul Abell and Dr. Mary Leakey, in volcanic ash dating to 3.6 million years ago. The height of the smallest of the seemingly three individuals was estimated to be 3 ft. 11 in.

Earliest of the genus Homo The earliest species of this genus is *Homo* *habilis,* or "Handy Man," from Olduvai Gorge, Tanzania, named by Louis Leakey, Philip Tobias and John Napier in 1964 after a suggestion from Prof. Raymond Arthur Dart (1893–1988).

The greatest age attributed to fossils of this genus is about 2.4 million years for a piece of cranium found in western Kenya in 1965. At the time it could not be positively identified, but scientists in the USA were able to confirm the identification in 1991. The date was provided by Alan Deino of the Geochronology Center of the Institute of Human Origins, Berkeley, CA, who analyzed volcanic material in a layer just above the fossil site.

The earliest stone tools are abraded core-choppers dating from *c.* 2.7 million years ago. They were found at Hadar, Ethiopia in November–December 1976 by Hélène Roche (France). Finger-held (as opposed to fist-held) quartz slicers found by Roche and Dr. John Wall (New Zealand) close to the Hadar site by the Gona River can also be dated to *c.* 2.7 million years ago.

Oldest human body The body of a late Stone Age man was found almost perfectly preserved in an Austrian glacier in September 1991. The man is thought to have died *c.* 3300 B.C.

Oldest mummy Mummification (from the Persian word *mūm,* wax) dates from 2600 B.C. or the 4th dynasty of the Egyptian pharaohs. The oldest-known mummy is that of a high-ranking young woman who was buried *c.* 2600 B.C. on a plateau near the Great Pyramid of Cheops at Giza, or Al-Gizeh, Egypt. Her remains, which appear to represent an early attempt at mummification, were discovered in a 6-ft.-deep excavation on 17 Mar. 1989, but only her skull was intact. She is believed to have lived in the lost kingdom of Ankh Ptah.

The oldest complete mummy is of Wati, a court musician of *c.* 2400 B.C. from the tomb of Nefer in Saqqâra, Egypt, found in 1944.

Earliest Homo erectus The oldest example of this species (upright man), the direct ancestor of *Homo sapiens,* was discovered by Kamoya Kimeu on the surface at the site of Nariokotome III to the west of Lake Turkana, Kenya in August 1985. The skeleton of this 5 ft. 5 in. 12-year-old boy is the most complete of this species yet found; only a few small pieces are missing. It is dated to 1.6 million years ago.

Earliest Homo sapiens Through the Pleistocene epoch (1.6 million to 10,000 years ago) the trend toward large brains continued. *Homo sapiens* ("wise man") appeared about 300,000 years ago as the successor to *Homo erectus.*

United States Over 500 artifacts 11,000 to 16,000 years old were found in Washington Co., PA in April 1973 after being brought to the attention of the University of Pittsburgh by Albert Miller, whose family owned the land. The dig, led by Dr. James Adovasio, started in June 1973 and lasted until June 1983. The artifacts consist mainly of unfluted lanceolate projectile points (either spearheads or darts), an assortment of bifacial and unifacial tools (knives and scrapers), polyhedral blade cores (long thin flakes from which blades are made), and blades struck from this core. These items are all made from chert, a flintlike rock.

The site dates to the Pre-Clovis Paleo-Indian culture and it is believed that the *Homo sapiens* Paleo-Indians were the initial inhabitants of the site. The tools, dated by the mass accelerator spectrometer (MAS) technique, which measures the carbon content present in the amino acids at the time of death, resembled tools found in Manchuria. This supports theories that North America was first inhabited by peoples coming across a natural land bridge between Siberia and Alaska that is now deep beneath the Bering Sea.

In 1968 a burial site containing bones of two individuals believed to be an infant and an adolescent were uncovered by construction workers in Wilsall, MT. This site, called the Anzick burial site, also contained 120 artifacts with a red ocher covering believed to be grave offerings. These were mainly flint and stone bifacial (flaked by percussion along both sides of the chopping edge) tools and the remains of spear shafts.

The bones were dated by the MAS technique to not less than 10,600 years ago. The remains are believed to be of members of the Paleo-Indian culture, with the artifacts in the style of the Clovis Age. When taking into account the cultural material found in the next six levels below, the average range widely accepted for the existence of humans at the site is from 13,955 to 14,555 years ago.

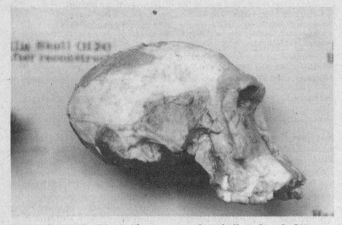

EARLIEST GENUS—HOMO. The most complete skull yet found of *Homo babilis* or "Handy Man." It was discovered at Olduvai Gorge, Tanzania in 1964, lying on the bentonitic clay of still-water lake deposits. (Photo: Ancient Art and Architecture Collection)

GOLIATH. David slaying the Philistine giant Goliath. In the left foreground of the picture is David's sling from which he hurled the stone that felled Goliath. (Photo: Ann Ronan Picture Library)

DIMENSIONS

GIANTS

Growth of the body is determined by growth hormone. This is produced by the pituitary gland, set deep in the brain. Overproduction in childhood produces abnormal growth, and true gigantism is the result. The true height of human giants is frequently obscured by exaggeration and commercial dishonesty. The only admissible evidence on the actual height of giants is that collected since 1870 under impartial medical supervision. Unfortunately, even medical authors are not always blameless and can include fanciful, as opposed to measured, heights.

TALLEST MEN

Earliest opinion is that the tallest man in medical history of whom there is irrefutable evidence was Robert Pershing Wadlow, born at 6:30 A.M. on 22 Feb. 1918 in Alton, IL. Weighing 8½ lbs. at birth, his abnormal growth started at the age of two following a double hernia operation. On his 13th birthday he stood 7 ft. 1¾ in. tall and by 17 he had reached 8 ft. ½ in.

On 27 June 1940 Dr. C.M. Charles, associate professor of anatomy at

Goliath of Gath   The Bible states that Goliath of Gath (*c.* 1060 B.C.) stood 6 cubits (approximately 9 ft.).

The Jewish historian Flavius Josephus (A.D. 37/38–*c.* 100) and some of the manuscripts of the Septuagint (the earliest Greek translation of the Old Testament) attribute to Goliath the wholly credible height of 4 Greek cubits (approximately 6 ft.).

Giants exhibited in circuses and exhibitions are routinely under contract not to be measured and are, almost traditionally, billed by their promoters at heights up to 18 in. in excess of their true heights.

Most variable stature   Adam Rainer (Austria; 1899–1950) measured 3 ft. 10.45 in. at the age of 21. He then suddenly started growing at a rapid rate, and by 1931 he had reached 7 ft. 1¾ in. He became so weak as a result that he was bedridden for the rest of his life. At the time of his death on 4 Mar. 1950, age 51, he measured 7 ft. 8 in. and was the only person in medical history to have been both a dwarf and a giant.

ROBERT WADLOW

Weighing 8½ lbs. at birth, Robert Wadlow started his abnormal growth at the age of two following a double hernia operation. His height progressed as follows:

AGE	HEIGHT ft.	in.	WEIGHT lbs.
5	5	4	105
8	6	0	169
9	6	2¼	180
10	6	5	210
11	6	7	–
12	6	10½	–
13	7	1¾	255
14	7	5	301
15	7	8	355
16	7	10¼	374
17[1]	8	0½	315
18	8	3½	–
19	8	5½	480
20	8	6¾	–
21	8	8¼	491
22[2]	8	11¹/₁₀	439

[1] *Following severe influenza and infection of the foot.*
[2] *Still growing during his terminal illness.*

Washington University's School of Medicine in St. Louis, MO, and Dr. Cyril MacBryde measured Robert Wadlow at 8 ft. 11.1 in. (arm span 9 ft. 5¾ in.) in St. Louis. Wadlow died 18 days later at 1:30 A.M. on 15 July 1940 weighing 439 lbs. in a hotel in Manistee, MI as a result of a septic blister on his right ankle caused by a poorly fitting brace. He was buried in Oakwood Cemetery, Alton, IL in a coffin measuring 10 ft. 9 in.

His greatest recorded weight was 491 lbs. on his 21st birthday. His shoes were size 37AA (18½ in.) and his hands measured 12¾ in. from the wrist to the tip of the middle finger (compare with the depth of this page at 10¾ in.).

TALLEST WOMEN

The tallest woman in medical history was the giantess Zeng Jinlian (b. 26 June 1964) of Yujiang village in the Bright Moon Commune, Hunan Province, central China, who measured 8 ft. 1¾ in. when she died on 13 Feb. 1982. This figure, however, represented her height with assumed normal spinal curvature, because she suffered from severe scoliosis (curvature of the spine) and could not stand up straight. She began to grow abnormally from the age of four months and stood 5 ft. 1½ in. before her fourth birthday and 7 ft. 1½ in. when she was 13. Her hands measured 10 in. and her feet 14 in. in length. Both her parents and her brother were of normal size.

The giantess Ella Ewing (1875–1913) of Gorin, MO was billed at 8 ft. 2 in., but this height was exaggerated. She measured 7 ft. 4½ in. at the age of 23, and may have attained 7 ft. 6 in. at the time of her death.

Living The world's tallest woman is Sandy Allen, born 18 June 1955 in Chicago, IL. A 6½ lb. baby, her abnormal growth began soon after birth. At 10 years of age she stood 6 ft. 3 in., and she measured 7 ft. 1 in. when she was 16. On 14 July 1977 this giantess underwent a pituitary gland operation, which inhibited further growth at 7 ft. 7¼ in. She now weighs 462 lbs. and takes a size 16 EEE shoe.

Married couple Anna Hanen Swan (1846–88) of Nova Scotia, Canada was said to be 8 ft. 1 in. but actually measured 7 ft. 5½ in. At the church of St. Martin-in-the-Fields, London, Great Britain on 17 June 1871 she married Martin van Buren Bates (1845–1919) of Whitesburg, KY, who stood 7 ft. 2½ in., making them the tallest married couple on record.

TALLEST TWINS

World The world's tallest identical twins are Michael and James Lanier (b. 27 Nov. 1969) from Troy, MI. They measured 7 ft. 1 in. at the age of 14 years and both now stand 7 ft. 4 in. Their sister Jennifer is 5 ft. 2 in. tall.

The world's tallest female identical twins are Heather and Heidi Burge (b. 11 Nov. 1971) from Palos Verdes, CA. They are both 6 ft. 4¾ in. tall.

Most dissimilar couple Nigel Wilks (b. 1963), 6 ft. 6 in. tall, of Kingston-upon-Hull, Great Britain, on 30 June 1984 married Beverley Russell (b. 1963), 4 ft. tall, who suffers from a skeletal disorder.

DWARFS

The strictures that apply to giants apply equally to dwarfs, except that exaggeration gives way to understatement. In the same way as 9 ft. may be regarded as the limit toward which the tallest giants tend, so 22 in. must be regarded as the limit toward which the shortest adult dwarfs or midgets tend (compare with the average length of newborn babies, which is 18–20 in.). In the case of child dwarfs, their *ages* are often exaggerated by their agents or managers.

There are many causes of short stature in humans. They include genetic abnormalities, lack of appropriate hormones, and malnutrition. Dwarfs of the past, whatever the cause of their condition, tended to be smaller because of lower nutritional standards.

Shortest person *Adult*   The shortest mature human of whom there is independent evidence is the still-living Gul Mohammad (b. 15 Feb. 1957) of Delhi, India. On 19 July 1990 he was examined at Ram Manohar Hospital, New Delhi, and found to measure 22½ in. in height and to weigh 37½ lbs. The other members of his immediate family are of normal height.

The shortest-ever female was Pauline Musters, a Dutch dwarf. She was born at Ossendrecht, Netherlands, on 26 Feb. 1876 and measured 11.8 in. at

SHORTEST PERSON.
Pauline Musters
("Princess Paulina";
1876–95), a Dutch
dwarf. On her death
a postmortem
examination showed
her height to be
exactly 24 in. (Photo:
Image Select)

birth. At nine years of age she was 21.65 in. tall and weighed only 3 lbs. 5 oz. She died on 1 Mar. 1895 in New York City at the age of 19. Although she was billed at 19 in., a postmortem examination showed her to be exactly 24 in. (there was some elongation after death). Her mature weight varied from 7½–9 lbs. and her measurements were 18½–19–17 in., which suggests she was overweight.

The shortest living female is Madge Bester (b. 26 Apr. 1963) of Johannesburg, South Africa, at 25½ in. She suffers from *Osteogenesis imperfecta* and is confined to a wheelchair. In this disease there is an inherited abnormality of collagen, which, with calcium salts, provides the rigid structure of bones. The disease is characterized by brittle bones and other deformities of the skeleton. Her mother, Winnie, is not much taller, measuring 27½ in., and she too is confined to a wheelchair.

Child In 1979 a height of 19.7 in. and a weight of 4 lbs. 6 oz. were reported for Stamatoula, a nine-year-old Greek girl (1969–85). When she died on 22 Aug. 1985 at the Lyrion Convent, Athens, Greece she measured 26.4 in. and weighed 11 lbs. The child, believed to be the survivor of twins, suffered from Seckel's syndrome, also known as "bird-headed dwarfism."

Most famous The most famous midget in history was Charles Sherwood Stratton, alias "General Tom Thumb," born on 4 Jan. 1838. When he joined up with Phineas T. Barnum, his birth date was changed to 4 Jan. 1832, so that when billed at 30½ in. at the age of 18 he was in fact 12.

Tom died of apoplexy on 15 July 1885 at his birthplace, Bridgewater, CT, age 47 (not 53) and was 3 ft. 4 in. (70 lbs.).

Twins The shortest twins ever recorded were the primordial dwarfs Matjus and Bela Matina (b. 1903–d. c.1935) of Budapest, Hungary, who later became American citizens. They both measured 30 in.

Living The world's shortest living twins are John and Greg Rice (b. 3 Dec. 1951) of West Palm Beach, FL, who both measure 34 in.

The shortest identical twin sisters are Dorene Williams of Oakdale and Darlene McGregor of Almeda, CA (b. 1949), who each stand 4 ft. 1 in.

Oldest There are only two centenarian dwarfs on record. The older was Hungarian-born Susanna Bokoyni ("Princess Susanna") of Newton, NJ, who died at the age of 105 years on 24 Aug. 1984. She was 3 ft. 4 in. tall and weighed 37 lbs.

The other was Miss Anne Clowes of Matlock, Derbyshire, Great Britain, who died on 5 Aug. 1784 at the age of 103 years. She was 3 ft. 9 in. tall and weighed 48 lbs.

TRIBES

Tallest The tallest major tribes in the world are the slender Tutsi (also known as the Watusi) of Rwanda and Burundi, Central Africa, and the Dinka of the Sudan. In the case of the Tutsi, average adult males and females among some groups stand 6 ft. 5 in. and 5 ft. 10 in. respectively.

Shortest The smallest pygmies are the Mbuti of the Ituri forest, Zaïre, Central Africa, with an average height of 4 ft. 6 in. for men and 4 ft. 5 in. for women.

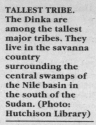

TALLEST TRIBE.
The Dinka are
among the tallest
major tribes. They
live in the savanna
country
surrounding the
central swamps of
the Nile basin in
the south of the
Sudan. (Photo:
Hutchison Library)

WEIGHT

Heaviest male   The heaviest human in medical history was Jon Brower
Minnoch (b. 29 Sep. 1941) of Bainbridge Island, WA, who had suffered from
obesity since childhood. The 6-ft.-1-in.-tall former taxi driver was 392 lbs.
in 1963, 700 lbs. in 1966, and 975 lbs. in September 1976.

In March 1978, Minnoch was rushed to University Hospital, Seattle, sat-
urated with fluid and suffering from heart and respiratory failure. It took a
dozen firemen and an improvised stretcher to move him from his home to a
ferryboat. When he arrived at the hospital he was put in two beds lashed together. It took 13 people just to roll him over. By extrapolating his intake
and elimination rates, consultant endocrinologist Dr. Robert Schwartz calculated that Minnoch must have weighed more than 1,387 lbs. when he was
admitted. A great deal of this was water accumulation due to his congestive
heart failure. After nearly 16 months on a 1,200-calorie-a-day diet, the chok-
ing fluid had gone, and he was discharged at 476 lbs. In October 1981 he had
to be readmitted, after having put on 197 lbs. When he died on 10 Sep. 1983
he weighed more than 798 lbs.

Heaviest living *Male*   The heaviest living man is T.J. Albert Jackson (b. 1941 Kent Nicholson), also known as "Fat Albert," of Canton, MS. He recently tipped the scales at 891 lbs. He has a 120-in. chest, a 116-in. waist, 70-in. thighs and a 29½-in. neck.

Heaviest female   The heaviest woman ever recorded was probably Rosie Carnemolla (b. 1944) of Poughkeepsie, NY, who registered a peak weight of 850 lbs. on 13 Mar. 1988. A week later she was put on a carefully controlled diet that reduced her weight by 250 lbs. in six months, and then she underwent an operation to reduce the size of her stomach. By September 1988 she was down to 350 lbs., during which time her waistline had declined from 98 in. to 46 in. and her dress size from 70 to 46. Her target weight is 150 lbs.

When Mrs. Percy Pearl Washington, who suffered from polydipsia (unrelenting thirst), died in a Milwaukee hospital on 9 Oct. 1972, the scales registered only up to 800 lbs., but she was credited with an unconfirmed weight of 880 lbs. She was 6 ft. tall and wore a size 62 dress.

Heaviest twins   Billy Leon (1946–79) and Benny Loyd (b. 7 Dec. 1946) McCrary, alias McGuire, of Hendersonville, NC were normal in size until the age of six when they both contracted German measles. In November 1978 they weighed 743 lbs. (Billy) and 723 lbs. (Benny) and had 84-in. waists. As professional tag-team wrestling performers they were billed at weights up to 770 lbs. Billy died at Niagara Falls, Ontario, Canada on 13 July 1979.

Weight gaining   The reported record for weight gain is held by Jon Brower Minnoch (see Heaviest male) at 196 lbs. in 7 days in October 1981 after readmittance to University Hospital, Seattle, WA. Arthur Knorr (USA; 1916–60), gained 294 lbs. in the last six months of his life.

Miss Doris James of San Francisco, CA is alleged to have gained 325 lbs. in the 12 months before her death in August 1965, age 38, at a weight of 675 lbs. She was only 5 ft. 2 in. tall.

Weight loss *Dieting*   The greatest recorded slimming feat by a male was that of Jon Brower Minnoch (see Heaviest male), who had reduced to 476 lbs. by July 1979, thus indicating a weight loss of at least 911 lbs. in 16 months.

The circus fat lady Mrs.. Celesta Geyer (b. 1901), alias Dolly Dimples, went from 552 lbs. to 152 lbs. in 1950–51, a loss of 400 lbs. in 14 months. Her "vital statistics" diminished from 79–84–84 in to a svelte 34–28–36 in. Her book *How I Lost 400 lbs.* was not a best-seller, perhaps because readers had difficulty in relating to the dressmaking and other problems of losing more than 400 lbs. when one is 4 ft. 11 in. tall. In December 1967 she was reportedly down to 110 lbs.

Operation   On 14 Mar. 1982 surgeons at a hospital in New York City removed 140 lbs. of adipose tissue from the abdominal wall of a 798-lb. man. They had to use a hoist to lift the layers of fat as they were removed.

Sweating   Ron Allen (b. 1947) sweated off 21½ lbs. of his weight of 239 lbs. in Nashville, TN in 24 hours in August 1984.

Greatest differential   The greatest weight difference recorded for a married couple is *c.* 1,300 lbs. in the case of Jon Brower Minnoch (See Heaviest male) and his 110-lb. wife Jeannette in March 1978.

Lightest   The thinnest recorded adults of normal height are those suffering from anorexia nervosa. Losses of up to 65 percent of original body weight have been recorded in females, with a low of 45 lbs. in the case of Emma Shaller (1868–90) of St. Louis, MO, who stood 5 ft. 2 in.

The lightest adult was Lucia Zarate (San Carlos, Mexico, 1863–89), an emaciated Mexican dwarf of 26½ in., who weighed 4.7 lbs. at the age of 17. She "fattened up" to 13 lbs. by her 20th birthday. At birth she had weighed 2½ lbs.

Edward C. Hagner (1892–1962), alias Eddie Masher (USA), is alleged to have weighed only 48 lbs. at a height of 5 ft. 7 in.

In August 1825 an unsubstantiated claim was made for Claude-Ambroise Seurat (1797–1826) of Troyes, France giving his biceps measurement as 4 in. and the distance between his back and his chest as less than 3 in. According to one report he stood 5 ft. 7½ in. and weighed 78 lbs., but in another account he was described as being 5 ft. 4 in. and only 36 lbs.

REPRODUCTIVITY

MOTHERHOOD

Most children   The greatest officially recorded number of children born to one mother is 69, by the wife of Feodor Vassilyev (b. 1707–*fl.* 1782), a peasant from Shuya, 150 miles east of Moscow, Russia. In 27 confinements she gave birth to 16 pairs of twins, seven sets of triplets and four sets of quadruplets. The case was reported to Moscow by the Monastery of Nikolskiy on 27 Feb. 1782. Only two of these who were born in the period *c.* 1725–65 failed to survive their infancy.

The world's most prolific mother is currently Leontina Albina (nee Espinosa; b. 1925) of San Antonio, Chile, who in 1981 produced her 55th and last child. Her husband Gerardo Secunda Albina (variously Alvina; b. 1921) states that they were married in Argentina in 1943 and had 5 sets of triplets (all boys) before coming to Chile. Only 40 (24 boys and 16 girls) survive. Eleven children died at birth or were lost in an earthquake.

It was reported on 31 Jan. 1989 that Mrs. Maria Olivera (b. 1939) of San Juan, Argentina had given birth to her 32nd child. All are believed to be still alive.

Oldest mother   Many apparently very late maternities may be cover-ups for illegitimate grandchildren. Post-menopausal women have been rendered fertile by recent hormonal techniques. Medical literature contains extreme but unauthenticated cases of septuagenarian mothers, such as Mrs. Ellen Ellis, age 72, of Four Crosses, Clwyd, Great Britain, who allegedly produced a stillborn 13th child on 15 May 1776 in her 46th year of marriage.

STUDENT'S NAME

John V. Kaiser

GIVE ORDER FORM AND
MONEY TO TEACHER BY

Total Items	Earn a FREE Book in December for every 4 you buy!	Total Cost
3		$7.85
47	Race for...IBM...3.5"-$19.95	
46	Race for...IBM...5.25"-$19.95	
45	Race for...Apple II 5.25"-$19.95	
44	Expert...IBM...3.5"-$14.95	
43	Expert...IBM...5.25"-$14.95	
42	Newbery Collection-$5.95	
41	Motel of the Mysteries-$3.95	
40	More Tales...Boxed Set-$5.95	
39	Jurassic Park-$3.95	1 $3.95
38	Hair Designs...-$5.95	
37	Garfield...3 Pack-$6.95	
36	File of Fun-$3.95	
35	Eyes of the Dragon-$3.95	
34	Dinotopia-$14.95	
33	Calligraphy Book...Pen-$5.95	
32	Webster's Dict. + Thes.-$2.50	
31	Wacky Mad Libs V-95¢	1 .95
30	Two Moons in August-$1.95	
29	Two-Minute Mysteries-$1.50	
28	True Story...Pigs-$2.50	
27	Tom and Jerry...-$2.50	
26	Somewhere in...Darkness-$2.50	
25	Solitary Blue-$2.50	
24	Silent Scream-$1.95	
23	Room Rules Poster-75¢	
22	Random House...Spanish-$1.95	
21	Random House...German-$1.95	
20	Random House...French-$1.95	
19	Pro Football...1993-$2.95	
18	Nothing But the Truth-$2.50	
17	Notebook...Atlas Pack-$2.50	
16	Monument-$2.95	
15	Molly By Any Other Name-$1.50	
14	Listening Silence-$1.95	
13	Last Action Hero-$2.95	
12	Guinness Book...1993-$2.95	1 2.95
11	Greek Gods-$1.95	
10	Free Fall...50	

1992 NEWBERY HONOR BOOK

...ay ...eroom. Sure, it bugs his teacher, but should he get suspended for it? Look at the evidence — diaries, letters, news reports — and you decide!

~~$3.99~~ $2.50

...oons ...just ...ooks

...onie's mother ...hing's been the ...en she meets ...who's got some big problems of his own. Can they work together to make the pain go away?

~~$3.25~~ $1.95

5. Cowboys of the Wild West

Russell Freedman

Just like the movies, but better! Go back in time to the Wild West and meet the *real* cowboys — on the open range, on the cattle trail, and back at the ranch. Find out what their lives were really like!

~~$5.95~~ $2.95

SAVE $3.00!

Cowboys of the Wild West
RUSSELL FREEDMAN

More than 50 real photos!

...PECIAL HARDCOVER BOOK

...inotopia

...s Gurney

...x 9¾"

...opia is a land ...from time. ...ing color pictures ...you a world ...e dinosaurs and ...le live together. ...Dinotopia's ...erfall City and Tree-Top ...wn...and wait till you see ...Dinosaur Races!

More than 50% off!

DINOTOPIA

~~$30.00~~ $14.95

The oldest recorded mother for whom the evidence satisfied medical verification was Mrs. Ruth Alice Kistler (nee Taylor), formerly Mrs. Shepard (1899–1982), of Portland, OR. A birth certificate indicated that she gave birth to a daughter, Suzan, at Glendale, near Los Angeles, CA on 18 Oct. 1956, when her age was 57 years 129 days.

In the *Gazette Médicale de Liège* (1 Oct. 1891) Dr. E. Derasse reported the case of one of his patients who gave birth to a healthy baby at the age of 59 years 5 months. The woman already had a married daughter age 40.

It was reported in the *British Medical Journal* (June 1991) that a mother gave birth at the age of 59 years.

BABIES

Heaviest single birth   Big babies (i.e., over 10 lbs.) are usually born to mothers who are large, overweight or have some medical problem such as diabetes. The heaviest baby born to a healthy mother was a boy weighing 22 lbs. 8 oz. who was born to Signora Carmelina Fedele of Aversa, Italy in September 1955.

Mrs. Anna Bates (nee Swan; 1846–88), the 7-ft.-5½-in. Canadian giantess, gave birth to a boy weighing 23 lbs. 12 oz. (length 30 in.) at her home in Seville, OH on 19 Jan. 1879, but the baby died 11 hours later.

Twins   The world's heaviest twins were born to Mrs. J.P. Haskin, Fort Smith, AR, collectively weighing 27 lbs. 12 oz. on 20 Feb. 1924.

Triplets   The unconfirmed report of the world's heaviest triplets was a case from Iran (two male, one female) collectively weighing 26 lbs. 6 oz. born on 18 Mar. 1968.

Quadruplets   The world's heaviest quadruplets (four girls) weighed 22 lbs. 13 oz. collectively and were born to Mrs. Ayako Takeda Tsuchihashi at the Maternity Hospital in Kagoshima, Japan on 4 Oct. 1978.

Quintuplets   Two cases have been recorded for heaviest quintuplets, both recording a total weight of 25 lbs. The first set was born on 7 June 1953 to Mrs. Lui Saulian of Zhejiang, China, and the second set to Mrs. Kamalammal of Pondicherry, India on 30 Dec. 1956.

Longest interval between twins   Mrs. Danny Petrungaro (nee Berg; b. 1953) of Rome, Italy, who had been on hormone treatment after suffering four miscarriages, gave birth normally to a girl, Diana, on 22 Dec. 1987, but the other twin, Monica, was delivered by cesarean on 27 Jan. 1988, 38 days later.

Lightest single birth   A premature baby girl weighing 9.9 oz. was reported to have been born in 1989 at the Loyola University Medical Center, IL.

Lightest twins   Mary, 16 oz., and Margaret, 19 oz., were born on 16 Aug. 1931 to Mrs. Florence Stimson of Old Fletton, Great Britain.

**LONGEST INTERVAL BETWEEN TWINS. Diana and Monica
Petrungaro, although twins, were born 36 days apart.
Diana was born on 22 Dec. 1987 and Monica on 27 Jan.
1988. (Photo: Fabrizio Di Giorgio)**

Test-tube babies There are various methods by which babies can be conceived outside of the mother's body. These children are usually known as "test-tube" babies and the technique as IVF (in-vitro fertilization).

First The world's first test-tube baby was born to Lesley Brown, age 31, who gave birth by cesarean section to Louise (5 lbs. 12 oz.) in Oldham General Hospital, Great Britain at 11:47 P.M. on 25 July 1978. Louise was externally conceived on 10 Nov. 1977.

The first test-tube baby in the United States was Elizabeth Jordan Carr (5 lbs. 12 oz.), who was delivered by cesarean section from Judy Carr, age 28, in Norfolk General Hospital, VA on 28 Dec. 1981. Elizabeth was externally conceived on 15 Apr. 1981. Dr. Howard Jones of Eastern Virginia Medical School performed the in-vitro procedure.

Twins The world's first test-tube twins, Stephen and Amanda, were delivered by cesarean section to Mrs. Radmila Mays, age 31, at the Queen Victoria Medical Centre, Melbourne, Australia on 5 June 1981. Amanda weighed in at 5 lbs. 6 oz. and Stephen at 5 lbs. 3 oz.

Triplets The world's first test-tube triplets (two girls and one boy) were born at Flinders Medical Centre, Adelaide, Australia on 8 June 1983. At the request of the parents, no names were released.

Quintuplets Alan, Brett, Connor, Douglas and Edward were born to Linda and Bruce Jacobssen at University College Hospital, London, Great Britain on 26 Apr. 1985.

Oldest mother to have delivered following IVF   A Cypriot woman 49 years 54 days gave birth by cesarean section to a girl weighing 96 oz. in October 1990. The fertilized egg had been implanted in the patient's womb under the supervision of Dr. Krinos Trokoudes, Director of the Pedieos IVF Center in Nicosia, Cyprus.

Longest interval between test-tube twins   Mrs. Mary Wright, age 38, gave birth to Amy and Elizabeth, 18 months apart, from eggs fertilized by her husband in March 1984. Elizabeth was born at Stoke-on-Trent, Great Britain on 22 Apr. 1987 from an egg which had been in frozen storage for 29 months.

First birth from frozen embryo   Zoe (last name withheld) was delivered by cesarean section weighing 5 lbs. 13 oz. on 28 Mar. 1984 in Melbourne, Australia. Scientists from Monash University announced the birth.

United States   A boy (9 lbs. 8 oz.) was delivered by cesarean section on 4 June 1986 from Monique (last name withheld), age 36, in Cottage Hospital, Santa Barbara, CA. A second child (name withheld) was born on 23 Oct. 1989 by the same procedure and it is believed that this is the only case of siblings from frozen embryos. Dr. Richard Marrs was in charge of the procedure.

Most-premature babies   James Elgin Gill was born to Brenda and James Gill on 20 May 1987 in Ottawa, Ontario, Canada 128 days premature and weighing 1 lb. 6 oz.

United States   In the United States the most premature baby is Ernestine Hudgins, who was born on 8 Feb. 1983 in San Diego, CA about 18 weeks premature and weighing 17 oz.

Twins   Joanne and Mark Holding (nonidentical twins) were born on 28 Feb. 1988 in Portsmouth, Great Britain 105 days premature. Joanne weighed 1 lb. 15 oz. and Mark 1 lb. 8 oz.

Quadruplets   Tina Piper of St. Leonards-on-Sea, Great Britain, had quadruplets on 10 Apr. 1988, after exactly 26 weeks of pregnancy. Oliver, 2 lbs. 9 oz. (d. Feb. 1989), Francesca, 2 lbs. 2 oz., Charlotte, 2 lbs. 4½ oz., and Georgina, 2 lbs. 5 oz., were all born at The Royal Sussex County Hospital, Brighton, Great Britain.

MULTIPLE BIRTHS

"Siamese" twins   Conjoined twins derive the name "Siamese" from the celebrated Chang and Eng Bunker ("Left" and "Right" in Thai), born at Meklong, Thailand on 11 May 1811 of Chinese parents. They were joined by a cartilaginous band at the chest. They married (in 1843) the Misses Sarah and Adalaide Yates of Wilkes County, NC, and fathered 10 and 12 children respectively. They died within three hours of each other on 17 Jan. 1874, age 62.

Rarest   The most extreme form of conjoined twins is dicephales tetra-brachius dipus (two heads, four arms and two legs). The only fully reported example is Masha and Dasha Krivoshlyapovy, born in Russia on 4 Jan. 1950.

Earliest successful separation   The earliest successful separation of Siamese twins was performed on xiphopagus (joined at the sternum) girls at Mount Sinai Hospital, Cleveland, OH by Dr. Jac S. Geller on 14 Dec. 1952.

Oldest surviving   The oldest surviving unseparated twins are the craniopagus (heads are fused at the crown) pair, Yvonne and Yvette McCarther (b. 1949) of Los Angeles, CA. They have rejected an operation to separate them.

Longest-parted twins   Through the help of New Zealand's television program *Missing* on 27 Apr. 1989, Iris (nee Haughie) Johns and Aro (nee Haughie) Campbell (b. 13 Jan. 1914) were reunited after 75 years' separation.

United States   Fraternal twins Lloyd Earl and Floyd Ellsworth Clark were born on 15 Feb. 1917 in Nebraska. They were parted when only four months old and lived under their adopted names Dewayne William Gramly (Lloyd) and Paul Edward Forbes (Floyd). Both men knew that they had been born twins but it wasn't until 16 June 1986 that they were reunited, after having been separated for over 69 years.

Fastest triplet birth   Bradley, Christopher and Carmon were born naturally to Mrs. James E. Duck of Memphis, TN in two minutes on 21 Mar. 1977.

Quindecaplets   It was announced by Dr. Gennaro Montanino of Rome that he had removed by hysterotomy after four months of pregnancy the fetuses of ten girls and five boys from the womb of a 35-year-old housewife on 22 July 1971. A fertility drug was responsible for this unique instance of quindecaplets.

Decaplets   The highest number reported at a single birth were two males and eight females at Bacacay, Brazil on 22 Apr. 1946. Reports were also received from Spain in 1924 and China on 12 May 1936.

Most sets of multiple births in a family   *Quintuplets*   There is no recorded case of more than a single set.

Quadruplets   Four sets to Mde. Feodor Vassilyev, Suya, Russia (died b. 1707) (see Motherhood).

Triplets   15 sets to Maddalena Granata, Italy (b. 1839–*fl.* 1886).

Twins   16 sets to Mde Vassilyev (see above). Note also that Mrs. Barbara Zulu of Barbeton, South Africa bore three sets of girls and three mixed sets in seven years (1967–73). Mrs. Anna Steynvaait of Johannesburg, South Africa produced two sets within 10 months in 1960.

Nonuplets   The world's only certain nonuplets were born to Mrs. Geraldine Broderick at Royal Hospital for Women, Sydney, Australia on 13 June 1971. None of the five boys (two stillborn) and four girls lived for more than 6 days.

It was reported that a patient at the University of Pennsylvania, Philadelphia, PA gave birth on 29 May 1971 to nonuplets; they all died. Nonuplets were also born to a 30-year-old mother from Bagerhat, Bangladesh *c.* 11 May 1977; none survived.

Septuplets   Septuplets were born on 21 May 1985 to Patti Jorgenson Frustaci of Orange, CA, a 30-year-old English teacher who had been taking a fertility drug. One baby was stillborn and the living infants weighed as little as 1 lb. In the weeks that followed, three more babies died, but three have survived.

Sextuplets   Mrs. Susan Jane Rosenkowitz (nee Scoones; b. 28 Oct. 1947, Colombo, Sri Lanka) gave birth to three males and three females at Mowbray, Cape Town, South Africa on 11 Jan. 1974. In order of birth they were David, Nicolette, Jason, Emma, Grant and Elizabeth. They totaled 24 lbs. 1 oz.

Mrs. Rosanna Giannini (b. 1952) gave birth to four males and two females at Careggi Hospital, Florence, Italy on 11 Jan. 1980.

DESCENDANTS

In polygamous countries (countries that allow a man to have more than one wife at a time), the number of a person's descendants can become incalculable. The last Sharifian emperor of Morocco, Moulay Ismail (1672–1727), known as "The Bloodthirsty," was reputed to have fathered a total of 525 sons and 342 daughters by 1703 and to have achieved a 700th son in 1721.

At his death in April 1984, Adam Borntrager, age 96, of Medford, WI, had 707 direct descendants, of whom all but 32 were living. The total extant comprised 11 children, 115 grandchildren, 529 great-grandchildren and 20 great-great-grandchildren.

Mrs. Peter L. Schwartz (1902–88) had 14 children, 13 of whom are still living; 175 grandchildren; 477 great-grandchildren; and 20 great-great-grandchildren.

Seven-generation family   Augusta Bunge (nee Pagel; b. 13 Oct. 1879) of Wisconsin learned that she was a greatgreat-great-great-grandmother when she received news of her great-great-great-great-grandson, Christopher John Bollig (b. 21 Jan. 1989).

Great-great-great-grandmother   Harriet Holmes of Newfoundland, Canada (b. 17 Jan. 1899) became the youngest living great-great-great-grandmother on 8 Mar. 1987 at the age of 88 years 50 days. The families' average generation was only 17.6 years.

Most living ascendants   Megan Sue Austin of Bar Harbor, ME had a full set of grandparents and great-grandparents and five great-great-grandparents, making 19 direct ascendants when born on 16 May 1982.

Family tree   The lineage of K'ung Ch'iu or Confucius (551–479 B.C.) can be traced back further than that of any other family. His great-great-great-great-grandfather K'ung Chia is known from the 8th century B.C. This man's 85th lineal descendants, Wei-yi (b. 1939) and Wei-ning (b. 1947), live today in Taiwan.

FAMILY TREE. Confucius, China's most famous teacher, philosopher and political theorist, whose ideas influenced the civilization of all eastern Asia. His family can be traced back further than any other; his 85th lineal descendants live today in Taiwan. (Photo: Archiv für Kunst und Geschichte)

LONGEVITY

No single subject is more obscured by vanity, deceit, falsehood and deliberate fraud than human longevity. Apart from the traces left by accidental markers (e.g. the residual effects of established dated events such as the Chernobyl incident), there is no known scientific method of checking the age of any part of the living body.

Centenarians surviving beyond their 113th year are in fact extremely rare, and the present absolute proven limit of human longevity does not yet admit of anyone living to celebrate his or her 121st birthday.

65 + POPULATION

STATE	TOTAL (1,000's)
California	3,136
Florida	2,369
New York	2,364
Pennsylvania	1,829
Texas	1,717

Data: AARP/AOA

From data on documented centenarians, actuaries have shown that only one 115-year life can be expected in 2.1 billion lives (note that the world population was estimated to be 5.48 billion by mid-1992).

The limits of credulity were reached on 5 May 1933, when a news agency filed a story from China with a Beijing source announcing that Li Zhongyun, the "oldest man on Earth," born in 1680, had just died after 253 years (*sic*).

The latest census in China revealed only 3,800 centenarians, of whom two-thirds were women. According to a 1985 census carried out in the Chinese province of Xinjiang Uygur, Zizhiqi there were 850 centenarians in the area, one of whom was listed at a highly improbable 125 years of age. In the United States as of 1 Apr. 1990 the figure was 35,808 centenarians.

In 1990 the United States population of people 65 and over was 31.2 million, representing 12.6 percent of the population. Since 1900 the American population 65 and over has increased tenfold from 3.1 million. It is projected that a child born in 1989 has a life expectancy of 75.2 years. In 1900 the figure was 46.9 years.

Oldest authentic centenarian   The greatest *authenticated* age to which any human has ever lived is 120 years 237 days in the case of Shigechiyo Izumi of Asan on Tokunoshima, an island 820 miles southwest of Tokyo, Japan. He was born in Asan on 29 June 1865 and was recorded as a 6-year-old in Japan's first census of 1871. He died in his ranch house at 12:15 GMT on 21 Feb. 1986 after developing pneumonia. He worked until the age of 105. His wife died when only 90 years of age. He drank *Sho-chu* (firewater) (distilled from sugar) and took up smoking when 70 years old. He attributed his long life to "God, Buddha and the Sun."

Oldest living   The oldest living person in the world whose date of birth can be reliably authenticated is Jeanne Louise Calment, who was born in France on 21 Feb. 1875. She now lives in a nursing home in Arles, Southern France, where she celebrated her 117th birthday with champagne. She met Vincent van Gogh (died 29 July 1890) in her father's shop.

Oldest twins   The chances of identical twins both reaching 100 are now probably about one in 50 million.

Eli Shadrack and John Meshak Phipps were born on 14 Feb. 1803 at Affinghton, VA. Eli died in Hennessey, OK on 23 Feb. 1911 at the age of 108 years 9 days, on which day John was still living in Shenandoah, IA.

AUTHENTIC NATIONAL LONGEVITY RECORDS

COUNTRY	YEARS	DAYS		BORN	DIED
Japan	120	237	Shigechiyo Izumi	29 June 1865	21 Feb. 1986
France	117	64	Jeanne Louise Calment	21 Feb. 1875	fl.* Apr. 1992
United States[1]	116	88	Carrie White (Mrs.; nee Joyner)	18 Nov. 1874	14 Feb. 1991
Great Britain[2]	114	213	Charlotte Hughes (Mrs., nee Milburn)	1 Aug. 1877	fl. Mar. 1992
Canada[3]	113	124	Pierre Joubert	15 July 1701	16 Nov. 1814
Australia	112	330	Caroline Maud Mockridge	11 Dec. 1874	6 Nov. 1987
Spain[4]	112	228	Josefa Salas Mateo	14 July 1860	27 Feb. 1973
Norway	112	61	Maren Bolette Torp	21 Dec. 1876	20 Feb. 1989
Morocco	112		El Hadj Mohammed el Mokri (Grand Vizier)		16 Sep. 1957
Poland	112	+	Roswlia Mielczarak (Mrs.)	1868	7 Jan. 1981
Netherlands[5]	111	354	Thomas Peters	6 Apr. 1745	26 Mar. 1857
Ireland	111	327	The Hon. Katherine Plunket	22 Nov. 1820	14 Oct. 1932
Scotland	111	238	Kate Begbie (Mrs.)	9 Jan. 1877	5 Sep. 1988
South Africa[6]	111	151	Johanna Booyson	17 Jan. 1857	16 June 1968
Sweden[7]	111	90	Wilhelmine Sande (Mrs.)	24 Oct. 1874	21 Jan. 1986
Czechoslovakia	111	+	Marie Bernatková	22 Oct. 1857	fl. Oct. 1968
Germany[8]	111		Maria Corba.	15 Aug. 1878	fl. Mar. 1990
Finland	111	+	Fanny Matilda Nystrom	30 Sep. 1878	1989
Channel Islands	110	321	Margaret Ann Neve (nee Harvey)	18 May 1792	4 Apr. 1903
Northern Ireland	110	234	Elizabeth Watkins (Mrs.)	10 Mar. 1863	31 Oct. 1973
Yugoslavia	110	150+	Demitrius Philipovitch	9 Mar. 1818	fl. Aug. 1928
Greece[9]	110	+	Lambrini Tsiatoura (Mrs.)	1870	19 Feb. 1981
USSR[10]	110	+	Khasako Dzugayev	7 Aug. 1860	fl. Aug. 1970
Italy	110	+	Damiana Sette (Sig.)	1874	25 Feb. 1985
Denmark	109	265	Maria Louise Augusta Bramsen	4 May 1878	23 Jan. 1988
Tasmania (State of)	109	179	Mary Ann Crow (Mrs.)	2 Feb. 1836	31 July 1945

Belgium	108	327	Mathilda Vertommen-Hellemans	12 Aug.	1868	4 July	1977
Iceland	108	45	Halldóra Bjarndóttir	14 Oct.	1873	28 Nov.	1981
Portugal[11]	108	+	Maria Luisa Jorge	7 June	1859	fl. July	1967
Malaysia	106	+	Hassan Bin Yusoff	14 Aug.	1865	fl. Jan.	1972
Luxembourg	105	228	Nicolas Wiscourt	31 Dec.	1872	17 Aug.	1978

[1] Ex-slave Mrs. Martha Graham died at Fayetteville, NC on 25 June 1959 apparently aged 117 or 118. Census research shows that she was apparently born in December 1844 and hence was aged 114 years 6 months. Mrs. Rena Glover Brailsford died in Summerton, SC on 6 Dec. 1977 reputedly aged 118 years. Mrs. Rosario Reina Vasquez, who died in California on 2 Sep. 1980, was reputedly born in Sonora, Mexico on 3 June 1866, which would have made her 114 years 93 days. The 1900 U.S. Federal Census for Crawfish Springs Militia District of Walker County, GA, records an age of 77 for a Mark Thrash. If the Mark Thrash (reputedly born in Georgia in December 1822) who died near Chattanooga, TN on 17 Dec. 1943 was he, and the age attributed was accurate, then he would have survived for 121 years. According to Jackson Pollard's Social Security payments, he was born on 15 Dec 1869 in Georgia, but no birth certificate or family bible are available.

[2] British-born Miss Isabella Shepheard was allegedly 115 years old when she died at St. Asaph, Clwyd, Great Britain, on 20 Nov. 1948, but her actual age was believed to have been 109 years 90 days.

[3] Mrs. Ellen Carroll died in North River, Newfoundland, Canada on 8 Dec. 1943, reputedly aged 115 years 49 days.

[4] Señor Benita Medrana of Avila died on 28 Jan. 1979, allegedly aged 114 years 335 days.

[5] Jean Michael Reskens died 7 Jan. 1990 aged 111 years 241 days.

[6] Mrs. Susan Johanna Deporter of Port Elizabeth, South Africa was reputedly 114 years old when she died on 4 Aug. 1954. Mrs. Sarah Lawrence of Cape Town, South Africa was reputedly 112 on 3 June 1968.

[7] Mrs. Sande was born in present-day Norway.

[8] An unnamed female died in Germany in 1979 aged 112 years, and an unnamed male, aged also 112 years, died in 1969. The Austrian record is 108 years (female d. 1975) and the Swiss record is also 108 years (female d. 1967).

[9] The claim that Liakon Efdokia died on 17 Jan. 1982 aged 118 years 13 days is not substantiated by the censuses of 1971 or 1981. Birth registration before 1920 was fragmentary.

[10] A figure of 21,700 centenarians has been quoted for the former USSR (compared with 54,000 in the United States). Of these, 21,000 are ascribed to the Georgian SSR, i.e., one in every 232. In July 1962 it was reported that 128, mostly male, were in the one village of Medini.

[11] Senhora Jesuina da Conceição of Lisbon was reputedly 113 years old when she died on 10 June 1965.

* Note: fl. is the abbreviation for the Latin floruit, meaning he or she was living at the relevant date.

Female   On 17 June 1984, identical twin sisters Mildred Widman Philippi and Mary Widman Franzini of St. Louis, MO celebrated their 104th birthday. Mildred died on 4 May 1985, 44 days short of the twins' 105th birthday.

Oldest living siblings   The oldest living siblings in the United States are Nellie Hardman Eby (b. 13 Apr. 1992) and Katherine Hardman Davenport (b. 31 Mar. 1883), who on 13 Apr. 1992 were 111 and 109 respectively.

Oldest living triplets   Faith, Hope and Charity Cardwell were born in Sweetwater, TX on 18 May 1899, and live together in a Sweetwater retirement home.

Oldest quadruplets   The Ottman quads of Munich, Germany—Adolf, Anne-Marie, Emma and Elisabeth—celebrated their 78th birthday on 5 May 1991.

ANATOMY AND PHYSIOLOGY

Hydrogen (63 percent) and oxygen (25.5 percent) constitute the most common of the 24 elements regarded as normally present in the human body. Carbon, sodium, potassium, calcium, sulfur, chlorine (as chlorides), phosphorus, iron and zinc are all present in significant quantities. Present in "trace" quantities, but generally regarded as normal in a healthy body (even if their "necessity" is a matter of controversy) are iodine, fluorine, copper, cobalt, chromium, manganese, selenium, molybdenum and probably vanadium, nickel, silicon, tin and arsenic.

HANDS, FEET AND HAIR

Touch   The extreme sensitivity of the fingers is such that a vibration with a movement of 0.02 microns can be detected.

Longest fingernails   Fingernails grow at a rate of about 0.02 in. a week—four times faster than toenails. The aggregate measurement of those of Shridhar Chillal (b. 1937) of Pune, Maharashtra, India, on 3 Mar. 1992 was 195 in. for the five nails on his left hand (thumb 46 in., index finger 34 in., second finger 37 in., third finger 40 in., and the pinkie 38 in.). He last cut his nails in 1952.

Fewest toes   The two-toed syndrome exhibited by some members of the Wadomo tribe of the Zambezi Valley, Zimbabwe and the Kalanga tribe of the eastern Kalahari Desert, Botswana is hereditary via a single mutated gene. They are not handicapped by their deformity, and can walk great distances without discomfort.

Largest feet   If cases of elephantiasis are excluded, then the biggest feet known are those of Haji Mohammad Alam Channa of Pakistan, who wears size 22 sandals.

Balancing on one foot   The longest recorded duration for balancing on one foot is 45 hrs. 25 min. by Leslie Silva at Negombo, Sri Lanka from 6–8 Apr. 1991. The disengaged foot may not be rested on the standing foot, nor may any object be used for support or balance.

Shaving   The fastest barbers on record are Denny Rowe, who shaved 1,994 men in 60 min. with a retractor safety razor in Herne Bay, Great Britain on 19 June 1988, taking on average 1.8 sec. per volunteer, and drawing blood four times; and Gerry Harley, of Gillingham, Great Britain, who on 13 Aug. 1984 shaved 235 even-braver volunteers in 60 min. with a cut-throat razor, averaging 15.3 sec. per face. He drew blood only once.

HAIR SPLITTING. Human hair magnified many times (above), showing the problem of "split ends"; the hair needs to be cut regularly in order for this not to happen. The greatest reported achievement in hair splitting was that of the former champion cyclist and craftsman Alfred West (Great Britain; 1901–85), who succeeded in splitting a human hair 17 times into 18 parts on eight occasions. (Photo: Science Photo Library)

Longest hair   Human hair grows at a rate of about 0.5 in. a month. If left uncut it will usually grow to a maximum of 2–3 ft.

In 1780 a head of hair measuring 12 ft. in length and dressed in a style known as the *plica candiforma* (hair forming matted spikes) was sent to Dresden after adorning the head of a Polish peasant woman for 52 years. The braid of hair had a circumference of 11.9 in.

The hair of Diane Witt of Worcester, MA measured over 12 ft. 2 in. in May 1992. This is the longest documented length of hair.

Most valuable hair   On 18 Feb. 1988 a bookseller from Cirencester, Great Britain, paid £5,575 ($10,035) for a lock of hair that had belonged to British naval hero Lord Nelson (1758–1805) at an auction held at Crewkerne, Great Britain.

Longest beard   The beard of Hans N. Langseth (b. 1846 near Eidsvoll, Norway) measured 17½ ft. at the time of his burial in Kensett, IA in 1927 after 15 years' residence in the United States. It was presented to the Smithsonian Institution, Washington, D.C., in 1967.

The beard of Janice Deveree, "the bearded lady" (b. Bracken Co., KY, 1842), was measured in 1884 at 14 in.

Longest mustache   The mustache of Birger Pellas (b. 21 Sep. 1934) of Malmö, Sweden, grown since 1973, reached a span of 10 ft. 2 in. in February 1992.

Karna Ram Bheel (1928–87) was granted permission by a New Delhi prison governor in February 1979 to keep the 7-ft.-10-in. mustache which he had grown since 1949 during his life sentence. He used mustard, oil, butter and cream to keep it in trim.

DENTITION

Earliest   Tooth enamel is the only part of the human body that remains basically unchanged throughout life. It is also the hardest substance in the body. The first deciduous or milk teeth normally appear in infants at 5–8 months, these being the upper and lower jaw first incisors. There are many records of children born with teeth, the most distinguished example being Prince Louis Dieudonné, later Louis XIV of France, who was born with two teeth on 5 Sep. 1638. Molars usually appear at 24 months, but in a case published in Denmark in 1970, a six-week premature baby was documented with eight teeth at birth, of which four were in the molar region.

Most teeth at birth   Shaun Keaney of Newbury, Great Britain was born

---

Lifting with teeth   Walter Arfeuille of Ieper-Vlamertinge, Belgium lifted weights totaling 621 lbs. a distance of 6¾ in. off the ground with his teeth in Paris, France, on 31 Mar. 1990.

Hercules John Massis (b. Wilfried Oscar Morbée; 1940–88) of Oostakker, Belgium prevented a helicopter from taking off using only a tooth bit harness in Los Angeles, CA on 7 Apr. 1979 for a *Guinness Spectacular* TV show.

---

on 10 Apr. 1990 with 12 teeth, but they were extracted a few days after his birth.

Most Cases of the growth in late life of a third set of teeth have been recorded several times. A reference to a case in France of a *fourth* dentition, known as Lison's case, was published in 1896.

Most dedicated dentist Brother Giovanni Battista Orsenigo of the Ospedale Fatebenefratelli, Rome, Italy, a dentist, conserved all the teeth he extracted during the time he practiced his profession from 1868 to 1904. In 1903 the number was counted and found to be 2,000,744 teeth, indicating an average of 185 teeth, or nearly six total extractions, a day.

Most valuable tooth In 1816 a tooth belonging to British scientist Sir Isaac Newton (1643–1727) was sold in London, Great Britain for £730 ($3,650). It was purchased by a nobleman who had it set in a ring, which he wore constantly.

Earliest false teeth From discoveries made in Etruscan tombs, partial dentures of bridgework type were being worn in what is now the Tuscany region of Italy as early as 700 B.C. Some were permanently attached to existing teeth and others were removable.

OPTICS

Highest visual acuity The human eye is capable of judging relative position with remarkable accuracy, reaching limits of between 3 and 5 seconds of arc.

In April 1984 Dr. Dennis M. Levi of the College of Optometry, University of Houston, TX, repeatedly identified the position of a thin white line within 0.85 sec. of arc. This is equivalent to a displacement of some ¼ in. at a distance of one mile.

Color sensitivity The unaided human eye, under the best possible viewing conditions, comparing large areas of color, in good illumination, using both eyes, can distinguish 10,000,000 different color surfaces. The most accurate photoelectric spectrophotometers possess a precision probably only 40 percent as good as this. About 7.5 percent of men and 0.1 percent of women are colorblind. The most extreme form, monochromatic vision, is very rare. The highest rate of red–green color-blindness is in Czechoslovakia, and the lowest rate is among Fijians and Brazilian Indians.

BONES

Longest Excluding a variable number of sesamoids (small rounded bones), there are 206 bones in the adult human body, compared with 300 in children (as they grow, some bones fuse together). The thigh bone or femur is the longest. It constitutes usually 27.5 percent of a person's stature, and may be expected to be 19¾ in. long in a 6-ft.-tall man. The longest recorded bone was the femur of the German giant Constantine, who died in Mons, Belgium, on 30 Mar. 1902, age 30. It measured 29.9 in. The femur of Robert Wadlow, the tallest man ever recorded, measured an estimated 29½ in. (See Tallest men.)

COLOR-BLINDNESS. The Czechs and Slovaks have the highest rate for red-green color-blindness in the world; therefore the owners of the parked cars in this picture might have difficulty in recognizing them. In the background is Hradčany Castle in Prague, the largest ancient castle in the world. (Photo: Spectrum Colour Library)

Smallest The stapes or stirrup bone, one of the three auditory ossicles in the middle ear, measures 0.10–0.17 in. in length and weighs from 0 .03–0.065 grains.

MUSCLES

Largest Muscles normally account for 40 percent of body weight. The bulkiest of the 639 named muscles in the human body is usually the gluteus maximus or buttock muscle, which extends the thigh. However, in pregnant women the uterus or womb can increase its weight from about 1 oz. to over 2.2 lbs. and becomes larger than even the most successful body-builder's buttock.

Smallest The stapedius, which controls the stapes (see above), is less than 0.05 in. long.

Longest The longest muscle in the human body is the sartorius, which is a narrow, ribbonlike muscle running from the pelvis across the front of the thigh to the top of the tibia below the knee. Its function is to draw the lower limb into the cross-legged sitting position, proverbially associated with tailors.

Most active   It has been estimated that the eye muscles move 100,000 times a day or more. Many of these eye movements take place during the dreaming phase of sleep. (See Longest and shortest dreams.)

Longest name   The muscle with the longest name is the *levator labii superioris alaeque nasi,* which runs inwards and downwards on the face, with one branch running to the upper lip and the other to the nostril. It is the muscle that everts or curls the upper lip and its action was particularly well demonstrated in the performances of Elvis Presley (1935–77).

Strongest   The strongest muscle in the human body is the masseter, of which there are two, one on each side of the mouth, which is responsible for the action of biting. In August 1986, Richard Hofmann (b. 1949) of Lake City, FL achieved a bite strength of 975 lbs. for approximately two seconds in a research test using a gnathodynamometer at the College of Dentistry, University of Florida. This figure is more than six times the normal biting strength.

Largest chest measurements   The largest are among endomorphs (those with a tendency toward a thick, chunky, well-rounded body). In the extreme case of Robert Earl Hughes (USA; 1926–58) the measurement was 124 in., and T.J. Albert Jackson, currently the heaviest living man, has a chest measurement of 120 in. (See Weight, Heaviest living.)

The largest muscular chest measurement recorded so far is that of American power-lifter Bruce Wayne Richardson (b. 23 Sep. 1948) of Salt Lake City, UT at 72½ in. He is 5 ft. 8 in. tall and weighs 252 lbs.

Largest and smallest biceps   Isaac "Dr. Size" Nesser (b. 21 Apr. 1962) of Greensburg, PA has biceps of 26⅛ in. "cold" (not pumped).

The biceps of Robert Thorn measured 4¼ in.

WAISTS

Largest   The largest waist ever recorded was that of Walter Hudson (1944–91) of New York, which measured 119 in. at his peak weight of 1,197 lbs.

Smallest   The smallest waist in someone of normal stature was that of Mrs. Ethel Granger (1905–82) of Peterborough, Great Britain, reduced from a natural 22 in to 13 in over the period 1929–39. A measurement of 13 in. was also claimed for the French actress Mlle Polaire (real name Emile Marie Bouchand; 1881–1939).

Queen Catherine de Medici (1519–89) decreed a waist measurement of 13¾ in. for ladies of the French court, but this was at a time when the human race was more diminutive.

NECKS

Longest   The maximum measured extension of the neck by the successive fitting of copper coils, as practiced by the women of the Padaung or Kareni tribe of Myanmar (formerly Burma), is 15¾ in. When the rings are removed, the muscles developed to support the head and neck shrink to their normal length.

BRAINS

Heaviest   In normal brains there is little correlation between intelligence and size.

The heaviest brain ever recorded was that of a 50-year-old male, which weighed 4 lbs. 8.3 oz. and was reported by Dr. Thomas F. Hegert, chief medical examiner for District 9, State of Florida, on 23 Oct. 1975.

Lightest   The lightest "normal" or non-atrophied brain on record was one weighing 2 lbs. 6.7 oz. reported by Dr. P. Davis and Prof. E. Wright of King's College Hospital, London, Great Britain in 1977. It belonged to a 31-year-old woman.

Most expensive skull   The skull of Emanuel Swedenborg (1688–1772), the Swedish natural philosopher and theologian, was bought in London, Great Britain by the Royal Swedish Academy of Sciences for £5,500 ($10,505) on 6 Mar. 1978.

Human computer   Mrs. Shakuntala Devi of India multiplied two 13-digit numbers ($7,686,369,774,870 \times 2,465,099,745,779$) randomly selected by the Computer Department of Imperial College, London, Great Britain on 18 June 1980, in 28 seconds. Her answer was 18,947,668,177,995,426,462,773,730 and was correct. Some experts on calculating prodigies refuse to give credence to Mrs. Devi on the grounds that her achievements are so vastly superior to the calculating feats of any other investigated prodigy that the authentication must have been defective.

Memory   Bhandanta Vicitsara recited 16,000 pages of Buddhist canonical texts in Yangon, Myanmar (formerly Rangoon, Burma) in May 1974.

Gon Yangling, 26, has memorized more than 15,000 telephone numbers in Harbin, China, according to the Xinhua News Agency. Rare instances of eidetic memory—the ability to re-project and hence "visually" recall material—are known to science.

Card memorizing   Dominic O'Brien of Buntingford, Great Britain memorized on a single sighting a random sequence of 35 separate decks of cards (1,820 cards in all) that had been shuffled together, with only two mistakes, at the Star Inn, Furneux, Great Britain on 22 July 1990.

Jonathan Hancock of Middlesbrough, Great Britain memorized a single deck of shuffled playing cards in a time of 2 min. 5 sec. with no errors on 6 Dec. 1991 at Oxford, Great Britain.

George Uhrin of Houston, TX memorized on a single sighting a random sequence of 30 separate decks of cards (1,560) that had been all shuffled together, with two errors, at the Texas Commerce Tower, Houston, TX on 16 July 1989.

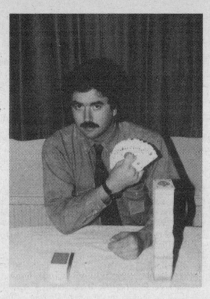

CARD MEMORIZING. Dominic O'Brien memorized a random sequence of 35 separate decks of playing cards, which had been shuffled together, on a single sighting, with only two errors. (Photo: Philip Crossley)

The greatest number of places of pi Hideaki Tomoyori (b. 30 Sep. 1932) of Yokohama, Japan recited pi from memory to 40,000 places in 17 hrs. 21 min. including breaks totaling 4 hrs. 15 min. on 9–10 Mar. 1987 at the Tsukuba University Club House.

Note: It is only the *approximation* of π at $^{22}/_7$ which recurs after its sixth decimal place and can, of course, be recited *ad nauseam*. The true value is a string of random numbers fiendishly difficult to memorize. The average capacity for memorizing random numbers is barely more than eight, as proved by the common inability to memorize nine- or ten-digit telephone numbers.

VOICE

Greatest range The normal intelligible outdoor range of the male human voice in still air is 600 ft. The *silbo*, the whistled language of the Spanish-speaking Canary Island of La Gomera, is intelligible across the valleys, under ideal conditions, at five miles. There is a recorded case, under optimal acoustic conditions, of the human voice being detectable at a distance of 10½ miles across still water at night.

Screaming The highest scientifically measured emission has been one of 128 decibels at 8 ft. 2 in. produced by the screaming of Simon Robinson of McLaren Vale, South Australia at The Guinness Challenge at Adelaide, Australia on 11 Nov. 1988.

Whistling Roy Lomas achieved 122.5 decibels at 8 ft. 2 in. in the Dead-room at the British Broadcasting Corporation studios in Manchester, Great Britain on 19 Dec. 1983.

Shouting   Donald H. Burns of St. George's, Bermuda achieved 119 decibels in shouting when he appeared on the Fuji TV film *Narvhodo the World* at Liberty State Park, NJ on 18 Jan. 1989.

Yodeling   Yodeling has been defined as "repeated rapid changes from the chest-voice to falsetto and back again." The most rapid recorded yodel is ten tones (six falsetto) in 0.88 sec., by Jim Whitman at Bethesda County, Great Britain on 16 Nov. 1990.

Lowest detectable sound   The intensity of noise or sound is measured in terms of pressure. The pressure of the quietest sound that can be detected by a person of normal hearing at the most sensitive frequency of *c.* 2,750 Hz is 2×10^{-5} pascal. One-tenth of the logarithm to this standard provides a unit termed a decibel (dB). A noise of 30 dB is negligible.

Hamlet's soliloquy   Sean Shannon, a Canadian residing in Oxford, Great Britain, recited Hamlet's soliloquy "To be or not to be" (259 words) in a time of 24 sec. (equivalent to 647.5 words per min.) on British Broadcasting Corporation's *Radio Oxford* on 26 Oct. 1990.

Backwards talking   Steve Briers of Kilgetty, Great Britain recited the entire lyrics of Queen's album *A Night at the Opera* backwards at British Broadcasting Corporation North-West Radio 4's *Cat's Whiskers* on 6 Feb. 1990 in a time of 9 min. 58.44 sec.

United States   David Fuhrer of California recited the entire lyrics of Queen's album *A Night at the Opera* at Trax Recording Studio, CA on 28 July 1989 in a time of 10 min. 19 sec.

Longest memory   The lymphocyte has probably the longest memory of any cell. As successive generations of lymphocytes are produced during life, the cells never forget an enemy. So, for example, once a measles virus has introduced itself to the lymphocytes in the first years of life, these stalwarts of the immune system will still be ready to recognize and destroy the measles virus 70 years later. This is why you cannot get measles twice.

Highest noise levels   Prolonged noise above 150 dB will cause permanent deafness, while above 192 dB a lethal over-pressure shock wave can be formed. Equivalent continuous sound levels (LEQ) above 90 dB are impermissible in factories in many countries, but this compares with 125 emitted by racing cars and 130 by amplified music.

Highest detectable pitch   The upper limit is calculated to be 20,000 Hz (cycles per sec.), although it has been alleged that children with asthma can detect sounds of 30,000 Hz. Bats emit pulses at up to 90,000 Hz. It was announced in February 1964 that experiments in the former USSR had conclusively proved that oscillations as high as 200,000 Hz can be detected if the oscillator is pressed against the skull.

Fastest talker   Few people are able to speak *articulately* at a sustained speed above 300 words per minute. The fastest broadcaster is thought to have been Gerry Wilmot (b. Victoria, British Columbia, Canada, 6 Oct. 1914), an ice hockey commentator of the late forties.

In public life the fastest speed recorded was a burst in excess of 300 words per min. in a speech made in December 1961 by President John Fitzgerald Kennedy (1917–63).

Steve Woodmore of Orpington, Great Britain spoke 595 words in a time of 56.01 sec., or 637.4 words per minute, on the ITV program *Motor Mouth* on 22 Sep. 1990.

United States   John Moschitta (USA) recited 545 words in 55.8 sec., or 586 words per minute, on 24 May 1988 in Los Angeles, CA.

BLOOD

Groups   The preponderance of blood groups varies greatly from one locality to another. On a world basis Group O is the most common (46 percent), but in some areas, for example Norway, Group A predominates.

The rarest type in the world is a type of Bombay blood (subtype h-h) found so far only in a Czechoslovak nurse in 1961, and in a brother (Rh positive) and sister (Rh negative) named Jalbert in Massachusetts, reported in February 1968.

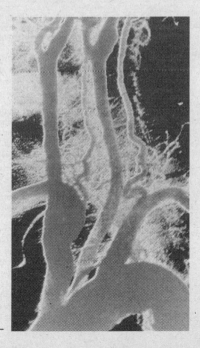

LARGEST ARTERY. The largest artery is the aorta, which is 1.18 in. in diameter. It is seen here at the bottom of the picture, where it curves over the heart. (Photo: Science Photo Library)

The most common subgroup in the United States is O+, which is found in 38.4 percent of the population. The rarest generic blood group is AB–, which occurs in only 0.7 percent of persons in the United States.

Recipient   A 50-year-old hemophiliac, Warren C. Jyrich, required 2,400 donor units of blood, equivalent to 1,900 pints of blood, when undergoing open heart surgery at the Michael Reese Hospital, Chicago, IL in December 1970.

Largest vein   The largest is the inferior vena cava, which returns the blood from the lower half of the body to the heart.

Largest artery   The largest is the aorta, which is 1.18 in. in diameter where it leaves the heart. By the time it ends at the level of the fourth lumbar vertebra it is about 0.68 in. in diameter.

Most alcoholic   The University of California Medical School, Los Angeles reported in December 1982 the case of a confused but conscious 24-year-old female, who was shown to have a blood alcohol level of 1.8 grains per 0.18 pt. After two days she discharged herself.

Tommy Johns of Brisbane, Queensland, Australia died in April 1988 from a brain tumor at the age of 66 years, after having been arrested nearly 3,000 times for being drunk and disorderly in a public place.

CELLS

Biggest   The biggest cell body is the ovum (egg cell) which comes from the female ovary. It is about the size of the period at the end of this paragraph.

Smallest   Some of the smallest cells are brain cells in the cerebellum that measure about 0.005 mm.

Longest   The longest cells are neurons of the nervous system. Motor neurons 4.26 ft. long have cell bodies (gray matter) in the lower spinal cord with axons (white matter) that carry nerve impulses from the spinal cord down to the big toe. Even longer are the cell systems that carry certain sensations (vibration and positional sense) back from the big toe to the brain. Their uninterrupted length, from the toe and up the posterior part of the spinal cord to the medulla of the brain, is about equal to the height of the body.

Fastest turnover of body cells   The fastest turnover of body cells—i.e., the shortest life—is in the lining of the alimentary tract (gut), where the cells are shed every three days.

Longest life   Those with the longest life are brain cells, which last for life. They may be three times as old as bone cells, which may live 25–30 years.

Largest blood cell   The largest blood cell is the megakaryocyte. It spends its life in the bone marrow, rarely venturing out into the main stream of the blood itself. In the marrow it produces the "stickiest" particles in the body—the platelets. There are about 250,000 platelets in each pin-prick (cu. mm) of blood. They have an important role in stopping bleeding. Once a hole is formed in a blood vessel the platelets quickly gather at the site and stick to it, thus sealing the breach.

BODY TEMPERATURE

Highest Willie Jones, 52, was admitted to Grady Memorial Hospital, Atlanta, GA on 10 July 1980 with heatstroke on a day when the temperature reached 90° F. with 44 percent humidity. His temperature was found to be 115.7° F. After 24 days he was discharged "at prior baseline status."

Lowest People may die of hypothermia with body temperatures of 95° F. There are three recorded cases of individuals surviving body temperatures as low as 60.8° F.: Dorothy Mae Stevens (1929–1974), who was found in an alley in Chicago, IL on 1 Feb. 1951 with a pulse that had dropped to 12 beats per min.; Vickie Mary Davis, age 2 years 1 month, discovered in an unheated house in Marshalltown, IA on 21 Jan. 1956; and 2-year old Michael Troke, found in the snow near his home in Milwaukee, WI on 19 Jan. 1985.

ILLNESS AND DISEASE

Commonest *Noncontagious* The commonest noncontagious diseases are periodontal diseases such as gingivitis (inflammation of the gums). In their lifetime few people completely escape the effects of tooth decay.

Contagious The commonest contagious disease in the world is coryza (acute nasopharyngitis), or the common cold.

Rarest Medical literature periodically records hitherto undescribed diseases. A disease as yet undiagnosed but predicted by a Norwegian doctor is podocytoma of the kidney. This is a potential of the cells lining that part of the kidney (glomerus) which acts as a sieve or filter for the blood.

Most recently eradicated scourge of humankind The last case of endemic smallpox was recorded in Ali Maow Maalin in Merka, Somalia on 26 Oct. 1977. This disease is now extinct. Its eradication was achieved by the World Health Organization, whose main weapon in the fight was a stable freeze-dried smallpox vaccine. (The liquid vaccine had often lost its potency by the time it came to be used in the tropics.) A systematic and progressive interruption of the chain of smallpox transmission included not just vaccination, but also rapid detection and isolation of cases so that the disease could not spread further. It has been estimated that the defeat of smallpox saved the developed world alone a billion dollars a year in vaccination costs, making it the most cost-effective application of technology ever.

Highest mortality The virus AIDS (Acquired Immune Deficiency Syndrome) was first reported in 1981. The virus attacks the body's immune defense system, leaving the body wide open to attack from infections which in a healthy person would be fought off without any problems. Many people who are carriers of the virus (HIV) may have none of the signs or symptoms of the disease AIDS, which may develop later. The World Health Organization (WHO) reported 446,691 HIV positive cases worldwide by 1 Jan. 1992. WHO estimates that there are actually 1.5 million AIDS cases worldwide.

By 30 Nov. 1991 the total number of HIV positive cases in the United States was 202,843. This total included 199,417 adults and 3,426 children under 13. The total number of deaths was 130,687, of which 128,857 were in adults and 1,830 were in children.

AIDS STATISTICS

STATE	CASES
New York	42,061
California	37,717
Florida	19,096
Texas	14,254
New Jersey	12,479

CITY	CASES
New York	36,545
Los Angeles	13,394
San Francisco	11,283
Miami	6,172
Houston	5,902

*Data: Centers for Disease Control
(30 Nov. 1991)*

Most infectious and most fatal   The pneumonic form of plague, as evidenced by the Black Death of 1347–51, had a mortality rate of 100 percent. A quarter of the population of Europe perished during the outbreak.

Leading cause of death   In industrialized countries, arteriosclerosis (thickening of the arterial wall) underlies much coronary and cerebrovascular disease. In 1990, the top five causes of death in the United States were: heart disease, 725,010; cancer, 506,000; strokes, 145,340; accidents, including automobile, 93,550; and lung disease and related conditions, 88,980.

MEDICAL EXTREMES

Longest coma   Elaine Esposito (1934–78) of Tarpon Springs, FL, never stirred after an appendectomy on 6 Aug. 1941, when she was 6 years old. She died on 25 Nov. 1978 at the age of 43 years 357 days, having been in a coma for 37 years 111 days.

Longest and shortest dreams   Dreaming sleep is characterized by rapid eye movements known as REM, first described in 1953 by William Dement of the University of Chicago. The longest recorded period of REM is one of 2 hrs. 23 min. on 15 Feb. 1967 at the Department of Psychology, University of Illinois, Chicago by Bill Carskadon, who had had his previous sleep interrupted. In July 1984 the Sleep Research Center, Haifa, Israel recorded no REM in a 33-year-old male who had a shrapnel brain injury. (See Most active muscle.)

g forces   Racing driver David Purley (1945–85) survived a deceleration from 108 mph to zero in 26 in. in a crash at Silverstone, Great Britain on 13 July 1977 that involved a force of 179.8 *g*. He suffered 29 fractures, three dislocations and six heart stoppages.

The highest *g* value endured on a water-braked rocket sled is 2.9 oz. for

0.04 sec. by Eli L. Beeding, Jr. at Holloman Air Force Base, NM on 16 May 1958. He was subsequently hospitalized for three days.

A land diver of Pentecost Island, Vanuatu (formerly the New Hebrides) dove from a platform 81 ft. 3 in. high with liana vines attached to his ankles on 15 May 1982. His body speed was 50 ft. per sec., or 34 mph. The jolt transmitted a momentary *g* force in excess of 110.

Heart arrest   The longest is four hours in the case of a Norwegian fisherman, Jan. Egil Refsdahl (b. 1936), who fell overboard in the icy waters off Bergen on 7 Dec. 1987. He was rushed to nearby Haukeland Hospital after his body temperature fell to 77° F. and his heart stopped beating, but he made a full recovery after he was connected to a heart–lung machine normally used for heart surgery.

United States   On 9 Oct. 1986, Allen Smith, age 2, fell into the swollen waters of the Stanislaus River in Oakdale, CA. He was spotted 90 minutes later and rushed to Modesto Memorial Hospital, where two hours later his heart began beating again spontaneously.

Hiccupping   The longest recorded attack of hiccupping was that which afflicted Charles Osborne (1894–1991) of Anthon, IA, who had hiccupped continuously for 69 years 5 months, since 1922. He began hiccupping when he was slaughtering a hog and was unable to find a cure, but led a reasonably normal life in which he had two wives and fathered eight children. He hiccupped every 1½ seconds until a morning in February 1990. He died on 1 May 1991.

Fire-breather   Reg Morris blew a flame from his mouth to a distance of 31 ft. at the Miner's Rest, Chasetown, Great Britain on 29 Oct. 1986.

Fire extinguishers   Inge Widar Svingen, alias "Benifax" of Norway, on 10 Aug. 1990 extinguished 25,270 torches of flame in his mouth in 2 hrs at Kolvereid in Nord-Trøndelag, Norway.

On 26 July 1986 at Port Lonsdale, Victoria, Australia, Sipra Ellen Lloyd set a female record by extinguishing 8,357 torches. *Note: Fire-eating is potentially a highly dangerous activity*.

Lung power   The inflation of a standardized meteorological balloon to a diameter of 8 ft. against time was achieved by Nicholas Berkeley Mason in 45 min. 8 sec. at the British Broadcasting Corporation TV Centre, London, Great Britain on 25 Sep. 1989.

Most potent poison   The rickettsial disease Q-fever can be instituted by a *single* organism, though it is fatal in only 1 in 1,000 cases. About 10 organisms of *Francisella tularenesis* (formerly *Pasteurella tularenesis*) can initiate tularemia, variously called alkali disease, Francis disease or deerfly fever. This disease is fatal in upwards of 10 cases in 1,000.

Hospital stay   The longest stay in a hospital was by Miss Martha Nelson, who was admitted to the Columbus State Institute for the Feeble-Minded in Ohio in 1875. She died in January 1975 at the age of 103 years 6 months in the Orient State Institution, OH after spending more than 99 years in hospitals.

Human salamanders   The highest dry-air temperature endured by naked men in US Air Force experiments in 1960 was 400° F., and by heavily clothed men 500° F. (Steaks require only 325° F. to cook.) Temperatures of 284° F. have been found quite bearable in saunas.

Hunger strike   Doctors estimate that a well-nourished individual can survive without adverse medical consequences on a diet of sugar and water for 30 days or more. The longest period for which anyone has gone without solid food is 382 days in the case of Angus Barbieri (b. 1940) of Tayport, Great Britain, who lived on tea, coffee, water, soda water and vitamins in Maryfield Hospital, Dundee, Great Britain, from June 1965 to July 1966. His weight declined from 472 lbs. to 178 lbs. *Note: Records claimed without continuous medical surveillance are inadmissible.*

The longest recorded case of survival without food *and* water is 18 days by Andreas Mihavecz, then 18, of Bregenz, Austria, who was put in a holding cell on 1 Apr. 1979 in a local government building in Höchst, and then was totally forgotten by the police. On 18 Apr. 1979 he was discovered close to death, having had neither food nor water. He had been a passenger in a car that crashed.

The longest recorded hunger strike was 385 days, from 28 June 1972 to 18 July 1973, by Denis Galer Goodwin in Wakefield Prison, Great Britain, protesting his innocence of a rape charge. He was fed orally by tube.

Motionlessness   The longest that anyone has continuously remained motionless is 24 hours, by William Fuqua at Glendale, CA, on 17–18 May 1985 while sitting on a motorcycle.

António Gomes dos Santos of Zare, Portugal stood motionless for 15 hrs. 2 min. 55 sec. on 30 July 1988 at the Amoreiras Shopping Center, Lisbon.

Fastest nerve impulses   The results of experiments published in 1966 have shown that messages transmitted by the human nervous system can travel at 180 mph. With advancing age, impulses are carried 15 percent more slowly.

Heaviest organ   The skin is medically considered to be an organ. It weighs around 5.9 lbs. in an average adult. The heaviest internal organ is the liver at 3.3 lbs. This is four times heavier than the heart.

Pill-taking   The highest recorded total of pills swallowed by a patient is 565,939 between 9 June 1967 and 19 June 1988 by C.H.A. Kilner (1926–88) of Bindura, Zimbabwe.

Postmortem birth   The longest gestation interval in a postmortem birth was one of 84 days in the case of a girl born on 5 July 1983 to a brain-dead woman in Roanoke, VA who had been kept on a life support machine since April.

Pulse rates   A normal adult rate is 70–78 beats per min. at rest for males

MOTIONLESSNESS. António Gomes dos Santos stood still for 15 hrs. 2 min. 55 sec. No facial movements are allowed other than the involuntary blinking of the eyes.

and 75–85 for females. (The abnormal heart may beat as fast as 300 times per min., or the beat may be so slow as to be virtually undetectable). The heart rate may increase to 200 or more during violent exercise in the unfit. Super-fit athletes do not have to increase their heart rates nearly as much as this. The reason is that with training the fit heart can put out much more blood with each contraction. Thus it is able to produce the necessary increase of blood during exercise by raising its rate to perhaps only 140 beats per minute.

Sleeplessness   Victims of the very rare condition known as chronic colestites (total insomnia) have been known to go without definable sleep for many years.

Sneezing   The longest-lasting sneezing fit ever recorded is that of Donna Griffiths (b. 1969) of Pershore, Great Britain. She started sneezing on 13 Jan. 1981 and surpassed the previous duration record of 194 days on 27 July 1981. She sneezed an estimated million times in the first 365 days. She achieved her first sneeze-free day on 16 Sep. 1983—the 978th day.

The fastest speed at which particles expelled by sneezing have ever been measured to travel is 103.6 mph.

Snoring   The highest sound level recorded by any chronic snorer peaked at 90 decibels, measured at the Department of Medicine, University of British Columbia, Vancouver, Canada during the evening of 3 Nov. 1987. The meter was placed 2 ft. above the head of Mark Thompson Hebbard (b. 28 Feb. 1947) of Richmond, British Columbia, Canada, who maintained an overall level of 85 decibels. Since a Vancouver city traffic bylaw for acceptable noise stipulates a maximum of 80 decibels, he wonders if he is legally entitled to sleep there.

Standing   The longest period on record that anyone has continuously stood is more than 17 years in the case of Swami Maujgiri Maharaj when performing the *Tapasya* or penance from 1955 to November 1973 in Shahjahanpur, Uttar Pradesh, India. When sleeping he would lean against a plank. He died at the age of 85 in September 1980.

Swallowing   The worst reported case of compulsive swallowing of objects involved an insane female, Mrs. H., who at the age of 42 complained of a "slight abdominal pain." She proved to have 2,533 objects, including 947 bent pins, in her stomach. These were removed by Drs. Chalk and Foucar in June 1927 at the Ontario Hospital, Canada. In a more recent case, 212 objects were removed from the stomach of a man admitted to Groote Schuur Hospital, Cape Town, South Africa in May 1985. They included 53 toothbrushes, two telescopic aerials, two razors and 150 handles of disposable razors.

A compulsive swallower in the United States, a 24-year-old psychoneurotic woman, gulped down a 5-in.-long iron hinge bolt from a hospital door, which amazingly passed through the curve of the duodenum and the intestinal tract and broke the bedpan when the patient successfully passed the object.

Most tattoos   The ultimate in being tattooed is represented by Tom Leppard of the Isle of Skye, Scotland. He has chosen a leopard-skin design, with all the skin between the dark spots tattooed saffron yellow. The area of his body covered is approximately 3,002 in.², 99.2 percent of totality.

Bernard Moeller of Pennsylvania has the most separate designs, with 14,000 individual tattoos up to 3 Jan. 1992.

The world's most decorated woman is strip artiste "Krystyne Kolorful" (b. 5 Dec. 1952, Alberta, Canada). Her 95 percent bodysuit took 10 years to complete.

Under water   In 1986 two-year-old Michelle Funk of Salt Lake City, UT, made a full recovery after spending 66 minutes under water. The toddler fell into a swollen creek near her home while playing. When she was eventually discovered, rescue workers found she had no pulse or heartbeat. Her life was saved by the first successful bypass machine; it warmed her blood, which had dropped to 66° F. Doctors at the hospital described the time she had spent underwater as the "longest documented submergence with an intact neurological outcome."

Most injections   A diabetic, Mrs. Phyllis Lush (b. 25 Oct. 1916) of Darlington Point, New South Wales, Australia has given herself over 65,000 insulin injections during the past 69 years.

Longest in "iron lung"   Mrs. Laurel Nisbet (1912–85) of La Crescenta, CA was in an "iron lung" for 37 years 58 days continuously until her death.

OPERATIONS

Longest   The most protracted reported operation was one of 96 hrs. performed from 4–8 Feb. 1951 in Chicago, IL on Mrs. Gertrude Levandowski for the removal of an ovarian cyst. During the operation her weight fell from 616 lbs. to 308 lbs. The patient suffered from a weak heart and surgeons had to exercise the utmost caution during the operation.

Most performed   Dr. M.C. Modi, a pioneer of mass eye surgery in India since 1943, together with assistants, has performed as many as 833 cataract operations in one day, visited 45,416 villages and 10,094,632 patients, performing a total of 595,019 operations to February 1990.

Dr. Robert B. McClure (b. 1901) of Toronto, Ontario, Canada performed a career total of 20,423 major operations from 1924 to 1978.

Most endured Since 22 July 1954 Charles Jensen of Chester, SD has had 889 operations to remove the tumors associated with basal cell nevus syndrome. This is a rare genetically determined disorder characterized by multiple skin lesions which are usually first noticed in childhood and increase in size and number in late adolescence.

Stretcher bearing The record for carrying a stretcher case with a 140-lb. "body" is 142.3 miles in 38 hrs. 39 min. by two four-man teams from 1 Field Ambulance, Canadian Forces Base, Calgary, Canada on 5–7 Apr. 1989.

The record limited to youth organizations (under 20 years of age) and 8-hr. carrying is 42.02 miles by eight members of the Henry Meoles School, Moreton, Great Britain on 13 July 1980.

Eating Michel Lotito (b. 15 June 1950) of Grenoble, France, known as Monsieur Mangetout, has been eating metal and glass since 1959. Gastroenterologists have X-rayed his stomach and described his ability to consume 2 lbs. of metal per day as unique. His diet since 1966 has included 10 bicycles, a supermarket cart (in 4½ days), seven TV sets, six chandeliers, a low-calorie Cessna light aircraft and a computer. He is said to have provided the only example in history of a coffin (handles and all) ending up inside a man.

Oldest patient The greatest recorded age at which anyone has undergone an operation is 111 years 105 days in the case of James Henry Brett, Jr. (1849–1961) of Houston, TX. He underwent a hip operation on 7 Nov. 1960.

Earliest general anesthesia The earliest recorded operation under general anesthesia was for the removal of a cyst from the neck of James Venable by Dr. Crawford Williamson Long (1815–78), using diethyl ether $(C_2H_5)_2O$, in Jefferson, GA on 30 Mar. 1842.

Hemodialysis patient Raymond Jones (1929–91) of Slough, Great Britain suffered from kidney failure from the age of 34, and received continuous hemodialysis for 28 years. He averaged three visits per week to the Royal Free Hospital, London, Great Britain.

Munchausen's syndrome The most extreme recorded case of the rare and incurable condition known as Munchausen's syndrome (a continual desire to have medical treatment) was William McIloy (b. 1906), who cost Britain's National Health Service an estimated £2.5 million ($4 million) during his 50-year career as a hospital patient. During that time he had 400 major and minor operations, and stayed at 100 different hospitals using 22 aliases. The longest period he was ever out of the hospital was six months. In 1979

FASTEST AMPUTATION. A time of 13–15 seconds was recorded by French military surgeon Dominique Jean Larrey (1766–1842), for the amputation of a leg without anesthetic. Here he is shown demonstrating muscular contractions in a recently amputated leg due to galvanic effects. (Photo: Ann Ronan Picture Library)

he hung up his bedpan for the last time, saying he was sick of hospitals, and retired to an old people's home in Birmingham, Great Britain, where he died in 1983.

Fastest amputation   The shortest time recorded for a leg amputation in the pre-anesthetic era was 13–15 sec. by Napoleon's chief surgeon, Dominique Larrey. There could have been no ligation of blood vessels.

Largest tumor   The largest tumor ever recorded was Spohn's case of an ovarian cyst weighing 328 lbs. taken from a woman in Texas in 1905. She made a full recovery.

Largest gallbladder   On 15 Mar. 1989 at the National Naval Medical Center in Bethesda, MD, Prof. Bimal C. Ghosh removed a gallbladder that weighed 23 lbs. from a 69-year-old woman. The patient had been complaining of increasing swelling around the abdomen, and after removal of this enlarged gallbladder, which weighed more than three times as much as the average newborn baby, the patient felt perfectly well and left the hospital 10 days after the operation.

Gallstones   The largest gallstone reported in medical literature was one of 13 lbs. 14 oz. removed from an 80-year-old woman by Dr. Humphrey Arthure at Charing Cross Hospital, London, Great Britain on 29 Dec. 1952.
    In August 1987 it was reported that 23,530 gallstones had been removed

from an 85-year-old woman by Mr. K. Whittle Martin at Worthing Hospital, Sussex, Great Britain, after she complained of severe abdominal pain.

Surgical instruments   The largest instruments are robot retractors used in abdominal surgery, introduced by Abbey Surgical Instruments of Chingford, Great Britain in 1968 and weighing 11 lbs. Some bronchoscopic forceps measure 23½ in. in length.

   The smallest instrument is the microcystotome, a super microknife for cutting the lens capsule in eye microsurgery. The working part is 0.011 in. long and 2.03 in. wide. The instrument is licensed by the Research and Technology Complex of the Russian Ministry of Health, Moscow.

TRANSPLANTS

Heart   The first heart transplant operation was performed on Louis Washkansky, age 55, at the Groote Schuur Hospital, Cape Town, South Africa between 1 A.M. and 6 A.M., on 3 Dec. 1967, by a team of 30 headed by Professor Christiaan Neethling Barnard. The donor was Miss Denise Ann Darvall, age 25. Washkansky lived for 18 days.

United States   The first operation was performed on a 2½-week-old baby boy at Maimonides Hospital, Brooklyn, NY on 6 Dec. 1967 by a team of 22 headed by Dr. Adrian Kantrowitz. The donor was a newborn infant. The baby boy lived 6½ hours. The first adult transplant took place at the Stanford Medical Center in Palo Alto, CA on 6 Jan. 1968 by Dr. Norman E. Shumway and was performed on 54-year-old Mike Kasperak. Mr. Kasperak, a retired steelworker, lived 14 days. From December 1967 until February 1992 there have been 11,720 heart transplants. The greatest number of transplants in the United States in one year is 2,080, in 1990.

Double heart transplant   The first double heart transplant operation in the United States was performed on Darrell Hammarley, age 56, at the Stanford Medical Center in Palo Alto, CA on 20 Nov. 1968 by Dr. Norman E. Shumway. The first heart implanted failed to beat steadily and was replaced by a second transplant two hours later.

Longest surviving   William George van Buuren of California (1929–91) received an unnamed person's heart at the Stanford Medical Center, Palo Alto, CA on 3 Jan. 1970, and survived for 22 years 10 months 24 days. The surgeon who performed the operation was Dr. Edward Stinson.

Currently living   Arthur F. Gay (b. 3 Oct. 1936) is the longest-surviving heart transplant patient currently alive. His operation was performed at the Medical College of Virginia on 11 Jan. 1973 by Dr. Richard Lower.

> **Five-organ**   Tabatha Foster (1984–88) of Madisonville, KY, at 3 years 143 days of age, received a transplanted liver, pancreas, small intestine, portions of stomach and large intestine in a 15-hour operation at the Children's Hospital, Pittsburgh, PA on 31 Oct. 1987. Before the operation, she had never eaten solid food.

Youngest   Paul Holt of Vancouver, British Columbia, Canada underwent a heart transplant at Loma Linda Hospital in California on 16 Oct. 1987 at the age of 2 hrs. 34 min. He was born six weeks premature weighing 6 lbs. 6 oz.

First transplantee to give birth   Betsy Sneith, 23, gave birth to a girl, Sierra (7 lbs. 10 oz.), at the Stanford Medical Center, Palo Alto, CA on 17 Sep. 1984. She had received a donor heart in Feb. 1980.

Animal-to-human transplant   The first operation in the United States was carried out on 23 Jan. 1964 at the University of Mississippi Medical Center in Jackson, MS by a team of 12 headed by Dr. James D. Hardy. The patient, age 64, received the heart of a chimpanzee, which beat for 90 minutes.

Heart–lung–liver   The first triple transplant took place on 17 Dec. 1986 at Papworth Hospital, Cambridge, Great Britain when Mrs. Davina Thompson (b. 28 Feb. 1951) of Rawmarsh, Great Britain underwent surgery for seven hours by a team of 15 headed by chest surgeon Dr. John Wallwork and Prof. Sir Roy Calne.

Artificial heart   On 1–2 Dec. 1982 at the Utah Medical Center, Salt Lake City, UT, Dr. Barney B. Clark, 61, of Des Moines, WA was the first recipient of an artificial heart. The surgeon was Dr. William C. DeVries. The heart was a Jarvik-7 designed by Dr. Robert K. Jarvik. Dr. Clark died on 23 Mar. 1983, 112 days later. William J. Schroeder survived 620 days with an artificial heart in Louisville, KY from 25 Nov. 1984 to 7 Aug. 1986. The Food and Drug Administration (FDA) recalled the Jarvik-7 on 11 Jan. 1990. At the time of the recall it was the only artificial heart approved by the FDA and thus the only one allowed in the United States.

First synthetic heart implant   Haskell Karp, age 47, of Skokie, IL received the first synthetic heart implant on 4 Apr. 1969, at St. Luke's Episcopal Hospital, Houston, TX. Dr. Denton A. Cooley led the team of doctors, which included the developer of the heart, Dr. Domingo Liotta. The artificial heart was replaced by a human transplant on 7 April.

Kidney   Dr. Richard H. Lawler (USA; b. 1895) performed the first transplant of a kidney in a human at Little Company of Mary Hospital, Chicago, IL, on 17 June 1950. The first successful kidney transplant operation was performed at Peter Bent Brigham Hospital (now Brigham and Women's Hospital) in Boston, MA on 23 Dec. 1954 by a team of surgeons headed by Dr. John P. Merrill. The patient, Richard Herrick, age 23, received a kidney from his identical twin, Ronald. The longest surviving kidney transplant patient is Kathleen Severson (b. 25 July 1943) of Minnesota, whose operation was performed with her brother as donor on 8 July 1964, at the University of Minnesota Hospital. From 1977, when figures were first gathered, until 1989, there have been a total of 81,200 kidney transplants in the United States.

Lung   The first lung transplant operation in the United States took place on 11 June 1963 at the University of Mississippi Medical Center in Jackson, MS. The surgery, which was headed by Dr. James D. Hardy, lasted three hours and involved the replacement of the patient's left lung. The patient, John Richard Russell, survived 18 days.

SCIENCE AND TECHNOLOGY

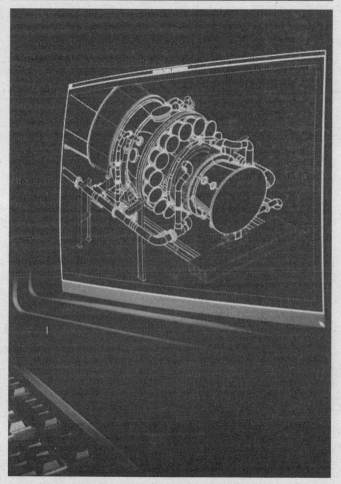

Computer-aided design. (Photo: Zefa Picture Library)

ELEMENTS

All known matter in, on and beyond the Earth is made up of chemical elements. It is estimated that there are 10^{87} electrons (the stable elementary particle present in all atoms) in the known universe. The total of naturally occurring elements is 92, comprising, at ordinary temperatures, two liquids, 11 gases and 79 solids.

Hydrogen (H) is the most common element, accounting for 90 percent of all known matter in the universe and 70.68 percent by mass in the solar system.

The so-called fourth state of matter is plasma, when negatively charged electrons and positively charged ions are in flux; 99 percent of all visible matter is in this form.

SUBNUCLEAR PARTICLES

Quarks are a set of at least six (up, down, charmed, strange, top and bottom) elementary particles and their corresponding antiparticles postulated to be the basic constituents of all baryons and mesons. Evidence for all except the top quark is now available. The lightest is the up quark with a short-range (current) mass of 6 MeV and a long-range mass of 350 MeV, and the heaviest is the as-yet unobserved top quark with a predicted mass of 140 GeV.

It is currently thought that there are only three "families" of quarks and leptons. The theoretical masses of the graviton (the as-yet unobserved gravitational gauge boson), the photon, and the three neutrino leptons should all be zero. Current experimental limits are less than 7.6×10^{-67} g for the gravi-

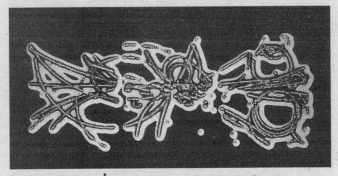

HEAVIEST PARTICLE. A Z° particle is too short-lived to be seen, but its existence is deduced from the "signature" of the electron–positron pair seen here emerging from the high-energy collision of a proton and an antiproton in the Super-Proton-Synchrotron (SPS) collider at CERN, Geneva, Switzerland. Debris of other particles with visible tracks also resulted from the collision. (Photo: Science Photo Library)

ton, less than 5.3×10^{-60} g for the photon, and less than 10 eV (less than 1.8×10^{-32} g) for the electron neutrino.

As of April 1990, physicists accepted the existence of three gauge bosons, six leptons and 136 hadron multiplets (77 meson multiplets and 59 baryon multiplets), representing the eventual discovery of 256 particles and an equal number of antiparticles.

Heaviest The heaviest particle accepted is the neutral weak gauge boson, the Z°, of mass 91.18 GeV and lifetime 2.64×10^{-25} sec., which was discovered in May 1983 by the UA1 Collaboration, CERN, Geneva, Switzerland.

Most stable The "Grand Unified Theory" of the weak, electromagnetic, and strong forces predicts that the proton will not be stable, but experiments indicate that the lifetime of the most likely decay mode (to a positron and a neutral pion) has a lower limit of 3.1×10^{32} years, which is over 40 times longer than the maximum lifetime predicted by the theory.

Least stable The shortest-lived subatomic particle is the neutral weak gauge boson Z° particle with a lifetime of 2.64×10^{-25} sec. (See Heaviest particle).

THE 109 ELEMENTS

There are 92 confirmed naturally occurring elements (up to plutonium), while to date 17 transuranic elements (atomic numbers 93 to 109) have been claimed, of which 10 are undisputed. The names for elements 104 (unnilquadium) to 109 (unnilennium) are provisional.

Most common The commonest element in the atmosphere is nitrogen (N), which is present at 78.08 percent by volume (75.52 percent by mass).

Rarest (natural) The least abundant element in the atmosphere is the radioactive gas radon (Rn), with a volume of 6×10^{-20} parts per million (ppm). This is only 5.3 lbs. overall, but concentrated amounts of this radioactive gas in certain granite areas have been blamed for a number of cancer deaths.

Most dense *Solid* The densest solid at room temperature is osmium (Os) at 0.8161 lb./in.^{3}.

Gas The heaviest gas is radon (Rn) at 0.6274 lb./ft.^{3}.

Least dense *Solid* The least dense element at room temperature is the metal lithium (Li) at 0.01927 lb./in.^{3}, although the density of solid hydrogen at its melting point of -434.546 °F. is only 0.00315 lb./in.^{3}.

Gas The lightest gas at NTP (Normal Temperature and Pressure, 0°C and one atmosphere) is hydrogen (H) at 0.005612 lb./ft.^{3}.

Melting/boiling point *Highest* The metallic element tungsten (or Wolfram) (W) melts at 6,188° F. On the assumption that graphite transforms to carbyne forms above 4,172° F., the nonmetal with the highest melting and boiling points would be carbon (C) at 6,386° F. and 6,998° F. respectively. However, this is disputed; an alternative suggestion is that graphite remains stable at high temperatures, sublimes directly to vapor at 6,728° F. and cannot be obtained in a liquid form unless the temperature exceeds 8,006° F. at a pressure of 10 MPa.

Lowest   Mercury (Hg) has the lowest melting (and boiling) point of the metals, at −37.892°F.

The gas helium (He) cannot be obtained as a solid at atmospheric pressure. The minimum pressure necessary is 24.985 atm (2.532 MPa), for solidification at a temperature of −458.275°F.

Boiling point   *Highest*   In addition to the highest melting point, tungsten has the highest boiling point at 10,580°F.

Lowest   The lowest boiling point is −452.070°F. for helium. The lowest for a metal is 673.92°F. for mercury.

Purest   In April 1978 P.V.E. McClintock of the University of Lancaster, Great Britain, reported success in obtaining the isotope helium 4 (He4) with impurity levels at less than two parts in 10^{15}.

Hardest substance   The carbon (C) allotrope diamond has a Knoop value of 8,400.

Thermal expansion   The metal with the highest expansion is cesium (Cs), at 94×10^{-5} per deg. C., while the diamond allotrope of carbon (C) has the lowest expansion at 1.0×10^{-6} per deg. C.

Most ductile   1 oz. of gold (Au) can be drawn to a length of 43 miles.

Highest tensile strength   The element with the highest tensile strength is boron (B) at 5.7 GPa 8.3 × 10^5 lbs./in.² as redetermined at the Technical Research Center of Finland.

Newest   The discovery of element 108 or unniloctium (Uno) (provisional IUPAC name) was announced in April 1984 by G. Münzenberg *et al.* and was based on the observation of only three atoms at the Gesellschaft für Schwerionenforschung (GSI), Darmstadt, Germany. A less-substantiated claim was made in June of the same year by Yu.Ts. Oganessian *et al.* of the Joint Institute for Nuclear Research, Dubna, Russia.

The single atom of the provisionally-named unnilennium (Une) produced at GSI on 29 Aug. 1982 represents the highest atomic number (109) and the heaviest atomic mass (266) obtained.

Isotopes   *Most*   The highest number is 36, shared by the gas xenon (Xe), with nine stable and 27 radioactive isotopes, and cesium (Cs; one stable and 35 radioactive).

The greatest number of stable isotopes is 10, for the metallic element tin (Sn).

Least   Hydrogen (H) has only three confirmed isotopes, including two stable (protium and deuterium) and one radioactive (tritium). Twenty elements exist naturally only as single nuclides.

Most stable   The most stable radioactive isotope is the double-beta decaying tellurium 128 (Te-128), with a half-life of 1.5×10^{24} years, a property confirmed in 1968, 44 years after its identification.

The alpha-decay record is 8×10^{15} years for samarium 148 (Sm-148) and the beta-decay record is 9×10^{15} years for cadmium 113 (Cd-113).

Least stable   Lithium 5 (Li-5) has a lifetime of 4.4×10^{-22} sec., determined in 1950.

Liquid range   Based on the differences between melting and boiling points, the element with the shortest liquid range (on the Celsius scale) is the inert gas neon (Ne) at only 2.5 degrees (from –248.6 to –246.1°C. [–415.5°F. to –411°F.]). The radioactive transuranic element neptunium (Np) has the longest liquid range, at 3,453 degrees (from 637 to 4,090°C. [1,179° F. to 7,394°F.]). However, based on the true range of liquids from their melting points to their critical points, the shortest range is for helium (He) at 5.19 degrees C. (9.351 degrees F.) from absolute zero (i.e., –273.15°C. to –267.95°C. [–459.67°F. to –450.32°F.]), and the largest range is for tungsten (W) at 10,200 degrees C. (8,360 degrees F.) (from 3,420 to 13,620°C. [from 6,188°F. to 24,548°F.]).

Toxicity   The most stringent restriction placed on a nonradioactive element is for beryllium (Be), with a threshold limit value in air of only 2 µg./m.^{3}. For radioactive isotopes, which occur naturally or are produced in nuclear installations and have ecologically significant half-lives (i.e., in excess of six months), the severest restriction in air is placed on thorium 228 (Th-228) or radiothorium, at 2.4×10^{-16} grams/m.^{3} (equivalent radiation intensity 0.0074 becquerel/m.^{3}).

The severest restriction in water is placed on radium 228 (Ra-228) or mesothorium I, at 1.1×10^{-13} grams/liter (equivalent radiation intensity 1.1 becquerel/liter).

PHYSICAL EXTREMES

Highest temperature   Temperatures produced in the center of a thermonuclear fusion bomb are of the order of 400,000,000°C. This temperature was attained in 1990 under controlled experimental conditions in the Tokamak Fusion Test Reactor at the Princeton Plasma Physics Laboratory, Princeton, NJ, by deuterium injection into a deuterium plasma.

Lowest temperature   The absolute zero of temperature, 0 K on the Kelvin scale, corresponds to –459.67°F. The lowest temperature ever reached is 2×10^{-9} Kelvin, i.e., two billionths of a degree above absolute zero. This was achieved at the Low Temperature Laboratory, Helsinki University of Technology, Finland in a nuclear demagnetization device and announced in October 1989.

Highest pressures   A sustained laboratory pressure of 1.70 megabars (11,000 tons force/in.^{2}) was achieved in the giant hydraulic diamond-faced press at the Carnegie Institution's Geophysical Laboratory, Washington, D.C.

and reported in June 1978. Using dynamic methods and impact speeds of up to 18,000 mph, momentary pressures of 75 million atmospheres (490,000 tons/in.^{2}) were reported from the United States in 1958.

Lowest friction   The lowest coefficient of static and dynamic friction of any solid is 0.04, in the case of polytetrafluoroethylene, or PTFE, ($[-C_2F_4-]$ñ), which is equivalent to wet ice on wet ice. It was first manufactured in quantity by E.I. du Pont de Nemours & Co. Inc. in 1943, and is marketed in the United States as Teflon.

In the centrifuge at the University of Virginia a 30-lb. rotor magnetically supported has been spun at 1,000 Hz in a vacuum of 10^{-6} mm. of mercury pressure. It loses only one revolution per second per day, thus spinning for years.

Highest velocity   The highest velocity at which any solid visible object has been projected is 93 miles/sec. (334,800 mph) in the case of a plastic disc at the Naval Research Laboratory, Washington, D.C., reported in August 1980.

Finest balance   The Sartorius Model 4108 manufactured in Göttingen, Germany can weigh objects of up to 0.018 oz. to an accuracy of 3.5×10^{-10} oz., equivalent to little more than one sixtieth of the weight of the ink on this period.

Largest bubble chamber   The $7 million installation, completed in Oct. 1973 at Batavia, IL, is 15 ft. in diameter. It contains 8,718 gallons of liquid hydrogen at a temperature of –413° F. and has a superconducting magnet of 3 tesla (a unit of magnetic induction). The last trackway was recorded on 1 Feb. 1988, in conjunction with Experiment 632.

Fastest centrifuge   Ultra-centrifuges were invented by Theodor Svedberg (Sweden; b. 30 Aug. 1884) in 1923.

The highest man-made rotary speed ever achieved and the fastest speed of any earthbound object is 4,500 mph by a swirling tapered 6-in. carbon fiber rod in a vacuum at Birmingham University, Great Britain reported on 24 Jan. 1975.

Finest cut   The $13 million large optics diamond turning machine at the Lawrence Livermore National Laboratory, CA was reported in June 1983 to be able to sever a human hair 3,000 times lengthwise.

Most powerful electric current   If fired simultaneously, the 4,032 capacitors comprising the Zeus capacitor at the Los Alamos Scientific Laboratory, NM would produce, for a few microseconds, twice as much current as that generated anywhere else on Earth.

Highest measured frequency   The highest *directly* measured frequency is a visible yellow-green light at 520.2068085 terahertz (a terahertz being a million million hertz or cycles per second) for the o-component of the 17–1 P (62) transition line of iodine-127.

The highest measured frequency determined by precision metrology is a green light at 582.491703 terahertz for the b_{21} component of the R (15) 43–0 transition line of iodine-127.

LARGEST BUBBLE CHAMBER. The 15-ft. Fermilab bubble chamber in Batavia, IL was decommissioned in 1988 after 15 years and was the world's last operational large cryogenic bubble chamber. (Photo: Fermilab Visual Media Services)

Thinnest glass   The thinnest glass, type D263, has a minimum thickness of 0.000984 in. and a maximum thickness of 0.00137 in. It is made by Deutsche Spezialglas AG, Grünenplan, Germany for use in electronic and medical equipment.

Smallest hole   In May 1983 it was reported from the University of Illinois that an electron microscope beam had accidentally bored a hole measuring 20 Å (2×10^{-9} m) in diameter in a sample of sodium beta-alumina.

Most powerful laser beams   The first illumination of another celestial body was achieved on 9 May 1962, when a beam of light was successfully reflected from the moon by the use of a laser attached to a 48 in. telescope at the Massachusetts Institute of Technology, Cambridge, MA. The spot was estimated to be 4 miles in diameter on the moon. The device was propounded in 1958 by the American Dr. Charles Hard Townes (b. 1915). Such a flash for $1/5000$th of a second can bore a hole through a diamond by vaporization at 18,032° F., produced by 2×10^{23} photons. The "Shiva" laser was reported at the Lawrence Livermore Laboratory, CA to be concentrating 2.6×10^{13} watts into a pinhead-sized target for 9.5×10^{-11} sec. in a test on 18 May 1978.

Brightest light   The brightest artificial sources are "laser" pulses generated at the Los Alamos National Laboratory, NM, announced in March 1987. An ultraviolet flash lasting one picosecond (1 trillionth sec.) is intensified to a power of 5×10^{15} watts.

The most powerful searchlight ever developed was one produced during World War II by the General Electric Company Ltd. at the Hirst Research Center in London, Great Britain. It had a consumption of 600 kW and gave an arc luminance of 300,000 candles/in.^{2} and a maximum beam intensity of 2.7 billion candles from its parabolic mirror (diameter 10 ft.).

Of continuously burning sources, the most powerful is a 313 kW high-pressure argon arc lamp of 1.2 million candlepower, completed by Vortek Industries Ltd. of Vancouver, British Columbia, Canada in March 1984.

Shortest light pulse   In 1988 it was announced that Charles V. Shank and colleagues at the AT&T Laboratories in New Jersey generated light pulses lasting just 6 femtoseconds (6×10^{-15} sec.). These pulses comprised three or four optical cycles (wavelengths of visible light).

Largest electromagnet   The world's largest electromagnet is part of the L3 detector, another experiment on LEP (large electron–positron collider). The octagonal-shaped magnet consists of 6,400 tons of low carbon steel yoke and 1,100 tons of aluminum coil. The yoke elements are welded pieces of up to 30 tons each and the coil consists of 168 turns welded together to form an eight-sided frame. Thirty thousand amperes of current flow through the aluminum coil to create a uniform magnetic field of 5 kilogauss. The magnet is higher than a four-story building of about 59,320 ft.^{3} volume. The total weight of the magnet, including the frame, coil and inner support tube, is 7,810 tons, and it is composed of more metal than the Eiffel Tower.

Magnetic fields   The strongest continuous field strength achieved was a total of 35.3 ± 0.3 teslas at the Francis Bitter National Magnet Laboratory, Massachusetts Institute of Technology in Cambridge, MA, on 26 May 1988, employing a hybrid magnet with holmium pole pieces. These had the effect of enhancing the central magnetic field of 31.8 teslas generated in the hybrid magnet.

The weakest magnetic field measured is one of 8×10^{-15} teslas in the heavily shielded room at the same laboratory. It is used by Dr. David Cohen for research into the very weak magnetic field generated in the heart and brain.

Most powerful microscope   The scanning tunneling microscope (STM) invented at the IBM Zürich research laboratory, Switzerland, in 1981 has a magnifying ability of 100 million and is capable of resolving down to one-hundredth the diameter of an atom (3×10^{-10} m). The fourth generation of the STM now being developed is said to be "about the size of a fingertip."

By using field ion microscopy, the tips of probes of scanning tunneling microscopes have been shaped to end in a single atom—the last three layers constituting the world's smallest man-made pyramid, consisting of 7, 3 and 1 atoms. Since the announcement in January 1990 that D.M. Eigler and E.K. Schweizer of the IBM Almaden Research Center, San Jose, CA had used an STM to move and reposition single atoms of xenon on a nickel surface in order to spell out the initials "IBM," other laboratories around the world have used similar techniques on single atoms of other elements.

Smallest optical prism Researchers at the National Institute of Standards and Technology laboratories in Boulder, CO have created a glass prism with sides 0.001 in.—barely visible to the naked eye. This should find application in fiber optics and instrumentation research.

Largest scientific instrument The largest scientific instrument so far (and arguably the world's largest machine) is the electron–positron storage ring "LEP" at CERN, housed in a ring tunnel 16.8 mile in circumference. The tunnel, 12½ ft. in diameter, runs between 164 and 492 ft. under the Earth's surface, and is accessible through 18 vertical shafts. Over 60,000 tons of technical equipment have been installed in the tunnel and its eight

---

Largest barometer An oil-filled barometer, of overall height 42 ft., was constructed by Allan Mills and John Pritchard of the Department of Physics and Astronomy, University of Leicester, Great Britain in 1991. It attained a standard height of 40 ft. (at which pressure mercury would stand at 2 ft. 6 in.).

Smallest thermometer Dr. Frederich Sachs, a biophysicist at the State University of New York at Buffalo, has developed an ultra-microthermometer for measuring the temperature of single living cells. The tip is one micron in diameter, about one-fiftieth the diameter of a human hair.

Hottest flame The hottest is carbon subnitride (C_4N_2), which, at one atmosphere pressure, can produce a flame calculated to reach 9,010°F.

Heaviest magnet The heaviest magnet is in the Joint Institute for Nuclear Research at Dubna, near Moscow, Russia, for the 10 GeV synchrophasotron measuring 196 ft. in diameter and weighing 42,518 tons.

Highest note A laser beam striking a sapphire crystal at the Massachusetts Institute of Technology, Cambridge, MA in September 1964 generated a note of 60 gigahertz.

Longest echo The longest echo in any building is one of 15 sec. following the closing of the door of the Chapel of the Mausoleum, Hamilton, Scotland, built 1840–55.

Smallest microphone Prof. Ibrahim Kavrak of Bogazici University, Istanbul, Turkey developed a microphone for a new technique of pressure measurement in fluid flow in 1967. It has a frequency response of 10 Hz–10 kHz and measures 0.06 × 0.03 in.

Scientific instrument The highest auction price paid for a scientific instrument is £385,000 ($654,500) for a 13½ in. Dutch gilt-brass astrolabe of 1559 by Walter Arsenius, sold at Christie's, London on 29 Sep. 1988.

underground work zones. It is intended to be a "Z° factory" producing up to 10,000 of these neutral weak gauge bosons every day in order to obtain a deeper understanding of the subatomic nature of matter. (See Heaviest particle.)

Most powerful particle accelerator The 1.25-mile diameter proton synchrotron at the Fermi National Accelerator Laboratory near Batavia, IL is the highest energy "atom smasher" in the world. On 14 May 1976 an energy of 500 GeV (5×10^{11}) was achieved for the first time. On 13 Oct. 1985 a center of mass energy of 1.6 TeV (1.6×10^{12} electron volts) was achieved by colliding beams of protons and antiprotons. This involves 1,000 superconducting magnets maintained at a temperature of $-452°$ F. by means of the world's largest (1,188 gallons per hour) helium liquefying plant, which began operating on 18 Apr. 1980.

On 16 Aug. 1983 the US Department of Energy set up a study for the superconducting supercollider (SSC) 1995 with two 20 TeV proton and antiproton colliding beams with a diameter of 52 miles at Waxahachie, TX.

Sharpest objects and smallest tubes The sharpest objects yet made are glass micropipette tubes used in intracellular work on living cells. Techniques were developed and applied in 1977 by Prof. Kenneth T. Brown and Dale G. Flaming of the Department of Physiology, University of California, San Francisco. The beveled tips achieved an outer diameter of 0.02 µm and an 0.01 µm inner diameter. The latter is 6,500 times thinner than a human hair.

Highest vacuum The highest vacuum was obtained at the IBM Thomas J. Watson Research Center, Yorktown Heights, NY in Oct. 1976 in a cryogenic system with temperatures down to $-452°$ F. This is equivalent to depopulating baseball-sized molecules from 1 yard to 50 miles apart.

Lowest viscosity The California Institute of Technology first announced on 1 Dec. 1957 that there was no measurable viscosity, i.e., perfect flow, in liquid helium II, which exists at temperatures close to absolute zero (-459.67 °F.).

Highest voltage The highest-ever potential difference obtained in a laboratory was 32 ± 1.5 million volts by the National Electrostatics Corporation at Oak Ridge, TN on 17 May 1979.

Most absorbent substance The US Department of Agriculture Research Service announced on 18 Aug. 1974 that "H-span" or Super Slurper, composed of one-half starch derivative and one-fourth each of acrylamide and acrylic acid, can, when treated with iron, retain water 1,300 times its own weight.

Finest powder The ultimate is solid helium, which was first postulated to be a monatomic powder as early as 1964.

Most refractory substance The most refractory substance is tantalum carbide ($TaC_{0.88}$), which melts at 7,214°F.

Least dense solids These are the silica aerogels in which tiny spheres of bonded silicon and oxygen atoms are joined into long strands separated by pockets of air. In February 1990 the lightest of these aerogels, with a density of only 5 oz./ft.^{3}, was produced at the Lawrence Livermore Laboratory, CA. The main use will be in space to collect micrometeoroids and the debris present in comets' tails.

Highest superconducting temperature
In May 1991, bulk superconductivity with a transition to zero resistance at $-231.3°$ F. was obtained by T. Kankeko, H. Yamauchi and S. Tanaka of the Superconducting Research Laboratory, International Superconducting Technology Center, in Tokyo, Japan for a mixed oxide of thallium, barium, calcium and copper ($Tl_{1.7}Ba_2Ca_{2.3}Cu_3O_z$).

Most magnetic substance
The most magnetic substance is neodymium iron boride ($Nd_2Fe_1B_4$) with a maximum energy product (the highest energy that a magnet can supply when operating at a particular operating point) of up to 280 kJ/m^3.

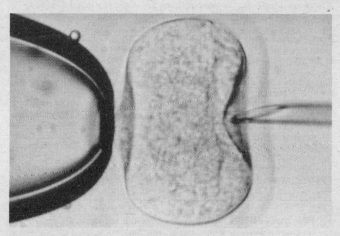

SMALLEST TUBE. The beveled tip (right) being used here to inject sperm cells directly into a human egg (center) during IVF (in-vitro fertilization) research has an inner diameter of just 0.01 μm. The relatively broad pipette used to hold the egg steady gives some idea of the minute scale. (Photo: Science Photo Library)

CHEMICAL EXTREMES

Smelliest substance   The most evil of the 17,000 smells so far classified must be a matter of opinion, but ethyl mercaptan (C_2H_5SH) and butyl seleno-mercaptan (C_4H_9SeH) are pungent claimants, each with a smell reminiscent of a combination of rotting cabbage, garlic, onions, burned toast and sewer gas.

Most powerful nerve gas   VX, 300 times more toxic than phosgene ($COCl_2$), used in World War I, was developed at the Chemical Defense Experimental Establishment, Porton Down, Great Britain, in 1952. Patents were applied for in 1962 and published in Feb. 1974 showing it to be ethyl S-2-diisopropylaminoethylmethylphosphonothiolate. The lethal dosage is 10 mg-minute/m^3 airborne or 0.3 mg. orally.

Most lethal man-made chemical   TCDD (2, 3, 7, 8-tetrachlorodibenzo-p-dioxin), the most deadly of the 75 known dioxins, is admitted to be 150,000 times more deadly than cyanide, at 3.1 trillion moles/kg.

Strongest acid and alkaline solutions   Normal solutions of strong acids such as perchloric acid ($HCLO_4$) and strong alkalis such as sodium hydroxide (NaOH), potassium hydroxide (KOH) and tetramethylammonium hydroxide ($N[CH_3]_4OH$), tend towards pH values of 0 and 14 respectively. However, this scale is inadequate for describing the "superacids," the strongest of which is estimated to be an 80 percent solution of antimony pentafluoride in hydrofluoric acid (fluoroantimonic acid HF: SbF_5). The acidity function, H_0, of this solution has not been measured but even a 50 percent solution has an acidity function of -30, so that this acid mixture is a quintillion (10^{18}) times stronger than concentrated sulfuric acid.

Pharmaceuticals   The world's largest pharmaceutical company is Johnson & Johnson of New Brunswick, NJ. The company employed a workforce of 82,200, generating sales of $12.44 billion in 1991. Total assets for the year were $10.5 billion.

Longest index   The 11th collective index of *Chemical Abstracts,* completed in December 1987, contains 29,406,094 entries in 162,992 pages and 93 volumes and weighs 407 lbs. It provides references to 2,812,413 published documents in the field of chemistry.

Chemicals   The largest manufacturer of chemicals in the United States is E. I. Du Pont de Nemours & Co. Inc. of Wilmington, DE. As of 31 December 1991, DuPont had sales of $38.7 billion, net income of $1.4 billion and a workforce of 133,000.

Sweetest substance Talin from arils (appendages found on certain seeds) of katemfe (*Thaumatococcus daniellii*), discovered in West Africa, is 6,150 times as sweet as a one percent sucrose solution.

MATHEMATICS

In dealing with large numbers, scientists use the notation of 10 raised to various powers to eliminate a profusion of zeros. For example, 19.16 trillion miles would be written 1.916×10^{13} miles. Similarly, a very small number, for example 0.0000154324 of a gram, would be written $1.543\ 24 \times 10^{-5}$. Of the prefixes used before numbers the smallest is "yocto," symbol Y, of power 10^{-24}, and the largest is "yotta," symbol Y, of power 10^{24}. Both are based on the Greek *octo*, eight (for the eighth power of 10^3).

Highest numbers The highest lexicographically accepted named number in the system of successive powers of ten is the centillion, first recorded in 1852. It is the hundredth power of a million, or 1 followed by 600 zeros.

The number 10^{100} is designated a googol. The term was suggested by the nine-year-old nephew of Dr. Edward Kasner (USA). Ten raised to the power of a googol is described as a googolplex. Some conception of the magnitude of such numbers can be gained when it is considered that the number of electrons in some models of the observable universe is believed to be of the order of 10^{87}. The highest named number outside the decimal notation is the Buddhist *asankhyeya*, which is equal to 10^{140} and is mentioned in Jain works of *c*. 100 B.C.

The highest number ever used in a mathematical proof is a bounding value published in 1977 and known as Graham's number. It concerns bichromatic hypercubes and is inexpressible without the special "arrow" notation, devised by Knuth in 1976, extended to 64 layers.

Prime numbers A prime number is any positive integer (excluding unity

---

Most innumerate The Nambiquara of the northwest Matto Grosso of Brazil lack any system of numbers. They do, however, have a verb that means "they are alike."

Oldest mathematical puzzle Apart from slight differences in wording, the following puzzle is identical to one found in the Rhind papyrus, an Egyptian scroll bearing mathematical tables and problems, copied by the scribe Ahmes *c*. 1650 B.C.:

As I was going to St. Ives, I met a man with seven wives. Every wife had seven sacks, every sack had seven cats, every cat had seven kits. Kits, cats, sacks and wives, how many were going to St. Ives?

1) having no integral factors other than itself and unity, e.g., 2, 3, 5, 7 or 11. The lowest prime number is thus 2.

The highest *known* prime number (known as a Mersenne prime) is $2^{756,839}-1$, discovered in February 1992 by analysts at AEA Technology's Harwell Laboratory, Great Britain. The number contains 227,832 digits (enough to fill over 18 pages of *The Guinness Book of Records*) and was found on a CRAY-2 supercomputer. (See Perfect numbers.)

The largest-known twin primes are $1,706,595 \times 2^{11,235} -1$ and $1,706,595 \times 2^{11,235} + 1$, found on 6 Aug. 1989 by a team in Santa Clara, CA using an Amdahl 1200 supercomputer.

MOST PROVED THEOREM. Part of a manuscript written by the Greek philosopher and mathematician Pythagoras (c. 580–500 B.C.), whose theorem has at least 370 different published proofs. (Photo: Science Photo Library)

Composite numbers   The lowest nonprime or composite number (excluding 1) is 4.

Perfect numbers   A number is said to be perfect if it is equal to the sum of its divisors other than itself, e.g., $1 + 2 + 4 + 7 + 14 = 28$. The lowest perfect number is 6 ($=1 + 2 + 3$).

The highest known perfect number, and the 32nd so far discovered, is $(2^{756,839}-1) \times 2^{756,838}$. It has a total of 455,663 digits, a consequence of the largest Mersenne prime (also the largest prime known) being $2^{756,839}-1$, discovered in February 1992. (See Prime numbers.)

Newest mathematical constant   The study of turbulent water, the weather and other chaotic phenomena has revealed the existence of a new universal constant, the Feigenbaum number. Named after its discoverer, Mitchell Feigenbaum (USA), it equals approximately 4.669201609102990.

Most-proved theorem   A book published in 1940 entitled *The Pythagorean Proposition* contained 370 different proofs of Pythagoras' theorem, including one by President James Garfield.

Longest proof   The proof of the classification of all finite simple groups is spread over more than 14,000 pages in nearly 500 papers in mathematical journals, contributed by more than 100 mathematicians over a period of more than 35 years.

Most prolific mathematician   Leonard Euler (Switzerland; 1707–83) was so prolific that his papers were still being published for the first time more than 50 years after his death. His collected works have been printed bit by bit since 1910 and will eventually occupy more than 75 large quarto volumes.

Largest mathematical prize   Dr. Paul Wolfskell left prize money in his will for the first person to solve the last theorem of Pierre Fermat (1601–65). This prize was worth 100,000 deutsch marks in 1908. As a result of inflation, the prize is now worth just over 10,000 deutsch marks.

Most accurate version of pi   On 19 Nov. 1989 the greatest number of decimal places to which *pi* (π) had been calculated was 1,073,740,000 by Yasumasa Kanada and Yoshiaki Tamura of the University of Tokyo, Japan using a Hitac S-820/80E computer.

Most inaccurate version of pi   In 1897 the General Assembly of Indiana enacted Bill No. 246 stating that *pi* was *de jure* 4. In 1853 William Shanks published his calculation of π to 707 decimal places, all calculated by hand. Ninety-two years later, in 1945, it was discovered that the last 180 digits were in fact all incorrect.

Earliest measures   The earliest known measure of weight is the *beqa* of the Amratian period of Egyptian civilization *c.* 3800 B.C., found at Naqada, Egypt. The weights are cylindrical, with rounded ends, and weigh 6.65–7.45 oz.

The unit of length used by the megalithic tomb-builders in northwestern Europe *c.* 3500 B.C. appears to have been 2.72 ± 0.003 ft. This was deduced by Prof. Alexander Thom (1894–1985) in 1966.

Time measure Because of variations in the length of a day, which is estimated to be increasing irregularly at an average rate of about a millisecond per century due to the moon's tidal drag, the second has been redefined. Instead of being 1/86,400th part of a mean solar day, it has, since 1960, been reckoned as 1/315,569,259,747th part of the solar (or tropical) year at A.D. 1900, January 0.12 hr., Ephemeris time. In 1958 the second of Ephemeris time was computed to be equivalent to $9,192,631,770 \pm 20$ cycles of the radiation corresponding to the transition of cesium-133 atoms when unperturbed by exterior fields. The greatest diurnal change recorded was 10 milliseconds on 8 Aug. 1972, due to the most violent solar storm recorded in 370 years of observations.

The accuracy of the cesium beam frequency standard approaches eight parts in 10^{14}, compared to two parts in 10^{13} for the methane-stabilized helium-neon laser and six parts in 10^{13} for the hydrogen maser.

The longest measure of time is the *kalpa* in Hindu chronology. It is equivalent to 4,320 million years. In astronomy a cosmic year is the period of rotation of the sun around the center of the Milky Way galaxy, i.e., 225 million years. In the Late Cretaceous Period of *c.* 85 million years ago the Earth rotated faster, resulting in 370.3 days per year, while in Cambrian times, *c.* 600 million years ago, there is evidence that the year comprised 425 days.

COMPUTING

Earliest The earliest programmable electronic computer was the 1,500-valve Colossus formulated by Prof. Max H.A. Newman (1897–1985) and built by T.H. Flowers. It was run in December 1943 at Bletchley Park, Great Britain to break the German coding machine Enigma. It arose from a concept published in 1936 by Dr. Alan Mathison Turing (Great Britain; 1912–54) in his paper *On Computable Numbers with an Application to the Entscheidungsproblem*. Colossus was declassified on 25 Oct. 1975.

The world's first stored-program computer was the Manchester University (Great Britain) Mark I, which incorporated the Williams storage cathode ray tube (patented 11 Dec. 1946). It ran its first program, by Prof. Tom Kilburn (b. 1921), for 52 min. on 21 June 1948.

Computers were greatly advanced by the invention of the point-contact transistor by John Bardeen and Walter Brattain announced in July 1948, and the junction transistor by R.L. Wallace, Morgan Sparks and Dr. William Bradford Shockley (1910–89) in early 1951.

The concept of the integrated circuit, which has made micro-miniaturization possible, was first published on 7 May 1952 by Geoffrey W.A. Dummer (Great Britain; b. 1909) in Washington, D.C.

The invention of the microcomputer was attributed to a team led by M.E. Hoff, Jr. of Intel Corporation with the production of the microprocessor chip "4004" in 1969–71. However, on 17 July 1990 priority was accorded to Gilbert Hyatt (b. 1938), who devised a single chip microcomputer at Micro Computer Inc. of Van Nuys, Los Angeles, CA in 1968–71 with the award of US Patent No. 4942516.

Most powerful The world's most powerful computer is the liquid-cooled

CRAY-2, from Cray Research Inc., Minneapolis, MN. Its memory has a capacity of 256 million 64-bit words, resulting in a capacity of 2.12 gigabytes of central memory. (A "byte" is a unit of storage comprising eight "bits" that are collectively equivalent to one alphabetic symbol or two numericals; "giga" denotes 10^9.) It attains speeds of 250 million floating point operations per second.

Fastest In 1992 it was reported that Cray Research had developed a parallel vector system, the Y-MP C90 supercomputer, with 2 gigabytes of central memory and with 16 CPUs (central processing units), giving a combined peak performance of 16 gigaflops/sec. (16 billion floating point operations per second).

Sandia National Laboratory, NM on 18 Mar. 1988 announced a "massively parallel" hypercube computer with 1,024 parallel processors, which, by breaking down problems into parts for simultaneous solution, proved 1,019 times faster than any conventional mainframe computer.

Smallest modem Modems are devices that allow electron signals to be transmitted over large distances by MOdulating the signal at one end, and DEModulating the signal back to its original form at the destination, hence the name. The smallest is the SRM-3A, which is 2.4 in. long, 1.2 in. wide, and 0.8 in. high, and weighs 1.1 oz. It is currently manufactured by RAD Data Communications Ltd. of Tel Aviv, Israel.

Fastest chip In March 1992 it was reported that DEC of Maynard, MA had developed an all-purpose computer chip, a 64-bit processor known as Alpha, which could run at speeds of up to 150 MHz (compared with 25 MHz for many modern personal computers). One Alpha chip is claimed to have about the same processing power as a CRAY-1, which went on sale in 1976 as the Cray company's first supercomputer, at a cost of $7.5 million.

Fastest transistor A transistor capable of switching 230 billion times per second was announced by Illinois State University on 5 Oct. 1986.

Longest computer computation for a yes–no answer
The twentieth Fermat number, $2^{2^{20}} + 1$, was tested on a CRAY-2 supercomputer in 1986 to see if it was a prime number. After 10 days of calculation the answer was no.

Computer company The world's largest computer firm is International Business Machines (IBM) Corporation of Armonk, NY. As of 31 Dec. 1991, gross revenues were $64.792 billion, net earnings were $2.827 billion and assets were $92.473 billion. The company has 344,396 employees worldwide and 772,047 stockholders.

Earliest atomic pile The world's first atomic pile was built in a disused squash court at Stagg Field, University of Chicago, IL. It went "critical" at 3:25 P.M. local time on 2 Dec. 1942.

POWER

Largest power plant   Currently, the most powerful installed power station is the Raul Leoni hydro-electric plant in Guri, Venezuela, which has a capacity of 10,300 MW.

The $11-billion Itaipu power station on the Paraná River near the Brazil–Paraguay border began generating power formally on 25 Oct. 1984 and will attain 13,320 MW from 18 turbines. Construction began in 1975 with a work force approaching 28,000. A 20,000 MW power station project on the Tunguska River, Russia was announced in February 1982.

Nuclear power stations *Earliest*   The first nuclear power station producing electricity was the EBR-1 (Experimental Breeder Reactor) in Shippingport, PA on 20 Dec. 1951. The station had a capacity of 60 MW. It was shut down in 1974, then resumed operation in 1977 before it was retired in 1984.

As of 31 December 1990, there were 111 nuclear power plants operating in the United States, with a total net summer capability of 99,588 MW. Illinois has the greatest number of stations, at 13.

Largest   The world's largest nuclear power station, with 10 reactors and net output of 8,814 MW, is the station in Fukushima, Japan.

The largest nuclear power complex in the United States is at Wintersburg, AZ. The three Palo Verde, CA units have a net summer capability of 3,663 MW. The largest unit in the country is found in Bay City, TX. The South Texas 1 unit has a capability of 1,251 MW; the South Texas 2 unit's capability is 1,250 MW.

Nuclear reactors   The largest single nuclear reactor in the world is the Ignalina station, Lithuania, which came fully in stream in January 1984 and has a net capacity of 1,380 MW.

The largest under construction is the CHOOZ-B1 reactor in France. Work began on site in July 1982 and the first reactor became operational in 1991 with a planned net capacity of 1,455 MW.

Fusion power   Tokamak-7, the experimental thermonuclear apparatus, was declared in January 1982 by the then Soviet academician Velikhov to be operating "reliably for months on end." An economically viable thermonuclear reactor is not anticipated anywhere in the world in this millennium.

The first significant controlled fusion power production was achieved on 9 Nov. 1991 at the Joint European Torus (JET) at Culham, Great Britain by tritium injection into a deuterium plasma. Optimum fusion was sustained for about 2 sec. and produced a power rating of 1.7 megawatts. Temperatures at the center of thermonuclear fusion explosions have been found to be about 400,000,000° C. (See Physical Extremes, Highest temperature.)

Solar power   The largest solar furnace in the world is the LUZ plant, located in the Mojave Desert, 140 miles northeast of Los Angeles, CA. It is currently operating the world's nine largest solar electric generating systems (SEGS), which account for more than 92 percent of the the world's solar electricity. LUZ is now producing 354 MW. SEGS IX is the second phase in a six-plant, $1.5 billion solar development program due for completion in 1994 that will bring the total to 675 MW.

The $30 million thermal solar energy system at the Packerland Packing Co. Bellevue Plant, Green Bay, WI, completed in January 1984, comprises 9,7504 × 8 ft. collectors covering 7.16 acres. It can yield up to 8,000 million BTUs a month.

There were seven solar-powered and 16 wind-powered electric generating plants in the United States as of 1990, owned and operated by public utility companies. California had the most solar plants, with three, while Minnesota had the most wind-powered plants, also three.

Tidal power station   The world's first major station is the *Usine maré-motrice de la Rance*, officially opened on 26 Nov. 1966 on the Rance estuary in the Golfe de St.-Malo, Brittany, France. It has a net annual output of 544 million kW. The 2,640 ft. barrage contains 24 turbo alternators.

Largest boilers   The largest boilers ever designed were those ordered in the United States from Babcock & Wilcox (USA), with a capacity of 1,330 MW, involving the evaporation of 9.33 million lbs. of steam per hour.

Largest generators   The largest operational is a turbo generator of 1,450 MW (net) being installed at the Ignalina atomic power station in southern Lithuania. However, dynamos in the 2,000,000 kW (or 2,000 MW) range are now in the planning stages both in Great Britain and the United States.

Turbines   The largest hydraulic turbines are those rated at 815,000 kW (equivalent to 1.1 million hp), 32 ft. in diameter with a 449 ton runner and a 350 ton shaft installed by Allis-Chalmers at the Grand Coulee Third Power-plant, WA.

Pump   The world's largest reversible pump-turbine is that made by Allis-Chalmers for the Bath County project, VA. It has a maximum rating of 457 MW as a turbine and maximum operating head of 1,289 ft. The impeller/run-ner diameter is 20 ft. 9 in., with a synchronous speed of 257.1 rev./min.

Gas   The largest gas turbine is type GT 13 E from BBC Brown Boveri AG, with a maximum output of 140 MW. The first machine installed in Holland was to increase the general output of a 500 MW steam-powered plant (Hemweg 7) by more than 46 percent.

The smallest self-sustaining gas turbine is one with 2 in. compressor and turbine wheels built by Geoff Knights of London, Great Britain. It has an operating speed of 50,000 rev./min.

Battery *Largest*   The 10 MW lead-acid battery at Chino, CA has a de-sign capacity of 40 MW/h. It will be used at an electrical substation for lev-eling peak demand loads. This $13 million project is a cooperative effort by Southern California Edison Company Electric Power Research Institute and International Lead Zinc Research Organization Inc.

Most durable   The zinc foil and sulfur dry-pile batteries made by Watlin and Hill of London, Great Britain in 1840 have powered ceaseless tintinnab-ulation inside a bell jar at the Clarendon Laboratory, Oxford, Great Britain since that year.

BIGGEST BLACKOUT. About 30 million people across the US and Canada were affected by the world's largest power failure on 9–10 Nov. 1965. This filtered image, taken from the Defense Meteorological Satellite Program spacecraft, shows normal electricity usage and provides an accurate indication of population densities across several time zones. By extrapolation, one can imagine the scope of that November power failure. (Photo: Science Photo Library)

Biggest blackout   The greatest power failure in history struck seven northeastern US states and Ontario, Canada on 9–10 Nov. 1965. About 30 million people in 80,000 miles² were plunged into darkness. Only two people died as a result of the blackout. In New York City the power failed at 5:27 P.M. and was not fully restored for 13½ hrs.

The total losses in the 52-min. New York City power failure of 13 July 1977, including looting, were put at $1 billion.

Windmills *Earliest*   The earliest recorded windmills were those used for grinding corn in Persia (now Iran) in the 7th century A.D.

Tallest   The De Noord windmill in Schiedam, Netherlands at 109 ft. 4 in. is the tallest in Europe.

Most powerful   The world's first 3,000 kW wind generator was the 492 ft. tall turbine built by Grosse Windenergie–Anlage, which was set up in 1982 on the Friesian coast of Germany.

The $14.2 million GEC MOD-5A installation on the north shore of Oahu, HI produces 7,300 kW when the wind reaches 32 mph with 400 ft. rotors. Installation was started in March 1984.

Oldest water mill   The water mill with the oldest continuous commercial use is at Priston Mill near Bath, Great Britain, first mentioned in A.D. 931 in a charter to King Athelstone (924/5–939). It is driven by the Conygre Brook and is the only remaining working water mill of the 5,700 recorded in the Domesday Book of 1085.

Tidal mill   On 12 Nov. 1989 the Eling Tide Mill, Great Britain attained 16 hr. 7 min. rotation of the waterwheel in one day. It is the only surviving mill in the world harnessing the power of the tide for regular production of wholemeal flour.

ENGINEERING

Oldest machinery   The earliest mechanism still in use is the *dâlu*—a water-raising instrument known to have been in use in the Sumerian civilization, which originated *c.* 3500 B.C. in what is now lower Iraq.

Blast furnace   The world's largest blast furnace has an inner volume of 185,224 ft.^{3} and a 49 ft. diameter hearth at ZBF at the Oita Works, Kyūshū, Japan, completed in October 1976 with 4.2 tons annual capacity.

Catalytic cracker   The world's largest catalytic cracker is Exxon's Bayway Refinery plant at Linden, NJ, with a fresh feed rate of 5.04 million gals. per day.

Concrete pumping   The world record distance for pumping ready-mixed concrete without a relay pump is 4,986 ft., set on the Lake Chiemsee, Bavaria, Germany sewage tunnels project in the summer of 1989.

Conveyor belts   The world's longest single-flight conveyor belt is one of 18 miles in Western Australia installed by Cable Belt Ltd. of Camberley, Great Britain.

The world's longest multiflight conveyor was one of 62 miles between the phosphate mine near Bucraa and the port of El Aiún, Morocco, built by Krupps and completed in 1972. It had 11 flights of 5.6–6.8 miles and was driven at 10.06 mph. It has since been closed down.

Most powerful cranes   The greatest single load lifted by cranes is over 10,750 metric tons during the positioning of an integrated module onto the Piper Bravo platform in the North Sea off Aberdeen, Scotland in December 1991. The record lift was carried out by twin AmClyde 6000 cranes, designed and built by AmClyde Engineered Products Inc. of St. Paul, MN and installed onboard the vessel *Derrick Barge 102*.

Gantry crane   The 92.3 ft. wide Rahco (R.A. Hanson Disc Ltd.) gantry crane at the Grand Coulee Dam Third Powerplant was tested to lift a load of 2,460 tons in 1975. It lowered a 1,972 ton generator rotor with an accuracy of 1.32 in.

Tallest mobile crane   The 890-ton Rosenkranz K10001, with a lifting capacity of 1,100 tons, and a combined boom and jib height of 663 ft., is carried on 10 trucks, each limited to a length of 75 ft. 8 in. and an axle weight of 130 tons. It can lift 33 tons to a height of 525 ft.

The Taklift 4 craneship of the Smit International fleet based in Rotterdam, the Netherlands has a boom and jib height of 312 ft.

Most powerful diesel engines   Five 12RTA84 type diesel engines have been constructed by Sulzer Brothers of Winterthur, Switzerland, for containerships built for the American President Lines. Each 12-cylinder power unit gives a maximum continuous output of 57,000 bhp at 95 rev./min. The first of these ships, the *President Truman*, was handed over in April 1988.

Draglines   The Ural Engineering Works in Yekaterinburg (formerly Sverdlovsk), Russia, completed in March 1962, has a dragline known as the ES-25 (100), with a boom of 328 ft., and a bucket with a capacity of 848 ft.[3]

The world's largest walking dragline is "Big Muskie," the Bucyrus-Erie 4250W with an all-up weight of 13,200 tons and a bucket capacity of 5,933 ft.[3] on a 310 ft. boom. This is the largest mobile land machine and is now operating on the Central Ohio Coal Co. Muskingum site in Ohio.

Earthmover   The giant wheeled loader developed for open-air coal mining in Australia by SMEC, a consortium of 11 manufacturers in Tokyo, Japan, is 55.1 ft. in length, weighs 198 tons, and has rubber tires 11.5 ft. in diameter. The bucket has a capacity of 671 ft.[3]

Escalators   The term "escalator" was registered in the United States on 28 May 1900, but the earliest "inclined escalator" was installed by Jesse W. Reno on the pier at Coney Island, NY in 1896. The escalators at the station formerly named Lenin Square on the St. Petersburg (Leningrad), Russia underground have 729 steps and a vertical rise of 195 ft. 9½ in.

The world's longest *ride* is on the four-section outdoor escalator at Ocean Park, Hong Kong, which has an overall length of 745 ft. and a total vertical rise of 377 ft.

Moving walkways   The world's longest "moving sidewalks" are those installed in 1970 in the Neue Messe Center, Dusseldorf, Germany, which measure 738 ft. between comb plates.

The ultimate in pampering for weary shoppers is the escalator at the shopping mall at Kawasaki-shi, Japan. It has a vertical height of 32.83 in. and was installed by Hitachi Ltd.

Forging   The largest forging on record is one of a 225-ton, 55-ft.-long generator shaft for Japan, forged by the Bethlehem Steel Corporation of Pennsylvania in October 1973.

Forklift trucks   Kalmar LMV of Sweden in 1985 manufactured ten counterbalanced forklift trucks capable of lifting loads up to 99 tons at a load center of 90.5 in. They were built to handle the Libyan Great Man-made River Project, comprising two separate pipelines, one 620 miles long running from Sawir to Gulf of Sirte and the other 575 miles from Tazirbu to Benghazi, Libya.

Lathe   The largest is the 126-ft.-long 460-ton giant lathe built by Waldrich

Siegen of Germany in 1973 for the South African Electricity Supply Commission at Rosherville. It has a capacity for 330-ton workpieces and a swing-over bed of 16 ft. 5 in. in diameter.

Greatest load raised   The heaviest lifting operation in engineering history was the raising of the entire 0.745 mile long offshore Ekofisk complex in the North Sea, Great Britain, owing to subsidence of the seabed. The complex consists of eight platforms weighing some 44,090 tons. During 17–18 Aug. 1987 it was raised 21 ft. 4 in. by 122 hydraulic jacks requiring a computer-controlled hydraulic system developed and supplied by Hydraudyne Systems & Engineering bv of Boxtel, Netherlands.

Escalator riding   The record distance traveled on a pair of "up" and "down" escalators is 133.18 miles, by David Beattie and Adrian Simons at Top Shop in London, Great Britain, from 17 to 21 July 1989. They each completed 7,032 circuits.

Top-spinning   The duration record for spinning a clock-balance wheel by unaided hand is 5 min. 26.8 sec. by Philip Ashley, 16, of Leigh, Great Britain on 20 May 1968.
    The record using 36 in. of string with a 7¼-oz. top is 58 min. 20 sec., by Peter Hodgson at Southend-on-Sea, Great Britain on 4 Feb. 1985.
    A team of 25 from the Mizushima Plant of Kawasaki Steel Works in Okayama, Japan spun a giant top 6 ft. 6¾ in. tall and 8 ft. 6¾ in. in diameter, weighing 793.6 lbs., for 1 hr. 21 min. 35 sec. on 3 Nov. 1986.

Slowest machine   A nuclear environmental machine for testing stress corrosion has been developed by Nene Instruments of Wellingborough, Great Britain that can be controlled at a speed as slow as one million millionth of a millimeter per minute, or one meter (3.28 ft.) in about 2 billion years.

Largest nuts   The largest nuts ever made weigh 5 tons each with an outside diameter of 52 in. and a 25 in. thread. Known as "Pilgrim Nuts," they are manufactured by Pilgim Moorside Ltd. of Oldham, Great Britain for use on the columns of a large forging press.

Oil tanks   The largest oil tanks ever constructed are the five ARAMCO 1½-million-barrel storage tanks at Ju'aymah, Saudi Arabia. They are 72 ft. tall with a diameter of 386 ft. and were completed in March 1980.

Passenger elevators   The fastest domestic passenger elevators in the world are the express elevators to the 60th floor of the 787.4 ft. tall "Sunshine 60" building, Ikebukuro, in Tokyo, Japan, completed 5 Apr. 1978. They were built by Mitsubishi Corporation and operate at a speed of 2,000 ft./min. or 22.7 mph.
    Much higher speeds are achieved in the winding cages of mine shafts. A

hoisting shaft 6,800 ft. deep, owned by Western Deep Levels Ltd. in South Africa, winds at speeds of up to 40.9 mph (3,595 ft./min.). Otitis media (popping of the ears) presents problems above even 10 mph.

Pipelines *Earliest* The world's earliest pipeline, of 2 in. diameter cast iron, was laid at Oil Creek, PA in 1863, but was torn up by Luddites (opponents of industrial change or innovation).

Oil The longest crude oil pipeline in the world is the Interprovincial Pipe Line Company installation from Edmonton, Alberta, Canada to Buffalo, NY, a distance of 1,775 miles. Along the length of the pipe, 13 pumping stations maintain a flow of 8.3 million gals. of oil per day.

The ultimate length of the Trans-Siberian pipeline will be 2,319 miles, running from Tuimazy through Omsk and Novosibirsk to Irkutsk. The first 30-mile section was opened in July 1957.

Gas The longest natural gas pipeline in the world is the Trans-Canada pipeline, which by 1974 had 5,654 miles of pipe up to 42 in. in diameter. The world's longest submarine pipeline is 264 miles long and carries natural gas from the Union Oil platform to Rayong, Thailand. It opened on 12 Sep. 1981.

Water The world's longest water pipeline runs a distance of 350 miles to the Kalgoorlie goldfields from near Perth in Western Australia. Engineered in 1903, the system has since been extended fivefold by branches.

Most expensive The world's most expensive pipeline is the Alaska pipeline running 800.3 miles from Prudhoe Bay to Valdez. On completion of the first phase in 1977, it had cost $8 billion. The pipe is 48 in. in diameter and its capacity is now 2.1 million barrels per day.

Presses The world's two most powerful production machines are forging presses in the United States. The Loewy closed-die forging press, in a plant leased from the US Air Force by the Wyman-Gordon Company at North Grafton, MA, weighs 10,438 tons and stands 114 ft. 2 in. high, of which 66 ft. is sunk below the operating floor. It has a rated capacity of 49,163 tons and became operational in October 1955. A similar press is at the plant of the Aluminum Company of America in Cleveland, OH.

The greatest press force of any sheet metal forming press is 116,844 tons for a QUINTUS fluid cell press delivered by ASEA to BMG AG in Munich, Germany in January 1986. The Bêché & Grohs counter-blow forging hammer, manufactured in Germany, is rated at 66,138 tons.

Printer The world's fastest printer was the Radiation Inc. electro-sensitive system at the Lawrence Radiation Laboratory, Livermore, CA. It printed up to 36,000 lines per minute, each containing 120 alphanumeric characters per minute, attained by controlling electronic pulses through chemically impregnated recording paper that was moving rapidly under closely spaced fixed styli. It could thus print the entire wordage of the Bible (773,692 words) in 65 seconds—3,048 times as fast as the peak rate of the world's fastest typist. (See Literature, The Bible, and Miscellaneous Endeavors, Fastest typist.)

Radar installations The largest of the three installations in the US Ballistic Missile Early Warning System (BMEWS) is that near Thule, in Greenland, 931 miles from the North Pole. It was completed in 1960 at a cost of $500 million. Its sister stations are one at Cape Clear, AK, which was completed in 1961, and the $115 million radar installation at Fylingdales Moor, Great Britain, which was completed in June 1963.

The largest scientific radar installation is the 21-acre ground array at Jicamarca, Peru.

Ropes The largest rope ever made was a coil fiber launching rope with a circumference of 47 in. made in 1858 for the British liner *Great Eastern* by John and Edwin Wright of Birmingham, Great Britain. It consisted of four strands, each of 3,780 yarns. The longest fiber rope ever made without a splice was one of 11.36 miles of 6½ in. circumference manila by Frost Brothers (now British Ropes Ltd.) in London, Great Britain in 1874.

Wire ropes The longest wire ropes in the world are the four made at British Ropes Ltd., Wallsend, Great Britain, each measuring 14.9 miles. The ropes are 1.3 in. in diameter, weigh 120 tons each, and were ordered by the CEGB for use in the construction of the 2,000 MW cross-Channel power cable.

The suspension cables on the Seto Grand Bridge, Japan, completed in 1988, are 41 in. in diameter. The thickest ever manufactured are spliced crane strops from wire ropes 11¼ in. thick with 2,392 individual wires made in Mar. 1979 by British Ropes Ltd. of Doncaster at Willington Quay, Great Britain, and designed to lift loads of up to 3,307 tons.

The heaviest-ever wire ropes (four in number) are each of 143 tons, made for the twin shaft system of Western Deep Levels gold mine, South Africa by Haggie Rand Ltd. of Johannesburg.

The strongest cable-laid wire rope lifting strop made is one 15½ in. in diameter with a breaking strain of 8,300 tons manufactured by ScanRope Ltd. of Norway. The sling was used to lift the steel jacket for the Veslefrikk Offshore Field in the Norwegian sector of the North Sea in 1989.

Ropeway or téléphérique The longest ropeway in the world is the *Compagnie Minière de l'Ogooué*, or COMILOG, installation built in 1959–62 for the Moanda manganese mine in Gabon, which extends 47.2 miles. It has 858 towers and 2,800 buckets, with 96.3 miles of wire rope running over 6,000 idler pulleys. The longest single-span ropeway is the 13,500 ft. span from the Coachella Valley to Mt. San Jacinto (10,821 ft.), CA, inaugurated on 12 Sep. 1963.

The highest and longest passenger-carrying aerial ropeway in the world is the *Teleférico Mérida* in Venezuela, from Mérida City (5,379 ft.) to the summit of Pico Espejo (15,629 ft.), a rise of 10,250 ft. The ropeway is in four sections, involving three car changes in the eight-mile ascent in one hour. The fourth span is 10,070 ft. in length. The two cars work on the pendulum system—the carrier rope is locked and the cars are hauled by means of three pull ropes powered by a 233 hp motor. They have a maximum capacity of 45 persons and travel at 32 ft./sec. (21.8 mph).

Shovel The Marion 6360 has a reach of 236.75 ft., a dumping height of 153 ft. and a bucket capacity of 4,860 ft.^{3}. Manufactured in 1964 by the Marion Power Shovel Co., Marion, OH, it weighs 24.3 million lbs. and uses 20 electric motors that generate 45,000 hp to operate its 220.5-ft.-long boom arm. It is operated for open-cast coal mining near Percy, IL by the Arch Mineral Corporation.

Snow-plow blade   A blade measuring 32 ft. 3 in. in length was designed and constructed by the Thomas Sedgwick Construction Co., Inc. of Syracuse, NY for use at Hancock International Airport. With a 6 in. snowfall the plow can push away 229,500 ft.³ of snow in one hour.

Steel companies   The Pohang works of the Pohang Iron & Steel Co. Ltd. (POSCO) of South Korea produced 9.9 million tons of crude steel in 1988, the highest amount produced by a single integrated works.

The largest producer of steel in the United States in 1991 was USX Corporation, of Pittsburgh, PA, which produced 10.5 million tons of raw steel. The 1991 sales figure for the US Steel Group of USX was $4.86 billion and assets stood at $5.63 billion. The number of employees for the year was 22,234.

Transformers   The world's largest single-phase transformers are rated at 1,500,000 kVA. Eight of these are in service with the American Electric Power Service Corporation. Of these, five step down from 765 to 345 kV.

Transmission lines   The longest span between pylons of any power line in the world is that across the Sogne Fjord, Norway, between Rabnaberg and Fatlaberg. Supplied in 1955 by Whitecross of Warrington, Great Britain, and projected and erected by A.S. Betonmast of Oslo as part of the high-tension power cable from Refsdal power station at Vik, it has a span of 16,040 ft. and a weight of 13.3 tons. In 1967 two further high-tensile steel/aluminum lines 16,006 ft. long, and weighing 36.4 tons, manufactured by Whitecross and BICC, were erected there.

Highest   The world's highest transmission lines are those across the Straits of Messina, Italy, with towers of 675 ft. (Sicily side) and 735 ft. (Calabria side) 11,900 ft. apart.

Highest voltages   The highest voltages now carried are 1,330,000 volts for 1,224 miles on the D.C. Pacific Inter-tie in the United States. The Ekibastuz D.C. transmission lines in Kazakhstan are planned to be 1,490 miles long with 1,500,000 volt capacity.

Valve   The world's largest valve is the 32-ft. diameter, 187-ton butterfly valve designed by Boving & Co. Ltd. of London, Great Britain for use at the Arnold Air Force Base engine test facility in Tennessee.

Wind tunnel   The world's largest wind tunnel is that of the NASA Ames Research Center in Mountain View, Palo Alto, CA. The tunnel, 40 × 80 ft., was opened on 11 Dec. 1989 and powered by six 22,500 hp motors allowing a best speed of 345 mph.

BORINGS AND MINES

Deepest　The deepest penetration into the Earth's crust is a geological exploratory drilling near Zapolarny in the Kola Peninsula of Arctic Russia, begun on 24 May 1970 and reported in April 1992 to have surpassed a depth of 40,230 ft. The eventual target of 49,212 ft. was expected in 1995 but now looks increasingly unlikely. The drill bit is mounted on a turbine driven by a mud pump. The temperature at 7.45 miles was already 229° F. The Germans announced the test drilling of the Erbendorf hole, Upper Bavaria on 9 Oct. 1986. The planned depth of the $263 million project is 8.6 miles or 45,900 ft.

Ocean drilling　The deepest recorded drilling into the seabed by the *Glomar Challenger* of the US Deep Sea Drilling Project is one of 5,709 ft. off northwest Spain in 1976. The deepest site is now 23,077 ft. below the surface on the western wall of the Mariana Trench, Pacific Ocean.

Ice-core drilling　The deepest borehole in ice was drilled at the Vostok station (Central Antarctica) by specialists of the Leningrad Mining Institute in September 1989, when a depth of 8,333 ft. was achieved. The 18th Expedition drilled the deepest "dry" borehole (without antifreeze) in 1972; it reached 3,125 ft.

OIL

Production　The world's largest oil producer is the former USSR, with a production in 1991 of 10.26 million barrels per day (b/d—compared with a peak 12.5 million b/d), followed by Saudi Arabia with 8.2 million b/d. The United States was third with 7.4 million b/d.

Fields　The world's largest oil field is the Ghawar field, Saudi Arabia, developed by ARAMCO, which measures 150 × 22 miles.

United States　The largest oil field in the United States is the Permian Basin, which covers approximately 100,000 miles^2 in southeast New Mexico and western and northwestern Texas.

In 1989, the United States imported 7,979,000 barrels of oil per day. In 1990, Texas produced 702.16 million barrels of oil, more than any other state.

Refineries　The world's largest refinery is the Petroleos de Venezuela S.A. refinery in Judibana, Falcón, Venezuela. It is operated by the Lagoven subsidiary of Petroleos and in 1991 produced 530,000 barrels of crude oil per day.

United States　The largest refinery in the United States is Amoco Oil Co.'s Texas City, TX refinery, which has a capacity of 433,000 barrels per day.

MINE RECORDS

EARLIEST
World [1] • 41,250 B.C. ± 1,600 Lion Cavern, Haematite (red iron ore) at Ngwenya, Hhohho, Swaziland.

DEEPEST
World [2] • 11,749 ft., Gold, Western Deep Levels (temp 131 °F) at Carletonville, South Africa.

COAL
Largest (US) • 27.9 million short tons per annum, ARCO Coal Co.'s Black Thunder Mine in Wright, WY.

Oldest (US) [3] • c. 1750 at James River coalfield near Richmond, VA. This site is now abandoned.

Deepest (exploratory shaft) • 6,700 ft., Donbas field, Ukraine.

(open cast, lignite) • 1,066 ft., near Bergheim, Germany.

COPPER
Deepest (open pit) • 2,625 ft. Bingham Canyon (begun 1906), location near Salt Lake City, UT.

Longest (underground) • 994 miles of tunnels, Division El Teniente of Codelco, Chile.

United States • 356 miles of tunnels, San Manuel Mine, Magma Copper Co. in AZ.

GOLD
Largest [4] • 12,100 acres, East Rand Proprietary Mines Ltd. at Boksburg, Transvaal, South Africa.

Richest • 49.4 million fine oz., Crown Mines (all-time yield) in Transvaal, South Africa.

IRON
Largest • 22.4 billion tons rich ore, Lebedinsky (45–65% ore), Kursk region, Russia.

United States [5] • 13.708 million metric tons at Mountain Iron, MN.

LEAD
Largest • 10 percent of world output, Viburnum Trend in southeast Missouri.

PLATINUM
Largest • 30.8 tons per annum, Rustenburg Platinum Mines Group, Rustenburg Platinum, mine location Western Transvaal, South Africa.

QUARRY

Largest ● 2.81 miles², 3,698 million tons extracted, Bingham Canyon, UT.
● 1,066 ft. deep, 8 mile² area, Fortuna-Garsdorf (lignite) (begun 1955), near Bergheim, Germany.

SPOIL DUMP

Largest ● 275 million yds.³, New Cornelia Tailings at Ten Mile Wash, AZ.

TUNGSTEN

Largest ● 2,205 tons per day, Union Carbide Mount Morgan mine, near Bishop, CA.

URANIUM

Largest[6] ● 5,600 tons of uranium oxide, Rio Tinto Zinc open cast pit at Rössing, Namibia.

---

[1] Carbon dated as such, but generally accepted as c. 110,000 B.C.

[2] Sinking began in July 1957. Scheduled to reach 12,370 ft. by 1992, with 14,000 ft. or 2.65 miles regarded as the limit. No. 3 vertical ventilation shaft is the world's deepest shaft at 9,675 ft. This mine requires 141,150 tons of air per day and refrigeration, which uses the energy it would take to make 41,440 short tons of ice. An underground shift comprises 11,150 men.

[3] The first recorded discovery of coal in the United States was in 1679 by French explorers, who reported a "coal mine" on the Illinois River.

[4] The world's most productive gold mine may be Muruntau, Kyzyl Kum, Uzbekistan. According to one Western estimate it produces 88 tons of gold in a year. It has been estimated that South Africa has produced in 96 years (1886–1982) 40,768 tons or more than 31 percent of all gold mined since 3900 B.C. The United States produced 290.2 metric tons of gold during 1990, the most since national yearly records were first kept in 1835. The largest gold mine currently in the United States is the Newmont Gold Company's Mine Complex in Eureka County and Elko County, NV.

[5] Minnesota produced the most iron in the United States in 1990, at 45.160 metric tons. The greatest year for iron production for the entire country was 1953, with 119.888 million metric tons.

[6] The biggest mill currently active in the United States is Gas Hills, WY, operated by the Pathfinder Mines Corp. It produces 2,800 short tons of ore per day. The mill with the greatest capacity is in Grant, NM, which can produce 7,000 short tons of ore per day. Although shut down several years ago, it remains on standby.

Fastest drilling   The most footage drilled in one month is 34,574 ft. in June 1988 by Harkins & Company Rig Number 13 during the drilling of four wells in McMullen County, TX.

Oil gushers   The greatest wildcat ever recorded blew at Alborz No. 5 well, near Qum, Iran on 26 Aug. 1956. The uncontrolled oil gushed to a height of 170 ft. at 120,000 barrels per day at a pressure of 9,000 lbs./in.^{2}. It was closed after 90 days' work by B. Mostofi and Myron Kinley of Texas.

   The Lake View No. 1 gusher in California on 15 Mar. 1910 may have yielded 125,000 barrels in its first 24 hours.

Crude oil imports   During the period January–December 1991, the United States imported 7.6 million barrels of crude oil and its by-products per day. In 1990 this figure was 7.8 million. Saudi Arabia was the leading supplier at 1.8 million barrels per day, which represented 23.8 percent of US imports. OPEC countries supplied the US with 4.1 million barrels per day, or 53.6 percent of the total, while Persian Gulf countries supplied 1.7 million, or 24.5 percent.

Platforms *Heaviest*   The world's heaviest oil platform is the *Gullfaks C* in the North Sea, Great Britain, built and operated by the Norwegian oil company Statoil. The platform is of the Condeep type, with a steel deck and modules on top of a concrete gravity base. Total dry weight of the $2.3 billion structure is 933 tons. Total height is 115.82 ft. The gravity base was built by Norwegian contractors, Stavanger, and the deck by Aker, Stord.

Tallest   The world's tallest production platform stands in water 1,760 ft. deep about 100 miles off the Louisiana coast. It is operated by Conoco and co-owned by Conoco, Texas and Occidental Petroleum.

Rigs   On 31 January 1990, the all-time lowest number of oil rigs in the United States was 653. This number includes all land rigs, those on inland barges and offshore rigs.

Spills   The world's worst oil spill occurred as a result of a marine blow-out beneath the drilling rig *Ixtoc I* in the Gulf of Campeche, Gulf of Mexico, on 3 June 1979. The slick reached 400 miles by 5 Aug. 1979. It was eventually capped on 24 Mar. 1980 after a loss of 3,000,000 barrels (599,200 tons).

   The worst single assault ever made on the environment was released on 19 Jan. 1991 by the Iraqi president, Saddam Hussein, who ordered the pumping of Gulf crude oil from Kuwait's Sea Island terminal and from seven large tankers into the Persian Gulf. The best estimate of the outflow is between 4–6 million barrels (168–252 million gallons). It required nine months of intense work to extinguish the fires.

   The worst oil spill in history from a marine collision was of 260,140 tons of oil from two supertankers, *Atlantic Empress* and *Aegean Captain*, when they collided off Tobago on 19 July 1979.

   The *Exxon Valdez* in Prince William Sound, AK struck a reef on 24 Mar. 1989, spilling 10 million gallons of crude. The slick spread over 2,600 miles^2.

CRUDE OIL IMPORTS*

(January–December 1991)

COUNTRY	BARRELS 1,000 PER DAY
Saudi Arabia	1,795
Canada	1,031
Venezuela	1,014
Mexico	801
Nigeria	702
Angola	254
Algeria	252
Virgin Islands*	243
Colombia	162
United Kingdom	136
OPEC Countries	4,060
Persian Gulf Countries	1,843

*Supplier of products made from crude oil.
American Petroleum Institute.

GAS

Production   The world's largest producer of natural gas is the former USSR, with 28.8 trillion ft.^{3} in 1990, followed by the United States with 18.4 trillion ft.^{3}.

Deposits   The largest gas deposit in the world is at Urengoi, Russia, with an eventual production of 261.6 billion yds.^{3} per year through six pipelines from proved reserves of 9.156 trillion yds.^{3}.

Flare   The greatest gas fire was the one that burned at Gassi Touil in the Algerian Sahara from noon on 13 Nov. 1961 to 9:30 A.M. on 28 Apr. 1962. The pillar of flame rose 450 ft. and the smoke 600 ft. It was eventually extinguished by Paul Neal ("Red") Adair (b. 1916) of Houston, TX, using 550 lbs. of dynamite. His fee was reported to be about $1 million plus expenses.

Water wells   The world's deepest water bore is the Stensvad Water Well 11-W1 of 7,320 ft., drilled by the Great Northern Drilling Co. Inc. in Rosebud County, MT in October–November 1961. The Thermal Power Co. geothermal steam well, begun in Sonoma County, CA in 1955, is down to 9,029 ft.

TIMEPIECES

Most accurate   The most accurate timekeeping device is a commercially available atomic clock manufactured by Hewlett-Packard of Palo Alto, CA, unveiled in December 1991. Designated the HP 5071A primary frequency standard with cesium II technology, the device, costing $54,000 and about the size of a desktop computer, is accurate to one second in 1.6 million years.

Mechanical   The Olsen clock, completed for the Copenhagen Town Hall, Denmark in Dec. 1955, has more than 14,000 units, and took 10 years to make; the mechanism functions in 570,000 different ways. The celestial pole motion will take 25,753 years to complete a full circle and is the slowest-moving designed mechanism in the world. The clock is accurate to 0.5 sec. in 300 years—50 times more accurate than the previous record.

Largest sundials   The world's largest sundial is the Samrat Yantra, with a gnomon height (rod of sundial that shows time by its shadow on marked surface) of 88.5 ft. and a vertical height of 118 ft. It was built in 1724 at Jaipur, India.

On 1 Mar. 1991, Walt Disney World in Orlando, FL unveiled the largest cylindrical sundial, measuring 120 ft. high, 122 ft. in diameter at the base. The sundial was designed by Arata Isozaki of Tokyo, Japan.

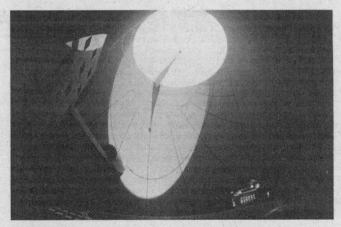

LARGEST SUNDIAL. Designed by Arata Isozaki of Tokyo, Japan as the centerpiece of the Walt Disney World Company headquarters in Orlando, FL, this sundial has a base diameter of 122 ft. and is 120 ft. high, with a gnomon (projecting arm) of the same length. (Photo: Esto Photographics/Peter Aaron)

CLOCKS

Earliest   The earliest mechanical clock—that is, one with an escapement—was completed in China in A.D. 725 by Y. Xing and Liang Lingzan.

Oldest   The oldest surviving working clock in the world is the faceless clock, dating from 1386, or possibly earlier, at Salisbury Cathedral, in Great Britain, which was restored in 1956, having struck the hours for 498 years and ticked more than 500 million times. Earlier dates, ranging back to *c.* 1335, have been attributed to the weight-driven clock in Wells Cathedral, Great Britain, but only the iron frame is original.

A model of Giovanni de Dondi's heptagonal astronomical clock of 1348–64 was completed in 1962.

Pendulum   The longest pendulum in the world is a reconstruction of Foucault's experiment. It swings from a cable 90 ft. long and 23 ft. above the heads of visitors to the Convention Center in Portland, OR and weighs 900 lbs.

Most expensive   The highest price paid for any clock is $1,540,000 for a rare "Egyptian Revival" clock made by Cartier in 1927. Designed as an ancient Egyptian temple gate, with figures and hieroglyphs, the exotic clock is made of mother-of-pearl, coral and lapis lazuli. It was sold at Christie's, New York on 24 Apr. 1991 to a private bidder.

Smallest   The smallest watches are those produced by Jaeger le Coultre of Switzerland. Equipped with a 15-jeweled movement, they measure just over ½ in. long and ³/₁₆ in. in width. Movement and case weigh under 0.25 oz.

Largest   The world's most massive clock is the astronomical clock in the Cathedral of St.-Pierre, Beauvais, France, constructed between 1865 and 1868. It contains 90,000 parts and is 40 ft. high, 20 ft. wide and 9 ft. deep.

The Su Song clock, built in China at Kaifeng in 1088–92, had a 23-ton bronze armillary sphere for 1.7 tons of water. It was removed to Beijing in 1126 and was last known to be working in its 40 ft. high tower in 1136.

"Timepiece," a clock that measures $51 \times 51 \times 51$ ft., is suspended over five stories in the atrium of the International Square building in Washington, D.C. Computer-driven and accurate to within 1/100th of a second, it weighs 2.3 tons. It is lit by 400 ft. of neon tube lighting and requires 1,500 ft. of cable and wiring. Twelve tubes at its base light up to tell the hour and the minute. The clock, designed by the sculptor John Safer, also indicates when the sun is at its zenith in 12 international cities.

Clock faces   The world's largest is that of the floral clock constructed at Matsubara Park, Toi, Japan. The clock face is 101 ft. in diameter and the large hand is 41 ft. long.

The digital, electronic, two-sided clock that revolves on top of the Texas Building in Fort Worth, TX has dimensions of $44 \times 44 \times 28$ ft.

The largest vertical outdoor clock face is the octagonal Colgate clock in Jersey City, NJ, with a diameter of 50 ft. and a minute hand 27 ft. 3 in. in length. In 1989 it was dismantled from the position it had occupied since 1908 at the top of the company's factory, which is being redeveloped. There are plans to relocate it at another site.

The largest four-faced clock in the world is that on the building of the Allen Bradley Co. of Milwaukee, WI. Each face has a diameter of 40 ft. 3½ in. with a minute hand 20 ft. in overall length.

Tallest   The tallest two-sided clock in the world is at the top of the Morton International Building, Chicago, IL. It is 580 ft. above street level.

WATCHES

Oldest   The oldest portable clockwork timekeeper is one of iron made by Peter Henlein in Nürnberg (Nüremberg), Germany, c. 1504.

The earliest wristwatches were those of Jacquet-Droz and Leschot of Geneva, Switzerland, dating from 1790.

Largest   The largest watch was a "Swatch" 531 ft. 6 in. long and 65 ft. 7½ in. in diameter, made by D. Tomas Feliu, which was set up on the site of the Bank of Bilbao building, Madrid, Spain from 7–12 Dec. 1985.

Heaviest   The Eta "watch" on the Swiss pavilion at Expo 86 in Vancouver, British Columbia, Canada from May–October weighed 38.5 tons and stood 80 ft. high.

Astronomical   The entirely mechanical Planetarium Copernicus, made by Ulysse Nardin of Switzerland, is the only wristwatch that indicates the time of day, the date, the phases of the moon, and the astronomical position of the sun, Earth, moon and the planets known in Copernicus' day. It also represents the Ptolemaic universe showing the astrological "aspects" at any given time.

Most expensive   The record price paid for a watch is £1,894,304 ($3,315,000) at Habsburg Feldman, Geneva, Switzerland on 9 Apr. 1989 for a Patek Philippe "Calibre '89" with 1,728 separate parts.

Excluding watches with jeweled cases, the most expensive standard man's pocket watch is Heaven at Hand, known to connoisseurs as the Packard and made in 1922 by Patek Philippe for the American automobile magnate James Packard. The timepiece is the most outstanding example of a "complicated" pocket watch in the world and was bought back by Patek Philippe in September 1988 for $1,200,000. To satisfy Packard's eccentric demands, Patek Philippe created a perfect celestial chart in enamel on the watch in gold casing to show the heavens as they moved over Packard's hometown of Warren, OH—in fact, exactly as he could see them from his bedroom window.

TELECOMMUNICATIONS

Telephones   There were approximately 423,619,000 telephones in the world on 1 Jan. 1989. The country with the greatest number was the United States, with 118,400,662.

The city with the most telephones in the world is Tokyo, Japan with 5,511,000. The greatest number of calls made in any country is in the United States with 421,022 million per year. The American Telephone and Telegraph (AT&T) "Worldwide Intelligent Network" handled a record 41 billion calls in 1991, with the busiest day on 2 Dec., when 157.8 million calls were handled.

Longest telephone cable   The world's longest submarine telephone cable is ANZCAN, which runs for 9,415 miles (8,181 nautical miles) from Port Alberni, Canada to Auckland, New Zealand and Sydney, Australia via Fiji and Norfolk Island. It cost some $379 million and was inaugurated by Queen Elizabeth II in Nov. 1984.

Largest telecommunications company   The largest telecommunications company in the United States is AT&T of New York, NY. As of 31 Dec. 1991, gross revenues were $44.651 billion and net earnings were $522 million. The company has 317,100 employees and 2.42 million stockholders.

Longest terrestrial call   A telephone call around the world, over an estimated 98,700 miles, was made on 28 Dec. 1985 from, and back to, the Royal Institute, London, Great Britain, during one of the Christmas lectures given by David Pye, Prof. of Zoology, University of London. The international telecommunications "rule," that only one communication satellite be used at a time, was suspended for the demonstration so that both geostationary Intelsats, one over the Indian Ocean and one over the Pacific, could be employed. The two "telephonists," Anieka Russell and Alison Risk, experienced a delay in their conversation of 530 milliseconds.

Morse code   The highest recorded speed at which anyone has received Morse code is 75.2 words per minute—over 17 symbols per second. This was achieved by Ted R. McElroy of the United States in a tournament at Asheville, NC on 2 July 1939.

The fastest speed recorded for hand-key transmitting is 175 symbols a minute by Harry A. Turner of the US Army Signal Corps at Camp Crowder, MO on 9 Nov. 1942.

Busiest telephone exchange   GPT (GEC Plessey Telecommunications Ltd.) demonstrated the ability of the "System X" telephone exchange to handle 1,558,000 calls in an hour through one exchange at Beeston, Great Britain on 27 June 1989.

Telephones *Largest*   The world's largest operational telephone was exhibited at a festival on 16 Sep. 1988 to celebrate the 80th birthday of Centraal Beheer, an insurance company based in Apeldoorn, the Netherlands. It was 8 ft. 1 in. high and 19 ft. 11 in. long, and weighed 3.8 tons. The handset, being 23 ft. 5 in. long, had to be lifted by crane in order for a call to be made.

Smallest   The smallest operational telephone was created by Jeff Smith of GTE Northwest, Everett, WA in 1988 and measured $4\frac{1}{8} \times \frac{3}{4} \times 1\frac{1}{2}$ in.

Largest switchboard   The world's biggest switchboard is the one in the Pentagon, Washington, D.C., with 25,000 lines handling over 200,000 calls per day through 100,000 miles of telephone cable.

Facsimile machine *Largest*   The largest facsimile (fax) machine is manufactured by WideCom Group Inc. of Ontario, Canada. "Wide Fax 36" has scanning and printing facilities to 36 in.

Smallest   The world's smallest fax machine is the NEC portable cellular fax machine NECi300, which can send and receive A4-size documents, and has an error correction mode. It measures $11\frac{3}{4} \times 8\frac{1}{4} \times 1\frac{1}{2}$ in. and weighs 4 lbs. 9½ oz.

SMALLEST TELEPHONE. The smallest operational telephone was created by Jeff Smith of GTE Northwest, Everett, WA. It was made in 1988 to honor the company's centennial and measured $4\frac{1}{8} \times \frac{3}{4} \times 1\frac{1}{2}$ in. Next to it is one of the more usual size with the various functions that telephones often have these days.

TELESCOPES

Earliest   The refractive properties of lenses were certainly known in ancient times, and spectacles were in use in the 13th century. Roger Bacon (*c.* 1214–92) in England wrote extensively about lenses, and claims have been made on behalf of others, notably the Elizabethan scientists Digges (father and son), and Dee. Leonardo da Vinci (1452–1519) is said to have used some sort of reflecting device to "make the moon seem larger," though this is not fully authenticated. It is very probable that the first telescope actually constructed was a refractor made by H. Lippershey in Holland in October 1608. The first astronomical observations with telescopes were made shortly afterward, notably in 1609 by Thomas Harriot (Great Britain; 1560–1621), who even drew a telescopic map of the moon—though the first really systematic telescopic observations were made by Galileo from January 1610.

The first reflecting telescope was made by Isaac Newton, and was presented to the Royal Society in 1671 and thought to have been constructed by him in 1668 or 1669.

Largest reflector   The largest single-mirror telescope now in use is the 19 ft. 8 in. reflector sited on Mount Semirodriki, near Zelenchukskaya in the Caucasus Mountains, Russia, at an altitude of 6,830 ft., completed in 1976. It has never come up to expectations, partly because it is not set up on a really good observing site. The largest satisfactory single-mirror telescope is the 200 in. Hale reflector at Mount Palomar, CA. Though the Hale was completed in 1948, it is now much more efficient than it was, as it is used with electronic devices that are more sensitive than photographic plates. The CCD (Charged-Coupled Device) increases the sensitivity by a factor of around 100.

Metal-mirror   This 72 in. reflector was made by the third Earl of Rosse, and set up at Birr Castle, Ireland in 1845. The mirror was of speculum metal (an alloy of copper and tin). With it, Lord Rosse discovered the spiral forms of the galaxies. It was last used in 1909.

Largest partially completed telescope   The Keck telescope on Mauna Kea, HI now being constructed will have a 394 in. mirror, made up of 36 segments fitted together to produce the correct curve. Each segment is 72 in. in aperture. An active support system holds each segment in place, and ensures that the images produced are brought to the same focus. The first image of the spiral galaxy NGC 1232 was obtained on 24 Nov. 1990, when nine of the segments were in place. All segments were in place by the end of 1991, and the first observational programs began in 1992. A twin Keck telescope is to be set up close to the first. When completed, Keck I and Keck II will be able to work together as an interferometer. Theoretically they would be able to see a car's headlights separately from a distance of 15,500 miles.

Largest planned   The largest telescope of the century should be the VLT (Very Large Telescope) being planned by the European Southern Observatory. It will consist of four 26 ft. 3 in. telescopes working together, providing a light-grasp equal to a single 52 ft. 6 in. mirror. The chosen site is

Paranal in northern Chile, well to the north of the La Silla Observatory in the Atacama Desert of northern Chile (see First telescope to use active optics). It is hoped to have the first units working by 1995, and the complete telescope by 2000.

Multiple-mirror The MMT (Multiple-Mirror Telescope) at the Whipple Observatory at Mount Hopkins, AZ uses six 72 in. mirrors together, giving a light-grasp equal to a single 176 in. mirror. There are, however, considerable operational problems, and it is now planned to replace the six separate mirrors with a single large mirror.

Infrared The largest infrared reflector in Great Britain is the UKIRT (United Kingdom Infrared Telescope) on Mauna Kea, HI with a 147 in. mirror. It is so good that it can be used for visual work as well as infrared.

Solar The McMath solar telescope at Kitt Peak, AZ has a 6 ft. 11 in. primary mirror; the light is sent to it via a 32° inclined tunnel from a coelostat (rotatable mirror) at the top end. Extensive modifications to it are now being planned.

Southern The largest southern hemisphere telescope is the 157⅞ in. reflector at Cerro Tololo in the Atacama Desert, northern Chile. The Anglo-Australian Telescope (AAT) at Siding Spring in New South Wales has a 153⅛ in. mirror.

Submillimeter The James Clark Maxwell telescope on Mauna Kea, HI has a 49 ft. 3 in. paraboloid primary, and is used for studies of the submillimeter part of the electromagnetic spectrum (0.01–0.03 in.). It does not produce a visual image.

Largest refractor A 62 ft. long 40 in. refractor completed in 1897 is situated at the Yerkes Observatory, Williams Bay, WI and belongs to the University of Chicago, IL. Although nearly 100 years old, it is still in full use on clear nights. A larger refractor measuring 59 in. was built in France and shown at the Paris Exhibition in 1900. However, it was a failure and was never used for scientific work.

Largest radio dish Radio waves from the Milky Way galaxy were first detected by Karl Jansky of Bell Telephone Laboratories, Holmdel, NJ in 1931 when he was investigating static with an improvised 100 ft. aerial. The only radio telescope built for that purpose before the outbreak of the war in 1939 was made by an amateur, Grote Reber, who detected radio emissions from the sun. The diameter of the dish was 31 ft. 2 in.

The pioneer large "dish" was the 250 ft. telescope at Jodrell Bank, Great Britain, now known as the Lovell Telescope, completed in 1957. It is part of the MERLIN network, which includes other dishes in various parts of Britain.

The world's largest fully steerable dish is the 328-ft.-diameter, 3,360-ton assembly at the Max Planck Institute for Radio Astronomy of Bonn in the Effelsberger Valley, Germany; it was completed in 1971.

Largest radio installation The largest radio installation is the Australian Telescope, which includes dishes at Parkes (210 ft.), Siding Spring (72 ft.) and Culgoora (also 72 ft.). There are also links with tracking stations at Usuada and Kashima, Japan, and with the TDRS (Tracking and Data Relay

Satellite), which is in a geosynchronous orbit. This is equivalent to a radio telescope with an effective diameter of 2.16 Earth diameters (17,102 miles).

The VLA (Very Large Array) of the US National Science Foundation is Y-shaped, with each arm 13 miles long and with 27 mobile antennae (each of 82 ft. diameter) on rails. It is 50 miles west of Socorro in the Plains of San Augustin, NM. It was completed on 10 Oct. 1980.

First telescope to use active optics   Active optics involves automatic correction of the mirror curve as the telescope is moved around. It gives a great increase in resolution. The first major telescope to use active optics was the New Technology Telescope (NTT) at La Silla in the Atacama Desert of northern Chile, the observing site of the ESO (European Southern Observatory). The NTT, like all modern telescopes, has an altazimuth mount, and is probably the most effective ground-based telescope in use in the world today. It will shortly incorporate adaptive optics, which involves compensating the shape of the mirror for minor short-term variations in the atmosphere.

Planetaria   The ancestor of the modern planetarium is the rotatable Gottorp Globe, built by Andreas Busch in Denmark about 1660. It was 34 ft. 7 in. in circumference, weighed nearly 3.9 tons and is now preserved in St. Petersburg, Russia. The stars were painted on the inside. The first modern planetarium was opened in 1923 in Jena, Germany; it was designed by Walther Bauersfelt of the Carl Zeiss company.

The world's largest planetarium is in Miyazaki, Japan, and was completed on 30 June 1987. The dome has a diameter of 88 ft. 7 in.

The Rueben H. Fleet Space Theater & Science Center in San Diego, CA and The Ethyl Universe Planetarium & Space Theater in Richmond, VA both have dome diameters of 75.5 ft.

The American Museum–Hayden Planetarium, New York City has a dome diameter of 75.1 ft., but has the largest seating capacity of any planetarium in the United States with 650 seats.

The Adler Planetarium in Chicago, IL, which opened on 12 May 1930, is the oldest planetarium in the United States. Its dome is 68 ft. in diameter and it seats 450 people.

Observatory *Oldest*   The oldest observatory building extant is the "Tower of the Winds" used by Andronichus of Cyrrhus in Athens, Greece *c.* 100 B.C., and equipped with sundials and clepsydra (water clock).

Highest   The high-altitude observatory at Denver, CO is at 14,100 ft. and was opened in 1973. The main instrument is a 24 in. reflector. It is slightly higher than the observatory at the summit of Mauna Kea in Hawaii at 13,760 ft.

Lowest   The lowest "observatory" is at Homestake Mine, SD, where the "telescope" is a tank of cleaning fluid (perchloroethylene), which contains chlorine, and can trap neutrinos from the sun. The installation is 1.1 miles below ground level, in the shaft of a gold mine; the detector has to be at this depth, as otherwise the experiments would be confused by cosmic rays. The

PROGRESSIVE ROCKET ALTITUDE RECORDS

HEIGHT (MILES)	ROCKET	PLACE	LAUNCH DATE
0.71	A 3 in. rocket	London, Great Britain	Apr. 1750
1.25	Reinhold Tiling[1] (Germany) solid fuel rocket	Osnabruck, Germany	Apr. 1931
3.04	GIRD-X semi-liquid fuel (USSR)	Moscow, USSR (now Russia)	25 Nov. 1933
52.46	A.4 rocket (Germany)[2]	Peenemünde, Germany	3 Oct. 1942
c. 85	A.4 rocket (Germany)	Heidelager, Poland	early 1944
118	A.4 rocket (Germany)	Heidelager, Poland	mid 1944
244	V2/WAC Corporal (2-stage) Bumper No. 5 (USA)	White Sands, NM[3]	24 Feb. 1949
682	Jupiter C (USA)	Cape Canaveral, FL	20 Sep. 1956
>800	ICBM test flight R-7 (USSR)	Tyuratam, USSR (now Kazakhstan)	21 Aug. 1957
>2,700	Farside No. 5 (4-stage; USA)	Eniwetok Atoll	20 Oct. 1957
70,700	Pioneer 1-B Lunar Probe (USA)	Cape Canaveral, FL	11 Oct. 1958
215,300,000*	Luna 1 or Mechtá (USSR)	Tyuratam, USSR (now Kazakhstan)	2 Jan. 1959
242,000,000*	Mars 1 (USSR)	Tyuratam, USSR (now Kazakhstan)	1 Nov. 1962
3,666,000,000[4]	Pioneer 10 (USA)	Kennedy Space Center, Cape Canaveral, FL	2 Mar. 1972

* Apogee in solar orbit.

[1] There is some evidence that Tiling may shortly after have reached 5.90 miles with a solid fuel rocket at Wangerooge, East Friesian Islands, Germany.

[2] The A.4 rocket was later referred to as the V2 rocket, a code for second revenge weapon (vergeltungswaffe) following upon the V1 "flying bomb."

[3] The V2/WAC height of 244 miles may have been exceeded during the period 1950–56 before the Jupiter C flight, as the Soviets reported in 1954 that a rocket had reached 240 miles at an unspecified date.

[4] Distance on crossing Pluto's orbit on 17 Oct. 1986. It is now much deeper into space and will be surpassed by Voyager 1. Pioneer II and Voyager 2 are also leaving the solar system.

Homestake Observatory has been operating since 1964 and has provided results of tremendous value.

Largest Schmidt telescope   A Schmidt telescope uses a spherical mirror with a correcting plate and can cover a very wide field with a single exposure. The largest is the 6 ft. 6 in. instrument at the Karl Schwarzschild Observatory at Tautenberg, Germany. It has a clear aperture of 53 in. with a 78¾ in. mirror, focal length 13 ft. It was brought into use in 1960.

Space telescope *Largest*   The largest is the $1.55 billion NASA Edwin P. Hubble Space Telescope of 12 tons and 43 ft. in overall length with a 94.5 in. reflector. It was placed in orbit at 381 miles altitude aboard a US space shuttle on 24 Apr. 1990. When it had been launched, it was found to have a defective mirror, because of a mistake in the original construction, leading to spherical aberration. It can still outperform any ground-based telescope in some areas of astronomy.

ROCKETRY

Earliest uses   War rockets, propelled by gunpowder (charcoal-saltpeter-sulfur), were described by Zeng Gongliang of China in 1042. This early form of rocket became known in Europe by 1258.

The first launching of a liquid-fueled rocket (patented 14 July 1914) was by Dr. Robert Hutchings Goddard (1882–1945; USA), at Auburn, MA, on 16 Mar. 1926, when his rocket reached an altitude of 41 ft. and traveled a distance of 184 ft.

The earliest rocket in the former USSR was the semiliquid-fueled GIRD-IX (Gruppa Izucheniya Reaktivnogo Dvizheniya), begun in 1931 and tested on 17 Aug. 1933.

Highest velocity   The first space vehicle to achieve the Third Cosmic velocity—sufficient to break out of the solar system—was *Pioneer 10*. The Atlas SLV-3C launcher with a modified Centaur D second stage and a Thiokol TE-364-4 third stage left the Earth at an unprecedented 32,114 mph on 2 Mar. 1972. However, the fastest escape velocity from Earth was 34,134 mph, achieved by the ESA *Ulysses* spacecraft, powered by an IUS–PAM upper stage after deployment from the Space Shuttle *Discovery* on 18 Oct. 1989, en route to a solar polar orbit via Jupiter.

Mariner 10 reached a recorded solar system speed of 131,954 mph as it passed Mercury in September 1974, but the fastest speed of approximately 158,000 mph is recorded by the NASA-German *Helios B* solar probe each time it reaches the perihelion of its solar orbit. Sister spaceship *Helios A* will also exceed *Mariner 10* 's velocity. (See Closest approach to the sun by a rocket.)

Most powerful rocket   The NI booster of the former USSR, first launched from Baikonur, Kazakhstan (then USSR) on 21 Feb. 1969, had a thrust of 5,090 tons but exploded at takeoff + 70 secs. Three other launch attempts also failed. Its current booster *Energya*, first launched on 15 May 1987

> **Most powerful rocket engine** The most powerful rocket
> engine was built in the former USSR by Scientific Industrial
> Corporation of Energetic Engineering in 1980. The engine has a
> thrust of 2,645.5 tons in open space and a thrust of 4,409.5 tons at
> the Earth's surface. The RD-170 has a turbopump of 190 MW and
> burns liquid oxygen and kerosene.

from the Baikonur Cosmodrome, when fully loaded weighed 2,645 tons and
had a thrust of 3,840 tons. It was capable of placing 116 tons into low Earth
orbit and measured 192 ft. 7 in. tall with a maximum diameter of 52 ft. 6 in.
It comprised a core stage powered by four liquid oxygen and hydrogen engines—the first cryogenic units flown by the Russians. Four strap-on boost-
ers powered by single RD-170 engines burning liquid oxygen and kerosene
were used.

Closest approach to the sun by a rocket The research spacecraft *Helios B* approached within 27 million miles of the sun, carrying both US and
German instrumentation, on 16 Apr. 1976. (See Highest velocity.)

Remotest man-made object *Pioneer 10*, launched from Cape Canaveral,
FL, crossed the mean orbit of Pluto on 17 Oct. 1986, being then at a distance
of 3.67 billion miles from Earth. In A.D. 34,593 it will make its nearest approach to the star *Ross 248*, 10.3 light-years distant. *Voyager 1*, traveling
faster, will surpass *Pioneer 10* in remoteness from the Earth. *Pioneer 11* and
Voyager 2 are also leaving the solar system.

SPACE FLIGHT

The physical laws controlling the flight of artificial satellites were first postulated by Sir Isaac Newton (1642–1727) in his *Philosophiae Naturalis Prin-
cipia Mathematica* ("Mathematical Principles of Natural Philosophy"), begun
in March 1686 and first published in July 1687.

The first artificial satellite was successfully put into orbit from the
Baikonur Cosmodrome at Tyuratam, Kazakhstan 170 miles east of the Aral
Sea and 155 miles south of the town of Baikonur on the night of 4 Oct. 1957.
It reached an altitude of between 142 miles (perigee or nearest point to Earth)
and 588 miles (apogee or furthest point from Earth) and a velocity of more
than 17,750 mph. This spherical satellite, called *Sputnik 1* ("Fellow Traveler"), was officially designated "Satellite 1957 Alpha 2." It weighed 184.3
lbs., with a diameter of 22¾ in.; its lifetime is believed to have been 92 days,
ending on 4 Jan. 1958. The 96 ft. 9 in. SL–4 launcher was designed under the
direction of former Gulag prisoner Dr. Sergei Pavlovich Korolyov (1907–66).

Earliest manned satellite The earliest manned spaceflight ratified by
the world governing body, the *Fédération Aéronautique Internationale* (FAI,
founded 1905), was by Cosmonaut Flight Major (later Col.) Yuri Alekseye-

vich Gagarin (1934–68) in *Vostok 1* on 12 Apr. 1961. Details filed showed takeoff to be from the Baikonur Cosmodrome, Kazakhstan at 6:07 A.M. GMT and the landing near Smelovka, near Engels, in the Saratov region, of Russia, 108 minutes later. Col. Gagarin landed separately from his spacecraft, by parachute, after ejecting as planned, as did all the *Vostok* pilots.

The maximum altitude during *Vostok 1*'s 25,394½ mile flight was listed at 203 miles, with a maximum speed of 17,560 mph. Col. Gagarin, invested a Hero of the Soviet Union and awarded the Order of Lenin and the Gold Star Medal, was killed in a jet plane crash near Moscow on 27 Mar. 1968.

There were 151 manned spaceflights to 7 May 1992, of which 77 were American and 73 Soviet.

United States   On 5 May 1961, aboard *Mercury 3,* Cdr. Alan B. Shepard, Jr. (USN) became the first American to man a spaceflight. The suborbital flight, which lasted 15 min. 28 sec., covered 302 miles and reached an altitude of 116.5 miles.

John H. Glenn was the first American to orbit the Earth. His flight aboard *Mercury 6* (*Friendship 7*) was launched at 9:47 A.M. EST on 20 Feb. 1962 and splashed down into the Atlantic Ocean at 2:43 P.M. EST that same day. Glenn completed three orbits of the Earth and traveled approximately 81,000 miles.

First woman in space   The first woman to orbit the Earth was Junior Lt. (now Lt.-Col. Eng) Valentina Vladimirovna Tereshkova (b. 6 Mar. 1937), who was launched in *Vostok 6* from the Baikonur Cosmodrome, Kazakhstan at 9:30 A.M. GMT on 16 June 1963, and landed at 8:16 A.M. on 19 June, after a flight of 2 days 22 hrs. 50 min., during which she completed over 48 orbits (1.23 million miles) and passed momentarily within three miles of *Vostok 5.* As of 31 Mar. 1992 a total of eighteen women had flown into space—14 Americans, two Soviets, one from Great Britain and one Canadian.

United States   The first American woman in space was Sally Ride, who was launched in the US space shuttle *Challenger STS–7* on 18 June 1983, and returned to Earth 24 June.

Space fatalities   The greatest published number to perish in any of the 151 attempted spaceflights to 7 May 1992 is seven (five men and two women) aboard the *Challenger 51L* on 28 Jan. 1986, when an explosion occurred 73 sec. after liftoff, at a height of 47,000 ft. *Challenger* broke apart under extreme aerodynamic overpressure. Four people, all Soviet, have been killed during actual spaceflight—Vladimir Komarov on 24 Apr. 1967 on *Soyuz 1,* which crashed on landing; and the un-spacesuited Georgi Dobrovolsky, Viktor Patsayev and Vladislav Volkov, who died when their *Soyuz 11* spacecraft depressurized during reentry on 29 June 1971.

Astronauts   *Oldest*   The oldest astronaut of the 270 people in space (to 7 May 1992) was Vance DeVoe Brand (USA; b. 9 May 1931), age 59, while on the space shuttle mission aboard the *Columbia STS 35* 2–10 Dec. 1990. The oldest woman was Shannon Lucid (USA), aged 48 years on space shuttle mission *Discovery STS 43* in July 1991. Lucid is also the first woman to make three space flights.

Youngest   The youngest was Major (later Lt.-Gen.) Gherman Stepanovich Titov (b. 11 Sep. 1935), who was 25 years 329 days when launched in *Vos-*

tok 2 on 6 Aug. 1961. The youngest woman in space was Valentina Tereshkova, 26. (See First woman in space.)

The youngest American astronaut was astrophysicist Tamara Jernigan, who on 5 June 1991, aged 32 years, was launched aboard *STS 40 Columbia*.

Duration record on the moon   The crew of *Apollo 17* collected a record 253 lbs. of rock and soil during their three EVAS of 22 hrs. 5 min. They were Capt. Eugene A. Cernan, USN (b. 14 Mar. 1934) and Dr. Harrison H. (Jack) Schmitt (b. 3 July 1935), who became the 12th man on the moon. The crew were on the lunar surface for 74 hrs. 59 min. during this longest of lunar missions, which took 12 days 13 hrs. 51 min. on 7–19 Dec. 1972.

Longest and shortest manned spaceflight   The longest manned flight was by Col. Vladimir Georgeyevich Titov (b. 1 Jan. 1947) and Flight Engineer Musa Khiramanovich Manarov (b. 22 Mar. 1951), who were launched to the Mir space station aboard *Soyuz TM4* on 21 Dec. 1987, and landed, in *Soyuz TM6* (with French spationaut Jean-Loup Chretien), at a secondary recovery site near Dzhezkazgan, Kazakhstan, on 21 Dec. 1988, after a spaceflight lasting 365 days 22 hrs. 39 min. 47 sec. The shortest manned flight was made by Cdr. Alan B. Shepard, Jr. (b. 18 Nov. 1923; USN) aboard *Mercury Redstone 3* on 5 May 1961. His suborbital mission lasted 15 min. 28 sec.

The most experienced space traveler is the Soviet flight engineer Musa Manarov, who clocked 541 days 31 min. 10 sec. on two space flights in 1987–88 and 1990–91.

United States   Gerald P. Carr, Edward G. Gibson and William R. Pogue manned the longest American flight aboard *Skylab SL–4*, which was launched 16 Nov. 1974 and splashed down 8 Feb. 1975, after 2,017 hrs. 15 min. 32 sec. in space.

Most journeys   Capt. John Watts Young (USN ret.) (b. 24 Sep. 1930) completed his sixth spaceflight on 8 Dec. 1983, when he relinquished command of *Columbia STS 9/Spacelab* after a space career of 34 days 19 hrs. 41 min. 53 sec. Young flew *Gemini 3, Gemini 10, Apollo 10, Apollo 16, STS 1* and *STS 9*. The greatest number of flights by a Soviet cosmonaut is five, by Vladimir Dzhanibekov (between 1978 and 1985). The most by a woman is three, by Shannon Lucid (*STS 51 9, 34* and *43*) and Kathryn Sullivan (*STS 41 9, 31* and *45*). Lucid is scheduled to make a fourth flight in 1993.

Largest crew   The largest crew on a single space mission was eight. This included one female and was launched on space shuttle *Challenger 9 STS 61A*, the 22nd shuttle mission, on 30 Oct. 1985, carrying the German *Spacelab D1* laboratory. The mission, commanded by Henry W. "Hank" Hartsfield, lasted 7 days 44 min. 51 sec. The greatest number of women in a space crew is three (of seven) on *Columbia STS 40* in June 1991.

Most in space   The greatest number of people in space at any one time has been 12, on two occasions. Seven Americans were aboard the space shuttle *Columbia STS 35*, two Soviet cosmonauts were aboard the *Mir* space station, and two cosmonauts and one Japanese journalist were aboard *Soyuz TM11* on 2–10 Dec. 1990. On 23–24 Mar. 1992, six Americans and one Belgian were on space shuttle *Atlantis*, two Soviet cosmonauts were on *Mir* and two Soviet cosmonauts and a German were on *Soyuz TM14*.

Spacewalks   Lt.-Col. (now Maj. Gen.) Aleksey Arkhipovich Leonov (b. 20 May 1934) from *Voskhod 2* was the first person to engage in EVA ("extravehicular activity") on 18 Mar. 1965. Capt. Bruce McCandless II (b. 8 June 1937; USN), from the space shuttle *Challenger,* was the first to engage in untethered EVA, at an altitude of 164 miles above Hawaii, on 7 Feb. 1984. His MMU (Manned Maneuvering Unit) back-pack cost $15 million to develop. The first woman to perform an EVA was Svetlana Savitskaya (b. 8 Aug. 1948) from *Soyuz T12/Şalyut 7* on 25 July 1985.

The greatest number of spacewalks is eight by Soviet cosmonauts Leonid Kizim and Vladimir Solovyov during two missions in 1984 and 1986.

The first American to "walk" in space was Edward H. White II (1930–67) from the spacecraft *Gemini 4* on 3 June 1965. Between 3–7 June, White and James McDivitt completed 62 circuits in orbit around the Earth, and it was during the third orbit that White left the capsule and, using a 25-ft. lifeline, maneuvered for 20 minutes in space.

The first American woman to "walk" in space was Kathryn D. Sullivan, on 11 Oct. 1984, as part of the space shuttle *Challenger* mission 5–13 Oct. 1984.

Lunar conquest   Neil Alden Armstrong (b. 5 Aug. 1930), command pilot of the *Apollo 11* mission, became the first human to set foot on the moon, on the Sea of Tranquility, at 02:56 and 15 sec. GMT on 21 July 1969. He was followed out of the lunar module *Eagle* by Col. Edwin Eugene "Buzz" Aldrin, Jr., USAF (b. 20 Jan. 1930) while the command module *Columbia*, piloted by Lt. Col. Michael Collins, USAF (b. 31 Oct. 1930), orbited above.

Eagle landed at 20:17 and 42 sec. GMT on 20 July and lifted off at 17:54 GMT on 21 July, after a stay of 21 hrs. 36 min. *Apollo 11* had blasted off from Cape Canaveral, FL at 13:32 GMT on 16 July and was a culmination of the US space program, up to that point, which, at its peak, employed 376,600 people and attained in 1966–67 a record budget of $5.9 billion.

There were six lunar landings altogether, and twelve people made a total of 14 EVAs on the moon totalling 79 hrs. 35 min. between July 1969 and December 1972.

Altitude   The greatest altitude attained by humans was when the crew of the *Apollo 13* were at apocynthion (i.e., their furthest point) 158 miles above the lunar surface, and 248,655 miles above the Earth's surface at 1:21 A.M. EST on 14 Apr. 1970. The crew were Capt. James Arthur Lovell, Jr., USN (b. 25 Mar. 1928), Fred Wallace Haise, Jr. (b. 14 Nov. 1933) and John L. Swigert (1931–82).

The greatest altitude attained by an American woman is 330 miles by astronaut Kathryn D. Sullivan (b. 3 Oct. 1951; USA) during her flight in space shuttle *Discovery* on 24 Apr. 1990.

Speed   The fastest speed at which humans have traveled is 24,791 mph when the command module of *Apollo 10* carrying Col. (now Brig. Gen.) Thomas Patten Stafford, USAF (b. 17 Sep. 1930), and Cdr. Eugene Andrew

Cernan, USN (b. 14 Mar. 1934) and Cdr. (now Capt.) John Watts Young, USN (b. 24 Sep. 1930), reached this maximum value at the 75.7 mile altitude interface on its trans-Earth round-trip flight on 26 May 1969.

The fastest speed recorded by a woman is 17,864 mph by Kathryn Sullivan at the start of reentry at the end of the *Discovery STS 31* shuttle mission on 29 Apr. 1990. The highest recorded by a Soviet space traveler was 17,470 mph by Valentina Tereshkova of the USSR (see First woman in space) in *Vostok 6* on 16 June 1963, although because orbital injection of Soyuz spacecraft occurs at a marginally lower altitude, it is probable that Tereshkova's speed was exceeded twice by Svetlana Savitskaya aboard *Soyuz TM7* and *TM12* on 19 Aug. 1982 and 17 July 1984.

First extraterrestrial vehicle   The first wheeled vehicle landed on the moon was the unmanned *Lunokhod 1*, which began its Earth-controlled travels on 17 Nov. 1970. It moved a total of 6.54 miles on gradients up to 304° in the Mare Imbrium and did not break down until 4 Oct. 1971. The lunar speed and distance record was set by the manned *Apollo 16* Rover, with 11.2 mph downhill and 22.4 miles.

Heaviest and largest space objects   The heaviest object orbited is the *Saturn V* third stage of the *Apollo 15* spacecraft, which, prior to translunar injection into parking orbit, weighed 309,690 lbs. The 440 lb. US RAE (Radio Astronomy Explorer) B, or *Explorer 49*, launched on 10 June 1973, was, however, larger, with antennae 1,500 ft. from tip to tip.

Most expensive projects   The total cost of the US manned space program as of 14 Feb. 1992 was $78.3 billion. The first 15 years of the Soviet space program, from 1958 to September 1973, are estimated to have cost $45 billion. The aggregate cost of the NASA Shuttle program is $42.8 billion.

First reusable spacecraft   The US space shuttle *Columbia STS 1*, the world's first reusable spacecraft, lifted off from its launch pad at Cape Canaveral, FL, on 12 Apr. 1981 at 7 A.M. EST. After 36 orbits and 54 hours in space, the craft glided to a perfect landing on a dry lake bed at Edwards Air Force Base in the Mojave Desert, CA on 14 Apr. at 1:21 P.M. EST. The craft was manned by John W. Young, USN and Robert L. Crippen. As of 14 Feb. 1992 there have been 44 space shuttle flights using four shuttle craft: *Columbia*, *Challenger*, *Discovery* and *Atlantis*. *Discovery* has flown the most times with 13 missions.

BUILDINGS AND STRUCTURES

Neuschwanstein Castle, Bavaria.
(Photo: Spectrum Colour Library)

EARLIEST STRUCTURES

The earliest-known human structure may be the footings of a windbreak. It is a rough circle of loosely piled lava blocks found on the lowest cultural level at the Lower Paleolithic site at Olduvai Gorge in Tanzania, revealed by Dr. Mary Leakey in January 1960. The ring of several hundred stones was associated with artifacts and bones on a work-floor, dating from *c.* 1,750,000 B.C.

The earliest evidence of *buildings* yet discovered is that of 21 huts with hearths or pebble-lined pits and delimited by stake-holes found in October 1965 at the Terra Amata site in Nice, France, thought to belong to the Acheulian culture of *c.* 400,000 years ago. Excavation carried out between 28 June and 5 July 1966 revealed one hut with palisaded walls with axes of 49 ft. and 20 ft.

The remains of a stone tower 20 ft. high originally built into the walls of Jericho have been excavated and are dated to 5000 B.C. The foundations of the walls themselves have been dated to as early as 8350 B.C.

The oldest freestanding structures in the world are now believed to be the megalithic temples at Mgarr and Skorba in Malta. With those at Ggantija in Gozo, they date from *c.* 3250 B.C., some 3½ centuries earlier than the earliest Egyptian pyramid.

BUILDINGS FOR WORKING

LARGEST

Construction project   The Madinat Al-Jubail Al-Sinaiyah project in Saudi Arabia is the largest public works project in modern times. Construction started in 1976 for an industrial city covering 250,705 acres. At the peak of construction nearly 52,000 workers were employed, representing 62 nationalities. The total earth dredging and moving volume has reached 953.5 billion ft.³, enough to construct a 3-foot high belt around the Earth at the equator seven times.

The seawater cooling system is believed to be the world's largest canal system, bringing 353 million ft.³ of seawater per day to cool the industrial establishment.

Urban development   The largest urban regeneration project in the world is that of the London Docklands, which covers 8½ miles². By 1992 £8 billion had been invested by the private sector together with a further £1.1 billion injected by the London Docklands Development Corporation. Over 27 million ft.³ of commercial development space and over 17,000 new homes have been completed or are under construction, and £3.5 billion is being invested in new public transport. More than 40,000 jobs have been created since

URBAN PROJECT—DOCKLANDS. An aerial view of the largest regeneration project in the world, the London Docklands, which covers an area 8½ sq. miles. (Photo: Images Colour Library)

LARGEST INDUSTRIAL BUILDING. This photo-montage shows the Asia Terminals Ltd. container freight station at Kwai Chung, Hong Kong with a representation of the uncompleted work superimposed on the existing structure. The total floor area on completion at the end of 1992 will be 9,321,171.7 ft.². (Photo: Asia Terminals)

1981. The Canary Wharf development in the London Docklands is also the world's largest commercial development.

Industrial The largest multilevel industrial building that is one discrete structure is the container freight station of Asia Terminals Ltd. at Hong Kong's Kwai Chung container port. The gross floor area completed by April 1992 was 6,148,660 ft.^{2}, and the total area on completion of the 15-story building, scheduled for the end of 1992, will be 9,321,171.7 ft.^{2}. The building plan area is 905.5 × 958 ft. and 359.25 ft. high. It has a total floor area of 21.4 acres and its height is 359 ft. The building's volume will be 206,698.87 ft.^{3}. The entire area in each floor is directly accessible by 46 ft. container trucks, and the building includes 16.67 miles of roadway and 2,609 container truck parking bays.

Hod carrying Russell Bradley of Worcester, Great Britain carried bricks totaling 456 lbs. 6 oz. up a ladder of the minimum specified length of 12 ft. on 28 Jan. 1991 at Worcester City Football Club.

He also carried bricks with a total weight of 574.1 lbs. in a 105.8 lb. hod a distance of 16 ft. 5 in. on level ground before ascending a runged ramp to a height of 7 ft. at Worcester Rugby Club on 17 Mar. 1991.

Brick carrying The greatest distance achieved for carrying a 9-lb. brick in a nominated ungloved hand in an uncradled downward pincer grip is 61¾ miles, by Reg Morris of Walsall, Great Britain on 16 July 1985.

The women's record for a 9-lb.-12-oz. brick is 22½ miles, by Wendy Morris of Walsall, Great Britain on 28 Apr. 1986.

Commercial The greatest ground area covered by any commercial building in the world under one roof is the flower auction building of the Co-operative VBA (Verenigde Bloemenveilingen Aalsmeer), Aalsmeer, Netherlands, with dimensions of 2,546 × 2,070 ft. The original floor surface of 84.82 acres was extended in 1986 to 91.05 acres.

The assembly plant with the largest cubic capacity in the world is that of the Boeing Company at Everett, WA, completed in 1968, with a volume capacity of 2,440,000 ft.^{2}.

Scientific The most capacious scientific building is the Vehicle Assembly Building (VAB) at Complex 39, the selected site for the final assembly and launching of the *Apollo* spacecraft on the Saturn V rocket, at the John F. Kennedy Space Center on Merritt Island, Cape Canaveral, FL. Construction was begun in April 1963 by the Ursum Consortium. It is a steel-framed building measuring 716 ft. in length, 518 ft. in width and 525 ft. high. The building contains four bays, each with its own door 460 ft. high. Its floor area is 7.88 acres and its capacity is 129.5 million ft.^{3}. The building was "topped out" on 14 Apr. 1965, the cost then amounting to $108,700,000.

Administrative The largest ground area covered by any office building is that of the Pentagon, in Arlington, VA. Built to house the US Defense Department's offices, it was completed on 15 Jan. 1943 and cost an estimated $83 million. Each of the outermost sides is 921 ft. long and the perimeter of the building is about 4,610 ft. Its five stories enclose a floor area of 149.2 acres. The corridors total 17 miles in length and there are 7,748 windows to be cleaned. There are 29,000 people working in the building, which has over 44,000 telephones connected by 160,000 miles of cable. There are 220 employees to handle 280,000 calls a day. Two restaurants, six cafeterias, ten snack bars and a staff of 675 form the catering department.

Office   The complex with the largest rentable space is the World Trade Center in New York City with a total of 100.32 acres in each of the twin towers. Tower Two is 1,377 ft. high, incorporating the observation deck on top. The tip of the TV antenna on Tower One is 1,710 ft. above street level and is thus 3 ft. taller than the antennae on top of the Sears Tower (see Tallest, below). There are 99 elevators in each tower building and 43,600 windows comprising 600,000 ft.^{2} of glass. There are 50,000 people working in the complex and 90,000 visitors daily.

Rentals   The highest rentals in the world for prime offices, according to *World Rental Levels* by Richard Ellis of London, Great Britain, are in Tokyo, Japan at $224.78 per sq. ft. per year (December 1991). With added service charges and rates this is increased to $243.01 per sq. ft. The highest rates ever were in June 1991 at $206.68 per sq. ft. per year.

TALLEST

The tallest office building in the world is the Sears Tower, national headquarters of Sears, Roebuck & Co. on Wacker Drive, Chicago, IL, with 110 stories, rising to 1,454 ft. Its gross area is 103.3 acres. Construction was started in August 1970 and it was "topped out" on 4 May 1973, having surpassed the World Trade Center in New York City in height at 2:35 P.M. on 6 Mar. 1973 with the first steel column reaching to the 104th story. It does not, however, surpass the World Trade Center for most rentable space. The addition of two TV antennae brought the total height to 1,707 ft.

HABITATIONS

Greatest altitude   The highest inhabited buildings in the world are those in the Indo-Tibetan border fort of Bāsisi by the Māna Pass (Lat. 31° 04′N, Long. 79° 24′E) at *c*. 19,700 ft.

In April 1961 a three-room dwelling was discovered at 21,650 ft. on Cerro Llullaillaco (22,057 ft.), on the Argentina–Chile border, believed to date from the late pre-Columbian period *c*. 1480. A settlement on the T'e-li-mo trail in southern Tibet is sited at an altitude of 19,800 ft.

Northernmost   The Danish scientific station set up in 1952 in Pearyland, northern Greenland is over 900 miles north of the Arctic Circle and is manned every summer. Inuit hearths dated to before 1000 B.C. were discovered there in 1969. Polar Inuits were discovered in Inglefield Land, northwest Greenland in 1818.

The former USSR's drifting research station "North Pole 15" passed within 1¼ miles of the North Pole in December 1967.

The most northerly continuously inhabited place is the Canadian Depart-

THICKEST WALLS–UR. Urnammu's city walls, destroyed by the Elamites in 2006 B.C., were 88 ft. thick. (Photo: Spectrum Colour Library)

ment of National Defense outpost at Alert on Ellesmere Island, Northwest Territories at Lat. 82° 30′ N, Long. 62° W, set up in 1950.

Southernmost   The most southerly permanent human habitation is the United States' Amundsen–Scott South Polar Station, completed in 1957 and replaced in 1975.

EMBASSIES AND CIVIC BUILDINGS

Largest   The embassy of the former USSR, now the Russian embassy, on Bei Xiao Jie, Beijing, China, in the northeastern corner of the northern walled city, occupies the whole 45 acre area of the old Orthodox Church Mission (established 1728), now known as the *Beiguan*. It was handed over to the USSR in 1949.

United States   The largest American embassy is in Bonn, Germany, at 6.6 acres.

SHOPPING CENTERS

The world's first shopping center was built in 1896 at Roland Park, Baltimore, MD.

The world's largest center is the $1.1 billion West Edmonton Mall in Alberta, Canada, which was opened on 15 Sep. 1981 and completed four years later. It covers 5.2 million ft.² on a 121 acre site and encompasses over 800 stores and services as well as 11 major department stores. Parking is provided for 20,000 vehicles for more than 500,000 shoppers per week.

The world's largest wholesale merchandise mart is the Dallas Market Center on Stemmons Freeway, Dallas, TX, with nearly 213.5 acres in eight buildings; technically, six comprise the Dallas Market Center, one is Infomart, and one is Design District. The three segments together are still called by the original name; however, they are managed by different companies. The complex covers 175 acres and houses some 2,580 permanent showrooms displaying merchandise of more than 30,000 manufacturers. The center attracts 760,000 buyers each year to its 107 annual markets and trade shows.

The longest mall in the world is part of the £40 million ($68 million) shopping center at Milton Keynes, Great Britain. It measures 2,133 ft.[2].

INDUSTRIAL STRUCTURES

Tallest chimneys   The Ekibastuz, Kazakhstan coal power plant No. 2 stack is 1,377 ft. tall and was built at a cost of 7.89 million rubles. It was started on 15 Nov. 1983 and completed on 15 Oct. 1987 by the Soviet Building Division of the Ministry of Energy. The diameter tapers from 144 ft. at the base to 46.6 ft. at the top. It weighs 42,996 tons and became operational in 1991.

The world's most massive chimney is one of 1,148 ft. at Puentes de Garcia Rodriguez, northwest Spain, built by M.W. Kellogg Co. It contains 549,840 ft.[3] of concrete and 2.9 million lbs. of steel and has an internal volume of 6.7 million ft.[3].

Tallest unbuilt structure   The tallest unbuilt structure yet designed is the proposed "Millennium Tower" planned by the Japanese Ohbuyashi building conglomerate for a reclaimed site in Tokyo Bay. The design by Sir Norman Foster calls for a conical tower 2,624.6 ft. tall.

Largest brickworks   The largest brickworks in the world is the London Brick Co. Ltd. plant at Stewartby, Great Britain. Established in 1898, the site now covers 221 acres and has a weekly production capacity of 10.5 million bricks and brick equivalent.

Largest exhibition centers   The International Exposition Center in Cleveland, OH, the world's largest, is situated on a 188 acre site adjacent to Cleveland's Hopkins International Airport in a building that measures 57.39 acres. An indoor terminal provides direct rail access and parking for 10,000 cars.

Largest grain elevator   The single-unit elevator operated by the C-G-F Grain Co. at Wichita, KS consists of a triple row of storage tanks, 123 on each side of the central loading tower or "head house." The unit is 2,717 ft. long and 100 ft. wide. Each tank is 120 ft. high, with an inside diameter of 30 ft., giving a total storage capacity of 20 million bushels of wheat.

The world's largest collection of grain elevators are the 23 at Thunder Bay, Ontario, Canada, on Lake Superior, with a total capacity of 103.9 million bushels.

Cooling towers   The largest is that adjacent to the nuclear power plant at Uentrop, Germany, which is 590 ft. tall, completed in 1976.

HANGARS

Largest   Hangar 375 ("Big Texas") at Kelly Air Force Base, San Antonio, TX, completed on 15 Feb. 1956, has four doors, each 250 ft. wide, 60 ft. high and weighing 598 tons. The high bay area measures 2,000 × 300 × 90 ft. and is surrounded by a 44-acre concrete apron. It is the largest freestanding hangar in the world.

Delta Airlines' jet base on a 175-acre site at Hartsfield International Airport, Atlanta, GA has a 36-acre roof area. An addition to the hangar has just been completed. The high bay area is 1,041 × 242 × 90 ft.

SEWAGE WORKS

Largest   The Stickney Water Reclamation Plant (formerly the West-Southwest Sewage Treatment Works), in Stickney, IL began operation in 1939 on a 570-acre site and serves an area containing 2,193,000 people. It treated an average of 791 million gals. of waste per day in 1991 and the capacity of its sedimentation and aeration tanks is 1.7 million yds.^{3}.

Refuse electrical generation plants   As of 1990 there were 13 refuse electrical generation plants in the United States, with an aggregate capacity of 276 Mw. The biggest plant in the country is the South Meadow, Hartford County, CT plant, which has a capacity of 90 Mw.

WOODEN BUILDINGS

Largest   Between 1942 and 1943, 16 Navy airship wooden blimp hangers were built at various locations throughout the United States. They measure 1,040 ft. long, 150 ft. 4 in. high at the crown and 296 ft. 6 in. wide at the base. There are only nine remaining—two each at Tillamook, OR, Moffett Field and Santa Ana, CA and Lakehurst, NJ, and one at Elizabeth City, NC.

AIR-SUPPORTED BUILDINGS

Largest   The 80,638-capacity octagonal Pontiac Silverdome Stadium, Pontiac, MI is 522 ft. wide and 722 ft. long. The air pressure is 5 lbs./ft.^{2} supporting the 10 acre translucent Fiberglas roofing. The main floor is 402 ft. × 240 ft. and the roof is 202 ft. high. Geiger-Berger Associates of New York City were the structural engineers.

The largest standard size air hall (air-supported structure) is one 860 ft. long, 140 ft. wide and 65 ft. high. One was first sited at Lima, OH, made by Irvin Industries of Stamford, CT.

BUILDINGS FOR LIVING

WOODEN BUILDINGS

Oldest   The oldest extant wooden buildings in the world are those comprising the Pagoda, Chumanar Gate and Temple of Horyu (Horyu-ji) at Nara, Japan, dating from *c.* A.D. 670 and completed in 715. The wood used was from 1,000-year-old Hinoki trees. The nearby Daibutsuden, built in 1704–11, once measured 285.4 ft. long, 167.3 ft. wide and 153.3 ft. tall. Presently the dimensions are 188 × 165.3 × 159.4 ft.

CASTLES

Earliest   The castle at Gomdan in Yemen originally had 20 stories and dates from before A.D. 100.

Largest   The largest inhabited castle in the world is the royal residence of Windsor Castle at Windsor, Great Britain. It is primarily of 12th-century construction and is in the form of a waisted parallelogram measuring 1,890 × 540 ft.

The total area of Dover Castle, Kent, Great Britain, however, covers 34 acres, with a width of 1,100 ft. and a curtain wall of 1,800 ft., or if underground works are included, 2,300 ft.

The largest ancient castle in the world is Hradçany Castle, Prague, Czechoslovakia, originating in the 9th century. It is an oblong irregular polygon with an axis of 1,870 ft. and an average transverse diameter of 420 ft. for a surface area of 18 acres.

Thickest walls   Urnammu's city walls at Ur (now Muqayyar, Iraq), destroyed by the Elamites in 2006 B.C., were 88 ft. thick and made of mud brick.

PALACES

Largest   The Imperial Palace (Gu gong) in the center of Beijing, China, covers a rectangle 3,150 × 2,460 ft., an area of 178 acres. The outline survives from the construction of the third Ming emperor, Yongle (1402–24), but due to constant reconstruction work most of the intramural buildings are from the 18th century. These consist of five halls and 17 palaces.

The Palace of Versailles, 14 miles southwest of Paris, France, has a façade

---

Sand castle   The tallest sand castle on record, constructed only with hands, buckets and shovels, was 19 ft. 6 in. high and was made by Team Totally in Sand and Freddie and the Sandblasters at Harrison Hot Springs, British Columbia, Canada on 15 Oct. 1991.

The longest sand castle was 5.2 miles long, and was made by staff and pupils of Ellon Academy, near Aberdeen, Great Britain on 24 Mar. 1988.

1,902 ft. in length, with 375 windows. The building, completed in 1682 for Louis XIV, (1643–1715) occupied over 30,000 workmen under Jules Hardouin-Mansert (1646–1708).

Residential   The palace (Istana Nurul Iman) of HM the Sultan of Brunei in the capital Bandar Seri Begawan, completed in January 1984 at a reported cost of $350 million, is the largest residence in the world, with 1,788 rooms and 257 lavatories. The underground garage accommodates the sultan's 110 cars.

Largest moat   From plans drawn by French sources it appears that those that surround the Imperial Palace in Beijing (see above) measure 162 ft. wide and have a total length of 10,800 ft. In all, the city's moats total 23½ miles.

HOTELS

Largest   The $290-million Excalibur Hotel/Casino, NV, opened in April 1990, is built on a 117 acre site. It has 4,032 deluxe rooms and employs a staff of 4,000. Its facilities include seven theme restaurants and a total of 11 food outlets throughout the hotel and casino.

The Las Vegas Hilton, Reno, NV, built on a 63 acre site in 1974–81, has 3,174 rooms, 13 international restaurants and a staff of 3,600. It has a 10 acre

THE PALACE OF VERSAILLES. The largest palace in the world is the beautiful Palace of Versailles, which was completed in 1682 to the designs of the great architects Le Vau, Charles Le Brun and J.H. Mansart, for Louis XIV, the King of France (1643–1715). (Photo: Images Colour Library)

rooftop recreation deck, a 48,000 ft.² pillar-free ballroom and 125,000 ft.² of convention space.

The Hotel Rossiya in Moscow, Russia opened in 1967 with 3,200 rooms, but because of its high proportion of dormitory accommodations, it is not on the international list of the largest hotels. The Izmailovo Hotel complex, opened in July 1980 for the 22nd Olympic Games in Moscow, was designed to accommodate 9,500 people.

Hoteliers   Following its acquisition of Holiday Inns North America in February 1990, Bass plc, Great Britain's largest brewing company, took ownership of the world's largest hotel chain. The company now owns, manages and franchises 1,655 hotels totaling 326,843 rooms in 53 countries. (See Business World—Brewers.)

United States   The largest hotel operator in the United States for 1991, based on number of properties, was Best Western International of Phoenix, AZ, with 1,774. The largest hotel operator based on number of rooms was Holiday Inn Worldwide, which operates 270,050.

Largest lobby   The lobby at the Hyatt Regency, San Francisco, is 350 ft. long and 160 ft. wide, and at 170 ft. is the height of a 17-story building.

Tallest   Measured from the street level of its main entrance to the top, the 73-story Westin Stamford in Raffles City, Singapore "topped out" in March 1985 at 741.9 ft. tall. The $235 million hotel is operated by Westin Hotel Co. and owned by Raffles City Pte Ltd. However, the Westin at the Renaissance Center in Detroit, MI, is 748 ft. tall when measured from the rear entrance.

LARGEST HOTEL. The Excalibur Hotel/Casino, Las Vegas, NV opened in April 1990. The architect was Veldon Simpson and the interior designer Yates Silverman. The design is based on the theme of King Arthur, Camelot and the Knights of the Round Table. (Photo: Excalibur Hotel)

Most expensive   The Penthouse Suite in the Fairmont Hotel, San Francisco, CA can be rented for $6,000 per night, plus tax. The price includes an around-the-clock butler and maid, and airport limousine service. The suite was built in 1927 atop the Fairmont's main building. It has an immense drawing room with grand piano, a dining room accommodating up to 50, a two-story circular library with the celestial constellations in gold on a domed ceiling, a game room, three bedrooms and four bathrooms with 24-carat gold-plated fittings.

In May 1989 the 92-room Hotel Bel-Air in Los Angeles was sold for a record $1.2 million per room, for a total cost of $110 million, to the Sekitei Kaihatsu Co. of Tokyo, Japan.

Most mobile   The three-story brick Hotel Fairmount (built 1906) in San Antonio, TX, which weighed 1,600 tons, was moved on 36 dollies with pneumatic tires over city streets approximately five blocks and over a bridge, which had to be reinforced. The move by Emmert International of Portland, OR took six days, 30 Mar.–4 Apr. 1985, and cost $650,000.

Spas   Spas are named after the town of Spa, a watering place in the Liège province of Belgium, where hydropathy was developed from 1626. The largest spa, measured by number of available hotel rooms, is Vichy, Allier, France, with 14,000 rooms. The highest French spa is Barèges, Hautes-Pyrénées, at 4,068 ft. above sea level.

LARGEST SPA. The Thermalisme in Vichy Spa, Allier Département, France. Vichy is the largest spa in the world, with 14,000 hotel rooms. Its alkaline springs first became famous in the 17th century. (Photo: Gamma Presse Images)

HOUSING

According to the National Association of Realtors, as of November 1991 the median price of existing homes sold in the 83 largest metropolitan areas in the United States is $97,800. The metropolitan area with the highest median price is Honolulu, HI, at $345,000.

Largest house   The 250-room Biltmore House in Asheville, NC is owned by George and William Cecil, grandsons of George Washington Vanderbilt II (1862–1914). The house was built between 1890 and 1895 in an estate of 119,000 acres, at a cost of $4.4 million; it is now valued at $5.5 million, with 12,000 acres.

Most expensive house   The most expensive private house ever built is the Hearst Ranch at San Simeon, CA. It was built from 1922–39 for William Randolph Hearst (1863–1951), at a total cost of more than $30 million. It has more than 100 rooms, a 104-ft.-long heated swimming pool, an 83-ft.-long assembly hall and a garage for 25 limousines. The house was maintained by 60 servants.

The highest price for any house on the global presidential property mar-

---

Camping out   The silent Indian *fakir* Mastram Bapu ("contented father") remained on the same spot by the roadside in the village of Chitra for 22 years from 1960–82.

Pole sitting   Modern records do not come close to that of St. Simeon the Younger (*c.* A.D. 521–97), called Stylites, a monk who spent his last 45 years atop a stone pillar on the Hill of Wonders, near Antioch, Syria.

The "standards of living" at the tops of poles can vary widely. Mellissa Sanders lived in a shack measuring 6 ft. × 7 ft. at the top of a pole in Indianapolis, IN from 26 Oct. 1986–24 Mar. 1988, a total of 516 days.

Pat Bowen stayed in a barrel (maximum capacity 150 gals.) at the top of a pole 18 ft. high outside the Bull Hotel, Ludlow, Great Britain for 40 days 1 hr. from 28 May–7 July 1986.

Longest continuous home construction   Winchester House in San Jose, CA has been under construction for 38 years. The original house was an eight-room farmhouse with separate barn on the 161-acre estate of Oliver Winchester, who did not invent the Winchester rifle, but owned its patent. Sarah Winchester, widowed in 1886, consulted a psychic in Boston, who told her that she alone could balance the ledger for those killed by Winchester firearms by never stopping construction of the estate.

Mrs. Winchester moved to California, where she transformed the farmhouse into a mansion, which now has 13 bathrooms, 52 skylights, 47 fireplaces, 10,000 windows, 40 staircases, 2,000 doorways and closets opening into blank walls, secret passageways, trapdoors, three $10,000 elevators and more. The house remodeling is intended to confuse the resident ghosts.

---

ket is £50 million asked in 1992 for the Casa Batlló in central Barcelona, Spain. It was built by José Batlló in 1887 and extensively remodeled by Antonio Gaudí (d. 1926).

Largest non-palatial residence   St. Emmeram Castle, Regensburg, Germany, valued at more than $177 million, contains 517 rooms with a floor space of 231,000 ft.². Only 95 rooms are personally used by the family of the late Prince Johannes von Thurn und Taxis.

APARTMENTS

Tallest   The 716-ft. Metropolitan Tower on West 57th Street, New York City is 78 stories; the upper 48 are residential.

The tallest purely residential apartment house is Lake Point Tower, Chicago, IL, which has 879 units consisting of 70 stories, standing 639.4 ft. high.

BUILDINGS FOR ENTERTAINMENT

STADIUMS

Largest   The open Strahov Stadium in Prague, Czechoslovakia was completed in 1934 and could accommodate 240,000 spectators for mass displays of up to 40,000 Sokol gymnasts.

Soccer   The Maracaña Municipal Stadium in Rio de Janeiro, Brazil, has a normal capacity of 205,000, of whom 155,000 can be seated. A crowd of 199,854 was accommodated for the World Cup final between Brazil and Uruguay on 16 July 1950. A dry moat, 7 ft. wide and more than 5 ft. deep, protects players from spectators and vice versa.

The largest stadium in the United States is the Rose Bowl, Pasadena, CA, which has a current seating capacity of 102,083. The largest crowd ever to attend an event there was 106,869 for the Rose Bowl game on New Year's Day, 1973. USC defeated Ohio State 42–27.

Covered   The Azteca Stadium, Mexico City, opened in 1968, has a capacity of 107,000. Nearly all seats are under cover.

Retractable roof   The world's largest covers the 54,000-seating-capacity SkyDome, Toronto. Ontario, Canada, completed in June 1989. The diameter is 679 ft.

Indoor   The $173-million 273-ft. tall Louisiana Superdome in New Orleans, LA, covering 13 acres, was completed in May 1975. Its maximum seating capacity for conventions is 97,365, or 76,791 for football. A gondola with six 312 in. TV screens produces instant replay.

Largest roof   The transparent acrylic glass "marquee" roof over the Munich Olympic Stadium, Germany measures 914,940 ft.² in area, resting on a steel net supported by masts.

The longest roof span in the world is that of the Louisiana Superdome in New Orleans, LA at 680 ft. diameter. The major axis of the elliptical Texas Stadium, completed in 1971 at Irving, TX, is, however, 787 ft. 4 in.

RESORTS

Amusement resort *Largest*   Disney World is set in 28,000 acres of Orange and Osceola counties, 20 miles southwest of Orlando in central Florida. It was opened on 1 Oct. 1971 after a $400 million investment.

Most attended   Disneyland, Anaheim, CA (opened 1955) received its 250-millionth visitor on 24 Aug. 1985 at 9:52 A.M. Disneyland welcomed its 300-millionth visitor in 1989.

Largest pleasure beach   Virginia Beach, VA has 28 miles of beach-front on the Atlantic and 10 miles of estuary frontage. The area embraces 310 miles² with 157 hotels, motels and condos with 11,189 rooms. There are also 2,230 campsites.

Piers *Origins*   The origin of piers goes back to the origin of man-made harbors. The one at Caesarea reputedly had the first freestanding breakwaters in 13 B.C. However, it is possible that the structures associated with the "great harbors" of the ancient world in Crete, Alexandria and Carthage predate this.

LONGEST PIER. The longest pleasure pier in the world is Southend Pier, Essex, Great Britain, which is 1.34 miles in length. Its attractions include a narrow-gauge railway, theaters, shops, and amusement arcades. (Photo: Spectrum Colour Library)

Longest   The longest pleasure pier in the world is Southend Pier at Southend-on-Sea, Great Britain. The original wooden pier was opened in 1830 and extended in 1846. The present pier is 1.34 miles in length and was first opened in August 1889, with final extensions made in 1929. In 1949–50 the pier had a peak 5.75 million visitors. The pier railroad closed in October 1978, and reopened on 2 May 1986.

Most piers   The resort with the most piers was Atlantic City, NJ with seven, though currently only five remain: the Garden Pier (1912), Million Dollar (1906; now called Shops on Ocean One), Auditorium (1900; now the Steeplechase), Steel (1898), and Applegates (1883), now known as Central.

FAIRS

Earliest   The earliest major international fair was the Great Exhibition of 1851 in the Crystal Palace, London, Great Britain, which in 141 days attracted 6,039,195 admissions.

Largest   The site of the Louisiana Purchase Exposition at St. Louis, MO in 1904 covered 1,271.76 acres and there was an attendance of 19,694,855. Events of the 1904 Olympic Games were staged in conjunction with the fair.

Big wheels   The original Ferris Wheel, named after its constructor, George W. Ferris (1859–96), was erected in 1893 at the Midway at the Chicago World's Fair for $385,000. It was 250 ft. in diameter, 790 ft. in circumference, weighed 1,283.8 tons and carried 36 cars, each seating 60 people, making a total of 2,160 passengers. The structure was removed in 1904 to St. Louis, MO for the Louisiana Purchase Exposition (see above) and was eventually sold as scrap for $1,800.

In 1897 a Ferris Wheel with a diameter of 248 ft. was erected for the Earl's Court Exhibition, London, Great Britain. It had ten 1st-class and 30 2nd-class cars.

The largest-diameter wheel now operating is the Cosmoclock 21 at Yokohama City, Japan. It is 344½ ft. high and 328 ft. in diameter, with 60 gondolas, each with eight seats. There are such features as illumination by laser beams and acoustic effects by sound synthesizers. The 60 arms holding the gondolas each serve as a second hand for the 42½-ft.-long electric clock mounted at the hub.

ROLLER COASTERS

The maximum speeds claimed for switchbacks, scenic railroads or roller coasters have long been exaggerated for commercial reasons.

Oldest operating   A *Rutschbahnen* (Russian Switchback) Mk.2 was constructed at the Tivoli Gardens, Copenhagen, Denmark, in 1913. This coaster opened to the public in 1914, and has remained open ever since.

The oldest operating roller coaster in the United States is the *Zippin Pippin*, constructed at Libertyland Amusement Park, Memphis, TN in 1915.

Longest   The longest roller coaster in the world is *The Ultimate* at Lightwater Valley, Ripon, Great Britain. The run is 1.42 miles.

The longest roller coaster in the United States is *The Beast* at Kings Island near Cincinnati, Ohio. The run of 1.40 miles incorporates 800 ft. of tunnels and a 540-degree banked helix.

Greatest drop and fastest   The *Steel Phantom*, opened in April 1991 at Kennywood Amusement Park, West Mifflin, PA, has a vertical drop of 225 ft. into a natural ravine, with a speed of 80 mph.

Tallest *Steel*   The tallest above ground is the *Moonsault Scramble* at the Fujikyu Highland Park, near Kawaguchi Lake, Japan, opened on 24 June 1983. It is 207 ft. tall.

Most loops   At its highest point 188 ft. above the ground the *Viper* at Six Flags Magic Mountain, Valencia, CA sends riders upside-down seven times over a 3,830 ft. track.

Longest slide   The Bromley Alpine Slide on Route 11 in Peru, VT, has a length of 4,000 ft. and a vertical drop of 700 ft.

NIGHT CLUBS AND RESTAURANTS

Night clubs   The earliest night club (*boîte de nuit*) was "Le Bal des Anglais" at 6 rue des Anglais, Paris, France. Established in 1843, it closed *c*. 1960.

Largest   Gilley's Club (formerly Shelly's), built in 1955, was extended in 1971 on Spencer Highway, Houston, TX, with a seating capacity of 6,000 under one roof covering 4 acres.

The largest night club in the world in the more classic sense of the term is The Mikado in the Akasaka district of Tokyo, Japan, with a seating capacity of 2,000. Binoculars can be essential to an appreciation of the floor show.

Lowest   The Minus 206 in Tiberias, Israel, on the shores of the Sea of Galilee, is 676 ft. below sea level. An alternative candidate has been the oft-raided "Outer Limits," opposite the Cow Palace, San Francisco, CA. It has been called "The Most Busted Joint" and "The Slowest to Get the Message."

Restaurants *Earliest*   The Casa Botin was opened in 1725 in Calle de Cuchilleros 17, Madrid, Spain.

Largest casino   The Trump Taj Mahal, Atlantic City, NJ, which opened in April 1990, has a casino area of 2.75 acres.

Slot machines   The biggest beating handed to a "one-armed bandit" was $6,814,823.48 by Cammie Brewer, 61, at the Club Cal-Neva, Reno, NV on 14 Feb. 1988.

House of cards   The greatest number of stories achieved in building freestanding houses of standard playing cards is 68, to a height of 12 ft. 10 in., built by John Sain, 15, of South Bend, IN in May 1984.

Largest   The Tump Nak restaurant in Bangkok, Thailand consists of 65 adjoining houses built on 10 acres. A thousand waiters are available to serve the 3,000 potential customers.

Highest   The highest restaurant in the world is in the Chacaltaya ski resort, Bolivia, at 17,519 ft.

Restaurateurs   The world's largest restaurant chain is operated by McDonald's Corporation of Oak Brook, IL, founded in 1955 by Ray A. Kroc (1902–84) after buying out the brothers Dick and "Mac" McDonald, pioneers of the fast-food drive-in. By April 1992 McDonald's licensed and owned 12,500 restaurants in 60 countries. Its largest outlet opened in Beijing, China on 23 Apr. 1992, with almost 1,000 specially trained local staff at the 28,000 ft.², 700-seater restaurant. Worldwide sales in 1991 were $19.9 billion.

Fish and chip restaurant   The world's largest fish and chip eatery is Harry Ramsden's at White Cross, Guiseley, Great Britain, with 140 employees serving 1 million customers per year, who consume 235 tons of fish and 392 tons of potatoes. On 30 Oct. 1988, between 11:30 A.M. and 10:00 P.M., Harry Ramsden's celebrated its Diamond Jubilee by selling 10,182 servings of fish and chips at 1928 prices.

BARS

Largest   The largest beer-selling establishment in the world is the "Mathäser," Bayerstrasse 5, Munich, Germany, where daily sales reach 84,470 pints. It was established in 1829, demolished in World War II and rebuilt by 1955. It now seats 5,500 people.

The beer consumption at the Dube beer halls in Soweto, Johannesburg, South Africa may, however, be higher on some Saturdays when the average daily consumption of 48,000 pints is far exceeded.

Tallest   Humperdink's Seafood and Steakhouse Bar in Dallas, TX is 25 ft. 3 in. high with two levels of shelving containing over 1,000 bottles. The lower level has four rows of shelves approximately 40 ft. across and can be reached from floor level. If an order has to be met from the upper level, which has five rows of shelves, it is reached by climbing a ladder.

Longest   The world's longest permanent bar is the 340-ft.-long bar in "Lulu's Roadhouse," Kitchener, Ontario, Canada, opened on 3 Apr. 1984. The "Bar at Erickson's," on Burnside Street, Portland, OR, in its heyday (1883–1920) possessed a bar measuring 684 ft. that ran continuously around and across the main saloon. The chief bouncer, Edward "Spider" Johnson, had an assistant named "Jumbo" Reilly, who weighed 322 lbs. and was said to resemble "an ill-natured orangutan." Beer was five cents for 16 fluid ounces. Temporary bars of greater length have been erected.

TOWERS AND MASTS

TALLEST STRUCTURES

World   The tallest-ever structure in the world was the guyed Warszawa Radio mast at Konstantynow, 60 miles northwest of the capital of Poland. Prior to its fall during renovation work on 10 Aug. 1991 it was 2,120⅔ ft. tall or more than four-tenths of a mile. It was completed on 18 July 1974 and put into operation on 22 July 1974. It was designed by Jan Polak and weighed 606 tons. The mast was so high that anyone falling off the top would reach terminal velocity and hence cease to be accelerating before hitting the ground. Work was begun in July 1970 on this tubular steel construction, with its 15 steel guy ropes. It recaptured for Europe, after 45 years, a record held in the United States since the Chrysler Building surpassed the Eiffel Tower in 1929. After 1991 it was described by the Poles as the "world's longest tower."

TALLEST TOWERS

The tallest self-supporting tower (as opposed to a guyed mast) in the world is the $44 million CN Tower in Metro Center, Toronto, Ontario, Canada, which rises to 1,815 ft. 5 in. Excavation began on 12 Feb. 1973 for the erection of the 143,300 ton reinforced, post-tensioned concrete structure, which was "topped out" on 2 Apr. 1975. The 416-seat restaurant revolves in the Sky Pod at 1,140 ft., from which the visibility extends to hills 74½ miles distant. Lightning strikes the top about 200 times (30 storms) per year.

The tallest tower built before the era of television masts is the Eiffel Tower in Paris, France, designed by Alexandre Gustav Eiffel (1832–1923) for the Paris Exhibition and completed on 31 Mar. 1889. It was 985 ft. 11 in. tall,

---

HIGHEST STRUCTURES IN THE UNITED STATES

FEET	STORIES	BUILDING	YEAR COMPLETED
1,454	110	Sears Tower, Chicago, IL	1974
1,377	110	World Trade Center (North), New York City	1972
1,362	110	World Trade Center (South), New York City	1973
1,250	102	Empire State Building, New York City	1931
1,136	80	Amoco Building, Chicago, IL	1973
1,127	100	John Hancock Center, Chicago, IL	1968
1,046	77	Chrysler Building, New York City	1930
1,012	75	Library Square Tower, Los Angeles, CA	1989
1,000	79	Texas Commerce Plaza, Houston, TX	1982
970	71	Allied Bank Plaza, Houston, TX	1983

Council of Tall Buildings and Urban Habitat; Lehigh University, Bethlehem, PA

now extended by a TV antenna to 1,052⅓ ft., and weighs 8,090 tons. The maximum sway in high winds is 5 in. The whole iron edifice, which has 1,792 steps, took 2 years, 2 months and 2 days to build and cost 7,799,401 francs 31 centimes.

BRIDGES

Oldest   Arch construction was understood by the Sumerians as early as 3200 B.C., and a reference exists to a Nile bridge in 2650 B.C.

The oldest surviving datable bridge in the world is the slab stone single-arch bridge over the River Meles in Izmir (formerly Smyrna) Turkey, which dates from *c*. 850 B.C.

Clapper bridges   The clapper bridges of Dartmoor and Exmoor, Great Britain (e.g., the Tarr Steps over the River Barle, Exmoor, Great Britain) are thought to be of prehistoric types although none of the existing examples can be dated with certainty. They are made of large slabs of stone placed over boulders.

LONGEST

Cable suspension   The world's longest bridge span is the main span of the Humber Estuary Bridge, Humberside, Great Britain, at 4,626 ft. Work began on 27 July 1972, after a decision announced on 22 Jan. 1966. The towers are 533 ft. 1⅝ in. tall and are 1⅜ in. out of parallel to allow for the curvature of the Earth. Including the Hessle and the Barton side spans, the bridge stretches 1.37 miles. It was structurally completed on 18 July 1980 at a cost of £96 million ($192 million) and was opened by Queen Elizabeth II on 17 July 1981.

The Akashi-Kaikyo road bridge linking Honshū and Shikoku, Japan was started in 1988 and completion is planned for 1998. The main span will be 6,528 ft. in length with an overall suspended length, with side spans, totaling 12,828 ft. Two towers will rise 974.40 ft. above water level, and the two main supporting cables will be 43.3 in. in diameter, making both tower heights at span world records.

The Seto-Ohashi double-deck road and rail bridge linking Kojima, Honshū with Sakaide, Shikoku, Japan opened on 10 Apr. 1988 at a cost of $8.33 billion and 17 lives. The overall length of the bridge is 7.64 miles, making it the longest combined road/railway bridge in the world. The tolls for cars are $43 each way. The Minami Bisan-seto Bridge on this link has the world's longest suspension bridge span—3,609 ft. for combined road-railroad traffic.

Cable-stayed   The longest cable-stayed bridge span in the world is the 1,739 ft. Skarnsundet Bridge over the Trondheim Fjord in Norway, completed in 1991.

The Tatara Bridge on the Onomichi-Imabari Route, Japan, is due for completion in 1997, and will be the leading long-span cable-stayed bridge in the world, with a main span of 2,920 ft.

GOLDEN GATE BRIDGE. The Golden Gate suspension bridge is the tallest in the world. It connects San Francisco and Marin County, CA. Opened to traffic in May 1937, its 4,200-ft. span made it the world's longest suspension bridge until surpassed by the Verrazano–Narrows Bridge in New York City in 1964. It carries six lanes of roadway and two footways on a deck 90 ft. wide. Its towers extend 747 ft. above the water level. (Photo: Spectrum Colour Library)

The Mackinac Straits Bridge between Mackinac City and St. Ignace, MI is the longest suspension bridge between anchorages (1.58 miles), and has an overall length, including approaches, of 5 miles.

United States   The longest suspension bridge in the USA is the Verrazano–Narrows Bridge, which measures 4,260 ft. The bridge spans Lower New York Bay and connects Staten Island to Brooklyn. Construction was completed in 1964.

Cantilever   The Quebec Bridge (Pont de Québec) over the St. Lawrence River in Canada has the longest cantilever truss span of any in the world—1,800 ft. between the piers and 3,239 ft. overall. It carries a railroad track and two carriageways. Begun in 1899, it was finally opened to traffic on 3 Dec. 1917 at a cost of 87 lives and Can$22.5 million.

United States   The longest cantilever bridge in the USA is the John Barry Bridge, in Chester, PA. It spans the Delaware River and measures 1,644 ft. Work was completed in 1974.

Bridge building   British soldiers from the 35th Engineer Regiment based at Hameln, Germany constructed a bridge across a 26 ft. gap using a five-bay single-story MGB (medium girder bridge) in 8 min. 31 sec. at Quebec Barracks, Osnabruck, Germany on 17 Oct. 1989.

Bridge sale   The largest antique ever sold was London Bridge in Great Britain in March 1968. The sale was made by Ivan F. Luckin (d. 1992) of the Court of Common Council of the Corporation of London to the McCulloch Oil Corporation of Los Angeles, CA for £1,029,000 ($2,469,600). The 11,810.5 tons of façade stonework were reassembled at a cost of $7.2 million at Lake Havasu City, AZ and rededicated on 10 Oct. 1971.

Bicycle bridge   The longest bicycle bridge is over the 17 railroad tracks of Cambridge Station, Great Britain. It has a tower 115 ft. high and two 164-ft.-long approach ramps, and is 779.5 ft. in length.

Floating bridge   The longest is the Second Lake Washington Bridge, Evergreen, Seattle, WA. Its total length is 12,596 ft. and its floating section measures 7,518 ft. It was built at a total cost of $15 million and completed in August 1963.

Steel arch   The longest is the New River Gorge bridge, near Fayetteville, WV, completed in 1977, with a span of 1,700 ft.

Concrete arch   The longest concrete arch is the Jesse H. Jones Memorial Bridge, which spans the Houston Ship Canal in Texas. Completed in 1982, the bridge measures 1,500 ft.

Covered   The longest is that at Hartland, New Brunswick, Canada, measuring 1,282 ft. overall, completed in 1899.

Railway   The world's longest railway bridge is the 43,374-ft.-long Seto-Ohashi double-deck road and rail bridge linking Kojima, Honshū with Sakaide, Shikoku, Japan, which opened on 10 Apr. 1988 (see Bridges, Longest).

United States   The longest is the Huey P. Long Bridge, Metairie, LA, with a railroad section 23,235 ft. long (4.4 miles), including approach roads. It has a 3-span tress: 529 ft., 790 ft. and 531 ft., followed by a single span of 531.5 ft. It was completed on 16 Dec. 1935.

Longest bridging   The Second Lake Pontchartrain Causeway was completed on 23 Mar. 1969, joining Lewisburg and Mandeville, LA. It has a length of 126,055 ft. It cost $29.9 million and is 228 ft. longer than the adjoining First Causeway, completed in 1956.

Longest railway viaduct   The longest railway viaduct is the rock-filled Great Salt Lake Railroad Trestle, carrying the Southern Pacific Railroad 11.85 miles across the Great Salt Lake, UT. It was opened as a pile and trestle bridge on 8 Mar. 1904, but converted to rock fill in 1955–60.

Stone arch   The longest stone arch bridge is the 3,810 ft.-long Rockville Bridge north of Harrisburg, PA, with 48 spans containing 216,051 tons of stone. It was completed in 1901.
   The longest stone arch span is the Planen Bridge in Germany at 295 ft.

Widest   The widest long-span bridge is the 1,650 ft. Sydney Harbor Bridge, Australia (160 ft. wide). It carries two electric overhead railroad tracks, eight lanes of roadway and bicycle and pedestrian lanes. It was officially opened on 19 Mar. 1932.
   The Crawford Street Bridge in Providence, RI has a width of 1,148 ft.

HIGHEST

The highest bridge in the world is over the Royal Gorge of the Arkansas River in Colorado, at 1,053 ft. above the water level. It is a suspension bridge with a main span of 880 ft. and was constructed in six months, ending on 6 Dec. 1929.

Railway   The highest railroad bridge in the world is the Mala Rijeka viaduct of Yugoslav Railways at Kolasin on the Belgrade–Bar line. It is 650 ft. high and was opened on 1 June 1976. It consists of steel spans mounted on concrete piers.

Road   The road bridge at the highest altitude in the world, 18,380 ft., is the 98.4-ft.-long Bailey Bridge, designed and constructed by Lt. Col. S.G. Vombatkere and an Indian Army team in August 1982 near Khardung-La, in Ladakh, India.

AQUEDUCTS

Longest ancient   The greatest of ancient aqueducts was the aqueduct of

Carthage in Tunisia, which ran 87.6 miles from the springs of Zaghouan to Djebel Djougar. It was built by the Romans during the reign of Publius Aelius Hadrianus (A.D. 117–138). In 1895, 344 arches still survived. Its original capacity has been calculated at 7 million gals. per day.

The triple-tiered aqueduct Pont du Gard, built in A.D. 19 near Nimes, France, is 157 ft. high.

The tallest of the 14 arches of the Aguas Livres aqueduct, built in Lisbon, Portugal, in 1784 is 213 ft.

Longest modern   The world's longest aqueduct, in the nonclassical sense of water conduit, excluding irrigation canals, is the California State Water Project aqueduct, completed in 1974, with a length of 826 miles, of which 385 miles is canalized.

CANALS

Earliest   Relics of the oldest canals in the world, dated by archaeologists c. 4000 B.C., were discovered near Mandali, Iraq early in 1968.

Longest   The longest canal in the ancient world was the Grand Canal of China from Beijing to Hangzhou. It was begun in 540 B.C. and not completed until A.D. 1327, by which time it extended (including canalized river sections) for 1,107 miles. The estimated work force c. A.D. 600 reached 5 million on the Bian section. By 1950 it had been allowed to silt up to the point that it was nowhere more than 6 ft. deep; however, it is now plied by vessels of up to 2,205 tons.

The Beloye More (White Sea) Baltic Canal from Belomorsk to Povenets, Karelian Republic, Russia is 141 miles long and has 19 locks. It was completed with the use of forced labor in 1933 but cannot accommodate ships of more than 16 ft. in draft

The world's longest big-ship canal is the Suez Canal linking the Red Sea with the Mediterranean, opened on 16 Nov. 1869 but inoperative from June 1967 to June 1975. It is 100.6 miles in length from Port Said lighthouse to Suez Roads, and 197 ft. wide. The canal was planned by the French diplomat Comte Ferdinand de Lesseps (1805–94) and work began on 25 Apr. 1859. The work force consisted of 8,213 men and 368 camels.

The largest vessel to transit the Suez Canal has been SS *Settebello*, of 355,432 tons (length 1,110.3 ft.; beam 188.1 ft. at a maximum draft of 73.3 ft.). This was southbound in ballast on 6 Aug. 1986. The USS *Shreveport* transited southbound on 15–16 Aug. 1984 in a record 7 hrs. 45 min. There are over 20,000 transits annually or some 55 per day.

United States   The longest canal in the USA is the Erie Barge Canal, connecting the Hudson River at Troy, NY, with Lake Erie at Buffalo, NY. It is 365 miles long, 150 ft. wide and 12 ft. in depth. The Erie Barge is part of the main waterway of the New York State Barge Canal System, which covers a distance of 525 miles.

LARGEST CUT. The Corinth Canal, Greece links the Aegean and
Ionian seas. With its towering and almost vertical rock walls
its extreme depth is 1,505 ft. (Photo: Spectrum Colour Library)

Longest irrigation   The Karakumsky Kanal stretches 745 miles from Haun-Khan to Ashkhabad, Turkmenistan. The "navigable" length is 497 miles.

LOCKS

Largest   The Berendrecht lock, which links the River Scheldt with docks at Antwerp, Belgium, is the largest sea lock in the world. First used in April 1989, it has a length of 1,640 ft., a width of 223 ft. and a sill level of 44.3 ft. Each of its four sliding lock gates weighs 1,771.5 tons. The cost of construction was approximately BFr 12,000 million.

Highest rise and longest flight   The world's highest lock elevator overcomes a head of 225 ft. at Ronquières on the Charleroi–Brussels Canal, Belgium. Two 236-wheeled caissons are each able to carry 1,510 tons, and take 22 minutes to cover the 4,698-ft.-long inclined plane.

Largest cut   The Corinth Canal, Greece, opened in 1893, is 3.94 miles long, 26 ft. deep, with an average depth of cutting of 1,003 ft. over some 2.6 miles, and an extreme depth of 1,505 ft.

The Gaillard Cut (known as "the Ditch") on the Panama Canal is 270 ft. deep between Gold Hill and Contractor's Hill with a bottom width of 500 ft. In one day in 1911 as many as 333 trains, each carrying 400 tons of earth, left this site—a total of more than 130,000 tons of soil.

Longest artificial seaway   The St. Lawrence Seaway is 189 miles in length along the New York State–Ontario border from Montreal to Lake Ontario. It enables ships up to 728 ft. long and 26.2 ft. draft (some of which weigh 29,100 tons) to sail 2,342 miles from the North Atlantic up the St. Lawrence estuary and across the Great Lakes to Duluth, MN. The project, begun in 1954, cost $470 million and was opened on 25 Apr. 1959.

Busiest   The busiest ship canal is the Kiel Canal linking the North Sea with the Baltic Sea in Germany. Over 45,000 transits were recorded in 1987. The busiest in terms of tonnage of shipping is the Suez Canal, with nearly 440 million grt.

Deepest   The deepest lock is the Zaporozhe on the Dnieperbug Canal, Ukraine which can raise or lower barges at 128 ft.

The deepest lock in the United States is the John Day dam lock on the River Columbia, in Oregon and Washington State, that was completed in 1963. It can raise or lower barges 113 ft. and is served by a 1,100-ton gate.

DAMS

Earliest   The earliest-known dams were those uncovered by the British School of Archaeology in Jerusalem in 1974 and at Jawa in Jordan in 1975. These stone-faced earthen dams are dated to *c*. 3200 B.C.

Most massive   Measured by volume, the earth- and rock-filled Pati Dam on the Paraná River, Argentina has a volume of 8.4 billion ft.^{3}. It is 108.6 miles in length and 118 ft. high. This volume will be surpassed by the Syncrude Tailings dam in Canada with 19 billion ft.^{3}.

Largest concrete   The Grand Coulee Dam on the Columbia River, WA was begun in 1933 and became operational on 22 Mar. 1941. It was finally completed in 1942 at a cost of $56 million. It has a crest length of 4,173 ft. and is 550 ft. high. The volume of concrete poured was 285 million ft.^{3} to the weight of 21.5 million tons.

Highest   The highest will be the 1,098-ft.-high Rogunskaya earth-filled dam across the river Vakhsh, Tadzhikistan, with a crest length of only 1,975 ft. and a volume of 2.5 billion ft.^{3}. Preparations for building started in 1976, and construction began in March 1981. The completion date was set for early 1992, but it will probably not be met. Meanwhile the tallest dam ever completed is the 984-ft.-high Nurek dam, of 2.05 billion ft.^{3} volume.

United States   The embankment–earthfill Oroville Dam is the United States' highest dam, reaching 754 ft. and spanning the Feather River of California. It was completed in 1968.

Coal shoveling   The record for filling a 1,120 lb. hopper with coal is 29.4 sec., by Piet Groot at the Inangahua A and P Show, New Zealand on 1 Jan. 1985.

Largest polder   Of the five great polders (lands reclaimed from the sea) in the old Zuider Zee, Netherlands, the largest will be the Markerwaard, of 148,250 acres (231 miles^2). Work on the 65-mile-long surrounding dike began in 1957. The water area remaining after the erection of the dam (20 miles in length), built between 1927–32, is called IJsselmeer, and will have a final area of 487½ miles^2.

Largest levees   The most massive ever built are the Mississippi levees, begun in 1717 but vastly augmented by the federal government after the disastrous floods of 1927. They extend for 1,732 miles along the main river from Cape Girardeau, MO to the Gulf of Mexico and comprise more than 27 billion ft.^{3} of earthworks. Levees on the tributaries comprise an additional 2,000 miles.

Longest   The 134½-ft.-high Yacyreta–Apipe Dam across the Paraná on the Paraguay–Argentina border will extend for 43.2 miles. It was due for completion in 1992.

The Kiev Dam across the Dnieper, Ukraine, completed in 1964, has a crest length of 256 miles.

In the early 17th century an impounding dam of moderate height was built in Lake Hongze, Jiangsu, China, of a reputed length of 62 miles.

The longest sea dam in the world is the Afsluitdijk, stretching 20.2 miles across the mouth of the Zuider Zee in two sections of 1.6 miles (mainland of North Holland to the Isle of Wieringen) and 18.6 miles from Wieringen to Friesland. It has a sea-level width of 293 ft. and a height of 24 ft. 7 in.

Strongest   On completion, the strongest will be the 803.8-ft.-high Sayano-Shushenskaya Dam on the River Yenisey, Russia, which is designed to bear a load of 19.8 million tons from a fully filled reservoir of 1.1 trillion ft.^{3} capacity.

Largest reservoir   The most voluminous man-made reservoir is the Bratskoye reservoir, on the Angara River in Siberia, Russia, with a volume of 40.6 miles^3 and an area of 2,112 miles^2. It extends for 372 miles with a width of 21 miles. It was filled in 1961–67.

The world's largest artificial lake measured by surface area is Lake Volta, Ghana, formed by the Akosombo Dam, completed in 1965. By 1969 the lake had filled to an area of 3,275 miles^2, with a shoreline 4,500 miles in length.

The completion in 1954 of the Owen Falls Dam near Jinja, Uganda, across the northern exit of the White Nile from the Victoria Nyanza, marginally raised the level of that natural lake by adding 218.9 million acre-feet, and technically turned it into a reservoir with a surface area of 17.2 million acres.

The $4-billion Tucurui Dam in Brazil by 1984 converted the Tocantins River into a 1,180-mile-long chain of lakes.

United States   The largest wholly artificial reservoir in the USA is Lake Mead in Nevada. It was formed by the Hoover Dam, which was completed in 1936. The lake has a capacity of 1,241,445 million ft.^{3} and a surface area of 28,255,000 acre-ft.

TUNNELS

LONGEST

Water-supply tunnel   The longest tunnel of any kind is the New York City West Delaware water-supply tunnel, begun in 1937 and completed in 1944. It has a diameter of 13½ ft. and runs for 105 miles from the Rondout Reservoir into the Hillview Reservoir, on the border of Yonkers, NY and New York City.

Rail   The 33.46-mile-long Seikan Rail Tunnel was bored to 787 ft. beneath sea level and 328 ft. below the seabed of the Tsugaru Strait between Tappi Saki, Honshū, and Fukushima, Hokkaidō, Japan. Tests started on the subaqueous section (14½ miles) in 1964 and construction began in June 1972. It was holed through on 27 Jan. 1983 after a loss of 34 lives. The first test run took place on 13 Mar. 1988.

Proposals for a Brenner Pass Tunnel between Innsbruck, Austria and Italy envisage a rail tunnel 36–39 miles long.

The Channel Tunnel, an electric railroad under the English Channel, is being constructed as a joint Anglo-French project at an estimated cost of $13.5 billion. Nonstop through trains, operated by the national railroads, will carry passengers and freight. The system will consist of three bored tunnels—two main tunnels each carrying a single railroad track and a central tunnel containing essential services such as electricity, ventilation and drainage. Some 23 miles will be under the sea and the journey will take about 35 minutes. The project is due for completion in 1993. (See also Channel Tunnel feature).

United States   The longest main-line tunnel railroad in the USA is the Moffat Tunnel, which cuts through a 6.2 mile section of the Rocky Mountains in Colorado. Tunnel construction was completed in 1928.

Continuous subway   The Moscow Metro underground railroad line from Medvedkovo to Bittsevsky is *c.* 23.5 miles long and was completed in early 1990.

Road tunnel   The 10.14-mile-long two-lane St. Gotthard road tunnel from Göschenen, Switzerland to Airolo, Italy opened to traffic on 5 Sep. 1980. Nineteen lives were lost during its construction, begun in fall 1969, at a cost of SFr 686 million (then $414 million).

United States   The longest road tunnel in the USA is the 2.5 mile Lincoln Tunnel, linking New York City and New Jersey. The tunnel was dug beneath the Hudson River and was completed in 1937.

Largest   The largest-diameter road tunnel in the world is the one blasted through Yerba Buena Island, San Francisco, CA. It is 77 ft. 10 in. wide, 56 ft. high and 540 ft. long. More than 90 million vehicles pass through on its two decks every year.

Hydroelectric irrigation   The 51½-mile-long Orange–Fish Rivers tunnel, South Africa, was bored between 1967 and 1973 at an estimated cost of £60 million ($144 million). The lining to a minimum thickness of 9 in. gave a completed diameter of 17½ ft.

The Majes dam project in Peru involves 60.9 miles of tunnels for hydroelectric and water-supply purposes. The dam is at 13,780 ft. altitude.

Tunneling   The longest unsupported example of a machine-bored tunnel is the Three Rivers water tunnel, 30,769 ft. long with a 10.5 ft. diameter, constructed for the city of Atlanta, GA from April 1980 to February 1982.

The Channel Tunnel

The Channel Tunnel, an electric railway under the English Channel, is being constructed as a joint Anglo-French project at an estimated cost of $13.5 billion. It is the largest single civil engineering project undertaken in this century in Europe, and will provide the first fixed links between the railway and road systems of Great Britain and France. Nonstop through-trains, operated by the national rail system, will carry passengers and freight. Cars, buses and trucks will be carried on shuttle trains and will run on a continuous loop line between Cheriton, near Folkestone, Great Britain and Sangatte, near Calais, France. The system will consist of three bored tunnels—two main tunnels, each carrying a single railway track, and a central tunnel containing essential services such as electricity, ventilation

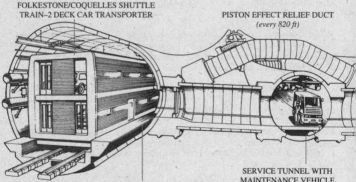

FOLKESTONE/COQUELLES SHUTTLE TRAIN–2 DECK CAR TRANSPORTER

PISTON EFFECT RELIEF DUCT *(every 820 ft)*

SOUTH (UP) RUNNING TUNNEL

SERVICE TUNNEL WITH MAINTENANCE VEHICLE

Above: an artist's impression of a typical cross section of the Channel tunnel and shuttle train (locomotive and loader wagon not shown).

and drainage. The north-running tunnel is the lowest point on the railways in Europe, 9.5 miles from the English shore, where the rails are 417 ft below mean sea-level. Some 23.5 miles of the tunnel will be under the sea and the journey will take about 35 minutes. The project is due for completion in 1993. Freight trains are scheduled to start running in November 1993, with passenger trains beginning mid-1994.

Tunnel History
For nearly 200 years engineers have put forward various schemes for
the building of a Channel tunnel. The first person to conceive the
idea was a Frenchman, Albert Mathieu-Favier, a mining engineer,
who in 1802 suggested horse-drawn vehicles, with candles for
lighting and air shafts for ventilation. In 1851 Hector Horeau
proposed the idea of an iron tube to rest on the sea bed. In 1867
Thomé de Gamond exhibited a version at the Universal Exhibition of
Paris, France, but unfortunately other projects, such as the Suez
Canal, the London Underground and St Gotthard Alpine tunnel, were
being constructed, and the Channel tunnel was once more pushed
into the background. From then on, wars and financial obstacles
prevented further progress.

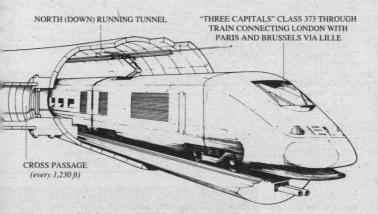

NORTH (DOWN) RUNNING TUNNEL

"THREE CAPITALS" CLASS 373 THROUGH
TRAIN CONNECTING LONDON WITH
PARIS AND BRUSSELS VIA LILLE

CROSS PASSAGE
(every 1,230 ft)

The project eventually got under way when the British Prime
Minister Margaret Thatcher and the French President François
Mitterand signed a treaty on 12 Feb 1986, agreeing to the conditions
under which the tunnel was to be built and operated. Excavation
began on 1 Jul 1987, and on 30 Oct 1990 the two countries were
linked with a British bore hole 2 in in diameter.

Tunneling
The longest unsupported example of a machine-bored tunnel is the Three Rivers water tunnel, 30,769 ft long with a 10.5 ft diameter, constructed for the city of Atlanta, GA from April 1980 to February 1982.

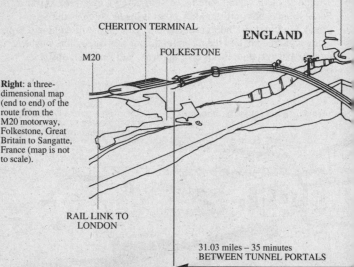

DOVER

SHAKESPEARE CLIFF

CHERITON TERMINAL

ENGLAND

FOLKESTONE

M20

Right: a three-dimensional map (end to end) of the route from the M20 motorway, Folkestone, Great Britain to Sangatte, France (map is not to scale).

RAIL LINK TO LONDON

31.03 miles – 35 minutes
BETWEEN TUNNEL PORTALS

Tunnel boring machine
Eleven tunnel boring machines were ordered from a variety of manufacturers. The machines used in England and France were fundamentally different because of the differing geological conditions. This is one of the British machines maufactured by Howden & Co. of Glasgow, Scotland. The boring machines weigh over 600 metric tons and can advance at a rate of 26 ft an hour.

First channel tunnel scheme
Right: Albert Mathieu-Favier's plan was for two tunnels. This picture depicts the one designed to carry horse-drawn vehicles.

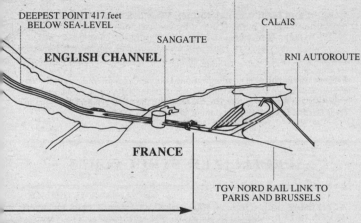

COQUELLES SHUTTLE TERMINAL

DEEPEST POINT 417 feet BELOW SEA-LEVEL

CALAIS

SANGATTE

ENGLISH CHANNEL

RNI AUTOROUTE

FRANCE

TGV NORD RAIL LINK TO PARIS AND BRUSSELS

Size comparison of the Eiffel Tower and material excavated in building the Channel Tunnel. The amount of material excavated for the tunnel is estimated at 246 million ft^3. The Eiffel Tower in Paris weighs 7,340 metric tons and stands 1,052.5 ft high.

Sewerage   The Chicago TARP (Tunnels and Reservoir Plan) in Illinois, when complete, will involve 130 miles of sewerage tunneling. Phase I will comprise 109 miles when completed. As of August 1991, 50.5 miles are operational, 24.9 miles are under construction, and the remaining 33.8 miles are unfunded. The system will provide pollution control to the area and will service 3.9 million people in 52 communities over a 375 mile^2 area. The estimated cost for the project is $3.7 billion ($2.5 billion for Phase I, $1.2 billion for Phase II).

The Viikinmäki Central Treatment Plant in Helsinki, Finland is the world's first major waste-water plant to be built underground. It will involve the excavation of nearly 35,314 ft.^{3} of rock before its completion in 1993.

Bridge-tunnel   The Chesapeake Bay Bridge-Tunnel extends 17.65 miles from the Eastern Shore peninsula to Virginia Beach, VA. It cost $200 million and was completed in 42 months. It opened to traffic on 15 Apr. 1964. The longest bridged section is Trestle C (4.56 miles long) and the longest tunnel section is the Thimble Shoal Channel Tunnel (1.09 miles).

Longest and largest canal-tunnel   The Rove Tunnel on the Canal de Marseille au Rhône in the south of France was completed in 1927 and is 23,359 ft. long, 72 ft. wide and 37 ft. high. Built to be navigated by seagoing ships, it was closed in 1963 following a collapse and has not been reopened.

Oldest navigable   The Malpas tunnel on the Canal du Midi in southwest France was completed in 1681 and is 528 ft. long. Its completion enabled vessels to navigate from the Atlantic Ocean to the Mediterranean Sea via the river Garonne to Toulouse and the Canal du Midi to Sète.

SPECIALIZED STRUCTURES

Advertising signs *Highest*   The highest is the logo "I" at the top of the 73-story 1,017-ft.-tall First Interstate World Center building, Los Angeles, CA.

The most conspicuous sign ever erected was the electric Citroën sign on the Eiffel Tower, Paris, France. It was switched on on 4 July 1925, and could be seen 24 miles away. It was in six colors with 250,000 lamps and 56 miles of electric cables. The letter "N" that terminated the name "Citroën" between the second and third levels measured 68 ft. 5 in. in height. The sign was dismantled in 1936.

Neon   The longest is the letter "M" installed on the Great Mississippi River Bridge, Old Man River at Memphis, TN. It is 1,800 ft. long and comprises 200 high-intensity lamps.

The largest neon sign measures 210 × 55 ft. and was built for Marlboro cigarettes at Hung Hom, Kowloon, Hong Kong in May 1986. It contains 35,000 ft. of neon tubing and weighs approximately 126 tons.

An interior-lit fascia advertising sign in Clearwater, FL completed by the Adco Sign Corp in April 1983 measured 1,168 ft. 6½ in. in length.

Billboards   The world's largest billboard is that of the Bassat Ogilvy Promotional Campaign for Ford España, measuring 475 ft. 9 in. in length and 78 ft. 9 in. in width. It is sited at Plaza de Toros Monumental de Barcelona, Barcelona, Spain.

Illuminated   The world's longest illuminated sign measures 196½ ft. × 65½ ft. It is lit by 62,400 W metal-halide projectors and was erected by Abudi Signs Industry Ltd. of Israel.

Animated   The world's most massive is the one outside the Circus Circus Hotel, Reno, NV, which is named Topsy the Clown. It is 127 ft. tall and weighs over 45 tons, with 1.4 miles of neon tubing. Topsy's smile measures 14 ft. across.

Longest airborne   Reebok International Ltd. of Massachusetts flew a banner from a single-seater plane that read "Reebok Totally Beachin." The banner measured 50 ft. in height and 100 ft. in length, and was flown from 13–16 and 20–23 Mar. 1990 for four hours each day at Daytona Beach, FL.

Bonfire   The largest was constructed in Espel, in the Noordoost Polder, Netherlands. It stood 91 ft. 5 in. high with a base circumference of 276 ft. 11 in. and was lit on 19 Apr. 1987.

Breakwater   The world's longest breakwater is the one that protects the Port of Galveston, TX. The granite South Breakwater is 6.74 miles in length.

Cemeteries *Largest*   Rookwood Necropolis, New South Wales, Australia is the largest cemetery, covering an area of 728 acres, with over 575,536 interments and 177,542 cremations. It has been in continuous use since 1867.

The United States' largest cemetery is Arlington National Cemetery, which is situated on the Potomac River in Virginia, directly opposite from Washington, D.C. It is 612 acres in extent and more than 200,000 members of the armed forces are buried there. Presidents William Howard Taft and John Fitzgerald Kennedy are also buried there.

Tallest   The permanently illuminated Memorial Necropole Ecuméncio, located in Santos, near São Paulo, Brazil is 10 stories high, occupying an area of 4.448 acres. When full, its final capacity will be 20,000.

Tallest columns   The tallest are the thirty-six 90-ft.-tall fluted pillars of Vermont marble in the colonnade of the Education Building, Albany, NY. Their base diameter is 6½ ft.

The tallest load-bearing stone columns in the world are those measuring 69 ft. in the Hall of Columns of the Temple of Amun at Karnak, opposite Thebes on the Nile, the ancient capital of Upper Egypt. They were built in the 19th dynasty in the reign of Rameses II *c.* 1270 B.C.

Crematorium   The largest crematorium in the world is at the Nikolo-Arkhangelskoye Cemetery, east Moscow, Russia with seven twin cremators of British design, completed in March 1972. It has several Halls of Farewell for atheists.

Domes   The largest is the Louisiana Superdome, New Orleans, which has a diameter of 680 ft.

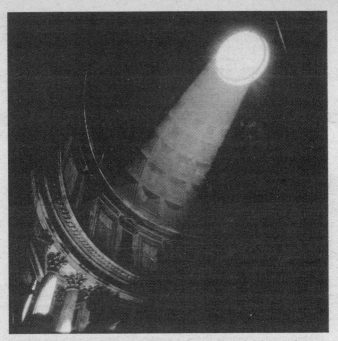

LARGEST ANCIENT DOME, ROME. The concrete dome of the Pantheon, Rome was the largest built until modern times, with a diameter of 142½ ft. and rising to a height of 71 ft. Built as a temple, it was dedicated in A.D. 609 as the church of the Sta. Maria Rotonda. (Photo: Spectrum Colour Library)

The largest dome of ancient architecture is that of the Pantheon, built in Rome in A.D. 112, with a diameter of 142½ ft.

Doors *Largest* The four doors in the Vehicle Assembly Building near Cape Canaveral, FL have a height of 460 ft.

Heaviest The heaviest is that of the laser target room at Lawrence Livermore National Laboratory, CA. It weighs 360 tons, is up to 8 ft. thick and was installed by Overly.

Largest dry dock With a maximum shipbuilding capacity of 1.34 million tons dwt, the Daewoo Okpo No. 1 Dry Dock, Koje Island in South Korea measures 1,740 ft. long × 430 ft. wide and was completed in 1979. The dock gates, 46 ft. high and 33 ft. thick at the base, are the world's most massive.

Earthworks The largest prior to the mechanical era were the Linear Earth Boundaries of the Benin Empire in the Bendel state of Nigeria. Their existence was first reported in 1900 and they were partially surveyed in 1967. In April 1973 it was estimated by Patrick Darling that the total length of the earthworks was probably between 4,000 and 8,000 miles, with the amount of earth moved estimated at 13.4–16 billion ft.[3]

Fences *Longest* The dingo-proof wire fence enclosing the main sheep areas of Australia is 6 ft. high, 1 ft. underground and stretches for 3,437 miles. The Queensland state government discontinued full maintenance in 1982.

Tallest The world's tallest fences are security screens 65 ft. high erected by Harrop-Allin of Pretoria, South Africa in November 1981 to protect fuel depots and refineries at Sasolburg from terrorist rocket attack.

Tallest flagpoles Erected outside the Oregon Building at the 1915 Panama-Pacific International Exposition in San Francisco, CA, and trimmed from a Douglas fir, this flagpole stood 299 ft. 7 in. in height and weighed 51.8 tons.

The tallest unsupported flagpole in the world is the 282-ft.-tall steel pole, weighing 120,000 lbs., that was erected on 22 Aug. 1985 at the Canadian Expo 86 exhibition in Vancouver, British Columbia and supports a gigantic ice hockey stick 205 ft. in length. Sherrold Haddad of Flag Chevrolet Oldsmobile Ltd. was instrumental in moving and reconstructing the flagpole at its present location at the company's premises on 104th Avenue, Surrey, British Columbia.

Tallest fountain The tallest is the fountain at Fountain Hills, AZ, built at a cost of $1.5 million for McCulloch Properties Inc. At full pressure of 375 lbs./in.[2] and at a rate of 5,828 gals./min., the 562 ft. tall column of water weighs more than 8 tons. When all three pumps are on, it can reach 625 ft., if weather conditions are favorable. The nozzle speed achieved by the three 600 hp pumps is 46.7 mph.

Largest gas tanks The largest gas tanks are at Fontaine L'Eveque, Belgium, where disused mines have been adapted to store up to 17.6 billion ft.[3] of gas at ordinary pressure.

The largest known remaining conventional gas tank is that at Wien-Simmering, Vienna, Austria, completed in 1968, with a height of 275 ft. and a capacity of 10.6 million ft.[3]

Longest deep-water jetty The Quai Hermann du Pasquier at Le Havre, France, with a length of 5,000 ft., is part of an enclosed basin and has a constant depth of water of 32 ft. on both sides.

Lampposts The tallest lighting columns are the four made by Petitjean & Cie of Troyes, France and installed by Taylor Woodrow at Sultan Qaboos Sports Complex, Muscat, Oman. They stand 208 ft. 4 in. high.

Lighthouses *Tallest* The 348 ft. steel tower near Yamashita Park in Yokohama, Japan has a power of 600,000 candelas and a visibility range of 20 miles.

Greatest range The lights with the greatest range are those 1,089 ft. above the ground on the Empire State Building, New York City. Each of the four-arc mercury bulbs has a rated candlepower of 450 million, visible 80 miles away on the ground and 300 miles away from aircraft.

Marquee *Largest*   A marquee covering an area of 188,368 ft.^{2} (4.32 acres) was erected by the firm of Deuter of Augsburg, Germany for the 1958 "Welcome Expo" in Brussels, Belgium.

Buildings demolished by explosives   The largest was the 21-story Traymore Hotel, Atlantic City, NJ on 26 May 1972 by Controlled Demolition Inc. of Towson, MD. This 600-room hotel had a cubic capacity of 6.5 million ft.^{3}.

The tallest chimney ever demolished by explosives was the Matla Power Station chimney, Kriel, South Africa, on 19 July 1981. It stood 902 ft. and was brought down by the Santon (Steeplejack) Co. Ltd. of Greater Manchester, Great Britain.

Grave digging   It is recorded that Johann Heinrich Karl Thieme, sexton of Aldenburg, Germany, dug 23,311 graves during a 50-year career. In 1826 his understudy dug *his* grave.

Demolition work   Fifteen members of the Black Leopard Karate Club demolished a seven-room wooden farmhouse west of Elnora, Alberta, Canada in 3 hrs. 18 min. by foot and unaided hand on 13 June 1982.

Largest revolving globe   The 33-ton 33-ft.-diameter sphere called "Globe of Peace" was built in five years, from 1982 to 1987, by Orfeo Bartolucci from Apecchio, Pesaro, Italy.

Largest fumigation   Carried out during the restoration of the Mission Inn complex in Riverside, CA on 28 June–1 July 1987 to rid the buildings of termites, the fumigation was performed by Fume Masters Inc. of Riverside. Over 350 tarpaulins were used, each weighing up to 350 lbs., and the operation involved completely covering the 70,000 ft.^{2} site and buildings—domes, minarets, chimneys and balconies, some of which exceeded 100 ft. in height.

Garbage dump   Reclamation Plant No. 1, Fresh Kills, Staten Island, NY, opened in March 1974, is the world's largest sanitary landfill. In its first four months of operation 503,751 tons of refuse from New York City carried by 700 barges was dumped on the site.

Mazes   The oldest datable representation of a labyrinth is that on a clay tablet from Pylos, Greece *c.* 1200 B.C.

The world's largest hedge maze is the one at Longleat, near Warminster, Great Britain, designed for Lord Weymouth by Greg Bright, which has 1.69 miles of paths flanked by 16,180 yew trees. It was opened on 6 June 1978 and measures 381 × 187 ft.

STONEHENGE. The largest trilithons are at Stonehenge, Salisbury Plain, Great Britain. They are made up of two standing stones with a linking lintel. Stonehenge is generally thought to have been constructed for religious purposes. (Photo: Spectrum Colour Library)

"Il Labirinto" at Villa Pisani, Stra, Italy, in which Napoleon was "lost" in 1807, had 4 miles of pathways.

Menhir (prehistoric upright monolith)   The tallest known is the 418.8 ton Grand Menhir Brisé, now in four pieces, which originally stood 72 ft. high at Locmariaquer, Brittany, France. Recent research suggests a possible 75 ft. for the height of a menhir, in three pieces, weighing 280 tons, also at Locmariaquer.

Monuments *Tallest*   The stainless-steel Gateway to the West arch in St. Louis, MO, completed on 28 Oct. 1965 to commemorate the westward expansion after the Louisiana Purchase of 1803, is a sweeping arch spanning 630 ft. and rising to the same height of 630 ft. It cost $29 million. It was designed in 1947 by the Finnish-American architect Eero Saarinen (1910–61).

Tallest column   Constructed from 1936–39, at a cost of $1.5 million, the tapering column that commemorates the Battle of San Jacinto (21 Apr. 1836), on the bank of the San Jacinto River near Houston, TX, is 570 ft. tall, 47 ft. square at the base, and 30 ft. square at the observation tower, which is surmounted by a star weighing 220 tons. It is built of concrete with buff limestone, and weighs 35,150 tons.

Largest trilithons   The largest trilithons exist at Stonehenge, to the south of Salisbury Plain, Wiltshire, Great Britain, with single sarsen blocks weighing over 49.6 tons and requiring over 550 men to drag them up a 9 degree gradient. The earliest stage of the construction of the ditch has been dated to 2800 B.C. Whether Stonehenge, which required some 30 million man-years, was built as a place of worship, as a lunar calendar, or as an eclipse predictor is still debated.

Largest artificial mound   The gravel mound built as a memorial to the Seleucid King Antiochus I (r. 69–34 B.C.) stands on the summit of Nemrud Dagi (8,182 ft.), southeast of Malatya, eastern Turkey. It measures 197 ft. tall and covers 7.5 acres.

Naturist resorts *Oldest*   The oldest resort is Der Freilichtpark, Klingberg, Germany, established in 1903.

The center Helio-Marin at Cap d'Agde, southern France, which covers 222 acres, is visited by 100,000 people each year.

Largest standing obelisks (monolithic)   The "skewer" or "spit" (from the Greek *obeliskos*) of Tuthmosis III brought from Aswan, Egypt by Emperor Constantius in the spring of A.D. 357 was repositioned in the Piazza San Giovanni in Laterane, Rome on 3 Aug. 1588. Once 118.1 ft. tall, it now stands 107.6 ft. and weighs 501.5 tons.

The unfinished obelisk, probably commissioned by Queen Hatshepsut *c.* 1490 B.C., and *in situ* at Aswan, Egypt is 136.8 ft. in length and weighs 1,287 tons.

The obelisk that has remained upright *in situ* for the longest time is the one still standing at Heliopolis, near Cairo, erected by Senwosret I *c.* 1750 B.C.

Tallest   The world's tallest obelisk is the Washington Monument in Washington, D.C. Situated in a 106 acre site and standing 555 ft. 5⅛ in. high, it was built to honor George Washington (1732–99), the first President.

Longest piers   The Dammam Pier, Saudi Arabia, on the Persian Gulf, with an overall length of 6.79 miles, was begun in July 1948 and completed on 15 Mar. 1950. The area was subsequently developed by 1980 into the King Abdul Aziz Port, with 39 deep-water berths. The original causeway, greatly widened, now extends to 7.95 miles including other port structures.

Longest covered promenade   The Long Corridor in the Summer Palace in Beijing, China is a covered promenade running for 2,388½ ft. It is built entirely of wood and divided by crossbeams into 273 sections. These crossbeams, as well as the ceiling and side pillars, have over 10,000 paintings of famous Chinese landscapes, episodes from folk tales, and flowers and birds.

Pyramids *Largest*   The largest pyramid, and the largest monument ever constructed, is the Quetzalcóatl at Cholula de Rivadabia, 63 miles southeast of Mexico City. It is 177 ft. tall and its base covers an area of nearly 45 acres. Its total volume has been estimated at 116.5 million ft.³ compared with 88.2 million ft.³ for the Pyramid of Khufu or Cheops (a fourth-dynasty Egyptian pharaoh).

The largest-known single block in pyramid-building is from the Third Pyramid (Pyramid of Mycerinus) at El Gizeh, Egypt and weighs 320 tons.

Oldest   The Djoser step pyramid at Saqqâra, Egypt dates from *c.* 2680 B.C. It was constructed by Imhotep to a height of 204 ft., and originally had a Tura limestone casing.

The oldest New World pyramid is that on the island of La Venta in southeastern Mexico, built by the Olmec people *c.* 800 B.C. It stands 100 ft. tall with a base dimension of 420 ft.

Scaffolding   The tallest scaffolding was 174.8 ft. high, erected around

TALLEST OBELISK.
The Washington
Monument, located at
the west end of the
Mall, Washington,
D.C. Standing 555 ft.
5⅛ in. high, it was
completed in 1884 to
honor George
Washington, the first
President. (Photo:
Images/Horizon
Colour Library)

the statue of the Albert Memorial in London, Great Britain. It was free-standing and clad with plastic sheeting and could resist wind forces of up to 90 mph.

United States The largest freestanding scaffolding in the United States is believed to be the one erected for the restoration of the Goldstone antenna in California. It was 170 ft. high, 70 ft. deep and went 180 ft. around the circumference of the structure.

Snow and ice constructions
A snow palace 87 ft. high, one of four structures which together spanned 702.7 ft., was unveiled on 7 Feb. 1987 at Asahikawa City, Hokkaidō, Japan.

The world's largest ice construction was the ice palace built in January 1986, using 9,000 blocks of ice, at St. Paul, MN during the Winter Carnival. Designed by Ellerbe Associates Inc., it stood 128 ft. 9 in. high—the equivalent of a 13-story building.

Snowman A snow structure 74 ft. high and named "Yukichian, the Snow Girl" was built by villagers of Sumon and Niigata, Japan on 3 Mar. 1991.

"Super Frosty," the largest snowman in the United States, was built by a

LONGEST COVERED PROMENADE. This covered way is located at the southern side of the Longevity Hill skirting the shoreline of the Kunming Lake, Beijing, China. Built entirely from wood, the 273 sections are 2,388.5 ft. in length. (Photo: Hu Chuei)

team in Anchorage, AK led by Myron L. Ace between 20 Feb. and 5 Mar. 1988, and stood 63.56 ft.

Longest stairways The service staircase for the Niesenbahn funicular near Spiez, Switzerland rises to 7,759 ft. It has 11,674 steps and a banister.

The stone-cut Tai Chan temple stairs of 6,600 steps in the Shandong Mountains, China ascend 4,700 ft.

The tallest spiral staircase is on the outside of the chimney Bobila Almirall located in Angel Sallent in Tarrasa, Barcelona, Spain. Built by Mariano-Masana i Ribas in 1956, it is 207 ft. high and has 217 steps.

The longest spiral staircase is one 1,103 ft. deep with 1,520 steps installed in the Mapco-White County Coal Mine, Carmi, IL by Systems Control Inc. in May 1981.

Kitchen An Indian government field kitchen set up in April 1973 at Ahmadnagar, Maharashtra, a famine area, daily provided 1.2 million subsistence meals.

Scarecrow The tallest scarecrow ever built was "Stretch II," constructed by the Speers family of Paris, Ontario, Canada and a crew of 15 at the Paris, Ontario Fall Fair on 2 Sep. 1989. It measured 103 ft. 6¾ in. in height.

Largest Lego statue The sculpture of the Indian chief Sitting Bull, at the Legoland Park, Billund, Denmark, measures 25 ft. to the top of the feather. The largest statue ever constructed from Lego, it required 1.5 million bricks, individually glued together to withstand the weather.

Statues *Longest* Near Bamiyan, Afghanistan there are the remains of the recumbent Sakya Buddha, built of plastered rubble, which was "about 1,000 ft." long and is believed to date from the 3rd or 4th century A.D.

Tallest A full-figure statue, that of "Motherland," a prestressed concrete female figure on Mamayev Hill, outside Volgograd, Russia, was designed in 1967 by Yevgeny Vuchetich, to commemorate victory in the Battle of Stalingrad (1942–43). The statue from its base to the tip of the sword clenched in the right hand measures 270 ft.

The statue of Maitreya is carved out of a single piece of wood from a white sandalwood tree and it stands 85.30 ft. high. It is located northwest of Beijing, China at the Lama Temple (Yonghegong), built in 1649. The Imperial Court allowed two years for the carving of the statue in the Pavilion House of Ten Thousand Fortunes and finished the project in 1750.

United States The Statue of Liberty, originally named Liberty Enlightening the World, is the tallest statue in the United States. Designed and built in France to commemorate the friendship of the two countries, the 152 ft. statue was shipped to New York City, where its copper sheets were assembled. President Grover Cleveland accepted the statue for the USA on 28 Oct. 1886.

The statue, which became a national monument in 1924, stands on Liberty Island in Upper New York Bay. The base of the statue is an eleven-pointed star; a 150 ft. pedestal is made of concrete faced with granite. The statue was closed to the public on 23 June 1985 in order to complete restoration work, at a cost of $698 million. The statue was officially reopened by President Ronald Reagan on 4 July 1986 during a weekend-long celebration of the statue's 100th birthday.

SEVEN WONDERS OF THE WORLD

The Seven Wonders of the World were first designated by Antipater of Sidon in the second century B.C. They included the Pyramids of Giza, built by three fourth-dynasty Egyptian pharaohs, Khwfw (Khufu or Cheops), Kha-f-Ra (Khafre, Khefren or Chepren) and Menkaure (Mycerinus) near El Giza (El Gizeh), southwest of El Qâhira (Cairo) in Egypt.

THE GREAT PYRAMID

The "Horizon of Khufu" was finished under Rededef *c.* 2580 B.C. Its original height was 480 ft. 11 in. (now, since the loss of its topmost stones and the pyramidion, reduced to 449 ft. 6 in.) with a base line of 756 ft. and thus covering slightly more than 13 acres. It has been estimated that a permanent work force of 4,000 required 30 years to maneuver into position the 2.3 million limestone blocks averaging 2.76 tons each, totaling about 6,437,432 tons and a volume of 88.2 million ft.^{3}. Some blocks weighed 15 tons. A cost estimate published in December 1974 indicated that it would take 405 men six years to build it at a cost of $1.13 billion.

FRAGMENTS REMAIN OF:

The Temple of Artemis (Diana) of the Ephesians, built *c.* 350 B.C. at Ephesus, Turkey (destroyed by the Goths in A.D. 262); The Tomb of King Mausolus of Caria, at Halicarnassus, now Bodrum, Turkey, c. 325 B.C.

NO TRACE REMAINS OF:

The Hanging Gardens of Semiramis, at Babylon, Iraq c. 600 B.C.;

The statue of Zeus (Jupiter), by Phidias (fifth century B.C.), at Olympia, Greece (lost in a fire in Istanbul) in marble, gold and ivory and 40 ft. tall;

The figure of the god Helios (Apollo), the 117-ft.-tall statue by Chares of Lindus called the Colossus of Rhodes (sculptured 292–280 B.C., destroyed by an earthquake in 224 B.C.);

The 400-ft.-tall lighthouse, the world's earliest lighthouse, built by Sostratus of Cnidus (c. 270 B.C.) as a pyramidically shaped tower of white marble (finally destroyed by earthquake in A.D. 1375), on the island of Pharos (Greek, *pharos* = lighthouse), off the coast of El Iskandariya (Alexandria), Egypt.

Tallest swing   A glider swing 30 ft. high was constructed by Kenneth R. Mack, Langenburg, Saskatchewan, Canada for Uncle Herb's Amusements. The swing is capable of taking its four sides 25 ft. off the ground.

Largest tombs   The Mount Li tomb, the burial place of Qin Shi Huangdi, the 1st Emperor of Qin, dates to 221 B.C. and is situated 25 miles east of Xianyang, China. The two walls surrounding the grave measure 7,129 × 3,195 ft. and 2,247 × 1,896 ft. Several pits in the tomb contained a vast army of an estimated 8,000 life-sized terracotta soldiers.

A tomb housing 180,000 World War II dead on Okinawa, Japan was enlarged in 1985 to accommodate another 9,000 bodies thought to be buried on the island.

Totem pole   A 173-ft.-tall pole was raised on 6 June 1973 at Alert Bay, British Columbia, Canada. It tells the story of the Kwakiutl tribe and took 36 man-weeks to carve.

Vats *Largest*   The largest wooden winecask in the world is the Heidelberg Tun, completed in 1751, in the cellar of the Friedrichsbau, Heidelberg, Germany. Its capacity is 40,790 gals.

"Strongbow," used by H. P. Bulmer Ltd., the English cider-makers of Hereford, Great Britain, measures 64½ ft. in height and 75½ ft. in diameter, with a capacity of 1.63 million gals.

Oldest   The world's oldest-known vat still in use is at Hugel et Fils (founded 1639), Riqueweihr, Haut-Rhin, France. Twelve generations of the family have used it since 1715.

Longest wall   The Great Wall of China has a main-line length of 2,150 miles. Completed during the reign of Qin Shi Huangdi (221–210 B.C.), it has a further 1,780 miles of branches and spurs. Its height varies from 15–39 ft. and it is up to 32 ft. thick. It runs from Shanhaiguan, on the Gulf of Bohai, to Yumenguan and Yanguan, and was kept in repair up to the 16th century. Some 32 miles of the wall have been destroyed since 1966 and part of the wall was blown up to make way for a dam in July 1979. On 6 Mar. 1985 a report from China stated that a five-year survey proved that its total length was once 6,200 miles. In October 1990 it was reported that after two years of exertion Lin Youdian had become the first person to walk its entire length.

Indoor waterfall   The tallest indoor waterfall measures 114 ft. in height and is backed by 2,525 ft.^{2} of marble. It is situated in the lobby of Greektown's International Center Building, Detroit, MI.

Water tower   The Union water tower in New Jersey, built in 1965, rises to a height of 210 ft., with a capacity of 250,000 gals. The tower is owned and operated by the Elizabethtown Water Co.

Largest waterwheel   The Mohammadieh Noria wheel at Hamah, Syria has a diameter of 131 ft. and dates from Roman times.

Largest windows   The largest sheet of glass ever manufactured was one of 540 ft.^{2}, or 65 ft. 7 in. by 8 ft. 2¼ in., exhibited by the Saint Gobin Co. in France at the *Journées Internationales de Miroiterie* in March 1958.

The largest single windows in the world are those in the Palace of Industry and Technology at *Rondpoint de la Défense*, Paris, France, with an extreme width of 715.2 ft. and a maximum height of 164 ft.

The largest sheet of tempered (safety) glass ever processed was one made by P.T. Sinar Rasa Kencana of Jakarta, Indonesia. It measures 22.96 ft. long by 7.02 ft. wide and is 0.05 in. thick.

Largest wine cellars   The cellars at Paarl of the Ko-operative Wijnbouwers Vereeniging, known as KWV, Cape Province, in the center of the wine-growing district of South Africa, cover an area of 25 acres and have a capacity of 30 million gals.

United States   The Cienega Winery of the Almaden Vineyards in Hollister, CA covers 4 acres and can house 37,300 oak barrels containing 1.83 million gallons of wine.

Ziggurat   The largest ziggurat (from the Assyrian *ziqqurata*, meaning summit, height) ever built was that of the Elamite King Untas, *c.* 1250 B.C., known as the Ziggurat of Choga Zanbil, 18.6 miles from Haft Tepe, Iran. The outer base was 344 × 344 ft. and the fifth "box" 91.8 × 91.8 ft., nearly 164 ft. above.

Stair climbing   The 100-story record for stair climbing was set by Dennis W. Martz in the Detroit Plaza Hotel, Detroit, MI on 26 June 1978 at 11 min. 23.8 sec.

Brian McCauliff ran a vertical mile (ascending and descending eight times) on the stairs of the Westin Hotel, Detroit, MI in 1 hr. 38 min. 5 sec. on 2 Feb. 1992.

Steve Silva climbed 45,708 steps of the Westin Peachtree Plaza Hotel, Atlanta, GA (a vertical height of 26,676 ft.) in 9 hrs. 50 min. 43 sec. on 27–28 Jan. 1992. He made a total of 39 ascents, descending by elevator.

The record for the 1,760 steps (vertical height 1,122 ft.) in the world's tallest freestanding structure, Toronto's CN Tower, Canada, is 7 min. 52 sec. by Brendan Keenoy on 29 Oct. 1989.

The record for the 1,336 stairs of the world's tallest hotel, the Westin Stamford Hotel, Singapore, is 6 min. 55 sec. by Balvinder Singh, in its third Vertical Marathon on 4 June 1989.

Scott Elliott raced up the 1,575 steps of the Empire State Building, New York City on 14 Feb. 1990 in 10 min. 47 sec.

Window cleaning   Keith Witt of Amarillo, TX cleaned three standard 42½ × 47 in. office windows with an 11.8-in.-long squeegee and 1.98 gals. of water in 10.50 sec. on 21 Jan. 1990 at the International Window Cleaning Association convention in Orlando, FL. Smears are not tolerated and are penalized.

TRANSPORT

The Cumbres and Toltec Railway, CO.
(Photo: Images Colour Library)

SHIPS

EARLIEST SEAGOING BOATS

Aborigines are thought to have been able to cross the Torres Strait from New Guinea to Australia, then at least 43½ miles across, as early as 55,000 B.C. It is believed that they used double canoes.

The earliest surviving "vessel" is a pinewood dugout found in Pesse, Netherlands and dated to c. 6315 B.C.± 275, now in the Provincial Museum, Assen.

The earliest representation of a boat is a matter for dispute; there are possible rock-art outlines of Mesolithic skin-boats in Høgnipen, Norway (c. 8000–7000 B.C.); in Minateda, Spain (7000–3000 B.C.); and in Kobystan, Russia (8000–6000 B.C.).

An 18-in.-long paddle was found at the Star Carr site in Great Britain in 1948. It has been dated to c. 7600 B.C. and is now in the Cambridge Museum of Archaeology, Great Britain.

The oldest surviving boat is a 27-ft.-long 2½-ft.-wide wooden eel-catching canoe discovered at Tybrind Vig on the Baltic island of Fünen, which is dated to c. 4490 B.C.

A fleet of 12 funerary boats discovered in 1991 at Abydos, Egypt have been tentatively dated to about 3000 B.C.; they measure up to 60 ft. in length.

The oldest shipwreck ever found is one of a Cycladic trading vessel located off the islet of Dhókós, near the Greek island of Hydra, reported in May 1975 and dated to 2450 B.C. ± 250.

Earliest power Marine propulsion by steam engine was first achieved when in 1783 the Marquis Claude-François-Dorothée Jouffroy d'Abbans (1751–1832) ascended a reach of the river Saône near Lyons, France, in the 198-ton paddle wheeler *Pyroscaphe*.

The tug *Charlotte Dundas* was the first successful power-driven vessel. She was a stern paddle wheel steamer built for the Forth and Clyde Canal, Great Britain in 1801–02 by William Symington (1763–1831), using a double-acting condensing engine constructed by James Watt (1736–1819).

The world's oldest active paddle wheeler continuously operated as such is *Skibladner*, which has plied Lake Mjøsa, Norway since 1856. She was built in Motala, Sweden and has had two major refits.

Oldest active The world's oldest active oceangoing ship is the *MV Doulos* (Greek for "servant"), built in 1914 in the USA and first named *Medina*. She is currently operating as an international educational and Christian service vessel with approximately 300 crew members, personnel and passengers on board from 30 different nations.

Earliest turbine The *Turbinia*, built in 1894 at Wallsend-on-Tyne, Great Britain to the design of Sir Charles Parson (1854–1931), was 100 ft. long and of 46 tons displacement with machinery consisting of three steam turbines totaling about 2,000 shp. At her first public demonstration in 1897 she reached 34.5 knots and is now preserved at Newcastle upon Tyne, Great Britain.

WARSHIPS

Largest battleships   The largest battleship in active service is the USS *Missouri*, an IOWA class battleship. The remaining three ships in this class were recently deactivated. It is 887 ft., has a beam of 108 ft., and its displacement is 58,000 tons. Her complement is 1,573 crewmen, including 58 Marines. The ship can attain a maximum speed of over 40 mph (35 knots). Armament includes nine 16 in./50 caliber guns, twelve 5 in./38 caliber guns, four 20 mm. Phalanx CIWS (Close In Warfare System), 32 Tomahawk cruise missiles from eight armored box launchers, and 16 Harpoon missiles fired from four quad cell launchers. Four SH-3 or SH-60 helicopters are on deck.

Two other ships of the same class, USS *New Jersey* and USS *Iowa*, are now in reserve. *New Jersey* last saw action off Lebanon in 1983–84.

The Japanese battleships *Yamato* (completed on 16 Dec. 1941 and sunk southwest of Kyūshū, Japan by US planes on 7 Apr. 1945) and *Musashi* (sunk in the Philippine Sea by 11 bombs and 16 torpedoes on 24 Oct. 1944) were the largest battleships ever commissioned, each with a full-load displacement of 81,545 tons. With an overall length of 863 ft., a beam of 127 ft. and a full-load draft of 35½ ft., they mounted nine 18.1-in. guns in three triple turrets. Each gun weighed 181.5 tons and was 75 ft. in length, firing a 3,200 lb. projectile.

Fastest warship   A US Navy hovercraft, the 78-ft.-long 110-ton test vehicle SES-100B, achieved a speed of 91.9 knots (105.8 mph). (See Hovercraft, fastest.)

Fastest destroyer   The fastest speed attained by a destroyer was 45.25 knots (51.83 mph) by the 3,120 ton French destroyer *Le Terrible* in 1935.

LARGEST BATTLESHIP. The USS *New Jersey* was one of four IOWA class battleships built during World War II. Although all are now deactivated, she most recently saw action off Lebanon in 1983–84. Her armaments include 32 Tomahawk cruise missiles and nine 16-inch guns. (Photo: US Navy)

She was built in Blainville, France and was powered by four Yarrow small-tube boilers and two Rateau geared turbines, giving 100,000 shp. She was removed from the active list at the end of 1957.

The fastest destroyers in the US Navy arsenal are the Spruance class and Kidd class ships, which attain a maximum speed of 38 mph (33 knots).

Fastest shipbuilding   The fastest times in which complete ships of more than 10,000 tons were ever built were achieved at Kaiser's Yard, Portland, OR during the wartime program for building 2,742 liberty ships in 18 shipyards from 27 Sep. 1941. In 1942 No. 440, named *Robert E. Peary,* had her keel laid on 8 November, was launched on 12 November and was operational after 4 days 15½ hrs. on 15 November. She was broken up in 1963.

Most aircraft landings   The greatest number of landings on an aircraft carrier in one day was 602, achieved by Marine Air Group 6 of the United States Pacific Fleet Air Force aboard the USS *Matanikau* on 25 May 1945 between 8 A.M. and 5 P.M.

AIRCRAFT CARRIERS

Largest   The warships with the largest full-load displacement in the world are the Nimitz class US Navy aircraft carriers USS *Nimitz, Dwight D. Eisenhower, Carl Vinson, Theodore Roosevelt, George Washington*, and *Abraham Lincoln*, the last two of which displace 100,846 tons. They are 1,092 ft. in length overall, with 4½ acres of flight deck, and have a speed well in excess of 30 knots from their four nuclear-powered 260,000 shp geared steam turbines. They have to be refueled after about 900,000 miles of steaming. Their full complement of personnel is 5,986.

SUBMARINES

Largest   The world's largest submarines are of the Russian Typhoon class. The launch of the first at the covered shipyard at Severodvinsk in the White Sea was announced by NATO on 23 Sep. 1980. They are believed to have a dive displacement of 27,557 tons, to measure 558 ft. overall and to be armed with 20 SS NX 20 missiles with a 4,800-nautical-mile range, each with seven warheads. By late 1987 two others built in St. Petersburg, Russia (formerly Leningrad, USSR) were operational, each deploying 140 warheads.

The largest submarines in the US Navy are of the Ohio class. Each of the nine ships in active service has a displacement of 18,700 tons. At 560 ft., they are the longest submarines in the fleet at 42 ft., and also have the largest crew, at 165.

The longest submarine patrol that ever dove unsupported (of those that have been made public) is 111 days by HM Submarine *Warspite* in the South Atlantic from 25 Nov. 1982 to 15 Mar. 1983. She sailed 30,804 nautical miles.

Fastest   The Russian Alfa class nuclear-powered submarines have a reported maximum speed of 45 knots plus (51.8 mph). With the use of titanium alloy in the hull, they are believed to be able to dive to 2,500 ft. A US spy satellite over Leningrad's naval yard on 8 June 1983 showed they were being lengthened and are now 260.1 ft. long.

Deepest   The US Navy deep submergence vessel *Sea Cliff* (DSV 4), 30 tons, commissioned in 1973, reached a depth of 20,000 ft. in March 1985.

PASSENGER LINERS

Largest   The RMS *Queen Elizabeth* (finally 82,998 but formerly 83,673 grt), of the Cunard fleet, was the largest passenger vessel ever built and had the largest displacement of any liner in the world. She had an overall length of 1,031 ft., was 118 ft. 7 in. in breadth and was powered by steam turbines that developed 168,000 hp. Her last passenger voyage ended on 15 Nov. 1968. In 1970 she was removed to Hong Kong to serve as a floating marine university and renamed *Seawise University*. She was burned out on 9 Jan. 1972 when three *simultaneous* outbreaks of fire strongly pointed to arson. The gutted hull had been cut up and removed by 1978. *Seawise* was a pun on the owner's initials—C.Y. Tung (1911–82).

The largest in current use, and the longest ever, is the *Norway*, 76,049 tons and 1,035 ft. 7½ in. in overall length, with a capacity of 2,400 passengers. She was built as the *France* in 1960 and renamed after purchase in June 1979 by Norwegian Knut Kloster. She normally cruises in the Caribbean and is based at Miami, FL. Work undertaken during an extensive refit, including two new decks, during the fall of 1990 increased the number of passenger decks to 11. Her draft is 34½ ft. and her speed is 18 knots.

TANKERS

Largest   The *Jahre Viking*, formerly the *Happy Giant*, had the all-time record for any ship with a deadweight of 622,420 tons. She is 1,504 ft. long overall, with a beam of 225 ft. 11 in., and has a draft of 80 ft. 9 in. She was lengthened by Nippon Kokan in 1980 by adding a 265 ft. 8 in. midship section. She was attacked by Iraqi Mirage jets off Larak Island in the Persian Gulf on 22 Dec. 1987 and was severely damaged in another attack on 14 May 1988. Despite this damage, she was bought by a Norwegian, and is to be returned to service after refitting in Singapore.

The largest tanker and ship of any kind in service today is the 611,839 ton dwt *Hellas Fos*, a steam turbine tanker built in 1979. Of 254,582 grt and 227,801 nrt, she is managed by the Bilinder Marine Corporation of Athens, Greece but has been laid up in Piraeus, Greece since April 1991.

CARGO VESSELS

Largest   The largest ship carrying dry cargo is the Norwegian ore carrier *Berge Stahl*, 402,082.6 tons dwt, built in South Korea for the Norwegian owner Signora Bergesen. She has a length of 1,125 ft., a beam measuring 208 ft. and was launched on 5 Nov. 1986.

Largest whale factory   The former USSR's *Sovietskaya Ukraina* (35,878 tons), with a summer deadweight of 51,519 tons, was completed in October 1959. She is 714½ ft. in length and 84 ft. 7 in. abeam.

Barges   The world's largest RoRo (roll-on, roll-off) ships are four *El Rey* class barges, weighing 18,408 tons and measuring 580 ft. in length. They were built by the FMC Corp of Portland, OR and are operated by Crowley Maritime Corp of San Francisco between Florida and Puerto Rico with tri-level lodging for up to 376 truck-trailers.

Containership   *Earliest*   Shipborne containerization began in 1955 when the tanker *Ideal X* was converted by Malcolm McLean (USA). She carried containers only on deck.

Largest   American President Lines has built five ships in Germany—*President Adams*, *President Jackson*, *President Kennedy*, *President Polk* and *President Truman*—that are termed post-Panamax, being the first container vessels too large for transit of the Panama Canal. They are 902.69 ft. in length and 129.29 ft. abeam; the maximum beam for the Panama transit is 105.97 ft. These vessels have a quoted capacity of 4,300 TEU (Standard length Twenty-foot Equivalent Unit Containers); they have in fact carried in excess of this in normal service.

Most powerful tugs   The *Nikolay Chiker* and *SB–134*, commissioned in April–May 1989, and built by Hollming Ltd. of Sweden for V/O Sudoiport, in the former USSR, have 24,480 hp and are capable of 250 tons bollard pull at full power. They are 324.8 ft. long and 63.8 ft. wide.

Largest rail ferry   The operating route of the biggest international rail ferries, *Klaipeda, Vilnius, Mukran* and *Greifswald,* is in the Baltic Sea, between the ports of Klaipeda, Lithuania and Mukran, Germany. Consisting of two decks 625 ft. in length, 301.4 ft. in breadth and 13,104 tons dwt, these ferries were built in Wismar, Germany. Each of them can lift 103 railcars of standard 48.65 ft. length and weighing up to 84 tons. The ferries can cover a distance of 273 nautical miles (314.2 miles) in 17 hours.

Car ferries   *Largest*   The world's largest car and passenger ferry is the 58,376 grt *Silja Serenade*, which entered service between Stockholm, Sweden and Helsinki, Finland in 1990 and is operated by the Silja Line. She is 666 ft. long and 103.34 ft. abeam, and can carry 2,500 passengers and 450 cars.

Fastest   The fastest is the 24,065 grt gas-turbine powered *Finnjet*, built in 1977, which operates in the Baltic Sea between Helsinki, Finland and Travemunde, Germany and is capable of exceeding 30 knots (34.47 mph).

Largest propeller   The largest propeller ever made is the triple-bladed screw of 36 ft. 1 in. diameter made by Kawasaki Heavy Industries, Japan, and delivered on 17 Mar. 1982 for the 233,787 ton bulk carrier *Hoei Maru* (now renamed *New Harvest*).

Largest hydrofoil   The 212-ft.-long *Plainview* (347 tons full-load) naval hydrofoil was launched by the Lockheed Shipbuilding and Construction Co. at Seattle, WA on 28 June 1965. She has a service speed of 57.2 mph.

Three 185-ton Supramar PTS 150 Mk III hydrofoils carry 250 passengers at 40 knots across the Öre Sound between Malmö, Sweden and Copenhagen, Denmark. They were built by Westermoen Hydrofoil Ltd. of Mandal, Norway.

Riverboat   The world's largest inland boat is the 382-ft. *Mississippi Queen*, designed by James Gardner of London, Great Britain. The vessel was commissioned on 25 July 1976 in Cincinnati, OH and is now in service on the Mississippi River.

Most powerful icebreakers   The most powerful icebreaker built for that purpose is the 28,000 ton 460-ft.-long *Rossiya*, powered by 75,000 hp nuclear engines, built in Leningrad (now St. Petersburg, Russia) and completed in 1985.

A 100,000 hp engined 636-ft.-long polar icebreaker of the Class 8 type was ordered by the Canadian government in October 1985. Her cost was $Can500 million.

The largest *converted* icebreaker was the 1,007-ft.-long SS *Manhattan* (43,000 shp), which was converted by the Humble Oil Co. into a 168,000 ton icebreaker. She made a double voyage through the Northwest Passage in Arctic Canada from 24 Aug. to 12 Nov. 1969.

The Northwest Passage was first navigated by Roald Engebereth Gravning Amundsen (Norway; 1872–1928) in the sealing sloop *Gjöa* in 1906.

Yacht *Largest (royal)*   The largest royal yacht in the world is the Saudi Arabian royal yacht *Abdul Aziz*, which is 482 ft. long. Built in Denmark and completed in 1984 at Vospers Yard, Southampton, Great Britain, it was estimated in September 1987 to be worth more than $100 million.

Largest (nonroyal)   The largest private (nonroyal) yacht is the *Alexander*, a former ferry converted to a private yacht in 1986, at 400 ft. overall.

Most powerful dredger   The 468.4-ft. long *Prins der Nederlanden* of 10,586 grt can dredge up 19,700 tons of sand from a depth of 115 ft. via two suction tubes in less than an hour.

Wooden ship *Heaviest*   The *Richelieu*, 333⅔ ft. long and weighing 8,534 tons, was launched in Toulon, France on 3 Dec. 1873.

HM Battleship *Lord Warden*, completed in 1869, displaced 7,940 tons.

Longest   The longest ever built was the New York-built *Rochambeau* (1867–72), formerly the *Dunderberg*, which measured 377 ft. 4 in. overall.

It should be noted that the biblical length of Noah's ark was 300 cubits, or, at 18 in. to a cubit, 450 ft.

Longest canoe   The 117-ft.-long Kauri wood Maori war canoe *Nga Toki Matawhaorua* was shaped with adzes at Kerikeri Inlet, New Zealand in 1940. The crew numbered 70 or more.

The "Snake Boat" *Nadubhagóm*, 135 ft. long, from Kerala, southern India, has a crew of 109 rowers and nine "encouragers."

SAILING SHIPS

Largest The largest vessel ever built in the era of sail was the *France II* (5,806 gross tons), launched at Bordeaux, France in 1911. This was a steel-hulled, five-masted barque (square-rigged on four masts and fore-and-aft rigged on the aftermost mast). Her hull measured 418 ft. overall. Although principally designed as a sailing vessel with a stump topgallant rig, she was also fitted with two auxiliary engines; however, these were removed in 1919 and she became a pure sailing vessel. She was wrecked off New Caledonia on 13 July 1922.

The only seven-masted sailing schooner ever built was the 375.6-ft.-long *Thomas W. Lawson* (5,218 gross tons), built at Quincy, MA in 1902 and wrecked off the Isles of Scilly, Great Britain on 15 Dec. 1907. (See Largest junks, below.)

Largest in service The largest now in service is the 357-ft.-long *Sedov*, built in 1921 in Kiel, Germany and used for training by the Russians. She is 48 ft. wide, with a displacement of 6,300 grt (4,267.2 tons) and a sail area of 45,123 ft.[2].

The world's only surviving first rate ship-of-the-line is the Royal Navy's 104-gun battleship HMS *Victory*, laid down at Chatham, Great Britain on 23 July 1759 and constructed from the wood of some 2,200 oak trees. She bore the body of Admiral Nelson from Gibraltar to Portsmouth, Great Britain, arriving 44 days after serving as his victorious flagship at the Battle of Trafalgar on 21 Oct. 1805. In 1922 she was moved to No. 2 dock, Portsmouth—site of the world's oldest graving dock. The length of her cordage (both standing and running rigging) is 19.12 miles.

Oldest active The oldest active square-rigged sailing vessel in the world is the restored SV *Maria Asumpta* (formerly the *Ciudad de Inca*), built near Barcelona, Spain in 1858. She is 98 ft. overall and weighs 142.3 tons. She was restored in 1981–82 and is used for film work, promotional appearances at regattas and sail training. She is operated by The Friends of *Maria Asumpta* of Lenham, Great Britain.

Longest The longest is the 613-ft.-long French-built *Club Med I* with five aluminum masts. The 2,500 ft.[2] polyester sails are computer-controlled. She is operated as a Caribbean cruise vessel for 425 passengers bound for Club Med. With her small sail area and powerful engines she is really a motor-sailer. A sister ship, *Club Med II*, is now being commissioned.

Largest junks The largest on record was the seagoing *Cheng Ho*, flagship of Admiral Cheng Ho's 62 treasure ships, *c.* 1420, with a displacement of 3,472 tons and a length variously estimated up to 538 ft. She is believed to have had nine masts.

A river junk 361 ft. long, with treadmill-operated paddle wheels, was recorded in A.D. 1161.

In *c.* A.D. 280 a floating fortress 600 ft. square, built by Wang Jun on the Yangzi River, took part in the Jin-Wu river war. Present-day junks do not, even in the case of the Jiangsu traders, exceed 170 ft. in length.

HMS *VICTORY*. Nelson's flagship at the Battle of Trafalgar in 1805. This 104-gun ship of the line was launched at Chatham, Great Britain on 7 May 1765. She is constructed from the wood of 2,200 oak trees. (Photo: Spectrum Colour Library)

Longest day's run under sail   Calculated for any commercial vessel under sail, the longest day's run was one of 462 nautical miles by the clipper *Champion of the Seas* (3,048.7 tons) of the Liverpool Black Ball Line, running before a northwesterly gale in the south Indian Ocean under the command of Capt. Alex Newlands in 1854. The elapsed time between the fixes was 23 hrs. 17 min., giving an average of 19.97 knots (23 mph).

Largest sails   Sails are known to have been used for marine propulsion since 3500 B.C. The largest spars ever carried were those in HM

Battleship *Temeraire*, completed at Chatham, Great Britain, on 31 Aug. 1877. She was broken up in 1921. The fore and main yards measured 115 ft. in length. The foresail contained 5,100 ft. of canvas weighing 2.23 tons, and the total sail area was 25,000 ft.².

HM Battleship *Sultan* was ship-rigged when completed at Chatham, Great Britain on 10 Oct. 1871 and carried 34,100 ft.² of sails plus 15,300 ft.² of stunsails. She was broken up in 1946.

Tallest mast   The *Velsheda*, a J-class sailing vessel, is the tallest known single-masted yacht in the world. Measured from heel fitting to the mast truck, she is 169¼ ft. in height. Built in 1933, the second of the four British J-class yachts, she is unusual in that she was the only one ever built that was not intended to race for the America's Cup. With a displacement of 160 tons, she supports a sail area of 7,500 ft.².

Largest wreck   The 312,186 dwt very large crude carrier (VLCC) *Energy Determination* blew up and broke in two in the Straits of Hormuz on 12 Dec. 1979. Her full value was $58 million.

The largest wreck removal was carried out in 1979 by Smit Tak International, which removed the remains of the French tanker *Betelgeuse*, 120,000 tons, from Bantry Bay, Republic of Ireland, within 20 months.

Most massive collision   The closest an irresistible force has come to striking an immovable object occurred on 16 Dec. 1977, 22 miles off the coast of southern Africa, when the tanker *Venoil* (330,954 dwt) struck her sister ship *Venpet* (330,869 dwt).

Message in a bottle   The longest recorded interval between drop and pickup is 73 years in the case of a message thrown from the SS *Arawatta* out of Cairns, Queensland, Australia on 9 June 1910 in a lotion bottle and reported as found on Moreton Island, Queensland on 6 June 1983.

Riveting   The world record for riveting is 11,209 rivets in 9 hrs., by John Moir at the Workman Clark Ltd. shipyard, Belfast, Northern Ireland in June 1918. His peak hour was his 7th, with 1,409 rivets, an average of nearly 23½ per min.

Largest human-powered   The giant ship *Tessarakonteres,* a three-banked catamaran galley with 4,000 rowers, built for Ptolemy IV *c.* 210 B.C. in Alexandria, Egypt, measured 420 ft. with up to eight men to an oar of 38 cubits (57 ft.) in length.

OCEAN CROSSINGS

Earliest Atlantic The earliest crossing of the Atlantic by a power vessel, as opposed to an auxiliary-engined sailing ship, was a 22-day voyage begun in April 1827, from Rotterdam, Netherlands, to the West Indies, by the *Curaçao*. She was a 127-ft. wooden paddle boat of 490.5 tons, built as the *Calpe* in Dover, Great Britain in 1826 and purchased by the Dutch government for a West Indian mail service.

The earliest Atlantic crossing entirely under steam (with intervals for desalting the boilers) was by HMS *Rhadamanthus*, from Plymouth, Great Britain to Barbados in 1832.

The earliest crossing under continuous steam power was by the condenser-fitted packet ship *Sirius* (787 tons) from Queenstown (now Cóbh), Ireland to Sandy Hook, NJ, in 18 days 10 hrs., from 4–22 Apr. 1838.

Fastest Atlantic Under the rules of the Hales Trophy or "Blue Riband," which recognizes the highest average speed rather than the shortest duration, the record is held by *Hoverspeed Great Britain* with an average speed of 36.966 knots (46.02 mph) between the Nantucket Light Buoy, Nantucket, MA and Bishop Rock Lighthouse, Cornwall, Great Britain on 20–23 June 1990. However, although she is a passenger vessel, *Hoverspeed Great Britain* is not intended for the North Atlantic, and traditionalists still feel that the Blue Riband should be held by the vessel making the best passage in regular liner service.

That distinction goes to the *United States* (then 51,988, now 38,216 grt), former flagship of the United States Lines. On her maiden voyage between 3–7 July 1952 from New York to Le Havre, France and Southampton, Great Britain, she averaged 35.39 knots (40.75 mph) for three days 10 hrs. 40 min. (6:36 P.M. GMT, 3 July to 5:16 A.M., 7 July) on a route of 2,949 nautical miles from the Ambrose Light Vessel to the Bishop Rock Lighthouse, Isles of Scilly, Great Britain. During this run, on 6–7 July, she steamed the greatest distance ever covered by any ship in a day's run (24 hrs.)—868 nautical miles (998.9 miles), thus averaging 36.17 knots (41.65 mph). The maximum speed attained from her 240,000 shp engines was 44.13 mph in trials on 9–10 June 1952.

Fastest Pacific The fastest crossing from Yokohama, Japan to Long Beach, CA—4,840 nautical miles (5,567.64 miles)—took 6 days 1 hr. 27 min. (30 June–6 July 1973) by the containership *Sea-Land Commerce* (56,353 tons), at an average speed of 33.27 knots (38.31 mph).

Water speed The fastest speed ever achieved on water is an estimated 300 knots (345.48 mph) by Kenneth Peter Warby (b. 9 May 1939) on the Blowering Dam Lake, New South Wales, Australia on 20 Nov. 1977 in his unlimited hydroplane *Spirit of Australia*.

The official world water speed record is 277.57 knots (319.63 mph) set on 8 Oct. 1978 by Warby on Blowering Dam Lake.

Fiona, Countess of Arran (b. 1918) drove her 15-ft. three-point hydroplane *Stradag* (Gaelic "The Spark") to the first world water speed record for electrically propelled powerboats at a speed of 45.13 knots (51.97 mph), at the National Water Sports Center, Nottingham, Great Britain, on 22 Nov. 1989.

TRANSATLANTIC MARINE RECORDS

(Compiled by Nobby Clarke and Richard Boehmer)

CATEGORY	VESSEL	SKIPPER	START	FINISH	DURATION
FIRST SOLO SAILING E–W	15-ton gaff sloop	Josiah Shackford (USA)	Bordeaux, France, 1786	Surinam (Guiana)	35 days
FIRST ROWING	Ship's boat 20 ft.	John Brown and 5 British deserters from garrison	St. Helena 10 June 1799	Belmonte, Brazil (fastest-ever row)	28 days (83 mpd)
FIRST SOLO SAILING W–E	*Centennial* 20 ft.	Alfred Johnson (USA)	Sag Harbor, ME, 1876	Wales	46 days
FIRST MOTORBOAT	*Abiel Abbott Low* 38 ft. (engine: 10hp kerosene)	William C. Newman (USA) Edward (son)	New York, 1902	Falmouth Great Britain	36 days (83.3 mpd)
FIRST WOMAN SOLO E–W	*Felicity Ann* 23 ft.	Ann Davison (Great Britain) Canary Islands	Las Palmas, 20 Nov. 1952	Dominica 1953	65 days
FIRST SOLO ROWING E–W	*Britannia* 22 ft.	John Fairfax (Great Britain)	Las Palmas, 20 Jan. 1969 Canary Islands	Ft. Lauderdale, FL, 19 July 1969	180 days
FIRST SOLO ROWING W–E	*Super Silver* 20 ft.	Tom McClean (Ireland)	St. John's, Newfoundland 1969	Black Sod Bay, Ireland 27 July 1969	70.7 days
FIRST OUTBOARD	*Trans-Atlantic* 26 ft. (2.65 hp Evinrudes)	Al Grover (USA) Dante (son)	St. Pierre, Newfoundland 1985 (via Azores) –	Lisbon, Portugal	34 days (88 mpd approx.)
FIRST ROW BOTH DIRECTIONS	*QE III* 19 ft. 10 in.	Don Allum (Great Britain)	Canary Islands 1986 St. John's, Newfoundland, Canada	Nevis, West Indies Ireland 1987	114 days 77 days
YOUNGEST SOLO SAILING	*Sea Raider* 35 ft.	David Sandeman (Great Britain) (17 years 176 days)	Jersey, Channel Islands, 1976	Newport, RI	43 days
OLDEST SOLO SAILING	*Tawny Pipit* 25 ft.	Stefan Szwarnowski (Great Britain)(76 years 165 days)	New Jersey 2 June 1989	Bude, Great Britain 13 Aug. 1989	72 days
YOUNGEST SOLO ROWING	*Finn Again* 20 ft. 6 in.	Sean Crowley (Great Britain; 25 years 306 days)	Halifax, Nova Scotia, 17 June 1988	Co. Galway, Ireland, 21 Sep. 1988	95 days 22 hrs.

OLDEST SOLO ROWING	*Khaggavisana* 19¾ ft.	Sidney Genders (Great Britain; 51 years)	Penzance, Great Britain, 1970	Miami, FL via Antigua	160 days 8 hrs.
FASTEST POWER W-E	*Gentry Eagle* 110 ft.	Tom Gentry (USA)	Ambrose Light Tower, NJ 13:49 BST 24 July 1989	Bishop Rock Light, Great Britain 03:56 BST 27 July 1989	2 days 14 hrs. 7 min. 47 sec. (45.7 knots smg)
FASTEST SAIL W-E Non-solo	*Jet Services 5* 75 ft. catamaran sloop	Serge Madec (France)	Ambrose Light Tower, NJ 9 June 1990	Lizard Lighthouse, Great Britain 2 June 1990	6 days 13 hrs. 3 min. 32 sec. (18.4 knots smg)
FASTEST SAIL W-E Solo	*Pierre Ier* 60 ft. trimaran sloop	Florence Arthaud (France)	Ambrose Light Tower, NJ 24 July 1990	Lizard Lighthouse, Great Britain 3 Aug. 1990	9 days 21 hrs. 42 min. (12.2 knots smg)
FASTEST SAIL E-W Solo in multihull	*Fleury Michon (IX)* 60 ft. trimaran	Philippe Poupon (France)	Plymouth, Great Britain (STAR) 5 June 1988	Newport, RI 15 June 1988	10 days 9 hrs. 15 min. 9 sec. (11.6 knots smg)

TRANSPACIFIC MARINE RECORDS

FIRST RAFT Shore to Shore	*La Balse* 42 ft. (balsa logs)	Vital Alsar (Spain) and 3 crew	Guayaquil, Ecuador, 1970	Mooloolaba, Australia	160 days
FIRST ROWING	*Britannia II* 35 ft.	John Fairfax (Great Britain) Sylvia Cook (Great Britain)	San Francisco, CA 26 Apr. 1971	Hayman Island, Australia 22 Apr. 1972	362 days
FIRST ROWING SOLO E-W	*Hele-on-Britannia* 32 ft.	Peter Bird (Great Britain)	San Francisco, CA 23 Aug. 1982	Great Barrier Reef, Australia 14 June 1983	294 days 9,000 miles
FIRST ROWING SOLO W-E	*Sector* 26 ft.	Gérard d'Aboville (France)	Chōshi, Japan 11 July 1991	Ilwaco, WA, 21 Nov. 1991	133 days, 6,300 miles
FASTEST SAIL CALIFORNIA–JAPAN	*Pen Duick V* 35-ft. sloop	Eric Tabarly (France)	San Francisco, CA 15 Mar. 1969	Tokyo, Japan 24 Apr. 1969	39 days 15 hrs. 44 min. (4.66 knots smg)

Notes: The earliest single-handed Pacific cross ngs were achieved East–West by Bernard Gilboy (USA) in 1882 in the 18 ft. double-ender Pacific to Australia, and West–East by Fred Rebel (Latvia) in the 18 ft. *Elaine* (from Australia) and Edward Miles (USA) in the 36¾-ft. *Sturdy II* (from Japan), both in 1932, the latter via Hawaii. All mileages are nautical miles. smg = speed made good.

MARINE CIRCUMNAVIGATION RECORDS

(Compiled by Nobby Clarke and Richard Boehmer)

Strictly speaking, a circumnavigation involves someone passing through a pair of antipodal points. Of the records listed below, only those with an asterisk are actually known to have met this requirement. A nonstop circumnavigation is entirely self-maintained; no water supplies, provisions, equipment or replacements of any sort may be taken aboard en route. Vessel may anchor, but no physical help may be accepted apart from passing mail or messages.

CATEGORY	VESSEL	SKIPPER	START	FINISH
*FIRST	*Victoria* Expedition of Fernão de Magalhães (Ferdinand Magellan)	Juan Sebastián de Elcano or del Cano (d. 1526) and 17 crew	Seville, Spain 20 Sep. 1519	San Lucar, Spain 6 Sep. 1522 30,700 nm
FIRST WOMAN	*Etoile* (Storeship for Bougainville's La Boudeuse)	Crypto-female valet of M. de Commerson, named Jeanne Baret	St. Malo, France 1766	1769 (revealed as female on Hawaii)
*FIRST SOLO	*Spray* 36 ft. 9 in. gaff yawl	Capt. Joshua Slocum, 51 (USA) (a nonswimmer)	Newport, RI, via Magellan Straits 24 Apr. 1895	3 July 1898 46,000 nm
FIRST MOTORBOAT	*Speejacks* 98 ft.	Albert Y. Gowen (USA) plus wife and crew	New York City 1921	New York City 1922
*FIRST SUBMERGED	*Triton* Nuclear submarine	Capt. Edward L. Beach USN plus 182 crew	New London, CT 16 Feb. 1960	84 days 19 hrs., 36,300 nm 10 May 1960
*FIRST NONSTOP SOLO W-E	*Suhaili* 32.4 ft. Bermudan ketch	Robin Knox-Johnston (Great Britain)	Falmouth, Great Britain 14 June 1968	22 Apr. 1969 (312 days)
*FIRST NONSTOP SOLO E-W	*British Steel* 59 ft. ketch	Chay Blyth (Great Britain)	Hamble River, Great Britain 18 Oct. 1970	6 Aug. 1971 (292 days)

Category	Vessel	Skipper	Start	Finish	Duration
* FIRST WOMAN SOLO	Express Crusader 53 ft. cutter	Dame Naomi James (New Zealand)		Dartmouth, Great Britain 9 Sep. 1977	Dartmouth, Great Britain 8 June 1978 265 sailing days + 7 days in port
* FIRST BY NORTHWEST PASSAGE	Mabel E. Holland 42 ft. rnotor lifeboat	David Scott Cowper (Great Britain)		Newcastle-upon-Tyne, Great Britain 14 July 1986	Newcastle-upon-Tyne, Great Britain. 24 Sep. 1990 (approx. 260 days motoring)
* FIRST SOLO IN BOTH DIRECTIONS (via Cape Horn)	Ocean Bound 41 ft. Eermudan sloop	David Scott Cowper (Great Britain)		Plymouth, Great Britain 1979 (W–E) Plymouth 1981 (E–W)	Plymouth 1980 Plymouth 1982
FIRST SOLO ROUND THREE TIMES (same yacht)	Tarmin. 24 ft. 7 in. Bermudan sloop	John Sowden (USA)		Various ports 1966, 1974, 1983	1970, 1977, 1986
FASTEST SAIL NONSTOP W–E Solo in monohull	Ecureuil d'Aquitaine II 60 ft. ULDB cutter	Titouan Lamazou (France)		Les Sables, France (VGC) 26 Nov. 1989	Les Sables, France (via 5 capes) 16 Mar. 1990 109 days 8 hrs. 48 min. 50 sec. (205.7 mpd)
* FASTEST SAIL WITH STOPS W–E Solo in multihull	Un Autre Regard 75 ft. tr.maran	Olivier de Kersauson (France)		Brest, France 28 Dec. 1988	Brest, France (via 5 capes and 2 stops) 5 May 1989 125 days 19 hrs. 32 min. 33 sec. + 2 days in port

OTHER MARINE RECORDS

CATEGORY	VESSEL	SKIPPER	START	FINISH	DURATION
LONGEST TIME AND DISTANCE NONSTOP BY SAIL	Parr' Endeavour 44 ft. Bermudan sloop	Jon Sanders (Australia)	Fremantle, Australia 25 May 1986	Fremantle, Australia 13 Mar. 1988	(71,000 nm in 658 days) (4.5 knots)
GOLD RUSH ROUTE Fastest multihull	Grea American 60 ft. trimaran	Georgs Kolesnikows (Canada)	New York 10 Mar. 1989	San Francisco 26 May 1989	76 days 23 hrs. 20 min. (7.36 knots smg.)

(continued)

CATEGORY	VESSEL	SKIPPER	START	FINISH	DURATION
GOLD RUSH ROUTE Fastest monohull	Thursday's Child 60 ft. ULDB cutter	Warren Luhrs (USA)	New York 24 Nov. 1988	San Francisco 12 Feb. 1989	80 days 18 hrs. 39 min. (includes 3-day stop)
BEST DAY'S RUN Non-solo in multihull	Jet Services 5 60 ft. catamaran sloop	Serge Madec (France)	42.638° N 62.626° W 22:22 GMT 3 June 1990	45.750° N 51.480° W 21:58 GMT 4 June 1990	514.01 nm (GCD)/23 hrs. 36 min. (21.8 knots smg)
BEST DAY'S RUN Non-solo in monohull	Phocea 243 ft. ULDB schooner	Philippe Mornay (France)	During transatlantic record run in 1988		490 nm/24 hrs. (20.4 knots smg)
BEST DAY'S RUN Solo in multihull	Laiterie Mont St. Michel 60 ft. trimaran	Olivier Moussy (France)	50° 13' N 11° 30' W 18:18 GMT 6 June 1988	21:17 GMT 7 June 1988 48° 18' N 23° 30' W	430.8 nm (GCD)/24 hrs. (18.0 knots smg)
BEST DAY'S RUN Solo in monohull	Generali Concorde 60 ft. sloop	Alain Gautier (France)	50.300° S 42.550° E 15:39 GMT 2 Dec. 1990	51.800° S 50.617° E 15:16 GMT 3 Dec. 1990	317.1 nm (GCD)/23 hrs. 37 min. (13.43 knots smg)
BEST DAY'S RUN Sailboard	Fanatic board Gaastra sail	Françoise Canetos (France)	Sète, France 13 July 1988	14 July 1988	227 nm/24 hrs. (9.46 knots smg)
ONE NAUTICAL MILE Fastest sail	Crédit Agricole (II) 74 ft. catamaran	Philippe Jeantot (France)	Martinique January 1985		2 min. 13 sec. (27.1 knots smg)
500 METERS Fastest	Naish sailboard with ART sail	Pascal Maka (France)	Saintes Maries-de-la-Mer, France, 27 Feb. 1990		22.65 sec. (42.91 knots)
500 METERS Fastest sailboat	Longshot 20 ft. 9 in. trifoiler	Russell Long (USA)	Lethbridge, Canada 12 Oct. 1990		26.17 sec. (37.14 knots)

Eduard Roditi, author of *Magellan of the Pacific*, advances the view that Magellan's slave, Enrique, was the first circumnavigator. He had been purchased in Malacca and it was shown that he already understood the Filipino dialect Vizayan when he reached the Philippines from the east. He "tied the knot" off Limasawa on 28 Mar. 1521. ULDB = Ultra-light displacement boat. VGC = Vendée Globe Challenge Race. GCD = Great circle distance. All mileages are nautical miles. smg = speed made good.

TRANS-PACIFIC ROWING. Peter Bird (Great Britain) (top) was the first person to row solo east to west across the Pacific Ocean from San Francisco to the Great Barrier Reef, Australia. He began his journey on 23 Aug. 1982 and arrived in Australia on 14 June 1983 after traveling a distance of 9,000 miles in his 32-ft.-long *Hele-on-Britannia* boat. French oarsman Gérard d'Aboville (bottom) set out from Choshi, Japan on 11 July 1991 to row alone across the Pacific Ocean. After battling with storms and capsizing many times, he ended his grueling journey after 134 days when he landed at the fishing village of Ilwaco, WA, having covered 6,300 miles. (Photos: Peter Bird, Gérard d'Aboville)

LARGEST PORT. Rotterdam is the second-largest town in the Netherlands but it has the world's largest artificial harbor and is the busiest port, dealing with cargo from all over the world. It covers an area of 38 miles². (Photo: Spectrum Colour Library)

MERCHANT SHIPPING

Total The world total of merchant shipping, excluding vessels of less than 100 gross tonnage, sailing vessels and barges, was 80,030 ships of 423,026,858 gross tonnage on 1 July 1991.

As of September 1991, there were 395 privately owned deep draft merchant ships with a gross tonnage of 1,000 or more in the United States. These ships are either oceangoing or Great Lakes motor carriers. Their carrying capacity is 19.949 million deadweight tons.

Shipbuilding Worldwide production completed in 1991 was 16.1 million gross tonnage of ships, excluding sailing ships, nonpropelled vessels and vessels of less than 100 gross tonnage. The figures for the Commonwealth of Independent States (formerly part of the USSR), Romania and the People's Republic of China are incomplete. Japan completed 7.2 million gross tonnage (45 percent of the world total) in 1991.

The world's leading shipbuilder in 1991 was Hyundai of South Korea, which completed 30 ships of 1.9 million gross tonnage.

Biggest owner   The largest ship owners are the Japanese NYK Group, whose fleet of owned vessels totaled 11,374,977 gross tons on 1 Feb. 1992.

United States   The largest shipping owner and operator in the United States is Exxon Corporation, whose fleets of owned/managed and chartered tankers in 1987 totaled a daily average of 10.42 million deadweight tons.

Largest fleet   The largest merchant fleet in the world in mid-1991 was that under the flag of Liberia with a fleet totaling 52,426,516 gross tonnage.

PORTS

Largest   The largest port in the world is the Port of New York and New Jersey. The port has a navigable waterfront of 755 miles (295 miles in New Jersey), stretching over 92 miles². A total of 261 general cargo berths and 130 other piers gives a total berthing capacity of 391 ships at any one time. The total warehousing floor space is 422.4 acres.

Busiest   The world's busiest port and largest artificial harbor is Rotterdam-Europoort in the Netherlands, which covers 38 miles², with 76 miles of quays. It handled 317.1 million tons of seagoing cargo.

   Although the port of Singapore handled less tonnage in total seaborne cargo (than Rotterdam), it handled the greatest number of containers, making it the No.1 container port in the world, with a record of 6.35 million TEUs in 1991.

United States   The busiest port in the USA is New Orleans, LA, which handled 1.775 million tons of cargo in 1989.

HOVERCRAFT
(Skirted air-cushion vehicles)

Fastest   The world's fastest warship is the 78-ft.-long 110.2 ton US Navy test hovercraft SES-100B. She attained a world record 91.9 knots (105.8 mph) on 25 Jan. 1980 on the Chesapeake Bay Test Range, MD. As a result of the success of this test craft, a 3,307 ton US Navy Large Surface Effect Ship (LSES) was built by Bell Aerospace under contract from the Department of Defense in 1977–81.

Longest journey   The longest hovercraft journey was one of 5,000 miles, by the British Trans-African Hovercraft Expedition, under the leadership of David Smithers, through eight West African countries in a Winchester class SRN6, between 15 Oct. 1969 and 3 Jan. 1970.

Highest   The highest altitude reached by a hovercraft was on 11 June 1990 when *Neste Enterprise* and her crew of ten reached the navigable source of the Yangzi River, China at 16,050 ft.

   The greatest altitude at which a hovercraft is operating is on Lake Titicaca, Peru, where since 1975 an HM2 Hoverferry has been hovering 12,506 ft. above sea level.

ROAD VEHICLES

AUTOMOBILES

The total number of vehicles constructed worldwide in 1991 was 46,420,410, of which 34,998,534 were automobiles.

In 1991 the number of automobiles constructed in the United States was 5,438,579. The leading manufacturer was General Motors Corporation, which produced 2,496,006. The number of trucks manufactured in 1991 was 3,366,943; Ford was the leading manufacturer with 1,255,076.

The world's largest manufacturer of motor vehicles and parts (and the largest manufacturing company) is General Motors Corporation of Detroit, MI. The company has on average 756,300 employees. The company's highest annual income was $126 billion in 1989.

Largest plant The largest single automobile plant in the world is the Volkswagenwerk at Wolfsburg, Germany, with 64,000 employees and a capacity for producing 4,000 vehicles every week. The factory buildings cover an area of 371 acres and the whole plant covers 1,878 acres, with 46 miles of rail sidings.

The largest automobile plant in the United States, as calculated by its "straight-time capacity" (the number of cars or trucks built using two eight-hour shifts, five days per week), is Honda of America Manufacturing Inc.'s Marysville, OH plant with a capacity of 370,000 cars per year. It is estimated that Nissan Motor Manufacturing Corp.'s Smyrna, TN plant will have a capacity of 450,000 cars and compact pickup trucks at the end of 1992. The GM Lordstown, OH plant will also be capable of producing 450,000 cars by 1993.

Earliest automobiles *Model* The earliest "automobile" of which there is a record was a two-foot-long steam-powered model constructed by Ferdinand Verbiest (d. 1687), a Belgian Jesuit priest, and described in his *Astronomia Europaea*. His model of 1668 was possibly inspired either by Giovanni Branca's description of a steam turbine, published in his *La Macchina* in 1629, or even by *Nan Huairen* (writings on "fire carts") in the Chu kingdom (*c.* 800 B.C.).

The earliest full-scale automobile was the first of two military steam tractors completed at the Paris Arsenal in October 1769 by Nicolas-Joseph Cugnot (1725–1804). This reached 2¼ mph. Cugnot's second, larger tractor, completed in May 1771, today survives in the *Conservatoire Nationale des Arts et Métiers* in Paris, France.

Passenger-carrying The world's first passenger-carrying automobile was a steam-powered road vehicle carrying eight passengers and built by Richard Trevithick (1771–1833). It first ran on 24 Dec. 1801 in Camborne, Great Britain.

Internal combustion The Swiss Isaac de Rivaz (d. 1828) built a carriage powered by his "explosion engine" in 1805. The first practical internal combustion engined vehicle was that built by the Londoner Samuel

Brown (British Patent Number 5350, 25 Apr. 1826), whose 4 hp two-cylinder atmospheric gas 88-liter engined carriage climbed Shooters Hill, Kent, Great Britain in May 1826.

The first successful gasoline-driven car, the Motorwagen, built by Karl-Friedrich Benz (1844–1929) of Karlsruhe, Germany, ran at Mannheim, Germany in late 1885. It was a 3 cwt three-wheeler reaching 8–10 mph. Its single-cylinder engine (bore 3.6 in., stroke 6.3 in.) delivered 0.85 hp at 400 rpm. It was patented on 29 Jan. 1886. Its first 1.6 mile road test was reported in the local newspaper, the *Neue Badische Landeszeitung*, of 4 June 1886, under the heading "Miscellaneous."

FASTEST CARS

Land speed The *official* one-mile land-speed record is 633.468 mph, set by Richard Noble (b. 1946) on 4 Oct. 1983 over the Black Rock Desert, NV in his 17,000 lb. thrust Rolls-Royce Avon 302 jet-powered *Thrust 2*, designed by John Ackroyd.

Rocket-engined The fastest speed attained by any wheeled land vehicle is 631.367 mph by *The Blue Flame*, a rocket-powered four-wheeled vehicle driven by Gary Gabelich (USA; b. 23 Aug. 1940) on the Bonneville Salt Flats, UT on 23 Oct. 1970. Momentarily Gabelich exceeded 650 mph. The car was powered by a liquid natural gas/hydrogen peroxide rocket engine developing a maximum 22,000 lb. s.t. and thus theoretically capable of 900 mph.

The fastest reputed land speed figure in one direction is 739.666 mph, or Mach 1.0106, by Stan Barrett (USA) in the *Budweiser Rocket*, a rocket-engined three-wheeled car, at Edwards Air Force Base, CA on 17 Dec. 1979. *This published speed of Mach 1.0106 is not officially sanctioned by the USAF, as the Digital Instrument Radar was not calibrated or certified. The radar information was not generated by the vehicle directly but by an operator aiming a dish by means of a TV screen.*

The fastest land speed recorded by a woman is 524.016 mph by Mrs. Kitty Hambleton (nee O'Neil; USA) in the 48,000 hp rocket-powered three-wheeled SM1 *Motivator* over the Alvard Desert, OR on 6 Dec. 1976. Her official two-way record was 512.710 mph and she probably touched 600 mph momentarily.

Piston-engined The fastest speed measured for a wheel-driven car is 432.692 mph by Al Teague in *Speed O-Motive/Spirit of '76* at Bonneville Salt Flats, UT on 21 Aug. 1991 over the final 132 ft. of a mile run (av. 425.230 mph for the whole mile).

For a flying start over a distance of 666.386 yds., Donald Malcolm Campbell (1921–67) attained an average speed of 403.10 mph in his 30-ft.-long *Bluebird*, weighing 9,600 lbs., on the salt flats at Lake Eyre, South Australia, on 17 July 1964. The car was powered by a Bristol-Siddeley Proteus 705 gas-turbine engine developing 4,500 shp. Its peak speed was *c.* 445 mph.

Diesel-engined The prototype 3-liter Mercedes C 111/3 attained 203.3 mph in tests on the Nardo Circuit, southern Italy on 5–15 Oct. 1978, and in Apr. 1978 averaged 195.4 mph for 12 hours, thus covering a world record 2,399.76 miles.

FASTEST CARS (above). A unique collection of record-breaking cars. In the foreground is Richard Noble's *Thrust 2*, in which the official one-mile land-speed record was set at 633.468 mph on 4 Oct 1983. (Far left) *Bluebird*, which held the land-speed record in 1964 at 403.10 mph when driven by Donald Campbell (1921–67). (Front center) *The Sunbeam*, driven in 1922 by Kenelm Lee Guinness at a record speed of 133.75 mph. (Far back) 1929 *Golden Arrow*, driven by Henry Segrave (1896–1930) at 231.44 mph. He was knighted for his achievement in 1929 but was fatally injured the following year immediately after setting a water-speed record. (Right) *Red Sunbeam*, also driven by Segrave in 1927 at a speed of 203.79 mph.

(Below) Al Teague built *Speed-O-Motive/Spirit of '76* between January 1974 and August 1976, adding further modifications thereafter. On 21 Aug. 1991 he broke his own world record for a wheel-driven, single-piston-engine car at Bonneville Salt Flats, Wendover, UT with a speed of 432.692 mph. (Photos: National Motor Museum and Rasco)

Rocket-powered sleds   The fastest speed recorded on ice is 247.93 mph by *Oxygen*, driven by Sammy Miller (b. 15 Apr. 1945) on Lake George, NY on 15 Feb. 1981.

Steam car   On 19 Aug. 1985 Robert E. Barber broke the 79-year-old record for a steam car driving No. 744, *Steamin' Demon*, built by the Barber-Nichols Engineering Co., which reached 145.607 mph at Bonneville Salt Flats, UT.

Road cars   Various revved up track cars have been licensed for road use but are not normal production models.

A Jaguar XJ 220 built by Jaguar Sports at Bloxham, Great Britain attained a speed of 212.3 mph during tests in the United States in July 1991, making it the fastest production car in the world. It has a sale price of over $580,000.

The highest road-tested acceleration reported for a standard production car is 60 mph in 3.98 sec. for a Ferrari F40 owned by Nick Mason and driven by Mark Hales of *Fast Lane* magazine at Millbrook, Great Britain on 9 Feb. 1989.

Carriage driving   The only man to drive 48 horses in a single hitch is Dick Sparrow of Zearing, IA, between 1972 and 1977. The lead horses were on reins 135 ft. long.

Coaching   The longest horse-drawn procession was a cavalcade of 68 carriages that measured 3,018 ft. "nose to tail," organized by the Spies Traveling Company of Denmark on 7 May 1986. It carried 810 people through the woods around Copenhagen to celebrate the coming of spring.

Car registrations *Earliest*   The world's first license plates were introduced by the Paris police in France in 1893.

License plate No. 8 was sold at a Hong Kong government auction for HK$5 million (approximately $602,250) on 13 Feb. 1988 to Law Tingpong, a textile manufacturer. The number 8 is considered a lucky number.

As of October 1991, it was estimated that there were 145.043 million automobiles and 45.698 million trucks registered in the United States.

Longest car   A 100-ft.-long 26-wheeled limo was designed by Jay Ohrberg of Burbank, CA. It has many special features, including a swimming pool, a diving board and a king-sized water bed. It is designed to be driven as one piece, or it can be changed to bend in the middle. Its main purpose is for use in films and exhibitions.

Car wrecking   The greatest number of cars wrecked in a stunting career is 1,997 through April 1992 by Dick Sheppard of Gloucester, Great Britain.

LARGEST CARS

Of cars produced for private use, the largest was the Bugatti Royale type 41, of which only six were assembled (although it is believed that seven were built) at Molsheim, France by the Italian Ettore Bugatti. First built in 1927, this machine has an eight-cylinder engine of 12.7 liters' capacity, and measures over 22 ft. in length. The hood is over 7 ft. long.

Largest engines The largest car ever used was the White Triplex, sponsored by J.H. White of Philadelphia, PA. Completed early in 1928, after two years' work, the car weighed about 4.5 tons and was powered by three Liberty V12 aircraft engines with a total capacity of 81,188 cc, developing 1,500 brake horsepower (bhp) at 2,000 rpm. It was used to break the world speed record but crashed at Daytona, FL on 13 Mar. 1929.

Most powerful *Production car* The highest engine capacity of a production car was 2.5 gallon, for the US Pierce-Arrow 6–66 Raceabout of 1912–18, the US Peerless 6–60 of 1912–14 and the Fageol of 1918.

The most powerful current production car is the Bugatti GB110 Super Sports, which develops in excess of 610 bhp.

Heaviest The heaviest car recently in production (up to 25 were made annually) appears to be the Russian-built Zil–41047 limousine with a 12.72 ft. wheelbase. It weighs 7,352 lbs. (3.3 tons). The "stretched" Zil (four to five made annually) was used by former USSR President Mikhail Gorbachev until December 1991. It weighed 6.6 tons and was made of three-inch armor-plated steel. The eight-cylinder, 7-liter engine guzzled fuel at a rate of 6 miles to the gallon.

MISCELLANEOUS CARS

Highest mileage The highest recorded mileage for a car was 1,402,515 authenticated miles up to 23 June 1992 for a 1963 Volkswagen "Beetle" owned by Albert Klein of Pasadena, CA.

Longest in production Among mass-production models, the Volkswagen "Beetle" dates from 1938. The 21 millionth "Beetle" rolled off the last remaining production line, at Puebla, Mexico in Dec. 1991. It is still Mexico's best-selling car.

The Morgan 4/4 celebrated its 56th birthday on 27 Dec. 1991. Built by the Morgan Motor Car Co. of Malvern, Great Britain (founded 1910), there is still a six- to eight-year waiting list.

United States The luxury model Cadillac Fleetwood has been in continuous production since 1936. The oldest mass-production model still in production is the Chrysler Imperial, which was in production from 1926–84 and 1990–present.

Lightest Louis Borsi of London, Great Britain has built and driven a 21 lb. car with a 2.5 cc engine. It is capable of 15 mph.

Parade of Rolls-Royces A parade of 114 Rolls-Royce motor cars assembled on the northbound carriageway of the Tolo Harbour Highway in the New Territories of Hong Kong on 8 Sep. 1991. The average length of the cars participating was 17 ft. 2 in. and the total length of the parade was 1 mile 22 yds.

PRICE EXTREMES

Most expensive The most expensive car ever built was the US Presidential 1969 Lincoln Continental Executive delivered to the US Secret Service on 14 Oct. 1968. It has an overall length of 21 ft. 6¼ in. with a 13 ft. 4 in. wheelbase, and with the addition of 2.2 tons of armor plate weighs 6 tons (12,000 lbs.). The estimated cost of research, development and manufacture was $500,000, but it is rented at $5,000 per year. Even if all four tires were shot out it could travel at 50 mph on inner rubber-edged steel discs.

Used Although higher prices have been reported for sales by private treaty, the greatest price paid at a public auction was £6.4 million ($10.83 million), including commission, for a 1962 Ferrari 250 GTO sold by Sotheby's on 22 May 1990 at Monte Carlo, Monaco. It was bought by Hans Thulin (Sweden).

Most inexpensive The cheapest car of all time was the 1922 Red Bug Buckboard, built by the Briggs & Stratton Co. of Milwaukee, WI, listed at $125 $150. It had a 62 in. wheelbase and weighed 245 lbs. Early models of the King Midget cars were sold in kit form for self-assembly for as little as $100 in 1948.

DRIVING

Around the world The fastest circumnavigation embracing more than an equator's length of driving (24,901 miles) is one of 39 days 23 hrs. 35 min. Driving two Rover 827Si Saloon cars, six members (three male and three female) of the Transworld Venture, organized by the Royal Army Ordnance Corps, left the Tower of London, Great Britain on 13 May 1990 and returned to the same place on 22 June. On their journey they traveled through six continents and covered 25 countries. The distance covered was 25,187.8 miles.

Amphibious circumnavigation The only circumnavigation by an amphibious vehicle was by Ben Carlin (Australia; d. 7 Mar. 1981) in the amphibious jeep *Half-Safe*. He completed the last leg of the Atlantic crossing (the English Channel) on 24 Aug. 1951. He arrived back in Montreal, Canada on 8 May 1958, having completed a circumnavigation of 39,000 miles over land and 9,600 miles by sea and river. He was accompanied on the transatlantic stage by his ex-wife Elinore (USA) and on the long transpacific stage (Tokyo, Japan to Anchorage, AK) by Broye Lafayette De-Mente (USA; b. 1928).

One-year duration record The greatest distance ever covered in one year is 354,257 miles by two Opel Rekord 2-liter passenger sedans, both of which covered this distance between 18 May 1988 and the same date in 1989 without any major mechanical breakdowns. The vehicles were manufactured by the Delta Motor Corporation, Port Elizabeth, South Africa, and were driven on tar and gravel roads in the Northern Cape by a team of company drivers from Delta. The entire undertaking was monitored by the Automobile Association of South Africa.

Trans-Americas Garry Sowerby (Canada), with Tim Cahill (USA) as co-driver and navigator, drove a 1988 GMC Sierra K3500 four-wheel-drive pickup truck powered by a 6.2 liter V8 Detroit diesel engine from Ushuaia, Tierra del Fuego, Argentina to Prudhoe Bay, AK, a distance of 14,739 miles, in a total elapsed time of 23 days 22 hrs. 43 min. from 29 Sep. to 22 Oct. 1987. The vehicle and team were surface-freighted from Cartagena, Colombia to Balboa, Panama so as to bypass the Darién Gap.

The Darién Gap was first traversed by the Land Rover *La Cucaracha Carinosa* (The Affectionate Cockroach) of the Trans-Darién Expedition 1959–60, crewed by Richard E. Bevir (Great Britain) and engineer Terence John Whitfield (Australia). They left Chepo, Panama on 3 Feb. 1960 and reached Quibdó, Colombia on 17 June, averaging 660 ft. per hour of indescribable difficulty.

Trans-America Jeremiah L. Burr (driver/leader), Kurt E. Detlefsen (driver) and Thaddeus E. Burr (navigator) of Connecticut completed the first documented traverse of all the contiguous 48 states of the United States from 13 May to 19 May 1991, in a total elapsed time of 5 days, 7 hours and 15 minutes and a total distance of 7,217.8 miles. The team drove a 1990 Chevrolet Astro Van and stopped only for fuel. Dehydrated foods and nine gallons of water made the team self-sufficient.

Gasoline consumption An experimental Japanese vehicle achieved the equivalent of 6,409 mpg in the Shell Mileage Marathon at Silverstone, Great Britain on 30 June 1988.

Longest fuel range The greatest distance driven without refueling on a single fuel fill in a standard vehicle (38.2 gals. carried in factory-optional twin fuel tanks) is 1,691.6 miles by a 1991 Toyota LandCruiser diesel station wagon. Driven by Ewan Kennedy with Ian Lee (observer) from Nyngan, New South Wales, Australia to Winton, Queensland and back between 18–21 May 1992, the average speed 37.3 mph giving 044.2 mpg.

Driving in reverse Charles Creighton (1908–70) and James Hargis of Maplewood, MO drove their Model A Ford 1929 roadster in reverse from New York 3,340 miles to Los Angeles, CA, from 26 July–13 Aug. 1930 without once stopping the engine. They arrived back in New York in reverse on 5 September, having completed 7,180 miles in 42 days.

Brian "Cub" Keene and James "Wilbur" Wright drove their Chevrolet Blazer 9,031 miles in reverse in 37 days (1 Aug.–6 Sep. 1984) through 15 American states and Canada. Though it was prominently named "Stuck in Reverse," law-enforcement officers in Oklahoma refused to believe it and insisted they drive in reverse reverse—i.e., forward—out of the state.

The highest average speed attained in any nonstop reverse drive exceeding 500 miles was achieved by Gerald Hoagland, who drove a 1969 Chevrolet Impala 501 miles in 17 hrs. 38 min. at Che-mung Speed Drome, NY on 9–10 July 1976, to average 28.41 mph.

Two-side-wheel driving *Car* Bengt Norberg (b. 23 Oct. 1951) of Äppelbo, Sweden drove a Mitsubishi Colt GTi-16V on two side wheels nonstop for a distance of 192.873 miles in a time of 7 hrs. 15 min. 50 sec. He also achieved a distance of 30.328 miles in 1 hr. at Rattvik Horse Track, Sweden on 24 May 1989.

Sven-Erik Söderman (Sweden; b. 26 Sep. 1960) achieved a speed of 102.14 mph over a 100 m (328.1 ft.) flying start on the two wheels of an Opel Kadette at Mora Siljan airport, Mora, Sweden on 2 Aug. 1990. Söderman achieved a record speed for the flying kilometer at 152.96 km (95.04 mph) at the same venue on 24 Aug. 1990.

Truck Sven-Erik Söderman drove a Daf 2800 7.5 ton truck on two wheels for a distance of 6.73 miles at Mora Siljan airport, Mora, Sweden on 19 May 1991.

Bus Bobby Ore (Great Britain; b. Jan. 1949) drove a double-decker bus a distance of 810 ft. on two wheels at North Weald airfield, Great Britain on 21 May 1988.

Wheelie Steve Murty, driving a Pirelli High Performer, established the record for the longest wheelie in a truck, covering 1,794.9 ft. at the National Power Sports Festival in Blackpool, Great Britain on 28 June 1991.

Car collection The unrivaled collector of Rolls-Royces was Bhagwan Shree Rajneesh (Osho; ne Chandra Mohan Jain [1931–90]), the Indian mystic of Rajneeshpuram, OR. His disciples bestowed 93 of these upon him before his deportation from the USA in November 1985.

Smallest street-legal car The smallest registered street-legal car in the United States has an overall length of 88¾ in. and a width of 40½ in. It was built by Arlis Sluder and is now owned by Jeff Gibson.

Ramp jumping The longest ramp jump in an automobile, with the car landing on its wheels and being driven on, is 232 ft., by Jacqueline De Creed (nee Creedy) in a 1967 Ford Mustang at Santa Pod Raceway, Bedfordshire, Great Britain on 3 Apr. 1983.

Tire supporting The greatest number of tires supported in a free-standing lift is 96, by Gary Windebank of Romsey, Great Britain in February 1984. The total weight was 1,440 lbs. The tires used were Michelin XZX 155 × 13.

Worst driver It was reported that a 75-year-old male driver received ten traffic tickets, drove on the wrong side of the road four times, committed four hit-and-run offenses and caused six accidents, all within 20 minutes, in McKinney, TX on 15 Oct. 1966.

Most durable driver   Goodyear Tire and Rubber Co. test driver Weldon C. Kocich drove 3,141,946 miles from 5 Feb. 1953 to 28 Feb. 1986, thus averaging 95,210 miles per year.

Oldest drivers   Roy M. Rawlins (b. 10 July 1870) of Stockton, CA was given a warning for driving at 95 mph in a 55 mph zone in June 1974. On 25 Aug. 1974 he was awarded a California State license valid until 1978, but he died on 9 July 1975, one day short of his 105th birthday.

Mrs. Maude Tull of Inglewood, CA, who took to driving at the age of 91 after her husband died, was issued a renewal on 5 Feb. 1976 when she was 104.

Driving tests   The world's easiest tests are those in Egypt, in which the ability to drive 19.64 ft. forward and the same in reverse has been deemed sufficient. In 1979 it was reported that accurate reversing between two rubber traffic cones had been added. "High cone attrition" soon led to the substitution of white lines.

Mrs. Fannie Turner (b. 1903) of Little Rock, AR passed the *written* test for drivers on her 104th attempt in Oct. 1978.

Drivers' licenses   Regular drivers' licenses are issued to 15-year-olds without a driver-education course only in Hawaii and Mississippi. Thirteen states issue restricted juvenile licenses at 14.

SERVICES

Filling stations   The largest concentration of pumps is 204—96 of them Tokheim Unistar (electronic) and 108 Tokheim Explorer (mechanical)—in Jeddah, Saudi Arabia.

The highest filling station in the world is at Leh, Ladakh, India, at 12,001 ft., operated by the Indian Oil Corporation.

Garages   The largest private garage is one of two stories built outside Bombay, India for the private collection of 176 cars owned by Pranlal Bhogilal (b. 1939).

The KMB Overhaul Center, operated by the Kowloon Motor Bus Co. (1933) Ltd., Hong Kong, is the world's largest multi-story service center. Built expressly for double-decker buses, it has four floors occupying more than 11.6 acres.

Parking lots   The world's largest is the one in the West Edmonton Mall, Edmonton, Alberta, Canada, which can hold 20,000 vehicles. There are overflow facilities on an adjoining lot for 10,000 more cars.

Skid marks   The skid marks made by the jet-powered *Spirit of America*, driven by Norman Craig Breedlove, after the car went out of control at Bonneville Salt Flats, UT, on 15 Oct. 1964, were nearly six miles long.

Tires *Largest*   The largest ever manufactured were by Goodyear Tire & Rubber Co. for giant dump trucks. They measure 12 ft. in diameter, weigh 12,500 lbs. and cost $74,000. A tire 17 ft. in diameter is believed to be the limit of what is practical.

Tows The longest on record was one of 4,759 miles from Halifax, Nova Scotia to Canada's Pacific coast, when Frank J. Elliott and George A. Scott of Amherst, Nova Scotia, Canada persuaded 168 passing motorists in 89 days to tow their Model T Ford (in fact engineless) to win a $1,000 bet on 15 Oct. 1927.

After his 1969 MGB broke down in the vicinity of Moscow, Russia (formerly USSR), the late Eddie McGowan of Chipping Warden, Great Britain was towed by Mark Steven Morgan, driving his 1968 MGC, a distance of 1,456 miles from Moscow to Berlin, Germany on a single 7-ft. nylon tow rope from 12–17 July 1987.

MISCELLANEOUS VEHICLES

Land *Largest* The most massive automotive land vehicle is "Big Muskie," the 12,004 ton mechanical shovel built by Bucyrus Erie for the Musk mine. It is 487 ft. long, 151 ft. wide and 222 ft. high, with a grab capacity of 364 tons.

Longest The Arctic Snow Train owned by the world famous tightrope-walker Steve McPeak (USA) has 54 wheels and is 572 ft. long. It was built by R.G. Le Tourneau Inc. of Longview, TX for the US Army. Its gross train weight is 441 tons, with a top speed of 20 mph, and it was driven by a crew of six when used as an "overland train" for the military. McPeak undertook all repairs, including every punctured wheel, single-handedly in often sub-zero temperatures in Alaska. It generates 4,680 shp and has a fuel capacity of 7,832 gals.

Largest ambulance The world's largest are the 59-ft.-long articulated Alligator Jumbulances Marks VI, VII, VIII and IX, operated by the ACROSS Trust to convey the sick and handicapped on vacations and pilgrimages across Europe. They are built by Van Hool of Belgium with Fiat engines, cost $350,000 and carry 44 patients and staff.

Crawler The most massive vehicle ever constructed is the Marion eight-caterpillar crawler used for conveying Saturn V rockets to their launch pads at Cape Canaveral, FL. It measures 131 ft. 4 in. × 114 ft. and the two built cost $12.3 million. The loaded train weight is 9,000 tons. The windshield wiper blades are 42 in. long and are the world's largest.

Buses *Earliest* The first municipal bus service in the world was inaugurated on 12 Apr. 1903 and ran between Eastbourne railroad station and Meads, Great Britain.

Longest The longest are the articulated buses, with 121 passenger seats and room also for 66 "strap-hangers," built by the Wayne Corporation of Richmond, IN for use in the Middle East. They are 76 ft. long and weigh 23,957 lbs.

The longest rigid single bus is 49 ft. long and carries 69 passengers. It was built by Van Hool of Belgium.

LARGEST CAMPER. The world's largest camper has five stories, stands 39 ft. high, is 66 ft. long and 39 ft. wide. There are eight bedrooms, each with a bathroom, and garage space for four cars. It was manufactured for H.E. Sheik Hamad Bin Hamdan Al Nahyan, a member of the ruling family of Abu Dhabi, United Arab Emirates. (Photo: Peter Beattie, Australian Arab Agriculture Co.)

Largest fleet   The 6,580 single-decker buses in Rio de Janeiro, Brazil make up the world's largest bus fleet.

Longest route   The longest regularly scheduled bus route is 3,559 miles long, operated by Group Ormeño, which since August 1978 has run a regular scheduled service between Tumbes, Peru and Buenos Aires, Argentina. The route takes 116 hrs., with two hours stopover in Lima and 12 hours in Santiago, Chile.

The longest scheduled bus route currently in use in the United States is by Greyhound from Los Angeles to St. Louis. It runs twice per day, is 1,680 miles long, and takes 42 hours to complete employing six drivers, with no change of bus.

Greatest passenger volume   The city with the greatest passenger volume in the United States as of December 1991 was New York City, with 715.403 million unlinked passenger trips. In 1989 the city with the highest aggregate for passenger miles traveled was Los Angeles, CA, where bus riders logged 1.660 billion miles.

Campers *Largest*   The largest two-wheeled five-story camper was built in 1990 by H.E. Sheik Hamad Bin Hamdan Al Nahyan of Abu Dhabi, United Arab Emirates. It is 66 ft. long, 39 ft. wide and stands 39 ft. Weighing 120 tons, it comprises eight bedrooms, eight bathrooms, four garages and water storage for 6,340 gals.

Longest journey   The continuous motor camper journey of 143,716 miles by Harry B. Coleman and Peggy Larson in a Volkswagen Camper from 20 Aug. 1976 to 20 Apr. 1978 took them through 113 countries.

Fastest   The world speed record for a camper is 126.76 mph by a Roadster camper towed by a 1990 Ford EA Falcon, driven by Charlie Kovacs, at Mangalore Airfield, Seymour, Victoria, Australia on 18 Apr. 1991.

Dump truck   The world's largest is the Terex Titan 33–19 manufactured by General Motors Corporation and now in operation at Westar Mine, British Columbia, Canada. It has a loaded weight of 604.7 tons and a capacity of 350 tons. When tipped its height is 56 ft. The 16 cylinder engine delivers 3,300 hp. The fuel tank holds 1,300 gals.

Fire engines   The fire appliance with the greatest pumping capacity is the 860 hp eight-wheel Oshkosh firetruck, weighing 66 tons and used for aircraft and runway fires. It can discharge 41,600 gals. of foam through two turrets in just 150 sec.

Fastest   The fastest on record is the Jaguar XJ12 "Chubb Firefighter," which on 2 Nov. 1982 attained a speed of 130.57 mph in tests when servicing the *Thrust 2* land-speed record trials. (See Fastest cars—Land speed.)

Fire pumping   The greatest gallonage stirrup-pumped by a team of eight in an 80 hr. charity pump is 27,414 gals. by fire fighters representing Grampian Fire Brigade, from 17–20 Aug. 1989 at Aberdeen, Great Britain.

Fire pump handling   The longest unaided tow of a fire appliance in excess of 1,120 lbs. in 24 hrs. on a closed circuit is 223 miles, by a 32-man team of the Dublin Fire Brigade with a 1,144-lb. fire pump on 20–21 June 1987.

Go karts   The highest mileage recorded in 24 hours on an outdoor circuit by a four-man team is 1,018 miles on a one mile track at the Erbsville Kartway, Waterloo, Ontario, Canada on 4–5 Sep. 1983. The 5-hp 140 cc Honda engined kart was driven by Owen Nimmo, Gary Ruddock, Jim Timmins and Danny Upshaw.

The greatest distance recorded in a 48-hour marathon is 1,696.3 miles by Denis Wedes, Stephen Mantle, Len Nicholson and Janice Bennett, driving a Yamaha RC100SE kart powered by a KT100J 100 cc engine at Mount Sugarloaf Circuit, Newcastle, New South Wales, Australia on 25–27 Mar. 1983. They averaged 70.67 mph.

A record distance achieved in six hours in the 100 cc non-gearbox category is 194.81 miles by Emily Newman at Rye House Raceway, Hoddesdon, Great Britain on 25 June 1986.

Solar-powered   The fastest speed attained by a solely solar-powered land vehicle is 48.71 mph by Molly Brennan driving the General Motors

TAXIS. Mexico City has the largest taxi fleet in the world with over 60,000. Seen here in Reforma Avenue are the yellow taxis of the city passing the famous statue of Cuauhtémoc (1495–1522), the 11th and last Aztec emperor. (Photo: Spectrum Colour Library)

Sunraycer at Mesa, AZ on 24 June 1988. The fastest speed of 83.88 mph using solar/battery power was achieved by Star Micronics' solar car *Solar Star* driven by Manfred Hermann on 5 Jan. 1991 at Richmond RAAF Base, Richmond, New South Wales, Australia.

Taxis The largest taxi fleet is that in Mexico City, with 60,000 "normal" taxis, *pesaros* (communal fixed-route taxis) and *settas* (airport taxis).

The city with the largest taxi fleet in the USA is New York City, which on 1 Jan. 1992 had 11,787 registered yellow medallion cabs and 38,000 drivers. In addition, there are approximately 28,000 rental service vehicles in New York City. Both figures for 1992 show a significant drop from previous years.

Taxi drivers   Carmen Fasanella (b. 19 Feb. 1903) was continuously licensed as a taxicab owner and driver in the Borough of Princeton, NJ for 68 years 243 days, from 1 Feb. 1921 to 2 Nov. 1989.

The longest taxicab ride on record is one of 14,414 miles with the meter running at a cost of 70,000 FIM (approximately $16,000). Mika Lehtonen and Juhani Saramies left Nokia, Finland on 2 May 1991, traveling through Scandinavia down to Spain, and arrived back in Nokia on 17 May 1991.

Snowmobile   John W. Outzen of Derry (expedition organizer and leader), Andre, Carl and Dennis Boucher, traveled 10,252.3 miles across North America, from Anchorage, AK to Dartmouth, Nova Scotia, Canada, in 62 days (56 riding days) from 2 Jan. to 3 Mar. 1992 on four Arctic Cat Panther Deluxe Snowmobiles. The team averaged 183 miles per day on the first documented transcontinental drive from the Pacific to the Atlantic oceans entirely on snow.

Longest distance   The longest drive on a power lawn mower was 3,034 miles, when Ian Ireland of Harlow, Great Britain drove an Iseki SG15 between Harlow and Southend Pier, Great Britain from 13 Aug. to 7 Sep. 1989. He was assisted by members of 158 Round Table, Luton, Great Britain and raised over £15,000 ($26,250) to aid the Leukemia Research Fund.

Pedal car   The record from Marble Arch, London, Great Britain to the Arc de Triomphe, Paris, France, including a Channel crossing by ferry, is 21 hrs. 24 min. 0 sec., for a distance of 238 miles, by a team of six members of the national childcare charity in Great Britain on 30 Aug. 1991.

Lawn mowers   The widest gang mower in the world is the 5.6 ton 60 ft. wide 27-unit "Big Green Machine" used by the turf farmer Jay Edgar Frick of Monroe, OH. It mows an acre in 60 sec.

Tractors   The world's largest tractor is a $459,000 US Department of Agriculture Wide Tractive Frame Vehicle completed by Ag West of Sacramento, CA in June 1982. It measures 33 ft. between its wheels, which are designed to run on permanent paths, and weighs 24.5 tons.

The sport of tractor-pulling was put on a national US championship basis in 1967 at Bowling Green, OH, where the winner was "The Purple Monster" built and driven by Roger E. Varns. Today there are 12 classes ranging up to "12,200 lbs. unlimited."

Longest journey   The longest journey by tractor on record is 14,500 miles. The Young Farmers Group of Devon, Great Britain left their native country on 18 Oct. 1990 and drove overland to Zimbabwe, arriving on 4 Mar. 1991.

Trams *Longest journey*   The longest tram journey now possible is from Krefeld St. Tönis to Witten Annen Nord, Germany. With luck at the eight interconnections, the 65.5 mile trip can be completed in 5½ hours.

By early 1991, St. Petersburg, Russia had the most extensive tramway system, with 2,402 cars on 64 routes and 429.13 miles of track.

Oldest   The oldest trams in revenue service in the world are motor cars 1 and 2 of the Manx Electric Railway, dating from 1893. These run regularly on the 17¾ mile railroad between Douglas and Ramsey, Isle of Man, Great Britain.

Most powerful truck   A 1987 Ford LTL 9000 truck, owned and driven by Ken Warby of Cincinnati, OH, is outfitted with a General Electric J 79 engine tuned to produce 20,000 lbf. of thrust. Weighing 4.8 tons, it has achieved 210.2 mph in 7.7 sec. over a quarter-mile course from a standing start.

Wrecker   The world's most powerful wrecker is the Twin City Garage and Body Shop's 22.7-ton, 36-ft.-long International M6-23 "Hulk" 1969 stationed at Scott City, MO. It can lift in excess of 325 tons on its short boom.

LOADS

Heaviest load   On 14–15 July 1984 John Brown Engineers & Contractors BV moved the Conoco Kotter Field production deck with a roll-out weight of 325 tons for the Continental Netherlands Oil Co. of Leidsenhage, Netherlands.

MODEL CARS

Nonstop duration   A Scalextric Jaguar XJ8 ran nonstop for 866 hrs. 44 min. 54 sec. and covered a distance of 1,771.2 miles from 2 May to 7 June 1989. The event was organized by the Rev. Bryan G. Apps and church members of Southbourne, Great Britain.

24-hour slot car racing   On 5–6 July 1986 the North London Society of Model Engineers team at the ARRA club in Southport, Great Britain achieved a distance record for a 1:32 scale car of 305.949 miles in 24 hours, 11,815 laps of the track, driving a Rondeau M482C Group C Sports car, built by Ian Fisher. This was under the rules of the BSCRA (British Slot Car Racing Association).

The longest slot car track measures 958 ft. and was built at Mallory Park Circuit, Great Britain on 22 Nov. 1991 using pieces collected from enthusiasts. One lap was successfully completed by a car.

MOTORCYCLES

As of October 1991 it was estimated that there were 4.156 million registered motorcycles in the United States.

Earliest   The earliest internal combustion-engined motorized bicycle was a wooden-framed machine built at Bad Cannstatt, Germany in October–November 1885 by Gottlieb Daimler (1834–1900) and first ridden by Wilhelm Maybach (1846–1929). It had a top speed of 12 mph and developed one-half of one horsepower from its single-cylinder 264 cc four-cycle engine at 700 rpm. Known as the "Einspur," it was lost in a fire in 1903.

The earliest factory that made motorcycles in quantity was opened in 1894 by Heinrich and Wilhelm Hildebrand and Alois Wolfmüller in Munich, Germany. In its first two years this factory produced over 1,000 machines, each having a water-cooled 1,488 cc twin-cylinder four-cycle engine developing about 2.5 bhp at 600 rpm—the highest-capacity motorcycle engine ever put into production.

Fastest production road machine The 151 hp 1-litre Tu Atara Yamaha Bimota 6th edition E1 has a road-tested top speed of 186 mph.

Fastest racing machine There is no satisfactory answer to the identity of the fastest track machine other than to say that the current Honda, Suzuki and Yamaha machines have all been geared to attain speeds marginally in excess of 186.4 mph under race conditions.

Fastest speeds *Official world speed records must be set with two runs over a measured distance made in opposite directions within a time limit of 1 hr. for FIM records and of 2 hrs. for AMA records.*

Donald A. Vesco (USA; b. 8 Apr. 1939), riding his 6.4 m long *Lightning Bolt* streamliner, powered by two 1,016 cc Kawasaki engines, on Bonneville Salt Flats, UT on 28 Aug. 1978 set AMA and FIM absolute records with an overall average of 318.598 mph and had a fastest run at an average of 318.865 mph.

The world record for 1,093.6 yds. (1 km) from a standing start is 16.68 sec. by Henk Vink (Netherlands; b. 24 July 1939) on his supercharged 984 cc four-cylinder Kawasaki, at Elvington Airfield, North Yorkshire, Great Britain on 24 July 1977. The faster run was made in 16.09 sec.

The world record for 1,320 ft. from a standing start is 8.805 sec. by Henk Vink on his supercharged 1,132 cc four-cylinder Kawasaki at Elvington Airfield, Great Britain on 23 July 1977. The faster run was made in 8.55 sec.

The fastest time for a single run over 1,320 ft. (1 km) from a standing start is 7.08 sec. by Bo O'Brechta (USA) riding a supercharged 1,200 cc Kawasaki-based machine in Ontario, CA in 1980.

The highest terminal velocity recorded at the end of a 1,320 ft. (1 km) run from a standing start is 199.55 mph by Russ Collins (USA) in Ontario, CA on 7 Oct. 1978.

Longest Gregg Reid of Atlanta, GA designed and built a Yamaha 250 cc motorcycle that measures 15 ft. 6 in. long and weighs 520 lbs. It is street legal and has been insured.

Smallest Simon Timperley and Clive Williams of Progressive Engineering Ltd., Ashton-under-Lyne, Lancashire, Great Britain designed and constructed a motorcycle with a wheelbase of 4.25 in., a seat height of 3¾ in. and a wheel diameter of 0.75 in. for the front and 0.95 in. for the back. The bike was ridden a distance of 3.2 ft.

Magnor Mydland of Norway constructed a motorcycle with a wheelbase of 4.72 in., a seat height of 5.82 in. and wheel diameters of 1.49 in. for the front and 3.39 in. for the back. He rode a distance of 1,870 ft., reaching a speed of 7.2 mph.

Duration   The longest time a motor scooter, a Kinetic Honda DX 100 cc, has been kept in nonstop motion is 1,001 hrs. It was ridden by Har Parkash Rishi, Amarjeet Singh and Navjot Chadha, covering a distance of 49,831 miles at Traffic Park, Pune, Maharashtra, India between 22 Apr. and June 1990.

Longest tour   Jim Rogers and Tabitha Estabrook traveled 57,022 miles on motorcycle from New York through Europe, Africa, Asia, South America and ending in New York, from March 1990 to November 1991. If other modes of transportation are counted, they journeyed 99,422 miles in total.

The first woman to circumnavigate the world solo was Moniika Vega (b. 9 May 1962) of Rio de Janeiro, Brazil, riding her Honda 200 cc motorcycle. Her journey began in Milan, Italy on 7 Mar. 1990 and she returned to Italy on 24 May 1991, having covered a distance of 51,885 miles and visited 53 countries.

Trans-Americas   Kurt Nerlich and Hans Shirmer traveled 67,000 miles (55,400 by motorcycle) around the Americas (North, South and Central) in 27 months from July 1954 to September 1956. Travel to and through Central and South America was much more primitive then than it is today.

Trans-America   Ken Hatton of Chicago, IL completed a solo motorcycle trek across the United States, in September 1988, in a record time of 42 hrs. 17 min.

Biggest pyramid   The ASC Tornadoes, a motorcyle display team of the Indian Army, established a world record with a pyramid of 45 men on eight motorcycles. The pyramid was held together by muscle and determination only, with no straps, harnesses or other aids. It traveled a distance of 874 yds. on 6 June 1992 at Manekshaw Parade Ground, Bangalore, India.

Backwards riding   Steering a motorcycle facing backwards from the top of a 10 ft. ladder, over a continuous period of 1 hr. 30 min., Signalman Dewi Jones of the Royal Signals White Helmets covered a distance of 20.505 miles at Catterick Airfield, Great Britain on 30 Nov. 1988.

Wall of death   The greatest endurance feat on a "wall of death" was 7 hrs. 0 min. 13 sec., by Martin Blume, Berlin, Germany on 16 Apr. 1983. He rode over 12,000 laps on the 33-ft. diameter wall on a Yamaha XS400, averaging 30 mph for the 181½ miles.

Ramp jumping   The longest distance ever achieved by a motorcycle long-jumping is 251 ft., by Doug Danger on a 1991 Honda CR500 at Loudon, NH on 22 June 1991.

Wheelie *Distance* Yasuyuki Kudoh at the Japan Automobile Research Institute, Tsukuba City, Ibaragi-prefecture, Japan covered 205.7 miles nonstop on the rear wheel of his Honda TLM 220 R 216 cc motorcycle on 5 May 1991.

United States Doug Domokos on the Alabama International Speedway, Talladega on 27 June 1984 covered 145 miles nonstop on the rear wheel of his Honda XR 500. He stopped only when the gasoline ran out.

Speed The highest speed attained on a rear wheel of a motorcycle is 150 mph by Steve Burns on 3 July 1989 at Bruntingthorpe Proving Ground, Great Britain on his Suzuki GXS 1100 engine Spondon 1425 turbo.

Two-wheel sidecar riding Graham John Martin drove a distance of 198.9 miles on a Yamaha XS 1,100 cc bike in a time of 3 hrs. 5 min. at Gerotek Test Track, Pretoria, South Africa on 21 Aug. 1988.

Most on one machine The record for the most people on a single machine is 46 members of the Illawarra Mini Bike Training Club, New South Wales, Australia. They rode on a 1,000 cc motorcycle and traveled a distance of one mile on 11 Oct. 1987.

BICYCLES

Earliest The first design for a machine propelled by cranks and pedals with connecting rods has been attributed to Leonardo da Vinci (1452–1519) or one of his pupils, *c.* 1493.

The earliest such design actually built was in 1839–40 by Kirkpatrick Macmillan (1810–78) of Dumfries, Great Britain. The machine is now in the Science Museum, London, Great Britain.

The first practical bicycle was the *vélocipède* built in March 1861 by Pierre Michaux and his son Ernest of Rue de Verneuil, Paris, France.

In 1870, James Starley of Coventry, Great Britain constructed the first "penny-farthing" or ordinary bicycle. It had wire-spoked wheels for lightness and was later available with an optional-speed gear.

Bicycle parade The greatest participation was one involving 30,000 cyclists (2.75 percent of the population of Puerto Rico) at San Juan on 17 Apr. 1988. It was organized by TV personality "Pacheco" Joaquín Monserrat.

Trishaw The longest parade on record was when 177 trishaw peddlers rode in single file in Penang, Malaysia on 23 Nov. 1986.

Longest The longest true tandem bicycle ever built (i.e., without a third stabilizing wheel) is one of 66 ft. 11 in. for 35 riders built by Pedaalstompers Westmalle of Belgium. The riders covered *c.* 195 ft. in practice on 20 Apr. 1979. The machine weighed 2,425 lbs.

Terry Thessman of Pahiatua, New Zealand designed and built a bike measuring 72.96 ft. long and weighing 340 lbs. It was ridden by four riders a distance of 807 ft. on 27 Feb. 1988. Turning corners is a problem.

Smallest Jacques Puyoou of Pau, Pyrénées-Atlantiques, France has built a tandem of 14.1 in. wheel diameter, which has been ridden by him and Madame Puyoou.

Largest The largest bicycle as measured by the front-wheel diameter is "Frankencycle," built by Dave Moore of Rosemead, CA and first ridden by Steve Gordon of Moorpark, CA, on 4 June 1989. The wheel diameter is 10 ft. and it is 11 ft. 2 in. high.

HPVs *Fastest land* The world speed records for human-powered vehicles (HPVs) over a 200 m (656.2 ft.) flying start (single rider), are 65.484 mph by Fred Markham at Mono Lake, CA on 11 May 1986 and 62.92 mph (multiple riders) by Dave Grylls and Leigh Barczewski at the

PENNY-FARTHING. In 1870 James Starley, an inventive foreman at Rowley B. Turner of Coventry, set out to reduce the weight of the first practical bicycle, the *vélocipède*. He made a bicycle with a large front wheel and a small rear wheel, which was nicknamed the "penny-farthing" after the largest and smallest English copper coins of the period. (Photo: Spectrum Colour Library)

Ontario Speedway, CA, on 4 May 1980. The one-hour standing start (single rider) record is held by Pat Kinch, riding *Kingcycle Bean*, averaging a speed of 46.96 mph on 8 Sep. 1990 at Millbrook Proving Ground, Great Britain.

Water cycle   The men's 6,562 ft. (single rider) record is 12.84 mph by Steve Hegg in *Flying Fish* at Long Beach, CA on 20 July 1987.

Wheelie   A duration record of 5 hrs. 12 min. 33 sec. was set by David Robilliard at the Beau Sejour Leisure Center, St. Peter Port, Guernsey, Channel Islands on 28 May 1990.

Unicycles *Tallest*   The tallest unicycle ever mastered is one 101 ft. 9 in. tall ridden by Steve McPeak (with a safety wire suspended by an overhead crane) for a distance of 376 ft. in Las Vegas, NV in October 1980. The freestyle riding (i.e., without a safety harness) of ever-taller unicycles would inevitably lead to serious injury or fatality.

Smallest   Peter Rosendahl of Las Vegas, NV rode a unicycle with a wheel diameter of 2.99 in. in a radius of 4 ft. for 30 sec. at Circus Circus Hotel, Las Vegas, NV on 4 Aug. 1990.

Endurance   Deepak Lele of Maharashtra, India unicycled 3,963 miles from New York to Los Angeles from 6 June–25 Sep. 1984.
Takayuki Koike of Kanagawa, Japan set a unicycle record for 100 miles in 6 hrs. 44 min. 21.84 sec. on 9 Aug. 1987 (average speed 14.83 mph).

Backwards   Peter Rosendahl of Las Vegas, NV rode his 24-in.-wheel unicycle backwards for a distance of 46.7 miles in 9 hrs. 25 min. on 19 May 1990.

Sprint   Peter Rosendahl set sprint records from a standing start over 100 m (328.1 ft.) of 12.74 secs. (17.55 mph), and from a flying start for the same distance of 12.43 secs. (17.99 mph), at the Wet 'N Wild Show, Las Vegas on 1 July 1990.

Underwater tricycling   A team of 32 divers pedaled a distance of 116.66 miles in 75 hrs. 20 min. on a standard tricycle at Diver's Den, Santa Barbara, CA on 16–19 June 1988 to raise money for the Muscular Dystrophy Association.

ROADS

Road mileages   The country with the greatest length of road is the United States (all 50 states), with 3,880,151 miles of graded road. The state with the most miles of road is Texas (305,951), while Hawaii has the least, with 4,099 miles.

Longest driveable road   The Pan-American Highway, from northwest Alaska to Santiago, Chile, then eastward to Buenos Aires, Argentina and terminating in Brasilia, Brazil is over 15,000 miles in length. There remains a gap known as the Tapon del Darién in Panama and another at the Atrato Swamp, Colombia. The first all-land crossing was achieved by Loren Lee Uption and Patricia Mercier in a 1966 CJ 5 Jeep. Their journey began at Yavisa, Republic of Panama on 22 Feb. 1985 and ended on 4 Mar. 1987 at Rio Suico, Colombia.

The longest highway solely in the United States is US-20, which runs 3,370 miles from Boston, MA to Newport, OR. The longest highway in the interstate system is I-90, 3,107 miles from Boston, MA to Seattle, WA.

Highest roads   The highest trail in the world is an eight-mile stretch of the Kang-ti-suu between Khaleb and Xingi-fu, Tibet, which in two places exceeds 20,000 ft.

The highest traversable road in the world is one 733.2 miles long between Tibet and southwestern Xinjiang, China, completed in October 1957, which takes in passes at altitudes up to 18,480 ft. above sea level.

Lowest roads   The lowest road is along the Israeli shores of the Dead Sea at 1,290 ft. below sea level.

The world's lowest named "pass" is Rock Reef Pass, Everglades National Park, FL, which is 3 ft. above sea level.

Widest roads   The widest road in the world is the Monumental Axis, running for 1½ miles from the Municipal Plaza to the Plaza of the Three Powers in Brasilia, the capital of Brazil. The six-lane boulevard, opened in April 1960, is 820.2 ft. wide.

The San Francisco–Oakland Bay Bridge Toll Plaza has 23 lanes (17 westbound) serving the bridge in Oakland, CA.

Greatest traffic volume   The most heavily traveled stretch of road is Interstate 10, at Normandie Avenue Interchange (Junction Route 13.30) and at Vermont Avenue Interchange (Junction Route 13.80) in Los Angeles, CA, which both had a rush-hour traffic volume of 22,400 vehicles in 1990. The Vermont Avenue Interchange has a monthly average number of vehicles per day of 355,000 and a yearly average number of 341,000. These averages are the highest anywhere in the United States.

The territory with the highest traffic density in the world is Hong Kong. By 1 Jan. 1987 there were 300,000 motor vehicles on 867 miles of serviceable roads, giving a density of 4.53 yds. per vehicle.

Worst exit to miss   The longest distance between controlled access exits in the United States is 51.1 miles from Florida Turnpike exit 193 (Yeehaw Junction, FL) to exit 244 (Kissimee, FL). The worst exit to miss on any interstate highway is 37.7 miles from I-80 exit 41 (Knolls, UT) to exit 4 (Bonneville Speedway, UT).

Parking tickets   Mrs. Silvia Matos of New York City has set what must be a world record in unpaid parking tickets, totaling $150,000. She collected the 2,800 tickets between 1985 and 1988, but authorities have been unable to collect any money; she registered her car under 19 addresses and 36 license plates and cannot be found.

Parking meters   The earliest ever installed, put in the business district of Oklahoma City, OK on 19 July 1935, were the invention of Carl C. Magee (USA).

LOWEST ROAD. Seen here at the right of the picture is the lowest road in the world at 1,290 ft. below sea level. It runs along the Israeli shores of the Dead Sea in the Judean desert. (Photo: Spectrum Colour Library)

Bridge The world's busiest bridge is the Howrah Bridge across the river Hooghly in Calcutta, India. In addition to 57,000 vehicles per day it carries an incalculable number of pedestrians across its 1,500-ft.-long 72-ft.-wide span.

Longest traffic jams The longest ever reported was that of 16 Feb. 1980, which stretched northwards from Lyons 109.3 miles towards Paris, France.

A record traffic jam was reported for 1½ million cars crawling bumper-to-bumper over the East–West German border on 12 Apr. 1990.

Streets *Longest* The longest designated street in the world is Yonge Street, running north and west from Toronto, Ontario, Canada. The first stretch, completed on 16 Feb. 1796, ran 34 miles. Its official length, now extended to Rainy River on the Ontario–Minnesota border, is 1,178.3 miles.

Narrowest The world's narrowest street is in the village of Ripatransone in the Marche region of Italy. It is called *Vicolo della Virilita* ("Virility Alley") and is 16.9 in. wide.

Shortest The title for "The Shortest Street in the World" is claimed by the town of Bacup, Great Britain, where Elgin Street, situated by the old market ground, measures just 17 ft.

Steepest The steepest street in the world is Baldwin Street, Dunedin, New Zealand, which has a maximum gradient of 1 in 1.266.

The crookedest and steepest street in the United States is Lombard Street, San Francisco, CA. It has eight consecutive 90-degree turns of 20-ft. radius.

Squares *Largest* Tiananmen ("Gate of Heavenly Peace") Square in Beijing, described as the navel of China, covers 98 acres.

The Maiden e Shah Square in Isfahan, Iran extends over 20.1 acres.

RAILROADING

TRAINS

Earliest Wagons running on wooden rails were used for mining as early as 1550 at Leberthal, Alsace.

Richard Trevithick built his first steam locomotive for the 3-ft.-gauge iron plateway at Coalbrookdale, Great Britain in 1803, but there is no evidence that it ran. His second locomotive drew wagons in which men rode on a demonstration run at Penydarren, Great Britain on 22 Feb. 1804, but it broke the plate rails.

The earliest commercially successful steam locomotive worked in 1812 on the Middleton Colliery Railway to Leeds, Great Britain, and was authorized by Britain's first Railway Act of 9 June 1758.

The first practical electric railroad was Werner von Siemens' oval meter-gauge demonstration track, about 984 ft. long, at the Berlin Trades Exhibition in Germany on 31 May 1879.

Fastest   The fastest speed attained by a railed vehicle is 6,121 mph, or Mach 8, by an unmanned rocket sled over the 9½ mile long rail track at White Sands Missile Range, NM on 5 Oct. 1982.

The fastest speed recorded on any national rail system is 320 mph by the French SNCF high-speed train TGV (*Train à Grande Vitesse*) between Courtalain and Tours on 18 May 1990. It was brought into service on 27 Sep. 1981. By September 1983 it had reduced its scheduled time for the Paris–Lyons run in France of 264 miles to exactly 2 hours, thus averaging 132 mph.

The highest speed ever ratified for a steam locomotive was 125 mph over 1,320 ft., by the LNER 4-6-2 No. 4468 *Mallard* (later numbered 60022), which hauled seven coaches weighing 267.9 tons down Stoke Bank, near Essendine, Great Britain on 3 July 1938. Driver Joseph Duddington was at the controls with Fireman Thomas Bray. The engine suffered some damage.

Most powerful   The world's most powerful steam locomotive, measured by tractive effort, was No. 700, a triple-articulated or triplex six-cylinder 2-8-8-8-4 engine built by the Baldwin Locomotive Works in 1916 for the Virginian Railway. It had a tractive force of 166,300 lbs. when working compound and 199,560 lbs. when working simple.

Probably the heaviest train ever hauled by a single engine was one of 17,135 tons made up of 250 freight cars stretching 1.6 miles by the *Matt H. Shay* (No. 5014), a 2-8-8-8-2 engine, which ran on the Erie Railroad from May 1914 until 1929.

Greatest load   The world's strongest rail carrier, with a capacity of 838 tons, is the 36-axle "Schnabel," 301 ft. 10 in. long, built for a US railroad by Krupp, Germany in March 1981.

The heaviest load ever moved on rails is the 11,971 ton Church of the Virgin Mary (built in 1548 in the village of Most, Czechoslovakia), in October–November 1975, moved because it was in the way of coal operations. It was moved 2,400 ft. at 0.0013 mph over four weeks, at a cost of $17 million.

Freight trains   The world's longest and heaviest freight train on record, with the largest number of cars recorded, made a run on the 3-ft.-6-in. gauge Sishen–Saldanha railroad in South Africa on 26–27 Aug. 1989. The train consisted of 660 cars each loaded to 105 tons gross, a tank car and a caboose, moved by nine 50 kV electric and seven diesel-electric locomotives distributed along the train. The train was 4½ miles long and weighed 77,720 tons excluding locomotives. It traveled a distance of 535 miles in 22 hrs. 40 min.

United States   The longest and heaviest freight train on record was about 4 miles in length. It comprised 500 coal motor cars with three 3,600 hp diesels pulling and three more in the middle, on the Iaeger, WV, to Portsmouth, OH stretch of 157 miles on the Norfolk and Western Railway on 15 Nov. 1967. The total weight was nearly 47,040 tons.

Rail Speed through the Ages

The first big advance in speed was the introduction of electric trains–the German *Siemens und Halske* electric train set numerous rail speed records in 1903. The next big advance in speed was by the Japanese *Shinkansen* (bullet) trains, which established the first regular scheduled service averaging over 100 mph on 1 Nov 1965. Trains traveling between Tokyo and Osaka (321 miles) made the trip in 3 hr 10 min at an average speed of 103.3 mph, with a maximum speed of 130 mph.

The most recent advance was in the 1980s, with the French *Train à Grande Vitesse* (TGV), which is the fastest commercial train ever to operate, reaching peak running speeds of 180 mph. The fastest train service currently scheduled is from Paris to Le Mans, where the TGV *Atlantique* averages 137 mph–a speed limited only by the amount of straight track available.

Rail speeds will continue to be challenged in the future. Although the TGV is currently the fastest train, the Japanese are working on an experimental bullet train that they believe will reach a maximum speed of 219 mph.

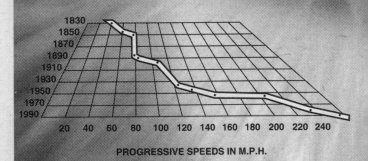

PROGRESSIVE SPEEDS IN M.P.H.

George Stephenson's *Rocket* of 1829
On 8 Oct 1829 Stephenson's *Rocket* established a rail
speed of 29.1 mph at the Rainhills Trials on the
Liverpool & Manchester Railway, Great Britain. One
hundred sixty
years later,
trains now
reach peak
running
speeds of up
to 180 mph,
over five
times as fast.

The French TGV
reaching speeds of
200 mph

Passenger train   The longest passenger train was 1,894 yds., consisted of 70 coaches, and had a total weight of over 2,800 tons. The National Belgium Railway Company's train was powered by one electric locomotive and took 1 hr. 11 min. 5 sec. to complete the 38.5 mile journey from Ghent to Ostend on 27 Apr. 1991.

TRACKS

Longest   The world's longest run is one of 5,864½ miles on the Trans-Siberian line from Moscow to Nakhodka, Russia, on the Sea of Japan. There are 97 stops on the journey, which is scheduled to take 8 days 4 hrs. 25 min.

The longest cross-country railway in the world is the 1,954 mile Baikal–Amur Mainline (BAM), begun in 1938, restarted in 1974 and put into service on 27 Oct. 1984. It runs from Ust-Kut, Eastern Siberia to Komsomolsk on the Pacific coast. The volume of earth and rock which had to be moved was estimated at 13.5 billion ft.^{3}.

Longest straight   The Commonwealth Railways Trans-Australian line over the Nullarbor Plain, from Mile 496 between Nurina and Loongana, Western Australia to Mile 793 between Ooldea and Watson, South Australia, is 297 miles dead straight, although not level.

United States   The longest straight track in the United States is 78.86 miles on CSX Railroad, between Wilmington and Hamlet, NC.

Spike driving   In the World Championship Professional Spike Driving Competition held at the Golden Spike National Historic Site in Utah, Dale C. Jones, 49, of Lehi, UT, drove six 7-in. railroad spikes in a time of 26.4 sec. on 11 Aug. 1984. He incurred no penalty points under the official rules.

Suggestion boxes   The most prolific example on record of the use of a suggestion box is that of John Drayton (1907–87) of Newport, Great Britain, who plied the British rail system with a total of 31,400 suggestions from 1924 to August 1987. More than one in seven were adopted, and 100 were accepted by London Transport. In 1983 he was presented with a chiming clock by British Rail to mark almost 60 years of suggestions.

Widest and narrowest gauge   The widest in standard use is 5 ft. 6 in. This width is used in Spain, Portugal, India, Pakistan, Bangladesh, Sri Lanka, Argentina and Chile.

The narrowest gauge on which public services are operated is 10¼ in. on the Wells Harbor (0.7 mile) and the Wells-Walsingham Railways (4 miles) in Norfolk, Great Britain.

Highest line   At 15,806 ft. above sea level, the standard gauge (4 ft. 8½ in.) track on the Morococha branch of the Peruvian State Railways at La Cima is the highest in the world.

Lowest line The world's lowest is in the Seikan Tunnel between Honshu and Hokkaido, Japan. The rails are 786 ft. below the Tsugaro Straits. The tunnel was opened on 13 Mar. 1988 and is 33.4 miles long. The lowest in Europe is in the Channel Tunnel, where the rails are 417 ft. below mean sea level. (See also Buildings and Structures, Channel tunnel feature.)

Steepest railway The world's steepest railway is the Katoomba Scenic Railway in the Blue Mountains of NSW, Australia. It is 1,020 ft. long with a gradient of 1 in. 0.82. A 220 hp electric winding machine hauls the car by twin steel cables of 22 mm diameter. The ride takes about 1 min. 40 sec. and carries about 420,000 passengers a year.

Steepest gradient The world's steepest standard-gauge gradient by adhesion is 1:11, between Chedde and Servoz on the meter-gauge SNCF Chamonix line, France.

Busiest system The railroad carrying the largest number of passengers is the East Japan Railway Co., which in 1989 carried 14,660,000 passengers daily. Among articles lost in 1989 were 377,712 umbrellas, 141,200 clothing items, 143,761 books and stationery items, 4,359 accessories and 89,799 purses.

Greatest length of railroad As of 1990, the country that has the greatest length of railroad is the United States, with 178,223 miles for all classes of track. There were 200,074 miles of class I track (freight only) owned.

RAIL TRAVEL

Most countries in 24 hours The greatest number of countries traveled through entirely by train in 24 hours is 10, by Aaron Kitchen on 16–17 Feb. 1987. His route started in Yugoslavia and continued through Austria, Italy, Liechtenstein, Switzerland, France, Luxembourg, Belgium and the Netherlands, ending in Germany 22 hrs. 42 min. later.

Longest issued rail ticket A rail ticket measuring 111 ft. 10½ in. was issued to Ronald, Norma and Jonathan Carter for journeys traveled on British Rail between 15–23 Feb. 1992.

Smallest model railroad The smallest model railroad ever built is one of 1:1000 scale by Jean Damery (b. 1923) of Paris, France. The engine runs on a 4½ volt battery and measures ⁵/₁₆ in. overall.

Model trains—nonstop duration A standard lifelike BL2 HO scale electric train pulled six eight-wheel coaches for 1,207.5 hrs. from 4 Aug. to 23 Sep. 1990 and covered a distance of 909.5 miles. The event was organized by Ike Cottingham and Mark Hamrick of Mainline Modelers of Akron, OH.

Handpumped railcars A speed of 20.51 mph for a 984 ft. course was achieved by Gold's Gym, Surrey, British Columbia, Canada at the Annual World Championship Handcar Races, Port Moody, British Columbia with their five-man team (one pusher, four pumpers) in a time of 32.71 sec. on 2 July 1986.

STATIONS

Largest The world's largest is Grand Central Terminal, Park Avenue and 42nd Street, New York City, built from 1903–13. It covers 48 acres on two levels with 41 tracks on the upper level and 26 on the lower. On average there are more than 550 trains and 200,000 commuters, in addition to 300,000 who pass through the terminal. The Main Room is 80,000 ft.^{2} and is 250 ft. tall.

In 1993, five new platforms will open for international trains using the Channel Tunnel with additional face of 6,594 ft.

Busiest The busiest railroad junction in the world is Clapham Junction, London, Great Britain, in the Southern Region of British Rail, with an average of 2,200 trains passing through each 24 hours.

Highest The Condor station in Bolivia at 15,705 ft. on the meter-gauge Rio Mulato-to-Potosi line is the highest in the world.

Waiting rooms The world's largest waiting rooms are the four in Beijing Station, Chang'an Boulevard, Beijing, China, opened in September 1959, with a total standing capacity of 14,000.

Platforms The longest railroad platform in the world is the Kharagpur platform, West Bengal, India, which measures 2,733 ft. in length.
The State Street Center subway platform on "The Loop" in Chicago, IL measures 3,500 ft. in length.
The two platforms comprising the New Misato railroad station on the Musashino line, Saitama, Japan are 984 ft. apart and are connected by a bridge.

SUBWAY SYSTEMS

Most extensive The subway with most stations in the world is the New York City Metropolitan Transportation Authority subway (first section opened on 27 Oct. 1904). The network covers 231.73 route miles, comprising 469 subway stations, and serves an estimated 5 million subway and bus riders per day. In 1991, there were an average 3.3 million commuters, and the estimate for 1992 is 3.2 million.

Traveling *New York subway* The record for traveling the whole system is 26 hrs. 21 min. 08 sec., set by Kevin Foster (USA) on 25–26 Oct. 1989.

Moscow Metro The record transit on 9 Dec. 1988 (all 123 named stations) was 9 hrs. 39 min. 50 sec. by Peter Altman and Miss Jackie Smith (both Great Britain).

Busiest The world's busiest metro system has been the Greater Moscow

Metro (opened 1935) in Russia, with as many as 3.3 billion passengers per year at its peak. There are 141 stations (18 of which have more than one name, being transfer stations) and 140 miles of track. The 5 kopek fare was maintained for the first 55 years from 1935 to 1990.

Worst subway disaster   The worst subway accident in the United States occurred on 1 Nov. 1918, in Brooklyn, NY when a BRT Line train derailed on a curve on Malbone St. in the Brighton Beach section. There were 97 fatalities on the scene and five more people died later from injuries sustained in the crash. The BRT line went bankrupt on 31 Dec. 1918 as a result of the tragedy.

AIRCRAFT

The use of the Mach scale for aircraft speeds was introduced by Prof. Ackeret of Zürich, Switzerland. The Mach number is the ratio of the velocity of a moving body to the local velocity of sound. This ratio was first employed by Dr. Ernst Mach (1838–1916) of Vienna, Austria in 1887. Mach 1.0 equals 760.98 mph at sea level at 59° F., and is assumed, for convenience, to fall to a constant 659.78 mph in the stratosphere, i.e., above 36,089 ft.

EARLIEST FLIGHTS

The first controlled and sustained power-driven flight occurred near Kill Devil Hill, Kitty Hawk, NC, at 10:35 A.M. on 17 Dec. 1903, when Orville Wright (1871–1948) flew the 12 hp chain-driven *Flyer I* for a distance of 120 ft. at an airspeed of 30 mph, a ground speed of 6.8 mph and an altitude of 8–12 ft. for about 12 seconds, watched by his brother Wilbur (1867–1912), four men and a boy. Both brothers, from Dayton, OH, were bachelors because, as Orville put it, they had not the means to "support a wife as well as an airplane." The *Flyer* was first exhibited in the National Air and Space Museum at the Smithsonian Institution, Washington, D.C. on 17 Dec. 1948.

The first hop by a passenger-carrying airplane entirely under its own power was made when Clément Ader (1841–1925) of France flew in his *Éole* for about 164 ft. at Armainvilliers, France on 9 Oct. 1890. It was powered by a lightweight steam engine of his own design, which developed about 20 hp.

The earliest "rational design" for a flying machine, according to the Royal Aeronautical Society, London, Great Britain was that published by Emanuel Swedenborg (1688–1772) in Sweden in 1717.

Jet-engined   Proposals for jet propulsion date back to Capt. Marconnet (1909) of France, and Henri Coanda (1886–1972) of Romania, and to the turbojet proposals of Maxime Guillaume (France) in 1921.

The first flight by an airplane powered by a turbojet engine was made by the Heinkel He 178, piloted by Flug Kapitän Erich Warsitz, at Marienehe, Germany on 27 Aug. 1939. It was powered by a Heinkel He S3b engine weighing 834 lbs. (as installed with long tailpipe) designed by Dr. Hans Pabst von Ohain, whose first bench tests were made at an unrecorded date in 1937.

Transatlantic   The first crossing of the North Atlantic by air was made by Lt.-Cdr. Albert Cushion Read (1887–1967) and his crew (Stone, Hinton, Rodd, Rhoads and Breese) in the 84 knot US Navy/Curtiss flying boat NC-4 from Trepassey Harbor, Newfoundland, Canada, via the Azores, to Lisbon, Portugal from 16–27 May 1919. The whole flight of 4,717 miles, originating from Rockaway Air Station, Long Island, NY on 8 May, required 53 hrs. 58 min., terminating at Plymouth, Great Britain on 31 May. The Newfoundland–Azores flight of 1,200 miles took 15 hrs. 18 min. at 81.7 knots (94.1 mph).

Nonstop   The first nonstop transatlantic flight was achieved 18 days later. The pilot, Capt. John Williams Alcock (1892–1919), and navigator, Lt. Arthur Whitton Brown (1886–1948) left Lester's Field, St. John's, Newfoundland, Canada at 4:13 P.M. GMT on 14 June 1919, and landed at Derrygimla Bog near Clifden, Republic of Ireland, at 8:40 A.M. GMT, 15 June, having covered a distance of 1,960 miles in their Vickers Vimy, powered by two 360 hp Rolls-Royce Eagle VIII engines.

Solo   The first solo transatlantic flight was achieved by Capt. Charles Augustus Lindbergh (USA; 1902–74), who took off in his 220 hp Ryan monoplane *Spirit of St. Louis* at 12:52 P.M. GMT on 20 May 1927 from Roosevelt Field, Long Island, NY. He landed at 10:21 P.M. GMT on 21 May 1927 at Le Bourget Airfield, Paris, France. His flight of 3,610 miles lasted 33 hrs. 29½ min. and he won a prize of $25,000. The *Spirit of St. Louis* is now in the National Air and Space Museum at the Smithsonian Institution, Washington, D.C.

Most flights   Between March 1948 and his retirement on 1 Sep. 1984, Flight Service Manager Charles M. Schimpf logged a total of 2,880 Atlantic crossings—a rate of 6.4 per month.

Transpacific   The first nonstop flight was by Major Clyde Pangborn and Hugh Herndon in the Bellanca cabin monoplane *Miss Veedol*. They took off from Sabishiro Beach, Japan and covered the distance of 4,558 miles to Wenatchee, WA in 41 hrs. 13 min. from 3–5 Oct. 1931. (For earliest crossing, see Circumnavigational flights.)

Circumnavigational flights   Strict circumnavigation of the globe requires the aircraft to pass through two antipodal points, thus covering a minimum distance of 24,859.73 miles.

Earliest   The earliest such flight, of 26,345 miles, was by two US Army Douglas DWC amphibians in 57 "hops" between 6 April and 28 Sep. 1924, beginning and ending in Seattle, WA. The *Chicago* was piloted by Lt. Lowell H. Smith and Lt. Leslie P. Arnold, and the *New Orleans* by Lt. Erik H. Nelson and Lt. John Harding. Their flying time was 371 hrs. 11 min.

Fastest   The fastest flight under the FAI (*Fédération Aéronautique Internationale*) rules, which permit flights that exceed the length of the

Tropic of Cancer or Capricorn (22,858.8 miles), was that of the eastbound flight of 36 hrs. 8 min. 34 sec. by the Gulfstream IV, N400GA (Capt. Allen E Paulson) from Houston, TX via Lake Charles, Shannon (Ireland), Dubai, Hong Kong, Taipei (Taiwan), Honolulu and Miami on 26–28 Feb. 1988. The average speed was 637.7 mph.

A Boeing 747SP *Friendship One* (Capt. Clay Lacy) with 141 passengers achieved an eastbound flight in 36 hrs. 54 min. 15 sec., covering 23,125 miles from Seattle, WA from 28–30 Jan. 1988. The plane reached 803 mph over the Atlantic and refueled only in Athens, Greece and Taipei, Taiwan.

First without refueling   Richard G. "Dick" Rutan and Jeana Yeager, in their specially constructed aircraft *Voyager*, designed by Dick's brother Burt Rutan, flew from Edwards Air Force Base, CA from 14–23 Dec. 1986. Their flight took 9 days 3 min. 44 sec. and they covered a distance of 25,012.665 miles, averaging 115.65 mph. The plane, with a

---

Around the world   The fastest time for a circumnavigation on scheduled flights is 44 hrs. 6 min. by David J. Springbett (b. 2 May 1938) of Taplow, Great Britain. His route took him from Los Angeles, CA eastward via London, Bahrain, Singapore, Bangkok, Manila, Tokyo and Honolulu from 8–10 Jan. 1980 over a 23,068 mile course.

Round the world—antipodal points   Brother Michael Bartlett of Balham, London, Great Britain traveled 26,868 miles on scheduled flights. He visited antipodal points at Madrid, Spain and Ti Tree Point, on Highway 52, New Zealand in a time of 95 hrs. 44 min. He achieved the second point by flying to Wellington and journeying by car to Ti Tree Point, the exact antipodal point to Madrid.

London–New York   The record from central London, Great Britain to downtown New York City by helicopter and Concorde is 3 hrs. 59 min. 44 sec., and for the return, 3 hrs. 40 min. 40 sec., both by David J. Springbett and David Boyce on 8–9 Feb. 1982.

Fastest transcontinental flight   The record aircraft time from coast to coast (Los Angeles to Washington, D.C.) is 68 min. 17 sec. by Lt. Col. Ed Yeilding, pilot, and Lt. Col. J.T. Vida, reconnaissance systems officer, aboard the SR–71 Blackbird spy plane during its Air Force retirement flight to the Smithsonian Institution on 6 Mar. 1990. The Blackbird was refueled over the Pacific Ocean at 27,000 ft. before starting a climb to above 80,000 ft., heading east from the California coastline and crossing the finish line near Salisbury, MD. The plane averaged 2,145 mph between Los Angeles and Washington, and 2,190 mph between St. Louis and Cincinnati. This is the first (and only) time that a sonic boom has traveled uninterrupted from coast to coast across the continental United States.

wingspan of 110.8 ft., was capable of carrying 1,240 gals. of fuel weighing 8,934 lbs. It took over two years and 22,000 man-hours to construct. The pilot flew from a cockpit measuring 5.6 × 1.8 ft. and the off-duty crew member occupied a cabin 7½ × 2 ft. *Voyager* is now in the National Air and Space Museum at the Smithsonian Institution, Washington, D.C.

First circumpolar   Capt. Elgen M. Long, 44, achieved the first circumpolar flight in a Piper PA-31 Navajo from 5 Nov.–3 Dec. 1971. He covered 38,896 miles in 215 flying hours. The cabin temperature sank to –40° F. over Antarctica.

First single-engined circumpolar   Richard Norton, an American airline captain, and Calin Rosetti, head of satellite navigation systems at the European Space Agency, made the first single-engined circumpolar flight in a Piper PA-46-310P Malibu. This began and finished at Le Bourget Airport, Paris, France, from 21 Jan.–15 June 1987. They traveled 34,342 miles in a flying time of 185 hrs. 41 min.

AIRCRAFT

Largest wingspan   The aircraft with the largest wingspan ever constructed is the $40-million Hughes H.4 Hercules flying boat (*Spruce Goose*). She was raised 70 ft. into the air in a test run of 3,000 ft., piloted by Howard Hughes (1905–76), off Long Beach Harbor, CA, on 2 Nov. 1947, but after this she never flew again. The eight-engined 212 ton aircraft had a wingspan of 319 ft. 11 in. and a length of 218 ft. 8 in. In a delicate engineering feat she was moved bodily by the Goldcoast Corporation, aided by the US Navy barge crane YD-171, on 22 Feb. 1982, to her final resting place 6 miles across the harbor under a 415-ft.-diameter, clear-span aluminum dome, the world's largest.

Among current aircraft, the Russian Antonov An-124 has a span of 240 ft. 5¾ in., and the Boeing 747-400 one of 213 ft. The USAF C-5B cargo plane has a wingspan of 222 ft. 8½ in., which is the greatest for any United States military aircraft

A modified six-engine version of the An-124, known as An-225 and built to carry the former Soviet space shuttle *Buran*, has a wingspan of 290 ft. (see Heaviest aircraft).

The $34-million Piasecki Heli-Stat, comprising a framework of light alloy and composite materials, to mount four Sikorsky SH-34J helicopters and the envelope of a Goodyear ZPG-2 patrol airship, was exhibited on 26 Jan. 1984 at Lakehurst, NJ. Designed for use by the US Forest Service and designated Model 94-37J Logger, it had an overall length of 343 ft. and was intended to carry a payload of 24 tons. It crashed on 1 July 1986.

Heaviest   The aircraft with the highest standard maximum takeoff weight is the Russian Antonov An-225 *Myira* ("Dream") at 660 tons (1,322,750 lbs.). (See Most capacious.) The aircraft lifted a payload of 344,579 lbs. to a height of 40,715 ft. on 22 Mar. 1989. This flight was achieved by Capt. Alexander Galunenko and his crew of seven pilots, and was made along the route Kiev–St. Petersburg–Kiev without landing at a range of 1,305 miles and lasted 3 hrs. 47 min. (See Most capacious.)

Electric plane The MB-E1 is the first electrically propelled aircraft. A Bosch 10.7 hp motor is powered by Varta FP25 nickel-cadmium 25 Ah batteries. The aircraft, with a wingspan of 39.4 ft., is 23 ft. long and weighs 882 lbs. It was designed by the model aircraft constructor Fred Militky (USA) and made its maiden flight on 21 Oct. 1973.

Ultralight On 3 Aug. 1985 Anthony A. Cafaro (b. 30 Nov. 1951) flew an ultralight aircraft (ULA; maximum weight 245 lbs., maximum speed 65 mph, fuel capacity 5 gals.) single-seater Gypsy Skycycle for 7 hrs. 31 min. at Dart Field, Mayville, NY. Nine fuel "pickups" were completed during the flight.

Smallest The smallest plane ever flown is the *Bumble Bee Two*, designed and built by Robert H. Starr of Arizona. It was 8 ft. 10 in. long, with a wingspan of 5 ft. 6 in., and weighed 396 lbs. empty. The fastest speed attained was 190 mph. On 8 May 1988, after flying to a height of approximately 400 ft., it crashed, and was totally destroyed.

The smallest monoplane ever flown is the *Baby Bird*, designed and built by Donald R. Stits. It is 11 ft. long, with a wing span of 6 ft. 3 in., and weighs 252 lbs. empty. It is powered by a 55-hp two-cylinder Hirth engine, giving a top speed of 110 mph. It was first flown by Harold Nemer on 4 Aug. 1984 at Camarillo, CA.

The smallest twin-engined aircraft may be the Colombian MGI5 Cricri (first flown 19 July 1973), which has a wingspan of 16 ft. and measures 12 ft. 10 in. long overall. It is powered by two JPX PUL engines, and it is rated at 15 hp.

The smallest jet is the 280 mph Silver Bullet, weighing 432 lbs., with a 17 ft. wingspan, built by Bob Bishop (USA).

Bombers *Heaviest* The eight-jet swept-wing Boeing B-52G/H Stratofortress has a maximum takeoff weight of over 244 tons (488,000 lbs.), a wingspan of 185 ft., and is 157 ft. 6¾ in. in length. It has a speed of over 650 mph. Of the two series in active service, the B-52G is the longest bomber in the USAF at 160 ft. 11 in. The B-52H has the greatest thrust of a bomber in the US fleet at 136,000 lbs. and the greatest unrefueled range of over 8,800 miles. The B-52 can carry 12 SRAM thermonuclear short-range attack missiles or 24 750-lb. bombs under its wings and eight more SRAMs, or 84 500-lb. bombs, in the fuselage.

The ten-engined Convair B-36J, weighing 204 tons, had a greater wingspan at 230 ft., but it is no longer in service. Its top speed was 435 mph. The use of both piston engines (driving propellers) and jet engines (providing thrust) led to the epithet "six turning, four burning."

Fastest The world's fastest operational bombers include the French Dassault Mirage IV, which can fly at Mach 2.2 (1,450 mph) at 36,000 ft.

The American variable-geometry or "swing-wing" General Dynamics FB111A has a maximum speed of Mach 2.5, and the Soviet swing-wing Tupolev Tu-22M, known to NATO as "Backfire," has an estimated over-target speed of Mach 2.0 but could be as fast as Mach 2.5.

Largest airliner The highest-capacity jet airliner is the Boeing 747 "Jumbo Jet," first flown on 9 Feb. 1969, which has a capacity of from 385 to more than 650 passengers and a maximum speed of 602 mph. Its wingspan is 231.8 ft. and its length 195.7 ft. It entered service on 22

Jan. 1970. The first 747-400 entered service with Northwest Airlines on 26 Jan. 1988 with a wingspan of 213 ft., a range exceeding 8,000 miles and a capacity for 660 passengers. Theoretical accommodation is available for 516 passengers seated 10 abreast in the main cabin plus up to 69 in the stretched upper deck in the 747-300.

A stretched version of the McDonnell Douglas MD-11 airliner was being contemplated, with accommodation for 515 passengers in the main cabin and up to 96 in a lower "panorama deck" forward of the wing. This has given way to the MD-12, proposed in early 1990 and revised by the manufacturer in April 1992, when it was portrayed in a double-deck configuration with capacity for 511 passengers. Growth options include a 26-ft. stretch (to more than 233 ft. in length) to accommodate up to 700 people in two classes.

Stowaway   The most rugged stowaway was Socarras Ramirez, who escaped from Cuba on 4 June 1969 by stowing away in an unpressurized wheel well in the starboard wing of a Douglas DC-8 from Havana, Cuba to Madrid, Spain in a 5,600-mile Iberian Airlines flight.

Longest air ticket   A ticket 39 ft. 4½ in. long was issued for $4,500 to M. Bruno Leunen of Brussels, Belgium in December 1984 for a 53,203-mile trip on 80 airlines with 109 layovers.

Passenger load   The greatest passenger load carried by any single commercial airliner was 1,087 during *Operation Solomon*, which began on 24 May 1991 when Ethiopian Jews were evacuated from Falasha to Israel on a Boeing 747 belonging to El Al airline.

Fastest airliner   The supersonic BAC/Aérospatiale Concorde, first flown on 2 Mar. 1969, with a designed capacity of 128 (and potentially 144) passengers, cruises at up to Mach 2.2 (1,450 mph). It has a maximum takeoff weight of 408,000 lbs. It flew at Mach 1.05 on 10 Oct. 1969, exceeded Mach 2 for the first time on 4 Nov. 1970, and became the first supersonic airliner used in passenger service on 21 Jan. 1976. In service with Air France and British Airways, Concorde has now been laid out to carry 100 passengers. The New York–London, Great Britain record is 2 hrs. 55 min. 15 sec., set on 14 Apr. 1990.

Most capacious   The Aero Spacelines Super Guppy has a cargo hold with a usable volume of 49,790 ft.³ and a maximum takeoff weight of 87.5 tons. Its wingspan is 156 ft. 3 in. and its length 141 ft. 3 in. Its cargo compartment is 108 ft. 10 in. long with a cylindrical section 25 ft. in diameter.

The Russian Antonov An-124 *Ruslan* has a cargo hold with a usable volume of 35,800 ft.³ and a maximum takeoff weight of 446 tons. It is powered by four Lotarev D-18T turbofans giving a cruising speed of up to 528 mph at 39,370 ft. and a range of 2,796 miles. A special-purpose heavy-lift version of the An-124, known as An-225 *Myira* ("Dream"), has been developed with a stretched fuselage providing as much as

**MOST FLIGHTS BY PROPELLER-DRIVEN AIRCRAFT. The CV-580
is a turboprop conversion of the earlier piston engined CV-340
and CV-440. The conversion was developed by Pacific Airmotive
of Burbank, CA using Allison 504-D13 turboprop engines.
In 1991 it was reported that 139,368 flights had been achieved
by one of these aircraft. (Photo: Austin J. Brown)**

42,000 ft.^{3} usable volume. A cargo compartment includes an unobstructed
141 ft. hold length, with maximum width and height of 21 ft. and 14 ft.
5¼ in. respectively. A new wing center section carries an additional two
engines, permiting an estimated total 310,000 lb. thrust. Having flown first
on 21 Dec. 1988, the aircraft was used to carry the Soviet space shuttle
Buran for the first time on 13 May 1989, when it was airborne for 13
hrs. 13 min. (See Heaviest aircraft.)

Heaviest commercial cargo movement   Russian manufacturer Antonov
and British charter company Air Foyle claim a record for the heaviest
commercial air cargo movement after carrying three transformers weighing 47.4 tons each and other equipment weighing 147.14 tons, from
Barcelona, Spain to Noumea, New Caledonia, between 10–14 Jan. 1991.

Antonov and the former Soviet state airline Aeroflot carried a one-
piece newsprint press weighing 60.6 tons from Helsinki, Finland to Melbourne, Australia in November 1989 on behalf of forwarding agent
Röhlig Australia. The total payload was 134.5 tons.

Largest propeller   The largest ever used was the 22 ft. 7½ in. diameter Garuda propeller, fitted to the Linke-Hofmann R II built in Breslau, Germany (now Wroclaw, Poland), which flew in 1919. It was driven
by four 260-hp Mercedes engines and turned at only 545 rpm.

Most flights by propeller-driven airliner   A Convair CV-580 turboprop airliner was reported by the manufacturer in April 1991 to have
achieved 139,368 flights. Its exact age was not announced, but even if

it were the first such airliner, the figure equates to more than nine flights a day since 1952.

Most flights by jet airliner A survey of aging airliners or so-called "geriatric jets" in *Flight International* Magazine for April 1992 reported a McDonnell Douglas DC-9 still in service that had logged 94,159 flights in less than 26 years. This comes to 10 flights a day and 11 daily flights on weekends, but after allowing for "downtime" for maintenance, the real daily average is higher.

The most hours recorded by a jet airliner still in service is 89,236 hours reported for a Boeing 747 in the same issue of *Flight International* (see above).

Oldest jet airliner According to the British-based aviation insurance service company Airclaims, two first-generation airliners built in 1958— a deHavilland DH106 Comet and a Boeing 707—were still in service on 1 Jan. 1992.

Scheduled flights *Longest* The nonstop flights by airlines Air New Zealand, Northwest, United Airlines and Qantas from Los Angeles, CA to Sydney, Australia last 14 hrs. 50 min. in a Boeing 747SP, a journey of over 7,487 miles.

The longest nonstop delivery flight by a commercial jet is 11,250 miles from London, Great Britain to Sydney, Australia by a Qantas Boeing 747-400 *Longreach*, using 176.6 tons of specially formulated Shell Jet A-1 high-density fuel, in 20 hrs. 9 min. on 16–17 Aug. 1989. It is the first time this route has been completed nonstop by an airliner.

Shortest The shortest scheduled flight is by Loganair between the Orkney Islands of Westray and Papa Westray, Great Britain, which has been flown with Britten-Norman Islander twin-engined 10-seat transports since September 1967. Though scheduled for two minutes, in favorable wind conditions it was once completed in 58 sec. by Capt. Andrew D. Alsop. The check-in time for the 2 min. flight is 20 min.

Alaska Airlines provides the shortest scheduled flight by jet, by McDonnell Douglas MD-80 between San Francisco and Oakland, CA. There is one daily return flight six days a week; the time averages 5 minutes for the 12 mile journey. Some 25 minutes are allowed in the airline timetable.

Most flights in 24 hours Brother Michael Bartlett of London, Great Britain, an "Eccentric Globetrotter," made 42 scheduled passenger flights with Heli Transport of Nice, Southern France between Nice, Sophia, Antipolis, Monaco and Cannes in 13 hrs. 33 min. on 13 June 1990.

FASTEST SPEED

Official record The airspeed record is 2,193.2 mph, by Capt. Eldon W. Joersz and Major George T. Morgan, Jr., in a Lockheed SR-71A "Blackbird" near Beale Air Force Base, CA over a 15½ mile course on 28 July 1976.

Air-launched record The fastest fixed-wing aircraft in the world was the US North American Aviation X-15A-2, which flew for the first time (after modification from the X-15A) on 25 June 1964, powered by a liquid oxygen and ammonia rocket-propulsion system. Ablative materials on the airframe enabled it to withstand a temperature of 3,000°F. The landing speed was momentarily 242 mph. The fastest speed attained was 4,520 mph (Mach 6.7) when piloted by Major William J. Knight, USAF (b. 1930), on 3 Oct. 1967.

An earlier version piloted by Joseph A. Walker (USAF; 1920–66) reached 354,200 ft. also over Edwards Air Force Base, CA on 22 Aug. 1963. The final flight was on 24 Oct. 1968, after which the program was suspended. Each X-15 was carried aloft by a Boeing B-52 "mother" aircraft

US NASA Rockwell International space shuttle orbiter *Columbia*, commanded by Capt. John W. Young, USN and piloted by Capt. Robert L. Crippen, USN, was launched from the Kennedy Space Center, Cape Canaveral, FL on 12 Apr. 1981 after expenditure of $9.9 billion since 1972. *Columbia* broke all records in space by a fixed-wing craft, with 16,600 mph at main engine cutoff. After reentry from 75.8 miles, experiencing temperatures of 3,920° F., she glided home weighing 107 tons, and with a landing speed of 216 mph, on Rogers Dry Lake, CA on 14 Apr. 1981.

Under the FAI (*Fédération Aéronautique Internationale*) Category P for aerospacecraft, the *Columbia* is holder of the current absolute world record for duration—10 days 2 hrs. 0 min. 38 sec. to main touchdown—when on its 33rd mission, STS 32, with five crewmen, on 9 Jan. 1990.

Orbiter *Discovery* holds the shuttle altitude record of 332 miles, achieved on 24 Apr. 1990 on its 10th flight.

The greatest mass lifted by the shuttle and placed in orbit was 293,019 lbs. This was lift-off weight of *Discovery STS 41*, launched on 6 Oct. 1990 carrying the *Ulysses* solar polar orbiter and an IUS/PAM solid propellant upper stage.

Supersonic flight The first was achieved on 14 Oct. 1947 by Capt. (later Brig. Gen.) Charles ("Chuck") Elwood Yeager (b. 13 Feb. 1923), over Edwards Air Force Base, Muroc, CA, in a Bell XS-1 rocket plane (*Glamorous Glennis*—named for Yeager's wife) at Mach 1.015 (670 mph) at an altitude of 42,000 ft. The XS-1 is now in the National Air and Space Museum at the Smithsonian Institution, Washington, D.C.

First supersonic airliner The former Soviet Tupolev TU-144 was first flown on 31 Dec. 1968 as the world's first supersonic airliner, although it entered service initially as a cargo plane.

Fastest jet The USAF Lockheed SR-71, a reconnaissance aircraft, has been the world's fastest jet (see official record). First flown in its definitive form on 22 Dec. 1964, it was reportedly capable of attaining an altitude ceiling of close to 100,000 ft. It has a wingspan of 55.6 ft. and a length of 107.4 ft. and weighs 85 tons at takeoff. Its reported range at Mach 3 was 2,982 miles at 78,750 ft. At least 30 are believed to have been built before the plane was retired by the US Air Force.

Fastest combat jets   The fastest combat jet is the Russian Mikoyan MiG-25 fighter (NATO code name "Foxbat"). The reconnaissance aircraft "Foxbat-B" has been tracked by radar at about Mach 3.2 (2,110 mph). When armed with four large underwing air-to-air missiles known to NATO as "Acrid," the fighter "Foxbat-A" is limited to Mach 2.8 (1,845 mph). The single-seat "Foxbat-A" has a wingspan of 45 ft. 9 in., is 278 ft. 2 in. long and has an estimated maximum takeoff weight of 82,500 lbs.

United States   The fastest combat jets in the United States' arsenal are the F-111 and the F-15, both of which fly at Mach 2.5, although the F.-15 is listed in one official release as flying at Mach 2.5 plus. The F-15E is a two-seat craft that is 63 ft. 9 in. long, has a wingspan of 42 ft. 9¾ in., and has a gross takeoff weight of 81,000 lbs.

Fastest biplane   The fastest is the Italian Fiat CR42B, with a 1,010 hp Daimler-Benz DB601A engine, which attained 323 mph in 1941. Only one was built.

Fastest piston-engined aircraft   On 21 Aug. 1989, in Las Vegas, NV, the *Rare Bear*, a modified Grumman Bearcat F8F2 piloted by Lyle Shelton, set the FAI approved world record for a 3 km run of 528.33 mph.

Fastest propeller-driven aircraft   The fastest propeller-driven aircraft in use is the former Soviet Tu-95/142 "Bear" with four 14,795 hp engines driving eight blade counter-rotating propellers with a maximum level speed of Mach 0.82 575 mph.

The turboprop-powered Republic XF84H prototype US Navy fighter that flew on 22 July 1955 had a top *design* speed of 670 mph, but was abandoned.

FASTEST PISTON-ENGINED AIRCRAFT. Lyle Shelton at the controls of *Rare Bear*, a modified F8F2 Grumman Bearcat in which he set a world record for a 3 km run of 528.33 mph on 21 Aug 1989. (Photo: Chuck Aro)

McDonnell Douglas expected its projected MD-91X, powered by counter-rotating multi-bladed fans, to cruise at about Mach 0.78 (514 mph). In tests during 1987–88 with an MD-80 experimentally fitted with a General Electric GE36 engine driving two fans (in place of one of the two standard Pratt & Whitney JT8D turbofans) a maximum speed of Mach 0.865 was attained before development was discontinued.

Fastest transatlantic flight   The flight record is 1 hr. 54 min. 56.4 sec. by Major James V. Sullivan, 37, and Major Noel F. Widdifield, 33, flying a Lockheed SR-71A "Blackbird" eastward on 1 Sep. 1974. The average speed, slowed from refueling by a KC-135 tanker aircraft, for the New York–London stage of 3,461.53 miles was 1,806.96 mph.

The solo record (Gander to Gatwick) is 8 hrs. 47 min. 32 sec., an average speed of 265.1 mph, by Capt. John J.A. Smith in a Rockwell Commander 685 twin-turboprop on 12 Mar. 1978, achieving an average speed of 265.214 mph.

Fastest climb   Heinz Frick of British Aerospace took a Harrier GR5 powered by a Rolls-Royce Pegasus 11-61 engine from a standing start to 39,370 ft. in 2 min. 6.63 sec. above the Rolls-Royce flight test center, Filton, Bristol, Great Britain on 15 Aug. 1989.

Aleksandr Fedotov (USSR) in a Mikoyan E 266M (MiG-25) aircraft established the fastest time-to-height record on 17 May 1975, reaching 114,830 ft. in 4 min. 11.7 sec. after takeoff from Podmoscovnoe, Russia.

United States   The fastest time-to-height record for a United States aircraft is to 62,000 ft. in 2 min. 2.94 sec., by Major Roger J. Smith, USAF, in an F-15 Eagle on 19 January 1975.

Duration   The longest flight on record is 64 days 22 hrs. 19 min. 5 sec., set by Robert Timm and John Cook in the Cessna 172 *Hacienda*. They took off from McCarran Airfield, Las Vegas, NV just before 3:53 P.M. local time on 4 Dec. 1958 and landed at the same airfield just before 2:12 P.M. on 7 Feb. 1959. They covered a distance equivalent to six times around the world, being refueled without any landings.

AIRPORTS

Largest   The largest is the $3.6 billion King Khalid International Airport outside Riyadh, Saudi Arabia, which covers an area of 87 miles^2 (55,040 acres). It was opened on 14 Nov. 1983. It also has the world's largest control tower, 266 ft. in height.

The Hajj Terminal at the $4.76 billion King Abdul-Aziz Airport near Jeddah, Saudi Arabia is the world's largest roofed structure, covering 370 acres.

The present six runways and four terminal buildings of Dallas/Fort Worth Airport, TX are planned to be extended to eight runways, 13 terminals, and 260 gates, with an ultimate capacity for 150 million passengers.

The world's largest airport terminal is at Hartsfield Atlanta International Airport, GA, opened on 21 Sep. 1980, with floor space covering 2.4 million ft.^{2} (50½ acres) and still expanding. It had 146 gates handling 48,024,566 passengers in 1990, but has capacity for 75 million.

Busiest   The busiest airport is Chicago International Airport, O'Hare Field, IL, with a total of 59,130,007 passengers and 780,658 operation movements in the year 1989. This represents a takeoff or landing every 40.4 sec. around the clock.

The busiest landing area ever was Bien Hoa Air Base, South Vietnam, which handled approximately 1,000,000 takeoffs and landings in 1970.

Helipad   The world's largest helipad was at An Khe, South Vietnam. The heliport at Morgan City, LA, one of a string used by helicopters flying energy-related offshore operations into the Gulf of Mexico, has pads for 46 helicopters.

Landing fields *Highest*   The highest is La Sa (Lhasa) Airport, Tibet, People's Republic of China, at 14,315 ft.

Lowest   The lowest landing field is El Lisan on the east shore of the Dead Sea, 1,180 ft. below sea level, but during World War II BOAC Short C-class flying boats operated from the surface of the Dead Sea at 1,292 ft. below sea level.

The lowest international airport is Schiphol, Amsterdam, Netherlands, at 15 ft. below sea level.

Furthest and nearest to city or capital   The airport furthest from the city center it allegedly serves is Viracopos, Brazil, which is 60 miles from São Paulo. Gibraltar Airport is a mere 2,625 ft. from the city center.

BUSIEST AIRPORT. Aircraft waiting for flight clearance at Chicago International Airport, O'Hare Field, IL, the busiest airport in the world. There are a total of 780,658 operation movements per year, with planes landing or taking off every 40.4 sec. (Photo: Austin J. Brown)

Longest runways   The longest runway in the world is at Edwards Air Force Base on the west side of Rogers dry lakebed at Muroc, CA. which measures 39,104 ft., or 7.4 miles. The *Voyager* aircraft, taking off on its around-the-world unrefueled flight (see Circumnavigational flights), used 14,200 ft. of the 15,000-ft.-long main base concrete runway.

The world's longest civil airport runway is one of 3.04 miles at Pierre van Ryneveld Airport, Upington, South Africa, constructed in five months from August 1975 to January 1976.

The most southerly major runway (1.6 miles) in the world is at Mount Pleasant, East Falkland (Lat 51° 50′ S), built in 16 months and completed in May 1985.

Plane pulling   Dave Gauder single-handedly pulled a Concorde 40 ft. across the tarmac at Heathrow Airport, London, Great Britain on 11 June 1987.

Wing walking   Roy Castle, the host of the British Broadcasting Corporation *Record Breakers* television program, flew on the wing of a Boeing Stearman airplane for 3 hrs. 23 min. on 2 Aug. 1990, taking off from Gatwick, Great Britain and landing at Le Bourget, near Paris, France.

Smallest helicopter   The Aerospace General Co. one-person rocket-assisted minicopter weighs about 160 lbs. and can cruise for 250 miles at 185 mph.

AIRLINES

Busiest   The country with the busiest airlines system is the United States, where the total number of passenger enplanements by large commercial air carriers in domestic operations in 1991 was 453 million. The overall total, including regional/commuter service, was 484.4 million.

Busiest international route   The city-pair with the highest international scheduled passenger traffic is London/Paris. In 1989, 3,046,000 passengers flew between the two cities, approximately equal to 4,186 each way each day (although London-bound traffic was 9.5 percent higher than that bound for Paris). The second busiest pair is London/New York (2,356,000 in 1989).

Largest   The Russian state airline Aeroflot, so named since 1932, was instituted on 9 Feb. 1923 and has been the largest airline of all time. In its last complete year of formal existence (1990) it employed 600,000 (more than the top 18 US airlines put together) and flew 139 million passengers, with 20,000 pilots, along 620,000 miles of domestic routes across 11 time zones. The peak size of its fleet remains unknown, with estimates ranging up to 14,700, if both aircraft and helicopters were included. By late 1991 the fleet was operated by at least 46 domestic operators.

United States   The largest US airline in terms of number of aircraft in 1991 was American, with 622. The airline also led in number of passenger enplanements, 74.864 million, and available seat miles, with 128.7 billion. United Airlines led in revenue passenger miles, at 80.2 billion *v.* American's 79.7 billion.

Oldest   The oldest airline, Koninklijke-Luchtvaart-Maatschappij NV (KLM), the national airline of the Netherlands, was established on 7 Oct. 1919. It opened its first scheduled service (Amsterdam–London, Great Britain) on 17 May 1920, seven months after its establishment.

Delag (Deutsche Luftschiffahrt AG) was founded at Frankfurt am Main, Germany on 16 Oct. 1909 and started a scheduled airship service on 17 June 1910.

Chalk's International Airline has been flying amphibious planes from Miami, FL to the Bahamas since July 1919. Albert "Pappy" Chalk flew from 1911–75.

Aerospace company   The world's largest aerospace company is Boeing of Seattle, WA. As of December 1991 its sales figures were $29.3 billion and its workforce was 158,500 worldwide. Cessna Aircraft Company of Wichita, KS had total sales of $818 million and a workforce of 5,400 in 1991. The company has produced over 177,000 aircraft since Clyde Cessna's first was built in 1911.

HELICOPTERS

Earliest   Leonardo da Vinci (1452–1519) proposed the idea of a helicopter-type craft, although it is known that the French had built helicopter toys before that time.

Igor Sikorsky built a helicopter in Russia in 1909, but the first practical machine was the Focke-Achgelis, first flown in 1936.

Fastest   Under FAI rules, the world's speed record for helicopters was set by John Trevor Eggington with co-pilot Derek J. Clews, who averaged 249.09 mph over Somerset, Great Britain on 11 Aug. 1986 in a Westland Lynx company demonstrator helicopter.

Largest   The former Soviet Mil Mi-12 (NATO code-name "Homer"), also known as the V-12, is powered by four 6,500 hp turboshaft engines and has a span of 219 ft. 10 in. over its rotor tips, with a length of 121 ft. 4½ in. It weighs 114 tons.

The largest helicopter in the western world is the USN CH/MH-53 Super Stallion, which weighs 73,500 lbs. and has an overall length including rotors of 99 ft. ½ in. The fuselage is 73 ft. 4 in. long and the rotor diameter is 79 ft.

Highest altitude   The record for helicopters is 40,820 ft. by an Aérospatiale SA315B Lama, over Istres, France on 21 June 1972 by John Boulet.

The highest recorded landing was at 23,000 ft., below the southeast face of Mt. Everest in. a rescue sortie in May 1971.

Longest hover   Doug Daigle, Brian Watts and Dave Meyer of Tridair Helicopters, together with Rod Anderson of Helistream, Inc. of California, maintained a continuous hovering flight in a 1947 Bell B model for 50 hrs. 50 sec. during 13 and 15 Dec. 1989.

Circumnavigation   H. Ross Perot, Jr. and Jay Coburn made the first helicopter circumnavigation in *Spirit of Texas* in 29 days 3 hrs. 8 min. 13 sec. on 1–30 Sep. 1982 from Dallas, TX.

The first solo around-the-world flight in a helicopter was completed by Dick Smith (Australia) on 22 July 1983. Taking off from and returning to the Bell Helicopter facility at Fort Worth, TX, in a Bell Model 206L, LongRanger III, his unhurried flight began on 5 Aug. 1982 and covered a distance of 35,258 miles.

AUTOGYROS

Earliest   The autogyro, or gyroplane, a rotorcraft with an unpowered rotor turned by the airflow in flight, preceded any practical helicopter with its engine-driven rotor.

Juan de la Cierva (Spain) designed the first successful gyroplane with his model C.4 (commercially named Autogiro), which flew at Getafe, Spain on 9 Jan. 1923.

Speed, altitude and distance records   Wing-Cdr. Kenneth H. Wallis (Great Britain) holds the straight-line distance record of 543.27 miles, set in his WA-116F autogyro on 28 Sep. 1975 with a nonstop flight from Lydd to Wick, Great Britain. On 20 July 1982, flying from Boscombe Down, Great Britain, he established a new autogyro altitude record of 18,516 ft. in his WA-121/Mc. Wing-Cdr. Wallis also flew his WA-116, with a 72-hp McCulloch engine, to a record speed of 120.3 mph over a 1.86 mile straight course at Norfolk, Great Britain, on 18 Sep. 1986.

Human-powered flight   The Daedalus Project achieved its goal of human-powered flight when Kanellos Kanellopoulos (b. 25 Apr. 1957) averaged 18.5 mph in his 112 ft. wingspan machine from Crete to the island of Santoríni, Greece on 23 Apr. 1988, flying 74 miles.

FLYING BOATS

Fastest   The fastest flying boat ever built was the Martin XP6M-1 Seamaster, the US Navy four-jet-engined minelayer flown in 1955–59, with a top speed of 646 mph. In September 1946 the Martin JRM-2 Mars flying boat set a payload record of 68,327 lbs.

The official flying boat speed record is 566.69 mph, set by Nikolay Andreievski and crew of two in a Soviet Beriev M-10, powered by two AL-7 turbojets, over a 9.3–15½ mile course at Joukovsky-Petrovskoye, Russia on 7 Aug. 1961.

The M-10 holds all 12 records listed for jet-powered flying boats, including an altitude record of 49,088 ft. set by Georgiy Buryanov and crew over the Sea of Azov in the former USSR on 9 Sep. 1961.

AIRSHIPS

Earliest flight   The earliest flight in an airship was by Henri Giffard from Paris to Trappes, France in his steam-powered coal-gas airship 88,300 ft.^{3} in volume and 144 ft. long, on 24 Sep. 1852.

Largest   *Rigid*   The largest was the 235-ton German *Graf Zeppelin II* (LZ 130), with a length of 804 ft. and a capacity of 7.06 million ft.^{3}. She flew her maiden flight on 14 Sep. 1938 and in May and August 1939 made radar spying missions in British air space. She was dismantled in April 1940. Her sister ship, *Hindenburg*, was 5 ft. 7 in. longer.

Non-rigid   The largest ever constructed was the US Navy ZPG 3-W, which had a capacity of 1.5 million ft.^{3}, a length of 403 ft., a diameter of 85.1 ft. and a crew of 21. She first flew on 21 July 1958 but crashed into the sea in June 1960.

Greatest passenger load   The most people ever carried in an airship was 207, in the US Navy *Akron* in 1931. The transatlantic record is 117, by the German *Hindenburg* in 1937. She exploded into a fireball at Lakehurst, NJ on 6 May 1937.

Distance records   The FAI accredited straight-line distance record for airships is 3,967.1 miles, set by the German *Graf Zeppelin LZ127*, captained by Dr. Hugo Eckener, between 29 Oct. and 1 Nov. 1928. From 21–25 Nov. 1917 the German *Zeppelin L59* flew from Yambol, Bulgaria to a point south of Khartoum, Sudan and returned, covering a minimum of 4,500 miles.

Duration record   The longest recorded flight by a non-rigid airship (without refueling) is 264 hrs. 12 min. by a US Navy Goodyear-built ZPG-2 class ship (Cdr. J.R. Hunt, USN) that flew 9,448 miles from South Weymouth Naval Air Station, MA to Key West, FL, on 4–15 Mar. 1957.

BALLOONING

Earliest   The earliest recorded ascent was by a model hot-air balloon invented by Father Bartolomeu de Gusmão (ne Lourenço; 1685–1724), which was flown indoors at the Casa da India, Terreiro do Paço, Portugal on 8 Aug. 1709.

Distance record   The record distance traveled by a balloon is 5,208.68 miles, by the Raven experimental helium-filled balloon *Double Eagle V* (capacity 399.053 ft.^{3}) from 9–12 Nov. 1981. The journey started at Nagashima, Japan and ended at Covello, CA.

Abruzzo and Newman, with Maxie L. Anderson, set a duration record of 137 hrs. 5 min. in *Double Eagle II* in the first balloon crossing of the North Atlantic, from Presque Isle, ME to Miserey, France on 12–17 Aug. 1958.

Col. Joe Kittinger, USAF, (see Parachuting) became the first man to complete a solo transatlantic crossing by balloon. He lifted off from Caribou, ME on 14 Sep. 1984 and completed a distance of 3,543 miles before landing at Montenotte, near Savóna, Italy on 18 Sep. 1984.

Largest number to jump from a balloon   On 5 Apr. 1990 12 members of the Red Devils Free Fall Parachute Team together made a jump from a Cameron A210, hot-air balloon over Bath, Great Britain, at a height of 6,000 ft.

Distance record   The first crossing of the United States was by the helium-filled balloon *Super Chicken III* (pilots Fred Gorell and John Shoecraft), flying 2,515 miles from Costa Mesa, CA to Blackbeard's Island, GA from 9–12 Oct. 1981.

Mass ascent   The greatest mass ascent of hot-air balloons from a single site took place within one hour on 15 Aug. 1987 when 128 participants at the Ninth Bristol International Balloon Festival in Bristol, Great Britain took off.

Highest   *Unmanned*   The highest altitude attained by an unmanned balloon was 170,000 ft. by a Winzen balloon, with a 47.8 million ft.^{3} capacity, launched at Chico, CA in October 1972.

Manned   The highest altitude reached in a manned balloon is an unofficial 123,800 ft. by Nicholas Piantanida (1933–66) of Bricktown, NJ, from Sioux Falls, SD on 1 Feb. 1966. He landed in a cornfield in Iowa but did not survive.

The official record (closed gondola) is 113,740 ft. by Cdr. Malcolm D. Ross, USNR, and the late Lt. Cdr. Victor A. Prother, USN, in an ascent from the deck of the USS *Antietam* over the Gulf of Mexico on 4 May 1961 in a balloon of 12 million ft.^{3} capacity.

Largest   The largest balloons ever built have an inflatable volume of 70 million ft.^{3} and stand 1,000 ft. tall. They are unmanned. The manufacturers are Winzen Research Inc. of Minnesota.

Hot-air   *Atlantic crossing*   Richard Branson (Great Britain) and his pilot, Per Lindstrand (Great Britain), were the first to cross the Atlantic in a hot-air balloon, on 2–3 July 1987. They ascended from Sugarloaf, ME and covered the distance of 3,075 miles to Limavady, Northern Ireland in 31 hours 41 minutes.

Pacific crossing   Richard Branson and Per Lindstrand crossed the Pacific in the *Virgin Otsuka Pacific Flyer* from the southern tip of Japan to Lac la Matre, Yukon, northwestern Canada on 15–17 Jan. 1991 in a 2.6 million ft.^{3} capacity hot-air balloon (the largest ever flown) to set FAI records for duration (46 hrs. 15 min.) and distance (great circle 4,768 miles). Unofficial world best performances were also set for the fastest speed from takeoff to landing, 147 mph. A speed of 239 mph was sustained for over one hour.

Altitude   Per Lindstrand (Great Britain) achieved the altitude record of 65,000 ft. in a Colt 600 hot-air balloon over Laredo, TX on 6 June 1988.

The FAI endurance and distance record for a gas and hot-air balloon is 96 hrs. 24 min. and 2,074.817 miles by *Zanussi*, crewed by Donald Allan Cameron (Great Britain) and Major Christopher Dafey (Great Britain). The balloon failed by only 103 miles to achieve the first balloon crossing of the Atlantic on 30 July 1978, going from St. Johns, Newfoundland, Canada to the Bay of Biscay.

PERSONAL AVIATION RECORDS

Oldest pilots The world's oldest pilot was Ed McCarty (b. 18 Sep. 1885) of Kimberley, ID, who in 1979 was flying his rebuilt 30-year-old Ercoupe at the age of 94.

Most flying hours *Pilot* John Edward Long (USA; b. 10 Nov. 1915) between 1 May 1933 and 17 Sep. 1991 logged 56,400 hrs. 5 min. of flight time as a pilot—cumulatively more than six years airborne.

Most planes flown James B. Taylor, Jr. (1897–1942) flew 461 different types of powered aircraft during his 25 years as an active experimental test and demonstration pilot for the US Navy and a number of American aircraft manufacturing companies.

MODEL AIRCRAFT

Altitude, speed and duration Maynard L. Hill (USA), flying radio-controlled models, established the world record for altitude of 26,922 ft. on 6 Sep. 1970, and on 4 July 1983 he set a closed-circuit distance record of 1,231 miles.

The free-flight speed record is 213.70 mph, achieved by V. Goukoune and V. Myakinin, with a radio-controlled model at Klementyevo, Russia on 21 Sep. 1971.

The record duration flight is one of 33 hrs. 32 min. 30 sec. by A. Smolentsev flying a radio-controlled glider at Planerskoye, Ukraine on 2–4 Sep. 1983.

An indoor model with a wound rubber motor designed by J. Richmond (USA) set a duration record of 52 min. 14 sec. on 31 Aug. 1979.

Jean-Pierre Schiltknecht flew a solar-driven model aircraft for a duration of 10 hrs. 43 min. 51 sec. at Wetzlar, Germany on 10 July 1991.

Paper aircraft The level flight duration record for a hand-launched paper aircraft is 16.89 sec., by Ken Blackburn in the Reynolds Coliseum, North Carolina State University, on 29 Nov. 1983.

Largest The largest flying paper airplane, with a wingspan of 30 ft. 6 in., was constructed by pupils of various schools in Hampton, VA and

---

Smallest model aircraft The smallest to fly is one weighing 0.004 oz., powered by an attached horsefly and designed by insectonaut Don Emmick of Seattle, WA. On 24 July 1979 an Emmick flew for 5 minutes at Kirkland, WA.

flown on 25 Mar. 1992. It was launched indoors from a 10-ft.-high platform and flown for a distance of 114 ft. 9 in.

KITE FLYING

The following records are all recognized by *Kite Lines* Magazine.

Longest   The longest kite flown was 3,394 ft. in length. It was made and flown by Michel Trouillet and a team of helpers at Nîmes, France on 18 Nov. 1990.

Largest   The largest kite flown was one of 5,952 ft.^{2}. It was first flown by a Dutch team on the beach at Scheveningen, Netherlands on 8 Aug. 1981.

Highest   A record classic height of 31,955 ft. was reached by a train of eight kites over Lindenberg, Germany on 1 Aug. 1919.
   The altitude record for a single kite is 12,471 ft., in the case of a kite flown by Henry Helm Clayton and A.E. Sweetland at the Blue Hill Weather Station, Milton, MA on 28 Feb. 1898.

Fastest   The fastest speed attained by a kite was 120 mph for a kite flown by Pete Di Giacomo at Ocean City, MD on 22 Sep. 1989.

Greatest lift   The greatest lift by a single kite was one of 728 lbs., achieved by a kite flown by G. William Tyrrell, Jr., also at Ocean City, MD on 23 Sep. 1984.

Most on a single line   The greatest number of kites flown on a single line is 11,284, by Sadao Harada and a team of helpers at Sakurajima, Kagoshima, Japan on 18 Oct. 1990.

Longest duration   The longest recorded flight is one of 180 hrs. 17 min. by the Edmonds Community College team at Long Beach, WA from 21–29 Aug. 1982. Managing the flight of this J-25 parafoil was Harry N. Osborne.

BUSINESS WORLD

**BANKNOTES. A selection of banknotes from
around the world. (Photo: Images Colour Library)**

COMMERCE

Oldest industry   The oldest-known industry is flint knapping, involving the production of chopping tools and hand axes, dating from 2.5 million years ago in Ethiopia. The earliest evidence of trading in exotic stone and amber dates from *c.* 28,000 B.C. in Europe. Agriculture is often described as "the oldest industry in the world," but in fact there is no firm evidence yet that it was practiced before *c.* 11,000 B.C.

Oldest company   The Faversham Oyster Fishery Co. is referred to in the Faversham Oyster Fishing Act of 1930 as having existed "from time immemorial," i.e., in English law, from before 1189.

The oldest existing documented company is Stora Kopparbergs Bergslags of Falun, the Swedish industrial and forestry enterprise, which has been in continuous operation since the 11th century. It is first mentioned in historical records in the year 1288, when a Swedish bishop bartered an eighth share in the enterprise, and it was granted a charter in 1347. Originally concerned with the mining and processing of copper, it is now the largest privately-owned power producer in Sweden. In June 1991 it was reported, however, that the company was closing down its 1,000-year-old copper mine at Falun.

Largest company   The largest manufacturing company in the world is General Motors Corporation of Detroit, MI, with operations throughout the world and a workforce of 756,300. In addition to its core business of motor vehicles and components, the company produces defense and aerospace materials and provides computer and communication services. Its assets in 1991 were $184.3 billion, with sales totaling $123.8 billion. Despite these figures, however, the company announced a loss of $4.45 billion for the year, representing the largest loss in US history and the second largest ever. (See Greatest loss.)

Largest employer   The world's largest employer is Indian Railways, with 1,646,704 employees on 31 Mar. 1990.

Greatest sales   The first company to surpass the $1 billion mark in annual sales was the United States Steel (now USX) Corporation of Pittsburgh, PA in 1917.

The *Fortune 500* list of leading industrial corporations in April 1992 is headed by the General Motors Corporation of Detroit, MI, with sales of $123.8 billion for 1991.

Greatest profit   The greatest net profit ever made by a corporation in 12 months is $7.6 billion, by American Telephone and Telegraph Co. (AT&T) from 1 Oct. 1981 to 30 Sep. 1982.

Greatest loss   The Argentine-government-owned oil company Yacimientos Petrolíferos (YPF) was reported to have had a trading loss of $4.6 billion in 1983.

The record private company deficit, and the greatest loss reported by an American company, was $4.45 billion, posted by General Motors Corporation for 1991. (See Largest company.)

Takeover The highest bid in a corporate takeover was $21 billion, for RJR Nabisco Inc., the tobacco, food and beverage company, by the Wall Street leveraged buyout firm Kohlberg Kravis Roberts (KKR), which offered $90 a share on 24 Oct. 1988. By 1 Dec. 1988 the bid, led by Henry Kravis, had reached $109 per share to then total $25 billion.

Bankruptcies Rajendra Sethia (b. 1950) was arrested in New Delhi, India on 2 Mar. 1985 on charges including criminal conspiracy and forgery. He had been declared bankrupt by the High Court in London, Great Britain on 18 Jan. 1985, when Esal Commodities was said to be in debt for a record £170 million ($177 million). His personal debts were estimated at £140 million ($146 million).

William G. Stern (b. 1936) of London, Great Britain, a US citizen since 1957, who set up the Wilstar Group Holding Co. in the London property market in 1971, was declared bankrupt for £104 million ($235 million) in February 1979. This figure rose to £143 million ($272 million) by February 1983.

Accountants The world's largest firm of accountants and management consultants is KPMG Peat Marwick McLintock, whose worldwide fee income totaled $6.0 billion at 30 Sep. 1991. The company had over 76,000 employees and 819 offices at the end of April 1992. In the United States KPMG also had the most offices at 135. Arthur Andersen & Co., SC, had the most sales in the United States, at $2.5 billion and had 26,790 employees.

Banks *Largest* The world's largest multilateral development bank is the International Bank for Reconstruction and Development, founded on 27 Dec. 1945 and known as the World Bank. Based in Washington, D.C., the bank had an authorized share capital of $174.7 billion on 30 June 1991. There were 156 members with a subscribed capital of $139.1 billion on 30 June 1991, at which time the World Bank also had unallocated reserves and accumulated net income of $11.9 billion.

The International Monetary Fund (IMF), also in Washington, D.C., had 156 members with an aggregate quota or special drawing rights of $92 billion as of 19 Oct. 1991.

Commercial The world's biggest commercial bank is the Dai-Ichi Kangyo Bank Ltd. of Japan, with assets on 31 Mar. 1990 of $428.2 billion.

The largest commercial bank in the United States is Citibank, N.A., located in New York City, with total assets of $216.9 billion and deposits of $146.5 billion as of 31 Dec. 1991.

Most branches The bank with most branches is the State Bank of India, which had 12,462 outlets on 1 Jan. 1991 and assets of $37.4 billion.

Oldest The oldest bank in the United States in continuous operation is The Bank of New York, founded in 1834 by Alexander Hamilton.

Confectioners The largest chocolate and confectionary factory is the one built by Hershey Chocolate United States in Hershey, PA in 1903–05. It has 2 million ft.^{2} of floor space.

Department stores   Woolworth Corporation now operates more than 8,700 general stores worldwide. Frank Winfield Woolworth opened his first store, "The Great Five Cent Store," in Utica, NY on 22 Feb. 1879. The net income for 1990 was $317 million.

The world's largest department store is R.H. Macy & Co. Inc. at Herald Square, New York City. It covers 50.5 acres and its employees handle 400,000 items. Total sales for the company's 150 stores in 1990 were $7.3 billion. Rowland Hussey Macy's sales on his first day in his fancy goods store on Sixth Avenue, on 27 Oct. 1858, were recorded as $11.06.

Drug stores   The largest chain of drug stores in the world is Rite Aid Corporation of Shiremanstown, PA, which in 1991 had 2,452 branches throughout the United States. The Walgreen Co. of Deerfield, IL has fewer stores, but a larger volume of sales, totaling $6.9 billion in 1991.

Employment agency   The world's largest employment services group is Manpower, with worldwide sales of all their brand units of $3.5 billion.

Grocery stores   The largest grocery chain in the United States is American Stores, of Salt Lake City, UT, with 1991 sales of $22.2 billion. Kroger Co. of Cincinnati, OH has the most stores in the United States with 2,214.

Sales per unit area   Stew Leonard's Supermarket in Norwalk, CT has the greatest sales per unit area in the United States, with sales of $3,636 per ft.^{2} for the calendar year 1991 (total sales $120,501,770).

Insurance   The company with the highest volume of insurance in force in the world is the Metropolitan Life Insurance Co. of New York City, with $1.0271 trillion at year end 1991. The Prudential Insurance Company of America of Newark, NJ has the greatest volume of consolidated assets, totaling $189.1 billion in 1991. The largest single insurance association in the world is the Blue Cross and Blue Shield Association, the American-based hospital insurance organization. It had a membership of 68.1 million in 1991, and benefits paid out totaled $60 billion.

Policies   The largest life insurance policy ever issued was for $100 million, bought by a major American entertainment corporation on the life of a leading American entertainment industry figure. The policy was sold in July 1990 by Peter Rosengard of London, Great Britain and was placed by Shel Bachrach of Albert G. Ruben & Co. Inc. of Beverly Hills, CA and Richard Feldman of the Feldman Agency, East Liverpool, OH with nine insurance companies to spread the risk.

The highest payout on a single life was reported on 14 Nov. 1970 to be some $18 million to Linda Mullendore, widow of an Oklahoma rancher. Her murdered husband had paid $300,000 in premiums in 1969.

Marine insurance   The largest-ever marine insurance loss was approximately $836 million for the Piper Alpha Oil Field in the North Sea,

Great Britain. On 6 July 1988 a leak from a gas compression chamber underneath the living quarters ignited and triggered a series of explosions that blew Piper Alpha apart. Of the 232 people on board, only 65 survived. The largest sum claimed for consequential losses was approximately $1.7 trillion against owning, operating and building corporations and Claude Phillips, resulting from the 55-million-gallon oil spill from MT *Amoco Cadiz* on the Brittany coast, France on 16 Mar. 1978.

Greatest auction   The greatest auction was of the Hughes Aircraft Co. for $5 billion by General Motors of Detroit, MI on 5 June 1985.

Greatest barter deal   The biggest barter in trading history was 30 million barrels of oil, valued at $1,710 million, exchanged for ten Boeing 747s for the Royal Saudi Airline in July 1984.

Greatest faux pas   If measured by financial consequence, the greatest *faux pas* on record was that of the young multimillionaire James Gordon Bennett (1841–1918), committed on 1 Jan. 1877 at the family mansion of his demure fiancée, one Caroline May, on Fifth Avenue in New York City. Bennett arrived in a two-horse carriage, late and obviously drunk. By dint of intricate footwork, he entered the drawing room, where he was the center of attention. He mistook the fireplace for a plumbing fixture more usually reserved for another purpose. The May family broke the engagement and Bennett was obliged to spend the rest of his footloose and fancy-free life based in Paris, France, with the resultant noncollection of millions of dollars in tax by the US Treasury.

Rummage sale   The Cleveland Convention Center, OH White Elephant Sale (instituted 1933) on 18–19 Oct. 1983 raised $427,935.21. The greatest amount of money raised at a one-day sale was $195,388.53 at the 59th one-day rummage sale organized by the Winnetka Congregational Church, IL on 9 May 1991.

Largest piggy bank   The largest piggy bank in the United States measures 6 ft. 11 in. high × 10 ft. × 17 ft. 2 in. and answers to the name of Penny the Pig. Created by Mary Ann Spanagel and Coldwell Banker Real Estate of Pittsburgh, PA, Penny is used to raise money for the homeless in Pennsylvania.

Menswear store   The world's largest store selling only men's suits and accessories is Slater Menswear of Glasgow, Great Britain, which has a weekly turnover in excess of 2,000 suits. The store covers 40,250 ft.² and stocks over 17,000 suits at any one time.

Toy store   The world's biggest toy store is Hamleys, founded in 1760 in London, Great Britain. Its selling space covers 45,000 ft.² on six floors, and it employs 400 staff during the Christmas season.

Law firms The world's largest law firm in terms of billings is Skadden, Arps, Slate, Meagher & Flom, based in New York, which as of 31 Dec. 1991 had sales of about $500 million. As of 30 Apr. 1992 they had 1,000 lawyers, of whom 230 are partners, and there are 19 offices worldwide.

The largest firm in terms of offices and lawyers is Baker & McKenzie, which was founded in Chicago, IL in 1949 and now has 1,637 lawyers, 509 of whom are partners, and 44 offices in 27 countries. Billings for fiscal year 1991 were $478 million.

Paper company The world's largest producer of paper, fiber and wood products is International Paper of Purchase, NY, with sales in 1991 of $12.7 billion, a net income of $638 million and assets of $14.9 billion. The company employs 70,500 workers.

Pharmaceuticals The world's largest pharmaceutical company is Johnson & Johnson of New Brunswick, NJ. The company employed a work force of over 82,000, generating sales of $12.5 billion, net income of $1.5 billion in 1991. Total assets for the year were $10.5 billion.

Real estate *Landowners* The world's largest landowner is the United States government, with a holding of 728 million acres, which is bigger than the world's eighth largest country, Argentina, and 12 times larger than Indiana.

Price, most expensive The most expensive piece of property ever recorded, the land around the central Tokyo retail food store Mediya Building in the Ginza district, was quoted in October 1988 by the Japanese National Land Agency at 358.5 million yen per ft.^{2} (then equivalent to $248,000).

Retailer The largest retailer in the United States was Wal-Mart, Inc. of Bentonville, AR with a sales volume of $44 billion and a net income of $1.6 billion, as of 31 Jan. 1992. Wal-Mart was founded by Samuel Moore "Sam" Walton (1918–92) in Rogers, AR in 1962, and as of April 1992 Wal-Mart had over 1,720 retail locations employing 365,000 workers.

The largest retailing firm in the United States based on current assets is Sears, Roebuck and Co. (founded by Richard Warren Sears in North Redwood, MN in 1886) of Chicago, IL, with $45.775 billion. Sears Merchandise Group had 956 retail stores, including 88 specialty stores, 33 catalog sales offices and 2,178 independent catalog merchants in the United States as of 31 Dec. 1991.

Savings and loan association The world's biggest lender is the Japanese-government-controlled House Loan Corporation.

The largest savings and loan association (S&L) in the United States is Home Savings of America, FA in Irwindale, CA. As of 30 Sep. 1991 the company had total assets of $47.7 billion and total deposits of $39.2 billion. Home Savings also has the most branch offices of any S&L, with 333. Great Western Bank Association in Beverly Hills, CA has the most deposit accounts, with 2.813 million.

ECONOMICS

MONETARY AND FINANCIAL

Largest budget   The greatest governmental expenditure ever made by any country was $1.323 trillion by the United States government for the fiscal year 1991. The highest-ever revenue figure was $1.0543 trillion in the same fiscal year. An expenditure budget of $1.5 trillion was sent to Congress on 29 Jan. 1992 for the fiscal year 1993, which starts on 1 Oct. 1992.

The greatest fiscal surplus ever was $8,419,469,844 in the United States in 1947/48. The worst deficit was $268.7 billion in the US fiscal year 1991, but this may be exceeded by the anticipated $399 billion for the fiscal year 1992.

Foreign aid   The greatest donor of foreign aid has been the United States—the total net foreign aid given by its government between 1 July 1945 and 1 Jan. 1991 was $312.7 billion.

The country receiving most US aid in 1990 was Israel with $3.65 billion. Egypt was second with $2.25 billion. These totals are for both economic and military aid. US foreign aid began with $50,000 to Venezuela for earthquake relief in 1812.

Least taxed   The sovereign countries with the lowest income tax in the world are Bahrain and Qatar, where the rate is zero, regardless of income. No tax is levied on the Sarkese (inhabitants of Sark), in the Channel Islands, Great Britain. There is no taxation in Tristan da Cunha apart from a nominal 65p a year paid by all males between the ages of 18 and 65.

United States   The lowest income tax rate in United States history was 1 percent between 1913 and 1915.

Highest taxation rates   The country with the highest taxation is Norway, where the highest rate of income tax in 1992 is 65 percent, although additional personal taxes make it possible to be charged in excess of 100 percent. In January 1974 the 80 percent limit was abolished there and some 2,000 citizens were then listed in the *Lignings Boka* as paying more than 100 percent of their taxable income. The shipping magnate Hilmar Reksten (1897–1980) was assessed at 491 percent.

In Denmark the highest rate of income tax is 68 percent, but a net wealth tax of 1 percent can result in tax of over 100 percent on income in extreme situations.

United States   The highest income tax rate in United States history was implemented in 1944 by the Individual Tax Act with a 91 percent bracket. The current highest income tax bracket is 33 percent.

Highest tax levy   The highest recorded personal tax levy is one for $336 million on 70 percent of the estate of Howard Hughes.

Balance of payments (current account)   The record balance of payments deficit for any country for a fiscal year is $143.7 billion in 1987 by the United States. The preliminary estimate for the United States balance of payments deficit for the year ending 1991 was $8.6 billion. The record balance of payments surplus is $87.0 billion in 1987 by Japan.

National debt   The largest national debt of any country in the world is that of the United States, where the gross federal public debt of the federal government surpassed the trillion dollar mark on 30 Sep. 1981. By the end of 1991 it had reached $3.81 trillion, with net interest payments on the debt of $286.02 billion on 30 Sep. 1991.

Most foreign debt   The country most heavily in overseas debt at the end of fiscal year 1991 was the United States, with $443.4 billion, although the size of its debt is small relative to its economic strength. Among developing countries, Brazil has the highest foreign debt, with $123 billion at the end of 1990.

Gross national product   The country with the largest gross national product is the United States, which, having reached $3 trillion in 1981, was running at $5.67 trillion for the year ending 31 Dec. 1991.

National wealth   The richest country as listed in the 1990 *World Bank Atlas* ranking is Switzerland, which in 1988 had an average gross national product (GNP) per capita of $27,370. The United States, which had held the lead from 1910 to 1973, was sixth. It has been estimated that the value of all physical assets in the United States on 1 Jan. 1983 was $12.5 trillion. By 31 December 1991 the per capita income for the United States was $19,135.

According to figures released by the Commerce Department's Bureau of Economic Analysis, in 1991 Connecticut enjoyed the highest per capita income level of any state ($25,881), while Mississippi continued to be the lowest ($13,343). Personal income totaled $19,135 per person for 1991.

The median household income in the United States in 1990 was $28,906. Connecticut enjoyed the highest level at $42,000 and Mississippi was the lowest at $19,774.

Poorest country   Mozambique had the lowest GNP per capita in 1990, with $100, although there are several sovereign countries for which the *World Bank Atlas* is not able to include data.

Gold reserves   The country with the greatest monetary gold reserves is the United States, whose Treasury held 261.88 million fine oz. as of 31 Dec. 1991. At $341.90 per fine oz. (30 Mar. 1992, NY COMEX closing price), their value was $89.54 billion.

The United States Bullion Depository at Fort Knox, 30 miles southwest of Louisville, KY, has been the principal federal depository of US gold since December 1936. Gold is stored in 446,000 standard mint bars of 400 troy ounces measuring $7 \times 3\frac{5}{8} \times 1\frac{5}{8}$ in. Gold's peak price was $875 per fine oz. on 21 Jan. 1980.

Inflation   The United States Department of Labor measures changes in the Consumer Price Index (CPI) in twelve-month periods ending in December. The Bureau of Labor Statistics first began keeping the CPI in 1913. Since that time the change of the greatest magnitude was a 20.4 percent increase for the twelve-month period ending December 1918, and the largest decline was −10.8 percent in December 1921. The largest peacetime increase, recorded in December 1979, was 13.3 percent. Figures are based on the United States city average CPI for all urban consumers.

Worst The world's worst inflation occurred in Hungary in June 1946, when the 1931 gold pengö was valued at 130 million trillion (1.3 × 1020) paper pengös. Notes were issued for "Egymillard billion" (one sextillion or 10^{21}) pengös on 3 June and withdrawn on 11 July 1946. Vouchers for 1 billion trillion (10^{27}) pengös were issued for taxation payment only. On 6 Nov. 1923 Germany's Reichsbank marks circulation reached 400,338,326,350,700,000,000 and inflation was 755,700 million-fold at 1913 levels.

The country with the worst inflation in 1990, the last year that has comparable figures, was Nicaragua, where the rate was 13,500 percent, according to *Latin American Weekly Report*. Inflation in the CIS (formerly part of the USSR) in April 1992 was variously reported to be running at 200 to 300 percent per month.

Least The countries with least inflation in 1990 were Burkina Faso and Niger, where the rate was 0.8 percent.

WEALTH AND POVERTY

Comparisons and estimates of extreme personal wealth are beset with intractable difficulties. Quite apart from reticence and the element of approximation in the valuation of assets, as Jean Paul Getty (1892–1976) once said: "If you can count your millions you are not a billionaire." The term millionaire was invented *c*. 1740 and billionaire in 1861. The earliest dollar centimillionaire was Cornelius Vanderbilt (1794–1877), who left $100 million in 1877. The first billionaires were John Davison Rockefeller (1839–1937) and Andrew William Mellon (1855–1937), with Rockefeller believed to be the first to have a billion dollars.

Richest men Much of the wealth of the world's monarchs represents national rather than personal assets. The least fettered and most monarchical is HM Sir Muda Hassanal Bolkiah Mu'izzaddin Waddaulah (b. 15 July 1946) of Brunei. He appointed himself Prime Minister, Finance Minister and Home Affairs Minister on 1 Jan. 1984. *Fortune* Magazine reported in September 1991 that his fortune was $31 billion.

Of private citizens, the richest would appear to be Robson Walton (USA; b. 1946), son of Sam Walton (1918–92), who built up the sales of the over 1,720 store chain Wal-Mart to $44 billion in 1991. Provided Robson, one of four children, receives over 20 percent of his late father's reputed fortune of $23 billion to add to his own $9.9 billion, he will become the richest American with in excess of $10 billion. The only other estimated deca-billionaire is Taikichiro Mori of Japan, 88 years of age, with assets of $10 billion. (See also Retailer.)

Richest women Her Majesty Queen Elizabeth II is asserted by some to be the wealthiest woman, and *The Sunday Times* of London, Great

Britain estimated in April 1992 that she had assets worth £6.5 billion ($10.1 billion). However, few of her assets under the perpetual succession of the Crown are either personal or disposable, and her personal wealth was estimated at £500 million ($900 million). An alternative estimate published by British magazine *The Economist* in January 1992 placed her personal wealth at much closer to £150 million ($270 million).

The cosmetician Madame C.J. Walker (nee Sarah Breedlove [USA]; 1867–1919) is reputed to have been the first self-made millionairess. She was an uneducated black orphan whose fortune was founded on a hair relaxer.

POOREST COUNTRY. Mozambique, which achieved its independence from Portugal in 1975, is the poorest country in the world. Its economy has been devastated by civil war and drought; famine is widespread. (Photo: Rex Features/K. Nomachi)

Greatest miser If meanness is measurable as a ratio between expendable assets and expenditures, then Henrietta (Hetty) Howland Green (nee Robinson; 1835–1916), who kept a balance of over $31.4 million in one bank alone, was the all-time world champion. Her son had to have his leg amputated because of her delays in finding a *free* medical clinic. She herself ate cold cereal because she was too thrifty to heat it. Her estate proved to be worth $95 million.

Longest pension Miss Millicent Barclay was born on 10 July 1872, three months after the death of her father, Col. William Barclay, and became eligible for a Madras Military Fund pension to continue until her marriage. She died unmarried on 26 Oct. 1969, having drawn the pension every day of her life of 97 years 3 months.

Richest families It has been tentatively estimated that the combined value of the assets nominally controlled by the Du Pont family of some 1,600 members may be on the order of $150 billion. The family arrived in the United States from France on 1 Jan. 1800. Capital from Pierre Du Pont (1730–1817) enabled his son Eleuthère Irénée Du Pont to start his explosives company in the United States.

Youngest millionaires The youngest person ever to accumulate a million dollars was the American child film actor Jackie Coogan (1914–84), who co-starred with Charlie Chaplin (1889–1977) in *The Kid*, made in 1920.

The youngest of the 71 billionaires reported in the United States in 1992 was William Gates, 36, cofounder of Microsoft of Seattle, WA, whose *MS/DOS* operating system enables an estimated 72 million of the United States' 90 million *PCs* (Personal Computers) to work. Gates was 20 when he set up his company in 1976 and was a billionaire by 31.

The youngest millionairess was Shirley Temple (b. 23 Apr. 1928), now Mrs. Charles Black, who accumulated wealth exceeding $1 million before she was 10. Her childhood acting career spanned the years 1934 to 1939.

Highest incomes The largest incomes derive from the collection of royalties per barrel by rulers of oil-rich sheikhdoms who have not formally revoked personal entitlement. Shaikh Zayid ibn Sultan an-Nuhayan (b. 1918), head of state of the United Arab Emirates, arguably has title to some $9 billion of the country's annual gross national product.

Largest dowry The largest recorded dowry was that of Elena Patiño, daughter of Don Simón Iturbi Patiño (1861–1947), the Bolivian tin millionaire, who in 1929 bestowed $39 million from a fortune at one time estimated to be worth $607.5 million.

Return of cash The largest amount of cash ever found and returned to its owners was $500,000, discovered by Lowell Elliott, 61, on his farm in Peru, IN. It had been dropped in June 1972 by a parachuting hijacker.

Jim Priceman, 44, assistant cashier at Doft & Co. Inc., returned an envelope containing $37.1 million in *negotiable* bearer certificates found outside 110 Wall Street to A.G. Becker Inc. of New York on 6 Apr. 1982. In announcing a reward of $250, Becker was acclaimed as being "all heart."

Greatest bequests The largest single bequest in the history of philanthropy was of the art collection belonging to the American publisher Walter Annenberg, which was worth $1 billion. He announced on 12 Mar. 1991 that he would be leaving the collection to the Metropolitan Museum of Art in New York City.

The largest single cash bequest was the $500 million gift, announced on 12 Dec. 1955, to 4,157 educational and other institutions by the Ford Foundation (established 1936) of New York.

Highest salary It was reported by the US government that Michael Milken, the "junk bond king" at Drexel Burnham Lambert Inc., was paid $550 million in salary and bonuses in 1987. (See Judicial, Fines.)

The world's highest-paid executive in 1991 was Anthony "Tony" O'Reilly, chairman of Heinz, who received $75,085,000. This total included a salary of $1.1 million, stock options of $71.5 million (granted ten years ago and now considered income to the IRS), and bonuses. If stock-incentives are included, Leon Hirsch, chief executive of U.S. Surgical, would have a total pay of $118 million, but this includes $109 million for stock options that cannot be exercised until later years.

Highest fees The highest-paid investment consultant in the world is Harry D. Schultz, who lives in Monte Carlo and Zurich, Switzerland. His standard consultation fee for 60 minutes is $2,400 on weekdays and $3,400 on weekends. Most popular are the five-minute phone consultations at $200 (i.e., $40 a minute). His "International Harry Schultz Letter," instituted in 1964, sells for $50 per copy. A life subscription costs $2,400.

Golden handshake *Business Week* Magazine reported in May 1989 that the largest "golden handshake" ever given was one of $53.8 million, to F. Ross Johnson, who left RJR Nabisco as chairman in February 1989.

PAPER MONEY

The Department of the Treasury reported that in fiscal year 1991, 3.21 billion $1 bills were printed, the most of any denomination. Other bills were printed as follows: $5 (1.04 billion), $10 (0.81 billion), $20 (2.08 billion), $50 (0.13 billion) and $100 (0.74 billion).

Earliest Paper money was an invention of the Chinese, first tried in A.D. 812 and prevalent by A.D. 970. The world's earliest banknotes (*bancosedler*) were issued in Stockholm, Sweden in July 1661, the oldest survivor being one of five dalers dated 6 Dec. 1662.

Largest and smallest The largest paper money ever issued was the one-guan note of the Chinese Ming Dynasty issue of 1368–99, which measured 9 × 13 in.

The smallest national note ever issued was the 10-bani note of the Ministry of Finance of Romania, in 1917. It measured (printed area) $1^1/_{16}$ × $1^1/_2$ in. Of German *Notgeld*, the smallest were the 1–3 pfg notes of Passau (1920–21), measuring $^{11}/_{16}$ × $^3/_4$ in.

Highest values   The highest-value notes in circulation are US Federal Reserve $10,000 banknotes, bearing the head of Salmon P. Chase (1808–73). It was announced in 1969 that no further notes higher than $100 would be issued, and only 345 $10,000 bills remain in circulation or unretired. The highest value ever issued by the US Federal Reserve System is a note for $100,000, bearing the head of Woodrow Wilson (1856–1924), which is only used for transactions between the Federal Reserve and the Treasury Department.

Lowest values   The lowest value (and the lowest denomination) legal tender bank note is the 1-sen (or $^1/_{100}$ th of a rupiah) Indonesian note. Its exchange value in early 1992 was more than 201,000 to the dollar.

Most expensive   The record price paid for a single lot of banknotes was £240,350 ($478,900 including buyer's premium) by Richard Lobel, on behalf of a consortium, at Phillips, London, Great Britain on 14 Feb. 1991. The lot consisted of a cache of British military notes which were found in a vault in Berlin, Germany, and contained more than 17 million notes.

Bank note collection   Colin Dealey of Berkhamsted, Great Britain has accumulated banknotes from 184 different countries in the four years since he started collecting in 1988.

Coin snatching   The greatest number of British 10p pieces clean-caught from being flipped from the back of a forearm into the same downward palm is 254, by Dean Gould of Felixstowe, Great Britain on 12 July 1991.

CHECKS AND COINS

Largest   The greatest amount paid by a single check in the history of banking was £1.425 trillion ($2.494 trillion). Issued on 11 July 1989 and signed by three treasurers, the check represented a payment from the expiring Abbey National Building Society in favor of the newly created Abbey National plc. A larger one, for $4,176,969,623.57, was drawn on 30 June 1954, although this was an internal US Treasury check.

Collection—record price   The highest price ever paid for a coin collection was $25,235,360 for the Garrett family collection of US and colonial coins, which had been donated to Johns Hopkins University, Baltimore, MD. The sales were made at a series of four auctions held on 28–29 Nov. 1979 and 25–26 Mar. 1981 at the Bowers & Ruddy Galleries in Wolfeboro, NH. The collection was put together by members of the Garrett family between 1860 and 1942.

Hoards The most valuable hoard of coins was one of about 80,000 aurei found in Brescello near Modena, Italy in 1714, and believed to have been deposited *c.* 37 B.C. The largest deliberately buried hoard ever found was the Brussels hoard of 1908 containing *c.* 150,000 coins.

The largest accidental hoard on record was the 1715 Spanish Plate Fleet, which sank off the coast of Florida. A reasonable estimate of its contents would be some 60 million coins, of which about half were recovered by Spanish authorities shortly after the event. Of the remaining 30 million pieces, perhaps 500,000 have been recovered by modern salvagers. The other 29½ million coins are, presumably, still on the bottom of the sea, awaiting recovery.

The record in terms of weight is 47 tons of gold, from the White Star

---

COINS

OLDEST
c. 670 B.C. electrum staters of King Gyges of Lydia, Turkey.[1]

EARLIEST DATED
Samian silver tetradrachm struck in Zankle (now Messina), Sicily, dated year 1, *viz.* 494 B.C.—shown as "A." *Christian Era:* MCCXXXIIII (1234) Bishop of Roskilde coins, Denmark (6 known).

HEAVIEST
43 lb. 7¼ oz. Swedish 10-daler copper plate 1644.[2]

LIGHTEST
14,000 to the oz. Nepalese silver ¼ jawa *c.* 1740.

MOST EXPENSIVE
Set: $3,190,000 for the King of Siam Proof Set, a set of 1804 and 1834 US coins which had once been given to the King of Siam, purchased by Iraj Sayah and Terry Brand at Superior Galleries, Beverly Hills, CA on 28 May 1990. Included in the set of nine coins was the 1804 silver dollar, which had an estimated value of about $2,000,000.

Individual: $1,500,000 for the US 1907 Double Eagle Ultra High Relief $20 gold coin, sold by MTB Banking Corporation of New York to a private investor on 9 July 1990.

[1] Chinese uninscribed "spade" money of the Zhou dynasty has been dated to *c.* 770 B.C.
[2] The largest coinlike medallion was completed on 21 Mar. 1986 for the World Exposition in Vancouver, British Columbia, Canada, Expo 86—a $1,000,000 gold piece. Its dimensions were 37.5 in. diameter and ¾ in. thick and it weighed 365 lbs. 15 oz., or 5,337 oz. (troy) of gold.

Liner HMS *Laurentic*, which was mined in 132 ft. of water off Fanad Head, Donegal, Ireland in 1917. The Royal Navy, Cossum Diving Syndicate and Consortium Recovery Ltd. have since recovered 3,191 of the 3,211 gold ingots.

Mints *Largest*   The largest mint in the world is that of the US Treasury. It was built from 1965–69 on Independence Mall, Philadelphia and covers 11½ acres, with an annual production capacity on a three-shift seven-day week of 15 billion coins. A new high-speed stamping machine (called the "Graebner Press") can produce coins at a rate of 42,000 per hour. It can produce up to 310 million coins per week or over 15 billion coins in a year. In recent history, the record production for coins was in 1982, when 19.5 billion were produced between the Philadelphia and Denver mints.

Smallest   The smallest issuing mint in the world belongs to the smallest state in the world—The Headquarters of the Sovereign Military Hospitaller Order of Saint John of Jerusalem—a recognized sovereign state with less than one acre of territory within the City of Rome. The state is recognized by no less than 35 countries throughout the world and has issued proof coins since 1961. The single-press mint is housed in one small room within the main building.

Most popular coin   More than 250 billion pennies with Lincoln's head have been minted in the 80 years since the première issue of this coin in 1909 for the 100th anniversary of Lincoln's birth. If lined up, the 250 billion coins would stretch 2,808,586 miles, and if piled up (17 to an inch) they would tower 220,851 miles into space.

Charity fund-raising   The "Sport Aid" event, conceived by Chris Long and organized by Bob Geldof, took place in 277 cities in 78 countries on 25 May 1986 and raised a worldwide figure of over $100 million.

The greatest recorded amount raised by a charity walk or run is $Cdn24.7 million by Terry Fox (1958–81) of Canada who, with an artificial leg,

---

Coin balancing   Hiem Shda of Kiriat Mozkien, Israel stacked a pyramid of 847 coins on the edge of a coin free-standing vertically on the base of a coin that was on a table on 30 July 1989.

The tallest single column of coins ever stacked on the edge of a coin was made up of 253 Indian one-rupee pieces on top of a vertical five-rupee coin, by Dipak Syal of Yamuna Nagar, India on 3 May 1991. He also balanced 10 one-rupee coins and 10 ten-paise coins alternately horizontally and vertically in a single column on 1 May 1991.

Column of coins   The most valuable column of coins was worth £15,606 ($30,338) and was 6 ft. 1½ in. high. It was built by pupils of Middlecroft School, Staveley, Great Britain at Ringwood Hall Hotel, Brimington, Great Britain on 26 Aug. 1990.

ran from St. John's, Newfoundland to Thunder Bay, Ontario in 143 days from 12 Apr.–2 Sep. 1980. He covered 3,339 miles.

Line of coins   The most valuable line of coins was made up of 662,353 quarters to a value of $165,588.25. It was 10 miles 5 ft. 7 in. long, and was laid at Central City Park, Atlanta, GA on 16 Mar. 1985.

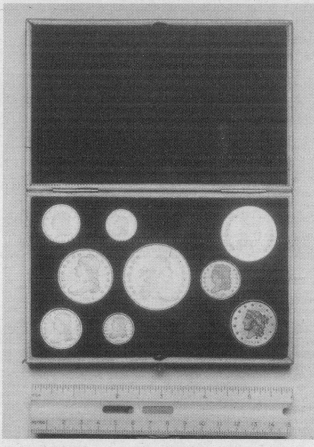

MOST EXPENSIVE COINS. The most valuable set of coins is valued at $3,190,000. These nine US coins from 1804 and 1834 were once given to the King of Siam, and include an 1804 silver dollar with an estimated value of $2 million. On 28 May 1990 the coins were purchased by Iraj Sayah and Terry Brand. (Photo: Numismatic News, Iola, WI)

The longest line of coins on record had a total length of 27.33 miles and was made using 1,698,073 two-pence coins. It was laid by representatives from St. John Ambulance, Cranleigh Division and helpers at Cranleigh, Great Britain on 10 Aug. 1991.

Pile of coins   The Copper Mountain, devised by Terry Pitts Fenby for the National Society for the Prevention of Cruelty to Children, at Selfridges, Oxford Street, in London, Great Britain, consisted of over 3 million coins accumulated in 350 days (24 May 1984–7 May 1985), with a total value of £57,051.34 ($69,032).

LABOR

First labor union   The first officially recognized labor organization in the United States was formed by the Shoemakers and Coopers of Boston, MA. They were granted a three-year charter by King Charles II in 1648. The charter was not renewed.

Largest labor union   The world's largest union is Professionalniy Soyuz Rabotnikov Agro-Promyshlennogo Kompleksa (Agro-Industrial Complex Workers' Union) in the former Soviet Union, with 15,000,000 members on 1 Apr. 1992.

United States   As of 31 Aug. 1991 the largest union in the United States was the National Education Association (NEA), which has 2.11 million members.

Smallest labor union   The ultimate in small unions was the Jewelcase and Jewelry Display Makers Union (JJDMU), founded in 1894. It was dissolved on 31 Dec. 1986 by its general secretary, Charles Evans. The motion was seconded by Fergus McCormack, its only other surviving member.

Longest name   The union with the longest name is the International Association of Marble, Slate and Stone Polishers, Rubbers and Sawyers, Tile and Marble Setters' Helpers and Marble, Mosaic and Terrazzo Workers' Helpers, or the IAMSSPRSTMSHMMTWH, of Washington, D.C.

Earliest labor dispute   A labor dispute concerning monotony of diet and working conditions was recorded in 1153 B.C. in Thebes, Egypt. The earliest recorded strike was one by an orchestra leader named Aristos from Greece, in Rome *c.* 309 B.C. The dispute concerned meal breaks.

Longest strike   The world's longest recorded strike ended on 4 Jan. 1961, after 33 years. It concerned the employment of barbers' assistants in Copenhagen, Denmark.

The longest recorded major strike in the world was that at the plumbing fixtures factory of the Kohler Co. in Sheboygan, WI, between April 1954 and October 1962. The strike is alleged to have cost the United Automobile Workers' Union about $12 million to sustain.

According to the Bureau of Labor Statistics, the most work stoppages occurred in 1952, with 470 strikes. In this same year 2.75 million workers, the highest ever, were involved in work stoppages employing 1,000 or more. The peak year for most days idle was 1959, with 60.85 million.

Unemployment *Lowest* In December 1973 in Switzerland (population 6.6 million), the total number of unemployed was reported to be 81.

United States The highest annual unemployment average in United States history was 24.9 percent, or 12,830,000 people, in 1933 during the Great Depression, and the lowest average was 1.2 percent, or 670,000 people, in 1944 during World War II. These figures are based on a labor force aged fourteen and older. Since 1948 the United States Department of Labor has kept statistics based on household members aged sixteen and older. According to these figures, the highest annual unemployment average since 1948 was 9.7 percent, or 10,717,000 people, in 1982, and the lowest was 2.9 percent, or 1,834,000 people, in 1953.

Longest working career The longest working life was one of 98 years by Mr. Izumi (see Human Being, Oldest authentic centenarian), who began work goading draft animals at a sugar mill at Isen, Tokunoshima, Japan in 1872. He retired as a sugar cane farmer in 1970 at the age of 105.

Longest working week A case of a working week of 142 hours (with an average each day of 3 hrs. 42 min. 51 sec. for sleep) was recorded in June 1980 by Dr. Paul Ashton, 32, the anesthetics registrar at Birkenhead General Hospital, Merseyside, Great Britain. He described the week in question as "particularly bad but not untypical."

ENERGY CONSUMPTION

To express the various forms of available energy (coal, liquid fuels, water power, etc., but omitting vegetable fuels and peat), it is the practice to convert them all into terms of coal.

The highest consumption in the world is in the US Virgin Islands, with an average of 597.4 cwt. per person per year. The highest in a sovereign country is 430.7 cwt. in Qatar.

The lowest average is 28.6 lbs. per person, most recently recorded in Bhutan in 1987.

United States The Energy Information Administration reports that in 1990, total consumption of energy in the United States was 81.508 quadrillion Btu (British thermal units—the amount of energy needed to raise the temperature of 1 lb. of water one degree at 39.2° F.). Total consumption of coal was 18.807 quadrillion Btu; natural gas, 20.156 quadrillion Btu; petroleum, 32.720 quadrillion Btu; hydroelectric power, 3.082 quadrillion Btu, and nuclear electric power, 6.543 quadrillion Btu.

STOCK EXCHANGES

The oldest stock exchange of the 138 listed throughout the world is that of Amsterdam, Netherlands, founded in 1602 with dealings in printed shares of the United East India Company of the Netherlands in the Oude Zijds Kapel. The largest in trading volume in 1990 was Tokyo, with

LOWEST ENERGY CONSUMPTION. A view of Paro Valley and Rimpung Dzon, Bhutan. Despite its valleys being wide and fertile, Bhutan is one of the poorest and least-developed countries in the world. About 90 percent of its labor force is involved in producing food crops. (Photo: Spectrum Colour Library)

LARGEST MINT. The Mint of the US Treasury at Independence Mall, PA was created by an act of Congress on 2 Apr. 1792, although the current building was only completed in 1969. The Mint manufactures all US coins and distributes them through the Federal Reserve banks and branches. It produces over 15 billion coins a year. (Photo: Spectrum Colour Library)

$1.45 trillion, ahead of New York City with $957 billion and London, Great Britain with $608.5 billion.

New York Stock Exchange The market value of stocks listed on the New York Stock Exchange reached an all-time high of $3.2 trillion at the end of March 1991. The record day's trading was 608,148,710 shares on 20 Oct. 1987, compared with 16,410,030 shares on 29 Oct. 1929, the "Black Tuesday" of the famous "crash," a record unsurpassed until April 1968.

The largest stock trade in the history of the New York Stock Exchange was a 48,788,800-share block of Navistar International Corporation stock at $10 in a $487,888,000 transaction on 10 Apr. 1986.

The highest price paid for a seat on the New York Stock Exchange was $1.15 million in 1987. The lowest 20th-century price was $17,000 in 1942.

Closing prices The highest index figure on the Dow Jones Industrial average (instituted 8 Oct. 1896) of selected stocks at the close of a day's trading was 3,413.21 on 1 June 1992. The index closed above 3,000 points for the first time on 17 Apr. 1991, at 3,004.46, although it had edged past the 3,000 barrier on Friday 13 July 1990 after a strong run.

The Dow Jones Industrial average, which reached 381.71 on 3 Sep. 1929, plunged 30.57 points on 29 Oct. 1929, on its way to the Depression's lowest point of 41.22 on 2 July 1932. The largest decline in a day, 508 points (22.6 percent), occurred on 19 Oct. 1987.

The total lost in security values from 1 Sep. 1929 to 30 June 1932 was $74 billion. The greatest paper loss in a year was $210 billion in 1974.

The record daily increase on 21 Oct. 1987 was 186.84 points to 2,027.85.

Largest stock offering On 19 May 1992 General Motors Corp. offered the biggest common-stock issue in the United States, with 55 million shares at $39 per share for a total offering of $2.15 billion.

Largest flotation The largest-ever flotation in stock market history was the £5.2 billion ($9.9 billion) sale of the 12 British regional electricity companies to 5.7 million stockholders at the end of 1990.

The earlier flotation of British Gas plc in 1986 had an equity offer that produced the higher sum of £7.75 billion ($10.85 billion), but to only 4.5 million stockholders.

Most valued company The greatest aggregate market value of any corporation at 6 Mar. 1992 was $125 billion for Exxon of Irving, TX.

Stockholders attendance, greatest A total of 20,109 stockholders attended the annual general meeting in April 1961 of the American Telephone and Telegraph Co. (AT & T), thereby setting a world record.

Public trading in stocks and shares originated in 1602 in Amsterdam, the Netherlands with the issue of printed shares in the United Dutch East India Company.

The chart shows the world's top exchanges, based on the capitalization of listed stocks on the total market at year end 1991, and is headed by New York, Tokyo and London.

The graphs represent weekly movements since 1987 of the world's three largest exchanges. In a period of apparent global recession, several markets around the world have registered record closing figures. New York's Dow Jones Industrial average has achieved some 21 record highs in the year to May 1992, the latest being 3,398.43 on 28 May. This trend was mirrored closely by the London Financial Times Stock Exchange 100 index (FT-SE), which reached peak trading volumes in April and a new high of 2,737.8 on 11 May.

In contrast, over the past few years Tokyo has lost its place as world market leader, with a series of political and financial scandals and the relaxation of the country's fiscal and monetary policies resulting in record low figures on the Nikkei-225. The index figure has fallen from 38,876.94 on 28 Dec 1989 to 16,598.15 on 9 Apr 1992 (a 57.3 percent drop), prompting the fear of economic disaster and widespread major bankruptcies should prices fall below 15,000.

In addition to the Dow Jones and the FT-SE 100 index, records were also broken by several other (often emerging) markets, with two performing particularly well in the year. From a low of 3,565.14 on 21 Jun 1991, Hong Kong's Hang Seng index reached several new peaks, touching 6,101.89 points on 27 May before closing at 6,082.70, an increase of 70.6 percent.

The sharpest increase in 1991, achieved mainly through a series of major privatizations, was by the IFC index of Buenos Aires, Argentina, at 370 percent in dollar terms. This brought its market capitalization up to $18.5 billion, or about 13 percent of the country's GDP.

Other countries reaching record highs included India, Pakistan, Brazil, Portugal, South Africa and Zimbabwe.

Stocks and Shares

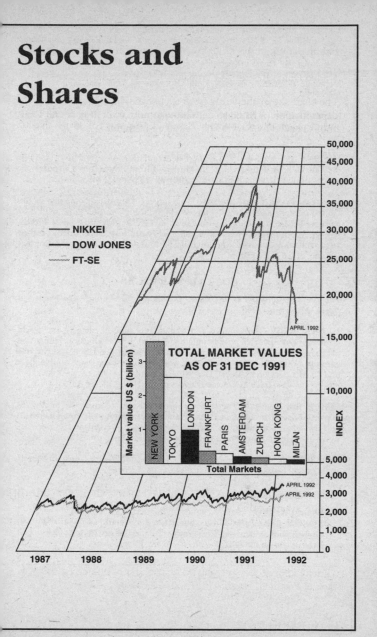

- NIKKEI
- DOW JONES
- FT-SE

APRIL 1992

TOTAL MARKET VALUES
AS OF 31 DEC 1991

Market value US $ (billion)

NEW YORK
TOKYO
LONDON
FRANKFURT
PARIS
AMSTERDAM
ZURICH
HONG KONG
MILAN

Total Markets

INDEX

APRIL 1992
APRIL 1992

50,000
45,000
40,000
35,000
30,000
25,000
20,000
15,000
10,000
5,000
4,000
3,000
2,000
1,000
0

1987 1988 1989 1990 1991 1992

Largest rights issue   The largest recorded rights issue was one of £921 million ($1.57 billion) by Barclays Bank, Great Britain, announced on 7 Apr. 1988.

Gold prices   The highest closing spot price for gold on the Commodities Exchange (COMEX) in New York City was $875.00 per fine oz. on 21 Jan. 1980.

Silver prices   The highest closing spot price for silver on the Commodities Exchange (COMEX) in New York City was $50.35 per fine oz. on 18 Jan. 1980.

Highest par value   The highest denomination of any share quoted in the world is a single share in Moeara Enim Petroleum Corporation, worth 165,000 Dutch florins ($75,500) on 17 Aug. 1989.

Largest investment house   The largest securities company in the United States, and formerly the world's largest partnership, with 124 partners before becoming a corporation in 1959, is Merrill Lynch, Pierce, Fenner & Smith Inc. (founded 6 Jan. 1914) of New York. At the end of 1991, the company had a net revenue of $7.3 billion, together with a net income of $696.1 million.

POSTAL SERVICES

The practice of numbering houses began on the Pont Notre Dame, in Paris, France in 1463.

Largest mail   The country with the largest mail service in the world is the United States, whose population mailed 165.851 billion letters and packages at the end of the fiscal year 1991, when the US Postal Service employed 748,961 people, with the world's largest civilian vehicle fleet of 185,513 cars and trucks. The average number of letters and packages per capita was 661. There are 39,985 post offices in the US.

Oldest mailboxes   The first organized system of roadside mailboxes was established in 1653 in Paris, France, to facilitate the interchange of correspondence in the city. The mailboxes were erected at the intersections of main thoroughfares and were emptied three times a day.

Post offices   The country with the greatest number of post offices is India, with 144,829 in 1988.

Stamp licking   John Kenmuir of Hamilton, Strathclyde, Scotland, Great Britain licked and affixed 393 stamps in 4 min. at the British Broadcasting Corporation TV studios on 26 Sep. 1990, later shown on the BBC *Record Breakers* TV program.

POSTAGE STAMPS

EARLIEST
Put on sale at GPO 1 May 1840. 1 d Penny Black of Great Britain, Queen Victoria, 68,158,080 printed.

USA
Put on sale in New York City 1 July 1847. 5-cent red-brown Benjamin Franklin, 3,712,200 issued, and 10-cent black George Washington, 891,000 issued.

EARLIEST ADHESIVE STAMP
Earliest adhesive stamps were those used for local delivery by the City Dispatch Post established in New York City 15 Feb. 1842.

HIGHEST PRICE (AUCTION)
Sw.Fr. 3,400,000 ($2,400,000), including buyer's premium. Penny Black, 2 May 1840 cover, bought at Harmers, Lugano, Switzerland, on behalf of a Japanese buyer on 23 May 1991.

£203,500 ($350,000), including buyer's premium, for a philatelic item. Bermuda 1854 Perot Postmasters' Stamp affixed to a letter, 1d red on bluish wove paper, sold by Christie's Robson Lowe, London, Great Britain on 13 June 1991.

USA
$1.1 million (including buyer's premium). "Curtiss Jenny" plate block of four 24-cent stamps from 1918 with inverted image of an airplane, bought by an unnamed American executive at Christie's, New York on 12 Oct. 1989.

LARGEST PURCHASE
$11 million. Marc Haas collection of 3,000 US postal and pre-postal covers to 1869 by Stanley Gibbons International Ltd. of London, Great Britain in August 1979.

LARGEST (SPECIAL)
9¾ × 2¾ in. Express Delivery of China, 1913.

USA
3¾ × 2 in. 1865 newspaper stamps.

LARGEST (STANDARD)
6.3 × 4.33 in. Marshall Islands 75-cent issued 30 Oct. 1979.

USA
$^1/_{11}$ × $^5/_{11}$ in. 5-cent blue and carmine Air Beacon issued 25 July 1928, and 2-cent black and carmine George Rogers Clark issued 25 Feb. 1929.

SMALLEST
0.31 × 0.37 in. 10-cent and 1-peso Colombian State of Bolivar, 1863–66.

HIGHEST DENOMINATION
$10,000. Documentary and Stock Transfer stamps, 1952–58.

USA
$100. Indian Maiden, 1895–97

LOWEST DENOMINATION
3,000 pengö of Hungary. Issued 1946 when 604.5 trillion pengö = 1 cent.

USA
½ cent. Earliest sepia Nathan Hale, 1925; George Washington, 1932; Benjamin Franklin, 1938 and 1954.

RAREST
Unique examples include: British Guiana (now Guyana) 1-cent black on magenta of 1856; Swedish 3-skilling banco yellow color error of 1855. Gold Coast provisional of 1885 and US postmaster stamp from Boscowen, NH and Lockport, NY.

AGRICULTURE

Origins   It has been estimated that about 21 percent of the world's land surface is cultivable and that only 7.6 percent is actually under cultivation.

Evidence adduced in 1971 from Nok Nok Tha and Spirit Cave, Thailand tends to confirm that plant cultivation was part of the Hoabinhian culture *c.* 11,000 B.C., but it is still likely that hominids (humans and their human-like ancestors) probably survived for 99.93 percent of their known history without cultivating plants or domesticating animals.

A village site found near Nineveh, Iraq, dated provisionally to 9000 B.C., shows evidence of agricultural practices. The earliest evidence for maize cultivation comes from samples taken of sediments in Lake Ayauchi, near the Rio Santiago tributary of the Amazon, which were dated to at least 5,300 years ago. Rice was grown in China by *c.* 5000 B.C. at Hemudu, near Shanghai.

Animal husbandry   It has been suggested that reindeer (*Rangifer tarandus*) may have been domesticated as early as 18,000 B.C., but definite proof is still lacking. The earliest definite date for the horse (*Equus caballus*) is *c.* 4350 B.C. from Dereivka, Ukraine, but evidence from southern France indicates that horses may have been tethered earlier than 30,000 B.C. The oldest evidence for the possible domestic use of camels (*Camelus*) came from a site at Sihi, Saudi Arabia, where a jawbone has been carbon-dated to *c.* 7200–7100 B.C.

The earliest-known animals domesticated for food were probably descendants of the wild goats of Bezoar (*Capra aegagrus = hircus*), which were herded at Asiah, Iran *c.* 7700 B.C. Sheep (*Ovisaries*) have been dated to *c.* 7200 B.C. at Argissa Magula in Thessaly, Greece, and pigs (*Sus domestica*) and cattle (*Bos primigenius = taurus*) to *c.* 7000 B.C. at the same site. Chickens were domesticated before 6000 B.C. in Indochina, and by 5900–5400 B.C. had spread to North China, as shown by radiocarbon dating from a Neolithic site at Peiligang, near Zhengzhou, and also at Wu'an Cishan and Tengxian Beixin.

FISHERIES

United Nations Food and Agricultural Organization figures for 1989 (the last year for which comparable data is available) showed the world's leading fishing nation to be the former USSR, with a total catch of 12.46 million tons, followed by China (12.35 million tons) and Japan (12.35 million tons). The United States was in sixth place with 6.3 million tons from a worldwide level of 100.7 million tons.

The record value for a catch by a single trawler is $473,957 from a 41,776 ton catch by the Icelandic vessel *Videy* at Hull, Great Britain on 11 Aug. 1987. The greatest catch ever recorded from a single throw is 2,724 tons by the purse seine-net boat M/S *Flømann* from Hareide, Norway in the Barents Sea on 28 Aug. 1986. It was estimated that more than 120 million fish were caught in this shoal.

FISHING NATIONS. Japan, although no longer the world's foremost fishing nation, still leads the world in imports, with $10 billion worth of marine and freshwater fish imported annually. (Photo: Rex Features/K. Nomachi)

FARMS

Largest The largest farms in the world were *kolkhozy* collective farms in the former USSR. These were reduced in number from 235,500 in 1940 to 26,900 in 1988 and represented a total cultivated area of 417.6 million acres. Units of over 60,000 acres were not uncommon.

The pioneer farm owned by Laucidio Coelho near Campo Grande, Mato Grosso, Brazil *c*. 1901 covered 3,358 miles^2 and supported 250,000 head of cattle at the time of the owner's death in 1975.

Cattle ranch Until 1915 the Victoria River Downs Station in Northern Territory, Australia had an area of 35,000 miles^2. The world's largest cattle ranch is currently the 11,600 miles^2 Anna Creek ranch in South Australia owned by the Kidman family. The biggest component is Strangway at 5,500 miles^2.

Chicken farm The Croton Egg Farm in Ohio has 4.8 million hens laying some 3.7 million eggs daily.

Community garden The largest such project is the one operated by the City Beautiful Council and the Benjamin Wegerzyn Garden Center in Dayton, OH. It comprises 1,173 plots, each measuring 812 ft.^{2}.

Hop farm The world's leading hop growers are John I. Haas Inc., with farms in Idaho, Oregon and Washington; Tasmania, Australia; and Kent, Great Britain, covering a total net area of 5,163 acres. The largest field covers 1,715 acres near Toppenish, WA.

RICE CULTIVATION. Contrasting view of fields in India (above and opposite), which uses 42.6 million hectares of its land to farm rice. About half of the world's population is totally dependent on rice as the staple food. (Photo: Zefa)

Mushroom farm The world's largest mushroom farm is owned by Moonlight Mushrooms Inc. and was founded in 1937 in a disused limestone mine near Worthington, PA. The farm employs over 1,000 people who work in a maze of underground galleries 110 miles long, producing over 22,500 tons of mushrooms per year. The French annual consumption is unrivaled at 7 lbs. per capita.

Pig farm The world's largest pig farm is the Sljeme pig unit in Yugoslavia, which is able to process 300,000 pigs in a year.

Rice farm The largest wild rice (*Zizania aquatica*) farm in the world is that of Clearwater Rice Inc. in Clearbrook, MN, covering 2,000 acres. In 1986 it yielded 577,000 lbs., the largest amount to date.

Sheep ranch The largest sheep ranch in the world is Commonwealth Hill, in the northwest of South Australia. It grazes between 50,000 and 70,000 sheep, along with 24,000 uninvited kangaroos, in an area of 4,080 miles^2 enclosed by 138 miles of dog-proof fencing. The head count on Sir William Stevenson's 40,970 acre Lochinver station in New Zealand was 114,016 on 1 Jan. 1992.

The largest sheep move on record occurred when 27 horsemen moved a flock of 43,000 sheep 40 miles from Barcaldine to Beaconsfield station, Queensland, Australia in 1886.

Turkey farm The world's largest turkey farm is that of Bernard Matthews plc in Norfolk, Great Britain, where 2,600 employees tend 9 million turkeys.

CROP PRODUCTION

Barley The total amount of land farmed for barley production in the 1991/92 season was estimated to be 78.4 million hectares, with total production of 169.0 million metric tons and an average yield of 2.2 metric tons per hectare.

United States In 1991 3.4 million hectares of barley were farmed in the United States, with an average yield of 2.97 metric tons per hectare and a total production of 10.1 million metric tons.

Corn The total amount of land used for growing corn in 1991/92 was estimated to be 130.6 million hectares, producing 520 metric tons, of which 97 million metric tons was produced by China from an estimated 21.5 million hectares.

United States In 1991 27.9 million hectares of corn were farmed in the United States, yielding 6.82 metric tons of corn per hectare, for a total of 189.9 million metric tons.

Cotton The total area of land used for cotton production in 1991/92 was estimated to be 33 million hectares, giving a total production of 87 million bales, each weighing 480 lbs. The leading cotton producer is China, with figures estimated at 20.7 million such bales from 5.6 million hectares.

United States In 1991 4.7 million hectares were planted for cotton production in the United States. The average yield per hectare was 0.71 metric tons, with a total production of 15.5 million 480-lb. bales.

Oats The worldwide production of oats in 1991/92 was an estimated 32.5 million metric tons harvested from about 20.4 million hectares.

United States In 1991 1.9 million hectares of oats were farmed in the United States, with an average yield of 1.81 metric tons per hectare and a total production of 3.5 million metric tons.

Potatoes In 1991 1.4 million acres of potatoes were farmed in the United States with an average yield of 13.8 metric tons per acre and a total production of 18.97 million metric tons.

Rice About half of the world's population, including virtually the whole of East Asia, is totally dependent on rice as the staple food. The estimated total amount of land used for rice production in 1991/92 was 147 million hectares, with India leading in the area farmed, at 42.6 million hectares. The world's leading producer, however, is China, with estimated yields of 189.3 million metric tons from 33.1 million hectares.

United States In 1991 1.1 million hectares of rice were planted in the United States, with an average yield of 6.2 metric tons per hectare and a total production of 7.1 million metric tons.

Sugar beets The highest recorded yield for sugar beets is 62.4 tons per acre by Andy Christensen and Jon Giannini in the Salinas Valley, CA.

Sugar cane In 1991 898,000 acres of sugar cane were planted in the United States, with an average yield per acre of 30.6 metric tons and a total production of 27.5 million metric tons.

Wheat An estimated 222.1 million hectares of land was used for wheat production worldwide in 1991/92, giving a yield of 541.6 million metric tons.

The largest single fenced field sown with wheat measured 35,000 acres and was sown in 1951 southwest of Lethbridge, Alberta, Canada.

United States   In 1991/92 23.3 million hectares of wheat were farmed in the United States, with an average yield of 2.31 metric tons per hectare and a total production of 53.9 million metric tons.

Plowing   The world championship (instituted 1953) has been staged in 18 countries and won by competitors from 12 nations. Great Britain has been most successful, winning ten championships. The only person to take the title three times is Hugh B. Barr of Northern Ireland, in 1954–56.

The fastest recorded time for plowing an acre by the Society of Ploughmen (Great Britain) rules is 9 min. 49.88 sec. by Joe Langcake at Hornby Hall Farm, Brougham, Great Britain on 21 Oct. 1989. He used a Case IH 7140 Magnum tractor and a Kverneland four-furrow plow.

The greatest area plowed with a six-furrow plow to a depth of 9 in. in 24 hours is 173 acres. This was achieved by Richard Gaisford and Peter Gooding of Wiltshire Young Farmers, using a Case IH tractor and a Lemken plow, at Manor Farm, Pewsey, Great Britain on 25–26 Sep. 1990.

Bale rolling   Michael Priestley and Marcus Stanley of Heckington Young Farmers Club rolled a 3-ft.-11-in.-wide cylindrical bale over a 164-ft. course in 18.06 sec. at the Lincolnshire Federation of Young Farmers' Clubs annual sports day at Sleaford, Great Britain on 25 June 1989.

Baling   A rick of 40,400 bales of straw was built between 22 July and 3 Sep. 1982 by Nick and Tom Parsons with a gang of eight at Cuckoo Pen Barn Farm, Birdlip, Great Britain. It measured 150 × 30 × 60 ft. high and weighed some 784 tons. The team baled, hauled and ricked 24,200 bales in seven consecutive days from 22–29 July.

Svend Erik Klemmensen of Trustrup, Djursland, Denmark baled 220 tons of straw in 9 hrs. 54 min. using a Hesston 4800 baling machine on 30 Aug. 1989.

Combine harvesting   Philip Baker of West End Farm, Merton, Great Britain harvested 182.5 tons of wheat in eight hours using a Massey Ferguson MF 38 combine on 8 Aug. 1989. On 9 Aug. 1990 an international team from CWS Agriculture, led by estate manager Ian Hanglin, harvested 394.73 tons of wheat in eight hours from 108.72 acres at Cockayne Hatley Estate, Sandy, Great Britain. The equipment consisted of a Claas Commandor 228 combine fitted with a Shelbourne Reynolds SR 6000 stripper head.

Field to loaf   The fastest time for producing 13 loaves (a baker's dozen) from growing wheat is 21 min. 22 sec., by Wheat Montana at Three Forks, MT on 29 Aug. 1991.

LIVESTOCK PRICES

Some exceptionally high livestock auction prices are believed to result from collusion between buyer and seller to raise the ostensible price levels of the breed concerned. Others are marketing and publicity exercises with little relation to true market prices.

Cattle   The highest price ever paid was $2.5 million for the beefalo (a ⅜ Bison, ⅜ Charolais, ¼ Hereford) Joe's Pride, sold by D.C. Basalo of Burlingame, CA to the Beefalo Cattle Co. of Calgary, Canada on 9 Sep. 1974.

Cow   The highest price paid for a cow is $1.3 million for a Holstein at auction in East Montpelier, VT in 1985.

Goat   On 25 Jan. 1985 an Angora buck bred by Waitangi Angoras of Waitangi, New Zealand was sold to Elliott Brown Ltd. of Waipu, New Zealand for NZ $140,000.

Horse   The highest price paid for a draft horse is $47,000 by C.G. Good of Ogden, IA for the seven-year-old Belgian stallion Farceur at Cedar Falls, IA on 16 Oct. 1917.

Pig   The highest price ever paid for a pig is $56,000 for a cross-bred barrow named Bud, owned by Jeffrey Roemisch of Hermleigh, TX and bought by E.A. Bud Olson and Phil Bonzio on 5 Mar. 1983.

Sheep   The highest price ever paid for a sheep is $A450,000 ($358,750) by Willogoleche Pty Ltd. for the Collinsville stud "JC&S 43" at the 1989 Adelaide Ram Sales, South Australia.

Wool   The highest price ever paid for wool is $A3,008.5 per kg greasy wool for a bale of Tasmania superfine at the wool auction in Tasmania, Australia on 23 Feb. 1989 by Fujii Keori Ltd. of Osaka, Japan—top bidders since 1973.

Lowest price   The lowest price ever realized for livestock was at a sale at Kuruman, Cape Province, South Africa in 1934, where donkeys were sold for less than 2 p (less than 5 cents) each.

CATTLE

As of 1990 the world's leading producer of cattle was India, with 271.4 million head from a world total of 1 billion head, in 1991. The leading producer of milk in 1991 was the former USSR, with preliminary estimates of 99 million tons.

In 1991 there were 100.1 million head of cattle farmed in the United States. The leading cattle producer was Texas with 13.6 million head.

Largest   The heaviest breed of cattle is the Chianini, which was brought to the Chiana Valley in Italy from the Middle East in pre-Roman times. Four types of the breed exist, the largest of which is the Val di Chianini, found on the plains and low hills of Arezzo and Sienna. Bulls average 5 ft. 8 in. at the forequarters and weigh 2,865 lbs. (compare with

1,873 lbs. for cows), but Chianini oxen have been known to attain heights of 6 ft. 2¾ in. The sheer expense of feeding such huge cattle has put the breed under threat of extinction in Italy, but farmers in North America, Mexico and Brazil are still enthusiastic buyers of the breed.

The heaviest cattle on record was a Holstein–Durham cross named Mount Katahdin, exhibited by A.S. Rand of Maine from 1906–10, which frequently weighed in at an even 5,000 lbs. He was 6 ft. 2 in. at the shoulder with a 13 ft. girth, and died in a barn fire c. 1923.

Smallest The smallest breed of domestic cattle is the Ovambo of Namibia. Bulls and cows average 496 lbs. and 353 lbs. respectively.

Oldest Big Bertha, a Dremon owned by Jerome O'Leary of Blackwatersbridge, County Kerry, Republic of Ireland celebrated her 48th birthday in 1992. (See also Reproductivity.)

Reproductivity On 25 Apr. 1964 it was reported that a cow named Lyubik had given birth to seven calves in Mogilev. A case of five live calves at one birth was reported in 1928 by T.G. Yarwood of Manchester, Great Britain. The lifetime breeding record is 39 in the case of Big Bertha. (See Oldest.)

Sires Soender Jylland's Jens, a Danish black-and-white bull, left 220,000 surviving progeny by artificial insemination when he was put away at the age of 11 in Copenhagen in September 1978. Bendalls Adema, a Friesian bull, died at the age of 14 in Clondalkin, Dublin, Republic of Ireland on 8 Nov. 1978, having sired an estimated 212,000 progeny by artificial insemination.

Hand-milking of cows Andy Faust at Collinsville, OK in 1937 achieved a yield of 88.2 gals. in 12 hours.

Birth weights The heaviest recorded live birth weight for a calf is 225 lbs. for a British Friesian cow at Rockhouse Farm, Bishopston, Great Britain in 1961. On 28 May 1986 a Holstein cow owned by Sherlene O'Brien of Simitar Farms, Henryetta, OK gave birth to a perfectly formed stillborn calf weighing 270 lbs. The sire was an Aberdeen-Angus bull that had "jumped the fence."

Lightest The lowest live birth weight recorded for a calf is 16 lbs. 7½ oz. for an Angus bull born on the Utz family farm in Madison, VA on 6 Oct. 1991. It stood 17½ in. at the hindquarters and measured 23 in. overall. Another crossbred Angus calf owned by Leroy and Jo Seiner of Humansville, MO weighed 16 lbs. 12 oz. at two weeks old and an estimated 9 lbs. at birth on 12 Sep. 1991.

Milk yields As of 1991, the world's leading producer of cow's milk was the former USSR, with 99 million tons. The United States produced 74.27 million tons in 1991. Wisconsin led the country, producing 12.2

million tons. The highest recorded world lifetime yield of milk is 465,224 lbs. by the unglamorously named cow No. 289 owned by M.G. Maciel & Son of Hanford, CA, to 1 May 1984.

The greatest recorded yield for one lactation (maximum 365 days) is 55,661 lbs. in 1975 by the Holstein Beecher Arlinda Ellen, owned by Mr. and Mrs. Harold L. Beecher of Rochester, IN. The highest reported milk yield in a day is 241 lbs. by a cow named Urbe Blanca in Cuba on or about 23 June 1982.

Butterfat yields The world record lifetime yield is 16,370 lbs. by the US Holstein Breezewood Patsy Bar Pontiac in 3,979 days.

The world record for 365 days is 3,126 lbs. by Roybrook High Ellen, a Holstein owned by Yashuhiro Tanaka of Tottori, Japan.

Cheese The oldest and most primitive cheeses are the Arabian *kishk*, made of the dried curd of goats' milk. Today there are 450 named cheeses in 18 major varieties, but many are merely named after different towns and differ only in shape or the method of packing. France has 240 varieties. The world's biggest producer of cheese is the United States, with an estimated factory production of 223 million tons in 1991.

The most active cheese-eaters are the people of France, with an annual average of 43.6 lbs. per person.

GOATS

Largest The largest goat ever recorded was a British Saanen named Mostyn Moorcock, owned by Pat Robinson of Ewyas Harold, Great Britain, which reached a weight of 400 lbs. (shoulder height 44 in. and overall length 66 in.). He died in 1977 at the age of four.

Smallest Some pygmy goats weigh only 33–44 lbs.

Oldest The oldest goat on record is a Toggenburg feral cross named Hongi (b. August 1971), belonging to April Koch of Glenorchy, near Otago, New Zealand, which was still alive in mid-March 1989 at the age of 17 years 8 months.

Reproductivity According to the British Goat Society, at least one or two cases of quintuplets are recorded annually out of the 10,000 goats registered, but some breeders only record the females born.

On 14 Jan. 1980 a nanny goat named Julie, owned by Galen Cowper of Nampah, ID, gave birth to septuplets, but they all died, including the mother.

Milk yields The highest recorded milk yield for any goat is 7,714 lbs. in 365 days by Osory Snow-Goose, owned by Mr. and Mrs. G. Jameson of Leppington, New South Wales, Australia, in 1977.

Snowball, a goat owned by Don Papin of Tipton, CA, lactated continuously for 12 years 10 months between 1977 and 1989.

PIGS

The world's leading producer of hogs in 1991 was China, with 365 million head from a world total of 768.1 million. As of 1 Dec. 1991 there were 57 million head of hogs farmed in the United States. The leading state was Iowa with 14.8 million head.

Largest   The heaviest pig ever recorded was a Poland–China hog named Big Bill, who was so obese that his belly dragged along the ground. Bill weighed an astonishing 2,552 lbs. just before he was put away after suffering a broken leg in an accident en route to the Chicago World's Fair for exhibition in 1933. Other statistics included a shoulder height of 5 ft. and a length of 9 ft. At the request of his owner, W.J. Chappall, this prized possession was mounted and put on display in Weekly County, TN until 1946, when the exhibit was acquired by a traveling carnival. On the death of the carnival's proprietor his family reportedly donated Big Bill to a museum, but no trace has been found of him since.

Smallest   The smallest breed of pig is the Mini Maialino, developed by Stefano Morini of St. Golo d'Enza, Italy, after 10 years of experimentation with Vietnamese pot-bellied pigs. The piglets weigh 14 oz. at birth and 20 lbs. at maturity.

Reproductivity   A breeding sow will live 12 years or more before it is slaughtered, but the maximum potential lifespan is 20 years. The highest recorded number of piglets in one litter is 34, farrowed on 25–26 June 1961 by a sow owned by Aksel Egedee of Denmark. In February 1955 a Wessex sow belonging to E.C. Goodwin of Paul's Farm, Leigh, Great Britain also had a litter of 34, of which 30 were stillborn.

A Large White owned by H.S. Pedlingham farrowed 385 pigs in 22 litters from December 1923 to September 1934. A Newsham Large White × Landrace sow of Meeting House Farm, Staintondale, Great Britain had farrowed 189 piglets (seven stillborn) in nine litters up to 22 Mar. 1988. Between 6 May 1987 and 9 Feb. 1988 she gave birth to 70 piglets.

Birth weights   The average birth weight for a piglet is 3 lbs. A Hampshire × Yorkshire sow belonging to Rev. John Schroeder of Mountain Grove, MO farrowed a litter of 18 on 26 Aug. 1979. Five were stillborn, including one male that weighed 5 lbs. 4 oz.

The highest recorded weight for a piglet at weaning (eight weeks) is 81 lbs. for a boar, one of a litter of nine farrowed on 6 July 1962 by the Landrace gilt Manorport Ballerina 53rd, alias "Mary," and sired by a Large White named Johnny at Kettle Lane Farm, West Ashton, Great Britain.

In November 1957 a total weight of 1,134 lbs. was reported at weaning for a litter of 18 piglets farrowed by an Essex sow owned by Mrs. B. Ravel of Seaton House, Thorugumbald, Great Britain.

POULTRY

Figures for 1991 showed the United States to be the largest producer of chicken meat, or broiler, with a total of 12.8 million tons. The most produced by a state was 2 million tons, by Arkansas. The leading egg producer, however, is China, where 159 billion were laid in 1991. United States egg production in 1991 was 69 billion. The greatest state production was in California, with 7.4 billion eggs.

Most abundant   The most abundant domesticated bird is the chicken, the tame version of the wild red jungle fowl (*Gallus gallus*) of southeast Asia. According to the FAO (Food and Agriculture Organization of the United Nations), the world's chicken population stood at 8,295,760,000 in 1985; that means there are 1.6 chickens for every member of the human race.

Chicken *Largest*   The heaviest breed of chicken is the White Sully, developed by Grant Sullens of West Point, CA by crossing and recrossing large Rhode Island Reds with other varieties. One monstrous rooster named Weirdo reportedly weighed 22 lbs. in January 1973 and was so aggressive that he killed two cats and crippled a dog that ventured too close. The heaviest chicken is currently a White Ross 1 rooster named Bruno, owned by John Steele of Kirkhills Farms, Boyndie, Great Britain. On 4 July 1989 this outsized bird recorded a weight of 22 lbs. 1 oz.

Reproductivity   The highest authenticated rate of egg-laying is by a White Leghorn, No. 2988, which laid 371 eggs in 364 days in an official test conducted by Prof. Harold V. Biellier ending on 29 Aug. 1979 at the College of Agriculture, University of Missouri.

The highest recorded annual average per bird for a flock is 313 eggs in 52 weeks from 1,000 Warren-Stadler SSL layers (from 21 weeks of age), owned by Eric Savage of White Lane Farm, Albury, Great Britain in 1974–75.

Largest egg   The heaviest egg reported was one of 16 oz., with double yolk and double shell, laid by a White Leghorn at Vineland, NJ on 25 Feb. 1956. The largest egg recorded was one of nearly 12 oz. for a five-yolked egg measuring 12¼ in. around the long axis and 9 in. around the short, laid by a Black Minorca at Mr. Stafford's Damsteads Farm, Mellor, Great Britain in 1896.

Most yolks   The highest claim for the number of yolks in a hen's egg is nine, reported by Diane Hainsworth of Hainsworth Poultry Farms, Mount Morris, NY in July 1971, and also from a hen in Kyrgyzstan in August 1977.

Chicken and turkey plucking   Ernest Hausen (1877–1955) of Fort Atkinson, WI died undefeated after 33 years as champion chicken plucker. On 19 Jan. 1939 he was timed at 4.4 sec.

Vincent Pilkington of Cootehill, Co. Cavan, Republic of Ireland killed and plucked 100 turkeys in 7 hrs. 32 min. on 15 Dec. 1978. His record for a single turkey is 1 min. 30 sec. in Dublin on 17 Nov. 1980.

Egg shelling   Two kitchen hands, Harold Witcomb and Gerald Harding, shelled 1,050 dozen eggs in a 7¼-hr. shift at Bowyers, Great Britain on 23 Apr. 1971. Both men were blind.

Egg dropping   The greatest height from which fresh eggs have been dropped (to the ground) and remained intact is 650 ft., by David S. Donoghue from a helicopter on 2 Oct. 1979 on a golf course in Tokyo, Japan.

Flying   Sheena, a barnyard bantam owned by Bill and Bob Knox, flew 630 ft. 2 in. at Parkesburg, PA on 31 May 1985.

Duck *Reproductivity*   An Aylesbury duck belonging to Annette and Angela Butler of Princes Risborough, Great Britain laid 457 eggs in 463 days, including an unbroken run of 375 in as many days. The duck died on 7 Feb. 1986. Another duck of the same breed owned by Edmond Walsh of Gormanstown, Republic of Ireland laid eggs every year right up to her 25th birthday. She died on 3 Dec. 1978 at the age of 28 yrs. 6 months.

Goose   The heaviest goose egg on record was one of 24 oz. that measured 13½ in. around the long axis and had a maximum circumference of 9½ in. around the short axis. It was laid on 3 May 1977 by a white goose named Speckle, owned by Donny Brandenberg of Goshen, OH. The average weight is 10–12 oz.

Turkey   The greatest dressed weight recorded for a turkey is 86 lbs. for a stag named Tyson reared by Philip Cook of Leacroft Turkeys Ltd., Peterborough, Great Britain. It won the annual "heaviest turkey" competition held in London, Great Britain on 12 Dec. 1989 and was auctioned for charity for a record £4,400 ($7,480). Stags of this size have been so overdeveloped for meat production that they are unable to mate because of their shape and the hens have to be artificially inseminated.

SHEEP

The world's leading producer of sheep is Australia, with a total of 177.8 million head in 1990. As of 1 Jan. 1992 there were 10.9 million head of sheep farmed in the United States. The leading state was Texas, with 2.14 million head.

Largest   The largest sheep ever recorded was a Suffolk ram named Stratford Whisper 23H, which weighed 545 lbs. and stood 43 in. tall in March 1991. It is owned by Joseph and Susan Schallberger of Boring, OR.

Smallest   The smallest breed of sheep is the Soay, which is now confined to the island of Hirta in the St. Kilda group, Outer Hebrides, Great Britain. Adults weigh 55–60 lbs.

Oldest   A crossbred sheep owned by Griffiths & Davies of Dolclettwr Hall, Taliesin, Great Britain gave birth to a healthy lamb in the spring of 1988 at the grand old age of 28, after lambing successfully more than 40 times. She died on 24 Jan. 1989 just one week before her 29th birthday.

Reproductivity   The record for lambs at a single birth is eight (five rams and three ewes) on 4 Sep. 1991 from a Finnish Landrace ewe owned by the D.M.C. Partnership of Feilding, Manawatu, New Zealand. The partnership is made up of Trevor and Diane Cooke, Stephen and Mary Moss and Ken and Carole Mihaere. Eight lambs were also reported from Gwent, Great Britain in June 1956 and Humberside, Great Britain in March 1981, but none survived.

Seven live lambs (four rams and three ewes) were reported for a Finn × Targhoe ewe owned by Elsward Meine of Crookston, MN on 24 Mar. 1980.

Birth weights *Heaviest* The highest recorded birth weight for a lamb is 38 lbs. at Clearwater, Sedgwick County, KS in 1975, but neither lamb nor ewe survived. Another lamb of the same weight was born on 7 Apr. 1975 on the Gerald Neises Farm, Howard, SD but died soon afterward.

Combined weight A four-year-old Suffolk ewe owned by Gerry H. Watson of Augusta, KS gave birth to two live sets of triplets on 30–31 Jan. 1982. The total weight of the lambs was 49½ lbs.

Lowest The lowest live birthweight recorded for a lamb is 1 lb. 15¾ oz. for a female badger-faced Welsh mountain lamb named Lyle, born on 8 June 1991 at Thorpe Park, Great Britain. Her larger male twin, "Tate," weighed 2 lbs. 14 ¹⁄₅ oz.

Shearing The fastest speed for sheep shearing in a working day was that recorded by Alan McDonald, who machine-sheared 805 lambs in nine hours (an average of 40.2 seconds per lamb) at Waitnaguru, New Zealand on 20 Dec. 1990. Peter Casserly of Christchurch, New Zealand achieved a solo blade (i.e., hand-shearing) record of 353 lambs in nine hours on 13 Feb. 1976. The women's record is 390 Merino lambs in eight hours, set by Deanne Sarre of Pingrup, Western Australia at Yealering, also in Western Australia, on 1 Oct. 1989.

In a 24-hour shearing marathon, Alan MacDonald and Keith Wilson machine-sheared 2,220 sheep at Warkworth, Auckland Province, New Zealand on 26 June 1988. Lavor Taylor (1896–1989) of Ephraim, UT claimed to have sheared 515,000 sheep to May 1984.

Fine spinning The longest thread of wool, hand-spun and plied to weigh 0.35 oz., was one with a length of 1,815 ft. 3 in., achieved by Julitha Barber of Bull Creek, Western Australia, at the International Highland Spin-In, Bothwell, Tasmania, Australia on 1 Mar. 1989.

Sheep's survival On 24 Mar. 1978 Alex Maclennan found one ewe still alive after he had dug out 16 sheep buried in a snowdrift for 50 days near the river Skinsdale on Mrs. Tyser's Gordonbush Estate in Sutherland, Great Britain after the great January blizzard. The sheep's hot breath creates airholes in the snow, and the animals gnaw their own wool for protein, enabling them to survive in a snowdrift for a considerable length of time.

Sheep to shoulder At the International Wool Secretariat Development Center, Ilkley, West Yorkshire, Great Britain, a team of eight using commercial machinery produced a sweater—from shearing sheep to the finished article—in 2 hrs. 28 min. 32 sec. on 3 Sep. 1986.

ARTS AND ENTERTAINMENT

Theatrical mask.

PAINTING

Origins The world's oldest examples of art are possibly pieces of bone bearing geometric engraved marks, dated to *c*. 350,000 years ago from an Old Stone Age site at Bilzingsleben, near Erfurt, Germany. The oldest known extant and dated examples of representational art are from layers dated to *c*. 25,000 B.C. from La Ferrassie, near Les Eyzies in the Périgord, France, where blocks of stone engraved with animals and female symbols were found. Some blocks were also decorated with symbols painted in red ocher.

Largest The largest-ever painting measures 72,437 ft.^{2} after allowing for shrinkage of the canvas. It is made up of brightly colored squares with a Smiley face superimposed, and was painted by students of Robb College at Armidale, New South Wales, Australia, aided by local schoolchildren and students from neighboring colleges. The canvas was completed by its designer, Australian artist Ken Done, and unveiled at the University of New England at Armidale on 10 May 1990.

"Old Master" The largest "Old Master" is *Il Paradiso*, by Jacopo Robusti, alias Tintoretto (1518–94), and his son Domenico (1565–1637), on the east wall of the Sala del Maggior Consiglio in the Palazzo Ducale (Doge's Palace) in Venice, Italy between 1587 and 1590. The work is 72 ft. 2 in. long, 22 ft. 11½ in. high and contains some 350 human figures.

Auction The largest painting ever auctioned was Carl Larsson's *Midvinterblot*, painted in Stockholm, Sweden from 1911 to 1915 and sold at Sotheby's, London, on 25 Mar. 1988 for £880,000 ($1,496,000) to the Umeda Gallery of Japan. The painting measured 44 × 9 ft.

Most valuable The "Mona Lisa" (*La Gioconda*) by Leonardo da Vinci (1452–1519) in the Louvre, Paris, France, was assessed for insurance purposes at $100 million for its move to Washington, D.C. and New York City for exhibition from 14 Dec. 1962 to 12 Mar. 1963. However, insurance was not purchased because the cost of the closest security precautions was less than that of the premiums. It was painted *c*. 1503–07 and measures 30.5 × 20.9 in. It is believed to portray either Mona (short for Madonna) Lisa Gherardini, the wife of Francesco del Giocondo of Florence, or Constanza d'Avalos, coincidentally nicknamed La Gioconda, mistress of Giuliano de Medici. King Francis I of France bought the painting for his bathroom in 1517 for 4,000 gold florins, or 92 oz. of gold.

Most prolific painter Pablo Diego José Francisco de Paula Juan Nepomuceno Crispin Crispiano de la Santisima Trinidad Ruiz y Picasso (1881–1973) of Spain was the most prolific of all painters in a career that lasted 78 years. It has been estimated that Picasso produced about 13,500 paintings or designs, 100,000 prints or engravings, 34,000 book illustrations and 300 sculptures or ceramics. His lifetime *oeuvre* has been valued at over $800 million.

Finest standard paintbrush The finest standard brush sold is the 000 in Series 7 by Winsor and Newton, known as a "triple goose." It is made of 150–200 Kolinsky sable hairs weighing 0.000529 oz.

Largest poster A poster measuring 215,280 ft.^{2} was made by the Sendai Junior Chamber Inc. of Sendai City, Japan on 18 Aug. 1991.

Largest galleries The world's largest art gallery is the Winter Palace and the neighboring Hermitage in St. Petersburg, Russia. One has to walk 15 miles to visit each of the 322 galleries, which house nearly 3 million works of art and objects of archaeological interest.

Most heavily endowed The J. Paul Getty Museum at Malibu, CA, was established with an initial $1.4 billion budget in January 1974 and now has an annual budget of $180 million for acquisitions to stock its 38 galleries.

MOSAICS

Largest The world's largest mosaic is on the walls of the central library of the Universidad Nacional Autónoma de Mexico in Mexico City. Of the four walls, the two largest measure 12,949 ft.^{2}, and the scenes on each represent the pre-Hispanic past.

MURALS

Earliest The earliest-known murals on man-made walls are the clay relief leopards at Catal Hüyük in southern Anatolia, Turkey, discovered by James Malaart at level VII in 1961 and dating from *c.* 6200 B.C.

Largest A mural on the 23-story Vegas World Hotel, Las Vegas, NV covers an area of 95,442 ft.^{2}.

HIGHEST PRICES

Painting On 15 May 1990, *Portrait of Dr. Gachet* by Vincent "Willem" van Gogh (1853–90) was sold within three minutes for $82.5 million at Christie's, New York. The painting depicts van Gogh's physician and was completed only weeks before the artist's suicide in 1890. The new owner was subsequently identified as Ryoei Saito, Japan's second-largest paper manufacturer.

Art collection The most valuable art collection of a single owner sold at auction realized $131,297,870 at Sotheby's, New York in October 1990. The collection was formed by John T. Dorrance, Jr., and included *Femme a l'Ombrelle Rouge Assise de Profil* (1921), by Henri Matisse, which raised $12.375 million.

Miniature The record price is the £352,000 ($621,632) paid by the

Alexander Gallery of New York at Christie's, London on 7 Nov. 1988 for a 2⅛-in.-high miniature of George Washington. It was painted by the Irish-American miniaturist John Ramage (c. 1748–1802) in 1789.

Twentieth-century painting   The record bid at auction for a 20th-century painting is $47.8 million for a self-portrait by Pablo Picasso (1881–1973), *Yo Picasso* (1901), at Sotheby's, New York on 9 May 1989.

Living artist   The highest price paid at auction for a work by a living artist is $20.68 million for *Interchange*, an abstract by the American painter Willem de Kooning (b. Rotterdam, Netherlands, 1904) at Sotheby's, New York on 8 Nov. 1989. Painted in 1955, it was bought by Japanese dealer-cum-collector "Mountain Tortoise."

Print   The record price for a print at auction was £561,600 ($786,000) for a 1655 etching of *Christ Presented to the People* by Rembrandt (1606–69) at Christie's, London on 5 Dec. 1985. It was sold by the Chatsworth Settlement Trustees.

Drawing   The ·highest price ever paid for a drawing is $8.36 million

LARGEST ART GALLERY. The Winter Palace and neighboring Hermitage in St. Petersburg, Russia house nearly three million works of art in 322 galleries. The views below and opposite show the magnificent façade, the lighted hall and some of the classical exhibits in the Dionysus Room. (Photos: Zefa Picture Library)

for the pen-and-ink scene *Jardin de Fleurs*, drawn by Vincent van Gogh in Arles, France in 1888 and sold at Christie's, New York on 14 Nov. 1990 to an anonymous buyer.

Poster   The record price for a poster is £62,000 ($74,400) for an advertisement for the 1902 Vienna Exhibition by Koloman Moser (1868–1918), sold at Christie's, London on 1 Apr. 1985.

SCULPTURE

Earliest A piece of ox rib found in 1973 at Pech de l'Aze, Dordogne, France in an early Middle Paleolithic layer of the Riss glaciation of *c.* 105,000 B.C. has several engraved lines on one side, thought to be possibly intentional.

The earliest-known examples of sculpture date from the Aurignacian culture of *c.* 28,000–22,000 B.C. and include the so-called "Venus" figurines from Austria and numerous figurines from northern Italy and central France.

Most expensive The record price for a sculpture at auction is £6.82 million ($12 million) at Sotheby's, London on 7 Dec. 1989 for a bronze garden ornament, *The Dancing Faun*, made by the Dutch-born sculptor Adrien de Vries (1545/6–1626). London dealer Cyril Humpris bought the figure from an unnamed couple who had paid £100 ($240) in the 1950s and in whose garden it had stood undiscovered for 40 years.

The highest price paid for the work of a sculptor during his lifetime is the $1,265,000 at Sotheby's, New York on 21 May 1982 for the 75-in.-long elmwood *Reclining Figure* by Henry Moore (Great Britain; 1898–1986).

United States The highest price paid at auction for a sculpture by an American sculptor is $4.4 million for *Coming Through the Rye*, by Frederic Remington (1861–1909), at Christie's, New York on 25 May 1989.

Sand sculpture The longest sand sculpture ever made—with the sculpture meticulously carved—was the 86,535-ft.-6-in.-long sculpture named "The GTE Directories Ultimate Sand Castle" built by more than 10,000 volunteers at Myrtle Beach, SC on 31 May 1991.

The tallest was the "Invitation to Fairyland," which was 56 ft. 2 in. high, and was built by 2,000 local volunteers at Kaseda, Japan on 26 July 1989 under the supervision of Gerry Kirk of Sand Sculptors International of San Diego and Shogo Tashiro of Sand Sculptors International of Japan.

Largest The mounted figures of Jefferson Davis (1808–89), Gen. Robert Edward Lee (1807–70) and Gen. Thomas Jonathan (Stonewall) Jackson (1824–63) cover 1.33 acres on the face of Stone Mountain, near Atlanta, GA. They are 90 ft. high. Roy Faulkner was on the mountain face for 8 years 174 days with a thermo-jet torch, working with the sculptor Walker Kirtland Hancock and other helpers, from 12 Sep. 1963 to 3 Mar. 1972.

The largest scrap-metal sculpture was built by Sudhir Deshpande of Nashik, India and unveiled in February 1990. Named *Powerful*, the colossus weighs 29.8 tons and stands 55¾ ft. tall.

Ground figures In the Nazca Desert, 185 miles south of Lima, Peru, there are straight lines (one more than 7 miles long), geometric shapes, and outlines of plants and animals drawn on the ground some time between 100 B.C. and A.D. 600 for an uncertain but probably religious, astronomical or even economic purpose by an imprecisely identified civilization. They were first detected from the air c. 1928 and have been described as the world's longest works of art.

Hill figures A 330-ft.-tall figure was found on a hill above Tarapacá, Chile in August 1968.

ANTIQUES

All prices quoted are inclusive of the buyer's premium.

Auctioneers The oldest continuous firm of art auctioneers in the world is the Stockholms Auktionsverk of Sweden, which was established on 27 Feb. 1647. The largest firm of art auctioneers in the world is the Sotheby Group of London, Great Britain and New York City, founded in 1744, which until 1778 traded primarily in books. Sotheby's turnover in 1989 was a record $2.9 billion. A single-session record of $360.4 million was set at Sotheby's, New York in 17 May 1990.

Art nouveau The highest auction price for any piece of art nouveau is $1.78 million for a standard lamp in the form of three lotus blossoms by the Daum Brothers and Louis Majorelle of France, sold at Sotheby's, New York on 2 Dec. 1989.

Baseball card The most valuable card is one of the six known baseball series cards of Honus Wagner, which was sold at Sotheby's, New York for $451,000 on 22 Mar. 1991. The buyers were Bruce McNall, owner of the Los Angeles Kings hockey club, and team member Wayne Gretzky, the game's most successful player.

Blanket The most expensive blanket was a Navajo Churro hand-spun serape of c. 1852 sold for $115,500 at Sotheby's, New York on 22 Oct. 1983.

Bottle A cobalt-blue bottle made by the Isabella Glassworks of New Jersey c. 1855–65 was sold for $26,400 at the Robert W. Skinner Galleries in Bolton, MA on 7 Oct. 1989.

Carpet In 1946 the Metropolitan Museum in New York City privately paid $1 million for the 26.5 × 13.6 ft. Anhalt Medallion carpet, made in Tabriz or Kashan, Persia (now Iran) c. 1590.
   The highest price paid at auction for a carpet is $672,400 for a Louis XV Savonnerie at Christie's, Monaco in June 1989.

Ceramics The highest auction price for any ceramic is £3.74 million ($6.4 million) for a Chinese Tang dynasty (A.D. 681–907) horse sold by the British Rail Pension Fund and bought by a Japanese dealer at Sotheby's, London, on 12 Dec. 1989. The horse was stolen from a warehouse in Hong Kong on 14 November, but was recovered on 2 December in time for the sale.

Chamber pot   A 33 oz. silver pot, made by David Willaume and engraved for the 2nd Earl of Warrington, Great Britain, sold for £9,500 ($13,300) at Sotheby's, London on 14 June 1984.

Doll   The highest price paid at auction for a doll is £90,200 ($153,340) for a 1909 bisque Kämmer and Reinhardt doll at Sotheby's, London, on 16 Feb. 1989. It was bought by Mme. Dina Vierny, who planned to open a Museum of Childhood in France.

Auctioneering   The longest one-man auction on record was of 60 hrs., conducted by Reg Coates at Gosport, Great Britain from 9–11 Sep. 1988.

Icon   The record price for an icon is $150,000, paid at Christie's, New York on 17 Apr. 1980 for the *Last Judgment* (from the George R. Hann collection, Pittsburgh, PA), made in Novgorod, Russia in the 16th century.

Furniture   The highest price ever paid for a single piece of furniture is £8.58 million ($15 million) at Christie's, London on 5 July 1990 for the 18th-century Italian "Badminton Cabinet" owned by the Duke of Beaufort. It was bought by Barbara Piasecka Johnson of Princeton, NJ.

United States   The highest price ever paid for a single piece of American furniture is $12.1 million at Christie's, New York on 3 June 1989 for a mahogany desk-cum-bookcase, made in the 1760s by master craftsman John Goddard of Newport, RI for the eminent statesman Nicholas Brown. It was bought by Israel Sack, one of New York's leading dealers in American furniture.

Glass   The auction record is £520,000 ($1,175,200) for a Roman glass cage-cup of *c*. A.D. 300, measuring 7 in. in diameter and 4 in. in height, sold at Sotheby's, London, on 4 June 1979 to Robin Symes.

Gold plate   The record for any gold artifact is £950,400 ($1,140,000) for the 22-carat font made by Paul Storr to the design of Humphrey Repton in 1797. It was sold at Christie's, London by Lady Anne Cavendish-Bentinck and bought by Armitage of London, Great Britain on 11 July 1985.

Guns   A .45 caliber Colt single-action army revolver, Serial No. 1 from 1873 was sold for $242,000 at Christie's New York on 14 May 1987.
  A set of rare, 24-carat gold-inlaid Colt 1851 model Navy presentation revolvers was sold for $352,000 at Christie's, New York on 26 Jan. 1991.

Helmet   The highest price ever paid for an item of headwear is $66,000 by the Alaska State Museum at an auction in New York City in November 1981 for a native North American Tlingit Kiksadi ceremonial frog helmet dating from *c.* 1600.

Jewelry   The world's largest jewelry auction, which included a Van Cleef and Arpels 1939 ruby and diamond necklace, realized over $50 million when the collection belonging to the Duchess of Windsor (1896–1986) was sold at Sotheby's, Geneva, Switzerland on 3 Apr. 1987.

The highest auction price for individual items of jewelry is $6.2 million for two pear-shaped diamond drop earrings of 58.6 and 61 carats bought and sold anonymously at Sotheby's, Geneva on 14 Nov. 1980.

Music box   The highest price paid for a music box is £20,900 ($22,990) for a Swiss example made for a Persian prince in 1901 and sold at Sotheby's, London on 23 Jan. 1985.

Playing cards   The highest price for a deck of playing cards is $143,352 paid by the Metropolitan Museum of Art, New York City at Sotheby's, London on 6 Dec. 1983.

Sculpture   The *Cycladic Marble Head of a Goddess*, from the early Bronze Age II, *c.* 2,600–2,500 B.C., was sold at Sotheby's, New York in December 1988 for $2,090,000.

Toys   The most expensive antique toy was sold for $231,000, by the trustees in bankruptcy of London dealers Mint & Boxed to an anonymous telephone bidder at Christie's, New York on 14 Dec. 1991. The work is a hand-painted tinplate replica of the "Charles" hose reel, a piece of fire-fighting equipment pulled by two firemen, measuring 15 × 23 in. and built *c.* 1870 by George Brown & Co. of Forestville, CT. Claims that this toy had been sold privately for $1 million in 1991 were subsequently refuted.

The highest price paid for a single toy soldier is £3,375 ($5,714) for a uniformed scale figure of Hitler's deputy, Rudolf Hess, made by the Lionel company of Brandenburg, Germany. The figure was among several sold by the Danish auction house Boyes in London, Great Britain on 23 Apr. 1991.

Silver   The record for English silver is £1,485,000 ($2,578,700) for the "Maynard" sideboard dish made by the Huguenot silversmith Paul de Lamerie in 1736, which was sold at Christie's, London on 22 May 1991.

Sword   The highest price paid for a sword is $1,316,800 for the Duke of Windsor's Royal Navy officer's sword (presented to him by King George V in 1913) at Sotheby's, Geneva, Switzerland on 3 Apr. 1987.

Tapestry   The highest auction price for a tapestry is £638,000 ($1,124,794), paid by Swiss dealer Peter Kleiner at Christie's, London on 3 July 1990 for a fragment of a rare Swiss example woven near Basle in the 1430s. The tapestry was in the Benedictine Abbey at Muri until 1840 before descending through the Vischer family.

Teddy bear   The highest price paid for a teddy bear at auction is £55,100 ($86,350). The dual-plush brown bear, made by Steiff of Germany *c.* 1920, was bought at Sotheby's, London on 19 Sep. 1989 by dealer James Fox.

Thimble   The record auction price for a thimble is £8,000 ($17,600) paid by London dealer Winifred Williams at Christie's, London on 3 Dec. 1979 for a Meissen dentil-shaped porcelain piece dated *c.* 1740.

LANGUAGE

There is no actual agreement on the number of languages spoken today. Most reference books give a figure of 4,000–5,000, but estimates have varied from 3,000 to as many as 10,000.

Earliest   The ability to speak is believed to be dependent upon physiological changes in the height of the larynx between *Homo erectus* and *Homo sapiens sapiens* as developed *c.* 45,000 B.C. The discovery of a hyoid bone (from the base of the tongue) from a cave site on Mt. Carmel, Israel shows that Neanderthal man may have been capable of speech 60,000 years ago, but the usual dating is 50,000–30,000 B.C.

Oldest English words   It was first suggested in 1979 that languages ancestral to English and to Latvian (both Indo-European) split *c.* 3,500 B.C. According to researches completed in 1989, about 40 words of a pre–Indo-European substratum survive in English, among them apple (apal), bad (bad), gold (gol) and tin (tin). The parent language is thought to have been spoken before 3,000 B.C. and to have split into different languages over the period 3,000–2,000 B.C.

Commonest language   The language used by more people than any other is Chinese, spoken by an estimated 1 billion people. The so-called "common language" (*putonghua*) is the standard form of Chinese, with a pronunciation based on that of Beijing. It is known in Taiwan as *guoyu* ("national speech") and in the West as Mandarin. After various attempts to write Chinese in the Roman alphabet, *Hanyu Pinyin*, the term used on mainland China and meaning "spell sound," was finally adopted on 11 Feb. 1958 as a writing system of 58 symbols.

The next most commonly spoken language, and the most widespread, is English, with an estimated 330–350 million native speakers and 700–1,400 million as many using it as a second or third language.

Most languages   About 845 of the world's languages and dialects are spoken in India. The former Australian territory of Papua New Guinea has, because of its many isolated valleys, the greatest concentration of separate languages in the world, with an estimated 869; each language has about 4,000 speakers.

Most complex   The following extremes of complexity have been noted: the Ample language of Papua New Guinea has the most verb forms, with over 69,000 finite forms and 860 infinitive forms of the verb; Haida, the North American Indian language, has the most prefixes, with 70; Tabassaran, a language of Daghestan, Azerbijan, uses the most noun cases, 48; and Inuit uses 63 forms of the present tense, and simple nouns have as many as 252 inflections.

Fewest irregular verbs   Esperanto, with no irregular verbs, was first published by its inventor, Dr. Ludwig Zamenhof (1859–1917) of Warsaw, in 1887. It is now estimated (by textbook sales) to have a million speakers. The even earlier interlanguage Volapük, invented by Johann Martin Schleyer (1831–1912), also has absolutely regular configuration.

The Turkish language has a single irregular verb — *olmak*, meaning "to be."

Most irregular verbs   According to *The Morphology and Syntax of Present-day English* by Prof. Olu Tomori, English has 283 irregular verbs, 30 of which are formed merely by adding prefixes.

Commonest sound   No language is known to be without the vowel "a" (as in the English "father").

Vocabulary   The English language contains about 616,500 words plus another 400,000 technical terms, the most in any language, but it is

MOST COMPLEX LANGUAGE. The Eskimo language used by the Inuit people of North America and Greenland has 63 forms of the present tense, and simple nouns may have up to 252 inflections. (Photo: Rex Features)

doubtful if any individual speaker uses more than 60,000. The members of the International Society for Philosophical Enquiry (no admission for IQs below 148) have an average vocabulary of 36,250 words. Shakespeare employed a vocabulary of *c.* 33,000 words.

Greatest linguist If the yardstick of ability to speak with fluency and reasonable accuracy is maintained, it is doubtful whether any human being could maintain fluency in more than 20 to 25 languages concurrently or achieve fluency in more than 40 in a lifetime.

The world's greatest linguist is believed to be have been Dr. Harold Williams of New Zealand (1876–1928), a journalist. Self-taught in Latin, Greek, Hebrew and many of the European and Pacific island languages as a boy, Dr. Williams spoke 58 languages and many dialects fluently. He was the only person to attend the League of Nations (1920–46) in Geneva, Switzerland and converse with every delegate in their own language.

In terms of oral fluency, the most multilingual living person is Derick Herning of Lerwick, Great Britain, whose command of 22 languages earned him victory in the inaugural "Polyglot of Europe" contest held in Brussels, Belgium in May 1990.

The 1975 edition of *Who's Who in the United Nations* listed "only" 19 languages for Georges Schmidt (1914–90), Chief of the UN Terminology Section in 1965–71, because he was then unable to find time to "revive" his former fluency in 12 others. Louis Jay Herman of New York City *worked* with 25 languages as a translator for the United Nations between 1958 and 1980.

Rarest sounds The rarest speech sound is probably that written "ř" in Czech and termed a "rolled post-alveolar fricative." It occurs in very few languages and is the last sound mastered by Czech children. In the southern Bushman language !xo there is a click articulated with both lips, which is written ⊙. This character is usually referred to as a "bull's eye" and the sound, essentially a kiss, is termed a "velaric ingressive bilabial stop." In some contexts the "l" sound in the Arabic word *Allah* is pronounced uniquely in that language.

Debating Students at University College, Dublin, Republic of Ireland debated the motion that "Every Dog Should Have Its Day" for 503 hrs. 45 min., from 16 Nov.–7 Dec. 1988.

The longest debate in the United States was 109 hrs. 35 min., from 16–21 Nov. 1989, by students at St. Andrews Presbyterian College, Laurinburg, NC. They debated the motion: "World Hunger: Solvable or Unsolvable?"

ALPHABET

There are 65 alphabets in use worldwide.

Earliest The earliest-known example of alphabetic writing was found at Ugarit (now Ras Sharma), Syria, dated to *c.* 1450 B.C. It comprised a clay tablet of 32 cuneiform letters.

Oldest letter The letter "O" is unchanged in shape since its adoption in the Phoenician alphabet *c.* 1,300 B.C.

Newest letters The newest letters to be added to the English alphabet are "j" and "v," which are of post-Shakespearean use (*c.* 1630). Formerly they were used only as variants of "i" and "u."

Longest The language with the most letters in its alphabet is Cambodian (now usually referred to as Khmer), with 74 (including some without any current use).

Shortest Rotokas of central Bougainville Island, Papua New Guinea has the fewest letters, with 11 (a, b, e, g, i, k, o, p, r, t and u).

Most and least consonants The language with the greatest number of distinct consonantal sounds is Ubykhs in the Caucasus, with 80–85. Rotokas has the least, with six consonants.

Most and least vowels The language with the most vowels is Sedang, a central Vietnamese language with 55 distinguishable vowel sounds,

LONGEST ALPHABET. These Cambodian schoolchildren would do well to pay attention, as their alphabet, now usually referred to as Khmer, consists of 74 letters. (Photo: Rex Features)

and the one with the fewest is the Caucasian language Abkhazian, with two.

Smallest letters   Scanning tunneling microscope (STM) techniques pioneered in April 1990 by physicists Donald Eigler and Erhard Schweizer at IBM's Almaden Research Center in San Jose, CA have enabled single atoms of various elements to be manipulated to form characters and pictures.

WORDS

Longest   Lengthy concatenations and some compound or agglutinative words or nonce words are or have been written in the closed-up style of a single word. The longest known example is a compound "word" of 195 Sanskrit characters (which transliterates into 428 letters in the Roman alphabet) describing the region near Kanci, Tamil Nadu, India that appears in a 16th-century work by Tirumalāmbā, Queen of Vijayanagara.

English   The longest word in the *Oxford English Dictionary* is *pneumonoultramicroscopicsilicovolcanoconiosis (-koniosis)*, which has 45 letters and allegedly means "a lung disease caused by the inhalation of very fine silica dust." It is, however, described as "factitious" by the editors of the dictionary.

Longest scientific name   The systematic name for *deoxyribonucleic acid* (DNA) of the human mitochondria contains 16,569 nucleotide residues and is thus *c.* 207,000 letters long. It was published in key form in *Nature* on 9 Apr. 1981.

Longest palindromes   The longest-known palindromic word (a word that reads the same backward or forward) is *saippuakivikauppias* (19 letters), which is Finnish for "a dealer in lye" (caustic soda). The longest in English is *tattarrattat*, with 12 letters, which appears in the *Oxford English Dictionary*.
  Some baptismal fonts in Greece and Turkey bear the circular 25-letter inscription NIΨON ANOMHMATA MH.M.ONAN OΨIN, meaning "wash (my) sins not only (my) face."

Longest anagrams   The longest non-scientific English words that can form anagrams are the 19-letter transpositions *representationalism* and

---

Most succinct word   The most challenging word for any lexicographer to define briefly is the Fuegian (southernmost Argentina and Chile) word *mamihlapinatapai*, meaning "looking at each other hoping that either will offer to do something which both parties desire but are unwilling to do."

Most synonyms   The condition of being inebriated has more synonyms than any other condition or object. Delacorte Press of New York City has published a selection of 1,224 from a list of 2,241 compiled by Paul Dickson of Garrett Park, MD.

LONGEST WORDS

JAPANESE[1]	Chi-n-chi-ku-ri-n (12 letters) *a very short person (slang)*
SPANISH	Superextraordinarisimo (22) *extraordinary*
FRENCH	Anticonstitutionnellement (25) *anticonstitutionally*
CROATIAN	Prijestolonasljednikovica (25) *wife of an heir apparent*
ITALIAN	Precipitevolissimevolmente (26) *as fast as possible*
PORTUGUESE	Inconstitucionalissimamente (27) *with the highest degree of unconstitutionality*
ICELANDIC	Haecstaréttarmálautningsmaôur (29 Icelandic letters, transliterating as 31) *supreme court barrister*
RUSSIAN	Ryentgyenoelyektrokardiograchyeskogo (33 Cyrillic letters, transliterating as 38) *of the X-ray electrocardiographic*
HUNGARIAN	Megszentségtelenithetetlenségeskedéseitekért (44) *for your unprofanable actions*
DUTCH[2]	Kindercarnavalsoptochtvoorbereidingswerkzaamheden (49) *preparation activities for a children's carnival procession*
MOHAWK[3]	Tkanuhstasrihsranuhwe'tsraaksahsrakaratattsrayeri' (50) *the praising of the evil of the liking of the finding of the house is right*
TURKISH[2]	Cekoslovakyallastrabilemediklerimizlerdenmisiniz (50) *"are you not of that group of persons that we were said to be unable to Czechoslovakianize?"*
GERMAN[2,4]	Donaudampfschiffahrtselektrizitaetenhauptbetriebswerkbauunterbeamtengesellschaft (80) *The club for subordinate officials of the head office management of the Danube steamboat electrical services (name of a pre-war club in Vienna)*
SWEDISH[2]	Nordöstersjökustartilleriflygspaningssimulatoranläggningsmaterielunderhållsuppföljningssystemdiskussionsinläggsförberedelsearbeten (130) *Preparatory work on the contribution to the discussion on the maintaining system of support of the material of the aviation survey simulator device within the northeast part of the coast artillery of the Baltic*

[1] Patent applications sometimes harbor long compound "words." An extreme example is one of 13 kana (Japanese syllabary) which transliterates to the 40-letter Kyukitsurohekimenfuchakunenryōsekisanryō meaning "the accumulated amount of fuel condensed on the wall face of the air intake passage."

[2] Agglutinative words are limited only by imagination and are not found in standard dictionaries. The first 100-letter such word was published in 1975 by the late Eric Rosenthal in Afrikaans.

[3] Lengthy concatenations are a feature of Mohawk.

[4] The longest dictionary word in everyday usage is Rechtsschutzversicherungsgesellschaften (39) meaning "insurance companies which provide legal protection."

misrepresentational. The longest scientific transposals are *hydroxydes-oxycorticosterone* and *hydroxydeoxycorticosterones*, with 27 letters.

Abbreviations *Longest* The initials S.K.O.M.K.H.P.K.J.C.D.P.W.B., which stand for the Syarikat Kerjasama Orang-orang Melayu Kerajaan Hilir Perak Kerana Jimat Cermat Dan Pinjam-meminjam Wang Berhad, are the Malay name for The Cooperative Company of the Lower State of Perak Government's Malay People for Money Savings and Loans Ltd., in Teluk Anson, Perak, West Malaysia (formerly Malaya). The abbreviation for this abbreviation is Skomk.

Shortest The 55-letter full name of Los Angeles (El Pueblo de Nuestra Señora la Reina de los Angeles de Porciuncula) is abbreviated to L.A., or 3.63 percent of its length.

Longest acronym The longest acronym is NIIOMTPLABOPARM-BETZHELBETRABSBOMONIMONKONOTDTEKHSTROMONT with 56 letters (54 in Cyrillic) in the *Concise Dictionary of Soviet Terminology,* meaning: the Laboratory for Shuttering, Reinforcement, Concrete and Ferroconcrete Operations for Composite-monolithic and Monolithic Constructions of the Department of the Technology of Building-Assembly Operations of the Scientific Research Institute of the Organization for Building Mechanization and Technical Aid of the Academy of Building and Architecture of the USSR.

Commonest words and letters The most frequently used words in written English are, in descending order of frequency: *the, of, and, to, a, in, that, is, I, it, for* and *as.* The most commonly used in conversation is "*I.*" The commonest letter is "e." More words begin with the letter "s" than with any other, but the most commonly *used* initial letter is "t" as in "the," "to," "that" or "there."

Most meanings The most overworked word in English is "set," to which Dr. Charles Onions (1873–1965) of Oxford University Press gave 58 uses as a noun, 126 uses as a verb and ten as a participial adjective.

PERSONAL NAMES

Earliest The earliest personal name that has survived seems to be that of a predynastic king of Upper Egypt *ante* 3,050 B.C., who is represented by the hieroglyphic sign for a scorpion. It has been suggested, that the name should be read as Sekhen.

Longest personal name The longest name appearing on a birth certificate is that of Rhoshandiatellyneshiaunneveshenk Koyaanfsquatsiuty

---

Most contrived name In the United States the determination to derive commercial or other benefit from being the last listing in the local telephone book has resulted in self-given names starting with up to nine "Z's" — an extreme example being Zachary Zzzzzzzzzra in the San Francisco book.

Will'ams, born to Mr. and Mrs. James Williams in Beaumont, TX on 12 Sep. 1984. On 5 Oct. 1984 the father filed an amendment that expanded his daughter's first name to 1,019 letters and her middle name to 36 letters.

Most first names Laurence Watkins (b. 9 June 1965) of Auckland, New Zealand claims a total of 2,310 first names, added by deed poll in 1991 after official opposition by the registrar and a prolonged court battle. The great-great-grandson of Carlos III of Spain, Don Alfonso de Borbón y Borbón (1866–1934), had 94 first names, several of which were lengthened by hyphenation.

Shortest family names The commonest single-letter surname is "O," prevalent in Korea but with 52 examples in US telephone books (1973–81) and 12 in Belgium. This name causes great distress to those concerned with the prevention of cruelty to computers. Every other letter, except "Q," has been traced as a surname in US telephone books by A. Ross Eckler.

Commonest family name The Chinese name Zhang is borne, according to estimates, by between 9.7 and 12.1 percent of the Chinese population. Even at the lower estimate this means that there are at least some 104 million Changs—more than the entire population of all but seven of the other 170 sovereign countries of the world.

The commonest surname in the English-speaking world is Smith. There are an estimated 2,382,509 Smiths in the United States.

PLACE-NAMES

Earliest The world's earliest-known place-names are pre-Sumerian, e.g., Kish, Ur and the now-lost Attara, and therefore earlier than *c.* 3,600 B.C.

Longest The official name for Bangkok, the capital city of Thailand, is Krungthep Mahanakhon. However, the full name is Krungthep Mahanakhon Bovorn Ratanakosin Mahintharayutthaya Mahadilokpop Noparatratchathani Burirom Udomratchanivet mahasathan Amornpiman Avatarnsathit Sakkathattiyavisnukarmprasit (167 letters), which in its most scholarly transliteration emerges with 175 letters.

The longest place-name now in use in the world is Taumatawhakatangihangakoauauotamateaturipukakapikimaungahoro-nukupokai-whenuakitanatahu, the unofficial 85-letter version of the name of a hill (1,002 ft. above sea level) in the Southern Hawke's Bay district of North Island, New Zealand. The Maori translation means "The place where Tamatea, the man with the big knees, who slid, climbed and swallowed mountains, known as landeater, played his flute to his loved one."

Shortest The shortest place-names consist of just single letters, and examples can be found in various countries around the world.

There was once a town called "6" in West Virginia.

Most spellings The spelling of the Dutch town of Leeuwarden has been recorded in 225 versions since A.D. 1046. Bromesberrow, Great Britain is recorded in 161 spellings since the 10th century as reported by local historian Lester Steynor.

LITERATURE

Earliest   Tokens or tallies from Tepe Asiab and Ganji-I-Dareh Tepe in Iran have been dated to 8,500 B.C. The earliest written language discovered is on Yangshao culture pottery from Paa-t'o in the Shaanxi province of China, found in 1962. This bears proto-characters for the numbers 5, 7 and 8 and has been dated to 5,000–4,000 B.C.

Encyclopedias   The earliest known encyclopedia was compiled by Speusippus (*post* 408–*c.* 388 B.C.), a nephew of Plato, in Athens c. 370 B.C.

Printing   The oldest surviving printed work is the Dharani scroll or *sutra* from wooden printing blocks found in the foundations of the Pulguk Sa pagoda, Kyongju, South Korea on 14 Oct. 1966. It has been dated to no later than A.D. 704.

Paper dated to between 71 B.C. and A.D. 21, i.e., 100 years earlier than the previous presumed date for paper's invention, has been found in northwest China.

Oldest mechanically printed   It was claimed in November 1973 that a 28-page book of Tang dynasty poems at Yonsei University, Korea was printed from metal type *c.* 1160. Work on watermarks published in 1967 indicates that a copy of a surviving printed "Donatus" Latin grammar was made from paper *c.* 1450.

It is widely accepted that the earliest mechanically printed full-length book was the 42-line-per-page Gutenberg Bible, printed in Mainz, Germany *c.* 1454 by Johann Henne zum Gensfleisch zur Laden, called "zu Gutenberg" (*c.* 1398–1468). The earliest exactly dated printed work is the Psalter completed on 14 Aug. 1457 by Johann Fust (*c.* 1400–66) and Peter Schöffer (1425–1502), who had been Gutenberg's chief assistant.

The earliest printing by William Caxton (*c.* 1422–91), though undated, would appear to be *The Recuyel of the Historyes of Troye* in Cologne in late 1473 to spring 1474.

Smallest book   The smallest marketed bound printed book is one printed on 22 gsm paper measuring $\frac{1}{25} \times \frac{1}{25}$ in., comprising the children's story *Old King Cole!* and published in 85 copies in March 1985 by The Gleniffer Press of Paisley, Great Britain. The pages can be turned (with care) only by the use of a needle.

Largest publications   The largest publication ever compiled was the *Yongle Dadien* (the great thesaurus of the Yongle reign) of 22,937 manuscript chapters (370 still survive) in 11,095 volumes. It was written by 2,000 Chinese scholars in 1403–08.

The entire Buddhist scriptures are inscribed on 729 marble slabs measuring $5 \times 3\frac{1}{2}$ ft. housed in 729 stupas in the Kuthodaw Pagoda, south of Mandalay, Myanmar (formerly Burma). They were incised in 1860–68.

Dictionaries   *Deutsches Wörterbuch*, started by Jacob and Wilhelm

Grimm in 1854, was completed in 1971 and consists of 34,519 pages and 33 volumes.

The largest English-language dictionary is the 20-volume *Oxford English Dictionary*, with 21,728 pages. The first edition was published between 1884 and 1928. A first Supplement of 964 pages appeared in 1932, and a second one in four volumes, between 1972 and 1986. Work on the second edition began in 1984, and the work involved represented 500 person-years. Published in March 1989, it defines a total of 616,500 word-forms, with 2,412,400 illustrative quotations and approximately 350 million letters and figures. Now computerized, the dictionary required 625 million bytes to store in machine-readable form. The longest entry in the second edition is that for the verb *set*, with over 75,000 words of text.

The largest English-language dictionary published in the United States is *Webster's Third New International Dictionary Unabridged*, published in 1986 by Merriam-Webster Inc. It defines 470,000 word-forms, with 99,943 illustrative quotations and approximately 60 million letters and numerics. The longest entry is for the verb *turn*, with over 5,500 words of text.

The best-selling dictionary in the United States is *Webster's Ninth New Collegiate Dictionary*, published in 1983 and 1990 by Merriam-Webster Inc. The 1983 edition has reportedly sold over one million copies each year.

The *New Grove Dictionary of Music and Musicians*, edited by Stanley Sadie (b. 30 Oct. 1930) and published in 20 volumes by Macmillan in February 1981, contains over 22 million words and 4,500 illustrations and is the largest specialized dictionary.

Longest literary gestation The standard German dictionary *Deutsches Wörterbuch* was begun by the brothers Grimm (Jacob and Wilhelm, 1785–1863 and 1786–1859 respectively) in 1854 and finished in 1971. *Acta Sanctorum,* begun by Jean Bolland in 1643, arranged according to saints' days, reached the month of November in 1925, and an introduction for December was published in 1940.

Oxford University Press received back its proofs of *Constable's Presentments* from the Dugdale Society in December 1984. They had been sent out for correction 35 years earlier, in December 1949.

Encyclopedias *Largest* The largest encyclopedia ever compiled was the Chinese *Yongle Dadian* (See Largest publications.)

Currently, the largest encyclopedia is *La Enciclopedia Universal Ilustrada Europeo-Americana* (J. Espasa & Sons, Madrid and Barcelona) totaling 105,000 pages with an annual supplement since 1935. The encyclopedia comprises 165.2 million words. The number of volumes in the set in August 1983 was 104, and the price $2,325.

The most comprehensive English-language encyclopedia is *The New Encyclopaedia Britannica*, first published in Edinburgh, Great Britain in December 1768. A group of booksellers in the United States acquired reprint rights in 1898 and completed ownership in 1899. The current 32-volume 15th edition contains 32,330 pages and 44 million words from more than 4,000 contributors. It is now edited in Chicago, IL.

Fiction   The novel *Tokuga-Wa Ieyasu* by Sohachi Yamaoka has been serialized in Japanese daily newspapers since 1951. Now completed, it will require nearly 40 volumes.

The longest novel of note ever published is *Les hommes de bonne volonté* by Louis-Henri-Jean Farigoule (1885–1972), alias Jules Romains, of France, published in 27 volumes in 1932–46. The English version, *Men of Good Will*, was published in 14 volumes in 1933–46 as a "novel-cycle." The 4,959-page edition published by Peter Davies Ltd. has an estimated 2,070,000 words, excluding the 100-page index.

Who's Who   The longest of the 79,400 entries in *Who's Who in America* (46th edition) is that of Mr. Thomas Capper Eakin (b. 16 Dec. 1933), with an all-time record of 128 lines.

MAPS

Oldest   A clay tablet depicting the river Euphrates flowing through northern Mesopotamia (Iraq) dates to *c.* 2250 B.C. The earliest printed map in the world is one of western China dated to 1115.

Largest   A giant relief map of California, *Paradise in Panorama* by Reuben Hall, measuring 45 × 18 ft. and weighing 43 tons, was displayed in the Ferry Building, San Francisco from 1924–60. It required 29 person-years and $147,000 to build and is now stored at the Hamilton Air Force Base in Novato, CA.

Most expensive   The highest price paid for an atlas is $1,925,000 for a copy of Ptolemy Cosmographia, which was sold at Sotheby's, New York City on 31 Jan. 1990.

HIGHEST PRICES

Book   The highest price paid for any book is £8.14 million ($12 million) for the 226-leaf manuscript *The Gospel Book of Henry the Lion, Duke of Saxony* at Sotheby's, London on 6 Dec. 1983. The book, which measures 13½ × 10 in., was illuminated *c.* 1170 by the monk Herimann at Helmershansen Abbey, Germany with 41 full-page illustrations. The book was bought by Hans Kraus for the Hermann Abs consortium.

The highest price ever paid for a *printed* book is $5.39 million for an Old Testament (Genesis to the Psalms) Gutenberg Bible printed in 1455 in Mainz, Germany. It was bought by Tokyo booksellers Maruzen Co. Ltd. at Christie's New York on 22 Oct. 1987.

Broadsheet   The highest price ever paid for a broadsheet was $2,420,000 for one of the 24 known copies of *The Declaration of Independence*, printed by John Dunlap in Philadelphia, PA in 1776, and sold to Donald J. Scheer of Atlanta, GA on 13 June 1991.

Manuscript   The highest price ever paid for a complete manuscript is £2.97 million ($11.4 million) by London dealers Quaritch at Sotheby's,

London on 29 Nov. 1990 for the 13th-century Northumberland Bestiary, a colorful and heavily illustrated encyclopedia of real and imaginary animals.

Musical The auction record for a musical manuscript is $4,394,500 at Sotheby's, London on 22 May 1987 for a 510-page, 8½ × 6½ in. bound volume of nine complete symphonies in Mozart's hand. The manuscript is owned by Robert Owen Lehman and is on deposit at the Pierpont Morgan Library in New York City.

The record price paid for a single musical manuscript is £1.1 million paid at Sotheby's, London on 6 Dec. 1991 for the autographed copy of the Piano Sonata in E minor, opus 90, by Ludwig van Beethoven (1770–1827).

Scientific The highest price paid for a scientific manuscript was $1.16 million for a 72-page document by Albert Einstein, which explained his theory of relativity, on 2 Dec. 1987 at Sotheby's, New York.

BIBLE

Oldest The earliest biblical texts are from two silver amulets found under the Scottish Church, Jerusalem in 1979 bearing Numbers Chapter 6 verse 22–27 and dated to *c.* 587 B.C. In 1945 various papyrus texts were discovered at Nag Hammodi, Egypt, including gnostic gospels or secret books (apocrypha) ascribed to Thomas, James, John, Peter and Paul. They were buried *c.* A.D. 350 but the originals are thought to have been written *c.* A.D. 120–150.

The oldest-known Bible is the *Codex Vaticanus*, written in Greek *ante* A.D. 350 and preserved in the Vatican Museum, Rome. The earliest complete Bible *printed* in English was edited by Miles Coverdale, Bishop of Exeter (*c.* 1488 1569), while living in Antwerp, Belgium, and printed in 1535. William Tyndale's New Testament in English was, however, printed in Cologne and Worms, Germany in 1525, and John Wycliffe's first manuscript translation dates from 1382.

Longest and shortest book The longest book in the Authorized Version (King James) of the Bible is the Book of Psalms, and the longest book including prose is the Book of the Prophet Isaiah, with 66 chapters. The shortest is the Third Epistle of John, which has only 294 words in 14 verses. The Second Epistle of John has only 13 verses but 298 words.

Longest and shortest psalm Of the 150 psalms, the longest is the 119th, with 176 verses, and the shortest is the 117th, with two verses.

Longest and shortest verse The shortest verse in the Authorized Version (King James) of the Bible is verse 35 of Chapter XI of the Gospel according to St. John, consisting of the two words "Jesus wept." The longest is verse 9 of Chapter VIII of the Book of Esther, which extends to a 90-word description of the Persian empire.

Total letters and words The total number of letters in the Bible is 3,566,480. The total number of words depends on the method of counting hyphenated words, but is usually given as between 773,692 and 773,746. According to Colin McKay Wilson of the Salvation Army, the word *"and"* appears 46,227 times. According to the Interpreters Dictionary of the Bible, there are 212,916 references to "God" (in all forms) in the Bible.

Longest name   The longest actual name in English language bibles is the 18-letter Maher-shalal-hash-baz, the symbolic name of the second son of Isaiah (Isaiah, Chapter VIII, verses 1 and 3).

The caption of Psalm 22, however, contains a Hebrew title sometimes rendered as Al-Ayyeleth Hash-Shahar (20 letters).

DIARIES AND LETTERS

Longest-kept diary   Col. Ernest Loftus of Harare, Zimbabwe began his daily diary on 4 May 1896 at the age of 12 and continued it until his death on 7 July 1987 at the age of 103 years 178 days. George C. Edler (1889–1987) of Bethesda, MD kept a handwritten diary continuously from 20 Sep. 1909, a total of 78 years.

Longest and most letters   Uichi Noda, former vice minister of treasury and minister of construction in Japan, from July 1961 until his bedridden wife Mitsu's death in March 1985, wrote her 1,307 letters amounting to 5 million characters during his overseas trips. These letters have been published in 25 volumes totaling 12,404 pages.

Rev. Canon Bill Cook and his fiancée/wife Helen of Diss, Norfolk, Great Britain exchanged 6,000 love letters during their 4¼ year separation from March 1942–May 1946.

Longest letter to an editor   The *Upper Dauphin Sentinel* of Pennsylvania published a letter of 25,513 words spread over eight issues from August to November 1979, written by John Sultzbaugh of Lykens, PA.

Shortest correspondence   The shortest correspondence on record was that between Victor Marie Hugo (1802–85) and his publisher, Hurst and Blackett, in 1862. The author was on vacation and was anxious to know how his new novel *Les Misérables* was selling. He wrote "?" and received the reply "!"

Most personal mail   The highest confirmed amount of mail received by any private citizen in a year is 900,000 letters by the baseball star Henry Louis "Hank" Aaron (b. 5 Feb. 1934), reported by the US Postal Department in June 1974. About a third were letters of hate engendered by his bettering of George Herman "Babe" Ruth's career record for home runs. (See also Baseball.)

Pen pals   The longest sustained correspondence on record is one of 75 years between Mrs. Ida McDougall of Tasmania, Australia and Miss R. Norton of Sevenoaks, Kent, Great Britain from 11 Nov. 1904 until Mrs. McDougall's death on 24 Dec. 1979.

AUTOGRAPHS AND SIGNATURES

Earliest   The earliest surviving examples of autographs are those made by scribes on cuneiform clay tablets from Tell Abu Salābīkh, Iraq dated to the early Dynastic III A c. 2,600 B.C. A scribe named "a-du" has added "dub-sar" after his name, thus translating to "Adu, scribe." The earliest surviving signature on a papyrus is that of the scribe Amen-'aa, held in the St. Petersburg Museum, Russia and dated to the Egyptian Middle Kingdom, which began c. 2,130 B.C.

Most expensive   The highest price ever paid on the open market for a single signed autograph letter was $360,000 on 29 Oct. 1986 at Sotheby's, New York for a letter written by Thomas Jefferson in 1818 condemning prejudice against Jews. It was sold by Charles Rosenbloom of Pittsburgh, PA.

The highest price paid for an autographed letter signed by a living person is $12,500 at the Hamilton Galleries on 22 Jan. 1981 for a letter from President Ronald Reagan praising Frank Sinatra.

Rarest and most valuable   Only one example of the signature of Christopher Marlowe (1564–93) is known. It is in the County Archives in Kent, Great Britain on a will of 1583.

The only known document that bears ten US presidential signatures is a letter sent by President Franklin Delano Roosevelt to Richard C. Corbyn, then of Dallas (now of Amarillo), TX, dated 26 Oct. 1932. It was subsequently signed by Herbert Hoover, Harry S Truman, Dwight D. Eisenhower, Gerald Ford, Lyndon Johnson, Jimmy Carter, Ronald Reagan and George Bush. Richard Nixon's first signature was signed with an autopen but he later re-signed it.

Christmas cards   The earliest-known Christmas card was sent out by Sir Henry Cole (1808–82) in 1843, but this practice did not become an annual ritual until 1862.

The greatest number of personal Christmas cards sent by an individual is believed to be 62,824 by Werner Erhard of San Francisco, CA in December 1975. Many must have been to unilateral acquaintances.

Christmas card exchange   Frank Rose of Burnaby, British Columbia, Canada and Gordon Loutet of Lake Cowichan, British Columbia have exchanged the same Christmas card every year since 1929.

Warren Nord of Mesa, AZ and Thor (Tut) Andersen (d. 11 Sep. 1988) of Ashtabula, OH exchanged the same Christmas card every year from 1930–87.

AUTHORS

Most prolific A lifetime output of 72–75 million words has been calculated for Charles Harold St. John Hamilton, alias Frank Richards (1876–1961), the creator of Billy Bunter. In his peak years (1915–26) he wrote up to 80,000 words a week for the boys' school weeklies *Gem* (1907–39), *Magnet* (1908–40) and *Boys' Friend*.

Novels The greatest number of novels published is 904, by Kathleen Lindsay (Mrs. Mary Faulkner; 1903–73) of Somerset West, Cape Province, South Africa. She wrote under two other married names and eight pen names.

Baboorao Arnalkar (b. 9 June 1907) of Maharashtra State, India published 1,092 short mystery stories in book form and several nonfiction books between 1936 and 1984.

Greatest advance The greatest advance paid for any book is $5 million for *Whirlwind*, to James Clavell at auction in New York City on 11 Jan. 1986 by William Morrow & Co. and Avon Books. On 9 Feb. 1989 Stephen King was reported to have garnered over $30 million advance for his next four books.

Top-selling The world's top-selling writer of fiction is Dame Agatha Christie (nee Miller, later Lady Mallowan, 1890–1976), whose 78 crime novels have sold an estimated 2 billion copies in 44 languages. Her famous Belgian detective, Hercule Poirot, is featured in 33 books and 56 stories, while his English counterpart, Miss Marple, has appeared in 12 books and 20 stories. Agatha Christie also wrote 19 plays and six romantic novels under the pseudonym Mary Westmacott. Royalty earnings are estimated to be worth $4.25 million per year.

The top-selling female author is currently Dame Barbara Cartland, with global sales of over 600 million for some 564 titles published in 25 languages to date. She has averaged 23 titles per year for the last 18 years and was made a Dame of the Order of the British Empire by Her Majesty Queen Elizabeth II in the 1991 New Year's Honours List for services to literature and the community.

An estimated 600 million copies of Belgian novelist Georges Simenon's (1903–89) works have also been sold, but in 47 languages.

Highest-paid author In 1958 Mrs. Deborah Schneider of Minneapolis, MN wrote 25 words to complete a sentence in a competition for the best slogan for Plymouth cars. She beat about 1.4 million other entrants to win a prize of $500 every month for life. Based on normal life expectancy she should collect $12,000 per word. No known anthology includes Mrs. Schneider's deathless prose, but it is in her safe deposit box at her bank, "Only to be opened after death."

Most successful poem *If* by Rudyard Kipling (1865–1936), first published in 1910, has been translated into 27 languages and, according to Kipling, "anthologized to weariness."

Most pseudonyms The writer with greatest number of pseudonyms is the minor Russian humorist Konstantin Arsenievich Mikhailov (b. 1868), whose 325 pen names are listed in the *Dictionary of Pseudonyms* by I.F. Masanov, published in Moscow in 1960. The names, ranging from Ab. to Z, were mostly abbreviations of his real name.

Most rejections The record for rejections before publication is 176 (plus non-acknowledgement from many other publishers) in the case of Bill Gordon's *How Many Books Do You Sell in Ohio?* from October 1983 to November 1985. The record was then spoiled by Mr. Gordon's rejection of a written offer from Aames-Allen.

Oldest The oldest author in the world was Alice Pollock (nee Wykeham-Martin, 1868–1971) of Haslemere, Great Britain, whose first book, *Portrait of My Victorian Youth* (Johnson Publications), was published in March 1971 when she was aged 102 years 8 months. The oldest living author is Griffith R. Williams of Llithfaen, Great Britain, whose autobiography, *Cofio Canrif*, was published on his 102nd birthday on 5 June 1990.

Longest poem The longest poem ever published was the Kirghiz folk epic *Manas*, which appeared in printed form in 1958 but has never been translated into English. According to the *Dictionary of Oriental Literatures*, this three-part epic runs to about 500,000 lines. Short translated passages appear in *The Elek Book of Oriental Verse*.

The longest poem ever written in the English language is one on the life of King Alfred by John Fitchett (1766–1838) of Liverpool, Great Britain, which ran to 129,807 lines and took 40 years to write. His editor, Robert Riscoe, added the concluding 2,585 lines.

In contrast, the 24-line Kamassian poem *Lament* is the only known literary work in this Samoyed language (distantly related to Hungarian), spoken in the Sayan Mountains near Lake Baikal, Siberia, Russia but now on the verge of extinction. This little poem is chronicled in the Hungarian publication *Ancient Cultures of the Uralian Peoples* and is printed in International Phonetics because Kamassian has no written form of its own.

BEST-SELLING BOOKS

The world's most widely distributed book is the Bible, which has been translated into 318 languages, and portions of it into a further 1,628 languages. This compares with 222 languages for Lenin's works. It has been estimated that between 1815 and 1975 some 2.5 billion copies of the Bible were printed, of which 1.5 billion were handled by bible societies. Since 1976, combined global sales of Today's English Version (*Good News*) New Testament and Bible (which is copyrighted by the bible societies) have exceeded 111.3 million copies. Apart from the King James version (averaging some 13 million copies printed annually), there are at least 14 other copyrights on other versions of the Bible. The oldest publisher of bibles is the Cambridge University Press, which began with the Geneva version in 1591.

Excluding versions of the Bible, the world's all-time best-selling book is *The Guinness Book of Records,* first published in October 1955 by the

Guinness Brewery and edited by Norris Dewar McWhirter (b. 12 Aug. 1925) and his twin brother Alan Ross McWhirter (killed 27 Nov. 1975). Global sales in 40 languages surpassed 65 million in October 1990.

Best-seller lists The longest duration on the *New York Times* best-seller list (founded 1935) has been for *The Road Less Traveled* by M. Scott Peck, which on 2 Oct. 1988 had its 258th week on the lists.

Fiction It is difficult to state with certainty which single work has the highest sales, but two novels are considered contenders. *Valley of the Dolls* (first published March 1966) by Jacqueline Susann (Mrs. Irving Mansfield; 1921–74) sold a worldwide total of 28,712,000 to 30 Mar. 1987. In the first six months Bantam sold 6.8 million copies.

Alistair Stuart MacLean (1922–87) wrote 30 books that have been translated into 28 languages, and 13 have been filmed. It has been estimated that a MacLean novel is purchased every 18 seconds.

PUBLISHERS AND PRINTERS

Oldest publisher Cambridge University Press has a continuous history of printing and publishing since 1584. The University received a Royal Letters Patent to print and sell all manner of books on 20 July 1534.

In 1978 the Oxford University Press (OUP) celebrated the 500th anniversary of the printing of the first book in the City of Oxford, Great Britain in 1478. This was before OUP itself was in existence.

United States The firm of Lea Febiger of Malvern, PA (founded as Matthew Carey) has a continuous history of publishing since 1785.

Most prolific publisher At its peak in 1989, Progress Publishers (founded in 1931 as the Publishing Association of Foreign Workers in the former USSR) of Moscow, Russia printed over 750 titles in 50 languages annually.

Largest publisher The world's largest publishing company is Time Warner of New York. It has 9,600 employees, and sales in 1991 totaled $3.0 billion.

Fastest publisher A thousand bound copies of Sir Frederick Mason's village history *Ropley—Past and Present* were produced in 12 hrs. 26 min. from raw disk by publishers Scriptmate Editions in conjunction with printers Scan Laser Ltd.

Largest printer The largest printers in the world are believed to be R.R. Donnelley & Sons Co. of Chicago, IL. The company, founded in 1864, has nearly 100 manufacturing facilities, offices, service centers and subsidiaries worldwide, turning out $3.9 billion worth of work in 1991.

The largest printer under one roof is the United States Government Printing Office (founded 1861) in Washington, D.C. Encompassing 34.4 acres of floor space, the central office processes an average of 1,464 print orders daily, and uses 93.2 million lbs. of paper annually. The Superintendent of Documents sells approximately $83.2 million worth of

US government publications every year and maintains an inventory of over 16,000 titles in print.

HIGHEST PRINTINGS

It is believed that in the United States, Van Antwerp Bragg and Co. printed some 60 million copies of the 1879 edition of *The McGuffey Reader*, compiled by Henry Vail in the pre-copyright era for distribution to public schools.

The total dispersal through noncommercial channels by Jehovah's Witnesses of *The Truth that Leads to Eternal Life*, published by the Watchtower Bible and Tract Society of New York City on 8 May 1968, reached 107,073,279 in 117 languages by April 1991.

Largest print order   The initial print order for the 1990/91 Automobile Association (Great Britain) *Members' Handbook* was 6,153,000 copies. Stacked on top of each other, this would be seven times the height of Mt. Everest. The total printed since 1908 is 97,673,000, and it is currently printed by web offset by Petty & Sons Ltd. of Leeds, Great Britain and Jarrolds Printing Ltd. of Norwich, Great Britain.

Bookstore   The bookstore with the most titles and the longest shelving (30 miles) in the world is W. & G. Foyle Ltd. of London, Great Britain. First established in 1904 in a small store, the company now has a site of 75,825 ft.^{2}. The most capacious individual bookstore in the world measured by square footage is the Barnes & Noble Bookstore at 105 Fifth Ave at 18th Street, New York City. It covers 154,250 ft.^{2} and has 12.87 miles of shelving.

Public relations   The world's largest public relations firm is Burson Marsteller. Based in New York, the company had a net fee income of $210.372 million in 1990. Burson Marsteller operates 62 offices worldwide with a staff of 2,299.

Hill and Knowlton Inc. has most offices worldwide, with 68, in 25 countries. The company generated a net fee income solely within the United States of $119.66 million for 1990.

Slowest seller   The prize for the world's slowest-selling book (a category known in publishing as slooow sellers) probably belongs to David Wilkins' translation of the New Testament from Coptic into Latin, published by Oxford University Press (OUP) in 1716 in a printing of 500 copies. Selling an average of one each 20 weeks, it remained in print for 191 years.

Most durable advertiser   The Jos Neel Co., a clothing store in Macon, GA (founded 1880) has run an ad in the *Macon Telegraph* every day in the upper-left corner of page 2 since 22 Feb. 1889.

LIBRARIES

Earliest   One of the earliest-known collections of archival material was that of King Ashurbanipal at Nineveh (668–627 B.C.). He had clay tablets referring to events and personages as far back as the Dynasty of Agode *c.* 23rd century B.C.

United States   The first library in America was established at Harvard University in 1638. The first subscription library in the country was the Philadelphia Library Company in 1731. The first library in America that meets the definition of a modern public library was in Peterboro, NH, established on 9 Apr. 1833. The Peterboro Town Library was the first free public library in the country and was tax-supported with $750 from the New Hampshire State Literary Fund. The original collection contained 700 books, mainly religious, historical, biographical and educational works. The current collection of Peterboro Library numbers 49,000 books, and circulation is automated.

Largest   The United States Library of Congress (founded on 24 Apr. 1800) in Washington, D.C. contains 98,636,944 items, including 15,374,079 books in the classified collections and 83,262,865 items in the nonclassified collections. The library occupies approximately 2.85 million ft.^{2} of space in the three Capitol Hill buildings. Additionally, the library has some 350,000 ft.^{2} of space in six different remote locations. As of May 1991 there were 575 miles of shelving.

The largest nonstatutory library in the world is the New York Public Library (founded 1895) on Fifth Avenue, New York City with a floor space of 525,276 ft.^{2} and 88 miles of shelving, plus an underground extension with the capacity for an additional 92 miles. Its collection, including 82 branch libraries, embraces 13,887,774 volumes, 18,349,585 manuscripts and 381,645 maps.

The largest public library in the United States is the Harold Washington Library Center, Chicago, IL, which opened on 7 Oct. 1991. The tenstory, 750,000 ft.^{2} building contains 70.8 miles of bookshelves and cost $144 million. The collection includes 2 million books, 8,585 periodical titles, nearly 900,000 government documents, 100,000 pamphlets, 3.4 million microforms and 1.6 million recordings, audiovisual aids, picture files and sheet music.

Overdue books   The record for an unreturned and overdue library book was set when a book in German on the Archbishop of Bremen, published in 1609, was borrowed from Sidney Sussex College, Cambridge, Great Britain by Colonel Robert Walpole in 1667–68. It was found by Prof. Sir John Plumb in the library of the then-Marquess of Cholmondeley at Houghton Hall, Norfolk, Great Britain and returned 288 years later.

The most overdue book in the United States was a book on febrile diseases checked out in 1823 from the University of Cincinnati Medical Library and returned 7 Dec. 1968 by the borrower's great-grandson Richard Dodd. The calculated fine of $2,264 was waived.

MUSEUMS

Oldest   The world's oldest extant museum is the Ashmolean in Oxford, Great Britain, built between 1679 and 1683 and named after the collector Elias Ashmole (1617–92). Since 1924 it has housed an exhibition of historic scientific instruments.

Largest   The Smithsonian Institution comprises 15 museums containing over 139 million items and has 6,000 employees.

The American Museum of Natural History in New York City was founded in 1869 and comprises 22 interconnected buildings in an 18-acre park. The buildings of the museum and the planetarium contain 1.2 million ft.^{2} of floor space, accommodating more than 30 million artifacts and specimens. Its exhibits are viewed by more than 3 million visitors each year.

Most popular   The highest attendance for any museum is that at the Smithsonian's National Air and Space Museum, Washington, D.C., opened in July 1976. The record-setting day on 14 Apr. 1984, with an attendance of over 118,437, required the doors to be temporarily closed.

NEWSPAPERS

Oldest   A copy has survived of a news pamphlet published in Cologne, Germany in 1470. The oldest existing newspaper in the world is the Swedish official journal *Post och Inrikes Tidningar*, founded in 1645 and published by the Royal Swedish Academy of Letters. The oldest existing commercial newspaper is the *Haarlems Dagblad/Oprechte Haarlemsche Courant*, published in Haarlem, Netherlands, first issued as the *Weeckelycke Courante van Europa* on 8 Jan. 1656. A copy of issue No. 1 survives.

United States   The oldest continuously published newspaper in the United States is the *Hartford Courant*, established by Thomas Greene on 29 Oct. 1764. Originally a weekly four-page newspaper, it had an estimated circulation of 8,000 during the American Revolution, when it printed the Declaration of Independence and the Constitution. In 1836 the *Courant* became a daily newspaper and in 1913 started a Sunday edition. It was acquired by the Times Mirror organization in 1979 and has outlasted 40 other newspapers published at one time or another out of Hartford. Its current circulation figures are 234,285 daily and 326,884 Sunday papers, as of March 1992.

The oldest continuously published daily newspaper in the United States is the *New York Post*, established as the *New York Evening Post* by Alexander Hamilton on 16 Nov. 1801. Originally four pages, the newspaper had an estimated circulation of 600 in 1801. Its current circulation is 491,326, as of 30 Apr. 1992.

Largest   The most massive single issue of a newspaper has been of the Sunday *New York Times*, which weighed 12 lbs. and contained 1,612 pages, on 14 Sep. 1987. The largest page size ever used was 51 × 35 in. for *The Constellation*, printed in 1859 by George Roberts as part of the July 4th celebrations in New York City.

Smallest   The smallest original page size was the 3 × 3¾ in. of the

Daily Banner (25 cents per month) of Roseberg, OR, issues of which, dated 1 and 2 Feb. 1876, survive. The British Library Newspaper Library contains the *Watford News and Advertiser* of 1 Apr. 1899, which measures 2.9 × 3.9 in.

Longest editorship   Sir Etienne Dupuch (b. 16 Feb. 1899) of Nassau, Bahamas was editor-in-chief of *The Tribune* from 1 Apr. 1919 to 1972, and a contributing editor until his death on 23 Aug. 1991, a total of 72 years.

Most Pulitzer prizes   The *New York Times* has won 65 Pulitzer prizes, more than any other news organization. The Pulitzer is the highest award given annually for American journalism and arts.

Most durable feature   Eric Hardy of Liverpool, Great Britain is in his 65th year as a regular natural history contributor to the *Daily Post* of Liverpool, Great Britain, with a weekly "Countryside" feature.

Most syndicated columnist   Ann Landers (nee Eppie Lederer, b. 4 July 1918) appears in over 1,200 newspapers with an estimated readership of 90 million. Her only serious rival is "Dear Abby" (Mrs Pauline Phillips), her identical twin sister based in Beverly Hills, CA.

Cartoon strips *Earliest*   "The Yellow Kid" first appeared in the *New York Journal* on 18 Oct. 1896.

Most durable   The longest-lived newspaper comic strip is "The Katzenjammer Kids" (Hans and Fritz), created by Rudolph Dirks and first published in the *New York Journal* on 12 Dec. 1897.

Most successful   "Peanuts" by Charles Schulz of Santa Rosa, CA, first published in October 1950, currently appears in 2,300 newspapers in 68 countries and 26 languages. In 1990 Schulz's income was estimated at $5 million per month.

CIRCULATION

In 1991 the total number of morning and evening newspapers published in the United States was 1,586 with a total circulation of 60,689,183. There were 825 Sunday newspapers with a circulation of 62,067,820. The peak year for US newspapers was 1910, when there were 2,202.

The country with the leading number of newspaper readers in the world is Sweden, where 580 newspapers are sold for every 1,000 people.

Earliest million   The first newspaper to achieve a circulation of one million copies was *Le Petit Journal*, published in Paris, France, which reached this figure in 1886, when selling at 5 centimes.

Highest   The highest circulation for any newspaper in the world was that for *Komsomolskaya Pravda* (founded 1925), the youth paper of the former Soviet Communist Party, which reached a peak daily circulation of 21,975,000 copies in May 1990. The eight-page weekly newspaper *Argumenty i Fakty* (founded 1978) of Moscow, Russia attained a figure of 33,431,100 copies in May 1990 when it had an estimated readership of over 100 million.

United States The highest-circulation daily newspaper in the United States is the *Wall Street Journal* (founded 1889), published by Dow Jones & Co. As of March 1992, circulation was 1,852,863 copies.

Most read The national newspaper that achieves the closest to a saturation circulation is the *Sunday Post*, established in Glasgow, Great Britain in 1914. In 1989 its estimated readership in Scotland of 2,213,000 represented 54 percent of the entire population aged 15 and over. The *Arran Banner* (founded March 1974) has a readership of 97+ percent on Britain's seventh largest offshore island.

PERIODICALS

Oldest The oldest continuing periodical in the world is *Philosophical Transactions of the Royal Society*, published in London, Great Britain, which first appeared on 6 Mar. 1665.

United States The oldest continuously published periodical in the United States is *The Old Farmer's Almanac*, started in Massachusetts by Robert Thomas, a teacher and amateur astronomer, in 1792. *The Farmers Almanac*, as it was called originally, changed to its current title in 1848. The 200th edition was brought out in September, 1991. This anniversary edition required 3 million pounds of paper to produce a press run of 7.5 million, which is 3 million higher than last year's issue. The *Almanac* has an estimated readership of 70 million.

Largest circulations The peak circulation of any weekly periodical was achieved by *TV Guide*, which in 1974 became the first magazine to sell a billion copies in a year. As of March 1992 it had a circulation of 15.67 million. The world's highest-circulation magazine is currently *Modern Maturity*, with a figure as of March 1992 of 22.45 million.

In its 41 basic international editions, *Reader's Digest* (established February 1922) circulates 28.5 million copies monthly in 17 languages, including a US edition of more than 16.31 million copies and a Great Britain edition (established 1939) of over 1.5 million copies (ABC July–December 1990). *Parade*, the syndicated color magazine, is distributed with a record 343 US newspapers every Sunday, giving a peak circulation in July 1991 of 36.4 million.

Largest The bulkiest consumer magazine ever published was the January 1992 issue of *Hong Kong Toys*, running to 1,356 pages. Published by the Hong Kong Trade Development Council, it retails for HK$100 (about $12.50).

CROSSWORDS

Earliest Opinions differ on what constitutes a true crossword as distinct from other forms of word puzzle, but the earliest contender is considered to be a 25-letter acrostic of Roman provenance discovered on a wall in Cirencester, Great Britain in 1868. Another possible contender is an example of "blended squares," published in the women's magazine

The People's Home Journal in September 1904. The modern crossword is believed to have evolved from Arthur Wynne's "Word Cross," published in the Sunday *New York World* on 21 Dec. 1913.

Largest published   In July 1982 Robert Turcot of Québec, Canada compiled a crossword puzzle comprising 82,951 squares. It contained 12,489 clues across, 13,125 down and covered 38.28 ft.^{2}.

Compilers   The most prolific compiler is Roger F. Squires of Ironbridge, Great Britain, who compiles 42 published puzzles single-handedly each week. His total output to September 1991 was over 37,500 puzzles, and his millionth clue was published in the *Daily Telegraph* (London) on 6 Sep. 1989.

Fastest crossword solution   The fastest recorded time for completing *The Times* (London) crossword under test conditions is 3 min. 45 sec. by Roy Dean of Bromley, Great Britain, in the British Broadcasting Corporation *Today* radio studio on 19 Dec. 1970.

Dr. John Sykes won *The Times/Collins Dictionaries* championship ten times between 1972 and 1990, when he solved each of the four puzzles in an average time of 8 min. and beat the field by a record margin of 9½ min. on 8 Sep. at the Hilton Hotel, London, Great Britain. He set a championship best time of 4 min. 28 sec. in 1989.

Slowest solution   In May 1966 *The Times* of London received an announcement from a Fijian woman that she had just succeeded in completing their crossword No. 673, published in the issue of 4 Apr. 1932. As her husband, D.T. Lloyd disclosed in a letter to *The Times* on 8 Feb. 1990, he and his wife were stationed in Fiji by the British government. The problem wasn't that the puzzle was so fiendishly difficult—it was just that it had been used to wrap a package, and had subsequently lain uncompleted for 34 years.

MUSIC

Whistles and flutes made from perforated phalange bones (parts of fingers or toes) have been found at Upper Paleolithic sites of the Aurignacian period (c. 25,000–22,000 B.C.) at Istallóskö, Hungary and in Moldova.

A heptatonic scale deciphered from a clay tablet by Dr. Duchesne-Guillemin in 1966–67 was found at a site in Nippur, Sumer, now Iraq. Musical history can, however, be traced back to the third millennium B.C., when the yellow bell (*huang zhong*) had a recognized standard musical tone in Chinese temple music.

The human voice   Before this century the extremes were a staccato E in *altaltissimo* (e^{iv}) by Ellen Beach Yaw (1869–1947) in Carnegie Hall, New York City on 19 Jan. 1896, and an A_1 (55 Hz [cycles per sec.]) by Kasper Foster (1617–73).

Madeleine Marie Robin (1918–60), the French operatic coloratura, could produce and sustain the B above high C in the Lucia mad scene in Donizetti's *Lucia di Lammermoor*. Since 1950 singers have achieved high and low notes far beyond formerly accepted extremes. However, notes at the bass and treble extremities of the register tend to lack harmonics and are of little musical value. Ivan Rebroff, the German singer, has a voice which extends easily over four octaves from a low F to a high F, one and a quarter octaves above C.

The highest note put into song is G^{iv}, occurring in Mozart's *Popoli di Tessaglia*. The lowest vocal note in the classical repertoire is in Mozart's *Die Entführung aus dem Serail* in Osmin's aria, which calls for a low D (73.4 Hz).

Most durable musicians   The Romanian pianist Cual Delavrancea (1887–1991) gave her last public recital, receiving six encores, at the age of 103. The longest international career in the history of Western music is held by Polish pianist Mieczyslaw Horszowski (b. July 1892), who played for Emperor Franz-Joseph in Vienna, Austria in 1899 and was still playing in 1989.

The world's oldest active musician is Jennie Newhouse (b. 12 July 1889) of High Bentham, Great Britain, who has been the regular organist at the church of St. Boniface in Bentham since 1920.

INSTRUMENTS

Earliest piano   The earliest piano-forte in existence is one built in Florence, Italy in 1720 by Bartolommeo Cristofori (1655–1731) of Padua, and now preserved in the Metropolitan Museum of Art, New York City.

Grandest piano   The grandest grand piano was one of 1.4 tons and 11 ft. 8 in. in length made by Chas H. Challen & Son Ltd. of London, Great Britain in 1935. The longest bass string measured 9 ft. 11 in., with a tensile strength of 33 tons.

Most expensive piano   The highest price ever paid for a piano was $390,000 at Sotheby Parke Bernet, New York City on 26 Mar. 1980 for a Steinway grand of *c.* 1888 sold by the Martin Beck Theater. It was bought by a non-pianist.

Largest organ   The largest and loudest musical instrument ever constructed is the now only partially functional Auditorium Organ in Atlantic City, NJ. Completed in 1930, this instrument had two consoles (one with seven manuals and another movable one with five), 1,477 stop controls and 33,112 pipes, ranging in tone from $\frac{1}{5}$ in. to the 64 ft. tone. It had the volume of 25 brass bands, with a range of seven octaves.

The world's largest fully functional organ is the six manual 30,067 pipe Grand Court Organ installed in the Wanamaker Store, Philadelphia, PA in 1911 and enlarged between then and 1930. It has a 64 ft. tone gravissima pipe.

The world's largest church organ is that in Passau Cathedral, Germany. It was completed in 1928 by D.F. Steinmeyer & Co. and has 16,000 pipes and five manuals. The chapel organ at the United States Military Academy at West Point, NY has, since 1911, been expanded from 2,406 to 18,200 pipes.

The world's most powerful electronic organ is Robert A. Nye's 7,000-watt "Golden Spirit" organ, designed by Henry N. Hunsicker. It has 700 speakers and made its public concert debut in Trump Castle, Atlantic City, NJ on 9 Dec. 1988.

Loudest organ stop   The Ophicleide stop of the Grand Great in the Solo Organ in the Atlantic City Auditorium (see above) is operated by a pressure of water $3\frac{1}{2}$ lbs./in.^{2} and has a pure trumpet note of ear-splitting volume, more than six times the volume of the loudest locomotive whistles.

Largest pan pipes   The world's largest pan pipes, created by Simon Desorgher and Lawrence Casserley, consist of five contrabass pipes, each 4 in. in diameter, with lengths of 19 in., 16 in., 14 in., 12 in. and 10 in. respectively, and five bass pipes of 2 in. diameter with lengths of 9.5 in., 8 in., 7 in., 6 in. and 5 in. Their first public appearance was at Jubilee Gardens, London, Great Britain on 9 July 1988.

Largest brass instrument   The largest recorded brass instrument is a tuba standing $7\frac{1}{2}$ ft. tall, with 39 ft. of tubing and a bell 3 ft. 4 in. across. This contrabass tuba was constructed for a world tour by the band of American composer John Philip Sousa (1854–1932), *c*. 1896–98.

Largest stringed instrument   The largest movable stringed instrument ever constructed was a pantaleon with 270 strings stretched over 50 ft.^{2} used by George Noel in 1767. The greatest number of musicians required to operate a single instrument was the six required to play the gigantic orchestrion, known as the Apollonican, built in 1816 and played until 1840.

Largest double bass   A double bass measuring 14 ft. tall was built in 1924 in Ironia, NJ by Arthur K. Ferris, allegedly on orders from the Archangel Gabriel. It weighed 1,301 lbs. with a sound box 8 ft. across, and had leather strings totaling 104 ft. Its low notes could be felt rather than heard.

Guitar *Largest*   The largest playable guitar in the world is 38 ft. 2 in. tall, 16 ft. wide and weighs 1,865 lbs. Modeled on the Gibson "Flying V," it was made by students of Shakamak High School in Jasonville, IN. The instrument was unveiled on 17 May 1991 when, powered by six amplifiers, it was played simultaneously by six members of the school.

Most expensive   A Fender Stratocaster belonging to legendary rock guitarist Jimi Hendrix (1942–70) was sold by his former drummer Mitch

Mitchell to an anonymous buyer for £198,000 ($338,580) at Sotheby's, London on 25 Apr. 1990.

Most valuable violin   The highest price paid at auction for a violin is £902,000 ($1.7 million) for the 1720 "Mendelssohn" Stradivarius, named after the German banking family who were descendants of the composer. It was sold to a mystery buyer at Christie's, London on 21 Nov. 1990.

Most valuable cello   The highest auction price for a violoncello is £682,000 (approximately $1.2 million) at Sotheby's, London on 22 June 1988 for a Stradivarius known as "The Cholmondeley," which was made in Cremona, Italy *c.* 1698.

Largest drum   A drum with a 13 ft. diameter was built by the Supreme Drum Co., London, Great Britain and played at the Royal Festival Hall, London on 31 May 1987.

Double bass playing   Sixteen musicians from Blandford, Dorset, Great Britain played a double bass simultaneously (five fingering and eleven bowing) in a rendition of Strauss' *Perpetuum Mobile* at Blandford Town Hall on 6 June 1989.

Guitar playing   The fastest guitar playing ever was by Rick Raven (b. Gary Clarke), who played 5,400 notes in a minute at the Jacobean Nite Club, Stockport, Great Britain on 27 Apr. 1989.

Drumming   Four hundred separate drums were played in 31.78 sec. by Rory Blackwell at Finlake Country Park, Chudleigh, Great Britain on 30 May 1988.

Largest drum kit   A drum kit consisting of 81 pieces — 45 drums, including six bass drums, 15 cymbals, five temple blocks, two triangles, two gongs, two sets of wind chimes, one solid bar chime, six assorted cowbells, a drum set tambourine, a vibra slap and an icebell—is owned by Darreld MacKenzie of Calgary, Alberta, Canada.

Longest alphorn   A 154 ft. 8 in. (excluding mouthpiece) long alphorn weighing 227 lbs. was completed by Swiss-born Peter Wutherich, of Boise, ID in December 1989. The diameter at the bell is 24½ in. and the sound takes 105.7 milliseconds to emerge from the bowl after entry into the mouthpiece.

Highest and lowest notes   The extremes of orchestral instruments (excluding the organ) range from a handbell tuned to g^v (6,272 cycles/sec.) to the sub-contrabass clarinet, which can reach C_{11} or 16.4 cycles/sec. The highest note on a standard pianoforte is c^v (4,186 cycles/sec.), which is also the violinist's limit. In 1873 a sub-double bassoon able to reach $B_{111}\pm$ or 14.6 cycles/sec. was constructed, but no surviving specimen is known.

The extremes for the organ are g^{vi} (the sixth G above middle C)

(12.544 cycles/sec.) and C₁₁₁ (8.12 cycles/sec.) obtainable from ¾ in. and 64 ft. pipes respectively.

SONGS

Oldest   The *shaduf* chant has been sung since time immemorial by irrigation workers on the human-powered, pivoted-rod bucket raisers of the Nile water mills (or *saqiyas*) in Egypt. The world's earliest surviving musical notation dates from *c.* 1800 B.C. An Assyrian love song, also *c.* 1800 B.C., to an Ugaritic god from a tablet of notation and lyric was reconstructed for an 11-string lyre at the University of California, Berkeley on 6 Mar. 1974.

The oldest-known harmonized music performed today is the English song *Sumer is icumen in,* which dates from *c.* 1240.

National anthems   The oldest national anthem is the *Kimigayo* of Japan, the words of which date from the 9th century, although the music was written in 1881. The oldest music belongs to the anthem of the Netherlands, *Vilhelmus,* which was written *c.* 1570.

The shortest anthems are those of Japan, Jordan and San Marino, each with only four lines. Of the 11 wordless national anthems, the oldest is that of Spain, dating from 1770.

Top songs   The most frequently sung songs in English are *Happy Birthday to You* (based on the original *Good Morning to All*), by Kentucky Sunday school teachers Mildred Hill and Patty Smith Hill of New York (written in 1893 and under copyright from 1935 to 2010); *For He's a*

OLDEST NATIONAL ANTHEM. The words of the *Kimigayo,* the Japanese national anthem, date from the 9th century. It is played here as the Japanese Emperor Akihito and Empress Michiko with other dignitaries await former Soviet President Mikhail Gorbachev at the Akaska Palace, Tokyo. (Photo: Rex Features)

Jolly Good Fellow (originally the French *Malbrouk*), known at least as early as 1781; and *Auld Lang Syne* (originally the Strathspey *I Fee'd a Lad at Michaelmass*), some words of which were written by Robert Burns (1759–1796). *Happy Birthday* was sung in space by the *Apollo IX* astronauts on 8 Mar. 1969.

Songwriters   The most successful songwriters in terms of number-one singles are John Lennon (1940–80) and Paul McCartney (b. 18 June 1942). McCartney is credited as writer on 32 number-one hits in the United States to Lennon's 26 (with 23 co-written), whereas Lennon authored 29 Great Britain number-ones to McCartney's 28 (25 co-written).

In the United States Barry Gibb of the Bee Gees has written or co-written 16 number-ones. The most successful female songwriter in the United States is Carole King (nee Carole Klein, 9 Feb. 1942) with eight number-ones.

Singers   Of great fortunes earned by singers, the highest on record are those of Enrico Caruso (1873–1921), the Italian tenor, whose estate was worth about $9 million at his death.

David Bowie drew a fee of $1.5 million for a single show at the US Festival in Glen Helen Regional Park, San Bernardino County, CA on 26 May 1983. The four-man Van Halen rock band attracted a matching fee.

Longest rendering of a national anthem   "God Save the King" was played nonstop 16 or 17 times by a German military band on the platform of Rathenau railroad station, Brandenburg, Germany on the morning of 9 Feb. 1909. The reason was that King Edward VII was struggling inside the train to put on the uniform of a German field-marshal before he could emerge.

Bottle orchestra   In an extraordinary display of oral campanology (bell ringing), the Brighton Bottle Orchestra—Terry Garoghan and Peter Miller—performed a musical medley on 444 Gordon's gin bottles at the Brighton International Festival, Great Britain on 21 May 1991. It took 18 hours to tune the bottles, and about 10 times the the normal rate of puff (90 breaths/min.) to play them.

HYMNS

Earliest   There are more than 950,000 Christian hymns in existence. The music and parts of the text of a hymn in the *Oxyrhynchus Papyri* from the second century are the earliest known hymnody. The earliest exactly datable hymn is the *Heyr Himna Smióur* (*Hear, the Maker of Heaven*) from 1208 by the Icelandic bard and chieftain Kolbeinn Tumason (1173–1208).

Longest   The *Hora novissima tempora pessima sunt; vigilemus* by Bernard of Cluny (mid-12th century) runs to 2,966 lines. The longest in

English is *The Sands of Time Are Sinking* by Anne Ross Cousin (nee Cundell, 1824–1906), which runs to 152 lines in full, though only 32 lines appear in the Methodist Hymn Book.

Most prolific hymnist Frances (Fanny) Jane van Alstyne (nee Crosby, 1820–1915) of the United States wrote 8,500 hymns and is reputed to have knocked off one hymn in 15 minutes.

Oldest choral society The oldest active choral society in the United States is the Handel and Haydn Society of Boston, which gave its first concert performance on Christmas Day 1815 at Stone Chapel (now King's Chapel). The Handel and Haydn Society also gave the first complete performance of The Messiah in the United States on 25 Dec. 1818 at Boylston Hall, Boston. It celebrated its 175th anniversary in 1990.

BELLS

Oldest The world's oldest bell is the tintinnabulum found in the Babylonian Palace of Nimrod in 1849 by Mr. (later Sir) Austen Henry Layard (1817–94), dating from *c.* 1100 B.C. The oldest-known tower bell is one in Pisa, Italy dated MCVI (1106).

United States The oldest bell in the United States is located at St. Stephens Episcopal Church in East Haddam, CT. The bell was cast in Spain in A.D. 815 and shipped to the United States in 1834.

Heaviest The Tsar Kolokol, cast by Russian brothers I.F. and M.I. Motorin on 25 Nov. 1735 in Moscow, weighs 222.6 tons, measures 22 ft. in diameter and 20 ft. high, and is 24 in. at its thickest point. The bell was cracked in a fire in 1737 and a fragment, weighing about 12.91 tons, was broken from it. The bell has stood, unrung, on a platform in the Kremlin in Moscow since 1836 with the broken section alongside.

The heaviest bell still in use is the Mingun bell, weighing 101 tons with a diameter of 16 ft. 8½ in. at the lip, in Mandalay, Myanmar (formerly Burma). The bell is struck by a teak boom from the outside. It was cast at Mingun late in the reign of King Bodawpaya (1782–1819). The heaviest swinging bell in the world is the Petersglocke in the southwest tower of Cologne Cathedral, Germany, cast in 1923, with a diameter of 11 ft. 1¾ in., weighing 28 tons.

United States The largest bell in the United States weighs 17 tons and hangs at St. Francis de Scelle church in Cincinnati, OH. It was cast *c.* 1895. The heaviest ring in the United States is that of 10 bells cast in 1963 for the Washington National Cathedral, Washington, D.C. The total bell weight is 13,682 lbs.—the heaviest bell weighs 3,588 lbs.

Peals A ringing peal is defined as a diatonic "ring" of five or more bells hung for full-circle change ringing. Of 5,517 rings so hung, only 92 are outside the British Isles. The heaviest ring in the world is that of 13 bells cast in 1938–39 for the Anglican Cathedral in Liverpool, Great Britain. The total bell weight is 18.5 tons, of which Emmanuel, the tenor bell note *A*, weighs 9,195 lbs.

Bell ringing Eight bells have been rung to their full "extent" (40,320 unrepeated changes) only once without relays. This took place in a bell foundry at Loughborough, Great Britain, beginning at 6:52 A.M. on 27 July 1963 and ending at 12:50 A.M. on 28 July, after 17 hrs. 58 min. The peal was composed by Kenneth Lewis of Altrincham, Great Britain, and the eight ringers were conducted by Robert B. Smith of Marple, Great Britain. Theoretically it would take 37 years 355 days to ring 12 bells (maximus) to their full extent of 479,001,600 changes.

The greatest number of peals (minimum of 5,000 changes, all in tower bells) rung in a year is 303, by Colin Turner of Abingdon, Great Britain in 1989.

The late George E. Fearn rang 2,666 peals from 1928 to May 1974. Matthew Lakin (1801–1899) was a regular bell-ringer at Tetney Church near Grimsby, Great Britain for 84 years.

Largest carillon The largest carillon (minimum of 23 bells) in the world is at Kirk in the Hills Presbyterian Church, Bloomfield, MI. The carillon is made up of 77 bells. *M*, the largest, weighs 8 tons.

ORCHESTRAS

Oldest The first modern symphony orchestra—basically four sections consisting of woodwind, brass, percussion and bowed string instruments—was founded at the court of Duke Karl Theodor at Mannheim, Germany in 1743. The oldest existing symphony orchestra, the Gewandhaus Orchestra of Leipzig, Germany, was also established in 1743. Originally known as the Grosses Concert and later as the Liebhaber-Concerte, its current name dates from 1781.

United States The oldest orchestra in the United States is the Philharmonic-Symphony Society of New York, which was founded by Ureli Corelli Hill in 1842. It was established in the same year as the Vienna Symphony Orchestra and both will celebrate their sesquicentennial in 1992/93.

Largest On 17 June 1872, Johann Strauss the younger (1825–99) conducted an orchestra of 987 pieces supported by a choir of 20,000, at the World Peace Jubilee in Boston, MA. The number of first violinists was 400.

On 4 Nov. 1990 a 1,500-piece orchestra consisting of 13 youth orchestras from Mexico and Venezuela gave a full concert, including works by Handel, Tchaikovsky, Beethoven and Dvorak, under the baton of Mexican conductor Fernando Lozano at the Magdalena Mixhiuca Sports Center, Mexico City.

Largest band The most massive band ever assembled was one of 20,100 players at the Ullevaal Stadium, Oslo, Norway from Norges Musikkorps Forbund bands on 28 June 1964.

One-man band Rory Blackwell, of Starcross, Great Britain, aided by his double left-footed perpendicular percussion-pounder, plus his three-tier right-footed horizontal 22-pronged differential beater, and his 12-outlet bellow-powered horn-blower, played 108 different instruments (19 melody and 89 percussion) simultaneously in Dawlish, Great Britain on

29 May 1989. He also played 314 instruments in a single rendition in 1 min. 23.07 sec., again at Dawlish, on 27 May 1985.

Marching band   The largest marching band was one of 4,524, including 1,342 majorettes, under the direction of entertainer Danny Kaye (1913–87) at Dodger Stadium, Los Angeles, CA on 15 Apr. 1985.

Musical march   The longest recorded musical march was one of 46.7 miles, by members of showband Marum, a Dutch marching band, who walked from Assen to Marum, Netherlands on 9 May 1992. Of the 60 people who started, 52 managed to complete the march in 13 hrs. 50 min.

Conductors   The Austrian conductor Herbert von Karajan (1908–89), principal conductor of the Berlin Philharmonic Orchestra for 35 years before his retirement from the position shortly before his death, was the most prolific conductor ever, having made over 800 recordings of all the major works. In addition to Berlin, Karajan had also led the Philharmonia of London, the Vienna State Opera and La Scala Opera of Milan.
    The 1991–92 season was the 58th for the Cork Symphony Orchestra (Cork, Republic of Ireland) under the baton of Dr. Aloys Fleischmann.
    Sir Georg Solti (b. 22 Oct. 1912), the Hungarian-born principal conductor of the Chicago Symphony Orchestra, has won a record 29 Grammy awards for his recordings. (See also Grammy awards.)

United States   The Chicago Symphony Orchestra was directed by Frederic Stock from 1905 until his death in 1942, a total of 37 seasons.

Largest choir   Excluding "singalongs" by stadium crowds, the greatest choir is one of 60,000, which sang in unison as a finale of a choral contest among 160,000 participants in Breslau, Germany on 2 Aug. 1937.

Singer's pulling power   In 1850, up to $653 was paid for a single seat at the US concerts of Johanna ("Jenny") Maria Lind (1820–87), the "Swedish nightingale." She had a range from g to e''', of which the middle register is still regarded as unrivaled.

CONCERT ATTENDANCES

Estimating the size of audiences at open-air events where no admission is paid is often left to the police, media reporters, promoters and publicity agents. Estimates therefore vary widely and there is no way to check the accuracy of claims.

Classical   An estimated record 800,000 attended a free open-air concert by the New York Philharmonic conducted by Zubin Mehta, on the Great Lawn of Central Park, New York City on 5 July 1986, as part of the Statue of Liberty Weekend.

Rock/pop festival   The best claim is believed to be 725,000 for Steve Wozniak's 1983 US Festival in San Bernardino, CA. The Woodstock Music and Art Fair held on 15–17 Aug. 1969 at Bethel, NY is thought to have attracted an audience of 300,000–500,000.

Solo performer The largest *paying* audience ever attracted by a solo performer was an estimated 180,000–184,000 in the Maracaña Stadium, Rio de Janeiro, Brazil to hear Paul McCartney (b. 1942) on 2 Apr. 1990. Jean-Michel Jarre, the *son et lumière* specialist, entertained an estimated audience of two million in Paris, France at a free Bastille Day concert in 1990.

Most successful concert tour The Rolling Stones' 1989 "Steel Wheels" North American tour earned an estimated $310 million and was attended by 3.2 million people in 30 cities.

Most successful concert series Michael Jackson sold out for seven nights at Wembley, London, Great Britain in the summer of 1988. The stadium has a capacity of 72,000, so a total of 504,000 people saw Jackson perform 14–16, 22–23 July and 26–27 Aug. 1988.

Largest concert On 21 July 1990, Potsdamer Platz, straddling East and West Berlin, was the site of the largest single rock concert in terms of participants and organization ever staged. Roger Waters' production of Pink Floyd's "The Wall" involved 600 people performing on a stage measuring 551 × 82 ft. at its highest point. An estimated 200,000 people gathered for the symbolic building and demolition of a wall made of 2,500 styrofoam blocks.

Musical chairs The largest game on record was one starting with 8,238 participants, ending with Xu Chong Wei on the last chair, which was held at the Anglo-Chinese School, Singapore on 5 Aug. 1989.

Baton twirling The greatest number of complete spins done between tossing a baton into the air and catching it is 10, by Donald Garcia, on the British Broadcasting Corporation *Record Breakers* TV program on 9 Dec. 1986.
  The record for women is seven, shared by Lisa Fedick on the same program; Joanne Holloway, at Great Britain National Baton Twirling Association Championships in Paignton, Great Britain on 29 Oct. 1987; and Rachel Hayes on 18 Sep. 1988, also later shown on the British Broadcasting Corporation *Record Breakers* TV program.

Fastest rapper Tung Twista rapped 597 syllables in under 60 sec. at INS recording studio in New York City on 20 May 1992.

Longest silence The longest interval between the known composition of a piece by a major composer and its performance in the manner intended is from 3 Mar. 1791 until 9 Oct. 1982 (over 191 years), in the case of Mozart's *Organ Piece for a Clock,* a fugue fantasy in F minor (K 608), arranged by the organ builders Wm. Hill & Son and Norman & Beard Ltd. at Glyndebourne, Great Britain.

COMPOSERS

Most prolific   The most prolific composer of all time was probably Georg Philipp Telemann (1681–1767) of Germany. He composed 12 complete sets of services (one cantata every Sunday) for a year, 78 services for special occasions, 40 operas, 600 to 700 orchestral suites, 44 passions, plus concertos and chamber music. The most prolific symphonist was Johann Melchior Molter (*c.* 1695–1765) of Germany, who wrote 169 symphonies. Franz Joseph Haydn (1732–1809) of Austria wrote 108 numbered symphonies, many of which are regularly played today.

Longest symphony   The longest single classical symphony is the orchestral Symphony No. 3 in D minor by Gustav Mahler (1860–1911) of Austria. This work, composed in 1896, requires a contralto, a women's and a boys' choir in addition to a full orchestra. A full performance requires 1 hr. 40 min., of which the first movement alone takes between 30 and 36 min.

The Symphony No. 2 (the Gothic), composed from 1919–22 by British-born William Havergal Brian (1876–1972), was played by over 800 performers (four brass bands) in the Victoria Hall, Hanley, Staffordshire, Great Britain on 21 May 1978 (conductor Trevor Stokes). A recent broadcast required 1 hr. 45½ min. Brian wrote an even vaster work based on Shelley's "Prometheus Unbound" lasting 4 hrs. 11 min., but the full score has been missing since 1961.

The symphony *Victory at Sea*, written by US composer Richard Rodgers (1902–1979) and arranged by Robert Russell Bennett for NBC TV in 1952, lasted 13 hours.

Longest piano composition   The longest continuous nonrepetitious piano piece ever published is *The Well-Tuned Piano* by La Monte Young, first presented by the Dia Art Foundation at the Concert Hall, Harrison St., New York City on 28 Feb. 1980. The piece lasted 4 hrs. 12 min. 10 sec.

Symphonic Variations, composed in the 1930s for piano and orchestra by the British-born Kaikhosru Shapurji Sorabji (1892–1988) on 500 pages of close manuscript in three volumes, would last for six hours at the prescribed tempo.

PERFORMERS

Highest-paid pianists   Wladziu Valentino Liberace (1917–87) earned more than $2 million each 26-week season, with a peak of $138,000 for a single night's performance at Madison Square Garden, New York City in 1954. The highest-paid classical concert pianist was Ignace Jan Paderewski (1860–1941), Prime Minister of Poland (1919–20), who accumulated a fortune estimated at $5 million, of which $500,000 was earned in a single season in 1922/23.

The pianist Artur Rubinstein (1887–1982) between 1937 and 1976 commanded 70 percent of the gross from his concerts.

Largest contracts   It was reported on 21 Mar. 1991 that Michael Jackson (b. 29 Aug. 1958) had signed a 15-year contract worth $890 million with the Sony Corporation of Japan for a series of music, television and film projects. Not wanting to be left out, in the same month Michael's sister Janet signed a deal with Virgin Records reportedly worth $32 million for as few as two albums.

OPERA

Longest The longest of commonly performed operas is *Die Meistersinger von Nürnberg* by Wilhelm Richard Wagner (1813–83) of Germany. A normal uncut performance of this opera as performed by the Sadler's Wells company between 24 Aug. and 19 Sep. 1968 entailed 5 hrs. 15 min. of music. *The Heretics* by Gabriel von Wayditch (1888–1969), a Hungarian-American, is orchestrated for 110 pieces and lasts 8½ hrs.

Shortest The shortest opera published was *The Deliverance of Theseus* by Darius Milhaud (1892–1972), first performed in 1928, which lasted for 7 min. 27 sec.

Longest aria The longest single aria, in the sense of an operatic solo, is Brünnhilde's immolation scene in Wagner's *Götterdämmerung*. A well-known recording of this has been precisely timed at 14 min. 46 sec.

Youngest opera singer Ginetta Gloria La Bianca, born in Buffalo, NY on 12 May 1934, sang Rosina in *The Barber of Seville* at the Teatro dell' Opera, Rome, Italy on 8 May 1950 at the age of 15 years 361 days, having appeared as Gilda in *Rigoletto* at Velletri 45 days earlier.

Oldest opera singers The tenor Giovanni Martinelli sang Emperor Altoum in *Turandot* in Seattle, WA on 4 Feb. 1967 when he was 81. Danshi Toyotake (b. Yoshie Yokota, 1891–1989) of Hyogo, Japan sang *Musume Gidayu* (traditional Japanese narrative) for 91 years from the age of seven. Her professional career spanned 81 years.

Largest opera houses The Metropolitan Opera House, Lincoln Center, New York City, completed in September 1966 at a cost of $45.7 million, has a standing and seating capacity of 4,065 with 3,800 seats in an auditorium 451 ft. deep. The stage is 230 ft. wide and 148 ft. deep.

The tallest opera house is in a 42-story building on Wacker Drive in Chicago, IL, which houses the Chicago Lyric Opera Company. The Teatro della Scala (La Scala) in Milan, Italy shares with the Bolshoi Theatre in Moscow, Russia the distinction of having the greatest number of tiers.

Clapping The duration record for continuous clapping (sustaining an average of 160 claps per min., audible at 120 yds.) is 58 hrs. 9 min. by V. Jeyaraman of Tamil Nadu, India from 12–15 Feb. 1988.

Most curtain calls On 24 Feb. 1988 Luciano Pavarotti (b. 12 Oct. 1935) received 165 curtain calls and was applauded for 1 hr. 7 min. after singing the part of Nemorino in Gaetano Donizetti's *L'elisir d'Amore* at the Deutsche Oper in Berlin, Germany.

Classical Records

Music originated as far back as 3000 B.C. with the recognized standard musical tone of the bell in Chinese temple music, and the earliest surviving example of musical notation dates from *c.* 1800 B.C.

Compositionally speaking, the Classical period in music is usually defined as the "Viennese school" of the late 18th and early 19th centuries, but a certain degree of artistic license is exercised here.

Recordings
The best-selling classical album is *In Concert*, recorded by José Carreras, Placido Domingo and Luciano Pavarotti at the 1990 World Cup Finals in Rome, Italy, with global sales of five million copies.

Instruments The harp is the only solely finger-plucked instrument capable of creating enough sound to merit a regular place in a symphony orchestra. Tension in the strings can reach over 1,000 lb and the sound board is often up to 0.4 in thick to withstand this.

Conductors The most prolific conductor was Herbert von Karajan (1908–89), principal conductor of the Berlin Philharmonic Orchestra for 35 years, who made over 800 recordings of all the major works. He was also with the Philharmonia of London, the Vienna State Opera and La Scala Opera of Milan during his extensive career.

The most honored conductor is Sir Georg Solti (b. 22 Oct 1912), formerly with the Chicago Symphony Orchestra, who has won a record 29 Grammy awards (including a special Trustees' award) for his recordings since 1958.

The record for durability among professionals is held by Prof. Aloys Fleischmann, who has been principal conductor of the Cork Symphony Orchestra, Ireland, since 1935.

Most valuable instrument The auction record for any musical instrument is $1.7 million for the 1720 "Mendelssohn" Stradivarius violin sold at Christie's, London, Great Britain on 21 Nov 1990. The instrument is named after the German banking family who are descendants of the composer Felix Mendelssohn (1809–47).

Most recordings As the largest-ever recording project, in 1990–91 Philips Classics released the complete authenticated works of Wolfgang Amadeus Mozart (1765–91) on a set of 180 compact discs, representing over 200 hours of music. This was just part of a year-long tribute to the composer in the bicentennial of his death.

Orchestras The basic structure of the modern symphony orchestra dates from the court of Duke Karl Theodor at Mannheim, Germany in 1743, which is also the founding date of the oldest existing symphony—the Gewandhaus of Leipzig in Germany.

the Bach Family

JOHANN SEBASTIAN (20)
(1685–1750)

By Maria Barbara (7)   By Anna Magdalena (13)

WILHELM FRIEDEMANN
(1710–84)

CARL PHILIPP EMANUEL
(1714–88)

JOHANN GOTTFRIED BERNHARD
(1715–39)

JOHANN CHRISTOPH FRIEDRICH
(1732–95)

JOHANN CHRISTIAN
(1735–82)

WILHELM FRIEDRICH ERNST
(1759–1845)

Most extensive family The largest musical family is the Bach family, some 76 members of which are known, of whom 53 were named Johann. The most famous is undoubtedly Johann Sebastian (1685–1750), five of whose six surviving sons (from a total of 20 children from two marriages) were accomplished musicians and composers.

Composers The most prolific composer is Georg Philipp Telemann (1681–1767), who wrote over 2,000 works, including about 1,000 orchestral suites and even operas. He was considered Germany's leading composer during his lifetime, with a reputation far exceeding that of his friend and contemporary Johann Sebastian Bach.

The record for symphonic output is held by Johann Melchior Molter (1696–1765), Kapellmeister at the Karlsruhe court at Baden-Durlach and later at Eisenach, Germany, whose surviving instrumental works include over 170 symphonies. Almost as prolific and perhaps better known is Franz Joseph Haydn (1732–1809) of Austria, who wrote 108 numbered symphonies, many of which are still played regularly, the highest-numbered usually being 104.

Most durable musicians The Romanian pianist Cella Delavrancea (1887–1991) gave her last public recital, receiving six encores, at the age of 103. The oldest living concert performer is the Polish pianist Mieczyslaw Horszowski (b. July 1892), who played before Emperor Franz-Joseph in Vienna, Austria in 1899.

RECORD BREAKING COMPOSERS

Telemann

Mozart

Haydn

Molter

Above: The group of record-breaking composers is completed by the most valued, Ludwig van Beethoven (1770–1827), whose autograph copy of the Piano Sonata in E minor, opus 90 set the auction record for a single musical work when bought for $1.97 million at Sotheby's, London, Great Britain on 6 Dec 1991. This is surpassed only by the $4,394,500 paid at the same auction house on 22 May 1987 for a bound volume of nine complete symphonies in Mozart's hand.

First opera company   The first opera company in the United States was The American Company, founded in 1752 by Lewis Hallam. The oldest continuously performing opera company in the United States is the Metropolitan Opera Company of New York City; its first season was in 1883.

Longest operatic encore   The longest operatic encore listed in the *Concise Oxford Dictionary of Opera* was of the entire opera *Il Matrimonio Segreto* by Cimarosa at its premiere in 1792. This was at the command of the Austro-Hungarian emperor Leopold II (r. 1790–92).

BALLET

Fastest "entrechat douze"   In the *entrechat* (a vertical spring from the fifth position with the legs extended criss-crossing at the lower calf), the starting and finishing position each count as one, so that in an *entrechat douze* there are five crossings and uncrossings. This feat was performed by Wayne Sleep for the British Broadcasting Corporation *Record Breakers* TV program on 7 Jan. 1973. He was in the air for 0.71 sec.

Grands jetés   On 28 Nov. 1988, Wayne Sleep completed 158 grands jetés along the length of Dunston Staiths, Great Britain in 2 min.

Most turns   The greatest number of spins called for in classical ballet choreography is 32 *fouettés rond de jambe en tournant* in *Swan Lake* by Piotr Ilyich Tchaikovsky (1840–93). Delia Gray (Great Britain; b. 30 Oct. 1975) achieved 166 such turns during the Harlow Ballet School's summer workshop at The Playhouse, Harlow, Great Britain on 2 June 1991.

Most curtain calls   The greatest recorded number of curtain calls ever received is 89, by Dame Margot Fonteyn de Arias (nee Margaret Evelyn Hookham; 1919-91) and Rudolf Hametovich Nureyev (born on a train near Irkutsk, USSR, 17 Mar. 1938) after a performance of *Swan Lake* at the Vienna Staatsoper, Austria in October 1964.

DANCING

Marathon dancing must be distinguished from choreomania (dancing mania), or tarantism, which is a pathological condition. The worst outbreak of the latter was at Aachen, Germany in July 1374, when hordes of men and women broke into a frenzied and compulsive choreomania in the streets. It lasted for many hours until injury or complete exhaustion ensued.

Largest and longest dances   An estimated 30,000 people took part in a Madison/Electric Slide line dance held during the 1991 Comin' Home African American Holiday Celebration in Columbus, OH on 12 July 1991.

The most taxing marathon dance staged as a public spectacle was one by Mike Ritof and Edith Boudreaux, who logged 5,148 hrs. 28½ min. to win $2,000 at Chicago's Merry Garden Ballroom, Belmont and Sheffield, IL from 29 Aug. 1930 to 1 Apr. 1931. Rest periods were progressively cut from 20 to 10 to 5 to zero minutes per hour, with 10-inch steps and a maximum of 15 seconds for closure of eyes.

"Rosie Radiator" (Rose Marie Ostler) led an ensemble of 14 tap dancers through the streets of San Francisco, CA on 18 July 1987, covering a distance of 7¾ miles.

Ballroom   The world's most successful professional ballroom dancing champions have been Bill and Bobbie Irvine, who won 13 world titles between 1960 and 1968. The oldest competitive ballroom dancer was Albert J. Sylvester (1889–1989) of Corsham, Great Britain, who retired at the age of 94.

Conga   The longest recorded conga was the Miami Super Conga, held in conjunction with Calle Ocho—a party to which Cuban-Americans invite the rest of Miami for a celebration of life together. Held on 13 Mar. 1988, the conga line consisted of 119,986 people.

Country dancing   The largest Scottish country dance ever held was a 512-person reel, held in Toronto, Ontario, Canada on 17 Aug. 1991 and organized by the Toronto branch of the Royal Scottish Country Dance Society.

Dancing dragon   The longest dancing dragon, created for the 3rd International Abilympics in 1991, measured 3,023 ft. from the end of its tongue to the tip of its tail and took four months to construct. A total of 1,024 people brought the dragon to life, making it dance for two minutes at the Happy Valley racecourse, Hong Kong on 11 Aug. 1991.

Square dance calling   Alan Covacic called for 26 hrs. 2 min. for the Wheelers and Dealers Square Dance Club at RAF Halton, Aylesbury, Great Britain from 18–19 Nov. 1988.

Flamenco   The fastest flamenco dancer ever measured is Solero de Jerez, age 17, who in Brisbane, Australia in September 1967 attained 16 heel taps per second, in an electrifying routine.

Limbo   The lowest height for a bar (flaming) under which a limbo dancer has passed is 6 in. off the floor, by Dennis Walston, alias King Limbo, at Kent, WA on 2 Mar. 1991. Junior J. Renaud (b. 7 June 1954) became the first Official World Limbo Champion at the inaugural International Limbo Competition on 19 Feb. 1974 at Port of Spain, Trinidad.

The record for a performer on roller skates is 5⅛ in., achieved by Amitesh Durohit at the National sub-junior school championships held at Indore, Madhya Pradesh, India on 19 July 1991.

Tap   The fastest *rate* ever measured for tap dancing is 32 taps per second by Stephen Gare of Sutton Coldfield, Great Britain, at the Grand Hotel, Birmingham, Great Britain on 28 Mar. 1990.

Roy Castle (b. 1933), host of the British Broadcasting Corporation *Record Breakers* TV program, achieved one million taps in 23 hrs. 44 min. at the

Guinness World of Records exhibition, London, Great Britain on 31 Oct.–1 Nov. 1985.

The greatest-ever assemblage of tap dancers in a single routine numbered 5,622 outside Macy's department store at 34th Street and Sixth Avenue, New York City on 11 Aug. 1991.

RECORDED SOUND

Origins   The phonograph was first conceived by Charles Cros (1842–88), a French poet and scientist, who described his idea in sealed papers deposited with the French Academy of Sciences on 30 Apr. 1877. However, the realization of a practical device was first achieved by Thomas Alva Edison (1847–1931) of the United States.

The first successful wax cylinder machine was constructed by his mechanic, John Kruesi, on 4–6 Dec. 1877, demonstrated on 7 Dec. and patented on 19 Feb. 1878. The horizontal disc was introduced by Emile Berliner (1851–1929) and first demonstrated in Philadelphia on 18 May 1888.

Earliest recordings   The earliest voice recording is believed to be a speech made by Lord Stanley of Preston, governor-general of Canada, during the opening of the Toronto Industrial Exhibition on 11 Sep. 1888. Copies of this speech are held in the National Sound Archive, London, Great Britain.

Tape recording   Magnetic recording was invented by Valdemar Poulsen (1869–1942) of Denmark with his steel wire Telegraphone in 1898 (US Pat. No. 661619). Fritz Pfleumer (German Patent 500900) introduced tape in 1928. Tapes were first used at the Blattner Studios, Elstree, Great Britain in 1929. Plastic tapes were devised by BASF of Germany in 1932–35, but were first marketed in 1950 by Recording Associates of New York.

Oldest records   The British Broadcasting Corporation record library contains over one million recordings, with the oldest being white wax cylinders dating from 1888. The earliest commercial disc recording was manufactured in 1895.

Smallest functional record   Six titles of $1^5/_{16}$ in. diameter were recorded by HMV's studio at Hayes, Great Britain on 26 Jan. 1923 for Queen Mary's Doll House. Some 92,000 of these miniature records were pressed, including 35,000 of *God Save The King*.

Number one in most countries   The most successful singer on records is Madonna (Madonna Louise Veronica Ciccone, b. 16 Aug. 1959). Her album *True Blue*, with sales of over 17 million, was number one in 28 countries.

Most successful solo recording artist   No independently audited figures have ever been published for Elvis Aron Presley (1935–77). In view of Presley's worldwide tally of over 170 major hit singles and over 80 top-selling albums from 1956 continuing after his death, it may be assumed he must have succeeded Bing Crosby as the top-selling solo artist of all time.

On 9 June 1960 the Hollywood Chamber of Commerce presented Harry Lillis (alias Bing) Crosby Jr. (1904–77) with a platinum disc to commemorate the alleged sale of 200 million records from the 2,600 singles and 125 albums he had recorded. On 15 Sep. 1970 he received a second platinum disc when Decca claimed a sale of 300.6 million discs. No independently audited figures of his global lifetime sales have ever been published, and the figures are believed to be exaggerated.

Largest record store   HMV opened the world's largest record store at 150 Oxford Street, London, Great Britain on 24 Oct. 1986. Its trading area measures 36,684 ft.²

Phonographic identification   Dr. Arthur B. Lintgen (b. 1932) of Rydal, PA, has an as-yet unique and proven ability to identify the music on phonograph records purely by visual inspection without hearing a note.

Smallest recorder   In April 1983 Olympic Optical Industry Co. of Japan marketed a micro-cassette recorder measuring $4^1/_5 \times 2 \times \frac{1}{2}$ in. and weighing 4.4 oz.

Most successful group   The singers with the greatest sales of any group have been the Beatles. This group from Liverpool, Great Britain was comprised of George Harrison (b. 25 Feb. 1943), John Ono (formerly John Winston) Lennon (1940–1980), James Paul McCartney (b. 18 June 1942) and Richard Starkey, alias Ringo Starr (b. 7 July 1940). The all-time Beatles sales up to May 1985 have been estimated by EMI at over one billion discs and tapes. All four ex-Beatles sold many million more records as solo artists.

Earliest golden discs   The first actual golden disc was one sprayed by RCA Victor for the US trombonist and bandleader Alton "Glenn" Miller (1904–44) for his *Chattanooga Choo Choo* on 10 Feb. 1942.

The first record eventually to aggregate a total sale of a million copies was of performances by Enrico Caruso (b. Naples, Italy, 1873, d. 2 Aug. 1921) of the aria "*Vesti la giubba*" ("On with the Motley") from the opera *I Pagliacci* by Ruggiero Leoncavallo (1858–1919), the earliest version of which was recorded with piano on 12 Nov. 1902. The first single recording to surpass the million mark was *Carry Me Back to Old Virginny*, sung by Alma Gluck, on the Red Seal Victor label on the twelve-inch single-faced (later backed) record No. 74420.

Most golden discs   The only *audited* measure of gold, platinum and multiplatinum singles and albums within the United States is certification by the Recording Industry Association of America (RIAA), introduced on 14 Mar. 1958.

Out of the 5,943 RIAA awards (1,206 gold singles, 3,433 gold albums, 98 platinum singles and 1,206 platinum albums) made to 31 Dec. 1990, the Rolling Stones, with 55 (34 gold, 15 platinum, 6 multi-platinum) have the most for any group. The group with the most gold albums is the Rolling Stones, with 34. The group with the most multiplatinum albums is the Beatles with 11.

The individual artist to receive the most gold and platinum discs is Paul McCartney, with 75 (48 as a member of the Beatles, and 27 as a member of Wings, as a solo artist, and from duets with Stevie Wonder and Michael Jackson). The solo artist to receive the most awards is Elvis Presley (1935–77), with 56 (16 gold singles, 33 gold albums and 8 platinum albums). It is estimated that Presley's total of million-selling singles is 80 worldwide. The female solo artist to receive the most awards is Barbra Streisand, with 56 (7 gold singles, 30 gold albums and 19 platinum albums).

The first platinum album was awarded to the Eagles for *Greatest Hits, 1971–75* in 1976. The group Chicago holds the record for most platinum albums, with 17. Barbra Streisand holds the record for a solo artist, with 19, and the record for most multiplatinum, with seven. Paul McCartney holds the record for a male solo artist, with 12, while Billy Joel holds the record for the most multiplatinum albums for an individual, with eight.

Most recordings   In what is believed to be the largest-ever recording project devoted to a single composer, 180 compact discs containing the complete set of authenticated works by Mozart were produced by Philips Classics for release in 1990/91 to commemorate the bicentennial of the composer's death. The complete set comprises over 200 hours of music and would occupy 6½ ft. of shelving.

MOST GOLDEN DISCS. The Rolling Stones have received 55 awards from the Recording Industry Association of America (RIAA). This total is the most for any group and includes 34 gold albums, 15 platinum and six multiplatinum (for sales of two million or more). The current lineup is (from left to right) Ronnie Wood, Mick Jagger, Keith Richard, Charlie Watts and Bill Wyman. (Photo: Rex Features/Eugene Adebari)

Biggest sellers (singles)   The greatest seller of any phonograph record to date is *White Christmas* by Irving Berlin (b. Israel Bailin, 1888–1989), recorded by Bing Crosby on 29 May 1942. It was announced on Christmas Eve 1987 that North American sales alone reached 170,884,207 copies by 30 June 1987.

The highest claim for any "rock" record is an unaudited 25 million for *Rock Around the Clock*, copyrighted in 1953 by James E. Myers under the name Jimmy De Knight and the late Max C. Freedmann and recorded on 12 Apr. 1954 by Bill Haley (1927–1981) and the Comets.

Biggest sellers (albums)   The best-selling album of all time is *Thriller* by Michael Jackson (b. Gary, IN 29 Aug. 1958), with global sales of over 40 million copies by May 1990. The best-selling album by a group is Fleetwood Mac's *Rumours* with over 21 million sales by May 1990.

In Concert is the best-selling classical album, with sales of five million to date. It was recorded by José Carreras, Placido Domingo and Luciano Pavarotti at the 1990 Soccer World Cup Finals in Rome, Italy.

Whitney Houston by Whitney Houston, released in 1985, is the best-selling debut album of all time. It has sold over 14 million copies, including over nine million in the United States, one million in Great Britain, and a further million in Canada.

Soundtrack   The best-selling movie soundtrack is *Saturday Night Fever*, with sales of over 26.5 million by May 1987.

The charts (US singles)   Singles record charts were first published by *Billboard* on 20 July 1940, when the No. 1 single was *I'll Never Smile Again* by Tommy Dorsey (1905–56). *Near You* by Francis Craig stayed at the No. 1 spot for 17 weeks in 1947.

The Beatles have had the most No. 1's (20), Conway Twitty the most Country No. 1's (35) and Aretha Franklin the most Rhythm and Blues No. 1's (20). Aretha Franklin is also the female solo artist with the most million-selling singles, with 14 between 1967 and 1973. Elvis Presley has had the most hit singles on *Billboard*'s Hot 100—149 from 1956 to May 1990.

Bing Crosby's *White Christmas* spent a total of 72 weeks on the chart between 1942 and 1962, while *Tainted Love* by Soft Cell stayed on the chart for 43 *consecutive* weeks from January 1982.

The charts (US albums)   *Billboard* first published an album chart on 15 Mar. 1945, when the No. 1 was *King Cole Trio* featuring Nat "King" Cole (1919–65). *South Pacific* was No. 1 for 69 weeks (non-consecutive) from May 1949. *Dark Side of the Moon* by Pink Floyd enjoyed 730 weeks on the *Billboard* charts to April 1989.

Most Grammy awards   An all-time record 30 awards (including a special Trustees' award presented in 1967) have been won since 1958 by the British conductor Sir Georg Solti (b. Hungary; 21 Oct. 1912), while the Chicago Symphony now has 45. The greatest number won in a year is eight by Michael Jackson in 1984.

The Beatles had the most No. 1's (15), Elvis Presley was the most successful male soloist (nine), and Simon and Garfunkel the top duo with three. Elvis Presley has had the most hit albums (94 from 1956 to April 1989).

The woman with the most No. 1 albums (six), and most hit albums in total (40 between 1963 and April 1992), is Barbra Streisand, 30 of whose albums have been certified gold (500,000 sales) and 19 platinum (one million sales) by the RIAA, making Streisand the best-selling female singer of all time. (See Most golden discs.)

Fastest-selling   The fastest-selling non-pop record of all time is *John Fitzgerald Kennedy—A Memorial Album* (Premium Albums), recorded on 22 Nov. 1963, the day of President Kennedy's assassination, which sold 2.1 million copies at 99 cents in six days (7–12 Dec. 1963).

Advance sales   The greatest advance sale for a single worldwide is 2.1 million for *Can't Buy Me Love* by the Beatles, released on 21 Mar. 1964.

Compact discs   Announced by Philips in 1978 and introduced by the same company in 1982, the compact disc (CD) increasingly challenges the LP and cassette as a recording medium. The first CD to sell a million copies worldwide was Dire Straits' *Brothers in Arms* in 1986. It subsequently topped a million sales in Europe alone.

THEATER

Oldest   Theater in Europe has its origins in Greek drama performed in honor of a god, usually Dionysus. The earliest amphitheaters date from the 5th century B.C. The first stone-built theater in Rome, erected in 55 B.C., could accommodate 40,000 spectators.

Oldest indoor theater   The oldest indoor theater in the world is the Teatro Olimpico in Vicenza, Italy. Designed in the Roman style by Andrea di Pietro, alias Palladio (1508–80), it was begun three months before his death and finished by his pupil Vicenzo Scamozzi (1552–1616) in 1583. It is preserved today in its original form.

Largest   The world's largest building used for theater is the National People's Congress Building (*Ren min da hui tang*) on the west side of Tiananmen Square, Beijing, China. It was completed in 1959 and covers an area of 12.9 acres. The theater seats 10,000 and is occasionally used as such, as in 1964 for the play *The East Is Red*.

The theater with the largest capacity is the Perth Entertainment Center, Western Australia, completed in November 1976, with 8,003 seats. The stage area is 12,000 ft.^{2}.

United States   The highest-capacity theater currently in use on Broadway is the Gershwin Theater (formerly the Uris Theater), with 1,933 seats. Designed by Ralph Alswang, the theater opened on 28 Nov. 1972. Its name was changed on 5 June 1983 to honor the famed composer George Gershwin.

Most ardent theatergoer   Dr. H. Howard Hughes (b. 1902), Prof. Emeritus of Texas Wesleyan College, Fort Worth, TX attended 6,136 shows in the period 1956–87.

Gladiatorial combat   Emperor Trajan of Rome (A.D. 98–117) staged a display involving 4,941 pairs of gladiators over 117 days. Publius Ostorius, a freedman, survived 51 combats in Pompeii.

Lowest theater attendance   The ultimate in low attendance was in December 1983, when the comedy *Bag* in Grantham, Great Britain opened to a zero attendance.

Smallest   The smallest regularly operated professional theater in the world is the Piccolo in Juliusstrasse, Hamburg, Germany. It was founded in 1970 and has a maximum capacity of 30 seats.

Largest amphitheater   The Flavian amphitheater or Colosseum of Rome, Italy, completed in A.D. 80, covers five acres and has a capacity of 87,000. It has a maximum length of 612 ft. and a maximum width of 515 ft.

Largest stage   The largest stage in the world is in the Ziegfeld Room, Reno, NV, with 176 ft. passerelle, three main elevators each capable of raising 1,200 show girls (72 tons), two 62½-ft.-circumference turntables and 800 spotlights.

Longest runs   The longest continuous run of any show in the world is *The Mousetrap* by Dame Agatha Christie (nee Miller; 1890–1976). This thriller opened on 25 Nov. 1952 at the Ambassadors Theatre, London, Great Britain (capacity 453) and moved after 8,862 performances to the St. Martin's Theatre next door on 25 Mar. 1974. The 16,000th performance was on 6 May 1991, and the box office total was £20 million ($36 million) from more than nine million attenders.

The Vicksburg Theater Guild, MS has been playing the melodrama *Gold in the Hills* by J. Frank Davis discontinuously but every season since 1936.

Revue   The greatest number of performances of any theatrical presentation is 47,250 (to April 1986) in the case of *The Golden Horseshoe Revue*, a show staged at Disneyland, Anaheim, CA. It started on 16 July 1955 and closed on 12 Oct. 1986 after being seen by 16 million people. The main performers were Fulton Burley, Dick Hardwick (who replaced Wally Boag, who had appeared from the opening day until his retirement in 1983) and Betty Taylor, who played to as many as five houses a day in a routine that lasted 45 minutes.

Broadway   *A Chorus Line* opened on 25 July 1975 and closed on 28 Apr. 1990 after a record run of almost 15 years and 6,137 performances. It was created by Michael Bennett (1943–87).

Musical shows   The off-Broadway musical show *The Fantasticks* by Tom Jones and Harvey Schmidt opened on 3 May 1960, and the total number of performances to 26 Apr. 1992 is 13,270 at the Sullivan Street Playhouse, Greenwich Village, New York City.

Shortest runs   The shortest theatrical run on record was that of *The Intimate Revue* at the Duchess Theatre, London, Great Britain, on 11 Mar. 1930. Anything that could go wrong did. With scene changes taking up to 20 min. apiece, the management scrapped seven scenes to get the finale on before midnight. The run was described as "half a performance."

Greatest loss   The greatest loss sustained by a theatrical show was by the Royal Shakespeare Company's musical *Carrie*, which closed after five performances on Broadway on 17 May 1988 at a cost of $7 million. *King*, the musical about Martin Luther King, incurred a loss of £3 million ($5.04 million) in a six-week run ending on 2 June 1990, thus matching the record losses of *Ziegfeld* in 1988 in London, Great Britain.

Tony awards   Harold (Hal) S. Prince (b. 1928) has won 16 "Tonys"— the awards of the American Theater Wing, instituted on 6 Apr. 1947—the most of any individual. Prince has won eight awards as a producer, seven as a director and one special award. Three plays share the record for most Tonys, with five: *A Man for All Seasons* (1962), *Who's Afraid of Virginia Woolf?* (1963) and *Amadeus* (1981).

The only person to win five Tonys in a starring role is Julie Harris, in *I Am a Camera* (1952), *The Lark* (1956), *Forty Carats* (1969), *The Last of Mrs. Lincoln* (1973) and *The Belle of Amherst* (1977).

The record number of awards for a starring role in a musical is four, by Angela Lansbury: *Mame* (1966), *Dear World* (1969), *Gypsy* (1975) and *Sweeney Todd* (1979). Gwen Verdon has also won four Tonys; three in leading roles: *Damn Yankees* (1956), *New Girl in Town* (1958), *Redhead* (1959), and one in a supporting role, *Can-Can* (1954). The musical that has won the most awards is *Hello Dolly!* (1964), with 10.

One-man shows   The longest run of one-man shows is 849, by Victor Borge (b. Copenhagen, 3 Jan. 1909) in his *Comedy in Music* from 2 Oct. 1953 to 21 Jan. 1956 at the Golden Theater, Broadway, New York City.

The world aggregate record for one-man shows is 1,700 performances of *Brief Lives* by Roy Dotrice (b. Guernsey, 26 May 1923), including 400 straight at the Mayfair Theatre, London, Great Britain ending on 20 July 1974. He was on stage for more than 2½ hrs. per performance of this 17th-century monologue and required 3 hrs. for makeup and 1 hr. for removal of makeup, thus aggregating 40 weeks in the chair.

Most durable performer   Kanmi Fujiyama (b. 1929) played the lead role in 10,288 performances by the comedy company Sochiku Shikigeki from November 1966 to June 1983.

Advance sales   The musical *Miss Saigon*, produced by Cameron Mackintosh and starring Jonathan Pryce and Lea Salonga, opened on Broadway in April 1991 after generating record advance sales of $36 million.

Most roles   The greatest recorded number of theatrical, film and television roles portrayed is 3,385, from 1951 to March 1989, by Jan Leighton (USA).

GREATEST ADVANCE. The musical show *Miss Saigon* opened on Broadway in April 1991 after setting a box-office record of $36 million in advance ticket sales. (Photo: Rex Features/Le Poer Trench)

Theatrical roles   Kanzaburo Nakamura (b. July 1909) has performed in 806 Kabuki titles from November 1926 to January 1987. Since each title in this classical Japanese theatrical form lasts 25 days, he has therefore played 20,150 performances.

Shakespeare   The first all-amateur company to have staged all 37 plays was The Southsea Shakespeare Actors, Hampshire, Great Britain (founded 1947) in October 1966 when, under K. Edmonds Gateley, they presented *Cymbeline*. The longest Shakespeare play is *Hamlet*, with 4,042 lines and 29,551 words. Of Shakespeare's 1,277 speaking parts, the longest is Hamlet with 11,610 words.

Longest chorus line   The longest chorus line in performing history numbered up to 120 in some of the early *Ziegfeld Follies*. In the finale of *A Chorus Line* on the night of 29 Sep. 1983, when it broke the record as the longest-running Broadway show ever, 332 top-hatted "strutters" performed on stage. An even tighter squeeze was achieved by 369 dancers—including the original Tiller Girls and a number of British TV personalities—in a specially choreographed routine performed on the British Broadcasting Corporation *Record Breakers* TV program broadcast on 14 Dec. 1990.

Highest cabaret fee   Dolly Parton (b. 19 Jan. 1946) received up to $400,000 per live concert. Johnny Carson's fee for the non-televised Sears Roebuck Centennial Gala in October 1984 was set at $1 million.

Arts festival   The world's largest arts festival is the annual Edinburgh Fringe Festival (instituted in 1947). In 1990, 537 groups gave 9,504 performances of 1,103 shows between 12 Aug. and 1 Sep. Prof. Gerald Berkowitz of Northern Illinois University attended a record 145 separate performances at the 1979 Festival from 15 Aug.–8 Sep.

Beauty contests   The first international beauty contest was staged by P.T. Barnum (with the public as the judges) in the United States in June 1855. The world's largest annual beauty pageants are the Miss World and Miss Universe contests (inaugurated in 1951 and 1952 respectively). The most successful country in the latter contest has been the USA, with winners in 1954, 1956, 1960, 1967, 1980 and 1982. The greatest number of countries represented in the Miss Universe contest was 81 in 1983.

The country that has produced the most winners in the Miss World contest is Great Britain, with five. The maximum number of contestants was 84 in November 1988. The shortest reign as Miss World, was 18 hrs., by Miss Germany (Gabriella Brum) in 1980.

Fashion shows   The greatest distance covered by female models on a catwalk is 71.1 miles, by Roberta Brown and Lorraine McCourt at Parke's Hotel, Dublin, Republic of Ireland from 19–21 Sep. 1983. Male model Eddie Warke covered a further 11.9 miles on the catwalk.

CIRCUS

The oldest permanent circus building is Cirque d'Hiver (originally Cirque Napoléon), which opened in Paris, France on 11 Dec. 1852. The largest traveling circus tent was that of Ringling Bros. and Barnum & Bailey, which was used on tours in the United States from 1921 to 1924. It covered 91,415 ft.², consisting of a round top 200 ft. in diameter with five middle sections 60 ft. wide.

The largest audience for a circus was 52,385 for Ringling Bros. and Barnum & Bailey, at the Superdome, New Orleans, LA on 14 Sep. 1975, and the largest in a tent was 16,702 (15,686 paid), also for Ringling Bros. and Barnum & Bailey, at Concordia, KS on 13 Sep. 1924.

Aerial acts   The highest trapeze act was performed by Ian Ashpole (Great Britain) at a height of 16,420 ft., suspended from a hot-air balloon between St. Neots, Great Britain and Newmarket, Suffolk on 16 May 1986. Janet May Klemke (USA) performed a record 305 one-arm planges at Medina Shrine Circus, Chicago, IL on 21 Jan. 1938. A single-heel hang on a swinging bar was first performed by Angela Revelle in Australia in 1977.

Flying return trapeze   A flying return trapeze act was first performed by Jules Léotard (France) at Cirque Napoléon, Paris, France on 12 Nov. 1859. A triple back somersault on the flying trapeze was first performed by Lena

Jordan (Latvia) to Lewis Jordan (USA) in Sydney, Australia in April 1897. The back somersault record is a quadruple back, by Miguel Vasquez (Mexico) to Juan Vasquez at Ringling Bros. and Barnum & Bailey Circus, Tucson, AZ on 10 July 1982. The greatest number of consecutive triple back somersaults successfully carried out is 135, by Janńe Ibarra (Mexico) to Alejandro Ibarra, between 23 July–12 Oct. 1989, at various locations in the United States.

Flexible pole   Corina Colonelu Mosoianu (Romania) is the only person to have performed a triple full twisting somersault, at Madison Square Garden, New York City, USA on 17 Apr. 1984.

High wire   A seven-person pyramid (three layers) was achieved by the Great Wallendas (Germany) at Wallenda Circus in the United States in 1947. The highest high-wire act (ground supported) was at a height of 1,350 ft. by Philippe Petit (France) between the towers of the World Trade Center, New York City on 7 Aug. 1974.

Horseback riding   The record for consecutive somersaults on horseback is 23, by James Robinson (USA) at Spalding & Rogers Circus, Pittsburgh, PA in 1856. Willy, Beby and Rene Fredianis (Italy) performed a three high column (no mechanic) at Nouveau Cirque, Paris, France in 1908, a feat not since emulated. "Poodles" Hanneford (Ireland, b. England) holds the record for running leaps on and off, with 26 at Barnum & Bailey Circus, New York City in 1915.

Human cannonball   The first human cannonball was Eddie Rivers (USA), billed as "Lulu," from a Farini cannon at Royal Cremorne Music Hall, London, Great Britain in 1871. The record distance a human has been fired from a cannon is 175 ft. in the case of Emanuel Zacchini (Italy) in the USA in 1940.

Human pyramid   The weight record is 1,700 lbs., when Tahar Douis supported twelve members of the Hassani Troupe (three levels in height) at the BBC TV studios, Birmingham, Great Britain on 17 Dec. 1979. The height record is 39 ft., when Josep-Joan Martinez Lozano of the Colla Vella dels Xiquets mounted a nine-high pyramid at Valls, Spain on 25 Oct. 1981.

Risley   A back somersault feet to feet was first performed by Richard Risley Carlisle and son (USA) at the Theatre Royal, Edinburgh, Scotland in February 1844.

Teeter board   The Kehaiovi Troupe (Bulgaria) achieved a seven-person high perch pole column at Blackpool Tower Circus, Blackpool, Great Britain on 16 July 1986.

Trampoline   Marco Canestrelli (USA) performed a septuple twisting back somersault to bed at Ringling Bros. and Barnum & Bailey Circus, St. Petersburg, FL on 5 Jan. 1979. He also managed a quintuple twisting back somersault to a two high column, to Belmonte Canestrelli at Ringling Bros. and Barnum & Bailey Circus, New York City, on 28 Mar. 1979. Richard Tison (France) achieved a triple twisting triple back somersault at Berchtesgaden, Germany on 30 June 1981.

Lion-taming   The greatest number of lions mastered and fed in a cage by an unaided lion-tamer was 40, by "Captain" Alfred Schneider in 1925. Clyde Raymond Beatty handled more than 40 "cats" (lions and tigers) simultaneously. Beatty (1903–1965) was the featured attraction at every show he appeared in for more than 40 years. He insisted upon being called a lion-trainer. More than 20 lion-tamers have died of injuries since 1900.

Stilt-walking   The fastest stilt-walker on record is Roy Luiking, who covered 328 ft. on 1 ft. high stilts in 13.14 sec. at Didam, Netherlands on 2 June 1991. Over a long distance, the fastest is M. Garisoain of Bayonne, France, who in 1892 walked the 4.97 miles from Bayonne to Biarritz on stilts in 42 min., an average speed of 7.10 mph.

The greatest distance ever walked on stilts is 3,008 miles, from Los Angeles, CA to Bowen, KY by Joe Bowen from 20 Feb.–26 July 1980.

In 1891 Sylvain Dornon stilt-walked from Paris, France to Moscow, Russia in 50 stages, covering 1,830 miles. Another source gives his time as 58 days. Either way, although Bowen's distance was greater, Dornon walked at a much higher speed.

Even with a safety or Kirby wire, very high stilts are *extremely* dangerous—25 steps are deemed to constitute "mastery." The tallest stilts ever mastered measured 40 ft. 9½ in. from ground to ankle. Eddy Wolf ("Steady Eddy") of Loyal, WI walked a distance of 25 steps without touching his safety handrail wires on 3 Aug. 1988 using aluminum stilts of this length.

The heaviest stilts ever mastered weighed 57 lbs. each, and were the ones used by Eddy Wolf in his successful attempt on the height record (see above).

Fastest magician   Eldon D. Wigton, alias Dr. Eldoonie, performed 225 different tricks in 2 min. at Kilbourne, OH on 21 Apr. 1991.

Plate spinning   The greatest number of plates spun simultaneously is 84, by Dave Spathaky on British Broadcasting Corporation *Record Breakers* TV program on 21 Oct. 1986.

High diving   Col. Harry A. Froboess (Switzerland) jumped 394 ft. into the Bodensee from the airship *Graf Hindenburg* on 22 June 1936.

The greatest height reported for a dive into an air bag is 326 ft., by stuntman Dan Koko, who jumped from the top of Vegas World Hotel and Casino onto a $20 \times 40 \times 14$ ft. target on 13 Aug. 1984. His impact speed was 88 mph.

Kitty O'Neil dove 180 ft. from a helicopter over Devonshire Downs, CA on 9 Dec. 1979 onto an air cushion measuring 30×60 ft. for a TV film stunt.

PHOTOGRAPHY

Origins   The earliest reference to a photograph on glass taken in a camera was in a letter dated 19 July 1822 to French scientist Joseph Niépce (1765–1833) from his brother Claude (1763–1828), referring to a photograph of a copper engraving of Pope Pius VII taken at Gras, near Chalon-sur-Saône, France.

Earliest photographs   The earliest known surviving photograph, also by Niépce, was taken in 1827 using a camera obscura and shows the view from the window of his home. Rediscovered by Helmut Gernsheim in 1952, it is now in the Gernsheim Collection at the University of Texas, Austin, TX.

Aerial photograph   The world's earliest aerial photograph was taken in 1858 by Gaspard Félix Tournachon (1820–1910), alias Nadar, from a balloon near Villacoublay, on the outskirts of Paris, France.

CAMERAS

Largest   The largest and most expensive industrial camera ever built is the 30 ton Rolls-Royce camera now owned by BPCC Graphics Ltd. of Derby, commissioned in 1956. It measures 8 ft. 10 in. high, 8¼ ft. wide and 46 ft. in length. The lens is a 63 in. f 16 Cooke Apochromatic and the bellows were made by Camera Bellows Ltd. of Birmingham, Great Britain.

A pinhole camera was created from a Portakabin unit measuring 34 × 9½ × 9 ft. by photographers John Kippen and Chris Wainwright at the National Museum of Photography, Film and Television at Bradford, Great Britain on 25 Mar. 1990. The unit produced a direct positive measuring 33 × 6 ft.

Largest lens   The National Museum of Photography, Film and Television, Bradford, Great Britain has the largest lens on display, made by Pilkington Special Glass Ltd., St. Asaph, Clwyd, Great Britain. Its dimensions are: focal length 333 in., diameter 54 in., weight 474 lbs. Its focal length allows writing on the museum's walls to be read from a distance of 40 ft.

Smallest   Apart from cameras built for intracardiac surgery and espionage, the smallest that has been marketed is the circular Japanese "Petal" camera, with a diameter of 1.14 in. and a thickness of 0.65 in. It has a focal length of 0.47 in. A functional replica Edwardian field camera (complete with tripod) measuring 1 × 1 × 2 in. with bellows extended was designed and built by William Pocklington of Ascot, Great Britain in 1989, with the bellows made by Camera Bellows Ltd.

Fastest   A camera built for research into high-power lasers by The Blackett Laboratory of Imperial College of Science and Technology, London, Great Britain registers images at a rate of 33 billion per sec. The fastest production camera is currently the Imacon 675, made by Hadland Photonics Ltd. of Bovingdon, Great Britain, at up to 600 million frames per sec.

Most expensive   The most expensive complete range of camera equipment in the world is that of Nikon Corporation of Tokyo, Japan, which in May 1991 marketed its complete range of 26 cameras with 84 lenses and 617 accessories at a total cost of $225,174.49 excluding tax.

The highest auction price for a camera is £26,400 ($44,880) for a Leica R6 sold at Christie's, London on 9 Nov. 1989 to De Liugi Garibaldi.

Longest negative   On 1 July 1988 Christopher Creighton of Port Hope, Ontario, Canada, using a 24 in. focal length Turner-Reich lens, fitted to a Kodak 8 Cirkut camera, made a portrait of an estimated 1,500 inhabitants of Port Hope, achieving a 355 degree view in a single shot. The resulting negative measured 11 ft. 10½ in. × 7¾ in.

CINEMA

FILMS

The earliest motion pictures were made by Louis Aimé Augustin Le Prince (1842–90), who was attested to have achieved dim moving outlines on a whitewashed wall at the Institute for the Deaf, Washington Heights, New York City as early as 1885–87. The earliest surviving film (sensitized 2⅛ in. wide paper roll) is from his camera, taken in early October 1888, of the garden of his father-in-law, Joseph Whitley, in Roundhay, Great Britain at 10 to 12 frames per second.

The first commercial presentation of motion pictures was at Holland Bros.' Kinetoscope Parlor at 1155 Broadway, New York City on 14 Apr. 1894. Viewers could see five films for 25 cents or ten for 50 cents from a double row of Kinetoscopes developed by William Kennedy Laurie Dickson (1860–1935), assistant to Thomas Edison (1847–1931), in 1889–1891.

The earliest publicly presented film on a *screen* was *La Sortie des Ouvriers de l'Usine Lumière*, probably shot in August or September 1894 in Lyons, France. It was exhibited at 44 rue de Rennes, Paris, France on 22 Mar. 1895 by the Lumière brothers, Auguste-Marie-Louis-Nicholas (1862–1954) and Louis-Jean (1864–1948).

Earliest "talkie"   The earliest sound-on-film motion picture was achieved by Eugene-Augustin Lauste (1857–1935), who patented his process on 11 Aug. 1906 and produced a workable system using a string galvanometer in 1910 at Benedict Road, London, Great Britain. The earliest public presentation of sound on film was by the Tri-ergon process at the Alhambra Theater, Berlin, Germany on 17 Sep. 1922.

United States   The earliest screening of a sound-on-picture motion picture in the United States before a paying audience was at the Rivoli Theater in New York City on 15 Apr. 1923. The first all-talking motion picture was Warner Brothers' *Lights of New York*, shown at the Strand Theater, New York City on 6 July 1928.

Country with largest output   India's production of feature-length films was a record 948 in 1990, and its annual output has exceeded 700 every year since 1979. In the United States, 330 films were produced in 1991; 479 were produced in 1988, the most in a year since 1968.

Most expensive film   At the time of its release in July 1991, *Terminator 2: Judgment Day*, was reported to have cost Carolco Pictures $104 million, plus print and advertising costs of about $20 million. Its star, Arnold Schwarzenegger, was believed to have received a fee of $15 million for the film.

Largest number of extras   It is believed that over 300,000 extras appeared in the funeral scene of Sir Richard Attenborough's *Gandhi* (1982).

Most films seen   Gwilym Hughes of Dolgellau, Great Britain had seen 20,064 films by March 1991. He saw his first film in 1953 while in the hospital.

Albert E. van Schmus (b. 1921) saw 16,945 films in 32 years (1949–1982) as a rater for the Motion Picture Association of America Inc.

Fastest film production   The shortest time ever taken to make a feature-length film from the announcement of the title to the screening was 13 days for *The Fastest Forward,* produced by Russ Malkin and directed by John Gore. The all-star British cast, the crew, technicians and film suppliers accepted the charity challenge, and the 75-minute thriller was given a gala premiere in London, Great Britain on 27 May 1990 to raise money for the British Telethon '90.

Most expensive photograph   The platinum print *Roses, Mexico* taken by Tina Modotti in 1925 was sold at Sotheby's, New York on 17 Apr. 1991 for a record $165,000.

Most portrayed character   The character most frequently recurring on the screen is Sherlock Holmes, created by Sir Arthur Conan Doyle (1859–1930). The Baker Street sleuth has been portrayed by some 72 actors in over 197 films since 1900.

In horror films the character most often portrayed is Count Dracula, created by the Irish writer Bram Stoker (1847–1912). Representations of the Count or his immediate descendants outnumber those of his closest rival, Frankenstein's monster, by 160 to 112.

Biggest screen   The largest permanently installed theater screen, with an area of 96 × 70½ ft., is located at the Keong Emas Imax Theatre, Taman Mini Park, Jakarta, Indonesia, opened on 20 Apr. 1984. The Six Flags Great America Pictorium, Gurnee, ID, opened in 1979, has a screen of equal size, but it is 3D. A temporary screen measuring 297 × 33 ft. was used at the 1937 Paris Exposition in France.

Least expensive full-length feature film The total cost of production for the 1927 film *The Shattered Illusion*, by Victorian Film Productions, was £300 ($1,458).

Highest box office gross The box office gross champion is Steven Spielberg's *ET: The Extra-Terrestrial*, released on 11 June 1982, which had grossed over $700 million (including videos) by December 1989.

Batman Returns (Warner Bros) set a new opening day record of $16.1 million on 19 June 1992 and also a single-day record of $16.8 million on 20 June during its US opening weekend at a record 2,644 cinemas.

Largest loss Michael Cimino's 1980 production *Heaven's Gate* earned $1.5 million in North American rentals against an estimated negative cost of $44 million and a total cost, including distribution and overheads, of $57 million.

Highest earnings Jack Nicholson stood to receive up to $60 million for playing "The Joker" in Warner Brothers' $50 million *Batman*, through a percentage of the film's receipts in lieu of salary.

The highest-paid actress is Barbra Streisand, who received $6 million for *Prince of Tides*.

The highest-paid child performer is Macauley Culkin (b. 28 Aug. 1980), who was paid $1 million for *My Girl* (1991). This was followed by a contract for $5 million (plus 5 percent of ticket sales) for *Home Alone II: Lost in New York* (1992), the sequel to his 1990 box office hit, *Home Alone*.

Stuntman Dar Robinson was paid $100,000 for the 1,100 ft. leap from the CN Tower, Toronto, Ontario, Canada in November 1979 for *High Point*. His parachute opened just 300 ft. above the ground.

Longest series still continuing Japan's *Tora-San* films have now stretched from *Tora-San I* in August 1969 to *Tora-San XLIII* in 1991, with Kiyoshi Atsumi (b. 1929) starring in each for Shochiku Co.

Largest studios The largest complex of film studios in the world is the one at Universal City, Los Angeles, CA. The back lot contains 573 buildings and there are 34 sound stages on the 420-acre site.

Largest studio stage The world's largest studio stage is the 007 stage at Pinewood Studios, Buckinghamshire, Great Britain. It was designed by Ken Adam and Michael Brown and built in 1976 for the James Bond film *The Spy Who Loved Me*. It measures 336 × 139 × 41 ft., and accommodates 1.2 million gallons of water, a full-scale 672,000 ton oil tanker and three nuclear submarines.

Largest film set The largest film set ever built was the 1,312 × 754 ft. Roman Forum designed by Veniero Colosanti and John Moore for Samuel Bronston's production of *The Fall of the Roman Empire* (1964). It was built on a 55-acre site outside Madrid, Spain, where 1,100 workmen spent seven months laying the surface of the Forum with 170,000 cement blocks, erecting 22,000 ft. of concrete stairways, 601 columns and 350 statues, and constructing 27 full-size buildings.

Longest directorial career The directorial career of King Vidor (1894–1982) lasted for 66 years, beginning with the two-reel comedy *The*

Tow (1914) and culminating in another short, a documentary called *The Metaphor* (1980).

Oldest director   The Dutch director Joris Ivens (1898–1989) made the Franco-Italian co-production *Le Vent* in 1988 at the age of 89. He made his directorial debut with the Dutch film *De Brug* in 1928. Hollywood's oldest director was George Cukor (1899–1983), who made his 50th and final film, MGM's *Rich and Famous*, in 1981 at the age of 81.

HIGHEST EARNINGS (above). Laughing all the way to the bank is Jack Nicholson, whose role as "The Joker" in Tim Burton's *Batman* (1987) was worth up to $60 million based on a percentage of the film's box-office receipts. (Photo: Gamma)

LARGEST LOSS (right). The greatest loss in cinema box-office history was incurred by *Heaven's Gate,* directed by Michael Cimino and starring Kris Kristofferson and Isabelle Huppert, which earned only $1.5 million in North American rentals against an estimated total cost of $57 million. (Photo: Image Select)

Oldest performers The oldest screen performer of all time is the French actress Jeanne Louise Calment (b. 1875–*fl.* May 1992), who portrayed herself in the 1990 French-Canadian film *Vincent and Me*. (See Human Being, Oldest living person.)

Most durable performers The record for the longest screen career is held by German actor Curt Bois (b. 1900), who made his debut in *Mutterliebe* at the age of nine and whose most recent films include *Wings of Desire* (1988). American actress Helen Hayes (b. 10 Oct. 1900) first appeared on screen at the age of 10 in *Jean and the Calico Doll*, but much of her later work has been on the stage. The most enduring stars of the big screen are French actor Charles Vanel (b. 1892), who marked his 75th anniversary as a film actor in *Les Saisons du Plaisir* (1988), and Lillian Gish (b. 14 Oct. 1893) — although her birthdate is usually given as 1896. She made her debut in *An Unseen Enemy* (1912) and most recently appeared in *The Whales of August* (1987).

Most generations of screen actors in a family There are four generations of screen actors in the Redgrave family. Roy Redgrave (1872–1922) made his screen debut in 1911 and continued to appear in Australian films until 1920. His son, Sir Michael Redgrave, married actress Rachel Kempson, and their two daughters Vanessa and Lynn and son Corin are all actors. Vanessa's two daughters, Joely and Natasha, and Corin's daughter Jemma, are already successful actresses with films such as *Wetherby*, *A Month in the Country* and *The Dream Demon* to their respective credit.

Costumes The largest number of costumes used for any one film was 32,000 for the 1951 film *Quo Vadis*.

Most changes Elizabeth Taylor changed costume 65 times in *Cleopatra* (1963). The costumes were designed by Irene Sharaff and cost $130,000.

Most expensive Constance Bennett's sable coat in *Madam X* was valued at $50,000. The most expensive costume designed and made specially for a film was Edith Head's mink and sequins dance costume worn by Ginger Rogers in *Lady in the Dark*. It cost Paramount $35,000 (See Oscar winners). The ruby slippers, a personal prop worn by Judy Garland in the 1939 film *The Wizard of Oz*, were sold on 2 June 1988 to a mystery buyer at Christie's, New York for $165,000.

Oscar winners Walter (Walt) Elias Disney (1901–66) won more "Oscars"—the awards of the United States Academy of Motion Picture Arts and Sciences, instituted on 16 May 1929—than any other person. The physical count comprises 20 statuettes and 12 other plaques and certificates, including posthumous awards.

The only person to win four Oscars in a starring role is Katharine Hepburn (b. Hartford, CT, 8 Nov. 1909) for *Morning Glory* (1932/33), *Guess Who's Coming to Dinner* (1967), *The Lion in Winter* (1968) and *On Golden Pond* (1981). She has been nominated 12 times. Edith Head (1907–81) won eight individual awards for costume design.

Fifteen performers have won two Oscars in starring roles (the year the award was presented is given in each case): Ingrid Bergman (1945 and 1956), Marlon Brando (1955 and 1973), Gary Cooper (1942 and 1953), Bette Davis (1936 and 1939), Olivia de Havilland (1947 and 1950), Sally Field (1980 and

1985), Jane Fonda (1972 and 1979), Jodie Foster (1989 and 1992), Dustin Hoffman (1980 and 1989), Glenda Jackson (1971 and 1974), Vivien Leigh (1940 and 1952), Frederic March (1933 and 1947), Luise Rainer (1937 and 1938), Elizabeth Taylor (1961 and 1967) and Spencer Tracy (1938 and 1939).

The film with the most awards is *Ben Hur* (1959) with 11. The film with the most nominations was *All About Eve* (1950) with 14. It won six (Best Supporting Actor: George Sanders; Best Picture; Best Costume Design: Edith Head, Charles Le Maire; Best Director: Joseph L. Mankiewicz; Best Sound Recording; Best Screenplay: Joseph L. Mankiewicz).

Youngest winners   The youngest winner in competition was Tatum O'Neal (b. 5 Nov. 1963), who was 10 when she received the award in 1974 for Best Supporting Actress in *Paper Moon* (1973). Shirley Temple (b. 23 Apr. 1928) was awarded an honorary Oscar at the age of five in 1934.

Oldest winners   The oldest recipients, George Burns (b. 20 Jan. 1896) for *The Sunshine Boys* in 1976 and Jessica Tandy (b. 7 June 1909) for *Driving Miss Daisy* in 1990, were both 80 at the time of the presentation.

Most honored entertainer   The most honored entertainer in history is Bob Hope (ne Leslie Townes Hope; London, Great Britain, 29 May 1903). He has been uniquely awarded the USA's highest civilian honors—the Medal of Freedom (1969); Congressional Gold Medal (1963); Medal of Merit (1966); Distinguished Public Service Medal (1973); Distinguished Service Gold Medal (1971)—and is also an Hon. CBE (1976) and was appointed Hon. Brigadier of the US Marine Corps. He also has 44 honorary degrees.

MOVIE THEATERS

Earliest   The earliest structure designed and used exclusively for exhibiting projected films is believed to be one erected at the Atlanta Show, GA in October 1895 to exhibit C.F. Jenkins's phantoscope.

Largest   The largest theater in the world is the Radio City Music Hall, New York City, opened on 27 Dec. 1932, with 5,945 (now 5,874) seats. Kinepolis, the first eight screens of which opened in Brussels, Belgium in 1988, is the world's largest theater complex. It has 24 screens and a total seating capacity of 7,000.

Highest movie theater attendance   The Chinese Ministry of Culture reported in September 1987 that there were 21 billion movie theater attendances in 1986—or nearly 21 per person per year.

Highest box office gross   In 1991, domestic gross box office receipts (USA only) were $4.803 billion. In 1989 there was an all-time high of $5.033 billion.

RADIO

In the United States, the most popular formats for listeners (12 years and older) as of November 1991, per a survey conducted by M. Street Journal, were country (26.6 percent), adult contemporary (19.2 percent), religious (8.6 percent), oldies (7.7 percent) and top 40 (7.2 percent).

Earliest patent   The earliest patent for telegraphy without wires (wireless) was received by Dr. Mahlon Loomis (USA; 1826–86). It was entitled "Improvement in Telegraphy" and was dated 20 July 1872 (US Pat. No. 129,971). He in fact demonstrated only potential differences on a galvanometer between two kites 14 miles apart in Loudoun County, VA in October 1866.

The authentic first patent for a system of communication by means of electromagnetic waves, numbered No. 12039, was granted on 2 June 1896 to the Italian-Irish Marchese Guglielmo Marconi (1874–1937). A public demonstration of wireless transmission of speech was, however, given in the town square of Murray, KY in 1892 by Nathan B. Stubblefield. He died destitute on 28 Mar. 1928. The first permanent wireless installation was constructed at The Needles on the Isle of Wight, Great Britain, by Marconi's Wireless Telegraph Co. Ltd., in November 1897.

Earliest broadcast   The world's first advertised broadcast was made on 24 Dec. 1906 by the Canadian-born Prof. Reginald Aubrey Fessenden (1868–1932) from the 420 ft. mast of the National Electric Signalling Company at Brant Rock, MA. The transmission included Handel's *Largo*. Fessenden had achieved the broadcast of speech as early as November 1900 but it was highly distorted.

Transatlantic transmissions   The earliest claim to have received wireless signals (the letter S in Morse Code) across the Atlantic was made by Marconi, George Stephen Kemp and Percy Paget from a 10 kW station at Poldhu, Cornwall, Great Britain, to Signal Hill, St. John's, Newfoundland, Canada, at 12:30 P.M. on 12 Dec. 1901.

Human speech was first heard across the Atlantic in November 1915 when a transmission from the US Navy station at Arlington, VA was received by US radiotelephone engineers on the Eiffel Tower, Paris, France.

Earliest radio-microphones   The radio-microphone, which was in essence also the first "bug," was devised by Reg Moores (Great Britain) in 1947 and first used on 76 MHz in the ice show *Aladdin* at Brighton Sports Stadium, Great Britain in September 1949.

Most durable programs   *Rambling with Gambling,* the early morning program on WOR, New York City, was first broadcast in March 1925 and celebrated its 20,969th show as of 30 Apr. 1992. The show has been hosted by three generations of the Gambling family: John B. Gambling (1925–59), John A. Gambling (1959–present) and John R. Gambling 1985–present). The show currently airs six days per week, year round.

The weekly sports report "The Tenpin Tattler" was first broadcast on

WCFL, Chicago, IL on 24 Aug., 1935. Fifty-three years and over 2,900 broadcasts later it still continues on WGN, Chicago with the original host, Sam Weinstein, who is probably the longest continuing host of a program.

Most hours broadcast per week   Larry King's radio and television programs are broadcast a combined 46 hours per week, the most of any broadcaster heard nationwide. He has been broadcasting ten hours per week on CNN since 1985, and his program is aired in 130 countries. He has broadcast 36 hours per week on Mutual Broadcasting since 1978.

Most stations   The country with the greatest number of radio broadcasting stations is the United States, where there were 9,555 authorized broadcast stations as of year end 1991, made up of 4,985 AM (amplitude modulation) stations and 4,570 FM (frequency modulation) stations.

Largest audience   Surveys carried out in 90 countries showed that, in 1990, the global estimated audience for the British Broadcasting Corporation World Service, broadcast in 38 languages, was 120 million regular listeners—greater than the combined listenership of Voice of America, Radio Moscow and *Deutsche Welle*. This is, however, a conservative estimate because figures are unavailable for several countries, including China, Cuba, Myanmar (formerly Burma), Iran, Afghanistan and Vietnam.

The peak recorded listenership on British Broadcasting Corporation Radio was 30 million on 6 June 1950 for the boxing match between Lee Savold (USA) and Bruce Woodcock (Great Britain; b. 1921).

Largest response   The largest recorded response to a radio show occurred on 27 Nov. 1974 when, on a 5-hr. talk show on WCAU, Philadelphia, PA, astrologer Howard Sheldon registered a call count of 388,299 on the *Bill Corsair Show*.

Most durable program   The grand 'Ole Opry has broadcast continuously from November 1925 to May 1992, a total of more than sixty-six years.

Longest continuous radio broadcast   Radio Telefís Éireann transmitted an unedited reading of *Ulysses* by James Joyce (1882–1941) for 29 hrs. 38 min. 47 sec. on 16–17 July 1982.

Most assiduous radio ham   The late Richard C. Spenceley of KV4AA at St. Thomas, VI built his contacts (QSOs) to a record level of 48,100 in 365 days in 1978.

TELEVISION

At the end of 1991 there were 1,132 commercial and educational licensed television stations in the United States.

Invention   The invention of television, the instantaneous viewing of distant objects by electrical transmission, was not an act but a process of successive and interdependent discoveries.

The first commercial cathode ray tube was introduced in 1897 by Karl Ferdinand Braun (1850–1918), but was not linked to "electric vision" until 1907 by Prof. Boris Rosing (disappeared 1918) of Russia, in St. Petersburg. A.A. Campbell Swinton (1863–1930) published the fundamentals of television transmission on 18 June 1908 in a brief letter to the publication *Nature* entitled "Distant Electric Vision."

The earliest public demonstration of television was given on 27 Jan. 1926 by John Logie Baird (1888–1946) of Scotland, using a development of the mechanical scanning system patented by Paul Gottlieb Nipkow (1860–1940) on 6 Jan. 1884. He had achieved the transmission of a Maltese Cross over 10 ft. at 8 Queen's Arcade, Hastings, Great Britain, by February 1924, and the first facial image (of William Taynton, 15) at 22 Frith Street, London, Great Britain on 30 Oct. 1925.

A patent application for the Iconoscope had been filed on 29 Dec. 1923 by Dr. Vladimer Kosma Zworykin (1889–1982) but was not issued until 20 Dec. 1938.

Earliest service   Baird launched his first television "service" via a British Broadcasting Corporation transmitter on 30 Sep. 1929 and marketed the first sets, Baird Televisors, in May 1930. The world's first high-definition (i.e., 405 lines) television broadcasting service was opened from Alexandra Palace, London, Great Britain on 2 Nov. 1936, when there were about 100 sets in all of Great Britain.

First transatlantic transmissions   On 9 Feb. 1928 the image of J.L. Baird and of a Mrs. Howe was transmitted from Station 2 KZ at Coulsdon, Great Britain to Station 2 CVJ, Hartsdale, NY.

The earliest transatlantic transmission by satellite was achieved at 1 A.M. on 11 July 1962, via the active satellite *Telstar 1* from Andover, ME to Pleumeur Bodou, France. The picture was of Frederick R. Kappell, chairman of the American Telephone and Telegraph Company, which owned the satellite. The first "live" broadcast was made on 23 July 1962.

Longest telecast   The longest pre-scheduled telecast on record was a continuous transmission for 163 hrs. 18 min. by GTV 9 of Melbourne, Australia, covering the *Apollo XI* moon mission from 19–26 July 1969.

Earliest videotape recording   Alexander M. Poniatoff first demonstrated videotape recording, known as Ampex (his initials plus "ex" for excellence), in 1956.

The earliest demonstration of a home video recorder was on 24 June 1963 at the British Broadcasting Corporation News Studio at Alexandra Palace,

London, Great Britain, of the Telcan, developed by Norman Rutherford and Michael Turner of the Nottingham Electronic Valve Co.

Most durable shows   The world's most durable TV show is NBC's *Meet the Press*, first transmitted on 6 Nov. 1947 and broadcast weekly since 12 Sep. 1948. As of 26 Apr. 1992, 2,238 shows had been broadcast. The show was originated by Lawrence E. Spivak, who served as host and chief analyst through 1975.

On 1 June 1986 Joe Franklin presented the 21,700th version of his show, started in 1951. Since 1949 over 150,000 individual episodes of the TV show *Bozo the Clown*, by Larry Harmon Pictures, have been aired daily on 150 stations in the United States and abroad.

The greatest number of hours on camera on US national television is 10,190 hrs. 30 min. by the TV personality Hugh Downs in over 46 years up to 7 June 1991.

Most sets   The United States had, by September 1991, 91,788,100 TV households, with 56,189,000, or 61.2 percent, receiving cable. A total 71,140,000 homes, 77.5 percent, owned a videocassette recorder as of April 1991. The global total of homes with television surpassed 500 million in 1987, led by the USA with 89,130,000. More than 60 percent of homes in the United States have two or more TV sets.

On 15 Feb. 1988 the New China News Agency announced that China's number of TV viewers had risen to 600 million from 100 million sets.

TV watching   In June 1988 it was reported that the average US child sees at least 26,000 murders on TV by his or her 18th birthday. Between the ages of 2 and 11 the average viewing time is 31 hours 52 minutes per week. There are 8,250 TV transmitting stations worldwide, of which 1,241 are in the United States.

Greatest audience   The estimated global audience for the 1990 Soccer World Cup finals played in Italy from 8 June to 8 July was 26.5 billion. An estimated 2.5 billion viewers tuned in to the live and recorded transmissions of the XXIIIrd Olympic Games in Los Angeles, CA from 27 July to 13 Aug. 1984. The American Broadcasting Co. airing schedule comprised 187½ hours of coverage on 56 cameras.

The estimated viewership for the Live Aid concerts organized by Bob Geldof and Bill Graham (1931–91), via a record 12 satellites, was 1.6 billion, or nearly one-third of the world's population.

The program that attracted the highest-ever viewership was the "Goodbye, Farewell and Amen" final episode of M*A*S*H (the acronym for Mobile Army Surgical Hospital 4077), transmitted by CBS on 28 Feb. 1983 to 60.3 percent of all households in the United States. It was estimated that some 125 million people tuned in, taking a 77 percent share of all viewing.

The *Muppet Show* is the most widely viewed program in the world, with an estimated audience of 235 million in 106 countries as of August 1989.

Emmy awards   Instituted on 25 Jan. 1949 by the Academy of Television Arts & Sciences, the Emmy is awarded for achievement in national nighttime television programming.

Most   The most Emmys won by any individual is 16, by television producer Dwight Arlington Hemion (b. 14 Mar. 1926). He also holds the record for most nominations, with 37. *The Mary Tyler Moore Show* (CBS) has won the most awards for a series, with 29. *Cheers* has received the most nominations, with 101. The most Emmys awarded to a miniseries was nine, to *Roots* (ABC) in 1977. In 1977 *Eleanor and Franklin: The White House Years* (ABC) received the most Emmys, 11, for a television movie. Columbia Broadcasting System (CBS) holds the record for most Emmys won by a network in a single season, with 44 in 1973–74.

Most expensive production   *The Winds of War,* a seven-part Paramount World War II saga aired by ABC, was the most-expensive-ever TV production, costing $42 million over 14 months' shooting. The final episode on 13 Feb. 1983 attracted a rating of 41 percent of the total number of viewers, and a 56 percent share of total sets that were turned on.

Largest contract   John William "Johnny" Carson (b. 23 Oct. 1925), the former host of *The Tonight Show*, had a contract with NBC reportedly calling for an annual payment of $5 million for his one-hour evening shows, aired four times weekly. He retired on 22 May 1992. He first appeared as guest host in 1958 and became the regular host on 1 Oct. 1962.

Most successful telethon   The world record for a telethon is $78,438,573 in pledges in 21½ hours by the 1989 Jerry Lewis Labor Day Telethon on 4 September.

Biggest sale   The greatest number of episodes of any TV program ever sold was 1,144 episodes of *Coronation Street* by Granada Television to CBKST Saskatoon, Saskatchewan, Canada, on 31 May 1971. This constituted 20 days 15 hrs. 44 min. of continuous viewing. A further 728 episodes (January 1974–January 1981) were sold to CBC in August 1982.

Most prolific scriptwriter   The most prolific television writer in the world is the Rt. Hon. Lord Willis (b. 13 Jan. 1918). Since 1949 he has created 41 series, including the first seven years and 2.25 million words of *Dixon of Dock Green*, which ran on British Broadcasting Corporation television from 1955 to 1976; 36 stage plays; and 39 feature films. He has had 29 plays produced and his total output since 1942 is estimated to be 20 million words.

TV producers   The most prolific producer in television history is game show producer Mark Goodson (b. 1915). Since 1948, Goodson has produced 38,000 episodes totaling more than 20,800 hours of air-time. Since February 1950, a Mark Goodson-produced show has appeared on national television at least once every week.

Aaron Spelling (b. 1928) has produced more than 2,633 TV episodes totaling 2,642.5 hours of air time. The total 2,642.5 broadcast hours is equal to 14 million ft. of film and, projected 24 hours a day, it would take 109 days to screen it all. The average American TV is turned on six hours per day. At this rate, Spelling has produced enough film to last 436 days.

Highest TV advertising rates   The highest TV advertising rate was $800,000 per 30 sec. for ABC network prime time during the transmission of Super Bowl XXV on 27 Jan. 1991.

Commercial records   It was reported in March 1988 that Pepsi Cola had paid Michael Jackson $12 million to do four TV commercials for them.

Largest sets   The Sony Jumbo Tron color TV screen at the Tsukuba International Exposition '85 near Tokyo, Japan in March 1985 measured 80 ft. × 150 ft. The largest cathode ray tubes for color sets are 37 in. models manufactured by Mitsubishi Electric of Japan.

Smallest sets   The Seiko TV-Wrist Watch, launched on 23 Dec. 1982 in Japan, has a 1.2 in. screen and weighs only 2.8 oz. Together with the receiver unit and headphones, the entire black and white system, costing 108,000 yen, weighs only 11.3 oz. The smallest single-piece set is the Casio-Keisanki TV-10, weighing 11.9 oz. with a 2.7 in. screen, launched in Tokyo in July 1983. The smallest color set is the liquid crystal display (LCD) Japanese Epson, launched in 1985, with dimensions of 3 × 6¾ × 1⅛ in., weighing, with batteries and its 52,800 crystals, only 16 oz.

TV's most frequent clapper   It has been estimated that *Wheel of Fortune* hostess Vanna White claps 720 times per show, or 28,080 times in one year.

Longest-running commercial character in TV history The longest-running commercial characters in American television history are Dick Wilson, alias "Mr. Whipple," from 1964 to 1989, and Jan Miner as "Madge the Manicurist" from 1965 to 1991.

Most expensive television rights   In November 1991 it was reported that a group of US and European investors, led by CBS, had paid $8 million for the television rights to *Scarlett,* the sequel to Margaret Mitchell's *Gone With the Wind,* written by Alexandra Ripley. The proposed eight-hour mini-series is scheduled for screening in 1993.

Fastest video production   Tapes of the Royal Wedding of HRH Prince Andrew and Miss Sarah Ferguson on 23 July 1986 were produced by Thames Video Collection. Live filming ended with the departure of the honeymoon couple from Chelsea Hospital by helicopter at 4:42 P.M. The first fully edited and packaged VHS tapes were purchased 5 hrs. 41 min. later by Fenella Lee and Lucinda Burland of London at the Virgin Megastore in Oxford Street, London, Great Britain at 10:23 P.M.

Most takes   The highest number of takes for a TV commercial is 28 in 1973 by Pat Coombs, the British comedienne. Her explanation was: "Every time we came to the punch line I just could not remember the name of the product."

Highest-paid entertainer   The highest-paid television performer is currently Bill Cosby, who was reported by *Forbes* Magazine in October 1990 to have earned an estimated $115 million in 1990 and 1991.

HUMAN WORLD

King Bhumibol Adulyadej (Rama IX) of Thailand,
currently the longest-serving monarch. (Photo: Gamma)

POLITICAL AND SOCIAL

COUNTRIES

The world comprises 188 sovereign countries and 62 nonsovereign or other territories (dependencies of sovereign states, territories claimed in Antarctica and disputed territories), making a total of 250 as of June 1992.

Largest   The country with the greatest area is Russia, with a total area of 6,592,800 miles^2, or 11.5 percent of the world's total land area. It is 1.8 times the size of the United States, but with a population in 1991 of 148.54 million has less than 60 percent of the people in the United States.

The United States covers 3,787,425 miles^2, with a land area of 3,536,342 miles^2 and a water area of 251,083 miles^2. It ranks fifth in the world in area behind Russia, Canada, China and Brazil.

Smallest   The smallest independent country in the world is the State of Vatican City or Holy See (Stato della Città del Vaticano), which was made an enclave within the city of Rome, Italy on 11 Feb. 1929. The enclave has an area of 108.7 acres. The maritime sovereign country with the shortest coastline is Monaco, with 3½ miles, excluding piers and breakwaters. The world's smallest republic is Nauru, less than 1 degree south of the equator in the western Pacific, which became independent on 31 Jan. 1968. It has an area of 5,263 acres and a population of 9,350 (latest estimate 1991).

Colony   The smallest colony in the world is Gibraltar (since 1969, the City of Gibraltar), with an area of 2¼ miles^2 (1,440 acres). However, Pitcairn Island, the only inhabited island (59 people in mid-1991) of a group of four (total area 18½ miles^2), has an area of 960 acres/1½ miles^2. It was named after Midshipman Robert Pitcairn of HMS *Swallow* in July 1767. Until it was forcibly incorporated into Dahomey (now Benin) in 1961, the smallest colony was the Portuguese enclave of Ouidah, consisting of the Fort of St. John the Baptist of Ajuda, with an area of just 5 acres.

The official residence, since 1834, of the Grand Master of the Order of the Knights of Malta, totaling 3 acres and comprising the Villa del Priorato di Malta on the lowest of Rome's seven hills, the 151-ft. Aventine, retains certain diplomatic privileges, as does 68 via Condotti, also in Rome. The Order has accredited representatives to foreign governments and its legal status is the same as other states, hence it is sometimes cited as the world's smallest "state."

Flattest and most elevated   The country with the lowest "high point" is Maldives; it attains 8 ft. The country with the highest "low point" is Lesotho, where the egress of the Senqu (Orange) riverbed is 4,530 ft. above sea level.

Largest political division   The Commonwealth, a free association of 50 independent states and their dependencies that are, or have been at some time, ruled by Great Britain, covers an area of 11,310,000 miles^2 with a population estimated in 1989 to be 1,435,484,000. The British Empire began to expand when Henry VII patented trade monopolies to John Cabot in Mar. 1496 and when the East India Co. was incorporated on 31 Dec. 1600.

National boundaries   There are 266 national land boundaries in the world. The continent with the greatest number is Africa, with 107. Of the estimated 420 maritime boundaries, only 140 have so far been ratified. The ratio of boundaries to area of land is greatest in Europe.

The frontier which is crossed most frequently is that between the United States and Mexico. In the year to 30 Sep. 1991 there were 265,109,145 crossings.

Longest boundaries   The longest *continuous* boundary in the world is that between Canada and the United States, which (including the Great Lakes boundaries) extends for 3,987 miles (excluding the frontier of 1,538 miles with Alaska). If the Great Lakes boundary is excluded, the longest land boundary is that between Chile and Argentina, which is 3,265 miles in length.

Shortest boundaries   The "frontier" of the Holy See in Rome measures 2.53 miles. The land frontier between Gibraltar and Spain at La Linea, closed between June 1969 and February 1985, measures 1 mile. Zambia, Zimbabwe, Botswana and Namibia, in Africa, almost meet at a single point.

SMALLEST COLONY. The smallest colony in the world is Gibraltar (since 1969, the City of Gibraltar). It has an area of 2¼ miles² and an estimated population of 31,000.

Most boundaries China has the most land frontiers, with 16—Mongolia, Russia, North Korea, Hong Kong, Macau, Vietnam, Laos, Myanmar (formerly Burma), India, Bhutan, Nepal, Pakistan, Afghanistan, Tajikistan, Kyrgyzstan and Kazakhstan. These extend for 14,900 miles. The country with the largest number of maritime boundaries is Indonesia, with 19. The longest maritime boundary is that between Greenland and Canada at 1,676 miles.

POPULATIONS

World The average daily increase in the world's population is rising towards 258,700 or an average of approximately 180 per minute. There are, however, seasonal variations in the numbers of births and deaths throughout the year. (For past, present and future estimates, see World Population table.)

Matej Gaspar, born 11 July 1987 in Yugoslavia, was symbolically named the world's 5-billionth inhabitant by the United Nations Secretary-General.

United States According to the Census Bureau, as of 1 July 1992 there were 248,709,873 million people in the United States. New York City has the highest minority group representation, comprising 2.1 million blacks, 1.78 million of Hispanic origin (any race), .51 million Asian or Pacific Islander, .03 million American Indian, Inuit or Aleut, and .85 million of other races. By 1 July 2000 the Census Bureau predicts that the country's population will be 268.3 million.

Most populous country The most populated country is China, which in *pinyin* is written Zhongguo (meaning "central land"). It had an estimated population of 1,151,300,000 in mid-1991 and had a rate of natural increase of about 16.1 million per year or just over 44,000 per day. India (mid-1991 population of 871,200,000) is expected to overtake China in size of population by A.D. 2050, with 1.591 billion against 1.555 billion for China.

Least populous country The independent state with the smallest population is Vatican City or the Holy See (see Smallest country, above), with 750 inhabitants in 1991 and no births.

Most densely populated The most densely populated territory in the world is the Portuguese province of Macau, on the southern coast of China. It has an estimated population of 474,000 (1991) in an area of 6.5 miles², giving a density of 69,706/mile².

The principality of Monaco, on the south coast of France, has a population of 30,200 (1991) in an area of just 473 acres, a density equal to 40,112/mile².

Of countries over 1,000 miles² the most densely populated is Bangladesh, with a population of 115,555,000 (1991) living in 55,598 miles² at a density of 2,078/mile². The Indonesian island of Java (with an area of 51,073 miles²) had a population of 104,565,00 in 1990, giving a density of 2,049/mile².

Most sparsely populated Antarctica became permanently occupied by relays of scientists from 1943 on. The population varies seasonally and reaches 2,000 at times.

The least populated territory, apart from Antarctica, is Greenland, with a population of 56,500 (1991) in an area of 840,000 miles², giving a density of one person to every 14.87 miles². Some 84.3 percent of the island is made up of an ice cap.

Emigration More people emigrate from Mexico than from any other country, mainly to the United States. The Soviet invasion of Afghanistan in December 1979 caused an influx of 2.9 million refugees into Pakistan and a further 2.2 million into Iran. By 1989 the number of Afghan refugees in Pakistan had increased to 3,622,000. In 1991 there were some 25 million refugees worldwide.

Immigration The country that regularly receives the most legal immigrants is the United States. During fiscal year 1991 (October 1990–September 1991) 1,827,167 people legally entered the United States. Of these, 893,301 were from Mexico, by far the largest intake from a single country.

In fiscal year 1991 a total of 1,197,875 people were apprehended for immigration violations. The largest group by nationality were 1,131,510 from Mexico. The most common violation is people entering without inspection

WORLD POPULATION

DATE	MILLIONS	DATE	MILLIONS
8000 B.C.	c. 6	1970	3,698
A.D. 1	c.255	1975	4,080
1000	c.254	1980	4,450
1250	416	1985	4,854
1500	460	1986	4,936
1600	579	1987	5,023
1700	679	1988	5,111
1750	770	1989	5,201
1800	954	1990	5,292
1900	1,633	1991	5,385
1920	1,862	1992	5,480
1930	2,070	2000†	6,261
1940	2,295	2025†	8,504
1950	2,515	2050†	10,019
1960	3,019		

†*These projections are from the UN publication* World Population Prospects 1990.

Note: *The all-time peak annual increase of 2.06 percent in the period 1965–70 had declined to 1.74 percent by 1985–90. By 2025 this should decline to 0.99 percent. In spite of the reduced percentage increase, world population is currently growing by 97 million people every year. Projections issued by the UN Population Fund on 29 Apr. 1992 estimated that the population would stabilize at around 11.6 billion c. 2150.*

Using estimates made by the French demographer J.N. Biraben and others, A.R. Thatcher, former Director of the Office of Population Censuses and Surveys, has calculated that the number of people who died between 40,000 B.C. and A.D. 1990 was nearly 60 billion. This estimate implies that the current world population is about one eleventh of all those who have ever lived.

(EWI), and of these, 1,145,691 were apprehended crossing the Mexican border, 5,868 at the Canadian border and 9,936 at other parts of the United States border.

Tourism The most popular tourist destination is France, which in 1990 received 51,462,000 foreign tourists. The country with the greatest receipts from tourism is the United States, with $40.6 billion in 1990. The biggest spenders on foreign tourism are Americans, who in the same year spent $38.7 billion abroad.

Birthrate *Highest and lowest* The crude birthrate—the number of births per 1,000 population—for the whole world was estimated to be 27.1 per 1,000 in the period 1985–90. The highest rate estimated by the United Nations for the period 1985–90 was 56.3 per 1,000 for Malawi. Excluding Vatican City, where the rate is zero, the lowest recorded rate was 9.5 per 1,000 for San Marino.

US CENSUS

STATE	POPULATION 1990	STATE	POPULATION 1990
California	29,760,021	Connecticut	3,287,116
New York	17,990,455	Oklahoma	3,145,585
Texas	16,986,510	Oregon	2,842,321
Florida	12,937,926	Iowa	2,776,755
Pennsylvania	11,881,643	Mississippi	2,573,216
Illinois	11,430,602	Kansas	2,477,574
Ohio	10,847,115	Arkansas	2,350,725
Michigan	9,295,297	West Virginia	1,793,477
New Jersey	7,730,188	Utah	1,722,850
North Carolina	6,628,637	Nebraska	1,578,385
Georgia	6,478,216	New Mexico	1,515,069
Virginia	6,187,358	Maine	1,227,928
Massachusetts	6,016,425	Nevada	1,201,833
Indiana	5,544,159	New Hampshire	1,109,252
Missouri	5,117,073	Hawaii	1,108,229
Wisconsin	4,891,769	Idaho	1,006,749
Tennessee	4,877,185	Rhode Island	1,003,464
Washington	4,866,692	Montana	799,065
Maryland	4,781,468	South Dakota	696,004
Minnesota	4,375,099	Delaware	666,168
Louisiana	4,219,973	North Dakota	638,800
Alabama	4,040,587	District of Columbia	606,900
Kentucky	3,685,296	Vermont	562,758
Arizona	3,665,228	Alaska	550,043
South Carolina	3,486,703	Wyoming	453,588
Colorado	3,294,394	*Census Bureau*	

United States   The National Center for Health Statistics (NCHS) estimates that 4.111 million babies were born in 1991. The estimated United States crude birthrate (the number of babies for every 1,000 people) is 16.2 percent. The most recent official statistics issued by the NCHS show that in 1988, 3,909,510 live births took place in the United States (2,002,424 boys, 1,907,086 girls), which works out to an official birthrate of 15.9 percent. California led with 605,694 births, while Wyoming had the least, with 6,801. The most live births registered in the United States in any year were 4,300,000 in 1957. The highest birthrate recorded after 1909, the first year official records were recognized, was 30.1 percent in 1910.

Death rate   The crude death rate—the number of deaths per 1,000 population of all ages—for the whole world was an estimated 9.8 per 1,000 in the period 1985–90. East Timor had a rate of 45.0 per 1,000 from 1975–80, although this had subsided to 21.5 in 1985–90. The highest estimated rate for 1985–90 was 23.4 for Sierra Leone. The lowest estimated rate for 1985–90 was 3.8 deaths per 1,000 for Bahrain and the United Arab Emirates.

United States   The crude death rate for the United States in 1991 was 8.5 per 1,000 persons or 2,165,000 people.

Natural increase   The rate of natural increase (crude birthrate minus crude death rate) for the whole world was estimated to be 17.3 (27.1 minus 9.8) per 1,000 in the period 1985–90 compared with a peak 22 per 1,000 in 1965. The highest of the latest available recorded rates was 37.4 (51.1 less 13.7) for Zambia in 1985–90. The lowest rate of natural increase in any major independent country in recent times was in the former West Germany, which experienced a decline in the same period, with a figure of 1.5 per 1,000 (10.7 births and 12.2 deaths).

Suicide   The estimated daily rate of suicide throughout the world surpassed 1,000 in 1965. The country with the highest suicide rate is Hungary, with a rate of 40 per 100,000 in 1989. The country with the lowest recorded rate is Jordan, with just a single case in 1970 and hence a rate of 0.04 per 100,000. The number in China rose to 382 per day, or 16 per hour, in 1987–88.

Marriage and divorce   The marriage rate for the Northern Mariana Islands, in the Pacific Ocean, is 31.2 per 1,000 population.

United States   In the United States the median age at first marriage in 1989 was 26.2 years (bridegrooms) and 23.8 years (brides). In 1991 2,371,00 couples were married.
   The country with the most divorces is the United States, with a total of 2,187,000 million in 1990—a rate of 4.7 per 1,000 population. The all-time high rate was 5.4 per 1,000 population in 1979. In 1986 some 2 percent of all *existing* marriages in the United States broke up.

Sex ratio   There were estimated to be 1,012 males in the world for every 1,000 females in 1988. The country with the largest recorded shortage of males is Monaco, with an estimated 1,145 females to every 1,000 males. The country with the largest recorded shortage of women in 1988 was the United Arab Emirates, with an estimated 484 females to every 1,000 males.

Infant mortality   The world infant mortality rate—the number of deaths at ages under one year per 1,000 live births—in 1987 was 80.0 per 1,000 live births. Based on deaths before one year of age, the lowest of the latest recorded rates is 5.0 in Japan in 1987.

In Ethiopia the infant mortality rate was unofficially estimated to be nearly 550 per 1,000 live births in 1969. The highest rate recently estimated is 172.1 per 1,000 in Afghanistan (1985–90).

Housing   For comparison purposes, a dwelling unit is defined as a structurally separated room or rooms occupied by a private household of one or more people and having separate access or a common passageway to the street.

The country with the greatest number of dwelling units is China, with 276,947,962 in 1990.

At the end of the fiscal year 1991 there were 91,947,410 households in the United States. Of these, 59,024,811 were owner-occupied (64.19 percent) and 32,922,599 (35.81 percent) were rentals.

Largest hospital   The largest psychiatric hospital in the world is the Pilgrim State Hospital, West Brentwood, NY, with 3,816 beds. It formerly contained 14,200 beds. The largest psychiatric institute is at the University of California, Los Angeles (UCLA).

The busiest maternity hospital in the world has been the Mama Yemo Hospital, Kinshasa, Zaïre, with 42,987 deliveries in 1972. The record "birthquake" occurred on a day in May 1976, with 175 babies born. The hospital had 599 beds. India has the greatest number of midwives, with 181,000 registered in 1987.

Dentists   The country with the most dentists is the United States, where there were 150,300 registered members of the American Dental Association on 31 Dec. 1990.

Medical families   The Bauccia family of Valencia, Spain, has had the same medical practice for seven generations, since 1792.

The four sons and five daughters of Dr. Antonio B. Vicencio of Los Angeles, CA, all earned medical degrees during the period 1964–82.

Physicians   The country with the greatest number of physicians is China, which had 1,774,000 physicians in 1989, including those practicing dentistry and those practicing traditional Chinese medicine. The United States had 615,421 physicians on 1 Jan. 1990.

Mental health   The country with the most psychiatrists is the United States. The registered membership of the American Psychiatric Association (instituted in 1844) was 37,380 in early 1992, and the membership of the American Psychological Association (instituted in 1892) was 96,000.

United States   The infant mortality rate for the United States in 1991 was 8.9 per 1,000 live births, or 36,500. In 1990, California had most infant mortalities, with 4,722, while Vermont had the least, at 53.

Life expectancy   World life expectancy is rising from 47.5 years (1950–55) towards 63.9 years (1995–2000). In the decade 1890–1900, life expectancy among the population of India was 23.7 years.

The highest average life expectancy is in Japan, with 81.8 years for women and 75.9 years for men in 1990. The lowest life expectancy at birth for the period 1985–90 is 39.4 years for males in Ethiopia and Sierra Leone, and 42.0 years for females in Afghanistan.

United States   In the United States the average life expectancy is 75.4 years for men and 78.8 years for women.

POLITICAL UNREST

Biggest demonstration   A figure of 2.7 million was reported from China for a demonstration against the USSR in Shanghai on 3–4 Mar. 1969 following border clashes.

Saving of life   The greatest number of people saved from extinction by one person is estimated to be nearly 100,000 Jews in Budapest, Hungary from July 1944 to January 1945 by the Swedish diplomat Raoul Wallenberg (b. 4 Aug. 1912). After escaping an assassination attempt by the Nazis, he was imprisoned without trial in the Soviet Union. On 6 Feb. 1957, Deputy Foreign Minister Andrei Gromyko said that prisoner "Wallenberg" had died in a cell in Lubyanka Jail, Moscow on 16 July 1947. Sighting reports within the Gulag system persisted for years after his disappearance. He was made an Honorary Citizen of the United States on 5 Oct. 1981, and on 7 May 1987 a statue to him was unveiled in Budapest to replace an earlier one that had been removed.

Mass killings *China*   The greatest massacre ever imputed by the government of one sovereign nation to the government of another is that of 26.3 million Chinese during the regime of Mao Zedong (1893–1976) between 1949 and May 1965. This accusation was made by an agency of the Soviet government in a radio broadcast on 7 Apr. 1969. The broadcast broke down the figure into four periods: 2.8 million (1949–52); 3.5 million (1953–57); 6.7 million (1958–60); and 13.3 million (1961–May 1965).

The Walker Report, published by the US Senate Committee of the Judiciary in July 1971, placed the parameters of the total death toll within China since 1949 between 32.25 and 61.7 million. An estimate of 63.7 million was published by *Figaro* magazine, 19–25 Nov. 1978.

From the 13th through the 17th centuries there were three periods of wholesale massacre in China. The numbers of victims attributed to these events are assertions rather than reliable estimates. The figures given for the Mongolian invasions of northern China from 1210–19 and from 1311–40 are both on the order of 35 million, while the number of victims of the bandit leader Zhang Xianzhong (*c.* 1605–47), known as the "Yellow Tiger," from 1643–47 in the Siechuan province has been put at 40 million.

USSR   Scholarly estimates for the number of human casualties of Soviet communism hover around 40 million, excluding those killed in the "Great Patriotic War." Larger figures are claimed in Moscow today, but these are not necessarily more authoritative. Nobel laureate Alexander Solzhenitsyn (b. 11 Dec. 1918) put the total as high as 66,700,000 for the period between October 1917 and December 1959.

Nazi Germany   Reliable estimates of the number of victims of the Holocaust or the genocidal "Final Solution" (*Endlösung*) ordered by Adolf Hitler, before or at the latest by the fall of 1941 and continuing into May 1945, range from 5.1 to 6 million Jews. At the SS (*Schutzstaffel*) death camp (*Vernichtungslager*) at Auschwitz-Birkenau (Oświecim-Brzezinka), near Oświecim (Auschwitz) in southern Poland (annexed by Germany), it is estimated that over a million Jews and up to 2 million others were murdered from 14 June 1940 to 18 Jan. 1945. The greatest number killed in a day was 6,000.

Cambodia   As a percentage of a nation's total population the worst genocide appears to have been that in Cambodia (or Kampuchea). According to the Khmer Rouge Foreign Minister, Teng Sary, more than a third of the 7 million Khmers were killed between 17 Apr. 1975 and January 1979. The philosophy of class conflict induced indifference to individual suffering, serving as a warrant for massacre. Under the rule of Saloth Sar, alias Pol Pot, a founding member of the CPK (Communist Party of Kampuchea, formed in September 1960), towns, money and property were abolished, and economical execution by bayonet and club introduced. Deaths at the Tuol Sleng interrogation center reached 582 in a day.

STATES

Most populous   The most populous state in the United States in 1990 was California, with 29.76 million people.

Least populous   The least populous state was Wyoming, with 453,588 people in 1990.

Thirteen original states   The thirteen original states were Connecticut, Delaware, Georgia, Maryland, Massachusetts, New Hampshire, New Jersey, New York, North Carolina, Pennsylvania, Rhode Island, South Carolina and Virginia.

Confederate states   Eleven states seceded from the union between December 1860 and June 1861. They were (in order of secession): South Carolina, Mississippi, Florida, Alabama, Georgia, Louisiana, Texas, Virginia, Arkansas, North Carolina and Tennessee.

COUNTIES

As of year end 1991 there were 3,142 counties in the United States (in Alaska, counties are known as divisions, and in Louisiana they are called parishes). The largest in the lower 48 states is San Bernardino County, CA, with an area of 20,062 miles^2. The biggest legally established county is the North Slope Borough of Alaska at 87,860 acres. The state with the most counties is Texas with 254, and the state with the fewest is Delaware with three (Kent, New Castle and Sussex).

WORST DISASTERS IN THE WORLD

TYPE OF DISASTER	NUMBER KILLED	LOCATION	DATE
Pandemic	75,000,000	Eurasia: The Black Death (bubonic, pneumonic and septicemic plague)	1347–51
Genocide	c.35,000,000	Mongol extermination of Chinese peasantry	1311–40
Famine[1]	c. 30,000,000	Northern China	1959–61
Influenza	21,640,000	Worldwide	1918–19
Atomic Bomb	155,200	Hiroshima, Japan (including radiation deaths within year)	6 Aug. 1945
Conventional Bombing[2]	c. 140,000	Tokyo, Japan	10 Mar. 1945
Marine (Single Ship)	c. 7,700	Wilhelm Gustloff (28,542.1 tons) German liner torpedoed off Danzig by USSR submarine S-13 (only 903 survivors)	30 Jan. 1945
Panic	c. 4,000	Chongquig, China, air raid shelter	6 June 1941
Industrial (Chemical)	3,350	Union Carbide methylisocyanate plant, Bhopal, India	2–3 Dec. 1984
Tunneling (Silicosis)	c. 2,500	Hawk's Nest hydroelectric tunnel, West Virginia	1931–35
Explosion[3]	1,635	Halifax, Nova Scotia, Canada	6 Dec. 1917
Mining[4]	1,549	Honkeiko Colliery, (Benxihu) China (coal dust explosion)	26 Apr. 1942
Tornado	c. 1,300	Shaturia, Bangladesh	26 Apr. 1989
Riot	c. 1,200	New York anticonscription riots	13–16 July 1863
Mass Suicide[5]	960	Jewish Zealots, Masada, Israel	73
Railway	>800	Bagmati River, Bihar, India	6 June 1981
Fireworks	>800	Dauphin's wedding, Seine, Paris, France	16 May 1770
Aircraft (Civil)[6]	583	KLM-Pan Am Boeing 747 ground crash, Tenerife, Canary Islands, Spain	27 Mar. 1977
Man-eating Animal	1436	Champawat district, India, tigress shot by Col. Jim Corbet (died 1955)	1902–10
Terrorism	329	Bomb aboard Air-India Boeing 747, crashed into Atlantic southwest of Ireland. Sikh extremists suspected	23 June 1985

Road[7]	176	Gas tanker explosion inside Salang Tunnel, Afghanistan	3 Nov. 1982
Offshore Oil Platform	167	Piper Alpha oil production platform, North Sea	6 July 1988
Submarine	130	Le Surcouf rammed by US merchantman Thomas Lykes in Caribbean	18 Feb. 1942
Helicopter	54	Israel, military Sea Stallion, West Bank	10 May 1977
Ski Lift (Cable car)	42	Cavalese resort, northern Italy	9 Mar. 1976
Nuclear Reactor[8]	31	Chernobyl No. 4, Ukraine (then USSR)	26 Apr. 1986
Elevator (Lift)	23	Vaal Reefs gold mine lift fell 1.2 miles	27 Mar. 1980
Yacht Racing	19	28th Fastnet Race—23 boats sank or abandoned in Force 11 gale	13–15 Aug. 1979
Space Exploration	7	US Challenger 51L Shuttle, Cape Canaveral, FL	28 Jan. 1986
Nuclear Waste Accident[9]	high but undisclosed	Venting of plutonium extraction wastes, Kyshtym, Russia (then USSR)	c.Dec. 1957

FOOTNOTES

1 It has been estimated that more than 5 million died in the post–World War I famine of 1920–21 in the USSR. The USSR government in July 1923 informed Mr. (later President) Herbert Hoover that the ARA (American Relief Administration) had since August 1921 saved 20 million lives from famine and famine-related diseases.

2 The number of civilians killed by the bombing of Germany has been put variously at 593,000 and "over 635,000," including some 35,000 deaths in the raids on Dresden, Germany from 13–15 Feb. 1945. Total Japanese fatalities were 600,000 (conventional) and 220,000 (nuclear).

3 Some sources maintain that the final death toll was over 3,000 on 6–7 December. Published estimates of the 11,000 killed at the BASF chemical plant explosion at Oppau, Germany on 21 Sep. 1921 were exaggerated. The most reliable estimate is 561 killed.

4 The worst gold-mining disaster in South Africa was when 182 were killed in Kinross gold mine on 16 Sep. 1986.

5 As reported by the historian Flavius Josephus (c. 37–100). In modern times, the greatest mass suicide was on 18 Nov. 1978 when 913 members of the People's Temple cult died of mass cyanide poisoning near Port Kaituma, Guyana. In June 1943,

6 The crash of JAL's Boeing 747, flight 123, near Tokyo on 12 Aug. 1985, in which 520 passengers and crew perished, was the worst single plane crash in aviation history.

7 Western estimates gave the number of deaths at c. 1,100. Suriname has the highest fatality rate in road accidents, 33.5 deaths per 100,000 population, and Malta the lowest, with 1.6 per 100,000. The worst year for road deaths in the United States was 1972 (56,278).

8 Explosion at 0123 hrs local time. Thirty-one was the official Soviet total of immediate deaths. It is not known how many of the c. 200,000 people involved in the cleanup died in the five-year period following the disaster since no systematic records were kept. The senior scientific officer, Vladimir Chernousenko, who is expected to die in two to four years, put the death toll at between 7,000 and 10,000 in a statement on 13 Apr. 1992.

9 More than 30 small communities in a 460 mile² area have been eliminated from USSR maps since 1958, with 17,000 people evacuated. Possibly an ammonium nitrate-hexone explosion was the cause.

22,000 Japanese jumped off a cliff to their deaths during the US Marines' assault on the island of Tarawa (now in Kiribati).

TOWNS AND CITIES

Oldest The oldest-known walled town in the world is Arihā (Jericho). Radiocarbon dating on specimens from the lowest levels reached by archaeologists indicates habitation there by perhaps 2,700 people as early as 7800 B.C. The settlement of Dolní Vestonice, Czechoslovakia has been dated to the Gravettian culture *c.* 27,000 B.C. The oldest capital city in the world is Dimashq (Damascus), Syria. It has been continuously inhabited since *c.* 2500 B.C.

United States The oldest town of European origin in the United States is St. Augustine, St. John's County, FL (present population 12,000), founded on 8 Sep. 1565, on the site of Seloy by Pedro Menendez de Aviles.

The oldest incorporated city is York, ME (present population 14,000), which received an English charter in March 1642, and was incorporated under the name Georgiana.

Most remote town from the sea The large town most remote from the sea is Urumqi (Wu-lu-mu-ch'i) in Sinkiang, the capital of China's Sinkiang Uighur Autonomous Region, at a distance of about 1,500 miles from the nearest coastline. Its population was estimated to be 1,110,000 in late 1989.

Most populous The most populous urban agglomeration in the world is Mexico City, which was listed in the United Nations *Prospects of World Urbanization, 1990* as having a population of 20,200,000. By 2000 it is expected to have increased to 25,600,000. Tokyo-Yokohama, Japan, which in the late 1980s had been the most populous, is expected to have declined to third in the list by the turn of the century, with São Paulo in Brazil second.

United States The 1990 United States census shows that 76 percent of all Americans live in metropolitan areas—central cities and their surrounding suburbs—up from 56 percent in 1950. The largest metropolitan area is that of New York City with 8,087,251 residents.

Smallest incorporated place The smallest incorporated place in the United States in 1990 was Valley Park, OK, with one resident.

Largest in area The world's largest city (defined as a densely populated settlement), in area, is Mount Isa, Queensland, Australia. The area administered by the City Council is 15,822 miles^2.

Highest The new town of Wenzhuan, founded in 1955 on the Qinghai–Tibet road north of the Tangla range, is the highest city in the world at 16,730 ft. above sea level.

United States The highest incorporated city in the United States is Leadville, CO, at an elevation of 10,152 ft. Founded in 1878, Leadville has a current population of 2,629.

Capital city   The highest capital in the world, before the domination of Tibet by China, was Lhasa, at an elevation of 12,087 ft. above sea level. La Paz, administrative and *de facto* capital of Bolivia, stands at an altitude of 11,916 ft. above sea level. Its airport, El Alto, is at 13,385 ft. The city was founded in 1548 by Capt. Alonso de Mendoza on the site of an Indian village named Chuquiapu. It was originally called Ciudad de Nuestra Señora de La Paz (City of Our Lady of Peace), but in 1825 was renamed La Paz de Ayacucho, its present official name. Sucre, the legal capital of Bolivia, stands at 9,301 ft. above sea level.

Lowest   The Israeli settlement of Ein Bokek, which has a synagogue, on the shores of the Dead Sea is the lowest in the world, at 1,291 ft. below sea level.

United States   The lowest incorporated city in the United States is Calipatria, CA, at 184 ft. below sea level. Founded on 28 Feb. 1919, it has a current population of 2,696. The flagpole outside city hall is 184 ft. tall, allowing "Old Glory" to fly at sea level.

Northernmost   The northernmost village is Ny Ålesund (78° 55′ N), a coal-mining settlement on King's Bay, Vest Spitsbergen, in the Norwegian territory of Svalbard. The northernmost capital is Reykjavik, Iceland (64° 08′ N). Its population was 97,569 in 1990.

United States   The northernmost city in the United States is Barrow, AK (71° 17′ N).

Southernmost   The world's southernmost village is Puerto Williams (population about 1,000) on the north coast of Isla Navarino, Tierra del Fuego, Chile, 680 miles north of Antarctica. Wellington, North Island, New Zealand, with a 1989 population of 324,600, is the southernmost capital city (41° 17′ S). The world's southernmost administrative center is Port Stanley, Falkland (Malvinas) Islands (51° 43′ S), with a population of 1,643 in 1991.

United States   The southernmost city in the United States is Hilo, HI (19° 43′ N).

HEADS OF STATE AND ROYALTY

Forty-five of the world's 188 sovereign states are not republics. They are headed by 1 emperor, 13 kings, 3 queens, 2 sultans, 1 grand duke, 2 princes, 3 emirs, an elected monarch, the Pope, a president chosen from and by 7 hereditary sheiks, a head of state currently similar to a constitutional monarch, and 2 nominal nonhereditary "princes" in one country. Queen Elizabeth II is head of state of Great Britain and 16 other Commonwealth countries.

LONGEST-REIGNING QUEEN. Her Majesty Queen Elizabeth II of the United Kingdom of Great Britain and Northern Ireland is currently the longest-reigning queen, having succeeded to the throne on 6 Feb. 1952. She is seen during a tour of India in 1961 (opposite top), at her coronation in Westminster Abbey on 2 June 1953 (opposite bottom), reviewing the Trooping of the Colour ceremony in June 1987 (below) and meeting with other world leaders at Buckingham Palace on the occasion of the G7 (Group of Seven) summit in July 1991 (above). (Photos: Popperfoto and Hulton Picture Company)

Oldest ruling house   The Emperor of Japan, Akihito (b. 23 Dec. 1933), is the 125th in line from the first Emperor, Jimmu Tenno or Zinmu, whose reign was traditionally from 660 to 581 B.C., but more probably dates from *c*. 40 B.C. to *c*. 10 B.C.

Reigns   *Longest all-time*   The longest recorded reign of any monarch is that of Phiops II (also known as Pepi II), or Neferkare, a Sixth Dynasty pharaoh of ancient Egypt. His reign began *c*. 2281 B.C., when he was 6 years of age, and is believed to have lasted *c*. 94 years. Musoma Kanijo, chief of the Nzega district of western Tanganyika (now part of Tanzania), reputedly reigned for more than 98 years, from 1864, when he was 8 years old, until his death on 2 Feb. 1963. Minhti, King of Arakan (now part of Myanmar, formerly Burma), is reputed to have reigned for 95 years between 1279 and 1374. The longest reign of any European monarch was that of Afonso I Henriques of Portugal, who ascended the throne on 30 Apr. 1112 and died on 6 Dec. 1185 after a reign of 73 years 220 days, first as a count and then as king.

Longest current   The King of Thailand, Bhumibol Adulyadej (Rama IX; b. 5 Dec. 1927), is currently the world's longest-reigning monarch, having succeeded to the throne following the death of his older brother on 9 June 1946. The longest-reigning queen is Queen Elizabeth II of the United Kingdom, who succeeded to the throne on 6 Feb. 1952 on the death of her father.

Shortest   Crown Prince Luis Filipe of Portugal was mortally wounded at the same time that his father was killed by a bullet that severed his carotid artery (one of the two great arteries carrying blood to the head), in the streets of Lisbon on 1 Feb. 1908. He was thus technically King of Portugal (Dom Luis III) for about 20 minutes.

Longest-lived royal   The longest-lived European royal on record was Zita, Empress of Austria and Queen of Hungary, whose husband reigned as Emperor Charles I of Austria and King Charles IV of Hungary from 1916–18; she died on 14 Mar. 1989 at the age of 96 years 309 days, after living in exile from 23 Mar. 1919.

Youngest king and queen   The country with the youngest king is Swaziland, where King Mswati III was crowned on 25 Apr. 1986 at the age of 18 years 6 days. He was born Makhosetive, the 67th son of King Subhusa II. The country with the youngest queen is Denmark, with Queen Margrethe II (b. 16 Apr. 1940).

Heaviest monarch   The world's heaviest monarch is the 6-ft.-3-in.-tall King Taufa'ahau of Tonga, who in September 1976 was weighed on the only adequate scales in the country, at the airport, recording 462 lbs. By 1985 he was reported to have slimmed down to 308 lbs. but by late 1991 he was up to 360½ lbs. His embassy car in London, Great Britain has the license plate "1 TON," although this is an abbreviated reference to his status as king of Tonga rather than to his weight.

Heads of state   *Oldest and youngest*   The oldest head of state in the world is Félix Houphouët-Boigny, president of Ivory Coast (b. 18 Oct. 1905). The youngest is King Mswati III of Swaziland (b. 19 Apr. 1968). (See Youngest King and Queen, above.)

First female presidents   Isabel Perón (b. 4 Feb. 1931) of Argentina became the world's first female president when she succeeded her husband on his death on 1 July 1974. She held office until she was deposed in a bloodless coup on 24 Mar. 1976. President Vigdis Finnbogadottir (b. 15 Apr. 1930) of Iceland became the world's first democratically elected female head of state on 30 June 1980.

Largest meeting   The largest meeting of heads of state and heads of government took place on the occasion of the World Summit for Children, held on 29–30 Sep. 1990. The conference at the headquarters of the United Nations in New York City was attended by 71 world leaders and dealt with the plight of children worldwide.

Most prolific   The most prolific monogamous "royals" were Prince Hartmann of Liechtenstein (1613–86), who had 24 children, of whom 21 were born alive, by Countess Elisabeth zu Salm-Reifferscheidt (1623–88). HRH Duke Roberto I of Parma (1848–1907) also had 24 children, but by two wives.

Highest post-nominal numbers   The highest post-nominal number ever used to designate a member of a royal house was 75, briefly enjoyed by Count Heinrich LXXV Reuss zu Schleiz (1800–1801). All male members of this branch of the German family are called Heinrich and are successively numbered from I upwards in three sequences. The first began in 1695 (and ended with Heinrich LXXV), the second began in 1803 (and ended with Heinrich XLVII) and the third began in 1910. These are purely *personal* numbers and should not be confused with *regnal* numbers (years of a royal reign).

LEGISLATURES—UNITED STATES

PRESIDENTS

Youngest   The youngest president to assume office was Theodore Roosevelt. Vice-President Roosevelt became president at the age of 42 years, 10 months when President William McKinley was assassinated in 1901.

Shortest term of office   The shortest term in office was 32 days (4 Mar.–4 Apr. 1841) by William Henry Harrison.

Most ex-presidents living   Between 4 Mar. 1861 (the inauguration of Abraham Lincoln) and the death of ex-president John Tyler on 18 Jan. 1862, there were five ex-presidents living: Martin Van Buren, Millard Fillmore, Franklin Pierce, James Buchanan and John Tyler.

Path to the Presidency

Prior to the late 19th century there were often candidates from more than two parties. The third party candidate with the highest percentage of the popular vote in the 20th century to date was Theodore Roosevelt running as the candidate for the Progressive Party. He won 27.4 percent in 1912.

Ronald Reagan received the highest total for electoral votes in 1984, with 525.

Campaign Costs

1988 was the most expensive campaign year in US history. Spending on candidates during the campaign (from the primaries through the general election) was $148.07 million for the Democrats and $168.99 million for the Republicans. It is widely expected that these figures will be surpassed in the 1992 election.

The most votes cast in one year is 92,628,458 in 1984.

National Conventions

The national convention is the gathering of party delegates to elect their parties' presidential and vice-presidential nominees. The winning candidate requires a simple majority of delegate votes to gain the nomination.

The highest number of delegates ever sent by a state to a national party convention will be the 383 from California's delegation to the 1992 Democratic National Convention.

Franklin Delano Roosevelt served the longest term as president—12 years 39 days (1933–45).

Primary Campaign
In order to win the party nomination for president the candidate must receive a majority of delegate votes at the party's national convention. These votes are earned in the primary campaign, a series of state elections (either a primary or a caucus) held over a period of five months. Election procedures vary among states, but in general, in a primary election the voters register their preference for an individual candidate by ballot, whereas in a caucus, they register their preference by a public display at an open meeting. The number of delegate votes alloted to each state depends on the population of the state, but in most cases the delegates are bound to vote at the national convention in the manner determined by the results of the primary or caucus.

Ronald Reagan was the oldest president (69 years 349 days old when he took the oath of office). He was re-elected at age 73.

George Washington was the only president to run unopposed (in 1788 and 1792). James Monroe also ran unopposed in 1820, but one elector cast his ballot for John Quincy Adams so that Washington's record would not be matched.

Woodrow Wilson (left) was elected by the smallest percentage of the popular vote, with 41.8 percent in 1912. Richard Nixon was next lowest with 43.4 percent in 1968.

(Note: before 1872, presidential electors were not chosen by popular vote in all states.)

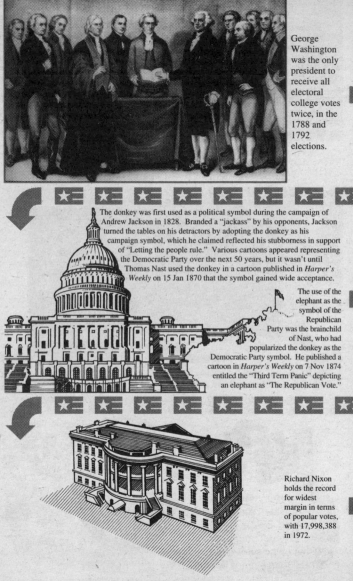

George Washington was the only president to receive all electoral college votes twice, in the 1788 and 1792 elections.

The donkey was first used as a political symbol during the campaign of Andrew Jackson in 1828. Branded a "jackass" by his opponents, Jackson turned the tables on his detractors by adopting the donkey as his campaign symbol, which he claimed reflected his stubborness in support of "Letting the people rule." Various cartoons appeared representing the Democratic Party over the next 50 years, but it wasn't until Thomas Nast used the donkey in a cartoon published in *Harper's Weekly* on 15 Jan 1870 that the symbol gained wide acceptance.

The use of the elephant as the symbol of the Republican Party was the brainchild of Nast, who had popularized the donkey as the Democratic Party symbol. He published a cartoon in *Harper's Weekly* on 7 Nov 1874 entitled the "Third Term Panic" depicting an elephant as "The Republican Vote."

Richard Nixon holds the record for widest margin in terms of popular votes, with 17,998,388 in 1972.

INAUGURATION

Electoral College

The Electoral College is a body of electors, appointed by each of the states, whose responsibility is to select the president and vice-president of the United States. The Electoral College was created by Article II, sections 2 and 3, of the Constitution. On Election Day the voters choose the electors who make up the Electoral College when they vote for their choice for president and vice-president. Each state is represented by a number of electors equal to its full delegation in Congress. The electors vote on the first Monday after the second Wednesday in December. In modern times the electors vote for the nominee who gets the largest popular vote in their state. The results are sent to the president of the United States Senate, and to various other federal and state officials. The sealed state ballots are opened and counted at a joint session of Congress on January 6 of the year following the election.

California has 54 electoral votes for the 1992 election, the most ever enjoyed by any state.

Lyndon Johnson won the highest percentage of the popular vote, with 61.05 % in 1964. (Note: records have been kept from 1824 onwards.)

Jimmy Carter was the first president to walk the inaugural parade route from the Capitol Building to the White House.

The youngest president ever elected was John Fitzgerald Kennedy, who took the oath of office at age 43 years 236 days in 1961.

Largest gathering   The largest gathering of men who had been or would become president was eight, on 30 Dec. 1834 in the old House Chamber of the Capitol: ex-president John Quincy Adams; ex-president Andrew Jackson; Vice-president Martin Van Buren; Senator John Tyler; Senator James Buchanan; and Representatives James K. Polk, Millard Fillmore and Franklin Pierce.

For additional presidential records, see Path to the Presidency feature.

VICE-PRESIDENTS

Fourteen men have held the offices of both president and vice-president. Eight became president following the death of the incumbent: John Tyler (1841–45); Millard Fillmore (1850–53); Andrew Johnson (1865–69); Chester Arthur (1881–85); Theodore Roosevelt (1901–09); Calvin Coolidge (1923–29); Harry Truman (1945–53); Lyndon Johnson (1963–69). Five gained the presidency via election: John Adams (1797–1801); Thomas Jefferson (1801–1809); Martin Van Buren (1837–41); Richard Nixon (1969–74); George Bush (1989–present). Gerald Ford (1974–77) became president following the resignation of the incumbent, Richard Nixon.

Longest term of office   Only five vice-presidents have served two full four-year terms in office: John Adams (1789–97), Thomas R. Marshall (1913–1921), John Nance Garner (1933–41), Richard Nixon (1953–61) and George Bush (1981–89).

Handshaking   The record number of hands shaken by a public figure at an official function was 8,513 by President Theodore Roosevelt (1858–1919) at a New Year's Day White House presentation in Washington, D.C. in 1907.

Loman Brophy shook 21,276 different hands in 8 hours as part of UCD (University College Dublin) Science Day in Dublin, Republic of Ireland on 15 Feb. 1992.

Highest-paid legislators   The most highly paid of all the world's legislators are members of the US Congress. The annual salary for members of the House of Representatives is $129,500. The basic annual salary for members of the Senate is $101,900. The President of the United States has an annual salary of $200,000, a $50,000 per year expense account, and a lifetime pension of $138,900 per year.

Most roll calls   Senator William Proxmire (D-Wisconsin) did not miss a single one of the 9,695 roll calls from Apr. 1966 to 27 Aug. 1987. Rep. William H. Natcher (D-Kentucky) has cast 13,190 consecutive roll call votes and responded in person to 4,210 recorded quorum calls, for a total of 17,400 votes to 21 May 1992. He has not missed a roll call or quorum call since being sworn in as a House member on 6 Jan. 1954, a total of 38 years.

Youngest to hold office   The youngest man to become vice-president was John Cabell Breckinridge (Democrat; b. 21 Jan. 1821), who took office on 4 Mar. 1857 at the age of 36 years 1 month.

Oldest to hold office   Alben William Barkley (Democrat; b. 24 Nov. 1877) took office on 20 Jan. 1949 at the age of 71 years 40 days. He served a full four-year term.

Longest-lived   The longest-lived vice-president was John Nance Garner, who served under Franklin D. Roosevelt from 1933 to 1941. He was born in 1868 and died on 7 Nov. 1967 at the age of 98.

CONGRESS

Speaker of the House of Representatives   In 1947 Congress enacted a law placing the Speaker of the House first in line to the presidency should both the president and vice-president die, become incapacitated or be disqualified from office. James K. Polk is the only person to hold the offices of speaker (1835–89) and president (1845–49).

Longest term   The longest term served by any speaker was 17 yrs. by Sam Rayburn (1882–1961; D-Texas). Rayburn served three terms: 1940–47, 1949–53, 1955–61.

Shortest term   The shortest term of any speaker is one day, 3 Mar. 1869, served by Theodore Medad Pomeroy (1824–1905; R-New York).

Oldest speaker   The oldest speaker was Sam Rayburn (D-Texas), who was reelected speaker for the 87th Congress on 3 Jan. 1961 at age 78 years 11 months.

Youngest speaker   The youngest speaker was Robert Mercer Taliaferro Hunter (1809–87; D-Virginia), who was chosen Speaker for the 26th Congress on 2 Dec. 1839 at age 30 years 7 months.

House of Representatives   The longest any representative has ever served is 50 years 6 months (as of June 1992), by Rep. Jamie L. Whitten (D-Mississippi). He began his career on 4 Nov. 1941.

Youngest elected   The youngest man ever to serve in the House was William Charles Cole Claiborne (1775–1817; Jeffersonian Democrat-Tennessee), who, in contravention of the 25-year age requirement of the Constitution, was elected in August 1797 at the age of 22.

Oldest elected   The oldest man ever elected representative was Claude Denson Pepper (1900–89; D-Florida), who was reelected on 8 Nov. 1988 at age 88 years 2 months.

Senate   The longest any senator has ever served is 42 years by Carl Trumbull Hayden (1877–1972; D-Arizona). Hayden served in the Senate from 1927–69. (See also Congressional service.)

The current longest-serving member of the Senate is James Strom Thurmond (b. 5 Dec. 1902; R-South Carolina). As of June 1992 Thurmond has served for 37 years. He was originally elected as a Democrat in December 1954, but changed to the Republican Party in 1964.

PRESIDENTIAL RECORDS

Article II of the Constitution provides for the office of the presidency. The President is head of all executive agencies, has full responsibility for the execution of the laws, is commander in chief of the armed forces, conducts foreign affairs, and with the advice and consent of Congress appoints cabinet members and any other executive officials. The Constitution sets the term of office at four years and requires that the position be filled by election through the Electoral College. The Twenty-second Amendment (1951) limits a president to two consecutive four-year terms. To be eligible for the presidency one must be a native-born citizen, over 35 years old, and at least 14 years resident in the United States.

LONGEST TERM IN OFFICE	12 years 39 days	Franklin Delano Roosevelt	1933–45
SHORTEST TERM IN OFFICE	32 days	William Henry Harrison	4 Mar.–4 Apr. 1841
YOUNGEST TO ASSUME OFFICE	42 years 10 months	Theodore Roosevelt	1901–09
YOUNGEST ELECTED	43 years 236 days	John Fitzgerald Kennedy	1961–63
OLDEST ELECTED	69 years 349 days	Ronald Wilson Reagan	1981–89
TALLEST	6 ft. 4 in.	Abraham Lincoln	1861–65
SHORTEST	5 ft. 4 in.	James Madison	1809–17
LONGEST LIVED	90 years 258 days	John Adams	1797–1801
SHORTEST LIVED	46 years 6 months	John Fitzgerald Kennedy	1961–63
LONGEST LIFE AFTER PRESIDENCY	31 years 7 months	Herbert Clark Hoover	1929–33
SHORTEST LIFE AFTER PRESIDENCY	105 days	James K. Polk	1845–49
HEAVIEST	354 lbs.	William Howard Taft	1909–13
MOST CHILDREN	15	John Tyler	1841–45
MOST CHILDREN (one spouse)	10	William Henry Harrison	1841
BACHELOR		James Buchanan	1857–61
RESIGNED		Richard M. Nixon	1969–74
ASSASSINATED	14 Apr. 1865	Abraham Lincoln	1861–65
	2 July 1881	James A. Garfield	1881
	6 Sep. 1901	William H. McKinley	1897–1901
	22 Nov. 1963	John Fitzgerald Kennedy	1961–63

FIRST LADIES

Barbara Bush is the 37th first lady. The term itself dates only from the time of Lucy Ware Webb Hayes, who was the 16th first lady in 1887–81.

FIRST AND EARLIEST BORN	21 June 1731	Martha Dandridge Custis (1731–1802)	m George Washington
LONGEST TENURE	12 years 39 days	(Anna) Eleanor Roosevelt (1884–1962)	m Franklin D. Roosevelt 1933–45
SHORTEST TENURE	32 days in 1841	Anna Tuthill Symmes (1775–1864)	m William H. Harrison
MOST CHILDREN	6 sons, 4 daughters	Anna Tuthill Symmes	m William H. Harrison
LEAST CHILDREN	None	Five first ladies were childless: Martha Dandridge Custis Washington (1731–1802), Dorothea "Dolley" Payne Madison (1768–1849), Sarah Childress Polk (1803–91), Edith Bolling Galt Wilson (1872–1961) and Florence (Kling) De Wolfe Harding (1860–1924).	
LARGEST GATHERING	8	At inauguration of John F. Kennedy (1917–63) in Washington, D.C. on 20 Jan. 1961—his wife, 4 past and 3 future first ladies.	
COMMONEST HOME STATE	New York (8)	18 other states represented. Only foreign-born First Lady has been Louisa Catherine Johnson (1775–1852), in London, England on 12 Feb 1775 and there married John Quincy Adams on 26 July 1797.	
COMMONEST ANCESTRY		All 37 have British ancestry; 25 have purely English ancestry.	
RAREST ANCESTRY		Only 1 has Native American ancestry—Edith Bolling Galt Wilson (see above) was a ninth-generation descendant of Princess Pocahontas (c. 1595–1617).	

GOVERNORS

STATE	YOUNGEST*	OLDEST*
Alabama	Thomas Bibb (1820–21)............36 yrs.	Hugh McVay (1837)............71 yrs.
Alaska	Keith Miller (1969–70)............44 yrs. 2 mo.	Walter J. Hickell (191–)............71 yrs. 5 mo.
Arizona	Bruce E. Babbitt (1978–87)............39 yrs. 9 mo.	George W.P. Hunt (1930–32)............71 yrs.
Arkansas	Bill Clinton (1979–81, 1983–)............32 yrs. 5 mo.	Thomas C. McRae (1921–25)............69 yrs. 22 days
California	J. Neely Johnson (1856–58)............30 yrs. 5 mo.	Frank Merriam (1934–39)............68 yrs. 5 mo.
Colorado	James B. Grant (1883–85)............35 yrs. 7 days	Edwin C. Johnson (1955–57)............71 yrs. 10 days
Connecticut	Joseph R. Hawley (1866–67)............39 yrs. 6 mo.	Simeon E. Baldwin (1911–15)............72 yrs. 10 mo.
Delaware	William Temple (1846–47)............31 or 32 yrs.	Caleb Prew Bennett (1833–36)............74 yrs.
Florida	Park Trammell (1913–17)............37 yrs.	Frederick P. Cone (1937–41)............66 yrs.
Georgia	Herman E. Talmadge (1947–55)............33 yrs.	Lamartine G. Hardman (1927–31)............73 yrs.
Hawaii	William Quinn (1959–62)............40 yrs.	John A. Burns (1962–73)............61 yrs.
Idaho	Frank Steunenberg (1897–1900)............35 yrs. 4 mo.	James H. Hawley (1911–12)............63 yrs. 11 mo.
Illinois	John M. Hamilton (1883–84)............35 yrs. 8 mo.	Louis L. Emmerson (1929–33)............65 yrs. 18 days
Indiana	James B. Ray (1825–31)............30 yrs.	James D. Williams (1877–80)............68 yrs. 11 mo.
Iowa	Terry Branstad (1983–)............36 yrs. 2 mo.	Francis M. Drake (1896–98)............65 yrs. 1 mo.
Kansas	Samuel J.G. Crawford (1865–68)............29 yrs. 8 mo.	Joan Finney (1991–)............65 yrs. 11 mo. 2 days
Kentucky	J.C.W. Beckham (1900–07)............30 yrs. 5 mo.	James B. McCreary (1875–79, 1911–15)............73 yrs. 5 mo.
Louisiana	Henry C. Warmouth (1868–72)............26 yrs. 1 mo.	Joshua Baker (1868)............68 yrs.
Maine	William Tudor (1929–33)............27 yrs.	S.S. Marble (1887–89)............69 yrs.
Maryland	Edward Lloyd (1809–11)............29 yrs.	Robert M. McLane (1884–85)............68 yrs.
Massachusetts	William E. Russell (1891–94)............33 yrs.	Samuel Adams (1793–97)............71 yrs.
Michigan	Stevens T. Mason (1835–40)............24 yrs.	Lauren D. Dickinson (1939–40)............79 yrs. 11 mo.
Minnesota	Harold E. Stassen (1939–43)............31 yrs. 8 mo.	Samuel Van Sant (1901–05)............58 yrs. 7 mo.
Mississippi	Albert G. Brown (1844–48)............30 yrs.	Henry L. Whitfield (1924–27)............65 yrs.
Missouri	Joseph W. Folk (1905–09)............35 yrs. 2 mo.	Forrest Smith (1949–53)............62 yrs. 10 mo.
Montana	Joseph K. Toole (1889–93, 1901–08)............38 yrs. 5 mo.	John E. Erickson (1925–33)............69 yrs. 9 mo.

State	Youngest Governor	Age	Oldest Governor	Age
Nebraska	Albinus Nance (1879–83)	30 yrs. 9 mo.	John M. Thayer (1887–91, 1891–92)	67 yrs.
Nevada	Emet D. Boyle (1915–22)	35 yrs. 6 mo.	Lewis R. Bradley (1871–78)	69 yrs. 2 mo.
New Hampshire	Levi Woodbury (1823–24)	34 yrs.	Mooly Currier (1885–)	79 yrs.
New Jersey	Rodman M. Price (1854–57)	37 yrs. 7 mo.	Charles S. Olden (1860–63)	61 yrs.
New Mexico	David E. Cargo (1967–71)	37 yrs. 11 mo.	Bruce King (1971–75, 1979–83, 1991–)	66 yrs. 8 mo.
New York	Daniel D. Tompkins (1807–17)	33 yrs.	John Taylor (1817–75)	74 yrs. 7 mo.
North Carolina	David L. Swain (1832–35)	31 yrs.	Samuel Ashe (1795–98)	70 yrs.
North Dakota	Joseph M. Devine (1898)	37 yrs. 5 mo.	Walter Welford (1935–36)	66 yrs. 8 mo.
Ohio	Thomas W. Barkley (1844)	32 yrs.	William Allen (1874–76)	71 yrs.
Oklahoma	J. Howard Edmondson (1959–63)	33 yrs. 3 mo.	Henry Bellmon (1963–67, 1987–91)	65 yrs. 4 mo.
Oregon	Jay Bowerman (1910–11)	33 yrs. 10 mo.	Gen. Charles H. Martin (1935–39)	71 yrs. 3 mo.
Pennsylvania	Robert E. Pattison (1883–87, 1891–95)	32 yrs.	David L. Lawrence (1959–63)	69 yrs.
Rhode Island	William Sprague (1860–63)	29 yrs.	James Fenner (1807–11, 1824–31, 1843–45)	73 yrs.
South Carolina	John G. Evans (1894–97)	31 yrs.	James F. Byrnes (1951–55)	71 yrs.
South Dakota	Richard Kneip (1971–78)	37 yrs. 11 mo.	Warren Green (1931–33)	60 yrs. 9 mo.
Tennessee	James C. Jones (1841–45)	32 yrs. 4 mo.	Alfred A. Taylor (1921–23)	72 yrs. 5 mo.
Texas	Dan Moody (1927–31)	33 yrs. 7 mo.	William Clements Jr (1979–83, 1987–91)	69 yrs. 9 mo.
Utah	Heber M. Wells (1896–1905)	36 yrs.	Simon Bamberger (1917–21)	70 yrs.
Vermont	F. Ray Keyser Jr. (1961–63)	34 yrs.	Erastus Fairbanks (1852–53, 1860–61)	78 yrs.
Virginia	William H. Cabel (1805–08)	32 yrs. 11 mo.	William H. Mann (1910–14)	66 yrs. 6 mo.
Washington	Daniel J. Evans (1965–77)	39 yrs. 2 mo.	Elisha P Ferry (1889–93)	64 yrs. 3 mo.
West Virginia	Cecil H. Underwood (1957–61)	34 yrs.	Mathew M. Neeley (1941–45)	66 yrs.
Wisconsin	Edward Salomon (1862–64)	33 yrs.	Walter S. Goodland (1943–47)	84 yrs.
Wyoming	John E. Osborne (1893–95)	34 yrs. 11 mo.	Joseph M. Carey (1911–15)	65 yrs. 11 mo.

Records are for the youngest and oldest governors per state at the time of election.

Oldest elected   The greatest age at which anyone has been returned as a senator is 87 years 11 months, the age at which Strom Thurmond (R-South Carolina) was reelected in November 1990.

Youngest elected   The youngest person ever elected senator was Brig. Gen. Armistead Thomson Mason (1787–1819; D-Virginia), who was elected on 3 Jan. 1816 and was sworn in on 22 January at the age of 28 years 5 months 18 days.

The youngest-ever senator was John Henry Eaton (1790–1856; D-Tennessee), who was appointed on 5 Sep. 1818 and sworn in on 16 November at age 28 years 4 months 29 days.

Filibusters   The longest continuous speech in the history of the US Senate was that of Senator Wayne Morse (1900–74; D-Oregon) on 24–25 Apr. 1953, when he spoke on the Tidelands Oil Bill for 22 hrs. 26 min, without resuming his seat. Interrupted only briefly by the swearing-in of a new senator, Senator Strom Thurmond (b. 1902) (R-South Carolina) spoke against a civil rights bill for 24 hrs. 19 min. on 28–29 Aug. 1957. The US national duration record on a state level is 43 hrs., by Texas State Senator Bill Meier, who spoke against nondisclosure of industrial accidents, in May 1977.

Fastest amendment   The constitutional amendment that took the shortest time to ratify after congressional approval was the 26th Amendment in 1971, which gave 18-year-olds the right to vote.

POLITICAL OFFICE HOLDERS

Congressional service   Carl Hayden (1877–1972; D-Arizona) holds the record for the longest congressional service, a total of 57 consecutive years (1912–69), of which 42 years were spent as a senator and the remainder as a representative.

LEGISLATURES—WORLD

PARLIAMENTS

Earliest and oldest   The earliest-known legislative assembly or *ukkim* was a bicameral one in Erech, Iraq, *c.* 2800 B.C. The oldest recorded legislative body is the Althing of Iceland, founded in A.D. 930. This body, which originally comprised 39 local chieftains at Thingvellir, was abolished in 1800, but restored by Denmark to a consultative status in 1843 and a legislative status in 1874. The legislative assembly with the oldest continuous history is the Isle of Man Tynwald, Great Britain, which may have its origins in the late ninth century and possibly predates the Althing.

Largest   The largest legislative assembly in the world is the National People's Congress of the People's Republic of China, which has 2,978 single-party members who are indirectly elected for a five-year term. The seventh congress convened in March 1988.

Smallest quorum   The House of Lords has the smallest quorum, expressed as a percentage of members eligible to vote, of any legislative body in the world—less than one-third of 1 percent. To transact business, there must be three peers present, including the lord chancellor or his deputy. The House of Commons' quorum of 40 MPs (out of 651 members), including the Speaker or his deputy, is 13 times as exacting.

Greatest petitions   The greatest petition has been supposed to be the Great Chartist Petition of 1848, but of the 5,706,000 "signatures" only 1,975,496 were valid. Consequently the largest one was in support of Lithuania's independence from the USSR. A total of 5,218,520 signatures were collected worldwide in four months during the summer of 1990 and presented to the Lithuanian president, Vytautas Landsbergis, on 4 Dec. 1990.

Longest membership   The longest span as a legislator was 83 years, by József Madarász (1814–1915). He first attended the Hungarian Parliament from 1832–36 as *oblegatus absentium* (i.e., on behalf of an absent deputy). He was a full member from 1848–50 and from 1861 until his death on 31 Jan. 1915.

Longest UN speech   The longest speech made in the United Nations was one of 4 hrs. 29 min. on 26 Sep. 1960 by President Fidel Castro Ruz (b. 13 Aug. 1927) of Cuba.

Oldest treaty   The oldest treaty still in force is the Anglo-Portuguese Treaty, which was signed in London, Great Britain over 619 years ago on 16 June 1373. The text was confirmed "with my usual flourish" by John de Banketre, Clerk.

Constitutions   The world's oldest national constitution still in force is that of the United States of America, ratified by the necessary ninth state (New Hampshire) on 21 June 1788 and declared to be in effect on 4 Mar. 1789.

Woman's suffrage   The earliest legislature with female voters was that of the Territory of Wyoming in 1869, followed by that of the Isle of Man, Great Britain in 1881. The earliest country to have universal woman's suffrage was New Zealand in 1893.

United States   In 1920 the 19th Amendment to the Constitution granted nationwide suffrage to women.

ELECTIONS

Largest   The largest elections in the world were those beginning on 20 May 1991 for the Indian *Lok Sabha* (Lower House), which has 543 elective seats. A total of 315,439,908 people cast their votes in the 511 constituencies where the seats were being contested, out of an eligible electorate of 488,678,993. The elections were contested by 359 parties, and there were nearly 565,000 polling stations manned by 3 million staff. As a result of the election a new government was formed under the leadership of P.V. Narasimha Rao of the Congress (I) Party.

Closest   The ultimate in close general elections occurred in Zanzibar (now

LARGEST PETITION. Excluding the Great Chartist petition with its huge number of invalid signatures, the largest one was in support of Lithuania's independence from the USSR. In four months during the summer of 1990 a total of 5,218,520 signatures were collected worldwide and presented to the Lithuanian president, Vytautas Landsbergis. In this photograph he is holding the official manuscript of the letter addressed to him.

COMMUNIST PARTIES. The largest national communist party is the Chinese Communist Party, formed in 1920, with an estimated membership of 50,320,000 in 1991. This was some three times greater than that of the former USSR at the same time. In both countries, membership in the youth branch of the party was widely encouraged. This photograph is of a Komsomol (youth party) card belonging to a 21-year-old Soviet woman. It was found lying in the streets of Berlin shortly after the breakup of her country. (Photo: Image Select) part of Tanzania) on 18 Jan. 1961, when the Afro-Shirazi Party won by a single seat, after the seat of Chake-Chake on Pemba Island had been gained by a single vote.

The narrowest recorded percentage win in an election would seem to be for the office of Southern District Highway Commissioner in Mississippi on 7 Aug. 1979. Robert E. Joiner was declared the winner over W.H. Pyron, with 133,587 votes to 133,582. The loser thus obtained more than 49.999 percent of the votes.

Most decisive   North Korea recorded a 100 percent turnout of electors and a 100 percent vote for the Workers' Party of Korea in the general election of 8 Oct. 1962. The closest to a unanimous vote was in Albania on 14 Nov. 1982, when a single voter spoiled national unanimity for the official (and only) Communist candidates, who consequently obtained 99.99993 percent of the vote in a reported 100 percent turnout of 1,627,968.

Most crooked   In the Liberian presidential election of 1927, President Charles D.B. King (1875–1961) was returned with an officially announced majority of 234,000 over his opponent, Thomas J.R. Faulkner of the People's Party. President King thus claimed a "majority" more than 15½ times greater than the entire electorate.

Highest personal majority   The highest-ever personal majority for any politician was 4,726,112 by Boris Yeltsin, the unofficial Moscow candidate, in the parliamentary elections held in the former Soviet Union on 26 Mar. 1989. Yeltsin received 5,118,745 votes out of the 5,722,937 that were cast in the Moscow constituency, his closest rival obtaining 392,633 votes. In 1956 W.R.D. Bandaranaike achieved 91.82 percent of the vote, with 45,016 votes, in the Attanagalla constituency of Sri Lanka (then Ceylon).

Communist parties   The largest national communist party is the Chinese Communist Party, formed in 1920, with a membership estimated to be 50,320,000 in 1991. This was some three times more than that of the former USSR at the same time. The largest in a non-Communist or non-Socialist country has been the Partito Communista Italiano, with 2,300,000 members in 1946. By 1990 its membership had declined to 1,320,000, and on 3 Feb. 1991 it changed its name to Partito Democratico della Sinistra (Democratic Party of the Left).

Largest field of candidates   There were 301 candidates running to represent Belgaum City in the State Assembly (Vidhan Sabha) elections in Karnataka, India held on 5 Mar. 1985.

Most coups   Statisticians contend that Bolivia, since it became a sovereign country in 1825, has had 191 coups, the latest on 30 June 1984, when President Hernan Siles Zuazo, age 70, was temporarily kidnapped from his official residence by more than 60 armed men masquerading as police officers.

PRIME MINISTERS
AND STATESMEN

Oldest   The longest-lived prime minister of any country was Naruhiko Higashikuni (Japan), who was born on 3 Dec. 1887 and died on 20 Jan. 1990, at age 102 years 48 days. He was his country's first prime minister after World War II, but held office for less than two months, resigning in October 1945.

El Hadji Muhammad el Mokri, Grand Vizier of Morocco, died on 16 Sep. 1957 at a reputed age of 116 Muslim (*Hijri*) years, equivalent to 112½ Gregorian years.

The oldest age at first appointment was 81, in the case of Morarji Ranchhodji Desai of India (b. 29 Feb. 1896) in March 1977.

Youngest   Currently the youngest head of government is HM Druk Gyalpo ("Dragon King") Jigme Singye Wangchuk of Bhutan (b. 11 Nov. 1955), who has been head of government since March 1972 when he was 16 years of age.

Longest term of office   The longest-serving prime minister of a sovereign state is currently Khalifa bin Sulman al-Khalifa (b. 3 July 1933) of Bahrain, who has held office since Bahrain became independent in August 1971. By then he had already been in office for 1½ years. The prime minister of the Bahamas, Sir Lynden Pindling (b. 22 Mar. 1930), has been in office since January 1967, but the Bahamas only gained independence in July 1973.

Marshall Kim Il Sung (ne Kim Sung Chu; b. 15 Apr. 1912) has been head of government or head of state of the Democratic People's Republic of Korea since 25 Aug. 1948.

Andrei Andreievich Gromyko (1909–89) had been Minister of Foreign Affairs of the USSR since 15 Feb. 1957 (having been Deputy Foreign Minister since 1946), when he was elected President of the USSR on 2 July 1985, a position he held until 30 Sep. 1988. Piotr Lomako (1904–90) served in the government of the former USSR as Minister for Non-Ferrous Metallurgy from 1940–86. He was relieved of his post on 1 Nov. 1986 after 46 years at age 82, having served on the Central Committee of the Communist Party of the Soviet Union (CPSU) since 1952.

Woman   Sirimavo Bandaranaike (b. 1916) of Ceylon (now Sri Lanka) became the first woman prime minister of any country when her party, the Sri Lanka ("Blessed Ceylon") Freedom Party, won the general election in July 1960.

JUDICIAL

LEGISLATION AND LITIGATION

Statutes *Oldest*   The earliest surviving judicial code was that of King Ur Hammu during the third dynasty of Ur, Iraq, *c.* 2250 B.C.

Most protracted litigation   The dispute over the claim of the Prior and

Convent (now the Dean and Chapter) of Durham Cathedral in Great Britain to administer the diocese during a vacancy in the See grew fierce in 1283. It flared up again in 1672 and 1890; an attempt in November 1975 to settle the issue, then 692 years old, was unsuccessful. Neither side admits the legitimacy of writs of appointment issued by the other even though identical persons are named.

Gaddam Hanumantha Reddy, a civil servant, brought a series of legal actions against the Hyderabad state government and the Indian government covering a total period of 44 years 9 months and 8 days from April 1945 through to January 1990. The litigation outlasted the entire period of his employment in the Indian Administration Service. He complained that his results in the entrance examination for the Hyderabad Civil Service entitled him to greater seniority and higher pay.

Longest hearing   The longest civil case heard before a jury is *Kemner* v. *Monsanto Co.*, which concerned an alleged toxic chemical spill in Sturgeon, MO in 1979. The trial started on 6 Feb. 1984, at St. Clair County Court House, Belleville, IL before Circuit Judge Richard P. Goldenhersh, and ended on 22 Oct. 1987. The testimony lasted 657 days, following which the jury deliberated for two months. The verdict was returned on 22 October when the plaintiffs secured sums of $1 nominal compensatory damage and $16,250,000 punitive damage.

Litigants in person   Dr. Mark Feldman, a chiropodist, of Lauderhill, FL became the first litigant in person to secure seven figures ($1 million) before a jury in compensatory and punitive damages, in September 1980. The case concerned conspiracy and fraud alleged against six other doctors.

Greatest damages   *Personal injury*   The greatest personal injury damages ever awarded were $78,183,000, to the model Marla Hanson, 26, on 29 Sep. 1987. Her face was slashed with razors in Manhattan, New York City in June 1987. The award was uncontested and included $4 million in punitive damages. The three men convicted and now serving 5–15 years have no assets, but Miss Hanson is entitled to 10 percent of their post-prison earnings.

The greatest sum awarded in compensatory personal injury damages was $65,086,000, awarded on 18 July 1986 to Mrs. Agnes Mae Whitaker against the New York City Health and Hospitals Corporation for medical malpractice. A misdiagnosis of food poisoning led to major surgery and severe disablement.

The compensation for the disaster on 2–3 Dec. 1984 at the Union Carbide Corporation plant in Bhopal, India was set at $470 million. The Supreme Court of India passed the order for payment on 14 Feb. 1989 after a settlement between the corporation and the Indian government, which represented the interests of more than 500,000 claimants, including the families of 3,350 people who died. On 27 Mar. 1992 the Bhopal Court put the death toll at more than 4,000, with 20,000 injured and the number of claimants rising to 600,000.

Civil damages   The largest damages awarded in legal history were $11.12 billion to Pennzoil Company against Texaco Inc. concerning the latter's allegedly unethical tactics in January 1984 in attempting to break up a merger between Pennzoil and Getty Oil Company. The verdict was handed down by Judge Solomon Casseb, Jr. in Houston, TX on 10 Dec. 1985. An out-of-court settlement of $5.5 billion was reached after a 48-hour negotiation on 19 Dec. 1987.

Defamation   The largest amount awarded in a libel case is $58 million, to Vic Feazell, a former district attorney, on 20 Apr. 1991 at Waco, TX. He claimed that he had been libeled by a Dallas-based television station and one of its reporters in 1985, and that this had ruined his reputation. The parties reached a settlement on 29 June 1991, but neither side would disclose the amount.

The U.S. Supreme Court on 4 Apr. 1988 let stand a $3,050,000 libel award against CBS Inc., its Chicago station WBBM and anchorman Walter Jacobsen. The damages awarded to Brown & Williamson Tobacco Corp. were the largest against a news media defendant in the United States.

Greatest compensation for wrongful imprisonment   Robert McLaughlin, 29, was awarded $1,935,000 in October 1989 for wrongful imprisonment as a result of a murder in New York City in 1979 which he did not commit. He had been sentenced to 15 years in prison and had actually served six years, from 1980 to 1986, when he was released after his foster father succeeded in showing the authorities that he had had nothing to do with the crime.

Largest alimony suit   Belgian-born Sheika Dena Al-Fassi, 23, filed the highest-ever alimony claim of $3 billion against her former husband, Sheik Mohammed Al-Fassi, 28, of the Saudi Arabian royal family, in Los Angeles, CA in February 1982. Attorney Marvin Mitchelson, explaining the size of the settlement claim, alluded to the Sheik's wealth, which included 14 homes in Florida alone and numerous private aircraft. On 14 June 1983 the claimant was awarded $81 million and declared she would be "very very happy" if she were able to collect.

Largest divorce settlement   The largest publicly declared settlement, achieved in 1982 by the lawyers for Soraya Khashóggi, was £500 million ($950 million) plus property from her husband Adnan. Mrs. Anne Bass, former wife of Sid Bass of Texas, was reported to have rejected $535 million as inadequate to live in the style to which she had been made accustomed.

Patent case   Polaroid Corporation was awarded $909.5 million in Boston, MA on 12 Oct. 1990 in a suit involving Eastman Kodak Company for infringing patents on instant photography cameras and films. Polaroid had filed suit in 1976, claiming that Kodak had infringed patents used in Polaroid's 1972 SX-70 system. Both companies filed appeals and eventually it was agreed that Kodak would pay $925 million.

Largest suit   The highest amount of damages ever sought to date is $675 trillion (then equivalent to 10 times the US national wealth) in a suit by Mr. I. Walton Bader brought in the US District Court, New York City on 14 Apr. 1971 against General Motors and others for polluting all 50 states.

Highest costs   The Blue Arrow trial, involving the illegal support of the company's shares during a rights issue in 1987, is estimated to have cost approximately £35 million (c. $60 million). The trial at the Old Bailey, London, Great Britain, lasted a year and ended on 14 Feb. 1992 with four of the defendants being convicted. They were subsequently given suspended prison sentences.

United States   The McMartin Preschool case in Los Angeles, CA is estimated to have cost $15 million. The trial, concerning the alleged abuse of children at the school in Manhattan Beach, CA, had begun with jury selection on 20 Apr. 1987 and resulted in the acquittal on 18 Jan. 1990 of the two defendants on 52 counts of child molestation and conspiracy.

LARGEST DIVORCE SETTLEMENT. The reported settlement achieved in 1982 by the lawyers of British-born Soraya Khashóggi after her divorce from her Saudi millionaire husband Adnan was £500 million plus property. In the photograph (left) he is in the middle of the shot. Soraya is with her son Omar in the picture above. (Photos: Gamma)

Wills *Shortest*   The shortest valid will in the world consists of the words "Vše zene," the Czech for "All to wife," written and dated 19 Jan. 1967 by Herr Karl Tausch of Langen, Germany. President Calvin Coolidge, who was known for his taciturn nature, left a will of 23 words: "Not unmindful of my son John, I give all my estate both real and person to my wife, Grace Coolidge, in fee simple."

Longest   The longest will on record was that of Mrs. Frederica Evelyn Stilwell Cook (b. USA), proved in London, Great Britain on 2 Nov. 1925. It consisted of four bound volumes containing 95,940 words, primarily concerning some $100,000 worth of property.

Oldest   The oldest written will dates from 2061 B.C. and is that of Nek'ure, the son of the Egyptian pharaoh Khafre. The will was carved onto the walls of his tomb, and indicated that he would bequeath 14 towns, 2 estates and other property to his wife, another woman and three children.

Codicils   The largest number of codicils (supplements modifying the details) to a will admitted to probate is 21, in the case of the will of J. Paul Getty. The will was dated 22 Sep. 1958 and it had 21 codicils dating from 18 June 1960 through 11 Mar. 1976. Getty died on 6 June 1976.

Most patents   Thomas Alva Edison (1847–1931) has had the most patents, with 1,093 either on his own or jointly. They included the microphone, the motion-picture projector and the incandescent electric lamp.

Most inexplicable legislation   Certain pieces of legislation have always defied interpretation, and the most inexplicable must be a matter of opinion. A judge of the Court of Session of Scotland once sent the Editor his candidate for most confusingly worded law, which reads: *"In the Nuts (unground), (other than ground nuts) Order, the expression nuts shall have reference to such nuts, other than ground nuts, as would but for this amending Order not qualify as nuts (unground) (other than ground nuts) by reason of their being nuts (unground)."*

Best-attended trial   The greatest attendance at any trial was at that of Major Jesús Sosa Blanco, age 51, for an alleged 108 murders. At one point in the 12½-hr. trial (5:30 P.M. to 6 A.M., 22–23 Jan. 1959), 17,000 people were present in the Havana Sports Palace, Cuba. He was executed on 18 Feb. 1959.

Longest lease   There is a lease concerning a plot for a sewage tank adjoining Columb Barracks, Mullingar, Ireland, which was signed on 3 Dec. 1868 for 10 million years. It is to be assumed that a future civil servant will bring up the matter for review early in A.D. 10,001,868. Leases in Ireland lasting "forever" are quite common.

Most durable judge   The oldest recorded active judge was Judge Albert R. Alexander (1859–1966) of Plattsburg, MO. He was the magistrate and probate judge of Clinton County until his retirement at the age of 105 years 8 months on 9 July 1965.

Narrowest margin   Judge Clarence Thomas was elected to the Supreme Court in 1991 by the narrowest margin ever recorded, 52 votes to 48.

Lawyers   In the United States, there was one lawyer for every 329 people in 1990.

Youngest judge   No collated records on the ages of judicial appointments exist. However, David Elmer Ward had to await the legal age of 21 before taking office after nomination in 1932 as judge of the County Court in Fort Myers, FL.

Muhammad Ilyas passed the examination enabling him to become a civil judge in July 1952 at the age of 20 years 9 months, although formalities such as medicals meant that it was not until eight months later that he started work as a civil judge in Lahore, Pakistan.

Most judges   Lord Balmerino was found guilty of treason by 137 of his peers on 28 July 1746. In the 20th century, 24 judges of the European Court of Human Rights in Strasbourg, France passed judgment in *The Sunday Times* v. *the United Kingdom (no. 2)* and *Observer* and *Guardian* v. *the United Kingdom* ("the Spycatcher case") on 26 Nov. 1991. The verdict was unanimous in favor of the newspapers.

CRIME

Largest criminal organizations   In terms of profit, the largest syndicate in organized crime is the Mafia or La Cosa Nostra. The Mafia consists of some 3,000 to 5,000 individuals in 25 "families" federated under "The Commission," with an annual turnover in vice, gambling, protection rackets, tobacco, bootlegging, hijacking, narcotics, loan-sharking and prostitution that was estimated by *US News & World Report* in Dec. 1982 at $200 billion, and a profit estimated in Mar. 1986 by US District Attorney Rudolph Giuliani at $75 billion. Its origin in the United States dates from 1869 in New Orleans, LA.

In terms of numbers, the Yamaguchigumi gang of the *yakuza* in Japan is the largest, with 30,000 members. There are some 90,000 *yakuza* or gangsters altogether, in more than 3,000 groups. They go about their business openly and even advertise for new recruits. On 1 Mar. 1992 Japan instituted new laws to combat their activities, which include drug trafficking, smuggling, prostitution and gambling.

There are believed to be more than 250,000 triad members worldwide, but they are fragmented into many groups which often fight each other, competing for crime territories in certain areas. Hong Kong alone has some 100,000 triads.

Assassinations   The most frequently assassinated heads of state in modern times have been the Tsars of Russia. In the two hundred years from 1718 to 1918 four Tsars and two heirs apparent were assassinated, and there were many other unsuccessful attempts.

Most prolific murderers   It was established at the trial of Behram, the Indian Thug, that he had strangled at least 931 victims with his yellow and white cloth strip or *ruhmal* in the Oudh district between 1790 and 1840. It has been estimated that at least 2 million Indians were strangled by Thugs (*burtotes*) during the reign of the Thugee (pronounced tugee) cult from 1550 until its final suppression by the British raj in 1853.

The greatest number of victims ascribed to a murderess was 610, in the case of Countess Erzsébet Báthory (1560–1614) of Hungary. At her trial, which began on 2 Jan. 1611, a witness testified to seeing a list of her victims in her own handwriting totaling this number. All were alleged to be young girls from near her castle at Csejthe, where she died on 21 Aug. 1614. She had been walled up in her room for 3½ years after being found guilty.

Twentieth century   A total of 592 deaths was attributed to one Colombian bandit leader, Teófilo ("Sparks") Rojas, between 1948 and his death in an ambush near Armenia, Colombia on 22 Jan. 1963. Some sources attribute 3,500 slayings to him during *La Violencia* of 1945–62.

United States   The greatest mass murder committed in the United States was the New York Social Club fire, which resulted in the deaths of 87 individuals. The fire was set by Julio Gonzalez, a 36-year-old Cuban immigrant, on 25 Mar. 1990 at an illegal social club, The Happy Land, in revenge for being thrown out of the club after an argument with a former girlfriend, Lydia Feliciano, who worked at the club. Ms. Feliciano was one of six survivors.

In a drunken rampage lasting eight hours on 26–27 Apr. 1982, policeman Wou Bom-Kon, 27, killed 57 people and wounded 35 with 176 rounds of rifle ammunition and hand grenades in the Kyong Sang-Namdo province of South Korea. He then blew himself up with a grenade.

Lynching   The worst year in the 20th century for lynchings in the United States was 1901, with 130 lynchings, of which 125 were of blacks and 5 were of whites. The first year with no reported cases was 1952. The year in which lynchings were last reported was on June 21, 1964, in Philadelphia, Mississippi. Three men, 2 white (Michael Schwerner and Andrew Goodman), and 1 black (James Chaney), were lynched in the Neshoba County town.

Mass poisoning   On 1 May 1981 the first of more than 600 victims of the Spanish cooking oil scandal died. On 12 June it was discovered that the cause of this 8-year-old boy's death was the use of "denatured" industrial oil from rape-seed. The trial of 38 defendants, including the manufacturers, Ramón and Elias Ferrero, lasted from 30 Mar. 1987 to 28 June 1988. The 586 counts on which the prosecution demanded jail sentences totaled 60,000 years.

Robbery   The greatest robbery on record was that of the Reichsbank following Germany's collapse in April–May 1945. The Pentagon in Washington described the event, first mentioned in *The Guinness Book of Records* in 1957, as "an unverified allegation." The book *Nazi Gold* by Ian Sayer and Douglas Botting, published in 1984, however, finally revealed full details and estimated the total haul at what were then current values as £2.5 billion ($3.75 billion).

The government of the Philippines announced on 23 Apr. 1986 that it had succeeded in identifying $860.8 million salted away by former President Fer-

MOST PROLIFIC MURDERESS. Countess Erzsébet Báthory of Hungary is believed to have tortured and murdered a total of 610 people. At her trial, which began on 2 Jan. 1611, a witness testified to seeing a list of Countess Báthory's victims in her own handwriting totaling this number. All were alleged to have been young girls from near her castle at Csejthe, Hungary. Although sentenced to death, she was not executed, but condemned to perpetual imprisonment.

dinand Edralin Marcos (1917–89) and his wife Imelda. The total since November 1965 was believed to be $5–$10 billion.

Treasury bills and certificates of deposit worth £292 million ($484.72 million) were stolen when a mugger attacked a money-broker's messenger in the financial sector of London, Great Britain on 2 May 1990. Because details of the documents stolen were quickly flashed on market dealing screens and given to central banks worldwide, the chances of anyone being able to benefit from the theft were considered to be very remote.

Art   It is arguable that the *Mona Lisa*, though never valued, is the most valuable object ever stolen. It disappeared from the Louvre, Paris, France on 21 Aug. 1911. It was recovered in Italy in 1913, when Vincenzo Perugia was charged with its theft

On 14 Apr. 1991 twenty paintings, estimated to be worth $500 million, were stolen from the van Gogh Museum in Amsterdam, Netherlands. However, only 35 min. later they were found in an abandoned car not far from the museum. Just over a year earlier, on 18 Mar. 1990, 11 paintings by Rembrandt, Vermeer, Degas, Manet and Flinck, plus a Chinese bronze beaker (also known as a *Ku*) of about 1200 B.C., worth in total an estimated $200 million, were stolen from the Isabella Stewart Gardner Museum in Boston, MA. Unlike the van Gogh paintings, these have not been recovered. Three corporations (Citibank, Chase Manhattan, and Chubb Corp.) have joined Christie's and Sotheby's in pledging a $1 million reward for any information that would lead to their recovery.

On 24 Dec. 1985, 140 priceless gold, jade and obsidian artifacts were stolen from the National Museum of Anthropology, Mexico City. The majority of the stolen objects were recovered in June 1989 from the Mexico City home of a man described by officials as the mastermind of the theft.

Bank   During the extreme civil disorder prior to 22 Jan. 1976 in Beirut, Lebanon, a guerrilla force blasted the vaults of the British Bank of the Middle East in Bab Idriss and cleared out safe deposit boxes with contents valued by former Finance Minister Lucien Dahdah at $50 million and by another source at an "absolute minimum" of $20 million.

Train   The greatest recorded train robbery occurred between 3:03 A.M. and 3:27 A.M. on 8 Aug. 1963, when a General Post Office mail train from Glasgow, Great Britain was ambushed at Sears Crossing and robbed at Bridego Bridge near Mentmore, Great Britain. The gang escaped with about 120 mailbags containing £2,631,784 ($7.41 million) worth of banknotes being taken to London for destruction. Only £343,448 ($961,654) was recovered.

Jewels   The greatest recorded theft of jewels was from the bedroom of the "well-guarded" villa of Prince Abdel Aziz bin Ahmed Al-Thani near Cannes, France on 24 July 1980. The jewels were valued at $16 million.

Greatest kidnapping ransom   Historically the greatest ransom paid

Greatest bank note forgery   The greatest forgery was the German Third Reich's forging operation, code name "Bernhard," engineered by SS Sturmbannführer Alfred Naujocks of the Technical Dept. of the German Secret Service Amt VI F in Berlin in 1940–41. It involved £150 million worth ($604.5 million) of £5 notes (worth $20.15).

Biggest bank fraud   The Banca Nazionale del Lavoro, Italy's leading bank, admitted on 6 Sep. 1989 that it had been defrauded of an estimated $3 billion, with the disclosure that its branch in Atlanta, GA had made unauthorized loan commitments to Iraq. Both the bank's chairman, Nerio Nesi, and its director general, Giacomo Pedde, resigned following the revelation.

Computer fraud   Between 1964 and 1973, 64,000 fake insurance policies were created on the computer of the Equity Funding Corporation in the United States, involving $2 billion.
   Stanley Mark Rifkin (b. 1946) was arrested in Carlsbad, CA by the FBI on 6 Nov. 1978 and charged with defrauding a Los Angeles bank of $10.2 million by manipulation of a computer system. He was sentenced to eight years' imprisonment in June 1980.

Maritime fraud   A cargo of 198,414 tons of Kuwaiti crude oil on the supertanker *Salem* at Durban was sold without title to the South African government in December 1979. The ship mysteriously sank off Senegal on 17 Jan. 1980, leaving the government to pay £148 million ($318.2 million) to Shell International, which owned the shipment.

was that for Atahualpa by the Incas to Francisco Pizarro in 1532–33 at Cajamarca, Peru, which constituted a hall full of gold and silver, worth some $170 million on today's market.

The greatest ransom ever reported in modern times was 1,500 million pesos ($60 million) for the release of the brothers Jorge Born, 40, and Juan Born, 39, of the firm Bunge and Born, paid to the left-wing urban guerrilla group Montoneros in Buenos Aires, Argentina on 20 June 1975.

Greatest hijack ransom   The highest amount ever paid to aircraft hijackers was $6 million, by the Japanese government, in the case of a JAL DC-8 at Dacca Airport, Bangladesh on 2 Oct. 1977, with 38 hostages. Six convicted criminals were also exchanged. The Bangladesh government had refused to sanction any retaliatory action.

Largest narcotics haul   The greatest haul in a drug seizure was on 28 Sep. 1989, when cocaine with an estimated street value of $6–7 billion was seized in a raid on a warehouse in Los Angeles, CA. The haul of 22 tons was prompted by a tip-off from a local resident who had complained about heavy truck traffic and people leaving the warehouse "at odd hours and in a suspicious manner."

The greatest haul in terms of weight was by the authorities in Bilo, Pakistan on 23 Oct. 1991. The seizure comprised 85,846 lbs. of hashish and 7,128 lbs. of heroin.

Largest narcotics operation   The bulkiest haul was 3,200 tons of Colombian marijuana in the 14-month-long "Operation Tiburon," carried out by the Drug Enforcement Administration. The arrest of 495 people and the seizure of 95 vessels was announced on 5 Feb. 1982.

CAPITAL PUNISHMENT

The discovery of Tollund man (found with a leather noose around his neck) in a bog near Silkeborg, Denmark in 1950 showed that capital punishment dates at least from the Iron Age. The countries in which capital punishment is still prevalent include China, South Africa, Turkey, Iran, Iraq, Saudi Arabia, Malaysia, United States (36 states) and some independent countries which were until recently in the USSR. Capital punishment was first abolished de facto in 1798 in Liechtenstein.

To 22 May 1992, 176 people have been put to death in the United States since the Supreme Court permitted states to restore the death penalty. Executions have been permitted in 20 states; Texas has executed 50 men, the most of any state.

Earliest   The earliest recorded execution among white settlers in the United States was that of John Billington for murder at Plymouth, MA on 30 Sep. 1630. The earliest judicial electrocution was of William Kemmler at Auburn Prison, NY, on 6 Aug. 1890, for the murder of Matilda Zeigler 495 days before.

Largest hanging   The most people hanged from one gallows were 38 Sioux Indians by William J. Duly outside Mankato, MN on 26 Dec. 1862 for the murder of unarmed citizens. Approximately 300 Indians were captured and taken prisoner by the U.S. Army. Of these, 39 were sentenced to death, but one individual turned state's evidence, and for that his sentence was commuted by President Lincoln to a term of ten years. The remaining prisoners were set free from federal prison in 1866.

The Nazi Feldkommandant simultaneously hanged 50 Greek resistance fighters as a reprisal measure in Athens, Greece on 22 July 1944.

Last public hangings   The last public hanging in the United States occurred at Owensboro, KY on 14 August 1936, when Rainey Bethea, a black man convicted of the rape and murder of an elderly white woman, was hung in a field by the banks of the Ohio River. He was executed in the presence of a crowd of between 10,000 and 15,000, including young children. The following year a "private" hanging was performed, which was actually witnessed by some 500 people although the number of official witnesses was limited to just 12—Roscoe "Red" Jackson was hung on 21 May 1937 at Galena, MO.

Last from yardarm   The last naval execution at the yardarm was the hanging of Private John Dalliger, Royal Marines, aboard HMS *Leven* in Victoria Bay near Luda, China, on 13 July 1860. Dalliger had been found guilty of two attempted murders.

Last guillotinings   The last person to be publicly guillotined in France was the murderer Eugen Weidmann, before a large crowd at Versailles, near Paris, France at 4:50 A.M. on 17 June 1939. Dr. Joseph Ignace Guillotin (1738–1814) died a natural death. He had advocated the use of the machine designed by Dr. Antoine Louis in 1789 in the French constituent assembly.

The last use before abolition on 9 Sep. 1981 was on 10 Sep. 1977 at Baumettes Prison, Marseilles, for torturer and murderer Hamida Djandoubi, age 28.

Death row   The longest sojourn on death row was the 39 years of Sadamichi Hirasawa (1893–1987) in Sendai Jail, Japan. He was convicted in 1948 of poisoning 12 bank employees with potassium cyanide to effect a theft of $403, and died in prison at the age of 94.

On 31 Oct. 1987 Liong Wie Tong, 52, and Tan Tian Tjoen, 62, were executed for robbery and murder by firing squad in Jakarta, Indonesia after 25 years on death row.

United States   Howard Virgil Lee Douglas spent 17½ years on death row, more than any other person in American penal history. On 15 May 1991 he was resentenced to life in prison.

PRISON SENTENCES

Longest sentences   Chamoy Thipyaso, a Thai woman known as the queen of underground investing, and seven of her associates were each sentenced to serve 141,078 years in jail by the Bangkok Criminal Court, Thailand on 27 July 1989 for swindling the public through a multimillion-dollar deposit-taking business.

For failing to deliver 42,768 letters, a sentence of 384,912 years, or nine years per letter, was demanded at the prosecution of mailman Gabriel Mar Grandos, 22, at Palma de Mallorca, Spain on 11 Mar. 1972.

The longest sentence imposed on a mass murderer was 21 consecutive life sentences and 12 death sentences in the case of John Wayne Gacy Jr., who killed 33 boys and young men between 1972 and 1978 in Illinois. He was sentenced by a jury in Chicago, IL on 13 Mar. 1980.

Longest time served   Paul Geidel (1894–1987) was convicted of second-degree murder on 5 Sep. 1911 when he was a 17-year-old porter in a hotel in New York. He was released from the Fishkill Correctional Facility, Beacon, NY at the age of 85 on 7 May 1980, having served 68 years, 8 months and 2 days—the longest recorded term in US history. He first refused parole in 1974.

Oldest   Bill Wallace (1881–1989) was the oldest prisoner on record, spending the last 63 years of his life in Aradale Psychiatric Hospital, at Ararat, Victoria, Australia. He had shot and killed a man at a restaurant in Melbourne, Victoria in December 1925, and having been found unfit to plead, was transferred to the responsibility of the Mental Health Department in February 1926. He remained at Aradale until his death on 17 July 1989, shortly before his 108th birthday.

Most arrests   A record for arrests was set by Tommy Johns (1922–88) in Brisbane, Queensland, Australia on 9 Sep. 1982 when he faced his 2,000th conviction for drunkenness since 1957. His total at the time of his last drink on 30 Apr. 1988 was "nearly 3,000."

Greatest mass arrest   The greatest mass arrest reported in a democratic country was of 15,617 demonstrators on 11 July 1988, rounded up by South Korean police to ensure security in advance of the 1988 Olympic Games in Seoul.

FINES

Heaviest   The largest fine ever was one of $650 million, which was imposed on the US securities firm of Drexel Burnham Lambert in December 1988 for insider trading. This figure represented $300 million in direct fines, with the balance to be put into an account to satisfy claims of parties who could prove they were defrauded by Drexel's actions.

The record for an individual is $200 million, which Michael Milken (see also Business World, Highest salary) agreed to pay on 24 Apr. 1990. In addition, he agreed to settle civil charges filed by the Securities and Exchange Commission and is now serving a 10-year prison sentence. The payments were in settlement of a criminal racketeering and securities fraud suit brought by the US government.

PRISONS

Most secure prison   After it became a maximum security federal prison in 1934, no convict was known to have lived to tell of a successful escape from the prison on Alcatraz Island in San Francisco Bay, CA. A total of 23 men attempted it, but 12 were recaptured, five were shot dead, one drowned and five were presumed drowned. On 16 Dec. 1962, just before the prison was closed on 21 Mar. 1963, one man reached the mainland alive, only to be recaptured on the spot. John Chase held the record for the longest time spent in Alcatraz, 26 years.

Most expensive prison   Spandau Prison, Berlin, originally built in 1887

HIGHEST FINES. The record fine imposed on an individual is $200 million, which Michael Milken, the "junk bond king," agreed to pay on 24 Apr. 1990. In addition, he agreed to settle civil charges filed by the Securities and Exchange Commission. The payments were in settlement of a criminal racketeering and securities fraud suit brought by the US government. He was later given a ten-year prison term, and is seen in this photograph with his wife following the announcement of his sentence. (Photo: Gamma)

for 600 prisoners, was used solely for the Nazi war criminal Rudolf Hess (26 Apr. 1894–17 Aug. 1987) for the last twenty years of his life. The cost of maintenance of the staff of 105 was estimated in 1976 to be $415,000 per year. On 19 Aug. 1987 it was announced that Hess had strangled himself with a piece of electric cord and that he had left a note in old German script. Two months after his death, the prison was demolished.

Longest escape   The longest recorded escape by a recaptured prisoner was that of Leonard T. Fristoe, 77, who escaped from Nevada State Prison on 15 Dec. 1923 and was turned in by his son on 15 Nov. 1969 at Compton, CA. He had had 46 years of freedom under the name of Claude R. Willis. He had killed two sheriff's deputies in 1920.

Greatest jail breaks   In February 1979 a retired US Army colonel, Arthur Bull Simons, led a band of 14 to break into Gasre Prison, Tehran, Iran to rescue two fellow Americans. Some 11,000 other prisoners took advantage of this and the Islamic revolution in what became history's largest-ever jailbreak. It was arranged by H. Ross Perot, the employer of the two Americans.

In September 1971, Raúl Sendic and 105 other Tupamaro guerrillas, plus five nonpolitical prisoners, escaped from a Uruguayan prison through a tunnel 298 ft. long.

HONORS, DECORATIONS
AND AWARDS

Oldest order The earliest honor known was the "Gold of Honor" for extraordinary valor awarded in the 18th Dynasty *c.* 1440–1400 B.C. A statuette was found at Qan-el-Kebri, Egypt. The oldest true order was the Order of St. John of Jerusalem (the direct descendant of which is the Sovereign Military Order of Malta), legitimized in 1113.

Youngest awardee The youngest age at which an official gallantry award has ever been won is eight years in the case of Anthony Farrer, who was given the Albert Medal on 23 Sep. 1916 for fighting off a cougar at Cowichan Lake, Vancouver Island, Canada to save Doreen Ashburnham. She was also awarded the Albert Medal, which, in 1974, was exchanged for the George Cross.

Most valuable annual prize The value of each of the 1992 Nobel Prizes (see Nobel Prizes) was Sw Kr 6.5 million, which at the time of printing was equivalent to approximately $969,000. The ceremonial presentations for the annual prizes in physics, chemistry, physiology or medicine, literature, and economics take place in Stockholm, Sweden, and the presentations for peace take place in Oslo, Norway.

Most statues The world record for raising statues to oneself was set by Generalissimo Dr. Rafael Leónidas Trujillo y Molina (1891–1961), former president of the Dominican Republic. In March 1960 a count showed that there were "over 2,000." The country's highest mountain was named Pico Trujillo (later Pico Duarte). One province was called Trujillo and another Trujillo Valdez. The capital was named Ciudad Trujillo (Trujillo City) in 1936, but reverted to its old name of Santo Domingo de Guzmán on 23 Nov. 1961. Trujillo was assassinated in an automobile ambush on 30 May 1961, and 30 May is now celebrated as a public holiday.

The man to whom the most statues have been raised is Buddha. The 20th-century champion is Vladimir Ilyich Ulyanov, alias Lenin (1870–1924), busts of whom have been mass-produced. This also has been the case with Mao Zedong (Mao Tse-tung) (1893–1976); and with Ho Chi Minh (1890–1969).

MILITARY

United States The highest US military decoration is the Congressional Medal of Honor. Five Marines received both the Army and Navy Medals of Honor for the same deeds in 1918, and 14 officers and men received the medal on two occasions between 1864 and 1915 for two distinct acts. The Defense Department refuses to recognize any military hero as having the most awards, but various heroes have been nominated by unofficial groups. Since medals and decorations cannot be compared in value, the title of most decorated is a matter of subjective evaluation. General Douglas MacArthur (1880–1964), because of his high rank and his years of military service spanning three wars, would seem to hold the best claim to "Most Decorated American Soldier." In addition to the Congressional Medal of Honor, he received 58 separate awards and decorations with 16 Oak Leaf Clusters (for repeat awards), plus 18 campaign stars.

Germany   The Knight's Cross of the Iron Cross with swords, diamonds and golden oak-leaves was uniquely awarded to Col. Hans Ulrich Rudel (1916–82) for 2,530 operational flying missions on the Eastern Front in the period 1941–45. He destroyed 519 Soviet armored vehicles.

USSR   The USSR's highest award for valor is the Gold Star of a Hero of the Soviet Union, of which 12,709 have been awarded, 11,040 of them during World War II. The only wartime triple awards were to Marshal Georgi Konstantinovich Zhukov (1896–1974; subsequently awarded a fourth Gold Star), and to the leading air aces Guards Colonel (later Marshal of Aviation)

NOBEL PRIZES

Earliest   1901 for Physics, Chemistry, Physiology or Medicine, Literature and Peace.

Most Prizes   The United States has won outright or shared 206 prizes, including most for Physiology or Medicine (69); Physics (55); Chemistry (36), Peace (18); Economics (18). France has most for Literature (12).

Oldest Laureate   Professor Francis Peyton Rous (USA; 1879–1970) in 1966 shared in Physiology or Medicine prize at the age of 87.

Youngest Laureates   *At time of award:* Professor Sir Lawrence Bragg (Great Britain; 1890–1971) 1915 Physics prize at 25. *At time of work:* Bragg, and Theodore W. Richards (USA; 1868–1928) 1914 Chemistry prize at 23. Literature: Rudyard Kipling (Great Britain; 1865–1936) 1907 prize at 41. *Peace:* Mrs. Mairead Corrigan-Maguire (Republic of Ireland; b. 27 Jan. 1944) 1976 prize (shared) at 32.

Most   3 Awards: International Committee of the Red Cross, Geneva (founded 1863) Peace 1917, 1944 and 1963 (shared); 2 Awards: Dr. Linus Carl Pauling (USA; b. 28 Feb. 1901) Chemistry 1954 and Peace 1962; Mme. Marja Sklodowska Curie (Polish-French; 1867–1934) Physics 1903 (shared) and Chemistry 1911; Professor John Bardeen (USA; 1908–91) Physics 1956 (shared) and 1972 (shared); Professor Frederick Sanger (b. 13 Aug. 1918) Chemistry 1958 and 1980 (shared); Office of the United Nations' High Commissioner for Refugees, Geneva (founded 1951) Peace 1954 and 1981.

Highest Prize   Sw Kr 6,000,000 (for 1991), equivalent to $969,000.

Lowest Prize   Sw Kr 115,000 (1923).

Aleksandr Ivanovich Pokryshkin (1913–85) and Aviation Maj. Gen. Ivan Nikitovich Kozhedub (1920–91) (Order of the Red Banner, seven times). Zhukov also uniquely was awarded the Order of Victory (twice), the Order of Lenin (six times) and the Order of the Red Banner (three times). The highest award of civil honor is the Gold Star of Socialist Labor, 20,424 of which have been awarded since it was established in 1938. There have been 15 awards of a third Gold Star of Socialist Labor. Leonid Ilyich Brezhnev (1906–82) was four times Hero of the Soviet Union and Hero of Socialist Labor, Order of Victory (withdrawn in 1990), Order of Lenin (eight times) and Order of the Red Banner (twice).

Most titles   The most titled person in the world is the 18th Duchess of Alba (Alba de Tormes), Doña Maria del Rosario Cayetana Fitz-James Stuart y Silva. She is six times a duchess, once a viscountess, 18 times a marchioness, 19 times a countess and 17 times a Spanish grandee.

Most honorary degrees   The greatest number of honorary degrees awarded to any individual is 123, given to Rev. Father Theodore M. Hesburgh (b. 1917), president of the University of Notre Dame, IN. These have been accumulated since 1954.

Most parade ribbons   On 10 June 1991, at the massive "Operation Welcome Home" parade in New York City, 140 miles of waterproof yellow ribbon were donated by Berwick Industries, Inc. and New York's Operation Welcome Home committee.

MILITARY AND DEFENSE

WAR

Earliest conflict   The oldest-known offensive weapon is a broken wooden spear found in April 1911 at Clacton-on-Sea, Great Britain by S. Hazzledine Warren. It is much beyond the limit of radiocarbon dating but is estimated to have been fashioned before 200,000 B.C.

Longest   The longest war which could be described as continuous was the Thirty Years War, between various European countries from 1618 to 1648. As a result, the map of Europe was radically changed. The so-called Hundred Years War between England and France, which lasted from 1338 to 1453 (115 years), was in fact a succession of wars rather than a single one. The *Reconquista*—the series of campaigns in the Iberian Peninsula to recover the region from the Islamic Moors—began in 718 and continued intermittently until 1492, when Granada, the last Moorish stronghold, was finally conquered.

Bloodiest   By far the most costly war in terms of human life was World War II (1939–45), in which the total number of fatalities, including battle deaths and civilians of all countries, is estimated to have been 54.8 million, assuming 25 million Soviet fatalities and 7.8 million Chinese civilians killed. The country that suffered most was Poland, with 6,028,000 or 17.2 percent of its population of 35.1 million killed. The total combatant death toll from World War I was 9.7 million, compared with the 15.6 million from World War II.

In the Paraguayan war of 1864–70 against Brazil, Argentina and Uruguay, Paraguay's population was reduced from 1.4 million to 220,000 survivors, of whom only 30,000 were adult males.

Dr. William Brydon (1811–73) and two natives were the sole survivors of a seven-day retreat of 13,000 soldiers and camp-followers from Kabul, Afghanistan. Dr. Brydon's horse died two days after his arrival at Jellalabad, some 70 miles to the east on the route to the Khyber Pass, on 13 Jan. 1842.

Bloodiest civil   The bloodiest civil war in history was the *Taiping* ("Great Peace") rebellion, which was a revolt against the Chinese Ch'ing Dynasty between 1851 and 1864. The rebellion was led by the deranged Hong Xiuquan (later executed), who imagined himself to be a younger brother of Jesus Christ. His force was named *Taiping Tianguo* ("Heavenly Kingdom of Great Peace"). According to the best estimates the loss of life was some 20 million, including more than 100,000 killed by government forces in the sack of Nanjing on 19–21 July 1864.

Most costly   The material cost of World War II far transcended that of all the rest of history's wars put together and has been estimated at $1.5 trillion. The total cost to the Soviet Union was estimated in May 1959 at 2.5 trillion rubles, while a figure of $530 billion has been estimated for the United States.

Bloodiest battles   *Modern*   The battle with the greatest recorded number of *military* casualties was the first Battle of the Somme, France, from 1 July–19 Nov. 1916, with 1,043,896; of these, 623,907 were Allied and the rest German. The published German figure of *c.* 670,000 is no longer accepted. Gunfire was heard in London, Great Britain.

The greatest death toll in a single battle (military and civilian) has been estimated at *c.* 2.1 million in the Battle of Stalingrad, USSR (now Volgograd, Russia), ending with the German surrender on 31 Jan. 1943 by Field Marshal Friedrich von Paulus (1890–1957). The Soviet garrison commander was Gen. Vasiliy Chuikov. Only 1,515 civilians out of a prewar population of more than 500,000 were found alive after the battle. The final drive on Berlin, Germany by the Soviet Army and the battle for the city that followed, from 16 April–2 May 1945, involved 3.5 million men, 52,000 guns and mortars, 7,750 tanks and 11,000 aircraft on both sides.

Ancient   Modern historians give no credence, on logistic grounds, to the casualty figures attached to ancient battles, such as the 250,000 reputedly killed at Plataea (Greeks *v.* Persians) in 479 B.C. or the 200,000 allegedly killed in a single day at Châlons-sur-Marne, France (Huns *v.* Romans) in A.D. 451.

United States   The American Civil War (1861–65) is the bloodiest war fought on American soil. The bloodiest battles between the Northern (Union) and the Southern (Confederate) forces were at Shiloh Church, near Pittsburg Landing in Hardin Co., TN on 6–7 Apr. 1862, when each side reported casualties of over 10,000; at Fredricksburg, VA on 13 Dec. 1862, when Union losses were over 12,000, more than double those of the Confederacy; and at Gettysburg, PA on 1–3 July 1863, when the Union reported losses of 23,000 and the Confederacy 25,000 (a disputed figure). The Civil War officially ended when Confederate General Robert E. Lee surrendered to Union General Ulysses S. Grant at Appomattox Courthouse, VA on 9 Apr. 1865.

Shortest war   The shortest war on record was that between Great Britain and Zanzibar (now part of Tanzania), which lasted from 9:02 to 9:40 A.M. on 27 Aug. 1896. The British battle fleet under Rear-Admiral Harry Rawson (1843–1910) delivered an ultimatum to the self-appointed Sultan Sa'īd Khalid to evacuate his palace and surrender. This was not forthcoming until after 38 minutes of bombardment. It was proposed at one time that elements of the local populace should be compelled to defray the cost of the broadsides fired.

Youngest conscripts   President Francisco Macias Nguema of Equatorial Guinea (deposed in August 1979) in March 1976 decreed compulsory military service for all boys between the ages of 7 and 14. The edict stated that any parent refusing to hand over his or her son "will be imprisoned or shot."

Largest civilian evacuation   Following the Iraqi invasion of Kuwait in August 1990, Air India evacuated 111,711 of its nationals who were working in Kuwait. Beginning on 13 August, 488 flights took the expatriates back to India over a two-month period.

Speed march   A team of nine, representing II Squadron RAF Regiment from RAF Hullavington, Great Britain, each man carrying a 40 lb. pack, including a rifle, completed the London Marathon in 4 hrs. 33 min. 58 sec. on 21 Apr. 1991.
   John Hunter of Scarborough, Great Britain set an individual record in the Humber Bridge Marathon on 8 Sep. 1991 with a pack weighing 44½ lbs. His time was 4 hrs. 17 min. 3 sec.

Army drill   On 8–9 July 1987 a 90-man squad of the Queen's Color Squadron, Royal Air Force (RAF) performed a total of 2,722,662 drill movements (2,001,384 rifle and 721,278 foot) at RAF Uxbridge, Middlesex, Great Britain from memory and without a word of command in 23 hrs. 55 min.

Greatest naval battles *Modern*   The greatest number of ships and aircraft ever involved in a sea–air action was 231 ships and 1,996 aircraft in the Battle of Leyte Gulf, in the Philippines, during World War II. It raged from 22–27 Oct. 1944, with 166 Allied and 65 Japanese warships engaged, of which 26 Japanese and six US ships were sunk. In addition, 1,280 US and

MOST DESTRUCTIVE NAVAL BATTLE. The death toll at the Battle of Lepanto, in the Gulf of Patras, Greece on 7 Oct. 1571, has been estimated at 33,000. The battle was between allied Christian forces and the Ottoman Turks during an Ottoman campaign to take the island of Cyprus. The allies were victorious, capturing 117 galleys in the process. (Photo: Archiv für Kunst und Geschichte)

716 Japanese aircraft were engaged. The greatest purely naval battle of modern times was the Battle of Jutland on 31 May 1916, during World War I, in which 151 British Royal Navy warships were involved against 101 German warships. The Royal Navy lost 14 ships and 6,097 men and the German fleet lost 11 ships and 2,545 men.

Ancient   The greatest of ancient naval battles was the Battle of Salamis, Greece in Sep. 480 B.C. There were an estimated 800 vessels in the defeated Persian fleet and 380 in the victorious fleet of the Athenians and their allies, with a possible involvement of 200,000 men. The death toll at the Battle of Lepanto on 7 Oct. 1571 has been estimated at 33,000.

Greatest invasion *Seaborne*   The greatest invasion in military history was the Allied land, air and sea operation against the Normandy coast of France on D-Day, 6 June 1944. Thirty-eight convoys of 745 ships moved in during the first three days, supported by 4,066 landing craft, carrying 185,000 men, 20,000 vehicles and 347 minesweepers. The air assault comprised 18,000 paratroopers from 1,087 aircraft The 42 available divisions had air support from 13,175 aircraft Within a month 1.1 million troops, 200,000 vehicles and 840,000 tons of stores were landed. The Allied invasion of Sicily from 10–12 July 1943 involved the landing of 181,000 men in three days.

Airborne   The largest airborne invasion was the Anglo-American assault

of three divisions (34,000 men), with 2,800 aircraft and 1,600 gliders, near Arnhem, in the Netherlands, on 17 Sep. 1944.

Greatest evacuation   The greatest evacuation in military history was that carried out by 1,200 Allied naval and civilian craft from the beachhead at Dunkerque (Dunkirk), France between 27 May and 4 June 1940. A total of 338,226 British and French troops were evacuated.

Longest march   The longest march in military history was the famous Long March by the Chinese Communists in 1934–35. In 368 days, of which 268 were days of movement, from October to October, their force of some 100,000 covered 6,000 miles from Ruijin, in Kiangsi, to Yan'an, in Shaanxi. They crossed 18 mountain ranges and 24 rivers, and eventually reached Yanan with only about 8,000 survivors, following continual rearguard actions against nationalist Kuomintang (KMT) forces.

Worst sieges   The worst siege in history was the 880-day siege of Leningrad, USSR (now St. Petersburg, Russia) by the German Army from 30 Aug. 1941 until 27 Jan. 1944. The best estimate is that between 1.3 and 1.5 million defenders and citizens died. This included 641,000 people who died of hunger in the city and 17,000 civilians killed by shelling. More than 150,000 shells and 100,000 bombs were dropped on the city.

The longest recorded siege was that of Azotus (now Ashdod), Israel, which according to Herodotus was besieged by Psamtik I of Egypt for 29 years, during the period 664–610 B.C.

Chemical warfare   The greatest number of people killed through chemical warfare were the estimated 4,000 Kurds who died at Halabja, Iraq in March 1988 when President Saddam Hussein used chemical weapons against

Iraq's Kurdish minority in revenge for the support it had given to Iran in the Iran–Iraq war.

DEFENSE SPENDING

In 1990 it was estimated that the world's spending on armaments was running at an annual rate of some $900 billion, according to the 1990 edition of the *United Nations Disarmament Yearbook*. In 1990 there were 25,320,000 full-time armed forces regulars or conscripts plus 37,586,000 reservists, totaling 62,906,000. The budgeted expenditure on defense by the US government for the fiscal year 1991 was $287.45 billion. The defense expenditure of the former USSR is given as 96.56 billion rubles in 1991, or $133.7 billion, but Western intelligence agencies still maintain that by NATO definition standards, spending is about twice as large as claimed.

LONGEST MARCH. The longest march in military history was the Long March by the Chinese Communists in 1934–35. In 368 days, from October to October, their force of some 100,000 covered 6,000 miles from Ruijin, in Kiangsi, to Yan'an, in Shaanxi. The march led to the Communist revolutionary base being relocated to the northwest of the country and resulted in the emergence of Mao Zedong (Mao Tse-tung) as the undisputed leader of the party. Mao, on the left, and Zhou En-lai (Chou En-lai), with him in the photograph, were to be leading figures in the party for the rest of their lives. (Photo: Hulton Picture Co.)

ARMED FORCES

Largest   Numerically the largest regular armed force in the world was that of the USSR prior to its breakup, with 3,400,000 (1991). It is too early to forecast the size of Russian armed forces following the breakup of the Soviet Union, but figures of between 1.25 and 1.5 million are frequently mentioned. China's People's Liberation Army's strength in 1991 was estimated to be 3,030,000 (comprising land, sea and air forces), with reductions in progress. Her reserves number around 1.2 million. The military forces of the United States for 1991 totaled 2,029,600. There were 702,100 active duty personnel in the United States Army as of 30 Sep. 1991.

Navies *Largest*   The largest navy in the world in terms of personnel is the United States Navy, with a total of 584,800 plus 195,700 Marines in mid-1991. The active strength in 1991 included six nuclear-powered aircraft carriers, nine conventionally powered aircraft carriers, two battleships, 34 ballistic missile submarines, 87 nuclear attack submarines, one diesel attack submarine, 46 cruisers, 49 destroyers, 97 frigates and 65 amphibious warfare ships.

The navy of the former USSR had a larger submarine fleet, comprising 281 vessels (including 60 ballistic missiles). It also had five aircraft carriers, 38 cruisers, 29 destroyers, 146 frigates and 78 amphibious warfare ships. This excludes the Black Sea Fleet, which has 28 submarines (none with ballistic missiles), and 46 surface combatants, and whose future is not yet decided, although it is likely to be split among Ukraine, Russia and Georgia. All of the former Soviet Navy is based at Russian ports.

Armies *Oldest*   The oldest army in the world is the 80–90 strong Pontifical Swiss Guard in Vatican City, founded 21 Jan. 1506. Its origins, however, predate 1400.

Largest   Numerically, the world's largest army is that of the People's Republic of China, with a total strength of some 2.3 million in mid-1991. The total size of the former USSR's army in mid-1991 was estimated by the International Institute for Strategic Studies, London, Great Britain at 1,400,000, believed to be organized into 139 divisions (tank, motor rifle and airborne).

Oldest soldier   The oldest "old soldier" of all time was probably John B. Salling of the Army of the Confederate States of America and the last accepted survivor of the Civil War (1861–65). He died in Kingsport, TN on 16 Mar. 1959, aged 113 years 1 day.

Youngest soldier   Marshall Duke of Caxias (25 Aug. 1803–7 May 1880), Brazilian military hero and statesman, entered his infantry regiment at the age of five in 1808.

Fernando Inchauste Montalvo (b. 18 June 1930), the son of a major in the Bolivian air force, went to the front with his father on his fifth birthday during the war between Bolivia and Paraguay (1932–35). He had received military training and was subject to military discipline.

Tallest soldier   The tallest soldier of all time was Väinö Myllyrinne (1909–63), who was conscripted into the Finnish Army when he was 7 ft. 3 in. and who later grew to 8 ft. 3 in.

Greatest mutiny   In World War I, 56 French divisions, comprising some 650,000 men and their officers, refused orders on the Western front sector of General Robert Nivelle in April 1917 after the failure of his offensive.

Air forces *Oldest*   The earliest autonomous air force is the Royal Air Force, which can be traced back to 1878, when the War Office commissioned the building of a military balloon. The Royal Engineers Balloon Section and Depot was formed in 1890 and the Air Battalion of the Royal Engineers followed on 1 Apr. 1911. On 13 May 1912 the Royal Flying Corps (RFC) was formed, with both Military and Naval Wings, the latter being renamed the Royal Naval Air Service (RNAS). The Royal Air Force was formed on 1 Apr. 1918 from the RFC and the RNAS, and took its place alongside the Royal Navy and the Army as a separate service with its own Ministry. The Prussian Army used a balloon near Strasbourg, France as early as 24 Sep. 1870.

Largest   The largest air force of all time was the United States Army Air Corps (now the US Air Force), which had 79,908 aircraft in July 1944 and 2,411,294 personnel in March 1944. The US Air Force, including strategic missile forces, had 571,400 personnel and 8,471 aircraft in mid-1991. The Air Force of the former USSR had 11,370 aircraft and 895,000 personnel (including some 200,000 manning strategic air missiles) in mid-1991. In addition, the USSR's Offensive Strategic Rocket Forces had about 164,000 operational personnel in mid-1991.

Anti-submarine successes   The highest number of U-boat kills attributed to one ship in World War II was 15, to HMS *Starling* (Capt. Frederic John Walker, RN). Captain Walker was in command at the sinking of a total of 25 U-boats between 1941 and the time of his death on 9 July 1944. The US destroyer escort *England* sank six Japanese submarines in the Pacific between 18 and 30 May 1944.

Most successful submarine captains   The most successful of all World War II submarine commanders was Lieutenant Otto Kretschmer, captain of the U.23 and U.99, who up to March 1941 sank one destroyer and 44 Allied merchantmen totaling 266,629 gross registered tons.

In World War I, Lieutenant (later Vice Admiral) Lothar von Arnauld de la Périère, in the U.35 and U.139, sank 195 Allied ships totaling 458,856 gross registered tons. The most successful boats were the U.35, which in World War I sank 54 ships of 90,350 gross registered tons in a single voyage and 224 ships of 539,711 gross registered tons all told, and the U.48, which sank 51 ships of 310,007 gross registered tons in World War II. The largest target ever sunk by a submarine was the Japanese aircraft carrier *Shinano* (66,131 tons) by USS *Archerfish* (Cdr. Joseph F. Enright, USN) on 29 Nov. 1944.

Top jet ace   The leading ace of World War I was Capt. Edward V. Rickenbacker, with 24.33 destroyed aircraft. The top ace of World War II, and the top overall, was Maj. Richard I. Borg, with 40 victories. The top ace of the Vietnam conflict was Capt. Charles B. DeBellevue, with six victories. The greatest number of kills in jet-to-jet battles is 16, a record shared by Lt.-Col. Heinz Bär (Germany) in 1945 and Capt. Joseph Christopher McConnell, Jr., USAF, in the Korean war (1950–53). Capt. McConnell was killed on 25 Aug. 1954. It is possible that an Israeli ace may have surpassed this total in the period 1967–70, but the identity of Israeli pilots is subject to strict security.

Top woman ace   The record score for any woman fighter pilot is 12, by Jnr.-Lt. Lydia Litvak (USSR; b. 1921) on the Eastern Front between 1941 and 1943. She was killed in action on 1 Aug. 1943.

BOMBS

Heaviest   The heaviest conventional bomb ever used operationally was the Royal Air Force's *Grand Slam*, weighing 22,000 lbs. and measuring 25 ft. 5 in. long, dropped on Bielefeld railroad viaduct, Germany on 14 Mar. 1945.

In 1949 the United States Air Force tested a bomb weighing 42,000 lbs. at Muroc Dry Lake, CA. The heaviest-known nuclear bomb was the MK 17 carried by US B-36 bombers in the mid-1950s. It weighed 42,000 lbs. and was 24 ft. 6 in. long.

Atomic   The first atom bomb dropped on Hiroshima, Japan by the United States at 8:16 A.M. on 6 Aug. 1945 had an explosive power equivalent to that of 12.5 kilotons of trinitrotoluene ($C_7H_5O_6N_3$), called TNT. Code-named *Little Boy*, it was 10 ft. long and weighed 9,000 lbs. It burst 1,850 ft. above the city center.

Thermonuclear   The most powerful thermonuclear device so far tested is one with a power equivalent to that of 57 megatons of TNT, detonated by the former USSR in the Novaya Zemlya area at 8:33 A.M. GMT on 30 Oct. 1961. The shock-wave circled the world three times, taking 36 hrs. 27 min. for the first circuit. Some estimates put the power of this device at between 62 and 90 megatons. The largest US H-bomb tested was the 18–22 megaton *Bravo* at Bikini Atoll, Marshall Islands on 1 Mar. 1954.

On 9 Aug. 1961, Nikita Khrushchev, then the Chairman of the Council of Ministers of the USSR, declared that the Soviet Union was capable of constructing a 100-megaton bomb, and announced the possession of one during a visit to what was then East Berlin, East Germany on 16 Jan. 1963. Such a device could make a crater in rock 355 ft. deep and 1.8 miles wide, with a fireball 8.6 miles in diameter.

Largest nuclear weapons   The most powerful ICBM (intercontinental ballistic missile) is the former USSR's SS–18 (Model 5), believed to be armed with ten 750-kiloton MIRVs (multiple independently targetable reentry vehicles). SS–18 ICBMs are located on both Russian and Kazakhstan territory—they are now controlled by the Commonwealth of Independent States. Earlier models had a single 20-megaton warhead. The US Titan II, carrying a W-53 warhead, was rated at 9 megatons but has now been withdrawn, leaving the 1.2 megaton W-56 as the most powerful US weapon.

Largest "conventional" explosion   The largest use of conventional explosives was for the demolition of the fortifications and U-boat pens at Helgoland, Germany on 18 Apr. 1947. A net charge of 7,122 tons gross was detonated by Commissioned Gunner E.C. Jellis of the naval team headed by Lt. F.T. Woosnam, RN, aboard HMS *Lasso* lying 9 miles out to sea.

TANKS

Earliest   The first tank was *No. 1 Lincoln*, modified to become *Little Willie*, built by William Foster & Co. Ltd. of Lincoln, Great Britain. It first ran on 6 Sep. 1915. Tanks were first taken into action by the Heavy Section, Machine Gun Corps, which later became the Royal Tank Corps, at the Battle of Flers-Courcelette in France on 15 Sep. 1916. The Mark I Male tank, armed with a pair of six-pounder guns and four machine guns, weighed 31.3 tons and was driven by a motor developing 105 hp, which gave it a maximum road speed of 3–4 mph.

Heaviest   The heaviest tank ever constructed was the German Panzer Kampfwagen Maus II, which weighed over 210 tons. By 1945 it had reached only the experimental stage and was not developed further.

The heaviest operational tank used by any army was the 83-ton 13-man French Char de Rupture 2C bis of 1922. It carried a 155-mm. howitzer and had two 250 hp engines giving a maximum speed of 8 mph. The world's most heavily armed tank since 1972 has been the Soviet T-72, with a 4⅞ in. high-velocity gun.

The heaviest tank in the United States Army is the M1A1 Abrams, which weighs 67 tons when combat loaded, is 32 ft. 3 in. long, and can reach a maximum speed of 41.5 mph.

Fastest   The fastest armored reconnaissance vehicle is the British *Scorpion*, which can reach 50 mph with a 75 percent payload. The American experimental tank M1936, built by J. Walter Christie, was clocked at 64.3 mph during official trials in Great Britain in 1938.

Most prolific   The greatest production of any tank was that of the Soviet T-54/55 series, of which more than 50,000 were built between 1954 and 1980 in the USSR alone, with further production in the one-time Warsaw Pact countries and China.

GUNS

Earliest   Although it cannot be accepted as proven, it is believed that the earliest guns were constructed in both China and North Africa in *c.* 1250. The earliest antiaircraft gun was an artillery piece on a high-angle mounting used in the Franco-Prussian War of 1870 by the Prussians against French balloons.

Most common   The most commonly used gun in the US Army is the M16A2 rifle, of which 270,000 have been fielded.

Largest   The largest gun ever constructed was used by the Germans in the siege of Sevastopol, USSR (now Russia) in July 1942. It was of a caliber of 31 in. with a barrel 94 ft. 8½ in. long. Internally it was named Schwerer Gustav, and was one of three guns that were given the general name of Dora, although the other two were not finished and so were not used in action. It was built by Krupp, and its remains were discovered near Metzenhof, Bavaria in August 1945. The whole assembly of the gun was 141 ft. long and weighed 1,481.5 tons, with a crew of 1,500. The range for an 8.9-ton projectile was 29 miles.

Lightest   The lightest gun in the US Army is the M9 9mm pistol, which weighs 2.6 lbs., has the shortest range, 55 yds., and has the smallest magazine capacity of 15 rounds.

Field gun pull   Three teams of eight members from 55 Ordnance Company (Volunteers) Royal Army Ordnance Corps pulled a 25-pounder field gun over a distance of 85.7 miles in 24 hrs. in Hounslow, Great Britain on 15–16 Apr. 1988.

Armor   The highest auction price paid for a suit of armor was £1,925,000 ($3,657,000), by B.H. Trupin (USA) on 5 May 1983 at Sotheby's, London, Great Britain for a suit made in Milan by Giovanni Negroli in 1545 for Henri II of France. It came from the Hever Castle Collection in Kent, Great Britain.

Military engines   The largest military catapults, or onagers, could throw a missile weighing 60 lbs. a distance of 500 yds.

Heaviest   The heaviest gun in the US Army is the MK19-3 40mm automatic grenade launcher, which weighs 72.5 lbs. and has both the greatest caliber and range of any US Army weapon: about 1,650 yds. at point targets, over 2,400 yds. at area targets. The bullets can penetrate 2 in. into armor at 2,400 yds.

Greatest range   The greatest range ever attained by a gun was achieved by the HARP (High Altitude Research Project) gun, consisting of two 16½ in. caliber barrels in tandem 119.4 ft. long and weighing 165 tons, at Yuma, AZ. On 19 Nov. 1966 an 185-lb. projectile was fired to an altitude of 111.8 miles or 590,550 ft. The static V3 underground firing tubes built in 50° shafts near Mimoyècques, near Calais, France by Germany during World War II, to bombard London, Great Britain, were never operative.

The famous long-range gun that shelled Paris, France in World War I was the *Kaiser Wilhelm Geschütz*, with a caliber of 8¼ in., a designed range of 79½ miles and an achieved range of 76 miles from the Forest of Crépy in March 1918. The *Big Berthas* were mortars of 16½ in. caliber and with a range of less than 9 miles.

Mortars   The largest mortars ever constructed were Mallet's mortar (Woolwich Arsenal, London, Great Britain, 1857); and the *Little David* of World War II, made in the United States. Each had a caliber of 36 in., but neither was ever used in action.

The heaviest mortar ever employed was the tracked German 23½ in. siege piece *Karl*; there were seven such mortars built. Only six of them were actually used in action, although never all at the same time—at Sevastopol, USSR in 1942; at Warsaw, Poland in 1944; and at Budapest, Hungary, also in 1944.

Largest cannon   The highest-caliber cannon ever constructed is the *Tsar Pushka* (*King of Cannons*), now housed in the Kremlin, Moscow, Russia. It was built in the 16th century with a bore of 35 in. and a barrel 17 ft. 6 in. long. It weighs 44 tons.

The Turks fired up to seven shots per day from a bombard 26 ft. long, with an internal caliber of 42 in., against the walls of Constantinople (now Istanbul) from 12 April–29 May 1453. The weapon was dragged by 60 oxen and 200 men and fired a 1,200-lb. stone cannonball.

United States   The largest cannon in the US Army is the M185 155 mm (6.05 in.) self-propelled howitzer. The M109A2/A3 unit has a range of 14.6 miles with a RAP (rocket assisted projectile), 11.2 miles unassisted. It is approximately 29 ft. 11 in. long, 10 ft. 9½ in. high, and 10 ft. 3½ in. wide. It weighs 28 tons, combat loaded, and carries a .50 caliber machine gun as well. This weapon is capable of firing nuclear munitions.

Nuclear delivery vehicles   As of September 1990 the USSR deployed 2,500 nuclear delivery launchers compared to the USA's 2,246, as counted under the START (Strategic Arms Reduction Talks) rules and compared to the START proposed limit of 1,600. Again under START counting rules, the former USSR could deliver a maximum of 10,271 warheads and the USA 10,563, but this is a theoretical total and not necessarily the number held. The START proposed limit for nuclear warheads is 6,000. There are four republics of the former USSR (Russia, Ukraine, Belarus and Kazakhstan) that hold strategic nuclear weapons.

EDUCATION

Compulsory education was introduced for the first time in Prussia in 1819.

University *Oldest*   The Sumerians had scribal schools or *é-Dub-ba* soon after 3500 B.C. The oldest existing educational institution in the world is the University of Karueein, founded in A.D. 859 in Fez, Morocco. The University of Bologna, the oldest in Europe, was founded in 1088.

United States   The oldest college in the United States is Harvard College in Cambridge, MA, founded in 1636 as Newtowne College and renamed in 1638 after its first benefactor, John Harvard. It was incorporated in 1650. The second oldest college in the US is the College of William and Mary, in Williamsburg, VA. It was chartered in 1693, opened in 1694, and acquired university status in 1779. However, its antecedents were in a university that was planned at Henrico, VA (1619–22) but was postponed because of the Indian massacre of 1622.

Largest   The largest existing university building in the world is the M.V. Lomonosov State University on the Lenin Hills, south of Moscow, Russia. It stands 787 ft. 5 in. tall, and has 32 stories and 40,000 rooms. It was constructed from 1949–53.

Greatest enrollment   The university with the greatest enrollment in the world is the State University of New York, which had 400,777 students at 64 campuses throughout the state in the fall of 1991. The greatest enrollment at a university centered in one city is at the University of Rome (La Sapienza), in Italy. It was built in the 1920s as a single-site campus, and still is mainly based there although some faculties are now outside the campus. Its record number of students was 180,000 in 1987, although the number had declined to 166,000 by 1990.

MOST GRADUATES IN A FAMILY. Mr. and Mrs. Harold Erickson of Naples, FL saw all of their 14 children—11 sons and three daughters—obtain university or college degrees between 1962 and 1978. Bringing them together for a family photograph more than ten years later required a great deal of work and organization, involving flights home from nine different cities. (Photo: Moment-In-Time Photography)

Most graduates in family   Mr. and Mrs. Harold Erickson of Naples, FL saw all of their 14 children—11 sons and three daughters—obtain university or college degrees between 1962 and 1978.

Youngest university students   Michael Tan (b. 4 Apr. 1984) of Christchurch, New Zealand took and passed his New Zealand bursary examination in Mathematics (equivalent to high school graduation exams in the United States) in November 1991 at the age of 7 years 7 months. He started studying for a BSc degree in Mathematics at Canterbury University, New Zealand in March 1992 at the age of 7 years 11 months.

United States   Adragon Eastwood De Mello (b. 5 Oct. 1976) of Santa Cruz, CA obtained his BA in mathematics from the University of California in Santa Cruz on 11 June 1988 at the age of 11 years 8 months.

Youngest doctorate   On 13 Apr. 1814 the mathematician Carl Witte of Lochau was made a Doctor of Philosophy of the University of Giessen, Germany at the age of 12.

Youngest college president   The youngest president of a major college was Ellen Futter, who was appointed to head Barnard College, New York City in May 1981 at the age of 31.

Schools *Most expensive*   The annual cost of keeping a pupil at the Gstaad International School, Gstaad, Switzerland (founded 1974) in 1991/92 was $55,000. It claims to be the most exclusive school in the world.

The annual cost of keeping a pupil at the most expensive school in the United States for the academic year 1992/93 will be $28,900 at the Oxford Academy (founded 1906), in Westbrook, CT.

Largest   In 1988/89 Rizal High School, Pasig, Manilla, Philippines had an enrollment of 16,458 regular students, although by the school year 1991/92 the number had declined to 16,419.

Most durable teacher   Medarda de Jesús León de Uzcátegui, alias La Maestra Chuca, has been teaching in Caracas, Venezuela for a total of 80 years. In 1911, at the age of 12, she and her two sisters set up a school there which they named *Modelo de Aplicación*. Since marrying in 1942, she has run her own school, which she calls the *Escuela Uzcátegui*, from her home in Caracas.

Highest endowment   The greatest single gift in the history of higher education was $125 million, to Louisiana State University by C.B. Pennington in 1983.

Most schools   The greatest documented number of schools attended by a pupil is 265, by Wilma Williams, now Mrs. R.J. Horton, from 1933–43 when her parents were in show business in the United States.

Lecture fees   Dr. Ronald Dante was paid $3,080,000 for lecturing students on hypnotherapy at a two-day course held in Chicago on 1–2 June 1986. He taught for 8 hrs. each day, and thus earned $192,500 per hr.

RELIGIONS

Oldest   Human burial, which has religious connotations, is known from *c.* 60,000 B.C. among *Homo sapiens neanderthalensis* in the Shanidar cave, northern Iraq.

Largest   Religious statistics are necessarily only tentative, since the test of adherence to a religion varies widely in rigor, while many individuals, particularly in the East, belong to two or more religions.

Christianity is the world's most widely practiced religion, with some 1,784 million adherents in 1991, or 33.1 percent of the world's population. There were 1,010 million Roman Catholics in the same year. The largest non-Christian religion is Islam (Muslim) with some 951 million followers in 1991.

The total of world Jewry is estimated to be 14.3 million. The highest concentration is in the United States, with 5,835,000. The total in Israel is 3,653,000. The total in Tokyo, Japan is only 750.

Largest clergies   The world's largest religious organization is the Roman Catholic Church—160 cardinals, 754 archbishops, 3,246 bishops, 401,479 priests and 885,645 nuns at the end of 1989.

PLACES OF WORSHIP

Earliest   Many archaeologists are of the opinion that the decorated Upper Paleolithic caves of Europe (*c.* 30,000–10,000 B.C.) were used as places of worship or religious ritual. Claims have been made that the El Juyo cave in northern Spain contains an actual shrine, dated to *c.* 12,000 B.C. Numerous Neolithic temples from various parts of Europe and the Near East are definite evidence for the worship of deities at a very early date, and from at least 6000 B.C.

The oldest surviving Christian church in the world is a converted house in Qal'at es Salihiye (formerly Douro-Europos) in eastern Syria, dating from A.D. 232.

Oldest *Church*   The oldest standing Protestant edifice in the United States and the only remaining example of Colonial Gothic is the Newport Parish Church, commonly known as St. Luke's, in Isle of Wight County, VA, four miles south of Smithfield, VA. The church was built *c.* 1632 and was originally called Warris-quioke Parish Church. In 1637 it was renamed the Isle of Wight Parish Church and its present name was instituted in 1957.

Synagogue   The oldest synagogue in the United States is Touro Synagogue, Newport, RI. Construction was started in 1759 and completed in 1763. The synagogue was dedicated during the Channukah celebration of 1763. Originally called the Jewish Synagogue of Newport, the synagogue was closed in 1820, but reopened in 1883, renamed Touro Synagogue.

Largest temple   The largest religious structure ever built is Angkor Wat ("City Temple"), enclosing 402 acres in Cambodia (or Kampuchea), Southeast Asia. It was built to the Hindu god Vishnu by the Khmer King Suryavarman II in the period A.D. 1113–50. Its curtain wall measures 4,199 × 4,199 ft. and its population, before it was abandoned in 1432, was 80,000. The whole complex of 72 major monuments, begun *c.* A.D. 900, extends over 15 × 5 miles.

The largest Buddhist temple in the world is Borobudur, near Jogjakarta, Indonesia, built in the eighth century. It is 103 ft. tall and 403 ft. square.

The largest Mormon temple is the Salt Lake Temple, UT, dedicated on 6 Apr. 1893, with a floor area of 253,015 ft.^{2} or 5.8 acres.

Largest cathedral   The world's largest cathedral is the cathedral church of the Diocese of New York, St. John the Divine, with a floor area of 121,000 ft.^{2} and a volume of 16,822,000 ft.^{3}. The cornerstone was laid on 27 Dec. 1892, and work on the Gothic building was stopped in 1941. Work was restarted in earnest in July 1979, but is still not finished. The nave is the longest in the world at 601 ft., with a vaulting 124 ft. in height.

The cathedral covering the largest area is that of Santa Mariá de la Sede in Sevilla (Seville), Spain. It was built in Spanish Gothic style between 1402 and 1519, and is 414 ft. long, 271 ft. wide and 100 ft. high to the vault of the nave.

Smallest cathedral   The smallest church in the world designated as a cathedral (the seat of a diocesan bishop) is that of the Christ Catholic Church, Highlandville, MO. It was consecrated in July 1983. It measures 14 × 17 ft. and has seating for 18 people.

Largest church   The largest church in the world is the Basilica of St. Peter, built between 1506 and 1614 in Vatican City, Rome, Italy. Its length, including the walls of the apse and façade, is 717 ft. 6 in. The area is 247,572 ft.^{2}. The inner diameter of the famous dome is 139 ft. 8 in. and its center is 393 ft. 4 in. high. The external height is 448 ft. 1 in. Taller, although not as tall as the cathedral in Ulm, Germany (see Tallest spire), is the Basilica of Our Lady of Peace (Notre Dame de la Paix) at Yamoussoukro, Ivory Coast, completed in 1989. Including its golden cross, it is 519 ft. high.

The elliptical Basilica of St. Pius X at Lourdes, France, completed in 1957 at a cost of $5.6 million, has a capacity of 20,000 under its giant span arches and a length of 660 ft.

Smallest church   The world's smallest church is the chapel of Santa Isabel de Hungría, in Colomares, a monument to Christopher Columbus at Benalmádena, Málaga, Spain. It is of irregular shape and has a total floor area of 21⅛ ft.^{2}.

The smallest church is the United States is Cross Island Chapel, at Oneida, NY, with a floor area of 29.1 ft.^{2} (6 ft. 9½ in. × 4 ft. 3½ in.).

Brasses   The world's oldest monumental brass is that commemorating Bishop Yso von Wölpe in the Andreaskirche, Verden, near Hannover, Germany, dating from 1231.

An engraved coffin plate of St. Ulrich (d. 973), laid in 1187, was found buried in the Church of SS Ulrich and Afra, Augsburg, Germany in 1979.

Singing   Rev. Acharya Prem Bhikshuji (d. 18 Apr. 1970) started chanting the Akhand Rama-Dhoon at Jamnagar, Gujarat, India on 1 Aug. 1964, and devotees were still continuing the chant in May 1992.

Undertakers   The world's largest undertaking business is SCI (Service Corporation International) of Houston, TX, with 551 funeral homes and 126 cemeteries. Its annual revenue in this most recession-proof of industries in the year ending 31 Dec. 1989 was $519 million.

Longest-serving chorister   John Love Vokins (1890–1989) was a chorister for 92 years. He joined the choir of Christ Church, Heeley, Great Britain in 1895 and that of St. Michael's, Hathersage, Great Britain 35 years later, and was still singing in 1987.

Longest   The crypt of the underground Civil War Memorial Church in the Guadarrama Mountains, 28 miles from Madrid, Spain, is 853 ft. in length. It took 21 years (1937–58) to build, at a reported cost of $392 million, and is surmounted by a cross 492 ft. tall.

Longest service   Rev. K.M. Jacob (1880–1984) was made a deacon in the Marthoma Syrian Church of Malabar in Kerala, southern India in 1897. He served his church for 87 years.

Largest synagogue   The largest synagogue in the world is Temple Emanu-El on Fifth Avenue at 65th Street, New York City. The temple, completed in September 1929, has a frontage of 150 ft. on Fifth Avenue and 253 ft. on 65th Street. The sanctuary proper can accommodate 2,500 people, and the adjoining Beth-El Chapel seats 350. When all the facilities are in use, more than 6,000 people can be accommodated.

Largest mosque   The largest mosque is Shah Faisal Mosque, near Islamabad, Pakistan. The total area of the complex is 48.87 acres, with the covered area of the prayer hall being 1.19 acres. It can accommodate 100,000 worshippers in the prayer hall and the courtyard, and a further 200,000 people in the adjacent grounds.

Tallest minaret   The tallest minaret in the world is that of the Great Hassan II Mosque, Casablanca, Morocco, measuring 576 ft. The cost of construction of the mosque was $381.5 million. Of ancient minarets, the tallest is the Qutb Minar, south of New Delhi, India, built in 1194 to a height of 238 ft. tall.

Tallest and oldest stupa   The now largely ruined Jetavanarama dagoba in the ancient city of Anuradhapura, Sri Lanka, measures 400 ft. in height. The 326-ft.-tall Shwedagon Pagoda, Yangon (formerly Rangoon), Myanmar (formerly Burma) is built on the site of a 27-ft.-tall pagoda of 585 B.C.

Sacred object   The sacred object with the highest intrinsic value is the 15th-century gold Buddha in Wat Trimitr Temple in Bangkok, Thailand. It is 10 ft. tall and weighs an estimated 6.06 tons. At the March 1992 price of $341.90 per fine ounce, its intrinsic worth was $34.02 million. The gold under the plaster exterior was found only in 1954.

Tallest spire   *Cathedral*   The tallest cathedral spire in the world is that of the Protestant Cathedral of Ulm in Germany. The building is early Gothic and was begun in 1377. The tower, in the center of the west façade, was not finally completed until 1890 and is 528 ft. high.

Church   The world's tallest church spire is that of the Chicago Temple of the First Methodist Church on Clark Street, Chicago, IL. The building consists of a 22-story skyscraper (erected in 1924) surmounted by a parsonage at 330 ft., a "Sky Chapel" at 400 ft. and a steeple cross at 568 ft. above street level.

Stained glass   *Oldest*   Pieces of stained glass dated before A.D. 850, some possibly even to the seventh century, excavated by Prof. Rosemary Cramp, were set into a window of that date in the nearby St. Paul's Church, Jarrow, Great Britain. The oldest complete stained-glass window in the world represents the Prophets in a window of the Cathedral of Augsburg, Germany, dating from the second half of the 11th century.

United States The oldest figured stained-glass window in the United States is in Christ Church, Pelham Manor, NY and was designed by William Jay Bolton and John Bolton in 1843.

Largest The largest stained-glass window is that of the Resurrection Mausoleum in Justice, IL, measuring 22,381 ft.^{2} in 2,448 panels, completed in 1971.

Although not one continuous window, the Basilica of Our Lady of Peace (Notre Dame de la Paix) at Yamoussoukro, Ivory Coast contains a number of stained-glass windows covering a total area of 80,000 ft.^{2}.

Tallest The tallest stained glass is the 135-ft.-high back-lit glass mural installed in 1979 in the atrium of the Ramada Hotel, Dubai.

CHURCH PERSONNEL

There are more than 2,000 "registered" saints, of whom around two-thirds are either Italian or French.

The first native-born American Roman Catholic saint was Mother Elizabeth Ann Bayley Seton (1774–1821), canonized 14 Sep. 1975.

Bishops *Oldest* The oldest Roman Catholic bishop in recent years was Archbishop Edward Howard, formerly Archbishop of Portland-in-Oregon (b. 5 Nov. 1877), who died at the age of 105 years 58 days on 2 Jan. 1983. He had celebrated mass about 27,800 times.

Youngest The youngest bishop of all time was HRH the Duke of York and Albany, the second son of George III, who was elected Bishop of Osnabrück, through his father's influence as Elector of Hanover, at the age of 196 days on 27 Feb. 1764. He resigned 39 years later.

United States The first consecrated Roman Catholic Bishop of the United States was John Carroll (1735–1815) of Baltimore, MD. In 1808, Carroll, a Jesuit, became the first Catholic archbishop of the United States, with suffragan sees at Boston, New York City, Philadelphia and Baidstown, KY. Carroll also founded Georgetown University in 1789.

Oldest parish priest Father Alvaro Fernandez (8 Dec. 1880–6 Jan. 1988) served as a parish priest at Santiago de Abres, Spain from 1919 until he was 107 years old.

The oldest Anglican clergyman, Rev. Clement Williams (b. 30 Oct. 1879), died at the age of 106 years 3 months on 3 Feb. 1986. He stood on the route at Queen Victoria's funeral and was ordained in 1904.

Sunday school The pioneer of the Sunday school movement is generally accepted to be Robert Raikes (1736–1811). In 1780 he engaged a number of women in his home city of Gloucester to teach children on Sundays. Reading and religious instruction were from the outset the main activities, and by 1785 the Sunday School Society had been formed.

F. Otto Brechel (1890–1990) of Mars, PA completed 88 years (4,576 Sundays) of perfect attendance at church school at three different churches in

POPES AND CARDINALS

LONGEST PAPAL REIGN
Pius IX—Giovanni Maria Mastai-Ferretti (1846–78).
31 years 236 days

SHORTEST PAPAL REIGN
Stephen II (died 752). 2 days

LONGEST-LIVED POPES
St. Agatho (d. 681; probably exaggerated), ?106 years.
Leo XIII—Gioacchino Pecci (1810–1903). 93 years 140 days

YOUNGEST ELECTED
John XII—Ottaviano (c. 937–64) in 955. 18 years old

LAST MARRIED
Adrian II (pre-celibacy rule). Elected 867

LAST WITH CHILDREN
Gregory XIII—Ugo Buoncompagni (1502–85). One son.
Elected 1572

LAST NON-CARDINAL
Urban VI—Bartolomeo Prignano (1318–89), Archbishop of Bari.
Elected 8 Apr. 1378

LAST PREVIOUS NON-ITALIAN
Adrian VI—Adrian Florensz Boeyens (Netherlands).
Elected 9 Jan. 1522

SLOWEST ELECTION
Gregory X—Teobaldi Visconti. 31 months,
Feb. 1269–1 Sep. 1271

FASTEST ELECTION
Julius II—on first ballot, 21 Oct. 1503

SLOWEST CANONIZATION
St. Leo III—over span of 857 years, 816–1673

OLDEST CARDINAL
(all-time) Georgio da Costa (b. Portugal 1406, d. Rome, Italy
aged 102 years). Elected 18 Sep. 1508
(current) Henri De Lubac (b. Cambrai, France, 20 Feb. 1896)

YOUNGEST CARDINAL
(all-time) Luis Antonio de Bourbon (b. 25 July 1727).
8 years 147 days. Elected 19 Dec. 1735
(current) Alfonso Lopez Trujillo of Colombia
(b. 18 Nov. 1935). 47 years 76 days

LONGEST-SERVING CARDINAL
Cardinal Duke of York, grandson of James VII of Scotland
and II of England. 60 years 10 days, 1747–1807

LONGEST-SERVING BISHOP
Bishop Louis François de la Baume de Suze (1603–90).
76 years 273 days from 6 Dec. 1613

Most rapidly canonized   The shortest interval that elapsed
between the death of a saint and his or her canonization was in the
case of St. Peter of Verona, Italy, who died on 6 Apr. 1252 and was
canonized 337 days later on 9 Mar. 1253. (For the other extreme of
857 years, see the table of Popes and Cardinals.)

Pennsylvania—the first from 1902 to 1931, the second from 1931 to 1954,
and the third from 1954 onward.

Bill Tom Adams (b. 30 Aug. 1898) of Monroe, LA is the current record-
holder; he has not missed Sunday school since June 1905, although there
have been occasions when ill health has meant that someone from his class
has come to his bedside and taught the lesson.

Largest crowds   The greatest recorded number of human beings assembled with a common purpose was an estimated 15 million at the Hindu festival of Kumbh mela, which was held at the confluence of the Yamuna
(formerly the Jumna), the Ganges and the invisible "Saraswathi" at Alla-
habad, Uttar Pradesh, India on 6 Feb. 1989. (See Largest funerals.)

Largest funerals   The funeral of the charismatic C.N. Annadurai (d. 3
Feb. 1969), Madras Chief Minister, was attended by 15 million people, according to a police estimate.

The line at the grave of the Russian singer and guitarist Vladimir Visot-
sky (died 28 July 1980) stretched for 6 miles.

HUMAN ACHIEVEMENTS

Parke Thompson, joint holder of the "most traveled person" record, at the South Pole.

ENDURANCE AND ENDEAVOR

Most traveled   The world's most traveled men are Parke G. Thompson, of Akron, OH, Giorgio Ricatto, of Turin, Italy and John Clouse, of Evansville, IN. All three had visited all of the sovereign countries and nonsovereign or other territories which existed at the end of 1991 (see Countries). Thompson and Ricatto have yet to go to the Heard and McDonald Islands, an island group in the southern Indian Ocean, while Clouse has not been to the Canton and Enderbury Islands, in the Pacific Ocean.

The most traveled couple is Dr. Robert and Carmen Becker of East Northport, NY, both of whom had visited all of the nonsovereign countries (the exception being Iraq) and all but eight of the nonsovereign or other territories.

Allen F. Zondlak visited 3,142 counties and county equivalents in the United States, completing his travels in 1991.

Most isolated   The farthest any human has been removed from his nearest living fellow human is 2,233.2 miles in the case of the command module pilot Alfred M. Worden on the US *Apollo 15* lunar mission of 30 July–1 Aug. 1971, while David Scott and James Irwin were at Hadley Base exploring the surface.

Longest walks   The first person reputed to have "walked around the world" is George Matthew Schilling (USA) from 3 Aug. 1897 to 1904, but the first *verified* achievement in this category was by David Kunst (b. 1939) from 20 June 1970 to 5 Oct. 1974. He wore out 21 pairs of shoes in the process.

Tomas Carlos Pereira (b. Argentina, 16 Nov. 1942) spent ten years, from 6 Apr. 1968 to 8 Apr. 1978, walking 29,800 miles around five continents. Steven Newman of Bethel, OH spent four years, from 1 Apr. 1983 to 1 Apr. 1987, walking 22,500 miles around the world, covering 20 countries and five continents.

Rick Hansen (b. Canada, 1957), who was paralyzed from the waist down in 1973 as a result of an auto accident, wheeled his wheelchair 24,901.55 miles through four continents and 34 countries. He started his journey from Vancouver, British Columbia on 21 Mar. 1985 and arrived back there on 22 May 1987.

George Meegan (b. 2 Oct. 1952) of Rainham, Great Britain walked 19,019 miles from Usuaia, in the southern tip of South America, to Prudhoe Bay in northern Alaska, taking 2,426 days from 26 Jan. 1977 to 18 Sep. 1983. He thus completed the first traverse of the Americas and the western hemisphere on foot.

Sean Eugene Maguire (USA; b. 15 Sep. 1956) walked 7,327 miles from the Yukon River, north of Livengood, AK to Key West, FL in 307 days, from 6 June 1978 to 9 Apr. 1979. The trans-Canada (Halifax to Vancouver) record walk of 3,764 miles is 96 days, by Clyde McRae, age 23, from 1 May to 4 Aug. 1973. John Lees (b. 23 Feb. 1945) of Brighton, Great Britain walked 2,876 miles across the United States from City Hall, Los Angeles to City Hall, New York City in 53 days 12 hrs. 15 min. (averaging 53.75 miles a day) between 11 April and 3 June 1972.

North Pole conquest The claims of the two Arctic explorers Dr. Frederick Albert Cook (1865–1940) and Cdr. (later Rear-Ad.) Robert Edwin Peary (1856–1920), of the US Naval Civil Engineering branch, to have reached the North Pole are not subject to irrefutable proof, and several recent surveys have produced conflicting conclusions. On excellent pack ice and modern sleds, Wally Herbert's 1968–69 expedition (see Arctic crossing, below) attained a best day's route mileage of 23 miles in 15 hrs. Cook (see above) claimed 26 miles twice, while Peary claimed an average of 38 miles per day over eight consecutive days, which many glaciologists regard as quite unsustainable.

The first people indisputably to have reached the North Pole at ground level—the exact point at Lat. 90° 00′ 00″ N (± 300 meters)—were Pavel Afanasyevich Geordiyenko, Pavel Kononovich Sen'ko, Mikhail Mikhaylovich Somov and Mikhail Yemel'yenovich Ostrekin (all of the former USSR), on 23 Apr. 1948. They arrived and departed by air.

The earliest indisputable attainment of the North Pole by surface travel over the sea-ice took place at 3 P.M. CST on 19 Apr. 1968, when expedition leader Ralph Plaisted (USA), accompanied by Walter Pederson, Gerald Pitzel and Jean Luc Bombardier, reached the Pole after a 42-day trek in four ski-doos (snowmobiles). Their arrival was independently verified 18 hrs. later by a US Air Force weather aircraft. The party returned by aircraft.

Naomi Uemura (1941–84), the Japanese explorer and mountaineer, became the first person to reach the North Pole in a solo trek across the Arctic ice cap at 4:45 A.M. GMT on 1 May 1978. He had traveled 450 miles, setting out on 7 March from Cape Edward, Ellesmere Island in northern Canada. He averaged nearly eight miles per day with his sled *Aurora* drawn by 17 huskies. He also left by aircraft.

The first people to ski to the North Pole were the seven members of a Soviet expedition, led by Dmitry Shparo. They reached the Pole on 31 May 1979 after a trek of 900 miles which took them 77 days.

Dr. Jean-Louis Etienne, age 39, was the first to reach the Pole solo and without dogs, on 11 May 1986 after 63 days. He left by aircraft.

On 20 Apr. 1987 Fukashi Kazami, age 36, of Tokyo, Japan reached the North Pole from Ward Hunt Island, northern Canada in 44 days, having started on his 250-cc motorcycle on 8 March. He also left by aircraft.

The first woman to set foot on the North Pole was Mrs. Fran Phipps (Canada) on 5 Apr. 1971. She traveled there by ski-plane with her husband, a bush pilot. Galina Aleksandrovna Lastovskaya (b. 1941) and Lilia Vladislavovna Minina (b. 1959) were crew members of the USSR atomic ice-breaker *Arktika*, which reached the Pole on 17 Aug. 1977.

South Pole conquest The first men to cross the Antarctic Circle (Lat. 66° 33′ S) were the 193 crew members and Capt. James Cook, Royal Navy (1728–79) of the *Resolution* (509 tons) and the *Adventure* (370 tons), captained by Lt. Tobias Furneaux, on 17 Jan. 1773 at 39° E.

The first person known to have sighted the Antarctic ice shelf was Capt. Thaddeus Thaddevich Bellingshausen (Russia; 1778–1852) on 27 Jan. 1820 from the vessel *Vostok* accompanied by the *Mirnyi*. The first people known to have sighted the mainland of the continent were Capt. William Smith (1790–1847) and Master Edward Bransfield, Royal Navy, in the brig *Williams*. They saw the peaks of Trinity Land three days later, on 30 Jan. 1820.

The South Pole (alt. 9,186 ft. on ice and 336 ft. bedrock) was first reached at 11 A.M. on 14 Dec. 1911 by a Norwegian party of five men led by Capt.

Roald Engebereth Gravning Amundsen (1872–1928), after a 53-day march with dog sleds from the Bay of Whales, to which he had penetrated in the vessel *Fram*. Subsequent calculations showed that Olav Olavson Bjaaland and Helmer Hanssen of the Amundsen party probably passed within 1,300–2,000 ft. of the exact location of the South Pole. The other two members of the party were Sverre H. Hassell (died 1928) and Oskar Wisting (died 1936).

The first woman to set foot on Antarctica was Mrs. Karoline Mikkelsen, a whaling captain's wife, on 20 Feb. 1935. It was not until 11 Nov. 1969 that a woman stood at the South Pole. On that day Lois Jones, Eileen McSaveney, Jean Pearson, Terry Lee Tickhill (all USA), Kay Lindsay (Australia) and Pam Young (New Zealand) arrived by air at Amundsen-Scott station and walked to the exact point from there.

First to visit both Poles   Dr. Albert Paddock Crary (USA; 1911–87) reached the North Pole in a Dakota aircraft on 3 May 1952. On 12 Feb. 1961

Most traveled man   The most traveled man in the era before motor vehicles was believed to be the Methodist preacher Bishop Francis Asbury (b. Handsworth, Great Britain, 1745), who traveled 264,000 miles in North America between 1771 and 1815. During this time he preached some 16,000 sermons and ordained nearly 3,000 ministers.

First to see both Poles   The first people to see both Poles were Amundsen and Oskar Wisting when they flew aboard the airship *Norge* over the North Pole on 12 May 1926, having previously been to the South Pole on 14 Dec. 1911.

Submergence   The *continuous* duration record (i.e., no rest breaks) for scuba (i.e., self-contained underwater breathing apparatus, used without surface air hoses) is 212 hrs. 30 min., by Michael Stevens of Birmingham, Great Britain in a Royal Navy tank at the National Exhibition Center, Birmingham from 14–23 Feb. 1986. Measures have to be taken to reduce the numerous health risks in such endurance trials.

Longest on a raft   The longest recorded survival alone on a raft is 133 days (4½ months) by Second Steward Poon Lim (b. Hong Kong) of Great Britain's Merchant Navy, whose ship, the SS *Ben Lomond*, was torpedoed in the Atlantic 565 miles west of St. Paul's Rocks at Lat. 00° 30′ N, Long. 38° 45′ W at 11:45 A.M. on 23 Nov. 1942. He was picked up by a Brazilian fishing boat off Salinópolis, Brazil on 5 Apr. 1943 and was able to walk ashore.

Tabwai Mikaie and Arenta Tebeitabu, two fishermen from the island of Nikunau in Kiribati, survived for 175 days adrift at sea in their fishing boat's 13-ft. open dinghy. They were caught in a cyclone shortly after setting out on a trip on 17 Nov. 1991 and were found washed ashore in Western Samoa, 1,200 miles away, on 14 May 1992. A third man had left with them but died a few days before they reached Western Samoa.

he arrived at the South Pole by Sno Cat on a scientific traverse party from the McMurdo Station.

First to walk to both Poles   The first man to walk to both the North and the South Poles was Robert Swan (Great Britain; b. 1956). He led the three-man Footsteps of Scott expedition, which reached the South Pole on 11 Jan. 1986, and three years later headed the eight-man Icewalk expedition, which arrived at the North Pole on 14 May 1989.

Arctic crossing   The first crossing of the Arctic sea-ice was achieved by the British Trans-Arctic Expedition, which left Point Barrow, AK on 21 Feb. 1968 and arrived at the Seven Island archipelago northeast of Spitzbergen, Svalbard, Norway 464 days later, on 29 May 1969. This involved a haul of 2,920 statute miles with a drift of 700 miles, compared with the straight-line distance of 1,662 miles. The team was made up of Wally Herbert (leader), 34, Major Ken Hedges, RAMC, 34, Allan Gill, 38, Dr. Roy Koerner (glaciologist), 36, and 40 huskies. The only crossing achieved in a single season was that by Fiennes and Burton (see Pole to Pole circumnavigation, below) from Alert via the North Pole to the Greenland Sea in open snowmobiles. Both reached the North Pole and returned by land.

Antarctic crossing   The first surface crossing of the Antarctic continent was completed at 1:47 P.M. on 2 Mar. 1958, after a trek of 2,158 miles lasting 99 days from 24 Nov. 1957, from Shackleton Base to Scott Base via the Pole. The crossing party of 12 was led by Dr. (now Sir) Vivian Ernest Fuchs (Great Britain; b. 11 Feb. 1908). The 2,600 mile trans-Antarctic leg from Sanae to Scott Base of the 1980–82 British Trans-Globe Expedition was achieved in 67 days, from 28 Oct. 1980 to 11 Jan. 1981, having reached the South Pole on 15 Dec. 1980. The three-man party on snowmobiles comprised Sir Ranulph Fiennes (b. 1944), Oliver Shepard and Charles Burton.

Pole to Pole circumnavigation   The first Pole to Pole circumnavigation was achieved by Sir Ranulph Fiennes and Charles Burton of the British Trans-Globe Expedition, who traveled south from Greenwich, Great Britain (2 Sep. 1979), via the South Pole (15 Dec. 1980) and the North Pole (10 Apr. 1982), and back to Greenwich, arriving on 29 Aug. 1982 after a 35,000 mile trek.

Longest sled journeys   The longest totally self-supporting polar sled journey ever made was one of 1,080 miles from west to east across Greenland from 18 June to 5 Sep. 1934 by Capt. M. Lindsay (later Sir Martin Lindsay of Dowhill, Great Britain; 1905–81), Lt. Arthur S.T. Godfrey (later Lt.-Col., killed 1942), Andrew N.C. Croft (later Col.), and 49 dogs. The Ross Sea Party of ten (three died) sledded over 2,000 miles in 300 days from 6 May 1915.

The International Trans-Antarctic Expedition (six members) sledded a distance of some 2,300 miles in 117 days from 7 Nov. 1989 (Patriot Hills) to 3 Mar. 1990 (Mirnyy). The journey had started at Seal Nunataks on 27 July 1989, but the dogs accompanying the expedition were flown out from Patriot Hills to South America for a period of rest before returning to the Antarctic. The expedition was supported by aircraft throughout its duration.

Greatest ocean descent   The record ocean descent was achieved in the Challenger Deep of the Mariana Trench, 250 miles southwest of Guam in the

Pacific Ocean, when the Swiss-built US Navy bathyscaphe *Trieste*, manned by Dr. Jacques Piccard (Switzerland; b. 1914) and Lt. Donald Walsh, USN, reached a depth of 35,813 ft. at 1:10 P.M. on 23 Jan. 1960. (See Oceans, deepest.) The pressure of the water was 16,883 lbf./in.^{2} and the temperature 37°F. The descent took 4 hrs. 48 min. and the ascent 3 hrs. 17 min.

Deep-diving records   The record depth for the *ill-advisedly* dangerous activity of breath-held diving is 351 ft., by Angela Bandini (Italy) on a marked cable off Elba, Italy on 3 Oct. 1989. She was underwater for 2 min. 46 sec.

The record dive with scuba (self-contained underwater breathing apparatus) is 437 ft., by John J. Gruener and R. Neal Watson (USA) off Freeport, Grand Bahama on 14 Oct. 1968.

The record dive utilizing gas mixtures (nitrogen, oxygen and helium) was a simulated dive of 2,250 ft. in a dry chamber by Stephen Porter, Len Whitlock and Erik Kramer at Duke University Medical Center in Durham, NC on 3 Feb. 1981, in a 43-day trial in a sphere of 8 ft. diameter.

A team of six divers (four Comex and two French Navy) descended and worked efficiently during a period of six days to a depth of 1,706 ft. off Marseilles, France, as part of the Hydra VIII operation in the spring of 1988. This involved the use of "hydreliox," a synthetic breathing mixture containing a high percentage of hydrogen. Arnaud de Nechaud de Feral performed a saturation dive of 73 days from 9 Oct.–21 Dec. 1989 in a hyperbaric chamber simulating a depth of 985 ft., as part of the Hydra IX operation carried out by Comex at Marseilles, France. He was breathing "hydrox," a mixture of hydrogen and oxygen.

High-altitude diving   The record for high-altitude diving is 16,200 ft. in Lake Donag-Tsho in the Himalayas, Nepal, by Frank B. Mee, Dr. John Leach and Dr. Andy McLean on 4 Mar. 1989. They dove to a depth of 92 ft., having first cut through 5 ft. of ice in temperatures of –18°F.

Deepest underwater escapes   The deepest underwater rescue ever achieved was of the *Pisces III*, in which Roger R. Chapman (28) and Roger Mallinson (35) were trapped for 76 hours when their vessel sank to 1,575 ft., 150 miles southeast of Cork, Republic of Ireland on 29 Aug. 1973. It was hauled to the surface on 1 September by the cable ship *John Cabot* after work by *Pisces V*, *Pisces II* and the remote-control recovery vessel US CURV.

The greatest depth from which an actual escape without any equipment has been made is 225 ft., by Richard A. Slater from the rammed submersible *Nekton Beta* off Catalina Island, CA on 28 Sep. 1970.

The record for an escape with equipment was by Norman Cooke and Hamish Jones on 22 July 1987. During a naval exercise they escaped from a depth of 601 ft. from the submarine HMS *Otus* in Bjornefjorden, off Bergen, Norway. They were wearing standard suits with a built-in life jacket, from which air expanding during the ascent passes into a hood over the escaper's head.

Deepest salvage   The greatest depth at which salvage has been successfully carried out is 17,251 ft., in the case of a helicopter that had crashed into the Pacific Ocean in August 1991 with the loss of four lives. Crew of the USS *Salvor* and personnel from East Port International managed to raise the wreckage to the surface on 27 Feb. 1992 so that the authorities could try to determine the cause of the accident.

HIGH-ALTITUDE DIVING. The record for high-altitude diving is 16,200 ft. in Lake Donag-Tsho in the Himalayas, Nepal, by Frank B. Mee, Dr. John Leach and Dr. Andy McLean on 4 Mar. 1989. They were accompanied by four ducks as mascots.

The deepest salvage operation ever achieved with divers was on the wreck of HM cruiser *Edinburgh*, sunk on 2 May 1942 in the Barents Sea off northern Norway, inside the Arctic Circle, in 803 ft. of water. Over 32 days (from 7 Sep.–7 Oct. 1981), 12 divers dove on the wreck in pairs, using a bell from the *Stephaniturm* (1,594 tons), under the direction of former Royal Navy officer Michael Stewart. A total of 460 gold ingots (the only 100 percent salvage to date) was recovered, John Rossier being the first person to touch the gold.

Greatest penetration into the Earth   The deepest penetration made into the ground by human beings is in the Western Deep Levels Mine at Carletonville, Transvaal, South Africa, where a record depth of 11,749 ft. was attained on 12 July 1977. The virgin rock temperature at this depth is 131° F. (See also Borings and mines.)

Shaft-sinking record   The one-month (31 days) world record is 1,251 ft. for a standard shaft 26 ft. in diameter at Buffelsfontein Mine, Transvaal, South Africa, in March 1962.

MARRIAGES

Most marriages   The greatest number of marriages contracted by one person in the monogamous world is 27, by former Baptist minister Glynn "Scotty" Wolfe (1908–91) of Blythe, CA, who first married in 1927. He believed that he had a total of 41 children.

The greatest number of monogamous marriages by a woman is 22, by Linda Lou Essex of Anderson, IN. She has been married to 15 different men since 1957, her most recent marriage being in October 1991. Less than a month later it was reported that she was seeking a divorce.

The record for bigamous marriages is 104, by Giovanni Vigliotto—one of many aliases used by either Fred Jipp (b. New York, 3 Apr. 1936) or Nikolai Peruskov (b. Siracusa, Sicily, 3 Apr. 1929) during 1949–81 in 27 states and 14 foreign countries. Four victims were aboard one ship in 1968 and two were in London, Great Britain. On 28 Mar. 1983 in Phoenix, AZ he received a sentence of 28 years for fraud and six for bigamy, and was fined $336,000. He died in February 1991.

Oldest bride and bridegroom   The oldest recorded bridegroom was Harry Stevens, age 103, who married Thelma Lucas, 84, at the Caravilla Retirement Home, WI on 3 Dec. 1984.

The oldest recorded bride is Minnie Munro, age 102, who married Dudley Reid, 83, at Point Clare, New South Wales, Australia on 31 May 1991.

Longest marriage   The longest recorded marriages were both of 86 years. Sir Temulji Bhicaji Nariman and Lady Nariman, who were married from 1853 to 1940, were cousins, and the marriage took place when both were age five. Sir Temulji (b. 3 Sep. 1848) died, at the age of 91 years 11 months, in August 1940 in Bombay, India. Lazarus Rowe (b. Greenland, NH in 1725) and Molly Webber were recorded as marrying in 1743. He died first, in 1829, also after 86 years of marriage.

Golden weddings   The greatest number of golden weddings in a family is ten, the six sons and four daughters of Joseph and Sophia Gresl of Manitowoc, WI all celebrating golden weddings between April 1962 and Sep-

Best man   The world champion "best man" is Ting Ming Siong, from Sibu, Sarawak, in Malaysia, who in March 1992 officiated at a wedding for the 737th time since 1976.

Longest engagement   The longest engagement on record was between Octavio Guillen and Adriana Martinez. They finally took the plunge after 67 years in June 1969 in Mexico City. Both were then 82 years old.

Most married   Ralph and Patsy Martin of Quartzsite, AZ have married each other a total of 51 times, their first wedding having been in 1960. Richard and Carole Roble of South Hempstead, NY have also married each other 51 times, with their first wedding being in 1969. Both couples have chosen different locations each time.

Youngest married   It was reported in 1986 that an 11-month-old boy was married to a 3-month-old girl in Bangladesh to end a 20-year feud between two families over a disputed farm.

tember 1988, and the six sons and four daughters of George and Eleonora Hopkins of Patrick County, VA all celebrating their golden weddings between November 1961 and October 1988.

Wedding ceremonies   The largest mass wedding ceremony was one of 6,516 couples officiated over by Sun Myung Moon (b. 1920) of the Holy Spirit Association for the Unification of World Christianity at a factory near Seoul, South Korea on 30 Oct. 1988. The answer to the question "Will you swear to love your spouse forever?" was "Ye."

Most expensive   The wedding of Mohammed, son of Shaik Rashid Bin Saeed Al Maktoum, to Princess Salama in Dubai in May 1981 lasted seven days and cost an estimated $44 million. It was held in a stadium built especially for the occasion, accommodating 20,000 wedding guests.

Greatest attendance   At the wedding of cousins Menachem Teitelbaum and Brucha Sima Melsels in Uniondale, NY on 4 Dec. 1984, the attendance of the Satmar sect of Hasidic Jews was estimated to be 17,000–20,000.

Oldest divorced   The oldest aggregate age of a couple being divorced is 188. On 2 Feb. 1984 a divorce was granted in Milwaukee, WI to Ida Stern, age 91, and her husband Simon, 97.

FEASTS AND CELEBRATIONS

Banquets   *Most lavish*   The most lavish menu ever served was for the main banquet at the Imperial Iranian 2,500th Anniversary gathering at Persepolis in October 1971. The feast, which lasted 5½ hrs., comprised quails' eggs stuffed with Iranian caviar, a mousse of crawfish tails in Nantua sauce, stuffed rack of roast lamb, a main course of roast peacock stuffed with *foie gras*, fig rings and raspberry sweet champagne sherbet. The wines included

Château Lafite-Rothschild 1945 at $160 (now $400) per bottle from Maxime's, Paris, France.

Largest   The largest feast was attended by 150,000 guests on the occasion of the renunciation ceremony of Atul Dalpatlal Shah, when he became a monk, at Ahmedabad, India on 2 June 1991.

Indoors   The greatest number of people served indoors at a single sitting was 18,000 municipal leaders at the Palais de l'Industrie, Paris, France on 18 Aug. 1889.

Military   It was estimated that some 30,000 guests attended a military feast given at Radewitz, Poland on 25 June 1730 by King August II (1709–33).

Dining out   The world champion for eating out was Fred E. Magel of Chicago, IL, who over a period of 50 years dined out 46,000 times in 60 countries as a restaurant grader. He claimed that the restaurant that served the largest helpings was Zehnder's Hotel, Frankenmuth, MI. Mr. Magel's favorite dishes were South African rock lobster and mousse of fresh English strawberries.

The greatest altitude at which a formal meal has been held is 22,205 ft., at the top of Mt. Huascaran, Peru, when nine members of the Ansett Social Climbers from Sydney, Australia scaled the mountain on 28 June 1989 with a dining table, chairs, wine and a three-course meal. At the summit they put on top hats and thermal evening attire for their dinner party, which was marred only by the fact that the wine turned to ice.

Party-giving   The International Year of the Child children's party in Hyde Park, London, Great Britain on 30–31 May 1979 was attended by the British royal family and 160,000 children.

The world's biggest birthday party was attended by 75,000 people at Buffalo, NY on 4 July 1991 as part of the 1991 Friendship Festival to celebrate the 215th birthday of the United States and Canada's 115th birthday.

The largest Christmas party ever staged was the one thrown by the Boeing Co. in the 65,000-seat Kingdome, Seattle, WA. The party was held in two parts on 15 Dec. 1979, and a total of 103,152 people attended.

During St. Patrick's week of 11–17 Mar. 1985, Houlihan's Old Place hosted St. Pat's Parties at the 48 Kansas City, MO-based Gilbert/Robinson restaurants, for a total of 206,854 documented guests.

Dish   The largest item on any menu in the world is roasted camel, prepared occasionally for Bedouin wedding feasts. Cooked eggs are stuffed into fish, the fish stuffed into cooked chickens, the chickens stuffed into a roasted sheep's carcass and the sheep stuffed into a whole camel.

MISCELLANEOUS ENDEAVORS

We intend to continue the process of phasing out those record categories in the "Human Achievements" chapter in which the duration of the event is the only criterion for inclusion. If you are planning an attempt on an endurance marathon you should contact us at a very early stage to check whether that category is likely to be retained in future editions of the book.

Barrel rolling The record for rolling a full 36-gallon metal beer barrel over a measured mile is 8 min. 7.2 sec., by Phillip Randle, Steve Hewitt, John Round, Trevor Bradley, Colin Barnes and Ray Glover of Haunchwood Collieries Institute and Social Club, Nuneaton, Great Britain on 15 Aug. 1982.

A team of ten rolled a 140 lb. barrel 150 miles in 30 hrs. 31 min. in Chlumcany, Czechoslovakia on 27–28 Oct. 1982.

Barrow pushing The heaviest loaded one-wheeled barrow pushed for a minimum 200 level feet was one loaded with bricks weighing a gross 8,275 lbs. It was pushed a distance of 243 ft. by John Sarich at London, Ontario, Canada on 19 Feb. 1987.

Barrow racing The fastest time attained in a 1 mile wheelbarrow race is 4 min. 48.51 sec., by Piet Pitzer and Jaco Erasmus at the Transvalia High School, Vanderbijlpark, South Africa on 3 Oct. 1987.

Bathtub racing The record for a 36 mile bathtub race is 1 hr. 22 min. 27 sec., by Greg Mutton at the Grafton Jacaranda Festival, New South Wales, Australia on 8 Nov. 1987. Tubs are limited to 75 in. and 6 hp motors. The greatest distance for paddling a hand-propelled bathtub in still water in 24 hrs. is 90½ miles, by 13 members of Aldington Prison Officers Social Club, near Ashford, Great Britain on 28–29 May 1983.

Bed making The pair record for making a bed with one blanket, two sheets, an undersheet, an uncased pillow, one bedspread and "hospital" corners is 17.3 sec., by Sister Sharon Stringer and Nurse Michelle Benkel of the Royal Masonic Hospital, London, Great Britain on 19 Sep. 1990, shown on the British Broadcasting Corporation's *Record Breakers* TV program.

The record time for one person to make a bed is 28.2 sec., by Wendy Wall, 34, of Hebersham, Sydney, Australia on 30 Nov. 1978.

Bed pushing The longest recorded push of a normally stationary object is of 3,233 miles, in the case of a wheeled hospital bed by a team of nine employees of Bruntsfield Bedding Center, Edinburgh, Great Britain from 21 June–26 July 1979.

Bed race The course record for a 10-mile bed race, is 50 min. as established by the Westbury Harrier's three-man bed team at Chew Valley, Avon, Great Britain.

Beer coaster flipping Dean Gould of Felixstowe, Great Britain flipped and caught a pile of 102 coasters (490 gsm wood pulp board) through 180 degrees in Hamburg, Germany on 18 Mar. 1988.

Beer keg lifting Tommy Gaskin raised a keg of beer weighing 137.8 lbs. above his head 656 times in the space of 6 hrs. at Newry, Northern Ireland on 28 Oct. 1989.

Beer stein carrying Barmaid Rosie Schedelbauer covered a distance of 49 ft. 2½ in. in 4 sec. with five full steins in each hand in a televised contest at Königssee, Germany on 29 June 1981.

Brick lifting Russell Bradley of Worcester, Great Britain lifted 30 bricks laid side by side off a table, raising them to chest height and holding them there for two seconds on 17 Nov. 1990. The greatest weight of bricks lifted was also by Russell Bradley on the same day, when he succeeded in lifting 26 far-heavier bricks weighing a total of 189 lbs. 9 oz., again holding them for two seconds.

Catapulting The greatest recorded distance for a catapult shot is 1,362 ft. by James M. Pfotenhauer, using a patented 17 ft. 1½ in. Monarch IV Supershot and a 53-caliber lead musket ball on Ski Hill Road, Escanaba, MI on 10 Sep. 1977.

Cigar box balancing Bruce Block balanced 213 cigar boxes (without modification) on his chin for 9.2 sec. at the Guinness World of Records exhibition, London, Great Britain on 5 Nov. 1990.

Crocheting Barbara Jean Sonntag (b. 1938) of Craig, CO crocheted 330 shells plus five stitches (equivalent to 4,412 stitches) in 30 min. at a rate of 147 stitches per min. on 13 Jan. 1981.

Ria van der Honing of Wormerveer, Netherlands completed a crochet chain 38.83 miles long on 14 July 1986.

Crawling The longest continuous voluntary crawl (progression with one or other knee in unbroken contact with the ground) on record is 31½ miles, by Peter McKinley and John Murrie, who covered 115 laps of an athletic track at Falkirk, Great Britain on 28–29 Mar. 1992. Over a space of 15 months ending on 9 Mar. 1985, Jagdish Chander, 32, crawled 870 miles from Aligarh to Jamma, India to propitiate his revered Hindu goddess, Mata.

Ducks and drakes (stone skipping) The video-verified record is 29 skips (14 plinkers and 15 pitty-pats), by Arthur Ring, 69, at Midway Beach, CA on 4 Aug. 1984; and Jerdone "Jerry" McGhee, 42, at Wimberley, TX on 18 Nov. 1986.

Egg and spoon racing Dale Lyons of Meriden, Great Britain ran 26 miles 385 yds. (the classic marathon distance) while carrying a dessert spoon with a fresh egg on it in 3 hrs. 47 min. on 23 Apr. 1990.

United States Chris Riggio of San Francisco, CA took 4 hrs. 9 min. 45 sec. to run 26 miles 385 yds. in a fresh egg and dessert spoon marathon on 7 Oct. 1979.

Egg hunt The greatest egg hunt on record in the United States involved

Bubble   David Stein of New York City created a 50-ft.-long bubble on 6 June 1988. He made the bubble using a bubble wand, dishwashing liquid and water.

Bubble-gum blowing   The greatest reported diameter for a bubble-gum bubble under the strict rules of this highly competitive activity is 22 in., by Susan Montgomery Williams of Fresno, CA in June 1985.

Crepe tossing   The greatest number of times a crepe has been tossed in 2 min. is 283, by Philip Artingstall of Portrush, Northern Ireland on 22 May 1992.

Largest garbage can   The world's largest garbage can was made by Natsales of Durban, South Africa for "Keep Durban Beautiful Association Week" from 16–22 Sep. 1991. The 19.71 ft. tall fiberglass can is a replica of Natsales' standard make and has a capacity of 11,493 gals.

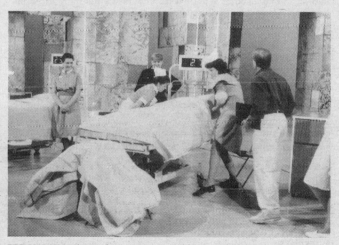

BED MAKING. Sister Sharon Stringer and Nurse Michelle Benkel of the Royal Masonic Hospital, London, Great Britain set a new two-person record for making a bed with a time of 17.3 sec. on 19 Sep. 1990.

120,000 plastic and candy eggs at a community Easter egg hunt at Coquina Beach in Manatee, FL on 23 Mar. 1991. The event, hosted by Meals on Wheels PLUS of Manatee, Inc., involved more than 40,000 children.

Footbag   This sport originated in Oregon in 1972 and was invented by John Stalberger (USA).

The world record for keeping a footbag airborne is 48,825 consecutive kicks or hacks by Ted Martin (USA) in Memphis, TN on 4 June 1988. The women's record is held by Francine Beaudry (Canada), with 15,458 on 28 July 1987 at Golden, CO.

The greatest number of kicks in five minutes is 912 by Kenny Shults (USA) at Golden, CO on 30 July 1991, and for women the record is 665 by Jody Welch (USA) on 31 July 1990, again at Golden, CO.

Garbage collection   The greatest number of volunteers involved in collecting garbage in one location in one day is 19,924, who cleaned up the city of Wellington, New Zealand in the "Keep Wellington Beautiful" campaign on 6 Oct. 1991.

United States   The greatest number of volunteers involved in collecting garbage in one location in the United States in one day is 18,143, along the coastline of Florida on 22 Sep. 1990 as part of the Center for Marine Conservation's National Beach Cleanup program.

Gold panning   The fastest time for "panning" eight planted gold nuggets in a 10 in. diameter pan is 7.55 sec. by Don Roberts of Diamond Bar, CA in the 27th World Gold Panning Championship on 16 Apr. 1989 at Dahlonega, GA.

The women's record is 10.03 sec., by Susan Bryeans of Fullerton, CA at the 23rd World Gold Panning Championship on 6 Mar. 1983 at Knott's Berry Farm, Buena Park, CA.

Grape catching   The greatest distance at which a grape thrown from level ground has been caught in the mouth is 327 ft. 6 in. by Paul J. Tavilla at East Boston, MA on 27 May 1991. The grape was thrown by James Deady.

Gum wrapper chain   The longest gum wrapper chain on record was 5,967 ft. in length, and was made by Cathy Ushler of Redmond, WA between 1969 and 1987.

Hopscotch   The greatest number of games of hopscotch successfully completed in 24 hrs. is 307, by Ashrita Furman of Jamaica, NY in Zürich, Switzerland on 5–6 Apr. 1991.

Hula-hooping, simultaneous   The record for simultaneous hula-hooping is 2,010 participants, at the St. John Labatt's Lite 24-Hour Relay in St. John, New Brunswick, Canada on 21 Sep. 1990.

Human centipede   The largest "human centipede" to move 98 ft. 5 in. (with ankles firmly tied together) consisted of 1,189 people at York, Great Britain on 16 Oct. 1991. Nobody fell over in the course of the walk.

Kissing   Alfred A.E. Wolfram of New Brighton, MN kissed 8,001 people in 8 hrs. at the Minnesota Rennaissance Festival on 15 Sep. 1990—one every 3.6 seconds.

Knitting   The world's most prolific hand-knitter has been Mrs. Gwen Matthewman of Featherstone, Great Britain. She attained a speed of 111 stitches per min. in a test at Phildar's Wool Shop, Leeds, Great Britain on 29 Sep. 1980.

The Exeter Spinners—Audrey Felton, Christine Heap, Eileen Lancaster, Marjorie Mellis, Ann Sandercock and Maria Scott—produced a sweater by hand from raw fleece in 1 hr. 55 min. 50.2 sec. on 25 Sep. 1983 at British Broadcasting Corporation Television Centre, London, Great Britain.

Knot-tying   The fastest recorded time for tying the six Boy Scout Handbook Knots (square knot, sheet bend, sheepshank, clove hitch, round turn and two half hitches, and bowline) on individual ropes is 8.1 sec. by Clinton R. Bailey, Sr., 52, of Pacific City, OR on 13 Apr. 1977.

Land rowing   The greatest distance covered by someone on a land rowing machine is 3,280 miles, by Rob Bryant of Fort Worth, TX, who "rowed" across the United States. He left Los Angeles, CA on 2 Apr. 1990, reaching Washington, D.C. on 30 July.

Lightning, most times struck   The only man in the world to be struck by lightning seven times is ex-park ranger Roy C. Sullivan (USA), the human lightning conductor of Virginia. His attraction for lightning began in 1942 (lost big toenail), and was resumed in July 1969 (lost eyebrows), in July 1970 (left shoulder seared), on 16 Apr. 1972 (hair set on fire), on 7 Aug. 1973 (hair set afire again and legs seared), on 5 June 1976 (ankle injured), and he was sent to Waynesboro Hospital with chest and stomach burns on 25 June 1977 after being struck while fishing. In September 1983 he died by his own hand, reportedly rejected in love.

Log rolling   The record number of International Championships won is 10, by Jubiel Wickheim of Shawnigan Lake, British Columbia, Canada, between 1956 and 1969. At Albany, OR on 4 July 1956 Wickheim rolled on a 14 in. log against Chuck Harris of Kelso, WA for 2 hrs. 40 min. before losing.

The youngest international log-rolling champion is Cari Ann Hayer (b. 23 June 1977), who won her first championship on 15 July 1984 at Hayward, WI.

Milk bottle balancing   The greatest distance walked by a person continuously balancing a full pint milk bottle on the head is 61 miles Ashrita Furman at Jamaica, NY on 23 May 1992. It took him 15 hr. 2 min. to complete the walk.

Milk crate balancing   Terry Cole managed to balance 25 crates on his chin for 10.3 sec. on the Isle of Dogs, London, Great Britain on 28 July 1991.

Needle threading   The record number of times that a strand of cotton has been threaded through a number 13 needle (eye ½ in. × ¹⁄₁₆ in.) in 2 hrs. is 11,796, set by Sujay Kumar Mallick of Bhopal, India on 5 Apr. 1992.

Sprinting stars

Carl Lewis set the 100-meter world record in August 1991, but what would happen if he were to compete against other people who have set records over the same distance?

Lewis ran 100 meters in 9.86 seconds. If **Florence Griffith-Joyner** had set her world record in the same race, she would have covered 94 meters by the time he crossed the finishing line, and she would be nearly three meters ahead of men running at the world record pace of 100 years ago. **Owen Morse** can juggle while he runs, and would be seven meters further back. The current stilt-walking record was set by **Roy Luiking** of the Netherlands. He would still have 25 meters to go, but would finish just ahead of **Ferdie Ato Adoboe**, who was running

backwards. Snowshoeing is more difficult (and would need a different track surface), but **Jeremy Badeau** is not far behind. Inevitably a person who walked on his hands could not keep up with the others, and does not even finish in the frame, but **Shin Don Mok** from South Korea would still have covered a quarter of the course.

Carl Lewis wins, but they are all winners in their own events.

United States The record number of times that a strand of cotton has been threaded through a number 13 needle (eye ½ in. × ¹⁄₁₆ in.) in 2 hrs. is 5,370, set by Diane Sharp on 1 Aug. 1987 at the Charitable Union's centennial event, Battle Creek, MI.

Oyster opening The record for opening oysters is 100 in 2 min. 20.07 sec., by Mike Racz in Invercargill, New Zealand on 16 July 1990.

Paper chain The Interact Club of Ivybridge, Great Britain, together with a team of helpers, made a paper chain 29 miles long at the National Shire Horse Center, Devon, Great Britain on 22–23 June 1991. The chain, which was made in under 24 hrs., consisted of more than 300,000 links.

Pogo stick jumping The greatest number of jumps achieved is 177,737, by Gary Stewart at Huntington Beach, Los Angeles, CA on 25–26 May 1990. Ashrita Furman of Jamaica, NY set a distance record of 14.99 miles in 5 hrs. 33 min. on 25 May 1991 in Seoul, South Korea.

Rope slide The greatest distance recorded in a rope slide is from the top of Blackpool Tower, Lancashire, Great Britain—a height of 454 ft. 11 in.—to a fixed point 1,120 ft. from the base of the tower. Set up by the Royal Marines, the rope was descended on 8 Sep. 1989 by Sgt. Alan Heward and Cpl. Mick Heap of the Royal Marines, John Herbert of Blackpool Tower, and Cheryl Baker and Roy Castle of the British Broadcasting Corporation's *Record Breakers* TV program. The total length descended was 1,202 ft.

Scarf The longest scarf ever knitted measured an amazing 20 miles 13 ft. long. It was knitted by residents of Abbeyfield Houses for the Abbeyfield Society in Great Britain and was completed on 29 May 1988.

OYSTER OPENING. Mike Racz opened 100 oysters in a record time of 2 min. 20.07 sec. at Invercargill, New Zealand on 16 July 1990. Frequent practice at home helps him to achieve such a speed.

Shorthand   The highest recorded speeds ever attained under championship conditions are 300 words per min. (99.64 percent accuracy) for five minutes and 350 wpm (99.72 percent accuracy—that is, two insignificant errors) for two minutes, by Nathan Behrin (USA) in tests in New York in December 1922. Behrin (b. 1887) used the Pitman system, invented in 1837.

Morris I. Kligman, official court reporter of the US Court House, New York City, has taken 50,000 words in 5 hrs. (a sustained rate of 166.6 wpm). Rates are much dependent upon the nature, complexity and syllabic density of the material. Mr. G.W. Bunbury of Dublin, Ireland held the unique distinction of writing at 250 wpm for 10 minutes on 23 Jan. 1894. Mr. Arnold Bradley achieved a speed of 309 wpm without error using the Sloan-Duployan system, with 1,545 words in 5 minutes in a test in Walsall, Great Britain on 9 Nov. 1920.

Spitting   Randy Ober of Bentonville, AR spat a tobacco wad 47 ft. 7 in. at the Calico 5th Annual Tobacco Chewing and Spitting Championships, held north of Barstow, CA on 4 Apr. 1982. The record for projecting a watermelon seed is 68 ft. 9⅛ in. by Lee Wheelis at Luling, TX on 24 June 1989. The greatest recorded distance for a cherry stone is 72 ft. 7½ in., by Rick Krause at Eau Claire, MI on 2 July 1988.

Stroller pushing   The greatest distance covered in pushing a stroller in 24 hrs. is 350.23 miles by 60 members of the Oost-Vlanderen branch of Amnesty International at Lede, Belgium on 15 Oct. 1988. A ten-man team from the Royal Marines School of Music, Deal, Great Britain, with an adult "baby," covered a distance of 271.7 miles in 24 hrs. from 22–23 Nov. 1990.

Tailoring   The fastest speed in which the manufacture of a three-piece suit has been executed from sheep to finished article is 1 hr. 34 min. 33.42 sec., by 65 members of the Melbourne College of Textiles, Pascoe Vale, Victoria, Australia on 24 June 1982. Catching and fleecing took 2 min. 21 sec., and carding, spinning, weaving and tailoring occupied the remaining time.

Tightrope walking   The oldest tightrope walker was "Professor" William Ivy Baldwin (1866–1953), who crossed the South Boulder Canyon, CO on a 320 ft. wire with a 125 ft. drop on his 82nd birthday on 31 July 1948.

The world tightrope endurance record is 185 days, by Henri Rochatain (b. 1926) of France, on a wire 394 ft. long, 82 ft. above a supermarket in Saint Etienne, France from 28 Mar.–29 Sep. 1973. Doctors were puzzled by his ability to sleep on a wire.

Ashley Brophy of Neilborough, Victoria, Australia walked 7.18 miles on a wire 147.64 ft. long and 32.81 ft. above the ground at the Adelaide Grand Prix, Australia on 1 Nov. 1985 in 3½ hrs.

The greatest drop over which anyone has walked on a tightrope is 10,335 ft., above the French countryside, by Michel Menin of Lons-le-Saunier, France, on 4 Aug. 1989.

Typewriting   The highest recorded speeds attained with a ten-word penalty per error on a manual machine are—five minutes: 176 wpm by Mrs. Carole Forristall Waldschlager Bechen at Dixon, IL on 2 Apr. 1959; one hour: 147 wpm by Albert Tangora (USA) on an Underwood Standard, 22 Oct. 1923.

The official hour record on an electric typewriter is 9,316 words (40 errors) on an IBM machine, giving a net rate of 149 words per min., by Margaret Hamma, now Mrs. Dilmore (USA), in Brooklyn, NY on 20 June 1941. In an official test in 1946, Stella Pajunas, now Mrs. Garnand, attained a rate of 216 words in a minute on an IBM machine.

Gregory Arakelian of Herndon, VA set a speed record of 158 wpm, with two errors, on a personal computer in the Key Tronic World Invitational Type-off, which attracted some 10,000 entrants worldwide. He recorded this speed in the semi-final, in a three-minute test, on 24 Sep. 1991.

Mihail Shestov set a numerical record by typing spaced numbers from 1 to 785 in 5 min. in Fredriksberg, Denmark on 17 Oct. 1991.

Les Stewart of Mudjimba Beach, Queensland, Australia has typed the numbers 1 to 730,000 in *words* on 14,500 quarto sheets as of 27 Feb. 1992. His target is to become a "millionaire."

WRITING, MINUSCULE. Surendra Apharya of Jaipur, India wrote 10,056 characters (from speeches by the first Indian Prime Minister, Jawaharlal Nehru) within the size of a definitive Indian postage stamp, measuring 0.78 × 0.70 in., in December 1990.

Writing, minuscule   Surendra Apharya of Jaipur, India wrote 10,056 characters (speeches by Nehru) within the size of a definitive Indian postage stamp, measuring 0.78 × 0.70 in., in December 1990. He also succeeded in writing 1,749 characters (names of various countries, towns and regions) on a single grain of rice on 19 May 1991.

Yo-yo   A yo-yo is said to have originated in the Philippines and means "come-come." The craze began when Donald F. Duncan of Chicago, IL initiated it in 1926. "Fast" Eddy McDonald of Toronto, Ontario, Canada completed 21,663 loops in 3 hrs. on 14 Oct. 1990 in Boston, MA, having previously set a 1 hr. speed record of 8,437 loops in Cavendish, Prince Edward Island, Canada on 14 July 1990. Dr. Allen Bussey in Waco, TX on 23 Apr. 1977 completed 20,302 loops in 3 hrs.

Leapfrogging   The greatest distance covered is 999.2 miles, by 14 students from Trancos dormitory at Stanford University, CA. They started leapfrogging on 16 May 1991 and stopped 244 hrs. 43 min. later on 26 May.

Quizzes   The greatest number of participants was 80,799 in the All-Japan High School Quiz Championship, televised by NTV on 31 Dec. 1983.

Unsupported circle   The highest recorded number of people who have demonstrated the physical paradox of all being seated without a chair is an unsupported circle of 10,323 employees of the Nissan Motor Co. at Komazawa Stadium, Tokyo, Japan on 23 Oct. 1982.

Whip cracking   The longest whip ever "cracked" is one of 184 ft. 6 in. (excluding the handle), wielded by Krist King of Pettisville, OH on 17 Sep. 1991.

Most objects aloft   Eight hundred and twenty-one jugglers kept 2,463 objects in the air simultaneously, each person juggling at least three objects, in Seattle, WA in 1990.

Pirouettes with 3 cigar boxes   Kris Kremo (Switzerland) performed a quadruple turn with 3 boxes in mid-air in 1977.

JUGGLING

12 rings (flashed)   Albert Lucas (USA), 1985.

11 rings (juggled)   Albert Petrovski (USSR), 1963–66; Eugene Belaur (USSR), 1968; Sergey Ignatov (USSR), 1973.

11 bean bags (flashed)   Bruce Serafian (USA), 1992.

10 balls   Enrico Rastelli (Italy), 1896–1931; Albert Lucas (USA), 1984.

8 plates   Enrico Rastelli (Italy), 1896–1931; Albert Lucas (USA), 1984.

8 clubs (flashed)   Anthony Gatto (USA), 1989.

7 clubs (juggled)   Albert Petrovski (USSR), 1963; Sorin Munteanu (Romania), 1975; Jack Bremlov (Czechoslovakia), 1985; Albert Lucas (USA), 1985; Anthony Gatto (USA), 1988.

7 flaming torches   Anthony Gatto (USA), 1989.

7 ping-pong balls with mouth   Tony Ferko (Czechoslovakia), 1987.

5 balls inverted   Bobby May (USA), 1953.

Ball spinning (on one hand)   François Chotard (France), 9 balls, 1990.

Basketball spinning   Bruce Crevier (USA), 15 basketballs (whole body), 1991.

Bounce juggling   Tim Nolan (USA), 10 balls, 1988.

Duration: 5 clubs without a drop   45 min. 2 sec., Anthony Gatto (USA), 1989.

Duration: 3 objects without a drop   Jas Angelo (Great Britain), 8 hrs. 57 min. 31 sec., 1989.

See also Jogging, Track and Field.

FOOD

Apple pie   The largest apple pie ever baked was made by chef Glynn Christian in a 40 × 23 ft. dish at Hewitts Farm, Chelsfield, Great Britain from 25–27 Aug. 1982. Over 600 bushels of apples were included in the pie, which weighed 30,115 lbs. It was cut by Rear-Admiral Sir John Woodward.

Banana split   The longest banana split ever created measured 4.55 miles in length, and was made by residents of Selinsgrove, PA on 30 Apr. 1988.

Barbecue   The record attendance at a one-day barbecue was 35,072, at the Iowa State Fairgrounds, Des Moines, IA on 21 June 1988. The greatest meat consumption ever recorded at a one-day barbecue was at the same event—20,130 lbs. of pork consumed in 5 hrs. The greatest quantity of meat consumed at any barbecue was 21,112 lbs. of beef at the Sertoma Club Barbecue, New Port Richey, FL, from 7–9 Mar. 1986.

Cakes *Largest*   The largest cake ever created weighed 128,238 lbs. 8 oz., including 16,209 lbs. of icing. It was made to celebrate the 100th birthday of Fort Payne, AL, and was in the shape of Alabama. The cake was prepared by a local bakery, EarthGrains, and the first cut was made by 100-year old resident Ed Henderson on 18 Oct. 1989.

Tallest   The tallest cake was 101 ft. 2½ in. high, created by Beth Cornell and her team of helpers at the Shiwassee County Fairgrounds, MI. It consisted of 100 tiers and work was completed on 5 Aug. 1990.

Oldest   The Alimentarium, a museum of food in Vevey, Switzerland, has on display the world's oldest cake, which was sealed and "vacuum-packed" in the grave of Pepionkh, who lived in ancient Egypt around 2200 B.C. The 4.3-in.-wide cake has sesame on it and honey inside, and was possibly made with milk.

Candy   The largest candy was a marzipan chocolate weighing 4,078.5 lbs., made at the Ven International Fresh Market, Diemen, Netherlands on 11–13 May 1990.

Cheese   The largest cheese ever created was a cheddar of 40,060 lbs., made on 13–14 Mar. 1988 at Simon's Specialty Cheese, Little Chute, WI. It was subsequently taken on tour in a specially designed, refrigerated "Cheese-mobile."

Cherry pie   The largest cherry pie on record weighed 37,740 lbs. 10 oz. and contained 36,800 lbs. of cherry filling. It measured 20 ft. in diameter, and was baked by members of the Oliver Rotary Club in Oliver, British Columbia, Canada on 14 July 1990.

Chocolate model   The largest chocolate model was one weighing 8,818 lbs. 6 oz. in the shape of a traditional Spanish sailing ship. It was made by

LARGEST CAKE. The largest cake ever created weighed 128,238 lbs. 8 oz., including 16,209 lbs. of icing. It measured 80 × 32 ft. and was made in the shape of Alabama to celebrate the 100th birthday of the town of Fort Payne, AL. (Photo: Gary Gengozian)

LARGEST CHOCOLATE MODEL. The largest chocolate model was one weighing 8,818 lbs. 6 oz., in the shape of a traditional Spanish sailing ship. It was made by Gremi Provincial de Pastissería, Confitería i Bollería school, Barcelona and measured 42 ft. 8 in. × 27 ft. 10½ in. × 8 ft. 2½ in. It was exhibited at an international food fair in the city in February 1991.

Gremi Provincial de Pastissería, Confitería i Bollería school, Barcelona in February 1991 and measured 42 ft. 8 in. × 27 ft. 10½ in. × 8 ft. 2½ in.

Cocktail   The largest cocktail on record was one of 1,321 gals., made by the Puerto Marina Benalmádena at Benalmádena Costa, Spain on 4 Aug. 1991. It contained gin, lemon and orange juice, banana liqueur and grenadine and was named "El 1992."

United States   The largest cocktail on record in the United States weighed 936.1 gals. and consisted of tequila, triple sec, sweet and sour concentrate and water. It was created by Chi Chi's Mexican Restaurant in Casselberry, FL on 21 Sep. 1991.

Crepe   The largest crepe was 41 ft. 2 in. in diameter and 1¼ in. deep, and weighed 5,908 lbs. It was baked and flipped at Bloemfontein, South Africa on 7 Mar. 1992.

Doughnut   The largest doughnut ever made was lemon-filled and weighed 2,099 lbs., with a diameter of 22 ft. It was baked by Ed Sanderson at Crystal River, FL on 10 Dec. 1988.

Easter eggs   The heaviest Easter egg on record, and also the tallest, was one weighing 10,482 lbs. 14 oz., 23 ft. 3 in. high, made by the staff of Cadbury Red Tulip at their factory at Ringwood, Victoria, Australia, and completed on 9 Apr. 1992.

Food, most expensive   The most expensive food is saffron from Spain, which comes from the stamen or stigma of a crocus.

Hamburger   The largest hamburger on record was one of 5,520 lbs., made at the Outgamie County Fairgrounds, Seymour, WI on 5 Aug. 1989. It was 21 ft. in diameter.

Ice-cream sundae   The largest ice-cream sundae was one weighing 54,914 lbs. 3 oz., made by Palm Dairies Ltd. under the supervision of Mike Rogiani in Edmonton, Alberta, Canada on 24 July 1988. It consisted of 44,689 lbs. 8 oz. of ice cream, 9,688 lbs. 2 oz. of syrup and 537 lbs. 3 oz. of topping.

Jello   The world's largest Jello, a 7,700 gal. watermelon-flavored pink Jello made by Paul Squires and Geoff Ross, worth $14,000, was set at Roma Street Forum, Brisbane, Queensland, Australia on 5 Feb. 1981 in a tank supplied by Pool Fab.

Kebab   The longest kebab ever was one 2,066 ft. 11 in. long, made by the Namibian Children's Home at Windhoek, Namibia on 21 Sep. 1991.

Lasagne   The largest lasagne was one weighing 3,609.6 lbs. and measuring 50 ft. × 5 ft. It was made at the Royal Dublin Society Spring Show in Dublin, Republic of Ireland on 11 May 1990.

United States   The largest lasagne in the United States weighed 3,477 lbs. and measured 63 ft. × 7 ft. It was made by Shade Pasta Inc. and Cornell University's Panhellenic and Interfraternity Councils in Ithaca, NY on 26 Oct. 1991.

Loaf   The longest loaf on record was a Rosca de Reyes 3,491 ft. 9in. long, baked at the Hyatt Regency Hotel in Guadalajara, Mexico on 6 Jan. 1991. If a consumer of the "Rosca," or twisted loaf, finds the embedded doll, that person has to host the Rosca party (held annually at Epiphany) the following year.

The largest pan loaf ever baked weighed 3,163 lbs. 10 oz. and measured 9 ft. 10 in. × 4 ft. 1 in. × 3 ft. 7 in., by the staff of Sasko in Johannesburg, South Africa on 18 Mar. 1988.

United States   The longest loaf on record in the United States was one 2,357 ft. 10 in. long, baked by the Northlands Job Corps, Vergennes, VT on 3 Nov. 1987. Some 35,840 lbs. of dough were required in the preparation of the loaf, and over 4,480 lbs. of charcoal and 4,700 ft. of aluminum foil were used to bake it.

Lollipop   The world's largest ice lollipop was one of 7,080 lbs., constructed by students and staff at Lawrence University, Appleton, WI on 17 Feb. 1990. The largest candy lollipop weighed 2,220.5 lbs. and was made by Lolly Pops/Johnson's Confectionary in Sydney, Australia on 18–19 Aug. 1990.

Meat pie   The largest meat pie on record weighed 19,908 lbs. and was the 9th in the series of pies baked in Denby Dale, Great Britain. It was baked on 3 Sep. 1988 to mark the bicentennial of Denby Dale pie-making, the first one having been made in 1788 to celebrate King George III's return to sanity. The fourth (Queen Victoria's Jubilee, 1887) went a bit "off" and had to be buried in quicklime.

Milk shake   The largest milk shake was a chocolate one of 1,575.2 gals., made by the Smith Dairy Products Co. at Orrville, OH on 20 Oct. 1989.

Omelet   The largest omelet in the world had an area of 1,324 ft.^{2} and was made in a skillet 41 ft. 1 in. in diameter. It was cooked by staff and pupils of the Municipal School for Special Education at Opwijk, Belgium on 10 June 1990.

United States   The largest omelet in the USA was one with an area of 706 ft. 8 in.^{2}, made with 54,763 eggs and 531 lbs. cheese in a skillet 30 ft. in diameter. It was cooked by Michael McGowan, assisted by his staff and the Sunrise Jaycees of Las Vegas, NV on 25 Oct. 1986.

Paella   The largest paella measured 52 ft. 6 in. in diameter and was made by Josep Gruges ("Pepitu") on 25 Aug. 1987 in the Playa de Aro, Gerona, Spain. The ingredients included 8,140 lbs. of rice, 6,600 lbs. of meat, 3,300 lbs. of mussels, 1,540 lbs. each of beans and peppers, 440 lbs. of garlic and 88 gals. of oil. The paella was eaten by 40,000 people, who washed it all down with 8,000 bottles of Catalan sparkling wine.

Pastry   The longest pastry in the world was an apple strudel 2,018 ft. 2 in. in length, made by Port Macquarie College of Technical and Further Education at Port Macquarie, New South Wales, Australia on 30 Sep. 1990.

United States   The longest pastry in the United States was a peach tart 1,683 ft. 2½ in. in length, made by chefs at the Hyatt Regency Ravinia, Atlanta, GA on 26 July 1986.

Pizza   The largest pizza ever baked was one measuring 122 ft. 8 in. in diameter with an area of 11,816 ft.², made at Norwood Hypermarket, Norwood, South Africa on 8 Dec. 1990.

United States   The largest pizza in the United States was one with an area of 10,057 ft.², organized by L. Amato and L. Piancone and completed at Highway 27, Havana, FL on 13 Oct. 1991.

Popcorn   The largest container full of popcorn was one with 5,979.33 ft.³ of popped corn. It was just over 19 ft. 6 in. in diameter and 19 ft. 1 in. in height. It took the staff of United Cinemas International in Derby, Great Britain three days to achieve the record, beginning their attempt on 23 Aug. 1991 and completing it on 26 August.

United States   The largest box of popcorn in the United States contained 5,438.16 ft.³ of popped corn. It measured 52 ft. 7¼ in. × 10 ft. 1½ in. and was filled by Stanly Community College, Albermarle, NC from 6–8 Aug. 1991. The average depth was 10 ft. 2½ in.

Potato chips   The Pringles plant in Jackson, TN produced a Pringle potato chip 23 in. × 14½ in. on 19 Apr. 1990. Pringles potato chips are made from potato flour.

Salami   The longest salami on record was one 61 ft. 3½ in. long with a circumference of 24 in., weighing 1,202.5 lbs., made by the Kutztown Bologna Co., PA and displayed at the Lebanon Bologna Fest in Kutztown on 11–13 Aug. 1989.

Burrito   Taco Tico of Nebraska, Inc. created the world's largest burrito, 1,597 ft. 9 in. long, on 29 June 1991 in Newton, Kansas. The burrito was constructed from 2,557 tortillas, 607 lbs. of refried beans and 75.75 lbs. of shredded cheese.

Condiment, rarest   The world's most prized condiment is Cà Cuong, a secretion recovered in minute amounts from beetles in North Vietnam. Because of war conditions, the price had risen to $100 per oz. before supplies virtually dried up in 1975.

Noodle making   Mark Pi made 4,096 noodle strings from a single piece of noodle dough in 54.8 sec. at the Thomas/SYSCO Food Show held at Columbus, OH on 25 Mar. 1992. This represented a speed of more than 74 noodles per second.

Omelet making   The greatest number of two-egg omelettes made in 30 min. is 427, by Howard Helmer at the International Poultry Trade Show held at Atlanta, GA on 2 Feb. 1990.

Sausage   The longest continuous sausage on record was one of 13⅛ miles, made at the premises of Keith Boxley at Wombourne, Great Britain in 15 hrs. 33 min. on 18–19 June 1988.

Soda float   The largest soda float ever made was one produced in a 2,000 gallon container, and consisted of 1,200 lbs. skim milk and 936 gallons Coca-Cola. It was made by Coleman Quality Chekd Dairy, Inc., Cool 95 FM, and Coca-Cola of Arkansas at the Arkansas State Fairgrounds, Little Rock, AR on 14 Oct. 1990.

Spice, "hottest"   The hottest of all spices is believed to be habanero, belonging to the genus *capsicum*, found mainly in the Caribbean and the Yucatán area of Mexico. A single dried gram will produce detectable "heat" in 440 lbs. of bland sauce.

Spice, most expensive   Prices for wild ginseng (root of *Panax quinquefolium*) from the Chan Pak Mountain area of China, thought to have aphrodisiac qualities, were reported in November 1979 to be as high as $23,000 per ounce in Hong Kong. Total annual shipments from Jilin Province do not exceed 140 oz. a year.

Strawberry bowl   The largest bowl of strawberries ever picked had a net weight of 4,832 lbs. The strawberries were picked at Walt Furlong's farm at New Ross, Republic of Ireland during the Enniscorthy Strawberry Fair on 9 July 1989.

DRINK

Since 1 Jan. 1981 the strength of spirits has been expressed only in terms of percentage volume of alcohol at 68° F. Absolute or "100 percent volume" alcohol was formerly expressed as 75.35° over proof, or 75.35° OP. In the USA proof is double the actual percentage of alcohol by volume at 60° F., so that absolute alcohol is 200 percent proof spirit. "Hangovers" are said to be aggravated by the presence of such toxic congenerics as amyl alcohol ($C_5H_{11}OH$).

Beer *Strongest*   Roger & Out, brewed at the Frog & Parrot in Sheffield, Great Britain, from a recipe devised by W.R. Nowill and G.B. Spencer, has an alcohol volume of 16.9 percent. It was first brewed in July 1985 and has been selling ever since.
   The strongest lager is Samichlaus Dark 1987, brewed by Brauerei Hürlimann of Zürich, Switzerland. It is 14.93 percent alcohol by volume at 68° F.

Bottles *Largest*   A bottle 6 ft. 11 in. tall and 5 ft. 4½ in. in circumference was displayed at the Laidley Tourist Festival, Laidley, Queensland, Australia on 2 Sep. 1989. The bottle was filled with 92 gals. of Laidley Gold, a wheat beer only available in Laidley.
   The largest bottles normally used in the wine and spirit trade are the Jeroboam (equal to 4 bottles of champagne or, rarely, of brandy, and from 5–6½

bottles of claret according to whether blown or molded) and the double magnum (equal, since *c.* 1934, to 4 bottles of claret or, more rarely, red Burgundy). A complete set of champagne bottles would consist of a quarter bottle, through a half bottle, bottle, magnum, Jeroboam, Rehoboam, Methuselah, Salmanazar and Balthazar, to the Nebuchadnezzar, which has a capacity of 28.14 pts., and is equivalent to 20 bottles.

A bottle containing 33.7 liters of Château Lalande Sourbet 1985, equal in volume to almost 45 standard wine bottles, was auctioned on 10 Oct. 1989 in Copenhagen, Denmark.

Smallest   The smallest bottles of liquor now sold are of White Horse Scotch Whisky; they stand just over 2 in. high and contain 22 minims. A mini case of 12 bottles costs about £8 ($14), and measures 2 $\frac{1}{16}$ × 1 $\frac{7}{8}$ × 1 $\frac{5}{16}$ in. The distributor is Cumbrae Supply Co., Linwood, Scotland.

Champagne cork flight   The longest flight of a cork from an untreated and unheated bottle 4 ft. from level ground is 177 ft. 9 in., reached by Prof. Emeritus Heinrich Medicus, RPI, at the Woodbury Vineyards Winery, NY on 5 June 1988.

Champagne fountain   The greatest number of stories achieved in a champagne fountain, successfully filled from the top and using traditional long-stem glasses, is 44 (height 24 ft. 8 in.), achieved by Pascal Leclerc with 10,404 glasses at the Biltmore Hotel, Los Angeles, CA on 18 June 1984.

Wine tasting   The largest ever reported was that staged by WQED on 22 Nov. 1986 in San Francisco, CA with 4,000 tasters, 260 bottle openers, 500 pourers and 9,360 bottles from 130 wineries.

Brewers   The oldest brewery in the world is the Weihenstephan Brewery, Freising, near Munich, Germany, founded in A.D. 1040.

The largest single brewing organization in the world is Anheuser-Busch Inc. of St. Louis, MO, with 12 breweries in the United States. In 1991 the company sold 2.66 billion gallons, the greatest annual volume ever produced by a brewing company in a year. The company's St. Louis plant covers 100 acres, and has an annual capacity of 403 million gallons. After the completion of current modernization projects in 1993, the plant will have an annual capacity of 416.6 million gallons.

The largest brewery on a single site is Coors Brewing Co. of Golden, CO, where 604 million gallons were produced in 1991.

Distillers   The world's largest distilling company is United Distillers, the spirits company of Guinness plc, which sells 56 million cases of "owned" distilled spirits brands per year. It is also the most profitable spirits company, having made £749 million ($1.3 billion) in 1991.

The largest blender and bottler of Scotch whiskey is also United Distillers, at their Shieldhall plant in Glasgow, Great Britain, which has the capacity to fill an estimated 144 million bottles of Scotch a year. This is equivalent to

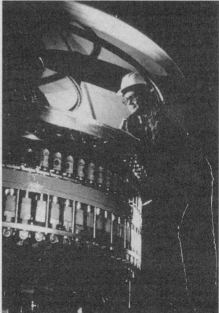

LARGEST BREWERS. The largest brewery on one single site is that of the Coors Brewing Co. at Golden, CO, where 604 million gals. were produced in 1991. This represented 19.5 million barrels. The photographs show the brewery (above) and an employee supervising the filling of cans (right). (Photos: PallasPhoto)

approximately 24 million gals., most of which is exported. The world's best-selling brands of Scotch and gin, Johnnie Walker Red Label and Gordon's, are both products of United Distillers.

Most alcoholic drinks During independence (1918–40) the Estonian Liquor Monopoly marketed 98 percent potato alcohol (196 proof US). In 31 states, Everclear, 190 proof or 95 percent volume alcohol, is marketed by the American Distilling Co. "primarily as a base for home-made cordials." The Royal New Zealand Navy still issues Navy rum at 4.5 Under Proof and is the last navy in the world to do so.

Spirits *Most expensive* The most expensive spirit is Springbank 1919 Malt Whisky, which is sold at Fortnum & Mason in London, Great Britain for £6,750 ($12,000; including tax) per bottle.

Vintners The world's oldest champagne firm is Ruinart Père et Fils, founded in 1729. The oldest cognac firm is Augier Frères & Cie, established in 1643.

Wine *Oldest* Evidence of wine dating from *c.* 3500 B.C. was detected at Godin Tepe, Iran in early 1991. Excavations there revealed the remains of a Sumerian jar containing a large red stain. This was analyzed, and the results showed the presence of tartaric acid, a chemical naturally abundant in grapes.

   The oldest bottle of wine sold at auction, was a bottle of 1646 Imperial Tokay, which was bought by John A. Chunko of Princeton, NJ and Jay Walker of Ridgefield, CT for SFr1250 at Sotheby's, Geneva, Switzerland on 16 Nov. 1984. At the time the sum paid was equivalent to $510.

Most expensive £105,000 ($131,250) was paid for a bottle of 1787 Château Lafite claret, sold to Christopher Forbes (USA) at Christie's, London, Great Britain on 5 Dec. 1985. The bottle was engraved with the initials of Thomas Jefferson (1743–1826), "Th J"—a factor that greatly affected the bidding. In November 1986 its cork, dried out by exhibition lights, slipped, making the wine undrinkable.

   The record price for a half bottle of wine is Fr180,000 ($30,600), for a 1784 Château Margaux, also bearing the initials of Thomas Jefferson, which was sold by Christie's at Vinexpo in Bordeaux, France on 26 June 1987.

   The record price for a glass of wine is $Cdn1,700 ($1,400), for the first glass of Beaujolais Nouveau 1991, bought in an auction in Toronto, Ontario, Canada by Joseph Neshoda, proprietor of a local restaurant and wine bar, on 21 Nov. 1991.

Auction The largest single sale of wine was conducted by Christie's of London, Great Britain on 10–11 July 1974 at Quaglino's Ballroom, London, when 2,325 lots comprising 432,000 bottles realized $2,400,000.

Soft drinks Pepsico of Purchase, NY topped the Fortune 500 list for beverage companies in April 1992, with total sales for 1991 of $19.7 billion, compared with $11.6 billion for the Coca-Cola Company of Atlanta, GA. Coca-Cola is, however, the world's most popular soft drink, with sales in 1991 of over 492 million drinks per day, representing an estimated 46 percent of the world market.

Mineral water The world's largest mineral water firm is Source Perrier, near Nîmes, France, with an annual production of more than 2.5 billion bottles, of which 1.1 billion now come from Perrier. The French drink about 136 pints of mineral water per person per year, although the highest average consumption is in Italy, with 185 pints per person per year.

MANUFACTURED ARTICLES

Because of the infinite number of objects it is possible to collect, we can include only a small number of claims that reflect proven widespread interest.
   We are more likely to consider claims for items accumulated on a personal basis over a significant period of time, made through appropriate organizations, established and recognized, as these organizations are often in a better position to comment authoritatively in record terms.

Ax   A steel ax measuring 60 ft. long, 23 ft. wide and weighing 7.7 tons was designed and built by BID Ltd. of Woodstock, New Brunswick, Canada. The ax was presented to the town of Nackawic, also in New Brunswick, on 11 May 1991 to commemorate the town's selection as Forestry Capital of Canada for 1991. Although calculations suggested it would take a 154-ton lumberjack to swing the ax, a crane was used to lift it into its concrete "stump."

United States   The largest ax in the United States was 36 ft. long with a 10 ft. 1 in. × 5 ft. 2 in. blade. It was designed and built by Moran Iron Works in May 1992.

Basket   The world's biggest basket measures 48 × 23 × 19 ft. It is a handwoven maple example made by the Longaberger Company of Dresden, OH in 1990.

Beer cans   Beer cans date from a test marketing by Krueger Beer of Newark, NJ, in Richmond, VA in 1935. The largest collection has been made by John F. Ahrens of Mount Laurel, NJ, with nearly 15,000 different cans.
   A Rosalie Pilsner can sold for $6,000 in the United States in April 1981. A collection of 2,502 unopened bottles and cans of beer from 103 countries was bought for A$25,000 by the Downer Club ACT of Australia at the Australian Associated Press Financial Markets Annual Charity Golf Tournament on 23 Mar. 1990.

Beer labels (labology)   Jan Solberg of Oslo, Norway has amassed 353,500 different labels from around the world to May 1992.

Blanket   The world's largest hand-knitted blanket was made by the Friends of St. Catherine's Hospice in Crawley, Great Britain. It measured 37,592 ft.² and was completed on 9 Aug. 1991 at Gatwick Airport.

Bottle caps   Since 1950 Helge Friholm (b. 1909) of Søborg, Denmark has amassed 67,330 different bottle caps from 170 countries.

LARGEST BLANKET. Seen here at Gatwick Airport are the Friends of St. Catherine's Hospice from Crawley, Great Britain, who made the blanket they are standing on. It measured 148 × 254 ft., giving an overall area of 37,592 ft.². It was made up of £20,000 ($38,000) worth of wool and weighed 1.7 tons. It was split up into more than 1,450 smaller blankets, which were donated to charity.

Pyramid A pyramid consisting of 338,500 bottle caps was constructed by Eddy Lenoir and Harald Prasse and a team of 21 from Frontwijk Blankenberge, Belgium from 20 Aug.–6 Sep. 1991.

Bottle collections George E. Terren of Southboro, MA had a collection of 31,804 miniature and distilled spirit and liquor bottles on 31 May 1992. Ted Shuler of Germantown, TN has a collection of 2,774 different bottled beers, including specimens from 101 countries.

Claive Vidiz of São Paulo, Brazil has a collection of 2,025 original Scotch Whiskey units.

David L. Maund of Upham, Great Britain, has a collection of unduplicated miniature Scotch whiskey bottles amounting to 9,347 as of November 1991.

The world's biggest collection of whiskey bottles is one of 4,800 unduplicated, assembled by Signor Edward Giaccone at his *whiskeyteca*, Salo, Lake Garda, Italy. The largest reported collection of spirits and liqueurs is 2,890 unduplicated bottles collected by Ian Boasman at Bistro French, Preston, Lancashire, Great Britain by February 1990.

Bowl, wooden The largest one-piece wooden bowl was made by Dan Cunningham, David Tarleton and Scott Hare in Kamuela, HI in September 1990. The bowl, which took 2,978 man-hours to complete, was constructed of monkeypod wood, stands 6 ft. 7 in. tall, and its widest diameter is 5 ft. 9⅝ in. with a circumference of 18 ft. 1 in.

Candles A candle 80 ft. high and 8½ ft. in diameter was exhibited at the

WHISKEY BOTTLE COLLECTION. Claive Vidiz, President of the Brazilian Whiskey Collector's Association, in his museum specially built to house his collection of 2,025 full original Scotch whiskey bottles.

1897 Stockholm Exhibition by the firm of Lindahls. Including the candlestick, the overall height was 127 ft.

A candle constructed by Enham Industries at the Charlton Leisure Center, Andover, Great Britain on 2 July 1989 measured 101.7 ft. high.

Carpets and rugs *Earliest* The earliest carpet known is a Seythian woolen pile-knotted carpet measuring 6 ft.² and dating from the 4th–3rd centuries B.C. It was discovered by the Russian archaeologist Sergei Ivanovich Rudenko in 1947 in the Pazyryk Valley in southern Siberia and is now preserved in the Hermitage, St. Petersburg, Russia.

Largest Of ancient carpets, the largest was a gold-enriched silk carpet of Hashim (dated A.D. 743) of the Abbasid caliphate in Baghdad, Iraq. It is reputed to have measured 180 × 300 ft. A 52,225 ft.², 31.4 ton red carpet was laid on 13 Feb. 1982, by the Allied Corporation, from Radio City Music Hall to the New York Hilton along the Avenue of the Americas, in New York City.

Most finely woven The most finely woven carpet known is one having 3,716 strands per in.², selected from 3,000 weaving specialists, for Ozipek Halicilik A.S. of Hereke, Turkey. The project took five years to complete, and the finished product, named *Hereke Treasure*, was sold to Gandhara Carpet Japan Co. Ltd., Tokyo in March 1988.

Most expensive   The most expensive carpet ever made was the Spring carpet of Khusraw, made for the audience hall of the Sassanian palace at Cte-siphon, Iraq. It was about 7,000 ft.^{2} of silk and gold thread, and was encrusted with emeralds. It was cut up as booty by looters in A.D. 635, and from the known realization value of the pieces must have had an original value of some $170 million.

Chair   An enlarged version, 53 ft. 4 in. tall, of the chair George Washington sat in while presiding at the Constitutional Convention was made by the NSA and brought to Washington, D.C. for the 1989 inauguration.

Chandeliers   The world's largest set of chandeliers was created by the Kookje Lighting Co. Ltd. of Seoul, South Korea. It is 39 ft. high, weighs 11.8 tons and has 700 bulbs. Completed in November 1988, it occupies three floors of the Lotte Chamshil Department Store in Seoul.

Check   The world's largest check was made by the Christmas Cracker project and measured 52½ × 26 ft. The £50 ($85) check, representing "One million hours of time and energy," was presented in London, Great Britain on 28 Sep. 1990.

Cigarettes   The world's largest collection of cigarettes was that of Robert E. Kaufman, of New York. It consisted of 8,390 different cigarettes made in 173 countries and territories. Upon his death in March 1992 his wife Naida took over the collection. The oldest brand represented is *Lone Jack*, made in the USA *c*. 1885.

Cigarette cards   The earliest known tobacco card is "Vanity Fair," dated 1876, issued by Wm. S. Kimball & Co., Rochester, NY. The earliest British example appeared *c*. 1883 in the form of a calendar issued by Allen & Ginter, of Richmond, VA, trading from Holborn Viaduct, City of London, Great Britain.
    The largest-known collection is that of Mr. Edward Wharton-Tigar (b. 1913) of London, Great Britain, with more than 1 million cigarette and trade cards in about 45,000 sets. This collection has been accepted as a bequest by the British Museum, where it will eventually be available for public study.

Cigarette packets   The earliest surviving cigarette packet is a Finnish Petit Canon packet for 25, made by Tollander & Klärich in 1860, from the Ventegodt Collection. The rarest is the Latvian 700-year anniversary (1201–1901) Riga packet, believed to be unique, from the same collection.

Cigars   The largest cigar ever made measures 16 ft. 8½ in. in length and weighs 577 lbs. 9 oz. It took 243 hours to make and used 3,330 full tobacco leaves. It was made by Tinus Vinke and Jan Weijmer in February 1983 and is in the Tobacco Museum in Kampen, Netherlands.
    The largest marketed cigar in the world is the 14 in. Valdez Emperador, manufactured by Fábrica de Puros Santa Clara of San Andrés Tuxtla, Veracruz, Mexico and exclusively distributed by Tabacos San Andrés.

Coasters (tegestology)   The world's largest collection of coasters is owned by Leo Pisker of Vienna, Austria, who has collected 135,480 different coasters from 154 countries to date.

Credit cards   The largest collection of valid credit cards to date is one of 1,356 (all different) by Walter Cavanagh (b. 1943) of Santa Clara, CA. The cost of acquisition for "Mr. Plastic Fantastic" was zero, and he keeps them in the world's longest wallet—250 ft. long, weighing 37½ lbs. and worth more than $1.6 million in credit.

Doll, rag   The largest rag doll in the United States is one 41 ft. 11 in. in total length, created by Apryl Scott at Autoworld in Flint, MI on 20 Nov. 1990.

Dress   A wedding outfit created by Helene Gainville with jewels by Alexander Reza is believed to be worth $7,301,587.20 precisely. The dress is embroidered with diamonds mounted on platinum and was unveiled in Paris, France on 23 Mar. 1989.

Dress train   The world's longest wedding dress train measured 171 ft. 3 in. and was made by Agnès Remaud of La Roche-sur-Yon, France in 1990.

Egg   The largest and most elaborate jeweled egg stands 2 ft. tall and was fashioned from 37 lbs. of gold studded with 20,000 pink diamonds. Designed by British jeweler Paul Kutchinsky, the Argyle Library Egg took six British craftsmen 7,000 hours to create and has a price tag of £7 million ($12 million). It was unveiled on 30 Apr. 1990 before going on display at the Victoria and Albert Museum, London, Great Britain.

Fabrics *Oldest*   The oldest surviving fabric, discovered from Level VI A at Çatal Hüyük, Turkey, has been radiocarbon dated to 5900 B.C.

Most expensive   The most expensive fabric is Vicuña cloth manufactured by Fujii Keori Ltd. of Osaka, Japan, retailing at 1 million yen ($7,600) per meter in January 1988.

Finest   The finest denier nylon yarn ever produced is the 5 denier produced by Nilit Ltd. of Tel Aviv, Israel and used by Pretty Polly for women's hosiery in Great Britain. The sheerest stockings normally available are 9 denier. A hair from the average human head is about 50 denier.

Fan   A handpainted Spanish fan made of fabric and wood, measuring 15.45 ft. when unfolded and 8 ft. high, was completed by D. Juan Reolid González of Torrent, Valencia, Spain in June 1991.

Fireworks *Largest*   The largest firework ever produced was Universe I Part II, exploded for the Lake Toya Festival, Hokkaidō, Japan on 15 July 1988. The 1,543 lb. shell was 1,354.7 in. in diameter and burst to a diameter of 3,937 ft.

Fireworks display   The longest firecracker display was produced by the Johor Tourism Department, the United Malaysian Youth Movement and Mr. Yap Seng Hock, and took place on 20 Feb. 1988 at Pelangi Garden, Johor Bahru, Johor, Malaysia. The total length of the display was 18,777 ft. and consisted of 3,338,777 firecrackers and 1,468 lbs. of gunpowder. It burned for 9 hrs. 27 min.

Flags *Oldest*   The oldest-known flag is one dated to *c*. 3000 B.C. found in 1972 at Khabis, Iran. It is of metal and measures 9 × 9 in. and depicts an eagle, two lions and a goddess, three women and a bull.

Largest   The largest flag in the world, one of the Republic of China presented to the city of Kaohsiung, Taiwan by Unichamps Inpe'l Corp. on 9 Apr. 1989, measured 413 × 275½ ft. and weighed 1,807.7 lbs. The largest flag *flown* from a flagpole is a Brazilian national flag measuring 229 ft. 8 in. × 328 ft. 1 in. in Brasilia.

Float   The largest float was the 155-ft.-long, 24-ft. wide "Merry Christmas America" float bearing three double arches, a 17-ft. Christmas tree, two 15-ft. peppermint candy sticks and 5,380 ft.^{2} of wrapping paper, used at the 40th Annual Christmas Parade, Baton Rouge, LA on 5 Dec. 1986.

Golden coffin   The gold coffin of the 14th-century B.C. Pharaoh Tutankhamun, discovered by Howard Carter on 16 Feb. 1923 in the Valley of the Kings, western Thebes, Egypt, weighed 243 lbs.

Jigsaw puzzles   The earliest jigsaws were made as "dissected maps" by John Spilsbury (1739–69) in Russell Court off Drury Lane, London, Great Britain *c.* 1762.

Largest   The world's largest jigsaw puzzle measures 11,302.2 ft.^{2} but consists of only 2,250 pieces. Assembled on 19 Mar. 1991, it was devised by J.N. Nichols (Vimto) plc of Manchester, Great Britain, and designed and built by students from Manchester Polytechnic.

A puzzle consisting of 204,484 pieces was made by BCF Holland b.v. of Almelo, Netherlands and assembled by students of the local Gravenvoorde School on 25 May–1 June 1991. The completed puzzle measured 1,036 ft.^{2}.

Most expensive   Custom-made Stave puzzles made by Steve Richardson of Norwich, VT of 2,640 pieces cost $8,680 in June 1992.

Kettle   The largest antique copper kettle was one standing 3 ft. high with a 6 ft. girth and a 20 gal. capacity, built in Taunton, Somerset, Great Britain, for the hardware merchants Fisher and Son *c.* 1800.

Knife   The penknife with the greatest number of blades is the Year Knife made by cutlers Joseph Rodgers & Sons, of Sheffield, Great Britain, whose trademark was granted in 1682. The knife was made in 1822 with 1,822 blades, and a blade was added every year until 1973 when there was no further space. It was acquired by Britain's largest hand tool manufacturers, Stanley Works (Great Britain) Ltd. of Sheffield, Great Britain, in 1970.

Lego tower   The world's tallest Lego tower, 65 ft. 2 in., was built by the people of Auckland, New Zealand on 22–23 Feb. 1992.

Needles   The longest needle is one 6 ft. 1 in. long made by George Davies of Thomas Somerfield, Bloxwich, Great Britain for stitching on mattress buttons lengthwise. One of these is preserved in the National Needle Museum at Forge Mill, Great Britain.

Pens   The most expensive writing pen is the 5003.002 Caran D'Ache 18-carat solid gold Madison slimline ballpoint pen incorporating white diamonds

Beds   Philip, Duke of Burgundy, Belgium had a bed 12½ ft. × 19 ft. erected for the perfunctory *coucher officiel* ceremony with Princess Isabella of Portugal in 1430.

Beer tankard   The largest tankard was made by the Selangor Pewter Co. of Kuala Lumpur, Malaysia and unveiled on 30 Nov. 1985. It measures 6½ ft. in height and has a capacity of 615 gals.

Greeting cards   Craig Shergold of Carshalton, Great Britain was reported to have collected a record 33 million get-well cards by May 1991, when his mother pleaded for no more. Jarrod Booth of Salt Spring Island, British Columbia, Canada had a collection of 205,120 Christmas cards in February 1990.

Catherine Wheel   On 3 Nov. 1991, as part of a fireworks display, a 45 ft. diameter catherine wheel was constructed on a fairground Ferris wheel by Celebration Fireworks and Deducated Micros of Bury, Lancashire, Great Britain. The wheel was flamed and ran for approximately one minute.

Matchbox labels   The oldest matchbox label of accepted provenance is that of Samuel Jones *c*. 1830. The finest collection of trademark matchbox labels (excluding any pub/bar or other advertising labels) is some 280,000 pieces collected by the phillumenist Robert Jones of Indianapolis, IN. Teiichi Yoshizawa (b. 1904) of Chiba-Ken, Japan has amassed 712,118 matchbox labels (including advertising labels) from 150 countries since 1925.

Quilt   The world's largest quilt was made by 7,000 citizens of North Dakota for the 1989 centennial of North Dakota. It measured 85 × 134 ft.

String ball, largest   The largest ball of string on record is one 12 ft. 9 in. in diameter, 40 ft. in circumference and weighing 11 tons, amassed by Francis A. Johnson of Darwin, MN between 1950 and 1978.

Tablecloth   The world's largest tablecloth is 1,502 ft. long, and 4½ ft. wide, and was made by the Sportex division of Artex International in Highland, IL on 17 Oct. 1990.

Stuffed toy, longest   A snake measuring 400 ft. was completed in Nov. 1991 by the Grove School Knit and Natter Club of Newark, Great Britain.

Yo-yo   The largest yo-yo ever constructed was one measuring 6 ft. in diameter made by the woodworking class of Shakamak High School in Jasonville, IN. It weighed 820 lbs. and was launched from a 160 ft. crane on 29 Mar. 1990, when it "yo-yoed" 12 times.

of 6.35 carats, exclusively distributed by Jakar International Ltd. of London, Great Britain. Its recommended retail price, including tax, in 1992 is £23,950 ($40,545).

A Japanese collector paid 1.3 million French francs ($2,340,000) in Feb. 1988 for the "Anémone" fountain pen made by Réden, France. It was encrusted with 600 precious stones, including emeralds, amethysts, rubies, sapphires and onyx, and took skilled craftsmen over a year to complete.

Piñata　The biggest piñata made in the United States measured 27 ft. high with a diameter of 30 ft., a circumference of 100 ft. and a weight of 10,000 lbs. It was built in March 1990 during the celebrations for Carnaval Miami in Miami, FL.

Pottery　The largest vase on record is one 11 ft. high, weighing 3,968 lbs., thrown by Aksel Krog and Jorgen Hansen of Denmark on 10–13 Feb. 1989. The Chinese ceramic authority Chingwah Lee of San Francisco, CA was reported in August 1978 to have appraised a unique 39-in. Kangxi four-sided vase then in a bank vault in Phoenix, AZ at $60 million.

Shoes　James Smith, founder of James Southall & Co. of Norwich, Great Britain, introduced sized shoes in 1792. The firm began making "Startrite" children's shoes in 1923.

Emperor Bokassa of the Central African Empire (now Republic) commissioned pearl-studded shoes from the House of Berluti, Paris, France for his self-coronation on 4 Dec. 1977 at a cost of $85,000.

The most expensive manufactured shoes are mink-lined golf shoes with 18-carat gold embellishments and ruby-tipped spikes made by Stylo Matchmakers International of Northampton, Great Britain, which retail for $23,000 per pair.

A pair of women's cream kid and braid high-heeled slap-soled shoes c. 1660 was sold by Lord Hereford at Sotheby's, London, Great Britain in September 1987 to Mrs. Sonia Bata for £21,000 ($33,600). An export license was reportedly refused on 20 June 1988.

Silver　The largest single pieces of silver are a pair of water jugs of 10,408 troy oz. (4.77 cwt.) made in 1902 for the Maharaja of Jaipur (1861–1922). They are 5 ft. 3 in. tall, with a circumference of 8 ft. 1½ in., and have a capacity of 1,800 gallons. They are now in the City Palace, Jaipur, India. The silversmith was Gorind Narain.

Sofa　The longest standard sofa manufactured is the Augustus Rex Sofa, 12 ft. 3 in. in length, made by Dodge & Son of Sherborne, Great Britain.

In April 1990 a 21 ft. 9 in. long jacquard fabric sofa was specially manufactured by Mountain View Interiors of Collingwood, Ontario, Canada with an estimated value of $8,000.

Suit　EVA suits for extravehicular activity, worn by space shuttle crews since 1982, have a unit cost of $3.4 million.

Table　The longest table was set up in Pesaro, Italy on 20 June 1988 by the US Libertas Scavolini Basketball team. It was 10,072 ft. in length and was used to seat 12,000 people.

Tapestry　The earliest-known examples of tapestry woven linen are three pieces from the tomb of the Egyptian pharaoh Thutmose IV dated to 1483–1411 B.C.

The largest tapestry ever woven is the *History of Irak*, with an area of 13,370.7 ft.². It was designed by the Yugoslavian artist Frane Delale and produced by the Zivtex Regeneracija Workshop in Zabok, Yugoslavia. The tapestry was completed in 1986 and it now adorns the wall of an amphitheater in Baghdad, Iraq.

LARGEST VASE. The largest thrown vase, named *Cleopatra*, stands 17½ ft. high including a 4¼ ft. tall lid. The potter was Joao Ramos Moraes and it was made in June 1991 by Faiarte Ceramics of Rustenburg, South Africa.

The famous Bayeux tapestry, *Telle du Conquest, dite tapisserie de la reine Mathilde*, a hanging tapestry 19½ in. × 23 ft., depicts events of 1064–66 in 72 scenes and was probably worked in Canterbury, Great Britain, *c.* 1086. It was "lost" for 2½ centuries, from 1476 until 1724.

The Overlord Embroidery of 34 panels, each 8 × 3 ft., commissioned by Lord Dulverton (b. 1915) from the Royal School of Needlework in London, Great Britain, was completed in 1979 after 100 person-years of work and is 41 ft. longer than the Bayeux. It has the largest area of any embroidery, 816 ft.². An uncompleted 8 in. deep 1,338 ft. long embroidery of scenes from C.S. Lewis's *Narnia* children's stories has been worked by Margaret S. Pollard of Truro, Great Britain to the order of Michael Maine.

Tartan   The earliest evidence of tartans is the so-called Falkirk tartan, found stuffed in a jar of coins in Bells Meadow, Scotland. It is of a dark and light brown pattern and dates from *c.* A.D. 245. The earliest reference to a specific named tartan is to a Murray tartan in 1618, although Mackay tartan was probably worn earlier. There are 2,179 tartans known to The Tartans Museum at the headquarters of the Scottish Tartans Society in Comrie, Perth, Tayside, Great Britain. HRH Prince of Wales is eligible to wear 11, including the Balmoral, which has been exclusive to the British royal family since 1852.

Time capsule   The world's largest time capsule is the Tropico Time Tunnel of 10,000 ft.³ in a cave in Rosamond, CA, sealed by the Kern Antelope Historical Society on 20 Nov. 1966 and intended for opening in A.D. 2866.

Wallet   The most expensive wallet ever made is a platinum-cornered, diamond-studded crocodile creation made by Louis Quatorze of Paris, France and Mikimoto of Tokyo, selling in September 1984 for $84,000.

Wreath   The most expensive wreath on record was that presented to Sri Chinmoy in New York on 11 July 1983 by Ashrita Furman and Pahar Meltzer. It was handled by the Garland of Divinity's Love Florist, contained 10,000 flowers, and cost $3,500.

Zipper   The world's longest zipper was laid around the center of Sneek, Netherlands on 5 Sep. 1989. The brass zipper, made by Yoshida (Netherlands) Ltd., is 9,353.56 ft. long and consists of 2,565,900 teeth.

SPORTS
AND GAMES

Anja Fichtel (Germany) (left), three-time world fencing champion, in action during the 1990 World Championship final. (Photo: Karina Hoskyns)

GENERAL RECORDS

Origins Sport stems from the time when self-preservation ceased to be the all-consuming human preoccupation. Archery, although a hunting skill in Mesolithic times (by *c.* 8000 B.C.), did not become an organized sport until later—possibly as early as *c.* 1150 B.C., since an archery competition is described in Homer's *Iliad*, and certainly by *c.* A.D. 300, among the Genoese. The earliest dated evidence for any sport is *c.* 2750–2600 B.C. for wrestling.

Fastest The fastest speed reached in a nonmechanical sport is in skydiving, in which a speed of 185 mph is attained in a head-down free-falling position, even in the lower atmosphere. In delayed drops, speeds of 625 mph have been recorded at high, rarefied altitudes.

The fastest projectile speed in any moving ball game is *c.* 188 mph, in jai alai. This compares with 170 mph (electronically timed) for a golf ball driven off a tee.

Slowest In wrestling, before the rules were modified to favor "brighter wrestling," contestants could be locked in holds for so long that a single bout once lasted for 11 hrs. 40 min.

In the extreme case of the 2 hr. 41 min. pull in the regimental tug o'war in Jubbulpore, India, on 12 Aug. 1889, the winning team moved a net distance of 12 ft. at an average speed of 0.00084 mph.

World record breakers *Youngest* The youngest age at which anybody has broken a nonmechanical world record is 12 yrs. 298 days for Gertrude Caroline Ederle (USA; b. 23 Oct. 1906), with 13 min. 19.0 sec. for women's 880 yd. freestyle swimming, at Indianapolis, IN on 17 Aug. 1919.

Oldest Gerhard Weidner (Germany; b. 15 Mar. 1933) set a 20-mile walk record on 25 May 1974, at age 41 yrs. 71 days, the oldest to set an official world record recognized by an international governing body.

Most prolific Between 24 Jan. 1970 and 1 Nov. 1977, Vasiliy Alekseiev (USSR; b. 7 Jan. 1942) broke 80 official world records in weightlifting.

Champions *Youngest* The youngest successful competitor in a world title event was a French boy, whose name is not recorded, who coxed the Netherlands' Olympic pair at Paris, France on 26 Aug. 1900. He was not more than ten and may have been as young as seven.

Fu Mingxia (China) won the women's world title for platform diving at Perth, Australia on 4 Jan. 1991, at the age of 12.

The youngest individual Olympic winner was Marjorie Gestring (USA; b. 18 Nov. 1922), who took the springboard diving title at the age of 13 yrs. 268 days at the Olympic Games in Berlin, Germany on 12 Aug. 1936.

Oldest Fred Davis (Great Britain; b. 14 Feb. 1913) won the world professional billiards title in 1980, at age 67.

All-Star game selection Bo Jackson is believed to be the only athlete selected to the All-Star games in two professional sports. He was the MVP of the baseball All-Star Game, on 11 July 1989 at Anaheim, CA. Jackson played for the American League; he hit a home run and had 2 RBI's. He was selected for the 1990 NFL Pro Bowl as a running back for the AFC team. However, because of an injury, he was unable to participate in the game, played 3 Feb. 1991 in Hawaii.

Largest contract   In March 1990, the National Football League concluded a deal worth $3.64 billion for four years' coverage by the five major TV and cable networks—ABC, CBS, NBC, ESPN and TBS. This represented $26.1 million for each league team in the first year, escalating to $39.1 million in the fourth.

Largest crowd   The greatest number of live spectators for any one-day sporting spectacle is the estimated 2.5 million who have lined the route of the New York City Marathon. However, spread over three weeks, it is estimated that more than 10 million see the annual Tour de France cycling race.

Olympics   The total attendance at the 1984 Summer Games, held at Los Angeles, CA, was 5,797,923 for all sports plus an estimated 275,000 spectators at road cycling and marathon events.

Stadium   A crowd of 199,854 attended the Brazil *v.* Uruguay World Cup Final soccer match, in the Maracaña Municipal Stadium, Rio de Janeiro, Brazil on 16 July 1950.

LARGEST ATTENDANCE. The Toronto SkyDome is home to the Toronto Blue Jays of the American League. In the 1991 season, the Blue Jays attracted an aggregate attendance for their 80 regular-season home games of 4,001,527. Seen here is the opening ceremony of the 1991 All-Star Game. (Photo: Ian Scott)

Most participants   On 15 May 1988 an estimated 110,000 (including unregistered athletes) ran in the *Examiner* Bay–to–Breakers 7.6-mile race in San Francisco, CA.

The 1988 Women's International Bowling Congress (WIBC) Championship tournament attracted 77,735 bowlers for the 96-day event, held 31 March–4 July at Reno/Carson City, NV.

Worst disasters   In recent history, the stands at the Hong Kong Jockey Club racetrack collapsed and caught fire on 26 Feb. 1918, killing an estimated 604 people.

During the reign of Antoninus Pius (A.D. 138–161), 1,112 spectators were killed when the upper wooden tiers in the Circus Maximus, Rome collapsed during a gladiatorial combat.

Youngest international winner   The youngest age at which any person has won international honors is eight, in the case of Joy Foster, the Jamaican singles and mixed doubles table tennis champion, in 1958.

Heaviest sportsman   Professional wrestler William J. Cobb of Macon, GA, who in 1962 was billed as "Happy Humphrey," weighed 802 lbs.

The heaviest player of any ball game was Bob Pointer, the 487-lb. football tackle formerly on the 1967 Santa Barbara High School team, CA.

Longest reign   Jacques Edmond Barre (France; 1802–73) was a world champion for 33 years (1829–62) at court tennis.

AEROBATICS

Origins   The first aerobatic "maneuver" is generally considered to be the sustained inverted flight in a Bleriot flown by Célestin-Adolphe Pégoud (1889–1915), at Buc, France on 21 Sep. 1913, but Lt. Capt. Petr Nikolayevich Nesterov (1887–1914), of the Imperial Russian Air Service, performed a loop in a Nieuport Type IV monoplane at Kiev, USSR on 27 Aug. 1913.

World Championships   This contest has been held biennially since 1960 (except 1974). Scoring is based on a system originally devised by Col. José Aresti of Spain. The competition consists of a known and unknown compulsory and a free program.

The USSR has won the men's team competition a record six times. Petr Jirmus (Czechoslovakia) is the only man to have become world champion twice, in 1984 and 1986. Betty Stewart (USA) won the women's competition in 1980 and 1982.

Speed in Sports

Speed is an essential factor in sports. This feature brings together the extremes of speed in a variety of activities in which there is no benefit from mechanical assistance

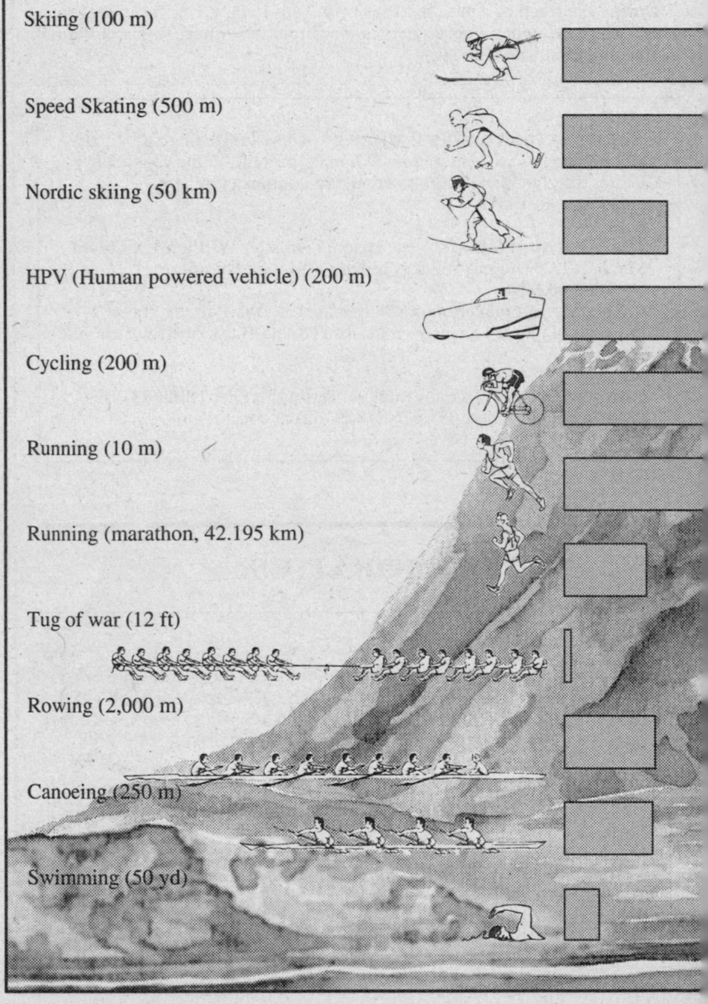

Skiing (100 m)

Speed Skating (500 m)

Nordic skiing (50 km)

HPV (Human powered vehicle) (200 m)

Cycling (200 m)

Running (10 m)

Running (marathon, 42.195 km)

Tug of war (12 ft)

Rowing (2,000 m)

Canoeing (250 m)

Swimming (50 yd)

142.165 mph
Michaël Prüfer (France)—Les Arcs, France 1992

30.68 mph
Uwe-Jens Mey (GDR)—Calgary, Canada 1988

15.57 mph
Bill Koch (USA)—Putney, VT 1981

65.484 mph
Fred Markham (USA)—Mono Lake, CA 1986

44.30 mph
Vladimir Adamashvili (USSR)—Moscow, USSR 1990

26.95 mph
Ben Johnson (Canada) Carl Lewis (USA)—Seoul, South Korea 1988

12.40 mph
Belayneh Dinsamo (Ethiopia)—Rotterdam, Netherlands 1988

0.00084 mph
*"H" Company v "E" Company, 2nd Battalion Sherwood Foresters
(Derbys Regiment)—Jubbulpore, India 1889*

13.68 mph
American eight—Lucerne, Switzerland 1984

13.29 mph
Norway (K4)—Seoul, South Korea 1988

5.37 mph
Tom Jager (USA)—Nashville, TN 1990

Lyubov Nemkova (USSR) won a record five medals: first in 1986, second in 1982 and 1984, and third in 1976 and 1978. The oldest-ever world champion has been Henry Haigh (USA; b. 12 Dec. 1924), age 63 in 1988.

Inverted flight   The duration record is 4 hrs. 38 min. 10 sec. by Joann Osterud (USA) from Vancouver to Vanderhoof, Canada on 24 July 1991.

Loops   Joann Osterud achieved 208 outside loops in a "Supernova" Hyperbipe over North Bend, OR on 13 July 1989. On 9 Aug. 1986, David Childs performed 2,368 inside loops in a Bellanca Decathlon over North Pole, Alaska.

ARCHERY

Origins   Though the earliest pictorial evidence of the existence of bows is seen in Mesolithic cave paintings in Spain, archery as an organized sport appears to have developed in the third century A.D. Competitive archery may, however, date back to the 12th century B.C. The National Archery Association of America was established in 1879. The inaugural National Outdoor Target Championship was held in 1884. The world governing body is the *Fédération Internationale de Tir à l'Arc* (FITA), founded in 1931.

United States   The date of the first use of the bow as a weapon in North America is unknown; however, it is believed that Native American tribes in the eastern part of North America were familiar with the bow by the 11th century. The National Archery Association was founded in 1879 in Crawfordsville, IN and is the oldest amateur sports organization in continuous existence in the United States.

Highest championship scores   The highest scores achieved in either a world or Olympic championship for Double FITA rounds are: men, 2,617 points (possible 2,880) by Darrell Owen Pace (USA; b. 23 Oct. 1956) and Richard Lee McKinney (USA; b. 20 Oct. 1963) at Long Beach, CA on 21–22 Oct. 1983; and for women, 2,683 points by Kim Soo-nyung (South Korea; b. 5 Apr. 1971) at Seoul, South Korea on 27–30 Sep. 1988.

World Championships   The most titles won by a man is four, by Hans Deutgen (Sweden; 1917–89) in 1947–50, and the most by a woman is seven, by Janina Spychajowa-Kurkowska (Poland; b. 8 Feb. 1901) in 1931–34, 1936, 1939 and 1947. The USA has a record 14 men's and eight women's team titles.

Oscar Kessels (Belgium; 1904–68) participated in 21 world championships.

The most individual world titles by a US archer is three, by Richard McKinney: 1977, 1983 and 1985. Jean Lee, 1950 and 1952, is the only US woman to have won two individual world titles. Luann Ryon (b. 13 Jan. 1953) was Olympic women's champion in 1976 and also world champion in 1977.

Olympic Games   Hubert van Innis (Belgium; 1866–1961) won six gold and three silver medals at the 1900 and 1920 Olympic Games.

Greatest draw on a longbow   Gary Sentmam, of Roseberg, OR drew a longbow weighing a record 176 lbs. to the maximum draw on the arrow of 28¼ in. at Forksville, PA on 20 Sep. 1975.

Longest flight   The farthest an arrow has been shot is 2,047 ft. 2 in. by Harry Drake (USA; b. 7 May 1915), using a crossbow at the "Smith Creek" Flight Range near Austin, NV on 30 July 1988.

WORLD ARCHERY RECORDS

MEN (Single FITA rounds)

EVENTS	POINTS	POSSIBLE	NAME AND COUNTRY	YEAR
FITA	1,352	1,440	Vladimir Yesheyev (USSR)	1990
90 m	330	360	Vladimir Yesheyev (USSR)	1990
70 m	344	360	Hiroshi Yamamoto (Japan)	1990
50 m	345	360	Richard McKinney (USA)	1982
30 m	357	360	Takayoshi Matsushita (Japan)	1986
Final	345	360	Vladimir Yesheyev (USSR)	1990
Team	3,963	4,320	USSR (Stanislav Zabrodskiy, Vadim Shikarev, Vladimir Yesheyev)	1989
Final	1,005	1,080	South Korea (Kim Sun-Bin, Yang Chang-hoon, Park Jae-pyo)	1990

WOMEN (Single FITA rounds)

EVENTS	POINTS	POSSIBLE	NAME AND COUNTRY	YEAR
FITA	1,370	1,440	Lee Eun-Kyung (South Korea)	1990
70 m	341*	360	Kim Soo-nyung (South Korea)	1990
60 m	347	360	Kim Soo-nyung (South Korea)	1989
50 m	337	360	Lee Eun-Kyung (South Korea)	1990
30 m	357	360	Joanne Edens (Great Britain)	1990
Final	346	360	Kim Soo-nyung (South Korea)	1990
Team	4,025	4,320	South Korea (Kim Soo-nyung, Wang Hee-nyung, Kim Kyung-wook)	1989
Final	1,030	1,080	South Korea (Kim Soo-nyung, Lee Eun-Kyung, Lee Seon-hee)	1991

* unofficial

Indoor Double FITA rounds at 25 meters

MEN	591	600	Erwin Verstegen (Netherlands)	1989
WOMEN	592	600	Petra Ericsson (Sweden)	1991

Indoor FITA rounds at 18 meters

MEN	591	600	Vladimir Yesheyev (USSR)	1989
WOMEN	587	600	Denise Parker (USA)	1989

The most successful US archer at the Olympic Games has been Darrell Pace, gold medalist in 1976 and 1984. He was also world champion in 1975 and 1979.

US Championships   The US National Championships were first held in Chicago, IL from 12–14 Aug. 1879, and are staged annually. The most US archery titles won is 17, by Lida Howell (nee Scott; 1859–1939), from 20 contested between 1883 and 1907. She won three Olympic gold medals in 1904, for Double National and Double Columbia rounds and for the US team.

The most men's titles is nine (three individual, six pairs), by Richard Mc-Kinney, 1977, 1979-83, 1985-87. The greatest span of title winning is 29 years, by William Henry Thompson (1848-1918), who was the first US champion in 1879, and won his fifth and last men's title in 1908.

Twenty-four hours—target archery   The highest recorded score over 24 hours by a pair of archers is 76,158, during 70 Portsmouth Rounds (60 arrows per round at 20 yds. at 2 ft. FITA targets) by Simon Tarplee and David Hathaway at Evesham, Great Britain on 1 Apr. 1991. During this attempt Tarplee set an individual record of 38,500.

AUTO RACING

Origins   There are various conflicting claims, but the first automobile race was the 201-mile Green Bay-to-Madison, WI race run in 1878, won by an Oshkosh steamer. In 1887 Count Jules Félix Philippe Albert de Dion de Malfiancé (1856–1946) won the *La Vélocipéde* 31 km (19.3 mile) race in Paris, France in a De Dion steam quadricycle in which he is reputed to have exceeded 37 mph. The first "real" race was in France, from Paris to Bordeaux and back (732 miles) on 11–13 June 1895. The first to finish was Emile Levassor (1844–97) of France, in a Panhard-Levassor two-seater, with a 1.2-liter Daimler engine producing 3½ hp. His time was 48 hrs. 47 min. (average speed 15.01 mph). The first closed-circuit race was held over five laps of a mile-long dirt track at Narragansett Park, Cranston, RI on 7 Sep. 1896. It was won by A.H. Whiting, driving a Riker electric.

The oldest race in the world still regularly run is the Royal Automobile Club (RAC) Tourist Trophy, first staged on 14 Sep. 1905, in the Isle of Man, Great Britain. The French Grand Prix was first held on 26–27 June 1906. The Coppa Florio, in Sicily, has been irregularly held since 1906.

Fastest circuits   The highest average lap speed attained on any closed circuit is 250.958 mph, in a trial by Dr. Hans Liebold (Germany; b. 12 Oct. 1926), who lapped the 7.85 mile high-speed track at Nardo, Italy in 1 min. 52.67 sec. in a Mercedes-Benz C111-IV experimental coupé on 5 May 1979. It was powered by a V8 engine with two KKK turbochargers, with an output of 500 hp at 6,200 rpm.

The fastest road circuit was the Francorchamps circuit near Spa, Belgium, then 8.76 miles in length, which was lapped in 3 min. 13.4 sec. (average speed 163.086 mph) on 6 May 1973, by Henri Pescarolo (France; b. 25 Sep. 1942) driving a 2,993-cc V12 Matra-Simca MS670 Group 5 sports car.

INDIANAPOLIS 500. Rick Mears (USA) won for a record-equaling fourth time in 1991, and he is seen here with the Borg-Warner Trophy that has been presented to the winner since 1936. The trophy, made of 80 lbs. of sterling silver, cost $10,000 originally and is now priceless. It displays the faces of all the winners of the race since 1911, so Mears gets to see himself more than most! (Photos: Allsport USA/B. Spurlock & Steve Swope)

Fastest race   The fastest race is the Busch Clash at Daytona, FL over 50 miles on a 2½-mile 31-degree banked track. In 1987 Bill Elliott (USA; b. 8 Oct. 1955) averaged 197.802 mph in a Ford Thunderbird. Al Unser, Jr. (USA; b. 19 Apr. 1962) set the world record for a 500 mile race when he won the Michigan 500 on 9 Aug. 1990 at an average speed of 189.727 mph.

INDIANAPOLIS 500

The Indianapolis 500 mile race (200 laps) was inaugurated in the USA on 30 May 1911. Three drivers have four wins: Anthony Joseph "A.J." Foyt, Jr. (USA; b. 16 Jan. 1935) in 1961, 1964, 1967 and 1977; Al Unser (USA; b. 29 May 1939) in 1970–71, 1978 and 1987; and Rick Mears (USA; b. 3 Dec. 1951) in 1979, 1984, 1988 and 1991. The record time is 2 hrs. 41 min. (185.981 mph) by Arie Luyendyk (Netherlands) driving a Lola-Chevrolet on 27 May 1990. The record average speed for four laps qualifying is 232.482 mph by Roberto Guerrero (Colombia) in a Lola-Buick (including a one-lap record of 232.618 mph) on 9 May 1992. The track record is 233.433 mph by Jim Crawford (Great Britain) on 4 May 1992 although this was only a practice run. A.J. Foyt, Jr. has started a record 35 races, 1958–92, and Rick Mears has started from pole position a record six times, 1979, 1982, 1986, 1988–89, and 1991. The record prize fund is $7,527,450, and the individual prize record is $1,244,184 by Al Unser Jr., both in 1992.

First woman driver   The first woman to compete in the Indianapolis 500 was Janet Guthrie (USA; b. 7 Mar. 1938). She passed her rookie test in May 1976, and earned the right to compete in the qualifying rounds, but was unable to win a place on the starting line when the Vollstedt-Offenhauser she drove was withdrawn from the race after repeated mechanical failures. In the 61st running of the Indianapolis 500, in 1977, Guthrie became the first woman to compete, although her car developed mechanical problems that forced her to retire after 27 laps. In 1978, she completed the race, finishing in ninth place after 190 laps.

Closest finish   The closest margin of victory was 0.043 sec. in 1992 when Al Unser Jr. edged Scott Goodyear.

Indy Car Championships (CART)   The first Indy Car Championship was held in 1909 under the auspices of the American Automobile Association (AAA). In 1959 the United States Automobile Club (USAC) took over the running of the Indy series. Since 1979 Championship Auto Racing Teams Inc. (CART) has organized the Indy Championship, which since 1979 has been called the PPG Indy Car World Series Championship.

Most wins *National Championships*   The most successful driver in Indy car history is A.J. Foyt Jr., who has won 67 races and seven championships (1960–61, 1963–64, 1967, 1975 and 1979). The record for the most victories in a season is ten, shared by two drivers: A.J. Foyt Jr. (1964) and Al Unser (1970). Mario Andretti (USA; 28 Feb. 1940) has the most laps (7,392) in Indy championships as of 9 June 1991; he also holds the record for most pole positions at 64.

Highest earnings *Career*   As of 5 July 1992, Rick Mears holds the career earnings mark for Indy drivers with $11,024,836.

Season   The single-season record is $2,461,734, set in 1991 by Michael Andretti.

NASCAR *(National Association for Stock Car Auto Racing)*

The National Association for Stock Car Auto Racing, Inc. was founded by Bill France, Sr. in 1947. The first NASCAR championship was held in 1949. Since 1971 the championship series has been called the Winston Cup Championship. The championship has been won a record seven times by Richard Lee Petty (USA; b. 2 July 1937)—1964, 1967, 1971–72, 1974–75 and 1979.

Petty won 200 NASCAR Winston Cup races in 1,169 starts from 1958 to 17 June 1992, and his best season was 1967, with 27 wins. Petty, on 1 Aug. 1971, was the first driver to pass $1 million in career earnings.

The NASCAR career money record is $15,671,709 to 31 May 1992, by Dale Earnhardt (USA; b. 29 Apr. 1952). Earnhardt won a season record $3,083,056 in 1990. Geoff Bodine (USA; b. 18 Apr. 1949) won 55 races in NASCAR Modified racing in 1978.

Daytona 500   The Daytona 500 has been held at the 2½ mile oval Daytona International Speedway in Daytona, FL since 1959. The race is the major event of the NASCAR season. Richard Petty has a record seven wins—1964, 1966, 1971, 1973–74, 1979 and 1981. The record average speed for the race is 177.602 mph, by Buddy Baker in an Oldsmobile in 1980. The qualifying speed record is 210.364, by Bill Elliott in a Ford Thunderbird in 1987.

MOST WINS. The most National Association for (NASCAR) Stock Car Auto Racing Inc. championships (first held 1947, since 1971 the Winston Cup Championship) is seven, by Richard Petty (USA), 1964, 1967, 1971–72, 1974–75 and 1979. Petty won a record 200 NASCAR Winston Cup races in 1,169 starts, 1958–92. (Photo: Allsport/Steve Swope)

FORMULA ONE GRAND PRIX MOTOR RACING

Most successful drivers The World Drivers' Championship, inaugurated in 1950, has been won a record five times by Juan-Manuel Fangio (Argentina; b. 24 June 1911) in 1951 and 1954–57. He retired in 1958, after having won 24 Grand Prix races (two shared) from 51 starts.

Alain Prost (France; b. 24 Feb. 1955) holds the records for both the most Grand Prix points in a career, 699.5, and the most Grand Prix victories, 44 from 184 races, 1980–91. The most Grand Prix victories in a year is eight, by Ayrton Senna (Brazil; b. 21 Mar. 1960) in 1988. The most Grand Prix starts is 233, by Ricardo Patrese (Italy; b. 17 Apr. 1954) from 1977–92. The greatest number of pole positions is 61, by Ayrton Senna from 135 races (34 wins), 1985–92.

Two Americans have won the World Drivers' Championship—Phil Hill in 1961, and Mario Andretti in 1978. Andretti has the most Grand Prix wins by a US driver: 12 in 128 races, 1968–82.

Oldest and youngest The youngest world champion was Emerson Fittipaldi, who won his first World Championship on 10 Sep. 1972 at the age of 25 yrs. 273 days.

The oldest world champion was Juan-Manuel Fangio, who won his last World Championship on 4 Aug. 1957 at the age of 46 yrs. 41 days.

The youngest Grand Prix winner was Bruce Leslie McLaren (1937–70) of New Zealand, who won the United States Grand Prix at Sebring, FL on 12 Dec. 1959, age 22 yrs. 104 days. Troy Ruttman (USA) was 22 yrs. 80 days when he won the Indianapolis 500 on 30 May 1952; the Indianapolis 500 was part of the World Championships at the time. The oldest Grand Prix winner (in pre–World Championship days) was Tazio Giorgio Nuvolari (Italy; 1892–1953), who won the Albi Grand Prix at Albi, France on 14 July 1946, age 53 yrs. 240 days. The oldest Grand Prix driver was Louis Alexandre Chiron (Monaco; 1899–1979), who finished sixth in the Monaco Grand Prix on 22 May 1955, age 55 yrs. 292 days. The youngest driver to qualify for a Grand Prix was Michael Christopher Thackwell (New Zealand; b. 30 Mar. 1961) at the Canadian Grand Prix on 28 Sep. 1980, age 19 yrs. 182 days.

Manufacturers Ferrari has won a record eight manufacturers' World Championships, 1961, 1964, 1975–77, 1979, 1982–83. Ferrari has 103 race wins in 492 Grands Prix, 1950–92.

The greatest dominance by one team since the Constructor's Championship was instituted in 1958 was by McLaren in 1988, when the team won 15 of the 16 Grands Prix. Ayrton Senna had eight wins and three seconds, Alain Prost had seven wins and seven seconds. The McLarens, powered by Honda engines, amassed over three times the points of their nearest rivals, Ferrari. Excluding the Indianapolis 500 race, then included in the World Drivers' Championship, Ferrari won all seven races in 1952 and the first eight (of nine) in 1953.

Fastest race The fastest overall average speed for a Grand Prix race on a circuit in current use is 146.284 mph, by Nigel Mansell (Great Britain) in a Williams-Honda at Zeltweg in the Austrian Grand Prix on 16 Aug. 1987. The qualifying lap record was set by Keke Rosberg (Finland) at 1 min. 05.59 sec., an average speed of 160.817 mph, in a Williams-Honda at Silverstone in the British Grand Prix on 20 July 1985.

BEST START. Nigel Mansell (Great Britain) won the first five Grands Prix of the 1992 season, a record he shares with Sienna. Here he is seen celebrating his third success, the Brazilian (left), and in action during the fourth, the Spanish (below). (Photos: Allsport/Pascal Rondeau & Vandystadt)

> **Fastest pit stop** Robert William "Bobby" Unser (USA; b. 20
> Feb. 1934) took 4 seconds to take on fuel on lap 10 of the
> Indianapolis 500 on 30 May 1976.
>
> **Most Le Mans wins** The race has been won by Porsche cars
> twelve times, in 1970–71, 1976–77, 1979, 1981–87. The most wins
> by one man is six, by Jacques Bernard "Jacky" Ickx (Belgium; b. 1
> Jan. 1945), 1969, 1975–77 and 1981–82.

Closest finish The closest finish to a World Championship race was
when Ayrton Senna (Brazil) in a Lotus beat Nigel Mansell (Great Britain) in
a Williams by 0.014 sec. in the Spanish Grand Prix at Jerez de la Frontera on
13 Apr. 1986. In the Italian Grand Prix at Monza on 5 Sep. 1971, 0.61 sec.
separated winner Peter Gethin (Great Britain) from the fifth-placed driver.

LE MANS

The greatest distance ever covered in the 24-hour *Grand Prix d'Endurance*
(first held on 26–27 May 1923) on the old Sarthe circuit at Le Mans, France
is 3,314.222 miles, by Dr. Helmut Marko (Austria; b. 27 Apr. 1943) and Gijs
van Lennep (Netherlands; b. 16 Mar. 1942) in a 4907-cc flat-12 Porsche 917K
Group 5 sports car, on 12–13 June 1971. The record for the greatest distance
ever covered for the current circuit is 3,313.241 miles (avg. speed 137.718
mph) by Jan. Lammers (Netherlands), Johnny Dumfries and Andy Wallace
(both from Great Britain) in a Jaguar XJR9 on 11–12 June 1988.

The race lap record (now 8.410 mile lap) is 3 min. 21.27 sec. (average
speed 150.429 mph) by Alain Ferté (France) in a Jaguar XRJ-9 on 10 June
1989. Hans Stück (West Germany) set the practice lap record of 3 min. 14.8
sec. (avg. speed 156.62 mph) on 14 June 1985.

RALLYING

The earliest long rally, from Beijing, China to Paris, France, over about 7,500
miles from 10 June 1907, was promoted by the Parisian daily *Le Matin*. The
winner, Prince Scipione Borghese (1872–1927) of Italy, arrived in Paris on
10 Aug. 1907 in his 40-hp Itala accompanied by his chauffeur, Ettore, and
Luigi Barzini.

Longest The longest-ever rally was the *Singapore Airlines* London–
Sydney Rally over 19,329 miles from Covent Garden, London, Great Britain
on 14 Aug. 1977 to Sydney Opera House, Australia, won on 28 Sep. 1977 by
Andrew Cowan, Colin Malkin and Michael Broad in a Mercedes 280E. The
longest held annually is the Safari Rally (first run in 1953 as the Coronation
Rally, through Kenya, Tanzania and Uganda, but now restricted to Kenya).
The race has covered up to 3,874 miles, as in the 17th Safari held from 8–12
Apr. 1971. It has been won a record five times by Shekhar Mehta (Kenya; b.
20 June 1945) in 1973, 1979–82.

The Paris-Cape Town rally in January 1992 was scheduled to be raced over
about 7,890 miles from Paris to Cape Town passing through twelve countries. However, due to civil war, flooding and environmental concerns, cer-

tain stages were cancelled or shortened and the rally covered just over 5,900 miles.

Monte Carlo The Monte Carlo Rally (first run in 1911) has been won a record four times by Sandro Munari (Italy; b. 27 Mar. 1940) in 1972, 1975, 1976 and 1977; and by Walter Röhrl (West Germany; b. 7 Mar. 1947) (with co-driver Christian Geistdorfer) in 1980, 1982–84, each time in a different car. The smallest car to win was an 851-cc Saab driven by Erik Carlsson (Sweden; b. 5 Mar. 1929) and Gunnar Häggbom (Sweden; b. 7 Dec. 1935) on 25 Jan. 1962, and by Carlsson and Gunnar Palm on 24 Jan. 1963.

World Championship The World Drivers' Championships (instituted 1979) have been won by Juha Kankkunen (Finland; b. 2 Apr. 1959), on a record three occasions, 1986–87 and 1991. The most wins in World Championship races is 19, by Hannu Mikkola and Markku Alen (Finland) to the start of 1991. Lancia has won a record ten manufacturers' World Championships between 1972 and 1991.

DRAG RACING

Piston-engined The lowest official elapsed time recorded by a piston-engined dragster from a standing start for 440 yds. is 4.801 sec., by Eddie Hill (USA) at Gainesville, FL on 22 Mar. 1992. The highest terminal velocity at the end of a 440 yds. run is 301.70 mph, by Kenny Bernstein (USA) at Gainesville, FL on 20 Mar. 1992. For a gasoline-driven piston-engined car the lowest elapsed time is 7.139 sec., by Scott Geoffrion (USA), driving a Dodge Daytona and the highest terminal velocity is 194.46 mph, by Warren Johnson (USA) in an Oldsmobile Cutlass, both at Gainesville, FL on 20 Mar.

FASTEST DRAGSTER. The first person to break the 300 mph barrier for terminal velocity at the end of the quarter mile was Kenny Bernstein (USA) at Gainesville, FL on 20 Mar. 1992. He clocked up 301.70 mph in his Budweiser King top fuel dragster. (Photo: Allsport USA/Ken Levine)

1992. The lowest elapsed time for a gasoline-driven piston-engined motorcycle is 7.615 sec., by John Myers (USA; b. 1958) at Dallas, TX on 11 Oct. 1991, and the highest terminal velocity is 177.54 mph, by Byron Hines (USA) at Houston, TX on 6 Mar. 1992.

Most wins   The greatest number of wins in National Hot Rod Association national events is 80, by Bob Glidden in Pro Stock, 1973–91.

BADMINTON

Origins   Badminton is a descendant of the children's game of battledore and shuttlecock, and a similar game was played in China more than 2,000 years ago. The modern game may have evolved *c.* 1870 at Badminton Hall in Avon, Great Britain, or from a game played in India. The first modern rules were codified in Pune, India in 1876. The world governing body is the International Badminton Federation, formed in 1934. Badminton became a full Olympic sport in 1992, following demonstrations in 1972 and 1988.

United States   A battledore shuttlecock is described in the 1864 *American Boy's Book of Sports and Games*. The first badminton club formed in the United States was the Badminton Club of New York, founded in 1878. The game was not organized at the national level until 1935, when the American Badminton Association (ABA) was founded in Boston, MA. In 1978 the ABA was renamed the United States Badminton Association.

World Championships *Individual*   In this competition, instituted in 1977, a record five titles have been won by Park Joo-bong (South Korea)—men's doubles, 1985 and 1991, and mixed doubles, 1985, 1989 and 1991. Three Chinese players have won two individual world titles: men's singles: Yang Yang, 1987 and 1989; women's singles: Li Lingwei in 1983 and 1989; Han Aiping in 1985 and 1987.

Team   The most wins at the men's International Team Badminton Championship for the Thomas Cup (instituted 1948) is eight, by Indonesia (1958, 1961, 1964, 1970, 1973, 1976, 1979 and 1984).
   The most wins at the women's International Team Badminton Champi-

---

Longest badminton rallies   In the men's singles final of the 1987 All-England Championships between Morten Frost (Denmark) and Icuk Sugiarto (Indonesia), there were two successive rallies of over 90 strokes.

Shortest game   In the 1969 Uber Cup in Tokyo, Japan, Noriko Takagi (later Mrs. Nakayama; Japan) beat Poppy Tumengkol (Indonesia) in 9 min.

---

onship for the Uber Cup (instituted 1956) is five, by Japan (1966, 1969, 1972, 1978 and 1981) and China (1984, 1986, 1988, 1990 and 1992).

United States   The USA has never won the Thomas Cup, but won the Uber Cup on the first three occasions that it was contested, 1957, 1960 and 1963. Judy Hashman (nee Devlin; b. 22 Oct. 1935) was the only player on all three teams.

United States Championships   The first competition was held in 1937.

Most titles   Judy Hashman won a record 31 US titles: 12 women's singles, 1954, 1956–63, 1965–67; 12 women's doubles, 1953–55, 1957–63, 1966–67 (11 with her sister Susan); and seven mixed doubles, 1956–59, 1961–62, 1967. David Freeman won seven singles titles: 1939–42, 1947–48, 1953.

BASEBALL

Origins   In 1908, the Spalding Commission, sponsored by Albert G. Spalding, a sporting goods tycoon, concluded that the game of baseball had been invented by Abner Doubleday in 1839 at Cooperstown, NY, and the legend of Doubleday's accomplishment has since become deeply embedded in American folklore. Despite this tradition, Spalding's official version of baseball history is disputed by sports historians. They argue that baseball in North America evolved from such English games as cricket, paddleball, trap ball and rounders. Printed references to "base ball" in England date to 1700 and in the USA to the mid-eighteenth century. It is uncontested that Alexander Cartwright, Jr. formulated the rules of the modern game in 1845, and that the first match under these rules was played on 19 June 1846 when the New York Nine defeated the New York Knickerbockers, 23–1, in four innings. On 17 Mar. 1871 the National Association of Professional Base Ball Players was formed—the first professional league in the United States. Today there are two main professional baseball associations, the National League (organized in 1876) and the American League (organized in 1901, recognized in 1903), which together form the major leagues, along with approximately 20 associations that make up the minor leagues. The champions of the two leagues first played for the World Series in 1903 and have played continuously since 1905. (For further details on World Series history, see below.)

MAJOR LEAGUE

Most games played   Peter Edward "Pete" Rose (b. 14 Apr. 1941) played in a record 3,562 games with a record 14,053 at-bats, for the Cincinnati Reds (NL), 1963–78 and 1984–86, the Philadelphia Phillies (NL), 1979–83, and the Montreal Expos (NL), 1984. Henry Louis "Lou" Gehrig (1903–41) played in 2,130 successive games for the New York Yankees (AL) from 1 June 1925 to 30 Apr. 1939.

Most home runs *Career*   Henry Louis "Hank" Aaron (b. 5 Feb. 1934) holds the major league career record with 755 home runs—733 for the Milwaukee (1954–65) and Atlanta (1966–74) Braves in the National League and 22 for the Milwaukee Brewers (AL) 1975–76. On 8 Apr. 1974 he bettered the previous record of 714 by George Herman "Babe" Ruth (1895–1948). Ruth hit his home runs from 8,399 times at bat, achieving the highest home run percentage of 8.5 percent. Joshua Gibson (1911–47) of the Homestead Grays and Pittsburgh Crawfords, Negro League clubs, hit an estimated 900 home runs in his career, including an unofficial season record of 84 in 1931. These totals are believed to include exhibition games.

Season   The major league record for home runs in a season is 61, by Roger Eugene Maris (1934–85) for the New York Yankees in 162 games in 1961. The most official home runs in a minor league season is 72, by Joe Bauman of the Roswell Rockets of the Longhorn League in 1954. Bauman hit his record "dingers" in 138 games, while batting .400 and driving in 224 runs.

Game   The most home runs in a major league game is four, first achieved by Robert Lincoln "Bobby" Lowe (1868–1951) for Boston *v.* Cinncinnati on 30 May 1894. The feat has been achieved a further ten times since then.

Consecutive games   The most home runs hit in consecutive games is eight, set by Richard Dale Long (b. 6 Feb. 1926) for the Pittsburgh Pirates (NL), 19–28 May 1956, and tied by Donald Arthur "Don" Mattingly (b. 21 Apr. 1961) for the New York Yankees (AL), on 18 July 1987.

Grand slams   Seven players have hit two grand slams in a single game. They are: Anthony Michael "Tony" Lazzeri (1903–46) for the New York Yankees (AL) on 24 May 1936, James Reubin "Jim" Tabor (1916–53) for the Boston Red Sox (AL) on 4 July 1939, Rudolph Preston "Rudy" York (1913–70) for the Boston Red Sox (AL) on 27 July 1946, James Edward "Diamond Jim" Gentile (b. 3 June 1934) for the Baltimore Orioles (AL) on 9 May 1961, Tony Lee Cloninger (b. 13 Aug. 1940) for the Atlanta Braves (NL) on 3 July 1966, James "Jim" Thomas Northrup (b. 24 Nov. 1939) for the Detroit Tigers (AL) on 24 June 1968, and Frank Robinson (b. 31 Aug. 1935) for the Baltimore Orioles (AL) on 26 June 1970.

Don Mattingly of the New York Yankees (AL) hit six grand slams in 1987. Lou Gehrig hit 23 grand slams during his 16 seasons with the New York Yankees (AL), 1923–39.

Most career hits   The career record for most hits is 4,256, by Pete Rose. Rose's record hits total came from a record 14,053 at-bats, which gave him a career batting average of .303.

Most consecutive hits   Michael Franklin "Pinky" Higgins (1909–69) had 12 consecutive hits for the Boston Red Sox (AL) in a four-game span, 19–21 June 1938. This was equaled by Walter "Moose" Dropo (b. 30 Jan. 1923) for the Detroit Tigers (AL), 14–15 July 1952. Joseph Paul "Joe" DiMaggio (b. 25 Nov. 1914) hit in a record 56 consecutive games for the New York Yankees (AL) in 1941; he went to bat 223 times, with 91 hits, totaling 56 singles, 16 doubles, 4 triples and 15 home runs.

Home runs and stolen bases   The only player to have hit 40 or more home runs and have 40 stolen bases in a season was José Canseco (b. 2 July

MOST RUNS. During 23 seasons in the major leagues, Henry Louis "Hank" Aaron surpassed batting records that had been set by some of the greatest hitters of the game. Aaron currently holds the major league career batting record for runs batted in (RBI's), 2,297, and the career record for most home runs, 755. (Photo: Allsport)

STOLEN BASES. Rickey Henderson of the Oakland Athletics successfully steals another base. Since passing Lou Brock's career record in 1991, he has continued to add to his total, passing the 1,000 mark early in the 1992 season. (Photo: Allsport USA/Otto Gruele)

1964) for the Oakland Athletics (AL) in 1988. His totals were 42 and 40 respectively.

Stolen bases   On 1 May 1991, Rickey Henley Henderson (b. 25 Dec. 1958) of the Oakland Athletics (AL) broke baseball's all-time record for stolen bases when he stole his 939th base, surpassing Lou Brock's mark. As of 31 May 1992, Henderson had extended his record to 1,016 stolen bases. Henderson also holds the mark for most stolen bases in a season, which he set in 1982 when he stole 130 bases.

Walks   Babe Ruth holds the record for career walks, 2,056, and the single-season record, 170 in 1923.
Two players share a record six walks for a single game: James E. "Jimmie" Foxx (1907–67) of the Boston Red Sox (AL) set the mark on 16 June 1938, and Andre Thornton (b. 13 Aug. 1949) of the Cleveland Indians (AL) tied the record on 2 May 1984 in a game that went 18 innings.

Strikeouts   The batter with the career strikeout record is Reginald Martinez "Reggie" Jackson (b. 18 May 1946), who struck out 2,597 times in 21 seasons with four teams. The season record is 189, by Bobby Lee Bonds (b. 15 Mar. 1946), right fielder for the San Francisco Giants in 1970. The longest run of games without striking out is 115, by Joseph Wheeler "Joe" Sewell (b. 9 Oct. 1898) while playing third base for the Cleveland Indians (AL) in 1929. He had a record seven seasons batting at least 500 times with less than ten strikeouts, and struck out only 114 times in his 14-year career.

Most games won by a pitcher   Denton True "Cy" Young (1867–1955) had a record 511 wins and a record 750 complete games from a total of 906 games and 815 starts in his career for the Cleveland Spiders (NL) 1890–98, the St. Louis Cardinals (NL) 1899–1900, the Boston Red Sox (AL) 1901–08, the Cleveland Indians (AL) 1909–11 and the Boston Braves (NL) 1911. He pitched a record total of 7,356 innings. The career record for most pitching appearances is 1,070, by James Hoyt Wilhelm (b. 26 July 1923) for a total of nine teams between 1952 and 1969; he set the career record with 143 wins by a relief pitcher. The season's record is 106 appearances, by Michael Grant Marshall (b. 15 Jan. 1943) for the Los Angeles Dodgers (NL) in 1974.

Most consecutive games won by a pitcher   Carl Owen Hubell (1903–88) pitched for the New York Giants (NL) to win 24 consecutive games, 16 in 1936 and eight in 1937.

Shutouts   The record for the most shutouts in a career is 110, pitched by Walter Perry Johnson (1887–1946) in his 21-season career with the Washington Senators (AL), 1907–27. Donald Scott "Don" Drysdale (b. 23 July 1936) pitched six consecutive shutouts for the Los Angeles Dodgers (NL) between 14 May and 4 June 1968. Orel Leonard Hershiser IV (b. 16 Sep. 1958) pitched a record 59 consecutive shutout innings for the Los Angeles Dodgers (NL) from 30 Aug. to 28 Sep. 1988.

No-hitters   Nolan Ryan, playing for the Texas Rangers (AL) against the Toronto Blue Jays (AL), pitched his record seventh no-hitter on 1 May 1991. Ryan also holds the record for greatest number of walks, giving up 2,718 through 15 July 1992. John Samuel "Johnny" Vander Meer (b. 2 Nov. 1914) of the Cincinnati Reds (NL) is the only player in baseball history to have pitched consecutive no-hitters, 11–15 June 1938.

Perfect game   A perfect nine-inning game, in which the pitcher allowed the opposition no hits, no runs and did not allow a man to reach first base, was first achieved by John Lee Richmond (1857–1929) for Worcester, MA against Cleveland in the NL on 12 June 1880. There have been 13 subsequent perfect games over nine innings, but no pitcher has achieved this feat more than once. On 26 May 1959 Harvey Haddix Jr. (b. 18 Sep. 1925) for Pittsburgh pitched a perfect game for 12 innings against Milwaukee in the National League, but lost in the 13th.

Saves   Robert Thomas "Bobby" Thigpen (b. 17 July 1963) saved a record 57 games for the Chicago White Sox (AL) in 1990. The career record for saves is 345 through 12 July 1992, by Jeffrey James "Jeff" Reardon (b. 1 Oct. 1955) in his 13 seasons playing for the New York Mets (NL), 1979–81; the Montreal Expos (NL), 1981–86; the Minnesota Twins (AL), 1987–89; and the Boston Red Sox (AL), 1990–92.

Longest throw   Glen Edward Gorbous (Canada; b. 8 July 1930) threw a baseball 445 ft. 10 in. on 1 Aug. 1957. Mildred Ella "Babe" Didrikson (USA [later Mrs. Zaharias]; 1914–56) threw a baseball 296 ft. at Jersey City, NJ on 25 July 1931.

Fastest base runner   The fastest time for circling bases is 13.3 sec., by Ernest Evar Swanson (1902–73) at Columbus, OH in 1932, at an average speed of 18.45 mph.

Longest home run   In a minor league game at Emeryville Ball Park, CA on 4 July 1929, Roy Edward "Dizzy" Carlyle (1900–56) hit a home run measured at 618 ft.
   The longest measured home run in a regular-season major league game was 573 ft., by Dave Nicholson (b. 29 Aug. 1939) for the Chicago White Sox *v.* Kansas City Athletics on 6 May 1964 at Comiskey Park in Chicago.

Holding 10 baseballs in one hand   James and Jason d'Amore of the Bronx, NY set a world record by holding 10 baseballs in one hand, 20 Oct. 1991.

Father and son   On 31 Aug., 1990, Ken Griffey, Sr. and Ken Griffey, Jr., of the Seattle Mariners (AL), became the first father and son to play for the same major league team at the same time. Griffey Sr., an 18-year veteran, was signed by Seattle on 29 Aug. In 1989 the Griffeys had been the first father/son combination to play in the major leagues at the same time–Griffey Sr. played for the Cincinnati Reds (NL) during that season, while Griffey, Jr. was in his first season with the Mariners.

MAJOR LEAGUE RECORDS
American League (AL), National League (NL)

CAREER BATTING RECORDS

Batting average	.367	Tyrus Raymond "Ty" Cobb (Detroit–AL, Philadelphia–AL)	1905–28
Runs scored	2,245	Ty Cobb	1905–28
Runs batted in (RBI's)	2,297	Henry Louis "Hank" Aaron (Milwaukee, Atlanta–NL, Milwaukee–AL)	1954–76
Base hits	4,256	Peter Edward "Pete" Rose (Cincinnati–NL, Philadelphia–NL, Montreal–NL)	1963–86
Total bases	6,856	Hank Aaron (Milwaukee, Atlanta–NL, Milwaukee–AL)	1954–76

SEASON BATTING RECORDS

Batting average	.438	Hugh Duffy (Boston–NL; 236 hits in 539 at-bats)	1894
modern record (1900–present)	.424	Rogers Hornsby (St. Louis–NL; 227 in 536 at-bats)	1924
Runs scored	196	William Robert Hamilton (Philadelphia–NL; in 131 games)	1894
modern record (1900–present)	177	George Herman "Babe" Ruth (New York–AL; in 152 games)	1921
Runs batted in (RBI's)	190	Lewis Robert "Hack" Wilson (Chicago–NL; in 155 games)	1930
Base hits	257	George Harold Sisler (St. Louis–AL; 631 times at bat, 143 games)	1920
Singles	202	William H. "Wee Willie" Keeler (Baltimore–NL; in 128 games)	1898
modern record (1900–present)	198	Lloyd James Waner (Pittsburgh–NL; in 150 games)	1927
Doubles	67	William Earl Webb (Boston–AL; in 151 games)	1931
Triples	36	John Owen Wilson (Pittsburgh–NL; in 152 games)	1912
Total bases	457	Babe Ruth (New York–AL; 85 singles, 44 doubles, 16 triples, 59 home runs	1921

SINGLE-GAME BATTING RECORDS

Runs batted in (RBI's) ....**12** James LeRoy Bottomley (St. Louis–NL) v. Brooklyn ....16 Sep. 1924
Base hits ....**9** John Henderson Burnett (Cleveland–AL; in 18 innings) ....10 July 1932
Total bases ....**18** Joseph Wilbur "Joe" Adcock (Milwaukee–AL); 1 double, 4 home runs ....31 July 1954

CAREER PITCHING RECORDS

Games won ....**511** Denton T. "Cy(clone)" Young (in 906 games; Cleveland 1890–1911
                                                  St. Louis, Boston–NL and Cleveland, Boston–AL)
Shutouts.......................................**110** Walter Perry Johnson (Washington–AL; in 802 games) 1907–27
Strikeouts.....................................***5,556** Lynn Nolan Ryan (New York–NL, California–AL, Houston–NL, Texas–AL) 1968–92
Through 7 June 1992

SEASON PITCHING RECORDS

Games won ....**60** Charles Gardner "Old Hoss" Radbourn (Providence–NL; and 12 losses) 1884
modern record (1900–present) ....**41** John Dwight "Jack" Chesbro (New York–AL) 1904
Shutouts..**16** George Washington Bradley (St. Louis–NL; in 64 games) 1876
modern record (1900–present) ....**16** Grover Cleveland "Pete" Alexander (Philadelphia–NL; 48 games) 1916
Strikeouts......................................**513** Matthew Aloysius Kilroy (Baltimore–AL)..1886
modern record (1900–present) ....**383** Lynn Nolan Ryan (California–AL) 1973

SINGLE-GAME PITCHING RECORDS

Strikeouts (9 innings)......................**20** William Roger Clemens (Boston–AL) v. Seattle..29 Apr. 1986
Strikeouts in extra innings...............**21** Thomas Edgar Cheney (Washington–AL) v. Baltimore (16 innings) ....12 Sep. 1962

Youngest player Frederick Joseph Chapman (1872–1957) pitched for Philadelphia in the American Association at 14 yrs. 239 days on 22 July 1887, but did not play again.

The youngest major league player of all time was the Cincinnati Reds (AL) pitcher Joseph Henry "Joe" Nuxhall (b. 30 July 1928), who played one game in June 1944, age 15 yrs. 314 days. He did not play again in the National League until 1952. The youngest player to play in a minor league game was Joe Louis Reliford (b. 29 Nov. 1939), who played for the Fitzgerald Pioneers against the Statesboro Pilots in the Georgia State League, age 12 yrs. 234 days on 19 July 1952.

Oldest player Leroy Robert "Satchel" Paige (1906–82) pitched for the Kansas City A's (AL) at 59 yrs. 80 days on 25 Sep. 1965.

Shortest and tallest players The shortest major league player was Eddie Gaedel, a 3 ft. 7 in., 65 lb. midget, who pinch-hit for the St. Louis Browns (AL) *v.* the Detroit Tigers (AL) on 19 Aug. 1951. Wearing number ⅛, the batter with the smallest-ever major league strike zone walked on four pitches. Following the game, major league rules were hastily rewritten to prevent the recurrence of such an affair. The tallest major leaguer of all time is Randy Johnson (b. 10 Sep. 1963) of the Seattle Mariners (AL), a 6 ft. 10 in. pitcher, who played in his first game for the Montreal Expos on 15 Sep. 1988.

Most Valuable Player Award The most selections in the annual vote (instituted in 1931) of the Baseball Writers' Association for Most Valuable Player of the Year (MVP) in the major leagues is three, won by: *National League*: Stanley Frank "Stan" Musial (b. 21 Nov. 1920; St. Louis), 1943, 1946, 1948; Roy Campanella (b. 19 Nov. 1921; Brooklyn), 1951, 1953, 1955; Mike Schmidt (b. 27 Sep. 1949; Philadelphia), 1980–81, 1986; *American League*: James Emory "Jimmie" Foxx (1907–67; Philadelphia), 1932–33, 1938; Joe DiMaggio (New York), 1939, 1941, 1947; Yogi Berra (New York), 1951, 1954–55; Mickey Mantle (b. 20 Oct. 1931; New York), 1956–57, 1962.

Cy Young Award In the competition for this prize, awarded annually from 1956 on to the outstanding pitcher in the major leagues, the most wins is four, by Stephen Norman "Steve" Carlton (b. 22 Dec. 1944; Philadelphia Phillies), 1972, 1977, 1980 and 1982.

Dwight Eugene Gooden (b. 16 Nov. 1964) of the New York Mets became the youngest pitcher to win the Cy Young Award in 1985 by unanimous vote of the 24 sportswriters who make the selection.

Longest and shortest games The most innings in a major league game were 26, when the Brooklyn Dodgers (NL) and the Boston Braves (NL) played to a 1–1 tie on 1 May 1920. The New York Giants (NL) beat the Philadelphia Phillies (NL), 6–1, in nine innings in 51 min. on 28 Sep. 1919. (A minor league game, Atlanta *v.* Mobile in the Southern Association on 19 Sep. 1910, took 33 min. [see below].) The Chicago White Sox (AL) played the longest ballgame in elapsed time—8 hours 6 min.—beating the Milwaukee Brewers, 7–6, in the 25th inning on 9 May 1984 in Chicago. The game started on Tuesday night and was still tied at 3–3 when the 1 A.M. curfew caused suspension until Wednesday night.

Longest baseball game The actual longest game was a minor league

STRIKEOUTS. In a career that has spanned four decades, Nolan Ryan (above) has set numerous major league records, the most notable being seven no-hitters and a career record 5,556 strikeouts as of 7 June 1992. (Photo: Allsport USA/D. Strohmeyer)

CY YOUNG AWARD. The only pitcher to have won the Cy Young award four times is Steve Carlton (right) of the Philadelphia Phillies: 1972, 1977, 1980 and 1982. (Photo: Allsport USA/B. Schwartzman)

game in 1981 that lasted 33 innings. At the end of nine innings the score was tied, 1–1, with the Rochester (NY) Red Wings battling the home team Pawtucket (RI) Red Sox. At the end of 21 innings it was tied 2–2, and at the end of 32 innings, the score was still 2–2, at which point the game was suspended. Two months later, play was resumed, and 18 minutes later, Pawtucket scored one run and won. The winning pitcher was the Red Sox's Bob Ojeda.

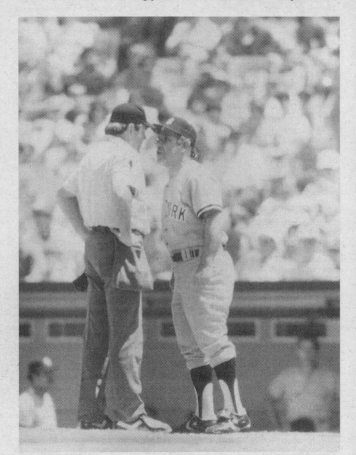

MOST VALUABLE PLAYER. Lawrence Peter "Yogi" Berra established two World Series records—most series played (14), and most base hits (71). He won the Most Valuable Player (MVP) award a record three times, in 1951, 1954–55. After retiring as a player, Berra went on to coach the New York Mets and then to manage the New York Yankees. He is seen here in a familiar stance, disputing the umpire's call. (Photo: Allsport)

Record attendances The all-time season record for attendance for both leagues is 56,888,512 in 1991. The record for an individual league is 32,117,588, for the American League in 1991, and this included an individual team record of 4,001,527 for the home games of the Toronto Blue Jays.

Managers Connie Mack (b. Cornelius Alexander McGillicuddy; 1862–1956) managed in the major leagues for a record 53 seasons and achieved a record 3,731 regular-season victories (and a record 3,948 losses)—139 wins and 134 losses for the Pittsburgh Pirates (NL) 1894–96, and 3,592 wins and 3,814 losses for the Philadelphia Athletics (AL), a team he later owned, 1901–50. The most successful in the World Series was Charles Dillon "Casey" Stengel (1890–1975), who managed the New York Yankees (AL) to seven wins in ten World Series, winning in 1949–53, 1956 and 1958, and losing in 1955, 1957 and 1960. Joseph Vincent "Joe" McCarthy (1887–1978) also coached the New York Yankees to seven wins, 1932, 1936–39, 1941, 1943, and his teams lost in 1929 (Chicago) and 1942 (New York). He had the highest win percentage of managers who achieved at least 1,500 regular-season wins, with .614—2,126 wins and 1,335 losses in his 24-year career with the Chicago Cubs (NL) 1926–30, the New York Yankees (AL) 1931–46, and the Boston Red Sox (AL) 1948–50, during which he never had an overall losing season.

WORLD SERIES

Origins Played annually between the winners of the National League and the American League championships, the World Series was first staged unofficially in 1903, and officially from 1905. The most wins is 22, by the New York Yankees between 1923 and 1978, during a record 33 Series appearances after winning the American League titles between 1921 and 1981. The most National League wins is 19, by the Dodgers—Brooklyn 1890–1957, Los Angeles 1958–88.

Most Valuable Player The only players to have won the award twice are Sandy Koufax (b. 30 Dec. 1935) (Los Angeles, NL, 1963, 1965), Bob Gibson (b. 9 Nov. 1935) (St. Louis, NL, 1964, 1967) and Reggie Jackson (b. 18 May 1946) (Oakland, AL, 1973, New York, AL, 1977).

Attendance The record attendance for a Series is 420,784, for the six games when the Los Angeles Dodgers beat the Chicago White Sox 4–2 between 1 and 8 Oct. 1959. The single-game record is 92,706, for the fifth game of this series at the Memorial Coliseum, Los Angeles on 6 Oct. 1959.

COLLEGE BASEBALL

Various forms of college baseball have been played throughout the 20th century; however, the National Collegiate Athletic Association (NCAA) did not organize a championship until 1947 and did not begin to keep statistical records until 1957.

NCAA Division I regular season *Hitting records* The most career home runs was 100, by Pete Incaviglia for Oklahoma State in three seasons, 1983–85. The most career hits was 418, by Phil Stephenson for Wichita State in four seasons, 1979–82.

WORLD SERIES RECORDS

American League (AL), National League (NL)

Most wins	**22** New York Yankees–AL	1923–78
Most series played	**14** Lawrence Peter "Yogi" Berra (New York Yankees–AL)	1947–63
Most series played by pitcher	**11** Edward Charles "Whitey" Ford (New York Yankees–AL)	1950–64

WORLD SERIES CAREER RECORDS

Batting average (min. 75 at-bats)	**.391** Louis Clark "Lou" Brock (St. Louis Cardinals–NL; 34 hits in 87 at-bats, 3 series)	1964–68
Runs scored	**42** Mickey Charles Mantle (New York Yankees–AL)	1951–64
Runs batted in (RBI's)	**40** Mickey Mantle (New York Yankees–AL)	1951–64
Base hits	**71** Yogi Berra (New York Yankees–AL)	1947–63
Home runs	**18** Mickey Mantle (New York Yankees–AL)	1951–64
Victories pitching	**10** Whitey Ford (New York Yankees–AL)	1950–64
Strikeouts	**94** Whitey Ford (New York Yankees–AL)	1950–64

WORLD SERIES SINGLE-SERIES RECORDS

Batting average (4 or more games) ...... .750   William Augustus "Billy" Hatcher (Cincinnati Reds–NL;
    9 hits in 12 at-bats in four-game series) 1990

Runs scored	10	Reginald Martinez "Reggie" Jackson (New York Yankees–AL)	1977
Runs batted in (RBI's)	12	Robert Clinton "Bobby" Richardson (New York Yankees–AL)	1960
Base hits (7-game series)	13	Bobby Richardson (New York Yankees–AL)	1960
	13	Lou Brock (St. Louis Cardinals–NL)	1968
	13	Martin "Marty" Barrett (Boston Red Sox–AL)	1986
Home runs	5	Reggie Jackson (New York Yankees–AL, in 20 at-bats)	1977
Victories pitching	3	Christopher "Christy" Matthewson (New York Yankees–AL; in five-game series)	1905
	3	John Wesley "Jack" Coombs (Philadelphia A's–AL; in five-game series)	1910

Ten other pitchers have won three games in more than five games.

Strikeouts	35	Robert "Bob" Gibson (St. Louis Cardinals–NL; in 7 games)	1968
	23	Sanford "Sandy" Koufax (Los Angeles Dodgers–NL; in 4 games)	1963

WORLD SERIES SINGLE-GAME RECORDS

Home runs	3	Babe Ruth (New York Yankees–AL) v. St. Louis Cardinals	6 Oct. 1926
	3	Babe Ruth (New York Yankees–AL) v. St. Louis Cardinals	9 Oct. 1928
	3	Reggie Jackson (New York Yankees–AL) v. Los Angeles Dodgers	18 Oct. 1977
Runs batted in (RBI's) in a game	6	Bobby Richardson (New York Yankees–AL) v. Pittsburgh Pirates	8 Oct. 1960
Strikeouts by pitcher in a game	17	Bob Gibson (St. Louis Cardinals–NL) v. Detroit Tigers	2 Oct. 1968
Perfect game (9 innings)		Donald James "Don" Larson (New York Yankees–AL) v. Brooklyn Dodgers	8 Oct. 1956

Pitching records   Don Heinkel won 51 games for Wichita State in four seasons, 1979–82. Derek Tatsumo struck out 541 batters for the University of Hawaii in three seasons, 1977–79.

College World Series   The first College World Series was played in 1947 in Kalamazoo, MI. The University of California at Berkeley defeated Yale University in a best-of-three game series, 2-0. In 1949 the series format was changed to a championship game. Since 1950 the College World Series has been played annually at Rosenblatt Stadium, Omaha, NE.

Most championships   The most wins in Division I is 11, by the University of Southern California (USC) in 1948, 1958, 1961, 1963, 1968, 1970–74 and 1978.

Hitting records   The record for most home runs in a College World Series is four, shared by five players: Bud Hollowell (University of Southern California), 1963; Pete Incaviglia (Oklahoma State), 1983–85; Ed Sprague (Stanford University), 1987–88; Gary Hymel (Louisiana State University), 1990–1991; and Lyle Mewton (Louisiana State University), 1990–91.
   Keith Moreland of the University of Texas holds the record for the most hits in a College World Series career, with 23 hits in three series, 1973–75.

Pitching records   The record for most wins in the College World Series is four games, shared by nine players: Bruce Gardner (University of Southern California), 1958, 1960; Steve Arlin (Ohio State), 1965–66; Bert Hooten (University of Texas at Austin), 1969–70; Steve Rogers (University of Tulsa), 1969, 1971; Russ McQueen (University of Southern California), 1972–73; Mark Bull (University of Southern California), 1973–74; Greg Swindell (University of Texas), 1984–85; Kevin Sheary (University of Miami of Florida), 1984–85; Greg Brummett (Wichita State), 1988–89.
   Carl Thomas of the University of Arizona struck out 64 batters in three College World Series, 1954–56.

World Amateur Championships   In this contest, instituted in 1938, the most successful nation has been Cuba, with 19 wins between 1939 and 1988. Baseball has been a demonstration sport at six Olympic Games, and American teams have won the tournament four times, 1912, 1956, 1964 and 1988.

BASKETBALL

Origins   The game of "Pok-ta-Pok" was played in the 10th century B.C. by the Olmecs in Mexico, and closely resembled basketball in its concept. "Ollamalitzli" was a variation of this game played by the Aztecs in Mexico as late as the 16th century. If the solid rubber ball was put through a fixed stone ring the player was entitled to the clothing of all the spectators. Modern basketball (which may have been based on the German game *Korbball*) was devised by the Canadian-born Dr. James Naismith (1861–1939) at the Training School of the International YMCA College in Springfield, MA in mid-December 1891. The first game played under modified rules was on 20 Jan. 1892. The International Basketball Federation (FIBA) was founded in 1932.

Highest score   In a senior international match, Iraq scored 251 points against Yemen (33) at New Delhi, India, in November 1982 at the Asian Games.

Largest attendance   The largest crowd for a basketball game was 80,000 for the final of the European Cup Winners' Cup between AEK Athens (89) and Slavia Prague (82) at the Olympic stadium, Athens, Greece on 4 Apr. 1968.

NATIONAL BASKETBALL ASSOCIATION

Origins   The Amateur Athletic Union (AAU) organized the first national tournament in the USA in 1897. The first professional league was the National Basketball League (NBL), founded in 1898, but this league only lasted two seasons. The American Basketball League was formed in 1925, but it declined, and the NBL was refounded in 1937. This organization merged with the Basketball Association of America in 1949 to form the National Basketball Association (NBA).

Most championships   The Boston Celtics have won a record 16 NBA titles—1957, 1959–66, 1968–69, 1974, 1976, 1981, 1984 and 1986.

MOST CHAMPIONSHIP WINS. The Boston Celtics have won the most NBA titles of any team, with 16. The picture shows the Celtics in action in the 1987 championships *v*. the Los Angeles Lakers, who hold the record for greatest winning streak, from 5 Nov. 1971 to 7 Jan. 1972. (Photo: Allsport USA)

Individual scoring　Wilton Norman "Wilt" Chamberlain (b. 21 Aug. 1936) set an NBA record with 100 points for Philadelphia *v.* New York at Hershey, PA on 2 Mar. 1962. This included a record 36 field goals and 28 free throws (from 32 attempts) and a record 59 points in a half (the second). The free throws game record was equaled by Adrian Dantley (b. 28 Feb. 1956) for Utah *v.* Houston at Las Vegas on 5 Jan. 1984. The most points scored in an NBA game in one quarter is 33, in the second quarter, by George Gervin for San Antonio *v.* New Orleans on 9 Apr. 1978.

Most games　Kareem Abdul-Jabbar (formerly Ferdinand Lewis Alcindor) (b. 16 Apr. 1947) took part in a record 1,560 NBA regular season games over 20 seasons, totaling 57,446 minutes played, for the Milwaukee Bucks, 1969–75, and the Los Angeles Lakers, 1975–89. He also played a record 237 playoff games. The most successive games is 906, by Randy Smith for the Buffalo Braves, the San Diego Clippers, the Cleveland Cavaliers and the New York Knicks from 18 Feb. 1972 to 13 Mar. 1983. The record for most complete games played in one season is 79, by Wilt Chamberlain for Philadelphia in 1962, when he was on court for a record 3,882 minutes. Chamberlain went through his entire career of 1,045 games without fouling out. On 21 Apr. 1991 Moses Malone played his 1,129th consecutive game without fouling out to the end of the 1991/92 season. In his career, Malone has played 1,246 games, fouling out on only five occasions.

MOST ASSISTS. Magic Johnson holds the career record for most assists in regular season play, with 9,921, and in the playoffs, with 2,142. (Photo: Allsport USA)

Most points   Kareem Abdul-Jabbar set NBA career records with 38,887 points, including 15,837 field goals, in regular-season games, and 5,762 points, including 2,356 field goals, in playoff games. The previous record holder, Wilt Chamberlain, had an average of 30.1 points per game for his total of 31,419 for the Philadelphia Warriors 1959–62, the San Francisco 76ers 1962–65, the Philadelphia Warriors 1964–68 and the Los Angeles Lakers 1968–73. He scored 50 or more points in 118 games, including 45 games in 1961/62 and 30 in 1962/63, to the next-best career total of 17. He set season records for points and scoring average with 4,029 at 50.1 per game, and also for field goals, 1,597, for Philadelphia in 1961/62. The highest career average for players exceeding 10,000 points is 32.3 points per game, by Michael Jordan (b. 17 Feb. 1963), 19,000 points in 589 games for the Chicago Bulls, 1984–92. Jordan also holds the career scoring average record for playoffs at 34.6, 3,184 points in 92 games 1984–92.

Kareem Abdul-Jabbar (Milwaukee, Los Angeles) had a record nine seasons scoring more than 2,000 points: 1970–74, 1976–77, 1980–81; and 19 scoring more than 1,000, 1970–88.

Steals   The most steals in an NBA game is 11, by Larry Kenon for San Antonio at Kansas City on 26 Dec. 1976. Alvin Robertson (b. 22 July 1962) set season records for San Antonio in 1985/86 with 301 at a record average of 3.67 steals per game.

Blocked shots   The record for most blocked shots in an NBA game is 17, by Elmore Smith for Los Angeles *v.* Portland at Los Angeles on 28 Oct. 1973.

Highest points   Mats Wermelin, 13 years old (Sweden), scored all 272 points in a 272–0 win in a regional boys' tournament in Stockholm, Sweden on 5 Feb. 1974.

The record score by a woman is 156 points by Marie Boyd (now Eichler) of Central High School, Lonaconing, MD in a 163–3 defeat of Ursaline Academy, Cumbria on 25 Feb. 1924.

Tallest basketball player   Tallest in NBA history has been Manute Bol (Sudan; b. 16 Oct. 1962) of the Washington Bullets, Golden State Warriors and Philadelphia 76ers, at 7 ft. 6¾ in. He made his pro debut in 1985.

Dribbling   Peter del Masto (USA) dribbled a basketball without "traveling" from near Lee to Provincetown, MA, a distance of 265.2 miles, from 12–25 Aug. 1989.

Bob Nickerson of Gallitzin, PA, Dave Davlin of Garland, TX and Jeremy Kable of Highspire, PA have each successfully demonstrated the ability to dribble four basketballs simultaneously.

Longest goal   Christopher Eddy (b. 13 July 1971) scored a field goal measured at 90 ft. 2¼ in. for Fairview High School *v.* Iroquois High School at Erie, PA on 25 Feb. 1989. The shot was made as time expired in overtime and it won the game for Fairview, 51–50.

NBA RECORDS

CAREER RECORDS

Points	.38,387	Kareem Abdul-Jabbar: Milwaukee ....1970–89 Bucks, Los Angeles Lakers
Field-goal percentage	599	Artis Gilmore: Chicago Bulls,.....................1977–88 San Antonio Spurs, Boston Celtics; min. 2,000 field goals
Free throws made	8,395	Moses Eugene Malone:.................................1976–92 Buffalo Braves, Houston Rockets, Philadelphia 76ers, Washington Bullets, Atlanta Hawks, Milwaukee Bucks
Free-throw percentage	900	Rick Barry: San Francisco/Golden ....1965–80 State Warriors, Houston Rockets; 3,818 from 4,243 attempts (technically .89983)
Field goals	15,837	Kareem Abdul-Jabbar 1970–89
Rebounds	23,924	Wilt Chamberlain: Philadelphia /San ....1960–73 Francisco Warriors, Philadelphia 76ers, Los Angeles Lakers
Assists	9,921	Earvin "Magic" Johnson: ....1980–91 Los Angeles Lakers
Steals	2,275	Maurice Cheeks: Philadelphia 76ers, ...1979–92 San Antonio Spurs, New York Knicks, Atlanta Hawks

SEASONS RECORDS

Points	4,029	Wilt Chamberlain: Philadelphia Warriors 1962
Field-goal percentage	727	Wilt Chamberlain: ....1972 Los Angeles Lakers; 426 of 586 attempts
Free throws made	840	Jerry West: Los Angeles Lakers;.......................1966 from 977 attempts
Free-throw percentage	958	Calvin Murphy: Houston Rockets; ....1981 206 of 215 attempts
Field goals	1,597	Wilt Chamberlain: Philadelphia Warriors 1962
Rebounds	2,149	Wilt Chamberlain: Philadelphia Warriors 1961
Assists	1,164	John Stockton: Utah Jazz 1991
Steals	301	Alvin Robertson: San Antonio Spurs..................1986

SINGLE-GAME RECORDS

Points	100	Wilt Chamberlain: Philadelphia ....2 Mar. 1962 Warriors v. New York Knicks
Field goals	36	Wilt Chamberlain ....2 Mar. 1962
Free throws made	28	Wilt Chamberlain ....2 Mar. 1962
	28	Adrian Dantley: Utah Jazz ....5 Jan. 1984 v. Houston Rockets
Rebounds	55	Wilt Chamberlain: Philadelphia............24 Nov. 1960 Warriors v. Boston Celtics
Assists	30	Scott Skiles: Orlando Magic ....30 Dec. 1990 v. Denver Nuggets
Steals	11	Larry Kenon: San Antonio ....26 Dec. 1976 Spurs v. Kansas City Kings

NBA PLAYOFF RECORDS

Most games played ....**237**   Kareem Abdul-Jabbar: Milwaukee 1970–89
Bucks, Los Angeles Lakers

CAREER RECORDS

Points ....**5,762**   Kareem Abdul-Jabbar 1970–89
(in 237 playoff games)

Field goals ....**2,356**   Kareem Abdul-Jabbar 1970–89
Free throws made ....**1,213**   Jerry West: Los Angeles Lakers; 1961–74
from 1,507 attempts

Assists ....**2,142**   Magic Johnson: Los Angeles Lakers 1980–91
Rebounds ....**4,104**   Bill Russell: Boston Celtics 1957–69

Series records

Points ....**284**   Elgin Baylor: Los Angeles Lakers.....................1962
(*v.* Boston Celtics); in 7 games

Field goals ....**113**   Wilt Chamberlain: San Francisco.....................1964
(*v.* St. Louis); in 6 games

Free throws made...................**86**   Jerry West: Los Angeles Lakers 1965
(*v.* Baltimore); in 6 games

Rebounds............................**220**   Wilt Chamberlain: Philadelphia 76ers...............1965
(*v.* Boston Celtics); in 7 games

Assists ....**115**   John Stockton: Utah Jazz 1988
(*v.* Los Angeles Lakers); in 7 games

SINGLE GAME RECORDS

Points ....**63**   Michael Jordan: Chicago Bulls..............20 Apr. 1986
(*v.* Boston Celtics); includes two
overtime periods

                     61   Elgin Baylor: Los Angeles ....14 Apr. 1962
Lakers (*v.* Boston Celtics)

Field goals ....**24**   Wilt Chamberlain: Philadelphia.............14 Mar. 1960
76ers *v.* Syracuse Nationals;
in 42 attempts

                     24   John Havlicek: Boston Celtics ....1 Apr. 1973
(*v.* Atlanta Hawks); in 36 attempts

                     24   Michael Jordan: Chicago Bulls ....1 May 1988
(*v.* Cleveland Cavaliers);
in 45 attempts

Free throws made...................**30**   Bob Cousy: Boston Celtics ....21 Mar. 1953
(*v.* Syracuse Nationals); includes
four overtime periods and 32 attempts

                     23   Michael Jordan: Chicago Bulls..............14 May 1989
(*v.* New York Knicks);
in 28 attempts

Rebounds..............................**41**   Wilt Chamberlain: Philadelphia ....5 Apr. 1967
76ers (*v.* Boston Celtics)

Assists ....**24**   Magic Johnson: Los Angeles................15 May 1984
Lakers (*v.* Phoenix Suns)

                     24   John Stockton: Utah Jazz ....17 May 1988
(*v.* Los Angeles Lakers)

Most Valuable Player   Kareem Abdul-Jabbar was elected the NBA's most valuable player a record six times, 1971–72, 1974, 1976–77 and 1980.

Highest score   The highest aggregate score in an NBA match is 370, when the Detroit Pistons (186) beat the Denver Nuggets (184) at Denver, CO on 13 Dec. 1983. Overtime was played after a 145–145 tie in regulation time. The record in regulation time is 318, when the Denver Nuggets beat the San Antonio Spurs 163–155 at Denver on 11 Jan. 1984. The most points in a half is 107, by the Phoenix Suns in the first half *v.* the Denver Nuggets on 11 Nov. 1990. The most points in a quarter is 58, in the fourth quarter, by Buffalo *v.* Boston on 20 Oct. 1972.

Winning margin   The greatest winning margin in an NBA game is 68 points, by which the Cleveland Cavaliers, 148, beat the Miami Heat, 80, on 17 Dec. 1991.

Winning streak   The Los Angeles Lakers won a record 33 NBA games in succession from 5 Nov. 1971 to 7 Jan. 1972, as during the 1971/72 season they won a record 69 games with 13 losses.

Coaches   The most successful coach in NBA history has been Arnold "Red" Auerbach (b. 1917) with 938 wins (1,037 including playoffs), with the Washington Capitols 1946–49, the Tri-Cities Blackhawks 1949–50, and the Boston Celtics 1950–66. He led the Boston Celtics to a record nine NBA titles, including eight in succession in 1959–66.

Pat Riley has won a record 108 playoff games, 102 with the Los Angeles Lakers (1981–90) and six with the New York Knicks (1992), to set the NBA all-time mark.

Richard "Dick" Motta has coached the most games, with 1,719 with the Chicago Bulls 1968–76, the Washington Bullets 1976–80, the Dallas Mavericks 1980–87 and the Sacramento Kings 1989–91. Motta's career totals are 856 wins and 863 losses.

NCAA RECORDS

Origins   In this competition, first held in 1939, the record for most Division I titles is 10, by the University of California at Los Angeles (UCLA), 1964–65, 1967–73, 1975. The only player to have been voted the most valuable player in the NCAA final three times has been Lew Alcindor of UCLA in 1967–69. He subsequently changed his name to Kareem Abdul-Jabbar.

Most points   The most points by an individual for an NCAA Division I team in a game is 100, by Frank Selvy for Furman *v.* Newberry on 13 Feb. 1954, including a record 41 field goals. Kevin Bradshaw scored 72 points for US International *v.* Loyola-Marymount, two Division I teams, on 5 Jan. 1991. In Division II, Clarence "Bevo" Francis scored 113 points for Rio Grande *v.* Hillsdale on 2 Feb. 1954.

Career and season scoring   Peter "Pistol Pete" Maravich (1947–88) set unmatched NCAA scoring records while at Louisiana State University: 1,138 points, an average 43.8 per game, in 1968; 1,148 at 44.2 per game in 1969; and the season record, 1,381 at 44.5 per game in 1970—the three highest season averages in NCAA history, for a total 3,667 points in 83 games. Maravich scored a career record 1,387 field goals. The career field goal

MARCH MACHINE. In 1992 Christian Laettner led Duke University to its second consecutive NCAA title. During the playoffs he set several NCAA tournament career records, among them: most points scored, 407, and most games played, 23. (Photo: Allsport/Phil Sears)

percentage record (minimum 400 scored) is 67.8 percent by Steve Johnson, 828 of 1,222 attempts for Oregon State, 1976–81. In Division II competition, Travis Grant of Kentucky State scored a record 4,045 points in 121 games, 1969–72, and a season average record was set at 46.5 points by Clarence "Bevo" Francis, with 1,255 points in 27 games for Rio Grande in 1954. In all collegiate competition, Philip Hutcheson of David Lipscomb University scored a record 4,106 points in his career, 1987–90.

Coaches The man to have coached most victories in NCAA Division I competition is Adolph Rupp (1901–77) at Kentucky, with 875 wins (and 190 losses), 1931–72. John Wooden (b. 1910) coached UCLA to all its ten NCAA titles.

Henry Iba coached the most games, 1,105, with Northwest Missouri State 1930–33, Colorado 1934, and Oklahoma State 1935–70. Iba's career record was 767 wins and 338 losses.

Record attendances The highest paid attendance for a college game is 66,144, for Louisiana State's 82–80 victory over Georgetown at the Louisiana Superdome, New Orleans, LA on 28 Jan. 1989.

Women's The record for a women's college game is 24,563, in Knoxville, TN for a game between the University of Tennessee and the University of Texas on 9 Dec. 1987.

NCAA MEN'S DIVISION I RECORDS
Through 1991/92 Season

CAREER RECORDS

Points	**3,667**	Peter "Pistol Pete" Maravich:	1968–70
		Louisiana State	
Field goals	**1,387**	Pistol Pete Maravich: Louisiana State	1968–70
Best percentage	**.685**	Stephen Sheffler: Purdue	1987–90
Rebounds	**2,243**	Tom Gola: La Salle	1952–55
Assists	**1,038**	Chris Corchiani, North Carolina State	1988–91

SEASON RECORDS

Points	**1,381**	Pistol Pete Maravich: Louisiana State	1970
Field goals	**522**	Pistol Pete Maravich: Louisiana State	1970
		(from 1,168 attempts)	
Best percentage	**.749**	Steve Johnson: Oregon State	1981
Three-point goals	**158**	Darrin Fitzgerald: Butler (in 362 attempts)	1987
Free throws	**355**	Frank Selvy: Furman (in 444 attempts)	1954
Best percentage	**.959**	Craig Collins: Penn State	1985
Rebounds	**734**	Walt Dukes: Seton Hall (in 33 games)	1953
Assists	**406**	Mark Wade: Nevada–Las Vegas	1987
Blocked shots	**207**	David Robinson: Navy (in 35 games)	1986

GAME RECORDS

Points	**100**	Frank Selvy: Furman (*v.* Newberry)	13 Feb. 1954
Field goals	**41**	Frank Selvy: Furman	13 Feb. 1954
Three-point goals	**14**	Dave Jamerson: Ohio (*v.* Charleston)	21 Dec. 1989
Free throws	**30**	Pistol Pete Maravich: Louisiana	22 Dec. 1969
		State (*v.* Oregon State)	
Rebounds	**51**	Bill Chambers: William and	14 Feb. 1953
		Mary (*v.* Virginia)	
Assists	**22**	Tony Fairly: Baptist	9 Feb. 1987
		(*v.* Armstrong State)	
	22	Avery Johnson: Southern–B.R.	25 Jan. 1988
		(*v.* Texas Southern)	
	22	Sherman Douglas: Syracuse	28 Jan. 1989
		(*v.* Providence)	
Blocked shots	**14**	David Robinson: Navy	4 Jan. 1986
		(*v.* North Carolina–Wilmington)	
	14	Shawn Bradley: BYU	7 Dec. 1990
		(*v.* Eastern Kentucky)	

WOMEN'S BASKETBALL

Origins Senda Berenson, a physical education instructor at Smith College, and Clara Baer, an instructor at Sophie Newcomb Memorial College, are generally credited as the pioneers of women's basketball. In 1892, Berenson adapted James Naismith's rules to make the game less physically demanding. Baer also adapted Naismith's game, and published her own set of

NCAA WOMEN'S DIVISION I CHAMPIONSHIP GAME RECORDS
Through 1991/92 Season

TEAM RECORDS

Most championships	2	Louisiana Tech (1982, 1988), USC (1983–84), Tennessee (1987, 1989)	
First championships		Louisiana Tech v. Cheyney State; 76–62	1982
Most points	97	Texas (v. USC)	1986
Most field goals	40	Texas (v. USC)	1986
Highest field-goal percentage	.588	Texas (v. USC; 40–68)	1986
Most 3-point field goals	11	Stanford (v. Auburn)	1990
Rebounds	57	Old Dominion (v. Georgia)	1985
Assists (since 1985)	22	Texas (v. USC)	1986
Blocked shots (since 1988)	7	Tennessee (v. Auburn)	1989
Steals (since 1988)	12	Louisiana Tech (v. Auburn)	1988

INDIVIDUAL RECORDS

Most points	27	Cheryl Miller, USC (v. Louisiana Tech)	1983
	27	Cynthia Cooper, USC (v. Texas)	1987
	27	Bridgette Gordon, Tennessee (v. Auburn)	1989
Most field goals	12	Erica Westbrooks, Louisiana Tech (v. Auburn)	1988
Highest field-goal percentage	.889	Jennifer White, Louisiana Tech (v. USC; 8–9)	1983
Most 3-point field goals (since 1988)	6	Katy Steding, Stanford (v. Auburn)	1990
Rebounds	20	Tracy Claxton, Old Dominion (v. Georgia)	1985
Assists (since 1985)	10	Kamie Ethridge, Texas (v. USC)	1986
	10	Melissa McCray, Tennessee (v. Auburn)	1989
Blocked shots (since 1988)	5	Sheila Frost, Tennessee (v. Auburn)	1989
Steals (since 1988)	6	Erica Westbrooks, Louisiana Tech (v. Auburn)	1988

rules in 1895; these became known as the Newcomb College rules. The game spread rapidly in the late 19th century, with the first women's collegiate game being contested between California and Stanford on 4 Apr. 1896. It was not until after World War II that women's basketball began to organize itself on a national level and bring its rules into line with the men's game. In 1969, Carol Eckman, coach at West Chester University, PA organized the first national invitational tournament. Under the auspices of the Association for In-

Shooting speed   The greatest goal-shooting demonstration was by Ted St Martin of Jacksonville, FL who, on 25 June 1977, scored 2,036 consecutive free throws. Also at Jacksonville, he scored 175 out of 185 free throws in 10 min. on 27 Jan. 1990, and 90 out of 97 attempts in five minutes on 24 Feb. 1990. On 14 Dec. 1990, Jeff Liles scored 224 out of 237 attempts in ten minutes at Southern Nazarene University, Bethany, OK. These speed records were both achieved with one ball and one rebounder.

In 24 hours Fred Newman scored 20,371 free throws from a total of 22,049 taken (92.39 percent) at Caltech, Pasadena, CA on 29–30 Sep. 1990.

Steve Bontrager (USA; b. 1 Mar. 1959) of Polycell Kingston scored 21 points in one minute from seven positions in a demonstration for the British Broadcasting Corporation's *Record Breakers* TV program on 29 Oct. 1986.

Vertical dunk height record   Joey Johnson of San Pedro, CA successfully dunked a basketball at a rim height of 11 ft. 7 in. at the One-on-One Collegiate Challenge on 25 June 1990 at Trump Plaza Hotel and Casino in Atlantic City, NJ.

Youngest and oldest player   The youngest NBA player has been Bill Willoughby (b. 20 May 1957), who made his debut for the Atlanta Hawks on 23 Oct. 1975 at 18 yrs. 156 days. The oldest NBA regular player was Kareem Abdul-Jabbar, who made his last appearance for the Los Angeles Lakers at age 42 yrs. 59 days in 1989.

NBA record attendance   The Minnesota Timberwolves set an NBA record for total attendance of 1,072,572 during the 1989/90 season, the Timberwolves' first in the league. The average crowd was 26,160 fans at the Metrodome in Minneapolis.

Highest score   The NCAA aggregate record is 399, when Troy State (258) beat De Vry Institute, Atlanta (141) at Troy, AL on 12 Jan. 1992. Troy's total was also the highest individual team score in a game.

tercollegiate Athletics for Women (AIAW), the national tournament was expanded, and in 1982 the NCAA was invited to take over the tournament.

Women's championships   In this competition, first held in 1982, the record for most Division I titles is three, by Tennessee, 1987, 1989 and 1991. The regular-season match aggregate record is 261, when St. Joseph's (Indiana) beat North Kentucky 131–130 on 27 Feb. 1988.

Coaches   Jody Conradt of the University of Texas has won the most games in Women's NCAA Division I competition with 598 victories through the 1991/92 season.

Most points   The women's record for most points scored in a college career is 4,061, by Pearl Moore. She scored 177 points in eight games for Anderson Junior College, Anderson, SC, and 3,884 points for Francis Marion College, Florence, SC, 1975–79. Francis Marion was a member of the Association of Intercollegiate Athletics for Women (AIWA) during Moore's career. The career points leader in NCAA Division I competition is Patricia Hoskins of Mississippi Valley State, with 3,122 points (1985–89). Two players hold the record for most points scored a championship game, 28, in the 1991 game between Virginia and Tennessee: Dawn Staley (Virginia) and Dena Head (Tennessee).

OTHER RECORDS

Olympic Games   Three men and two women have won two Olympic gold medals: Robert Albert "Bob" Kurland (b. 23 Dec. 1924) in 1948 and 1952; William Marion "Bill" Houghland (b. 20 June 1930) in 1952 and 1956; Burdette Eliele Haldorson (b. 12 Jan. 1934) in 1956 and 1960; Anne Theresa Donovan (b. 1 Nov. 1961) and Theresa Edwards, both in 1984 and 1988.

Most titles *Olympic*   The USA has won nine men's Olympic titles. From the time the sport was introduced to the Games in 1936 until 1972, the USA won 63 consecutive matches in the Olympic Games, until it lost 51–50 to the USSR in the disputed final match in Munich, Germany. The USA won its 8th and 9th titles in 1976 and 1984.

   The women's title was won by the USSR in 1976 and 1980, and by the USA in 1984 and 1988.

World   The USSR has won most titles at both the men's World Championships (instituted 1950) with three (1967, 1974 and 1982) and women's (instituted 1953), with six (1959, 1964, 1967, 1971, 1975 and 1983). Yugoslavia has also won three men's world titles: 1970, 1978 and 1990.

BIATHLON

Origins   Biathlon reflects one of the earliest techniques of human survival; rock carvings in Roedoey, Norway dating to 3000 B.C. seem to depict hunters stalking their prey on skis. Biathlon as a modern sport evolved from military ski patrol maneuvers, which tested the soldier's ability as a fast skier and accurate marksman.

   In 1958 the *Union Internationale de Pentathlon Moderne et Biathlon* (UIPMB) was formed as the international governing body of biathlon (consisting of cross-country skiing and shooting) and modern pentathlon. Biathlon was included in the Olympic Games for the first time in 1960, and World Championships were first held in 1958. Since 1984 there has been a women's World Championship, and women's biathlon was contested at the 1992 Olympics.

United States   The 1960 Olympic Games at Squaw Valley, CA, introduced biathlon to this country. National championships were first held in 1965. The United States Modern Pentathlon and Biathlon Association was established in 1971, but this body was split to create the US Modern Pentathlon Association in 1978. The current governing body of the sport is the United States Biathlon Association, founded in 1980 and based in Essex Junction, VT.

Most titles *Olympic*   Two Olympic individual titles have been won: by Magnar Solberg (Norway; b. 4 Feb. 1937), in 1968 and 1972; and Franz-Peter Rötsch (East Germany; b. 19 Apr. 1964) at both 10 km and 20 km in 1988. The USSR has won all six 4 × 7.5 km relay titles, from 1968 to 1988. Aleksandr Ivanovich Tikhonov (b. 2 Jan. 1947), who was a member of the first four teams, also won a silver in the 1968 20 km.

United States National Championships   In this competition, first held in 1965 in Rosendale, NY, men's events have been staged annually. Women's events were included in 1985.

Most titles   Lyle Nelson has won seven National Championships: five in the 10 km, 1976, 1979, 1981, 1985 and 1987; two in the 20 km, 1977 and 1985. Anna Sonnerup holds the women's record with five titles: two in the 10 km, 1986–87; two in the 15 km, 1989 and 1991; and one in the 7.5 km in 1989.

Biathlon   Frank Ullrich (East Germany; b. 24 Jan. 1958) has won a record six individual world titles, four at 10 km, 1978–81, including the 1980 Olympics, and two at 20 km, 1982–83. Aleksandr Tikhonov was in ten winning Soviet relay teams, 1968–80 and won four individual titles. The Biathlon World Cup (instituted 1979) was won four times by Frank Ullrich, 1978 and 1980–82. He was second in 1979 and third in 1983.

BILLIARDS

Origins   The earliest recorded mention of billiards was in France in 1429, and Louis XI, King of France 1461–83, is reported to have had a billiard table.

Most titles   The greatest number of World Championships (instituted 1870) won by one player is eight, by John Roberts Jr. (Great Britain; 1847–1919), in 1870 (twice), 1871, 1875 (twice), 1877 and 1885 (twice). The record for world amateur titles is four, by Robert James Percival Marshall (Australia; b. 10 Apr. 1910), in 1936, 1938, 1951 and 1962.

Youngest champion   The youngest winner of the world professional title is Mike Russell (b. 3 June 1969), age 20 yrs. 49 days, when he won at Leura, Australia on 23 July 1989.

Highest breaks   Tom Reece (1873–1953) made an unfinished break of 499,135, including 249,152 cradle cannons (two points each) in 85 hrs. 49 min. against Joe Chapman at Burroughes' Hall, Soho Square, London, Great Britain between 3 June and 6 July 1907. This was not recognized, because press and public were not continuously present.

The highest certified break made by the anchor cannon is 42,746, by William Cook (England) from 29 May to 7 June 1907.

The official world record under the then balkline rule is 1,784, by Joe Davis in the United Kingdom Championship on 29 May 1936.

Walter Albert Lindrum (Australia; 1898–1960) made an official break of 4,137 in 2 hrs. 55 min. against Joe Davis at Thurston's on 19–20 Jan. 1932, before the balkline rule was in force.

Davis had an unofficial personal best of 2,502 (mostly pendulum cannons) in a match against Tom Newman (England; 1894–1943) in Manchester, Great Britain in 1930.

The highest break recorded in amateur competition is 1,149, by Michael Ferreira (India) at Calcutta, India on 15 Dec. 1978.

Under the more stringent "two pot" rule, restored on 1 Jan. 1983, the highest break is Ferreira's 962 unfinished, in a tournament at Bombay, India on 29 Apr. 1986.

THREE CUSHION

Origins   This pocketless variation dates back to 1878. The world governing body, the *Union Mondiale de Billiard* (UMB), was formed in 1928.

Most titles   William F. "Willie" Hoppe (USA; 1887–1959) won 51 billiards championships in all forms, spanning the pre-and post-international era, from 1906 to 1952.

UMB   Raymond Ceulemans (Belgium; b. 12 July 1935) has won 20 world three-cushion championships (1963–73, 1975–80, 1983, 1985 and 1991).

Fastest century   Walter Lindrum made an unofficial 100 break in 27.5 sec. in Australia on 10 Oct. 1952. His official record is 100 in 46.0 sec., set in Sydney, Australia in 1941.

BOARD GAMES

BINGO

Bingo is a lottery game which, under the name of keno, was developed in the 1880s from lotto, whose origin is thought to be the 17th-century Italian game *tumbule*. The winner was the first to complete a random selection of numbers from 1 to 90. The US version called Bingo differs in that the selection is from 1 to 75.

Largest house The largest "house" in bingo sessions was 15,756, at the Canadian National Exhibition, Toronto on 19 Aug. 1983. Staged by the Variety Club of Ontario Tent Number 28, there was total prize money of $Cdn250,000 with a record one-game payout of $Cdn100,000.

Earliest and latest full house A "full house" call occurred on the 15th number by Norman A. Wilson at Guide Post Working Men's Club, Bedlington, Great Britain on 22 June 1978; by Anne Wintle of Brynrethin, Great Britain, on a coach trip to Bath, Great Britain on 17 Aug. 1982; and by Shirley Lord at Kahibah Bowling Club, New South Wales, Australia on 24 Oct. 1983.

"House" was not called until the 86th number at the Hillsborough Working Men's Club, Sheffield, Great Britain on 11 Jan. 1982. There were 32 winners.

Shortest backgammon game Alan Malcolm Beckerson (b. 21 Feb. 1938) devised a game of just 16 throws in 1982.

Domino toppling The greatest number set up single-handedly and toppled is 281,581 out of 320,236, by Klaus Friedrich, 22, at Fürth, Germany on 27 Jan. 1984. The dominoes fell within 12 min. 57.3 sec., having taken 31 days (10 hrs. daily) to set up.

Thirty students at Delft, Eindhoven and Twente Technical Universities in the Netherlands set up 1,500,000 dominoes representing all the European Community member countries. Of these, 1,382,101 were toppled by one push on 2 Jan. 1988.

Domino stacking David Coburn successfully stacked 291 dominoes on a single supporting domino on 19 Aug. 1988 in Miami, FL.

Biggest board game The world's biggest board game was a version of the game "Goose," and was organized by "Jong Nederland." It stretched for 2,090 ft. and was played by 1,631 participants at Someren, Netherlands on 16 Sep. 1989.

CHECKERS

Origins   Checkers, known as draughts in Europe, is believed to have originated on the French/Spanish border in the 12th century, when backgammon men were placed on a chessboard and moved as in the well-known game of the time, alquerque. The earliest book on the game was by Antonio Torquemada of Valencia, Spain in 1547.

World champions   Walter Hellman (USA; 1916–75) won a record eight world titles during his tenure as world champion, 1948–75.

Youngest and oldest national champion   Asa A. Long (b. 20 Aug. 1904) became the youngest US national champion, at age 18 yrs. 64 days, when he won in Boston, MA on 23 Oct. 1922. He became the oldest, age 79 yrs. 334 days, when he won his sixth title in Tupelo, MS on 21 July 1984. He was also world champion from 1934 to 1938.

Most opponents   Charles Walker played a record 229 games simultaneously, winning 227, drawing 1 and losing 1, at the International Checkers Hall of Fame, Petal, MS on 25 Jan. 1992.

The largest number of opponents played without a defeat or draw is 172, by Nate Cohen of Portland, ME at Portland on 26 July 1981. This was not a simultaneous attempt, but consecutive play over a period of four hours.

Newell W. Banks (1887–1977) played 140 games simultaneously, winning 133 and drawing seven, in Chicago, IL in 1933. His total playing time was 145 min., thus averaging about one move per sec. In 1947 he played blindfolded for 4 hrs. per day for 45 consecutive days, winning 1,331 games, drawing 54 and losing only two, while playing six games at a time.

Longest game   In competition the prescribed rate of play is not less than 30 moves per hour, with the average game lasting about 90 min. In 1958 a game between Dr. Marion Tinsley (USA) and Derek Oldbury (Great Britain) lasted 7 hrs. 30 min. (played under the 5-minutes-a-move rule).

CHESS

Origins   The game of chess is believed to have originated in ancient India under the name *Chaturanga* (literally "four-corps")—the name for the four traditional army divisions. The name *chess* is derived from the Persian word *shah* (a king or ruler). The earliest written reference is from the Middle Persian Chatrang Namak (*c*. A.D. 590–628). The oldest pieces identified as chess pieces were found at Nashipur, datable to *c*. A.D. 900. Chess reached Britain *c*. 1255. The *Fédération Internationale des Echecs* (FIDE) was established in 1924.

World championships   World champions have been officially recognized since 1886. The longest undisputed tenure was 26 yrs. 337 days, by Dr. Emanuel Lasker (1868–1941) of Germany, from 1894 to 1921.

The women's world championship title was held by Vera Francevna Stevenson-Menchik (USSR, later Great Britain; 1906–44) from 1927 until her death, and was successfully defended a record seven times.

The first American to be regarded as world champion was Paul Charles Morphy (1837–89) in 1858.

Most moves The Master chess game with the most moves on record was one of 269 moves, when Ivan Nikolić drew with Goran Arsović in a Belgrade, Yugoslavia tournament, on 17 Feb. 1989. The game took a total of 20 hrs. 15 min.

Slowest and longest chess games The slowest reported moving (before time clocks were used) in an official event is reputed to have been by Louis Paulsen (Germany; 1833–91) against Paul Charles Morphy (USA; 1837–84) at the first American Chess Congress, NY on 29 Oct. 1857. The game ended in a draw on move 56 after 15 hours of play, of which Paulsen used *c*. 11 hours.

Grand Master Friedrich Sämisch (Germany; 1896–1975) ran out of the allotted time (2 hrs. 30 min. for 45 moves) after only 12 moves, in Prague, Czechoslovakia, in 1938.

The slowest move played, since time clocks were introduced, was at Vigo, Spain in 1980 when Francisco R. Torres Trois (b. 3 Sep. 1946) took 2 hr. 20 min. for his seventh move *v*. Luis M.C.P. Santos (b. 30 June 1955).

Team The USSR has won the biennial men's team title (Olympiad) a record 18 times between 1952 and 1990, with a win in 1992 by Russia. The women's title has been won 11 times by the USSR from its introduction in 1957 to 1986, with Georgia winning in 1992.

The USA has won the men's title five times: 1931, 1933, 1935, 1937 and 1976.

Youngest Gary Kimovich Kasparov (USSR; b. 13 Apr. 1963) won the title on 9 Nov. 1985 at age 22 yrs. 210 days. Maya Grigoryevna Chiburdanidze (USSR; b. 17 Jan. 1961) won the women's title in 1978 when only 17.

Oldest Wilhelm Steinitz (Austria, later USA; 1836–1900) was 58 yrs. 10 days when he lost his title to Lasker on 26 May 1894.

Most active Anatoly Yevgenyevich Karpov (USSR; b. 23 May 1951) in his tenure as champion, 1975–85, averaged 45.2 competitive games per year, played in 32 tournaments and finished first in 26.

Grand Masters The youngest individual to qualify as an International Grand Master is Judit Polgar (Hungary; b. 25 July 1976), aged 15 yrs. 148 days on 20 Dec. 1991.

United States The youngest US Grand Master was Robert James "Bobby" Fischer (b. 9 Mar. 1943) in 1958.

Masters In August 1981, Stuart Rachels of Birmingham, AL became the youngest person in the history of the United States Chess Foundation to achieve a master rating, at the age of 11 yrs. 10 months.

Highest rating The highest rating ever attained on the officially adopted Elo System is 2,800, by Gary Kasparov (USSR) at the end of 1989.

The highest-rated woman player is Judit Polgar (Hungary; b. 25 July 1976), who is currently at 2,540 but has achieved a peak rating of 2,555.

Fewest games lost by a world champion   José Raúl Capablanca (Cuba; 1888–1942) lost only 34 games (out of 571) in his adult career, 1909–39. He was unbeaten from 10 Feb. 1916 to 21 Mar. 1924 (63 games) and was world champion 1921–27.

US Championships   The most wins since the US Championships became determined by match play competition in 1888 is eight, by Bobby Fischer, 1958–66. Fischer, world champion 1972–75, reached a rating on the Elo system of 2,785, the highest ever until surpassed by Gary Kasparov in 1989.

Most opponents   The record for most consecutive games played is 663, by Vlastimil Hort (Czechoslovakia, later Germany; b. 12 Jan. 1944) over 32½ hours at Porz, Germany on 5–6 Oct. 1984. He played 60–120 opponents at a time, scoring over 80 percent wins and averaging 30 moves per game. He also holds the record for most games played simultaneously, 201 during 550 consecutive games of which he only lost ten, in Seltjarnes, Iceland on 23–24 Apr. 1977.

Eric G.J. Knoppert (Netherlands; b. 20 Sep. 1959) played 500 games of ten-minute chess against opponents, averaging 2,002 on the Elo scale on 13–16 Sep. 1985. He scored 413 points (1 for win, ½ for draw), a success rate of 82.6 percent.

MONOPOLY

Monopoly, a real-estate trading game, of which Parker Brothers has sold in excess of 85 million copies worldwide in 19 languages (the most recent in Russian), was devised by Charles Darrow (1889–1967) of Germantown, PA, in 1935. While unemployed as a heating engineer during the Depression, he created the game using the street names of Atlantic City, NJ, where he spent his vacations.

World Champions   The current holder of the World Monopoly Championship trophy and medal is Ikuo Hiyakuta of Japan. He won the eighth World Monopoly Tournament (held every three years under the auspices of Parker Brothers) at the Park Lane Hotel, London, Great Britain in 1988 after two days of grueling play. His prize was $15,140 and a personal computer.

SCRABBLE *Crossword Game*

Origins   The crossword game was invented by Alfred M. Butts in 1931 and was developed, refined and trademarked as Scrabble Crossword Game by James Brunot in 1948.

Highest scores   The highest competitive game score is 1,049 by Phil Appleby (b. 9 Dec. 1957) in June 1989. His opponent scored 253, and the margin of victory, 796 points, is also a record. His score included a single turn of 374 for the word "OXIDIZERS."

The highest competitive single-turn score recorded, however, is 392, by Dr. Saladin Karl Khoshnaw (of Kurdish origin) in Manchester, Great Britain in April 1982. He laid down "CAZIQUES," which means "native chiefs of West Indian aborigines."

Most tournaments   Chuck Armstrong, a hospital worker from Saline, MI, has won the most tournaments—65 to the end of 1989.

BOBSLED AND LUGE

BOBSLEDDING

Origins   The oldest known sled is dated *c.* 6500 B.C. and came from Heinola, Finland. The first known bobsled race took place at Davos, Switzerland in 1889. The International Federation of Bobsled and Luge was formed in 1923, followed by the International Bobsled Federation in 1957.

United States   The United States Bobsled and Skeleton Federation was founded in 1941 and is still the governing body for the sport in this country.

Most titles   The Olympic four-man bob title (instituted 1924) has been won five times by Switzerland (1924, 1936, 1956, 1972 and 1988).
   The Olympic two-man bob title (instituted 1932) has been won three times by Switzerland (1948, 1980 and 1992).
   The most gold medals won by an individual is three, by Meinhard Nehmer (East Germany; b. 13 June 1941) and Bernhard Germeshausen (East Germany; b. 21 Aug. 1951) in the 1976 two-man, 1976 and 1980 four-man events.

MOST OLYMPIC TITLES. Switzerland has won the Olympic two-man bobsled title a record three times. Seen here in action during their 1992 success are Gustav Weder (driver) and Donat Acklin. (Photo: Allsport/Pascal Rondeau)

The most medals won is six (two gold, two silver, two bronze) by Eugenio Monti (Italy; b. 23 Jan. 1928), 1956 to 1968.

World and Olympic   The world four-man bob title (instituted 1924) has
been won 19 times by Switzerland (1924, 1936, 1939, 1947, 1954–57,
1971–73, 1975, 1982–83, 1986–90), including their five Olympic victories.
   Italy won the two-man title 14 times (1954, 1956–63, 1966, 1968–69, 1971
and 1975).
   Eugenio Monti was a member of 11 world championship crews, eight two-
man and three four-man, in 1957–68.

United States   Two American bobsledders have won two gold medals:
driver William Mead Lindsley "Billy" Fiske III (1911–40) and crewman Clif-
ford Barton Grey (1887–1941) in 1928 and 1932. At age 16 yrs. 260 days in
1928, Fiske was America's youngest-ever Winter Games gold medalist.

Oldest gold medalist   The oldest age at which a gold medal has been
won at any sport at the Winter Olympics is 49 yrs. 7 days, for James Jay
O'Brien (USA; 1883–1940) at four-man bob in 1932.

LUGEING

In lugeing the rider adopts a supine, as opposed to a sitting position. Official
international competition began at Klosters, Switzerland in 1881. The first
European championships were at Reichenberg, Germany in 1914 and the first
World Championships at Oslo, Norway in 1953. The International Luge Federation was formed in 1957. Lugeing became an Olympic sport in 1964.

United States   The United States has participated in all Olympic luge
events since the sport was sanctioned for the 1964 Olympic Games, but there
was no organized governing body for the sport in this country until 1979,
when the United States Luge Association was formed. The only luge run in
the United States accredited for international competition is the refrigerated
run used for the Lake Placid Olympics in 1980.

Most titles   The most successful rider in the World Championships was
Thomas Köhler (East Germany; b. 25 June 1940), who won the single-seater
title in 1962, 1964 (Olympic), 1967 and shared the two-seater title in 1965,
1967 and 1968 (Olympic). Margit Schumann (East Germany; b. 14 Sep.
1952) has won five women's titles, 1973–75, 1976 (Olympic) and 1977.
   Steffi Walter (nee Martin [East Germany]; b. 17 Sep. 1962) became the
first rider to win two Olympic single-seater luge titles, with victories at the
women's event in 1984 and 1988.

United States National Championships   This competition was inaugurated in 1974.

Fastest speed in lugeing   The fastest recorded photo-timed
speed is 85.38 mph, by Asle Strand (Norway) at Tandådalens
Linbana, Sälen, Sweden on 1 May 1982.

Most titles Frank Masley has won a record six men's championships, 1979, 1981–83 and 1987–88. Bonny Warner has won a record five women's titles, 1983–84, 1987–88 and 1990.

TOBOGGANING

Origins The word *toboggan* comes from the Micmac American Indian word *tobaakan*. The St. Moritz Luge Club, Switzerland, founded in 1887, is the oldest toboggan club in the world. It is notable for being the home of the Cresta Run, which dates from 1884, and for the introduction of the one-man skeleton racing toboggan.

Cresta Run The course is 3,977 ft. long with a drop of 514 ft., and the record is 50.91 sec. (avg. 53.26 mph) by Franco Gansser (Switzerland; b. 2 May 1945) on 22 Feb. 1987. On 20 Jan. 1991 Christian Bertschinger (Switzerland; b. 8 Feb. 1964) set a record from Junction (2,920 ft.) of 41.45 sec.

The greatest number of wins in the Grand National (instituted in 1885) is eight, by the 1948 Olympic champion Nino Bibbia (Italy; b. 15 Mar. 1922) in 1960–64, 1966, 1968 and 1973, and by Franco Gansser in 1981, 1983–86, 1988–89 and 1991. The greatest number of wins in the Curzon Cup (instituted 1910) is eight, by Bibbia in 1950, 1957–58, 1960, 1962–64 and 1969.

The only men to have won the four most important races (Curzon Cup, Brabazon Trophy, Morgan Cup and Grand National) in one season are Bruno Bischofberger (1972), Paul Felder (1974), Nico Baracchi (1982), Franco Gansser (1988) and Christian Bertschinger (1992), all from Switzerland.

The oldest person to have ridden the Cresta Run successfully is Robin Todhunter (Great Britain; b. 10 Mar. 1903), aged 83 yrs. 329 days on 2 Feb. 1987.

BOWLING

Origins The ancient German game of nine-pins (*Heidenwerfen*—"knock down pagans") was exported to the United States in the early 17th century. In 1841 the Connecticut State Legislature prohibited the game, and other states followed. Eventually a tenth pin was added to evade the ban; but there is some evidence of ten pins being used in Suffolk, Great Britain about 200 years ago.

The first body to standardize rules was the American Bowling Congress (ABC), established in New York City on 9 Sep. 1895.

World Championships The World (*Fédération Internationale des Quilleurs*) Championships were instituted for men in 1954 and for women in 1963.

The highest pinfall in the individual men's event is 5,963 (in 28 games) by Ed Luther (USA) at Milwaukee, WI on 28 Aug. 1971.

For the current schedule of 24 games the men's record is 5,261 by Richard Clay "Rick" Steelsmith (b. 1 June 1964), and the women's record is 4,894 by Sandra Jo Shiery (USA), both at Helsinki, Finland in June 1987.

Highest scores   The highest individual score for three sanctioned games (out of a possible 900) is 899, by Thomas Jordan (USA; b. 27 Oct. 1966) at Union, NJ on 7 Mar. 1989. He followed with a 299, setting a four-game series record of 1,198 pins.

The record by a woman is 864, by Jeanne Maiden (b. 10 Nov. 1957) at Sodon, OH on 23 Nov. 1986.

Youngest and oldest 300 shooters   The youngest bowler to score 300 is said to be Richard Daff, Jr. of Crownsville, MD (b. 28 Aug. 1978), who performed this feat at age 11, on 8 Apr. 1990. The oldest bowler to score 300 is Leo Sites of Wichita, KS, who performed the feat on 10 Apr. 1985 at age 80.

PROFESSIONAL BOWLERS
ASSOCIATION (PBA)

The PBA was founded in 1958 by Eddie Elias and is based in Akron, OH.

Most titles   Earl Anthony (b. 27 Apr. 1938) of Dublin, CA has won a lifetime total of 41 PBA titles. The record number of titles won in one PBA season is eight, by Mark Roth (b. 10 Apr. 1951) of Lake Heights, NJ, in 1978.

Consecutive titles   Only three bowlers have ever won three consecutive professional tournaments—Dick Weber (b. 23 Dec. 1929) (three times), in 1959, 1960 and 1961; Johnny Petraglia (b. 3 Mar. 1947) in 1971; and Mark Roth in 1977.

Perfect games   A total of 141 perfect (300-pin) games were bowled in PBA tournaments in 1990, the most ever for one year.

Dick Weber rolled three perfect games in one tournament (Houston, TX) in 1965, as did Billy Hardwick (b. 25 July 1941) of Louisville, KY (in the Japan Gold Cup competition) in 1968, John Wilcox (at Detroit, MI), in 1979, Norm Meyers of St. Louis (at Peoria, IL) in 1979, Ray Shackelford of Hartwood, VA (at St. Louis, MO) in 1982, Shawn Christensen of Denver (at Denver, CO) in 1984, and Amleto Monacelli (b. 27 Aug. 1961) of Venezuela (at Tucson, AZ) in 1989.

Amleto Monacelli rolled seven perfect games on the 1989 tour, and Guppy Troup (b. 18 Jan. 1950) of Savannah, GA, rolled six perfect games on the 1979 tour.

Triple Crown   The United States Open, the PBA National Championship and the Firestone Tournament of Champions comprise the Triple Crown of men's professional bowling. No bowler has won each of the three titles in the same year, and only three have managed to win all three during a career.

The first bowler to accumulate the three legs of the triple crown was Billy Hardwick: National Championship (1963); Firestone Tournament of Champions (1965); US Open (1969). Hardwick's feat was matched by Johnny Petraglia: Firestone (1971); US Open (1977); National (1980); and by Pete Weber: Firestone (1987); US Open (1988); National (1989).

US Open   Since its inauguration in 1942, the most wins in this tournament is four, by two bowlers: Don Carter in 1953–54 and 1957–58, and Dick Weber in 1962–63 and 1965–66.

Highest bowling score—24 hours   A team of six called the Brunswick Thursday Nite Stars, scored 209,072 at Brunswick Sharptown Lanes, Houston, TX on 20–21 June 1991. The highest individual total scored in 24 hours is 45,558 by Brian Larkin at Hollywood Bowl, Bolton, Great Britain on 27–28 Mar. 1992.

Largest bowling center   The Fukuyama Bowl, Osaka, Japan has 144 lanes. The Tokyo World Lanes Center, Japan, now closed, had 252 lanes.

Perfect scores   Les Schissler of Denver scored 300 in the Classic team event in 1967, and Ray Williams of Detroit scored 300 in regular team play in 1974, the first two perfect games bowled in team competition. In all, there have been only 160 perfect games in the regular ABC tournament through 1992.

Most tournament appearances   Bill Doehrman of Fort Wayne, IN competed in 71 consecutive ABC tournaments, beginning in 1908. (No tournaments were held 1943–45.)

Consecutive strikes, spares and splits   The record for most consecutive strikes is 40, by Jeanne Maiden (See Perfect games.) Mabel Henry of Winchester, KY had 30 consecutive spares in the 1986/87 season. Shirley Tophigh of Las Vegas, NV holds the unenviable record of rolling 14 consecutive splits in 1968/69.

PBA National Championship   Since its inauguration in 1960, the most wins in this tournament is six, by Earl Anthony in 1973–75 and 1981–83.

Firestone Tournament of Champions   Since its inauguration in 1965, the most wins in this tournament is three, by Mike Durbin in 1972, 1982 and 1984.

Highest earners   Marshall Holman (b. 29 Sep. 1954) won a record $1,583,921 in PBA competitions through 31 May 1992. Earl Roderick Anthony (b. 27 Apr. 1938) was the first to win $1 million.

Mike Aulby (b. 25 Mar. 1960) of Indianapolis, IN set a single-season earnings mark of $298,237 in 1989.

AMERICAN BOWLING CONGRESS (ABC)

Highest score   The highest individual score for three games is 899, by Thomas Jordan at Union, NJ on 7 Mar. 1989 (see Bowling—Highest scores). Highest three-game team score is 3,858, by Budweisers of St. Louis on 12 Mar. 1958.

The highest season average attained in sanctioned competition is 245.63, by Doug Vergouwen of Harrisonville, MO in the 1989/90 season.

The all-time ABC-sanctioned two-man single-game record is 600, held jointly by the teams of John Cotta (300) and Steve Larson (300) on 1 May

1981, at the Manteca, CA, Bowling Association Tournament; Jeff Mraz and Dave Roney of Canton, OH on 8 Nov. 1987 in the Ann Doubles Classic in Canton, OH; William Gruner and Dave Conway of Oceanside, CA on 27 Feb. 1990; and Scott Williams and Willie Hammar of Utica, NY on 7 Jan. 1990.

The two-man team series record is 1,655, by Thomas Jordon (899) and Ken Yorker, Jr. (856) in Union, NJ on 7 Mar. 1989.

Perfect scores   The highest number of sanctioned 300 games is 42, by Robert Learn, Jr. of Erie, PA.

Two perfect games were rolled back-to-back *twice* by Al Spotts of West Reading, PA on 14 Mar. 1982 and again on 1 Feb. 1985.

ABC CHAMPIONSHIPS
TOURNAMENT

Highest score   Highest three-game series in the ABC Championships tournament in singles is 826, by Ed Deines of Ft. Collins, CO in 1991. Best three-game total in any ABC event is 857, by Norm Duke of Albuquerque, NM in 1989. George Hall of Mundelein, IL holds the record for a nine-game All-Events total with 2,227 (747–747–733) set in Wichita, KS in 1989.

ABC Hall of Famers Fred Bujack of Detroit, MI, Bill Lillard of Houston, TX and Nelson Burton, Jr. of St. Louis, MO have won the most championships, with eight each. Bujack shared in three team and four team All-Events titles between 1949 and 1955, and also won the individual All-Events title in 1955. Lillard bowled with regular and team All-Events champions in 1955 and 1956 and with the Classic team champions in 1962 and 1971, and won regular doubles and All-Events titles in 1956. Burton shared in three Classic team titles, two Classic doubles titles and has won Classic singles twice and Classic All-Events.

Highest doubles   The ABC national tournament record of 561 was set in 1989 by Rick McCardy and Steve Mesmer of Redford, MI. The record score in a doubles series is 1,505, set in 1991 by Jimmy Johnson (784) of Columbus, OH and Dan Nadeau (721) of Las Vegas, NV.

Best finishes   Mike Newman of Buffalo, NY won the doubles, All-Events, and was on two winning teams in 1989 to tie Ed Lubanski of Detroit, MI and Bill Lillard of Houston, TX as the only men to win four ABC crowns in one year.

Youngest and oldest winners   The youngest champion was Ronnie Knapp of New London, OH, who was a member of the 1963 Booster team champions when he was 16 years old.

The oldest champion was Joe Detloff of Chicago, IL who, at the age of 72, was a winner in the 1965 Booster team event. The oldest doubles team in ABC competition totaled 165 years in 1955: Jerry Ameling (83) and Joseph Lehnbeutter (82), both from St. Louis, MO.

Strikes and spares in a row   In the greatest finish to win an ABC title, Ed Shay set a record of 12 strikes in a row in 1958, when he scored a perfect game for a total of 733 in singles. Most strikes in a row is 20, by Lou Veit of Milwaukee, WI in 1977. The most spares in a row is 23, by Lt. Hazen Sweet of Battle Creek, MI in 1950.

WOMEN'S INTERNATIONAL
BOWLING CONGRESS (WIBC)

Highest scores   Patty Ann of Appleton, WI, had a record five-year composite average of 227 through the 1985/86 season. She also had the best one-season average, 232, in the 1983/84 season.

The highest five-woman team score for a three-game series is 3,493, by Lisa's Flowers and Gift Shop, Franklin, WI in the 1989/90 season. The highest game score by a five-woman team is 3,437, by Goebel Beer of Detroit, MI in the 1988/89 season.

Championship Tournament   The highest score for a three-game series in the annual WIBC Championship Tournament is 773, by Debbie Kuhn of Baltimore, MD in the 1991 singles event. She also holds the record for highest All-Events score (nine games), with 2,036 in 1991.

The record for one game is 300, by Lori Gensch of Milwaukee, WI in the 1979 doubles event, by Rose Walsh of Pomona, CA in the 1986 singles event, and by Linda Kelly of Huber Heights, OH in the 1987 doubles event.

Dorothy Miller of Chicago, IL has won ten WIBC Championship Tournament events, the most by an individual.

Oldest and youngest players   Mary Covell of Chicago, IL participated in her 61st WIBC tournament in 1992. The oldest participant was Ethel Brunnick (b. 30 Aug. 1887) of Santa Monica, CA, at age 99 in 1987.

The youngest champion was Leila Wagner (b. 12 July 1960) of Annapolis, MD, who was 18 when she was a member of the championship five-woman team in 1979.

Perfect games   Jeanne Maiden of Tacoma, WA has rolled 20 perfect games to set the WIBC career record. She also set a record of 40 consecutive strikes in 1986 and rolled an 864 on games of 300–300–264. The most 300 games rolled in a career is 20, by Jeanne Maiden. The oldest woman to bowl a perfect game (12 strikes in a row) was Helen Duval of Berkeley, CA, at age 65 in 1982. Of all the women who rolled a perfect game, the one with the lowest average was Diane Ponza of Santa Cruz, CA, who had a 112 average in the 1977/78 season.

BOXING

Origins   Boxing with gloves was depicted on a fresco dated c. 1520 B.C. from the Isle of Thera, Greece. The earliest prize-ring code of rules was formulated in England on 16 Aug. 1743 by the champion pugilist Jack Broughton (1704–89), who reigned from 1734 to 1750. In 1867 boxing came under the Queensberry Rules, formulated for John Sholto Douglas, 8th Marquess of Queensberry (1844–1900).

United States   New York was the first state to legalize boxing in the United States, in 1896. Today professional boxing is regulated in each state by athletic or boxing commissions.

Longest fights The longest recorded fight with gloves was between Andy Bowen of New Orleans (1867–94) and Jack Burke at New Orleans, LA on 6–7 Apr. 1893. It lasted 110 rounds, 7 hrs. 19 min. (9:15 P.M.–4:34 A.M.), and was declared a no-contest (later changed to a draw). Bowen won an 85-round bout on 31 May 1893.

The longest bare-knuckle fight was 6 hrs. 15 min., between James Kelly and Jack Smith at Fiery Creek, Dalesford, Victoria, Australia on 3 Dec. 1855.

The greatest number of rounds was 276, in 4 hrs. 30 min., when Jack Jones beat Patsy Tunney in Cheshire, Great Britain in 1825.

Shortest fights There is a distinction between the quickest knockout and the shortest fight. A knockout in 10½ sec. (including a 10 sec. count) occurred on 23 Sep. 1946, when Al Couture struck Ralph Walton while the latter was adjusting a gum shield in his corner at Lewiston, ME. If the time was accurately recorded it is clear that Couture must have been more than halfway across the ring from his own corner at the opening bell.

The shortest fight on record appears to have been one in a Golden Gloves tournament at Minneapolis, MN on 4 Nov. 1947, when Mike Collins floored Pat Brownson with the first punch and the contest was stopped, without a count, 4 sec. after the opening bell.

The shortest world title fight was 45 sec., when Lloyd Honeyghan (Great Britain; b. 22 Apr. 1960) beat Gene Hatcher (USA) in an IBF welterweight bout at Marbella, Spain on 30 Aug. 1987. Some sources also quote the Al McCoy (1894–1966) first-round knockout of George Chip in a middleweight contest on 7 Apr. 1914 as being in 45 sec.

The shortest-ever heavyweight world title fight was the James J. Jeffries (1875–1953)–Jack Finnegan bout at Detroit, MI on 6 Apr. 1900, won by Jeffries in 55 sec.

Eugene Brown, on his professional debut, knocked out Ian Bockes at Leicester, Great Britain, on 13 Mar. 1989. The fight was officially stopped after ten seconds of the first round. Bockes got up after a count of six, but the referee stopped the contest.

Tallest The tallest boxer to fight professionally was Gogea Mitu (b. 1914) of Romania, in 1935. He was 7 ft. 4 in. and weighed 327 lbs. John Rankin, who won a fight in New Orleans, LA in November 1967, was reputedly also 7 ft. 4 in. Jim Culley, "The Tipperary Giant," who fought as a boxer and wrestled in the 1940s, is also reputed to have been 7 ft. 4 in.

Most fights without loss Edward Henry "Harry" Greb (USA; 1894–1926) was unbeaten in a sequence of 178 bouts, but these included 117 "no decision," of which five were unofficial losses, in 1916–23.

Of boxers with complete records, Packey McFarland (USA; 1888–1936) had 97 fights (5 draws) in 1905–15 without a defeat.

Pedro Carrasco (Spain; b. 7 Nov. 1943) won 83 consecutive fights from 22 April 1964 to 3 Sep. 1970, drew once and had a further nine wins before his loss to Armando Ramos in a WBC lightweight contest on 18 Feb. 1972.

Most knockouts The greatest number of finishes classed as "knockouts" in a career (1936–63) is 145 (129 in professional bouts), by Archie Moore (USA; b. Archibald Lee Wright, 13 Dec. 1913 or 1916).

The record for consecutive KO's is 44, by Lamar Clark (USA; b. 1 Dec. 1934) from 1958 to 11 Jan. 1960. He knocked out six in one night (five in the first round) at Bingham, UT on 1 Dec. 1958.

Attendances *Highest* The greatest paid attendance at any boxing match was 120,757 (with a ringside price of $27.50) for the Gene T. Tunney *v.* Jack D. Dempsey world heavyweight title fight at the Sesquicentennial Stadium, Philadelphia, PA on 23 Sep. 1926.

The indoor record is 63,350, at the Muhammad Ali *v.* Leon Spinks (b. 11 July 1953) fight in the Superdome, New Orleans, LA on 15 Sep. 1978.

The highest nonpaying attendance is 135,132, at the Tony Zale *v.* Billy Pryor fight at Juneau Park, Milwaukee, WI on 16 Aug. 1941.

Lowest The smallest attendance at a world heavyweight title fight was 2,434, at the Cassius Clay (Muhammad Ali) *v.* Sonny Liston fight at Lewiston, ME on 25 May 1965.

WORLD HEAVYWEIGHT

Earliest title fight Long accepted as the first world heavyweight title fight, with gloves and 3-min. rounds, was that between John Lawrence Sullivan (1858–1918) and James John "Gentleman Jim" Corbett (1866–1933) in New Orleans, LA on 7 Sep. 1892. Corbett won in 21 rounds. However, the fight between Sullivan, then the world bare-knuckle champion, and Dominick F. McCafferey in Chester Park, Cincinnati, OH on 29 Aug. 1885 was staged under Queensberry Rules with the boxers wearing gloves over six rounds. The referee, Billy Tait, left the ring without giving a verdict, but when asked two days later said that Sullivan had won.

Reign *Longest* Joe Louis (USA; b. Joseph Louis Barrow, 1914–81) was champion for 11 years 252 days, from 22 June 1937, when he knocked out James Joseph Braddock in the eighth round at Chicago, IL, until announcing his retirement on 1 Mar. 1949. During his reign Louis made a record 25 defenses of his title.

Shortest The shortest reigns were 83 days for WBA champion James "Bonecrusher" Smith (USA; b. 3 Apr. 1955), 13 Dec. 1986 to 7 Mar. 1987, and for Ken Norton (USA; b. 9 Aug. 1945), recognized by the WBC as champion from 18 Mar.–9 June 1978. Tony Tucker (USA; b. 28 Dec. 1958) was IBF champion for 64 days, 30 May–2 Aug. 1987.

Most recaptures Muhammad Ali is the only man to have regained the heavyweight championship twice. Ali first won the title on 25 Feb. 1964, defeating Sonny Liston. He defeated George Foreman on 30 Oct. 1974, after having been stripped of the title by the world boxing authorities on 28 Apr. 1967. He won the WBA title from Leon Spinks on 15 Sep. 1978, having previously lost to him on 15 Feb. 1978.

Undefeated Rocky Marciano (USA; b. Rocco Francis Marchegiano, 1923–69) is the only world champion at any weight to have won every fight of his entire professional career from 17 Mar. 1947 to 21 Sep. 1955 (he announced his retirement on 27 Apr. 1956); 43 of his 49 fights were by knockouts or stoppages.

Oldest "Jersey Joe" Walcott (USA; b. Arnold Raymond Cream, 31 Jan. 1914) was 37 yrs. 168 days when he knocked out Ezzard Mack Charles (1921–75) on 18 July 1951 in Pittsburgh, PA. He was also the oldest holder, at 38 yrs. 236 days, losing his title to Rocky Marciano on 23 Sep. 1952.

Youngest   Mike Tyson (USA) was 20 yrs. 144 days when he beat Trevor Berbick (USA) to win the WBC version at Las Vegas, NV on 22 Nov. 1986. He added the WBA title when he beat James "Bone-crusher" Smith on 7 Mar. 1987 at 20 yrs. 249 days. He became universal champion on 2 Aug. 1987 when he beat Tony Tucker (USA) for the IBF title.

Tallest   There is uncertainty as to the tallest world champion. Ernest Terrell (USA; b. 4 Apr. 1939), WBA champion 1965–67, was reported to be 6 ft. 6 in. Slightly higher figures had been given for earlier champions, but, according to measurements by the physical education director of the Hemingway Gymnasium, Harvard University, Cambridge, MA, Primo Carnera was 6 ft. 5.4 in., although widely reported and believed to be up to 6 ft. 8½ in. Jess Willard (1881–1968), who won the title in 1915, often stated to be 6 ft. 6¼ in., was in fact 6 ft. 5¼ in.

WORLD CHAMPIONS *Any weight*

Reign   *Longest*   The Joe Louis heavyweight duration record of 11 yrs. 252 days stands for all divisions.

Shortest   Tony Canzoneri (USA; 1908–59) was world light-welterweight champion for 33 days, 21 May to 23 June 1933, the shortest period for a boxer to have won and lost the world title in the ring.

Youngest   Wilfred Benitez (b. New York, 12 Sep. 1958) of Puerto Rico was 17 yrs. 176 days when he won the WBA light-welterweight title in San Juan, Puerto Rico on 6 Mar. 1976.

Oldest   Archie Moore, who was recognized as a light-heavyweight champion up to 10 Feb. 1962 when his title was removed, was then believed to be between 45 and 48 years old.

Longest career   Bob Fitzsimmons had a career of over 31 years, from 1883 to 1914. He had his last world title bout on 20 Dec. 1905 at the age of 42 yrs. 208 days. Jack Johnson (USA; 1878–1946) also had a career of over 31 years, from 1897–1928.

Longest fight   The longest world title fight (under Queensberry Rules) was that between the lightweights Joe Gans (1874–1910), of the USA, and Oscar Matthew "Battling" Nelson (1882–1954), the "Durable Dane," at Goldfield, NV on 3 Sep. 1906. It was terminated in the 42nd round when Gans was declared the winner on a foul.

Most different weights   The first to have won world titles at four weight categories was Thomas Hearns (USA; b. 18 Oct. 1958), WBA welterweight in 1980, WBC super-welterweight in 1982, WBC light-heavyweight in 1987 and WBC middleweight in 1987. He added a fifth weight division when he won the super-middleweight title recognized by the newly created World Boxing Organization (WBO) on 4 Nov. 1988, and he won the WBA light-heavyweight title on 3 June 1991.

Sugar Ray Leonard (USA; b. 17 May 1956) has also claimed world titles in five weight categories. Having previously won the WBC welterweight in 1979 and 1980, WBA junior middleweight in 1981 and WBC middleweight in 1987, he beat Donny Lalonde (Canada) on 7 Nov. 1988, for both the WBC light-heavyweight and super-middleweight titles. However, despite the fact that the WBC sanctioned the fight, it is against their rules to contest two divisions in one fight. Therefore, although Leonard won, he had to relinquish one of the titles.

The only man to hold world titles at three weights *simultaneously* was Henry "Homicide Hank" Armstrong (USA; 1912–88), at featherweight, lightweight and welterweight from August to December 1938. It is argued, however, that Barney Ross (b. Barney David Rosofsky [USA]; 1909–67) held the lightweight, junior-welterweight and welterweight titles simultaneously, from 28 May to 17 Sep. 1934, although there is some dispute as to when he relinquished his lightweight title. In recent years there has been a proliferation of weight categories and governing bodies, but Armstrong was undisputed world champion at widely differing weights, which makes his achievement all the more remarkable.

Most recaptures   The only boxer to win a world title five times at one weight is "Sugar Ray" Robinson (USA; b. Walker Smith Jr., 1921–89), who beat Carmen Basilio (USA) in Chicago Stadium, IL on 25 Mar. 1958 to regain the world middleweight title for the fourth time.

Most title bouts   The record number of title bouts in a career is 37, of which 18 ended in "no decision," by three-time world welterweight champion Jack Britton (USA; 1885–1962) in 1915–22. The record containing no "no-decision" contests is 27 (all heavyweight), by Joe Louis between 1937–50.

Lightest heavyweight   Robert James "Bob" Fitzsimmons (1863–1917) from Great Britain weighed 167 lbs. when he won the title by knocking out James J. Corbett at Carson City, NV on 17 Mar. 1897.

Heaviest   Primo Carnera (Italy; 1906–67), the "Ambling Alp," who won the title from Jack Sharkey in New York City on 29 June 1933, scaled 260½ lbs. for this fight, but his peak weight was 270 lbs. He had an expanded chest measurement of 54 in. and the longest reach at 85½ in. (fingertip to fingertip).

Shortest boxer   Tommy Burns, world heavyweight champion from 23 Feb. 1906 to 26 Dec. 1908, stood 5 ft. 7 in. and weighed between 168–180 lbs.

Longest-lived boxer   Jack Sharkey (b. Joseph Paul Cukoschay, 26 Oct. 1902), champion boxer from 21 June 1932 to 29 June 1933, surpassed the previous record of 87 yrs. 341 days held by Jack Dempsey (1895–1983) on 3 Oct. 1990.

Most knockdowns in title fight   Vic Toweel (South Africa; b. 12 Jan. 1929) knocked down Danny O'Sullivan of London, Great Britain 14 times in ten rounds in their world bantamweight fight at Johannesburg, South Africa on 2 Dec. 1950, before the latter retired.

Greatest weight difference   When Primo Carnera (Italy), 270 lbs., fought Tommy Loughran (USA), 184 lbs., for the world heavyweight title at Miami, FL on 1 Mar. 1934, there was a weight difference of 86 lbs. between the two fighters. Carnera won the fight on points.

Greatest "tonnage"·   The greatest "tonnage" recorded in any fight is 700 lbs., when Claude "Humphrey" McBride (Oklahoma), 340 lbs., knocked out Jimmy Black (Houston, TX), 360 lbs., in the third round at Oklahoma City, OK on 1 June 1971.

The greatest "tonnage" in a world title fight was 488¾ lbs., when Carnera, then 259½ lb., fought Paolino Uzcudun (Spain), 229¼ lb., in Rome, Italy on 22 Oct. 1933.

AMATEUR

Olympic titles   Only two boxers have won three Olympic gold medals: southpaw László Papp (Hungary; b. 25 Mar. 1926), middleweight winner 1948, light-middleweight winner 1952 and 1956; and Teofilo Stevenson (Cuba; b. 23 Mar. 1952), heavyweight winner 1972, 1976 and 1980.

The only man to win two titles in one Olympic celebration was Oliver L. Kirk (USA), who won both bantam and featherweight titles in St. Louis, MO in 1904, but he needed only one bout in each class.

A record that will stand forever is that of the youngest Olympic boxing champion: Jackie Fields (ne Finkelstein [USA]; b. 9 Feb. 1908), who won the 1924 featherweight title at age 16 yrs. 162 days. The minimum age for Olympic boxing competitors is now 17.

MOST WORLD TITLES. Three Cuban boxers have won a record three amateur World Championships, although only one has won them within the same weight division. Félix Savon, seen here in action during the 1986 Championships, won the heavyweight title in 1986, 1989 and 1991. (Photo: Allsport/Mike Powell)

Oldest gold medalist   Richard Kenneth Gunn (Great Britain; 1871–1961) won the Olympic featherweight gold medal on 27 Oct. 1908 in London, Great Britain at the age of 37 yrs. 254 days.

World Championships   Three boxers have won three world titles (instituted 1974): Teofilo Stevenson (Cuba), heavyweight winner 1974, 1978 and super-heavyweight winner 1986; Adolfo Horta (Cuba; b. 3 Oct. 1957), bantam winner 1978, feather winner 1982 and lightweight winner 1986; and Félix Savon (Cuba), heavyweight winner 1986, 1989 and 1991.

Most US titles   US Amateur Championships were first staged in 1888. The most titles won is five, by middleweight W. Rodenbach, 1900–04.

·CANOEING

Origins   The acknowledged pioneer of canoeing as a modern sport was John Macgregor (1825–92), a British attorney, who founded the Canoe Club in Surrey, Great Britain on 26 July 1866.

United States   The oldest club in the United States is the New York Canoe Club, founded at St. George, Staten Island, NY in 1871. The American Canoe Association was formed on 3 Aug. 1880.

Most titles *Olympics*   Gert Fredriksson (Sweden; b. 21 Nov. 1919) won a record six Olympic gold medals, 1948–60. He added a silver and a bronze for a record eight medals.

The most by a woman is three, by Lyudmila Iosifovna Pinayeva (nee Khvedosyuk [USSR]; b. 14 Jan. 1936), 1964–72, and Birgit Schmidt (nee Fischer [East Germany]; b. 25 Feb. 1962), one in 1980 and two in 1988.

The most gold medals at one Games is three, by Vladimir Parfenovich (USSR; b. 2 Dec. 1958) in 1980 and by Ian Ferguson (New Zealand; b. 20 July 1952) in 1984.

World   Including the Olympic Games, a women's record 22 titles have been won by Birgit Schmidt, 1978–88.

The men's record is 13, by Gert Fredriksson, 1948–60, Rüdiger Helm (East Germany; b. 6 Oct. 1956), 1976–83, and Ivan Patzaichin (Romania; b. 26 Nov. 1949), 1968–84.

United States   The only American canoeist to have won two Olympic gold medals is Gregory Mark Barton (b. 2 Dec. 1959), who won at K1 and K2 1,000 m events in 1988. He also has a US record three medals, as he took bronze at K1 1,000 m in 1984.

Most US titles   Marcia Ingram Jones Smoke (b. 18 July 1941) won 35 US national titles between 1962 and 1981, as well as 24 North American Championships and three gold medals at the 1967 Pan-American Games. The men's record is 33 US titles, by Ernest Riedel (b. 13 July 1901) between 1930 and 1948, mostly at kayak events.

Fastest speed   The Hungarian four-man kayak Olympic champions in 1988 at Seoul, South Korea covered 1,000 m in 2 min. 58.54 sec. in a heat. This represents an average speed of 12.53 mph. In this same race the Norwegian four achieved a 250 m split of 42.08 sec. between 500 m and 750 m for a speed of 13.29 mph.

CANOE SLALOM. Seen here is action from the 1991 World Championships at Ljubljana, Slovenia. World Championships in canoe slalom have been held biennially since 1949, and the sport returned to the Olympic program in Barcelona, having been contested in 1972 at Munich. (Photo: Allsport USA/Dan Smith)

Longest journey   Father and son Dana and Donald Starkell paddled from Winnipeg, Manitoba, Canada by ocean and river to Belem, Brazil, a distance of 12,181 miles, from 1 June 1980 to 1 May 1982. All portages were human-powered.

Without portages or aid of any kind, the longest is one of 6,102 miles, by Richard H. Grant and Ernest "Moose" Lassy, circumnavigating the eastern USA via Chicago, New Orleans, Miami, New York City and the Great Lakes from 22 Sep. 1930 to 15 Aug. 1931.

24 hours   Zdzislaw Szubski paddled 157.1 miles in a Jaguar K1 canoe on the Vistula River, Wlocklawek to Gdansk, Poland, on 11–12 Sep. 1987.

Flat water   Marinda Hartzenberg (South Africa) paddled, without benefit of current, 137.13 miles on Loch Logan, Bloemfontein, South Africa on 31 Dec. 1990–1 Jan. 1991.

Open sea   Randy Fine (USA) paddled 120.6 miles along the Florida coast on 26–27 June 1986.

Canoe raft   A raft of 568 kayaks and canoes, organized by the Nottinghamshire County Scout Council with the help of scouts from other counties, was held together by hands only, while free floating for 30 seconds on the River Trent, Nottingham, Great Britain on 30 June 1991.

Longest race   The Canadian Government Centennial Voyageur Canoe Pageant and Race from Rocky Mountain House, Alberta to the Expo 67 site at Montreal, Quebec was 3,283 miles. Ten canoes represented Canadian provinces and territories. The winner of the race, which took from 24 May to 4 Sep. 1967, was the Province of Manitoba canoe *Radisson*.

Greatest lifetime distance in a canoe   Fritz Lindner of Berlin, Germany, totaled 64,278 miles of canoeing from 1928 to 1987.

Eskimo rolls   Ray Hudspith (b. 18 Apr. 1960) achieved 1,000 rolls in 34 min. 43 sec. at the Elswick Pool, Newcastle-upon-Tyne, Great Britain on 20 Mar. 1987. He completed 100 rolls in 3 min. 7.25 sec. at Killingworth Leisure Center, Great Britain on 3 Mar. 1991.

Randy Fine (USA) completed 1,796 continuous rolls at Biscayne Bay, Miami, FL on 8 June 1991.

"Hand rolls"   Colin Brian Hill (b. 16 Aug. 1970) achieved 1,000 rolls in 31 min. 55.62 sec. at Consett, County Durham, Great Britain on 12 Mar. 1987. He also achieved 100 rolls in 2 min. 39.2 sec. in London, Great Britain on 22 Feb. 1987. He completed 3,700 continuous rolls at Durham City Swimming Baths, Great Britain on 1 May 1989.

CARD GAMES

CONTRACT BRIDGE

Origins Bridge (a corruption of *biritch*, a now-obsolete Russian word whose meanings include "declarer") is thought either to be of Levantine origin, similar games having been played there in the early 1870s, or to have come from India.

Auction bridge (highest bidder names trump) was invented *c.* 1902. The contract principle, present in several games (notably the French game *plafond, c.* 1917), was introduced to bridge by Harold Stirling Vanderbilt (USA; 1884–1970) on 1 Nov. 1925 during a Caribbean voyage aboard the SS *Finland.* It became a worldwide craze after the USA *v.* Great Britain challenge match between Romanian-born Ely Culbertson (USA; 1891–1955) and Lt. Col. Walter Thomas More Buller (Great Britain; 1887–1938) at Almack's Club, London, Great Britain in September 1930. The USA won the 200-hand match by 4,845 points.

Biggest tournament The Epson World Bridge Championship, held on 7 June 1991, was contested by almost 90,000 players playing the same hands at centers in 95 countries.

Most world titles The World Championship (Bermuda Bowl) has been won a record 13 times by Italy's Blue Team (*Squadra Azzura*), 1957–59, 1961–63, 1965–67, 1969, 1973–75, and by the USA, 1950–51, 1953–54, 1970–71, 1976–77, 1979, 1981, 1983, 1985, 1987. Italy also won the team Olympiad in 1964, 1968 and 1972 and the US won in 1988. Giorgio Belladonna (b. 7 June 1923) was on all the Italian winning teams.

Card holding Georgios Stefanidis held 292 standard playing cards in a fan in one hand, so that the value and color of each one was visible, at Reutlingen, Germany on 16 Mar. 1991.

Card throwing Kevin St. Onge threw a standard playing card 185 ft. 1 in. at the Henry Ford Community College campus, Dearborn, MI on 12 June 1979.

Perfect deals The mathematical odds against dealing 13 cards of one suit are 158,753,389,899 to 1, while the odds against a named player receiving a "perfect hand" consisting of all 13 spades are 635,013,559,599 to 1. The odds against each of the four players' receiving a complete suit (a "perfect deal") are 2,235,197,406,895,366,368,301,559,999 to 1.

Possible auctions The number of possible auctions with North as dealer is 128,745,650,347,030,683,120,231,926,111,609,371,-363,122,697,557.

The USA has a record six wins in the women's world championship for the Venice Trophy, 1974, 1976, 1978, 1987, 1989 and 1991, and three women's wins at the World Team Olympiad, 1976, 1980 and 1984.

Most world championship hands   In the 1989 Bermuda Bowl in Perth, Australia, Marcel Branco and Gabriel Chagas, both of Brazil, played a record 752 out of a possible 784 boards.

Most Master Points   In the latest ranking list based on Master Points awarded by the World Bridge Federation during the last ten years, the leading players in the world are *(men)* Robert Hamman (b. 1938) of Dallas, TX, with 597 points, and *(women)* Sandra Landy (Great Britain), with 284.

The all-time leading Master Point winner was Giorgio Belladonna (Italy) with 1,821¼ points. The world's leading woman player was Jacqui Mitchell (USA), with 347 points.

CRIBBAGE

Origins   The invention of the game (once spelled cribbidge) is credited to the English dramatist Sir John Suckling (1609–42).

Rare hands   Four maximum 29-point hands have been achieved by William E. Johnson of Waltham, MA, 1974–81, and by Mrs. Mary Matheson of Springhill, Nova Scotia, Canada, 1974–85. Paul Nault of Athol, MA had two such hands within eight games in a tournament on 19 Mar. 1977.

Most points in 24 hours   The most points scored by a team of four, playing singles in two pairs, is 111,201, by Christine and Elizabeth Gill, Jeanette MacGrath and Donald Ward at Grannie's Healin' Hame, Embo, Great Britain on 2–3 May 1987.

CRICKET

Origins   Cricket originated in England in the Middle Ages. It is impossible to pinpoint its exact origin; however, historians believe that the modern game developed in the mid-16th century. The earliest surviving scorecard is from a match played between England and Kent, Great Britain on 18 June 1744. The Marylebone Cricket Club (MCC) was founded in 1787 and, until 1968, was the world governing body for the sport. The International Cricket Conference (ICC) is responsible for international (Test) cricket, while the MCC remains responsible for the laws of cricket. The first international match was played between Canada and the USA in 1844. Fifteen years later those countries were host to the first English touring team.

First-class records   *Career*   The most runs scored in a career is 61,237, by Sir John Berry "Jack" Hobbs (1882–1963) for Surrey and England, 1905–34. The most wickets taken by an individual is 4,187, by Wilfred Rhodes (1877–1973) for Yorkshire and England, 1898–1930. The most dismissals by a wicket-keeper is 1,649, by Robert William Taylor (b. 17 July

1941) for Derbyshire and England, 1960–88. The most catches by a fielder is 1,018, by Frank Edward Woolley (1887–1978) for Kent and England, 1906–38.

TEST CRICKET

Origins   The first match, now considered as a Test, was played at Melbourne, Australia on 15–19 Mar. 1877 between Australia and England. Neither side was representative of its country, and indeed such was the case for

WORLD CUP. Seen here during their vital partnership of 139 in the 1992 World Cup final are Imran Khan (left) and Javed Miandad of Pakistan. Both players hold the record for having appeared in all five World Cup tournaments and having played a record 28 games. Imran has taken a record 34 wickets in World Cup matches and Javed has a record aggregate of 1,029 runs. (Photo: Allsport/Adrian Murrell)

many matches, now accepted as Tests, played over the next 50 years or so. Eight nations have played Test cricket: Australia, England, India, New Zealand, Pakistan, South Africa, Sri Lanka and West Indies.

Career records   The most runs scored by an individual is 10,122, by Sunil Manohar Gavaskar (India; b. 10 July 1949) in 125 Tests, 1971–87. The most wickets taken by a bowler is 431, by Sir Richard John Hadlee (New Zealand; b. 3 July 1951) in 86 Tests, 1973–90. The most dismissals by a wicket-keeper is 355, by Rodney William Marsh (Australia; b. 11 Nov. 1947), in 96 Tests, 1970–84. The most catches by a fielder is 135, by Allan Robert Border (Australia; b. 27 July 1955) in 130 Tests, 1978–92.

The best all-round Test career record is that of Ian Terence Botham (b. 24 Nov. 1955) with 5,200 runs, 383 wickets and 120 catches in 102 matches for England, 1977–92.

NATIONAL CRICKET CHAMPIONSHIPS

Australia   The premier event in Australia is the Sheffield Shield, an interstate competition contested since 1891–92. New South Wales has won the title a record 40 times.

England   The major championship in England is the County Championships, an intercounty competition officially recognized since 1890. Yorkshire has won the title a record 30 times.

India   The Ranji Trophy is India's premier cricket competition. Established in 1934 in memory of K. S. Ranjitsinhji, it is contested on a zonal basis, culminating in a playoff competition. Bombay has won the tournament a record 30 times.

New Zealand   Since 1975, the major championship in New Zealand has been the Shell Trophy. Otago, Wellington and Auckland have each won the competition four times.

Pakistan   Pakistan's national championship is the Quaid-e-Azam Trophy, established in 1953. Karachi has won the trophy a record seven times.

South Africa   The Currie Cup, donated by Sir Donald Currie, was first contested in 1889. Transvaal has won the competition a record 28 times.

West Indies   The Red Stripe Cup, established in 1966, is the premier prize played for by the association of Caribbean islands (plus Guyana) that form the West Indies Cricket League. Barbados has won the competition a record 13 times.

CROQUET

Origins   Its exact origins are obscure, but croquet is probably derived from the French game *jeu de mail*, first mentioned in the 12th century. A game resembling croquet, possibly of foreign origin, was played in Ireland in the 1830s, and was introduced to England.

United States   Although croquet had been played in the United States for a number of years, a national body was not established until the formation of the United States Croquet Association (USCA) in 1976. The first United States Championship was played in 1977.

International trophy   The MacRobertson Shield (instituted 1925 and held every three years) has been won a record eight times by Great Britain, in 1925, 1937, 1956, 1963, 1969, 1974, 1982 and 1990. The United States will compete for the first time in 1993 with Australia, New Zealand and the UK/Ireland teams.

A record seven appearances have been made by John G. Prince (New Zealand), in 1963, 1969, 1975, 1979, 1982, 1986 and 1990; on his debut he was the youngest-ever international, at 17 yrs. 190 days.

USCA National Championships   J. Archie Peck has won the singles title a record four times, 1977, 1979–80 and 1982. Ted Prentis has won the doubles title four times with three different partners, 1978, 1980–81 and 1988. The teams of Ted Prentis and Ned Prentis (1980–81), Dana Dribben and Ray Bell (1985–86), and Reid Fleming and Debbie Cornelius (1990–91) have each won the doubles title twice. Fleming also won doubles in 1989 with Wayne Rodoni, so Fleming won three times, although with two different partners. The New York Croquet Club has won a record six National Club Championships, 1980–83, 1986 and 1988.

CROSS-COUNTRY RUNNING

Origins   The earliest recorded international cross-country race took place over 9 miles 18 yds. from Ville d'Avray, outside Paris, France on 20 Mar. 1898 between England and France (England won by 21 points to 69).

World Championships   The inaugural International Cross-Country Championships took place at the Hamilton Park Racecourse, Great Britain on 28 Mar. 1903.

The greatest margin of victory is 56 sec. or 390 yds. by John "Jack" Thomas Holden (England; b. 13 Mar. 1907) at Ayr Racecourse, Strathclyde, Great Britain on 24 Mar. 1934.

Since 1973 the events have been official World Championships under the auspices of the International Amateur Athletic Federation.

MOST TITLES. John Ngugi (Kenya) is seen here in action at Stavanger, Norway in 1989 when he won his fourth world cross-country championship. Three years later, he succeeded for a record fifth time, winning in Boston, MA. (Photo: Allsport/Gray Mortimore)

United States   The USA has never won the men's team race, but Craig Steven Virgin (b. 2 Aug. 1955) won the individual race twice, 1980–81.

Most wins   The greatest number of team victories has been by England, with 45 for men, 11 for junior men and seven for women. The USA and the USSR each have a record eight women's team victories.

The greatest team domination was by Kenya at Auckland, New Zealand on 26 Mar. 1988. Their senior men's team finished eight men in the first nine, with a low score of 23 (six to score), and their junior men's team set a record low score, 11 (four to score) with six in the first seven.

The greatest number of men's individual victories is five, by John Ngugi (Kenya; b. 10 May 1962), 1986–89 and 1992. The women's race has been won five times by Doris Brown-Heritage (USA; b. 17 Sep. 1942), 1967–71; and by Grete Waitz (nee Andersen [Norway]; b. 1 Oct. 1953), 1978–81 and 1983.

US championship   In this competition, first staged in 1890, the most wins in the men's race is eight, by Patrick Ralph Porter (b. 31 May 1959), 1982–89. The women's championship was first contested in 1972, and the most wins is five, by Lynn A. Jennings (b. 1 July 1960), 1985, 1987–90.

Most appearances   Marcel van de Wattyne (Belgium; b. 7 July 1924) ran in a record 20 races, 1946–65. The women's record is 16, by Jean Lochhead (Wales; b. 24 Dec. 1946), 1967–79, 1981, 1983–84.

Largest cross-country field   The largest recorded field in any cross-country race was 11,763 starters (10,810 finished), in the 18.6-mile Lidingöloppet, near Stockholm, Sweden on 3 Oct. 1982.

CURLING

Origins   Although a 15th-century bronze figure in the Florence Museum appears to be holding a curling stone, the earliest illustration of the sport was in one of the Flemish painter Pieter Brueghel's winter scenes *c.* 1560. The game was probably introduced into Scotland by Flemings in the 15th century. The earliest documented club is Muthill, Great Britain, formed in 1739. Organized administration began in 1838, with the formation in Edinburgh, Great Britain of the Grand (later Royal) Caledonian Curling Club, the international legislative body until the foundation of the International Curling Federation in 1966, which was renamed the World Curling Federation in 1991.

United States   The USA won the first Gordon International Medal series of matches, between Canada and the United States, at Montreal in 1884. In 1832, Orchard Lake Curling Club, MI, was founded, the first in the United States. The oldest club in continuous existence in the USA is Milwaukee Curling Club, WI, formed circa 1850. Regional curling associations governed the sport in the USA until 1947, when the United States Women's Curling Association was formed, followed in 1958 by the Men's Curling Association. In 1986, the United States Curling Association was formed and is the current governing body for the sport. In Canada, the Dominion Curling Association was formed in 1935, renamed the Canadian Curling Association in 1968. Curling has been a demonstration sport at the Olympic Games of 1924, 1932, 1964 and 1988. A specialized German version of the game was demonstrated in 1936.

Most titles   Canada has won the men's World Championships (instituted 1959) 20 times, 1959–64, 1966, 1968–72, 1980, 1982–83, 1985–87, 1989–90.
   The most Strathcona Cup (instituted 1903) wins is seven, by Canada (1903, 1909, 1912, 1923, 1938, 1957, 1965) against Scotland.
   The most women's World Championships (instituted 1979) is six, by Canada (1980, 1984–87, 1989).

United States   The US has won the men's world title four times, with Bud Somerville skip on the first two winning teams, 1965 and 1974.

United States National Championship *Men* In this competition, first held in 1957, two curlers have been skips on five championship teams: Bud Somerville (Superior Curling Club, WI in 1965, 1968–69, 1974, 1981), and Bruce Roberts (Hibbing Curling Club, MN in 1966–67, 1976–77, 1984). Bill Strum of the Superior Curling Club has been a member of five title teams, in 1965, 1967, 1969, 1974 and 1978.

Women In this competition, first held in 1977, Nancy Langley, Seattle, WA has been the skip of a record four championship teams, 1979, 1981, 1983 and 1988.

The Labatt Brier (formerly the Macdonald Brier 1927–79) The Brier is the Canadian Men's Curling championship. The competition was first held at the Granite Club, Toronto in 1927. Sponsored by Macdonald Tobacco Inc., it was known as the Macdonald Brier; since 1980 Labatt Brewery has sponsored the event. The most wins is 22, by Manitoba (1928–32, 1934, 1936, 1938, 1940, 1942, 1947, 1949, 1952–53, 1956, 1965, 1970–72, 1979, 1981, 1984). Ernie Richardson (Saskatchewan) has been winning skip a record four times (1959–60, 1962–63). His brothers Arnold and Sam Richardson were also members of each championship team.

"Perfect" game Stu Beagle, of Calgary, Alberta, Canada, played a perfect game (48 points) against Nova Scotia in the Canadian Championships (Brier) at Fort William (now Thunder Bay), Ontario on 8 Mar. 1960.

Fastest game in curling Eight curlers from the Burlington Golf and Country Club curled an eight-end game in 47 min. 24 sec., with time penalties of 5 min. 30 sec., at Burlington, Ontario, Canada on 4 Apr. 1986, following rules agreed on with the Ontario Curling Association. The time is taken from when the first rock crosses the near hogline until the game's last rock comes to a complete stop.

Largest bonspiel The largest bonspiel (curling tournament) in the world is the Manitoba Curling Association Bonspiel, held annually in Winnipeg, Canada. In 1988 there were 1,424 teams of four men, a total of 5,696 curlers, using 187 sheets of curling ice.

Largest rink The world's largest curling rink was the Big Four Curling Rink, Calgary, Alberta, Canada, opened in 1959 and closed in 1990. Ninety-six teams and 384 players are accommodated on two floors, each with 24 sheets of ice.

Longest throw The longest throw of a curling stone was a distance of 576 ft. 4 in., by Eddie Kulbacki (Canada) at Park Lake, Neepawa, Manitoba, Canada on 29 Jan. 1989. The attempt took place on a specially prepared sheet of curling ice on frozen Park Lake, a record 1,200 ft. long.

CYCLING

Origins   The earliest recorded bicycle race was a velocipede race over 1.24 miles at the Parc de St. Cloud, Paris, France on 31 May 1868, won by Dr. James Moore (Great Britain; 1847–1935) (later Chevalier de la Légion d'Honneur).

United States   The first recorded cycle race in the United States took place in September 1883 when G.M. Hendrie beat W.G. Rowe in a road race.

Fastest speed   The fastest speed ever achieved on a bicycle is 152.284 mph, by John Howard (USA) behind a windshield at Bonneville Salt Flats, UT on 20 July 1985. It should be noted that considerable help was provided by the slipstreaming effect of the lead vehicle.

The 24 hr. record behind pace is 1,216.8 miles, by Michael Secrest at Phoenix International Raceway, AZ on 26–27 Apr. 1990.

Most titles   *Olympic*   The most gold medals won is three, by Paul Masson (France; 1874–1945) in 1896, Francisco Verri (Italy; 1885–1945) in 1906, and Robert Charpentier (France; 1916–66) in 1936. Daniel Morelon (France) won two in 1968, and a third in 1972; he also won a silver in 1976 and a bronze in 1964. In the "unofficial" 1904 cycling program, Marcus Latimer Hurley (USA; 1885–1941) won four events.

Burton Cecil Down (1885–1929) won a record six medals at the 1904 Games, two gold, three silver and one bronze. The only American woman to win a cycling gold medal is Helen Constance "Connie" Carpenter-Phinney (b. 26 Feb. 1957), who won the individual road race in 1984. She became the first woman to compete in the winter and summer Olympics, as she had competed as a speed skater in 1972.

World   World Championships are contested annually. They were first staged for amateurs in 1893 and for professionals in 1895.

The most wins at a particular event is ten, by Koichi Nakano (Japan; b. 14 Nov. 1955), professional sprint 1977–86.

The most wins at a men's amateur event is seven, by Daniel Morelon (France; b. 28 July 1944), sprint 1966–67, 1969–71, 1973, 1975; and by Leon Meredith (Great Britain; 1882–1930), 100 km motor paced 1904–05, 1907–09, 1911, 1913.

The most women's titles is eight, by Jeannie Longo (France; b. 31 Oct. 1958), pursuit 1986 and 1988–89; road 1985–87 and 1989; and points 1989.

The most world titles won by a US cyclist is four, at women's 3 kilometers pursuit by Rebecca Twigg (b. 26 Mar. 1963), 1982, 1984–85 and 1987. The most successful man has been Greg LeMond (b. 26 June 1960), winner of the individual road race in 1983 and 1989.

United States   National cycling championships have been held annually since 1899. Women's events were first included in 1937.

Leonard Nitx has won the most titles, 16: five pursuit (1976 and 1980–83); eight team pursuit (1980–84, 1986 and 1988–89); two 1-km time-trial (1982 and 1984); and one criterium (1986). Connie Carpenter has won 11 titles in women's events: four road race (1976–77, 1979 and 1981); three pursuit (1976–77 and 1979); two criterium (1982–83); and two points (1981–82).

WORLD RECORDS. The current record holder for the men's indoor 5 km is Francis Moreau (France) (top) with a time of 5 min. 40.617 sec. (an average speed of 32.83 mph) at Stuttgart, Germany on 17 Aug. 1991.

Jeannie Longo (France) (bottom) holds numerous world records, both indoors and out. Here she can be seen during her record-breaking ride in the indoor 10 km at Paris, France on 19 Oct. 1989. (Photos: Allsport/Vandystadt)

WORLD RECORDS

Records are recognized by the Union Cycliste Internationale (UCI) for both professionals and amateurs on open-air and indoor tracks for a variety of distances at unpaced flying and standing starts and for motor-paced. In this list only the best are shown, with an asterisk * to signify those records set by a professional rather than an amateur.

OPEN-AIR TRACKS

MEN

DISTANCE	HR.MIN.SEC	NAME AND COUNTRY	VENUE	DATE
Unpaced standing start				
1 km	1:02.091	Maic Malchow (East Germany)	Colorado Springs, CO	28 Aug. 1986
4 km	4:31.160	Gintautas Umaras (USSR)	Seoul, South Korea	18 Sep. 1987
5 km	5:44.700	Gregor Braun (West Germany)*	La Paz, Bolivia	12 Jan. 1986
10 km	11:39.720	Francesco Moser (Italy)*	Mexico City, Mexico	19 Jan. 1984
20 km	23:21.592	Francesco Moser (Italy)*	Mexico City, Mexico	23 Jan. 1984
100 km	2:09:11.312	Kent Bostick (USA)	Colorado Springs, CO	13 Oct. 1989
1 hour	51.151 km	Francesco Moser (Italy)*	Mexico City, Mexico	23 Jan. 1984
Unpaced flying start				
200 meters	10.118	Michael Hübner (East Germany)	Colorado Springs, CO	27 Aug. 1986
500 meters	26.993	Rory O'Reilly (USA)	Colorado Springs, CO	23 Nov. 1985
1 km	58.269	Dominguez Rueda Efrain (Colombia)*	La Paz, Bolivia	13 Dec. 1986
Motor-paced				
50 km	35:21.108	Aleksandr Romanov (USSR)	Tbilisi, USSR	6 May 1987
100 km	1:10:29.420	Giovanni Renosto (Italy)	Bassano del Grappa, Italy	16 Sep. 1988
1 hour	85.067 km	Giovanni Renosto (Italy)	Bassano del Grappa, Italy	16 Sep. 1988

WOMEN

DISTANCE	HR.MIN.SEC	NAME AND COUNTRY	VENUE	DATE
Unpaced standing start				
1 km	1:13.899	Zhou Lingmei (China)	Beijing, China	27 Sep. 1990
3 km	3:38.190	Jeannie Longo (France)	Mexico City, Mexico	5 Oct. 1989
5 km	6:14.135	Jeannie Longo (France)	Mexico City, Mexico	27 Sep. 1989
10 km	12:59.435	Jeannie Longo (France)	Mexico City, Mexico	1 Oct. 1989

(continued)

20 km	25:59.883	Jeannie Longo (France)	Mexico City, Mexico	1 Oct. 1989
100 km	2:28:26.259	Francesca Galli (Italy)	Milan, Italy	26 Oct. 1987
1 hour	46.35270 km	Jeannie Longo (France)	Mexico City, Mexico	1 Oct. 1989

Unpaced flying start

200 meters	11.383	Isabelle Gautheron (France)	Colorado Springs, CO.	16 Aug. 1986
500 meters	30.59	Isabelle Gautheron (France)	Cali, Colombia	14 Sep. 1986
1 km	1:10.463	Erika Salumyae (USSR)	Tashkent, USSR.	15 May 1984

Many of the above venues, such as La Paz, Colorado Springs, Cali and Mexico City, are at high altitude. The UCI recognizes separate world records for the classic one-hour event at venues below 600 meters. These are: MEN: 49.80193 km, Francesco Moser on 3 Oct. 1986; WOMEN: 43.58789 km, Jeannie Longo on 30 Sep. 1986, both at Milan, Italy.

INDOOR TRACKS

MEN

Unpaced standing start

1 km	1:02.576	Aleksandr Kirichenko (USSR)	Moscow, USSR.	2 Aug. 1989
4 km	4:28.900	Vyachselav Yekimov (USSR)	Moscow, USSR.	20 Sep. 1986
5 km	5:40.617	Francis Moreau (France)	Stuttgart, Germany	17 Aug. 1991
10 km	11:31.968	Vyacheslav Yekimov (USSR)	Moscow, USSR.	7 Jan. 1989
20 km	23:14.553	Vyacheslav Yekimov (USSR)	Moscow, USSR.	3 Feb. 1989
100 km	2:10:08.287	Beat Meister (Switzerland)	Stuttgart, West Germany	22 Sep. 1989
4 km team	4:08.66	Germany	Stuttgart, Germany	Aug. 1991
		(Michael Glöckner, Jens Lehmann, Stefan Steinway, Andreas Walzer)		
1 hour	50.644 km	Francesco Moser (Italy)	Stuttgart, West Germany	21 May 1988

Unpaced flying start

200 meters	10.099	Vladimir Adamashvili (USSR)	Moscow, USSR.	6 Aug. 1990
500 meters	26.649	Aleksandr Kirichenko (USSR)	Moscow, USSR.	29 Oct. 1988
1 km	57.260	Aleksandr Kirichenko (USSR)	Moscow, USSR.	25 Apr. 1989

Motor-paced

50 km	32:56.746	Aleksandr Romanov (USSR)	Moscow, USSR.	21 Feb. 1987
100 km	1:05:58.031	Aleksandr Romanov (USSR)	Moscow, USSR.	21 Feb. 1987
1 hour	91.131 km	Aleksandr Romanov (USSR)	Moscow, USSR.	21 Feb. 1987

WOMEN

Unpaced standing start

1 km	1:11.708	Isabelle Nicoloso (France)	Bordeaux, France	17 Nov. 1991
3 km	3:41.290	Jeannie Longo (France)	Grenoble, France	4 Nov. 1991
5 km	6:17.608	Jeannie Longo (France)	Grenoble, France	1 Nov. 1991
10 km	12:54.26	Jeannie Longo (France)	Paris, France	19 Oct. 1989
20 km	26:51.222	Jeannie Longo (France)	Moscow, USSR	29 Oct. 1989
100 km	2:24:57.618	Tea Vikstedt-Nyman (Finland)	Moscow, USSR	30 Oct. 1990
1 hour	45.016 km	Jeannie Longo (France)	Moscow, USSR	29 Oct. 1989

Unpaced flying start

200 meters	11.164	Galina Yenyukhina (USSR)	Moscow, USSR	6 Aug. 1990
500 meters	29.655	Erika Salumyae (USSR)	Moscow, USSR	6 Aug. 1987
1 km	1:05.232	Erika Salumyae (USSR)	Moscow, USSR	30 May 1987

Long Distance Bests (unpaced)

24 hrs.	830.79 km	Michael L. Secrest (USA)	Montreal, Canada	13–14 Mar. 1985
1,000 km	32 hrs. 4 min	Herman de Munck (Belgium)	Keerbergen, Belgium	23–24 Sep. 1983
1,000 miles	51:12:32	Herman de Munck (Belgium)	Keerbergen, Belgium	23–25 Sep. 1983

Highest altitude cycling Canadians Bruce Bell, Philip Whelan and Suzanne MacFadyen cycled at an altitude of 22,834 ft. on the peak of Mt. Aconcagua, Argentina on 25 Jan. 1991.

Cycling the length of the Americas Daniel Buettner, Bret Anderson, Martin Engel and Anne Knabe cycled the length of the Americas, from Prudhoe Bay, AK to the Beagle Channel, Ushuaia, Argentina from 8 Aug. 1986 to 13 June 1987. They cycled a total distance of 15,266 miles.

Greatest distance in one hour The greatest distance covered in one hour is 76 miles 504 yds. by Leon Vanderstuyft (Belgium; 1890–1964) on the Montlhéry Motor Circuit, France, on 30 Sep. 1928, achieved from a standing start paced by a motorcycle.

Fastest rollercycling speed James Baker (USA) achieved a record speed of 153.2 mph at El Con Mall, Tucson, AZ on 28 Jan. 1989.

Tour de France   The world's premiere stage race was first contested in 1903. Held over a three-week period, the longest race ever staged was over 3,596 miles in 1926. The greatest number of wins in the Tour de France is five, by Jacques Anquetil (France; 1934–1987), 1957, 1961–64; Eddy Merckx (Belgium; b. 17 June 1945), 1969–72 and 1974; and Bernard Hinault (France; b. 14 Nov. 1954), 1978–79, 1981–82 and 1985. Greg LeMond (USA; b. 26 June 1960) became the first American winner in 1986, and returned from serious injury to win again in 1989 and 1990.

The closest race ever was in 1989, when after 2,030 miles over 23 days (1–23 July) Greg LeMond, who completed the Tour in 87 hrs. 38 min. 35 sec., beat Laurent Fignon (France; b. 12 Aug. 1960) in Paris, France by only 8 sec.

The fastest average speed was 24.547 mph by Miguel Indurain (Spain; b. 16 July 1964) in 1992.

The longest-ever stage was the 486 km from Les Sables d'Olonne to Bayonne in 1919. The most participants was 210 starters in 1986.

Women   The inaugural women's Tour de France was staged in 1984. Jeannié Longo (France) has won the event a record four times, 1987–90.

Six-day races   The most wins in six-day races is 88 out of 233 events, by Patrick Sercu (Belgium; b. 27 June 1944), 1964–83.

Longest one-day race   The longest single-day "massed start" road race is the 342–385 mile Bordeaux–Paris, France event. Paced over all or part of the route, the highest average speed was 29.32 mph, by Herman van Springel (Belgium; b. 14 Aug. 1943) for 363.1 miles in 13 hrs. 35 min. 18 sec., in 1981.

Cross-America   The trans-America solo record recognized by the Ultra-Marathon Cycling Association for men is 8 days 8 hrs. 45 min., by Paul Selon at age 35 from Costa, CA to New York, in the 1989 Race Across AMerica. Selon won the race while wearing a plastic neck brace. The women's record is 9 days 9 hrs. 9 min., by Susan Notorangelo at age 35, also in the 1989 Race Across AMerica. She clipped 16 hrs. 55 min. off the previous women's record.

Cross-Canada   The trans-Canada record is 13 days 9 hrs. 6 min., by William "Bill" Narasnek of Lively, Ontario, 3,751 miles from Vancouver, British Columbia to Halifax, Nova Scotia on 5–18 July 1991.

Endurance   Thomas Edward Godwin (Great Britain; 1912–75), cycling every day during the 365 days of 1939, covered 75,065 miles, or an average of 205.65 miles per day. He then completed 100,000 miles in 500 days to 14 May 1940.

Jay Aldous and Matt DeWaal cycled 14,290 miles on an around-the-world trip from Place Monument, Salt Lake City, UT in 106 days, from 2 Apr.–16 July 1984.

Nicholas Mark Sanders (b. 26 Nov. 1957) of Glossop, Great Britain circumnavigated the world (13,035 road miles) in 78 days 3 hrs. 30 min. between 5 July and 21 Sep. 1985.

Cycle touring   The greatest mileage amassed in a cycle tour was more than 402,000 miles, by the itinerant lecturer Walter Stolle (b. Sudetenland,

1926) from 24 Jan. 1959 to 12 Dec. 1976. Starting from Romford, Great Britain, he visited 159 countries. From 1922 to 25 Dec. 1973, Tommy Chambers (1903–84) of Glasgow, Great Britain rode a verified total of 799,405 miles.

Visiting every continent, John W. Hathaway (b. Great Britain, 13 Jan. 1925) of Vancouver, British Columbia, Canada covered 50,600 miles from 10 Nov. 1974 to 6 Oct. 1976. Veronica and Colin Scargill, of Bedford, Great Britain, traveled 18,020 miles around-the-world on a tandem, 25 Feb. 1974–27 Aug. 1975.

Ronald and Sandra Slaughter hold the US record for tandem bicycling, having traveled 18,077.5 miles around the world from 30 Dec. 1989 to 28 July 1991.

The most participants in a bicycle tour were 31,678, in the 56-mile London–to–Brighton Bike Ride (Great Britain) on 19 June 1988. However, it is estimated that 40,000 cyclists took part in the 44-mile Tour de l'Ile de Montréal in June 1991.

The most participants in a tour in excess of 1,000 km is 2,037 (from 2,157 starters) for the Australian Bicentennial Caltex Bike Ride from Melbourne to Sydney, from 26 Nov.–10 Dec. 1988.

CYCLO-CROSS

The greatest number of World Championships (instituted 1950) has been won by Eric de Vlaeminck (Belgium; b. 23 Aug. 1945), with the Amateur and Open in 1966 and six Professional titles in 1968–73.

DARTS

Origins   Darts can be dated from the use by archers of heavily weighted ten-inch throwing arrows for self-defense in close-quarters fighting. The "dartes" were used in Ireland in the 16th century, and darts was played on the *Mayflower* by the Pilgrims in 1620. The modern game dates from 1896, when Brian Gamlin of Bury, Lancashire, Great Britain is credited with inventing the present numbering system on the board. The first recorded highest possible score of 180 was achieved by John Reader at the Highbury Tavern in Sussex, Great Britain in 1902.

Most titles   Eric Bristow (Great Britain; b. 25 Apr. 1957) has the most wins in the World Masters Championship (instituted 1974) with five, 1977, 1979, 1981 and 1983–84; the most in the World Professional Championship (instituted 1978) with five, 1980–81 and 1984–86; and the most in the World Cup Singles (instituted 1977) with four, 1983, 1985, 1987 and 1989.

John Lowe (Great Britain; b. 21 July 1945) is the only man besides Eric Bristow to have won each of the four major titles: World Masters, 1976 and 1980; World Professional, 1979 and 1987; World Cup Singles, 1981; and *News of the World*, 1981.

Record prize   John Lowe won £102,000 (c. $175,000) for achieving the first 501 scored with the minimum nine darts in a major event, on 13 Oct.

1984 at Slough, Great Britain in the quarter-finals of the World Match-play Championships. His darts were six successive treble 20s, treble 17, treble 18 and double 18.

Fewest darts   Scores of 201 in four darts, 301 in six darts, 401 in seven darts and 501 in nine darts have been achieved on various occasions.

The lowest number of darts thrown for a score of 1,001 is 19, by Cliff Inglis (b. 27 May 1935) (160, 180, 140, 180, 121, 180, 40) at the Bromfield Men's Club, Devon, Great Britain on 11 Nov. 1975; and by Jocky Wilson (Great Britain) (140, 140, 180, 180, 180, 131, Bull) at The London Pride, Bletchley, Great Britain on 23 Mar. 1989.

A score of 2,001 in 52 darts was achieved by Alan Evans (Great Britain; b. 14 June 1949) at Ferndale, Great Britain on 3 Sep. 1976. A score of 3,001 in 73 darts was thrown by Tony Benson at the Plough Inn, Gorton, Great Britain on 12 July 1986. Linda Batten (b. 26 Nov. 1954) set a women's 3,001 record of 117 darts at the Old Wheatsheaf, London, Great Britain on 2 Apr. 1986. A score of 100,001 was achieved in 3,732 darts by Alan Downie of Stornoway, Great Britain on 21 Nov. 1986.

Speed records   The fastest time taken to complete three games of 301, finishing on doubles, is 1 min. 47 sec., by Keith Deller on British Broadcasting Corporation's *Record Breakers* TV program on 22 Oct. 1985.

The record time for going around the board clockwise in "doubles" at arm's length is 9.2 sec., by Dennis Gower at the Millers Arms, Hastings, Great Britain on 12 Oct. 1975, and 14.5 sec. in numerical order by Jim Pike (1903–60) at the Craven Club, Newmarket, Great Britain in Mar. 1944.

The record for this feat at the 9-ft. throwing distance, retrieving own darts, is 2 min. 13 sec. by Bill Duddy (b. 29 Sep. 1932) at The Plough, London, Great Britain on 29 Oct. 1972.

Fewest darts   Roy Edwin Blowes (Canada; b. 8 Oct. 1930) was the first person to achieve a 501 in nine darts, "double-on, double-off," at the Widgeons Pub, Calgary, Canada on 9 Mar. 1987. His scores were: bull, treble 20, treble 17, five treble 20s and a double 20 to finish.

EQUESTRIAN SPORTS

Origins   Evidence of horse riding dates from a Persian engraving dated *c.* 3000 B.C. Pignatelli's academy of horsemanship at Naples dates from the 16th century. The earliest jumping competition was at the Agricultural Hall, London, in 1869. Equestrian events have been included in the Olympic Games since 1912. The world governing body is the *Fédération Equestre Internationale* (FEI), founded in Brussels, Belgium in 1921.

SHOW JUMPING

Olympic Games   The most Olympic gold medals won by a rider is five, by Hans Günter Winkler (West Germany; b. 24 July 1926), four team wins in 1956, 1960, 1964 and 1972 and the individual Grand Prix in 1956. He also won team silver in 1976 and team bronze in 1968, for a record seven medals overall.

The most team wins in the Prix des Nations is six, by Germany in 1936, 1956, 1960, 1964 and as West Germany in 1972 and 1988.

The lowest score obtained by a winner is no faults, by Frantisek Ventura (Czechoslovakia; 1895–1969) on Eliot, 1928, and Alwin Schockemöhle (West Germany; b. 29 May 1937) on Warwick Rex, 1976.

Pierre Jonquères d'Oriola (France; b. 1 Feb. 1920) uniquely won the individual gold medal twice, in 1952 and 1964.

United States   Two US riders have won individual gold medals: William "Bill" Clark Steinkraus (b. 12 Oct. 1925) won in 1968 and also won two silver and a bronze medal, 1952–68; and Joseph Halpin "Joe" Fargis (b. 4 Feb. 1948) won both individual and team gold medals in 1984 as well as team silver in 1988.

World Championships   The men's World Championships (instituted 1953) have been won twice by Hans-Günter Winkler (1954–55) and Raimondo d'Inzeo (Italy; b. 8 Feb. 1925) (1956 and 1960).

The women's title (1965–74) was won twice by Jane "Janou" Tissot (nee Lefebvre [France]; b. Saigon, 14 May 1945) on Rocket (1970 and 1974).

President's Cup   The world team championship (instituted 1965) has been won a record 14 times by Great Britain, 1965, 1967, 1970, 1972–74, 1977–79, 1983, 1985–86, 1989 and 1991.

World Cup   In this competition, instituted in 1979, double winners have included Conrad Homfeld (USA; b. 25 Dec. 1951), 1980 and 1985; Ian Millar (Canada; b. 6 Jan. 1947), 1988 and 1989; and John Whitaker (Great Britain; b. 5 Aug. 1955), 1990–91.

Jumping records   The official *Fédération Equestre Internationale* records are: high jump, 8 ft. 1¼ in., by Huasó, ridden by Capt. Alberto Larraguibel Morales (Chile) at Viña del Mar., Santiago, Chile on 5 Feb. 1949; long jump over water, 27 ft. 6¾ in., by Something, ridden by André Ferreira (South Africa) at Johannesburg, South Africa on 25 Apr. 1975.

THREE-DAY EVENT

Olympic Games and World Championships   Charles Ferdinand Pahud de Mortanges (Netherlands; 1896–1971) won a record four Olympic gold medals—team 1924 and 1928, individual (riding Marcroix) 1928 and 1932; he also won a team silver medal in 1932.

Bruce Oram Davidson (USA; b. 13 Dec. 1949) is the only rider to have won two world titles (instituted 1966), on Irish Cap in 1974 and Might Tango in 1978.

United States   The most medals won for the USA is six, by John Michael

Plumb (b. 28 Mar. 1940): team gold 1976 and 1984, and four silver medals, team 1964, 1968 and 1972, and individual 1976. Edmund Sloane "Tad" Coffin (b. 9 May 1955) is the one US rider to have won both team and individual gold medals in 1976.

DRESSAGE

Olympic Games and World Championships   Germany (West Germany 1968–90) has won a record seven team gold medals, 1928, 1936, 1964, 1968, 1976, 1984 and 1988, and has the most team wins, six, at the World Championships (instituted 1966). Dr. Reiner Klimke (West Germany; b. 14 Jan. 1936) has won a record six Olympic golds (team 1964–88, individual, 1984). He won individual bronze in 1976, for a record seven medals overall, and is the only rider to have won two world titles, on Mehmed in 1974 and on Ahlerich in 1982. Henri St. Cyr (Sweden; 1904–79) won a record two individual Olympic gold medals, in 1952 and 1956.

World Cup   Instituted in 1986, this competition has had only one double winner: Christine Stückelberger (Switzerland; b. 22 May 1947) on Gauguin de Lully in 1987–88.

CARRIAGE DRIVING

World Championships were first held in 1972. Three team titles have been won by Great Britain, 1972, 1974, and 1980; by Hungary, 1976, 1978 and 1984; and by the Netherlands, 1982, 1986 and 1988.

Two individual titles have been won by György Bárdos (Hungary), 1978 and 1980, and by Tjeerd Velstra (Netherlands), 1982 and 1986.

FENCING

Origins   Fencing (fighting with single sticks) was practiced as a sport, or as a part of a religious ceremony, in Egypt as early as *c.* 1360 B.C. The modern foil was introduced in France as a practice weapon for the short court sword in the mid-17th century. In the late 19th century the épée was developed in France and the light fencing sabre in Italy.

Fencing was included in the first Olympic Games of the modern era at Athens in 1896. The *Fédération Internationale d'Escrime* (FIE), the world governing body, was founded in Paris, France, in 1913. The first European Championships were held in 1921 and were expanded into World Championships in 1935.

United States   In the United States the Amateur Fencers League of America (AFLA) was founded on 22 Apr. 1891 in New York City. This group assumed supervision of the sport in the United States. In June 1981 the AFLA changed its name to the United States Fencing Association (USFA).

Most titles *World*   The greatest number of individual world titles won is five, by Aleksandr Romankov (USSR; b. 7 Nov. 1953), at foil 1974, 1977, 1979, 1982 and 1983, but Christian d'Oriola (France) won four world foil titles, 1947, 1949, 1953–54, as well as two individual Olympic titles (1952 and 1956).

Five women foilists have won three world titles: Helene Mayer (Germany; 1910–53), 1929, 1931, 1937; Ilona Schacherer-Elek (Hungary; 1907–88), 1934–35, 1951; Ellen Müller-Preis (Austria; b. 6 May 1912), 1947, 1949–50; Cornelia Hanisch (West Germany; b. 12 June 1952), 1979, 1981, 1985; and Anja Fichtel (West Germany; b. 17 Aug. 1968), 1986, 1988 and 1990. Of these only Ilona Schacherer-Elek also won two individual Olympic titles (1936 and 1948). The longest time span for winning an individual world or Olympic title is 20 years, by Aladár Gerevich (Hungary; b. 16 Mar. 1910) at sabre, 1935–55. Gerevich also had a 28-year span for winning Olympic team gold medals.

Olympic   The most individual Olympic gold medals won is three, by Ramón Fonst (Cuba; 1883–1959) in 1900 and 1904 (two); and by Nedo Nadi (Italy; 1894–1952) in 1912 and 1920 (two). Nadi also won three team gold medals in 1920, making five gold medals at one celebration, the record for fencing and a record for any sport at that time.

Edoardo Mangiarotti (Italy; b. 7 Apr. 1919), with six gold, five silver and two bronze, holds the record of 13 Olympic medals in fencing. He won them for foil and épée from 1936 to 1960.

The most gold medals won by a woman is four (one individual, three team) by Yelena Dmitryevna Novikova (nee Byelova [USSR]; b. 28 July 1947) from 1968 to 1976, and the women's record for all medals is seven (two gold, three silver, two bronze) by Ildikó Sági (formerly Ujlaki, nee Retjö [Hungary]; b. 11 May 1937) from 1960 to 1976.

United States   The only US Olympic champion was Albertson Van Zo Post (1866–1938), who won the men's single sticks and team foil (with two Cubans) at the 1904 Games.

United States National Championships   The most US titles won at one weapon is 12 at sabre, by Peter J. Westbrook, in 1974, 1975, 1979–86, 1988 and 1989. The women's record is 10 at foil, by Janice Lee York Romary in 1950–51, 1956–57, 1960–61, 1964–66 and 1968.

The most men's individual foil championships won is seven, by Michael Marx in 1977, 1979, 1982, 1985–87 and 1990. L. G. Nunes won the most épée championships, with six—1917, 1922, 1924, 1926, 1928 and 1932. Vincent Bradford won a record number of women's épée championships with four in 1982–84 and 1986.

NCAA Championship Division I *(Men)*   Since this competition was inaugurated in 1941, two teams have won 12 titles: New York University (1947, 1954, 1957, 1960–61, 1966–67, 1970–71, 1973–74, 1976); and Columbia University (1951–52, 1954–55, 1964–65, 1968, 1971, 1987–89, 1992). The longest consecutive title streak is four wins by Wayne State (MI), 1982–85.

Michael Lofton, New York University, has won the most titles in a career, with four victories in the sabre, 1984–87. Abraham Balk, New York University, is the only man to win two individual titles in one year, 1947 (foil and épée).

(Women) Since this competition was inaugurated in 1982, Wayne State (MI) has won the most titles: three (1982, 1988–89).

Caitlin Bilodeaux (Columbia-Barnard) and Molly Sullivan (Notre Dame) have both won the individual title twice—Bilodeaux in 1985 and 1987; Sullivan in 1986 and 1988.

In 1990, the NCAA team competition was combined for the first time. Penn State won both the 1990 and 1991 titles.

FIELD HOCKEY

Origins A representation of two players with curved snagging sticks apparently in an orthodox "bully" position was found in Tomb No. 17 at Beni Hasan, Egypt, and has been dated to *c.* 2050 B.C. The modern game evolved in London, Great Britain in the 1870s.

The *Fédération Internationale de Hockey* was formed on 7 Jan. 1924.

United States The sport was introduced to the United States in 1921 by a British teacher, Constance M.K. Applebee. The Field Hockey Association of America (FHAA) was founded in 1928 by Henry Greer. The first game was staged between the Germantown Cricket Club and the Westchester Field Hockey Club, also in 1928.

Most Olympic medals India was Olympic champion from the reintroduction of Olympic hockey in 1928 until 1960, when Pakistan beat India 1–0 in Rome. India had its eighth win in 1980. Of the six Indians who have won three Olympic team gold medals, two have also won a silver medal—Leslie Walter Claudius (b. 25 Mar. 1927), in 1948, 1952, 1956 and 1960 (silver), and Udham Singh (b. 4 Aug. 1928), in 1952, 1956, 1964 and 1960 (silver).

A women's tournament was added in 1980, when Zimbabwe was the winner. The Netherlands won in 1984 and Australia in 1988.

United States US men won the bronze medal in 1932, but only three teams played that year; US women won the bronze in 1984.

MEN

The first international match was the Wales *v.* Ireland match at Rhyl, Clwyd, Great Britain on 26 Jan. 1895. Ireland won 3–0.

Highest international score The highest score was achieved when India defeated the USA 24–1 at Los Angeles, CA in the 1932 Olympic Games.

Most international appearances Heiner Dopp (b. 27 June 1956) represented West Germany 286 times between 1975 and 1990, indoors and out.

Greatest scoring feats The greatest number of goals scored in international hockey is 267, by Paul Litjens (Netherlands; b. 9 Nov. 1947) in 177 games.

Best goalkeeping Richard James Allen (India; b. 4 June 1902) did not concede a goal during the 1928 Olympic tournament and gave up a total of only three in 1936.

WOMEN

The first national association was the Irish Ladies' Hockey Union, founded in 1894. The first international match was an England v. Ireland game in Dublin in 1896. Ireland won 2–0.

Most international appearances Valerie Robinson made a record 144 appearances for England, 1963–84.

United States Sheryl Johnson has made a record 137 appearances for the USA from 1978 to 1990.

Highest scores The highest score in an international match was when England beat France 23–0 at Merton, London, Great Britain on 3 Feb. 1923.

NCAA Division I (women) In this competition, inaugurated in 1981, Old Dominion University, Norfolk, VA has won the most championships with six titles: 1982–84, 1988 and 1990–91.

Field Hockey Champions' Trophy In this competition, first held in 1978 and contested annually since 1980 by the top six men's teams in the world, the most wins is five, by Australia, 1983–85, 1989–90. The first women's Champions' Trophy was won by the Netherlands in 1987. South Korea won in 1989 and Australia in 1991.

Field Hockey World Cup The World Cup for men was first held in 1971, and for women in 1974. The most wins are: (*men*) three by Pakistan, 1971, 1978 and 1982; (*women*) five by the Netherlands, 1974, 1978, 1983, 1986 and 1990.

Fastest goal in an international field hockey match
John French scored 7 sec. after the bully-off for England v. West Germany at Nottingham, Great Britain on 25 Apr. 1971.

Highest attendance The highest attendance was 65,165 for the match between England and the USA at Wembley, London, Great Britain on 11 Mar. 1978.

WORLD RECORDS—FRESHWATER AND SALTWATER

A selection of All-Tackle records ratified by the International Game Fish Association as of 1 Jan. 1992

SPECIES	WEIGHT LBS.	OZ.	CAUGHT BY	LOCATION	DATE
ARAWANA	10	2	Gilberto Fernandes	Puraquequara Lake, Amazon, Brazil	3 Feb. 1990
BARRACUDA, BLACKFIN	15	0	Alejandron Caniz	Puerto Quetzal, Guatemala	29 Oct. 1988
BARRACUDA, GREAT	83	0	K. J. W. Hackett	Lagos, Nigeria	13 Jan. 1952
BARRACUDA, MEXICAN	21	0	E. Greg Kent	Phantom Isle, Costa Rica	27 Mar. 1987
BASS, GIANT SEA	536	8	James D. McAdam, Jr.	Anacapa Island, CA	20 Aug. 1968
BASS, LARGEMOUTH	22	4	George W. Perry	Montgomery Lake, GA	2 June 1932
BASS, SMALLMOUTH	11	15	David L. Hayes	Dale Hollow Lake, KY	9 July 1955
BASS, STRIPED	78	8	Albert R. McReynolds	Atlantic City, NJ	21 Sep. 1982
BASS, STRIPED (landlocked)	66	0	Theordore Furnish	O'Neill Forebay, Los Ramos, CA	29 June 1988
BASS, WHITEROCK	24	3	David N. Lambert	Lessville Lake, VA	12 May 1989
BLUEFISH	31	12	James M. Hussey	Hatteras, NC	30 Jan. 1972
BONEFISH	19	0	Brian W. Batchelor	Zululand, South Africa	26 May 1962
CARP	75	1	Leo van der Gugten	Lac de St. Cassien, France	21 May 1987
CATFISH, BLUE	97	0	Edward B. Elliot	Missouri River, SD	16 Sep. 1959
COD, ATLANTIC	98	12	Alphonse J. Bielevich	Isle of Shoals, NH	8 June 1969
CONGER	102	8	Raymond E. Stewart	Plymouth, Great Britain	18 July 1983
FLOUNDER, SUMMER	22	7	Charles Nappi	Montauk, NY	15 Sep. 1975
GROUPER, BLACK	112	6	Donald W. Bone	Dry Tortugas, FL	27 Jan. 1990
HALIBUT (Pacific)	356	8	Gregory C. Olsen	Juneau, AK	8 Nov. 1986
MARLIN, BLACK	1,560	0	Alfred C. Glassell, Jr.	Cabo Blanco, Peru	4 Aug. 1953
MARLIN, BLUE (Atlantic)	1,282	0	Larry Martin	St. Thomas, Virgin Islands	6 Aug. 1977

Species	lb	oz	Angler	Location	Date
MARLIN, BLUE (Pacific)	1,376	0	Jay Wm de Beaubien	Kaaiwi Point, Kona Coast, HI	31 May 1982
MARLIN, STRIPED	494	0	Bill Boniface	Tutukaka, New Zealand	16 Jan. 1986
MARLIN, WHITE	181	14	Evandro Luiz Coser	Vitoria, Brazil	8 Dec. 1979
MUSKELLUNGE	69	15	Arthur Lawton	St. Lawrence River, NY	22 Sep. 1957
PERCH, NILE	152	1	Kurt M. Fenster	Tende Bay, Entebbe, Uganda	4 June 1989
PIKE, NORTHERN	55	1	Lothar Louis	Lake of Grefeern, Germany	16 Oct. 1986
SAILFISH (Atlantic)	128	1	Harm Steyn	Luanda, Angola	27 Mar. 1974
SAILFISH (Pacific)	221	0	C. W. Stewart	Santa Cruz Island, Ecuador	12 Feb. 1947
SALMON, CHINOOK	97	4	Les Anderson	Kenia River, AK	17 May 1985
SALMON, COHO	33	4	Jerry Lifton	Pulaski, NY	27 Sep. 1989
SHARK, BLUE	437	0	Peter Hyde	Catherine Bay, NSW, Australia	2 Oct. 1976
SHARK, HAMMERHEAD	991	0	Allen Ogle	Sarasota, FL	30 May 1982
SHARK, MAKO	1,115	0	Patrick Guillanton	Black River, Mauritius	16 Nov. 1988
SHARK, TIGER	1,780	0	Walter Maxwell	Cherry Grove, SC	14 June 1964
SHARK, WHITE	2,664	0	Alfred Dean	Ceduna, South Australia	21 Apr. 1959
SNAPPER, CUBERA	121	8	Mike Hebert	Cameron, LA	5 July 1982
SNAPPER, RED	461	1	E. Lane Nicholls	Destin, FL	1 Oct. 1985
STINGRAY	294	0	Iain Foulger	River Gambia, The Gambia	4 Nov. 1988
STURGEON, WHITE	468	0	Joey Pallotta III	Benicia, CA	9 July 1983
SWORDFISH	1,182	0	L. Marron	Iquique, Chile	17 May 1953
TARPON	283	4	Yvon Viktor Sebag	Sherbo Islands, Sierra Leone	16 Apr. 1991
TROUT, BROWN	35	15	Eugenio Cavaglia	Nahuel Huapi, Argentina	16 Dec. 1952
TROUT, LAKE	66	8	Rodney Harbeck	Great Bear Lake, NWT, Canada	19 July 1991
TUNA, BIGEYE (Pacific)	435	0	Dr. Russel V. A. Lee	Cabo Blanco, Peru	17 Apr. 1957
TUNA, BIGEYE (Atlantic)	375	8	Cecil Browne	Ocean City, MD	26 Apr. 1977
TUNA, BLUEFIN	1,496	0	Ken Fraser	Aulds Cove, Nova Scotia, Canada	26 Oct. 1979
WAHOO	155	8	William Bourne	San Salvador, Bahamas	3 Apr. 1990
WALLEYE	25	0	Mabry Harper	Old Hickory Lake, TN	1 Apr. 1960

FISHING

Oldest existing club   The Ellem Fishing Club was formed by a number of Edinburgh and Berwickshire gentlemen in Scotland in 1829. Its first annual general meeting was held on 29 Apr. 1830.

World Freshwater Championship   *The Confédération Internationale de la Pêche Sportive* (CIPS) championships were inaugurated as European championships in 1953 and recognized as world championships in 1957.

France won the European title in 1956 and 12 world titles between 1959 and 1990. Robert Tesse (France) took the individual title a record three times, 1959–60 and 1965.

The record weight (team) is 76.52 lbs. in 3 hrs. by West Germany on the Neckar at Mannheim, Germany on 21 Sep. 1980. The individual record is 37.45 lbs. by Wolf-Rüdiger Kremkus (West Germany) at Mannheim on 20 Sep. 1980. The most fish caught is 652, by Jacques Isenbaert (Belgium) at Danaújváros, Hungary on 27 Aug. 1967.

Fly fishing   World fly fishing championships were inaugurated by the CIPS in 1981. The most team titles is four, by Italy, 1982–84, 1986. The most individual titles is two, by Brian Leadbetter (Great Britain), 1987 and 1991.

Casting   The longest freshwater cast ratified under ICF (International Casting Federation) rules is 574 ft. 2 in., by Walter Kummerow (Germany),

---

Longest fight   The longest recorded individual fight with a fish is 37 hrs. by Bob Ploeger (USA) with a King salmon on 12–13 July 1989.

Largest single catch   The largest officially ratified fish ever caught on a rod was a man-eating great white shark (*Carcharodon carcharias*) weighing 2,664 lbs. and measuring 16 ft. 10 in. long, caught on a 130 lb. test line by Alf Dean at Denial Bay, near Ceduna, South Australia on 21 Apr. 1959. A great white shark weighing 3,388 lbs. was caught by Clive Green off Albany, Western Australia on 26 Apr. 1976 but will remain unratified, as whale meat was used as bait.

In June 1978 a great white shark measuring 20 ft. 4 in. in length and weighing over 5,000 lbs. was harpooned and landed by fishermen in the harbor of San Miguel, Azores.

The largest marine animal killed by *hand* harpoon was a blue whale 97 ft. in length, by Archer Davidson in Twofold Bay, New South Wales, Australia in 1910. Its tail flukes measured 20 ft. across and its jawbone 23 ft. 4 in.

The largest fish ever taken underwater was an 804 lb. giant black grouper or jewfish by Don Pinder of the Miami Triton Club, FL in 1955.

---

for the Bait Distance Double-Handed 30 g event held at Lenzerheide, Switzerland in the 1968 Championships.

At the currently contested weight of 17.7 g, known as 18 g Bait Distance, the longest Double-Handed cast is 457 ft. ½ in., by Kevin Carriero (USA) at Toronto, Ontario, Canada on 24 July 1984.

The longest Fly Distance Double-Handed cast is 319 ft. 1 in., by Wolfgang Feige (Germany) at Toronto, Ontario, Canada on 23 July 1984.

IGFA world records   The International Game Fish Association (IGFA) recognizes world records for game fish—both freshwater and saltwater—for a large number of species of fish. Its thousands of categories include all-tackle, various line classes and tippet classes for fly fishing. New records recognized by the IGFA reached an annual peak of 1,074 in 1984.

The heaviest freshwater category recognized by the IGFA is for the sturgeon, record weight 468 lbs., caught by Joey Pallotta III on 9 July 1983 off Benicia, CA.

FOOTBALL

Origins   On 6 Nov. 1869, Princeton and Rutgers Universities staged what is generally regarded as the first intercollegiate football game at New Brunswick, NJ. In Oct. 1873 the Intercollegiate Football Association (comprising Columbia, Princeton, Rutgers and Yale) was formed, with the purpose of standardizing rules. At this point football was a modified version of soccer. The first significant move towards today's style of play came when Harvard accepted an invitation to play McGill University (Montreal, Canada) in a series of three challenge matches, the first being in May 1874, under modified rugby rules. Walter Camp (1859–1925) is credited with organizing the basic format of the current game. Between 1880 and 1906, Camp sponsored the concepts of scrimmage lines, 11-man teams, reduction in field size, "downs" and yards to gain and a new scoring system. In 1902 the first Rose Bowl game was played in Pasadena, CA, and has been played there continuously since 1916.

The first professional game was played on 31 Aug. 1895 at Latrobe, PA, Latrobe YMCA defeating Jeanette Athletic Club 12–0. In 1920 the American Professional Football Association (APFA) was formed in Canton, OH. This organization was reorganized a number of times and in 1922 was renamed the National Football League (NFL). In 1944 the All-America Conference League was established, but eventually merged with the NFL in 1949. In 1959 the American Football League (AFL) was formed and competed with the NFL until a merger was agreed on in 1966, which led to the creation of the Super Bowl game, first played in January 1967. In 1970 the AFL and the NFL merged to form the present NFL.

NATIONAL FOOTBALL
LEAGUE (NFL) RECORDS

Most championships   The Green Bay Packers have won a record 11 NFL titles, 1929–31, 1936, 1939, 1944, 1961–62, 1965–67.

NFL RECORDS

MOST POINTS
Career 2,002, George Blanda (Chicago Bears, Baltimore Colts, Houston Oilers, Oakland Raiders), 1949–75. **Season** 176, Paul Hornung (Green Bay Packers), 1960. **Game** 40, Ernie Nevers (Chicago Cardinals), 28 Nov. 1929.

MOST TOUCHDOWNS
Career 126, Jim Brown (Cleveland Browns), 1957–65. **Season** 24, John Riggins (Washington Redskins), 1983. **Game** 6, Ernie Nevers (Chicago Cardinals), 28 Nov. 1929; William "Dub" Jones (Cleveland Browns) 25 Nov. 1951; Gale Sayers (Chicago Bears), 12 Dec. 1965.

MOST YARDS GAINED RUSHING
Career 16,726, Walter Payton (Chicago Bears), 1975–87. **Season** 2,105, Eric Dickerson (Los Angeles Rams), 1984. **Game** 275, Walter Payton (Chicago Bears), 20 Nov. 1977. Highest career average 5.22 yds. per game (2,359 yds. from 12,312 attempts), Jim Brown (Cleveland Browns), 1957–65.

MOST YARDS GAINED RECEIVING
Career 13,089, Steve Largent (Seattle Seahawks), 1976–89. **Season** 1,746, Charley Hennigan (Houston Oilers), 1961. **Game** 336, Willie "Flipper" Anderson (Los Angeles Rams), 26 Nov. 1989.

MOST YARDS GAINED PASSING
Career 47,003, Fran Tarkenton (Minnesota Vikings, New York Giants), 1961–78. **Season** 5,084, Dan Marino (Miami Dolphins), 1984. **Game** 554, Norm Van Brocklin (Los Angeles Rams), 28 Sep. 1951.

PASSING ATTEMPTS
Career 6,467, Fran Tarkenton (Minnesota Vikings, New York Giants), 1961–78. **Season** 655, Warren Moon (Houston Oilers), 1991. **Game** 68, George Blanda (Houston Oilers), 1 Nov. 1964.

MOST PASSES COMPLETED
Career 3,686, Fran Tarkenton (Minnesota Vikings, New York Giants), 1961–78. **Season** 404, Warren Moon (Houston Oilers), 1991. **Game** 42 (from 59 attempts), Richard Todd (New York Jets), 21 Sep. 1980. **Consecutive** 22, Joe Montana (San Francisco 49ers), 29 Nov. 1987 *v.* Cleveland Browns (5); 6 Dec. 1987 *v.* Green Bay Packers (17).

PASS RECEPTIONS
Career 819, Steve Largent (Seattle Seahawks), 1976–89. **Season** 106, Art Monk (Washington Redskins), 1984. **Game** 18, Tom Fears (Los Angeles Rams), 3 Dec. 1950.

FIELD GOALS
Career 373, Jan. Stenerud (Kansas City Chiefs, Green Bay Packers, Minnesota Vikings), 1967–85. **Season** 35, Ali Haji-Sheikh (New York Giants), 1983. **Game** 7, Jim Bakken (St. Louis Cardinals), 24 Sep. 1967; Rich Karlis (Minnesota Vikings), 5 Nov. 1989.

PUNTING
Career 1,154, Dave Jennings (New York Giants, New York Jets), 1974–87. **Season** 114, Bob Parsons (Chicago Bears), 1981. **Game** 15, John Teltschik (Philadelphia Eagles *v.* New York Giants), 6 Dec. 1987.

SACKS
Career 121.5, Lawrence Taylor (New York Giants), 1982–91. **Season** 22, Mark Gastineau (New York Jets), 1984. **Game** 7, Derrick Thomas (Kansas City Chiefs *v.* Seattle Seahawks), 11 Nov. 1990.

MOST INTERCEPTIONS
Career 81, Paul Krause (Washington Redskins; Minnesota Vikings), 1964–79. **Season** 14, Dick "Night Train" Lane (Los Angeles Rams), 1952. **Game** 4; 16 players have achieved this feat.

MOST PASS COMPLETIONS. Warren Moon of the Houston Oilers completed a record 404 passes from a record 655 attempts in the 1991 NFL season. (Photo: Allsport USA/Briam Masck)

Most consecutive wins (regular season and playoffs)   The Chicago Bears have won 18 consecutive games twice, in 1933–34 and 1941–42. This was matched by the Miami Dolphins in 1972–73 and by the San Francisco 49ers in 1989–90. The most consecutive games without defeat is 25, by the Canton Bulldogs (22 wins and 3 ties) in 1921–23.

Most games played   George Frederick Blanda (b. 17 Sep. 1927) played in a record 340 games in a record 26 seasons in the NFL, for the Chicago Bears (1948–58), the Baltimore Colts (1950), the Houston Oilers (1960–66), and the Oakland Raiders (1967–75).

The most consecutive games played is 282, by Jim Marshall for the Cleveland Browns (1960) and the Minnesota Vikings (1961–79).

Longest run from scrimmage   Anthony Drew "Tony" Dorsett (b. 7 Apr. 1954) completed a touchdown after a run of 99 yards for the Dallas Cowboys *v.* the Minnesota Vikings on 3 Jan. 1983.

Longest field goal   63 yards by Thomas John "Tom" Dempsey (b. 12 Jan. 1947) for the New Orleans Saints *v.* the Detroit Lions, 8 Nov. 1970.

Longest pass completion   Pass completions for a touchdown of 99 yards were achieved by: Frank Filchok (to Andy Farkas), Washington Redskins *v.* Pittsburgh Steelers, 15 Oct. 1939; George Izo (to Bobby Mitchell), Washington Redskins *v.* Cleveland Browns, 15 Sep. 1963; Karl Sweetan (to

Pat Studstill), Detroit Lions v. Baltimore Colts, 16 Oct. 1966; Sonny Jurgensen (to Gerry Allen), Washington Redskins v. Chicago Bears, 15 Sep. 1968; Jim Plunkett (to Cliff Branch), Los Angeles Raiders v. Washington Redskins, 2 Oct. 1983; Ron Jaworski (to Mike Quick), Philadelphia Eagles v. Atlanta Falcons, 10 Nov. 1985.

Longest punt   98 yards by Steve O'Neal for the New York Jets v. the Denver Broncos, 21 Sep. 1969.

Consecutive games *Scoring*   181, by Jim Breech for the Oakland Raiders, 1979, and the Cincinnati Bengals, 1980–91.

Scoring touchdowns   18, by Lenny Moore for the Baltimore Colts, 1963–65.

Pass receptions   177, by Steve Largent for the Seattle Seahawks, 1977–89.

Field goals   24, by Kevin Butler for the Chicago Bears, 1988–89.

Greatest comeback in NFL history   On 7 Dec., 1980, the San Francisco 49ers, playing at home, trailed the New Orleans Saints 35–7 at halftime. In the 2nd half, the 49ers, led by Joe Montana, scored 31 unanswered points to win the game 38–35. The 49ers had overcome a deficit of 28 points, the largest in NFL history.

Coaches   The winningest coach in NFL history was George Stanley Halas (1895–1983), whose Chicago Bears teams won 325 games (and 7 NFL titles) to 151 losses and 31 ties while he was coach in 1920–29, 1933–42, 1946–55 and 1958–67. The highest winning percentage was .740 percent, achieved by Vincent Thomas "Vince" Lombardi (1913–70): 105 wins, 35 losses and 6 ties with the Green Bay Packers, 1959–67, and the Washington Redskins, 1969.

Most seasons   40, George Halas, with the Decatur/Chicago Staleys/ Chicago Bears (1920–29, 1933–42, 1946–55, 1958–67).

THE SUPER BOWL

The Super Bowl was first held in 1967 between the winners of the NFL and AFL championships. Since 1970 it has been contested by the winners of the National and American Conferences of the NFL. The most wins is four, by the Pittsburgh Steelers in 1974–75, 1978–79, coached by Chuck Noll on each occasion, and by the San Francisco 49ers in 1981, 1984, 1988 and 1989, coached by Bill Walsh (1981, 1984, 1988) and George Seifert (1989).

Most appearances   The most Super Bowl appearances is five, by the Dallas Cowboys (2 wins, 3 losses), 1970, 1971, 1975, 1977–78, and by the Miami Dolphins (2 wins, 3 losses), 1971–73, 1982, 1984.
   The most appearances by a player is also five, shared by seven players: Marv Fleming (Green Bay Packers 1966–67, Miami Dolphins 1971–73); Larry Cole (Dallas Cowboys 1970–71, 1975, 1977–78); Cliff Harris (Dallas Cowboys 1970–71, 1975, 1977–78); D.D. Lewis (Dallas Cowboys 1970–71, 1975, 1977–1978); Preston Pearson (Baltimore Colts 1968, Pittsburgh Steel-

ers 1974, Dallas Cowboys 1975, 1977–78); Charlie Waters (Dallas Cowboys 1970–71, 1975, 1977–1978); Rayfield Wright (Dallas Cowboys 1970–71, 1975, 1977–78).

Don Shula has coached six Super Bowls to set the all-time mark: Baltimore Colts, 1968; Miami Dolphins, 1971–73, 1982, 1984. He won two games and lost four.

Highest scores   The highest aggregate score was 66 points, when the Pittsburgh Steelers beat the Dallas Cowboys 35–31 on 21 Jan. 1979. The highest team score and record victory margin was when the San Francisco 49ers beat the Denver Broncos 55–10 in New Orleans, LA on 28 Jan. 1990. In their 42–10 victory over the Denver Broncos on 31 Jan. 1988, the Washington Redskins scored a record 35 points in the second quarter. The narrowest margin of victory was one point, when the New York Giants defeated the Buffalo Bills 20–19 on 27 Jan. 1991.

Most valuable player   Joseph C. "Joe" Montana, Jr. (b. 11 June 1956), quarterback of the San Francisco 49ers, has been voted the Super Bowl MVP on a record three occasions: Super Bowl XVI, XIX, and XXIV.

COLLEGE FOOTBALL (NCAA)

Origins   At the turn of the 20th century, football's popularity was rising rapidly; however, with the increased participation came a rise in serious injuries and even some deaths. In December 1905, 13 universities outlined a plan to establish an organization to standardize playing rules. On 28 Dec., the Intercollegiate Athletic Association of the United States (IAAUS) was founded in New York City with 62 charter members. The IAAUS was renamed the National Collegiate Athletic Assocation (NCAA) in 1910 and first began to keep statistics for football in 1937. The oldest collegiate series still contested is that between Yale and Princeton, first played in November 1873, three years before the formation of the Intercollegiate Football Association. The first Rose Bowl game was held in Pasadena, CA on 1 Jan. 1902, when Michigan beat Stanford 49–0. The National Collegiate Athletic Association began classifying college teams into Divisions I, II and III in 1973. Five years later Division I was subdivided into 1-A and 1-AA.

Career Records (Divisions 1-A, 1-AA, II and III)   *Points scored* 474, Joe Dudek, Plymouth State (Div. III), 1982–85.

Rushing (yards)   6,320, Johnny Bailey, Texas A&I (Div. II), 1986–89.

Passing (yards)   15,031, Ty Detmer, Brigham Young (Div I-A), 1988–91.

Receptions (yards)   4,693, Jerry Rice, Mississippi Valley (Div. 1-AA), 1981–84.

Receptions (most)   301, Jerry Rice, Mississippi Valley (Div. 1-AA), 1981–84.

NCAA DIVISION 1-A INDIVIDUAL RECORDS

POINTS

Game	48	Howard Griffith (Illinois v. Southern Illinois; 8 touchdowns)	22 Sep. 1990
Season	234	Barry Sanders (Oklahoma State; 39 touchdowns in 11 games)	1988
Career	423	Roman Anderson (Houston; 70 field goals, 213 point-after-touchdowns)	1988–91

TOTAL YARDAGE

Game	732	David Klingler (Houston v. Arizona State; 716 passing, 16 rushing)	1 Dec. 1990
Season	5,221	David Klingler (Houston; 5,140 passing, 81 rushing)	1990
Career	14,665	Ty Detmer (Brigham Young; 15,031 passing, −366 rushing)	1988–91

YARDS GAINED RUSHING

Game	396	Tony Sands (Kansas v. Missouri)	23 Nov. 1991
Season	2,628	Barry Sanders (Oklahoma State; 344 rushes in 11 games, record av. 238.9)	1988
Career	6,082	Tony Dorset (Pittsburgh; 1,074 rushes)	1973–76

YARDS GAINED PASSING

Game	716	David Klingler (Houston v. Arizona State)	1 Dec. 1990
Season	5,188	Ty Detmer (Brigham Young)	1990
Career	15,031	Ty Detmer (Brigham Young; completed 958 of 1,530)	1988–91

PASS COMPLETIONS

Game	48	David Klingler (Houston v. SMU)	20 Oct. 1990
Season	374	David Klingler (Houston)	1990
Career	958	Ty Detmer (Brigham Young; 1,530 attempts)	1988–91

TOUCHDOWN PASSES

Game	11	David Klingler (Houston v. Eastern Washington)	17 Nov. 1990
Season	54	David Klingler (Houston)	1990
Career	121	Ty Detmer (Brigham Young)	1988–91

PASS RECEPTIONS

Game ....22 Jay Miller (Brigham Young *v.* New Mexico; 263 yards)................................3 Nov. 1973
Season ....142 Emmanuel Hazard (Houston)..1969
Career ....263 Terance Mathis (New Mexico) 1985–87, 1989

YARDS GAINED RECEIVING

Game ....349 Chuck Hughes (UTEP *v.* North Texas; caught 10)..............................18 Sep. 1965
Season ......1,779 Howard Twilley (Tulsa; caught 134 in 10 games) 1965
Career ......4,254 Terance Mathis (New Mexico) 1985–87, 1989

PASS INTERCEPTIONS

Game ....5 Dan Rebsch (Miami [Ohio] *v.* Western Michigan; 88 yards; ....4 Nov. 1972
    three others with less yards)
Season ....14 Al Worley (Washington; 130 yards, in 10 games) 1968
Career ....29 Al Brosky (Illinois; 356 yards, 27 games) 1950–52

TOUCHDOWNS (Receiving)

Game ....6 Tim Delaney (San Diego State *v.* New Mexico State)..........................15 Nov. 1969
Season ....22 Emmanuel Hazard (Houston)..1989
Career ....38 Clarkston Hines (Duke) 1986–89

FIELD GOALS

Game ....7 Mike Prindle (West Michigan *v.* Marshall) ....29 Sep. 1984
    7 Dale Klein (Nebraska *v.* Missouri)..19 Oct. 1985
Season ....29 John Lee (UCLA)..1984
Career ....80 Jeff Jaeger (Washington)..1983–86
Consecutive ....30 Chuck Nelson (Washington) 1981–82

TOUCHDOWNS

Game ....8 Howard Griffith (Illinois *v.* Southern Illinois) ....22 Sep. 1990
Season ....39 Barry Sanders (Oklahoma State)..1988
Career ....65 Anthony Thompson (Indiana) 1986–89

Field goals (game) 8, Goran Lingmerth, Northern Arizona (Div. 1-AA). Booting 8 out of 8 kicks, Lingmerth set the record on 25 Oct. 1986 *v.* Idaho.

Longest plays *Run from scrimmage* 99 yards by four players: Gale Sayers (Kansas *v.* Nebraska), 1963; Max Anderson (Arizona State *v.* Wyoming), 1967; Ralph Thompson (West Texas State *v.* Wichita State), 1970; Kelsey Finch (Tennessee *v.* Florida), 1977.

Field goal 67 yards by three players: Russell Erxleben (Texas *v.* Rice), 1977; Steve Little (Arkansas *v.* Texas), 1977; Joe Williams (Wichita State *v.* Southern Illinois), 1978. Ove Johansson kicked a 69-yard field goal for Abilene Christian University *v.* East Texas State on 16 Oct. 1976, but this was in an NAIA game.

Pass completion 99 yards on eight occasions by seven players: Fred Owens (to Jack Ford), Portland *v.* St. Mary's, CA, 1947; Bo Burris (to Warren McVea), Houston *v.* Washington State, 1966; Colin Clapton (to Eddie Jenkins), Holy Cross *v.* Boston U, 1970; Terry Peel (to Robert Ford), Houston *v.* Syracuse, 1970; Terry Peel (to Robert Ford), Houston *v.* San Diego State, 1972; Chris Collingsworth (to Derrick Gaffney), Florida *v.* Rice, 1977; Scott Ankrom (to James Maness), TCU *v.* Rice, 1984; Gino Torretta (to Horace Copeland), Miami *v.* Arkansas, 1991.

Punt 99 yards by Pat Brady, Nevada-Reno *v.* Loyola, CA in 1950.

TY DETMER. Ty Detmer holds NCAA career records for most yards gained passing, 15,031; most pass completions, 958; most touchdown passes, 121; and most total yardage, 14,665. Here he is seen in action for Brigham Young in 1990, the year he won the Heisman Memorial Trophy as the top college football player. (Photo: Allsport/Mike Powell)

Highest score The most points ever scored in a college game is 222, by Georgia Tech *v*. Cumberland College (0) of Lebanon, TN on 7 Oct. 1916. Tech set records for 63 points in a quarter, 32 touchdowns, and 30 points after touch-down in this game.

Longest streak The University of Oklahoma won 47 successive games from 1953 to 1957, when they were beaten 7–0 by Notre Dame. The longest unbeaten streak is 63 (59 won, 4 tied) by Washington from 1907 to 1917, ended by a 27–0 loss to California.

ROSE BOWL (both photos above). The oldest college bowl game is the Rose Bowl, which was first played on 1 Jan. 1902 at Tournament Park, Pasadena, CA, when Michigan beat Stanford 49–0. The bowl has been won most times by the University of Southern California (USC), 19. (Photos: Allsport/Mike Powell/Tim Defrisco)

Coaches   In Division 1-A competition, Paul "Bear" Bryant (1913–83) won more games than any other coach, with 323 wins over 38 years: Maryland 1945, Kentucky 1946–53, Texas A&M 1954–57 and Alabama 1958–82. He led Alabama to five national titles and 15 bowl wins, including 7 Sugar Bowls. The best win percentage in Division 1-A was 0.881, by Knute Rockne (1888–1931), with 105 wins, 12 losses and 5 ties, 12,847 points for and 667 against, at Notre Dame 1918–30. In overall NCAA competition, Eddie Robinson, Grambling (Division 1-AA) holds the mark for most victories, with 371 through 1991. In overall NCAA competition, Mark Duffner compiled a .917 record (60 wins, 5 losses and one tie) in six seasons with Holy Cross (Div. I-AA), 1987–91.

Record attendances   The highest attendances at college football games were estimated crowds of 120,000 at Soldier Field, Chicago, IL on 26 Nov. 1927 when Notre Dame beat Southern California 7–6, and on 13 Oct. 1928 when Notre Dame beat Navy 7–0. The highest average attendance for home games is 105,588 for the six games played by Michigan in 1985.

National College Football Champions   The most wins in the national journalists' poll, established in 1936, to determine the college team of the year is eight by Notre Dame, 1943, 1946–47, 1949, 1966, 1973, 1977 and 1988.

Bowl games   The oldest college bowl game is the Rose Bowl. It was first played on 1 Jan. 1902 at Tournament Park, Pasadena, CA, when Michigan beat Stanford 49–0. The second game did not take place until 1916, and the game has been played continuously since. The University of Southern California (USC) has a record 19 wins in the Rose Bowl. The University of Alabama has made a record 44 bowl appearances and had 24 wins. Most wins in the other "big four" bowl games: Orange Bowl: 11, Oklahoma; Sugar Bowl: 7, Alabama; Cotton Bowl: 9, Texas.

Heisman Memorial Trophy   This award has been given annually since 1935 by the Downtown Athletic Club of New York to the top college football player as determined by a poll of journalists. It was originally called the D.A.C. Trophy but the name was changed in 1936. Its full title is the John W. Heisman Memorial Trophy and it is named after the first athletic director of the Downtown Athletic Club. The only double winner has been Archie Griffin of Ohio State, 1974–75. The University of Notre Dame has had more Heisman Trophy winners than any other school, with seven selections.

GAELIC FOOTBALL

Origins   The game developed from inter-parish "free for alls," with no time limit, specific playing area, or rules. The earliest reported match was Meath v. Louth, at Slane, Ireland in 1712. Standardization came with the formation of the Gaelic Athletic Association in Thurles, Ireland on 1 Nov. 1884.

All-Ireland Championships   The greatest number of All-Ireland Championships won by one team is 30, by Ciarraidhe (Kerry) between 1903 and 1986. The greatest number of successive wins is four, by Wexford (1915–18) and Kerry twice (1929–32, 1978–81).

The most finals contested by an individual is ten, including eight wins by the Kerry players Pat Spillane, Paudie O'Shea and Denis Moran, 1975–76, 1978–82, 1984–86.

The highest team score in a final was when Dublin, 27 (5 goals, 12 points), beat Armagh, Great Britain, 15 (3 goals, 6 points), on 25 Sep. 1977. The highest combined score was 45 points, when Cork (26) beat Galway (19) in 1973. A goal equals three points.

The highest individual score in an All-Ireland final has been 2 goals, 6 points by Jimmy Keaveney (Dublin) *v.* Armagh, Great Britain, in 1977, and by Michael Sheehy (Kerry) *v.* Dublin in 1979.

Largest crowd   The record crowd was 90,556 for the Down *v.* Offaly final at Croke Park, Dublin in 1961.

GOLF

Origins   The Chinese Nationalist Golf Association claims the game is of Chinese origin (*qui wan*—the ball-hitting game) in the third or second century B.C. There were official ordinances prohibiting a ball game with clubs in Belgium and Holland from 1360. Gutta percha balls succeeded feather balls in 1848, and by 1902 were in turn succeeded by rubber-cored balls, invented in 1899 by Coburn Haskell (USA). Steel shafts were authorized in the United States in 1925.

United States   The first evidence of golf in the United States is that the game was played in Charleston, NC and in Virginia, in the mid-18th century. The first club organized for the playing of golf in North America was in Canada, when the Royal Montreal Golf Club was formed on Nov. 4 1873. The United States Golf Association (USGA) was founded in 1894 as the governing body of golf in the United States.

Oldest club   The oldest club of which there is written evidence is the Gentlemen Golfers (now the Honourable Company of Edinburgh Golfers) formed in March 1744—ten years prior to the institution of the Royal and Ancient Club of St. Andrews, Fife, Scotland. However, the Royal Burgess Golfing Society of Edinburgh, Great Britain claims to have been founded in 1735.

United States   Two golf clubs claim to be the first established in the United States: the Foxberg Golf Club, Clarion Co., PA (1887) and St. Andrews Golf Club of Yonkers, NY (1888).

Highest course   The Tuctu Golf Club in Morococha, Peru, is 14,335 ft. above sea level at its lowest point. Golf has, however, been played in Tibet at an altitude of over 16,000 ft.

Longest course   The world's longest course is the par-77 8,325 yd International Golf Club (see also at right) in Bolton, MA from the "Tiger" tees, remodeled in 1969 by Robert Trent Jones.

Floyd Satterlee Rood used the entire United States as a course, when he played from the Pacific surf to the Atlantic surf from 14 Sep. 1963 to 3 Oct. 1964 in 114,737 strokes. He lost 3,511 balls on the 3,397.7 mile trail.

Lowest course   The Furnace Creek course in Death Valley, CA is 220 ft. below sea level.

Longest drives   In officially regulated long driving contests over level ground the greatest distance recorded is 437 yds. 2 ft. 4 in. by Jack L. Hamm (USA), at an altitude of 5,280 ft., on 25 Oct. 1989 in Denver, CO. The longest recorded drive in a regulated competition at sea level is 411 yds. by Cary B. Schuman (USA) at the Navy Marine Golf Course, Oahu, HI on 7 May 1989.

On an airport runway, Kelly Murray (Canada) drove a Wilson Ultra 432 ball 684.8 yds. at Fairmont Hot Springs, British Columbia, Canada on 25 Sep. 1990.

The women's record is held by Helen Dobson (Great Britain), who drove a Titleist Pinnacle 531 yds. at RAF Honnington, Suffolk, Great Britain on 31 Oct. 1987.

The longest recorded drive on an ordinary course is one of 515 yds. by Michael Hoke Austin (b. 17 Feb. 1910) of Los Angeles, CA, in the US National Seniors Open Championship at Las Vegas, NV on 25 Sep. 1974. Austin, 6 ft. 2 in. tall and weighing 210 lbs., drove the ball to within a yard of the green on the par-4 450-yd. fifth hole of the Winterwood Course and it rolled 65 yds. past the flagstick. He was aided by an estimated 35 mph tailwind.

A drive of 2,640 yds. (1½ miles) across ice was achieved by an Australian meteorologist named Nils Lied at Mawson Base, Antarctica in 1962.

On the moon the energy expended on a mundane 300 yd. drive would achieve, craters permitting, a distance of 1 mile.

Longest putt   The longest recorded holed putt in a major tournament was one of 86 ft. on the vast 13th green at the Augusta National, GA by Cary Middlecoff (USA; b. 6 Jan. 1921) in the 1955 Masters Tournament.

Robert Tyre "Bobby" Jones, Jr. (1902–71) was reputed to have sunk a putt in excess of 100 ft. at the fifth green in the first round of the 1927 Open at St. Andrews.

Bob Cook (USA) sank a putt measured at 140 ft. 2¾ in. on the 18th at St. Andrews in the International Fourball Pro Am Tournament on 1 Oct. 1976.

SCORES

Lowest nine holes   Nine holes in 25 (4, 3, 3, 2, 3, 3, 1, 4, 2) was recorded by A.J. "Bill" Burke in a round in 57 (32+25) on the 6,389 yd. par-71 Normandie course at St. Louis, MO on 20 May 1970.

The professional tournament record is 27, by Mike Souchak (USA; b. 10 May 1927) for the second nine (par-35), first round of the 1955 Texas Open (see Lowest 72 holes); Andy North (USA; b. 9 Mar. 1950), for the second nine (par-34), first round, 1975 B.C. Open at En-Joie Golf Club, Endicott, NY; José Maria Canizares (Spain; b. 18 Feb. 1947), for the first nine, third round, in the 1978 Swiss Open on the 6,811 yd. Crans Golf Club, Crans-sur-Seine; and Robert Lee (Great Britain; b. 12 Oct. 1961), for the first nine,

LOWEST SCORE. The lowest 18-hole total in a PGA Tour competition is 59, which has been achieved twice. The second player to shoot 59 was Chip Beck, in the third round of the Las Vegas Invitational, on the 72-par 6,979 yd. Sunrise GC course, Las Vegas, NV on 11 Oct. 1991. (Photo: Allsport)

first round, in the Monte Carlo Open on the 6,249 yd. Mont Agel course on 28 June 1985.

Lowest 18 holes *Men* At least four players have played a long course (over 6,561 yds.) in a score of 58, most recently Monte Carlo Money (USA; b. 3 Dec. 1954), at the par-72, 6,607 yd. Las Vegas Municipal Golf Club, NV on 11 Mar. 1981.

Alfred Edward Smith (1903–85) scored 55 (15 under par 70) on his 18-hole home course of 4,248 yds. on 1 Jan. 1936, scoring 4, 2, 3, 4, 2, 4, 3, 4, 3=29 out, and 2, 3, 3, 3, 3, 2, 5, 4, 1=26 in.

The PGA tournament record for 18 holes is 59 (30+29), by Al Geiberger (b. 1 Sep. 1937) in the second round of the Danny Thomas Classic, on the 72-par 7,249 yd. Colonial Golf Club course, Memphis, TN on 10 June 1977, and by Chip Beck in the third round of the Las Vegas Invitational, on the 72-par 6,979 yd. Sunrise Golf Club course, Las Vegas, NV on 11 Oct. 1991.

Other golfers to have recorded 59 over 18 holes in major non-PGA tournaments include: Samuel Jackson "Sam" Snead (USA; b. 27 May 1912), at the Sam Snead Festival (third round) at White Sulphur Springs, WV on 16 May 1959; Gary Player (South Africa; b. 1 Nov. 1935), in the second round of the Brazilian Open in Rio de Janeiro on 29 Nov. 1974; David Jagger (Great Britain; b. 9 June 1949) in a Pro-Am tournament prior to the 1973 Nigerian Open at Ikoyi Golf Club, Lagos; and Miguel Martin (Spain) in the Argentine Southern Championship at Mar. del Plata on 27 Feb. 1987.

Women The lowest recorded score on an 18-hole course (over 5,600 yds.) for a woman is 62 (30+32) by Mary Kathryn "Mickey" Wright (USA; b. 14

Feb. 1935) on the Hogan Park Course (par-71, 6,286 yds.) at Midland, TX, in November 1964; Vicki Fergon at the 1984 San Jose Classic, San Jose, CA; Janice Arnold (New Zealand) (31 + 31) on the Coventry Golf Course (5,815 yds.) on 24 Sep. 1990; and Laura Davies (Great Britain) (32 + 30) at the Rail Golf Club, Springfield, IL on 31 Aug. 1991.

Wanda Morgan (b. 22 Mar. 1910) recorded a score of 60 (31 + 29) on the Westgate and Birchington Golf Club course, Kent, Great Britain, over 18 holes (5,002 yds.) on 11 July 1929.

Lowest 36 holes   The record for 36 holes is 122 (59 + 63), by Sam Snead in the 1959 Sam Snead Festival on 16–17 May 1959.

Horton Smith (1908–63), twice US Masters Champion, scored 121 (63 + 58) on a short course on 21 Dec. 1928 (see Lowest 72 holes).

Lowest 72 holes   The lowest recorded score on a first class course is 255 (29 under par), by Leonard Peter Tupling (Great Britain; b. 6 Apr. 1950) in the Nigerian Open at Ikoyi Golf Club, Lagos in February 1981, made up of 63, 66, 62 and 64 (average 63.75 per round).

The lowest 72 holes in a PGA tour event is 257 (60, 68, 64, 65), by Mike Souchak in the 1955 Texas Open at San Antonio.

The 72 holes record on the European tour is 258 (64, 69, 60, 65) by David Llewellyn (Wales; b. 18 Nov. 1951) in the Biarritz Open on 1–3 Apr. 1988. This was equaled by Ian Woosnam (Wales; b. 2 Mar. 1958) (66, 67, 65, 60) in the Monte Carlo Open on 4–7 July 1990.

Trish Johnson scored 242 (64, 60, 60, 58; 21 under par) in the Bloor Homes Eastleigh Classic at the Fleming Park Course (4,402 yds.) at Eastleigh, Great Britain on 22–25 July 1987.

Horton Smith scored 245 (63, 58, 61 and 63) for 72 holes on the 4,700 yd. course (par-64) at Catalina Country Club, CA to win the Catalina Open on 21–23 Dec. 1928.

Most shots under par   31, by two players—Andrew Magee and D.A. Weibring—at the 90-hole 1991 Las Vegas Invitational, 9–13 Oct. 1991. Magee won the tournament in a playoff.

Fastest rounds *Individual*   With such variations in lengths of courses, speed records, even for rounds under par, are of little comparative value. The fastest round played with the golf ball coming to rest before each new stroke is 27 min. 9 sec., by James Carvill (b. 13 Oct. 1965) at Warrenpoint Golf Course, County Down, Northern Ireland (18 holes, 6,154 yds.) on 18 June 1987.

Team   Forty-eight players completed the 18-hole 7,108 yd. Kyalami course, near Johannesburg, South Africa in 9 min. 51 sec. on 23 Feb. 1988, using only one ball. They scored 73!

Slowest rounds   The slowest stroke-play tournament round was one of 6 hrs. 45 min., taken by South Africa in the first round of the 1972 World Cup at the Royal Melbourne Golf Club, Australia. This was a four-ball medal round; everything holed out.

Most holes in 24 hours *On foot*   Ian Colston, 35, played 22 rounds plus five holes (401 holes in all) at Bendigo Golf Club, Victoria, Australia (par-73, 6,061 yds.) on 27–28 Nov. 1971.

Largest green   Probably the largest green in the world is that of the par-6 695 yd. fifth hole at International Golf Club, Bolton, MA with an area greater than 28,000 ft.^{2}.

Longest hole   The longest hole in the world is the 7th hole (par-7) of the Sano Course, Satsuki Golf Club, Japan, which measures 909 yds.

Most shots for one hole   A woman player in the qualifying round of the Shawnee Invitational for Ladies at Shawnee-on-Delaware, PA, *c.* 1912, took 166 strokes for the short 130 yd. 16th hole. Her tee shot went into the Binniekill River and the ball floated. She put out in a boat with her helpful but statistically minded husband at the oars. She eventually beached the ball 1½ miles downstream but was not yet out of the woods. She had to play through one on the home run.

Ray Ainsley of Ojai, CA took 19 strokes for the par-4 16th hole during the second round of the US Open at Cherry Hills Country Club, Denver, CO on 10 June 1938. Most of the strokes were used in trying to extricate the ball from a brook.

Hans Merell of Mogadore, OH took 19 strokes on the par-3 16th (222 yd.) during the third round of the Bing Crosby National Tournament at Cypress Point Club, Del Monte, CA on 17 Jan. 1959.

World one-club record   Thad Daber (USA), with a 6-iron, played the 6,037 yd. Lochmore Golf Club course, Cary, NC in 70 to win the 1987 World One-club Championship.

Highest shot on Earth   Ian Evans (Canada) played a shot from near the Independencia refuge hut on Mt. Aconcagua (20,341), Argentina on 1 Apr. 1991.

Fastest round of golf played on the PGA tour   At the 1977 Heritage Classic at Hilton Head, SC, Gary McCord and Bill Mallon played their fourth round of golf in 1 hr. 27 min., still the fastest time ever played on the PGA tour.

Golf ball balancing   Lang Martin balanced seven golf balls vertically without adhesive at Charlotte, NC on 9 Feb. 1980.

Most balls hit in one hour   The most balls driven in one hour, over 100 yds. and into a target area, is 1,536, by Noel Hunt at Shrigley Hall, Pott Shrigley, Great Britain on 2 May 1990.

Using golf carts   David Cavalier played 846 holes at Arrowhead Country Club, North Canton, OH (9 holes, 3,013 yds.) on 6–7 Aug. 1990.

Eric Freeman played 429 holes in 12 hours on the 6,231 yd. course at Glen Head Country Club, New York City on 29 July 1991.

Most holes played in a week   Steve Hylton played 1,128 holes at the Mason Rudolph Golf Club (6,060 yds.), Clarksville, TN from 25–31 Aug. 1980. Using a golf cart for transport, Colin Young completed 1,260 holes at Patshull Park Golf Club (6,412 yds.), Pattingham, Shropshire from 2–9 July 1988.

MEN'S CHAMPIONSHIP RECORDS

Grand Slam   In 1930 Bobby Jones won the United States and British Opens and the United States and British Amateur Championships. These four victories were christened the Grand Slam of golf. In 1960 the professional Grand Slam (the Masters, US Open, British Open and Professional Golfers Association [PGA] Championships) gained recognition when Arnold Palmer won the first two legs, the Masters and the US Open. However, he did not complete the set of victories, and the Grand Slam has still not been attained. Ben Hogan came closest to succeeding in 1951, when he won the first three legs, but he could not return to the United States from Britain in time for the PGA Championship.

The four grand slam events are also known as "the majors." Jack Nicklaus (b. 21 Jan. 1940) has won the most major championships with 18 professional titles (6 Masters, 4 US Opens, 3 British Opens and 5 PGA Championships). Additionally, Nicklaus has won two US Amateur titles, which are often included in calculating major championship victories.

The Masters   (played on the 6,980 yd. Augusta National Golf Course, GA, first in 1934)

Most wins   Jack Nicklaus has won six green jackets (1963, 1965–66, 1972, 1975, 1986). Two players have won consecutive Masters: Jack Nicklaus (1965–66) and Nick Faldo (Great Britain; 1989–90).

Lowest score   The lowest score for any round is 63, by Nicholas Raymond Leige Price (Zimbabwe; b. 28 Jan. 1957) in 1986.

Lowest total aggregate   271, by: Jack Nicklaus (67, 71, 64, 69) in 1965, and Raymond Loran Floyd (65, 66, 70, 70) in 1976.

Oldest and youngest winners   The oldest winner of the Masters was Jack Nicklaus, age 46 years 81 days in 1986. Severiano Ballesteros (Spain) was the youngest player to win the Masters, at 23 years 2 days in 1980.

US Open   (inaugurated 1895)

Most wins   Four players have won the title four times: Willie Anderson (1901, 1903–05), Bobby Jones (1923, 1926, 1929–30), Ben Hogan (1948, 1950–51, 1953) and Jack Nicklaus (1962, 1967, 1972, 1980). The only player to gain three successive titles was Willie Anderson, from 1903 to 1905.

LOWEST SCORE. Raymond Floyd (b. 4 Sep. 1942) holds the record for lowest aggregate score for the Masters, with 271 in 1976. He continues to press for honors in the majors, notably being runner-up in the Masters in 1990 (seen here) and 1992. (Photo: Allsport/ David Cannon)

Lowest score The lowest score for any round is 63, by Johnny Miller (b. 29 Apr. 1947) on the 6,921 yd. par-71 Oakmont Country Club, PA on 17 June 1973; by Jack Nicklaus and Tom Weiskopf (USA; b. 9 Nov. 1942), both on 12 June 1980 at Baltusrol Country Club, Springfield, NJ.

Lowest total aggregate 272 (63, 71, 70, 68) by Jack Nicklaus on the lower course (7,015 yds.) at Baltusrol Country Club, 12–15 June 1980.

Oldest and youngest winners The oldest US Open champion was Hale Irwin (b. 3 June 1945), at 45 yrs. 15 days on 18 June 1990. The youngest winner of the Open was John J. McDermott at 19 years 317 days in 1911; this is also the record for the youngest winner of any PGA event in the United States.

British Open (inaugurated 1860, Prestwick, Strathclyde, Scotland)

Most wins Harry Vardon won a record six titles, in 1896, 1898–99, 1908, 1911 and 1914. Tom Morris, Jr. is the only player to win four successive British Opens, from 1868 to 1872 (the event was not held in 1871).

Lowest score The lowest score for the first nine holes is 28, by Denis Durnian (b. 30 June 1950), at Royal Birkdale, Southport, Great Britain in the second round on 15 July 1983. The lowest score for any round is 63, by Mark Stephen Hayes (USA; b. 12 July 1949) at Turnberry, Strathclyde, Scotland, on 7 July 1977; Isao Aoki (Japan; b. 31 Aug. 1942), at Muirfield, Lothian, Scotland on 19 July 1980; Gregory John Norman (Australia; b. 10 Feb. 1955), at Turnberry, on 18 July 1986; Paul Broadhurst (Great Britain; b. 14 Aug. 1965) at St. Andrews, Fife, Scotland on 21 July 1990 ; and Joseph Martin "Jodie" Mudd (USA; b. 23 Apr. 1960) at Royal Birkdale on 21 July 1991.

Lowest total aggregate   268 (68, 70, 65, 65) by Thomas Sturges Watson (USA; b. 4 Sep. 1949) at Turnberry, in July 1977.

Youngest and oldest winners   The youngest winner of the British Open was Tom Morris, Jr. (1851–75) at Prestwick, Strathclyde, Scotland, in 1868 at the age of 17 yrs. 249 days. The oldest British Open champion was "Old

PGA TOUR ALL-TIME SCORING RECORDS*

Lowest score (9 holes)	27	Mike Souchak, Texas Open (back nine)	1955
	27	Andy North, B.C. Open (back nine)	1975
Lowest score (18 holes)	59	Al Geiberger, Danny Thomas Memphis Classic (2nd round)	1977
	59	Chip Beck, Las Vegas Invitational (3rd round)	1991
Lowest score (36 holes)	125	Ron Streck, Texas Open (3rd and 4th rounds)	1988
	125	Blaine McCallister, Hardee's Golf Classic (2nd and 3rd rounds)	1988
Lowest score (54 holes)	189	Chandler Harper, Texas Open (2nd, 3rd and 4th rounds)	1954
Lowest score (72 holes)	257	Mike Souchak, Texas Open	1955
Most shots under par	27	Ben Hogan, Portland Invitational	1945
	27	Mike Souchak, Texas Open	1955
Most birdies in a row	8	Bob Goalby, St. Petersburg Open (4th round)	1961
	8	Fuzzy Zoeller, Quad Cities Open (1st round)	1976
	8	Dewey Arnette, Buick Open (1st round)	1987
Fewest putts (18 holes)	18	Sam Trahan, IVB-Philadelphia Golf Classic (4th round)	1979
	18	Mike McGee, Federal Express St. Jude Classic (1st round)	1987
	18	Kenny Knox, MCI Heritage Classic (1st round)	1989
	18	Andy North, Anheuser Busch Golf Classic (2nd round)	1990
Fewest putts (72 holes)	93	Kenny Knox, MCI Heritage Classic	1989

Source: PGA Tour
* All records listed are for 72-hole tournaments.

Tom" Morris (1821–1908), age 46 yrs. 99 days when he won at Prestwick in 1867. The oldest this century has been the 1967 champion, Roberto de Vicenzo (Argentina) at 44 yrs. 93 days.

Professional Golfers Association (PGA) Championship *Most wins*   Two players have won the title five times: Walter Hagen (1921, 1924–27) and Jack Nicklaus (1963, 1971, 1973, 1975, 1980). Walter Hagen won a record four consecutive titles from 1924 to 1927.

Lowest score   The lowest score for any round is 63, by Bruce Crampton (Australia; b. 28 Sep. 1935) at Firestone Country Club, Akron, OH in 1975; and by Raymond Loran Floyd (b. 4 Sep. 1942) at Southern Hills, Tulsa, OK in 1982.

Lowest total aggregate   271, by Bobby Nicholls (64, 71, 69, 67) at Columbus Country Club, OH in 1964.

Oldest and youngest winners   The oldest winner of the PGA was Julius Boros (USA; b. 3 Mar. 1920) at the age of 48 years 110 days in 1968. Eugene "Gene" Sarazen (USA; b. 27 Feb. 1902) was the youngest PGA winner in 1922 at the age of 20 years 170 days.

WOMEN'S CHAMPIONSHIP RECORDS

Grand Slam   The Grand Slam of women's golf has consisted of four tournaments since 1955. From 1955–66, the US Open, Ladies Professional Golfers Association (LPGA) Championship, Western Open and Titleholders Championship served as the "majors." From 1967 to 1982 the Grand Slam events changed, as first the Western Open (1967) and then the Titleholders Championship (1972) were discontinued.

Since 1983, the US Open, LPGA Championship, du Maurier Classic and Nabisco Dinah Shore have been the major events. Patty Berg has won 15 professional Grand Slam events: US Open (1), Titleholders (7), Western Open (7); the latter two are now defunct. She also won one US Amateur title.

US Open   This competition was first held in 1946 at Spokane, WA at match-play, but at 72 holes of stroke-play annually on different courses from 1947.

Most wins   The most wins is four, by Elizabeth Earle "Betsy" Rawls (b. 4 May 1928), 1951, 1953, 1957 and 1960, and by Mickey Wright (b. 14 Feb. 1935), in 1958–59, 1961 and 1964. The biggest margin of victory is 14 strokes, by Mae Louise Suggs (b. 7 Sep. 1923) with an aggregate of 291 in 1949.

Consecutive wins   Five players have won twice: Mickey Wright (1958–59); Donna Caponi (1969–70); Susie Berning (1972–73); Hollis Stacy (1977–78); Betsy King (1989–90).

Lowest score   The record for the lowest round is 65, by Sally Little (South Africa; b. 12 Oct. 1951) in the fourth round in 1978, and by Judy Dickinson (b. 4 Mar. 1950) in the third round in 1985.

Lowest total aggregate   The lowest 72 holes aggregate is 279, by Pat Bradley (b. 24 Mar. 1951) in 1981.

Oldest and youngest winners   The oldest winner has been Fay Crocker, at 40 yrs. 11 months in 1955, and the youngest Catherine Lacoste (France; b. 27 June 1945) at 22 yrs. 5 days in 1967.

Ladies Professional Golfers Association (LPGA) Championship
It was inaugurated in 1955 at Orchard Ridge Country Club, Fort Wayne, IN; since 1987 it has been officially called the Mazda LPGA Championship.

Most wins   four, Mickey Wright in 1958, 1960–61 and 1963.

Consecutive wins   Two, by two players: Mickey Wright (1960–61); Patty Sheehan (1983–84).

Lowest scores   The lowest score for 18 holes is 63, by Patty Sheehan at the Jack Nicklaus Sports Center at Kings Island, OH in 1984.

Lowest total aggregate   The lowest score for 72 holes is 267, by Betsy King at the Bethesda Country Club, MD in 1992.

Du Maurier Classic   (inaugurated 1973, Royal Montreal Golf Club, Montreal, Canada; formerly called La Canadienne [1973] and the Peter Jackson Classic [1974–83]).

Most wins   Pat Bradley holds the record for most wins, with three titles won in 1980, 1985–86.

Lowest score   The lowest score for 18 holes is 64, by JoAnne Carner at the St. Georges Country Club, Canada in 1978.

Lowest total aggregate   Pat Bradley and Ayako Okamoto share the record for the lowest score for 72 holes, 276, at the Board of Trade Country Club, Toronto, Ontario, Canada in 1986. Cathy Johnson matched Bradley and Okamoto in 1990 at Westmount Golf and Country Club, Kitchener, Ontario, Canada.

Nabisco Dinah Shore   (inaugurated 1972, Mission Hills Country Club, Rancho Mirage, CA, the permanent site)

Most wins   The most wins is three, by Amy Alcott (1983, 1988 and 1991).

Lowest score   Nancy Lopez holds the record for the lowest score for 18 holes, 64, in 1981.

Lowest total aggregate   The lowest score for 72 holes is 273, by Amy Alcott in 1991.

LPGA Tour   In 1944, three women golfers, Hope Seignious, Betty Hicks and Ellen Griffin, launched the Women's Professional Golf Association (WPGA). By 1947 the WPGA was unable to sustain the tour at the level that was hoped, and it seemed certain that women's professional golf would fade

away. However, Wilson Sporting Goods stepped in, overhauled the tour and called it the Ladies Professional Golf Association. In 1950 the LPGA received its official charter.

Lowest score   The lowest score for 18 holes is 62, by Mickey Wright on the Hogan Park course, Midland, TX in the first round of the 1964 Tall City Open, as did Vicki Fergon (b. 29 Sep. 1955) at Almaden Golf & Country Club in the second round of the 1984 San Jose Classic, and Laura Davies (Great Britain; b. 5 Oct. 1963) in the first round of the 1991 Rail Charity Golf Classic. The lowest score for 36 holes is 129 (64 + 65), by Judy Dickinson at Pasadena Yacht & Country Club, St. Petersburg, FL in the 1985 S&H Golf Classic.

Lowest total aggregate   Betsy King (b. 13 Aug. 1955) scored 267 (68, 66, 67, 66) at Bethesda Country Club, MD in the 1992 Mazda LPGA Championship.

Biggest bunker   The world's biggest bunker is Hell's Half Acre on the 585 yd. seventh hole of the Pine Valley course, Clementon, NJ, built in 1912 and generally regarded as the world's most trying course.

Throwing a golf ball   The lowest recorded score for throwing a golf ball around 18 holes (over 6,000 yds.) is 82, by Joe Flynn (USA), 21, at the 6,228 yd. Port Royal course, Bermuda on 27 Mar. 1975.

Most wins in a single event   Sam Snead won a record eight times at the Greater Greensboro Open—1938, 1946, 1949–50, 1955–56, 1960 and 1965.

Most times leading money winner   Jack Nicklaus has been the PGA Tour leading money winner eight times—1964–65, 1967, 1971–1973, 1975–76. Kathy Whitworth won eight times—1965–68, 1970–73.

Youngest LPGA winner   The youngest LPGA tour event winner was Marlene Hagge (b. 16 Feb. 1934), who won the 1952 Sarasota Open at the age of 18 yrs. 14 days.

Richest prize   The greatest first place prize money ever won is $1 million, awarded annually from 1987 to 1991 to the winners of the Sun City Challenge, Bophuthatswana, South Africa. Ian Woosnam (Wales) was the first winner. The greatest total prize money is $2.55 million (including a $525,000 first prize) for the Johnnie Walker World Championship at Tryall Golf Course, Montego Bay, Jamaica on 19–22 Dec. 1991.

TEAM COMPETITIONS

Ryder Cup   The biennial Ryder Cup professional match between the USA and Europe (British Isles or Great Britain prior to 1979) was instituted in 1927. The USA has won 22 to 5 (with 2 ties) to 1991.

Arnold Palmer has won the most Ryder Cup matches, with 22 out of 32 played, with two halved and 8 lost, in six contests from 1963 to 1973. Christy O'Connor, Sr. (Ireland; b. 21 Dec. 1924) played in a record ten contests, 1955–73. The most contests and matches for the USA is 8 and 37 (with 20 wins) by Billy Casper (b. 24 June 1931).

World Cup (formerly Canada Cup)   The World Cup (instituted as the Canada Cup in 1953) has been won most often by the USA, with 17 victories between 1955 and 1988. The only men to have been on six winning teams have been Arnold Palmer (b. 10 Sep. 1929; 1960, 1962–64, 1966–67) and Jack Nicklaus (1963–64, 1966–67, 1971 and 1973). Only Nicklaus has taken the individual title three times (1963–64, 1971).

The lowest aggregate score for 144 holes is 544, by Australia, Bruce Devlin (b. 10 Oct. 1937) and Anthony David Graham (b. 23 May 1946), at San Isidro, Buenos Aires, Argentina from 12–15 Nov. 1970. The lowest individual score was 269, by Roberto de Vicenzo (Argentina; b. 14 Apr. 1923), also in 1970.

Walker Cup   The series was instituted in 1921 (for the Walker Cup since 1922 and now held biennially). The USA has won 29 matches, Great Britain and Ireland three (in 1938, 1971 and 1989), and the 1965 match was tied.

Jay Sigel (USA; b. 13 Nov. 1943) has won a record 16 matches, with five halved and eight lost, 1977–91. Joseph Boynton Carr (Great Britain & Ireland; b. 18 Feb. 1922) played in ten contests, 1947–67.

Curtis Cup   The biennial ladies' Curtis Cup match between the USA and Great Britain and Ireland was first held in 1932. The USA has won 20 matches to 1992, Great Britain and Ireland five (1952, 1956, 1986 and 1988, 1992), and two matches have been tied.

Mary McKenna (Great Britain and Ireland; b. 29 Apr. 1949) played in a record ninth match in 1986, when for the first time she was on the winning team. Carole Semple Thompson (USA) has won a record 12 games in 7 matches, 1974–92. Anne Sander (nee Quast, later Decker, Welts; b. 31 Aug. 1937) played in a US record eighth match in 1990, when at 52 years 332 days she became the oldest-ever player in the series.

INDIVIDUAL RECORDS

Highest earnings   PGA and LPGA circuits: The all-time top professional money-winner is Tom Kite (USA; b. 9 Dec. 1949) with $7,164,440, to 15 June 1992. He also holds the earnings record for a year on the US PGA circuit, $1,395,278 in 1989. The record career earnings for a woman is by Pat Bradley (b. 24 Mar. 1951), with $4,294,838 to 15 June 1992. The season's record is $863,578, by Beth Daniel in 1990.

Most tournament wins   John Byron Nelson (USA; b. 4 Feb. 1912) won a record 18 tournaments (plus one unofficial) in one year, including a record 11 consecutively from 8 Mar. to 4 Aug. 1945.

The LPGA record is 13, by Mickey Wright (1963). She also holds the record for most wins in scheduled events, with four between August and September 1962 and between May and June 1963, a record matched by Kathrynne "Kathy" Ann Whitworth (b. 27 Sep. 1939) between March and April 1969.

Sam Snead, who turned professional in 1934, won 84 official PGA tour events, 1936–65. The ladies' PGA record is 88, by Kathy Whitworth from 1962 to 1985.

Consecutive wins   Four, by two players: Mickey Wright (1962); Kathy Whitworth (1969).

Successive wins   Between May and June 1978, Nancy Lopez won all five tournaments that she entered; however, these events did not follow each other and are therefore not considered consecutive tournament victories.

Oldest winner   Sam Snead won a PGA tournament at the age of 52 years 312 days at the 1965 Greater Greensboro Open.

Greatest winning margin   The greatest margin of victory in a professional tournament is 21 strokes, by Jerry Pate (USA; b. 16 Sep. 1953), who won the Colombian Open with 262, from 10–13 Dec. 1981.

Cecilia Leitch won the Canadian Ladies' Open Championship in 1921 by the biggest margin for a national title, 17 up and 15 to play.

Willie Smith won the US Open in 1899 by 11 strokes, with a score of 315. Jack Nicklaus won the US Masters in 1965 with a nine-stroke margin, scoring 271.

Arthur D'Arcy "Bobby" Locke (South Africa; 1917–87) achieved the greatest winning margin in a PGA tour event by 16 strokes in the Chicago Victory National Championship in 1948.

NCAA Championships   Two golfers have won three NCAA titles: Ben Daniel Crenshaw (b. 11 Jan. 1952) of the University of Texas in 1971–73, tying with Tom Kite in 1972; and Phil Mickelson of the Arizona State University in 1989–90, 1992.

Largest tournament   The Volkswagen Grand Prix Open Amateur Championship in the United Kingdom attracted a record 321,778 (206,820 men and 114,958 women) competitors in 1984.

HOLES IN ONE

Longest   The longest straight hole ever holed in one shot was, appropriately, the tenth (447 yds.) at Miracle Hills Golf Course, Omaha, NE, by Robert Mitera (b. 1944) on 7 Oct. 1965. Mitera stood 5 ft. 6 in. tall and weighed 165 lbs. He was a two-handicap player who normally drove 245 yds. A 50 mph gust carried his shot over a 290 yd. drop-off.

The longest "dog-leg" hole achieved in one shot is the 480 yd. fifth at Hope Country Club, AR by L. Bruce on 15 Nov. 1962.

The women's record is 393 yds., by Marie Robie on the first hole of the Furnace Brook Golf Club, Wollaston, MA on 4 Sep. 1949.

Consecutive   There are at least 19 cases of "aces" being achieved in two consecutive holes, of which the greatest was Norman L. Manley's unique "double albatross" on the par-4 330 yd. seventh and par-4 290 yd. eighth holes on the Del Valle Country Club course, Saugus, CA on 2 Sep. 1964.

The first woman to record consecutive "aces" was Sue Prell, on the 13th and 14th holes at Chatswood Golf Club, Sydney, Australia on 29 May 1977.

The closest to achieving three consecutive holes in one were Dr. Joseph Boydstone on the third, fourth and ninth at Bakersfield Golf Club, CA, on 10 Oct. 1962; and the Rev Harold Snider (b. 4 July 1900), who aced the 8th, 13th and 14th holes of the par-3 Ironwood course in Arizona on 9 June 1976.

Youngest and oldest   The youngest golfer recorded to have shot a hole-in-one is Coby Orr (5 years) of Littleton, CO on the 103 yd. fifth at the Riverside Golf Course, San Antonio, TX in 1975.

The youngest American woman to score an ace was Mrs. Shirley Kunde (nee Caley) in Aug. 1943, at age 13.

The oldest golfers to have performed this feat are: *(men)* 99 yrs. 244 days, Otto Bucher (Switzerland; b. 12 May 1885) on the 130 yd. 12th at La Manga Golf Club, Spain on 13 Jan. 1985; *(women)* 95 yrs. 257 days, Erna Ross (b. 9 Sep. 1890) on the 112 yd. 17th at The Everglades Club, Palm Beach, FL on 23 Apr. 1986.

The oldest player to score his age is C. Arthur Thompson (1869–1975) of Victoria, British Columbia, Canada, who scored 103, on the Uplands course of 6,215 yds. in 1973.

Youngest and oldest national golf champions   Thuashni Selvaratnam (b. 9 June 1976) won the 1989 Sri Lankan Ladies Amateur Open Golf Championship, aged 12 yrs. 324 days, at Nuwara Eliya Golf Course on 29 Apr. 1989. Maria Teresa "Isa" Goldschmid (nee Bevione; b. 15 Oct. 1925) won the Italian Women's Championship, aged 50 yrs. 200 days, at Oligata, Rome on 2 May 1976.

Most club championships   Helen Gray has been ladies champion at Tormorden Golf Course, Great Britain 37 times between 1952 and 1991. Bernard Charles Cusack (b. 24 Jan. 1920) was men's champion 34 times, including 33 consecutively, at the Narembeen Golf Course, Western Australia, between 1943 and 1982.

At different clubs, Peter Toogood (Australia; b. 11 Apr. 1930) has won 35 championships in Tasmania. At different clubs in the United States, Frances Miles-Maslon Hirsh (USA) was ladies champion 44 times between 1951–90.

GREYHOUND RACING

Origins The first greyhound meeting was staged at Hendon, London, Great Britain, with a railed hare operated by a windlass, in September 1876. Modern greyhound racing originated with the perfecting of the mechanical hare by Owen Patrick Smith at Emeryville, CA, in 1919. St. Petersburg Kennel Club, located in St. Petersburg, FL, which opened on 3 Jan. 1925, is the oldest greyhound track in the world still in operation on its original site.

Derby Two greyhounds have won the American Derby twice, at Taunton, MA: Real Huntsman in 1950–51, and Dutch Bahama in 1984–85.

Fastest greyhound The fastest speed at which any greyhound has been timed is 41.72 mph (410 yds. in 20.1 sec.) by The Shoe on the then-straight-away track at Richmond, New South Wales, Australia on 25 Apr. 1968. It is estimated that he covered the last 100 yds. in 4.5 sec. or at 45.45 mph.

United States Tiki's Ace ran a distance of $5/16$ mile in 29.61 sec. in Naples, Ft. Myers, FL in 1988. The fastest $3/8$ mile time was 36.43 sec. by P's Rambling in Hollywood, FL in 1987. Old Bill Drozd ran a $7/16$ mile track in 42.83 sec. in Tucson, AZ in 1973.

Most wins The most career wins is 143, by the American greyhound JR's Ripper of Multnomah, Fairview, OR and Tucson, AZ in 1982–86. The most wins in a year is 61, by Indy Ann in Mexico and the United States in 1966.

   The most consecutive victories is 32 in Great Britain, by Ballyregan Bob, owned by Cliff Kevern and trained by George Curtis, from 25 Aug. 1984 to 9 Dec. 1986, including 16 track record times. His race wins were by an average of more than nine lengths.

   Joe Dump of Greenetrack, Eutaw, AL holds the US record, with 31 consecutive wins from 18 Nov. 1978 to 1 June 1979.

Highest earnings The career earnings record is held by Homespun Rowdy with $297,000 in the United States, 1984–87.

   The richest first prize for a greyhound race is $125,000, won by Ben G Speedboat in the Great Greyhound Race of Champions at Seabrook, NH on 23 Aug. 1986.

Most stakes victories Real Huntsman achieved ten wins in 1949–51, including the American Derby twice.

Longest odds Apollo Prince won at odds of 250–1 at Sandown Greyhound Race Course, Springvale, Victoria, Australia on 14 Nov. 1968.

GYMNASTICS

Origins   A primitive form of gymnastics was practiced in ancient Greece and Rome during the period of the ancient Olympic Games (776 B.C. to A.D. 393) but Johann Friedrich Simon was the first teacher of modern gymnastics, at Basedow's School, Dessau, Germany in 1776.

World Championships   *Women*   The greatest number of titles won in the World Championships (including Olympic Games) is 12 individual wins and five team, by Larisa Semyonovna Latynina (USSR; b. 27 Dec. 1934) between 1956 and 1964. Kim Zmeskal was the first American woman to win an all-around world championship, on 13 Sep. 1991.

The USSR won the team title on 20 occasions (eleven world and nine Olympic).

Men   Boris Anfiyanovich Shakhlin (USSR; b. 27 Jan. 1932) won ten individual titles between 1954 and 1964. He also had three team wins.

The USSR won the team title a record 12 times (eight World Championships, four Olympics) between 1952 and 1991.

The most successful US gymnast has been Kurt Bittereaux Thomas (b. 29 Mar. 1952), who won three gold medals: floor exercises 1978 and 1979, horizontal bar 1979.

WORLD CHAMPION. The first world gymnastics championships at individual events were held in 1992. Kim Zmeskal (USA), who had won the all-around gymnastics world title in 1991, became the first woman to win two gold medals—on the beam and (here) in the floor exercise. (Photo: Allsport/Vandystadt)

Youngest champions Aurelia Dobre (Romania; b. 6 Nov. 1972) won the women's overall world title at age 14 yrs. 352 days on 23 Oct. 1987. Daniela Silivas (Romania) revealed in 1990 that she was born on 9 May 1971, a year later than previously claimed, so that she was age 14 yrs. 185 days when she won the gold medal for balance beam on 10 Nov. 1985.

The youngest male world champion was Dmitriy Bilozerchev (USSR; b. 17 Dec. 1966), at 16 yrs. 315 days at Budapest, Hungary on 28 Oct. 1983.

Olympics Japan has won the men's team title most often (in 1960, 1964, 1968, 1972 and 1976). The USSR won the women's title nine times (1952–80, 1988).

The most men's individual gold medals is six, by: Boris Shakhlin, one in 1956, four (two shared) in 1960 and one in 1964; and Nikolay Yefimovich Andrianov (USSR; b. 14 Oct. 1952), one in 1972, four in 1976 and one in 1980.

Vera Caslavska-Odlozil (Czechoslovakia; b. 3 May 1942) has won the most individual gold medals, with seven, three in 1964 and four (one shared) in 1968.

Larisa Latynina won six individual gold medals and was on three winning teams from 1956–64, earning nine gold medals. She also won five silver and four bronze, 18 in all—an Olympic record.

The most medals for a male gymnast is 15, by Nikolay Andrianov (USSR), seven gold, five silver and three bronze, from 1972–80.

Aleksandr Nikolaivich Dityatin (USSR; b. 7 Aug. 1957) is the only man to win a medal in all eight categories in the same Games, with three gold, four silver and one bronze at Moscow in 1980.

United States The best US performances were in the 1904 Games, when there was only limited foreign participation. Anton Heida (b. 1878) won five gold medals and a silver, and George Eyser (b. 1871), who had a wooden leg, won three gold, two silver and a bronze medal.

Mary Lou Retton (b. 24 Jan. 1968) won a women's record five medals in 1984, gold at all-around, two silver and two bronze.

The most medals won by a US male gymnast since 1904 is four, by Mitchell Jay "Mitch" Gaylord (b. 10 Mar. 1961), a team gold and a silver and two bronze in individual events in 1984, when both Bart Conner (b. 28 Mar. 1958) and Peter Glen Vidmar (b. 3 June 1961) won two gold medals.

Youngest international Pasakevi "Voula" Kouna (b. 6 Dec. 1971) was age 9 yrs. 299 days at the start of the Balkan Games at Serres, Greece on 1 Oct. 1981, when she represented Greece.

Highest score Nadia Comaneci (Romania; b. 12 Nov. 1961) was the first to achieve a perfect score (10.00) in the Olympics, and achieved seven in all at Montreal, Canada in July 1976.

World Cup Gymnasts who have won two World Cup (instituted 1975) overall titles are three men: Nikolay Andrianov, Aleksandr Dityatin and Li Ning (China; b. 8 Sep. 1963), and one woman: Maria Yevgenyevna Filatova (USSR; b. 19 July 1961).

US Championships Alfred A. Jochim (1902–81) won a record seven men's all-around US titles, 1925–30 and 1933, and a total of 34 at all exercises, between 1923 and 1934.

EXERCISES
Speed and Stamina

Records are accepted for the most repetitions of the following activities within the given time span.

CHINS (CONSECUTIVE)
370 Lee Chin-yong (South Korea; b. 15 Aug. 1925) at Backyon Gymnasium, Seoul, South Korea on 14 May 1988.

CHINS (ONE ARM) (FROM A RING)—CONSECUTIVE
22 Robert Chisnall (b. 9 Dec. 1952) at Queen's University, Kingston, Ontario, Canada on 3 Dec. 1982. (Also 18 two-finger chins, 12 one-finger chins).

PARALLEL BAR DIPS—1 HOUR
3,726 Kim Yang-ki (South Korea) at the Rivera Hotel, Seoul, South Korea on 28 Nov. 1991.

PUSH-UPS—24 HOURS
40,360 Charles Servizio (USA) at Gold's Gym, Fontana, CA on 18–19 Jan. 1992.

PUSH-UPS (ONE ARM)—5 HOURS
7,683 John Decker (Great Britain) at Congleton Cricket Club, Cheshire, Great Britain on 16 June 1991.

PUSH-UPS (FINGERTIP)—5 HOURS
7,011 Kim Yang-ki at the Swiss Guard Hotel, Seoul, South Korea on 30 Aug. 1990.

PUSH-UPS (ONE FINGER)—CONSECUTIVE
124 Paul Lynch at the Hippodrome, London, Great Britain on 21 Apr. 1992.

SIT-UPS—24 HOURS
65,001 Marc Scriven (Great Britain) at St. John's Sports Centre, Worcester, Great Britain on 21–22 June 1991.

LEG LIFTS—12 HOURS
41,788 Lou Scripa, Jr. at Jack La Lanne's American Health & Fitness Spa, Sacramento, CA on 2 Dec. 1988.

SQUATS—1 HOUR
3,196 Bhupinder Singh Negi at Himachal Pradesh University, Shimla, India on 26 May 1992.

SQUAT THRUSTS—1 HOUR
2,998 Paul Wai Man Chung at the Chung Sze Kung Fu (HK) Association, Kowloon, Hong Kong on 14 Apr. 1991.

BURPEES—1 HOUR
1,771 Patrick Doherty at Salford Quays, Manchester, Great Britain on 25 Oct. 1991.

PUMMEL HORSE DOUBLE CIRCLES—CONSECUTIVE
75 by Lee Thomas (Great Britain) on British Broadcasting Corporation on 12 Dec. 1985.

PUSH-UPS IN A YEAR
Paddy Doyle achieved a documented *1,500,230* push-ups from October 1988 to October 1989.

The women's record is six all-around, 1945–46 and 1949–52, and 39 at all exercises, including 11 in succession at balance beam, 1941–51, by Clara Marie Schroth Lomady (b. 5 Oct. 1920).

McDonald's American Cup

The American Cup was created by the USGF in 1976. It has been called the McDonald's American Cup since 1980.

Most wins Mary Lou Retton has won the title three times (1983–85), more than any other woman gymnast. Kurt Thomas has also won three consecutive times (1978–80), making him champion of the men's division.

NCAA Championships *Men*

The men's competition was first held in 1932. The most team championships won is nine, by two colleges: University of Illinois, 1939–42, 1950, 1955–56, 1958, 1989; Pennslyvania State University, 1948, 1953–54, 1957, 1959–61, 1965, 1976.

The most individual titles in a career is seven, by two gymnasts: Joe Giallombardo, University of Illinois, tumbling, 1938–40, all-around title, 1938–40, and floor exercise, 1938; Jim Hartung, University of Nebraska, all-around title, 1980–81, rings, 1980–82, and parallel bar, 1981–82.

Women The women's competition was first held in 1982. The most team championships is six, by University of Utah, 1982–86 and 1990.

The most individual titles in a career is four, by three gymnasts: Kelly Garrison-Steves, University of Oklahoma, all-around title, 1987–88, balance beam, 1988, uneven bars, 1988; Kim Hamilton, University of California at Los Angeles (UCLA), floor exercise, 1987–89, and vault, 1989; Penney Hauschild, University of Alabama, all-around title, 1985–86; uneven bars, 1985; and floor exercise, 1986.

Static wall "sit" Paddy Doyle stayed in an unsupported sitting position against a wall for 4 hrs. 40 min. at The Magnet Center, Erdington, Great Britain on 18 Apr. 1990.

Club swinging Albert Rayner set a world record of 17,512 revolutions (4.9 per sec.) in 60 min. at Wakefield, Great Britain on 27 July 1981.

Gymnastics/aerobics display The now-discontinued Czechoslovak Spartakiad featured gymnastics displays by about 180,000 participants. Held at the Strahov Stadium, Prague until 1989, the competition drew 200,000 spectators for each of the four days. On the 15-acre infield there were markers for 13,824 gymnasts at a time.

Somersaults Ashrita Furman performed 8,341 forward rolls in 10 hrs. 30 min. over 12 miles 390 yards from Lexington to Charleston, MA on 30 Apr. 1986.

Shigeru Iwasaki (b. 1960) somersaulted backward 54.68 yds. in 10.8 sec. at Tokyo, Japan on 30 Mar. 1980.

PERFECT MARKS. At the 1988 Olympic Games, Marina Lobach (USSR; b. 26 June 1970) won the rhythmic gymnastic title with perfect scores in all six disciplines. The exercises, which are all performed on the floor, are free, ball, rope, hoop, clubs and, as seen here, the ribbon. (Photo: Allsport/Roger Labrosse)

Modern rhythmic gymnastics   The most overall individual world titles in modern rhythmic gymnastics is three, by Maria Gigova (Bulgaria) in 1969, 1971 and 1973 (shared).

Bulgaria has a record seven team titles, in 1969, 1971, 1981, 1983, 1985, 1987 and 1989 (shared). Bianka Panova (b. 27 May 1960) of Bulgaria won all four apparatus gold medals, all with maximum scores, and won a team gold in 1987.

Marina Lobach (USSR; b. 26 June 1970) won the 1988 Olympic title with perfect scores for all events. Lilia Ignatova (Bulgaria) has won both of the individual World Cup titles that have been held, in 1983 and 1986.

HARNESS RACING

Origins   Trotting races were held in Valkenburg, Netherlands in 1554. In Great Britain the trotting gait (the simultaneous use of the diagonally opposite legs) was known in the 16th century. The sulky first appeared in 1829. Pacers thrust out their fore and hind legs simultaneously on one side.

United States   The sport became very popular in the United States in the 19th century, and the National Trotting Association was founded, originally as the National Association for the Promotion of the Interests of the Trotting Turf, in 1870. It brought needed controls to a sport which had been threatened by gambling corruption.

Most successful driver   The most successful sulky driver in North American harness racing history has been Herve Filion (b. 1 Feb. 1940) of Québec, Canada, who had achieved 13,510 wins and prize earnings of $76,323,494 through 25 May 1992, including a record 814 wins in a year, 1989.

John D. Campbell (USA; b. 8 Apr. 1955) has the highest career earnings, $102,830,916 through 3 June 1992. This includes a season record of $11,622,778 in 1990, when he won 543 races.

Hambletonian   The most famous trotting race in North America, the Hambletonian Stakes, run annually for three-year-olds, was first staged at Syracuse, NY in 1926. The race is named after the great sire Hambletonian, born in 1849, from whom almost all harness horses trace their pedigree. The race record time is 1 min. 53³/₅ sec., by Mack Lobell, driven by John Campbell in 1987.

HARNESS RACING MILE RECORDS

TROTTING	HORSE (DRIVER)	PLACE	DATE
World .... 1:52 ¹/₅	*Mack Lobell* .... (John Campbell)	Springfield, IL	21 Aug. 1987
PACING			
World .... 1:48 ²/₅	*Matt's Scooter* .... (Michel Lachance)	Lexington, KY	23 Sep. 1988
Race .... 1:49 ²/₅	*Artsplace* .... (Catello Manzi)	East Rutherford, NJ	20 June 1992

Greatest winnings   For any harness horse the record amount is $4,408,857, by the trotter Ourasi (France), who won 32 races to the end of 1990. The greatest amount won by a pacer is $3,225,653, by Nihilator, who won 35 of 38 races in 1984–85.

The single-season records are $2,217,222 by the pacer Precious Bunny in 1991, and $1,610,608 by the trotter Prakas in 1985.

The largest-ever purse was $2,161,000, for the Woodrow Wilson two-year-old race over one mile at The Meadowlands, East Rutherford, NJ on 16 Aug. 1984. Of this sum a record $1,080,500 went to the winner, Nihilator, driven by William O'Donnell (b. 4 May 1948).

Highest prices   The highest prices paid were $19.2 million for Nihilator (a pacer), who was syndicated by Wall Street Stable and Almahurst Stud Farm in 1984; and $6 million for Mack Lobell (a trotter) by John Erik Magnusson of Vislanda, Sweden in 1988.

Little Brown Jug   Pacing's three-year-old classic has been held annually·at Delaware, OH from 1946. The name honors a great 19th century pacer. The race record time is 1 min. 52¹/₅ sec. by Nihilator, driven by Bill O'Donnell in 1985.

HOCKEY

Origins   There is pictorial evidence that a hockey-like game (*kalv*) was played on ice in the early 16th century in the Netherlands. The game was probably first played in North America on 25 Dec. 1855 at Kingston, Ontario, Canada, but Halifax also lays claim to priority. The International Ice Hockey Federation was founded in 1908.

NATIONAL HOCKEY LEAGUE (NHL)

Origins   The National Hockey League (NHL) was founded on 22 Nov. 1917 in Montreal, Canada following the collapse of the National Hockey Association of Canada (NHA). Four teams formed the original league: the Montreal Canadiens, the Montreal Wanderers, the Ottawa Senators and the Québec Bulldogs. The Toronto Arenas were admitted as a fifth team, but the Bulldogs were unable to operate, and the league began as a four-team competition. The first NHL game was played on 19 Dec. 1917. The NHL is now comprised of 21 teams, seven from Canada and 14 from the United States, divided into two divisions within two conferences: Adams and Patrick Divisions in the Wales Conference; Norris and Smythe Divisions in the Campbell Conference. At the end of the regular season, 16 teams compete in the Stanley Cup playoffs to decide the NHL championship. (For further details of the Stanley Cup see page 677.)

Team records   The Montreal Canadiens won a record 60 games and 132 points (with 12 ties) in 80 games played in 1976/77; their eight losses were also a record, the least ever in a season of 70 or more games. The highest percentage of wins in a season was .875, achieved by the Boston Bruins, with 30 wins in 44 games in 1929/30.

The longest undefeated run during a season, 35 games (25 wins and ten ties), was established by the Philadelphia Flyers from 14 Oct. 1979 to 6 Jan. 1980.

The New York Islanders won 15 consecutive games from 21 Jan.–20 Feb. 1982.

The most goals scored in a season is 446, by the Edmonton Oilers in 1983/84, when they also achieved a record 1,182 points.

The most shutouts in a season is 22, in 1928/29 by the Montreal Canadiens, in just 44 games, all by George Hainsworth, who also achieved a record low for goals against percentage of .98 that season.

Most games played   Gordon "Gordie" Howe (Canada; b. 31 Mar. 1928) played in a record 1,767 NHL regular-season games (and 157 playoff games) over a record 26 seasons, from 1946 to 1971, for the Detroit Red Wings and in 1979/80 for the Hartford Whalers. He also played 419 games (and 78 playoff games) for the Houston Aeros and for the New England Whalers in the World Hockey Association from 1973 to 1979, for a grand total of 2,421 professional hockey games.

Most consecutive games played   A record of 962 consecutive games played was achieved by Doug Jarvis for the Montreal Canadiens, the Washington Capitals and the Hartford Whalers from 8 Oct. 1975–5 Apr. 1987.

Fastest goals   The fastest goal was after 4 sec. by Joseph Antoine Claude Provost (b. 17 Sep. 1933; Montreal Canadiens) *v.* Boston Bruins in the second period at Montreal on 9 Nov. 1957, and by Denis Joseph Savard (b. 4 Feb. 1961; Chicago Black Hawks) *v.* Hartford Whalers in the third period at Chicago on 12 Jan. 1986. From the opening whistle, the fastest is 5 sec., by Doug Smail (b. 2 Sep. 1957; Winnipeg Jets) *v.* St Louis Blues at Winnipeg on 20 Dec. 1981, and by Bryan John Trottier (b. 17 July 1956; New York Islanders) *v.* Boston Bruins at Boston on 22 Mar. 1984. Bill Mosienko (b. 2 Nov. 1921; Chicago Black Hawks) scored three goals in 21 sec. *v.* New York Rangers on 23 Mar. 1952. Toronto scored eight goals in 4 min. 52 sec. *v.* New York Americans on 19 Mar. 1938.

Most goals *Team*   The NHL record is 21 goals, when the Montreal Canadiens beat Toronto St. Patrick's, 14–7, at Montreal on 10 Jan. 1920, and the Edmonton Oilers beat the Chicago Black Hawks, 12–9, at Chicago on 11 Dec. 1985. The NHL single team record is 16, by the Montreal Canadiens *v.* the Québec Bulldogs (3), at Québec City on 3 Nov. 1920.

Most goals and points *Career*   The North American career record for goals is 1,071 (including a record 801 in the NHL) by Gordie Howe (Detroit Red Wings, Houston Aeros, New England Whalers and Hartford Whalers) from 16 Oct. 1946 in 32 seasons ending in 1979/80. He took 2,204 games to achieve the 1,000th goal, but Robert Marvin "Bobby" Hull (Great Britain; b. 3 Jan. 1939; Chicago Black Hawks and Winnipeg Jets) scored his 1,000th in 1,600 games on 12 Mar. 1978.

Wayne Gretzky (Edmonton Oilers 1979–88, Los Angeles Kings 1988–92) holds the NHL record for assists, 1,514, and points, 2,263.

Season   The most goals scored in a season in the NHL is 92, in the 1981/82 season by Wayne Gretzky (b. 26 Jan. 1961) for the Edmonton Oilers. He scored a record 215 points, including a record 163 assists, in 1985/86.

Game   The most goals in an NHL game is seven, by Michael Joseph "Joe" Malone (b. 28 Feb. 1890) in Québec's 10–6 win over Toronto St. Patricks at Québec City on 31 Jan. 1920.

The most assists in an NHL game is seven, by William "Billy" Taylor (b. 3 May 1919) for Detroit, 10–6 Chicago on 16 Mar. 1947, and three by Wayne Gretzky for Edmonton, 8–2 *v.* Washington on 15 Feb. 1980, 12–9 *v.* Chicago on 11 Dec. 1985, and 8–2 *v.* Québec on 14 Feb. 1986.

The record number of assists in one period is five, by Dale Hawerchuk, for the Winnipeg Jets *v.* the Los Angeles Kings on 6 Mar. 1984.

Consecutive games   Harry Broadbent scored in 16 consecutive games for Ottawa in the 1921/22 season.

Most hat tricks   The most hat tricks (three or more goals in a game) in a career is 49, by Wayne Gretzky through the 1991/92 season for the Edmonton Oilers and the Los Angeles Kings. Wayne Gretzky also holds the record for most hat tricks in a season, ten, in both the 1982 and 1984 seasons for the Oilers.

Most consecutive 50-or-more-goal seasons   Mike Bossy (New York Islanders) scored at least 50 goals in nine consecutive seasons from 1977/78 through 1985/86. Wayne Gretzky (Edmonton Oilers, Los Angeles Kings) has also scored at least 50 goals in one season nine times, but his longest streak is eight seasons.

Most points in one game   The North American major league record for most points scored in one game is ten, by Jim Harrison (b. 9 July 1947; three goals, seven assists) for Alberta, later Edmonton Oilers in a World Hockey Association match at Edmonton on 30 Jan. 1973; and by Darryl Sittler (b. 18 Sep. 1950; six goals, four assists) for the Toronto Maple Leafs *v.* the Boston Bruins in an NHL game at Toronto on 7 Feb. 1976.

Period   The most points in one period is six, by Bryan Trottier, three goals and three assists in the second period, for the New York Islanders *v.* the New York Rangers (9–4) on 23 Dec. 1978. Nine players have a record four goals in one period.

Longest hockey game   The longest game was 2 hrs. 56 min. 30 sec. (playing time) when the Detroit Red Wings beat the Montreal Maroons 1–0 in the sixth period of overtime at the Forum, Montreal, at 2:25 A.M. on 25 Mar. 1936. Norm Smith, the Red Wings goaltender, turned aside 92 shots for the NHL's longest single shutout.

Stanley Cup goaltending   Jacques Plante holds the record for most shutouts in a playoff career, with 14, with the Montreal Canadiens (1953–63) and the St. Louis Blues (1969–1970). The record for most victories in a playoff career is 88, by Billy Smith for the New York Islanders (1975–88).

Most consecutive points   The most consecutive games scoring points was 51, by Wayne Gretzky from 5 Oct. 1983–27 Jan. 1984 for the Edmonton Oilers.

Goaltending   *Career*   Terrance "Terry" Gordon Sawchuk (1929–70) played a record 971 games as a goaltender, for the Detroit Red Wings, the Boston Bruins, the Toronto Maple Leafs, the Los Angeles Kings and the New York Rangers, from 1949 to 1970. He achieved a record 435 wins (to 337 losses and 188 ties). Jacques Joseph Ormar Plante (1929–86), with 434 NHL wins, surpassed Sawchuk's figure by adding 15 wins in his one season in the WHA, for a total of 449 in 868 games.

Season   Bernie Parent (b. 3 Apr. 1945) achieved a record 47 wins in a season, with 13 losses and 12 ties, for Philadelphia in 1973/74.

Most successful goaltending   The most shutouts played by a goaltender in an NHL career is 103, by Terry Sawchuck of Detroit, Boston, Toronto, Los Angeles and New York Rangers, between 1949 and 1970. Gerry Cheevers (b. 2 Dec. 1940; Boston Bruins) went a record 32 successive games without a defeat in 1971/72. George Hainsworth completed 22 shutouts for the Montreal Canadiens in 1928/29. Alex Connell played 461 min. 29 sec. without conceding a goal for Ottawa in the 1928/29 season. Roy Worters saved 70 shots for the Pittsburgh Pirates *v.* the New York Americans on 24 Dec. 1925.

Defensemen   Paul Coffey (Edmonton Oilers 1980–87, Pittsburgh Penguins 1988–91, Los Angeles Kings 1992) set records for most goals (318), assists (796) and points (1,114) by a defensemen. He scored a record 48 goals in 1985/86. Bobby Orr (Boston Bruins) holds the single-season marks for assists (102) and points (139), both of which were set in 1970/71.

Player awards   The Hart Trophy, awarded annually starting with the 1923/24 season by the Professional Hockey Writers Association as the Most Valuable Player award of the NHL, has been won a record nine times by Wayne Gretzky, 1980–87, 1989. Gretzky has also won the Art Ross Trophy a record nine times, 1981–87 and 1990–91; this has been awarded annually since 1947/48 to the NHL season's leading scorer. Bobby Orr of Boston won the James Norris Memorial Trophy, awarded annually starting with the 1953/54 season to the league's leading defenseman, a record eight times, 1968–75.

Coaches   Scotty Bowman holds the records for most victories and highest winning percentage by an NHL coach. He won 778 games (110, St. Louis Blues 1967–71; 419, Montreal Canadiens 1971–79; 210, Buffalo Sabres 1979–87; 39, Pittsburgh Penguins, 1991–92). His career record is 778 wins, 359 losses, 219 ties for a record .655 winning percentage. Dick Irvine has coached a record 1,437 games with three teams: Chicago Blackhawks (1930–31; 1955–56); Toronto Maple Leafs (1931–40); Montreal Canadiens (1940–55). Irvin's career record was 690 wins, 521 losses, 226 ties.

STANLEY CUP

The top NHL teams compete annually for the Stanley Cup, which was first presented in 1893 by Lord Stanley of Preston, then Governor-General of Canada. The longest Stanley Cup final game was settled after 115 min. 13 sec., in the third period of overtime, when the Edmonton Oilers beat the Boston Bruins 3–2 on 15 May 1990. (For further details see the Stanley Cup feature.)

Most games played   Larry Robinson has played in 227 Stanley Cup playoff games for the Montreal Canadiens (1973–89) and the Los Angeles Kings (1990–92).

Scoring records   Wayne Gretzky (the Edmonton Oilers and the Los Angeles Kings) has scored a record 306 points in Stanley Cup games, a record 95 goals and a record 211 assists. Gretzky scored a playoff record 47 points (16 goals, record 31 assists) in 1985. The most goals in a season is 19, by Reggie Leach for Philadelphia in 1976 and by Jari Kurri (Finland; b. 18 May 1960) for Edmonton in 1985.

Stanley Cup

The 1992–93 National Hockey League (NHL) season will mark the 100th anniversary of the Stanley Cup, currently the oldest competition in North American professional sports. The cup is named for Frederick Arthur, Lord Stanley of Preston, who donated the trophy in 1893 for presentation to the amateur hockey champions of Canada. Originally competition for the Stanley Cup was on a challenger basis; the champions were required to defend the Cup against opponents approved by the Cup's trustees. During the first 30 years of the Cup's existence there were 53 challenges. Starting in 1926 Stanley Cup competition was limited to NHL teams, and in 1946 the Cup came under the complete control of the NHL. The Cup has been won most times by the Montreal Canadiens, with 23 wins.

Wayne Gretsky
Edmonton Oilers, 1979–1988;
Los Angeles Kings, 1988–92

"The Great One" dominates the Stanley
Cup record book, setting marks in all
offensive categories. He holds career
records for most points, 306; most
goals, 95; and most assists, 211. He
also holds the record for most points in
Stanley Cup finals series, 13, and assists, 10. He
shares the record for most assists in any playoff
game (with Mikko Leinonen), 6, and the record for most
points in a period (shared with nine other players), 4.

Paul Coffey
Edmonton Oilers, 1980–87; Pittsburgh Penguins,
1987–91; Los Angeles Kings, 1992

An offensive-minded defenseman, Coffey
holds several Stanley Cup defenseman
scoring records, including most points in a
season, 37; most goals in a season, 12; most
assists in a season, 25; and most points in a
game, 6.

Maurice Richard
Montreal Canadiens, 1942–60

An explosive goal-scorer,
"Rocket" Richard holds several
Stanley Cup records, including
most career overtime goals, 6;
the most career three-or-more
goal games (shared with Wayne
Gretsky and Jari Kurri), 7; and
most points in one period of a
Stanley Cup finals game (shared
with nine others), 4.

Scotty Bowman

Teams coached: St. Louis Blues (1967–71), Montreal Canadiens (1971–79), Buffalo Sabres (1979–85) and Pittsburgh Penguins (1991–92)

Bowman coached more playoff games (207) and won more playoff games (130) than any other coach in Stanley Cup history. During his career Bowman has coached six championship teams—the Montreal Canadiens 1973, 1976–79; and the Pittsburgh Penguins, 1992.

Billy Smith

Los Angeles Kings (1971–72)
New York Islanders (1972–89)

A feisty goaltender Smith anchored the New York Islanders championship teams of the early 1980s. He holds the goaltending records for most career playoff games, 132, and most career playoff minutes, 7,645.

Most Championships

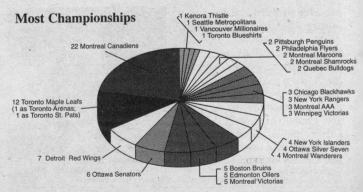

1 Kenora Thistle
1 Seattle Metropolitans
1 Vancouver Millionaires
1 Toronto Blueshirts

2 Pittsburgh Penguins
2 Philadelphia Flyers
2 Montreal Maroons
2 Montreal Shamrocks
2 Quebec Bulldogs

22 Montreal Canadiens

3 Chicago Blackhawks
3 New York Rangers
3 Montreal AAA
3 Winnipeg Victorias

12 Toronto Maple Leafs
(1 as Toronto Arenas;
1 as Toronto St. Pats)

4 New York Islanders
4 Ottawa Silver Seven
4 Montreal Wanderers

7 Detroit Red Wings

5 Boston Bruins
5 Edmonton Oilers
5 Montreal Victorias

6 Ottawa Senators

(Photos: Allsport USA/Fred Vuich/Tim Defrisco/Kevin Levine/Bruce Bennett Studios/M. DiGirolamo/Hockey Hall of Fame)

Five goals in a Stanley Cup game were scored by Maurice Richard (b. 14 Aug. 1924) in Montreal's 5–1 win over the Toronto Maple Leafs on 23 Mar. 1944; by Darryl Glen Sittler (b. 18 Sep. 1950) for Toronto's 8–5 victory over Philadelphia on 22 Apr. 1976; by Reggie Leach for Philadelphia's 6–3 victory over the Boston Bruins on 6 May 1976; and by Mario Lemieux (b. 1965) for the Pittsburgh Penguins' 10–7 victory over Philadelphia on 25 Apr. 1989. Reggie Leach (Philadelphia) scored at least one goal in nine consecutive playoff games in 1976. The streak started on 17 Apr. *v.* the Toronto Maple Leafs, and ended on 9 May when he was shut out by the Montreal Canadiens. Overall, Leach scored 14 goals during his record-setting run.

A record six assists in a game were achieved by Mikko Leinonen (Finland; b. 15 July 1955) for the New York Rangers in their 7–3 victory over Philadelphia on 8 Apr. 1982, and by Wayne Gretzky for Edmonton's 13–3 victory over Los Angeles on 9 Apr. 1987, when his team set a Stanley Cup game record of 13 goals. The most points in a game is eight, by Patrik Sundström (Sweden; b. 14 Dec. 1961), three goals and five assists, for the New Jersey Devils (10) *v.* the Washington Capitals (4) on 22 Apr. 1988, and by Mario Lemieux, five goals and three assists, for the Pittsburgh Penguins (10) *v.* the Philadelphia Flyers (7) on 25 Apr. 1989.

Point-scoring streak   Bryan Trottier (New York Islanders) scored a point in 27 playoff games over three seasons (1980–82), scoring 16 goals and 26 assists for 42 points.

Defensemen   During his career with the Edmonton Oilers, 1980–87, Paul Coffey set marks for the most points in a playoff game (6) and in a season (37)—both set in 1985. Also in 1985, Coffey set the record for most goals by a defenseman in a playoff season with 12 in 18 games. The record for most

MOST GAMES PLAYED. Larry Robinson has played in 227 Stanley Cup playoff games for the Montreal Canadiens (1973–89) and the Los Angeles Kings (1990–92). (Photo: Allsport/Mike Powell)

goals in a game by a defenseman is three, shared by five players: Bobby Orr (Boston Bruins v. Montreal Canadiens, 11 Apr. 1971); Dick Redmond (Chicago Blackhawks v. St. Louis Blues, 4 Apr. 1973); Denis Potvin (New York Islanders v. Edmonton Oilers, 17 Apr. 1981); Paul Reinhart twice (Calgary Flames v. Edmonton Oilers, 14 Apr. 1983; v. Vancouver Canucks, 8 Apr. 1984); Doug Halward (Vancouver Canucks v. Calgary Flames, 7 Apr. 1984).

Most valuable player   The Conn Smythe Trophy for the most valuable player in the playoffs has been awarded annually since 1965. The only players to win it twice have been Bobby Orr, 1970 and 1972; Bernie Parent (Philadelphia), 1974 and 1975; and Wayne Gretzky (Edmonton), 1985 and 1988. Henri Richard played on a record 11 winning teams for the Montreal Canadiens between 1956 and 1973.

Coaches   "Toe" Blake coached the Montreal Canadiens to eight championships (1956–60, 1965–66, 1968), the most of any coach. Scotty Bowman holds the record for most playoff wins at 130: (26, St. Louis Blues, 1967–71; 70, Montreal Canadiens, 1971–79; 18, Buffalo Sabres, 1979–87; 16, Pittsburgh Penguins, 1991–92).

WORLD CHAMPIONSHIPS AND OLYMPIC GAMES

World Championships were first held for amateurs in 1920 in conjunction with the Olympic Games, which were also considered world championships up to 1968. Since 1976, the World Championships have been open to professionals. The USSR won 22 world titles between 1954 and 1990, including the Olympic titles of 1956, 1964 and 1968. It has a record eight Olympic titles with a further five in 1972, 1976, 1984, 1988 and 1992 (as the CIS, with all players Russian). The longest Olympic career is that of Richard Torriani (Switzerland; 1911–88) from 1928 to 1948. The most gold medals won by any player is three, achieved by Soviet players Vitaliy Semyenovich Davydov, Anatoliy Vasilyevich Firsov, Viktor Grigoryevich Kuzkin and Aleksandr Pavlovich Ragulin in 1964, 1968 and 1972, and by Vladislav Aleksandrovich Tretyak in 1972, 1976 and 1984.

Women   The first two world championships were won by Canada, in 1990 and 1992.

Most goals   The greatest number of goals recorded in a world championship match was when Australia beat New Zealand 58–0 at Perth on 15 Mar. 1987.

Fastest goals   In minor leagues, Per Olsen scored two seconds after the start of the match for Rungsted against Odense in the Danish First Division at Hørsholm, Denmark on 14 Jan. 1990. Three goals in 10 seconds was achieved by Jørgen Palmgren Erichsen for Frisk v. Holmen in a junior league match in Norway on 17 Mar. 1991. The Skara Ishockeyclubb, Sweden, scored three goals in 11 seconds against Örebro IK at Skara on 18 Oct. 1981. The Vernon Cougars scored five goals in 56 seconds against the Salmon Arm Aces at Vernon, British Columbia, Canada on 6 Aug. 1982. The Kamloops Knights of Columbus scored seven goals in 2 min. 22 sec. v. the Prince George Vikings on 25 Jan. 1980.

MOST OLYMPIC TITLES. Seen here is action from the 1992 Olympic ice hockey final between the all-Russian team (competing under the title of the Unified Team of the National Olympic Committees of Russia, Belarus, Ukraine, Kazakhstan and Uzbekistan), and Canada. The Russians won 3–1 to add to the seven titles previously won by the former USSR. (Photo: Allsport/Vandystadt)

FASTEST HAT TRICK. Three goals in ten seconds was achieved by Jørgan Palmgren Erichsen for Frisk v. Holmen in a junior league match in Norway on 17 Mar. 1991. Erichsen can be seen here with the players who assisted him (from right): Bjørn Erik Mosknes, John Are Hårstad-Evjen, Andres Bastiansen and Eric Thuv.

HORSE RACING

Origins   Horsemanship was an important part of the Hittite culture of Anatolia, Turkey dating from 1400 B.C. The 33rd ancient Olympic Games of 648 B.C. in Greece featured horse racing. Horse races can be traced in England from the third century. The first sweepstakes race was originated by the 12th Earl of Derby at his estate in Epsom in 1780. The Epsom Derby is still run today, and is the classic race of the English flat racing season.

United States   Horses were introduced to the North American continent from Spain by Cortez in 1519. In colonial America, horse racing was common. Colonel Richard Nicholls, commander of English forces in New York, is believed to have staged the first organized race at Salisbury Plain, Long Island, NY in 1665. Thoroughbred racing was first staged at Saratoga Springs, NY in 1863. The first Jockey Club to be founded was at Charleston, SC in 1734.

Highest prizes   The highest prize money won for a day's racing is $10 million, for the Breeders' Cup series of seven races staged annually since 1984. Included each year is a record $3 million for the Breeders' Cup Classic.

Breeders' Cup   Two jockeys have won the most Breeders' Cup races: Laffit Pincay, Jr. with six from 1985 to 1990, and Pat Day with six from 1984 to 1991. The trainer with the most wins is D. Wayne Lukas, with ten.

● HORSES

Most successful   The horse with the best win–loss record was Kincsem, a Hungarian mare foaled in 1874, who was unbeaten in 54 races (1876–79) throughout Europe, including the Goodwood Cup of 1878.

Longest winning sequence   Camarero, foaled in 1951, was undefeated in 56 races in Puerto Rico from 19 Apr. 1953 to his first defeat on 17 Aug. 1955 (in his career to 1956, he won 73 of 77 races).

Career   Crossbar (foaled 1935) won 197 of his 325 races in Puerto Rico, 1937–47. Lenoxbar (foaled 1935) won 46 races in one year, 1940, in Puerto Rice from 56 starts.

The most career wins in the United States is 89, by Kingston in 138 starts, 1886–94. This included 33 in stakes races, but the horse with the most wins in stakes races in the USA is Exterminator (foaled 1915), with 34 between 1918 and 1923. John Henry (foaled 1975) won a record 25 graded stakes races, including 16 at Grade 1, 1978–84. On his retirement in 1984, his career prize money was $6,597,947, nearly twice as much as the next best. Of 83 races he won 39, was second 15 times and third 9 times.

Same race   Doctor Syntax (foaled 1811) won the Preston Gold Cup on seven successive occasions, 1815–21.

MOST SUCCESSFUL. The most successful horse in a single season, in money won, is *Sunday Silence* (seen here with the green noseband) in 1989. He won over $4.5 million from a mere nine races (seven wins), and this figure includes a $1 million bonus for his performances in the Triple Crown races (winning the Preakness Stakes and the Kentucky Derby, and coming in second in the Belmont Stakes). (Photo: Allsport USA/Ken Levine)

Triple Crown winners   The Triple Crown (Kentucky Derby, Preakness Stakes, Belmont Stakes) has been achieved 11 times, most recently by Affirmed in 1978. Eddie Arcaro is the only jockey to board two Triple Crown winners, Whirlaway in 1941 and Citation in 1948. Two trainers have schooled two Triple Crown winners: James Fitzsimmons, Gallant Fox in 1930 and Omaha in 1935; Ben A. Jones, Whirlaway in 1941 and Citation in 1948.

Greatest winnings   The career earnings record is $6,679,242, by the 1987 Kentucky Derby winner Alysheba (foaled 1984), from 1986–88. Alysheba's career record was 11 wins, 8 seconds and 2 thirds from 26 races. The most prize money earned in a year is $4,578,454, by Sunday Silence (foaled 1986) in the USA in 1989. His total included $1,350,000 from the Breeders' Cup Classic and a $1 million bonus for the best record in the Triple Crown races: he won the Kentucky Derby and Preakness Stakes and was second in the Belmont Stakes. The leading money-winning mare is Dance Smartly (foaled 1988) with $3,083,455 in North America, 1990–91. The one-race record is $2.6 million, by Spend A Buck (foaled 1982), for the Jersey Derby, Garden State Park, NJ on 27 May 1985, of which $2 million was a bonus for having previously won the Kentucky Derby and two preparatory races at Garden State Park.

World speed records   The fastest race speed recorded is 43.26 mph, by Big Racket, 20.8 sec. for ¼ mile, at Mexico City, Mexico on 5 Feb. 1945. The four-year-old carried 114 lbs. The record for 1½ miles is 37.82 mph by three-year-old Hawkster (carrying 121 lbs.) at Santa Anita Park, Arcadia, CA on 14 Oct. 1989, with a time of 2 min. 22.8 sec.

JOCKEYS

Most successful   Billie Lee "Willie" Shoemaker (USA; b. weighing 2½ lbs., 19 Aug. 1931, whose racing weight was 97 lbs. at 4 ft. 11 in.), rode a record 8,833 winners out of 40,350 mounts from his first ride on 19 Mar. 1949 and first winner on 20 Apr. 1949 to his retirement on 3 Feb. 1990. Laffit Pincay, Jr. (USA; b. 29 Dec. 1946) has earned a career record $165,452,089 from 1964 to May 1992.

The most races won by a jockey in a year is 597, in 2,312 rides, by Kent Jason Desormeaux (USA; b. 27 Feb. 1970) in 1989. The greatest amount won in a year is 2,356,280,400 yen (*c.* $16,250,000) by Yutaka Take (Japan; b. 1969) in Japan in 1990. The greatest amount won in the United States in a year is $14,877,298, by José Adeon Santos (USA; b. 26 Apr. 1961, Chile) in 1988. Pat Day (USA) rode a season record 60 stakes race winners in 1991.

Wins   The most winners ridden in one day is nine, by Chris Wiley Antley (USA; b. 6 Jan. 1966) on 31 Oct. 1987. They consisted of four in the afternoon at Aqueduct, NY and five in the evening at The Meadowlands, NJ.

One card   The most winners ridden on one card is eight, by six riders, most recently (and in fewest rides) by Pat Day, in only nine rides at Arlington, IL on 13 Sep. 1989.

Consecutive   The longest winning streak is 12, by: Sir Gordon Richards (Great Britain; 1904–86); one race at Nottingham, Great Britain on 3 October, six out of six at Chepstow on 4 October, and the first five races next day at Chepstow, in 1933; and Pieter Stroebel at Bulawayo, Southern Rhodesia (now Zimbabwe), 7 June–7 July 1958.

The longest consecutive winning streak for an American jockey is nine races, by Albert Adams (USA) at Marlboro Racetrack, MD over three days, 10–12 Sep. 1930. He won the last two races on 10 September, all six races on 11 September and the first race on 12 September.

TRAINERS

Jack Charles Van Berg (USA; b. 7 June 1936) has the greatest number of wins in a year, 496 in 1976. The career record is 5,750, by Dale Baird (USA; b. 17 Apr. 1935) from 1962 to 1991. The greatest amount won in a year is $17,842,358, by Darrell Wayne Lukas (USA; b. 2 Sep. 1935) in 1988.

The only trainer to saddle the first five finishers in a classic race is Michael William Dickinson (Great Britain; b. 3 Feb. 1950), in the Cheltenham Gold Cup on 17 Mar. 1983; he won a record 12 races in one day, 27 Dec. 1982.

OWNERS

The most lifetime wins by an owner is 4,775, by Marion H. Van Berg (1895–1971), in North America, in 35 years. The most wins in a year is 494, by Dan R. Lasater (USA) in 1974. The greatest amount won in a year is $6,881,902, by Sam-Son Farms (Canada) in 1991.

Biggest weight   The biggest weight ever carried is 420 lbs., by both Mr. Maynard's Mare and Mr. Baker's horse in a match won by the former over a mile at York, Great Britain on 21 May 1788.

Perfect card   The only recorded instance of a racing correspondent forecasting ten out of ten winners on a race card was at Delaware Park, Wilmington, DE on 28 July 1974, by Charles Lamb of the *Baltimore News American*.

Biggest payout   Anthony A. Speelman and Nicholas John Cowan (both Great Britain) won $1,627,084.40, after federal income tax of $406,768.00 was withheld, on a $64 nine-horse accumulator at Santa Anita racetrack, CA on 19 Apr. 1987. Their first seven selections won and the payout was for a jackpot, accumulated over 24 days.

Highest price   The most paid for a yearling is $13.1 million on 23 July 1985 at Keeneland, KY by Robert Sangster and partners for *Seattle Dancer*.

Oldest winners   The oldest horses to win on the flat have been the 18-year-olds Revenge, at Shrewsbury, Great Britain on 23 Sep. 1790; Marksman, at Ashford, Great Britain, on 4 Sep. 1826; and Jorrocks, at Bathurst, Australia on 28 Feb. 1851. At the same age Wild Aster won three hurdle races in six days in Mar. 1919 and Sonny Somers won two steeplechases in Feb. 1980.

MAJOR RACE RECORDS

RACE (instituted)	RECORD TIME	MOST WINS				LARGEST FIELD
		JOCKEY	TRIPLE CROWN	TRAINER	OWNER	
Kentucky Derby (1875) 1¼ miles Churchill Downs, Louisville, KY	1 min. 59.4 sec. *Secretariat* 1973	5–Eddie Arcaro 1938, 41, 45, 48, 52 5–Bill Hartack 1957, 60, 62, 64, 69		6–Ben Jones 1938, 41, 44, 48, 49, 52	8–Calumet Farm 1941, 44, 48, 49, 52, 57, 58, 68	23 (1974)
Preakness Stakes (1873) 1 mile 1½ furlongs Pimlico, Baltimore, MD	1 min. 53.2 sec. *Tank's Prospect* 1985	6–Eddie Arcaro 1941, 48, 50, 51, 55, 57		7–Robert Wyndham Walden 1875, 78, 79, 80, 81, 82, 88	5–George Lorillard 1878, 79, 80, 81, 82	18 (1928)
Belmont Stakes (1867) 1½ miles Belmont Park, New York	2 min. 24.0 sec. *Secretariat* 1973 (By a record 31 lengths)	6–Jimmy McLaughlin 1882, 83, 84, 86, 87, 88 6–Eddie Arcaro 1941, 42, 45, 48, 52, 55		8–James Rowe Sr. 1883, 84, 1901, 04, 07, 08, 10, 13	5–Dwyer Bros 1883, 84, 86, 87, 88 5–James R. Keene 1901, 04, 07, 08, 10 5–William Woodward Sr. (Belair Stud) 1930, 32, 35, 36, 39	15 (1983)

Derby (1780) 1½ miles Epsom Downs, Great Britain	2 min. 33.8 sec. *Mahmoud* 1936 2 min. 33.84 sec. *Kahyasi* 1988 (Electronically timed)	9–Lester Piggott 1954, 57, 60, 68, 70, 72, 76, 77, 83	7–Robert Robson 1793, 1802, 09, 10, 15, 17, 23 7–John Porter 1868, 82, 83, 86, 90, 91, 99 7–Fred Darling 1922, 25, 26, 31, 38, 40, 41	5–3rd Earl of Egremont 1782, 1804, 05, 07, 26 5–HH Aga Khan III 1930, 35, 36, 48, 52	34 (1862)
Prix de l'Arc de Triomphe (1920) 1 mile 864 yds. Longchamp, France	2 min. 26.3 sec. *Trempolino* 1987	4–Jacques Doyasbère 1542, 44, 50, 51 4–Frédéric "Freddy" Head 1966, 72, 76, 79 4–Yves Saint-Martin 1970, 74, 82, 84 4–Pat Eddery 1980, 85, 86, 87	4–Charles Semblat 1942, 44, 46, 49 4–Alec Head 1952, 59, 76, 81 4–François Mathet 1950, 51, 70, 82	6–Marcel Boussac 1936, 37, 42, 44, 46, 49	30 (1967)
VRC Melbourne Cup (1861) 1 mile 1739 yds. Flemington, Victoria, Australia	3 min. 16.3 sec. *Kingston Rule* 1990	4–Bobby Lewis 1902, 15, 19, 27 4–Harry White 1974, 75, 78, 79	9–Bart Cummings 1965, 66, 67, 74, 75, 77, 79, 90, 91	4–Etienne de Mestre 1861, 62, 67, 78	39 (1890)
Grand National (1839) 4½ miles Aintree, Liverpool, Great Britain	8 min. 47.8 sec. *Mr. Frisk* 1990	5–George Stevens 1856, 63, 64, 69, 70	4–Fred Rimell 1956, 61, 70, 76	3–James Machell 1873, 74, 76 3–Sir Charles Assheton-Smith 1893, 1912, 13 3–Noel Le Mare 1973, 74, 77	66 (1929)

HURLING

Origins   A game of very ancient origin, hurling was included in the Tail-teann Games (instituted 1829 B.C.). It only became standardized with the formation of the Gaelic Athletic Association in Thurles, Ireland on 1 Nov. 1884. The Irish Hurling Union was formed in 1879.

Most titles *All-Ireland*   The greatest number of All-Ireland Championships won by one team is 27, by Cork, between 1890 and 1990. The greatest number of successive wins is four, by Cork (1941–44).

Most appearances   The most appearances in All-Ireland finals is ten, shared by Christy Ring (Cork and Munster) and John Doyle (Tipperary). They also share the record of All-Ireland medals, won with eight each. Ring's appearances on the winning side were in 1941–44, 1946 and 1952–54, while Doyle's were in 1949–51, 1958, 1961–62 and 1964–65. Ring also played in a record 22 inter-provincial finals (1942–63), and was on the winning side 18 times.

Highest and lowest scores   The highest score in an All-Ireland final (60 min.) was in 1989, when Tipperary, 41 (4 goals, 29 points) beat Antrim (3 goals, 9 points). The record aggregate score was when Cork, 39 (6 goals, 21 points), defeated Wexford, 25 (5 goals, 10 points), in the 80-minute final of 1970. A goal equals three points. The highest recorded individual score was by Nick Rackard (Wexford), who scored 7 goals and 7 points against Antrim in the 1954 All-Ireland semifinal. The lowest score in an All-Ireland final was when Tipperary (1 goal, 1 point) beat Galway (zero) in the first championship at Birr in 1887.

Largest crowd   The largest crowd was 84,865 for the All-Ireland final between Cork and Wexford at Croke Park, Dublin in 1954.

ICE SKATING

Origins   The earliest reference to ice skating is in early Scandinavian literature referring to the second century, although its origins are believed, on archaeological evidence, to be ten centuries earlier than that. The earliest English account of ice skating in 1180 refers to skates made of bone. The earliest skating club was the Edinburgh Skating Club, formed in 1742.

The first recorded race was from Wisbech to Whittlesey, Great Britain in 1763. The first artificial rink in the world was opened in London, Great Britain on 7 Dec. 1842, although the surface was not of ice. The first artificial ice rink was called the Glaciarium and was opened in London, Great Britain on 7 Jan. 1876.

The International Skating Union was founded at Scheveningen, Netherlands in 1892.

FIGURE SKATING

In North America, the first national body was the Amateur Association of Canada, founded on 30 Nov. 1887. The Skating Club of the USA was founded in Philadelphia in 1887. Jackson Haines, a New Yorker, is regarded as the pioneer of the modern concept of figure skating, a composite of skating and dancing. Although his ideas were not initially favored in the United States, Haines moved to Europe in the mid-1860s, where his international style of figure skating was warmly received and promoted. The sport functioned informally in the United States until 1921, when the United States Figure Skating Assocation (USFSA) was formed to oversee skating in this country—a role it still performs.

Most titles *Olympic*   The most Olympic gold medals won by a figure skater is three: by Gillis Grafström (Sweden; 1893–1938) in 1920, 1924 and 1928 (also silver medal in 1932); by Sonja Henie (Norway; 1912–69) in 1928, 1932 and 1936; and by Irina Konstantinovna Rodnina (USSR; b. 12 Sep. 1949) with two different partners in the pairs in 1972, 1976 and 1980.

World   The greatest number of men's individual world figure skating titles (instituted 1896) is ten, by Ulrich Salchow (Sweden; 1877–1949) in 1901–05 and 1907–11. The women's record (instituted 1906) is also ten individual titles, by Sonja Henie between 1927 and 1936. Irina Rodnina won ten pairs titles (instituted 1908), four with Aleksey Nikolayevich Ulanov (b. 4 Nov. 1947), 1969–72, and six with her husband Aleksandr Gennadyevich Zaitsev (b. 16 June 1952), 1973–78. The most ice dance titles (instituted 1952) won is six, by Lyudmila Alekseyevna Pakhomova (1946–86) and her husband Aleksandr Georgiyevich Gorshkov (USSR; b. 8 Oct. 1946), 1970–74 and 1976. They also won the first-ever Olympic ice dance title in 1976.

Richard Totten "Dick" Button (b. 18 July 1929) set US records with two

---

Barrel jumping on ice skates   The official distance record is 29 ft. 5 in. over 18 barrels, by Yvon Jolin at Terrebonne, Quebec, Canada on 25 Jan. 1981. The women's record is 20 ft. 4¼ in. over 11 barrels, by Janet Hainstock in Wyandotte, MI on 15 Mar. 1980.

Greatest distance on ice skates   Robin John Cousins (Great Britain; b. 17 Aug. 1957) achieved 19 ft. 1 in. in an axel jump and 18 ft. with a back flip at Richmond Ice Rink, Surrey, Great Britain on 16 Nov. 1983.

Most mid-air rotations   Kurt Browning (Canada; b. 18 June 1966) was the first to achieve a quadruple jump in competition—a toe loop—in the World Championships at Budapest, Hungary on 25 Mar. 1988. The first woman to do so was Suruya Bonaly (France; b. 15 Dec. 1973) in the Women's World Championships at Munich, Germany on 16 Mar. 1991.

Olympic gold medals, 1948 and 1952, and five world titles, 1948–52. Five women's world titles were won by Carol Elizabeth Heise (b. 20 Jan. 1940), 1956–60, as well as the 1960 Olympic gold.

United States The US Championships were first held in 1914. The most titles won by an individual is nine, by Maribel Y. Vinson (1911–61), 1928–33 and 1935–37. She also won six pairs titles, and her aggregate of 15 titles is equaled by Therese Blanchard (nee Weld; 1893–1978), who won six individual and nine pairs titles between 1914 and 1927. The men's individual record is seven, by Roger Turner, 1928–34, and by Dick Button, 1946–52. At age 16 in 1946, Button was the youngest-ever winner.

Triple Crown Karl Schäfer (Austria; 1909–76) and Sonja Henie achieved double "Grand Slams," both in the years 1932 and 1936. This feat was repeated by Katarina Witt (East Germany; b. 3 Dec. 1965) in 1984 and 1988.

TRIPLE CROWN. Katarina Witt, with wins in 1984 and 1988, became the third skater to win the "Grand Slam" of World, Olympic and European titles twice. She followed Karl Schäfer and Sonja Henie in 1932 and 1936. (Photo: Allsport/Vandystadt)

Highest marks   The highest tally of maximum six marks awarded in an international championship was 29, to Jayne Torvill (Great Britain; b. 7 Oct. 1957) and Christopher Dean (Great Britain; 27 July 1958) in the World Ice Dance Championships at Ottawa, Canada on 22–24 Mar. 1984. This comprised seven in the compulsory dances, a perfect set of nine for presentation in the set pattern dance, and 13 in the free dance, including another perfect set from all nine judges for artistic presentation. They previously gained a perfect set of nine sixes for artistic presentation in the free dance at the 1983 World Championships in Helsinki, Finland and at the 1984 Winter Olympic Games in Sarajevo, Yugoslavia. In their career Torvill and Dean received a record total of 136 sixes.

The most by a soloist is seven: by Donald George Jackson (Canada; b. 2 Apr. 1940) in the World Men's Championship at Prague, Czechoslovakia in 1962; and by Midori Ito (Japan; b. 13 Aug. 1969) in the World Women's Championships at Paris, France in 1989.

Largest rink   The world's largest indoor ice rink is in the Moscow Olympic arena, which has an ice area of 86,800 ft.^{2}. The five rinks at Fujikyu Highland Skating Center in Japan total 285,243 ft.^{2}.

SPEED SKATING

Most titles *Olympic*   The most Olympic gold medals won in speed skating is six, by Lidiya Pavlovna Skoblikova (USSR; b. 8 Mar. 1939) in 1960 (two) and 1964 (four). The men's record is by Clas Thunberg (Finland; 1893–1973) with five gold (including one tied), and also one silver and one tied bronze, in 1924 and 1928. Eric Arthur Heiden (USA; b. 14 June 1958) also won five gold medals, uniquely at one Games at Lake Placid, NY in 1980.

SPEED SKATING. Bonnie Blair (USA) shown here with her two gold medals, won at Albertville, France in the 1992 Winter Olympics. (Photo: Allsport/Mike Powell)

SPEED SKATING

WORLD RECORDS

	min.:sec.	NAME AND COUNTRY	PLACE	DATE
MEN				
METERS				
500	36.45	Uwe-Jens Mey (East Germany)	Calgary, Canada	14 Feb. 1988
	36.23*	Nick Thometz (USA)	Medeo, USSR	26 Mar. 1987
1,000	1:12.58†	Pavel Pegov (USSR)	Medeo, USSR	25 Nov. 1983
	1:12.58	Igor Zhelozovskiy (USSR)	Heerenveen, Netherlands	25 Feb. 1989
	1:12.05*	Nick Thometz (USA)	Medeo, USSR	27 Mar. 1987
1,500	1:52.06	André Hoffmann (East Germany)	Calgary, Canada	20 Feb. 1988
3,000	3:57.52	Johann Olav Koss (Norway)	Heerenveen, Netherlands	13 Mar. 1990
	3:56.65*	Sergey Martyuk (USSR)	Medeo, USSR	11 Mar. 1977
5,000	6:41.73	Johann-Olav Koss (Norway)	Heerenveen, Netherlands	9 Feb. 1991
10,000	13:43.54	Johann-Olav Koss (Norway)	Heerenveen, Netherlands	10 Feb. 1991

Unofficial. †Set at high altitude.

WOMEN				
500	39.10	Bonnie Blair (USA)	Calgary, Canada	22 Feb. 1988
1,000	1:17.65	Christa Rothenburger (now Luding)(East Germany)	Calgary, Canada	26 Feb. 1988

1,500.........1:59.30† ...Karin Kania (East Germany)...............22 Mar. 1986
3,000.........4:10.80.......Gunda Kleeman (Germany).................9 Dec. 1990
5,000.........7:14.13.......Yvonne van Gennip (Netherlands)......28 Feb. 1988
10,000*......15:25.25.....Yvonne van Gennip (Netherlands)......Heerenveen, Netherlands.........19 Mar. 1988

Record not officially recognized for this distance. †Set at high altitude.

WORLD RECORDS—SHORT TRACK

MEN

500 ....43.43......Mark Lackie (Canada) ....Denver, CO .....3 Apr. 1992
1,000 ....1:28.47......Mike McMillen (New Zealand).......Denver, CO .....4 Apr. 1992
1,500 ....2:22.77......Andrew Nicholson (New Zealand).......Nobeyama, Japan.....7 Apr. 1992
3,000 ....5:04.24......Tatsuyoshi Ishihara (Japan).......Amsterdam, Netherlands .....17 Mar. 1985
5,000 relay ....7:14.02......South Korea ....Albertville, France .....18 Feb. 1992

WOMEN

500 ....46.72......Sylvie Daigle (Canada) ....Albertville, France .....16 Nov. 1991
1,000 ....1:38.93......Yulia Vlaxova ....Denver, CO .....4 Apr. 1992
1,500 ....2:28.26......Eden Donatelli (Canada).......Seoul, South Korea .....31 Mar. 1991
3,000 ....5:18.33......Maria-Rosa Candido (Italy) ....Budapest, Hungary .....17 Jan. 1988
3,000 relay........4:36.42......Canada ....Albertville, France .....18 Feb. 1992

WORLD RECORDS. Johann-Olav Koss (Norway) currently holds three speed skating records at the longer distances of 3,000, 5,000 and 10,000 m. The records set in the last two distances were at Heerenveen, Netherlands during the 1991 World Championships, when he won the title with a record score. Here he is seen in action at the 1992 Olympics, when he won gold in the 1,500 m. (Photo: Allsport/Shaun Botterill)

OLYMPICS. For the first time, at the 1992 Olympics, short-track speed skating was a full medal sport, and such was the level of competition that world records were set in three of the four events. The most successful skater was Kim Ki-hoon (South Korea), who won the 1,000 m (as seen here) in a then world record time of 1 min. 30.76 sec. and was a member of the winning 5,000 m relay team. (Photo: Allsport/Chris Cole)

World The greatest number of world overall titles (instituted 1893) won by any skater is five—by Oscar Mathisen (Norway; 1888–1954) in 1908–09 and 1912–14; and by Clas Thunberg in 1923, 1925, 1928–29 and 1931. The most titles won in the women's events (instituted 1936) is five, by Karin Kania (nee Enke [East Germany], b. 20 June 1961) in 1982, 1984, 1986–88. Kania also won a record six overall titles at the World Sprint Championships, 1980–81, 1983–84, 1986–1987. A record five men's sprint overall titles have been won by Igor Zhelezovskiy (USSR), 1985–86, 1989 and 1991–92.

The record score achieved for the world overall title is 157.396 points, by Johann-Olav Koss (Norway) at Heerenveen, Netherlands on 9–10 Feb. 1991. The record low women's score is 171.630 points, by Jacqueline Börner (East Germany) at Calgary, Canada on 10–11 Feb. 1990.

United States Eric Heiden won a US record three overall world titles, 1977–79. His sister Elizabeth Lee "Beth" Heiden (b. 27 Sep. 1959) became the only US women's overall champion in 1979. She completed a unique double championship when in the following year she became the first American woman to win the cycling road race world title. Later, at the University of Vermont, she took up cross-country skiing, and won the NCCA title.

World Short-track Championships The most successful skater in these championships (instituted 1978) has been Sylvie Daigle (Canada; b. 1 Dec. 1962), women's overall champion in 1979, 1983 and 1989–90.

Longest race The "Elfstedentocht" ("Tour of the Eleven Towns"), which originated in the 17th century, was held in the Netherlands from 1909–63, and again in 1985 and 1986, covering 200 km (124 miles 483 yds.). As the weather does not permit an annual race in the Netherlands, alternative "Elfstedentocht" take place at suitable venues. These venues have included Lake Vesijärvi, near Lahti, Finland; Ottawa River, Canada; and Lake Weissensee, Austria. The record time for 200 km is: *(men)* 5 hrs. 40 min. 37 sec., by Dries van Wijhe (Netherlands); and *(women)* 5 hrs. 48 min. 8 sec., by Alida Pasveer (Netherlands), both at Lake Weissensee (altitude 3,609 ft.), Austria on 11 Feb. 1989. Jan-Roelof Kruithof (Netherlands) won the race eight times— 1974, 1976–77, 1979–83. An estimated 16,000 skaters took part in 1986.

Twenty-four hours Martinus Kuiper (Netherlands) skated 339.681 miles in 24 hrs. in Alkmaar, Netherlands on 12–13 Dec. 1988.

ICE AND SAND YACHTING

Origins The sport originated in the Low Countries and along the Baltic coast in about 1600 (the year the earliest patent was granted). The earliest authentic record is Dutch, dating from 1768. Land or sand yachts of Dutch construction were first reported on beaches (now in Belgium) in 1595. The earliest international championship was staged in 1914.

Fastest speeds *Ice* The fastest speed officially recorded is 143 mph, by

John D. Buckstaff in a Class A stern-steerer on Lake Winnebago, WI in 1938. Such a speed is possible in a wind of 72 mph.

Sand   The official world record for a sand yacht is 66.48 mph, set by Christian-Yves Nau (France; b. 1944) in *Mobil* at Le Touquet, France on 22 Mar. 1981, when the wind speed reached 75 mph. A speed of 88.4 mph was attained by Nord Embroden (USA) in *Midnight at the Oasis* at Superior Dry Lake, CA on 15 Apr. 1976.

Largest ice yacht   The largest ice yacht was *Icicle,* built for Commodore John E. Roosevelt for racing on the Hudson River, NY in 1869. It was 68 ft. 11 in. long and carried 1,070 ft.² of canvas.

ICE YACHTING. The fastest official speed for ice yachting is currently 143 mph. Shown here are yachts racing in Finland. (Photo: Allsport/Mitch Carucci/Vandystadt)

JAI ALAI (PELOTA VASCA)

Origins   The game, which originated in Italy as *longue paume* and was introduced into France in the 13th century, is said to be the fastest of all ball games. The glove or *gant* was introduced *c.* 1840 and the *chistera* was invented by Jean "Gantchiki" Dithurbide of Ste. Pée, France. The *grand chis-*

tera was invented by Melchior Curuchague of Buenos Aires, Argentina in 1888. The world's largest *frontón* (enclosed stadium) is the Palm Beach Jai Alai, West Palm Beach, which has a seating capacity of 6,000 and covers three acres. The record attendance for a jai alai contest was 15,052 people at the World Jai Alai at Miami, FL, on 27 Dec. 1975. The frontón, which is the oldest in the United States (1926), has seating capacity for only 3,884.

United States   Jai alai was introduced in the United States at the St. Louis World's Fair in 1903. The sport took root in Miami, FL in 1924.

World Championships   The *Federacion Internacional de Pelota Vasca* stages World Championships every four years (the first in 1952). The most successful pair have been Roberto Elias and Juan Labat (Argentina), who won the *Trinquete Share* four times, 1952, 1958, 1962 and 1966. Labat won a record seven world titles in all between 1952 and 1966. Riccardo Bizzozero (Argentina) also won seven world titles in various *Trinquete* and *Frontón corto* events, 1970–82. The most wins in the long court game *Cesta Punta* is three, by José Hamuy (Mexico; 1934–83), with two different partners, 1958, 1962 and 1966.

Fastest speed   An electronically measured ball velocity of 188 mph was recorded by José Ramon Areitio (Spain; b. 6 July 1947) at the Newport Jai Alai, RI on 3 Aug. 1979.

Longest domination   The longest domination as the world's No. 1 player was enjoyed by Chiquito de Cambo (ne Joseph Apesteguy [France]; 1881–1955) from the beginning of the century until succeeded in 1938 by Jean Urruty (France; b. 19 Oct. 1913).

JUDO

Origins   Judo is a modern combat sport that developed out of an amalgam of several old Japanese martial arts, the most popular of which was ju-jitsu (jiu-jitsu), which is thought to be of Chinese origin. Judo has developed greatly since 1882, when it was first devised by Dr. Jigoro Kano (1860–1938). The International Judo Federation was founded in 1951.

Most titles *World and Olympic*   World Championships were inaugurated in Tokyo, Japan in 1956. Women's championships were first held in 1980 in New York. Yashiro Yamashita (b. 1 June 1957) won nine consecutive Japanese titles from 1977 to 1985; four world titles; Over 95 kg in 1979, 1981 and 1983; Open in 1981; and the Olympic Open category in 1984. He retired undefeated after 203 successive wins between 1977 and 1985. Three other men have won four world titles—Wilhelm Ruska (Netherlands; b. 29 Aug. 1940), Over 93 kg 1967, 1971, and 1972 Olympic and Open titles; Shozo Fujii (Japan; b. 12 May 1950), Under 80 kg 1971, 1973 and 1975, Under 75 kg 1979; and Naoya Ogawa (Japan), Open 1987, 1989, 1991 and Over 95 kg 1989. The only men to have won two Olympic gold medals are Wilhelm Ruska, Over 93 kg and Open in 1972; Peter Seisenbacher (Austria;

b. 25 Mar. 1960), 86 kg 1984 and 1988; and Hitoshi Saito (Japan; b. 2 Jan. 1961), Over 95 kg 1984 and 1988. Ingrid Berghmans (Belgium; b. 24 Aug. 1961) has won a record six women's world titles (first held 1980): Open 1980, 1982, 1984 and 1986 and Under 72 kg in 1984 and 1989. She has also won three silver medals and a bronze. She won the Olympic 72 kg title in 1988, when women's judo was introduced as a demonstration sport.

The only US judo players to win world titles have been Michael Swain (b. 21 Dec. 1960), at men's 71 kg class in 1987, and Ann-Maria Bernadette Burns (b. 15 Aug. 1958) at women's 56 kg in 1984.

Highest grades The efficiency grades in judo are divided into pupil (*kyu*) and master (*dan*) grades. The highest awarded is the extremely rare red belt *judan* (10th dan), given to only 13 men so far. The Judo protocol provides for an 11th dan (*juichidan*) who also would wear a red belt, a 12th dan (*junidan*) who would wear a white belt twice as wide as an ordinary belt, and the highest of all, *shihan* (ductor), but these have never been bestowed, except for the 12th dan, to the founder of the sport, Dr. Jigoro Kano.

Judo throws The brothers Carl and Peter Udry completed 18,779 judo throwing techniques in a ten-hour period at Hendra Sports Field, Truro, Great Britain on 29 Aug. 1987.

Jiu-Jitsu The World Council of Jiu-Jitsu Organization has staged World Championships biennially since 1984. The Canadian team has been the winner on each occasion.

KARATE

Origins Based on techniques devised from the sixth century Chinese art of Shaolin boxing (*kempo*), karate was developed by an unarmed populace in Okinawa as a weapon against armed Japanese oppressors *c.* 1500. Transmitted to Japan in the 1920s by Funakoshi Gichin, this method of combat was refined into karate and organized into a sport with competitive rules. The five major styles of karate in Japan are: *shotokan, wado-ryu, goju-ryu, shitoryu* and *kyokushinkai*, each of which places a different emphasis on speed, power, etc. Other styles include *sankukai, shotokai* and *shukokai*. *Wu shu* is a comprehensive term embracing all Chinese martial arts. *Gong fu* (kung fu) is one aspect of these arts popularized by the movies.

World Championships Great Britain has won a record six world titles (instituted 1970) at the kumite team event, in 1975, 1982, 1984, 1986, 1988 and 1990. Two men's individual kumite titles have been won by: Pat McKay (Great Britain) at Under 80 kg, 1982 and 1984; Emmanuel Pinda (France) at Open, 1984, and Over 80 kg, 1988; and Theirry Masci (France) at Under 70 kg, in 1986 and 1988. Four women's kumite titles have been won by Guus van Mourik (Netherlands) at Over 60 kg, in 1982, 1984, 1986 and 1988. Three individual kata titles have been won by: *(men)* Tsuguo Sakumoto (Japan) in 1984, 1986 and 1988; *(women)* Mie Nakayama (Japan) in 1982, 1984 and 1986.

Top exponents The leading exponents among karateka are a number of 10th dans in Japan.

KARATE. A contest at the International Karate competition in Paris, France in 1992. (Photo: Allsport/Vandystadt/Yann Guichadua)

LACROSSE

MEN

Origins The game is of Native American origin, derived from the inter-tribal game *baggataway*, and was played before 1492 by the Iroquois in lower Ontario, Canada and upper New York State. The French named it after their game of *chouler à la crosse*, known as far back as 1381.

Lacrosse was included in the Olympic Games of 1904 and 1908, and was featured as an exhibition sport in the 1928, 1932 and 1948 Games.

The first college team in the United States was that of New York University in 1877, and the US Amateur Lacrosse Association was founded in 1879.

Most titles *World* The USA has won five of the six World Championships, in 1967, 1974, 1982, 1986 and 1990. Canada won the other world title in 1978, beating the USA 17–16 after extra time; this was the first tied international match.

Highest lacrosse score The highest score in an international lacrosse match was the USA's 32–8 win over England at Toronto, Ontario, Canada in 1986.

The highest score by the women's team was by Great Britain and Ireland with their 40-0 defeat of Long Island during their 1967 tour of the United States.

Most international lacrosse appearances The record number of international appearances is 42, by Peter Daniel Roden (Great Britain; b. 8 Nov. 1954) from 1976–90.

United States National champions were determined by committee from 1936, and received the Wilson Wingate Trophy; since 1971 they have been decided by NCAA playoffs. Johns Hopkins University has the most wins overall: seven NCAA titles between 1974 and 1987, and six wins and five ties between 1941 and 1970.

Most points The record for most points in the NCAA lacrosse tournament is 25, by Eamon McEneaney (Cornell) in 1977 and Tim Goldstein (Cornell) in 1987. Both players played in three games.

Ed Mullen scored the most points in an NCAA championship game, with 12, for Maryland *v.* Navy in the 1976 championship game.

WOMEN

The first reported playing of lacrosse by women was in 1886. The women's game has evolved separately from the men's game, so the rules now differ considerably.

World Championships/World Cup The first World Cup was held in 1982, and the USA has won twice, in 1982 and 1989.

MICROLIGHTING

The *Fédération Aéronautique Internationale* has established two classes of aircraft for which records are accepted, C1 a/o and R 1-2-3, and the following are the overall best of the two classes (all in the C1 a/o class).

World records Distance in a straight line: 1,011.48 miles, Wilhelm Lischak (Austria), Volsau, Austria to Brest, France, 8 June 1988.

Distance in a closed circuit: 1,679.09 miles, Wilhelm Lischak (Austria), Wels, Austria, 18 June 1988.

Altitude: 30,147 ft., Eric S. Winton (Australia), Tyagarah Aerodrome, New South Wales, Australia, 8 Apr. 1989.

Speed over a 500 km closed circuit: 182 mph, C.T. Andrews (USA), 3 Aug. 1982.

Microlighting endurance Eve Jackson flew from Biggin Hill, Great Britain to Sydney, Australia from 26 Apr. 1986 to 1 Aug. 1987. Flying time was 279 hrs. 55 min. and the flight covered 13,639 miles. From 1 Dec. 1987 to 29 Jan. 1988, Brian Milton (Great Britain) flew from London, Great Britain to Sydney with a flying time of 241 hrs. 20 min. and covered 13,650 miles. Vijaypat Singhania (India) flew from Biggin Hill to Delhi, India, a distance of 5,420 miles, in 87 hrs. 55 min., from 18 Aug. to 10 Sep. 1988.

MODERN PENTATHLON

Point scores in riding, fencing, and cross-country, and hence overall scores, have no comparative value between one competition and another. In shooting and swimming (300 meters) the scores are of record significance.

The modern pentathlon (consisting of fencing, swimming, shooting, running and riding) was inaugurated at the Olympic Games in Stockholm in 1912. *L'Union Internationale de Pentathlon Moderne* (UIPM) was founded at Aldershot, Great Britain on 3 Aug. 1948. The United States Modern Pentathlon and Biathlon Association was established in 1971, but this body was split to create the US Modern Pentathlon Association in 1978.

Most titles *World* András Balczó (Hungary; b. 16 Aug. 1938) won the record number of world titles (instituted 1949), six individual and seven team. He won the world individual title in 1963, 1965–67 and 1969 and the Olympic title in 1972. His seven team titles (1960–70) comprised five world and two Olympic. The USSR has won a record 14 world and four Olympic team titles. Hungary has also won a record four Olympic team titles and ten world titles.

Women's World Championships were first held in 1981. Poland has won a record five women's world team titles: 1985, 1988–1991; Great Britain won three world titles and three World Cups, 1978–80, when this competition preceded the world championships. The only double individual champions have been Irina Kiselyeva (USSR), 1986–87, and Eva Fjellerup (Denmark), 1990–91.

The only US modern pentathletes to win world titles have been Robert Nieman (b. 21 Oct. 1947), 1979, when the men's team also won, and Lori Norwood (women's) in 1989.

Olympic The greatest number of Olympic gold medals won is three, by András Balczó, a member of the winning team in 1960 and 1968 and the 1972 individual champion. Lars Hall (Sweden; b. 30 Apr. 1927) has uniquely won two individual championships (1952 and 1956). Pavel Serafimovich Lednyev (USSR; b. 25 Mar. 1943) won a record seven medals (two team gold, one team silver, one individual silver, three individual bronze), 1968–80.

The only US individual Olympic medalist has been Robert Lee Beck, who won the bronze in 1960.

Probably the greatest margin of victory was by William Oscar Guernsey Grut (Sweden; b. 17 Sep. 1914) in the 1948 Games, when he won three events and placed fifth and eighth in the other two.

US National Championships   The men's championship was inaugurated in 1955. Mike Burley has won a record four titles (1977, 1979, 1981, 1985). The women's championship was first held in 1977; Kim Dunlop (née Arata) has won a record nine titles (1979–80, 1984–89 and 1991).

MODERN PENTATHLON

Highest scores in major competition

WORLD RECORDS

SHOOTING
200/200 (1,132 points): Charles Leonard (USA; b. 23 Feb. 1913)[1], Berlin, Germany, 3 Aug. 1936. Daniele Masala (Italy; b. 12 Feb. 1955), Jönkoping, Sweden, 21 Aug. 1978. George Horvath (Sweden; b. 14 Mar. 1960), Moscow, USSR, 22 July 1980.

SWIMMING
3 min. 08.22 sec. (1,368 points): John Scott (USA; b. 14 Apr. 1962), London, Great Britain, 27 Aug. 1982.

[1] *Points not given in 1936 Olympic Games.*

MOTORCYCLE RACING

Origins   The first motorcycle race was held over a mile on an oval track at Sheen House, Richmond, Great Britain on 29 Nov. 1897, won by Charles Jarrott (Great Britain; 1877–1944) on a Fournier. The oldest continuous motorcycle races in the world are the Auto-Cycle Union Tourist Trophy (TT) series, first held on the 15.81 mile "Peel" (St. John's) course in the Isle of Man, Great Britain on 28 May 1907, and still run in the island on the "Mountain" circuit.

Earliest race   The first reported race in the United States was won by George Holden of Brooklyn, NY in 1903, recording 14 min. 57.2 sec. for 10 miles.

Fastest circuits   The highest average lap speed attained on any closed circuit is 160.288 mph, by Yvon du Hamel (Canada; b. 1941) on a modified 903 cc four-cylinder Kawasaki Z1 at the 31-degree banked 2.5 mile Daytona International Speedway, FL in Mar. 1973. His lap time was 56.149 sec.

The fastest road circuit used to be Francorchamps circuit near Spa, Belgium, then 8.74 miles in length. It was lapped in 3 min. 50.3 sec. (average speed 137.150 mph) by Barry Stephen Frank Sheene (Great Britain; b. 11 Sep. 1950) on a 495 cc 4-cylinder Suzuki during the Belgian Grand Prix on 3 July 1977. On that occasion he set a record time for this ten-lap (87.74 mile) race of 38 min. 58.5 sec. (average speed 135.068 mph).

Most successful riders   Angel Roldan Nieto (Spain; b. 25 Jan. 1947) won a record seven 125 cc titles, 1971–72, 1979, 1981–84, and he also won a record six titles at 50 cc, 1969–70, 1972, 1975–77. Klaus Enders (Germany; b. 1937) won six world sidecar titles, 1967, 1969–70, 1972–74.

Giacomo Agostini (Italy; b. 16 June 1942) won 122 races (68 at 500 cc, 54 at 350 cc) in the World Championship series between 24 Apr. 1965 and 25 Sep. 1977, including a record 19 in 1970, a season's total also achieved by Mike Hailwood (Great Britain) in 1966.

World Championships   The most World Championship titles (instituted by the *Fédération Internationale Motocycliste* in 1949) won is 15, by Giacomo Agostini—seven at 350 cc, 1968–74, and eight at 500 cc in 1966–72, 1975. He is the only man to have won two World Championships in five consecutive years (350 cc and 500 cc titles, 1968–72).

In 1985 Freddie Burdette Spencer (USA; b. 20 Dec. 1961), riding for Honda, became the first man ever to win the 250 cc and 500 cc titles in the same year.

The most world titles won by an American motorcyclist is four, by Eddie Lawson (b. 11 Mar. 1958), at 500 cc in 1984, 1986, 1988–89.

Trials   A record four World Trials Championships have been won by Jordi Tarrés (Spain), 1987, 1989–91.

Most successful machines   Japanese Yamaha machines won 44 World Championships between 1964 and 1991.

Moto-cross   Joël Robert (Belgium; b. 11 Nov. 1943) won six 250 cc Moto-cross World Championships (1964, 1968–72). Between 25 Apr. 1964 and 18 June 1972 he won a record fifty 250 cc Grand Prix. The youngest moto-cross world champion was Dave Strijbos (Netherlands; b. 9 Nov. 1968), who won the 125 cc title at the age of 18 yrs. 296 days on 31 Aug. 1986. Eric Geboers (Belgium) has uniquely won all three categories of the Moto-cross World Championships, at 125 cc in 1982 and 1983, 250 cc in 1987 and 500 cc in 1988.

Youngest and oldest world champions   Loris Capirossi (Italy; b. 4 Apr. 1973) is the youngest to win a World Championship. He was 17 yrs. 165 days when he won the 125 cc title on 16 Sep. 1990. The oldest was Hermann-Peter Müller (1909–76) of West Germany, who won the 250 cc title in 1955 at the age of 46.

Longest circuit   The 37.73-mile "Mountain" circuit on the Isle of Man, Great Britain, over which the principal TT races have been run since 1911 (with minor amendments in 1920), has 264 curves and corners and is the longest used for any motorcycle race.

MOUNTAINEERING

Origins   Although Bronze-Age artifacts have been found on the summit of the Riffelhorn, Switzerland (9,605 ft.), mountaineering as a sport has a continuous history dating back only to 1854. Isolated instances of climbing for its own sake date back to the 13th century. The Atacamenans built sacrificial platforms near the summit of Llullaillaco (22,057 ft.) in late pre-Columbian times *c.* 1490.

Mount Everest   Everest (29,078 ft.) was first climbed at 11:30 A.M. on 29 May 1953, when the summit was reached by Edmund Percival Hillary (b. 20 July 1919), of New Zealand, and Sherpa Tenzing Norgay (1914–86, formerly called Tenzing Khumjung Bhutia). The successful expedition was led by Col. (later Hon. Brigadier) Henry Cecil John Hunt (b. 22 June 1910).

Most conquests   Ang Rita Sherpa (b. 1947), with ascents in 1983, 1984, 1985, 1987, 1988 and 1990, has scaled Everest six times, and all without the use of bottled oxygen.

Solo   Reinhold Messner (Italy; b. 17 Sep. 1944) was the first to make the entire climb solo, on 20 Aug. 1980. Also, Messner, with Peter Habeler (Austria; b. 22 July 1942), made the first entirely oxygen-less ascent, on 8 May 1978.

First woman   Junko Tabei (Japan; b. 22 Sep. 1939) reached the summit on 16 May 1975.

Oldest   Richard Daniel Bass (USA; b. 21 Dec. 1929) was age 55 yrs. 130 days when he reached the summit on 30 Apr. 1985.

Most successful expedition   The Mount Everest International Peace Climb, a team of American, Russian and Chinese climbers, led by James W. Whittaker (USA), in 1990 succeeded in putting the greatest number of people on the summit, 20, from 7–10 May 1990.

Most in a day   On 12 May 1992, 32 climbers (30 men and 2 women) from the USA, Russia, New Zealand, India, the Netherlands, Belgium, Israel, Hong Kong and Nepal, from five separate expeditions, reached the summit.

Sea level to summit   Timothy John Macartney-Snape (Australia; b. 30 Apr. 1963) traversed Everest's entire altitude from sea level to summit. He set off on foot from the Bay of Bengal near Calcutta, India on 5 Feb. 1990 and reached the summit on 11 May, having walked approximately 745 miles.

Mountaineer   Reinhold Messner was the first person to successfully scale all 14 of the world's mountains of over 26,250 ft., all without oxygen. With his ascent of Kanchenjunga in 1982, he became the first person to climb the world's three highest mountains, having earlier reached the summits of Everest and K2.

Oldest mountain climber   Teiichi Igarashi (Japan; b. 21 Sep. 1886) climbed Mt. Fuji (Fujiyama) (12,388 ft.) at the age of 99 yrs. 302 days on 20 July 1986.

Rappeling   Wilmer Pérez and Luis Aulestia set a rappeling record of 3,376 ft. by descending from above the Angel Falls in Venezuela down to its base on 24 Aug. 1989. The descent took 1¼ hrs.

The longest descent down the side of a building is one of 1,122 ft. by a team of eight men from the Code Four Rescue unit, who rappeled from the observation deck of the CN Tower in Toronto, Ontario, Canada to the ground on 26 June 1985.

The greatest distance rappeled by a team of ten in an eight-hour period is 27.74 miles, by members of the 63rd Airborne Squadron RCT from Aldershot, Great Britain. They achieved the record by rappeling 1,674 times down the side of Alexander House in Swindon, Great Britain on 14 Sep. 1991.

Human fly   The longest climb achieved on the vertical face of a building occurred on 26 June 1986 when Daniel Goodwin, 30, of California climbed a record 1,125 ft. up the outside of the 1,815 ft. 5 in. CN Tower in Toronto, Ontario, Canada (the tallest self-supporting tower in the world) using neither climbing aids nor safety equipment.

Greatest walls   The highest final stage in any wall climb is the one on the south face of Annapurna I (26,545 ft.). It was climbed by the British expedition led by Christian John Storey Bonington (b. 6 Aug. 1934) when from 2 Apr. to 27 May 1970, using 18,000 ft. of rope, Donald Whillans (1933–85) and Dougal Haston scaled to the summit. The longest wall climb is on the Rupal-Flank from the base camp, at 11,680 ft., to the South Point, at 26,384 ft., of Nanga Parbat—a vertical ascent of 14,704 ft. This was scaled by the Austro-German-Italian expedition led by Dr. Karl Maria Herrligkoffer (b. 13 June 1916) in April 1970.

The most demanding free climbs in the world are those rated at 5.13, the premier location for these being in the Yosemite Valley, CA.

Highest bivouac   Four Nepalese summiters bivouacked at more than 28,870 ft. in their descent from the summit of Everest on the night of 23 Apr. 1990. They were Ang Rita Sherpa, on his record-breaking sixth ascent of Everest; Ang Kami Sherpa (b. 1952); Pasang Norbu Sherpa (b. 1963); and Top Bahadur Khatri (b. 1960).

MOUNTAIN RACING

Mount Cameroon   Reginald Esuke (Cameroon) descended from the summit at 13,543 ft. to Buea at 3,002 ft. in 1 hr. 2 min. 15 sec. on 24 Jan. 1988, achieving a vertical rate of 167.5 ft. per min. Timothy Leku Lekunze (Cameroon) set the record for the race to the summit and back of 3 hrs. 46 min. 34 sec. on 25 Jan. 1987, when the temperature varied from 35° C. at the start to 0° C at the summit. The record time for the ascent is 2 hrs. 25 min. 20 sec., by Jack Maitland (Great Britain) in 1988. The women's record for the race is 4 hrs. 42 min. 31 sec., by Fabiola Rueda (Colombia; b. 26 Mar. 1963) in 1989.

NETBALL

Origins   The game of netball was invented in the United States in 1891 and introduced into England in 1895 by Dr. Toles.

Most titles *World*   Australia has won the World Championships (instituted 1963) a record six times—1963, 1971, 1975, 1979, 1983 and 1991.

Highest scores   On 9 July 1991, during the World Championships in Sydney, Australia, the Cook Islands beat Vanuatu 120–30. The record number of goals in the World Tournament is 402, by Judith Heath (England; b. 1942) in 1971.

Most international appearances   The record number of appearances is 100, by Jillian Hipsey of England, 1978–87.

OLYMPICS

These records include the Games, known as the Intercalated Games, held at Athens, Greece in 1906 to celebrate the tenth anniversary of the revival of the Olympics.

Origins   The earliest celebration of the ancient Olympic Games of which there is a definite record is that of July 776 B.C., when Coroibos, a cook from Elis, won the foot race, though the origin of the Games dates from perhaps as early as *c.* 1370 B.C. The ancient Games were terminated by an order issued in Milan in A.D. 393 by Theodosius I, "the Great" (*c.* 346–95), Emperor of Rome. At the instigation of Pierre de Fredi, Baron de Coubertin (1873–1937), the Olympic Games of the modern era were inaugurated in Athens on 6 Apr. 1896. In 1992, the XVI Winter Games took place in Albertville, France from 8–23 February, and the XXV Summer Games took place in Barcelona, Spain from 25 July–9 August.

Best attendance   Five countries have been represented at each of the 22 celebrations of the Summer Games: Australia, France, Greece, Great Britain and Switzerland (which only contested the equestrian events, held in Stockholm, Sweden, in 1956, and did not attend the Games in Melbourne, Australia). Of these, only Great Britain has been present at all Winter celebrations as well.

Largest crowd   The largest crowd at any Olympic site was 150,000 at the 1952 ski-jumping competition at the Holmenkollen, outside Oslo, Norway. Estimates of the number of spectators of the marathon race through Tokyo, Japan on 21 Oct. 1964 ranged from 500,000 to 1.5 million. The total spectator attendance at Los Angeles in 1984 was given as 5,797,923 (see General Records).

Olympic torch relay   The longest journey of the torch within one country was for the XV Olympic Winter Games in Canada in 1988. The torch arrived from Greece at St. John's, Newfoundland on 17 Nov. 1987 and was transported 11,222 miles (5,088 miles on foot, 4,419 miles by aircraft/ferry, 1,712 miles by snowmobile and 3 miles by dogsled) until its arrival at Calgary on 13 Feb. 1988.

Most participants   The greatest number of competitors at a Summer Games celebration was 8,465 (6,279 men, 2,186 women), who represented a record 159 nations, at Seoul, South Korea in 1988. The greatest number at the Winter Games was 1,808 (1,318 men, 490 women) representing 64 countries, at Albertville, France in 1992.

Ski orienteering   Eight World Championships in ski orienteering have been held. Sweden has won the men's relay five times (1977, 1980, 1982, 1984 and 1990) and Finland has won the women's relay five times (1975, 1977, 1980, 1988 and 1990).

Most medals   In the ancient Olympic Games, victors were given a chaplet of wild olive leaves. Leonidas of Rhodos won 12 running titles 164–152 B.C. The most individual gold medals won by a male competitor in the modern Games is ten, by Raymond Clarence Ewry (USA; 1874–1937) (see Track and Field). The female record is seven, by Vera Caslavska-Odlozil (Czechoslovakia) (see Gymnastics).

The most medals won by an American Olympian is 11, at shooting, by Carl Townsend Osburn (1884–1966) from 1912 to 1924—five gold, four silver, two bronze; and by Mark Andrew Spitz (b. 10 Feb. 1950), at swimming, 1968–72—nine gold, one silver, one bronze.

The most gold medals won by an American woman is four, by Patricia Joan McCormick (nee Keller, b. 12 May 1930), in both highboard and springboard diving, 1952 and 1956. The most medals won by an American woman is eight, by swimmer Shirley Babashoff (b. 31 Jan. 1957)—gold at 4 x 100 meters freestyle relay 1972 and 1976, and six silver medals 1972–76, a record for any competitor in Olympic history.

The only Olympian to win four consecutive individual titles in the same event has been Alfred Adolph Oerter (USA; b. 19 Sep. 1936), who won the discus, in 1956–68. However, Raymond Clarence Ewry (USA) won both the standing long jump and the standing high jump at four games in succession, 1900, 1904, 1906 (the Intercalated Games) and 1908. Also, Paul B. Elvström (Denmark; b. 25 Feb. 1928) won four successive gold medals at monotype yachting events, 1948–60, but there was a class change (1948 Firefly class, 1952–60 Finn class).

SKI JUMP. Toni Nieminen (Finland) became the youngest ever male gold medallist (16 yrs. 259 days) when he helped his Finnish team to success in the ski jumping team event with a final round jump of 123 m. He repeated this distance two days later to win the individual title on the 120 m hill. (Photo: Allsport)

ALPINE SKIING. Alberto Tomba (Italy) on his way to winning the giant slalom at the 1992 Winter Olympics, equaling Toni Sailer (Austria) and Jean-Claude Killy (France) in taking three Olympic titles in alpine skiing. He went on to win a silver in the slalom to make him the most successful male alpine skier in Olympic history. (Photo: Allsport)

Swimmer Mark Andrew Spitz (USA) won a record seven golds at one celebration, at Munich in 1972, including three in relays. The most won in individual events at one celebration is five, by speed skater Eric Arthur Heiden (USA; b. 14 June 1958) at Lake Placid, NY in 1980.

The only man to win a gold medal in both the Summer and Winter Games is Edward Patrick Francis Eagan (USA; 1898–1967), who won the 1920 light-heavyweight boxing title and was a member of the winning four-man bob in 1932. Christa Luding (nee Rothenburger [East Germany]; b. 4 Dec. 1959) became the first woman to win a medal at both the Summer and Winter Games when she won a silver in the cycling sprint event in 1988. She had previously won medals for speed skating—500 meter gold in 1984, and 1,000 meter gold and 500 meter silver in 1988.

Gymnast Larisa Latynina (USSR; b. 27 Dec. 1934) won a record 18 medals, and the men's record is 15, by Nikolay Andrianov (see Gymnastics). The record at one celebration is eight, by gymnast Aleksandr Dityatin (USSR; b. 7 Aug. 1957) in 1980.

Youngest and oldest gold medalist   The youngest-ever winner was a French boy (whose name is not recorded) who coxed the Netherlands pair in rowing in 1900. He was 7–10 years old and he substituted for Dr. Hermanus Brockmann, who coxed in the heats but proved too heavy. The youngest-ever female champion was Marjorie Gestring (USA; b. 18 Nov. 1922, now Mrs. Bowman), age 13 yrs. 268 days, in the 1936 women's springboard diving event. Oscar Swahn (Sweden) was on the winning running deer shooting team in 1912 at the age of 64 yrs. 258 days, and in this event was the oldest medalist—silver—at 72 yrs. 280 days in 1920.

The oldest American Olympic champion was retired minister Galen Carter Spencer (1840–1904), who assisted the Potomac Archers to an archery team medal two days after his 64th birthday in 1904. The oldest American medalist and Olympic participant was Samuel Harding Duvall (1836–1908), who was 68 yrs. 194 days when he was a member of the Cincinnati Archers silver medal team in 1904.

The youngest American medalist and participant was Dorothy Poynton (b. 17 July 1915), who won the springboard diving bronze medal at 13 yrs. 23 days in 1928. She went on to win the highboard gold in 1932 and 1936 (by then Mrs. Hill). The youngest American male medalist was Donald Wills Douglas, Jr. (b. 3 July 1917) with silver at 6-meter yachting in 1932, at 15 yrs. 40 days. He later became chief executive of the McDonnell-Douglas Corporation. The youngest American gold medalist was Jackie Fields, who won the 1924 featherweight boxing title at 16 yrs. 161 days (see Boxing).

Longest span   The longest span of an Olympic competitor is 40 years, by: Dr. Ivan Osiier (Denmark; 1888–1965) in fencing, 1908–32 and 1948; Magnus Konow (Norway; 1887–1972) in yachting, 1908–20, 1928 and 1936–48; Paul Elvström (Denmark) in yachting, 1948–1960, 1968–72 and 1984–88; and Durward Randolph Knowles (Great Britain 1948, then Bahamas; b. 2 Nov. 1917) in yachting, 1948–72 and 1988. Raimondo d'Inzeo (b. 8 Feb. 1925) competed for Italy in equestrian events at a record eight celebrations from 1948–76, gaining one gold, two silver and three bronze medals. This was equaled by Paul Elvström and Durward Knowles in 1988. The longest span by a woman is 28 years, by Anne Jessica Ransehousen (nee Newberry [USA]; b. 14 Oct. 1938) in dressage, 1960, 1964 and 1988. Fencer Kerstin Palm (Sweden; b. 5 Feb. 1946) competed in a women's record seven celebrations, 1964–88.

The US record for longest span of Olympic competition by a man is 28 years, by fencer Norman Cudworth Armitage (ne Cohn, 1907–72), who competed in the six Games held between 1928 and 1956; he won a team bronze at saber in 1948. He was also selected for the Games of 1940, which were canceled. Four other Americans contested six games: Frank Davis Chapot (b. 24 Feb. 1932), at show jumping 1956–76, winner of two team silver medals; Lt. Col. William Willard McMillan (b. 29 Jan. 1929) at shooting, 1952–76, missing 1956, winning gold at rapid-fire pistol in 1960; Janice Lee York Romary (b. 6 Aug. 1928), at fencing 1948–68; and John Michael Plumb (b. 28 Mar. 1940) at three-day event, 1960–84, winner of a gold and four silver medals. Plumb was also named for the 1980 Games, which the US boycotted.

ORIENTEERING

Origins   The first indications of orienteering as a competitive sport have been found in the Swedish army (1888) and the Norwegian army (1895). The first civilian competition seems to have been organized on 31 Oct. 1897 (with eight participants) by the sport club Tjalve, outside Oslo, Norway. In spite of a number of other small events up to 1910, the sport died out in Norway, but in Sweden it survived World War I. On 25 Mar. 1919, the first large competition with more than 200 participants was organized in the forest of Nacka, outside Stockholm. From there the sport spread rapidly throughout Sweden and later (about 1925) to Finland, Norway and (especially post-1945) to other countries in Europe and elsewhere. The initiator was Major Ernst Killander, who is known as "The Father of Orienteering." World Championships were instituted in 1966. The United States Orienteering Federation was founded in 1971.

Most titles   The men's relay has been won a record seven times by Norway—1970, 1978, 1981, 1983, 1985, 1987 and 1989. Sweden has won the women's relay nine times—1966, 1970, 1974, 1976, 1981, 1983, 1985, 1989 and 1991. Three women's individual titles have been won by Annichen Kringstad (Sweden; b. 15 July 1960), in 1981, 1983 and 1985. The men's title has been won twice by Åge Hadler (Norway; b. 14 Aug. 1944), in 1966 and 1972; Egil Johansen (Norway; b. 18 Aug. 1954), in 1976 and 1978; and Øyvind Thon (Norway; b. 25 Mar. 1958), in 1979 and 1981.

US National Championships   This competition was first held on 17 Oct. 1970. Sharon Crawford, New England Orienteering Club, has won a record 11 overall women's titles, 1977–82, 1984–87, 1989. Peter Gagarin, New England Orienteering Club, has won a record five overall men's titles, 1976–79, 1983.

Most competitors   The most competitors at a one-day event is 38,000, in the Ruf des Herbstes held in Sibiu, Romania in 1982. The largest event is the five-day Swedish O-Ring at Smaland, which attracted 120,000 competitors in 1983.

PARACHUTING

Origins   Parachuting became a regulated sport with the institution of World Championships in 1951. A team title was introduced in 1954 and women's events were included in 1956.

Most titles   *Team*   The USSR won the men's team title in 1954, 1958, 1960, 1966, 1972, 1976 and 1980, and the women's team title in 1956, 1958, 1966, 1968, 1972 and 1976.

Individual   Nikolay Ushamyev (USSR) has won the individual title twice, 1974 and 1980.

PARACHUTING. Parachuting in the Turquie Valley in the Euphrates. To the left of the photograph is the world's tallest mound. (Photo: Allsport/ Vandystadt)

Greatest accuracy   At Yuma, AZ, in March 1978, Dwight Reynolds scored a record 105 daytime dead centers, and Bill Wenger and Phil Munden tied with 43 night-time dead centers, competing as members of the US Army Golden Knights.

With electronic measuring, the official official *Fédération Aeronautique Internationale* (FAI) record is 50 dead centers, by Aleksandr Aasmiae (USSR) at Fergana, USSR in 1979 and by Linger Abdurakhmanov (USSR) at Fergana in 1988, when the women's record was set at 41, by Natalya Filinkova (USSR) in 1988.

PARACHUTING RECORDS

It is estimated that the human body reaches 99 percent of its low-level terminal velocity after falling 1,880 ft., which takes 13–14 sec. This is 117–125 mph at normal atmospheric pressure in a random posture, but up to 185 mph in a head-down position.

FIRST • Tower[1] • Louis-Sébastien Lenormand (1757–1839), quasi-parachute, Montpellier, France, 1783.

Balloon • André-Jacques Garnerin (1769–1823), 2,230 ft., Monceau Park, Paris, France, 22 Oct. 1797.

Aircraft • Man: "Captain" Albert Berry, an aerial exhibitionist, St. Louis, MI, 1 Mar. 1912. *Woman:* Mrs. Georgina "Tiny" Broadwick (b. 1893), Griffith Park, Los Angeles, CA, 21 June 1913.

LONGEST-DURATION FALL • Lt. Col. Wm. H. Rankin, USMC, 40 min. due to thermals, North Carolina, 26 July 1956.

LONGEST-DELAYED DROP • Man: Capt. Joseph W. Kittinger,[2] 84,700 ft. (16.04 miles), from balloon at 102,800 ft., Tularosa, NM, 16 Aug. 1960. *Woman:* E. Fomitcheva (USSR), 48,556 ft. over Odessa, USSR, 26 Oct. 1977.

MID-AIR RESCUE • Earliest • Miss Dolly Shepherd (1886-1983) brought down Miss Louie May on her single 'chute from balloon at 11,000 ft., Longton, Great Britain, 9 June 1908.

Lowest • Gregory Robertson saved Debbie Williams (unconscious), collision at 9,000 ft., pulled her ripcord at 3,500 ft.—10 secs. from impact, Coolidge, AZ, 18 Apr. 1987.

HIGHEST ESCAPE • Flt. Lt. J. de Salis, RAF and Fg. Off. P. Lowe, RAF, 56,000 ft., Moynash, Derby, Great Britain, 9 Apr. 1958.

LOWEST ESCAPE • S/Ldr. Terence Spencer DFC, RAF, 30–40 ft., Wismar Bay, Baltic, 19 Apr. 1945.

HIGHEST LANDING • Ten USSR parachutists[3], 23,405 ft., Lenina Peak, USSR, May 1969.

MOST SOUTHERLY • T/Sgt. Richard J. Patton (USA; d. 1973), Operation Deep Freeze, South Pole, 25 Nov. 1956.

The Men's Night Accuracy Landing record on an electronic score pad is 27 consecutive dead centers, by Cliff Jones (USA) in 1981. The women's record is 21, by Inessa Stepanova (USSR) at Fergana in 1988.

Paragliding   The greatest distance flown is 142.7 miles by Urs Harri (Switzerland), flying Nova Phantom, in Namibia on 15 Jan. 1992.

The greatest distance to a declared goal is 63.08 miles, by Sean Dougherty and Chris Muller (Canada) on 7 July 1991.

MOST NORTHERLY • Six members of the Canadian Armed Forces were the first people to jump at Lat. 90° 00′ N, 27 Apr. 1974.

CROSS-CHANNEL (LATERAL FALL) • Sgt. Bob Walters with three soldiers and two Royal Marines, 22 miles from 25,000 ft., Dover, Great Britain to Sangatte, France, 31 Aug. 1980.

TOTAL SPORT PARACHUTING DESCENTS • *Man:* Don Kellner (USA), 16,000, various locations up to 13 Sep. 1991. *Woman:* Valentina Zakoretskaya (USSR), 8,000, over USSR, 1964–Sep. 1980.

24-HOUR TOTAL • Dale Nelson (USA), 301 (in accordance with United States Parachute Association rules), PA, 26–27 May 1988.

MOST TRAVELED • Kevin Seaman from a Cessna Skylane (pilot Charles E. Merritt), 12,186 miles, jumps in all 50 US states, 26 Jul–15 Oct. 1972.

HEAVIEST LOAD • US Space Shuttle Columbia, external rocket retrieval, 80 ton capacity, triple array, each 120 ft. diameter, Atlantic, off Cape Canaveral, FL, 12 Apr. 1981.

HIGHEST COLUMN • 24, Royal Marine Team, Dunkeswell, Great Britain, 20 Aug. 1986.

LARGEST FREE-FALL FORMATION • 144, held for 8.8 sec., from 16,000 ft., Quincy, IL, 11 July 1988.

OLDEST • *Man:* Edwin C. Townsend (d. 7 Nov. 1987), 89 years, Vermillion Bay, LA, 5 Feb. 1986. *Woman:* Mrs. Sylvia Brett (GB), 80 years 166 days, Cranfield, Great Britain, 23 Aug. 1986.
Tandem: Corena Leslie (USA) 89 years 369 days, Sun Valley, AZ, 11 June 1992.

LONGEST FALL WITHOUT PARACHUTE • **World** • Vesna Vulovic (Yugoslavia), air hostess in DC–9 that blew up at 33,330 ft. over Serbska Kamenice, Czechoslovakia, 26 Jan. 1972.

[1] *The king of Ayutthaya, Siam in 1687 was reported to have been diverted by an ingenious athlete parachuting with two large umbrellas. Faustus Verancsis is reputed to have descended in Hungary with a framed canopy in 1617.*
[2] *Maximum speed in rarefied air was 625.2 mph at 90,000 ft.—marginally supersonic.*
[3] *Four were killed.*

The out and return distance record is 39.94 miles, by Hans Bachmayr (Austria) on 5 May 1990 flying Ailes de K Trilair.

The greatest triangle distance is 67.93 miles, by Willi Muller (Canada) on 4 July flying Apco Hilite III.

The height gain record is 10,170 ft. by Sepp Gschwendtner (Germany) on 17 Dec. 1989.

Nigel Horder scored four successive dead centers at the Dutch Open, Flevhof, Netherlands on 22 May 1983.

PÉTANQUE

Origins   The origins of pétanque or boules can be traced back over 2,000 years, but it was not until 1945 that the *Fédération Française de Pétanque et Jeu Provençal* was formed, and subsequently the *Fédération Internationale* (FIPJP).

World Championships   Winner of the most World Championships (instituted 1959) has been France, with 11 titles to 1991. Two women's World Championships were held in 1988 and 1990, and Thailand won on both occasions.

Highest score in 24 hours   Chris Walker (b. 16 Jan. 1942) and his son Richard (b. 26 Dec. 1966) scored a record 2,109 points in 24 hours (172 games) at the Gin Trap, Ringstead, Great Britain on 24–25 June 1988.

POLO

Origins   Polo can be traced to origins in Manipur state, India *c.* 3100 B.C., when it was played as *sagol kangjei*. It is also claimed to be of Persian origin, having been played as *pulu c.* 525 B.C. The game was introduced to British officers at Cachar by the Manipur Maharaja, Sir Chandrakirti Singh, and the earliest club was the Cachar Club (founded in 1859) in Assam, India. The oldest club still in existence is the Calcutta Polo Club (1862). The game was introduced into England from India in 1869 by the 10th Hussars at Aldershot, Great Britain, and the earliest match was one between the 9th Lancers and the 10th Hussars on Hounslow Heath, Great Britain in July 1871. The earliest international match between England and the USA was in 1886.

United States   Polo was introduced to the United States by James Gordon Bennett in 1876, when he arranged for the first indoor game at Dickel's Riding Academy, NY. The first game played outdoors was held on 13 May 1876 at the Jerome Park Racetrack in Westchester County, NY. The oldest existing polo club in the United States is Meadow Brook Polo Club, Jericho, NY, founded in 1879. The United States Polo Association was formed on 20 Mar.

1890. The United States Open Championship was inaugurated in 1904 and has been played continuously since then, with the exception of 1905–09, 1911, 1915, 1917–18 and 1942–45. The most wins is 28, by the Meadow Brook Polo Club, in 1916, 1920, 1923–1941, 1946–51 and 1953.

Most chukkas   The greatest number of chukkas played on one ground in a day is 43. This was achieved by the Pony Club on the Number 3 Ground at Kirlington Park, Great Britain on 31 July 1991:

LARGEST PLAYING FIELD. The largest playing field for any ball game is 12.4 acres for polo (top), or a maximum length of 300 yds. and a width, without side boards, of 200 yds. With boards the width is 160 yds. Here (bottom) the crowd is performing the traditional task of turf-treading. (Photos: Allsport)

Highest score   The highest aggregate number of goals scored in an international match is 30, when Argentina beat the USA 21–9 at Meadowbrook, Long Island, NY in September 1936.

World Championships   The first World Championships were held in Berlin, Germany in 1989. The USA won the title, defeating Great Britain 7–6 in the final.

Highest handicap   The highest handicap based on six 7½-min. "chukkas" is ten goals, introduced in the USA in 1891. A total of 55 players have received ten-goal handicaps.

A match of two 40-goal teams has been staged on three occasions—in Argentina in 1975, in the United States in 1990, and in Australia in 1991.

POOL

Origins   Pool traces its ancestry to billiards, an English game introduced in Virginia in the late 17th century. During the 19th century the game evolved from a game in which a mace was used to push balls around the table, to a game of precise skill using a cue, with the aim of pocketing numbered balls. The original form of pool in the United States was known as pocket billiards, with the object being to pocket eight out of the 15 balls on the table. From this game evolved "61-pool"; each of the 15 balls was worth points equal to its numerical value, and the first player to score 61 points was the winner.

In 1878 the first world championship was staged under the rules of 61-pool. In 1910, Jerome Keogh suggested that the rules be adjusted to make the game faster and more attractive; he proposed that the last ball be left free on the table to be used as a target on the next rack; the result was 14.1 continuous pool (also known as American straight pool). This was adopted as the championship form of pool from 1912 onward. In the last twenty years nine-ball pool and eight-ball pool have surpassed 14.1 in popularity. In 1990 the World Pool Billiard Authority inaugurated the nine-ball world championship.

14.1 CONTINUOUS POOL
(AMERICAN STRAIGHT POOL)

World Championship   The two most dominant 14.1 players have been Ralph Greenleaf (USA; 1899–1950), who won the "world" professional title six times and defended it 13 times (1919–37), and William "Willie" Mosconi (USA; b. 27 June 1913), who dominated the game from 1941 to 1956, and also won the title six times and defended it 13 times.

Longest consecutive run   The longest consecutive run in 14.1 recognized by the Billiard Congress of America (BCA) is 526 balls, by Willie Mosconi in March 1954 during an exhibition in Springfield, OH. Michael Eufemia is reported to have rocketed 625 balls at Logan's Billiard Academy, Brooklyn, NY on 2 Feb. 1960, but this run has never been ratified by the BCA.

Most balls pocketed   The greatest number of balls pocketed in 24 hrs. is 16,125, by James Abel at White Plains, NY on 17–18 Dec. 1991.

Pool pocketing speed   The record times for pocketing all 15 balls in a speed competition are: (*men*) 37.9 sec., by Rob McKenna at Blackpool, Great Britain on 7 Nov. 1987; (*women*) 44.5 sec., by Susan Thompson at Shrublands Community Centre, Gorleston, Great Britain on 20 Apr. 1990.

POWERBOAT RACING

Origins   A gasoline engine was first installed in a boat by Jean Joseph Etienne Lenoir (1822–1900) on the River Seine, Paris, France in 1865. Actual powerboat racing started in about 1900, the first prominent race being from Calais, France to Dover, Great Britain in 1903. International racing was largely established by the presentation of a Challenge Trophy by Sir Alfred Harmsworth in 1903. Thereafter, racing developed mainly as a "circuit," or short, sheltered course type competition. Offshore or sea-passage races also developed, initially for displacement (non-planing) cruisers. Offshore events for fast (planing) cruisers began in 1958, with a 170-mile passage race from Miami, FL to Nassau, Bahamas. Outboard motor racing, i.e., the combined motor/transmission detachable propulsion unit type racing, began in the United States in about 1920. Both inboard and outboard motorboat engines are mainly gasoline fueled, but since 1950 diesel (compression ignition) engines have appeared and are widely used in offshore sport.

United States   The American Power Boat Association (APBA) was founded on 22 Apr. 1903 in New York City. In 1913 the APBA issued the "Racing Commission" rules, which created its powers for ruling the sport and sanctioning races in North America. In 1924 the APBA set rules for boats propelled by "Outboard Detachable Motors" and became the governing body for both inboard and outboard racing in North America.

APBA Gold Cup   The American Power Boat Association (APBA) held its first Gold Cup race at the Columbia Yacht Club on the Hudson River, NY in 1904, when the winner was *Standard*, piloted by C.C. Riotto at an average speed of 23.6 mph. The most wins by a pilot is eight, by Bill Muncey, 1956–57, 1961–62, 1972, 1977–79. The most successful boat has been *Atlas Van Lines*, piloted by Muncey to victory in 1972, 1977–79 and by Chip Hanauer in 1982–84. Hanauer went on to complete a record seven successive victories to 1988. Hanauer won again in 1992 to equal his record.

Fastest speeds   The fastest speed recorded by a propeller-driven boat is 229 mph, by *The Texan*, a Kurtis Top Fuel Hydro Drag boat, driven by Eddie Hill (USA) on 5 Sep. 1982 at Chowchilla, CA. He also set a 440 yd. elapsed time record of 5.16 sec. in this boat at Firebird Lake, AZ on 13 Nov. 1983. The official American Drag Boat Association record is 223.88 mph, by *Final Effort*, a Blown Fuel Hydro boat driven by Robert T. Burns at Creve Coeur Lake, St. Louis, MO on 15 July 1985 over a 440 yd. course.

The fastest speed recognized by the *Union Internationale Motonautique* for an outboard-powered boat is in Class (e): 177.61 mph by P.R. Knight in a Chevrolet-engined Lautobach hull on Lake Ruataniwha, New Zealand in 1986. Robert F. Hering (USA) set the world Formula One record at 165.338 mph in *Second Effort* at Parker, AZ on 21 Apr. 1986.

The fastest speed recognized for an offshore boat is 154.438 mph for one way and 148.238 mph for two runs by Tom Gentry (USA), in his 49-ft. catamaran *Gentry Turbo Eagle*, powered by four Gentry Turbo Eagle V8 Chevrolets on 8 Mar. 1987.

The fastest speed recorded for a diesel (compression ignition) boat is 135.532 mph by the hydroplane *Iveco World Leader*, powered by an Aifo-Fiat engine, driven by Carlo Bonomi at Venice, Italy on 4 Apr. 1985.

Fastest race speeds   The fastest speed recorded in an offshore race is 103.29 mph, by Tony Garcia (USA) in a Class I powerboat at Key West, FL in Nov. 1983.

Longest races   The longest offshore race has been the Port Richborough London, Great Britain to Monte Carlo Marathon Offshore international event. The race extended over 2,947 miles in 14 stages from 10–25 June 1972. It was won by *H.T.S.* (Great Britain), driven by Mike Bellamy, Eddie Chater and Jim Brooker, in 71 hrs. 35 min. 56 sec., for an average of 41.15 mph. The longest circuit race is the 24-hour race held annually since 1962 on the River Seine at Rouen, France.

PROJECTILES

Throwing   The longest independently authenticated throw of any inert object heavier than air is 1,257 ft., for a flying ring, by Scott Zimmerman on 8 July 1986 at Fort Funston, CA.

Greatest distances achieved with other miscellaneous objects:

Boomerang throwing   The greatest number of consecutive two-handed catches is 801, by Stéphane Marguerite (France) on 26 Nov. 1989 at Lyons, France.

The longest out-and-return distance is 440 ft. 3 in., by Jim Youngblood (USA) on 12 June 1989 at Gaithersburg, MD.

The longest flight duration (with self-catch) is one of 2 min. 59.94 sec. by Dennis Joyce (USA) at Bethlehem, PA on 25 June 1987.

Matthieu Weber (Switzerland) caught 73 boomerang throws in 5 min. at Lyons, France on 2 Nov. 1991.

The juggling record—the number of consecutive catches with two boomerangs, keeping at least one boomerang aloft at all times — is 207, by Michael Girvin (USA) at Elkton, MD on 6 July 1991.

Brick ....146 ft. 1 in.
(standard 5-lb. building brick)
Geoff Capes at Braybrook School, Orton, Great Britain on 19 July 1978.

Egg (fresh hen's)...317 ft. 10 in.
(without breaking it)
Risto Antikainen to Jyrki Korhonen at Siilinjärvi, Finland on 6 Sep. 1981.

Rolling pin...175 ft. 5 in.
(2 lbs.)
Lori La Deane Adams, 21, at Iowa State Fair, IA on 21 Aug. 1979.

Slingshot ....1,434 ft. 2 in.
(51-in.-long sling and a 2 oz. stone)
Lawrence L. Bray at Loa, UT on 21 Aug. 1981.

Spear throwing ....616 ft. 10 in.
(using an atlatl or hand-held device that fits onto a short spear)
Wayne Brian at Overton, NV on 11 Apr. 1992.

Flying disc throwing (formerly Frisbee)   The World
Flying Disc Federation distance records are: (*men*) 623 ft. 7 in., by
Sam Ferrans (USA) on 2 July 1988 at La Habra, CA; (*women*) 426
ft. 10 in., by Amy Bekken (USA) on 25 July 1990 at La Habra, CA.

The throw, run and catch records are: (*men*) 303 ft. 11 in., by
Hiroshi Oshima (Japan) on 20 July 1988 at San Francisco, CA;
(*women*) 196 ft. 11 in., by Judy Horowitz (USA) on 29 June 1985
at La Mirada, CA.

The 24-hour distance records for a pair are: (*men*) 362.40 miles,
by Leonard Muise and Gabe Ontiveros (USA) on 21–22 Sep. 1988
at Carson, CA; (*women*) 115.65 miles, by Jo Cahow and Amy
Berard (USA) on 30–31 Dec. 1979 at Pasadena, CA.

The records for maximum time aloft are: (*men*) 16.72 sec., by
Don Cain (USA) on 26 May 1984 at Philadelphia, PA; (*women*) is
11.81 sec., by Amy Bekken (USA) on 1 Aug. 1991.

Cow chip tossing   The record distances in the country sport of
throwing dried cow pats or "chips" depend on whether or not the
projectile may be "molded into a spherical shape." The greatest
distance achieved under the "non-sphericalization and 100 percent
organic" rule (established in 1970) is 266 ft., by Steve Urner at the
Mountain Festival, Tehachapi, CA on 14 Aug. 1981.

RACKETS

Origins   There is a record of the sale of a racket court at Southernhay, Great Britain dated 12 Jan. 1798. The game, which is of 17th-century origin, was played by debtors in the Fleet Prison, London, Great Britain in the middle of the 18th century, and an inmate, Robert Mackay, claimed the first "world" title in 1820. The first closed court champion was Francis Erwood at Woolwich, London, Great Britain in 1860.

World Championships   Of the 22 world champions since 1820, the longest reign is by Geoffrey Willoughby Thomas Atkins (Great Britain; b. 20 Jan. 1927), who gained the title by beating the professional James Dear (Great Britain; 1910–81) in 1954, and held it until retiring, after defending it four times, in April 1972.

United States   The first American to be world champion was Jock Souter, and he had the longest span as champion, 1913–28.

RACQUETBALL

Origins   Racquetball, using a 40 ft. x 20 ft. court, was invented in 1950 by Joe Sobek at the Greenwich, CT YMCA. Sobek designed a "strung paddle racquet" and combined the rules of squash and handball to create the game of "paddle rackets." The International Racquetball Association (IRA) was founded in 1968 by Bob Kendler (USA), and renamed the American Amateur Racquetball Association (AARA) in 1979. The International Amateur Racquetball Federation (IARF) was founded in 1979 and staged its first world championships in 1981.

World Championships   First held in 1982, the IARF World Championships have been held biennially since 1984. The United States has won all five team titles, in 1981, 1984, 1986 (tie with Canada), 1988 and 1990. Egan Inoue (USA) has won the most men's singles titles with two, in 1986 and 1990. Two women have won the world singles championships twice: Cindy Baxter (USA) in 1981 and 1986; Heather Stupp (Canada) in 1988 and 1990.

US titles   In 1968, championships were initiated by the AARA (the governing body for the sport in the United States). A record four men's open titles have been won by Ed Andrews of California, 1980–81 and 1985–86, and a record four women's open titles by Cindy Baxter of Pennsylvania, 1981, 1983, 1985–86, and Michelle Gilman, 1989–92.

REAL/ROYAL TENNIS

Origins The game originated as *jeu de paume* in French monasteries *c.* 1050. A tennis court is mentioned in the sale of the Hôtel de Nesle, Paris, France, bought by King Philippe IV of France in 1308. The oldest of the surviving active courts in Great Britain is the one at Falkland Palace, Fife, Scotland built by King James V of Scotland in 1539.

Most titles *World* The first recorded world tennis champion was Clerge (France), *c.* 1740. Jacques Edmond Barre (France; 1802–73) held the title for a record 33 years from 1829 to 1862. Pierre Etchebaster (1893–1980), a Basque, holds the record for the greatest number of successful defenses of the title, with eight between 1928 and 1952.

The first two Women's World Championships in 1985 and 1987 were won by Judith Anne Clarke (Australia; b. 28 Dec. 1954) .

United States Jay Gould, Jr. (1888–1935) won his first US singles title in 1906, and retained the title until he retired from singles play in 1926. During his career he lost only one singles match. He also won 19 US doubles titles between 1909 and 1932.

RODEO

Origins Rodeo, which developed from 18th-century *fiestas,* came into being in the early days of the North American cattle industry. The sport originated in Mexico and spread from there into the cattle regions of the United States. A bronc-riding competition was held in Deer Trail, CO as early as 1869, and steer wrestling came in with Bill Pickett (1870–1932) of Texas in 1900. There are many claims to the first paying rodeo with spectators; The West of the Pecos Rodeo at Pecos, TX, first held in 1883, was the earliest documented, organized rodeo competition, and is now sanctioned by the Professional Rodeo Cowboys Association (PRCA), professional rodeo's largest organized association.

The largest rodeo in the world is the National Finals Rodeo, organized by the PRCA and the Women's Professional Rodeo Association (WPRA). The top 15 money-earning cowboys in each of the six PRCA events and the top 15 WPRA barrel racers compete at the Finals. The event was first held at Dallas, TX in 1959, and was held at Oklahoma City, OK for 20 years before moving to Las Vegas, NV in 1985. The 1990 Finals had a paid attendance of 171,368 for ten performances. In 1990 a record $2.3 million in prize money was offered for the event.

Most world titles The record number of all-around titles (awarded to the leading money winner in a single season in two or more events) in the

PRCA World Championships is six, by Larry Mahan (USA; b. 21 Nov. 1943) in 1966–70 and 1973, and, consecutively, 1974–79 by Tom Ferguson (b. 20 Dec. 1950). Jim Shoulders (b. 13 May 1928) of Henryetta, TX won a record 16 World Championships at four events between 1949 and 1959.

Earnings records   Roy Cooper (b. 13 Nov. 1955) holds the career rodeo earnings mark at $1,282,874 through 7 June 1992. The single-season record is $258,750, by Ty Murray in 1991. Ty Murray won a record $101,243 for one rodeo ($34,227 for saddle bronc-riding, $43,659 for bareback riding, and $23,357 for bull riding) at the 1991 National Finals Rodeo, Las Vegas, NV, 6–15 December.

Youngest champions   The youngest winner of a world title is Anne Lewis (b. 1 Sep. 1958), who won the WPRA barrel racing title in 1968, at 10 years of age. Ty Murray (b. 11 Oct. 1969) is the youngest cowboy to win the PRCA All-Around Champion title, at age 20, in 1989.

Time records   Records for PRCA timed events, such as calf-roping and steer-wrestling, are not always comparable, because of the widely varying conditions due to the sizes of arenas and amount of start given the stock. The fastest time recorded for calf-roping under the current PRCA rules is 6.7 sec., by Joe Beaver (b. 13 Oct. 1965) at West Jordan, UT in 1986, and the fastest time for steer wrestling is 2.4 sec., by James Bynum at Marietta, OK in 1955; Carl Deaton at Tulsa, OK in 1976; and Gene Melton at Pecatonica, IL in 1976. The fastest team roping time is 3.7 sec., by Bob Harris and Tee Woolman at Spanish Fork, UT in 1986.

Bull riding   Jim Sharp (b. 6 Oct. 1965) of Kermit, TX became the first rider to ride all ten bulls at a National Finals Rodeo at Las Vegas in December 1988. This feat was matched by Norm Curry of Deberry, TX at the 1990 National Finals Rodeo.

The highest score in bull riding was 100 points out of a possible 100, by Wade Leslie on Wolfman Skoal at Central Point, OR in 1991.

Saddle bronc-riding   The highest scored saddle bronc ride is 95 out of a possible 100, by Doug Vold at Meadow Lake, Saskatchewan, Canada in 1979. Descent, a saddle bronc owned by Beutler Brothers and Cervi Rodeo Company, received a record six PRCA Saddle Bronc of the Year awards, 1966–69, 1971–72.

Bareback riding   Joe Alexander of Cora, WY scored 93 out of a possible 100 at Cheyenne, WY in 1974. Sippin' Velvet, owned by Bernis Johnson, has been awarded a record five PRCA Bareback Horse of the Year titles between 1978 and 1987.

Top bull   The top bucking bull Red Rock dislodged 312 riders, 1980–88, and was finally ridden to the 8-sec. bell by Lane Frost (1963–89; world champion bull rider 1987) on 20 May 1988. Red Rock was retired at the end of the 1987 season but still continued to make guest appearances.

MOST SUCCESSFUL. Ty Murray was the youngest cowboy to win the Professional Rodeo Cowboys Association All-Around Champion title, aged 20, in 1989. He has continued to be highly successful, setting the record figure for prize money won in a single season in 1990, and surpassing this in 1991. (Photo: Allsport USA/Ken Levine)

ROLLER SKATING

Origins The first roller skate was devised by Jean Joseph Merlin (1735–1803) of Huy, Belgium in 1760 and was demonstrated by him in London, Great Britain, but with disastrous results. James L. Plimpton of New York produced the present four-wheeled type and patented it in January 1863. The first indoor rink was opened in London, Great Britain in about 1824.

Most titles *Speed* The most world speed titles won is 18, by two women: Alberta Vianello (Italy), eight track and ten road, 1953–65; and Annie Lambrechts (Belgium), one track and 17 road, 1964–81, at distances from 500 meters to 10,000 meters.

Figure The records for figure titles are: five by Karl Heinz Losch in 1958–59, 1961–62 and 1966; and four by Astrid Bader in 1965–68, both of West Germany. The most world pair titles is four, by Dieter Fingerle (West Germany) in 1959, 1965–67, with two different partners, and by John Arishita and Tammy Jeru (USA), 1983–86.

Speed skating The fastest speed posted in an official world record is 26.85 mph, when Luca Antoniel (Italy; b. 12 Feb. 1968) recorded 24.99 sec. for 300 meters on a road at Gujan-Mestras, France on 31 July 1987. The women's record is 25.04 mph, by Marisa Canofogilia (Italy; b. 30 Sep. 1965) for 300 meters on the road at Grenoble, France on 27 Aug. 1987. The world records for 10,000 meters on a road or track are: *(men)* 14 min. 55.64 sec., Giuseppe de Persio (Italy; b. 3 June 1959) at Gujan-Mestras, France on 1 Aug. 1988; *(women)* 15 min. 58.022 sec., Marisa Canofogilia (Italy) at Grenoble, France on 30 Aug. 1987.

Largest rink The largest indoor rink ever to operate was located in the Grand Hall, London, Great Britain. Opened in 1890 and closed in 1912, it had an actual skating area of 68,000 ft.². The current largest is the main arena of 34,981 ft.² at Guptill Roll-Arena, Boght Corner, NY. The total rink area is 41,380 ft.².

Skateboarding World championships have been staged intermittently since 1966. David Frank, 25, covered 270.5 miles in 36 hrs. 43 min. 40 sec. in Toronto, Ontario, Canada on 11–12 Aug. 1985.

The highest speed recorded on a skateboard is 78.37 mph in a prone position by Roger Hickey, 32, on a course near Los Angeles, CA on 15 Mar. 1990.

The stand-up record is 55.43 mph, also achieved by Roger Hickey, at San Demas, CA on 3 July 1990.

The high-jump record is 5 ft. 5¾ in., by Trevor Baxter (b. 1 Oct. 1962) of Burgess Hill, Great Britain at Grenoble, France on 14 Sep. 1982.

At the 4th US Skateboard Association Championship, at Signal Hill on 25 Sep. 1977, Tony Alva, 19, jumped 17 barrels (17 ft.).

ROWING

Origins The Sphinx Stela of Amenhotep (Amonophis) II (1450–1425 B.C.) records that he *stroked* a boat for some three miles. The earliest established sculling race is the Doggett's Coat and Badge, which was first rowed on 1 Aug. 1716 from London Bridge to Chelsea as a race for apprentices, and is still contested annually. Although rowing regattas were held in Venice in 1300, the first English regatta probably took place on the river Thames, London, Great Britain, by the Ranelagh Gardens near Putney, in 1775.

United States The first organized boat races in the United States were reported to be races staged between New York City boatmen in New York harbor in the late 18th century. The first rowing club formed in the United States was the Castle Garden Amateur Boat Club Association, New York City in 1834. The oldest active club is the Detroit Boat Club, founded in 1839. The first and oldest collegiate boat club was formed at Yale University in 1843. The National Association of Amateur Oarsmen (NAAO) was formed in 1872 and merged with the National Women's Rowing Association in 1982 to form the United States Rowing Association.

Most Olympic medals   Six oarsmen have won three gold medals: John Brendan Kelly (USA; 1889–1960), father of the late Princess Grace of Monaco, who won at Single Sculls (1920) and Double Sculls (1920 and 1924); his cousin, Paul Vincent Costello (USA; b. 27 Dec. 1894), Double Sculls (1920, 1924 and 1928); Jack Beresford, Jr. (Great Britain; 1899–1977), Single Sculls (1924), Coxless Fours (1932) and Double Sculls (1936); Vyacheslav Nikolayevich Ivanov (USSR; b. 30 July 1938), Single Sculls (1956, 1960 and 1964); Siegfried Brietzke (East Germany; b. 12 June 1952), Coxless Pairs (1972) and Coxless Fours (1976, 1980); and Pertti Karppinen (Finland; b. 17 Feb. 1953), Single Sculls (1976, 1980 and 1984).

World Championships   World rowing championships distinct from the Olympic Games were first held in 1962, and were held four times a year at first, but from 1974 were held annually, except in Olympic years.

The most gold medals won at World Championships and Olympic Games is nine, at coxed pairs by the Italian brothers Giuseppe (b. 24 July 1959) and Carmine (b. 5 Jan. 1962) Abbagnale, World 1981–82, 1985, 1987, 1989–91, Olympics 1984 and 1988. At women's events Jutta Behrendt (nee Hahn [East Germany]; b. 15 Nov. 1960) has won a record six golds.

The most wins at Single Sculls is five, by Peter-Michael Kolbe (West Germany; b. 2 Aug. 1953), 1975, 1978, 1981, 1983 and 1986; and by Pertti Karppinen, 1979 and 1985, and with his three Olympic wins (above); and in the women's events by Christine Hahn (nee Scheiblich [East Germany]; b. 31 Dec. 1954), 1974–75, 1977–78 (and the 1976 Olympic title).

Longest race   The longest annual rowing race is the annual Tour du Lac Leman, Geneva, Switzerland for coxed fours (the five-man crew taking turns as cox) over 99 miles. The record winning time is 12 hrs. 52 min., by LAGA Delft, Netherlands on 3 Oct. 1982.

Collegiate Championships   The first intercollegiate boat race in the United States was between Harvard and Yale in 1852. The Intercollegiate Rowing Association (IRA) was formed in 1895, and in 1898 inaugurated the Varsity Challenge Cup, which was recognized as the national championship. In 1982, the United States Rowing Assocation introduced the National Collegiate Championships, and this race now decides the national champion. Overall, Cornell University has won the most national championships, with 25 titles (all Varsity Cup wins). Since 1982, Harvard University has won five titles (1983, 1985, 1987–89).

The women's national championship was inaugurated in 1979. The University of Washington has won a record seven times (1981–85, 1987–88).

Henley Royal Regatta   The annual regatta at Henley-on-Thames, Great Britain was inaugurated on 26 Mar. 1839. Since then the course, except in 1923, has been about 1 mile 550 yds., varying slightly according to the length of the boat. In 1967 the shorter craft were "drawn up" so all bows start level.

The most wins in the Diamond Challenge Sculls (instituted 1844) is six consecutively, by Stuart A. Mackenzie (Australia and Great Britain; b. 5 Apr. 1937), 1957–62. The record time is 7 min. 23 sec., by Vaclav Chalupa (Czechoslovakia; b. 7 Dec. 1967) on 2 July 1989. The record time for the Grand Challenge Cup (instituted 1839) event is 5 min. 58 sec., by Hansa Dortmund, West Germany on 2 July 1989.

Fastest speed   The highest recorded speed on non-tidal water for 2,187 yds. is by an American eight in 5 min. 27.14 sec. (13.68 mph) at Lucerne, Switzerland on 17 June 1984. A crew from Penn AC was timed in 5 min. 18.8 sec. (14.03 mph) in the FISA Championships on the River Meuse, Liège, Belgium on 17 Aug. 1930.

Twenty-four hours   The greatest distance rowed in 24 hours (upstream and downstream) by an eight is 135.22 miles, by a coxed quad (Peter Halliday, Paul Turnbull, Mike Skerry, Belinda Goglia and Margaret Munneke) on the Yarra River, Melbourne, Australia on 26–27 Jan. 1992.

International Dragon Boat Race   Instituted in 1975 and held annually in Hong Kong, the fastest time achieved for the 700 yd. course is 2 min. 27.45 sec., by the Chinese Shun De team on 30 Jan. 1985. Teams have 28 members—26 rowers, one steersman and one drummer.

RUGBY

Records are determined in terms of present-day scoring values, i.e., a try at 4 points; a dropped goal, penalty or goal from a mark at 3 points; and a conversion at 2 points. The actual score, in accordance with whichever of the eight earlier systems was in force at the time, is also given, in parentheses.

Although there are records of a game with many similarities to rugby dating back to the Roman occupation of Britain, the game is traditionally said to have originated from a breach of the rules of soccer by William Webb Ellis (later the Rev.; *c.* 1807–72) in a match played at Rugby School in November 1823. This handling style of soccer evolved gradually and was known to have been played at Cambridge University, Great Britain in 1839. The Rugby Football Union was founded on 26 Jan. 1871. The International Rugby Football Board (IRFB) was founded in 1886.

In competitions held at four Olympic Games from 1900 to 1924, the only double gold medalist was the United States, which won in 1920 and 1924, defeating France in the final on both occasions.

WORLD CUP

The World Cup has been held on two occasions, 1987 and 1991, with the winners being New Zealand and Australia respectively. The highest team score was New Zealand's 74–13 victory over Fiji at Christchurch, New Zealand on 27 May 1987. New Zealand scored 10 goals, 2 tries and 2 penalty goals. The individual match record was 30 (3 tries, 9 conversions), by Didier Camberabero (France; b. 9 Jan. 1961) *v.* Zimbabwe at Auckland on 2 June 1987. The leading scorer in the tournament was the New Zealand goal-kicker,

Grant James Fox (b. 6 June 1962), with 170 points (including a record 126 in 1987).

INTERNATIONAL CHAMPIONSHIPS

The International Championship was first contested by England, Ireland, Scotland and Wales in 1884. France first played in 1910.

Wales has won the championship a record 21 times outright and tied for first a further 11 times up to 1988. The most Grand Slams, winning all four matches, is ten, by England, 1913–14, 1921, 1923–24, 1928, 1957, 1980 and 1991–92.

Highest team score The highest score in any full international was when New Zealand beat Japan by 106–4 at Tokyo, Japan on 1 Nov. 1987. France beat Paraguay 106–12 at Asunción, Paraguay on 28 June 1988.

MOST INTERNATIONAL RUGBY APPEARANCES

FRANCE	93	Serge Blanco	1980–92
		(b. 31 Aug. 1958)	
IRELAND	69	Cameron Michael Henderson Gibson)	1964–79
		(b. 3 Dec. 1942	
AUSTRALIA	67	David Ian Campese	1982–92
		(b. 21 Oct. 1962)	
NEW ZEALAND	58	Gary William Whetton	1981–92
		(b. 15 Dec. 1959)	
WALES	55†	John Peter Rhys "JPR" Williams	1969–81
		(b. 2 Mar. 1949)	
ENGLAND	55	Rory Underwood	1984–92
		(b. 19 June 1963)	
SCOTLAND	52	James Menzies "Jim" Renwick	1972–84
		(b. 12 Feb. 1952)	
	52	Colin Thomas Deans	1978–87
		(b. 3 May 1955)	
SOUTH AFRICA	38	Frederick Christoffel Hendrick Du Preez	1960–71
		(b. 28 Nov. 1935)	
	38	Jan Hendrik Ellis	1965–76
		(b. 5 Jan. 1943)	
UNITED STATES	29	Kevin Swords	1985–92
		(b. 1 July 1960)	

† *Gareth Owen Edwards (b. 12 July 1947) made a record 53 consecutive international appearances, never missing a match throughout his career for Wales, 1967–78. Willie John McBride also had 53 consecutive appearances during his 63 games for Ireland, 1962–75. Note: The criteria used to decide which games are classed as full internationals vary between countries.*

HIGHEST INDIVIDUAL SCORES

Internationals Phil Bennett (Wales; b. 24 Oct. 1948) scored 34 points (2 tries, 10 conversions, 2 penalty goals) for Wales *v*. Japan at Tokyo on 24 Sep. 1975, when Wales won 82–6. A record eight penalty goals were kicked by Mark Andrew Wyatt (b. 12 Apr. 1961) when he scored all Canada's points in their 24–19 defeat of Scotland at St. John, New Brunswick, Canada on 25 May 1991.

Career In all internationals, Michael Patrick Lynagh (b. 25 Oct. 1963) scored a record 737 points in 57 matches for Australia, 1984–92. The most tries is 49, by David Campese (b. 21 Oct. 1962) in 68 internationals for Australia, 1982–92.

Seven-a-sides Seven-a-side rugby dates from 28 Apr. 1883, when Melrose RFC Borders (Scotland), in order to compensate for the poverty of a club in such a small town, staged a seven-a-side tournament. The idea was that of Ned Haig, the town's butcher.

Hong Kong Sevens This, the world's most prestigious international tournament for seven-a-side teams, was first held in 1976. The record of seven wins is held by Fiji, 1977–78, 1980, 1984,1990–92.

Women's rugby The first women's World Cup was contested by 12 teams in 1991, with the USA beating England 19–6 in the final at Cardiff, Great Britain on 14 Apr. 1991.

MOST PENALTIES. A record eight penalty goals were kicked by Mark Andrew Wyatt when he scored all of Canada's points in their 24–19 defeat of Scotland at St. John, New Brunswick, Canada on 25 May 1991. (Photo: Allsport/Ken Levine)

All-arounder   Canadian international Barrie Burnham scored all possible ways—try, conversion, penalty goal, drop goal, goal from mark—for Meralomas *v.* Georgians (20–11) at Vancouver, British Columbia, Canada on 26 Feb. 1966.

Highest rugby posts   The world's highest rubgy union goal posts are 110 ft. ½ in. high, at the Roan Antelope Rugby Union Club, Luanshya, Zambia.

Highest shooting score in 24 hours   The Easingwold Rifle and Pistol Club (Yorkshire, Great Britain) team of John Smith, Edward Kendall, Phillip Kendall and Paul Duffield scored 120,242 points (averaging 95.66 per card) on 6–7 Aug. 1983.

Bench rest shooting   The smallest area on record into which a group of shots have been fired at 1,000 yds. is 4.375 in., by Earl Chronister with a .30–378 Weatherby Mag at Williamsport, PA on 12 July 1987.
 The smallest at 500 m (546 yds.) is 2.297 in., by Dennis Tobler (Australia) using a .30–06 rifle of his own design at Canberra, Australia on 28 Mar. 1992.

SHOOTING

The Lucerne Shooting Guild (Switzerland) was formed *c.* 1466 and the first recorded shooting match was at Zurich in 1472.

United States   The National Rifle Association (NRA) was founded in 1871, and is designated as the national governing body for shooting sports in the United States by the US Olympic Committee.

Most Olympic medals   Carl Townsend Osburn (USA; 1884–1966) won 11 medals, in 1912, 1920 and 1924—five gold, four silver and two bronze. Six other marksmen have won five gold medals. Gudbrand Gudbrandsönn Skatteboe (Norway; 1875–1965) is the only marksman to win three individual gold medals, in 1906. Separate events for women were first held in 1984.
 Six other marksmen have won five gold medals, including three Americans: Alfred P. Lane (b. 26 Sep. 1891), 1912–20; Willis Augustus Lee, Jr. (1888–94), all in 1920; and Morris Fisher (1890–1968), 1920–24. In 1920 a record seven medals were won by both Willis Lee, who also won a silver and bronze, and Lloyd S. Spooner—four gold, a silver and two bronze.
 The first US woman to win an Olympic medal was Margaret L. Murdock (nee Thompson; b. 25 Aug. 1942), who took the silver at small-bore rifle (three positions) in mixed competition in 1976. The first to win an Olympic gold medal was Patricia Spurgin (b. 10 Aug. 1965), at women's air rifle in 1984.

SHOOTING–INDIVIDUAL WORLD RECORDS

In 1986, the International Shooting Union (UIT) introduced new regulations for determining major championships and world records. Now the leading competitors undertake an additional round with a target subdivided to tenths of a point for rifle and pistol shooting, and an extra 25 shots for trap and skeet. Harder targets have since been introduced, and the table below shows the world records, as recognized by the UIT on 1 Jan. 1992, for the 13 Olympic shooting disciplines, giving in brackets the score for the number of shots specified plus the score in the additional round.

MEN

FREE RIFLE 50 m 3 × 40 shots	1,276.7	(1,179 + 97.7)	Rajmond Debevec (Yugoslavia)	Munich, Germany ... 2 June 1990
	1,276.7	(1,177 + 99.7)	Rajmond Debevec (Yugoslavia)	Zürich, Switzerland ... 7 June 1991
FREE RIFLE 50 m 60 shots prone	703.5	(599 + 104.5)	Jens Harskov (Denmark)	Zürich, Switzerland ... 6 June 1991
AIR RIFLE 10 m 60 shots	699.4	(596 + 103.4)	Rajmond Debevec (Yugoslavia)	Zürich, Switzerland ... 8 June 1990
FREE PISTOL 50 m 60 shots	671	(579 + 92)	Sergey Pyzhyanov (USSR)	Munich, Germany ... 31 May 1990
	671	(577 + 94)	Spas Koprinkov (Bulgaria)	Moscow, USSR ... 9 Aug. 1990
RAPID-FIRE PISTOL 25 m 60 shots	891	(594 + 297)	Ralf Schumann (West Germany)	Munich, Germany ... 3 June 1989
AIR PISTOL 10 m 60 shots	695.1	(593 + 102.1)	Sergey Pyzhyanov (USSR)	Munich, Germany ... 13 Oct. 1989
RUNNING TARGET 50 m 30 + 30 shots	679	(582 + 97)	Lubos Racansky (Czechoslovakia)	Munich, Germany ... 30 May 1991

WOMEN

STANDARD RIFLE 50 m 3 × 20 shots	684.9	(584 + 100.9)	Vessela Letcheva (Bulgaria)	Munich, Germany ... 29 Aug. 1991
AIR RIFLE 10 m 40 shots	500.8	(399 + 101.8)	Valentina Cherkasova (USSR)	Los Angeles, CA ... 23 Mar. 1991
SPORT PISTOL 25 m 60 shots	693	(593 + 100)	Nino Salukvadse (USSR)	Zagreb, Yugoslavia ... 13 July 1989
AIR PISTOL 10 m 40 shots	492.4	(392 + 100.4)	Lieslotte Breker (West Germany)	Zagreb, Yugoslavia ... 18 May 1989

OPEN

TRAP 200 targets	224	(200 + 24)	Jörg Damme (West Germany)	Moscow, USSR ... 18 Aug. 1990
	225	(200 + 25)	Axel Wegner (Germany)	Munich, Germany ... 31 Aug. 1991
SKEET 200 targets	225	(200 + 25)	Hennie Dompeling (Netherlands)	Munich, Germany ... 31 Aug. 1991

WORLD RECORD. Seen here in action in one of the few mixed sports contested at the Olympics is skeet world record holder Axel Wegner (Germany). He won the 1988 title with a score of 222 and set the current world record, a maximum 225, at Munich on 31 Aug. 1991. (Photo: Allsport/Russell Cheyne)

World record   The first world record by a woman at any sport for a category in direct and measurable competition with men was by Margaret Murdock, who set a world record for small-bore rifle (kneeling position) of 391 in 1967.

Clay pigeon   The most world titles have been won by Susan Nattrass (Canada; b. 5 Nov. 1950) with six, 1974–75, 1977–79, 1981. The record number of clay birds shot in an hour is 3,172, by Dan Carlisle (USA) at Norco, CA on 20 May 1990.

The maximum 200/200 was achieved by Ricardo Ruiz Rumoroso at the Spanish Clay Pigeon Championships at Zaragossa on 12 June 1983.

Noel D. Townend achieved the maximum 200 consecutive down-the-line targets at Nottingham, Great Britain on 21 Aug. 1983.

SKIING

The most ancient ski in existence was found well-preserved in a peat bog at Hoting, Sweden, dating from *c.* 2500 B.C. The earliest recorded military use of skiing was at the Battle of Isen, near Oslo, Norway in 1200. The Trysil Shooting and Skiing Club, founded in Norway in 1861, claims it is the world's oldest. The oldest ski competitions are the Holmenkøllen Nordic events, which were first held in 1866. The first downhill races were staged in Australia in the 1850s. The International Ski Federation (FIS) was founded on 2 Feb. 1924, succeeding the International Skiing Commission, founded at Christiania (Oslo), Norway on 18 Feb. 1910.

United States   The first ski club in the United States was formed at Berlin, NH in January 1872, and later became known as the Nansen Ski Club. The US Ski Association was originally founded as the National Ski Association in 1905. In 1962 it was renamed the USA Ski Association, and was renamed US Skiing in May 1990.

Longest ski run   The longest all-downhill ski run in the world is the Weissfluhjoch-Küblis Parsenn course, near Davos, Switzerland, which measures 7.6 miles. The run from the Aiguille du Midi top of the Chamonix lift (vertical lift 9,052 ft.) across the Vallée Blanche is 13 miles.

Snowshoeing   The IASSRF (International Amateur SnowShoe Racing Federation) record for covering one mile is 5 min. 56.7 sec., by Nick Akers of Edmonton, Alberta, Canada on 3 Feb. 1991. The 100 m record is 14.07 sec., by Jeremy Badeau at Canaseraga, NY on 31 May 1991.

Most titles   *World/Olympic Championships—Alpine*   The World Alpine Championships were inaugurated at Mürren, Switzerland in 1931. The greatest number of titles won has been by Christel Cranz (b. 1 July 1914) of Germany, with seven individual—four slalom (1934, 1937–39) and three downhill (1935, 1937, 1939), and five combined (1934–35, 1937–39). She also won the gold medal for the combined in the 1936 Olympics. The most won by a man is seven, by Anton "Toni" Sailer (Austria; b. 17 Nov. 1935), who won all four in 1956 (giant slalom, slalom, downhill and the non-Olympic Alpine combination) and the downhill, giant slalom and combined in 1958.

The only US skier to win two Olympic gold medals has been Andrea Mead-Lawrence (b. 19 Apr. 1932), at slalom and giant slalom in 1952.

World/Olympic Championships—Nordic   The first World Nordic Championships were those of the 1924 Winter Olympics in Chamonix, France. The greatest number of titles won is 11, by Gunde Svan (Sweden; b. 12 Jan. 1962), seven individual—15 km 1989, 30 km 1985 and 1991, 50 km 1985 and 1989, and Olympics, 15 km 1984, 50 km 1988; and four relays—4 × 10 km, 1987 and 1989, and Olympics, 1984 and 1988. The most titles won by a woman is nine, by Galina Alekseyevna Kulakova (USSR; b. 29 Apr. 1942), in 1970–78. The most medals is 23, by Raisa Petrovna Smetanina (USSR; b. 29 Feb. 1952), including six gold, 1974–92. Johann Grøttumsbraaten (1899–1942) of Norway also won six individual titles (two 18 km cross-country, four Nordic combined) in 1926–32. Ulrich Wehling (East Germany) has also won four Nordic combined, winning the World Championship in 1974 and the Olympic title, 1972, 1976 and 1980—the first skier to win the same event at three successive Olympics. The record for a jumper is five, by Birger Ruud (b. 23 Aug. 1911) of Norway, in 1931–32 and 1935–37. Ruud is the only person to win Olympic events in each of the dissimilar Alpine and Nordic disciplines. In 1936 he won the ski-jumping and the Alpine downhill (which was not then a separate event, but only a segment of the combined event).

MOST TITLES (right). Carole Merle (France) has won the Super-G World Cup title a record four times, 1989–92. (Photo: Allsport/David Cannon)

SPEED SKIING (below). At the 1992 Olympics, speed skiing was a demonstration sport, with world records being set in both the men's and women's event. The men's title was won by Michaël Prüfer (France), who bettered his own world record. (Photo: Allsport/Vandystadt)

MOST OLYMPIC SKIING TITLES

MEN

ALPINE 3   Anton "Toni" Sailer (Austria; b. 17 Nov. 1935) ....Downhill, slalom, giant slalom, 1956

       3   Jean-Claude Killy (France; b. 30 Aug. 1943) ....Downhill, slalom, giant slalom 1968

     3*   Alberto Tomba (Italy) ....Slalom, giant slalom, 1988; giant slalom, 1992

NORDIC ....4*   Sixten Jernberg (Sweden; b. 6 Feb. 1929) ....50 km 1956; 30 km 1960; 50 km and 4 × 10 km 1964

      4   Gunde Svan (Sweden; b. 12 Mar. 1962) ....15 km and 4 × 10 km 1984; 50 km and 4 × 10 km 1988

      4   Thomas Wassberg (Sweden; b. 27 Mar. 1956) ......15 km 1980; 50 km 1984; 4 × 10 km 1984, 1988

Jumping 4   Matti Nykänen (Finland; b. 17 July 1963) ....70 m hill 1988; 90 m hill 1984, 1988; team 1988

WOMEN

ALPINE 2   Andrea Mead-Lawrence (USA; b. 19 Apr. 1932) ......Slalom, giant slalom 1952

      2   Marielle Goitschel (France; b. 28 Sep. 1945) ....Giant slalom 1964; slalom 1968

      2   Marie-Thérèse Nadig (Switzerland; b. 8 Mar. 1954) ....Downhill, giant slalom 1972

      2   Rosi Mittermaier ....Downhill, slalom 1976

         (now Neureuther [West Germany]; b. 5 Aug. 1950)

     2*   Hanni Wenzel (Liechtenstein; b. 14 Dec. 1956) ......Giant slalom, slalom 1980

      2   Vreni Schneider (Switzerland; b. 26 Nov. 1964) .....Giant slalom, slalom 1988

      2   Petra Kronberger (Austria; b. 21 Feb. 1969) ....Slalom, combined, 1992

NORDIC 4   Galina Kulakova (USSR; b. 29 Apr. 1942) ....5 km, 10 km and 3 × 5 km relay 1972; 4 × 5 km relay 1976

     4*   Raisa Smetanina (USSR/CIS; b. 29 Feb. 1952) ....10 km, 4 × 5 km, 1976; 5 km, 1980; 4 × 5 km, 1992

(individual) ...3   Marja-Liisa Hämäläinen (Finland; b. 10 Aug. 1955) ...5 km, 10 km and 20 km 1984

* Most medals *(women)* 10, Raisa Smetanina, four gold, five silver and one bronze

               (men) 9, Sixten Jernberg, four golds, three silver and two bronze.

In Alpine skiing, the record is four; Hanni Wenzel won a silver in the 1980 downhill and a bronze in the 1976 slalom, and Tomba won a silver in the 1992 slalom.

World Cup   The World Cup was introduced for Alpine events in 1967 and for Nordic events in 1981. The most individual event wins is 86 (46 giant slalom, 40 slalom from a total of 287 races) by Ingemar Stenmark (Sweden; b. 18 Mar. 1956) in 1974–89, including a men's record 13 in one season in 1978/79, of which 10 were part of a record 14 successive giant slalom wins from 18 Mar. 1978, his 22nd birthday, to 21 Jan. 1980. Franz Klammer (Austria; b. 3 Dec. 1953) won a record 25 downhill races, 1974–84. Annemarie Moser (nee Pröll [Austria]; b. 27 Mar. 1953) won a women's record 62 individual event wins, 1970–79. She had a record 11 consecutive downhill wins from Dec. 1972 to Jan. 1974. Vreni Schneider (Switzerland; b. 26 Nov. 1964) won a record 13 events and a combined including all seven slalom events in 1988/89.

The Nation's Cup, awarded on the combined results of the men and women in the World Cup, has been won a record 14 times by Austria—1969, 1973–82, 1990–92.

United States   The most successful US skier has been Phillip Ferdinand Mahre (b. 10 May 1957), winner of the overall title three times, 1981–83, with two wins at giant slalom and one at slalom. The most successful US woman has been Tamara McKinney (b. 16 Oct. 1962), overall winner 1983, giant slalom 1981 and 1983, and slalom 1984.

The only American to win a Nordic skiing World Cup title has been William Koch (b. 7 June 1955), at cross-country in 1982.

Ski-jumping   The longest ski-jump ever recorded is one of 636 ft., by Piotr Fijas (Poland) at Planica, Yugoslavia on 14 Mar. 1987. The women's record is 361 ft., by Tiina Lehtola (Finland; b. 3 Aug. 1962), at Ruka, Finland on 29 Mar. 1981. The longest dry ski-jump is 302 ft., by Hubert Schwarz (West Germany) at Berchtesgarten, Germany on 30 June 1981.

Fastest speed   The official world record, as recognized by the International Ski Federation for a skier, is 142.165 mph, by Michaël Prüfer (France), and the fastest by a woman is 133.234 mph, by Tarja Mulari (Finland), both at Les Arcs, France on 22 Feb. 1992. On 16 Apr. 1988 Patrick Knaff (France) set a one-legged record of 115.309 mph.

The fastest average speed in the Olympic downhill race was 64.95 mph, by William D. Johnson (USA; b. 30 Mar. 1960), at Sarajevo, Yugoslavia on 16 Feb. 1984. The fastest in a World Cup downhill is 67.00 mph, by Harti Weirather (Austria; b. 25 Jan. 1958), at Kitzbühel, Austria on 15 Jan. 1982.

Fastest speed—cross-country   Bill Koch (USA; b. 13 Apr. 1943), on 26 Mar. 1981 skied ten times around a 3.11 mile loop on Marlborough Pond, near Putney, VT. He completed the 50 km (31.07 mile) course in 1 hr. 59 min. 47 sec., an average speed of 15.57 mph. A race includes uphill and downhill sections; the record time for a race in World Championships or Olympic Games is 2 hrs. 3 min. 31.6 sec., by Torgny Mogren (Sweden) in 1991, an average speed of 15.09 mph.

Longest races   The world's longest Nordic ski race is the Vasaloppet, which commemorates an event of 1521 when Gustav Vasa (1496–1560), later King Gustavus Eriksson, fled 53.3 miles from Mora to Sälen, Sweden. He was overtaken by loyal, speedy scouts on skis, who persuaded him to return eastward to Mora to lead a rebellion and become the king of Sweden. The reenactment of this return journey is now an annual event at 55.3 miles. There were a record 10,934 starters on 6 Mar. 1977 and a record 10,650 finishers on 4 Mar. 1979. The fastest time is 3 hrs. 48 min. 55 sec., by Bengt Hassis (Sweden) on 2 Mar. 1986.

The Finlandia Ski Race, 46.6 miles from Hämeenlinna to Lahti, on 26 Feb. 1984, had a record 13,226 starters and 12,909 finishers.

The longest downhill race is the Inferno in Switzerland, 9.8 miles from the top of the Schilthorn to Lauterbrunnen. The record number of entries was 1,401 in 1981, and the record time was 13 min. 53.40 sec. by Urs von Allmen (Switzerland) in 1991.

Long-distance (Nordic)   In 24 hours Seppo-Juhani Savolainen covered 258.2 miles at Saariselkä, Finland on 8–9 Apr. 1988. The women's 24 hr. record is 205.05 miles, by Sisko Kainulaisen at Jyväskylä, Finland on 23–24 Mar. 1985.

In 48 hours Bjørn Løkken (Norway; b. 27 Nov. 1937) covered 319 miles 205 yds. on 11–13 Mar. 1982.

Freestyle skiing   The first World Championships were held at Tignes, France in 1986, titles being awarded in ballet, moguls, aerials and combined. A record two titles have been won by Lloyd Langlois (Canada), aerials, 1986 and 1989; Jan Buchner (USA), ballet, 1986 and 1989; and Edgar Grospiron (France), moguls, 1989 and 1991. The three separate disciplines were included in the 1988 Olympics but only as demonstration events. Moguls were contested with full status at the 1992 Olympics, when Grospiron won the men's gold medal. Donna Weinbrecht (USA) won the women's moguls title in 1991 and at the Olympics in 1992.

Longest ski-lift   The longest gondola ski lift is 3.88 miles long, at Grindelwald-Männlichen, Switzerland (in two sections, but one gondola). The longest chair lift in the world was the Alpine Way–to–Kosciusko Chalet lift above Thredbo, near the Snowy Mountains, New South Wales, Australia. It took from 45 to 74 min. to ascend the 3.5 miles, depending on the weather. The chair lift has now collapsed. The highest lift is at Chacaltaya, Bolivia, rising to 16,500 ft.

Ski-bob   *Origins*   The ski-bob was the invention of J.C. Stevenson of Hartford, CT in 1891, and patented (No. 47334) on 19 Apr. 1892 as a "bicycle with ski-runners." The *Fédération Internationale de Skibob* was founded on 14 Jan. 1961 in Innsbruck, Austria, and the first World Championships were held at Bad Hofgastein, Austria in 1967.

The fastest speed attained is 103.4 mph, by Erich Brenter (Austria; b. 1940), at Cervinia, Italy in 1964.

World Championships   The only ski-bobbers to retain a world championship are: *(men)* Alois Fischbauer (Austria; b. 6 Oct. 1951), 1973 and 1975; Robert Mühlberger (West Germany), 1979 and 1981; *(women)* Gerhilde Schiffkorn (Austria; b. 22 Mar. 1950), 1967 and 1969; Gertrude Geberth (Austria; b. 18 Oct. 1951), 1971 and 1973.

GRASS SKIING

Grass skis were first manufactured by Josef Kaiser (Germany) in 1963. World Championships (now awarded for Super G, giant slalom, slalom and combined) were first held in 1979. The most titles won is ten, by Ingrid

Hirschhofer (Austria), 1979–89. The most by a man is seven, by Erwin Gansner (Switzerland), 1981–87.

The speed record is 53.99 mph, by Erwin Gansner at Owen, Germany on 5 Sep. 1982.

SKIPPING ROPE

Ten mile skip-run   Vadivelu Karunakaren (India) skipped rope ten miles in 58 min. at Madras, India, 1 Feb. 1990.

Most turns *One hour*   14,628, by Park Bong Tae (South Korea) at Pusan, South Korea, 2 July 1989. Robert Commers holds the US record, with 13,783, at Woodbridge, NJ, 13 May 1989.

On a single rope, team of 90   160, by students from the Nishigoshi Higashi Elementary School, Kumamoto, Japan, 27 Feb. 1987.

On a tightrope   358 (consecutive), by Julian Albulet (USA) at Las Vegas, NV, 2 July 1990.

Most on a rope *(minimum 12 turns obligatory)*   220, by a team at the International Rope Skipping Competition, Greeley, CO, 28 June 1990.

SLED DOG RACING

Longest trail   Racing between harnessed dog teams (usually huskies) had been practiced by the Inuits and the northern Indians of North America and in Scandinavia, but the first formal record of a race was in 1908, when the All-Alaskan Sweepstakes were contested on a run of 408 miles from Nome to Candle and back.

Now established as the world's most prestigious sled dog race, the Iditarod trail has existed since 1910 and has been raced annually since 1967 by dog

---

Longest trail   On 8 Feb. 1988 Rev. Donald Ewen McEwen, owner-musher of Nekanesu Kennels, Eldorado, Ontario, Canada drove a 76-dog sled for 2 miles single-handedly on the ice and around the shore of Lingham Lake. The team, consisting of 25 Siberian huskies and 51 Alaskan huskies, was assembled for the filming of a British TV commercial.

---

teams, 1,049 miles from Anchorage to Nome, AK. The inaugural winner, Dick Wilmarth, took 20 days 49 min. and 41 sec. to complete the course, beating 33 other racers.

The fastest time was set by Martin Buser of Switzerland in 1992 with 10 days 19 hrs. 36 min. 15 sec. Rick Swenson (US) has won the race a record five times (1977, 1979, 1981–82 and 1991).

SLED DOG RACING. The Iditarod trail has existed since 1910, and has been raced annually since 1967 by dog teams, 1,049 miles from Anchorage to Nome, AK. The photograph shows the start of the 1988 race in Anchorage, AK. (Photo: Allsport/Ronna)

SNOOKER

Origins   Research shows that snooker was originated by Colonel Sir Neville Francis Fitzgerald Chamberlain (1856–1944) as a hybrid of pool and pyramids, in Jubbulpore, India in 1875. Chamberlain added a set of colored balls to the 15 red ones used in pyramids and devised a scoring system based on pocketing the balls in sequence: red, color, red, color until all the reds have been cleared, leaving the colored balls to be pocketed in numerical order. The modern scoring system (a red ball is worth one point, yellow—2, green—3, brown—4, blue—5, pink—6 and black—7) was adopted in England in 1891. The sequence of pocketing the balls is called a break, the maximum possible break being 147. The name *snooker* comes from the term coined for new recruits at the Woolwich Military Academy and was Chamberlain's label for anyone who lost at his game. Championships were not started until 1916. The World Professional Championship was instituted in 1927.

Most world titles The world professional title was won a record 15 times by Joe Davis, on the first 15 occasions it was contested, 1927–40 and 1946. The most wins in the Amateur Championships have been two—by Gary Owen (England) in 1963 and 1966; Ray Edmonds (England) 1972 and 1974; and Paul Mifsud (Malta) 1985–86.

Maureen Baynton (nee Barrett) won a record eight Women's Amateur Championships between 1954 and 1968, as well as seven at billiards.

World Championships The youngest man to win a world title is Stephen O'Connor (Ireland; b. 16 Oct. 1972), who was 18 yrs. 40 days when he won the World Amateur Snooker Championship in Colombo, Sri Lanka on 25 Nov. 1990. Stephen Hendry (Scotland; b. 13 Jan. 1969) became the youngest World Professional champion, at 21 yrs. 106 days on 29 Apr. 1990. He had been the youngest winner of a major professional title, at 18 yrs. 285 days, when he won the Rothman's Grand Prix on 25 Oct. 1987.

Stacey Hillyard (Great Britain; b. 15 Sep. 1969) won the Women's World Amateur Championship in October 1984 at the age of 15.

Highest breaks Over 200 players have achieved the maximum break of 147. The first to do so was E.J. "Murt" O'Donoghue (b. New Zealand 1901) at Griffiths, New South Wales, Australia on 26 Sep. 1934. The first officially ratified 147 was by Joe Davis against Willie Smith in London, Great Britain on 22 Jan. 1955. Cliff Thorburn (Canada; b. 16 Jan. 1948) has scored two tournament 147 breaks, (the World Professional Championship), on 23 Apr. 1983 and 8 Mar. 1989.

The first century break by a woman in competitive play was 114, by Stacey Hillyard in a league match at Bournemouth, Great Britain on 15 Jan. 1985. The highest break by a woman in competition is 116, by Allison Fisher in the British Open at Solihull, Great Britain on 7 Oct. 1989.

Longest unbroken run From 17 Mar. 1990 to his defeat by Jimmy White (b. 2 May 1962) on 13 Jan. 1991, Stephen Hendry won five successive titles and 36 consecutive matches in ranking tournaments.

SOARING

Origins Research by Isadore William Deiches has shown evidence of the use of gliders in ancient Egypt c. 2500–1500 B.C. Emanuel Swedenborg (1688–1772) of Sweden made sketches of gliders c. 1714. The earliest human-carrying glider was designed by Sir George Cayley (1773–1857) and carried his coachman (possibly John Appleby) about 500 yds. across a valley in Brompton Dale, Great Britain in the summer of 1853.

Most titles The most World Individual championships (instituted 1937) won is four, by Ingo Renner (Australia) in 1976 (Standard class), 1983, 1985 and 1987 (Open).

The most titles won by a US pilot is two, by George Moffat, in the Open category, 1970 and 1974.

Women's altitude records   The women's single-seater world record for absolute altitude is 41,460 ft., by Sabrina Jackintell (USA) in an Astir GS on 14 Feb. 1979.

The height gain record is 33,506 ft., by Yvonne Loader (New Zealand) at Omarama, New Zealand on 12 Jan. 1988.

HANG GLIDING

Origins   In the 11th century the monk Eilmer is reported to have flown from the 60-ft. tower of Malmesbury Abbey, Wiltshire, Great Britain. The earliest modern pioneer was Otto Lilienthal (Germany; 1848–96) with about 2,500 flights in gliders of his own construction between 1891 and 1896. In the 1950s Professor Francis Rogallo of the National Space Agency developed a flexible "wing" from his space capsule reentry research.

World Championships   The World Team Championships (officially instituted in 1976) have been won most often by Great Britain (1981, 1985, 1989 and 1991).

World records   The *Fédération Aéronautique Internationale* recognizes world records for rigid-wing, flex-wing and multiplace flex-wing. The following records are the greatest in each category—all by flex-wing gliders.

Men   Greatest distance in straight line and declared goal distance: 303.35 miles, Larry Tudor (USA), Wills Wing Hobbs Airpark, NM to Elkhart, KS, 3 July 1990.

Height gain: 14,250 ft., Larry Tudor (USA), Owens Valley, CA, 4 Aug. 1985.

Out and return distance: 192.818 miles, Larry Tudor (USA) and Geoffrey Loyns (Great Britain), Owens Valley, 26 June 1988.

Triangular course distance: 121.81 miles, James Lee (USA), San Pedro, Mesa, CA, 4 July 1991.

Women   Greatest distance: 208.63 miles, Kari Castle (USA), Horseshoe-Mid, NV, 22 July 1991.

Height gain: 11,998.62 ft., Tover Buas-Hansen (Norway) and Keven Kline-felder (USA), Owens Valley, 6 July 1989.

Out and return distance in a single turn: 181.47 miles, Kari Castle (USA), Hobbs Airpark, 3 July 1990.

Declared goal distance: 132.04 miles, Liavan Mallin (Ireland), Owens Valley, 13 July 1989.

Triangular course distance: Judy Leden, 70.904 miles, Konsen, Austria, 22 June 1991.

SOCCER

Origins A game with some similarities called *Zu-qui* ("to kick a ball of stuffed leather") was played in China in the fourth and third centuries B.C. However, the ancestry of the modern game is traced to England. In 1314, King Edward II prohibited the game because of excessive noise. Three subsequent monarchs also banned the game. Nevertheless, "football," the name by which soccer is known outside the USA, continued its development in England. In 1848, the first rules were drawn up at Cambridge University, Great Britain; in 1863, the Football Association (FA) was founded in England. The sport grew in popularity worldwide, and the *Fédération Internationale de Football Association* (FIFA), the world governing body, was formed in Paris, France in 1904. FIFA currently has more than 160 members.

THE FIFA WORLD CUP

FIFA, which was founded on 21 May 1904, instituted the first World Cup on 13 July 1930, in Montevideo, Uruguay. It is now held quadrennially. Three wins have been achieved by Brazil, in 1958, 1962 and 1970; Italy, in 1934, 1938 and 1982; and West Germany, in 1954, 1974 and 1990.

Team records *Most appearances* Brazil is the only country to qualify for all 14 World Cup tournaments.

Most goals The highest score by one team in a game is ten, by Hungary in a 10–1 defeat of El Salvador at Elche, Spain on 15 June 1982. The most goals in tournament history is 148 (in 66 games) by Brazil.

Highest-scoring game The highest-scoring game took place on 26 June 1954 when Austria defeated Switzerland 7–5.

Individual records *Most wins* Pelé (Brazil) is the only player to have played on three winning teams, 1958, 1962 and 1970. He played during the 1962 Finals, but was injured before the final match and was therefore unable to play in it. Mario Zagalo (Brazil) was the first man to play (in 1958 and 1962) and be manager (1970) of a World Cup winning team. Franz Beckenbauer emulated Zagalo when he managed the West German team to victory in 1990. He had previously captained the 1974 winning team. Beckenbauer is the only man to have both captained and managed a winning side.

Most goals The most goals scored in a final is three, by Geoff Hurst for England *v.* West Germany on 30 July 1966.

Most games played Two players have appeared in 21 games in the finals tournament: Uwe Seeler (West Germany; b. 5 Nov. 1936) 1958–70; and Wladyslaw Zmuda (Poland; b. 6 June 1954) 1974–86.

Most goals scored The most goals scored by a player in a game is four; this has occurred nine times. The most goals scored in one tournament is 13, by Just Fontaine (France) in 1958, in six games. The most goals scored in a career is 14, by Gerd Muller (West Germany), ten goals in 1970 and four in 1974.

NCAA DIVISION I CHAMPIONSHIPS

Men   In this competition, first held in 1959, the University of St. Louis has won the most Division I titles with ten victories, including one tie: 1959–60, 1962–63, 1965, 1967, 1969–70, 1972–73.

Women   In this competition, first held in 1982, the University of North Carolina has won a record nine Division I titles. Its victories came in 1982–84, 1986–91.

MAJOR SOCCER LEAGUE (MSL)

The Major Soccer League (MSL) was founded in 1978 as the Major Indoor Soccer League (MISL), and renamed for the 1990/91 season.

Most championships   The San Diego Sockers have won a record eight MSL championships, 1983, 1985–86, 1988–92.

Individual records   Steve Zungul holds the career MSL records for the most goals scored, 652; most assists, 471; most power play goals, 89; most hat tricks, 99; and most points scored, 1,123. Zungul played 11 seasons for four teams: New York Arrows, 1978–83; Golden Bay Earthquakes, 1983; San Diego Sockers, 1984–86; Tacoma Stars, 1986–88; San Diego Sockers, 1989–90.

Kim Roentved has played the most games in MSL history, 494 in 12 seasons. Roentved has played for three teams: Wichita Wings, 1980–87; Kansas City Comets, 1987–91; Wichita Wings, 1991–92.

Most international appearances   Bruce Murray (b. 25 June 1966) has played a record 74 times for the United States in full international games as of 30 June 1992.

Olympic games   Soccer has been an official sport at the Olympics since 1908, except for 1932, when it was not staged in Los Angeles. The leading gold medal winner is Hungary, with three wins (1952, 1964, 1968). The highest Olympic score is 17, by Denmark *v.* France in 1908. A record 126 nations took part in qualifying for the 1992 tournament.

Largest soccer crowds   The top attendance for a soccer match in the USA was 101,799, for France's 2–0 Olympic final win over Brazil at the Rose Bowl, Pasadena, CA on 11 Aug. 1984.

The highest attendance for an MSL game was 21,728 at the Tacoma Dome on 20 June 1987 for the seventh game of the championship series. The Dallas Sidekicks defeated the Tacoma Stars 4-3 in overtime and won the title.

SOFTBALL

Origins Softball, a derivative of baseball, was invented by George Hancock at the Farragut Boat Club of Chicago, IL in 1887. Rules were first codified in Minneapolis, MN in 1895 under the name kitten ball. The name softball was introduced by Walter Hakanson at a meeting of the National Recreation Congress in 1926. The name was adopted throughout the United States in 1930. Rules were formalized in 1933 by the International Joint Rules Committee for Softball and adopted by the Amateur Softball Association of America. The International Softball Federation was formed in 1950 as the governing body for both fast pitch and slow pitch. It was reorganized in 1965. Women's fast pitch softball has been added to the Olympic program for 1996.

Most titles The USA has won the men's World Championship (instituted 1966) five times, 1966, 1968, 1976 (shared), 1980 and 1988, and the women's title (instituted 1965) three times, in 1974, 1978 and 1986. The world's first slow pitch championships for men's teams were held in Oklahoma City in 1987, when the winner was the USA.

US National Championships The most wins in the fast pitch championships (first held in 1933) for men is 10, by the Clearwater (Florida) Bombers between 1950 and 1973, and for women is 21, by the Raybestos Brakettes of Stratford, CT, between 1958 and 1990.
   Slow pitch championships have been staged annually since 1953 for men and since 1962 for women. Three wins for men have been achieved by Skip Hogan A.C. of Pittsburgh, 1962, 1964–65, and by Joe Gatliff Auto Sales of Newport, KY, 1956–57, 1963. At super slow pitch, four wins have been achieved by Steele's Silver Bullets, Grafton, OH, 1985–87 and 1990. The Dots of Miami, FL have a record five women's titles, playing as the Converse Dots, 1969; Marks Brothers; North Miami Dots, 1974–75; and Bob Hoffman Dots, 1978–79.

SPEEDWAY

Motorcycle racing on large dirt track surfaces has been traced back to 1902 in the United States. The first fully documented motorcycle track races were at the Portman Road Ground, Ipswich, Great Britain on 2 July 1904. Two heats and a final were contested, F.E. Barker winning in 5 min. 54.2 sec. for three miles. Modern speedway has developed from the "short track" races held at the West Maitland Agricultural (New South Wales, Australia) Show on 22 Dec. 1923, by Johnnie Hoskins (New Zealand; 1892–1987).

World Championships The World Speedway Championship was inaugurated at Wembley, London, Great Britain on 10 Sep. 1936. The most wins have been six, by Ivan Gerald Mauger (New Zealand; b. 4 Oct. 1939) in 1968–70, 1972, 1977 and 1979. Barry Briggs (New Zealand; b. 30 Dec. 1934) made a record 18 appearances in the finals (1954–70, 1972) and won the world title in 1957–58, 1964 and 1966. He also scored a record 201 points in world championship competition in 87 races.

Ivan Mauger also won four World Team Cups (three for Great Britain), two World Pairs (including one unofficial) and three world long track titles. Ove Fundin (Sweden; b. 23 May 1933) won 12 world titles: five individual, one pairs, and six World Team Cup medals in 1956–70. In 1985 Erik Gundersen (Denmark) became the first man to hold world titles at individual, pairs, team and long-track events simultaneously.

The World Pairs Championships (instituted unofficially 1968, officially 1970) have been won a record eight times by Denmark, 1979, 1985–91. The

MOST WINS (above and right). Denmark has won the World Speedway Pairs Championships eight times and the World Team Cup nine times, both records. Playing an integral part in most of these successes has been Hans Hollen Nielsen. He was a member of the winning Pairs team six times, and of the Team Cup eight times. (Photos: Per Kjærbye)

most successful individual in the World Pairs has been Hans Hollen Nielsen (b. 26 Dec. 1959) with six wins for Denmark. He won with Erik Gundersen, 1986–89, and with Jan O. Pederson, 1990–91. Maximum points (then 30) were scored in the World Pairs Championship by: Jerzy Szczakiel (b. 28 Jan. 1949) and Andrzej Wyglenda (Poland) at Rybnik, Poland in 1971; and Arthur Dennis Sigalos (b. 16 Aug. 1959) and Robert Benjamin ("Bobby") Schwartz (USA; b. 10 Aug. 1956) at Liverpool, New South Wales, Australia on 11 Dec. 1982.

The World Team Cup (instituted 1960) has been won a record nine times by England/Great Britain (Great Britain 1968, 1971–73; England 1974–75, 1977, 1980, 1989); and Denmark 1978, 1981, 1983–88, 1991. Hans Nielsen (Denmark) has ridden in a record eight Team wins.

Maximum points   The only speedway rider to have scored maximum points in every test series was Arthur "Bluey" Wilkinson (1911–40) in five matches for Australia *v.* England in Sydney in 1937/38.

SQUASH

At Harrow School, London, from 1817 on, boys waiting to play racquets knocked a ball around a confined space adjoining the racquets court. Its small area necessitated the use of a softer and smaller ball—one that could be squashed—hence the name. There was no recognized champion of any country until John A. Miskey of Philadelphia, PA won the American Amateur Singles Championship in 1907.

The first organized game in the United States was held in 1882 at St. Paul's School, Concord, NH.

World Championships   Jahangir Khan (Pakistan; b. 10 Dec. 1963) won six World Open (instituted 1976) titles, 1981–85 and 1988, and the ISRF world individual title (formerly World Amateur, instituted 1967) in 1979, 1983 and 1985. Geoffrey B. Hunt (Australia; b. 11 Mar. 1947) won four World Open titles, 1976–77 and 1979–80, and three World Amateur, 1967, 1969 and 1971. The most women's World Open titles is four, by Susan Devoy (New Zealand; b. 4 Jan. 1964), 1985, 1987 and 1990–91.

Australia (1967, 1969, 1971, 1973, 1989 and 1991) has won six men's world titles. England won the women's title in 1985, 1987, 1989 and 1990, following Great Britain's win in 1979.

Most titles   *Open Championship*   The most wins in the Open Championship held annually in Britain is ten, by Jahangir Khan, in successive years, 1982–91. Hashim Khan (Pakistan; b. 1915) won seven times, 1950–55 and 1957, and also won the Vintage title six times in 1978–83.

The most British Open women's titles is 16, by Heather Pamela McKay (nee Blundell [Australia]; b. 31 July 1941) from 1961 to 1977. She also won the World Open title in 1976 and 1979.

United States   The US amateur squash championships were first held for men in 1907 and for women in 1928; the most singles wins is six, by Stanley W. Pearson, 1915–17 and 1921–23; G. Diehl Mateer won a record 11 men's doubles titles between 1949 and 1966 with five different partners. Sharif Khan (Pakistan) won a record 13 North American Open Championships (instituted 1953), 1969–74 and 1976–82. Alicia McConnell has won a record seven women's national championships (1982–88).

Unbeaten sequences   Heather McKay was unbeaten from 1962 to 1980. Jahangir Khan was unbeaten from his loss to Geoff Hunt at the British Open on 10 Apr. 1981 until Ross Norman (New Zealand) ended his sequence in the World Open final on 11 Nov. 1986.

Longest and shortest championship matches   The longest recorded competitive match was one of 2 hrs. 45 min. when Jahangir Khan beat Gamal Awad (Egypt; b. 8 Sep. 1955) 9–10, 9–5, 9–7, 9–2, the first game lasting a record 1 hr. 11 min., in the final of the Patrick International Festival at Chichester, Great Britain on 30 Mar. 1983. Philip Kenyon (England) beat Salah Nadi (Egypt) in just 6 min. 37 sec. (9–0, 9–0, 9–0) in the British Open at Lamb's Squash Club, London, Great Britain on 9 Apr. 1992.

MOST SQUASH TITLES. The most women's World Open squash titles is four, by Susan Devoy (New Zealand), 1985, 1987, 1990–91. (Photo: Allsport/Bob Martin)

Most international squash appearances The men's record is 122, by David Gotto (b. 25 Dec. 1948) for Ireland. Marjorie Croke (nee Burke; b. 31 May 1961) made 103 appearances for Ireland, 1981–91.

Fastest squash ball speed In tests at Wimbledon Squash and Badminton Club, London, Great Britain in Jan. 1988, Roy Buckland hit a squash ball by an overhead service at a measured speed of 144.6 mph over the distance to the front wall. This is equivalent to an initial speed off the racket of 150.8 mph.

Largest squash crowd The finals of the ICI World Team Championships at the Royal Albert Hall, London, Great Britain had a record attendance for squash of 3,526 on 30 Oct. 1987.

SURFING

The traditional Polynesian sport of surfing in a canoe (*ehorooe*) was recorded by Capt. James Cook (1728–79) on his first voyage to Tahiti in December 1771. Surfing on a board (*Amo Amo iluna ka lau oka nalu*) was first described as "most perilous and extraordinary. . . altogether astonishing and is scarcely to be credited" by Lt. (later Capt.) James King, in March 1779 at Kealakekua Bay, Hawaii Island. The first depiction of a surfer was by this voyage's official artist, John Webber. The sport was revived at Waikiki by 1900. Hollow boards were introduced in 1929 and the light plastic foam type in 1956.

Most titles World Amateur Championships were inaugurated in May 1964 at Sydney, Australia. The most titles is three, by Michael Novakov (Australia), who won the Kneeboard event in 1982, 1984 and 1986. A World Professional series was started in 1975. The men's title has been won five times, by Mark Richards (Australia), 1975 and from 1979 to 1982, and the women's title (instituted 1979) four times, by Freida Zamba (USA), 1984–86, 1988.

Longest ride About four to six times each year, ridable surfing waves break in Matanchen Bay near San Blas, Nayarit, Mexico, which makes rides of *c.* 5,700 ft. possible.

Highest waves ridden Waimea Bay, HI reputedly provides the most consistently high waves, often reaching the ridable limit of 30–35 ft. The highest wave ever ridden was the *tsunami* of "perhaps 50 ft." that struck Minole, HI on 3 Apr. 1868, and was ridden to save his life by a Hawaiian named Holua.

MOST SURFING TITLES. Freida Zamba (USA) shows the poise and technique that have won her a record four World Professional surfing titles. (Photo: Allsport USA/Ken Levine)

SWIMMING

In Japan, swimming in schools was ordered by imperial edict of Emperor Go-Yozei (1586–1611) in 1603, but competition was known from 36 B.C. Seawater bathing was fashionable at Scarborough, Great Britain as early as 1660. The earliest pool was Pearless Pool, London, Great Britain, opened in 1743.

United States The first United States Swimming Championships were staged by the Amateur Athletic Union on 25 Aug. 1888 in New York City. The international governing body for swimming, diving and water polo—the *Fédération Internationale de Natation Amateur* (FINA)—was founded in 1908.

Fastest swimmer   In a 25-yd. pool, Tom Jager (USA; b. 6 Oct. 1964) achieved an average speed of 5.37 mph for 50 yards in 19.05 sec. at Nashville, TN on 23 Mar. 1990. The women's fastest is 4.48 mph, by Yang Wenyi (China) in her 50 m world record (see World Records table).

Most world records   *Men:* 32, Arne Borg (Sweden; 1901–87), 1921–29. *Women:* 42, Ragnhild Hveger (Denmark; b. 10 Dec. 1920), 1936–42. For currently recognized events (only metric distances in 50 m pools) the most is 26 by Mark Andrew Spitz (USA; b. 10 Feb. 1950), 1967–72, and 23 by Kornelia Ender (East Germany; b. 25 Oct. 1958), 1973–76. The most by a US woman is 15, by Deborah "Debbie" Meyer (b. 14 Aug. 1952), 1967–70.

The most world records set in a single pool is 86, in the North Sydney pool, Australia between 1955 and 1978. This total includes 48 imperial distance records, which ceased to be recognized in 1969. The pool, which was built in 1936, was originally 55 yards long but was shortened to 50 meters in 1964.

Most world titles   In the World Championships (instituted 1973) the most medals won is 13, by Michael Gross (West Germany; b. 17 June 1964)—five gold, five silver and three bronze, 1982–90. The most medals won by a woman is ten, by Kornelia Ender, with eight gold and two silver in 1973 and 1975. The most gold medals won is six (two individual and four relay) by James Paul Montgomery (USA; b. 24 Jan. 1955) in 1973 and 1975. The most medals won at a single championship is seven, by Matthew Nicholas "Matt" Biondi (USA; b. 8 Oct. 1965)—three gold, one silver, three bronze, in 1986.

The most gold medals by an American woman is five, by Tracy Caulkins, all in 1978, as well as a silver. The most medals overall is nine, by Mary Terstegge Meagher (b. 27 Oct. 1964)—two gold, five silver, two bronze, 1978–82.

US Championships   Tracy Caulkins (b. 11 Jan. 1963) won a record 48 US swimming titles and set 60 US records in her career, 1977–84. The men's record is 36 titles, by Johnny Weissmuller (ne Janos Weiszmuller; 1904–84), between 1921 and 1928.

Sponsored swim   The greatest amount of money collected in a charity swim was £119,735.85 (c. $204,000) in "Splash '92," organized by the Royal Bank of Scotland Swimming Club and held at the Royal Commonwealth Pool, Edinburgh, Great Britain on 25–26 Jan. 1992 with 3,218 participants.

Largest pools   The largest swimming pool in the world is the seawater Orthlieb Pool in Casablanca, Morocco. It is 1,574 ft. long and 246 ft. wide, and has an area of 8.9 acres. The largest land-locked swimming pool with heated water was the Fleishhacker Pool on Sloat Boulevard, near Great Highway, San Francisco, CA. It measured 1,000 × 150 ft. and up to 14 ft. deep and contained 7.5 million gals. of heated water. It was opened on 2 May 1925 but has now been abandoned. The largest land-locked pool in current use is Willow Lake in Warren, OH. It measures 600 × 150 ft. The greatest spectator accommodation is 13,614 at Osaka, Japan.

SWIMMING WORLD RECORDS (set in 50 meter pools)

MEN

EVENT	min.sec.	NAME AND COUNTRY	PLACE	DATE
FREESTYLE				
50 meters	21.81	Thomas "Tom" Jager (USA; b. 6 Oct. 1964)	Nashville, TN	24 Mar. 1990
100 meters	48.42	Matthew Nicholas "Matt" Biondi (USA; b. 8 Oct. 1965)	Austin, TX	10 Aug. 1988
200 meters	1:46.69	Giorgio Lamberti (Italy; b. 28 Jan. 1969)	Bonn, Germany	15 Aug. 1989
400 meters	3:46.47	Kieren John Perkins (Australia; b. 14 Aug. 1973)	Canberra, Australia	3 Apr. 1992
800 meters	7:46.60	Kieren John Perkins (Australia)	Sydney, Australia	16 Feb. 1992
1,500 meters	14:48.40	Kieren John Perkins (Australia)	Canberra, Australia	5 Apr. 1992
4 × 100 meter relay	3:16.53	United States (Christopher Jacobs, Troy Dalbey, Tom Jager, Matt Biondi)	Seoul, South Korea	23 Sep. 1988
4 × 200 meter relay	7:12.51	United States (Troy Dalbey, Matthew Cetlinski, Douglas Gjertsen, Matt Biondi)	Seoul, South Korea	21 Sep. 1988
BREASTSTROKE				
100 meters	1:01.29	Norbert Rozsa (Hungary; b. 9 Feb. 1972)	Athens, Greece	20 Aug. 1991
200 meters	2:10.60	Michael Ray Barrowman (USA; b. 4 Dec. 1968)	Fort Lauderdale, FL	13 Aug. 1991
BUTTERFLY				
100 meters	52.84	Pedro Pablo Morales (USA; b. 5 Dec. 1964)	Orlando, FL	23 June 1986
200 meters	1:55.69	Melvin Stewart (USA; b. 16 Nov. 1968)	Perth, Australia	12 Jan. 1991
BACKSTROKE				
100 meters	53.93	Jeff Rouse (USA; b. 6 Feb. 1970—relay leg)	Edmonton, Canada	25 Aug. 1991
200 meters	1:56.57	Martin Lopez-Zubero (Spain; b. 23 Apr. 1964)	Tuscaloosa, AL	24 Nov. 1991
MEDLEY				
200 meters	1:59.36	Tamás Darnyi (Hungary; b. 3 June 1967)	Perth, Australia	13 Jan. 1991
400 meters	4:12.36	Tamás Darnyi (Hungary)	Perth, Australia	8 Jan. 1991
4 × 100 meter relay	3:36.93	United States (David Berkoff, Richard Schroeder, Matt Biondi, Christopher Jacobs)	Seoul, South Korea	25 Sep. 1988

WOMEN

FREESTYLE

Event	Time	Name	Location	Date
50 meters	24.98	Yang Wenyi (China; b. 11 Jan. 1972)	Guangzhou, China	11 Apr. 1988
100 meters	54.48	Jenny Thompson (USA; b. 26 Feb. 1973)	Indianapolis, IN	1 Mar. 1992
200 meters	1:57.55	Heike Friedrich (East Germany; b. 18 Apr. 1970)	Berlin, Germany	18 June 1986
400 meters	4:03.85	Janet B. Evans (USA; b. 28 Aug. 1971)	Seoul, South Korea	22 Sep. 1988
800 meters	8:16.22	Janet B. Evans (USA)	Tokyo, Japan	20 Aug. 1989
1,500 meters	15:52.10	Janet B. Evans (USA)	Orlando, FL	26 Mar. 1988
4 × 100 meter relay	3:40.57	East Germany (Kristin Otto, Manuela Stellmach, Sabina Schulze, Heike Friedrich)	Madrid, Spain	19 Aug. 1986
4 × 200 meter relay	7:55.47	East Germany (Manuela Stellmach, Astrid Strauss, Anke Möhring, Heike Friedrich)	Strasbourg, France	18 Aug. 1987

BREASTSTROKE

Event	Time	Name	Location	Date
100 meters	1:07.91	Silke Hörner (East Germany; b. 12 Sep. 1965)	Strasbourg, France	21 Aug. 1987
200 meters	2:25.35	Anita Nall (USA; b. 21 July 1976)	Indianapolis, IN	2 Mar. 1992

BUTTERFLY

Event	Time	Name	Location	Date
100 meters	57.93	Mary Terstegge Meagher (USA; b. 27 Oct. 1964)	Milwaukee, WI	16 Aug. 1981
200 meters	2:05.96	Mary Terstegge Meagher (USA)	Milwaukee, WI	13 Aug. 1981

BACKSTROKE

Event	Time	Name	Location	Date
100 meters	1:00.31	Krizstina Egerszegi (Hungary; b. 16 Aug. 1974)	Athens, Greece	22 Aug. 1991
200 meters	2:06.62	Krizstina Egerszegi (Hungary)	Athens, Greece	25 Aug. 1991

MEDLEY

Event	Time	Name	Location	Date
200 meters	2:11.73	Ute Geweniger (East Germany; b. 24 Feb. 1964)	East Berlin, Germany	4 July 1981
400 meters	4:36.10	Petra Schneider (East Germany; b. 11 Jan. 1963)	Guayaquil, Ecuador	1 Aug. 1982
4 × 100 meter relay	4:03.69	East Germany (Ina Kleber, Sylvia Gerasch, Ines Geissler, Birgit Meineke [now Heukrodt])	Moscow, USSR	24 Aug. 1984

SHORT-COURSE SWIMMING WORLD BESTS (set in 25 meter pools)

MEN

EVENT	min.:sec.	NAME AND COUNTRY	PLACE	DATE
FREESTYLE				
50 meters	21.76	Nils Rudolph (East Germany; b. 18 Aug. 1965)	Bonn, Germany	11 Feb. 1990
100 meters	48.2†	Michael Gross (West Germany; b. 17 June 1964)	Offenbach, Germany	11 Feb. 1988
	48.33	Tommy Werner (Sweden; b. 31 Mar. 1966)	Malmö, Sweden	19 Mar. 1989
200 meters	1:43.64	Giorgio Lamberti (Italy; b. 28 Jan. 1969)	Bonn, Germany	11 Feb. 1990
400 meters	3:40.81	Anders Holmertz (Sweden; b. 1 Dec. 1968)	Paris, France	4 Feb. 1990
800 meters	7:38.75	Michael Gross (West Germany)	Bonn, Germany	8 Feb. 1985
1,500 meters	14:32.40	Kieren Perkins (Australia; b. 14 Aug. 1973)	Canberra, Australia	2 Feb. 1992
4 × 50 meters	1:27.95	West Germany	Bonn, Germany	14 Feb. 1988
4 × 100 meters	3:14.00	Sweden	Malmö, Sweden	19 Mar. 1989
4 × 200 meters	7:05.17	West Germany	Bonn, Germany	9 Feb. 1986
BACKSTROKE				
50 meters	25.06	Mark Tewksbury (Canada; b. 2 July 1968)	Saskatoon, Canada	2 Mar. 1990
100 meters	52.50	Mark Tewksbury (Canada)	Winnipeg, Canada	23 Feb. 1992
200 meters	1:56.60	Tamás Darnyi (Hungary; b. 3 June 1967)	Bonn, Germany	8 Feb. 1987
BREASTSTROKE				
50 meters	27.15	Dmitriy Volkov (USSR; b. 3 Mar. 1966)	Saint-Paul de la Réunion	30 Dec. 1989
100 meters	59.30	Dmitriy Volkov (USSR)	Bonn, Germany	11 Feb. 1990
200 meters	2:07.93	Nicholas Gillingham (Great Britain; b. 22 Jan. 1967)	Birmingham, Great Britain	20 Oct. 1991
BUTTERFLY				
50 meters	24.05	Nils Rudolph (Germany)	Sheffield, Great Britain	30 Mar. 1991
100 meters	52.07	Marcel Gery (Canada; b. 15 Mar. 1965)	Leicester, Great Britain	23 Feb. 1990
200 meters	1:54.67	Franck Esposito (France; b. 13 Apr. 1971)	Paris, France	1 Feb. 1992
MEDLEY				
100 meters	54.66	Josef Hladky (Germany; b. 18 June 1962)	Bonn, Germany	16 Mar. 1991
200 meters	1:57.19	Jani Sievinen (Finland)	Kuopio, Finland	17 Jan. 1992
400 meters	4:08.77	Luca Sacchi (Italy; b. 10 Jan. 1968)	Palma de Mallorca, Spain	28 Feb. 1992
4 × 50 meters	1:38.72	United States	Bonn, Germany	14 Feb. 1988

WOMEN

FREESTYLE

Event	Time	Name	Location	Date
50 meters	24.81	Livia Copariu (Romania; b. 1973)	Sibiu, Romania	8 Apr. 1989
100 meters	53.48	Livia Copariu (Romania)	Sibiu, Romania	7 Apr. 1989
200 meters	1:56.35	Birgit Meineke (East Germany; b. 4 July 1964)	Indianapolis, IN	7 Jan. 1983
400 meters	4:02.05	Astrid Strauss (East Germany; b. 24 Dec. 1968)	Bonn, Germany	8 Feb. 1987
800 meters	8:15.34	Astrid Strauss (East Germany)	Bonn, Germany	6 Feb. 1987
1,500 meters	15:43.31	Petra Schneider (East Germany; b. 11 Jan. 1963)	Gainesville, FL	10 Jan. 1982
4 × 50 meters	1:42.13	West Germany	Bonn, Germany	13 Feb. 1988
4 × 100 meters	3:38.77	East Germany	Monte Carlo, Monaco	12 Dec. 1987

BACKSTROKE

Event	Time	Name	Location	Date
50 meters	28.91	Svenja Schlicht (West Germany; b. 26 June 1966)	Bonn, Germany	8 Feb. 1987
100 meters	59.89	Betsy Mitchell (USA; b. 15 Jan. 1966)	Los Angeles, CA	26 Apr. 1987
200 meters	2:06.78	Nicole Stevenson (Australia)	Melbourne, Australia	7 Mar. 1992

BREASTSTROKE

Event	Time	Name	Location	Date
50 meters	31.22	Peggy Hartung (Germany)	Paris, France	2 Feb. 1992
100 meters	1:07.05	Silke Hörner (East Germany; b. 12 Sep. 1965)	Bonn, Germany	8 Feb. 1986
200 meters	2:22.92	Susanne Börnike (East Germany; b. 13 Aug. 1968)	Bonn, Germany	4 Feb. 1989

BUTTERFLY

Event	Time	Name	Location	Date
50 meters	27.30	Qian Hong (China; b. 1971)	Perth, Australia	6 Jan. 1991
100 meters*	58.91	Mary Terstegge Meagher (USA; b. 27 Aug. 1964)	Gainesville, FL	3 Jan. 1981
200 meters	2:05.65	Mary Meagher (USA)	Gainesville, FL	2 Jan. 1981

MEDLEY

Event	Time	Name	Location	Date
100 meters	1:01.61	Li Lin (China; b. 1970)	Palma de Mallorca, Spain	1 Mar. 1992
200 meters	2:10.60	Petra Schneider (East Germany)	Gainesville, FL	8 Jan. 1982
400 meters	4:31.36	Noemi Lung (Romania; b. 16 May 1968)	Paris, France	31 Jan. 1987
4 × 50 meters	1:54.37	East Germany	Bonn, Germany	14 Feb. 1988
4 × 100 meters	4:02.85	East Germany	Indianapolis, IN	8 Jan. 1983

Slower than long-course bests. † Hand-timed for first leg.

US NATIONAL SWIMMING RECORDS (set in 50 meter pools)

—— MEN ——

EVENT	TIME	NAME	PLACE	DATE
FREESTYLE				
50 meters	21.81	Thomas "Tom" Jager (b. 6 Oct. 1964)	Nashville, TN	24 Mar. 1990
100 meters	48.42	Matthew Nicholas "Matt" Biondi (b. 8 Oct. 1965)	Austin, TX	10 Aug. 1988
200 meters	1:47.72	Matt Biondi	Austin, TX	8 Aug. 1988
400 meters	3:48.06	Matthew Cetlinski (b. 4 Oct. 1964)	Austin, TX	11 Aug. 1988
800 meters	7:52.45	Sean Killion (b. 24 Oct. 1967)	Clovis, CA	27 July 1987
1,500 meters	15:01.51	George Thomas DiCarlo (b. 13 July 1963)	Indianapolis, IN	30 June 1984
4 × 100 meter relay	3:16.53	United States (Christopher Jacobs, Troy Dalbey,	Seoul, South Korea	23 Sep. 1988
		Tom Jager, Matt Biondi)		
4 × 200 meter relay	7:12.51	United States (Troy Dalbey, Matthew Cetlinski,	Seoul, South Korea	21 Sep. 1988
		Douglas Gjertsen, Matt Biondi)		
BREASTSTROKE				
100 meters	1:01.40	Nelson Diebel (b. 9 Nov. 1970)	Indianapolis, IN	1 Mar. 1992
200 meters	2:10.60	Michael Ray Barrowman (b. 4 Dec. 1968)	Ft. Lauderdale, FL	13 Aug. 1991
BUTTERFLY				
100 meters	52.84	Pedro Pablo Morales (b. 5 Dec. 1964)	Orlando, FL	23 June 1986
200 meters	1:55.69	Melvin Stewart (b. 16 Nov. 1968)	Perth, Australia	12 Jan. 1991
BACKSTROKE				
100 meters	53.93	Jeff Rouse	Edmonton, Canada	25 Aug. 1991
200 meters	1:58.66	Royce Sharp (b. 25 May 1972)	Indianapolis, IN	2 Mar. 1992
MEDLEY				
200 meters	2:00.11	David Wharton (b. 16 May 1969)	Tokyo, Japan	20 Aug. 1989
400 meters	4:15.21	Eric Namesnik (b. 7 Aug. 1970)	Perth, Australia	8 Jan. 1991
4 × 100 meter relay	3:36.93	United States (David Berkoff, Richard Schroeder,	Seoul, South Korea	25 Sep. 1988
		Matt Biondi, Christopher Jacobs)		

WOMEN

FREESTYLE

50 meters	25.20	Jenny Thompson (b. 26 Feb. 1973)	Indianapolis, IN	6 Mar. 1992
100 meters	54.48	Jenny Thompson	Indianapolis, IN	1 Mar. 1992
200 meters	1:58.23	Cynthia Woodhead (b. 7 Feb. 1964)	Tokyo, Japan	3 Sep. 1979
400 meters	4:03.85	Janet B. Evans (b. 28 Aug. 1971)	Seoul, South Korea	22 Sep. 1988
800 meters	8:16.22	Janet B. Evans	Tokyo, Japan	20 Aug. 1989
1,500 meters	15:52.10	Janet B. Evans	Orlando, FL	26 Mar. 1988
4 × 100 meter relay	3:43.26	United States World Championship Team (Nicola Haislett, Julie Cooper, Whitney Hedgepeth, Jenny Thompson)	Perth, Australia	9 Jan. 1991
4 × 200 meter relay	8:02.12	United States (Betsy Mitchell, Mary Terstegge Meagher, Kim Brown, Mary Alice Wayte)	Madrid, Spain	22 Aug. 1986

BREASTSTROKE

100 meters	1:08.91	Tracey McFarlane (b. 20 July 1966)	Austin, TX	11 Aug. 1988
200 meters	2:25.35	Anita Nall (b. 21 July 1976)	Indianapolis, IN	2 Mar. 1992

BUTTERFLY

100 meters	57.93	Mary Terstegge Meagher (b. 27 Oct. 1964)	Brown Deer, WI	16 Aug. 1981
200 meters	2:05.96	Mary Terstegge Meagier	Brown Deer, WI	13 Aug. 1981

BACKSTROKE

100 meters	1:00.84	Janie Wagstaff (b. 22 Aug. 1974)	Indianapolis, IN	3 Mar. 1992
200 meters	2:08.60	Betsy Mitchell (b. 15 Jan. 1966)	Orlando, FL	27 June 1986

MEDLEY

200 meters	2:12.64	Tracy Anne Caulkins (b. 11 Jan. 1963)	Los Angeles, CA	3 Aug. 1984
400 meters	4:37.76	Janet B. Evans	Seoul, South Korea	19 Sep. 1988
4 × 100 meter relay	4:05.98	United States (Janie Wagstaff, Keli King, Crissy Ahmann-Leighton, Nicole Haislett)	Edmonton, Canada	25 Aug. 1991

WORLD RECORDS. Canadian Mark Tewksbury (top) set short-course world records in both the 50 m backstroke and 100 m backstroke. Jenny Thompson (bottom) (USA) set the world record for the women's 100 m freestyle with 54.48 seconds at Indianapolis, IN on 1 Mar. 1992. (Photos: Allsport/Allsport USA/Daemmrich/Simon Bruty)

OLYMPIC RECORDS

Most medals *Men* The greatest number of Olympic gold medals won is nine, by Mark Spitz (USA): 100 m and 200 m freestyle, 1972; 100 m and 200 m butterfly, 1972; 4 × 100 m freestyle, 1968 and 1972; 4 × 200 m freestyle, 1968 and 1972; 4 × 100 m medley, 1972. All but one of these performances (the 4 × 200 m freestyle of 1968) were also new world records. He also won a silver (100 m butterfly) and a bronze (100 m freestyle) in 1968 for a record 11 medals. His record seven medals at one Games in 1972 was equaled by Matt Biondi (USA), who took five gold, a silver and a bronze in 1988.

Women The record number of gold medals won by a woman is six, by Kristin Otto (East Germany; b. 7 Feb. 1965) at Seoul in 1988: 100 m freestyle, backstroke and butterfly, 50 m freestyle, 4 × 100 m freestyle and 4 × 100 m medley. Dawn Fraser (Australia; b. 4 Sep. 1937) is the only swimmer to win the same event, the 100 m freestyle, on three successive occasions (1956, 1960 and 1964). The most gold medals won by a US woman is three, by 14 swimmers.

The most medals won by a woman is eight, by: Dawn Fraser—four golds (100 m freestyle, 1956, 1960 and 1964, 4 × 100 m freestyle, 1956) and four silvers (400 m freestyle, 1956, 4 × 100 m freestyle, 1960 and 1964, 4 × 100 m medley, 1960); by Kornelia Ender—four golds (100 m and 200 m freestyle, 100 m butterfly, and 4 × 100 m medley in 1976) and four silvers (200 m individual medley, 1972, 4 × 100 m medley, 1972, 4 × 100 m freestyle, 1972 and 1976); and by Shirley Babashoff (USA; b. 3 Jan. 1957), who won two golds (4 × 100 m freestyle, 1972 and 1976) and six silvers (100 m freestyle, 1972, 200 m freestyle, 1972 and 1976, 400 m and 800 m freestyle, 1976, 4 × 100 m medley 1976).

Most individual gold medals The record number of individual gold medals won is four, by: Charles Meldrum Daniels (USA [1884–1973]; 100 m freestyle, 1906 and 1908, 220 yd. freestyle 1904, 440 yd. freestyle 1904); Roland Matthes (East Germany; b. 17 Nov. 1950) with 100 m and 200 m in backstroke 1968 and 1972; Mark Spitz and Kristin Otto; and the divers Pat McCormick and Greg Louganis (see Diving).

DIVING

Origins Diving traces its roots to the gymnastics movement that developed in Germany and Sweden in the 17th century. During the summer, gymnasts would train at the beach, and acrobatic techniques would be performed over water as a safety measure. From this activity the sport of diving developed. The world governing body for diving is the *Fédération Internationale de Natation Amateur* (FINA), founded in 1908. FINA is also the governing body for swimming and water polo.

United States Ernst Bransten and Mike Peppe are considered the two main pioneers of diving in the United States. Bransten, a Swede, came to the United States following World War I. He introduced Swedish training methods and diving techniques, which revolutionized the sport in this country. Peppe's highly successful program at Ohio State University, 1931–68, produced several Olympic medalists and helped promote the sport in the United States.

Most Olympic medals   The most medals won by a diver is five, by: Klaus Dibiasi (Austria; b. 6 Oct. 1947 [Italy]), three gold, two silver, 1964–76; and Gregory Efthimios "Greg" Louganis (USA; b. 29 Jan. 1960), four golds, one silver, 1976, 1984–88. Dibiasi is the only diver to win the same event (highboard) at three successive Games (1968, 1972 and 1976). Two divers have won the highboard and springboard doubles at two Games: Patricia Joan McCormick (nee Keller; b. 12 May 1930), 1952 and 1956, and Greg Louganis, 1984 and 1988.

Most world titles   Greg Louganis (USA) won a record five world titles— highboard in 1978, and both highboard and springboard in 1982 and 1986, as well as four Olympic gold medals, in 1984 and 1988. Three gold medals at one event have also been won by Philip George Boggs (USA; 1949–90), springboard, 1973, 1975 and 1978.

United States Championships   The Amateur Athletic Union (AAU) organized the first national diving championships in 1909. Since 1981, United States Diving has been the governing body of the sport in this country, and thus responsible for the national championships.

Most titles   Greg Louganis has won a record 47 national titles: 17 at 1-meter springboard; 17 at 3-meter springboard; 13 at platform. In women's competition Cynthia Potter has won a record 28 titles.

High diving   The highest regularly performed head-first dives are those of professional divers from La Quebrada ("The Break in the Rocks") at Acapulco, Mexico, a height of 87½ ft. The base rocks, 21 ft. out from the take-off, necessitate a leap of 27 ft. out. The water is 12 ft. deep.

The world record high dive from a diving board is 176 ft. 10 in., by Olivier Favre (Switzerland) at Villers-le-Lac, France on 30 Aug. 1987.

The women's record is 120 ft. 9 in., by Lucy Wardle (USA) at Ocean Park, Hong Kong on 6 Apr. 1985.

Highest scores   Greg Louganis achieved record scores at the 1984 Olympic Games in Los Angeles, CA, with 754.41 points for the 11-dive springboard event and 710.91 for the highboard. At the world championships in Guayaquil, Ecuador in 1984 he was awarded a perfect score of 10.0 by all seven judges for his highboard inward 1½ somersault in the pike position.

The first diver to be awarded a score of 10.0 by all seven judges was Michael Holman Finneran (b. 21 Sep. 1948) in the 1972 US Olympic Trials, in Chicago, IL, for a backward 1½ somersault, 2½ twist, from the 10 m board.

LONG-DISTANCE SWIMMING

Longest swims   The greatest recorded distance ever swum is 1,826 miles down the Mississippi River between Ford Dam near Minneapolis, MN and Carrollton Ave, New Orleans, LA, by Fred P. Newton (b. 1903) of Clinton, OK from 6 July to 29 Dec. 1930. He was in the water for 742 hrs.

In 1966 Mihir Sen of Calcutta, India uniquely swam the Palk Strait from Sri Lanka to India (in 25 hrs. 36 min. on 5–6 Apr.); the Straits of Gibraltar (in 8 hrs. 1 min. on 24 Aug.); the length of the Dardanelles (in 13 hrs. 55 min. on 12 Sep.); the Bosphorus (in 4 hrs. on 21 Sep.); and the length of the Panama Canal (in 34 hrs. 15 min. on 29–31 Oct.).

Twenty-four hours　Anders Forvass (Sweden) swam 63.3 miles at the 25 meter Linköping public swimming pool, Sweden on 28–29 Oct. 1989. In a 50 meter pool, Evan Barry (Australia) swam 60.08 miles, at the Valley Pool, Brisbane, Australia on 19–20 Dec. 1987.

The women's record is 51.01 miles, by Irene van der Laan (Netherlands) at Amersfoort, Netherlands on 20–21 Sep. 1985. The longest distance swum by an American woman is 45.45 miles, by Jill Oviatt at the University of Michigan pool in Ann Arbor, MI on 24–25 Nov. 1988.

Long-distance relays　The New Zealand national relay team of 20 swimmers swam a record 113.59 miles in Lower Hutt, New Zealand in 24 hours, passing 100 miles in 20 hrs. 47 min. 13 sec. on 9–10 Dec. 1983. The 24-hour club record by a team of five is 96.27 miles, by the City of Newcastle ASC on 16–17 Dec. 1986. A women's team from the club swam 88.93 miles on the same occasion. The most participants in a one-day swim relay is 2,145, each swimming a length, organized by Jeff D. VanBuren and David W. Thompson at Hamilton College in Clinton, NY on 8 Apr. 1989.

Underwater swimming　Paul Cryne (Great Britain) and Samir Sawan al Awami (Qatar) swam 49.04 miles in a 24-hr. period from Doha, Qatar to Umm Said and back on 21–22 Feb. 1985 using sub-aqua equipment. They were swimming under water for 95.5 percent of the time. A relay team of six swam 94.44 miles in a swimming pool at Olomouc, Czechoslovakia on 17–18 Oct. 1987.

Manhattan swim　The fastest swim around Manhattan Island in New York City was in 6 hrs. 12 min. 29 sec., by Shelley Taylor (Australia; b. 1961) on 15 Oct. 1985. Drury J. Gallagher set the men's record, 6 hrs. 41 min. 35 sec., on 7 Sep. 1983.

CHANNEL SWIMMING

The first to swim the English Channel from shore to shore (without a life jacket) was the Merchant Navy captain Matthew Webb (1848–83), who swam an estimated 38 miles to make the 21 mile crossing from Dover, Great Britain to Calais Sands, France, in 21 hrs. 45 min. from 12:56 P.M. to 10:41 A.M., 24–25 Aug. 1875. Paul Boyton (USA) had swum from Cap Gris-Nez, France to the South Foreland, Great Britain in his life-saving suit in 23 hrs. 30 min. on 28–29 May 1875. It is reported that Jean-Marie Saletti, a French soldier, escaped from a British prison hulk off Dover by swimming to Boulogne in July or August 1815.

The first woman to succeed was Gertrude Caroline Ederle (USA; b. 23 Oct. 1906), who swam from Cap Gris-Nez, France to Deal, England on 6 Aug. 1926, in the then-overall record time of 14 hrs. 39 min.

Fastest　The official Channel Swimming Association (founded 1927) record is 7 hrs. 40 min. by Penny Dean (b. 21 Mar. 1955) of California, from Shakespeare Beach, Dover, Great Britain to Cap Gris-Nez, France on 29 July 1978.

TABLE TENNIS

Origins   The earliest evidence relating to a game resembling table tennis has been found in the catalogs of London, Great Britain sports goods manufacturers in the 1880s. The old Ping Pong Association was formed in 1902, but the game proved only a temporary craze until resuscitated in 1921. The International Table Tennis Federation was founded in 1926 and the United States Table Tennis Association was established in 1933. Table tennis was included at the Olympic Games for the first time in 1988.

Most titles   *World (instituted 1926)*   G. Viktor Barna (1911–72; b. Hungary, Győző Braun) won a record five singles, 1930, 1932–35, and eight men's doubles, 1929–35, 1939, in the World Championships (first held in 1926). Angelica Rozeanu (Romania; b. 15 Oct. 1921) won a record six women's singles, 1950–55, and Maria Mednyanszky (Hungary; 1901–79) won seven women's doubles, 1928, 1930–35. With two more at mixed doubles, Viktor Barna won 15 world titles in all, while 18 have been won by Maria Mednyanszky.

With the staging of championships biennially, the breaking of the above records would now be very difficult.

The most men's team titles (Swaythling Cup) is 12, by Hungary, 1927–31, 1933–35, 1938, 1949, 1952 and 1979. The women's record (Marcel Corbillon Cup) is nine, by China, 1965 and eight successive from 1975 to 1989 (biennially).

United States   The US won the Swaythling Cup in 1937 and the Corbillon Cup in 1937 and 1949. Ruth Aarons was the women's world champion in 1936 and 1937, sharing the title in the latter year. No American has won the men's world singles title, but James McClure won three men's doubles titles, with Robert Blattner in 1936–37 and with Sol Schiff in 1938.

English Open (instituted 1921)   Richard Bergmann (Austria, then Great Britain; 1920–70) won a record six singles, 1939–40, 1948, 1950, 1952, 1954,

---

Youngest table tennis player   The youngest-ever international contender was Joy Foster, who represented Jamaica in the West Indies Championships at Port of Spain, Trinidad in Aug. 1958 at the age of 8.

Counter hitting in table tennis   The record number of hits in 60 sec. is 172, by Thomas Busin and Stefan Renold, both of Switzerland, on 4 Nov. 1989. The women's record is 168, by the sisters Lisa (b. 9 Mar. 1967) and Jackie (b. 9 Sep. 1964) Bellinger, at Crest Hotel, Luton, Great Britain on 14 July 1987. With a paddle in each hand, Gary D. Fisher of Olympia, WA completed 5,000 consecutive volleys over the net in 44 min. 28 sec. on 25 June 1975.

and Viktor Barna won seven men's doubles titles, 1931, 1933–35, 1938–39, 1949. The women's singles record is six, by Maria Alexandru (Romania; b. 1941), 1963–64, 1970–72, 1974, and Diane Rowe (Great Britain, now Scholer; b. 14 Apr. 1933) won 12 women's doubles titles, 1950–56, 1960, 1962–65. Viktor Barna won 20 titles in all, and Diane Rowe won 17. Her twin Rosalind (now Mrs. Cornett) has won nine (two in singles).

US Championships   US national championships were first held in 1931. Leah Neuberger (nee Thall) won a record 21 titles between 1941 and 1961: 9 women's singles, 12 women's doubles. Richard Mills won a record ten men's singles titles between 1945 and 1962.

TAEKWONDO

Taekwondo is a martial art, with all activities based on defensive spirit, developed over 20 centuries in Korea. It was officially recognized as part of Korean tradition and culture on 11 Apr. 1955. The first World Taekwondo Championships were organized by the Korean Taekwondo Association and were held at Seoul in 1973. The World Taekwondo Federation was then formed, and has organized biennial championships. Women's events were first contested in 1987.

Most titles   The most world titles won is four, by Chung Kook-hyun (South Korea), light-middleweight 1982–83, welterweight 1985, 1987. Taekwondo was included as a demonstration sport at the 1988 Olympic Games.

United States   Three American women won gold medals at the 1988 Olympics; one of them, Lynette Love (b. 21 Sep. 1957), at heavyweight (over 70 kg), was also world champion in 1987.

TEAM HANDBALL

Origins   Team handball, or handball, as it is known outside of North America, was first played *c.* 1895 in Germany. It was introduced into the Olympic Games at Berlin in 1936 as an 11-a-side outdoor game, with Germany winning, but when reintroduced in 1972 it was an indoor game with seven-a-side, the standard team size since 1952.

The International Handball Federation was founded in 1946. The first international match was held at Halle/Saale on 3 Sep. 1925, when Austria beat Germany 6–3.

United States   Team handball was first introduced to the United States in the 1920s, and a national team entered the 1936 Olympic demonstration competition. In 1959 the United States Team Handball Federation (USTHF) was formed.

Most Championships *Olympic*   The USSR has won four titles—men, 1976 and 1988; women, 1976 and 1980. Yugoslavia has also won two men's titles, in 1972 and 1984.

World Championships (instituted 1938)   Romania has won four men's and three women's titles (two outdoor, one indoor) from 1956 to 1974. Three women's titles have also been won by East Germany, in 1971, 1975 and 1978, and the USSR, 1982, 1986 and 1990.

East Germany has also won three women's titles, in 1971, 1975 and 1978.

Highest Score   The highest score in an international match was recorded when the USSR beat Afghanistan 86–2 in the "Friendly Army Tournament" at Miskolc, Hungary in August 1981.

TENNIS

Origins   The modern game is generally agreed to have evolved as an outdoor form of the indoor game of tennis (see Real/Royal Tennis). "Field tennis" is mentioned in an English magazine—*Sporting Magazine*—of 29 Sep. 1793. The earliest club for such a game, variously called pelota or lawn rackets, was the Leamington Club, founded in 1872 by Major Harry Gem. The earliest attempt to commercialize the game was by Major Walter Clopton Wingfield (1833–1912), who patented a form called "sphairistike"—on 23 Feb. 1874. It soon came to be called lawn tennis. Amateur players were permitted to play with and against professionals in "open" tournaments in 1968.

Grand Slam   The grand slam for a tennis player is to hold all four of the world's major championship singles titles at the same time: the Australian Open, French Open, Wimbledon and US Open. The traditional slam is winning the four events in one year. The first man to have won all four was Frederick John Perry (Great Britain; b. 18 May 1909) when he won the French title in 1935. The first man to hold all four championships simultaneously, and thus achieve a grand slam, was John Donald "Don" Budge (USA; b. 13 June 1915) in 1938, and with Wimbledon and US in 1937, he won six successive grand slam tournaments. The first man to achieve the grand slam twice was Rodney George "Rod" Laver (Australia; b. 9 Aug. 1938), as an amateur in 1962 and again in 1969, when the titles were open to professionals.

Four women have achieved the grand slam, and the first three won six successive grand slam tournaments: Maureen Catherine Connolly (USA; 1934–69), in 1953; Margaret Jean Court (nee Smith [Australia]; b. 16 July 1942) in 1970; and Martina Navratilova (USA; b. 18 Oct. 1956) in 1983–84. The fourth was Stefanie Maria "Steffi" Graf (Germany; b. 14 June 1969) in 1988, when she also won the women's singles Olympic gold medal. Pamela

Howard "Pam" Shriver (USA; b. 4 July 1962) with Navratilova won a record eight successive grand slam tournament women's doubles titles and 109 successive matches in all events from April 1983 to July 1985.

The first doubles pair to win the grand slam were the Australians Frank Allan Sedgeman (b. 29 Oct. 1927) and Kenneth Bruce McGregor (b. 2 June 1929) in 1951.

The most singles championships won in grand slam tournaments is 24, by Margaret Court (11 Australian, 5 US, 5 French, 3 Wimbledon), 1960–73. She also won the US Amateur in 1969 and 1970 when this was held, as well as the US Open. The men's record is 12, by Roy Stanley Emerson (Australia; b. 3 Nov. 1936), 6 Australian, 2 each French, US, Wimbledon, 1961–67.

The most grand slam tournament wins by a doubles partnership is 20, by Althea Louise Brough (USA; b. 11 Mar. 1923) and Margaret Evelyn du Pont (nee Osborne [USA]; b. 4 Mar. 1918), 12 US, 5 Wimbledon, 3 French, 1942–57; and by Martina Navratilova and Pam Shriver, 7 Australian, 5 Wimbledon, 4 French, 4 US, 1981–89.

United States   The most singles wins in grand slam tournaments by a US player is 19, by Helen Wills Moody (b. 6 Oct. 1905), 8 Wimbledon, 7 US and 4 French. Martina Navratilova (formerly of Czechoslovakia) has won a total of 54 grand slam titles—18 singles, a world record 31 women's doubles and 5 mixed doubles. Billie Jean King (nee Moffit; b. 22 Nov. 1942) has the most of US-born players, with 39 titles—12 singles, 16 women's doubles and 11 mixed doubles.

Largest tennis crowd   The record crowd for one day at Wimbledon was 39,813, on 26 June 1986. The record for the whole championship was 403,706, in 1989.

"Golden set"   The only known example of a "golden set" (winning a set 6–0 without dropping a single point, i.e., winning 24 consecutive points) in professional tennis was achieved by Bill Scanlon (USA) against Marcos Hocevar (Brazil) in the first round of the WCT Gold Coast Classic at Del Ray, FL on 22 Feb. 1983. Scanlon won the match, 6–2, 6–0.

Fastest tennis service   The fastest service timed with modern equipment is 138 mph, by Steve Denton (USA; b. 5 Sep. 1956) at Beaver Creek, CO on 29 July 1984.

WIMBLEDON CHAMPIONSHIPS

Most wins *Women*   Billie Jean King won a record 20 titles between 1961 and 1979—six singles, ten women's doubles and four mixed doubles. Elizabeth Montague Ryan (USA; 1892–1979) won a record 19 doubles (12 women's, 7 mixed) titles from 1914 to 1934.

Men   The greatest number of titles by a man has been 13, by Hugh Laurence Doherty (Great Britain; 1875–1919) with five singles titles (1902–06) and a record eight men's doubles (1897–1901, 1903–05) partnered by his brother Reginald Frank (Great Britain; 1872–1910).

The most titles won by a US man is eight, by John Patrick McEnroe (b. 16 Feb. 1959), singles 1981, 1983 and 1984; men's doubles (all with Peter Fleming) 1979, 1981, 1983–84, and 1992 (with Michael Stich).

Singles   Martina Navratilova won a record nine titles, 1978–79, 1982–87 and 1990. The most men's singles wins since the Challenge Round was abolished in 1922 is five consecutively, by Bjørn Rune Borg (Sweden) in 1976–80. William Charles Renshaw (Great Britain; 1861–1904) won seven singles in 1881–86 and 1889.

Mixed doubles   The male record is four titles, shared by: Elias Victor "Vic" Seixas (USA; b. 30 Aug. 1923), in 1953–56; Kenneth Norman Fletcher (Australia; b. 15 June 1940), in 1963, 1965–66, 1968; and Owen Keir Davidson (Australia; b. 4 Oct. 1943) in 1967, 1971, 1973–74. The women's record is seven, by Elizabeth Ryan (USA) between 1919 and 1932.

Most appearances   Arthur William Charles "Wentworth" Gore (Great Britain; 1868–1928) made a record 36 appearances at Wimbledon between 1888 and 1927. In 1964, Jean Borotra (b. 13 Aug. 1898) of France made his 35th appearance since 1922. In 1977 he appeared in the Veterans' Doubles at the age of 78.

Youngest champions   The youngest champion was Charlotte "Lottie" Dod (Great Britain; 1871–1960), who was 15 yrs. 285 days when she won in 1887. The youngest male champion was Boris Becker (West Germany; b. 22 Nov. 1967), who won the men's singles title in 1985 at 17 yrs. 227 days. The youngest-ever player at Wimbledon was reputedly Mita Klima (Austria), who was 13 yrs. in the 1907 singles competition. The youngest seed was Jennifer Capriati (USA; b. 29 Mar. 1976) at 14 yrs. 89 days at the time of her first match on 26 June 1990. She won this match, making her the youngest-ever winner at Wimbledon.

Oldest champions   The oldest champion was Margaret Evelyn du Pont at 44 yrs. 125 days when she won the mixed doubles in 1962 with Neale Fraser (Australia). The oldest singles champion was Arthur Gore (Great Britain) in 1909 at 41 yrs. 182 days.

US OPEN CHAMPIONSHIPS

Most wins   Margaret Evelyn du Pont won a record 25 titles between 1941 and 1960. She won a record 13 women's doubles (12 with Althea Louise Brough), nine mixed doubles and three singles. The men's record is 16, by William Tatem "Bill" Tilden (1893–1953), including seven men's singles, 1920–25, 1929—a record for singles shared with: Richard Dudley Sears (1861–1943), 1881–87; William A. Larned (1872–1926), 1901–02, 1907–11; and at women's singles by: Molla Mallory (nee Bjurstedt; 1892–1959), 1915–16, 1918, 1920–22, 1926; and Helen Wills Moody, 1923–25, 1927–29, 1931.

Youngest and oldest   The youngest champion was Vincent Richards (1903–59), who was 15 yrs. 139 days when he won the men's doubles with Bill Tilden in 1918. The youngest singles champion was Tracy Ann Austin

(b. 12 Dec. 1962), who was 16 yrs. 271 days when she won the women's singles in 1979. The youngest men's singles champion was Pete Sampras (USA; b. 12 Aug. 1971), who was 19 yrs. 28 days when he won the 1990 title. The oldest champion was Margaret du Pont, who won the mixed doubles at age 42 yrs. 166 days in 1960. The oldest singles champion was William Larned at 38 yrs. 242 days in 1911.

FRENCH CHAMPIONSHIPS

Most wins (from international status 1925)   Margaret Court won a record 13 titles—five singles, four women's doubles and four mixed doubles, 1962–73. The men's record is nine, by Henri Cochet (France; 1901–1987)—four singles, three men's doubles and two mixed doubles, 1926–30. The singles record is seven, by Christine Marie "Chris" Evert (USA; b. 21 Dec. 1954), 1974–75, 1979–80, 1983, 1985–86. Bjørn Borg won a record six men's singles, 1974–75, 1978–81.

Youngest and oldest   The youngest doubles champions were the 1981 mixed doubles winners Andrea Jaeger (b. 4 June 1965), at 15 yrs. 339 days, and Jimmy Arias (b. 16 Aug. 1964), at 16 yrs. 296 days. The youngest singles winners have been Monica Seles (Yugoslavia; b. 2 Dec. 1973), who won the 1990 women's title at 16 yrs. 169 days in 1990, and Michael Chang (USA; b. 22 Feb. 1972), who won the men's title at 17 yrs. 109 days in 1989. The oldest champion was Elizabeth Ryan, who won the 1934 women's doubles with Simone Mathieu (France) at 42 yrs. 88 days. The oldest singles champion was Andrés Gimeno (Spain; b. 3 Aug. 1937) in 1972 at 34 yrs. 301 days.

GREATEST WINNINGS. Monica Seles, uniquely the youngest winner of two Grand Slam singles titles (French and Australian), won a season's record $2,457,758 in 1991. (Photo: Allsport/Simon Bruty)

AUSTRALIAN OPEN CHAMPIONSHIPS

Most wins Margaret Jean Court won the women's singles 11 times (1960–66, 1969–71 and 1973) as well as eight women's doubles and two mixed doubles, for a record total of 21 titles. A record six men's singles were won by Roy Stanley Emerson, 1961 and 1963–67. Thelma Dorothy Long (nee Coyne; b. 30 May 1918) won a record 12 women's doubles and four mixed doubles for a record total of 16 doubles titles. Adrian Karl Quist (b. 4 Aug. 1913) won ten consecutive men's doubles from 1936 to 1950 (the last eight with John Bromwich) and three men's singles.

Longest span, oldest and youngest Thelma Long won her first (1936) and last (1958) titles 22 years apart. Kenneth Robert "Ken" Rosewall (b. 2 Nov. 1934) won the singles in 1953, and in 1972, 19 years later, at 37 yrs. 62 days, became the oldest singles winner. The oldest champion was (Sir) Norman Everard Brookes (1877–1968), who was 46 yrs. 2 months when he won the 1924 men's doubles. The youngest champions were Rodney W. Heath, age 17 when he won the men's singles in 1905, and Monica Seles (Yugoslavia), who won the women's singles at 17 yrs. 55 days in 1991.

ATP WORLD CHAMPIONSHIPS

The first Grand Prix Masters Championships were staged in Tokyo, Japan in 1970. They were held in New York City annually from 1977 to 1989, with qualification by relative success in the preceding year's Grand Prix tournaments. The event was replaced from 1990 by the ATP Tour Championship, held in Frankfurt, Germany. A record five titles have been won by Ivan Lendl (Czechoslovakia; b. 7 Mar. 1960), 1982–83, two in 1986 (January and December) and 1987, and he appeared in nine successive finals, 1980–88. Lendl has the highest earnings on the ATP Tour, with $18,211,061 through 1991. James Scott "Jimmy" Connors (USA; b. 2 Sep. 1952) uniquely qualified for 14 consecutive years, 1972–85. He chose not to play in 1975, 1976 and 1985, and won in 1977. He qualified again in 1987 and 1988, but did not play in 1988.

A record seven doubles titles were won by John McEnroe and Peter Fleming (USA; b. 21 Jan. 1955), 1978–84.

Virginia Slims Championships The women's tour finishes with the Virginia Slims Championship, first contested in 1971 (with Avon Products the sponsor, 1979–82). Since 1983 the Virginia Slims final has been the one women's match played over the best of five sets. Martina Navratilova has a record six singles wins, between 1978 and 1986. She also has a record nine doubles wins, one with Billie Jean King in 1980, and eight with Pam Shriver to 1991.

OLYMPIC GAMES

Tennis was reintroduced to the Olympic Games in 1988, having originally been included from 1896 to 1924. It was also a demonstration sport in 1968 and 1984.

A record four gold medals, as well as a silver and a bronze, were won by Max Decugis (France; 1882–1978), 1900–20. A women's record five medals (one gold, two silver, two bronze) were won by Kitty McKane (later Mrs. Godfree [Great Britain]; 1897–1992) in 1920 and 1924.

United States   Four US players have won two Olympic gold medals: Beals Coleman Wright (1879–1961) in 1904; Vincent Richards (1903–59) and Helen Wills Moody in 1924, all at both singles and doubles; and Hazel Virginia Hotchkiss Wightman (1886–1974), at ladies' and mixed doubles in 1924. Richards won a US record third medal, silver at mixed doubles (with Marion Jessup) in 1924.

INTERNATIONAL TEAM

Davis Cup (instituted 1900)   The most wins in the Davis Cup, the men's international team championship, has been 29, by the USA. The most appearances for Cup winners is eight, by Roy Emerson (Australia), 1959–62, 1964–67. Bill Tilden (USA) played in a record 28 matches in the final, winning a record 21—17 out of 22 singles and four out of six doubles. He was on seven winning sides, 1920–26, and then on four losing sides, 1927–30.

Nicola Pietrangeli (Italy; b. 11 Sep. 1933) played a record 163 rubbers (66 ties), 1954 to 1972, winning 120. He played 109 singles (winning 78) and 54 doubles (winning 42).

John McEnroe has played for the US team on 27 occasions, 1978 through 1 Feb. 1992. He also has the most wins—57 matches in Davis Cup competition (41 singles and 16 doubles).

Wightman Cup (instituted 1923)   The annual women's match was won 51 times by the United States and 10 times by Great Britain. The contest was suspended in 1990 after a series of wipeouts by the US team. Chris Evert won all 26 of her singles matches, from 1971 to 1985, and including doubles achieved a record 34 wins from 38 rubbers played. Virginia Wade (Great Britain; 10 July 1945) played in a record 21 ties and 56 rubbers, 1965–85. Jennifer Capriati became the youngest-ever Wightman Cup winner and player at 13 yrs. 168 days, when she beat Clare Wood (Great Britain) 6–0, 6–0 at Williamsburg, VA on 14 Sep. 1989.

Federation Cup (instituted 1963)   The most wins in the Federation Cup, the women's international team championship, is 14, by the USA between 1963 and 1990. Virginia Wade (Great Britain) played each year from 1967 to 1983, in a record 57 ties, playing 100 rubbers, including 56 singles (winning 36) and 44 doubles (winning 30). Chris Evert won her first 29 singles matches, 1977–86. Her overall record, 1977–89, is 40 wins in 42 singles and 16 wins in 18 doubles matches.

Longest span as national champion   Keith Gledhill (b. 17 Feb. 1911) won the US National Boys' Doubles Championship with Sidney Wood in Aug. 1926. Sixty-one years later, at Goleta, CA in Aug. 1987, he won the US National 75-and-over Men's Doubles Championship with Elbert Lewis.

Dorothy May Bundy-Cheney (USA; b. September 1916) won 180 US titles at various age groups from 1941 to March 1988.

International contest *Longest span*   Jean Borotra (France; b. 13 Aug. 1898) played in every one of the twice-yearly contests between the International Club of France and the International Club of Great Britain from the first in 1929 to his 100th match at Wimbledon on 1–3 Nov. 1985. On that occasion he played mixed doubles against Kitty Godfree (Great Britain). Both were former Wimbledon singles champions, and were age 87 and 88 respectively.

DAVIS CUP. The Davis Cup (properly known as the International Lawn Tennis Championship) arose from the intense rivalry between American and British players at the turn of the century. The first challenge took place at Longwood Cricket Club, Boston, MA on 8–10 Aug. 1900. The USA built up a winning 3–0 lead before thunderstorms intervened to end the match. Seen here are the triumphant US team, Malcolm Whitman (left), Holcombe Ward (right) and Dwight F. Davis (center), with the gold-lined silver punch bowl that he had commissoned and that bore his name. The format of the event (four singles and a doubles match) has not changed since that first match. (Photo: The Bettmann Archive Inc.)

Highest earnings   Monica Seles (Yugoslavia) won a season's record $2,457,758 in 1991. In the same year Stefan Edberg (Sweden; b. 19 Jan. 1966) won a men's season's record $2,363,575. Ivan Lendl had career earnings of $18,211,061, 1978–91. Martina Navratilova's lifetime earnings by 1991 reached $17,661,593 in prize money. Earnings from special restricted events and team tennis are not included.

The greatest first-place prize money ever won is $2 million by Pete Sampras when he won the Grand Slam Cup in Munich, Germany on 16 Dec. 1990. In the final he beat Brad Gilbert (USA; b. 9 Aug. 1961) 6–3, 6–4, 6–2. Gilbert received $1 million, also well in excess of the previous record figure. The highest total prize money was $6,349,250 for the 1990 US Open Championships.

Largest crowd   A record 30,472 people were at the Astrodome, Houston, TX on 20 Sep. 1973, when Billie Jean King beat Robert Larimore "Bobby" Riggs (USA; b. 25 Feb. 1918). The record for a standard tennis match is 25,578 at Sydney, New South Wales, Australia on 27 Dec. 1954, in the Davis Cup Challenge Round (first day), Australia v. USA.

Longest game   The longest-known singles game was one of 37 deuces (80 points) between Anthony Fawcett (Rhodesia) and Keith Glass (Great Britain) in the first round of the Surrey Championships at Surbiton, Great Britain on 26 May 1975. It lasted 31 min. Noëlle van Lottum and Sandra Begijn played a game lasting 52 min. in the semifinals of the Dutch Indoor Championships at Ede, Gelderland on 12 Feb. 1984.

The longest tiebreak was 26–24 for the fourth and decisive set of a first round men's doubles at the Wimbledon Championships on 1 July 1985. Jan Gunnarsson (Sweden) and Michael Mortensen (Denmark) defeated John Frawley (Australia) and Victor Pecci (Paraguay) 6–3, 6–4, 3–6, 7–6.

TRACK AND FIELD

The earliest evidence of organized running was at Memphis, Eygpt c. 3800 B.C. The earliest accurately dated Olympic Games were held in July 776 B.C., when Coroibos won the foot race. The oldest surviving measurements are a long jump of 23 ft. 1½ in. by Chionis of Sparta in c. 656 B.C. and a discus throw of 100 cubits (about 152 ft.) by Protesilaus.

Fastest speed   An analysis of split times at each ten meters in the 1988 Olympic Games 100 m final in Seoul, South Korea on 24 Sep. 1988, won by Ben Johnson (Canada) in 9.79 (average speed 22.85 mph but later disallowed as a world record due to his positive drug test for steroids) from Carl Lewis (USA) 9.92, showed that both Johnson and Lewis reached a peak speed (40 m–50 m and 80 m–90 m respectively) of 0.83 sec. for 10 m, i.e., 26.95 mph. In the women's final, Florence Griffith Joyner was timed at 0.91 sec. for each 10 m from 60 m–90 m, i.e., 24.58 mph.

Highest jump above own head   The greatest height cleared above an athlete's own head is 23¼ in., by Franklin Jacobs (USA; b. 31 Dec. 1957),

5 ft. 8 in. tall, who jumped 7 ft. 7¼ in. at New York City, on 27 Jan. 1978. The greatest height cleared by a woman above her own head is 12¾ in., by Yolanda Henry (USA; b. 2 Dec. 1964), 5 ft. 6 in. tall, who jumped 6 ft. 6¾ in. at Seville, Spain on 30 May 1990.

Most Olympic titles   The most Olympic gold medals won is ten (an absolute Olympic record), by Raymond Clarence Ewry (USA; 1873–1937) in the standing high, long and triple jumps in 1900, 1904, 1906 and 1908.

Women   The most gold medals won by a woman is four, shared by: Francina "Fanny" E. Blankers-Koen (Netherlands; b. 26 Apr. 1918), with 100 m, 200 m, 80 m hurdles and 4 × 100 m relay, 1948; Betty Cuthbert (Australia; b. 20 Apr. 1938), with 100 m, 200 m, 4 × 100 m relay, 1956 and 400 m, 1964; and Bärbel Wöckel (nee Eckert [East Germany]; b. 21 Mar. 1955), with 200 m and 4 × 100 m relay in 1976 and 1980.

Most wins at one Games   The most gold medals at one celebration is five, by Paavo Johannes Nurmi (Finland; 1897–1973) in 1924: 1,500 m, 5,000 m, 10,000 m cross-country, 3,000 m team and cross-country team. The most at individual events is four, by Alvin Christian Kraenzlein (USA; 1876–1928) in 1900: 60 m, 110 m hurdles, 200 m hurdles and long jump.

Most Olympic medals   The most medals won is 12 (nine gold and three silver), by Paavo Nurmi (Finland) in the Games of 1920, 1924 and 1928.

Women   The most medals won by a woman athlete is seven, by Shirley Barbara de la Hunty (nee Strickland [Australia]; b. 18 July 1925) with three gold, one silver and three bronze in the 1948, 1952 and 1956 Games. A reappraisal of the photo-finish indicates that she finished third, not fourth, in the 1948 200-meter event, thus unofficially increasing her medal haul to eight. Irena Szewinska (nee Kirszenstein [Poland]; b. 24 May 1946) won three gold, two silver and two bronze in 1964, 1968, 1972 and 1976, and is the only woman athlete to win a medal in four successive Games.

United States   The most Olympic medals won is five, by Delorez Florence Griffith Joyner (b. 21 Dec. 1959): 200 m silver in 1984, gold at 100 m, 200 m and 4 × 100 m relay, silver at 4 × 400 m relay in 1988. Wilma Glodean Rudolph (later Ward; b. 23 June 1940) won three gold medals: 100 m, 200 m and 4 × 100 m relay in 1960; by Wyomia Tyus (b. 29 Aug. 1945): 100 m in 1968, 4 × 100 m relay in 1964 and 1968; and by Valerie Ann Brisco (b. 6 July 1960) at 200 m, 400 m and 4 × 400 m relay. Rudolph and Tyus also won one silver medal each. Four gold medals at one Games were won by Alvin Kraenzlein (see above). Jesse Owens (1913–80) in 1936 and Frederick Carleton "Carl" Lewis (b. 1 July 1961) in 1984 both won four gold medals at one Games, both at 100 m, 200 m, long jump and the 4 × 100 m relay. Lewis won two more gold medals in 1988.

Olympic champions *Oldest and youngest*   The oldest athlete to win an Olympic title was Irish-born Patrick Joseph "Babe" McDonald (ne McDonnell; 1878–1954), who was age 42 yrs. 26 days when he won the 56 lb. weight throw at Antwerp, Belgium on 21 Aug. 1920. The oldest female champion was Lia Manoliu (Romania; b. 25 Apr. 1932), age 36 yrs. 176 days when she won the discus at Mexico City on 18 Oct. 1968. The youngest gold medalist was Barbara Pearl Jones (USA; b. 26 Mar. 1937), who at 15 yrs.

123 days was a member of the winning 4 × 100 m relay team, at Helsinki, Finland on 27 July 1952. The youngest male champion was Robert Bruce "Bob" Mathias (USA; b. 17 Nov. 1930), age 17 yrs. 263 days when he won the decathlon at the London Games on 5–6 Aug. 1948.

The oldest Olympic medalist was Tebbs Lloyd Johnson (Great Britain; 1900–84), age 48 yrs. 115 days when he was third in the 1948 50,000 m walk. The oldest woman medalist was Dana Zátopková (Czechoslovakia; b. 19 Sep. 1922), age 37 yrs. 348 days when she was second in the javelin in 1960.

World Championships   Quadrennial World Championships, distinct from the Olympic Games, were inaugurated in 1983, when they were held in Helsinki, Finland. The most medals won is nine, by Frederick Carleton "Carl" Lewis (USA; b. 1 July 1961), eight gold, at 100 m, long jump and 4 × 100 m relay in 1983; 100 m, long jump and 4 × 100 m relay in 1987; 100 m and 4 × 100 m relay, 1991; and silver at long jump in 1991. This is based on the assumption that Ben Johnson (Canada), the original winner of the 1987 100 m gold, who was stripped of his title by the IAAF in 1989 following his admission of drug taking, also loses the gold. Lewis has also won six Olympic golds, four in 1984 and two in 1988.

World record breakers   *Oldest and youngest*   For the greatest age at which anyone has broken a world record under IAAF jurisdiction, see General Records. The female record is 36 yrs. 139 days for Marina Styepanova (nee Makeyeva [USSR]; b. 1 May 1950) with 52.94 sec. for the 400 m hurdles at Tashkent, USSR on 17 Sep. 1986. The youngest individual record breaker is Wang Yan (China; b. 9 Apr. 1971), who set a women's 5,000 m walk record at age 14 yrs. 334 days with 21 min. 33.8 sec. at Jian, China on 9 Mar. 1986. The youngest male is Thomas Ray (Great Britain; 1862–1904) at 17 yrs. 198 days when he pole-vaulted 11 ft. 2¾ in. on 19 Sep. 1879 (prior to IAAF ratification).

US championships   The most American national titles won at all events, indoors and out, is 65, by Ronald Owen Laird (b. 31 May 1938) at various walks events between 1958 and 1976. Excluding the walks, the record is 41, by Stella Walsh (nee Walasiewicz, 1911–80), who won women's events between 1930 and 1954—33 outdoors and 8 indoors.

The most wins outdoors at one event in AAU/TAC history is 11, by James Sarsfield Mitchel (1864–1921) at 56 lb. weight in 1888, 1891–97, 1900, 1903, 1905; Stella Walsh, 220 y/200 m 1930–31, 1939–40, 1942–48, and long jump 1930, 1939–46, 1948 and 1951; Maren Seidler (b. 11 June 1951) in shot 1967–68, 1972–80; Dorothy Dodson (b. 28 Mar. 1919) in javelin 1939–49.

Longest winning sequence   Iolanda Balas (Romania; b. 12 Dec. 1936) won a record 150 consecutive competitions at high jump from 1956 to 1967. The record at a track event is 122, at 400 m hurdles, by Edwin Corley Moses (USA; b. 31 July 1955) between his loss to Harald Schmid (West Germany; b. 29 Sep. 1957) at Berlin, Germany on 26 Aug. 1977 and that to Danny Lee Harris (USA; b. 7 Sep. 1965) at Madrid, Spain on 4 June 1987.

Longest running races   The longest races ever staged were the 1928 (3,422 miles) and 1929 (3,665 miles) transcontinental races from New York City to Los Angeles, CA. The Finnish-born Johnny Salo (1893–1931) was the winner in 1929 in 79 days, from 31 Mar. to 18 June. His elapsed time of

525 hrs. 57 min. 20 sec. (averaging 6.97 mph) left him only 2 min. 47 sec. ahead of Englishman Pietro "Peter" Gavuzzi (1905–81).

The longest race staged annually is the New York 1,300 Mile race, held since 1987, at Flushing Meadows-Corona Park, Queens, NY. The fastest time to complete the race is 16 days 19 hrs. 31 min. 47 sec. by Al Howie, Great Britain, from 16 Sep.–3 Oct. 1991.

Longest runs   The longest run by an individual is one of 11,134 miles around the United States, by Sarah Covington-Fulcher (USA; b. 14 Feb. 1962), starting and finishing in Los Angeles, CA, 21 July 1987–2 Oct. 1988. Al Howie (Great Britain) ran across Canada, from St. Johns, Newfoundland to Victoria, British Columbia, a distance of 4,533.2 miles, in 72 days 10 hrs. 23 min., 21 June–1 Sep. 1991. Robert J. Sweetgall (USA; b. 8 Dec. 1947) ran 10,608 miles around the perimeter of the United States, starting and finishing in Washington, D.C., Oct. 1982–15 July 1983. Ron Grant (Australia; b. 15 Feb. 1943) ran around Australia, 8,316 miles in 217 days 3 hrs. 45 min., 28 Mar.–31 Oct. 1983. Max Telford (New Zealand; b. Hawick, Scotland 2 Feb. 1955) ran 5,110 miles from Anchorage, AK to Halifax, Nova Scotia, in 106 days 18 hrs. 45 min. from 25 July to 9 Nov. 1977.

The fastest time for the cross-America run is 46 days 8 hrs. 36 min., by Frank Giannino, Jr. (USA; b. 1952) for the 3,100 miles from San Francisco to New York from 1 Sep.–17 Oct. 1980. The women's trans-America record is 69 days 2 hrs. 40 min., by Mavis Hutchinson (South Africa; b. 25 Nov. 1942) from 12 Mar.–21 May 1978.

Most track records in a day   Jesse Owens (USA; 1913–80) set six world records in 45 min. at Ann Arbor, MI on 25 May 1935, with a 9.4 sec. 100 yds. at 3:15 P.M., a 26 ft. 8¼ in. long jump at 3:25 P.M., a 20.3 sec. 220 yds. (and 200 m) at 3:45 P.M., and a 22.6 sec. 220 yds. (and 200 m) low hurdles at 4 P.M.

Longest career span   Duncan McLean (1884–1980) of Scotland set a world age (92) record of 100 m in 21.7 sec. in Aug. 1977, over 73 years after his best-ever sprint of 100 yds. in 9.9 sec. in South Africa in Feb. 1904.

Roof of the world run   Ultra runner Hilary Walker ran the length of the Friendship Highway from Lhasa, Tibet to Kathmandu, Nepal, a distance of 590 miles, in 14 days 9 hrs. 36 min. from 18 Sep.–2 Oct. 1991. The run was made at an average altitude of 13,780 ft.

Most international appearances   The greatest number of international matches contested for any nation is 89, by shot-putter Bjørn Bang Andersen (b. 14 Nov. 1937) for Norway, 1960–81.

**WORLD RECORD. Mike Powell (USA) (above in all three photos) at
the 1991 World Championships in Tokyo breaking the longest-
standing field event world record. (Photo: Allsport/G. Vandystadt)**

WORLD RECORDS *MEN*

World records for the men's events scheduled by the International Amateur Athletic Federation.
Fully automatic electric timing is mandatory for events up to 400 meters.

RUNNING	min.:sec.	NAME AND COUNTRY	PLACE	DATE
100 meters	9.86*	Frederick Carleton "Carl" Lewis (USA; b. 1 July 1961)	Tokyo, Japan	25 Aug. 1991
200 meters	19.72†	Pietro Mennea (Italy; b. 28 June 1952)	Mexico City, Mexico	12 Sep. 1979
400 meters	43.29	Harry Lee "Butch" Reynolds, Jr. (USA; b. 8 Aug. 1964)	Zürich, Switzerland	17 Aug. 1988
800 meters	1:41.73	Sebastian Newbold Coe (Great Britain; b. 29 Sep. 1956)	Florence, Italy	10 June 1981
1,000 meters	2:12.18	Sebastian Newbold Coe (Great Britain)	Oslo, Norway	11 July 1981
1,500 meters	3:29.46	Saïd Aouita (Morocco; b. 2 Nov. 1959)	Berlin, Germany	23 Aug. 1985
1 mile	3:46.32	Steven Cram (Great Britain; b. 14 Oct. 1960)	Oslo, Norway	27 July 1985
2,000 meters	4:50.81	Saïd Aouita (Morocco)	Paris, France	16 July 1987
3,000 meters	7:29.45	Saïd Aouita (Morocco)	Cologne, Germany	20 Aug. 1989
5,000 meters	12:58.39	Saïd Aouita (Morocco)	Rome, Italy	22 July 1987
10,000 meters	27:08.23	Arturo Barrios (Mexico; b. 12 Dec. 1963)	Berlin, Germany	18 Aug. 1989
20,000 meters	56:55.6	Arturo Barrios (Mexico)	La Flèche, France	30 Mar. 1991
25,000 meters	1 hr. 13:55.8	Toshihiko Seko (Japan; b. 15 July 1956)	Christchurch, New Zealand	22 Mar. 1981
30,000 meters	1 hr. 29:18.8	Toshihiko Seko (Japan)	Christchurch, New Zealand	22 Mar. 1981
1 hour	13.111 miles	Arturo Barrios (Mexico)	La Flèche, France	30 May 1991

*Ben Johnson (Canada; b. 30 Dec. 1961) ran 100m in 9.79 sec. at Seoul, South Korea on 24 Sep. 1988, but was subsequently disqualified when he tested positive for steroids. He later admitted to having taken drugs over many years, and this also invalidated his 9.83 sec. at Rome, Italy on 30 Aug. 1987.
† This record was set at high altitude—Mexico City 7,349 ft. Best mark at low altitude: 200 m: 19.75 sec, Carl Lewis, Indianapolis, IN, 19 June 1983, and Joseph Nathaniel DeLoach (USA; b. 5 June 1967) at Seoul, South Korea on 28 Sep. 1988.

HURDLING				
110 meters (3′6″)	12.92	Roger Kingdom (USA; b. 26 Aug. 1962)	Zürich, Switzerland	16 Aug. 1989
400 meters (3′0″)	47.02	Edwin Corley Moses (USA; b. 31 Aug. 1955)	Koblenz, Germany	31 Aug. 1983
3,000 meter steeplechase	8:05.35	Peter Koech (Kenya; b. 18 Feb. 1958)	Stockholm, Sweden	4 July 1989

RELAYS

4 × 100 meters	37.50	USA	Tokyo, Japan	1 Sep. 1991
		(Andre Cason, Leroy Burrell, Dennis Mitchell, Carl Lewis)		
4 × 200 meters	1:19.11	Santa Monica Track Club (USA)	Philadelphia, PA	25 Apr. 1992
		(Mike Marsh, Leroy Burrell, Floyd Wayne Heard, Carl Lewis)		
4 × 400 meters	2:56.16*	United States	Mexico City, Mexico	20 Oct. 1968
		(Vincent Edward Matthews, Ronald John Freeman II, George Lawrence James, Lee Edward Evans)		
	2:56.16	United States	Seoul, South Korea	1 Oct. 1988
		(Daniel Everett, Steven Earl Lewis, Kevin Bernard Robinzine, Butch Reynolds)		
4 × 800 meters	7:03.89	Great Britain	London, Great Britain	30 Aug. 1982
		(Peter Elliot, Garry Peter Cook, Steven Cram, Sebastian Coe)		
4 × 1,500 meters	14:38.8	West Germany	Cologne, Germany	17 Aug. 1977
		(Thomas Wessinghage, Harald Hudak, Michael Lederer, Karl Fleschen)		

Set at high altitude.

FIELD EVENTS

	m	ft. in.			
High jump	2.44	8	Javier Sotomayor (Cuba; b. 13 Oct. 1967)	San Juan, Puerto Rico	29 July 1989
Pole vault	6.11	20 0¼	Sergey Nazarovich Bubka (Ukraine; b. 4 Dec. 1963)	Dijon, France	13 June 1992
Long jump	8.95	29 4¼	Michael Anthony "Mike" Powell (USA; b. 10 Nov. 1963)	Tokyo, Japan	30 Aug. 1991
Triple jump	17.97	58 11	William Augustus "Willie" Banks (USA; b. 11 Mar. 1956)	Indianapolis, IN	16 June 1985
Shot 16 lb.	23.12	75 10¼	Eric Randolph "Randy" Barnes (USA; b. 16 June 1966)	Los Angeles, CA	20 May 1990
Discus 4 lb. 8 oz.	74.08	243 0	Jürgen Schult (East Germany; b. 11 May 1960)	Neubrandenburg, Germany	6 June 1986
Hammer 16 lb.	86.74	284 7	Yuriy Georgiyevich Sedykh (USSR; b. 11 June 1955)	Stuttgart, Germany	30 Aug. 1986
Javelin	91.46	300 0	Stephen James Backley (Great Britain; b. 12 Feb. 1969)	Auckland, New Zealand	25 Jan. 1992

DECATHLON

8,847 points	Francis Morgan "Daley" Thompson (Great Britain; b. 30 July 1958)	Los Angeles, CA	8–9 Aug. 1984

(1st day: 100 m 10.44 sec., Long Jump 26'3½", Shot Put 51'7", High Jump 6'8", 400 m 46.97 sec.)
(2nd day: 110 m hurdles 14.33 sec., Discus 152'9", Pole vault 16'4¾", Javelin 214'0", 1,500 m 4:35.00 sec.)

WORLD RECORDS WOMEN

World records for the women's events scheduled by the International Amateur Athletic Federation.

RUNNING	min.sec.	NAME AND COUNTRY	PLACE		DATE
100 meters	10.49	Delorez Florence Griffith Joyner (USA: b. 21 Dec. 1959)	Indianapolis, IN	16	July 1988
200 meters	21.34	Delorez Florence Griffith Joyner (USA)	Seoul, South Korea	29	Sep. 1988
400 meters	47.60	Marita Koch (East Germany; b. 18 Feb. 1957)	Canberra, Australia	6	Oct. 1985
800 meters	1:53.28	Jarmila Kratochvílová (Czechoslovakia: b. 26 Jan. 1951)	Münich, Germany	26	July 1983
1,000 meters	2:30.6	Tatyana Providokhina (USSR; b. 26 Mar. 1953)	Podolsk, USSR	20	Aug. 1978
1,500 meters	3:52.47	Tatyana Kazankina (USSR: b. 17 Dec. 1951)	Zürich, Switzerland	13	Aug. 1980
1 mile	4:15.61	Paula Ivan (Romania: b. 20 July 1963)	Nice, France	10	July 1989
2,000 meters	5:28.69	Maricica Puică (Romania; b. 29 July 1950)	London, Great Britain	11	July 1986
3,000 meters	8:22.62	Tatyana Kazankina (USSR)	Leningrad, USSR	26	Aug. 1984
5,000 meters	14:37.33	Ingrid Kristiansen (nee Christensen [Norway]; b. 21 Mar. 1956)	Stockholm, Sweden	5	Aug. 1986
10,000 meters	30:13.74	Ingrid Kristiansen (Norway)	Oslo, Norway	5	July 1986

HURDLING					
100 meters (2' 9")	12.21	Yordanka Donkova (Bulgaria; b. 28 Sep. 1961)	Stara Zagora, Bulgaria	20	Aug. 1988
400 meters (2' 6")	52.94	Marina Styepanova (nee Makeyeva [USSR]; b. 1 May 1950)	Tashkent, USSR	17	Sep. 1986

RELAYS					
4 x 100 meters	41.37	East Germany (Silke Gladisch [now Möller], Sabine Rieger [now Günther], Ingrid Auerswald [nee Brestrich], Marlies Göhr [nee Oelsner])	Canberra, Australia	6	Oct. 1985
4 x 200 meters	1:28.15	East Germany (Marlies Göhr [nee Oelsner], Romy Müller [nee Schneider], Bärbel Wöckel [nee Eckert], Marita Koch)	Jena, Germany	9	Aug. 1980

4 × 400 meters ....3:15.17 ....USSR ....Seoul, South Korea....................1 Oct. 1988
(Tatyana Ledovskaya, Olga Nazarova [nee Grigoryeva], Maria Pinigina [nee Kulchunova], Olga Bryzgina [nee Vladykina])

4 × 800 meters ....7:50.17 ....USSR ....Moscow, USSR ....5 Aug. 1984
(Nadezhda Olizarenko [nee Mushta], Lyubov Gurina, Lyudmila Borisova, Irina Podyalovskaya)

FIELD EVENTS

	m	ft.	in.			
High jump	2.09	.6	10¼	Stefka Kostadinova (Bulgaria; b. 25 Mar. 1965)	Rome, Italy	30 Aug. 1987
Long jump	7.52	.24	8¼	Galina Chistyakova (USSR; b. 26 July 1962)	Leningrad, USSR	11 June 1988
Triple jump	14.95	.49	1	Inessa Kravets (USSR; b. 5 Oct. 1966)	Moscow, USSR	10 June 1991
Shot 8 lb. 13 oz.	22.63	.74	3	Natalya Lisovskaya (USSR; b. 16 July 1962)	Moscow, USSR	7 June 1987
Discus 2 lb. 3 oz.	76.80	.252	0	Gabriele Reinsch (East Germany; b. 23 Sep. 1963)	Neubrandenburg, Germany	9 July 1988
Javelin 24 lb. 7 oz.	80.00	.262	5	Petra Felke (East Germany; b. 30 July 1959)	Potsdam, Germany	9 Sep. 1988

HEPTATHLON

7,291 points.Jacqueline Joyner-Kersee (USA; b. 3 Mar. 1962)..Seoul, South Korea...................23–24 Sep. 1988
(100 m hurdles 12.69 sec.; High jump 6 ft. 1¼ in.;
Shot 51 ft. 10 in.; 200 m 22.56 sec.; Long jump 23 ft. 10 in.;
Javelin 149 ft. 9 in.; 800 m 2 min. 08.51 sec.)

ULTRA LONG DISTANCE WORLD RECORDS

MEN

TRACK	hr.:min.:sec.	NAME AND COUNTRY	PLACE	DATE
50 km	2:48:06	Jeff Norman (Great Britain)	Manchester, Great Britain	7 June 1980
50 miles	4:51:49	Don Ritchie (Great Britain)	London, Great Britain	12 Mar. 1983
100 km	6:10:20	Don Ritchie (Great Britain)	London, Great Britain	28 Oct. 1978
100 miles	11:30:51	Don Ritchie (Great Britain)	London, Great Britain	15 Oct. 1977
200 km	15:11:10*	Yiannis Kouros (Greece)	Montauban, France	15–16 Mar. 1985
200 miles	27:48:35	Yiannis Kouros (Greece)	Montauban, France	15–16 Mar. 1985
500 km	60:23:00	Yiannis Kouros (Greece)	Colac, Australia	26–29 Nov. 1984
500 miles	105:42:09	Yiannis Kouros (Greece)	Colac, Australia	26–30 Nov. 1984
1,000 km	136:17:00	Yiannis Kouros (Greece)	Colac, Australia	26 Nov.–1 Dec. 1984

kilometers				
24 hours	283.600	Yiannis Kouros (Greece)	Montauban, France	15–16 Mar. 1985
48 hours	452.270	Yiannis Kouros (Greece)	Montauban, France	15–17 Mar. 1985
6 days	1,023.200	Yiannis Kouros (Greece)	Colac, Australia	26 Nov.–1 Dec. 1984

ROAD	hr.:min.:sec.	NAME AND COUNTRY	PLACE	DATE
50 km	2:43:38	Thompson Magawana (South Africa)	Claremont–Kirstenbosch, South Africa	12 Apr. 1988
50 miles	4:50:21	Bruce Fordyce (South Africa)	London–Brighton, Great Britain	25 Sep. 1983
1,000 miles	10d. 10hr. 30min. 35sec.	Yiannis Kouros (Greece)	New York City	21–30 May 1988

kilometers				
24 hours	286.463	Yiannis Kouros (Greece)	New York City	28–29 Sep. 1985
6 days	1,028.370	Yiannis Kouros (Greece)	New York City	21–26 May 1988

WOMEN

TRACK

	hr.:min.:sec.			
15 km	49:44.0	Silvana Cruciata (Italy)	Rome, Italy	4 May 1981
20 km	1:06:55.5	Rosa Mota (Portugal)	Lisbon, Portugal	14 May 1983
25 km	1:29:30	Karolina Szabo (Hungary)	Budapest, Hungary	23 Apr. 1988
30 km	1:47:06	Karolina Szabo (Hungary)	Budapest, Hungary	23 Apr. 1988
50 km	3:35:31	Ann Transon (USA)	Santa Rosa, CA	28 Mar. 1992
50 miles	6:14:34†	Ann Transon (USA)	Hayward, CA	3–4 Aug. 1991
100 km	7:48:15†	Ann Transon (USA)	Hayward, CA	3–4 Aug. 1991
100 miles	14:29:44	Ann Transon (USA)	Santa Rosa, CA	18–19 Mar. 1989
200 km	19:28:48	Eleanor Adams (Great Britain)	Melbourne, Australia	19–20 Aug. 1989
200 miles	39:09:03	Hilary Walker (Great Britain)	Blackpool, Great Britain	5–6 Nov. 1988
500 km	77:53:46	Eleanor Adams (Great Britain)	Colac, Australia	13–15 Nov. 1989
500 miles	130:59:58	Sandra Barwick (New Zealand)	Campbelltown, Australia	18–23 Nov. 1990

kilometers

1 hour	18.084	Silvana Cruciata (Italy)	Rome, Italy	4 May 1981
24 hours	240.169	Eleanor Adams (Great Britain)	Melbourne, Australia	19–20 Aug. 1989
48 hours	366.512	Hilary Walker (Great Britain)	Blackpool, Great Britain	5–7 Nov. 1988
6 days	866.631	Sandra Barwick (New Zealand)	Campbelltown, Australia	18–24 Nov. 1990

ROAD*

	hr.:min.:sec.			
30 km	1:38:27	Ingrid Kristiansen (Norway)	London, Great Britain	10 May 1987
50 km	3:08:13	Frith van der Merwe (South Africa)	Claremont-Kirstenbosch, South Africa	25 Mar. 1989
50 miles	5:40:18	Ann Trason (USA)	Houston, TX	23 Feb. 1991
100 km	7:18:57	Birgit Lennartz (West Germany)	Hanua, Germany	28 Sep. 1989
100 miles	13:47:41	Ann Trason (USA)	Queens, NY	4 May 1991
200 km	19:22:05	Ann Trason (USA)	Queens, NY	16–17 Sep. 1989
(indoors)	19:00:31	Eleanor Adams (Great Britain)	Milton Keynes, Great Britain	3–4 Feb. 1990
1,000 km	7d. 1hr. 11min. 00 sec.	Sandra Barwick (New Zealand)	Queens, NY	16–23 Sep. 1991
1,000 miles	12d. 14hrs. 38min. 40 sec.	Sandra Barwick (New Zealand)	Queens, NY	16–29 Sep. 1991

* Where superior to track bests and run on properly measured road courses. It should be noted that road times must be assessed with care as course conditions can vary considerably.

†Timed on one running watch only.

WORLD INDOOR RECORDS

Track performances around a turn must be made on a track of circumference no longer than 200 meters.

MEN

RUNNING	hr.:min.:sec.	NAME AND COUNTRY	PLACE		DATE
50 meters	5.61*	Manfred Kokot (East Germany; b. 3 Jan. 1948)	East Berlin, Germany	4	Feb. 1973
	5.61*	James Sanford (USA; b. 27 Dec. 1957)	San Diego, CA	20	Feb. 1981
60 meters	6.41*	Andre Cason (USA; b. 13 Jan. 1969)	Madrid, Spain	14	Feb. 1992
200 meters	20.36	Bruno Marie-Rose (France; b. 20 May 1965)	Liévin, France	22	Feb. 1987
400 meters	45.02	Danny Everett (USA; b. 1 Nov. 1966)	Stuttgart, Germany	2	Feb. 1992
800 meters	1:44.84	Paul Ereng (Kenya; b. 22 Aug. 1967)	Budapest, Hungary	4	Mar. 1989
1,000 meters	(2:16.4 officially) 2:16.62	Robert Druppers (Netherlands; b. 29 Apr. 1962)	The Hague, Netherlands	20	Feb. 1988
1,500 meters	3:34.16	Noureddine Morceli (Algeria; b. 20 Feb. 1970)	Seville, Spain	28	Feb. 1991
1 mile	3:49.78	Eamonn Coghlan (Ireland; b. 21 Nov. 1952)	East Rutherford, NJ	27	Feb. 1983
3,000 meters	7:36.66	Saïd Aouita (Morocco; b. 2 Nov. 1959)	Athens, Greece	11	Mar. 1992
5,000 meters	13:20.4	Suleiman Nyambui (Tanzania; b. 13 Feb. 1953)	New York City	6	Feb. 1983
50 meter hurdles	6.25	Mark McKoy (Canada; b. 10 Dec. 1961)	Kobe, Japan	5	Mar. 1986
60 meter hurdles	7.36‡	Gregory "Greg" Foster (USA; b. 4 Aug. 1958)	Los Angeles, CA	16	Jan. 1987
	7.37	Roger Kingdom (USA; b. 26 Aug. 1962)	Piraeus, Greece	8	Mar. 1989

* Ben Johnson (Canada; b. 30 Dec. 1961) ran 50m in 5.55 sec. at Ottawa, Cananda on 31 Jan. 1987 and 60 m in 6.41 sec. at Indianapolis on 7 Mar. 1987, but these were invalidated due to his admission of having taken drugs over many years, following his disqualification at the 1988 Olympics.

‡ adjudged by observers to have been made with a rolling start, but officially ratified.

RELAYS					
4 × 200 meters	1:22.11	United Kingdom	Glasgow, Great Britain	3	Mar. 1991
		(Linford Christie, Darren Braithwaite, Ade Mafe, John Regis)			
4 × 400 meters	3:03.05	Germany	Seville, Spain	10	Mar. 1991
		(Rico Lieder, Jens Carlowitz, Karsten Just, Thomas Schönlebe)			

WALKING

| 5,000 meters | 18:11.41* | Ronald Weigel (East Germany; b. 8 Aug. 1959) | Vienna, Austria | 13 Feb. 1988 |
| 5,000 meters | 18:15.25 | Grigoriy Kornev (Russia; b. 14 Mar. 1961) | Moscow, Russia | 7 Feb. 1992 |

* not officially recognized.

FIELD EVENTS

	m	ft. in.			
High jump	2.43	7 11½	Javier Sotomayor (Cuba; b. 13 Oct. 1967)	Budapest, Hungary	4 Mar. 1989
Pole vault	6.13	20 1¼	Sergey Nazarovich Bubka (Ukraine; b. 4 Dec. 1963)	Berlin, Germany	21 Feb. 1992
Long jump	8.79	28 10¼	Frederick Carleton "Carl" Lewis (USA; b. 1 July 1961)	New York City	27 Jan. 1984
Triple jump	17.76	58 3¾	Michael Alexander Conley (USA; b. 5 Oct. 1962)	New York City	27 Feb. 1987
Shot	22.66	74 4¼	Eric Randolph "Randy" Barnes (USA; b. 16 June 1966)	Los Angeles, CA	20 Jan. 1989

| HEPTATHLON | 6,418 points | Christian Plaziat (France; b. 28 Oct. 1963) | Genoa, Italy | 28–29 Feb. 1992 |

(60 m 6.83 sec.; Long jump, 7.58 m; Shot, 14.53 m; High jump, 2.13 m; 60 m hurdles, 7.97 sec.; Pole vault, 5.20 m; 1,000 m 2:40.17)

WOMEN

RUNNING	hr.:min.:sec.	NAME AND COUNTRY	PLACE	DATE
50 meters	6.11	Marita Koch (East Germany; b. 18 Feb. 1957)	Grenoble, France	2 Feb. 1980
60 meters	6.96	Merlene Ottey (Jamaica; b. 10 May 1960)	Madrid, Spain	14 Feb. 1992
200 meters	22.24	Merlene Ottey (Jamaica)	Seville, Spain	10 Mar. 1991
400 meters	49.59	Jarmila Kratochvílová (Czechoslovakia; b. 26 Jan. 1951)	Milan, Italy	7 Mar. 1982
800 meters	1:56.40	Christine Wachtel (East Germany; b. 6 Jan. 1965)	Vienna, Austria	13 Feb. 1988
1,000 meters	2:33.93	Inna Yevseyeva (Ukraine; b. 14 Aug. 1964)	Moscow, Russia	7 Feb. 1992
1,500 meters	4:00.27	Doina Melinte (Romania; b. 27 Dec. 1956)	East Rutherford, NJ	9 Feb. 1990
1 mile	4:17.14	Doina Melinte (Romania)	East Rutherford, NJ	9 Feb. 1990
3,000 meters	8:33.82	Elly van Hulst (Netherlands; b. 9 June 1957)	Budapest, Hungary	4 Mar. 1989
5,000 meters	15:03.17	Elizabeth McColgan (Great Britain; b. 24 May 1964)	Birmingham, Great Britain	22 Feb. 1992
50 meter hurdles	6.58	Cornelia Oschkenat (East Germany; b. 29 Oct. 1961)	Berlin, Germany	20 Feb. 1988
60 meter hurdles	7.69	Lyudmila Narozhilenko (USSR; b. 21 Apr. 1964)	Chelyabinsk, USSR	4 Feb. 1990

† Angella Issajenko [nee Taylor (Canada); b. 28 Sep. 1958) ran 6.06 at Ottawa, Canada on 31 Jan. 1987. This was accepted as a world record, but subsequently invalidated when she admitted steroid usage.

(continued)

RELAYS	hr:min:sec.	NAME AND COUNTRY	PLACE	DATE
4 × 200 meters	1:32.55	S. C. Eintracht Hamm (West Germany) (Helga Arendt, Silke-Beate Knoll, Mechthild Kluth, Gisela Kinzel)	Dortmund, Germany	19 Feb. 1988
4 × 400 meters	3:27.22	Germany (Sandra Seuser, Katrin Schreiter, Annet Hesselbarth, Grit Breuer)	Seville, Spain	10 Mar. 1991

WALKING	hr:min:sec.	NAME AND COUNTRY	PLACE	DATE
3,000 meters	11:44.00	Alina Ivanova (Ukraine; b. 25 June 1969)	Moscow, Russia	7 Feb. 1992

FIELD EVENTS	m	ft. in.	NAME AND COUNTRY	PLACE	DATE
High jump	2.07	6 9½	Heike Henkel (Germany; b. 5 May 1964)	Karlsruhe, Germany	9 Feb. 1992
Long jump	7.37	24 2¼	Heike Drechsler (East Germany; b. 16 Dec. 1964)	Vienna, Austria	13 Feb. 1988
Triple jump	14.45	47 5	Galina Chistyakova (USSR; b. 26 July 1962)	Lipetsk, USSR	29 Jan. 1989
Shot	22.50	73 10	Helena Fibingerová (Czechoslovakia; b. 13 July 1959)	Jablonec, Czechoslovakia	19 Feb. 1977

PENTATHLON			NAME AND COUNTRY	PLACE	DATE
PENTATHLON	4,991 points		Irina Belova (Russia; b. 27 Mar. 1968) (60 m hurdles 8.22 sec.; High jump 1.93 m; Shot 13.25 m; Long jump 6.67 m; 800 m 2:10.26)	Berlin, Germany	14–15 Feb. 1992

Mass relay records   The record for 100 miles by 100 runners from one club is 7 hrs. 53 min. 52.1 sec., by the Baltimore Road Runners Club, Towson, MD on 17 May 1981. The women's record is 10 hrs. 47 min. 9.3 sec. on 3 Apr. 1977, by the San Francisco Dolphins Southend Running Club. The record for 100 × 100 m is 19 min. 14.19 sec., by a team from Antwerp at Merksem, Belgium on 23 Sep. 1989.

The longest relay ever run was 10,806 miles by 23 runners of the Melbourne Fire Brigade, around Australia on Highway No. 1, in 50 days 43 min., 6 Aug.–25 Sep. 1991. The most participants is 5,060—10 teams of 506—for the Mars Torch Appeal at the National Indoor Arena, Birmingham, Great Britain on 7 Oct. 1991. The greatest distance covered in 24 hrs. by a team of ten is 280.232 miles, by Oxford Striders RC at East London, South Africa on 5–6 Oct. 1990.

United States   The greatest distance covered by an American team of ten runners in 24 hrs. is 271.974 miles, by students of Marcus High School in Texas, 17–18 May 1991.

WORLD RECORD. Carl Lewis (USA) a stride away from winning the 1991 world Championships 100 m final in a world record time of 9.86 seconds. (Photo: Allsport/G. Vandystadt)

US NATIONAL RECORDS *MEN*

RUNNING	hr.min.:sec.	NAME AND COUNTRY	PLACE	DATE
100 meters	9.86	Frederick Carleton "Carl" Lewis (b. 1 July 1961)	Tokyo, Japan	25 Aug. 1991
200 meters	19.75	Carl Lewis	Indianapolis, IN	19 June 1983
	19.75	Joseph Nathaniel "Joe" DeLoach (b. 5 June 1967)	Seoul, South Korea	28 Sep. 1988
400 meters	43.29	Harry Lee "Butch" Reynolds, Jr. (b. 8 Aug. 1964)	Zürich, Switzerland	17 Aug. 1988
800 meters	1:42.60	John Lee "Johnny" Gray (b. 19 June 1960)	Koblenz, Germany	28 Aug. 1985
1,000 meters	2:13.9	Richard Charles "Rick" Wohlhuter (b. 23 Dec. 1948)	Oslo, Norway	30 July 1974
1,500 meters	3:29.77	Sydney Maree (b. 9 Sep. 1956)	Cologne, Germany	25 Aug. 1985
1 mile	3:47.69	Steven Michael Scott (b. 5 May 1957)	Oslo, Norway	7 July 1982
2,000 meters	4:52.44	James C. "Jim" Spivey (b. 7 Mar. 1960)	Lausanne, Switzerland	15 Sep. 1987
3,000 meters	7:35.37	Sydney Maree *	London, Great Britain	17 July 1982
	7:35.84	Douglas Floyd Padilla (b. 4 Oct. 1956)	Oslo, Norway	9 July 1983
5,000 meters	13:01.15	Sydney Maree	Oslo, Norway	27 July 1985
10,000 meters	27:20.56	Marcus James Nenow (b. 16 Nov. 1957)	Brussels, Belgium	5 Sep. 1986
15,000 meters	43:39.8	William Henry "Bill" Rodgers (b. 23 Dec. 1947)	Boston, MA	9 Aug. 1977
20,000 meters	58:25.0	Bill Rodgers	Boston, MA	9 Aug. 1977
25,000 meters	1 hr. 14:11.8	Bill Rodgers	Saratoga, NY	21 Feb. 1979
30,000 meters	1 hr. 31:49	Bill Rodgers	Saratoga, NY	21 Feb. 1979
1 hour	12 miles 135 yds.	Bill Rodgers	Boston, MA	9 Aug. 1977
Marathon	2 hrs. 08:52	Alberto Baudy Salazar (b. 7 Aug. 1958)	Boston, MA	19 Apr. 1982

* Prior to obtaining US citizenship

HURDLING				
110 meters	12.92	Roger Kingdom (b. 26 Aug. 1962)	Zürich, Switzerland	16 Aug. 1989
400 meters	47.02	Edwin Corley Moses (b. 31 Aug. 1955)	Koblenz, Germany	31 Aug. 1983
3,000 meter steeplechase	8:09.17	Henry Dinwoodey Marsh (b. 15 Mar. 1954)	Koblenz, Germany	28 Aug. 1985

RELAYS

4 × 100 meters	37.50	National Team	Tokyo, Japan	1 Sep. 1991
		(Andre Cason, Leroy Burrell, Dennis Mitchell, Carl Lewis)		
4 × 200 meters	1:19.11	Santa Monica Track Club	Koblenz, Germany	23 Aug. 1989
		(Daniel Joe Everett, Leroy Russell Burrell, Floyd Heard, Carl Lewis)		
4 × 400 meters	2:56.16*	National Team	Mexico City, Mexico	20 Oct. 1968
		(Vincent Edward Matthews, Ronald John Freeman, George Lawrence "Larry" James, Lee Edward Evans)		
4 × 400 meters	2:56.16	National Team	Seoul, South Korea	1 Oct. 1988
		(Daniel Everett, Steven Earl Lewis, Kevin Bernard Robinzine, Harry Lee "Butch" Reynolds)		
4 × 800 meters	7:06.5	Santa Monica Track Club	Walnut, CA	26 Apr. 1986
		(James Robinson, David Mack, Earl Jones, Johnny Gray)		
4 × 1,500 meters	14:46.3	National Team	Bourges, France	24 June 1969

* Set at high altitude

FIELD EVENTS

	ft.	in.			
High jump	7	10½	Charles Austin	Zürich, Switzerland	7 Aug. 1991
Pole vault	19	6½	Daniel Joe Dial (b. 26 Oct. 1962)	Norman, OK	18 June 1987
Long jump	29	4½*	Mike Powell	Tokyo, Japan	30 Aug. 1991
Triple jump	58	11½	William Augustus "Willie" Banks (b. 11 Mar. 1956)	Indianapolis, IN	16 June 1985
Shot	75	10¼	Earl Randolph "Randy" Barnes (b. 16 June 1966)	Westwood, LA	20 May 1990
Discus	237	4**	Walter "Ben" Plunkett (b. 13 Apr. 1953)	Stockholm, Sweden	7 July 1981
Hammer	268	8†	Judson Campbell Logan (b. 19 July 1959)	University Park, PA.	22 Apr. 1988
Javelin	280	1†	Thomas Alan Petranoff (b. 8 Apr. 1958)	Helsinki, Finland	7 July 1986

* Set at high altitude; the low altitude best: 28 ft. 10¼ in., Carl Lewis at Indianapolis, IN on 19 June 1983.

** Ratified despite the fact that it was achieved after a positive drug test.

† Petranoff has also thrown 292 ft. 6 in. at Potchefstroom, South Africa on 1 Mar. 1991.

DECATHLON

8,812 points	Dan O'Brien	Tokyo, Japan	29–30 Aug. 1991

(100 m, 10.41 sec.; Long jump, 25 ft. 11 in.; Shot put, 53 ft. 3½ in.; High jump, 6 ft. 3¾ in.; 400 m, 46.53 sec.; 110 m hurdles, 13.94 sec.; Discus, 154 ft. 10 in.; Pole vault, 17 ft. ¾ in.; Javelin, 199 ft. 0 in.; 1,500 m, 4:37.50).

US NATIONAL RECORDS *WOMEN*

RUNNING	hr.:min.:sec.	NAME AND COUNTRY	PLACE	DATE
100 meters	10.49	Delorez Florence Griffith Joyner (b. 21 Dec. 1959)	Indianapolis, IN	16 July 1988
200 meters	21.34	Florence Griffith Joyner	Seoul, South Korea	29 Sep. 1988
400 meters	48.83	Valerie Ann Brisco (b. 6 July 1960)	Los Angeles, CA	6 Aug. 1984
800 meters	1:56.90	Mary Thereza Slaney (nee Decker; b. 4 Aug. 1958)	Berne, Switzerland	16 Aug. 1985
1,000 meters	2:34.8	Mary Slaney	Eugene, OR	4 July 1985
1,500 meters	3:57.12	Mary Slaney	Stockholm, Sweden	26 July 1983
1 mile	4:16.71	Mary Slaney	Zürich, Switzerland	21 Aug. 1985
2,000 meters	5:32.7	Mary Slaney	Eugene, OR	3 Aug. 1984
3,000 meters	8:25.83	Mary Slaney	Rome, Italy	7 Sep. 1985
5,000 meters	15:00.00	Patricia Susan "Patti-Sue" Plumer (b. 27 Apr. 1962)	Stockholm, Sweden	3 July 1989
10,000 meters	31:28.92	Francis Larrieu-Smith (b. 23 Nov. 1952)	Austin, TX	4 Apr. 1991
Marathon	2 hrs. 21:21	Joan Samuelson (nee Benoit; b. 16 May 1957)	Chicago, IL	20 Oct. 1985

HURDLING				
100 meters	12.48	Yolanda Gail Devers (now Roberts; b. 19 Nov. 1966)	Berlin, Germany	10 Sep. 1991
400 meters	53.37	Sandra Marie Farmer-Patrick (b. 18 Aug. 1962)	New York, NY	22 July 1989

RELAYS				
4 × 100 meters	41.55	National Team (Alice Regina Brown, Diane Williams, Florence Griffith, Pam Marshall)	Berlin, Germany	21 Aug. 1987
4 × 200 meters	1:32.57	Louisiana State University (Tananjalyn Stanley, Sylvia Brydson, Esther Jones, Dawn Sowell)	Des Moines, IA	28 Apr. 1989
4 × 400 meters	3:15.51	National Team (Denean Howard, Diane Lynn Dixon, Valerie Brisco, Florence Griffith Joyner)	Seoul, South Korea	1 Oct. 1988
4 × 800 meters	8:17.09	Athletics West (Susan Addison, Lee Arbogast, Mary Decker, Chris Mullen)	Walnut, CA	24 Apr. 1983

FIELD EVENTS

	ft.	in.			
High jump	6	8¼	Dorothy Louise Ritter (b. 18 Feb. 1958)	Austin, TX	8 July 1988
	6	8½	Louise Ritter	Seoul, South Korea	30 Sep. 1988
Long jump	24	5½	Jacqueline Joyner-Kersee	Indianapolis, IN	13 Aug. 1987
Triple jump	46	8¼	Sheila Hudson (b. 30 June 1967)	New Orleans, LA	21 June 1992
Shot	66	2½	Ramona Lu Pagel (nee Ebert; b. 10 Nov. 1961)	San Diego, CA	25 June 1988
Discus	216	10½	Carol Therese Cady (b. 6 June 1962)	San Jose, CA	31 May 1986
Javelin	227	5½	Kathryn Joan "Kate" Schmidt (b. 29 Dec. 1963)	Fürth, Germany	11 Sep. 1977

HEPTATHLON

7,291 points	Jacqueline Joyner-Kersee	Seoul, South Korea	23–24 Sep. 1988

(100 m hurdles 12.69 sec.; High jump 6 ft. 1¼ in.; Shot 51 ft. 10 in.; 200 m 22.56 sec.; Long jump 23 ft. 10 in.; Javelin 149 ft. 9 in.; 800 m 2 min. 08.51 sec.)

HIGH JUMP. Heike Henkel (Germany), the 1991 high jump world champion, continued her good form in the indoor season. This culminated in setting the world indoor best (2.07 m) at Karlsruhe, Germany on 9 Feb. 1992. (Photo: Allsport/Mike Powell)

RUNNING CHAMPIONS. Andre Cason (center) set the record for the fastest indoor 60 m at Madrid on 12 Feb. 1992. He broke the record of Leroy Burrell (right), set a year earlier at the same venue. (Photo: Allsport USA/Tony Duffy)

Greatest mileage Douglas Alistair Gordon Pirie (Great Britain; 1931–91), who set five world records in the 1950s, estimated that he had run a total distance of 216,000 miles in 40 years up to 1981.

Dr. Ron Hill (Great Britain; b. 21 Sep. 1938), has not missed a day's training since 20 Dec. 1964. His meticulously compiled training log shows a total of 124,984 miles from 3 Sep. 1956 to 12 May 1992. He has finished 114 marathons, all in less than 2:52, and has raced in 53 nations.

Joggling *3 objects* Owen Morse (USA), 100 m in 11.68 sec., 1989, and 400 m in 57.32 sec., 1990. Albert Lucas (USA), 110 m hurdles in 20.36 sec., and 400 m hurdles in 1 min. 10.37 sec., 1989. Owen Morse, Albert Lucas, Tuey Wilson and John Wee (all USA), 1 mile relay in 3 min. 57.38 sec., 1990. Kirk Swenson (USA), 1 mile in 4 min. 43 sec., 1986, and 5,000 m (3.1 miles) in 16 min. 55 sec., 1986. Ashrita Furman (USA), marathon—26 miles 385 yds.—in 3 hrs. 22 min. 32.5 sec., 1988, and 50 miles in 8 hrs. 52 min. 7 sec., 1989.

5 objects Owen Morse (USA), 100 m in 13.8 sec., 1988. Bill Gillen (USA), 1 mile in 7 min. 41.01 sec., 1989, and 3.1 miles in 28 min. 11 sec., 1989. (See also Endurance and Endeavor, juggling.)

MARATHON

The marathon is run over a distance of 26 miles 385 yds. This distance was used for the race at the 1908 Olympic Games, run in Great Britain from Windsor to the White City Stadium, London, and became standard from 1924 on. The marathon (of 40 km) was introduced to the 1896 Olympic Games to commemorate the legendary run of Pheidippides (or Philippides) from the battlefield of Marathon to Athens in 490 B.C. The 1896 Olympic marathon was preceded by trial races that year. The first Boston Marathon, the world's longest-lasting major marathon, was held on 19 Apr. 1897 at 24 miles 1,232 yds., and the first national marathon championship was that of Norway in 1897.

The first championship marathon for women was organized by the Road Runners Club of America on 27 Sep. 1970.

Fastest There are as yet no official records for the marathon, and it should be noted that courses may vary in severity. The following are the best times recorded, all on courses whose distance has been verified:

Men: 2 hrs. 6 min. 50 sec., by Belayneh Dinsamo (Ethiopia; b. 28 June 1965) at Rotterdam, Netherlands on 17 Apr. 1988.

Women: 2 hrs. 21 min. 6 sec., by Ingrid Kristiansen (nee Christensen [Norway]; b. 21 Mar. 1956) at London, Great Britain on 21 Apr. 1985.

Boston Marathon First run by 15 men on 19 Apr. 1897 over a distance of 24 miles 1,232 yards, the Boston Marathon is the world's oldest annual race. The full marathon distance was first run in 1927. It is run every year from Hopkinton to Boston on or about April 19, Patriot's Day, which honors the famed ride of Paul Revere through Boston.

The most wins is seven, by Clarence DeMar (1888–1958), in 1911, 1922–24, 1927–28 and 1930.

Kathy Switzer (USA) contested the race in 1967, although the race director tried to prevent her from running, but pioneering efforts helped force the acceptance of women runners, and they were admitted officially for the first time in 1972. Rosa Mota (Portugal; b. 29 June 1958) has a record three wins, 1987–88 and 1990, in the women's competition.

The course record for men is 2 hrs. 7 min. 51 sec. by Rob de Castella (Australia) in 1986. The women's record is 2 hrs. 22 min. 43 sec., by Joan Benoit (USA; now Samuelson) in 1983.

John A. Kelley (USA; b. 6 Sep. 1907) finished the Boston Marathon 61 times through 1992, winning twice, in 1933 and 1945.

New York City Marathon   The race was run in Central Park each year from 1970 to 1976, when, to celebrate the US Bicentennial, the course was changed to a route through all five boroughs of the city. Since that year, when there were 2,090 runners, the race has become one of the world's great sporting occasions, and in 1991 there were a record 25,797 finishers.

William Henry "Bill" Rodgers (USA; b. 23 Dec. 1947) had a record four wins—1976–79; and Grete Waitz (nee Andersen [Norway]; b. 1 Oct. 1953) was the women's winner nine times—1978–80, 1982–86 and 1988.

The course record for men is 2 hrs. 8 min. 1 sec., by Juma Ikangaa (Tanzania; b. 19 July 1957), and for women it is 2 hrs. 25 min. 30 sec., by Ingrid Kristiansen (Norway; b. 21 Mar. 1956) in 1990. On a course subsequently remeasured as about 170 yds. short, Grete Waitz was the 1981 women's winner in 2 hrs. 25 min. 29 sec.

Greatest mileage   The greatest competitive distance run in a year is 5,502 miles, by Malcolm Campbell (Great Britain; b. 17 Nov. 1934) in 1985.

Pancake race record   Dominic M. Cuzzacrea (USA; b. 8 June 1960) of Lockport, NY ran the Buffalo, New York Nissan Marathon (26.2 miles) while flipping a pancake in a time of 3 hrs. 6 min. and 22 sec. on 6 May 1990.

Most competitors   The record number of confirmed finishers in a marathon is 25,797 for 26,900 starters in the New York City Marathon on 3 Nov. 1991. A record 105 men ran under 2 hrs. 20 min., and 46 ran under 2 hrs. 15 min. in the World Cup Marathon at London, Great Britain on 21 Apr. 1991, and a record six men ran under 2 hrs. 10 min. at Fukuoka, Japan on 4 Dec. 1983 and at London on 23 Apr. 1989. A record nine women ran under 2 hrs. 30 min. in the first Olympic marathon for women at Los Angeles on 5 Aug. 1984.

Most run by an individual   Thian K. "Sy" Mah (Canada; 1926–88) ran 524 marathons of 26 miles 385 yds. or longer from 1967 to his death in 1988. He paced himself to take 3½ hrs. for each run.

Three in three days   The fastest combined time for three marathons in three days is 8 hrs. 22 min. 31 sec. by Raymond Hubbard (Belfast, Northern Ireland: 2 hrs. 45 min. 55 sec.; London, Great Britain: 2 hrs. 48 min. 45 sec.; and Boston: 2 hrs. 47 min. 51 sec.) on 16–18 Apr. 1988.

Oldest finishers   The oldest man to complete a marathon was Dimitrion Yordanidis (Greece), age 98, in Athens, Greece on 10 Oct. 1976. He finished in 7 hrs. 33 min. Thelma Pitt-Turner (New Zealand) set the women's age record in August 1985, completing the Hastings, New Zealand Marathon in 7 hrs. 58 min. at the age of 82.

Highest altitude   The highest start for a marathon is the biennially held Everest Marathon, first run on 27 Nov. 1987. It begins at Gorak Shep at 17,100 ft. and ends at Namche Bazar, 11,300 ft. The fastest times to complete this race are *(men)* 3 hrs. 59 min. 4 sec., by Jack Maitland; *(women)* 5 hrs. 44 min. 32 sec., by Dawn Kenwright, both in 1989.

One thousand hours   Ron Grant (Australia) ran 1.86 miles within an hour, every hour, for 1,000 consecutive hours at New Farm Park, Brisbane, Queensland, Australia from 6 Feb.–20 Mar. 1991.

WALKING

Most Olympic medals   Walking races have been included in the Olympic events since 1906. The only walker to win three gold medals has been Ugo Frigerio (Italy; 1901–68) with the 3,000 m in 1920, and 10,000 m in 1920 and 1924. He also holds the record for most medals, with four (he won the bronze medal at 50,000 m in 1932), a total shared with Vladimir Stepanovich Golubnichiy (USSR; b. 2 June 1936), who won gold medals for the 20,000 m in 1960 and 1968, the silver in 1972 and the bronze in 1964.

Most titles   Four-time Olympian Ronald Owen Laird (b. 31 May 1938) of the New York AC won a total of 65 US national titles from 1958 to 1976, plus four Canadian Championships.

Longest race   The race from Paris to Colmar (until 1980 from Strasbourg to Paris) in France (instituted 1926 in the reverse direction), now about 325 miles, is the world's longest annual race walk.
  The fastest performance is by Robert Pietquin (Belgium; b. 1938), who walked 315 miles in the 1980 race in 60 hrs. 1 min. 10 sec. (after deducting 4 hrs. compulsory stops). This represents an average speed of 5.25 mph. Roger Quémener (France) has won a record seven times, 1979, 1983, 1985–89. The first woman to complete the race was Annie van der Meer (Netherlands; b. 24 Feb. 1947), who was tenth in 1983 in 82 hrs. 10 min.

Twenty-four hours   The greatest distance walked in 24 hrs. is 140 miles 1,229 yd, by Paul Forthomme (Belgium) on a road course at Woluwe, Belgium on 13–14 Oct. 1984. The best by a woman is 125.7 miles, by Annie van der Meer at Rouen, France on 30 Apr.–1 May 1984 over a 1.185 km lap road course.

TRACK WALKING *WORLD RECORDS*

The International Amateur Athletic Federation recognizes men's records at 20 km, 30 km, 50 km and 2 hours, and women's at 5 km and 10 km.

MEN
RUNNING

	hr: min: sec	NAME AND COUNTRY	PLACE	DATE
10 km	38:02.60	Jozef Pribilinec (Czechoslovakia; b. 6 July 1960)	Banská Bystrica, Czechoslovakia	30 Aug. 1985
20 km	1:18:35.2	Stefan Johansson (Sweden: b. 11 Apr. 1967)	Fana, Norway	18 May 1992
30 km	2:03:56.5	Thierry Toutain (France; b. 14 Feb. 1962)	Héricourt, France	24 Mar. 1991
50 km	3:41:38.4	Raul Gonzalez (Mexico; b. 29 Feb. 1952)	Fana, Norway	25 May 1979
1 hour	15,447 m	Josef Pribilinec (Czechoslovakia)	Hildesheim, Germany	6 Sep. 1986
2 hours	29,090 m	Thierry Toutain (France)	Héricourt, France	24 Mar. 1991

WOMEN

		NAME AND COUNTRY	PLACE	DATE
3 km	11:51.26	Kerry Ann Saxby (Australia; b. 2 June 1961)	Melbourne, Australia	7 Feb. 1991
5 km	20:07.52	Beate Anders (East Germany; b. 4 Feb. 1968)	Rostock, Germany	23 June 1990
10 km	41:56.23	Nadezhda Ryashkina (USSR; b. 22 Jan. 1967)	Seattle, WA	24 July 1990

Backwards running Timothy "Bud" Badyana (USA) ran the fastest backwards marathon in 4 hrs. 15 sec. at Columbus, OH on 10 Nov. 1991. He has also run 10 km backwards in 45 min. 37 sec. at Toledo, OH on 13 July 1991. Donald Davis (USA; b. 10 Feb. 1960) ran 1 mile backwards in 6 min. 7.1 sec. at the University of Hawaii on 21 Feb. 1983. Ferdie Ato Adoboe (Ghana) ran 100 yds. backwards in 12.7 sec. at Smith College, Northampton, MA on 25 July 1991.

Walking on hands The distance record for walking on hands is 870 miles, by Johann Hurlinger of Austria, who in 55 daily 10 hr. stints averaged 1.58 mph from Vienna, Austria to Paris, France in 1900. The four-man relay team of David Lutterman, Brendan Price, Philip Savage and Danny Scannell covered 1 mile in 24 min. 48 sec. on 15 Mar. 1987 at Knoxville, TN.

Backwards walking The greatest-ever distance was 8,000 miles, by Plennie L. Wingo, who walked backwards from Santa Monica, CA to Istanbul, Turkey from 15 Apr. 1931 to 24 Oct. 1932. The longest distance recorded for walking backwards in 24 hrs. is 95.40 miles, by Anthony Thornton (USA) in Minneapolis, MN on 31 Dec. 1988–1 Jan. 1989.

ROAD WALKING

It should be noted that the severity of road race courses and the accuracy of their measurement may vary, sometimes making comparisons of times unreliable.

WORLD BESTS
MEN
20 km: 1 hr. 18 min. 13 sec., Pavol Blazek (Czechoslovakia; b. 9 Jul 1958) at Hildesheim, Germany on 16 Sep. 1990.
30 km: 2 hrs. 2 min. 41 sec., Andrey Perlov (USSR; b. 12 Dec. 1961) at Sochi on 19 Feb. 1989.
50 km: 3 hrs. 37 min. 41 sec., Andrey Perlov (USSR) at Leningrad, USSR on 5 Aug. 1989.

WOMEN
10 km: 41 min. 30 sec., Kerry Ann Saxby (Australia; b. 2 June 1961) at Canberra, Australia on 27 Aug. 1988.
20 km: 1 hr. 29 min. 40 sec., Kerry Saxby at Värnamo, Sweden on 13 May 1988.
50 km: 4 hrs. 50 min. 51 sec., Sandra Brown (Great Britain; b. 1 Apr. 1949) at Bassildon, Great Britain on 13 July 1991.

TRAMPOLINING

Trampolines were used in show business at least as early as "The Walloons" of the period 1910–12. The sport of trampolining (from the Spanish word *trampolin*, a springboard) dates from 1936, when the prototype "T" model trampoline was developed by George Nissen (USA).

World Championships   World Championships were instituted in 1964. A record five titles were won by Judy Wills (USA; b. 1948) in the women's event, 1964–68. Five men have won two titles.

United States Championships   The American Trampoline & Tumbling Association staged the first national individual trampoline championships in 1947. The inaugural event was open only to men; a women's event was introduced in 1961.

Most titles   Stuart Ransom has won a record 12 national titles: six, individual (1975–76, 1978–80, 1982); three, synchronized (1975, 1979–80); and three, double mini-tramp (1979–80, 1982). Leigh Hennessy has won a record 10 women's titles: one, individual (1978); eight, synchronized (1972–73, 1976–78, 1980–82); and one, double mini-tramp (1978).

Somersaults   Christopher Gibson performed 3,025 consecutive somersaults at Shipley Park, Derbyshire, Great Britain on 17 Nov. 1989.

The most complete somersaults in one minute is 75, by Richard Cobbing of Lightwater, Great Britain, at British Broadcasting Corporation Television Centre, London, Great Britain on 8 Nov. 1989. The most baranis in a minute is 78, by Zoe Finn of Chatham, Great Britain at British Broadcasting Corporation Television Centre, London, Great Britain on 25 Jan. 1988.

TRIATHLON

The triathlon combines long-distance swimming, cycling and running. Distances for each of the phases can vary, but for the best-established event, the Hawaii Ironman (instituted 1978), competitors first swim 2.4 miles, then cycle 112 miles, and finally run a full marathon of 26 miles 385 yards. The fastest time recorded over the Ironman distances is 8 hrs. 1 min. 32 sec., by Dave Scott at Lake Biwa, Japan on 20 July 1989.

World Championships   After earlier abortive efforts, a world governing body, *L'Union Internationale de Triathlon* (UIT), was founded at Avignon, France on 1 Apr. 1989, staging the first official World Championships in August 1989.

A World Championship race has been held annually in Nice, France from 1982; the distances are 3,200 m, 120 km and 32 km respectively, with the swim increased to 4,000 m from 1988. Mark Allen (USA) has won nine times, 1982–86, 1989–92. Paula Newby-Fraser (Zimbabwe) has a record four women's wins, 1989–92. The fastest times are: *(men)* 5 hrs. 46 min. 10 sec. in 1988, by Mark Allen; *(women)* 6 hrs. 27 min. 6 sec. in 1988, by Erin Baker (New Zealand).

Hawaii Ironman   This is the first, and best known, of the triathlons. The first race, held on 18 Feb. 1978, was contested by 15 athletes. The Ironman grew rapidly in popularity, and 1,000 athletes entered the 1984 race. Dave Scott (USA) has won the Ironman a record six times—1980, 1982–84, 1986–87. Mark Allen (USA) holds the record for fastest time at 8 hrs. 9 min. 16 sec. on 15 Oct. 1989. The women's event has been won a record three times by Paula Newby-Fraser (Zimbabwe), in 1986, 1988–89. Newby-Fraser holds the course record for women at 9 hrs. 0 min. 56 sec. on 15 Oct. 1989.

MOST IRONMAN TITLES. Seen here during her 1991 success, Paula Newby-Fraser (Zimbabwe) has won the women's event of the famous Hawaiian Ironman a record four times. (Photo: Allsport USA/Gary Newkirk)

TUG OF WAR

Origins   Though ancient China and Egypt have been suggested as the originators of the sport, it is known that Neolithic flint miners in Great Britain practiced "rope-pulling." The first rules were those framed by the New York AC in 1879. Tug of War was an Olympic sport from 1900 until 1920. World Championships have been held annually, 1975–86, and biennially since, with a women's event introduced in 1986.

Most titles   The most successful team at the World Championships has been England, which has won 15 of the 25 titles in all categories, 1975–88. Sweden has won the 520 kg twice and the 560 kg category three times at the Womens' World Championships (held bienially since 1986).

The Wood Treatment team (formerly the Bosley Farmers) of Cheshire, Great Britain won 20 consecutive AAA Catchweight Championships 1959–78, two world titles (1975–76) and ten European titles at 720 kg Hilary Brown (b. 13 Apr. 1934) was on every team. Trevor Brian Thomas (Great Britain; b. 1943) of British Aircraft Corporation Club is the only holder of three winners' medals in the European Open club competitions and added a world gold medal in 1988.

Longest tug of war   The longest tug of war (in distance) is the 1.616 mile Supertug across Little Traverse Bay, Lake Michigan. It has been contested annually since 1980 between two teams of 20 from Bay View Inn and Harbor Inn.

Longest pulls   *Duration*   The longest recorded pull (prior to the introduction of AAA rules) is one of 2 hrs. 41 min. when "H" Company beat "E" Company of the 2nd Battalion of the Sherwood Foresters (Derbyshire Regiment) at Jubbulpore, India on 12 Aug. 1889. The longest recorded pull under AAA rules (in which lying on the ground or entrenching the feet is not permitted) is one of 24 min. 45 sec. for the first pull between the Republic of Ireland and England during the world championships (640 kg class) at Malmö, Sweden on 18 Sep. 1988. The record time for "The Pull" (instituted 1898), across the Black River, between freshman and sophomore teams at Hope College, Holland, MI, is 3 hrs. 51 min. on 23 Sep. 1977, but the method of bracing the feet precludes this replacing the preceding records.

VOLLEYBALL

Origins   The game was invented as *mintonette* in 1895 by William G. Morgan at the YMCA gymnasium at Holyoke, MA. The *Fédération Internationale de Volleyball* (FIVB) was formed in Paris, France in April 1947 and is now based in Switzerland.

United States   The United States Volleyball Association was founded in 1922 and remains the governing body for the sport in this country. The United States National Championships were inaugurated in 1928 for men and in 1949 for women.

Most Olympic titles   The sport was introduced to the Olympic Games for both men and women in 1964. The USSR won a record three men's (1964, 1968 and 1980) and four women's (1968, 1972, 1980 and 1988) titles. The only player to win four medals is Inna Valeryevna Ryskal (USSR; b. 15 June 1944), who won women's silver medals in 1964 and 1976 and golds in 1968 and 1972. The record for men is held by Yuriy Mikhailovich Poyarkov (USSR; b. 10 Feb. 1937), who won gold medals in 1964 and 1968 and a bronze in 1972; and by Katsutoshi Nekoda (Japan; b. 1 Feb. 1944), who won gold in 1972, silver in 1968 and bronze in 1964.

United States   The USA won the men's championship in 1984 and 1988. Three men played on each of the winning teams and on the only US teams to win the World Cup (1985) and World Championships (1986): Craig Buck (b. 24 Aug. 1958), Charles "Karch" Kiraly (b. 3 Nov. 1960), and Stephen Timmons (b. 29 Nov. 1958). David Saunders (b. 19 Oct. 1960) was a reserve on the 1984 team and played on those of 1986 and 1988. "Karch" Kiraly is the only player to win an Olympic gold medal and the World Championship of Beach Volleyball.

Most world titles in volleyball   World Championships were instituted in 1949 for men and in 1952 for women. The USSR won six men's titles (1949, 1952, 1960, 1962, 1978 and 1982) and five women's (1952, 1956, 1960, 1970 and 1990).

BEACH VOLLEYBALL

Origins   In professional beach volleyball, teams play two-a-side on the same size court as that used for indoor volleyball. The sport originated in California in the late 1940s and grew rapidly in the 1960s. The first world championships were staged in 1976. The Association of Volleyball Professionals (AVP) was formed in 1981 and the AVP/Miller Lite tour started that same year.

World Championships   Sinjin Smith has won a record 125 tour events, 1977–91. Sinjin Smith and Randy Stoklos (USA) have won a record five titles, 1987–88, 1990–92. In 1989 there were no world championships, but a world series was held, and was won by Karch Kiraly and Steve Timmons (USA).

Highest earnings   Randy Stoklos has the highest career earnings, reaching $1 million in February 1992.

WATER POLO

Water polo was developed in England as "water soccer" in 1869 and first included in the Olympic Games in Paris, France in 1900.

United States   Professor John Robinson, an Englishman hired as aquatics director of the Boston Athletic Association in 1888, is credited with introducing water polo to the United States. The first official game took place on 28 Jan. 1890 in Providence, RI, with the Syndenham Swimming Club of Providence defeating Boston AA, 2–1. The Amateur Athletic Association served as the sport's governing body from 1897 to 1978; since 1978 U.S. Water Polo, Inc. has run the sport in the United States.

Most Olympic titles   Hungary has won the Olympic tournament most often, with six wins, in 1932, 1936, 1952, 1956, 1964 and 1976.
   Five players share the record of three gold medals: Britons George Wilkinson (1879–1946), in 1900, 1908, 1912; Paulo "Paul" Radmilovic (1886–1968), and Charles Sidney Smith (1879–1951), in 1908, 1912, 1920; and Hungarians Desző Gyarmati (b. 23 Oct. 1927) and György Kárpáti (b. 23 June 1935), in 1952, 1956, and 1964. Paul Radmilovic also won a gold medal for 4 × 200 m freestyle swimming in 1908.

United States   US teams took all the medals in 1904, but there were no foreign contestants. Since then their best result has been silver in 1984.

World Championships   This competition was first held at the World Swimming Championships in 1973. The most wins is two, by the USSR, 1975 and 1982, and Yugoslavia, 1986 and 1991. A women's competition was introduced in 1986, when it was won by Australia. The Netherlands won the second women's world title in 1991.

Most goals   The greatest number of goals scored by an individual in an international match is 13, by Debbie Handley for Australia (16) *v.* Canada (10) at the World Championship in Guayaquil, Ecuador in 1982.

Most international appearances   The greatest number of international appearances is 412, by Aleksey Stepanovich Barkalov (USSR; b. 18 Feb. 1946), 1965–80.

US National Championships   In this competition, inaugurated in 1891, the New York Athletic Club has won a record 25 men's championships: 1892–96, 1903–04, 1906–08, 1922, 1929–31, 1933–35, 1937–39, 1954, 1956,

1960–61, 1971. The women's championship was first held in 1926; the Industry Hills Athletic Club (California) has won a record five titles: 1980–81, 1983–85.

WATERSKIING

The origins of waterskiing derive from walking on planks and aquaplaning. A 19th-century treatise on sorcerers refers to Eliseo of Tarentum, who, in the 14th century, "walks and dances" on the water. The first report of aquaplaning was on America's Pacific Coast in the early 1900s. At Scarborough, Great Britain on 15 July 1914, a single plank-gliding contest was won by H. Storry.

The present-day sport of waterskiing was pioneered by Ralph W. Samuelson (1904–77) on Lake Pepin, MN, on two curved pine boards in the summer of 1922, although claims have been made for the birth of the sport on Lake Annecy (Haute-Savoie), France at about the same time. The first world organization, the *Union Internationale de Ski Nautique*, was formed in Geneva on 27 July 1946.

The American Water Ski Association was founded in 1939 and held the first national championships that year.

Most titles   World Overall Championships (instituted 1949) have been won four times by Sammy Duvall (USA), in 1981, 1983, 1985 and 1987, and three times by two women, Willa McGuire (nee Worthington; USA), in 1949–50 and 1955, and Elizabeth "Liz" Allan-Shetter (USA), in 1965, 1969 and 1975. Liz Allan-Shetter has won a record eight individual championship events and is the only person to win all four titles—slalom, jumping, tricks and overall in one year, at Copenhagen, Denmark in 1969. The USA has won the team championship on 17 successive occasions, 1957–89.

United States   US national championships were first held at Marine Stadium, Jones Beach State Park, Long Island, NY on 22 July 1939. The most overall titles is nine, by Carl Roberge, 1980–83, 1985–88, and 1990. The women's record is eight titles, by Willa Worthington McGuire, 1946–51 and 1954–55, and by Liz Allan-Shetter, 1968–75.

Fastest speed   The fastest waterskiing speed recorded is 143.08 mph, by Christopher Michael Massey (Australia) on the Hawkesbury River, Windsor, New South Wales, Australia on 6 Mar. 1983. His drag boat driver was Stanley Charles Sainty. Donna Patterson Brice (b. 1953) set a women's record of 111.11 mph at Long Beach, CA on 21 Aug. 1977.

Longest run   The greatest distance traveled is 1,321.16 miles, by Steve Fontaine (USA) on 24–26 Oct. 1988 at Jupiter Hills, FL.

Barefoot   The first person to waterski barefoot is reported to be Dick Pope, Jr. at Lake Eloise, FL on 6 Mar. 1947. The barefoot duration record is 2 hrs. 42 min. 39 sec., by Billy Nichols (USA; b. 1964) on Lake Weir, FL on 19 Nov. 1978. The backward barefoot record is 1 hr. 27 min. 3.96 sec., by Steve Fontaine at Jupiter, FL, on 31 Aug. 1989.

WATERSKIING RECORDS

SLALOM
MEN: 3.5 buoys on a 10.25 m line, Andrew Mapple (Great Britain; b. 3 Nov. 1958), at Miami, FL on 6 Oct. 1991.
WOMEN: 1 buoy on a 10.75 m line, Susi Graham (Canada) and Deena Mapple (nee Brush; USA) at West Palm Beach, FL on 13 Oct. 1990.

TRICKS
MEN: 11,030 points, Tory Baggiano (USA) at Destin, FL on 15 Sep. 1990.
WOMEN: 8,530 points, Tawn Larsen (USA) at Sherman, TX on 20 July 1991.

JUMPING
MEN: 207 ft., Jaret Llewellyn (USA) at Pine Mountain, GA on 23 May 1992.
WOMEN: 156 ft., Deena Mapple (nee Brush; USA) at Charlotte, NC on 9 July 1988.

WORLD RECORD. Two-time world slalom champion Andy Mapple (Great Britain) is the current holder of the slalom record with 3.5 buoys on a 10.25 m line, set on 6 Oct. 1991. His wife, Deena, is also a top waterskiier, having won six world titles (two overall, four jumping). She also holds world records for jumping and slalom. (Photo: Allsport/Oli Tennant)

The official barefoot speed record is 135.74 mph, by Scott Michael Pellaton (b. 8 Oct. 1956) over a quarter-mile course at Chandler, AZ, in November 1989. The fastest by a woman is 73.67 mph, by Karen Toms (Australia) on the Hawkesbury River, Windsor, New South Wales on 31 Mar. 1984.

The fastest official speed backward barefoot is 62 mph, by Robert Wing (Australia; b. 13 Aug. 1957) on 3 Apr. 1982.

The barefoot jump record is: *(men)* 76 ft. 5 in., by Mike Seipel (USA) at Jacksonville, FL on 13 Oct. 1990; and *(women)* 54 ft. 1 in., by Debbie Pugh (Australia) in 1990.

Walking on water Wearing 11-ft. water ski shoes, called Skijaks, and using a twin-bladed paddle, David Kiner walked 155 miles on the Hudson River from Albany, NY to Battery Park, New York City. His walk took him 57 hrs., from 22–27 June 1987.

Rémy Bricka of Paris, France "walked" across the Atlantic Ocean on waterskis 13 ft. 9 in. long in 1988. Leaving Tenerife, Canary Islands on 2 Apr. 1988, he covered 3,502 miles, arriving at Trinidad on 31 May 1988.

Most skiers towed by one boat A record 100 water-skiers were towed on double skis over a nautical mile by the cruiser *Reef Cat* at Cairns, Queensland, Australia on 18 Oct. 1986. This feat, organized by the Cairns and District Powerboat and Ski Club, was then replicated by 100 skiers on single skis.

WEIGHTLIFTING

Competitions for lifting weights of stone were held at the ancient Olympic Games. The first championships entitled "world" were staged at the Café Monico, Piccadilly, London, Great Britain on 28 Mar. 1891 and then in Vienna, Austria on 19–20 July 1898, subsequently recognized by the IWF. Prior to that time, weightlifting consisted of professional exhibitions in which some of the advertised poundages were open to doubt.

The *Fédération Internationale Haltérophile et Culturiste*, now the International Weightlifting Federation (IWF), was established in 1905, and its first official championships were held in Tallinn, Estonia, USSR on 29–30 Apr. 1922.

There are two standard lifts: the "snatch" and the "clean and jerk" (or "jerk"). Totals of the two lifts determine competition results. The "press," which was a standard lift, was abolished in 1972.

MEN'S WEIGHTLIFTING RECORDS

BODYWEIGHT CLASS	LIFT	WEIGHT kg	WEIGHT lbs.	NAME AND COUNTRY	PLACE	DATE
52 kg ***114½ lbs.***	Snatch	121	266¾	H. Zhuoqiang (China)	Cardiff, Great Britain	31 May 1992
	Jerk	155.5	342¾	Ivan Ivanov (Bulgaria)	Donaueschingen, Germany	27 Sep. 1991
	Total	272.5	600¾	Ivan Ivanov (Bulgaria)	Athens, Greece	16 Sep. 1989
56 kg ***123¼ lbs.***	Snatch	135	297½	Liu Shoubin (China)	Donaueschingen, Germany	28 Sep. 1991
	Jerk	171	377	Neno Terziiski (Bulgaria)	Ostrava, Czechoslovakia	6 Sep. 1987
	Total	300	661¼	Naim Suleimanov (Bulgaria)	Varna, Bulgaria	11 May 1984
60 kg ***132¼ lbs.***	Snatch	152.5	336	Naim Suleymanoğlü (Turkey)*	Seoul, South Korea	20 Sep. 1988
	Jerk	190	418¾	Naim Suleymanoğlü (Turkey)*	Seoul, South Korea	20 Sep. 1988
	Total	342.5	755	Naim Suleymanoğlü (Turkey)*	Seoul, South Korea	20 Sep. 1988
67.5 kg ***148¾ lbs.***†	Snatch	160	352¾	Israil Militosyan (USSR)	Athens, Greece	18 Sep. 1989
	Jerk	200.5	442	Mikhail Petrov (Bulgaria)	Ostrava, Czechoslovakia	8 Sep. 1987
	Total	355	782½	Mikhail Petrov (Bulgaria)	Seoul, South Korea	5 Dec. 1987
75 kg ***165¼ lbs.***	Snatch	170	374¾	Angel Guenchev (Bulgaria)	Miskolc, Hungary	11 Dec. 1987
	Jerk	215.5	475	Aleksandr Varbanov (Bulgaria)	Seoul, South Korea	5 Dec. 1987
	Total	382.5	843¼	Aleksandr Varbanov (Bulgaria)	Plovdiv, Bulgaria	20 Feb. 1988
82.5 kg ***181¾ lbs.***	Snatch	183	403¼	Asen Zlatev (Bulgaria)	Melbourne, Australia	7 Dec. 1986
	Jerk	225	496	Asen Zlatev (Bulgaria)	Sofia, Bulgaria	12 Nov. 1986
	Total	405	892¾	Yurik Vardanyan (USSR)	Varna, Bulgaria	14 Sep. 1984
90 kg ***198¼ lbs.***	Snatch	195.5	431	Blagoi Blagoyev (Bulgaria)	Varna, Bulgaria	1 May 1983
	Jerk	235	518	Anatoliy Khrapatiy (USSR)	Cardiff, Great Britain	29 Apr. 1988
	Total	422.5	931¼	Viktor Solodov (USSR)	Varna, Bulgaria	15 Sep. 1984

100 kg ***220¼ lbs.***	Snatch	200.5	442	Nicu Vlad (Romania)	Sofia, Bulgaria	14 Nov. 1986
	Jerk	242.5	534½	Aleksandr Popov (USSR)	Tallinn, USSR	5 Mar. 1988
	Total	440	970	Yuriy Zakharevich (USSR)	Odessa, USSR	4 Mar. 1983
110 kg ***242½ lbs.***	Snatch	210	462¾	Yuriy Zakharevich (USSR)	Seoul, South Korea	27 Sep. 1988
	Jerk	250.5	552¼	Yuriy Zakharevich (USSR)	Cardiff, Great Britain	30 Apr. 1988
	Total	455	1,003	Yuriy Zakharevich (USSR)	Seoul, South Korea	27 Sep. 1988
Over 110 kg ***242½ lbs.***	Snatch	216	476	Antonio Krastev (Bulgaria)	Ostrava, Czechoslovakia	13 Sep. 1987
	Jerk	266	586¼	Leonid Taranenko (USSR)	Canberra, Australia	26 Nov. 1988
	Total	475	1,047	Leonid Taranenko (USSR)	Canberra, Australia	26 Nov. 1988

** Formerly Naim Suleimanov or Neum Shalamanov of Bulgaria.*

† Angel Guenchev (Bulgaria) achieved 160 kg snatch, 202.5 kg jerk for a 362.5 kg total at Seoul, South Korea on 21 Sep. 1988 but was subsequently disqualified on a positive drugs test.

WOMEN'S WEIGHTLIFTING RECORDS

BODYWEIGHT CLASS	LIFT	WEIGHT kg	lbs.	NAME AND COUNTRY	PLACE	DATE
44 kg ***97 lbs.***	Snatch	75	165¼	Guan Hong (China)	Varna, Bulgaria	16 May 1992
	Jerk	100	220¼	Guan Hong (China)	Varna, Bulgaria	16 May 1992
	Total	175	385½	Guan Hong (China)	Varna, Bulgaria	16 May 1992
48 kg ***105¾ lbs.***	Snatch	82.5	181¼	Liu Xiuhua (China)	Varna, Bulgaria	17 May 1992
	Jerk	105	231¼	Liu Xiuhua (China)	Varna, Bulgaria	17 May 1992
	Total	187.5	413¼	Liu Xiuhia (China)	Varna, Bulgaria	17 May 1992
52 kg ***114½ lbs.***	Snatch	87.5	192¾	Peng Liping (China)	Varna, Bulgaria	18 May 1992
	Jerk	115	253½	Peng Liping (China)	Varna, Bulgaria	18 May 1992
	Total	202.5	446¼	Peng Liping (China)	Varna, Bulgaria	18 May 1992

(continued)

BODYWEIGHT CLASS	LIFT	WEIGHT kg	lbs.	NAME AND COUNTRY	PLACE	DATE
56 kg *123½ lbs.*	Snatch	92.5	203¾	Sun Caiyan (China)	Varna, Bulgaria	19 May 1992
	Jerk	117.5	259	Sun Caiyan (China)	Varna, Bulgaria	19 May 1992
	Total	210	462¾	Sun Caiyan (China)	Varna, Bulgaria	19 May 1992
60 kg *132½ lbs.*	Snatch	97.5	214¾	Li Hongyun (China)	Varna, Bulgaria	20 May 1992
	Jerk	125	275½	Li Hongyun (China)	Varna, Bulgaria	20 May 1992
	Total	222.5	490¼	Li Hongyun (China)	Varna, Bulgaria	20 May 1992
67.5 kg *148½ lbs.*	Snatch	98	216	Milena Trendafilova (Bulgaria)	Varna, Bulgaria	21 May 1992
	Jerk	130	286½	Gao Lijuan (China)	Varna, Bulgaria	21 May 1992
	Total	222.5	490¼	Gao Lijuan (China)	Varna, Bulgaria	21 May 1992
75 kg *165½ lbs.*	Snatch	107.5	236¾	Hua Ju (China)	Varna, Bulgaria	22 May 1992
	Jerk	137.5	303	Zhang Xiaoli (China)	Donaueschingen, Germany	3 Oct. 1991
	Total	242.5	534½	Zhang Xiaoli (China)	Donaueschingen, Germany	3 Oct. 1991
82.5 kg *181½ lbs.*	Snatch	110	242½	Zhang Xiaoli (China)	Varna, Bulgaria	23 May 1992
	Jerk	142.5	314	Zhang Xiaoli (China)	Varna, Bulgaria	23 May 1992
	Total	252.5	556½	Zhang Xaioli (China)	Varna, Bulgaria	23 May 1992
+82.5 kg	Snatch	115	253½	Li Yajuan (China)	Varna, Bulgaria	24 May 1992
	Jerk	150	330½	Li Yajuan (China)	Varna, Bulgaria	24 May 1992
	Total	265	584	Li Yajuan (China)	Varna, Bulgaria	24 May 1992

Most titles *Olympic*   Norbert Schemansky (USA; b. 30 May 1924) won a record four Olympic medals: gold, middle heavyweight 1952; silver, heavyweight 1948; bronze, heavyweight 1960 and 1964. Three US lifters won two gold medals: John Henry Davis, Jr. (b. 12 Jan. 1921), heavyweight 1948 and 1952; Tommy Tamio Kono (b. 27 June 1930), lightweight 1952, light heavyweight 1956; Charles Thomas "Chuck" Vinci, Jr. (b. 28 Feb. 1933), bantamweight 1956 and 1960.

World   The most world title wins, including Olympic Games, is eight, by: John Henry Davis (USA; 1921–84) in 1938, 1946–52; Tommy Kono (USA; b. 27 June 1930) in 1952–59; and Vasiliy Alekseiev (USSR; b. 7 Jan. 1942), 1970–77.

The only American woman to win a world title has been Karyn Marshall, at 82 kg in 1987.

United States   The most US national titles won is 13, by Anthony Terlazzo (1911–66), at 137 lbs., 1932 and 1936 and at 148 lbs., 1933, 1935, 1937–45.

Youngest world record holder   Naim Suleimanov (later Neum Shalamanov [Bulgaria]; b. 23 Jan. 1967) (now Naim Suleymanoğlu of Turkey) set 56 kg world records for clean and jerk (160 kg) and total (285 kg), at 16 yrs. 62 days, at Allentown, NJ on 26 Mar. 1983.

Heaviest lift to body weight   The first man to clean and jerk more than three times his body weight was Stefan Topurov (Bulgaria), who lifted 396¾ lbs. at Moscow, USSR on 24 Oct. 1983. The first man to snatch two-and-a-half times his own body weight was Naim Suleymanoğlu (Turkey), who lifted 330½ lbs. at Cardiff, Great Britain, on 27 Apr. 1988. The first woman to clean and jerk more than two times her own body weight was Cheng Jinling (China), who lifted 198 lbs. in the class of the World Championships at Jakarta, Indonesia in December 1988.

Women's World Championships   These are held annually, first at Daytona Beach, FL in October 1987. Women's world records have been ratified for the best marks at these championships. Peng Liping (China) won a record 12 gold medals with snatch, jerk and total in the 52-kg class each year, 1988–91.

POWERLIFTING

The sport of powerlifting was first contested at a national level in Great Britain in 1958. The first US Championships were held in 1964. The International Powerlifting Federation was founded in 1972, a year after the first, unofficial world championships were held. Offical championships have been held annually for men from 1973 and for women from 1980. The three standard lifts are squat, bench press and dead lift, the totals from the three lifts determining the results.

Most world titles *World*   The winner of the most world titles is Hideaki Inaba (Japan) with 16, at 52 kg, 1974–83, 1985–90. Lamar Gant (USA) holds the record for an American with 15 titles, at 56 kg, 1975–77, 1979, 1982–84; and at 60 kg, 1978, 1980–81 and 1986–90. The most by a woman is six, by

WORLD POWERLIFTING RECORDS
(All weights in kilograms)

MEN

CLASS	SQUAT	BENCH PRESS	DEADLIFT	TOTAL
52 kg	243 Hideaki Inaba (Japan) 1986	155 Andrzej Stanashek (Poland) 1991	242.5 Dennis Thios (Indonesia) 1990	587.5 Hideaki Inaba 1987
56 kg	248 Magnus Karlsson (Sweden) 1991	166.5 Magnus Karlsson 1991	289.5 Lamar Gant (USA) 1982	625 Lamar Gant 1982
60 kg	295 Joe Bradley (USA) 1980	180 Joe Bradley 1980	310 Lamar Gant 1988	707.5 Joe Bradley 1982
67.5 kg	300 Jessie Jackson (USA) 1987	200 Kristoffer Hulecki (Sweden) 1985	316 Daniel Austin (USA) 1991	762.5 Daniel Austin 1989
75 kg	328 Ausby Alexander (USA) 1989	217.5 James Rouse (USA) 1980	333 Jarmo Virtanen (Finland) 1988	850 Rick Gaugler (USA) 1982
82.5 kg	379.5 Mike Bridges (USA) 1982	240 Mike Bridges 1981	357.5 Veli Kumpuniemi (Finland) 1980	952.5 Mike Bridges 1982
90 kg	375 Fred Hatfield (USA) 1980	255 Mike MacDonald (USA) 1980	372.5 Walter Thomas (USA) 1982	937.5 Mike Bridges 1980
100 kg	422.5 Ed Coan (USA) 1989	261.5 Mike MacDonald 1977	378 Ed Coan 1989	1,032.5 Ed Coan 1989
110 kg	393.5 Dan Wohleber (USA) 1981	270 Jeffrey Magruder (USA) 1982	395 John Kuc (USA) 1980	1,000 John Kuc 1980
125 kg	428.5 Kirk Karwoski (USA) 1991	278.5 Tom Hardman (USA) 1982	387.5 Lars Norén (Sweden) 1987	1,005 Ernie Hackett (USA) 1982
125+ kg	445 Dwayne Fely (USA) 1982	300 Bill Kazmaier (USA) 1981	406 Lars Norén 1988	1,100 Bill Kazmaier 1981

WOMEN

CLASS	SQUAT	BENCH PRESS	DEADLIFT	TOTAL
44 kg	147.5 Raija Koskinen (Finland) 1992	81 Ann Leverett (USA) 1991	165 Nancy Belliveau (USA) 1985	352.5 Marie-France Vassart (Belgium) 1985
48 kg	150 Claudine Cognac (France) 1990	82.5 Michelle Evris (USA) 1981	182.5 Majik Jones (USA) 1984	390 Majik Jones 1984
52 kg	177.5 Mary Jeffrey (USA: nee Ryan) 1991	105 Mary Jeffrey 1991	197.5 Diana Rowell (USA) 1984	452.5 Mary Jeffrey 1991
56 kg	191 Mary Jeffrey 1989	115 Mary Jeffrey 1988	200.5 Joy Burt (Canada) 1989	485 Mary Jeffrey 1988
60 kg	200.5 Ruthi Shafer 1983	105.5 Judith Auerbach (USA) 1989	213 Ruthi Shafer 1983	502.5 Vicki Steenrod (USA) 1985
67.5 kg	230 Ruthi Shafer 1984	120 Vicki Steenrod 1990	244 Ruthi Shafer 1984	565 Ruthi Shafer 1984
75 kg	235 Cathy Millen (New Zealand) 1991	142.5 Liz Odendaal (Netherlands) 1989	240 Cathy Millen 1991	602.5 Cathy Millen 1991
82.5 kg	240 Cathy Millen 1991	150 Beverley Francis (Aus) 1981	247.5 Cathy Millen 1991	612.5 Cathy Millen 1991
90 kg	252.5 Lorraine Constanzo (USA) 1988	130 Lorraine Constanzo 1988	227.5 Lorraine Constanzo 1988	607.5 Lorraine Constanzo 1988
90+ kg	262.5 Lorraine Constanzo 1987	137.5 Myrtle Augee (Great Britain) 1989	237.5 Lorraine Constanzo 1987	622.5 Lorraine Constanzo 1987

Beverley Francis (Australia; b. 15 Feb. 1955), at 75 kg 1980, 1982; 82.5 kg 1981, 1983–85.

Twenty-four-hr. and one-hr. lifts   A deadlifting record of 5,777,777 lbs. in 24 hrs. was set by a team of ten from Her Majesty's Prison, Long Lartin, Evesham, Great Britain on 17–18 Jan. 1991. The 24-hr. deadlift record by an individual is 818,121 lbs., by Anthony Wright at Her Majesty's Prison, Featherstone, Wolverhampton, Great Britain, on 31 Aug.–1 Sep. 1990.

A bench press record of 8,529,699 lbs. was set by a nine-man team from the Hogarth Barbell Club, Chiswick, London, Great Britain on 18–19 July 1987. An individual bench press record of 1,231,150 lbs. was set by Paul Goodall at the Copthorne Hotel, Plymouth, Great Britain on 12–13 Mar. 1991. A squat record of 4,780,994 lbs. was set by a ten-man team from St. Albans Weightlifting Club and Ware Boys Club, Hertfordshire, Great Britain on 20–21 July 1986. A record 133,380 arm-curling repetitions using three 48¼ lbs. weightlifting bars and dumbbells was achieved by a team of nine from Intrim Health and Fitness Club at Gosport, Great Britain on 4–5 Aug. 1989.

Powerlifting feats   Lamar Gant (USA) was the first man to deadlift five times his own body weight, lifting 661 lbs. when weighing 132 lbs. in 1985. The greatest powerlift by a woman is a squat of 628 lbs. by Lorraine Constanzo (USA) at Dayton, OH on 21 Nov. 1987. Cammie Lynn Lusko (USA; b. 5 Apr. 1958) became the first woman to lift more than her body weight with one arm, with 131 lbs. at a body weight of 128.5 lbs., at Milwaukee, WI on 21 May 1983.

WRESTLING

The earliest depictions of wrestling holds and falls on wall plaques and a statue indicate that organized wrestling dates from *c.* 2750–2600 B.C. It was the most popular sport in the ancient Olympic Games, and victors were recorded from 708 B.C. The Greco-Roman style is of French origin, and arose about 1860. The International Amateur Wrestling Federation (FILA) was founded in 1912.

Most titles *Olympic*   Three Olympic titles have been won by: Carl Westergren (Sweden; 1895–1958) in 1920, 1924 and 1932; Ivar Johansson (Sweden; 1903–79) in 1932 (two) and 1936; and Aleksandr Vasilyevich Medved (USSR; b. 16 Sep. 1937) in 1964, 1968 and 1972. Four Olympic medals were won by: Eino Leino (Finland; b. 7 Apr. 1891) at freestyle 1920–32; and by Imre Polyák (Hungary; b. 16 Apr. 1932) at Greco-Roman in 1952–64.

The one US wrestler to win two Olympic freestyle titles was George Nicholas Mehnert (1881–1948), flyweight in 1904 and bantamweight in 1908.

The first, and only, US men to win a Greco-Roman title were Steven Fraser (b. 23 Mar. 1953) at light-heavyweight and Jeffrey Blatnick (b. 27 July 1957) at super-heavyweight in 1984.

World   The freestyler Aleksandr Medved (USSR) won a record ten World Championships, 1962–64, 1966–72 at three weight categories. The only wrestler to win the same title in seven successive years has been Valeriy Grigoryevich Rezantsev (USSR; b. 2 Feb. 1947) in the Greco-Roman 90 kg class in 1970–76, including the Olympic Games of 1972 and 1976.

United States   The most world titles won by a US wrestler is four (three world, one Olympic), by John Smith (b. 9 Aug. 1965), featherweight 1987–90. Three world titles have been won by Leroy Kemp (b. 24 Dec. 1956), welterweight, 1978–79 and 1982; and two world and one Olympic title have been won by Mark Schultz (b. 26 Oct. 1960), middleweight, 1984, 1985 and 1987.

Most wins   In international competition, Osamu Watanabe (Japan; b. 21 Oct. 1940), the 1964 Olympic freestyle 63 kg champion, was unbeaten and unscored and unscored-upon in 189 consecutive matches. Outside of FILA sanctioned competition, Wade Schalles (USA) won 821 bouts from 1964 to 1984, with 530 of these victories by pin.

NCAA Division I Championship   Oklahoma State University was the first unofficial national champion in 1928. Including five unofficial titles, Oklahoma State has won a record 29 NCAA titles, in 1928–31, 1933–35, 1937–1942, 1946, 1948–49, 1954–56, 1958–59, 1961–62, 1964, 1966, 1968, 1971, 1989–90. The University of Iowa has won the most consecutive titles, with nine championships from 1978–86.

Longest bout   The longest recorded bout was one of 11 hrs. 40 min. when Martin Klein (Estonia representing Russia; 1885–1947) beat Alfred Asikáinen (Finland; 1888–1942) for the Greco-Roman 75 kg "A" event silver medal in the 1912 Olympic Games in Stockholm, Sweden.

Heaviest heavyweight   The heaviest wrestler in Olympic history was Chris Taylor (1950–79), bronze medalist in the super-heavyweight class in 1972, who stood 6 ft. 5 in. tall and weighed over 420 lbs. FILA introduced an upper weight limit of 286 lbs. for international competition in 1985.

SUMO WRESTLING

The sport's origins in Japan date from *c.* 23 B.C. The heaviest-ever *rikishi* is Samoan-American Salevaa Fuali Atisnoe of Hawaii, alias Konishiki, who weighed in at 559 lbs. at Tokyo's Ryogaku Kokugikau on 27 Aug. 1991. He is also the first foreign *rikishi* to attain the second highest rank of *ozeki*, or champion. Weight is amassed by over-alimentation with a high-protein stew called *chankonabe*.

The most successful wrestlers have been *yokozuna* Sadaji Akiyoshi (b. 1912), alias Futabayama, winner of 69 consecutive bouts in the 1930s; *yokozuna* Koki Naya (b. 1940), alias Taiho ("Great Bird"), who won the Emperor's Cup 32 times up to his retirement in 1971; and the *ozeki* Tameemon Torokichi, alias Raiden (1767–1825), who in 21 years (1789–1810) won 254 bouts and lost only ten for the highest-ever winning percentage of 96.2. Taiho and Futabayama share the record of eight perfect tournaments without a single loss. The youngest of the 62 men to attain the rank of *yokozuna* (grand champion) was Toshimitsu Ogata (b. 16 May 1953), alias Kitanoumi, in July 1974 at the age of 21 years and two months. He set a record in 1978, winning 82 of the 90 bouts that top *rikishi* fight annually.

Yokozuna Mitsugu Akimoto (b. 1 June 1955), alias Chiyonofuji, set a record for domination of one of the six annual tournaments by winning the Kyushu Basho for eight successive years, 1981–88. He also holds the record for most career wins, 1,045, and *Makunoiuchi* (top division) wins, 807. He retired in May 1991 but remains in sumo as a training coach.

Hawaiian-born Jesse Kuhaulua (b. 16 June 1944), now a Japanese citizen named Daigoro Watanabe, alias Takamiyama, and a stablemaster in the Japan Sumo Association with the sumo elder (*toshiyori*) name of Azumazeki Oyakaba, was the first non-Japanese to win an official top-division tournament, in July 1972, and in 1981 he set a record of 1,231 consecutive top-division bouts.

Yukio Shoji (b. 14 Nov. 1948), alias Aobajo, did not miss a single bout in his 22-year career, 1964–86, and contested a record 1,631 consecutive bouts. Kenji Hatano (b. 4 Jan. 1948), alias Oshio, contested a record 1,891 non-consecutive bouts in his 26-year career, 1962–88, the longest in modern sumo history.

Katsumi Yamanaka (b. 16 Mar. 1967), alias Akinoshima, set a new *kinboshi* (gold star) record of 13 upsets over *yokozuna* by a *maegashira*. Hawaiian-born Chad Rowan (b. 8 May 1969), alias Akebono, scored a majority of wins for a record 18 consecutive tournaments, March 1988–March 1991.

YACHTING

Sailing as a sport dates from the 17th century. Originating in the Netherlands, it was introduced to England by Charles II, who participated in a 23-mile race along the river Thames in 1661. The oldest yacht club in the world is the Royal Cork Yacht Club, which claims descent from the Cork Harbor Water Club, founded in Ireland in 1720. The oldest continuously existing yacht club in the United States is the New York Yacht Club, founded in 1844.

Olympic titles The first sportsman ever to win individual gold medals in four successive Olympic Games was Paul B. Elvström (Denmark; b. 25 Feb. 1928) in the Firefly class in 1948 and the Finn class in 1952, 1956 and 1960. He also won eight other world titles in a total of six classes. The lowest number of penalty points by the winner of any class in an Olympic regatta is three points (five wins, one disqualified and one second in seven starts) by *Superdocious* of the Flying Dutchman class (Lt. Rodney Stuart Pattisson [b. 5 Aug. 1943] and Iain Somerled Macdonald-Smith [b. 3 July 1945]), at Acapulco Bay, Mexico in Oct. 1968.

United States The only US yachtsman to have won two gold medals is Herman Frasch Whiton (1904–67), at six-meter class, in 1948 and 1952.

Admiral's Cup and ocean racing

The ocean racing series with the most participating nations (three boats allowed to each nation) is the Admiral's Cup, held by the Royal Ocean Racing Club. A record 19 nations competed in 1975, 1977 and 1979. Britain has a record nine wins.

Modern ocean racing (in moderate or small sailing yachts, rather than professionally manned sailing ships) began with a race from Brooklyn, NY to Bermuda, 630 nautical miles, organized by Thomas Fleming Day, editor of the magazine *The Rudder*, in June 1906. The race is still held today in every even-numbered year, though the course is now Newport, RI to Bermuda.

The oldest race for any type of craft and either kind of water (fresh or salt) still regularly held is the Chicago-to-Mackinac race on Lakes Michigan and Huron, first sailed in 1898. It was held again in 1904, then annually until the present day, except for 1917–20. The record for the course (333 nautical miles) is 1 day 1 hr. 50 min. (average speed 12.89 knots), by the sloop *Pied Piper*, owned by Dick Jennings (USA) in 1987.

The current record holder of the elapsed-time records for both the premier American and British ocean races (the Newport, RI, to Bermuda race and the Fastnet race) is the sloop *Nirvana*, owned by Marvin Green (USA). The record for the Bermuda race, 635 nautical miles, is 2 days 14 hrs. 29 min., in 1982; and for the Fastnet race, 605 nautical miles, the record is 2 days 12 hrs. 41 min., in 1985—an average speed of 10.16 knots and 9.97 knots respectively.

Longest race

The world's longest sailing race is the Vendée Globe Challenge, the first of which started from Les Sables d'Olonne, France on 26 Nov. 1989. The distance circumnavigated without stopping was 22,500 nautical miles. The race is for boats between 50–60 ft., sailed single-handedly. The record time on the course is 109 days 8 hrs. 48 min. 50 sec. by Titouan Lamazou (France; b. 1955) in the sloop *Ecureuil d'Aquitaine*, which finished at Les Sables on 19 Mar. 1990.

The oldest regular sailing race around the world is the quadrennial Whitbread Round the World race (instituted Aug. 1973) organized by the Royal Naval Sailing Association. It starts in England, and the course around the world and the number of legs with stops at specified ports are varied from race to race. The distance for 1989–90 was 32,000 nautical miles from Southampton, Great Britain and return, with stops and restarts at Punta del Este, Uruguay; Fremantle, Australia; Auckland, New Zealand; Punta del Este, Uruguay; and Fort Lauderdale, FL.

America's Cup

The America's Cup was originally won as an outright prize (with no special name) by the schooner *America* on 22 Aug. 1851 at Cowes and was later offered by the New York Yacht Club as a challenge trophy. On 8 Aug. 1870 J. Ashbury's *Cambria* (Great Britain) failed to capture the trophy from *Magic*, owned by F. Osgood (USA). The Cup has been challenged 28 times.

The United States was undefeated, winning 77 races and only losing eight, until 1983, when *Australia II*, skippered by John Bertrand and owned by a

Perth syndicate headed by Alan Bond, beat *Liberty* 4–3, the narrowest series victory, at Newport, RI.

Charlie Barr (USA; 1864–1911), who defended in 1899, 1901 and 1903, and Harold S. Vanderbilt (USA; 1884–1970) in 1930, 1934 and 1937, each steered the successful cup defender three times in succession. Dennis Walter Conner (USA; b. 16 Sep. 1942) has been helmsman of American boats four times in succession: in 1980, when he successfully defended; in 1983, when he steered the defender, but lost; in 1987, when the American challenger regained the trophy; and in 1988, when he again successfully defended. He was also starting helmsman in 1974, with Ted Hood as skipper.

The largest yacht to have competed in the America's Cup was the 1903 defender, the gaff rigged cutter *Reliance*, with an overall length of 144 ft., a record sail area of 16,160 ft.^{2} and a rig 175 ft. high.

Fastest speeds   The fastest speed reached under sail on water by any craft over a 500-meter timed run is by Thierry Bielak (France) on a boardsailer at 44.66 knots at Saintes Maries-de-la-Mer Canal, Camargue, France on 27 Feb. 1990. The women's record was set at the same location by Brigitte Gimenez (France; b. 6 Oct. 1961), who achieved 39.45 knots in December 1990.

The American with the best time under sail over a 500 meter run is Jimmy Lewis, with 38.68 knots at Saintes Maries-de-la-Mer in Feb. 1988.

Most competitors   The most boats ever to start in a single race was 2,072 in the Round Zeeland (Denmark) race on 21 June 1984, over a course of 235 nautical miles.

The largest transoceanic race was the ARC (Atlantic Rally for Cruisers), when 204 boats of the 209 starters from 24 nations completed the race from Las Palmas de Gran Canaria (Canary Islands) to Barbados in 1989.

Boardsailing (windsurfing)   The British High Court ruled on 7 Aug. 1982 that Peter Chilvers (when age 12) had devised a prototype of a boardsailer in 1958 in England. In 1968 Henry Hoyle Schweitzer and Jim Drake pioneered the sport, of ten termed windsurfing, in California. World Championships were first held in 1973 and the sport was added to the Olympic Games in 1984, when the winner was Stephan van den Berg (Netherlands; b. 20 Feb. 1962), who also won five world titles 1979–83.

Longest sailboard   The longest snake of sailboards was made by 70 windsurfers in a row at the Sailboard Show '89 event at Narrabeen Lakes, Manly, Australia on 21 Oct. 1989.

The world's longest sailboard, 165 ft., was constructed at Fredrikstad, Norway, and first sailed on 28 June 1986.

EXTRA! EXTRA!

EARTH AND SPACE

Largest scale model (p. 4) The largest scale model of the solar system was developed by the Lakeview Museum of Arts and Sciences in Peoria, IL and inaugurated in April 1992. The Sun, with a diameter of 36 ft., was painted on the exerior of the museum's planetarium, and the planets were situated in appropriate locations in accordance with their distance from the Sun, with Pluto some 40 miles away.

Largest diamond (p. 50) Currently the largest uncut stone is one of 1,462 carats, that belongs to the De Beers central selling organization in London, Great Britain. It is of low quality and is not expected to be cut.

LIVING WORLD

Largest organism (p. 55) The fungus *Armillaria bulbosa* has been dwarfed by a network of the closely related *Armillaria ostoyae*, reported in May 1992 to be covering some 1,500 acres in Washington State.

Most guide dogs placed In the United States the record for the most guide dogs placed with users is held by the Seeing Eye of Morristown, NJ, with a total of 230 placements in 1991.

Smallest adult cat (p. 73) "Peanut," owned by Jacob and Jamie Piekarski of North Haven, CT, weighs 1 lb. 8 oz. and is 10 in. long.

Tallest pepper (fruit and vegetable feature, p. 118) The tallest pepper in the United States was grown by Fred Melton of Jacksonville, FL and measured 10 ft. 6 in. as of 29 July 1992.

HUMAN BEING

Oldest mother to have given birth following IVF (p. 151) Giuseppina Maganuco (b. 26 Jan. 1938) of Italy gave birth by cesarean section to a girl, Anna Maria, on 18 Dec. 1991 when aged 53 years 326 days.

Oldest living person (p. 155) *United States* The oldest living person in the United States is Mrs. Margaret Skeete (nee Seward), who was born in Rockport, TX on 27 October 1878.

Lifting with teeth (p. 160) Robert Galstyan of Masis, Armenia pulled two railroad cars coupled together, weighing a total of 136,195 lbs., a distance of 23 ft. along a railroad track with his teeth on 21 July 1992.

Largest biceps (p. 163) Denis Sester (b. 1963) of Bloomington, MN has biceps 28⅛ in. cold (not pumped).

Memory (p. 164)   Dominic O'Brien memorized the order of a single deck of playing cards in 55.62 seconds at the *Guinness World of Records* in London, Great Britain on 29 May 1992.

Yodeling (p. 166)   The most rapid recorded is twenty-two tones in 1 sec., by Peter Hinnen of Zürich, Switzerland on 9 Feb. 1992.

Stretcher-bearing (p. 175)   The longest distance a stretcher with a 140 lb. "body" has been carried is 158.2 miles, in 46 hrs. 35 min. from 27–29 May 1992. This was achieved by two four-man teams from the 85th Medical Batallion, Ft. Meade, MD.

Kidney (p. 178)   The longest surviving kidney transplant patient is Johanna Leanora Rempel of Red Deer, Alberta, Canada, who received a kidney from her identical twin sister Lana Blatzon on 28 Dec. 1960 at the Peter Bent Brigham Hospital, Boston, MA.

SCIENCE AND TECHNOLOGY

Most in space (p. 222)   There were 12 people in space on 31 July 1992—four CIS cosmonauts and one Frenchman aboard *Mir*, and five US astronauts, one Swiss and one Italian on *STS46 Atlantis*.

Spacewalks (p. 223)   The longest spacewalk ever undertaken was one of 8 hrs. 29 min., by Pierre Thuot, Rick Hieb and Tom Akers of *STS 49 Endeavour* on 13 May 1992.

BUILDINGS AND STRUCTURES

Largest teepee   The largest teepee in the United States measures 43 ft. in height, 42 ft. in diameter and utilizes 42 teepee poles. The teepee, owned by M.P. Doss of Washington, D.C., was exhibited near the Little Big Horn National Cemetery in 1992.

House of cards (p. 241)   The greatest number of floors achieved in building freestanding houses of standard playing cards is 75, to a height of 14 ft. 6 in., by Bryan Berg of Spirit Lake, IA on 18–20 Apr 1992.

Longest slide (p. 241)   The Bromley Alpine Slide has a length of 4,000 ft. and a vertical drop of 700 ft.

Coal shoveling (p. 251)   The record for filling a 1,120 lb. hopper with coal is 29.22 sec., by W. Miller of Fingal, Tasmania, Australia at the Fingal Valley Festival on 29 Feb. 1992.

Snowman (p. 266)   Philip and Colleen Price, in coordination with 10 others, constructed a snowman, *Prince William*, 76 ft. 2 in. high at Prince William Sound Community College, Valdez, AK on 2 Apr 1992.

Window cleaning (p. 269)   Keith Witt beat his previous record with a time of 10.13 sec. on 31 Jan. 1992 at the International Window Cleaning Association convention in San Antonio, TX.

TRANSPORT

Road cars (p. 293)   The highest speed ever attained by a standard production car is 217.1 mph for a Jaguar XJ220, driven by Martin Brundle at the Nardo test track, Italy on 21 June 1992.

Karting (p. 301)   Matthew and Michael Jones, Andrew Miller and Emma Williams drove a distance of 812 miles in 24 hrs. in 140cc go karts on an indoor circuit at the Welsh Karting Centre, Newport, Great Britain between 21–22 Nov. 1991.

Unicycles (p. 309)   *Smallest*   Peter Rosenthal rode a 2½ in. wheel diameter unicycle for 38 seconds at the *Guinness World of Records*, Las Vegas, NV on 6 Oct. 1991.

Air-launched record (p. 327)   The space shuttle *Columbia* broke its own world record for duration at 13 days 19 hrs. 30 min. on its 12th mission, *STS 50*, on 9 July 1992.

Ballooning (p. 334)   *First flight over Mount Everest*   Two balloons— *Star Flyer 1*, piloted by Chris Dewhirst and Leo Dickinson, and *Star Flyer 2*, piloted by Andy Elson and Eric Jones (all British)—achieved the first overflight of the summit of Mount Everest on 21 Oct. 1991.

BUSINESS WORLD

Column of coins (p. 352)   The most valuable column of coins was worth £18,701 ($34,000) and was 6 ft. 3 in. high. It was built by Robert Young and a team of helpers at Notton, Great Britain on 18 June 1992.

Lightest calf (p. 369)   A healthy female calf weighing 14 lbs. 5 oz. was born on 27 Oct. 1991 on the farm of Ole Willumsgaard Lauridsen and Roos Verhoven in Hemmet, Denmark.

Largest chicken (p. 372)   "Big Snow," a rooster owned and bred by Ronald Alldridge of Deuchar, Queensland, Australia, weighed 23 lbs. on 27 May 1992.

ARTS AND ENTERTAINMENT

Debating (p. 386)   Students of St. Andrews Presbyterian College in Laurinburg, NC, together with staff and friends, debated the motion "There's No Place Like Home" for 517 hrs. 45 min. from 4–26 Apr. 1992.

Most versions of the national anthem in 24 hours   Susan R. Jeske sang the Star-Spangled Banner live at 17 official events, attended by approximately 60,000 people, in California within a 24-hr. period on 3–4 July 1992. She traveled to the functions by automobile, helicopter and boat.

Fastest rapper (p. 415)   J.C. 001 of London, Great Britain rapped 631 syllables in 60 sec. on the British Broadcasting Corporation's radio 5 station on 28 Oct. 1991.

Longest photograph negative (p. 436)   On 6 May 1992, Thomas Bleich of Austin, TX produced a negative image measuring 23 ft. 4½ × 10½ in. using a 10½ in. focal length Turner-Reich lens and a Kodak No. 10 Cirkut Camera.

HUMAN WORLD

Heads of state—largest meeting (p. 465)   The United Nations Conference on Environment and Development, or Earth Summit, which was held in Rio de Janeiro, Brazil from 3–14 June 1992, was attended by 118 heads of state and heads of government.

Handshaking (p. 470)   Dhirendra Tomar of Jehangirabad, Bhopal, India shook hands with 23,040 different people in eight hours during a holy festival that took place on 16 May 1992.

Greatest petitions (p. 477)   The greatest petition on record was signed by 13,078,935 people in South Korea between 11 Nov–23 Dec. 1991, protesting efforts by advanced countries to open their country's rice market to foreign imports.

HUMAN ACHIEVEMENTS

Most traveled (p. 516)   John Todd of London, Great Britain became the joint record holder in 1992. He still has to visit the Heard and McDonald Islands.

Beer keg lifting (p. 526)   George Olesen raised a keg of beer weighing 138 lbs. above his head 670 times in six hours at Horsens, Denmark on 25 June 1992.

Cigar box balancing (p. 526)   Terry Cole of London, Great Britain balanced 220 unmodified cigar boxes on his chin for 9 sec. on 24 Apr. 1992.

Paella (p. 540)   The largest paella measured 65 ft. 7 in. in diameter and was made by Juan Carlos Galbis and his helpers in Valencia, Spain on 8 Mar. 1992. It was eaten by 100,000 people.

Pastry (p. 540)   The longest pastry was a blueberry strudel 2,040 ft. in length, made by staff and friends of the Fredonia Hotel, Nacogdoches, TX on 5 June 1992.

Largest burrito (p. 541)   The largest burrito in the United States weighed 1,126 lbs. and was made by Freebird's of Santa Barbara, CA on 14 May 1991.

Bottle collections (p. 547)   David Maund's collection totaled 9,601 unduplicated miniature Scotch whisky bottles in June 1992.

SPORTS AND GAMES

† Denotes a record set at the Summer Olympic Games in Barcelona, Spain.

Archery † (table, p. 563)   Cho Youn-Jeong (South Korea) established a new world record of 1,375 points for women's FITA round on 1 Aug. 1992.

Auto racing (p. 564)   On 26 July, Nigel Mansell (Great Britain) won the German Grand Prix at Hockenheim, his eighth success of the 1992 season and equaling the record of most wins in a season. On the same occasion Ricardo Patrese started his 234th Grand Prix.

Largest baseball bat   The largest baseball bat in the United States measures 5 ft. 8¼ in. high, 22¾ in. in width and weighs 57½ lbs. The bat, owned by Stephen Koschal of Boynton Beach, FL, has genuine autographs of all living members of the Baseball Hall of Fame.

Basketball † (p. 597) *United States*   Three member of the "Dream Team" won their second gold medals: Michael Jordan, Patrick Ewing and Chris Mullen. They join three other players with double championships.

Canoeing †   Birgit Schmidt (Germany) won a record fourth gold medal, winning the 500 m (K1) on 7 Aug. 1992.

Card holding (p. 619)   Ralf Laue held 310 standard playing cards in a fan in one hand, so that the value and color of each one was visible, at Zürich, Switzerland on 6 Apr. 1991.

Golf, British Open (p. 659)   Lowest score Nick Faldo completed the first 36 holes at Muirfield, Lothian, Great Britain in 130 strokes (66, 64) on 16–17 July 1992. Faldo added a third round of 69 to equal the 54-hole record of 199.

Gymnastics † (p. 669)   Vitaly Shcherbo (Unified Team) won six gold medals, the most by any gymnast at one Games. His victories came in the team event, all-around, pommel horse, rings, vault and parallel bars.

Table (p. 670)   Paul Lynch performed 40,401 press-ups in a 24-hour period at the NatWest Tower, London, Great Britain on 18–19 July 1992.

Mountaineering (p. 707)   The longest descent down the side of a building is one of 1,465 ft., by two teams of 12, representing the Royal Marines from Great Britain and the Canadian School of Rescue Training. All 24 people rappeled from the Space Deck of the CN Tower in Toronto, Canada to the ground on 1 July 1992.

Olympics † (pp. 708–712) *Largest Games*   A record 172 nations competed in the Summer Games, several for the first time. The Games attracted the largest number of participants, with 10,617 official entrants, of which 3,028 were women. The 26 sports and 257 events were also records.

Most games contested   Equestrian J. Michael Plumb competed in his seventh Olympics, the most by an American athlete in the history of the games. He also holds the record for the longest span of competition, with 32 years.

Most medals Matt Biondi won his 11th career medal, tying the record for most successful US Olympian already held by Mark Spitz and Carl Osburn. Biondi won his 11th medal when the United States team won the 4 × 100 meter medley relay, even though he did not swim in the final. Biondi has won eight golds, two silvers and one bronze, 1984–92.

Evelyn Ashford (track and field) and Janet Evans (swimming) tied the US women's career record for most gold medals, four. Evans won the 800-meter freestyle, and Ashford was a member of the winning 4 × 100 meter relay team.

Parachuting (p. 714) The oldest tandem female parachutist is 89 years 362 days old—Corena Leslie of Arizona, who made her jump on 8 June 1992.

A free-fall formation of 150 people was held for 70 seconds from a height 19,192 ft. over Koksijde military base, Belgium in July 1992.

Rodeo (p. 723) Vince Bruce (USA) performed 4,001 Texas Skips (jumps back and forth through a large, vertically spun loop) on 22 July 1991 at the Empire State Building, New York City.

Rowing † (p. 727) Steve Redgrave (Great Britain) became the seventh oarsman to win three Olympic gold medals on 1 Aug. 1992. He won the coxless pairs title with Matthew Pinsent, having previously won coxed fours in 1984 and coxless pairs in 1988 with Andrew Holmes.

Rugby (p. 730) Highest individual career scores Michael Lynagh has scored a record 749 points in 58 matches for Australia. David Campese has played in a record 69 internationals for Australia.

Swimming *Men's world records † (table, p. 752)* 1,500-meter freestyle, 14:43.48—Kieren Perkins (Australia) on 31 July 1992. 400-meter freestyle, 3:45.00—Yevgeny Sadovyi (Unified Team) on 29 July 1992. 200-meter breaststroke, 2:10.16—Mike Barrowman (USA) on 29 July 1992. 100-meter backstroke, 53.86—Jeff Rouse (USA) on 31 July 1992.

Women's world records † (table, p. 752) 50-meter freestyle, 24.79—Yang Wenyi (China) on 30 July 1992. 4 × 100 meter freestyle relay, 3:39.46—United States (Nicole Haislett, Dara Torres, Angel Martino, Jenny Thompson) on 28 July 1992. 200-meter medley, 2:11.65—Li Lin (China) on 30 July 1992. 4 × 100 meter medley relay, 4:02.54—United States (Lea Loveless, Anita Nall, Christine Ahmann-Leighton, Jenny Thompson) on 30 July 1992.

Youngest gold medalist † Kyoko Iwasaki (Japan) won the 200-meter breaststroke at age 14 yrs. 6 days to become the youngest swimming champion in Olympic history.

Long-distance relays (p. 761) The Tuckahoe Family YMCA in Richmond, VA holds the United States record for the longest-duration relay swim, 300 hours, from 4–16 May 1992.

Track and field (table, p. 782) *World indoor* 3,000 meters—The 3,000-meter indoor world record set by Saïd Aouita was disallowed by the

IAAF. The new record is 7 min. 37.31 sec. by Moses Kiptanui (Kenya), set at Seville, Spain on 20 Feb. 1992.

World outdoor † 400-meter hurdles, 46.78—Kevin Young (USA) on 6 Aug. 1992. 4 × 100 meter relay, 37.40—United States (Mike Marsh, Leroy Burrell, Dennis Mitchell, Carl Lewis) on 8 Aug. 1992. 4 × 400 meter relay, 2:55.74—United States (Andrew Valmon, Quincy Watts, Michael Johnson, Steve Lewis) on 8 Aug. 1992.

United States outdoor † 200 meters—Mike Marsh set a new US record of 19.73 seconds on 6 Aug. 1992.

Weightlifting † **(men's table, p. 804)** Kakhi Kakhiachvili (Unified Team) tied the world record for the 90 kg jerk, with 235.0 kg (518 lbs.) on 1 Aug. 1992.

Wrestling, most titles † **(p. 809)** *United States* In winning the 130 kg class, Bruce Baumgartner became the most successful Olympic wrestler in United States history, having won two gold and one silver, 1984–92. John Smith and Kenny Monday also won their second gold medal, matching the record of George Mehnert.

SUBJECT INDEX

B

569, 570, 818*
fountains 261
fraud
  bank 488
  computer 488
  maritime 488
  securities 491, *492*
frequency (of light) 184
friction 184
Frisbee *See* flying disc
    throwing
frogs 87, 106
frontiers *See* boundaries
fruits and vegetables
    118–122
fumigation 262
funerals 514
fungi 131–132
  largest organisms 55,
    814*
furnaces, blast 199
furniture 382
fusion power 196

G

Gaelic football 652–653
galaxies 2, *3*, 3–4
gallbladder 176
galleries, art 377,
    378–379
gallstones 176–177
game reserves 134
garages 298
garbage
  cans 527
  collection 528
  dumps 262
  electricity from 232
gardens, community 363
garlic 118–121
gas, natural
  deposits 209
  flares 209
  pipelines 202
  production 209
  tanks 261
  turbines 197
gas, nerve 190
gasoline consumption
    296
gas stations *See* filling
    stations
gastropods 101
gauges, railroad 316
geese
  domesticated 78, 373
  wild 78
gems, jewels and
    precious stones

50–53
  auctions 383
  robberies 488
General Motors Corp.
    290, 339–340
generations *See* families
generators 197
genocide 456–457, 458
geography 17–37 *See*
    also specific
    geographic
    features (e.g.,
    lakes)
  extreme points 22
  high points 27
Georgia
  bank fraud 488
  governors 474
  high point 27
  original statehood 457
  populations 453
  secession 457
gerbils 72, 73
Germany, Nazi
  forgery 488
  genocide 457
  hanging of Greek
    resistance fighters
    490
  Reichsbank robbery
    486
gestation
  amphibian 84
  literary work 393
  mammal 60–61
Getty Museum, J. Paul
    (Malibu,
    California) 377
geysers 41–42
g force
  for bird 81
  for human being
    170–171
  for insect 95
giants, human, *141*, 141,
    142
giraffes 59
glaciers 36
gladiatorial combat 429
glass
  antique 382
  eating of 175
  stained 511–512
  thinness 185
  window size 269–270
globes, revolving 262
goats 370
  prices 368
go karts 301, 816*
gold
  antiques 382

sacred objects 511
coffins 551
discs (record sales)
    425–426, *426*
mines 206
  disasters 459
nuggets 53
panning 528
physical properties 182
prices (COMEX) 360
reserves 345
Golden Gate Bridge *245*
golden handshake 349
goldfish 89
golf 653–666, *655, 659*,
    818*
  holes in one 665–666
  PGA tour records 660
Goliath (Biblical giant)
    141
gorges *See* canyons
gorillas 63
Gospel Book of Henry the
    Lion, Duke of
    Saxony, The
    (book) 394
governors, U.S. 474–475
grain elevators 231
Grammy Awards 427
Grand Canyon (Arizona)
    35
grape catching 528
grapefruit 118–121
grapes *See* vines and
    vineyards
grasses 124
grass skiing 738–739
grave digging 262
Great Barrier Reef
    (Australia) 25, 92,
    102
Great Wall of China 269
Great Western Bank
    Association 343
greeting cards 552
greyhound racing 667
grocery stores 341
gross national product
    (GNP) 345
ground figures
    (sculpture) 381
guide dogs
  period of service 70
  placements 814*
guillotinings 490
guinea pigs 72, 73
Guinness Book of
    Records, The
    (book) 399–400
guitars
  cost 408–409

Polaroid Corp. 482
polders (lands reclaimed
    from sea) 251
poles
    flexible 433
    sitting on 237
    totem 269
political divisions
    449–450
political unrest 456–457
polo 716–718
    playing field *717*
ponies 69–70
pool (sport) 718–719
popcorn 541
popes 513
population 451–456
    65 and over (5 U.S.
        states) 155
    density 451
    sex ratio 454
    urban 460
    U.S. census 451, 453
    world growth 451, 452,
        454
porcupines 65
porpoises 60, 105
Portrait of Dr. Gachet
    (van Gogh
    painting) 377
ports *288, 289*
postage stamps *See*
    stamps
postal services 360
posters 377, 379
post-nominal numbers
    465
post offices 360
potato chips 541
potatoes
    production 366
    size 118–121
potato peeling 122
pot plants 117
pottery *See* vases
poultry 371–373
poverty (of country) 345,
    347
powder 188
power 196–199
    ships driven by 272
powerboat racing
    719–720
Powerful (Deshpande
    sculpture) 380
powerlifting 807–809
power plants 196, 197
    garbage-using 232
    nuclear 196
    solar 196–197
    tidal 197

prairie dogs 56–57
precious stones *See* gems
precipitation *See* rainfall;
    snowfall
pregnancy, duration of
    172
presidents (heads of
    state)
    United States 465–470,
        472
    salary 470
    wives 473
    women 465
presses (industrial) 202
pressures 183–184
priests 512
primates 63
    endangered species
        103–104
    prehistoric 113, 138
prime ministers 480
printing
    antiquity 392
    companies 400–401
    electronic 202
    mechanical 392
    orders 401
    volume 400
prints 378
prisms 187
prisons 491–492
    escapes 492
    sentences 490–491
prizes
    mathematical 193
    Nobel 493, 494
procaryota 132–133 *See
    also* bacteria;
    viruses
processions *See* parades
producers
    television 445–446
    theater 430
productivity, artistic *See*
    prolificacy
profits and losses
    339–340
projectiles 720–721
prolificacy, artistic
    composers 416,
        418–421
    painters 376
    scriptwriters 446
promenades, covered
    264, *266*
propellers
    aircraft 325
    ships 276
protista (protozoa and
    protophytes) 131
Prudential Insurance Co.

of America 341
psalms 395
pseudonyms 399
psychiatrists 455
psychologists 455
public relations firms 401
publishers 400
Pulitzer Prizes 404
pulsars 6
pulse rates 172–173
pumpkins 118–121
push-ups 670, 818*
puzzles
    crosswords 405–406
    jigsaw 551
    mathematical 191
pyramids 264, 268
    human 433
    motorcycle 306
pythons 85

Q

quadruplets 149, 151,
    152, 158
quarks 180
quarries 207
quasars 4
quilts 552
quindecaplets 152
quintuplets 149,
    150–151, 152
quizzes 535
quorums 477

R

rabbits 72, 73, 75–76
rackets (sport) 722
racquetball 722
radar 202–203
radio 442–443
    dishes 216
    hams 443
    installations 216–217
    microphones 442
Radio City Music Hall
    (New York City)
    441
radishes 118–121
raft
    survival on 518
    trans-Pacific crossing
        by 283
railroads 312–319
    bridges 244, 246, 247
    disasters 458
    gradients 317

YOU'VE READ
THE BOOK—

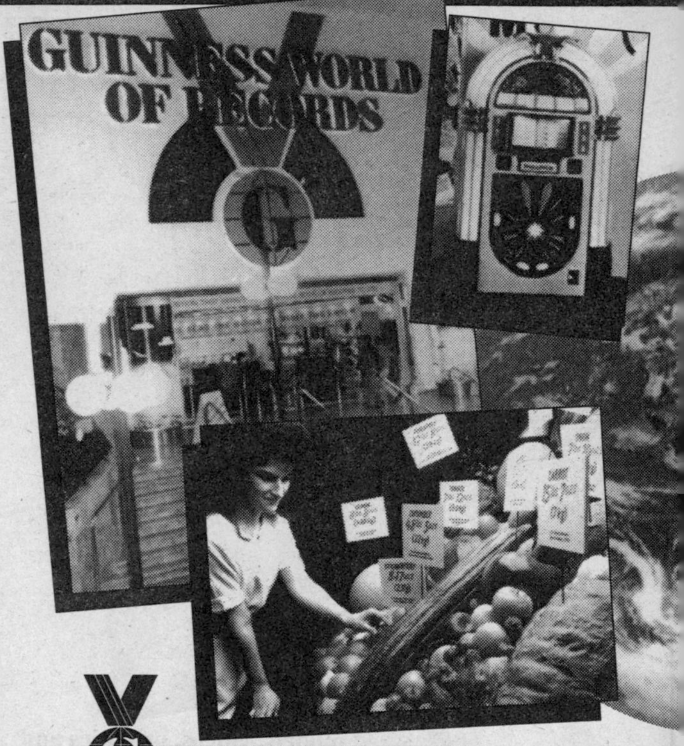

GUINNESS WORLD
OF RECORDS

GUINNESS
WORLD OF RECORDS

EXHIBITIONS

AT THE EMPIRE STATE BUILDING,
NEW YORK

NOW VISIT THE EXHIBITION

Through the use of life sized models, videos, graphics and audio technology, thousands of record breaking facts from the Guinness Book of Records come to life at these amazing Exhibitions. See the world's tallest, smallest, heaviest, fastest, loudest, richest and rarest. Open daily throughout the year.

and at the Trocadero, Piccadilly Circus, London –
Clifton Hill, Niagara Falls – Fisherman's Wharf, San Francisco –
Hollywood Boulevard – Las Vegas Boulevard – The Parkway, Gatlinburg Tenn. –
World Trade Centre, Singapore.